The Longman Anthology of World Literature

✦━❖━✦

VOLUME A

THE ANCIENT WORLD

David Damrosch

COLUMBIA UNIVERSITY

The Ancient Near East; Mesoamerica

David L. Pike

AMERICAN UNIVERSITY

Rome and the Roman Empire; Medieval Europe

❦

April Alliston

PRINCETON UNIVERSITY

The Age of the Enlightenment

Marshall Brown

UNIVERSITY OF WASHINGTON

The Nineteenth Century

Page duBois

UNIVERSITY OF CALIFORNIA, SAN DIEGO

Classical Greece

Sabry Hafez

UNIVERSITY OF LONDON

Arabic and Islamic Literatures

Ursula K. Heise

STANFORD UNIVERSITY

The Twentieth Century

Djelal Kadir

PENNSYLVANIA STATE UNIVERSITY

The Twentieth Century

Sheldon Pollock

COLUMBIA UNIVERSITY

South Asia

Bruce Robbins

COLUMBIA UNIVERSITY

The Nineteenth Century

Haruo Shirane

COLUMBIA UNIVERSITY

Japan

Jane Tylus

NEW YORK UNIVERSITY

Early Modern Europe

Pauline Yu

AMERICAN COUNCIL OF LEARNED SOCIETIES

China

The Longman Anthology of World Literature

SECOND EDITION

David Damrosch

David L. Pike

General Editors

VOLUME A

THE ANCIENT WORLD

Page duBois

Sheldon Pollock

David L. Pike

David Damrosch

Pauline Yu

PEARSON

Longman

New York   San Francisco   Boston
London   Toronto   Sydney   Tokyo   Singapore   Madrid
Mexico City   Munich   Paris   Cape Town   Hong Kong   Montreal

Editor-in-Chief: *Joseph Terry*
Associate Development Editor: *Erin Reilly*
Executive Marketing Manager: *Joyce Nilsen*
Senior Supplements Editor: *Donna Campion*
Production Manager: *Ellen MacElree*
Project Coordination, Text Design, and Page Makeup: *GGS Book Services PMG*
Senior Cover Design Manager: *Nancy Danahy*
On the Cover: Detail from a funerary shroud with a portrait of the deceased between Anubis
    and Osiris. Egypt, 2nd century C.E. Pushkin Museum of Fine Arts, Moscow. Copyright ©
    Scala/Art Resource, New York.
Image Permission Coordinator: *Joanne Dippel*
Senior Manufacturing Buyer: *Alfred C. Dorsey*
Printer and Binder: *RR Donnelley Crawfordsville,In*
Cover Printer: *The Lehigh Press, Inc.*

For permission to use copyrighted material, grateful acknowledgment is made to the copyright
holders on pages 1338–1342, which are hereby made part of this copyright page.

Library of Congress Cataloging-in-Publication Data

The Longman anthology of world literature / David Damrosch, David L. Pike, general
editors.—2nd ed.
    p.   cm.
    Includes bibliographical references and index.
    Contents: v. A. The ancient world—v. B. The medieval era—v. C. The early
modern period—v. D. The seventeenth and eighteenth centuries—v. E. The
nineteenth century—v. F. The twentieth century.
    ISBN 978-0-205-62595-6 (v. A).—ISBN 978-0-205-62596-3 (v. B).— 978-0-205-62597-0
    (v. C).— 978-0-205-62590-1 (v. D).— 978-0-205-62591-8 (v. E).— 978-0-205-62594-9 (v. F).
    1. Literature—Collections.   2. Literature—History and criticism.
I. Damrosch, David.   II. Pike, David L. (David Lawrence), 1963–
PN6013.L66   2009
808.8—dc22
                                                                    2008015921

Please visit us at http://www.ablongman.com/damrosch.

To place your order, please use the following ISBN numbers:

Volume One Package *The Ancient World to The Early Modern Period*
(includes Volumes A, B, and C): **ISBN 13: 978-0-205-62593-2; ISBN 10: 0-205-62593-2**

Volume Two Package *The Seventeenth Century to The Twentieth Century*
(includes Volumes D, E, and F): **ISBN 13: 978-0-205-62592-5; ISBN 10: 0-205-62592-4**

Or, to order individual volumes, please use the following ISBN numbers:

Volume A, *The Ancient World:* ISBN 13: 978-0-205-62595-6; ISBN 10: 0-205-62595-9
Volume B, *The Medieval Era:* ISBN 13: 978-0-205-62596-3; ISBN 10: 0-205-62596-7
Volume C, *The Early Modern Period:* ISBN 13: 978-0-205-62597-0; ISBN 10: 0-205-62597-5
Volume D, *The Seventeenth and Eighteenth Centuries:* ISBN 13: 978-0-205-62590-1;
    ISBN 10: 0-205-62590-8
Volume E, *The Nineteenth Century:* ISBN 13: 978-0-205-62591-8; ISBN 10: 0-205-62591-6
Volume F, *The Twentieth Century:* ISBN 13: 978-0-205-62594-9; ISBN 10: 0-205-62594-0

3 4 5 6 7 8 9 10—DOC—17 16 15 14

CONTENTS

═╪ PERSPECTIVES ╪═
Strangers in a Strange Land   145

Classical Greece   185

ARCHAIC LYRIC POETRY   559

ARKHILOKHOS (7th century B.C.E.)   560

SAPPHO (early 7th century B.C.E.)   562

ALKAIOS (7th-6th centuries B.C.E.)   568

⇒═ PERSPECTIVES ═⇐

The Culture of Rome and the Beginnings of Christianity 1244

On the Cover

Detail from a funerary shroud, tempera paint on linen, Saqqara, Egypt, c. 125–150 C.E. This shroud gives an almost life-sized portrait of the deceased, in a vivid meeting of Egyptian and Greco-Roman worlds. The man wears a Roman-style tunic and mantle, and his head is painted with the shaded, three-dimensional appearance favored by Roman portrait artists. He is being embraced, though, by the Egyptian god Anubis. The jackal-headed Anubis, patron of embalming and the soul's guide into the underworld, is shown in the stylized, flattened manner that Egyptian artists had used for three thousand years, while the deceased stands in a pose taken from Greek sculpture (see the full image on the back cover): his weight is on his left foot and his right knee angles forward as he prepares to cross from life to death. To the left in the full image is the god Osiris in mummified form; the deceased will be reborn in the underworld through union with Osiris, brought about by the spells in the Book of the Dead (the scroll the man is holding). His head is framed with a painting of a temple, whose hieroglyphics proclaim that he will be "given life forever by the good god."

ADDITIONAL AUDIO AND ONLINE RESOURCES

VOICES OF WORLD LITERATURE, DISK 1
(ISBN: 0-321-22517-1)

An audio CD to accompany *The Longman Anthology of World Literature*, Volume 1. Throughout most of history, literature was created to be read, recited, or sung aloud. The selections on this CD, which can be ordered/packaged with the anthology, present a range of the many voices of world literature from its beginnings to the end of the early modern period and open up a range of cultural contexts for student discussion and writing. The following selections are available for Volume A.

THE ANCIENT WORLD

1. Egyptian Harp Piece
Performed by the Ensemble De Organographia (1:24)

> *An Egyptian statuette from c. 600 B.C.E. portrays a harpist and a music director with a table showing basic notation of a melody. This performance interprets this notation using a harp and a full Egyptian orchestra including reed pipes, flute, and percussion.*

2. Oded Bouria from the Song of Songs: What is thy beloved more than another?
Performed by Hillel and Aviva (1:30)

> *A modern Israeli composer uses ancient instruments to set a lyric dialogue from the Song of Songs: "What is thy beloved more than another beloved, O thou fairest among women?" My beloved is white and ruddy. / Pre-eminent above ten thousand. / His head is as the finest gold, / His locks are curled, and black as a raven.*

3. Choral Ode from Euripides' Orestes
Performed by the Ensemble De Organographia (1:17)

> *Euripides and his contemporaries set their tragedies to music. This choral ode is one of only fifty ancient Greek compositions for which musical notation has been preserved. The ode is accompanied by two reed pipes played by a single musician. The text reads: "I lament, I lament, because your mother's blood drives you mad. Great fortune among mortals does not endure: a god upsets it like the sail of a fast boat overwhelmed in the rough frightful waves of dreadful calamity, as in the sea."*

4. Interlude from a Satyr Play
Performed by Philip Newman (2:43)

> *A haunting melody played on a classical Greek instrument, the syrinx, or panpipe.*

5. From the *Taittiriya Upanishad*: Never send away anyone who comes to the house.
Performed by Pandit Ramji Shastri Dravidya (1:38)

Vedic chanting has been preserved by priestly families in India for over 3,000 years. This selection concerns the religious duty of hospitality: "Never send away anyone who comes to the house. This is a meritorious discipline. Hence by some means or other one must secure a good stock of food. . . . The wise man offers in the best way the prepared food and he too gets in return the best of things."

6. From *Raga Kamavardhani*
Performed by Swami D. R. Parvatikar (1:34)

This Indian raga *(improvised melody) is known as "the instigator of desire" and is meant to be played in the early evening. The performer, a renowned wandering ascetic and musician, plays the* vina, *a seven-stringed instrument used for meditative sacred music.*

7. From the *Bhagavad Gita*
Recited in Sanskrit by T. M. P. Mahadevan (1:05)

The Bhagavad Gita *is a dialogue between the god Krishna and the great warrior Arjuna, who discuss sacred duty just before the climatic battle of the epic* Mahabharata. *In this passage, Arjuna asks to be told the qualities of a man of steady wisdom.*

8. From the *Bhagavad Gita*
Recited in English by Swami Nikhilananda (2:43)

A fuller selection of the dialogue on wisdom, performed in English infused with the spirit of traditional Sanskrit recitation.

9. Hellenistic Funeral Song
Performed by the Ensemble De Organographia (1:15)

Reed pipes, harp, and percussion accompany the singer, performing a Greek text from a burial stele from the first century C.E.: *"I am a portrait in stone. I was put here by Seikilos, where I remain forever, the symbol of timeless remembrance."*

10. Ovid: Invocation to Mercury
Recited by Giorgio Albertazzi (1:14)

Ovid chronicled the history of the gods in his Metamorphoses. *This invocation from his poem "The Fasti" praises Mercury, messenger of the gods and reported inventor of the lyre. The rolling Latin phrases urge Mercury: "Come, oh famous nephew of Atlantis . . . you who run through air with winged feet, thrilled with the sound of the lyre, . . . who with your teaching began to speak the tongue so eloquently."*

11. Early Christian Hymn: Third century C.E.
Performed by the Ensemble De Organographia (2:33)

This is the earliest Christian hymn to survive with musical notation. The Greek text begins: Father of the worlds, Father of the ages, let us and the remarkable bondmaids of God celebrate you. As many things as the cosmos holds at the holy command of the heavenly lights, let them be silent, and let the light-bringing stars dim . . . while we sing of the Father, the Son, and the Holy Ghost."

Companion Website for *The Longman Anthology of World Literature,* Second Edition

www.ablongman.com/damrosch

Our Companion Website for the second edition has been enhanced with the addition of an interactive timeline, practice quizzes for major periods and authors, author biographies, research links, a glossary of literary terms, an audio glossary that provides the accepted pronunciations of author, character, and selection names from the anthology, audio recordings of our Translations features, and sample syllabi.

RESOURCES FOR VOLUME A

Practice Quizzes

Period Quizzes
- The Ancient Near East
- Classical Greece
- Early South Asia
- China: The Classical Tradition
- Rome and the Roman Empire

Quizzes on Major Texts
- *The Epic of Gilgamesh*
- The Book of Job
- *The Iliad*
- *The Odyssey*
- *Agamemnon*
- *Oedipus the King*
- *Antigone*
- *The Medea*
- *Lysistrata*
- *The Tamil Anthologies*
- The Book of Songs
- *Aeneid*
- *Confessions*

Author Biographies

- Homer
- Sappho
- Aeschylus
- Sophocles
- Euripides
- Aristophanes
- Confucius
- Virgil
- Ovid
- Augustine

Research Links

Authors and Major Texts
- Aeschylus
- Aristophanes
- Aristotle
- Augustine
- The Bible
- Boethius
- The Book of Songs
- Confucius
- *The Descent of Ishtar to the Underworld*
- *Enuma Elish*
- *The Epic of Gilgamesh*
- Euripides
- Homer
- Kalidasa
- Love in a Courtly Language
- *Mahabharata* of Vyasa
- Ovid
- Pindar
- *Poetry of Love and Devotion*
- *Ramayana* of Valmiki
- *The Rig Veda*
- Sappho
- Sima Qian
- Sophocles
- Virgil

Perspectives

- Daoism and Its Ways
- Death and Immortality
- Strangers in a Strange Land
- The Culture of Rome and the Beginnings of Christianity
- Tyranny and Democracy
- What Is "Literature"?

Translations

- *Bhagavad Gita*
- Catullus
- Genesis

PREFACE

Our world today is both expanding and growing smaller at the same time. Expanding, through a tremendous increase in the range of cultures that actively engage with each other; and yet growing smaller as well, as people and products surge across borders in the process known as globalization. This double movement creates remarkable opportunities for cross-cultural understanding, as well as new kinds of tensions, miscommunications, and uncertainties. Both the opportunities and the uncertainties are amply illustrated in the changing shape of world literature. A generation ago, when the term "world literature" was used in North America, it largely meant masterworks by European writers from Homer onward, together with a few favored North American writers, heirs to the Europeans. Today, however, it is generally recognized that Europe is only part of the story of the world's literatures, and only part of the story of North America's cultural heritage. An extraordinary range of exciting material is now in view, from the earliest Sumerian lyrics inscribed on clay tablets to the latest Kashmiri poetry circulated on the Internet. Many new worlds—and newly visible *older* worlds of classical traditions around the globe—await us today.

How can we best approach such varied materials from so many cultures? Can we deal with this embarrassment of riches without being overwhelmed by it, and without merely giving a glancing regard to less familiar traditions? This anthology has been designed to help readers successfully navigate "the sea of stories"—as Salman Rushdie has described the world's literary heritage.

The enthusiastic reception of the first edition attests to the growing relevance of a truly global approach to world literature. Drawing from the insight of instructors across the country, we have updated and further improved our anthology. We've gone about this challenging, fascinating task in several ways.

NEW TO THIS EDITION

- In our new Translations features, a brief selection is presented in the original language accompanied by two or three translations, chosen to show differing strategies translators have used to convey the sense of the original in new and powerful ways.
- Each of the Perspectives sections is now followed by our new Crosscurrents feature, which will highlight additional connections for students to explore.
- In response to reviewer requests, we have reevaluated each selection and streamlined our coverage to focus on the readings most frequently taught in the world literature course. We have also added several important works in their entirety, including Sophocles' *Antigone,* Shakespeare's *Othello,* Moliere's *Tartuffe,* Tolstoy's *The Death of Ivan Ilych,* and Silko's "Yellow Woman."

- Pull-out quotations in our period introductions and new headings in our author introductions have been added to help draw student interest and highlight important information.
- We have enhanced our Companion Website with the addition of a multitude of resources, including an interactive timeline, practice quizzes for major periods and authors, author biographies, research links, a glossary of literary terms, an audio glossary that provides the accepted pronunciations of author, character, and selection names from the anthology, audio recordings of our translations features, and sample syllabi. Visit www.ablongman.com/damrosch to explore these and other resources.
- We have improved our table of contents through the addition of a new media index—enabling you to locate all available resources quickly.

Connecting Distinctive Traditions

Works of world literature engage in a double conversation: with their culture of origin and with the varied contexts into which they travel away from home. To look broadly at world literature is therefore to see patterns of difference as well as points of contact and commonality. The world's disparate traditions have developed very distinct kinds of literature, even very different ideas as to what should be called "literature" at all. This anthology uses a variety of means to showcase what is most distinctive and also what is commonly shared among the world's literatures. Throughout the anthology, we employ two kinds of grouping:

☞ Perspectives: **Groupings that provide cultural context for major works, illuminating issues of broad importance.**

☞ Resonances: **Sources for a specific text or responses to it, often from a different time and place.**

Throughout the anthology, our many "Perspectives" sections provide cultural context for the major works around them, giving insight into such issues as the representation of death and immortality (in the ancient Near East); the meeting of Christians, Muslims, and Jews in medieval Iberia; the idea of the national poet in the nineteenth century; and "modernist memory" in the twentieth. Perspectives sections give a range of voices and views, strategies and styles, in highly readable textual groupings. The Perspectives groupings serve a major pedagogical as well as intellectual purpose in making these selections accessible and useful within the time constraints of a survey course. New to the second edition is "Crosscurrents," a feature that concludes each "Perspectives" section with connections to related selections within the same volume and in other volumes of the anthologies. "Crosscurrents" opens up the focused grouping of the "Perspectives," facilitating the study of specific themes and issues across cultures and across time.

Our "Resonances" perform the crucial function of linking works across time as well as space. For Homer's *Iliad*, a Resonance shows oral composition as it is still practiced today north of Greece, while for the *Odyssey* we have Resonances giving modern responses to Homer by Franz Kafka, Derek Walcott, and the Greek poet George Seferis. Accompanying the traditional Navajo "Story of the Emergence" (Volume E) is an extended selection from *Black Elk Speaks* which shows how ancient imagery infused the dream visions of the Sioux healer and warrior Nicholas Black Elk, helping him deal with the crises of lost land and independence that his people were facing. Resonances for Conrad's *Heart of Darkness* (Volume F) give selections from Conrad's diary of his own journey upriver in the Congo, and a speech by Henry Morton Stanley, the explorer-journalist who was serving as publicist for King Leopold's exploitation of his colony in the years just before Conrad went there. Stanley's surreal speech—in which he calculates how much money the Manchester weavers can make providing wedding dresses and burial clothes for the Congolese—gives a vivid instance of the outlook, and the rhetoric, that Conrad grimly parodies in Mr. Kurtz and his associates.

PRINCIPLES OF SELECTION

Beyond our immediate groupings, our overall selections have been made with an eye to fostering connections across time and space: a Perspectives section on "Courtly Women" in medieval Japan (Volume B) introduces themes that can be followed up in "Court Culture and Female Authorship" in Enlightenment-era Europe (Volume D), while the ancient Mediterranean creation myths at the start of Volume A find echoes in later cosmic-creation narratives from Mesoamerica (Volume C) and indigenous peoples today (Volume E). Altogether, we have worked to create an exceptionally coherent and well-integrated presentation of an extraordinary variety of works from around the globe, from the dawn of writing to the present.

Recognizing that different sorts of works have counted as literature in differing times and places, we take an inclusive approach, centering on poems, plays, and fictional narratives but also including selections from rich historical, religious, and philosophical texts like Plato's *Apology* and the Qur'an that have been important for much later literary work, even though they weren't conceived as literature themselves. We present many complete masterworks, including *The Epic of Gilgamesh* (in a beautiful verse translation), Homer's *Odyssey,* Dante's *Inferno,* and Chinua Achebe's *Things Fall Apart,* and we have extensive, teachable selections from such long works as *The Tale of Genji, Don Quixote,* and both parts of Goethe's *Faust.*

Along with these major selections we present a great array of shorter works, some of which have been known only to specialists and only now are entering into world literature. It is our experience as readers and as teachers that the established classics themselves can best be understood when they're set in a varied literary landscape. Nothing is included here, though, simply to make a point: whether world-renowned or recently rediscovered, these are compelling works to read. Throughout our work on this book, we've tried to be highly inclusive in principle and yet carefully selective in practice, avoiding tokenism and also its inverse, the piling up of an unmanageable array of heterogeneous material. If we've succeeded as we hope, the result will be coherent as well as capacious, substantive as well as stimulating.

LITERATURE, ART, AND MUSIC

One important way to understand literary works in context is to read them in conjunction with the broader social and artistic culture in which they were created. Literature has often had a particularly close relation to visual art and to music. Different as the arts are in their specific resources and techniques, a culture's artistic expressions often share certain family resemblances, common traits that can be seen across different media—and that may even come out more clearly in visual or musical form than in translations of literature itself. This anthology includes dozens of black-and-white illustrations and a suite of color illustrations in each volume, chosen to work in close conjunction with our literary selections. Some of these images directly illustrate literary works, while others show important aspects of a culture's aesthetic sensibility. Often, writing actually appears on paintings and sculptures, with represented people and places sharing the space with beautifully rendered Mayan hieroglyphs, Arabic calligraphy, or Chinese brushstrokes.

Music too has been a close companion of literary creation and performance. Our very term "lyric" refers to the lyres or harps with which the Greeks accompanied poems as they were sung. In China, the first major literary work is the *Book of Songs*. In Europe too, until quite recent times poetry was often sung and even prose was usually read aloud. We have created two audio CDs to accompany the anthology, one for Volumes A through C and one for Volumes D through F. These CDs give a wealth of poetry and music from the cultures we feature in the anthology; they are both a valuable teaching resource and also a pure pleasure to listen to.

AIDS TO UNDERSTANDING

A major emphasis of our work has been to introduce each culture and each work to best effect. Each major period and section of the anthology, each grouping of works, and each individual author has an introduction by a member of our editorial team. Our goal has been to write introductions informed by deep knowledge worn lightly. Neither talking down to our readers nor overwhelming them with masses of unassimilable information, our introductions don't seek to "cover" the material but instead try to uncover it, to provide ways in and connections outward. Similarly, our footnotes and glosses are concise and informative, rather than massive or interpretive. Time lines for each volume, and maps and pronunciation guides throughout the anthology, all aim to foster an informed and pleasurable reading of the works. The second edition of *The Longman Anthology of World Literature* has added highlighted quotations in the period introductions and additional headings to the author introductions to help draw student interest and clarify key ideas.

GOING FURTHER

The second edition makes connections beyond its covers as well as within them. Bibliographies at the end of each volume point the way to historical and critical readings for students wishing to go into greater depth for term papers. The Companion Website we've developed for the course (www.ablongman.com/damrosch) gives a wealth of links to excellent Web resources on all our major texts and many related historical and cultural movements and events. The Website includes an audio version of our printed pronunciation guides: you can simply click on a name to hear it pronounced. Each of our new Translations features is also available on the Website, where you can listen to readings of works in their original language and in translation. This rich resource will give you extensive exposure to the aural dimension of many of the languages represented in the anthology. We have also enhanced the Website for this edition, with the addition of practice quizzes for each period and for major selections, an interactive timeline, author biographies, a searchable glossary of literary terms, and sample syllabi. For instructors, we have also created an extensive instructor's manual, written directly by the editors themselves, drawing on years of experience in

teaching these materials. Finally, our audio CDs remain available, providing a library
of music and readings to augment your world literature course.

TRANSLATION ACROSS CULTURES

The circulation of world literature is always an exercise in cultural translation, and one
way to define works of world literature is that they are the works that gain in translation.
Some great texts remain so intimately tied to their point of origin that they never read
well abroad; they may have an abiding importance at home, but don't play a role in the
wider world. Other works, though, gain in resonance as they move out into new contexts, new conjunctions. Edgar Allan Poe found his first really serious readers in France,
rather than in the United States. *The Thousand and One Nights,* long a marginal work in
Arabic traditions oriented toward poetry rather than popular prose, gained new readers
and new influence abroad, and Scheherazade's intricately nested tales now help us in
turn to read the European tales of Boccaccio and Marguerite de Navarre with new attention and appreciation. A Perspectives section on *"The Thousand and One Nights* in the
Twentieth Century" (Volume F) brings together a range of Arab, European, and American
writers who have continued to plumb its riches to this day.

As important as cultural translation in general is the issue of actual translation
from one language to another. We have sought out compelling translations for all our
foreign-language works, and periodically we offer our readers the opportunity to
think directly about the issue of translation. Sometimes we offer distinctively different translations of differing works from a single author or source: for the Bible, for
example, we give Genesis 1–11 in Robert Alter's lively, oral-style translation, while
we give selected psalms in the magnificent King James Version and the Joseph story
in the lucid New International Version. Our selections from Homer's *Iliad* appear in
Richmond Lattimore's stately older translation, while Homer's *Odyssey* is given in
Robert Fagles's eloquent new version.

At other times, we give alternative translations of a single work. So we have Chinese lyrics translated by the modernist poet Ezra Pound and by a contemporary
scholar; and we have Petrarch sonnets translated by the Renaissance English poet
Thomas Wyatt and also by contemporary translators. These juxtapositions can show
some of the varied ways in which translators over the centuries have sought to carry
works over from one time and place to another—not so much by mirroring and reflecting an unchanged meaning, as by refracting it, in a prismatic process that can add
new highlights and reveal new facets in a classic text. At times, when we haven't
found a translation that really satisfies us, we've translated the work ourselves—an
activity we recommend to all who wish to come to know a work from the inside.

To help focus on the many issues involved in translation, we have incorporated a
new Translations feature into the second edition. In each volume of the anthology, two
major works are followed by a selection in the original language and in several different
translations. By studying the different choices made by translators in different times and
cultural contexts, we not only discover new meaning in the original work but in the
ways in which literature is transformed as it is translated for each generation of readers.

We hope that the results of our years of work on this project will be as enjoyable
to use as the book has been to create. We welcome you now inside our pages.

David Damrosch
David L. Pike

ACKNOWLEDGMENTS

In the extended process of planning and preparing the second edition of this anthology, the editors have been fortunate to have the support, advice, and assistance of many people. Our editor, Joe Terry, and our publisher, Roth Wilkofsky, have supported our project in every possible way and some seemingly impossible ones as well, helping us produce the best possible book despite all challenges to budgets and well-laid plans in a rapidly evolving field. Their associates Mary Ellen Curley and Joyce Nilsen have shown unwavering enthusiasm and constant creativity in developing the book and its related Web site and audio CDs and in introducing the results to the world. Our development editors, first Adam Beroud and then Erin Reilly, have shown a compelling blend of literary acuity and quiet diplomacy in guiding thirteen far-flung editors through the many stages of work. Peter Meyers brought great energy and creativity to work on our CDs. Donna Campion and Dianne Hall worked diligently to complete the instructor's manual. A team of permissions editors cleared hundreds and hundreds of text permissions from publishers in many countries.

Once the manuscript was complete, Ellen MacElree, the production manager, oversaw the simultaneous production of six massive books on a tight and shifting schedule. Valerie Zaborski, managing editor in production, also helped and, along the way, developed a taste for the good-humored fatalism of Icelandic literature. Our copyeditor, Stephanie Magean, and then Doug Bell and his colleagues at GGS Book Services PMG, worked overtime to produce beautiful books accurate down to the last exotic accent.

Our plans for this edition have been shaped by the comments, suggestions, and thoughtful advice of our reviewers. Charles Bane (University of Central Arkansas); Laurel Bollinger (University of Alabama in Huntsville); Patricia Cearley (South Plains College); Ed Eberhart (Troy University); Fidel Fajardo-Acosta (Creighton University); Gene C. Fant (Union University); Kathy Flann (Eastern Kentucky University); Katona D. Hargrave (Troy University); Nainsi J. Houston (Creighton University); Marta Kvande (Valdosta State University); Wayne Narey (Arkansas State University); Kevin R. Rahimzadeh (Eastern Kentucky University); Elizabeth L. Rambo (Campbell University); Gavin Richardson (Union University); Joseph Rosenblum (University of North Carolina at Greensboro); Douglass H. Thomson (Georgia Southern University); and Tomasz Warchol (Georgia Southern University).

We remain grateful as well for the guidance of the many reviewers who advised us on the creation of the first edition: Roberta Adams (Fitchburg State College); Adetutu Abatan (Floyd College); Magda al-Nowaihi (Columbia University); Nancy Applegate (Floyd College); Susan Atefat-Peckham (Georgia College and State University); Evan Balkan (CCBC-Catonsville); Michelle Barnett (University of Alabama, Birmingham); Colonel Bedell (Virginia Military Institute); Thomas Beebee (Pennsylvania State University); Paula Berggren (Baruch College); Mark Bernier (Blinn College); Ronald Bogue (University of Georgia); Terre Burton (Dixie State College); Patricia Cearley (South Plains College); Raj Chekuri (Laredo Community College); Sandra Clark (University of Wyoming); Thomas F. Connolly (Suffolk University); Vilashini Cooppan (Yale University); Bradford Crain (College of the Ozarks); Robert W. Croft (Gainesville College); Frank Day (Clemson University); Michael Delahoyde (Washington State University); Elizabeth Otten Delmonico (Truman State University); Jo Devine (University of Alaska Southeast); Gene Doty (University of Missouri—Rolla); James Earle (University of Oregon); R. Steve Eberly (Western Carolina University); Walter Evans (Augusta State University); Fidel Fajardo-Acosta (Creighton University); Mike Felker (South Plains College);

Janice Gable (Valley Forge Christian College); Stanley Galloway (Bridgewater College); Doris Gardenshire (Trinity Valley Community College); Jonathan Glenn (University of Central Arkansas); Dean Hall (Kansas State University); Dorothy Hardman (Fort Valley State University); Elissa Heil (University of the Ozarks); David Hesla (Emory University); Susan Hillabold (Purdue University North Central); Karen Hodges (Texas Wesleyan); David Hoegberg (Indiana University-Purdue University—Indianapolis); Sheri Hoem (Xavier University); Michael Hutcheson (Landmark College); Mary Anne Hutchinson (Utica College); Raymond Ide (Lancaster Bible College); James Ivory (Appalachian State University); Craig Kallendorf (Texas A & M University); Bridget Keegan (Creighton University); Steven Kellman (University of Texas—San Antonio); Roxanne Kent-Drury (Northern Kentucky University); Susan Kroeg (Eastern Kentucky University); Tamara Kuzmenkov (Tacoma Community College); Robert Lorenzi (Camden County College—Blackwood); Mark Mazzone (Tennessee State University); David McCracken (Coker College); George Mitrenski (Auburn University); James Nicholl (Western Carolina University); Roger Osterholm (Embry-Riddle University); Joe Pellegrino (Eastern Kentucky University); Linda Lang-Peralta (Metropolitan State College of Denver); Sandra Petree (University of Arkansas); David E. Phillips (Charleston Southern University); Terry Reilly (University of Alaska); Constance Relihan (Auburn University); Nelljean Rice (Coastal Carolina University); Colleen Richmond (George Fox University); Gretchen Ronnow (Wayne State University); John Rothfork (West Texas A & M University); Elise Salem-Manganaro (Fairleigh Dickinson University); Asha Sen (University of Wisconsin Eau Claire); Richard Sha (American University); Edward Shaw (University of Central Florida); Jack Shreve (Allegany College of Maryland); Jimmy Dean Smith (Union College); Floyd C. Stuart (Norwich University); Eleanor Sumpter-Latham (Central Oregon Community College); Ron Swigger (Albuquerque Technical Vocational Institute); Barry Tharaud (Mesa State College); Theresa Thompson (Valdosta State College); Teresa Thonney (Columbia Basin College); Charles Tita (Shaw University); Scott D. Vander Ploeg (Madisonville Community College); Marian Wernicke (Pensacola Junior College); Sallie Wolf (Arapahoe Community College); and Dede Yow (Kennesaw State University).

We also wish to express our gratitude to the reviewers who gave us additional advice on the book's companion Web site: Nancy Applegate (Floyd College); James Earl (University of Oregon); David McCracken (Coker College); Linda Lang-Peralta (Metropolitan State College of Denver); Asha Sen (University of Wisconsin—Eau Claire); Jimmy Dean Smith (Union College); Floyd Stuart (Norwich University); and Marian Wernicke (Pensacola Junior College).

The editors were assisted in tracking down texts and information by wonderfully able research assistants: Kerry Bystrom, Julie Lapiski, Katalin Lovasz, Joseph Ortiz, Laura B. Sayre, and Lauren Simonetti. April Alliston wishes to thank Brandon Lafving for his invaluable comments on her drafts and Gregory Maertz for his knowledge and support. Marshall Brown would like to thank his research assistant Françoise Belot for her help and Jane K. Brown for writing the Goethe introduction. Sheldon Pollock would like to thank Whitney Cox, Rajeev Kinra, Susanne Mrozik, and Guriqbal Sahota for their assistance and Haruo Shirane thanks Michael Brownstein for writing the introduction to Hozumi Ikan, and Akiko Takeuchi for writing the introductions to the Noh drama.

It has been a great pleasure to work with all these colleagues both at Longman and at schools around the country. This book exists for its readers, whose reactions and suggestions we warmly welcome, as the second edition of *The Longman Anthology of World Literature* moves out into the world.

ABOUT THE EDITORS

David Damrosch (Columbia University). His books include *The Narrative Covenant: Transformations of Genre in the Growth of Biblical Literature* (1987), *Meetings of the Mind* (2000), *What Is World Literature?* (2003), and *How to Read World Literature* (2009). He has been president of the American Comparative Literature Association (2001–2003) and is founding general editor of *The Longman Anthology of British Literature* (third edition, 2006).

David L. Pike (American University). Author of *Passage Through Hell: Modernist Descents, Medieval Underworlds* (1997), *Subterranean Cities: The World Beneath Paris and London, 1800–1945* (2005), and *Metropolis on the Styx: The Underworlds of Modern Urban Culture* (2007). He is co-author of the forthcoming *A World of Writing: Poems, Stories, Drama, Essays.*

April Alliston (Princeton University). Author of *Virtue's Faults: Correspondences in Eighteenth-Century British and French Women's Fiction* (1996), and editor of Sophia Lee's *The Recess* (2000). Her book on concepts of character, gender, and plausibility in Enlightenment historical narratives is forthcoming.

Marshall Brown (University of Washington). Author of *The Shape of German Romanticism* (1979), *Preromanticism* (1991), *Turning Points: Essays in the History of Cultural Expressions* (1997), *The Gothic Text* (2005), and *The Tooth That Nibbles at the Soul: Essays on Music and Poetry* (forthcoming). Editor of *Modern Language Quarterly: A Journal of Literary History,* and the *Cambridge History of Literary Criticism,* Vol. 5: Romanticism.

Page duBois (University of California, San Diego). Her books include *Centaurs and Amazons* (1982), *Sowing the Body* (1988), *Torture and Truth* (1991), *Sappho Is Burning* (1995), *Trojan Horses* (2001), and *Slaves and Other Objects* (2003).

Sabry Hafez (University of London). Author of several books in Arabic on poetry, drama, the novel, and on a number of major Arab writers, including works on Mahfouz, Idris, and Mahmoud Darwish. His books in English include *The Genesis of Arabic Narrative Discourse* (1993), *The Quest for Identities: The Arabic Short Story* (2007), and the edited volumes *A Reader of Modern Arabic Short Stories* and *Modern Arabic Criticism.* He is the editor of the on-line bilingual Arabic/English monthly journal, *Al-Kalimah/The World.*

Ursula K. Heise (Stanford University). Author of *Chronoschisms: Time, Narrative, and Postmodernism* (1997) and of *Sense of Place and Sense of Planet: The Environmental Imagination of the Global* (2008).

Djelal Kadir (Pennsylvania State University). His books include *Columbus and the Ends of the Earth* (1992), *The Other Writing: Postcolonial Essays in Latin America's Writing Culture* (1993), and *Other Modernisms in an Age of Globalizations* (2002). He served in the 1990s as editor of *World Literature Today* and is coeditor of the *Comparative History of Latin America's Literary Cultures* (2004). He is the founding president of the International American Studies Association.

Sheldon Pollock (Columbia University). His books include *The Language of the Gods in the World of Men* (2006). He recently edited *Literary Cultures in History: Reconstructions from South Asia* (2003). He is general editor of the Clay Sanskrit Library.

Bruce Robbins (Columbia University). His books include *The Servant's Hand: English Fiction from Below* (1986), *Secular Vocations* (1993), *Feeling Global: Internationalism in Distress* (1999), and *Upward Mobility and the Common Good: Toward a Literary History of the Welfare State* (2007). Edited volumes include *Cosmopolitics: Thinking and Feeling Beyond the Nation* (1998).

Haruo Shirane (Columbia University). Author of *The Bridge of Dreams: A Poetics of "The Tale of Genji"* (1987) and of *Traces of Dreams: Landscape, Cultural Memory, and the Poetry of Bashō* (1998). He is coeditor of *Inventing the Classics: Modernity, National Identity, and Japanese Literature* (2000) and has recently edited *Early Modern Japanese Literature: An Anthology 1600–1900*.

Jane Tylus (New York University). Author of *Writing and Vulnerability in the Late Renaissance* (1993), coeditor of *Epic Traditions in the Contemporary World* (1999), and editor and translator of Lucrezia Tornabuoni de' Medici's *Sacred Narratives* (2001). Her study on late medieval female spirituality and the origins of humanism is forthcoming.

Pauline Yu (American Council of Learned Societies). President of the American Council of Learned Societies, she is the author of *The Poetry of Wang Wei* (1980) and *The Reading of Imagery in the Chinese Poetic Tradition* (1987), the editor of *Voices of the Song Lyric in China* (1994), and coeditor of *Culture and State in Chinese History* (1997) and *Ways with Words: Writing about Reading Texts from Early China* (2000).

Detail of stele inscribed with the Law Code of Hammurabi, c. 1750 B.C.E. The Babylonian king Hammurabi (reigned c. 1792–1750 B.C.E.) commissioned the major law code that bears his name, an ambitious effort to organize society under the rule of law. The seven-foot-tall stone column on which his laws are inscribed in cuneiform script is crowned with the scene showing Hammurabi conversing with the seated sun god, Shamash.

The Ancient World

The ancient world was shaped by great innovations. The first nations and the first empires were founded, several great world religions—including Hinduism, Buddhism, and Christianity—were established, the first organized law codes were drawn up, and in many respects the outlines of civilization as we know it today began to emerge. A common term in all of these developments was the invention of systems of writing. With writing came effective long-distance communication and the ability to build nations and empires. While great religious leaders like Gautama Buddha, Jesus, and later the prophet Muhammad didn't write their teachings down, the scriptures compiled by their disciples and adherents played a major role in the worldwide spread of the religions they founded. Writing also gave cultures the ability to record their history and to create the textual records of their societies, preserving their imaginative works as well as more practical documents for later generations to read: literature was born.

> *With writing came effective long-distance communication and the ability to build nations and empires.*

This volume includes major works from the cultures that created the world's first great bodies of literary texts between four thousand and a little less than two thousand years ago, in Mesopotamia, in the Mediterranean world, in India, and in China. These works often have a double focus: preserving ancient traditions with roots in the distant past, they also respond to their own present situations. Ancient writers looked to the past to understand their present. Stories of creation would lead to the present world order, epic accounts of ancient battles would celebrate the founding of a people or nation, and even very recent laws would be portrayed as the wisdom of the ancients. Traditions could be invented as well as preserved, and as written texts became numerous, competing traditions could be compared, analyzed, and creatively reimagined. The pleasures of imagination and of verbal beauty abound in these works as well, as ancient writers created the world's first written poems, dramas, and prose narratives. Their works became foundational for later writing in their own cultures and beyond, and have done much to shape our understanding and practice of literature to the present day. To read these texts now is to encounter a fascinating mixture of strangeness and immediacy, as the writers used the radically new technology of writing to convey ancient wisdom and to adapt it to their own changing times.

CITIES, NATIONS, AND EMPIRES

Ancient writing is largely urban in origin, for writing was employed mostly in courts and temples in the cities that grew rapidly in the second and first millennia B.C.E. The Greeks and Romans loved pastoral poems about shepherds and shepherdesses in the countryside, but the shepherds themselves couldn't write; with the possible exception of a few Egyptian love songs, the pastoral poetry we have was written by sophisticated urban poets dreaming of rural peace. Even so, the cities remained deeply dependent on the

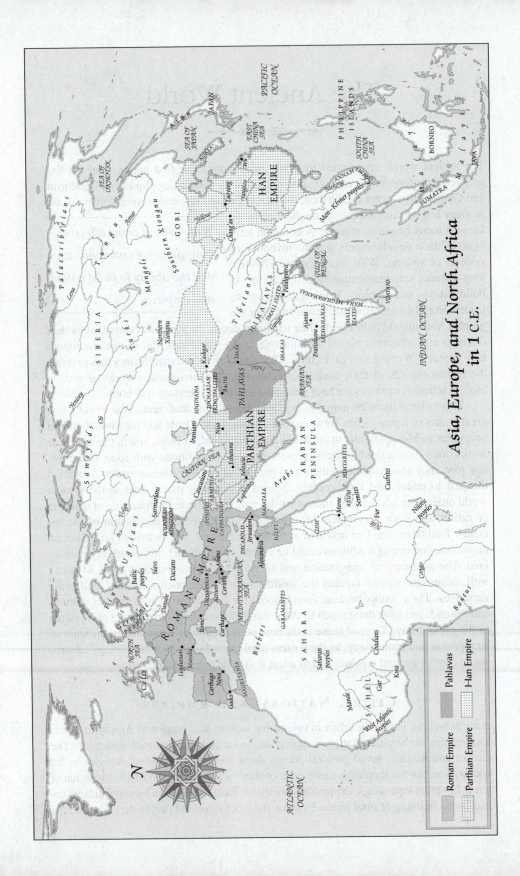

Asia, Europe, and North Africa
in 1 C.E.

Roman Empire

Pahlavas

Parthian Empire

Han Empire

Plate 1 *Tutankhamen and Ankhesenamen,* Egypt, c. 1320 B.C.E. This gold relief forms the back of a throne found in the tomb of the Egyptian king Tutankhamen, who died in 1324 at about age 19. The gold is inlaid with colored glass and semiprecious stones, with silver for the clothing. Tutankhamen and his wife (and half-sister) Ankhesenamen are shown in an intimate domestic moment, and at the same time the picture emphasizes the royal couple's direct link to the sun disk, the Aten, promoted by their father Akhenaten as the dominant god. The sun's rays stream down, equipped with hands giving strength and support. Some of the Aten's hands hold the *ankh,* the Egyptian hieroglyph for "life," which is a central element in both the king's and the queen's names. The couple is shown in the flattened, schematic style traditional in Egyptian art (shoulders turned sideways, every finger visible), but Tutankhamen's casually thrown-back arm reflects the lively realism promoted during his father's reign. *(Egyptian Museum, Cairo. Photo: AKG London / Francois Guenot.)*

Plate 2   The Ishtar Gate of Nebuchadnezzar II at Babylon, c. 600 B.C.E., reconstructed in Berlin's Vorderasiatisches Museum. Mesopotamian cities proclaimed their magnificence by the size and beauty of their walls. As *The Epic of Gilgamesh* urges its readers: "Look at [Uruk's] wall which gleams like copper, / inspect its inner wall, the likes of which no one can equal!" (page 59). The monumental gate of Ishtar, towering over all at a height of 50 feet, dramatizes the power of the city and its king to those who enter. Periodically, Nebuchadnezzar would sit beneath the arch to receive tribute, framed by the rows of watchful bulls, lions, and dragons shown in raised tiles of glazed brick. (*Vorderasiatisches Museum, Staatliche Museen, Berlin. Erich Lessing / Art Resource, New York.*)

Plate 3 Gold funeral mask, Mycenae, c. 1500 B.C.E. In 1876, the German archaeologist Heinrich Schliemann excavated the ruins of Mycenae on mainland Greece, home of Agamemnon, the legendary king who commanded the Greek forces against the Trojans. When he found this mask, Schliemann telegraphed a friend: "I have looked upon the face of Agamemnon." The actual identity of the mask's owner is unknown, but the finely shaped features convey a portrait of a distinctive individual still powerful in death. (*Scala / Art Resource, New York.*)

Plate 4 *Hercules and the Eryman-thian boar,* Greece, 6th century B.C.E. This black-figured vase shows Hercules completing one of the 12 labors imposed on him by his sickly brother and king, Eurystheus: to slay a wild boar ravaging the slopes of Mt. Erymanthus. Dressed in the skin of a lion (killed as his first la-bor), Hercules seems almost as wild as the boar he holds. Thanks to a trick by the goddess Hera, Eurys-theus had received the kingship that rightfully belonged to Hercules; the tension of the brothers' relationship can be seen as Hercules looms over Eurystheus, who seems about to be crushed by his brother's offering. (*The British Museum Images. © The British Museum.*)

Plate 5   The theater at Delphi, Greece, 4th century B.C.E. Seating five thousand spectators, the theater was built on the slopes of Mt. Parnassus at the sacred shrine at Delphi, regarded by the ancient Greeks as the center of the world. The site was dedicated to Apollo, and the springs on the slopes of Parnassus were said to bring poetic inspiration. The theater echoes the sweeping curves of the landscape around it, creating a harmonious order appropriate to the god of reason and of poetry. *(AKG London. Shutze / Rodemann.)*

Plate 6   Jain diagram of the universe, India. Like the theater at Delphi, this diagram creates a circular order centered on a sacred mountain. Jainism, which arose in the 6th century B.C.E., downplayed the elaborate ritual observances and social hierarchies developed in Vedic circles, emphasizing instead meditation and the achievement of inner knowledge. Yet the Jain view of the cosmos shared many features with those of the Buddhists and Hindus. This painted cloth diagram shows the universe centered on Meru, a mountain sacred to the gods, which stands in the middle of Jambudvipa, the Rose-Apple Island, or the known world (as even Chinese Buddhist pilgrims referred to it). The concentric circles that surround it are oceans teeming with fish and other creatures and dotted with inhabited islands. The whole map is surrounded in turn by Sanskrit texts identifying components of the Jain cosmography. (*British Library / Picture Desk, Inc. Kobal Collection.*)

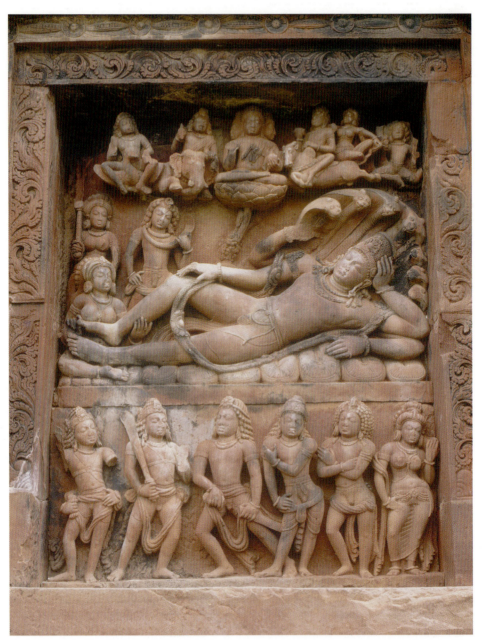

Plate 7   Reclining Vishnu, Hindu sculpture, Uttar Pradesh, India, c. 500 C.E. Vishnu is shown dreaming the universe into existence as he lies on the coiled serpent of infinity. Inspired by the goddess Lakshmi, who supports his leg, Vishnu creates the god Brahma, who floats above him on a lotus plant. Brahma in turn will create the earthly world by thinking, "May I become Many." Shown beneath Vishnu are the *Mahabharata*'s protagonists (see page 809): the five Pandava brothers and their shared wife, Draupadi. *(Jean Louis Nou / AKG Images, London.)*

Plate 8 Bronze incense burner from the tomb of Prince Liu Sheng, China, c. 120 B.C.E. Only ten inches tall, this artifact is a miniature vision of the Daoist paradise, the Island of the Immortals in the Eastern Sea. Daoism sought to perceive the path or Way (dao) of the universe and to help people blend with its current rather than struggle against it (see the *Dao De Jing,* page 1061). Waves inlaid in gold swirl around the island, whose mountain slopes are inhabited by tiny figures of enlightened people, animals, and birds. When it was in use, the burner would have given off clouds of incense, surrounding the island like the clouds that cover heaven from mortal sight. *(Hebei Provincial Museum, Shijazhuang, China. Wang Lui / ChinaStock.)*

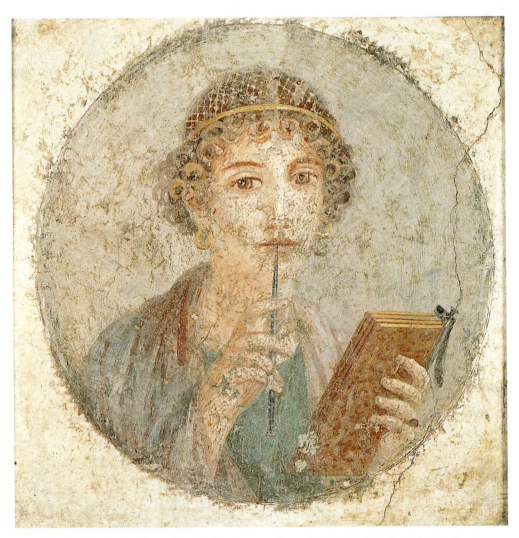

Plate 9 *Portrait of a Woman,* Pompeii, 1st century C.E. Preserved when the city of Pompeii was submerged in volcanic ash from Mt. Vesuvius in 79 C.E., this fresco shows the subtle shading and emphasis on individual character common in Roman portraiture. (Compare also the man on the cover of this volume, from Roman Egypt.) Apparently a poet, the woman shown here holds a set of wooden writing tablets, tapping her lips with her stylus as she searches for a word. *(Erich Lessing / Art Resource, New York.)*

countryside; the great majority of all people in antiquity were engaged in growing crops and raising livestock. Primitive peoples had subsisted through hunting, fishing, and foraging for whatever edible plants they might happen to encounter, but between around 8000 and 6000 B.C.E. the settled cultivation of crops began. Farming produced substantial new surpluses of food and allowed for specialized roles to emerge in the growing cities: rulers and administrators, soldiers, priests, craftsmen, painters, musicians, and poets. As early as 5000 B.C.E., the Sumerians in southern Mesopotamia were building large cities complete with public water supplies and drainage, and by around 3100 B.C.E. the Sumerians had pioneered the use of written notations to record their dealings.

The rulers of major cities extended their reach to create the first nations, often relying on rivers as conduits of trade and communication. "Mesopotamia" takes its name from the Greek phrase "between the rivers," referring to the Tigris and Euphrates rivers on whose banks were built the great early cities of Ur, Akkad, Nippur, and Babylon. The Nile formed the backbone of Egypt, united into a single country around 3100 B.C.E., and the hieroglyphic writing developed in Egypt around that time greatly aided the new country's administrators in knitting their new country together. In China, cities grew up along rivers like the Yangtse, while in India a major early civilization grew up in the fertile valley of the Indus River. Sea routes could serve as well as rivers: the early Greek cities of Knossos on Crete and Mycenae on the mainland became centers of trade and of cultural production.

Over time, the most powerful city-states vied for control of larger regions, and the first empires were born in the third and second millennia B.C.E. The Babylonian and Assyrian empires waxed and waned across Mesopotamia and regions north and west; the Egyptians had long periods of control over Nubia and the Sudan to the south, and much of Palestine to the north and east. India and China, unified countries today, were (and still are) made up of many different ethnic groups speaking unrelated languages, and the governments that came to extend across their territories were creating empires rather than homogeneous nations. In late antiquity, vast empires extended from centers in Persia, in Northern Greece, and then in Rome, and great writers like Virgil both celebrated and probed the empires ruled by their patrons.

TRAVEL, MIGRATION, AND TRADE

Armies of conquest weren't the only groups on the move in the ancient world. Populations expanded rapidly in periods of prosperity but could come under severe stress in times of drought, or simply through outgrowing their resources. Entire peoples journeyed in search of new grazing lands and new fields to farm, in waves of migration that periodically transformed the social landscape, creating mixed populations in formerly unified regions. On a smaller scale, caravans of traders crossed long distances along the "silk road" that grew up from China to India and into central Asia and Asia Minor, while Phoenician and Greek sailing ships established contacts around the Mediterranean. The pioneering *History* of Herodotus is as much a travel account as it is a history of the Greek and Persian wars, as the author describes his travels into lands around the eastern Mediterranean. Much ancient literature plays to people's fascination with hearing about distant peoples and their unusual customs, and many works explored what could happen when disparate cultures came into contact or conflict, either to comic effect or with tragic consequences.

LYRIC AND EPIC

The invention of writing allowed ancient singers to record their poems, both short lyrics and the sweeping poetic narratives we call epics, and over time poetry came to be composed in writing, independent of oral tradition. Even written literature, though, remained closely tied to public performance: "lyric" poetry gets its name from the Greek poets' custom of singing their poems to the accompaniment of a lyre or small harp. The great early Chinese poetry collection, *The Book of Songs,* is equally a collection of works made to be sung. The poetic impulse seems to be universal, and indeed in all of the ancient cultures presented here, lyric poetry was recorded long before prose fiction emerged. At the same time, the very fact that poetry is found everywhere means that it was composed in many different settings and with differing cultural assumptions, sometimes in close connection to religious ceremonies, other times purely as entertainment at banquets. Poets could be seen as powerful figures, verbal magicians whose words could have dangerous effects, or much more modestly as servants and entertainers. In China, poetry came to be regarded as an integral part of daily life; any educated person, male or female, was expected to be able to compose an apt poem for any occasion—the giving of a present, a friend's departure on a journey, or the downfall of a dynasty.

Poets could be seen as powerful figures, verbal magicians whose words could have dangerous effects.

By contrast with the universality of lyric poetry, epic poetry is found in some ancient cultures (Babylonia, India, Greece, and Rome) and not others (Egypt, China). Works labeled "epic" are long narrative poems, usually several thousand lines or more, concerning a series of great struggles or adventures of a hero or group of heroes, aided and opposed by different gods, often leading to the forming of a people or nation. Often an epic centers on a great battle, as with the *Mahabharata,* based on a war in northwest India, or Homer's *Iliad,* in which the war over Troy becomes a pivotal event in the shaping of Greek identity. Other epics, like the Babylonian *Epic of Gilgamesh* and Homer's *Odyssey,* center more on an individual's voyage and the return home. The oldest epics are collective compositions, long developed in oral tradition, but as time went on they became increasingly shaped through rewriting. Eventually they came to be composed by known individuals, like Virgil, whose *Aeneid* combines the two great themes of voyage and of battle. The epics presented in this volume give a range of forms and styles, through which their authors probe the fundamental limits and meaning of their culture.

MYTH, LEGEND, AND HISTORY

A distinct feature of ancient literature is the freedom with which it can mix kinds of material we usually think of as distinct, such as myths, legends, and verifiable historical facts. Most ancient cultures reckoned years by one monarch's reign and then the next, with spotty record-keeping if any, and no systematic marking of chronology. The dating of all the texts in this volume on the common scale of years B.C.E. ("before the common era") and C.E. ("common era") is based on efforts first made in the medieval era to date the year of Jesus's birth and organize history accordingly. (As is now common in world history texts, this anthology uses "B.C.E" and "C.E." in place of the traditional "B.C." and "A.D." with their direct theological emphasis.) With written records incomplete and inconsistent, the boundaries remained fluid in antiquity between what we would now separate as history versus legend or outright myth. "Myth" itself is a term with many meanings. Often today we call something a myth simply to say it isn't true, but in ancient Greek, the term *mythos* originally meant any speech or story. Gradually the term

"Myth" in the ancient world meant a story about ultimate truths.

came to refer especially to poetic legends about the early doings of the gods, or the gods and mortals together, in a distant, shadowy past. Far from signifying falsehood, then, "myth" in the ancient world meant a story about ultimate truths. Myths were sometimes told to explain the origins of the world as a whole or of a particular custom or feature of the landscape; at other times, they were used as background or charter for a ritual, as when the Babylonian creation myth was recited as part of an annual New Year's ceremony. Anonymous in origin, handed down over the years from one teller to another, a myth would vary in form and content as it circulated within a culture and beyond, and over time myths could be taken up and elaborated more for the sake of enjoyment than for any practical purpose.

The Greeks after Plato began to distinguish *mythos* from *logos* (word or report), considering myths as unverifiable legends not like the definite report about actual events that an observer could relate or a historian could reconstruct. Yet throughout ancient literature, mythic elements continually reappear even in sober historical writing, and human history—like the earthly landscape itself—continued to bear the marks of the gods' deeds and intentions. In between myth and history proper are legends, traditional tales of relatively recent people and events. Often a single work will blend mythic, legendary, and historical materials, challenging us to see the world in a new way, interfusing what we often think of as separate realms of fact and fiction.

Most ancient texts existed in only one manuscript or a few copies at most, and over time the majority were lost. The ancient works we have today are the rare exceptions, works so treasured that they circulated widely and were preserved through centuries of warfare and disruption, or else works that simply happened to be preserved in a tomb or a ruined royal library, where they could be rediscovered long after their world had vanished. In many ways these foundational works set the course for much later writing around the globe, and they convey the first writers' excitement as they captured their world on paper, on clay tablets, and on stone.

THE ANCIENT WORLD

YEAR	THE WORLD	LITERATURE
3500 B.C.E.		
	3200–3100 Development of cuneiform writing in Mesopotamia	
	c. 3100 Unification of Egypt; development of hieroglyphics	
3000		
	3000–2501 Neolithic settlements on Crete	
	c. 2700 Gilgamesh king of Uruk in southern Mesopotamia	
2500		
	2500–2001 Early Minoan culture on Crete	2500–2180 Pyramid Texts in Egypt
		2200–2000 Early Sumerian poems about Gilgamesh
2000		
	2000–1500 Greek–speakers begin to move from the East toward the eastern Mediterranean; Cecrops, legendary first king of Athens; Middle Minoan period of Crete; Decimal system on Crete; Late Minoan period of Crete (to 1400)	c. 1925 *The Story of Sinuhe*
	c. 1900 Hebrews begin to migrate from Babylonia to Palestine	
		c. 1600 Old Babylonian *Epic of Gilgamesh*
	c. 1550–1040 Shang dynasty in China	
1500		
	1500–1000 Wandering of pastoral nomadic groups across Eurasia	c. 1500–1000 Sanskrit *Vedas*
	1500–1200 Beginnings of Cretan–Mycenaean culture	
	c. 1372–1354 Reign of Akhnaten and "Amarna Revolution" in Egypt	c. 1360 Great Hymn to the Aten
		c. 1300–1200 Egyptian love poetry written down
	c. 1200 Traditional time of the Exodus of Israelites from captivity in Egypt	c. 1200 *Enuma Elish*; Sîn-liqe-unninni creates Standard Version of *The Epic of Gilgamesh*
	1193 Destruction of Troy, 6th level	
	c. 1100 According to legend, Aeneas arrives at Latium from Troy	
	c. 1040–256 Zhou dynasty in China	
	c. 1020 United Israel founded by King Saul	

YEAR	THE WORLD	LITERATURE
1000		
	1000–900 Ionians, displaced from mainland Greece, found cities in Asia Minor, including Ephesus and Miletus. Political unification of Athens. Greek alphabet based on Semitic–Phoenician characters adds vowels	**c. 950** Yahwists compose first version of the Torah, including Genesis
	c. 1000–960 Reign of King David in Israel	
	c. 960–931 Reign of King Solomon; after his death, Israel divided by civil war into Israel and Judah	
	900–700 Greek colonization throughout Mediterranean basin	**c. 900** The Book of Job
		c. 900–700 Composition of *Iliad, Odyssey, Theogony, Works and Days*
	800–600 Rise of urbanism in northern India	**c. 800–600** *Upanishads*
		c. 800–400 *Book of Songs,* China
	776 Legendary foundation of the Olympian games	
	753 Traditional date on which Romulus founds Rome	**c. 750** Kabti-ilani-Marduk, *Erra and Ishum*
	722 Israel conquered by Assyrians; Judah remains independent	
	722–481 Spring and Autumn Period in China	
		700–600 Arkhilokhos, Sappho, and other Greek lyric poets flourish
	594–593 Solon reforms Athenian government	
	586 Babylonians conquer Judah, deport many Hebrews to Babylon	**c. 550** Priestly writers among Hebrews in exile in Babylon revise Torah into canonical form
	c. 551–479 Life of Confucius	
	539 Cyrus the Great of Persia conquers Babylon and permits Hebrews to return to Israel. Founds Persian Empire	**c. 500–450** *Analects* of Confucius
	527 Death of Peisistratos, tyrant of Athens	**500–429** *Dao De Jing*
	510 Cleisthenes' democratic reforms	
	509 Rome becomes a republic	
500		
	500–429 Life of Athenian leader Pericles	
	500 Ionians revolt from Persia	
	490–449 Persian Wars	
	490 Battle of Marathon	
	480 Battles of Thermopylae and Salamis	**c. 475–450** Pindar, *Odes*
	470–399 Life of Socrates	**458** Aeschylus, *Oresteia*
	469–399 Hippocrates	**c. 450** *Discourses of the Buddha*
	448–433 Rebuilding of the Athenian Acropolis after Persian destruction	**431** Pericles' Funeral Oration
		431 Euripides, *Medea*
	431–404 Peloponnesian War between Athens and Sparta	**c. 430** Herodotus, *History*
	427–347 Life of Plato	**c. 426** Sophocles, *Oedipus the King*
	411 Oligarchic coup in Athens	**411** Aristophanes, *Lysistrata*
	405 Defeat of Athenians by Sparta	
	403–221 Warring States Period in China	

Year	The World	Literature
		c. 400 Thucydides, *History*
		c. 400 B.C.E.–400 C.E. *Mahabharata*
	399 Execution of Socrates	390 Plato, *Apology of Socrates*
	384–322 Life of Aristotle	
	369–286 Life of Zhuangzi	
	356–323 Alexander the Great conquers central Asia; 332 founds Alexandria in Egypt, dies in Babylon 323	
	352–336 Philip II of Macedon	
	338 Philip defeats Greeks at Chaeronea	
	c. 300 Rise of the Mauryan Empire in India (to 100 C.E.)	c. 300 B.C.E.–100 C.E. Kautilya, *Treatise on Power*
	250 Buddhism begins to spread beyond India	250 Asoka, *Inscriptions*
	221–206 Qin dynasty in China	
	206 B.C.E.–C.E. 220 Han dynasty in China	
		c. 200 Valmiki, *Ramayana*
	190 Palestine comes under Roman control	
	149–146 Third Punic War; Carthage is destroyed by Romans	
	147 Romans take control of Greece	
100		
	64–63 Conspiracy of Catiline in Rome against Cicero's consulship	
	58–50 Julius Caesar campaigns in Gaul	
		c. 55–54 Lucretius, *On the Nature of Things*
		c. 54 Catullus, *Poems*
	48 Caesar defeats Pompey at the battle of Pharsalus	
	44 Caesar murdered by Brutus and Cassius	
		39–29 Virgil, *Eclogues*
		35–30 Horace, *Satires*
	31 Octavian (Augustus) defeats Antony and Cleopatra at the battle of Actium, end of civil war; Egypt becomes a Roman province	
		29 B.C.E.–17 C.E. Livy, *History of Rome*
		19 Virgil, *Aeneid*
	c. 6 Birth of Jesus (traditionally estimated at 1 C.E.)	c. 1 B.C.E.–1 C.E. Ovid, *Art of Love, Remedy of Love*
1 C.E.		2–8 Ovid, *Metamorphoses*
	29 Augustus dies; succeeded after a month by Tiberius	
	c. 30 Jesus is crucified outside the walls of Jersualem	
		c. 45–64 Paul, *Epistles*

YEAR	THE WORLD	LITERATURE
		c. 60–90 Gospels according to Matthew, Mark, and Luke; Acts of the Apostles
	64 The great fire in Rome; Nero persecutes Christians	
	65 Failure of the Pisonian conspiracy against Nero; Lucan and Seneca compelled to suicide	
		c. 66 Petronius, *Satyricon*
	70 Jewish revolt against Rome; Temple in Jerusalem destroyed	
		c. 75 *Priapea*
	98–117 Reign of Trajan	
100		
		c. 101–127 Juvenal, *Satires*
		c. 117 Tacitus, *Annals*
		c. 120 Suetonius, *Lives of the Caesars*
	150 Rule of the Kushanas and Indo-Scythians	**150** Ashvaghosha, *Life of the Buddha*
	161–180 Reign of Marcus Aurelius	
	c. 200 Pandyas patronize Tamil culture in the south	**c. 200** *Tamil Anthologies*
		c. 200 Hala, *The Seven Hundred Songs*
	c. 200 End of the Satavahana Empire in south-central India	**c. 200–500** Early Buddhist *puranas,* including *Lore of the Dwarf Incarnation*
	200–500 End of Kushan rule and rise of the Gupta in northern India	
	313 Edict of Milan, Constantine proclaims toleration of the Christian religion	
	355–363 Reign of Julian "the Apostate"	
		384 Jerome, Vulgate Bible (New Testament)
		c. 400–425 Poetry of Tao Qian
		c. 400 Augustine, *Confessions*
		c. 400 Vatsyayana, *Kamasutra*
		406 Jerome, Vulgate Bible (Old Testament)
		413–427 Augustine, *City of God*
	420 Alaric sacks Rome	
	c. 450 Height of the Gupta Empire in India	**c. 450** Kalidasa, *Shakuntala*
500		

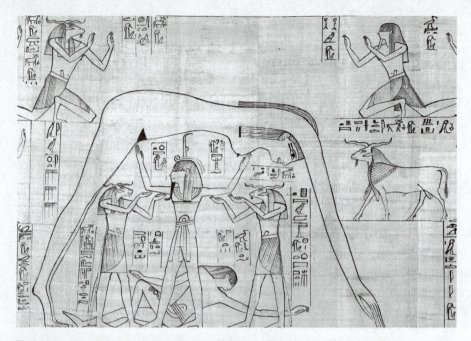

The creation of heaven and earth, Egyptian papyrus from c. 1025 B.C.E. The creator god Shu is shown raising up Nut, goddess of heaven, who arches over the reclining earth god, Geb.

The Ancient Near East

The story of world literature begins with the ancient cultures of Egypt and "the Fertile Crescent," a broad band of settled lands stretching from the Tigris and Euphrates rivers in what is now Iraq, up into Asia Minor and down through Palestine. Across this region a combination of favorable environmental conditions and human ingenuity led to the establishment of the world's first great cities, such as Thebes and Memphis in Egypt, and Ur and Babylon in Mesopotamia. As rulers sought to build empires and merchants created extensive trading networks, they began to develop the written means to communicate over large distances, settle their accounts, and extend their influence.

Near Eastern scribes achieved great authority as highly skilled counselors who could manage large-scale enterprises and conduct diplomacy with distant countries, representing monarchs who themselves were usually illiterate. In Egypt and Babylonia scribes became a sort of civil service elite, closely involved in the country's political and economic life, and scribes were immensely proud of their almost magical ability to write. As an Egyptian teacher exhorted students in a schoolbook known today as Papyrus Lansing: "Befriend the scroll, the palette. It pleases more than wine. . . . It is worth more than an inheritance in Egypt, than a tomb in the west." The writer goes on to extol the scribe's life as far better than harder kinds of work:

> Your boat is on the river; you are supplied with attendants. You stride about inspecting. A mansion is built in your town. . . . Put the writings in your heart, and you will be protected from all kinds of toil. You will become a worthy official. Do you not recall the fate of the unskilled man? His name is not known. He is burdened like a donkey in front of the scribe who knows what he is about.

This very writer, though, seems to admit that learning hieroglyphs was hard work itself: "Your heart is denser than an obelisk," he declares to his pupil; "though I beat you with every kind of stick, you do not listen . . . Though I spend the day telling you 'Write,' it seems like a plague to you. Writing"—the teacher sternly concludes—"is very pleasant!"

The first writing systems may have been pleasant to use, but they truly were hard to learn. Sometime around 3200 B.C.E., the Sumerian people of southern Mesopotamia began to inscribe clay tablets with symbolic representations of objects and then of sounds; around the same time or a little later, traders in Egypt developed their own, openly pictorial form of writing. By 3000 B.C.E. the world's first fully developed writing systems had emerged, capable of conveying detailed information and increasingly complex thoughts. The Mesopotamians used an intricate system of cuneiform ("wedge-shaped") signs, with hundreds of complex combinations of marks, each for a different syllable. Once baked or sun-dried, the clay tablets could easily be carried long distances, and to our good fortune they could last for thousands of years when buried in the region's dry, sandy soil.

By 3000 B.C.E. the Egyptians also had a fully developed script, carved on stone or written with a brush on scrolls made from the fiber of the papyrus plant (our

Portrait of Mereruka, Saqqara, Egypt, c. 2290 B.C.E. Mereruka was a scribe who reached the highest ranks in the Egyptian civil service, becoming Pharaoh Teti I's chief justice and vizier, as well as Inspector of Priests and Scribe of the Divine Books—and a son-in-law of the king himself. Mereruka's tomb had no fewer than 32 rooms, with beautifully carved and painted reliefs on the walls showing the deceased and his wife and son inspecting the elaborate preparations of goods and services for their use in the afterlife. The hieroglyphs above Mereruka have been carved as carefully and in as much detail as his own portrait. They serve as integral parts of the design, eternally providing the items they describe and testifying to Mereruka's prominence and to his accomplishments. His status as "royal scribe" is proclaimed in the hieroglyphs in the right-hand row of lettering, which twice shows the scribe's took kit: a pallette with circular depressions to hold black and red ink; a holder for reed pens; and small bag of powdered ink tied between them.

word "paper" comes from "papyrus"). Impressed by the word-pictures they saw delicately carved on temple and tomb walls, later Greek travelers called this writing hieroglyphics ("sacred carving"). Egyptian scribes created hundreds of hieroglyphic images of actual objects, and they found that they could employ these images to form many more words as well, via the "rebus" principle—using an image to signify just the initial sound of its object. Gradually, scribes began to favor a small number of hieroglyphs as the common stand-ins for most sounds (a serpent came to stand for "f," an owl for "m"), with the other hieroglyphs used in a secondary role to designate a specific object or class of objects (any word having to do with days or time would end with a sun disk). Eventually, during the second millennium B.C.E., some traders in Egypt and Palestine began to use a simplified version of the alphabetic symbols and dropped the visual signs altogether: the first phonetic alphabet was created, and soon after 1000 B.C.E. several area languages, including Hebrew, were being written in purely alphabetic scripts. Through traders in Phoenicia an early alphabet spread to Greece and beyond, eventually becoming the alphabet we use today.

LANGUAGES, CITIES, AND EMPIRES

The first writers faced the challenge of recording a complex reality. Mesopotamia was made up of distinct groups of widely different cultures. The earliest cuneiform texts were written by the Sumerians, who appear to have held the upper hand in the area until the rise of King Sargon of the now-lost city of Akkad in northern Babylonia. Around 2300 B.C.E., Sargon gained substantial control over Babylonia's city-states, and the Akkadian language became increasingly prevalent thereafter. Rather like Latin in later Europe, though, Sumerian retained prestige as a language for religious and literary composition long after

The first writers faced the challenge of recording a complex reality.

Akkadian became the language in general daily use. As one student lamented (in Sumerian) in a Babylonian school-text, "The Sumerian monitor said, 'You spoke in Akkadian!' and he beat me. My teacher said, 'Your handwriting is not at all good!' and *he* beat me."

The region's linguistic variety reflects its constantly shifting political and social history, as cities vied with each other and waves of migration occurred. During the second and early first millennia, major empires extended out from Babylon, then from Nineveh—capital of the Babylonians' perennial rivals the Assyrians—and then from Babylon once again. The Hittite Empire in Anatolia (modern Turkey) also reached down into the area, and the Hittites adapted Babylonian cuneiform for their own use, as did early scribes in Persia, whose ruler Cyrus the Great eventually conquered Babylonia in 539 B.C.E.; Greek culture came into the area after Alexander the Great conquered Babylon in 331. Over the centuries Mesopotamia's ethnic composition steadily evolved through the immigration of new groups such as the Aramaeans, whose language of Aramaic is a close cousin of Hebrew and is used at times in the Bible itself. The legendary father of the Hebrew people, Abraham, is identified in Genesis and Deuteronomy as an Aramaean whom God commanded to leave Mesopotamia in order to found a new nation.

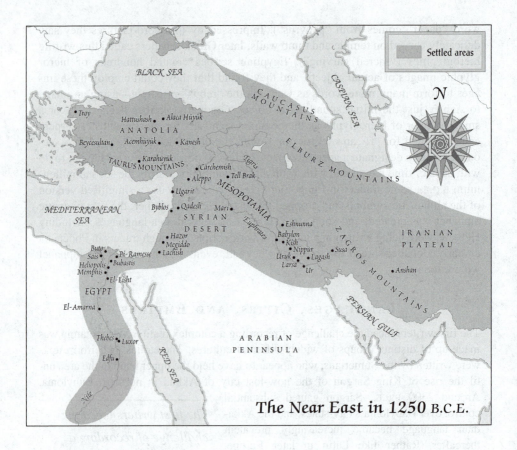

BLACK SEA

CAUCASUS MOUNTAINS

CASPIAN SEA

Troy

Hattushash • • Alaca Hüyük

ANATOLIA

Beycesultan • Acemhüyük • Kanesh

ELBURZ MOUNTAINS

TAURUS MOUNTAINS • Karahüyük

• Carchemish

Tigris

• Aleppo • Tell Brak

MESOPOTAMIA

• Ugarit

MEDITERRANEAN SEA

Byblos • • Qadesh   Mari •

SYRIAN DESERT

Euphrates

• Eshnunna

Babylon

• Hazor

• Kish

• Megiddo

Uruk • • Nippur

Buto • • Lachish

Larsa • • Lagash

Sais • • Pi-Ramesse

• Susa

Heliopolis • • Bubastis

Ur

Memphis •

ZAGROS MOUNTAINS

IRANIAN PLATEAU

• Anshan

• El-Lisht

EGYPT

El-Amarna •

PERSIAN GULF

ARABIAN PENINSULA

Thebes • • Luxor

RED SEA

Edfu •

Nile

Settled areas

N

The Near East in 1250 B.C.E.

South of the other end of the Fertile Crescent, Egypt achieved early unity as a country, supposedly through the efforts of a king named Menes who extended his sway over the previously separate regions of Upper and Lower Egypt in around 3100 B.C.E. Buffered by deserts on three sides and the Mediterranean to the north, Egypt remained a single country with an unbroken history for a remarkable period of more than three thousand years, a record matched only by China anywhere in the world. Egypt had imperial ambitions of its own, and over the centuries its reach waxed and waned up into Palestine and beyond, and southward into the Sudan. Yet for some thirty dynasties Egypt itself remained a highly unified culture, a unique and stable blend of African and eastern Mediterranean strands, and outsiders who settled in Egypt tended rapidly to adopt Egyptian ways rather than altering the culture they found.

For both the Mesopotamians and the Egyptians, the keys to prosperity and life itself were the great rivers that defined their lands: the Tigris and the Euphrates in Mesopotamia, the Nile in Egypt. These rivers provided water in a hot and dry climate. Some eight thousand years ago, farmers began to build canals, enabling them to irrigate large areas around their rivers. Their fields were famously fertile, and this rich agricultural base allowed for the growth and support of cities and for the development of urban culture starting in the fourth millennium B.C.E.

Those who lived in the cities considered them to be the greatest of human achievements, envied by their enemies and beloved of the gods. Their kings lavished wealth on public buildings and on city walls, which often became works of art in themselves, as with the magnificent (and deliberately intimidating) gates of Babylon, a reconstruction of which is shown in Color Plate 2. At the end of the *Epic of Gilgamesh,* the most famous Mesopotamian hero consoles himself in the face of mortality by proudly urging his companion to admire the towering wall he has built around his city of Uruk:

> O Ur-shanabi, climb Uruk's wall and walk back and forth!
> Survey its foundations, examine the brickwork!
> Were its bricks not fired in an oven?
> Did the Seven Sages not lay its foundation?

CITIES AND NOMADS

Magnificent though the great cities were, their very size rendered them vulnerable to environmental disruption and war. A city could be devastated if a flood swept through its baked-clay structures, a recurrent event in southern Mesopotamia that likely underlies the stories of the worldwide Flood described both in the *Epic of Gilgamesh* and in the Book of Genesis. Conversely, prolonged drought or warfare could destroy the vast acreage of surrounding fields whose produce was needed to support a city's population, in an age when long-distance trading was difficult and confined mostly to luxury goods. A city could be abandoned, never to be rebuilt, a fate that eventually overtook all the ancient cities of Mesopotamia. In a Babylonian poem from the eighth century B.C.E., *Erra and Ishum,* Babylon's patron god Marduk laments the destruction of his beloved city and fears that it may never be restored:

A city could be abandoned, never to be rebuilt . . .

> "Alas, Babylon," he cried, "whose head I ripened like a palm tree, now withered
>   by the wind!
> Alas, Babylon, which I filled with seeds like a pine-cone,
>   whose fulness I cannot enjoy!
> Alas, Babylon, which I planted like a lush garden, whose fruits I cannot taste!
> Alas, Babylon, which like a crystal seal I set at the throat of Anu!
> Alas, Babylon, which I held in my hands like the tablet of destiny,
>   and entrusted to no one else!"

Not everyone shared Marduk's civic pride, however. These lines lament the sacking of Babylon by raiding nomads, who were happy to seize the city's treasures but had no wish to stay. In much of the ancient Near East, many people lived by keeping sheep and cattle, often moving from place to place for grazing and water. In particular, there were many seminomadic herdsmen in the region variously called Palestine or Canaan, northeast of Egypt and west of Mesopotamia, where cities were small-scale affairs. The Book of Genesis symbolically records the tension between farmers and herdsmen in the mysterious, fatal struggle of the jealous farmer Cain against his shepherd brother Abel, whose meat offerings God prefers to Cain's produce.

The herdsmen often looked with suspicion upon cities and their dwellers, seeing them as corrupt and dissolute. They viewed the cities' kings as oppressive tyrants, as opposed to the fatherlike leaders of their own clans. Whereas the Babylonians considered their city the cornerstone of civilization and the prime meeting point for gods and mortals—"Babylon" means "Gate of God"—the formerly nomadic Hebrews placed human origins in an unpopulated garden and identified the first city builder as Enoch, son of the murderer Cain (Genesis 4:17). Babylon itself they described as the site of the Tower of Babel, an emblem of human pride, rightly destroyed by God (Genesis 11). A millennium later, clan-based nomadic life remained the setting among the pre-Islamic "brigand poets," and for centuries thereafter, city-based Arab poets would continue to celebrate and romanticize desert life and love.

COURTS AND TEMPLES

Cultural production in the Near East grew up around the dual centers of royal courts and temple priesthoods, which commissioned and created monuments and artworks along with written texts. Royal archives in Mesopotamian cities might contain tens of thousands of tablets, including literature and religious texts along with historical and administrative documents. Near Eastern societies were theocratic in nature: the king was the gods' representative on earth and could even be seen as divine himself. Egyptian pharaohs often went so far as to marry their sisters in order to conserve and strengthen their divine essence. In theory, court and temple were closely intertwined and mutually supportive; in practice, serious tensions could arise between them, if the priests came to feel that the court was falling away from right behavior, or if the king thought that the priests were gathering too much power to themselves (tensions comparable to those between later European popes and kings). In the middle centuries of the first millennium, a series of Hebrew prophets like Hosea and Jeremiah inveighed with particular eloquence against corrupt rulers and backsliding subjects alike.

Apart from such moments of bloody lyricism, the royal annals are often rather dry affairs.

So far as possible, though, Near Eastern monarchs presented themselves as the righteous and invincible servants of their gods, as in the scene carved atop the Law Code of Hammurabi (see illustration, facing page 1), in which the seated sun god bestows authority on the king. Similarly, the Assyrian king Shalmaneser III thanks three different patron gods for a victory in Palestine:

> I fought with them assisted by the mighty power of Nergal, my leader, by the ferocious weapons which Ashur, my lord, has presented to me, and I inflicted a defeat upon them. I slew their warriors with the sword, descending upon them like Adad when he makes a rainstorm pour down. In the moat of the town I piled them up, I covered the wide plain with the corpses of their fighting men, I dyed the mountains with their blood like red wool.

Apart from such moments of bloody lyricism, the royal annals are often rather dry affairs, but they could also include close observation and lively reported speech. Having overpowered a Canaanite chieftain who had conquered part of Egypt, the pharaoh Kamose (or rather his scribe, writing in his voice) doesn't stint himself in describing the climactic confrontation:

> I saw his women upon his roof peering from their loopholes toward the shore, without their bodies stirring when they heard me. They peered out with their noses on their walls like young rodents from inside their holes, while I was saying: "This is the attack! Here am I. I shall succeed. What is left over is in my hand; my lot is fortunate. As the valiant Amon endures, I will not leave you, I will not let you set foot in the fields unless I am upon you! So your wish has failed, miserable Canaanite!"

If scribes at court devoted themselves to extolling the king and his mighty deeds, different concerns were foremost within the temple precincts. These were often centers of learning, where scribes produced medical and astronomical texts as well as hymns and prayers. Extensive texts were written as early as the third millennium to guide deceased members of the Egyptian royal family safely into immortality among the gods; inscribed on pyramid walls, these have become known as the Pyramid Texts. Other spells were buried with mummified bodies in long scrolls known today as *The Book of the Dead,* one aspect of the enormously complex burial preparations and rituals that accompanied royal funerals—privileges that, as time went on, were extended to a growing number of the Egyptian upper classes.

The Egyptians lavished such attention on their tombs precisely because they loved earthly life so much. They prepared the deceased not for eternal rest but for eternal activity, plentifully supplied with the best in food, drink, furniture, and even board games. Most of the Egyptian stories and poems that we have today were placed in tombs as entertainment in the afterlife. Other peoples, though, were less confident of the pleasures of the next world: Babylonian texts like *The Descent of Ishtar* paint a gloomy picture of the House of Dust, "the house which those who enter cannot leave, / . . . Where dust is their food, clay their bread." References to the Hebrew underworld, Sheol, sound even more minimal, and Hebrew religion had no belief in resurrection after death. If earthly pleasures didn't necessarily carry over into the afterlife, though, the divine world was continually impinging on the human realm. Religion pervaded every aspect of Near Eastern life, most variously among the polytheistic societies, which developed elaborate pantheons of gods and goddesses, each often associated with a particular city, natural force, or animal, and each of whom expected appropriate sacrifices and could be appealed to for different purposes.

These divinities varied in name and number from one place to another, but there are family resemblances among the different Near Eastern pantheons, and between these groups and their Greek and Roman analogs. Typically a primordial generation of universal gods and goddesses was thought to have created the world and to have begotten further generations of divinities now in control of the world, usually with a large number of minor gods and

These divinities varied . . . from one place to another, but there are family resemblances.

goddesses ruled by a few major divinities: a god associated with the sun (called Utu in Sumerian, Shamash in Akkadian, Amon Re or Aten in Egypt, Apollo in Greece), a moon goddess associated with fertility and love (Inanna or Ishtar in Mesopotamia, Isis in Egypt, Aphrodite in Greece, Venus in Rome), and other divinities associated with such elemental forces as thunderstorms (Adad in Mesopotamia, Zeus in Greece) and water (Ea or Enki in Mesopotamia, Poseidon in Greece).

GODS AND GODDESSES, WOMEN AND MEN

Gods and goddesses were frequently paired as consorts in the polytheistic systems. Accounts of the creation of the universe expressed a cosmic interdependence of male and female principles, of a sort that would later be formalized in East Asian theories of the complementarity of yin and yang. Most Near Eastern societies were strongly patriarchal, but rulers were expected to appeal to the female deities upon whom earthly life depended; both in Sumer and in Egypt there were festivals in which the monarch would unite in a temple with a woman representing the country's most important goddess. Human fertility and the growth of crops were under the direct control of these goddesses; Egyptian reliefs often show the earth god, or the pharaoh, reaching up to a heaven represented as the overarching body of the sky goddess Nut, drawing sustenance and strength from her breasts and genitals. (See the illustration on page 10.)

The underworld too was doubly ruled, in Mesopotamia by Nergal and his consort Ereshkigal, precursors of Hades and Persephone in Greek myth. In surviving poems, it is Ereshkigal who is the dominant figure, notably in chilling accounts of the underworld descent of her sister, the goddess of love, who comes to visit her realm with nearly fatal results. As late as New Testament times, the ancient goddesses continued to inspire an intense devotion: in Acts 19, the apostle Paul's preaching is loudly opposed by devotees of "Diana of the Ephesians." In the second century, the north African writer Apuleius ended his comic narrative *The Golden Ass* by having his hero abandon his dissolute ways and join the priesthood of Isis, goddess of the moon and patroness of survival in a time of constant flux.

In the ancient Near East as in medieval and early modern Europe, noble and especially royal women could wield substantial power, though only very rarely ruling outright as Cleopatra did in Egypt in the first century B.C.E. Funerary stelae could record their lives, as with the monument to the mother of king Nabonidus of Babylon in the sixth century, who thanks the gods for allowing her a very long life of 104 years, during which "my eyesight remained good, my hearing was excellent, my hands and feet were sound, my words well chosen, food and drink agreed with me, my health was fine and my mind happy. I saw my great-great-grandchildren, up to the fourth generation, in good health, and had my fill of old age."

In Israel, women were powerful and sometimes dominant figures in clan-based life, and the Hebrew patriarchs are paired with imposing, and often cunning, matriarchs like Sarah, Rebekah, and Rachel. Women of modest circumstance are also represented at times, as in the moving relationship of Ruth and Naomi in the Book of Ruth, or in the Song of Songs and the lyric poetry that has survived from Egypt. In Hebrew wisdom tradition, wisdom itself—a female noun in Hebrew, *hokmah*—came to be personified as a prime agent of God's guiding power. According to the Book of Proverbs, "I, Wisdom, dwell in prudence. . . . By me kings reign, and nobles govern the earth." She prepares a banquet in her house of seven pillars and invites all to join her: "She has sent out her maidens to proclaim from the highest part of the town: 'Come in, you simpletons!' She says also to the fool, 'Come, dine with me and taste the wine that I have spiced. Cease to be foolish, and you will live, you will grow in understanding.'"

WISDOM AND ANTI-WISDOM

The wisdom tradition in which Hokmah came to prominence had ancient roots both in Egypt and Babylon, where proverbial wisdom was often presented in the form of an aging monarch's advice to his heir. At their most ambitious, these collections and related poetic texts sought to probe the mysteries of divine will, seeking the bases of justice in an often unjust world. Under polytheism, divinities were generally beneficent beings, supporting life on earth and human life in particular; when they withheld their favor and drought, disease, or defeat ensued, the problem was usually to be found in human misbehavior, and oracles and diviners would be consulted to determine the cause (as Sophocles later shows Oedipus doing). At the same time, the gods' multiplicity meant that some problems had to be seen as beyond human control altogether: the gods and goddesses often argued, and they might deceive mortals at will. Wisdom texts were intended to help humans navigate the shoals of human and divine relations alike, and writers in temple circles early began to compose poems on the gods' adventures among themselves and their often ambiguous interactions with humanity, usually seeking to justify the ways of the gods to humanity and to set out the principles of conduct that could restore good relations with the gods in troubled times.

Alongside such wisdom literature there could also be found what might be called *anti*-wisdom texts, works that questioned the possibility of true knowledge and even the value of moral behavior. The most famous of these works are the Bible's Book of Job, itself built on earlier Babylonian models, and the book of Ecclesiastes ("Vanity of vanities, says the Preacher . . . all is vanity"), which follows hard upon the confidently orthodox Book of Proverbs. Such concerns could be expressed in the most sacred of settings: a troubled poem has come down to us from Egypt, preserved on the wall of a tomb, where it is said to have been copied from the tomb of a king named Intef. In this song, a harper recalls the names of some famous wisdom writers and questions the value of their work:

> *Alongside such wisdom literature there could also be found. . . anti-*wisdom *texts.*

I have heard the words of Imhotep and Hardedef,
Whose sayings are recited whole.
What of their cult places?
Their walls have crumbled,
Their cult places are gone,
As though they had never been.
. . . .
Make holiday; do not weary of it.
Lo, none is allowed to take his goods with him,
Lo, none who departs comes back again.

Composed as early as 2000 B.C.E., this may be the oldest surviving example of a poem urging the listener to *carpe diem* ("seize the day"), a theme that would become prominent in Roman and later European poetry.

THE BIRTH OF MONOTHEISM

Throughout the Near East, the worship of many gods was often tempered by devotion to a particular god or group of gods. At times a patron deity might claim the almost exclusive attention of a city, tribe, or individual. For a number of years, the pharaoh Akhenaten (reigned c. 1372–1354) tried to enforce upon all Egypt a strong version of focused polytheism. He elevated his patron deity, the sun god Aten, to supreme authority, and radically reduced the privileges of other divinities and the wealth of their priesthoods. This movement, known as the "Amarna revolution" after the place where Akhenaten built a new capital, lasted only a few years, but this period remains famous for the delicate and unusually naturalistic art produced at this time, seen both on surviving buildings and in the magnificent artifacts recovered from the tomb of Akhenaten's young and short-lived successor, Tutankhamen (see Color Plate 1). Tutankhamen (or his counselors) reversed Akhenaten's reforms, and later rulers defaced the statues of Akhenaten and his wife Nefertiti and had their names chiseled off every monument they could find.

The seminomadic tribes of Palestine, however, had never developed the elaborate temple complexes and the multiple cults of their settled neighbors, and among the Hebrew tribes the worship of their patron god Yahweh gradually evolved into the world's first full-fledged monotheism. Passing references in the Psalms and elsewhere in the Bible indicate that Yahweh was originally seen as one god among many; he gradually came to be understood not simply as the Hebrew's patron god but as sole ruler over the whole universe, and rival deities were progressively demoted to the status of minor spirits or outright delusions. Over the course of the late second millennium, the Hebrew tribes achieved dominance over a wide area of Palestine, driving out or subordinating the several other groups in their territories. In 1020 B.C.E. a united nation of Israel was established under a king, Saul, despite opposition from priests who argued that only God should rule over Israel. The small Canaanite city of Jerusalem became a capital of substantial size under Israel's second king, David. His son Solomon built a great temple for Yahweh and a large palace for himself. He made his court into a cosmopolitan meeting-place, and Jerusalem became a crossroads for trade between Egypt, northern Palestine, and Mesopotamia. Solomon cemented relations beyond his borders by marrying many foreign brides—a policy that aroused sharp criticism in temple circles, as his wives often persisted in their devotion to the gods and goddesses of their homelands.

Israel's existence as a unified country was brief. Civil war broke out upon Solomon's death in around 931 B.C.E. and the country split into two, each with its own king: Israel to the north, and Judah (including Jerusalem) to the south. The divided country came under increasing pressure from outside powers, and Israel fell to the Assyrian king Sargon II in

Israel's existence as a unified country was brief.

722 B.C.E. Judah held out against the Assyrians, thanks to a plague that devastated the invading army. Eventually the Assyrian empire itself crumbled, and a renewed Babylonian empire took over its territories and conquered Judah in 586 B.C.E. The Israelite upper classes were deported to exile in Babylon. Seventy years later, the Babylonians were in turn subdued by Cyrus

Spoils from the Temple in Jerusalem. This scene comes from a triumphal arch built in Rome in 81 C.E. by the emperor Titus to commemorate his imperial victories, including his successful campaign to subdue the rebellious Jews in Palestine in 70 C.E., which culminated with the destruction of the Temple of Jerusalem. Roman troops are shown carrying off a large seven-branched menorah that was a central element in the temple's ritual equipment and a symbol for Judaism itself.

the Great of Persia, who allowed the exiles to return and rebuild their temple, but Judah never recovered full independence.

During the prosperous and expansive years of Solomon's reign, writers both at court and at the Temple had begun to compose chronicles and wisdom texts of their own, drawing inspiration from older Canaanite, Babylonian, and Egyptian sources and literary genres. Their work gained in extent and depth during the troubled years of the divided monarchy and the exile in Babylon, as they sought to account for the collapse of the united kingdom and to ascertain God's will for his people: a particularly difficult task, as monotheism denied them the option of blaming rival gods. The Hebrew Bible became an extraordinary compendium of historical writing, law, poetry, and profound reflection on fundamental questions of human existence.

Particularly after the destruction of the Temple and the onset of exile, to a unique extent the Hebrews came to center their culture on this central book or rather collection of books. (Our term "the Bible" comes from its Greek name, *ta biblia:* "the books.") The northern kingdom of Israel was no more, while Judah survived for several tenuous centuries as a semi-independent province of Persia, then Egypt, and then Rome. A series of rebellions against Roman authority led the Romans to destroy the rebuilt Temple in 70 C.E., and soon the Hebrews had lost anything resembling a nation of their own. They began to spread out across the Greek-speaking ("Hellenistic") world and then the Roman Empire, and their scriptures gained a still wider circulation as the young religion of Christianity reframed the Hebrew Bible as the Christian Old Testament. During the last centuries of the first millennium B.C.E. the old Mesopotamian cultures went into steep decline, followed in the Roman period by Egypt as well; their texts were forgotten and their very scripts ceased to be known. For nearly two thousand years, the Bible contained the only ancient Near Eastern literature that anyone could read.

THE REBIRTH OF THE PAST

For many centuries, the later peoples who lived in the Near East took no interest in the remains of the older societies that had preceded them; members of the newly dominant monotheistic religions of Christianity and then Islam disregarded the tombs and temples that were often the chief remaining monuments of a polytheistic past. Many of Egypt's pyramids and temples survived, having been built out in the unpopulated desert, and travelers would speculate on the hieroglyphs' mystical meanings but had no way to decipher them. Mesopotamia's ruined cities disappeared altogether, as baked clay bricks wore away or were reused for new buildings; sheep grazed on the large, flat hills that once were centers of ancient culture.

The situation began to change in the late eighteenth century, when thinkers in Enlightenment Europe began to debate the origins of society and to develop scientific methods to study the past. The discipline of archaeology was born, focused first on the surviving monuments of Greece and Rome. Interest turned eastward in 1798 when Napoleon invaded Egypt with an army of thirty thousand men, intending to wrest it from the Ottoman Empire and gain an advantage over the colonial interests of Great Britain. Along with his soldiers, he also brought a team of 167 scientists and scholars, who were charged with surveying Egypt's geography and its monuments. Napoleon's stay in Egypt was brief and bloody; within three years the French had been driven out of Egypt, with most of Napoleon's men having died in battle or from disease. His scholars, however, had made detailed studies of Egypt's antiquities, and a lavishly illustrated account by Baron Dominique Vivant Denon became a European best-seller and aroused great public interest.

Most significantly of all, one of Napoleon's soldiers uncovered the Rosetta Stone, a large slab of black basalt inscribed with texts commemorating the accession to the throne of Ptolemy V at the end of the second century B.C.E. The message was given in three versions: formal hieroglyphics, a cursive form of late Egyptian known as demotic, and Greek. Over the course of the following years, a young French scholar named Jean-François Champollion succeeded in using the Greek text to decipher the hieroglyphs, starting from the observation that royal names were enclosed in distinctive borders (cartouches). He could then analyze the Egyptian renderings of names whose pronunciation he knew from Greek. He gradually discovered the hieroglyphics' mixed phonetic and visual nature and established many of their sound values. From this basis he and others managed to decode the language itself, and by the middle of the nineteenth century it was once again possible to read Egyptian.

Champollion's exploits had inspired others to think about Mesopotamia as well, though little remained to see above ground. In the 1840s, however, an adventurous young Englishman named Austen Henry Layard fell under the spell of the mysterious mounds of Assyria and Babylonia. As he later wrote, a traveler viewing such a mound

> is now at a loss to give any form to the ruin before him. . . . the more he conjectures, the more vague the results appear. The scene around is worthy of the ruin he is contemplating; desolation meets desolation; a feeling of awe succeeds to wonder; for there is nothing to relieve the mind, to lead to hope, or to tell of what has gone by.

Spurred on rather than discouraged by this challenge, Layard managed to get a little funding from the British ambassador to Constantinople. He began to dig in a great mound outside the town of Mosul, some two hundred miles north of Baghdad. Within a day, he had discovered the palace of Sargon II of Assyria, complete with huge winged bulls that became a centerpiece of the British Museum's collection. A few years later, his Iraqi friend and associate Hormuzd Rassam discovered the royal library of Ashurbanipal, with over twenty thousand tablets, including what would prove to be the *Epic of Gilgamesh.* By then, a British army major named Henry Rawlinson had followed Champollion's lead and sought out a trilingual cuneiform inscription carved high on a cliff in western Persia. Perched upon a ladder on an eighteen-inch-wide ledge two hundred feet above the valley floor, Rawlinson painstakingly copied the inscription, and he and several other amateur linguists gradually managed to decipher the script and the principal languages that used it. Archaeologists working in Palestine similarly began to uncover the remains of Canaanite peoples of biblical times, and textual scholars undertook a kind of archaeology of the Bible itself, teasing out the several layers of composition that produced the received version of the Bible. An entire world could once again be seen and its literature read.

An entire world could once again be seen and its literature read.

The texts in this section are the result of a long-distance collaboration between their ancient creators and their modern discoverers. The very name we commonly use for the place of origin of these works—"the Near East"—reflects the European perspective of the nineteenth-century archaeologists who sought out and deciphered these materials. The original authors, of course, didn't think of themselves as living in the East at all, whether "near" or otherwise: the residents of great cities like Babylon and Thebes felt that they lived in the center of the world. The recovery of their large and varied world is one of the great intellectual achievements of the modern era, and it has given us new understandings of the biblical texts and a wealth of remarkable literature from the great ancient cultures at both ends of the Fertile Crescent.

PRONUNCIATIONS:

Akhenaten: akh-en-AH-ten
Euphrates: you-PHRAY-teas
Hammurabi: hahm-uhr-AH-bee
Mesopotamia: mess-oh-po-TAY-me-ah
Nefertiti: NEF-fer-TEE-tee
Shalmaneser: shahl-mahn-AY-zer
Tigris: TYE-gris
Tutankhamen: TOOT-ankh-AH-mun

━━◄═◊═►━━

A Babylonian Theogony

c. 2nd to 1st millennia B.C.E.

A "theogony" is a tale of the birth of the gods. In full versions, theogonies typically begin with a primordial god or pair of gods who then produce several younger generations, with the tale ending with the creation of humanity. Often, as here, such an account would be told from the perspective of a particular city, in this case a Mesopotamian city called "Dunnu of the twin towers." Its location is now unknown, and it doesn't seem to have ever been a prominent place, yet this poem proudly asserts that the very first gods built this city and served as its lords.

This text's ending is missing, and many lines are incomplete; brackets indicate gaps in the Babylonian tablet on which it was recorded in the middle of the first millennium B.C.E. The tablet includes a note saying that it was copied from an earlier copy in the city of Assur. The language of the text suggests that it was composed several centuries before Assur was destroyed in 614 B.C.E.; presumably the outlines of the story itself are far older. Our text describes with unembarrassed directness the process of incest and murder by which each generation of gods was first created and then supplanted by the next generation—themes that would be developed. There is still a lot of detail on Hesiod and this theme in the introduction to classical Greece (pages 185–197).

PRONUNCIATIONS:
Amakandu: ah-mah-KAHN-dou
Ga'um: gah-OOM
Ḫain: khayn
Ningeshtinna: neen-GESH-tee-nah

A Babylonian Theogony[1]

[..] in the beginning [. . .]
[..].. and . [. . .] . . . . [. . .]
They . . . [..] and .[..]. their plough
[With the] stroke of their plough they brought Sea into being.
5   [Second]ly, by themselves they bore Amakandu;[2]
[Third]ly, they built the city of Dunnu, the twin towers.
Ḫain dedicated the overlordship in the city of Dunnu to himself.
[Earth] cast her eyes on Amakandu, her son,
"Come, let me make love to you," she said to him.
10   Amakandu married Earth, his mother, and
Ḫain, his [father], he killed, and
Laid [him] to rest in the city of Dunnu, which he loved.
Then Amakandu took the overlordship of his father, [and]
Married Sea, his sister [. . .]
15   Laḫar,[3] son of Amakandu, went [and]
Killed Amakandu, and in the city of Dunnu
He laid [him] to rest in the [. . .] of his father.
He married Sea, his mother.
Then Sea murdered Earth, her mother.
20   In the month Chislev on the 16th day he took the overlordship and kingship.

[. . .], son of Laḫar, married River, his own sister, and
He killed [Laḫar], his father, and Sea, his mother, and
Laid them to rest [in . . . .]
[In the month . . .] on the first day [he] took the kingship and overlordship
    for himself.

1. Translated by W. G. Lambert.   3. God of cattle.
2. God of wild animals.

25 [. . . , son of . . .] married Ga'um, his sister
  [. . .] earth . . . [. . .]
  [. . .] . . . . [. . .]
  [. . .] . . fathers and .[. . .]
  [. . .] . . [. .]. for the . . . of the gods .[. . .]
30 [. . .] he killed River, his mother, [and]
  [. . .] he settled them.
  [In the month . . . on the _th day] he [took] the overlordship and kingship
   for himself.

  [. . . , son of . .] . , married Ningeshtinna, his sister, [and]
  Killed [. . . , his father, and] Ga'um, his mother.
35   [. . .] he settled them.
  [In the month . . .] on the 16th day, he took the kingship and overlordship.

━━ ⊯◆⊠ ━━

The Memphite Theology
c. 2500 B.C.E.

This vivid text was originally composed in Egypt in the early period known as the Old Kingdom. As the text tells us, a later king, Shabaka (c. 710 B.C.E.) found it worm-eaten and had it
engraved on granite to preserve it permanently. His efforts largely succeeded, though at some
point the stone slab was reused as a millstone and a hole was bored through its center, destroying the middle part of the text. In the well-preserved portions, given here, the earth god Geb is
having to decide on the rulership of Egypt after the death by drowning of his son Osiris. At
first, Geb divides the country between Osiris's two sons, the sky-god Horus and his younger
brother and rival, Seth. (Seth is often described as having actually killed his father, though
nothing is said about this here.) Geb then thinks better of this division, and awards the entire
country to Horus, who henceforth rules the distinct but united regions of Upper and Lower
Egypt—just as the pharaohs would do in historical times.

  Like the "Babylonian Theogony," this text centers on a particular city, here the Egyptian
capital of Memphis. It identifies Horus with a local earth god, Ta-tenen, and in turn identifies
both Horus and Ta-tenen with the creator-god Ptah, patron god of Memphis. Ptah is then identified with the sun god Atum. The whole council of nine great gods (the "Ennead") is represented as the mouth of Ptah/Atum, and they voice Ptah's will. This text shows Egyptian theology at its most exuberant; gods mingle and merge, at times seeming to create the very gods
who then create them in turn. As shifting and at times contentious as this situation is, it is ultimately under the control of Ptah in Memphis. Ptah's creative power is seen here as essentially
verbal in nature; like the God of Israel, he creates and establishes order by speaking his will.

from The Memphite Theology[1]

The living Horus: Who prospers the Two Lands; the Two Ladies: Who prospers the
Two Lands; the Golden Horus: Who prospers the Two Lands; the King of Upper and
Lower Egypt: Neferkare; the Son of Re: Sha[baka], beloved of Ptah-South-of-his-
Wall, who lives like Re forever.

  This writing was copied out anew by his majesty in the House of his father Ptah-
South-of-his-Wall, for his majesty found it to be a work of the ancestors which was

1. Translated by Miriam Lichtheim.

worm-eaten, so that it could not be understood from beginning to end. His majesty copied it anew so that it became better than it had been before, in order that his name might endure and his monument last in the House of his father Ptah-South-of-his-Wall throughout eternity, as a work done by the Son of Re [Shabaka] for his father Ptah-Ta-tenen, so that he might live forever.

[. . . King of Upper and Lower Egypt] is this Ptah, who is called by the great name: [Ta-te]nen [South-of-his-Wall, Lord of eternity. the joiner] of Upper and Lower Egypt is he, this uniter who arose as king of Upper Egypt and arose as king of Lower Egypt. [. . . . . .] "self-begotten," so says Atum: "who created the Nine Gods."

[HORUS AND PTAH ARE ONE]

[Geb, lord of the gods, commanded] that the Nine Gods gather to him. He judged between Horus and Seth; he ended their quarrel. He made Seth king of Upper Egypt in the land of Upper Egypt, up to the place in which he was born, which is Su. And Geb made Horus king of Lower Egypt in the land of Lower Egypt, up to the place in which his father was drowned, which is "Division-of-the-Two-Lands." Thus Horus stood over one region, and Seth stood over one region. They made peace over the Two Lands at Ayan. That was the division of the Two Lands.

Geb's words to Seth: "Go to the place in which you were born." Seth: Upper Egypt. Geb's words to Horus: "Go to the place in which your father was drowned." Horus: Lower Egypt. Geb's words to Horus and Seth: "I have separated you."—Lower and Upper Egypt.

Then it seemed wrong to Geb that the portion of Horus was like the portion of Seth. So Geb gave to Horus his inheritance, for he is the son of his firstborn son.

Geb's words to the Nine Gods: "I have appointed Horus, the firstborn." Geb's words to the Nine Gods: "Him alone, Horus, the heir." Geb's words to the Nine Gods: "To this heir, Horus, my inheritance." Geb's words to the Nine Gods: "To the son of my son, Horus, the Jackal of Upper Egypt—." Geb's words to the Nine Gods: "The firstborn, Horus, the Opener-of-the-ways." Geb's words to the Nine Gods: "The son who was born—Horus, on the Birthday of the Opener-of-the-ways."

Then Horus stood over the land. He is the uniter of this land, proclaimed in the great name: Ta-tenen, South-of-his-Wall, Lord of Eternity. Then sprouted the two Great Magicians upon his head. He is Horus who arose as king of Upper and Lower Egypt, who united the Two Lands in the Nome[2] of the Wall, the place in which the Two Lands were united.

Reed and papyrus were placed on the double door of the House of Ptah. That means Horus and Seth, pacified and united. They fraternized so as to cease quarreling in whatever place they might be, being united in the House of Ptah, the "Balance of the Two Lands" in which Upper and Lower Egypt had been weighed. * * *

Heart took shape in the form of Atum, Tongue took shape in the form of Atum. It is Ptah, the very great, who has given life to all the gods and their *ka*s[3] through this heart and through this tongue, from which Horus had come forth as Ptah, from which Thoth had come forth as Ptah.

Thus heart and tongue rule over all the limbs in accordance with the teaching that he, Ptah, is in every body and he, Ptah, is in every mouth of all gods, all men, all cattle, all creeping things, whatever lives, thinking whatever he wishes and commanding whatever he wishes.

---

2. Province. Memphis was known as "The White Wall."   3. The *ka* was a person's vital force.

His Ennead is before him as teeth and lips. They are the semen and the hands of Atum. For the Ennead of Atum came into being through his semen and his fingers. But the Ennead is the teeth and lips in this mouth which pronounced the name of every thing, from which Shu and Tefnut[4] came forth, and which gave birth to the Ennead.

Sight, hearing, breathing—they report to the heart, and it makes every understanding come forth. As to the tongue, it repeats what the heart has devised. Thus all the gods were born and his Ennead was completed. For every word of the god came about through what the heart devised and the tongue commanded.

Thus all the faculties were made and all the qualities determined, they that make all foods and all provisions, through this word. Thus justice is done to him who does what is loved, and punishment to him who does what is hated. Thus life is given to the peaceful, death is given to the criminal. Thus all labor, all crafts are made, the action of the hands, the motion of the legs, the movements of all the limbs, according to this command which is devised by the heart and comes forth on the tongue and creates the performance of every thing.

Thus it is said of Ptah: "He who made all and created the gods." And he is Ta-tenen, who gave birth to the gods, and from whom every thing came forth, foods, provisions, divine offerings, all good things. Thus it is recognized and understood that he is the mightiest of the gods. Thus Ptah was satisfied after he had made all things and all divine words.

> He gave birth to the gods,
> He made the towns,
> He established the nomes,
> He placed the gods in their shrines,
> He settled their offerings,
> He established their shrines,
> He made their bodies according to their wishes.
> Thus the gods entered into their bodies,
> Of every wood, every stone, every clay,
> Every thing that grows upon him
> In which they came to be.
> Thus were gathered to him all the gods and their *kas*,
> Content, united with the Lord of the Two Lands.

[MEMPHIS THE ROYAL CITY]

The Great Throne that gives joy to the heart of the gods in the House of Ptah is the granary of Ta-tenen, the mistress of all life, through which the sustenance of the Two Lands is provided, owing to the fact that Osiris was drowned in his water. Isis and Nephthys[5] looked out, beheld him, and attended to him. Horus quickly commanded Isis and Nephthys to grasp Osiris and prevent his drowning. They heeded in time and brought him to land. He entered the hidden portals in the glory of the lords of eternity, in the steps of him who rises in the horizon, on the ways of Re at the Great Throne. He entered the palace and joined the gods of Ta-tenen Ptah, lord of years.

Thus Osiris came into the earth at the Royal Fortress, to the north of the land to which he had come. His son Horus arose as king of Upper Egypt, arose as king of Lower Egypt, in the embrace of his father Osiris and of the gods in front of him and behind him.

---

4. Shu was the god of air; Tefnut was the daughter and "eye" of the sun god Re.

5. Isis, goddess of fertility, was Osiris's wife; Nephthys was her sister.

Genesis 1–11

1st millennium B.C.E.

The first eleven chapters of the Book of Genesis form a prologue for the entire Torah, the five books of Moses that begin the Hebrew Bible. In setting the stage for the national history that begins with Abraham in Genesis 12, the authors of Genesis reached back to old traditions of creation and of a primeval flood that was believed to have extinguished the ancient earthly order, after which modern societies began to be established. The biblical authors knew older versions of such stories, such as those found in the Babylonian *Enuma Elish* and the *Epic of Gilgamesh,* yet they wished to tell the stories differently. First and most importantly, the older accounts had assumed a polytheistic universe, in which humanity was created to serve an entire pantheon of gods, whose disputes could be seen as causing earthly disruptions. Second, the older stories typically stemmed from long-settled civilizations based around great cities—a social order foreign to the nomadic Hebrews, who remained deeply suspicious of city culture and of elaborate social hierarchies even after they had begun to form a united kingdom of Israel, centered on their capital city of Jerusalem.

In comparison to works like *Enuma Elish,* Genesis 1–11 is notable for the absence of war in heaven, or even any multiplicity of divine beings: Genesis 1 goes so far as to give no name at all to the sun and moon—major divinities in earlier systems—simply calling them "the great light" and "the small light." Similarly, the ocean goddess Tiamat is demoted to an impersonal watery abyss, her name made into a common noun, *tehom* in Hebrew. At the same time, the absence of rival divinities like Tiamat posed a challenge for the biblical writers: with the entire universe firmly ruled by a single and just God, how could evil ever have come into the world? The story of the Garden of Eden—one of the most resonant stories in the history of Judeo-Christian culture—explores this problem in an enigmatic tale of prohibition, confusion, and disobedience, with the human actors manipulated by a serpent who is "cunning" rather than evil. Going on to the Flood story, the biblical writers saw human wickedness as the cause of this natural disaster, in contrast to the older Babylonian account, in which the gods had simply gotten tired of the noise made by the growing earthly population. Noah himself, like the patriarchs and matriarchs of later Hebrew history, becomes a complex figure who fails to fully maintain his covenant with God. The primeval history concludes with the building of the Tower of Babel—not as the triumphal inauguration of human culture, as with the construction of Babylon in *Enuma Elish,* but as an impious act of defiance to God.

Most biblical scholars consider that this sequence of stories is the product of several stages of development, reflecting successive reworkings of the old stories. The initial account, known as the Yahwistic version (from God's name *Yahweh*), was probably written down around the time of King Solomon in the early tenth century B.C.E. This version was evidently revised by later writers, most notably a writer or group of writers whom modern scholars have named the Priestly source; Genesis 1 is a product of this source, which emphasizes God's serene ordering power. Genesis 2 then picks up the older Yahwistic creation account, portraying a more mysterious and tentative relationship between God and his creation.

The stories of Genesis are distinctive in form as well as in content. The older Babylonian epics are all written in verse, reflecting long histories of literacy and poetic development; Genesis is in prose, reflecting years of oral storytelling in tents and around campfires. Robert Alter's lively translation beautifully captures the oral immediacy of the biblical creation story.

from **Genesis 1–11**

Chapter 1

When God began to create heaven and earth, and the earth then was welter and waste and darkness over the deep and God's breath hovering over the waters, God said, "Let there be light." And there was light. And God saw the light, that it was good, and God divided the light from the darkness. And God called the light Day, and the darkness He called Night. And it was evening and it was morning, first day. And God said, "Let there be a vault in the midst of the waters, and let it divide water from water." And God made the vault and it divided the water beneath the vault from the water above the vault, and so it was. And God called the vault Heavens, and it was evening and it was morning, second day. And God said, "Let the waters under the heavens be gathered in one place so that the dry land will appear," and so it was. And God called the dry land Earth and the gathering of waters He called Seas, and God saw that it was good. And God said, "Let the earth grow grass, plants yielding seed of each kind and trees bearing fruit of each kind, that has its seed within it." And so it was. And the earth put forth grass, plants yielding seed of each kind, and trees bearing fruit that has its seed within it of each kind, and God saw that it was good. And it was evening and it was morning, third day. And God said, "Let there be lights in the vault of the heavens to divide the day from the night, and they shall be signs for the fixed times and for days and years, and they shall be lights in the vault of the heavens to light up the earth." And so it was. And God made the two great lights, the great light for dominion of day and the small light for dominion of night, and the stars. And God placed them in the vault of the heavens to light up the earth and to have dominion over day and night and to divide the light from the darkness. And God saw that it was good. And it was evening and it was morning, fourth day. And God said, "Let the waters swarm with the swarm of living creatures and let fowl fly over the earth across the vault of the heavens." And God created the great sea monsters and every living creature that crawls, which the water had swarmed forth of each kind, and the winged fowl of each kind, and God saw that it was good. And God blessed them, saying, "Be fruitful and multiply and fill the water in the seas and let the fowl multiply in the earth." And it was evening and it was morning, fifth day. And God said, "Let the earth bring forth living creatures of each kind, cattle and crawling things and wild beasts of each kind." And so it was. And God made wild beasts of each kind and cattle of every kind and crawling things on the ground of each kind, and God saw that it was good.

And God said, "Let us make a human in our image, by our likeness, to hold sway over the fish of the sea and the fowl of the heavens and the cattle and the wild beasts and all the crawling things that crawl upon the earth.

> And God created the human in his image,
> in the image of God He created him,
> male and female He created them.

And God blessed them, and God said to them, "Be fruitful and multiply and fill the earth and conquer it, and hold sway over the fish of the sea and the fowl of the heavens and every beast that crawls upon the earth." And God said, "Look, I have given you every seed-bearing plant on the face of all the earth and every tree that has fruit bearing seed, yours they will be for food. And to all the beasts of the earth and to all the fowl of the heavens and to all that crawls on the earth, which has the breath of life within it, the green plants for food." And so it was. And God saw all that He had done, and, look, it was very good. And it was evening and it was morning, the sixth day.

Chapter 2

Then the heavens and the earth were completed, and all their array. And God completed on the seventh day the work He had done, and He ceased on the seventh day from all the work He had done. And God blessed the seventh day and hallowed it, for on it He had ceased from all His work that He had done. This is the tale of the heavens and the earth when they were created.

On the day the Lord God made earth and heavens, no shrub of the field being yet on the earth and no plant of the field yet sprouted, for the Lord God had not caused rain to fall on the earth and there was no human to till the soil, and wetness would well from the earth to water all the surface of the soil, then the Lord God fashioned the human, humus from the soil,[1] and blew into his nostrils the breath of life, and the human became a living creature. And the Lord God planted a garden in Eden, to the east, and He placed there the human He had fashioned. And the Lord God caused to sprout from the soil every tree lovely to look at and good for food, and the tree of life was in the midst of the garden, and the tree of knowledge, good and evil. Now a river runs out of Eden to water the garden and from there splits off into four streams. The name of the first is Pishon, the one that winds through the whole land of Havilah, where there is gold. And the gold of that land is goodly, bdellium is there, and lapis lazuli. And the name of the second river is Gihon, the one that winds through all the land of Cush. And the name of the third river is Tigris, the one that goes to the east of Ashur. And the fourth river is Euphrates.[2] And the Lord God took the human and set him down in the garden of Eden to till it and watch it. And the Lord God commanded the human, saying, "From every fruit of the garden you may surely eat. But from the tree of knowledge, good and evil, you shall not eat, for on the day you eat from it, you are doomed to die."

And the Lord God said, "It is not good for the human to be alone, I shall make him a sustainer beside him." And the Lord God fashioned from the soil each beast of the field and each fowl of the heavens and brought each to the human to see what he would call it, and whatever the human called a living creature, that was its name. And the human called names to all the cattle and to the fowl of the heavens and to all the beasts of the field, but for the human no sustainer beside him was found. And the Lord God cast a deep slumber on the human, and he slept, and He took one of his ribs and closed over the flesh where it had been, and the Lord God built the rib He had taken from the human into a woman and He brought her to the human. And the human said:

> This one at last, bone of my bones
> and flesh of my flesh,
> This one shall be called Woman,
> for from man was this one taken.[3]

---

1. The punning "human/humus" reflects the play in Hebrew between *adam*, "person," and *adamah*, "earth."

2. These rivers place Eden in southern Mesopotamia.

3. In Hebrew, "man" is *ish*, "woman" is *ishshah*.

Therefore does a man leave his father and his mother and cling to his wife and they become one flesh. And the two of them were naked, the human and his woman, and they were not ashamed.

Chapter 3

Now the serpent was most cunning of all the beasts of the field that the LORD God had made. And he said to the woman, "Though God said, you shall not eat from any tree of the garden—" And the woman said to the serpent, "From the fruit of the garden's trees we may eat, but from the fruit of the tree in the midst of the garden God has said, 'You shall not eat from it and you shall not touch it, lest you die.' " And the serpent said to the woman, "You shall not be doomed to die. For God knows that on the day you eat of it your eyes will be opened and you will become as gods knowing good and evil." And the woman saw that the tree was good for eating and that it was lust to the eyes and the tree was lovely to look at, and she took of its fruit and ate, and she also gave to her man, and he ate. And the eyes of the two were opened, and they knew they were naked, and they sewed fig leaves and made themselves loincloths.

And they heard the sound of the LORD God walking about in the garden in the evening breeze, and the human and his woman hid from the LORD God in the midst of the trees of the garden. And the LORD God called to the human and said to him, "Where are you?" And he said, "I heard your sound in the garden and I was afraid, for I was naked, and I hid." And He said, "Who told you that you were naked? From the tree I commanded you not to eat have you eaten?" And the human said, "The woman whom you gave by me, she gave me from the tree, and I ate." And the LORD God said to the woman, "What is this you have done?" And the woman said, "The serpent beguiled me and I ate." And the LORD God said to the serpent, "Because you have done this,

> Cursed be you
> of all cattle and all beasts of the field.
> On your belly shall you go
> and dust shall you eat all the days of your life.
> Enmity will I set between you and the woman,
> between your seed and hers.
> He will boot your head
> and you will bite his heel."

To the woman He said,

> "I will terribly sharpen your birth pangs,
> in pain shall you bear children.
> And for your man shall be your longing,
> and he shall rule over you."

And to the human he said, "Because you listened to the voice of your wife and ate from the tree that I commanded you, 'You shall not eat from it,'

> Cursed be the soil for your sake,
> with pangs shall you eat from it all the days of your life.
> Thorn and thistle shall it sprout for you
> and you shall eat the plants of the field.
> By the sweat of your brow shall you eat bread

> till you return to the soil,
> for from there were you taken,
> for dust you are
> and to dust shall you return."

And the human called his woman's name Eve, for she was the mother of all that lives.[4] And the LORD God made skin coats for the human and his woman, and He clothed them. And the LORD God said, "Now that the human has become like one of us, knowing good and evil, he may reach out and take as well from the tree of life and live forever." And the LORD God sent him from the garden of Eden to till the soil from which he had been taken. And he drove out the human and set up east of the garden of Eden the cherubim and the flame of the whirling sword to guard the way to the tree of life.

Chapter 4

And the human knew Eve his woman and she conceived and bore Cain, and she said, "I have got me a man with the LORD." And she bore as well his brother, Abel, and Abel became a herder of sheep while Cain was a tiller of the soil. And it happened in the course of time that Cain brought from the fruit of the soil an offering to the LORD. And Abel too had brought from the choice firstlings of his flock, and the LORD regarded Abel and his offering but He did not regard Cain and his offering, and Cain was very incensed, and his face fell. And the LORD said to Cain.

> "Why are you incensed,
> and why is your face fallen?
> For whether you offer well,
> or whether you do not,
> at the tent flap sin crouches
> and for you is its longing
> but you will rule over it."

And Cain said to Abel his brother, "Let us go out to the field." And when they were in the field, Cain rose against Abel his brother and killed him. And the LORD said to Cain, "Where is Abel your brother?" And he said, "I do not know. Am I my brother's keeper?" And He said, "What have you done? Listen! your brother's blood cries out to me from the soil. And so, cursed shall you be by the soil that gaped with its mouth to take your brother's blood from your hand. If you till the soil, it will no longer give you its strength. A restless wanderer shall you be on the earth." And Cain said to the LORD, "My punishment is too great to bear. Now that You have driven me this day from the soil and I must hide from Your presence, I shall be a restless wanderer on the earth and whoever finds me will kill me." And the LORD said to him, "Therefore whoever kills Cain shall suffer sevenfold vengeance." And the LORD set a mark upon Cain so that whoever found him would not slay him.

And Cain went out from the LORD's presence and dwelled in the land of Nod[5] east of Eden. And Cain knew his wife and she conceived and bore Enoch. Then he became the builder of a city and called the name of the city, like his son's name, Enoch. And Irad was born to Enoch, and Irad begot Mehujael and Muhujael begot Methusael

---

4. "Eve" means "living."　　　　　5. "Wandering."

and Methusael begot Lamech. And Lamech took him two wives, the name of the one was Adah and the name of the other was Zillah. And Adah bore Jabal: he was the first of tent dwellers with livestock. And his brother's name was Jubal: he was the first of all who play on the lyre and pipe. As for Zillah, she bore Tubal-cain, who forged every tool of copper and iron. And the sister of Tubal-cain was Naamah. And Lamech said to his wives,

> "Adah and Zillah, O hearken my voice,
> You wives of Lamech, give ear to my speech.
> For a man have I slain for my wound,
> a boy for my bruising.
> For sevenfold Cain is avenged,
> and Lamech seventy and seven."

And Adam again knew his wife and she bore a son and called his name Seth,[6] as to say, "God has granted me other seed in place of Abel, for Cain has killed him." As for Seth, to him, too, a son was born, and he called his name Enosh. It was then that the name of the LORD was first invoked.

Chapter 5[7]

This is the book of the lineage of Adam: On the day God created the human, in the image of God He created him. Male and female He created them, and He blessed them and called their name humankind on the day they were created. And Adam lived a hundred and thirty years and he begot in his likeness by his image and called his name Seth. And the days of Adam after he begot Seth were eight hundred years, and he begot sons and daughters. And all the days Adam lived were nine hundred and thirty years. Then he died. And Seth lived a hundred and five years and he begot Enosh. And Seth lived after he begot Enosh eight hundred and seven years. Then he died. And all the days of Seth were nine hundred and twelve years. Then he died. And Enosh lived ninety years and he begot Kenan. And Enosh lived after he begot Kenan eight hundred and fifteen years, and he begot sons and daughters. And all the days of Enosh were nine hundred and five years. Then he died. And Kenan lived seventy years and he begot Mahalalel. And Kenan lived after he begot Mahalalel eight hundred and forty years, and he begot sons and daughters. And all the days of Kenan were nine hundred and ten years. Then he died. And Mahalalel lived sixty-five years and he begot Jared. And Mahalalel lived after he begot Jared eight hundred and thirty years, and he begot sons and daughters. And all the days of Mahalalel were eight hundred and ninety-five years. Then he died. And Jared lived a hundred and sixty-two years and he begot Enoch. And Jared lived after he begot Enoch eight hundred years, and he begot sons and daughters. And all the days of Jared were nine hundred and sixty-two years. Then he died. And Enoch lived sixty-five years and he begot Methuselah. And Enoch walked with God after he begot Methuselah three hundred years, and he begot sons and daughters. And all the days of Enoch were three hundred and sixty-five years. And Enoch walked with God and he was no more, for God took him. And Methuselah lived a hundred and eighty-seven years and he begot Lamech. And Methuselah lived after he begot Lamech seven hundred and eighty-two years,

---

6. "Granted."

7. This chapter gives a lineage of ten generations, linking Adam to Noah at the close of the primeval period.

and he begot sons and daughters. And all the days of Methuselah were nine hundred and sixty-nine years. Then he died. And Lamech lived a hundred and eighty-two years and he begot a son. And he called his name Noah,[8] as to say, "This one will console us for the pain of our hands' work from the soil which the LORD cursed." And Lamech lived after he begot Noah five hundred and ninety-five years, and he begot sons and daughters. And all the days of Lamech were seven hundred and seventy-seven years. Then he died. And Noah was five hundred years old and he begot Shem, Ham, and Japheth.

Chapter 6

And it happened as humankind began to multiply over the earth and daughters were born to them, that the sons of God saw that the daughters of man were comely, and they took themselves wives howsoever they chose. And the LORD said, "My breath shall not abide in the human forever, for he is but flesh. Let his days be a hundred and twenty years."

The Nephilim[9] were then on the earth, and afterward as well, the sons of God having come to bed with the daughters of man who bore them children: they are the heroes of yore, the men of renown.

And the LORD saw that the evil of the human creature was great on the earth and that every scheme of his heart's devising was only perpetually evil. And the LORD regretted having made the human on earth and was grieved to the heart. And the LORD said, "I will wipe out the human race I created from the face of the earth, from human to cattle to crawling thing to the fowl of the heavens, for I regret that I have made them." But Noah found favor in the eyes of the LORD. This is the lineage of Noah—Noah was a righteous man, he was blameless in his time, Noah walked with God—and Noah begot three sons, Shem and Ham and Japheth. And the earth was corrupt before God and the earth was filled with outrage. And God saw the earth and, look, it was corrupt, for all flesh had corrupted its ways on the earth. And God said to Noah, "The end of all flesh is come before me, for the earth is filled with outrage by them, and I am now about to destroy them, with the earth. Make yourself an ark of cypress wood, with cells you shall make the ark, and caulk it inside and out with pitch. This is how you shall make it: three hundred cubits, the ark's length; fifty cubits, its width; thirty cubits, its height.[1] Make a skylight in the ark, within a cubit of the top you shall finish it, and put an entrance in the ark on one side. With lower and middle and upper decks you shall make it. As for me, I am about to bring the Flood, water upon the earth, to destroy all flesh that has within it the breath of life from under the heavens, everything on the earth shall perish. And I will set up my covenant with you, and you shall enter the ark, you and your sons and your wife and the wives of your sons, with you. And from all that lives, from all flesh, two of each thing you shall bring to the ark to keep alive with you, male and female they shall be. From the fowl of each kind and from the cattle of each kind and from all that crawls on the earth of each kind, two of each thing shall come to you to be kept alive. As for you, take you from every food that is eaten and store it by you, to serve for you and for them as food." And this Noah did; as all that God commanded him, so he did.

---

8. "Comfort, rest."
9. Giants.

1. A cubit was about 18 inches.

Chapter 7

And the LORD said to Noah, "Come into the ark, you and all your household, for it is you I have seen righteous before me in this generation. Of every clean animal take you seven pairs, each with its mate, and of every animal that is not clean, one pair, each with its mate. Of the fowl of the heavens as well seven pairs, male and female, to keep seed alive over all the earth. For in seven days' time I will make it rain on the earth forty days and forty nights and I will wipe out from the face of the earth all existing things that I have made." And Noah did all that the LORD commanded him.

Noah was six hundred years old when the Flood came, water over the earth. And Noah and his sons and his wife and his sons' wives came into the ark because of the waters of the Flood. Of the clean animals and of the animals that were not clean and of the fowl and of all that crawls upon the ground two each came to Noah into the ark, male and female, as God had commanded Noah. And it happened after seven days, that the waters of the Flood were over the earth. In the six hundredth year of Noah's life, in the second month, on the seventeenth day of the month, on that day,

> All the wellsprings of the great deep burst
> and the casements of the heavens were opened.

And the rain was over the earth forty days and forty nights. That very day, Noah and Shem and Ham and Japheth, the sons of Noah, and Noah's wife, and the three wives of his sons together with them, came into the ark, they as well as beasts of each kind and cattle of each kind and each kind of crawling thing that crawls on the earth and each kind of bird, each winged thing. They came to Noah into the ark, two by two of all flesh that has the breath of life within it. And those that came in, male and female of all flesh they came, as God had commanded him, and the LORD shut him in. And the Flood was forty days over the earth, and the waters multiplied and bore the ark upward and it rose above the earth. And the waters surged and multiplied mightily over the earth, and the ark went on the surface of the water. And the waters surged most mightily over the earth, and all the high mountains under the heavens were covered. Fifteen cubits above them the waters surged as the mountains were covered. And all flesh that stirs on the earth perished, the fowl and the cattle and the beasts and all swarming things that swarm upon the earth, and all humankind. All that had the quickening breath of life in its nostrils, of all that was on dry land, died. And He wiped out all existing things from the face of the earth, from humans to cattle to crawling things to the fowl of the heavens, they were wiped out from the earth. And Noah alone remained, and those with him in the ark. And the waters surged over the earth one hundred and fifty days.

Chapter 8

And God remembered Noah and all the beasts and all the cattle that were with him in the ark. And God sent a wind over the earth and the waters subsided. And the wellsprings of the deep were dammed up, and the casements of the heavens, the rain from the heavens held back. And the waters receded from the earth little by little, and the waters ebbed. At the end of a hundred and fifty days the ark came to rest, on the

seventeenth day of the seventh month, on the mountains of Ararat.[2] The waters
continued to ebb, until the tenth month, on the first day of the tenth month, the mountaintops appeared. And it happened, at the end of forty days, that Noah opened the
window of the ark he had made. And he let out the raven and it went forth to and fro
until the waters should dry up from the earth. And he let out the dove to see whether
the waters had abated from the surface of the ground. But the dove found no resting
place for its foot and it returned to him to the ark, for the waters were over all the
earth. And he reached out and took it and brought it back to him into the ark. Then
he waited another seven days and again let the dove out of the ark. And the dove came
back to him at eventide and, look, a plucked olive leaf was in its bill, and Noah knew
that the waters had abated from the earth. Then he waited still another seven days and
let out the dove, and it did not return to him again. And it happened in the six hundred
and first year, in the first month, on the first day of the month, the waters dried up
from the earth, and Noah took off the covering of the ark and he saw and, look, the
surface of the ground was dry. And in the second month, on the twenty-seventh day of
the month, the earth was completely dry. And God spoke to Noah, saying, "Go out of
the ark, you and your wife and your sons and your sons' wives, with you. All the animals that are with you of all flesh, fowl and cattle and every crawling thing that
crawls on the earth, take out with you, and let them swarm through the earth and be
fruitful and multiply on the earth." And Noah went out, his sons and his wife and his
sons' wives with him. Every beast, every crawling thing, and every fowl, everything
that stirs on the earth, by families, came out of the ark. And Noah built an altar to the
LORD and he took from every clean cattle and every clean fowl and offered burnt offerings on the altar. And the LORD smelled the fragrant odor and the LORD said in His
heart, "I will not again damn the soil on humankind's score. For the devisings of the
human heart are evil from youth. And I will not again strike down all living things as
I did. As long as all the days of the earth—

> seedtime and harvest
> and cold and heat
> and summer and winter
> and day and night
> shall not cease."

Chapter 9

And God blessed Noah and his sons and He said to them, "Be fruitful and multiply and
fill the earth. And the dread and fear of you shall be upon all the beasts of the field and
all the fowl of the heavens, in all that crawls on the ground and in all the fish of the sea.
In your hand they are given. All stirring things that are alive, yours shall be for food,
like the green plants, I have given all to you. But flesh with its lifeblood still in it you
shall not eat. And just so, your lifeblood I will requite, from every beast I will requite
it, and from humankind, from every man's brother, I will requite human life.

> He who sheds human blood
> by humans his blood shall be shed,
> for in the image of God

2. A region in Armenia.

He made humankind.
As for you, be fruitful and multiply,
swarm through the earth, and hold sway over it."

And God said to Noah and to his sons with him, "And I, I am about to establish My covenant with you and with your seed after you, and with every living creature that is with you, the fowl and the cattle and every beast of the earth with you, all that have come out of the ark, every beast of the earth. And I will establish My covenant with you, that never again shall all flesh be cut off by the waters of the Flood, and never again shall there be a Flood to destroy the earth." And God said, "This is the sign of the covenant that I set between Me and you and every living creature that is with you, for everlasting generations: My bow I have set in the clouds to be a sign of the covenant between Me and the earth, and so, when I send clouds over the earth, the bow will appear in the cloud. Then I will remember My covenant, between Me and you and every living creature of all flesh, and the waters will no more become a Flood to destroy all flesh. And the bow shall be in the cloud and I will see it, to remember the everlasting covenant between God and all living creatures, all flesh that is on the earth." And God said to Noah, "This is the sign of the covenant I have established between Me and all flesh that is on the earth."

And the sons of Noah who came out from the ark were Shem and Ham and Japheth, and Ham was the father of Canaan. These three were the sons of Noah, and from these the whole earth spread out. And Noah, a man of the soil, was the first to plant a vineyard. And he drank of the wine and became drunk, and exposed himself within his tent. And Ham the father of Canaan saw his father's nakedness and told his two brothers outside.[3] And Shem and Japheth took a cloak and put it over both their shoulders and walked backward and covered their father's nakedness, their faces turned backward so they did not see their father's nakedness. And Noah woke from his wine and he knew what his youngest son had done to him. And he said,

> "Cursed be Canaan,
> the lowliest slave shall he be
> to his brothers."

And he said,

> "Blessed be the Lord
> the God of Shem,
> unto them shall Canaan be slave.
> May God enlarge Japheth,
> may he dwell in the tents of Shem,
> unto them shall Canaan be slave."

And Noah lived after the Flood three hundred and fifty years. And all the days of Noah were nine hundred and fifty years. Then he died.[4]

---

3. The story implies that Ham/Canaan had a sexual interest in Noah; later in the Bible (Leviticus 18), Canaanite sexual perversions are given as a reason God is displacing them in favor of the Hebrews.

4. Chapter 10, omitted here, gives a genealogy of Noah's descendants.

Chapter 11

And all the earth was one language, one set of words. And it happened as they journeyed from the east that they found a valley in the land of Shinar[5] and settled there. And they said to each other, "Come, let us bake bricks and burn them hard." And the brick served them as stone, and bitumen served them as mortar. And they said, "Come, let us build us a city and a tower with its top in the heavens, that we may make us a name, lest we be scattered over all the earth." And the LORD came down to see the city and the tower that the human creatures had built. And the LORD said, "As one people with one language for all, if this is what they have begun to do, nothing they plot will elude them. Come, let us go down and baffle their language there so that they will not understand each other's language." And the LORD scattered them from there over all the earth and they left off building the city. Therefore it is called Babel, for there the LORD made the language of all the earth babble. And from there the LORD scattered them over all the earth.

This is the lineage of Shem: Shem was a hundred years old when he begot Arpachshad two years after the Flood. And Shem lived after begetting Arpachshad five hundred years and he begot sons and daughters. And Arpachshad lived thirty-five years and he begot Shelah. And Arpachshad lived after begetting Shelah four hundred and three years and he begot sons and daughters. And Shelah lived thirty years and he begot Eber. And Shelah lived after begetting Eber four hundred and three years and he begot sons and daughters. And Eber lived thirty-four years and he begot Peleg. And Eber lived after begetting Peleg four hundred and thirty years and he begot sons and daughters. And Peleg lived thirty years and he begot Reu. And Peleg lived after begetting Reu two hundred and nine years and he begot sons and daughters. And Reu lived thirty-two years and he begot Serug. And Reu lived after begetting Serug two hundred and seven years and he begot sons and daughters. And Serug lived thirty years and he begot Nahor. And Serug lived after begetting Nahor two hundred years and he begot sons and daughters. And Nahor lived twenty-nine years and he begot Terah. And Nahor lived after begetting Terah one hundred and nineteen years and he begot sons and daughters. And Terah lived seventy years and he begot Abram, Nahor, and Haran. And this is the lineage of Terah: Terah begot Abram, Nahor, and Haran, and Haran begot Lot. And Haran died in the lifetime of Terah his father in the land of his birth, Ur of the Chaldees. And Abram and Nahor took themselves wives. The name of Abram's wife was Sarai and the name of Nahor's wife was Milcah daughter of Haran, the father of Milcah and the father of Iscah. And Sarai was barren, she had no child. And Terah took Abram his son and Lot son of Haran, his grandson, and Sarai his daughter-in-law, the wife of his son Abram, and he set out with them from Ur of the Chaldees toward the land of Canaan, and they came to Haran and settled there. And the days of Terah were two hundred and five years, and Terah died in Haran.[6]

5. The lowlands of the Tigris-Euphrates basin in Mesopotamia.
6. In northwest Mesopotamia; a substantial number of people migrated from this region into Canaan in the early 2nd millennium B.C.E.—a migration that begins the story of Israel's patriarchs and matriarchs in the next section of Genesis, which concludes with the story of Joseph in Egypt (see page 160).

❧ TRANSLATIONS: THE BIBLE ❧

The Hebrew Bible poses distinctive challenges for translators in two respects. First, it is the product of an ancient, predominantly oral culture, far removed from our modern print-based literary world. Second, it is a document of faith, and not of one but of two faiths, most widely read for many centuries as the Christian Old Testament. Translators therefore have difficult decisions to make in translating many of the books of the Bible. How oral or how literary in flavor should their rendering be? How strongly should the translation reflect a theological understanding of the text? Differing translations of two passages, one prose and the other poetry, can suggest the complexity of the issues that arise.

GENESIS 1:1–5, KING JAMES VERSION (1611)

In the beginning God created the heaven and the earth. And the earth was without form, and void; and darkness *was* upon the face of the deep. And the Spirit of God moved upon the face of the waters. And God said, Let there be light: and there was light. And God saw the light, that *it was* good: and God divided the light from the darkness. And God called the light Day, and the darkness he called Night. And the evening and the morning were the first day.

GENESIS 1:1–5, ROBERT ALTER TRANSLATION (1996)

When God began to create heaven and earth, and the earth then was welter and waste and darkness over the deep and God's breath hovering over the waters, God said, "Let there be light." And there was light. And God saw the light, that it was good, and God divided the light from the darkness. And God called the light Day, and the darkness He called Night. And it was evening and morning, first day.

The King James Version of the Bible, certainly the most widely read translation in the history of the English language, had a tremendous influence on English literature, and its phrasings are likely to seem natural and almost inevitable. The translators tried to stay as close as possible to the original, which is why they have italicized the verbs "was" and "it was," to indicate an addition to the text, simply because the Hebrew doesn't employ the verb "to be" at those points. The King James Version is stately and measured in tone. A theological choice underlies the phrase "the Spirit of God," which translates the Hebrew term *ruah 'elohim*; the term *ruah* means "breath" or "wind," but Christian theologians of the period identified this as the Holy Spirit. The translators rendered the term accordingly, even capitalizing "Spirit."

By contrast, Robert Alter's version reflects the Hebrew text's oral-style play of sounds, seen from the start in the piled-up phrases of his long opening sentence. Where the King James Version has the earth created "without form, and void," Alter has it being "welter and waste," a good approximation of the rhyming Hebrew phrase, "tohu wa-bohu." Alter's version is also notably untheological: it is simply "God's breath"—not God's "spirit," much less his "Spirit"—that hovers over the waters.

A somewhat different decision lies behind Alter's choice of "over the waters" where the King James Version has "upon the face of the waters." This translates the Hebrew preposition *al-peni*, "above, over," which literally means "on the face" or "on the surface." In opting for "over," Alter keeps his text as simple as possible, in keeping with a general project of reflecting a plainspoken, concise style. This pattern can also be seen at the end of the passage, where the King James Version has "the first day," in keeping with standard English usage, while Alter more abruptly has "first day," the direct equivalent of the Hebrew, *yom ahad.*

PSALM 22:14–17, KING JAMES VERSION

I am poured out like water, and all my bones are out of joint: my heart
    is like wax; it is melted in the midst of my bowels.
My strength is dried up like a potsherd; and my tongue cleaveth to my
    jaws; and thou hast brought me into the dust of death.
For dogs have compassed me: the assembly of the wicked have in-
    closed me: they pierced my hands and my feet.
I may tell all my bones: they look and stare upon me.

PSALM 22:14–17, ROBERT ALTER TRANSLATION

Like water I spilled out,
    all my limbs fell apart.
My heart was like wax,
    melting within my chest.
My palate turned dry as a shard
    and my tongue was annealed to my jaw,
        and to death's dust did You thrust me.
For the curs came all around me,
    a pack of the evil encircled me,
        they bound my hands and my feet.
They counted out all my bones.
    It is they who looked, who stared at me.

This psalm (whose full text can be found on page 142) has long been read by Christians as foreshadowing the trial and crucifixion of Jesus—quite understandably, as the gospel writers clearly had it in mind. Two of the gospels even record the dying Jesus as quoting the psalm's opening line, "My God, my God, why hast thou forsaken me?" The King James translation includes several details that reinforce this understanding: where the speaker's hands and feet are "bound" in Alter's version, the older version has them being "pierced" like Jesus's hands and feet on the cross.

If King James's translators were willing to shape the translation theologically, Alter is prepared to emend the text on more literary grounds. In the second verse above, the King James Version has the speaker's "strength" drying up, whereas Alter follows various older commentators and makes this the speaker's "palate." This change assumes an error in the biblical text, a reversal of two letters; making the change (or correcting the error) makes better sense of the image of drying out, and completes the parallelism with the line that follows, in which the speaker's tongue sticks to his jaw.

A further change seen in Alter is the updating of language: "I may tell all my bones" sounds today as though the speaker wants to say something to them, whereas in 1611 "to tell" often meant "to count." Alter has also more subtly modernized the speaker's body: where the older translation has the heart melting into the bowels (which is the term used in the Hebrew), Alter gives a more anatomically realistic—and poetically pleasing—reading: "My heart was like wax, melting within my chest." He also breaks the long lines of the Hebrew verses into short, indented lines, highlighting the parallelism of the verse.

As even these brief passages can show, translators undertake decisions with every word, decisions that are as much cultural as linguistic, profoundly shaping the way the work is read in a new time and place.

✦ ✦ ✦

Poetry of Love and Devotion
c. 3rd to 2nd millennia B.C.E.

The sacred and the secular were never clearly separate realms in the ancient Near East. The region's gods and goddesses pervaded their landscapes and every aspect of daily life, and they themselves were often portrayed, conversely, in markedly human terms. The poems collected here show something of the variety of ways in which divine and human love could intermingle, as piety mixed with familial love, political loyalty, and the erotic impulses of mortals and immortals alike.

The first work given here is an ancient Sumerian poem from the third millennium B.C.E.—the very dawn of writing. In this poem Inanna, goddess of love, celebrates her seduction by her consort Dumuzi. It was believed that their periodic union gave rise to seasonal fertility, and so this poem was performed at annual agricultural festivals. The many repetitions in the verses (typical in Sumerian poetry) would give the poem a resonant power when it was recited in public. For all its divine setting and ritual value, this poem is notable for the very human concern that Inanna shows: What will she tell her mother that she's been doing?

This intensely religious and public poem is followed by a selection of private Egyptian love poems. These are the closest thing to purely secular poetry that has survived from anywhere in the ancient Near East. Over the course of the period that modern scholars label Egypt's New Kingdom (1570–1090 B.C.E.), and probably before then as well, they were performed at banquets and sung in the fields; some fifty lyrics have survived, preserved on scraps of pottery and on scrolls deposited in tombs for the enjoyment of patrons who never wanted the party to end. Even in these romantic and erotic poems, the gods are ever present, as the poems call on them to guarantee the lovers' passion. One lyric paints an entire landscape as peopled with approving deities, while in another poem a young lover offers sacrifices to his sweetheart's door and its bolt, so that they will melt away before him. Other poems, though, make no religious reference, as in "The voice of the turtledove speaks out." This poem is the world's oldest surviving example of a "dawn-song" or aubade, in which lovers regret having to part at sunrise. The image of the turtledove is just one of many images in the Egyptian lyrics that recur in the biblical Song of Songs, which follows these poems. They can also be compared to later lyric mergings of sacred and secular, especially in India, where comparable lyric traditions extend from early times (see Volume B) to the present day.

Last night, as I, the queen, was shining bright[1]

Last night, as I, the queen, was shining bright,
Last night, as I, the queen of heaven, was shining bright,
As I was shining bright, as I was dancing about,
As I was uttering a song at the brightening of the oncoming night,
5   He met me, he met me,
The Lord Kuli-Anna met me,
The lord put his hand into my hand,
Ushumgalanna embraced me.

"Come now, wild bull, set me free, I must go home,
10   Kuli-Enlil, set me free, I must go home,
What shall I say to deceive my mother!
What shall I say to deceive my mother Ningal!"

"Let me inform you, let me inform you.
Inanna, most deceitful of women, let me inform you:
15   'My girl friend took me with her to the public square,
She entertained me there with music and dancing,
Her chant, the sweet, she sang for me.
In sweet rejoicing I whiled away the time there'—
Thus deceitfully stand up to your mother,
20   While we by the moonlight indulge our passion,
I will prepare for you a bed pure, sweet, and noble,
Will while away the sweet time with you in joyful fulfillment."

[*Several lines have been destroyed. When the text resumes, the lovers have
    decided to marry:*]

I have come to my mother's gate,
I, in joy I walk,
I have come to Ningal's gate,
I, in joy I walk.
5   To my mother he will say the word,
He will sprinkle cypress oil on the ground,
To my mother Ningal he will say the word,
He will sprinkle cypress oil on the ground,
He whose dwelling is fragrant,
10   Whose word brings deep joy.

---

1. Translated by S. N. Kramer. In this poem, Inanna addresses her lover Dumuzi by several different names, such as Kuli-Anna and Ushumgalanna in the first stanza.

My lord is seemly for the holy lap,
Amaushumgalanna, the son-in-law of Sin,[2]
The lord Dumuzi is seemly for the holy lap,
Amaushumgalanna, the son-in-law of Sin.
15 My lord, sweet is your increase,
Tasty your plants and herbs in the plain,
Amaushumgalanna, sweet is your increase,
Tasty your plants and herbs in the plain.

EGYPTIAN LOVE SONGS[1]

Distracting is the foliage of my pasture

Distracting is the [foliage] of my [pasture]:
[the mouth] of my girl is a lotus bud,
her breasts are mandrake apples,
her arms are [vines],
5 [her eyes] are fixed like berries,
her brow a snare of willow,
and I the wild goose!
My [beak] snips [her hair] for bait,
as worms for bait in the trap.

I sail downstream in the ferry by the pull of the current

I sail downstream in the ferry by [the pull of the current],
my bundle of reeds in my arms.
I'll be at Ankh-towy,[2]
and say to Ptah, the lord of truth,
5 give me my girl tonight.

The sea is wine,
Ptah its reeds,
Sekhmet° its [kelp],   *a Memphis goddess*
the Dew Goddess its buds,
10 Nefertum° its lotus flower.   *young sun god*

[The Golden Goddess°] rejoices   *sky goddess*
and the land grows bright at her beauty.
For Memphis is a flask of mandrake wine
placed before the good-looking god.°   *Ptah*

The voice of the turtledove speaks out

The voice of the turtledove speaks out. It says:
day breaks, which way are you going?

---

2. Inanna's father, the moon god.
1. Translated by W. K. Simpson. Words in brackets show what was most likely written in damaged parts of the papyrus manuscript.
2. "Life of the Two Lands," Memphis. The creator-god Ptah was patron god of Memphis.

Lay off, little bird,
must you so scold me?
5 I found my lover on his bed,
and my heart was sweet to excess,

We said:

I shall never be far away from you
while my hand is in your hand,
10 and I shall stroll with you
in every favorite place.

He set me as first of the girls
and he does not break my heart.

I embrace her, and her arms open wide

I embrace her, and her arms open wide,
I am like a man in Punt,[3]
like someone overwhelmed with drugs.
I kiss her,
5 her lips open,
and I am drunk
without a beer.

One, the lady love without a duplicate

One, the lady love without a duplicate,
more perfect than the world,
see, she is like the star rising
at the start of an auspicious year.

5 She whose excellence shines, whose body glistens,
glorious her eyes when she stares,
sweet her lips when she converses,
she says not a word too much.

High her neck and glistening her nipples,
10 of true lapis her hair,
her arms finer than gold,
her fingers like lotus flowers unfolding.

Her buttocks droop when her waist is girt,
her legs reveal her perfection;
15 her steps are pleasing when she walks the earth,
she takes my heart in her embrace.

She turns the head of every man,
all captivated at the sight of her;

---

3. A country south of Egypt, source of many spices.

20   everyone who embraces her rejoices,
            for he has become the most successful of lovers.

            When she comes forth, anyone can see
            that there is none like that One.

How well the lady knows to cast the noose

            How well the lady knows to cast the noose
            yet still escape the cattle tax.

            With her hair she throws lassoes at me,
            with her eyes she catches me,
5   with her necklace entangles me
            and with her seal ring brands me.

Why need you hold converse with your heart?

            Why need you hold converse with your heart?
            To embrace her is all my desire.
            As Amun lives, I come to you,
            my loin cloth on my shoulder.

I passed by her house in the dark

            I passed by her house in the dark,
            I knocked and no one opened.
            What a beautiful night for our doorkeeper!

            Open, door bolts!
5   Door leaves, you are my fate, you are my genie.
            Our ox will be slaughtered for you inside.
            Door leaves, do not use your strength.

            A long-horned bull will be slaughtered to the bolt,
            a short-horned bull to the door pin,
10   a wild fowl to the threshold,
            and its fat to the key.

            But all the best parts of our ox
            shall go to the carpenter's boy,
            so he'll make us a door of grass
15   and a door bolt of reeds.

            And any time when the lover comes
            he'll find her house open,
            he'll find beds made with linen sheets
            and in them a lovely girl.

20   And the girl will say to me:
            this place belongs to the captain's boy!

The Song of Songs

1st millennium B.C.E.

The phrase "song of songs," *shir ha-shirim* in Hebrew, means "best of all songs," a testimony to the power and beauty of the greatest love poem we have from the ancient Mediterranean world. Centuries of readers—and lovers—have relished the speakers' ecstatic praise of each other's bodies, the lyrical evocations of the beauties of nature and the landscape of Israel, and the mysterious episodes of abandonment and loss in the middle of the book. The title and opening line refer to it as a single song, and some editors over the centuries have inserted captions and dialogue markers to connect its parts into an extended dialogue between a woman, her beloved, and a chorus of her attendants or friends. The book can also be thought of, though, as a collection of older love poems. Many of these verses must have been sung individually, like the Egyptian poems they often resemble, long before they were collected together in around the third century B.C.E.

The Song of Songs was included in the Bible (after some ancient debate) thanks to the book's attribution to King Solomon. The rabbis who admitted it to the Bible interpreted the text allegorically as depicting the love of God for Israel. Later, Christian commentators adapted this line of interpretation, reading the collection as an allegory of the love of Christ for his Church. Modern scholarship tends instead to stress the poems' links to wedding songs and the older fertility myths that often underlay them. There was a developed tradition of "sacred marriage poetry" in the Near East, such as the poem in which the goddess Inanna celebrates her union with her lover Dumuzi, (see page 42). A list of hymn titles from the Mesopotamian city of Assur shows many that resemble verses in the Song of Songs:

> "How do I long for the beautiful one!"
> "The fragrance of cedar is thy love, O lord."
> "To the door of the lord she did come."
> "By night I thought of thee."
> "Thou hast caressed me; be thou my lord!"

In Mesopotamia, these hymns would have been performed in festivals associated with planting and harvest, with the king and the queen, or the king and a temple prostitute, enacting the roles of the goddess of love (Inanna or Ishtar) and her consort (Dumuzi or Tammuz), who takes her place in the underworld for six months of the year; their union was the mythic underpinning for the seasonal fertility of crops (see *The Descent of Ishtar to the Underworld,* page 99). Tammuz and Ishtar (known in Palestine as Astarte) were worshiped in Jerusalem before the establishment of Hebrew monotheism—and probably long afterward as well, to the dismay of the prophets who continually condemned persisting pagan practices.

No direct use of such old traditions is found in the Song of Songs, though some of the verses use the older imagery, either in the context of a wedding between Solomon and a bride, or in other stanzas that seem to tell of a quite different, private love affair. We can think of these verses as infusing theology back into daily life, for these lyrics endow the lovers with qualities of divine power and mystery, and the lovers' encounters are set against a panoramic backdrop of Israel's sacred landscape and history.

The Song of Songs[1]

Chapter 1

The Song of Songs, which is Solomon's.

Let him kiss me with the kisses of his mouth.
Your love is more delightful than wine;
delicate is the fragrance of your perfume,
5   your name is an oil poured out,
and that is why the maidens love you.
Draw me in your footsteps, let us run.
The King has brought me into his rooms;
you will be our joy and our gladness.
10   We shall praise your love above wine;
how right it is to love you.
I am black but lovely, daughters of Jerusalem,
like the tents of Kedar,
like the pavilions of Salmah.
15   Take no notice of my swarthiness,
it is the sun that has burnt me.
My mother's sons turned their anger on me,
they made me look after the vineyards.
Had I only looked after my own!

20   Tell me then, you whom my heart loves:
Where will you lead your flock to graze,
where will you rest it at noon?
That I may no more wander like a vagabond
beside the flocks of your companions.

25   If you do not know this, O loveliest of women,
follow the tracks of the flock,
and take your kids to graze
close by the shepherds' tents.

To my mare harnessed to Pharaoh's chariot
30   I compare you, my love.
Your cheeks show fair between their pendants
and your neck within its necklaces.
We shall make you golden earrings
and beads of silver.

35   —While the King rests in his own room
my nard yields its perfume.
My Beloved is a sachet of myrrh
lying between my breasts.
My Beloved is a cluster of henna flowers
40   among the vines of Engedi.

—How beautiful you are, my love,
how beautiful you are!

---

1. Jerusalem Bible translation.

Your eyes are doves.

—How beautiful you are, my Beloved,
45   and how delightful!
All green is our bed.

—The beams of our house are of cedar,
the paneling of cypress.

Chapter 2

—I am the rose of Sharon,[2]
50   the lily of the valleys.
—As a lily among the thistles,
so is my love among the maidens.
—As an apple tree among the trees of the orchard,
so is my Beloved among the young men.
55   In his longed-for shade I am seated
and his fruit is sweet to my taste.
He has taken me to his banquet hall,
and the banner he raises over me is love.
Feed me with raisin cakes,
60   restore me with apples,
for I am sick with love.
His left arm is under my head,
his right embraces me.

—I charge you, daughters of Jerusalem,
65   by the gazelles, by the hinds of the field,
not to stir my love, nor rouse it,
until it please to awake.

I hear my Beloved.
See how he comes
70   leaping on the mountains,
bounding over the hills.
My Beloved is like a gazelle,
like a young stag.
See where he stands
75   behind our wall.
He looks in at the window,
he peers through the lattice.

My Beloved lifts up his voice,
he says to me,
80   "Come then, my love,
my lovely one, come.
For see, winter is past,
the rains are over and gone.
The flowers appear on the earth.
85   The season of glad songs has come,
the cooing of the turtledove is heard in our land.

2. A rich plain along the Mediterranean coast.

The fig tree is forming its first figs
and the blossoming vines give out their fragrance.
Come then, my love,
90 my lovely one, come.
My dove, hiding in the clefts of the rock,
in the coverts of the cliff,
show me your face,
let me hear your voice;
95 for your voice is sweet
and your face is beautiful."

Catch the foxes for us,
the little foxes that make havoc of the vineyards,
for our vineyards are in flower.
100 My Beloved is mine and I am his.
He pastures his flock among the lilies.

Before the dawn-wind rises,
before the shadows flee,
return! Be, my Beloved,
105 like a gazelle,
a young stag,
on the rugged mountains.

Chapter 3

On my bed, at night, I sought him
whom my heart loves.
110 I sought but did not find him.
So I will rise and go through the City;
in the streets and the squares
I will seek him whom my heart loves.

I sought but did not find him.
115 The watchmen came upon me
on their rounds in the City:
"Have you seen him whom my heart loves?"

Scarcely had I passed them
than I found him whom my heart loves.
120 I held him fast, nor would I let him go
till I had brought him into my mother's house,
into the room of her who conceived me.

I charge you, daughters of Jerusalem,
by the gazelles, by the hinds of the field,
125 not to stir my love, nor rouse it,
until it please to awake.

What is this coming up from the desert
like a column of smoke,
breathing of myrrh and frankincense
130 and every perfume the merchant knows?

See, it is the litter of Solomon.
Around it are sixty champions,
the flower of the warriors of Israel;
all of them skilled swordsmen,
135   veterans of battle.
Each man has his sword at his side,
against alarms by night.

King Solomon has made himself a throne
of wood from Lebanon.
140   The posts he has made of silver,
the canopy of gold,
the seat of purple;
the back is inlaid with ebony.

Daughters of Zion,
145   come and see King Solomon,
wearing the diadem with which his mother crowned him
on his wedding day,
on the day of his heart's joy.

Chapter 4

How beautiful you are, my love,
150   how beautiful you are!
Your eyes, behind your veil, are doves;
your hair is like a flock of goats
frisking down the slopes of Gilead.
Your teeth are like a flock of shorn ewes
155   as they come up from the washing.
Each one has its twin,
not one unpaired with another.
Your lips are a scarlet thread
and your words enchanting.
160   Your cheeks, behind your veil,
are halves of pomegranate.
Your neck is the tower of David
built as a fortress,
hung round with a thousand bucklers,
165   and each the shield of a hero.
Your two breasts are two fawns,
twins of a gazelle,
that feed among the lilies.

Before the dawn-wind rises,
170   before the shadows flee,
I will go to the mountain of myrrh,
to the hill of frankincense.

You are wholly beautiful, my love,
and without a blemish.

175   Come from Lebanon, my promised bride,
come from Lebanon, come on your way.
Lower your gaze, from the heights of Amana,
from the crests of Senir and Hermon,
the haunt of lions,
180   the mountains of leopards.

You ravish my heart,
my sister, my bride,[3]
you ravish my heart
with a single one of your glances,
185   with one single pearl of your necklace.
What spells lie in your love,
my sister, my bride!
How delicious is your love, more delicious than wine!
How fragrant your perfumes,
190   more fragrant than all other spices!
Your lips, my promised one, distill wild honey.
Honey and milk are under your tongue;
and the scent of your garments
is like the scent of Lebanon.

195   She is a garden enclosed, my sister, my bride;
a garden enclosed, a sealed fountain.
Your shoots form an orchard of pomegranate trees,
the rarest essences are yours:
nard and saffron,
200   calamus and cinnamon,
with all the incense-bearing trees;
myrrh and aloes, with the subtlest odors.
Fountain that makes the gardens fertile,
well of living water,
205   streams flowing down from Lebanon.
Awake, north wind,
come, wind of the south!
Breathe over my garden,
to spread its sweet smell around.
210   Let my Beloved come into his garden,
let him taste its rarest fruits.

Chapter 5

I come into my garden,
my sister, my bride,
I gather my myrrh and balsam,
215   I eat my honey and my honeycomb,
I drink my wine and my milk.

---

3. As in Egyptian poetry, the lovers sometimes refer to each other as "sister" and "brother."

Eat, friends, and drink,
drink deep, my dearest friends.

I sleep, but my heart is awake.
220   I hear my Beloved knocking.
"Open to me, my sister, my love,
my dove, my perfect one,
for my head is covered with dew,
my locks with the drops of night."
225   —"I have taken off my tunic,
am I to put it on again?
I have washed my feet,
am I to dirty them again?"
My Beloved thrust his hand
230   through the hole in the door;
I trembled to the core of my being.
Then I rose to open to my Beloved,
myrrh ran off my hands,
pure myrrh off my fingers,
235   on to the handle of the bolt.

I opened to my Beloved,
but he had turned his back and gone!
My soul failed at his flight.
I sought him but I did not find him,
240   I called to him but he did not answer.
The watchmen came upon me
as they made their rounds in the City.
They beat me, they wounded me,
they took away my cloak,
245   they who guard the ramparts.
I charge you, daughters of Jerusalem,
if you should find my Beloved,
what must you tell him . . .?
That I am sick with love.

250   What makes your Beloved better than other lovers,
O loveliest of women?
What makes your Beloved better than other lovers,
to give us a charge like this?

My Beloved is fresh and ruddy,
255   to be known among ten thousand.
His head is golden, purest gold,
his locks are palm fronds and black as the raven.
His eyes are doves at a pool of water,
bathed in milk, at rest on a pool.
260   His cheeks are beds of spices,
banks sweetly scented.

His lips are lilies, distilling pure myrrh.
His hands are golden, rounded,
set with jewels of Tarshish.
265   His belly a block of ivory
covered with sapphires.
His legs are alabaster columns
set in sockets of pure gold.
His appearance is that of Lebanon,
270   unrivaled as the cedars.
His conversation is sweetness itself,
he is altogether lovable.
Such is my Beloved, such is my friend,
O daughters of Jerusalem.

Chapter 6

275   Where did your Beloved go,
O loveliest of women?
Which way did your Beloved turn
so that we can help you to look for him?

My Beloved went down to his garden,
280   to the beds of spices,
to pasture his flock in the gardens
and gather lilies.
I am my Beloved's, and my Beloved is mine.
He pastures his flock among the lilies.

285   You are beautiful as Tirzah,[4] my love,
fair as Jerusalem.
Turn your eyes away,
for they hold me captive.
Your hair is like a flock of goats
290   frisking down the slopes of Gilead.
Your teeth are like a flock of sheep
as they come up from the washing.
Each one has its twin,
not one unpaired with another.
295   Your cheeks, behind your veil,
are halves of pomegranate.

There are sixty queens
and eighty concubines
(and countless maidens).
300   But my dove is unique,
mine, unique and perfect.

---

4. A former capital of Israel.

She is the darling of her mother,
the favorite of the one who bore her.
The maidens saw her, and called her happy,
305   queens and concubines sang her praises:
"Who is this arising like the dawn,
fair as the moon,
resplendent as the sun,
terrible as an army with banners?"

310   I went down to the nut orchard
to see what was sprouting in the valley,
to see if the vines were budding
and the pomegranate trees in flower.
Before I knew . . . my desire had hurled me
315   on the chariots of my people, as their prince.

Chapter 7

Return, return, O maid of Shulam,[5]
return, return, that we may gaze on you!

Why do you gaze on the maid of Shulam
dancing as though between two rows of dancers?

320   How beautiful are your feet in their sandals,
O prince's daughter!
The curve of your thighs is like the curve of a necklace,
work of a master hand.
Your navel is a bowl well rounded
325   with no lack of wine,
your belly a heap of wheat
surrounded with lilies.
Your two breasts are two fawns,
twins of a gazelle.
330   Your neck is an ivory tower.
Your eyes, the pools of Heshbon,
by the gate of Bath-rabbim.
Your nose, the Tower of Lebanon,
sentinel facing Damascus.
335   Your head is held high like Carmel,
and its plaits are as dark as purple;
a king is held captive in your tresses.
How beautiful you are, how charming,
my love, my delight!
340   In stature like the palm tree,
its fruit-clusters your breasts.
"I will climb the palm tree," I resolved,

5. Perhaps a place name, or this may mean "Solomon's bride."

"I will seize its clusters of dates."
May your breasts be clusters of grapes,
345   your breath sweet-scented as apples,
your speaking, superlative wine.

Wine flowing straight to my Beloved,
as it runs on the lips of those who sleep.
I am my Beloved's,
350   and his desire is for me.
Come, my Beloved,
let us go to the fields.
We will spend the night in the villages,
and in the morning we will go to the vineyards.
355   We will see if the vines are budding,
if their blossoms are opening,
if the pomegranate trees are in flower.
Then I shall give you the gift of my love.
The mandrakes yield their fragrance,
360   the rarest fruits are at our doors;
the new as well as the old,
I have stored them for you, my Beloved.

Chapter 8

Ah, why are you not my brother,
nursed at my mother's breast!
365   Then if I met you out of doors, I could kiss you
without people thinking ill of me.
I should lead you, I should take you
into my mother's house, and you would teach me!
I should give you spiced wine to drink,
370   juice of my pomegranates.

His left arm is under my head
and his right embraces me.
I charge you, daughters of Jerusalem,
not to stir my love, nor rouse it,
375   until it please to awake.

Who is this coming up from the desert
leaning on her Beloved?
I awakened you under the apple tree,
there where your mother conceived you,
380   there where she who gave birth to you conceived you.

Set me like a seal on your heart,
like a seal on your arm.
For love is strong as Death,
jealousy relentless as Sheol.
385   The flash of it is a flash of fire,

a flame of Yahweh himself.
Love no flood can quench,
no torrents drown.[6]

The Epic of Gilgamesh
c. 1200 B.C.E.

The greatest literary composition of ancient Mesopotamia, *The Epic of Gilgamesh* can rightly be called the first true work of world literature. It began to circulate widely around the ancient Near East as early as 1000 B.C.E., and it was translated into several of the region's languages. Tablets bearing portions of the epic have been found not only around Mesopotamia but also in Turkey and in Palestine. We know of no other work that crossed so many borders so early, as people in many areas began to respond to the epic's searching exploration of the meaning of culture in the face of death.

The story of Gilgamesh developed over many centuries from a kernel of historical fact. Gilgamesh was an early king of the city-state of Uruk in southern Mesopotamia; he lived sometime around 2750 B.C.E. Early records credit him with building a great wall around his city, "spread out across the countryside like a net for birds." In the years following his death a cult grew up around his memory, and he was honored as a judge of the underworld. By around 2000 B.C.E. a loosely connected cycle of songs had been written in Sumerian about his life and legendary adventures. These old songs portray Bilgames (as they call him) as a great warrior, describe his journey to a distant mountain where he kills a monster and brings home cedar trees for his palace, and tell of a descent by his servant Enkidu into the grim regions of the underworld. These early poems already signal what would become the organizing theme of the full epic: its hero's fear of death and his quest for immortality. As he decides to journey to slay the monster guarding the Cedar Mountain, Bilgames voices his anguish to Enkidu:

> O Enkidu, since no man can escape life's end,
> I will enter the mountain and set up my name.
> ....
> In my city, a man dies, and the heart is stricken,
> a man perishes, and the heart feels pain.
> I raised my head on the rampart,
> my gaze fell on a corpse drifting down the river, afloat on the water:
> I too shall become like that, just so shall I be!

Over the course of the Old Babylonian period (2000–1600 B.C.E.) a poet or poets in Babylon took up this theme and adapted the Sumerian poems into a connected epic, written in Akkadian, the increasingly dominant language of the region. Finally, around 1200 B.C.E., the epic was revised into its definitive form by a Babylonian priest named Sîn-liqe-unninni, whose additions

---

6. The translators of the Jerusalem Bible consider that the poem proper ends here. Several miscellaneous paragraphs follow in a kind of appendix, beginning with an aphorism: "Were a man to offer all the wealth of his house to buy love, contempt is all he would purchase." Then follows an obscure passage that may be a veiled criticism of the worldly policies of a late Jewish ruler in the 2nd century B.C.E.:

> Our sister is little: her breasts are not yet formed. What shall we do for our sister on the day she is spoken for? If she is a rampart, on the crest we will build a battlement of silver; if she is a door, we will board her up with planks of cedar.—I am a wall, and my breasts represent its towers. And under his eyes I have found true peace.

> Solomon had a vineyard at Baal-hamon. He entrusted it to overseers, and each one was to pay him the value of its produce, a thousand shekels of silver. But I look after my own vineyard myself. You, Solomon, may have your thousand shekels, and those who oversee its produce their two hundred.

> You who dwell in the gardens, my companions listen for your voice: deign to let me hear it. Haste away, my Beloved. Be like a gazelle, a young stag, on the spicy mountains.

Impression from a stone cylinder seal, Babylonia, c. second millennium B.C.E. Scene showing Gilgamesh and Enkidu slaying the Bull of Heaven, as Ishtar angrily protests.

include the poem's preface, which summarizes Gilgamesh's accomplishments and reflects directly on the recovery of ancient tradition—as the Gilgamesh story itself was by then.

GILGAMESH AND EPIC

The term "epic" is sometimes used loosely to describe ancient narrative poems in general, but full-scale epics do more than tell a story in poetic language. Epics like Homer's *Iliad* often center on the founding or defense of a city and its society, with extensive battle scenes in which a great hero attempts to overcome heavy odds presented both by human opponents and divine antagonism. Other epics, like Homer's *Odyssey*, have to do chiefly with a voyage of travel, exploration, or escape. Like Virgil's *Aeneid*, *The Epic of Gilgamesh* combines both kinds of epic subject matter. Ancient though it is, *Gilgamesh* is also like the *Aeneid* in being a developed reworking of earlier epic texts. Where Virgil used Homer and other sources, Sîn-liqe-unninni drew on older poems of the Flood and of the underworld, as well as of Gilgamesh and his adventures, to create a broad exploration of the uses and limits of human culture, poised between the realms of nature and of the gods.

The poem presents Gilgamesh as a mixed figure himself; like Homer's hero Achilles, he has a human father and a divine mother, and like Achilles he is a great but flawed hero. As the epic begins, he has been oppressing his own people, who appeal to the gods for relief. The gods create Enkidu, no longer simply Gilgamesh's servant but now shown as a force of nature, a wild man who comes to Uruk and restrains Gilgamesh from his misbehavior. Becoming fast friends, Gilgamesh and Enkidu journey to a distant mountain and slay its guardian monster, and then enter into a fatal dispute with Ishtar, goddess of love. She tries to seduce Gilgamesh, who rejects her advances; she sends a great bull down from heaven to kill him, but Enkidu and Gilgamesh slaughter the bull. Then Enkidu goes too far: he rashly insults Ishtar, who decrees his death.

In despair at his friend's death, Gilgamesh sets off to find the distant, hidden home of his ancestor Utanapishtim, who with his wife was the sole survivor of a worldwide flood. Utanapishtim tells him the story of the Flood, in terms strikingly similar to the biblical account found in Genesis 6–9 (page 34–37). By weaving this formerly independent story into his epic, Sîn-liqe-unninni extends Gilgamesh's story to a wider context of the life and death of civilization itself. After telling his story, Utanapishtim gives Gilgamesh a plant that will give him immortality, but on his way home a serpent steals the plant, and Gilgamesh returns to Uruk distraught; his only comfort, in the poem's closing lines, is to survey his city's magnificent walls, in which he buries his story for later generations to read.

Gilgamesh is classically epic in its language as well as its story. The poem is written in an elevated style that moves with a grand, inexorable sweep, punctuated by haunting lyrical passages in which Gilgamesh and Enkidu voice their fears of the dangers they face and their grief at the prospect of death. Like later literary epics, *Gilgamesh* also makes thematic use of old patterns developed for earlier oral poetry. Sumerian poems like the hymn of Inanna (page 42) relied heavily on repetition for verbal effect and to aid listeners in understanding when they were recited in ritual settings. *Gilgamesh* is clearly a written composition rather than an oral one, intended for private reading and reflection rather than for any public use, but Sîn-liqe-unninni availed himself fully of the resources of repetition. Series of mysterious dreams foreshadow future events and build a sense of brooding uncertainty. Variations within lines allow the reader to see more fully into events and images, as when Utanapishtim tells Gilgamesh, "I will reveal to you a thing that is hidden, a secret of the gods I will tell you!"

GILGAMESH RECOVERED

In a fitting reflection of the poem's own themes of loss and recovery, *The Epic of Gilgamesh* itself vanished from human knowledge for over two thousand years, following the defeat and destruction of the major Mesopotamian cities by Persian invaders in the seventh and sixth centuries B.C.E. It was not until the 1850s that an Iraqi archaeologist, Hormuzd Rassam, discovered the ruins of the great royal library of Ashurbanipal, King of the World and King of Assyria in the mid-seventh century. Rassam shipped thousands of tablets back to the British Museum, where scholars began to piece fragments together and puzzle out their contents. A full twenty years later a young curator named George Smith began to study the eleven tablets that would turn out to contain *Gilgamesh*. Smith was electrified when he came upon the Noah-like Utanapishtim's account of the Flood. "I am the first man to read that after two thousand years of oblivion," he exclaimed, and, according to his associate E. A. W. Budge, "he jumped up and rushed about the room in a state of great excitement, and, to the astonishment of those present, began to undress himself!"

Ever since then, modern readers have been gripped by this epic poem, though they have differed widely about how it should be understood. Nineteenth-century readers debated whether it was a work of fiction or a genuine historical account. The parallels between Utanapishtim and Noah were taken by some to demonstrate the factual basis of the biblical version, while others drew an opposite conclusion, that Noah must be as fictional a figure as his Akkadian counterpart. Readers today focus on the epic as a poetic masterpiece rather than a historical document, yet the poem remains open to many interpretations. In part, it is open-ended simply because it is fragmentary: extensive gaps remain in the set of tablets that Rassam found in Nineveh and in other copies that have been recovered elsewhere. Some of these gaps can be filled in with parallel passages in earlier and later versions, and in this way a reasonably complete translation can be pieced together, as is presented here. The poem's great theme of the fragility of human life and culture is well illustrated by gaps and ellipses that continue to dot the text.

Even in the poem's many well-preserved episodes, mysteries remain. We first meet Enkidu living happily in the open countryside, naked, among the animals; when a temple prostitute seduces him and brings him to Uruk, does this episode celebrate city culture's riches or satirize them? Is Gilgamesh displaying heroic boldness in going off to slay the demon Humbaba, or is he being foolhardy, as his own counselors tell him? When he rejects the goddess Ishtar's advances, is Gilgamesh standing up for humanity or making the mistake of his—and

Enkidu's—life? What are we to make of the mysterious dreams that periodically visit both Gilgamesh and Enkidu? Does Utanapishtim sympathize with Gilgamesh's quest for immortality or mock him for believing he can transcend the human condition? Does the poem end in an affirmation of human culture or in despair?

First recorded a thousand years before either the Greeks or the Hebrews learned how to write, Gilgamesh's story circulated through the Near East and Asia Minor during the centuries in which both the legends of Genesis and the Homeric epics were developed and eventually written down. Both the Eden story and the Flood story have clear parallels in *Gilgamesh,* whose restless hero can also be well compared to Odysseus, even as his fated friendship with Enkidu can be related to the relationship of Achilles and his beloved friend Patroklos. Gilgamesh's story continued to live on in his own region in oral form, and his adventures have echoes in *The Thousand and One Nights* in such figures as Sindbad. Now that the epic itself has at last been recovered, its haunting images, its moving dialogues, and its engrossing drama make it once again, after two thousand years of oblivion, compelling reading today.

PRONUNCIATIONS:

Enkidu: AIN-key-dou
Gilgamesh: GILL-gah-mesh
Shamash: SHAY-mash
Shamhat: SHAHM-haht
Sîn-liqe-unninni: SEEN-LEE-kay-ooh-NEE-nee
Urshanabi: OOHR-sha-NAH-bee
Utanapishtim: ooh-TA-nah-PEASH-team

The Epic of Gilgamesh[1]
Tablet 1

He who has seen everything, I will make known to the lands.
I will teach about him who experienced all things.
Anu° granted him the totality of knowledge of all.   *the sky god*
He saw the Secret, discovered the Hidden,
5   he brought information of the time before the Flood.
He went on a distant journey, pushing himself to exhaustion,
but then was brought to peace.
He carved on a stone stela all of his toils,
and built the wall of Uruk-Haven,
10   the wall of the sacred Eanna Temple, the holy sanctuary.
Look at its wall which gleams like copper,
inspect its inner wall, the likes of which no one can equal!
Take hold of the threshold stone—it dates from ancient times!
Go close to the Eanna Temple, the residence of Ishtar,
15   such as no later king or man ever equaled!
Go up on the wall of Uruk and walk around,
examine its foundation, inspect its brickwork thoroughly.
Is not even the core of the brick structure made of kiln-fired brick,
and did not the Seven Sages[2] themselves lay out its plans?
20   One league city, one league palm gardens, one league lowlands, the open
     area of the Ishtar Temple,

1. Translated by Maureen Gallery Kovacs.   2. Sent by Ea, god of wisdom, to teach humanity the arts
                                                        of civilization.

three leagues and the open area of Uruk the wall encloses.
Find the copper tablet box,
open the hasp of its lock of bronze,
undo the fastening of its secret opening.
25   Take and read out from the lapis lazuli tablet
how Gilgamesh went through every hardship.

Supreme over other kings, lordly in appearance,
he is the hero, born of Uruk, the goring wild bull.
He walks out in front, the leader,
30   and walks at the rear, trusted by his companions.
Mighty net, protector of his people,
raging flood-wave who destroys even walls of stone!
Offspring of Lugalbanda, Gilgamesh is strong to perfection,
son of the august cow, Rimat-Ninsun, Gilgamesh is awesome to perfection.[3]
35   It was he who opened the mountain passes,
who dug wells on the flank of the mountain.
It was he who crossed the ocean, the vast seas, to the rising sun,
who explored the world regions, seeking life.
It was he who reached by his own sheer strength Utanapishtim, the Far-
      away,
40   who restored the sanctuaries that the Flood had destroyed!
Who can compare with him in kingliness?
Who can say like Gilgamesh: "I am King!"?
Whose name, from the day of his birth, was called "Gilgamesh"?
Two-thirds of him is god, one-third of him is human.
45   The Great Goddess designed the model for his body,
she prepared his form,[4]
                        . . .
beautiful, handsomest of men.
He walks around in the enclosure of Uruk,
like a wild bull he makes himself mighty, head raised over others.
50   There is no rival who can raise his weapon against him.
His fellows stand at the alert, attentive to his orders.
The men of Uruk become anxious:
Gilgamesh does not leave a son to his father;
Is Gilgamesh the shepherd of Uruk-Haven,
                        . . .
55   bold, eminent, knowing, and wise?
Gilgamesh does not leave a girl to her betrothed!
The daughter of the warrior, the bride of the young man,
the gods kept hearing their complaints, so
the gods of the heavens implored Anu, Lord of Uruk:
60   "You have indeed brought into being a mighty wild bull, head raised!
      There is no rival who can raise a weapon against him.
      His fellows stand at the alert, attentive to his orders,

---

3. Gilgamesh's father Lugalbanda was an earlier king of
Uruk; his mother is the goddess Ninsun, "Lady Wild
Cow."
4. Ellipses indicate missing lines and parts of lines.

Gilgamesh does not leave a son to his father,

. . .

Is he the shepherd of Uruk-Haven,

. . .

65   bold, eminent, knowing, and wise?

Gilgamesh does not leave a girl to her betrothed!"

The daughter of the warrior, the bride of the young man,

Anu listened to their complaints,

and called out to Aruru:°   *mother goddess*

70   "It was you, Aruru, who created this man,

now create a counterpart to him.

Let him be equal to Gilgamesh's stormy heart,

let them be a match for each other so that Uruk may find peace!"

When Aruru heard this she created within herself the counterpart of Anu.

75   Aruru washed her hands, she pinched off some clay, and threw it into the

wilderness.

In the wilderness she created valiant Enkidu,

born of Silence, endowed with strength by Ninurta.°   *god of war*

His whole body was shaggy with hair,

he had a full head of hair like a woman,

80   his locks billowed in profusion like Ashnan.°   *goddess of grain*

He knew neither people nor settled living,

but wore a garment like Sumukan.°   *goddess of cattle*

He ate grasses with the gazelles,

and jostled at the watering hole with the animals;

85   as with animals, his thirst was slaked with water.

A notorious trapper

came face-to-face with him opposite the watering hole.

A first, a second, and a third day

he came face-to-face with him opposite the watering hole.

90   On seeing him the trapper's face went stark with fear,

and he and his animals drew back home.

He was rigid with fear; though stock-still

his heart pounded and his face drained of color.

He was miserable to the core,

95   and his face looked like one who had made a long journey.

The trapper addressed his father saying:

"Father, a certain fellow has come from the mountains.

He is the mightiest in the land,

his strength is as mighty as the meteorite of Anu!

100   He continually goes over the mountains,

he continually jostles at the watering place with the animals,

he continually plants his feet opposite the watering place.

I was afraid, so I did not go up to him.

He filled in the pits that I had dug,

105   wrenched out my traps that I had spread,

released from my grasp the wild animals.

He does not let me make my rounds in the wilderness!"

The trapper's father spoke to him saying:

"My son, there lives in Uruk a certain Gilgamesh.
110   There is no one stronger than he,
        he is as strong as the meteorite of Anu.
        Go, set off to Uruk,
        tell Gilgamesh of this Man of Might.
        He will give you the harlot Shamhat, take her with you.
115   The woman will overcome the fellow as if she were strong.
        When the animals are drinking at the watering place
        have her take off her robe and expose her sex.
        When he sees her he will draw near to her,
        and his animals, who grew up in his wilderness, will be alien to him."
120 He heeded his father's advice.
    The trapper went off to Uruk,
    he made the journey, stood inside of Uruk,
    and declared to Gilgamesh:
        "There is a certain fellow who has come from the mountains—
125   he is the mightiest in the land,
        his strength is as mighty as the meteorite of Anu!
        He continually goes over the mountains,
        he continually jostles at the watering place with the animals,
        he continually plants his feet opposite the watering place.
130   I was afraid, so I did not go up to him.
        He filled in the pits that I had dug,
        wrenched out my traps that I had spread,
        released from my grasp the wild animals.
        He does not let me make my rounds in the wilderness!"
135 Gilgamesh said to the trapper:
        "Go, trapper, bring the harlot, Shamhat, with you.
        When the animals are drinking at the watering place
        have her take off her robe and expose her sex.
        When he sees her he will draw near to her,
140   and his animals, who grew up in his wilderness, will be alien to him."

    The trapper went, bringing the harlot, Shamhat, with him.
    They set off on the journey, making direct way.
    On the third day they arrived at the appointed place,
    and the trapper and the harlot sat down at their posts.
145 A first day and a second they sat opposite the watering hole.
    The animals arrived and drank at the watering hole,
    the wild beasts arrived and slaked their thirst with water.
    Then he, Enkidu, offspring of the mountains,
    who eats grasses with the gazelles,
150 came to drink at the watering hole with the animals,
    with the wild beasts he slaked his thirst with water.
    Then Shamhat saw him—a primitive,
    a savage fellow from the depths of the wilderness!
        "That is he, Shamhat! Release your clenched arms,
155   expose your sex so he can take in your voluptuousness.
        Do not be restrained—take his energy!
        When he sees you he will draw near to you.

Spread out your robe so he can lie upon you,
and perform for this primitive the task of womankind!
160 His animals, who grew up in his wilderness, will become alien to him,
and his lust will groan over you."
Shamhat unclutched her bosom, exposed her sex, and he took in her volup-
     tuousness.
She was not restrained, but took his energy.
She spread out her robe and he lay upon her,
165 she performed for the primitive the task of womankind.
His lust groaned over her;
for six days and seven nights Enkidu stayed aroused,
and had intercourse with the harlot
until he was sated with her charms.
170 But when he turned his attention to his animals,
the gazelles saw Enkidu and darted off,
the wild animals distanced themselves from his body.
Enkidu's body was utterly depleted,
his knees that wanted to go off with his animals went rigid;
175 Enkidu was diminished, his running was not as before.
But then he drew himself up, for his understanding had broadened.
Turning around, he sat down at the harlot's feet,
gazing into her face, his ears attentive as the harlot spoke.
The harlot said to Enkidu:
180 "You are beautiful, Enkidu, you are become like a god.
Why do you gallop around the wilderness with the wild beasts?
Come, let me bring you into Uruk-Haven,
to the Holy Temple, the residence of Anu and Ishtar,
the place of Gilgamesh, who is wise to perfection,
185 but who struts his power over the people like a wild bull."
What she kept saying found favor with him.
Becoming aware of himself, he sought a friend.
Enkidu spoke to the harlot:
"Come, Shamhat, take me away with you
190 to the sacred Holy Temple, the residence of Anu and Ishtar,
the place of Gilgamesh, who is wise to perfection,
but who struts his power over the people like a wild bull.
I will challenge him.
Let me shout out in Uruk: 'I am the mighty one!'
195 Lead me in and I will change the order of things;
he whose strength is mightiest is the one born in the wilderness!"
She replied: "Come, let us go, so he may see your face.
I will lead you to Gilgamesh—I know where he will be.
Look about, Enkidu, inside Uruk-Haven,
200 where the people show off in skirted finery,
where every day is a day for some festival,
where the lyre and drum play continually,
where harlots stand about prettily,
exuding voluptuousness, full of laughter,
205 and on the couch of night the sheets are spread.

Enkidu, you who do not know how to live,
I will show you Gilgamesh, a man of joy and sorrow.
Look at him, gaze at his face—
he is a handsome youth, with freshness,
210   his entire body exudes voluptuousness.
He has mightier strength than you,
without sleeping day or night!
Enkidu, it is your wrong thoughts you must change!
It is Gilgamesh whom Shamash° loves,   *the sun god*
215   and Anu, Enlil, and Ea[5] have enlarged his mind.
Even before you came from the mountain
Gilgamesh in Uruk had dreams about you."
Gilgamesh got up and revealed the dream, saying to his mother:
    "Mother, I had a dream last night.
220   Stars of the sky appeared,
and some kind of meteorite of Anu fell next to me.
I tried to lift it but it was too mighty for me,
I tried to turn it over but I could not budge it.
The Land of Uruk was standing around it,
225   the whole land had assembled about it,
the populace was thronging around it,
the Men clustered about it,
and kissed its feet as if it were a little baby.
I loved it and embraced it as a wife.
230   I laid it down at your feet,
and you made it compete with me."
The mother of Gilgamesh, the wise, all-knowing, said to her Lord;
Rimat-Ninsun, the wise, all-knowing, said to Gilgamesh:
    "As for the stars of the sky that appeared
235   and the meteorite of Anu which fell next to you,
which you tried to lift but it was too mighty for you,
which you tried to turn over but were unable to budge it,
which you laid down at my feet,
and I made it compete with you,
240   and you loved and embraced it as a wife:
There will come to you a mighty man, a comrade who saves his friend—
he is the mightiest in the land, he is strongest,
his strength is mighty as the meteorite of Anu!
You loved him and embraced him as a wife;
245   and it is he who will repeatedly save you.
Your dream is good and propitious!"
A second time Gilgamesh said to his mother:
    "Mother, I have had another dream:
At the gate of my marital chamber there lay an axe,
250   and people had collected about it.
The Land of Uruk was standing around it,

---

5. The sky god Anu is Uruk's patron god, Enlil is head of the younger generation of gods, Ea is god of wisdom.

the whole land had assembled about it,
the populace was thronging around it.
I laid it down at your feet,
255   I loved it and embraced it as a wife,
and you made it compete with me."
The mother of Gilgamesh, the wise, all-knowing, said to her son;
Rimat-Ninsun, the wise, all-knowing, said to Gilgamesh:
"The axe that you saw is a man,
260   whom you love and embrace as a wife,
but whom I have made compete with you.
There will come to you a mighty man, a comrade who saves his friend—
he is the mightiest in the land, he is strongest,
he is as mighty as the meteorite of Anu!"
265   Gilgamesh spoke to his mother saying:
"By the command of Enlil, the Great Counselor, so may it come to pass!
May I have a friend and adviser,
a friend and adviser may I have!
You have interpreted for me the dreams about him!"
270   After the harlot recounted the dreams of Gilgamesh to Enkidu
the two of them made love.

Tablet 2

Enkidu sits in front of her.[6]
Enkidu knew nothing about eating bread for food,
and of drinking beer he had not been taught.
The harlot spoke to Enkidu, saying:
5   "Eat the food, Enkidu, it is the way one lives.
Drink the beer, as is the custom of the land."
Enkidu ate the food until he was sated,
he drank the beer—seven jugs!—and became expansive and sang with joy!
He was elated and his face glowed.
10   He splashed his shaggy body with water,
and rubbed himself with oil, and turned into a human.
Shamhat pulled off her clothing,
and clothed him with one piece
while she clothed herself with a second.
15   She took hold of him as gods do
and brought him to the hut of the shepherds.

The shepherds gathered all around about him,
they marveled to themselves:
"How the youth resembles Gilgamesh—
20   tall in stature, towering up to the battlements over the wall!
Surely he was born in the mountains;
his strength is as mighty as the meteorite of Anu!"
They placed food in front of him,

6. Thirty-three lines are missing here. The next 15 lines are restored from parallels in the Old Babylonian version, as are several later passages.

they placed beer in front of him;
25   Enkidu did not eat or drink, but squinted and stared.
Enkidu scattered the wolves, he chased away the lions.
The herders could lie down in peace,
for Enkidu was their watchman.

Then he raised his eyes and saw a man.
30   He said to the harlot:
     "Shamhat, have that man go away!
     Why has he come? I will call out his name!"
The harlot called out to the man
and went over to him and spoke with him.
35   "Young man, where are you hurrying?
     Why this arduous pace?"
The young man spoke, saying to Enkidu:
     "They have invited me to a wedding,
     as is the custom of the people,
40   to make the selection of brides.
     I have heaped up tasty delights for the wedding on the ceremonial platter.
     For the King of Broad-Marted Uruk,
     open is the veil of the people for choosing a girl.
     For Gilgamesh, the King of Broad-Marted Uruk,
45   open is the veil of the people for choosing.
     He will have intercourse with the 'destined wife,'
     he first, the husband afterward.
     This is ordered by the counsel of Anu,
     from the severing of his umbilical cord it has been destined for him."
50   At the young man's speech Enkidu's face flushed with anger.
Enkidu walked in front, and Shamhat after him.[7]
He walked down the street of Uruk-Haven,
He blocked the way through Uruk the Sheepfold.
The land of Uruk stood around him,
55   the whole land assembled about him,
the populace was thronging around him,
and kissed his feet as if he were a little baby. . . .
For Ishara the bed of marriage is ready,
for Gilgamesh as for a god a counterpart is set up.
60   Enkidu blocked the entry to the marital chamber,
and would not allow Gilgamesh to be brought in.
They grappled with each other at the entry to the marital chamber,
in the street they attacked each other, the public square of the land.
The doorposts trembled and the wall shook.

[*The next seven lines are from the earlier version.*]

65   Gilgamesh bent his knees, with his other foot on the ground,
his anger abated and he turned his chest away.
After he turned his chest Enkidu said to Gilgamesh:

---

7. Several lines are missing, in which Enkidu evidently resolves to go and challenge Gilgamesh.

"Your mother bore you ever unique,
the Wild Cow of the Enclosure, Ninsun,
70   your head is elevated over other men,
Enlil has destined for you the kingship over the people."
. . .
They kissed each other and became friends.[8]
. . .
Enkidu made a declaration to Gilgamesh:
"In order to protect the Cedar Forest
75   Enlil assigned Humbaba as a terror to human beings—
Humbaba's roar is a Flood, his mouth is Fire, and his breath is Death!
He can hear 100 leagues away any rustling in his forest!
Who would go down into his forest?
Enlil assigned him as a terror to human beings,
80   and whoever goes down into his forest paralysis will strike!"
Gilgamesh spoke to Enkidu saying:
. . .
"Who, my Friend, can ascend to the heavens?
Only the gods can dwell forever with Shamash.
As for human beings, their days are numbered,
85   and whatever they keep trying to achieve is but wind!
Now you are afraid of death—
what has become of your bold strength?
I will go in front of you,
and your mouth can call out: 'Go on closer, do not be afraid!'
90   Should I fall, I will have established my fame.
They will say: 'It was Gilgamesh who locked in battle with Humbaba the
      Terrible!'
You were born and raised in the wilderness,
a lion leaped up on you, so you have experienced it all!'
. . .
I will undertake it and I will cut down the Cedar.
95   It is I who will establish fame for eternity!
Come, my friend, I will go over to the forge
and have them cast the weapons in our presence!"
Holding each other by the hand they went over to the forge.
The craftsmen sat and discussed with one another.
. . .
100   "The hatchet should be one talent in weight,[9]
Their swords should be one talent, and their armor as well. . . ."
Gilgamesh said to the men of Uruk:
"Listen to me, . . . you men of Uruk, . . .
I want to make myself more mighty, and will go on a distant journey!
105   I will face fighting such as I have never known,

---

8. A fragmentary passage describes Enkidu's sorrow at the decrease of his strength once he has left the wilderness. Gilgamesh proposes journeying to the Cedar Forest to kill its protector Humbaba and cut down the cedars. Enkidu reacts with fear.
9. About two-thirds of a pound.

I will set out on a road I have never traveled!
Give me your blessings!
I will enter the city gate of Uruk, . . .
I will devote myself to the New Year's Festival.
110   I will perform the New Year's ceremonies,
The New Year's Festival will take place, . . .
They will keep shouting 'Hurrah!' . . ."
Enkidu spoke to the Elders:
          . . .
"Say to him that he must not go to the Cedar Forest—
115   the journey is not to be made!"
          . . .
The Noble Counselors of Uruk arose and delivered their advice to
     Gilgamesh:
"You are young, Gilgamesh, your heart carries you off—
you do not know what you are talking about!
          . . .
Humbaba's roar is a Flood,
120   his mouth is Fire, his breath Death!
He can hear any rustling in his forest 100 leagues away!
Who would go down into his forest?
Who among even the Igigi gods can confront him?
In order to keep the Cedar safe, Enlil[1] assigned him as a terror to human
     beings."
125   Gilgamesh listened to the statement of his Noble Counselors.

Tablet 3

The Elders spoke to Gilgamesh, saying:
"Gilgamesh, do not put your trust in your vast strength,
but keep a sharp eye out, make each blow strike its mark!
     'The one who goes on ahead saves the comrade.'
5   'The one who knows the route protects his friend.'
Let Enkidu go ahead of you;
he knows the road to the Cedar Forest,
he has seen fighting, has experienced battle.
Enkidu will protect the friend, will keep the comrade safe.
10   Let his body urge him back to the wives."
[The Elders speak to Enkidu:]
"In our Assembly we have entrusted the King to you,
and on your return you must entrust the King back to us!"
Gilgamesh spoke to Enkidu, saying:
15   "Come on, my friend, let us go to the Egalmah Temple,
to Ninsun, the Great Queen;
Ninsun is wise, all-knowing.
She will put the advisable path at our feet."
Taking each other by the hand,

1. The chief Sumerian god.

20 Gilgamesh and Enkidu walked to the Egalmah,
   to Ninsun, the Great Queen.
   Gilgamesh arose and went to her.
       "Ninsun, even though I am extraordinarily strong,
       I must now travel a long way to where Humbaba is,
25   I must face fighting such as I have not known,
       and I must travel on a road that I do not know!
       Until the time that I go and return,
       until I reach the Cedar Forest,
       until I kill Humbaba the Terrible,
30   and eradicate from the land something baneful that Shamash hates,
       intercede with Shamash on my behalf!
       If I kill Humbaba and cut his Cedar
       let there be rejoicing all over the land,
       and I will erect a monument of the victory before you!"

35 The words of Gilgamesh, her son,
   grieving Queen Ninsun heard over and over.
   Ninsun went into her living quarters.
   She washed herself with the purity plant,
   she donned a robe worthy of her body,
40 she donned jewels worthy of her chest,
   she donned her sash, and put on her crown.
   She sprinkled water from a bowl onto the ground.

   She went up to the roof and set incense in front of Shamash,°   *the sun god*
   she offered fragrant cuttings, and raised her arms to Shamash.
45   "Why have you imposed—nay, inflicted!—a restless heart on my son,
           Gilgamesh?
       Now you have touched him so that he wants to travel,
       a long way to where Humbaba is!
       He will face fighting such as he has not known,
       and will travel on a road that he does not know!
50   Until he goes away and returns,
       until he reaches the Cedar Forest,
       until he kills Humbaba the Terrible,
       and eradicates from the land something baneful that you hate,
       on the day that you see him on the road
55   may Aja, the Bride,° without fear remind you,   *Shamash's wife*
       and command also the Watchmen of the Night,
       the stars, and at night your father, Sin."°   *moon god*

[*Long passage missing.*]

Ninsun banked up the incense and uttered the ritual words.
She called to Enkidu and would give him instructions:
60   "Enkidu the Mighty, you are not of my womb,
       but now I speak to you along with the sacred votaries of Gilgamesh,
       the high priestesses, the holy women, the temple servers."
   She laid a pendant on Enkidu's neck, . . . [saying]
       "I have taken Enkidu; Enkidu to Gilgamesh I have taken."

65   [The Elders said:]
        "Enkidu will protect the friend, will keep the comrade safe.
        Let his body urge him back to the wives.
        In our Assembly we have entrusted the King to you,
        and on your return you must entrust the King back to us!"[2]

Tablet 4

        At twenty leagues they broke for some food,
        at thirty leagues they stopped for the night,
        walking fifty leagues in a whole day,
        a walk of a month and a half.
5   On the third day they drew near to the Lebanon.
        They dug a well facing Shamash, the setting sun. . . .
        Gilgamesh climbed up a mountain peak,
        made a libation° of flour, and said: *offering*
            "Mountain, bring me a dream, a favorable message from Shamash."
10   Enkidu prepared a sleeping place for him for the night;
        a violent wind passed through so he attached a covering.
        He made him lie down. . . .
        While Gilgamesh rested his chin on his knees,
        sleep that pours over mankind overtook him.
15   In the middle of the night his sleep came to an end,
        so he got up and said to his friend:
            "My friend, did you not call out to me? Why did I wake up?
            Did you not touch me? Why am I so disturbed?
            Did a god pass by? Why are my muscles trembling?
20   Enkidu, my friend, I have had a dream—
            and the dream I had was deeply disturbing!
            In the mountain gorges, the mountain fell down on me!"

        He who was born in the wilderness,
        Enkidu, interpreted the dream for his friend:
25   "My friend, your dream is favorable,
            The dream is extremely important.
            My friend, the mountain which you saw in the dream is Humbaba.
            It means we will capture Humbaba, and kill him
            and throw his corpse into the wasteland.
30   In the morning there will be a favorable message from Shamash."

        At twenty leagues they broke for some food,
        at thirty leagues they stopped for the night,
        walking fifty leagues in a whole day,
        a walk of a month and a half.
35   They dug a well facing Shamash; . . .
        Gilgamesh climbed up a mountain peak,
        made a libation of flour, and said:
            "Mountain, bring me a dream, a favorable message from Shamash."

---

2. The rest of their speech is fragmentary.

Enkidu prepared a sleeping place for him for the night;
40   a violent wind passed through so he attached a covering.

While Gilgamesh rested his chin on his knees,
sleep that pours over mankind overtook him.
In the middle of the night his sleep came to an end,
so he got up and said to his friend:
45   "My friend, did you not call out to me? Why did I wake up?
Did you not touch me? Why am I so disturbed?
Did a god pass by? Why are my muscles trembling?
Enkidu, my friend, I have had a dream,
besides my first dream I have had a second.
50   And the dream I had—so striking, so . . . , so disturbing!
I was grappling with a wild bull of the wilderness,
with his bellow he split the ground, a cloud of dust rose to the sky.
I sank to my knees in front of him. . . .
My tongue hung out, My temples throbbed;
55   he gave me water to drink from his waterskin."
"My friend," Enkidu said, "the god to whom we go
is not the wild bull! He is totally different!
The wild bull that you saw is Shamash, the protector,
in difficulties he holds our hand.
60   The one who gave you water to drink from his waterskin
is your personal god, who brings honor to you, Lugalbanda.
We should join together and do one thing,
a deed such as has never before been done in the land."

At twenty leagues they broke for some food,
65   at thirty leagues they stopped for the night,
walking fifty leagues in a whole day,
a walk of a month and a half.
They dug a well facing Shamash; . . .
Gilgamesh climbed up a mountain peak,
70   made a libation of flour, and said:
          "Mountain, bring me a dream, a favorable message from Shamash."
Enkidu prepared a sleeping place for him for the night;
a violent wind passed through so he attached a covering.

While Gilgamesh rested his chin on his knees,
75   sleep that pours over mankind overtook him.
In the middle of the night his sleep came to an end,
so he got up and said to his friend:
          "My friend, did you not call out to me? Why did I wake up?
Did you not touch me? Why am I so disturbed?
80   Did a god pass by? Why are my muscles trembling?
Enkidu, my friend, I have had a third dream,
and the dream I had was deeply disturbing.
The heavens roared and the earth rumbled;
then it became deathly still, and darkness loomed.
85   A bolt of lightning cracked and a fire broke out,
and where it kept thickening, there rained death.

The white-hot flame dimmed, and the fire went out,
and everything that had been falling around turned to ash.
Let us go down into the plain so we can talk it over."

90   Enkidu heard the dream that he had presented and said to Gilgamesh:[3]

. . .

At twenty leagues they broke for some food,
at thirty leagues they stopped for the night,
walking fifty leagues in a whole day,
a walk of a month and a half.

95   They dug a well facing Shamash; . . .
Gilgamesh climbed up a mountain peak,
made a libation of flour, and said:
    "Mountain, bring me a dream, a favorable message from Shamash."
Enkidu prepared a sleeping place for him for the night;

100 a violent wind passed through so he attached a covering.

. . .

While Gilgamesh rested his chin on his knees,
sleep that pours over mankind overtook him.
In the middle of the night his sleep came to an end,
so he got up and said to his friend:

105   "My friend, did you not call out to me? Why did I wake up?
Did you not touch me? Why am I so disturbed?
Did a god pass by? Why are my muscles trembling?
Enkidu, my friend, I have had a fourth dream,
and the dream I had was deeply disturbing."[4]

. . .

110 Enkidu listened to his dream, and said:
    "The dream that you had is favorable, it is extremely important!
My friend, we will achieve victory over him,
Humbaba, against whom we rage, and triumph over him.
In the morning there will be a favorable message from Shamash."[5]

. . .

[*Gilgamesh appeals to Shamash:*]
His tears were running in the presence of Shamash.
    "What you said in Uruk, be mindful of it, stand by me!"
Gilgamesh, the offspring of Uruk-Haven,
Shamash heard what issued from his mouth,

120 and suddenly there resounded a warning sound from the sky.
    "Hurry, stand by him so that Humbaba does not enter the forest,
and does not go down into the thickets and hide!
He has not put on his seven coats of armor,
he is wearing only one, but has taken off six."

. . .

125 Gilgamesh spoke to Enkidu, saying:
    "Why, my friend, . . . we have crossed over all the mountains together, . . .

3. Enkidu's reply is missing.   5. A fragmentary fifth dream follows.
4. Gilgamesh's dream is missing.

my friend, you who are so experienced in battle, . . .
you need not fear death. . . .
Let your voice bellow forth like the kettledrum,
130 let the stiffness in your arms depart,
let the paralysis in your legs go away.
Take my hand, my friend, we will go on together.
Your heart should burn to do battle—
pay no heed to death, do not lose heart!
135 The one who watches from the side is a careful man,
but the one who walks in front protects himself and saves his comrade,
and through their fighting they establish fame!"
As the two of them reached the evergreen forest
they cut off their talk, and stood still.

Tablet 5[6]

They stood at the forest's edge,
gazing at the top of the Cedar Tree,
gazing at the entrance to the forest.
Where Humbaba would walk there was a trail,
5 the roads led straight on, the path was excellent.
Then they saw the Cedar Mountain, the Dwelling of the Gods, the throne
   dais of Irnini.[7]
Across the face of the mountain the Cedar brought forth luxurious foliage,
its shade was good, extremely pleasant.
The thornbushes were matted together, the woods were a thicket, . . .
10 the Forest was surrounded by a ravine two leagues long.[8]
          . . .
Humbaba spoke to Gilgamesh, saying:
   "An idiot and a moron should give advice to each other,
   but you, Gilgamesh, why have you come to me?
   Give advice, Enkidu, you 'son of a fish,' who does not even know his
      own father,
15 to the large and small turtles which do not suck their mother's milk!
   When you were still young I saw you but did not go over to you; . . .
   Now, you have brought Gilgamesh into my presence,
   Here you stand, an enemy, a stranger. . . .
   I would feed your flesh to the screeching vulture, the eagle, and the
      vulture!"
20 Gilgamesh spoke to Enkidu, saying:
   "My Friend, Humbaba's face keeps changing!"[9]
          . . .
Enkidu spoke to Gilgamesh, saying:
   "Why, my friend, are you whining so pitiably,
   hiding behind your whimpering?

---

6. This entire tablet is fragmentary. Several passages have been restored on the basis of Old Babylonian and Assyrian versions.
7. A war goddess associated with Ishtar.

8. In a fragmentary passage, Humbaba appears, frightening Enkidu anew, and Gilgamesh tries to reassure him.
9. In two missing lines, Gilgamesh in turn expresses fear.

25   Now there, my friend, . . . (it is time)
          to send the Flood, to crack the Whip.
          Do not snatch your feet away, do not turn your back;
          strike ever harder!"
                              . . .
        The ground split open with the heels of their feet,
30   as they whirled around in circles Mt. Hermon and Lebanon split.
        The white clouds darkened,
        death rained down on them like fog.
        Shamash raised up against Humbaba mighty tempests—
        Southwind, Northwind, Eastwind, Westwind, Whistling Wind,
35   Piercing Wind, Blizzard, Bad Wind, Wind of Simurru,
        Demon Wind, Ice Wind, Storm, Sandstorm—
        thirteen winds rose up against him and covered Humbaba's face.
        He could not butt through the front, and could not scramble out the back,
        so that Gilgamesh's weapons were in reach of Humbaba.
40   Humbaba begged for his life, saying to Gilgamesh:
          "You are young yet, Gilgamesh, your mother gave birth to you,
          and you are the offspring of Rimat-Ninsun
          It was at the instigation of Shamash, Lord of the Mountain,
          that you were roused to this expedition.
45   O scion of the heart of Uruk, King Gilgamesh!
                              . . .
        Gilgamesh, let me go,
        I will dwell with you as your servant.
        As many trees as you command me I will cut down for you,
        I will guard for you myrtle wood, wood fine enough for your palace!"
50   Enkidu addressed Gilgamesh, saying:
          "My friend, do not listen to Humbaba!"
                              . . .
        [Humbaba spoke to Enkidu:]
          "You understand the rules of my forest, . . .
          you are aware of all the things 'So ordered by Enlil.'
55   I should have carried you up, and killed you at the very entrance to the
              branches of my forest.
          I should have fed your flesh to the screeching vulture, the eagle, and the
              vulture.
          So now, Enkidu, clemency is up to you.
          Speak to Gilgamesh to spare my life!"
        Enkidu addressed Gilgamesh, saying:
60   "My friend, take Humbaba, Guardian of the Cedar Forest,
          grind up, kill, pulverize and . . . him!
          Humbaba, Guardian of the Forest, grind up, kill, pulverize and . . . him!"

        [*Long fragmentary passage deleted. Enkidu now speaks again to Gil-
          gamesh:*]
          "Before the Preeminent God Enlil hears,
65   and the gods are full of rage at us.
          Enlil is in Nippur, Shamash is in Sippar.

Erect an eternal monument proclaiming how Gilgamesh killed Humbaba."
Humbaba heard all this and said, . . .

"May he not live the longer of the two,

70   may Enkidu not have any old age more than his friend Gilgamesh!"
Enkidu spoke to Gilgamesh, saying:

"My friend, I have been talking to you but you have not been listening to me,
You have been listening to the curse of Humbaba!"

. . .

They pulled out his insides including his tongue.[1]

. . .

75   They cut through the Cedar
While Gilgamesh cuts down the trees, Enkidu searches through the stumps.
Enkidu addressed Gilgamesh, saying:

"My friend, we have cut down the towering Cedar whose top scrapes the sky.
Make from it a door 72 cubits high, 24 cubits wide,

80   one cubit thick, its fixture, its lower and upper pivots will be out of one piece.
Let them carry it to Nippur, the Euphrates will carry it down, Nippur will rejoice."
They tied together a raft, . . . Enkidu steered it,
while Gilgamesh held the head of Humbaba.

Tablet 6

Gilgamesh washed out his matted hair and cleaned up his equipment,
shaking out his locks down over his back,
throwing off his dirty clothes and putting on clean ones.
He wrapped himself in regal garments and fastened the sash.

5   When Gilgamesh placed his crown on his head,
Princess Ishtar raised her eyes to the beauty of Gilgamesh.

"Come along, Gilgamesh, be you my husband,
to me grant your lusciousness.
Be you my husband, and I will be your wife.

10   I will have harnessed for you a chariot of lapis lazuli and gold,
with wheels of gold and 'horns' of electrum.[2]
It will be harnessed with great storming mountain mules!
Come into our house, with the fragrance of cedar.
And when you come into our house the doorpost and throne dais will kiss your feet.

15   Bowed down beneath you will be kings, lords, and princes.
The Lullubu people will bring you the produce of the mountains and countryside as tribute.
Your she-goats will bear triplets, your ewes twins,
your donkey under burden will overtake the mule,
your steed at the chariot will be bristling to gallop,

1. This is the only complete line in a passage of 40 lines in   2. An alloy of gold and silver.
which Gilgamesh and Enkidu slay Humbaba.

20   your ox at the yoke will have no match."
      Gilgamesh addressed Princess Ishtar saying:
          "What would I have to give you if I married you?
          Do you need oil or garments for your body?
          Do you lack anything for food or drink?
25   I would gladly feed you food fit for a god,
          I would gladly give you wine fit for a king,
                              . . .
          You are an oven who [melts] ice,
          a half-door that keeps out neither breeze nor blast,
          a palace that crushes down valiant warriors,
30   an elephant who devours its own covering,
          pitch that blackens the hands of its bearer,
          a waterskin that soaks its bearer through,
          limestone that buckles out the stone wall,
          a battering ram that . . .
35   a shoe that bites its owner's feet!
          Where are your bridegrooms that you keep forever?
          Where is your 'Little Shepherd' bird that went up over you?
          See here now, I will recite the list of your lovers. . . .
          Tammuz, the lover of your earliest youth,
40   for him you have ordained lamentations year upon year![3]
          You loved the colorful 'Little Shepherd' bird
          and then hit him, breaking his wing, so
          now he stands in the forest crying 'My Wing'!
          You loved the supremely mighty lion,
45   yet you dug for him seven and again seven pits.
          You loved the stallion, famed in battle,
          yet you ordained for him the whip, the goad, and the lash,
          ordained for him to gallop for seven and seven hours,
          ordained for him drinking from muddied waters,
50   you ordained for his mother Silili to wail continually.
          You loved the Shepherd, the Master Herder,
          who continually presented you with bread baked in embers,
          and who daily slaughtered for you a kid.
          Yet you struck him, and turned him into a wolf,
55   so his own shepherds now chase him
          and his own dogs snap at his shins.
          You loved Ishullanu, your father's date gardener,
          who continually brought you baskets of dates,
          and brightened your table daily.
60   You raised your eyes to him, and you went to him:
              'Oh my Ishullanu, let us taste of your strength,
                  stretch out your hand to me, and touch our "date palm.'"[4]
          Ishullanu said to you:
              'Me? What is it you want from me?
65   Has my mother not baked, and have I not eaten

3. See *The Descent of Ishtar to the Underworld*, page 99,   underworld.
for Ishtar's use of her husband to redeem herself from the   4. A pun: "vulva" sounds like "date palm" in Akkadian.

that I should now eat food under contempt and curses
and that alfalfa grass should be my only cover against the cold?'
As you listened to these his words
you struck him, turning him into a dwarf,
70   and made him live in the middle of his garden of labors.
And now me! It is me you love, and you will ordain for me as for them!"

When Ishtar heard this
in a fury she went up to the heavens,
going to Anu, her father, and crying,
75   going to Antum, her mother, and weeping:
"Father, Gilgamesh has insulted me over and over,
Gilgamesh has recounted despicable deeds about me,
despicable deeds and curses!"
Anu addressed Princess Ishtar, saying:
80   "What is the matter? Was it not you who provoked King Gilgamesh?
So Gilgamesh recounted despicable deeds about you,
despicable deeds and curses!"
Ishtar spoke to her father, Anu, saying:
"Father, give me the Bull of Heaven,
85   so he can kill Gilgamesh in his dwelling.
If you do not give me the Bull of Heaven,
I will knock down the Gates of the Netherworld,
I will smash the door posts, and leave the doors flat down,
and will let the dead go up to eat the living!
90   And the dead will outnumber the living!"
Anu addressed Princess Ishtar, saying:
"If you demand the Bull of Heaven from me,
there will be seven years of empty husks for the land of Uruk.
Have you collected grain for the people?
95   Have you made grasses grow for the animals?"
Ishtar addressed Anu, her father, saying:
"I have heaped grain in the granaries for the people,
I made grasses grow for the animals,
in order that they might eat in the seven years of empty husks.
100   I have collected grain for the people,
I have made grasses grow for the animals."

. . .

When Anu heard her words,
he placed the nose-rope of the Bull of Heaven in her hand.
Ishtar led the Bull of Heaven down to the earth.
105   When it reached Uruk, . . . it climbed down to the Euphrates.
At the snort of the Bull of Heaven a huge pit opened up,
and a hundred Young Men of Uruk fell in.
At his second snort a huge pit opened up,
and two hundred Young Men of Uruk fell in.
110   At his third snort a huge pit opened up,
and Enkidu fell in up to his waist.
Then Enkidu jumped out and seized the Bull of Heaven by its horns.
The Bull spewed his spittle in front of him,

with his thick tail he flung his dung behind him . . .
115   Enkidu stalked and hunted down the Bull of Heaven.
He grasped it by the thick of its tail
and held onto it with both his hands,
while Gilgamesh, like an expert butcher,
boldly and surely approached the Bull of Heaven.
120   Between the nape, the horns, . . . he thrust his sword.
After they had killed the Bull of Heaven,
they ripped out its heart and presented it to Shamash.
They withdrew, bowing down humbly to Shamash.
Then the brothers sat down together.
125   Ishtar went up onto the top of the Wall of Uruk-Haven,
cast herself into the pose of mourning, and hurled her woeful curse:
        "Woe unto Gilgamesh who slandered me and killed the Bull of Heaven!"
When Enkidu heard this pronouncement of Ishtar,
he wrenched off the Bull's hindquarter and flung it in her face:
130   "If I could only get at you I would do the same to you!
        I would drape his innards over your arms!"
Ishtar assembled the cultic women of lovely-locks, joy-girls, and harlots,
and set them to mourning over the hindquarter of the Bull.
Gilgamesh summoned all the artisans and craftsmen.
135   All the artisans admired the thickness of its horns,
each fashioned from 30 minas° of lapis lazuli!   *pounds*
Two fingers thick is their casing.
Six vats of oil the contents of the two
he gave as ointment to his personal god Lugalbanda.
140   He brought the horns in and hung them in the bedroom of the family head.
They washed their hands in the Euphrates,
and proceeded hand in hand,
striding through the streets of Uruk.
The men of Uruk gathered together, staring at them.
145   Gilgamesh said to the palace retainers:
        "Who is the bravest of the men?
        Who is the boldest of the males?
        —Gilgamesh is the bravest of the men,
        the boldest of the males!
150   She at whom we flung the hindquarter of the Bull of Heaven in anger,
        Ishtar has no one that pleases her in the street!"
                                        . . .
Gilgamesh held a celebration in his palace.
The Young Men dozed off, sleeping on the couches of the night.
Enkidu was sleeping, and had a dream.
155   He woke up and revealed his dream to his friend.

Tablet 7

"My friend, why are the Great Gods in conference?
In my dream Anu, Enlil, and Shamash held a council,[5]

5. This account of Enkidu's dream is taken from a Hittite fragment.

and Anu spoke to Enlil:
    'Because they killed the Bull of Heaven and have also slain Humbaba,
5   the one of them who pulled up the Cedar of the Mountain must die!'
Enlil said: 'Let Enkidu die, but Gilgamesh must not die!'
But the Sun God of Heaven replied to valiant Enlil:
    'Was it not at my command that they killed the Bull of Heaven and
        Humbaba?
    Should now innocent Enkidu die?'
10   Then Enlil became angry at Shamash, saying:
    'It is you who are responsible because you traveled daily with them as
        their friend!'"
Enkidu was lying sick in front of Gilgamesh.
His tears flowing like canals, Gilgamesh said:
    "O brother, dear brother, why are they absolving me instead of my
        brother?"
15   Then Enkidu said: "So now must I become a ghost,
    to sit with the ghosts of the dead, to see my dear brother nevermore?"
            . . .

Enkidu raised his eyes, and spoke to the door as if it were human:
    "You stupid wooden door,
    with no ability to understand!
20   Already at twenty leagues I selected the wood for you, . . .
    your wood was without compare in my eyes.
    Seventy-two cubits° was your height,   *48 feet*
    Twenty-four cubits your width, one cubit your thickness; . . .
    I fashioned you, and I carried you to Nippur.
25   Had I known, O door, that this would be your gratitude . . .
    I would have taken an axe and chopped you up,
    and lashed your planks into a raft!
            . . .

    But yet, O door, I fashioned you, and I carried you to Nippur!
    May a king who comes after me reject you, . . .
30   may he remove my name and set his own name there!" . . .
Gilgamesh kept listening to his words, and retorted quickly,
Gilgamesh listened to the words of Enkidu, his Friend, and his tears flowed.
Gilgamesh addressed Enkidu, saying:
    "Friend, the gods have given you a mind broad and deep.
35   Though it behooves you to be sensible, you keep uttering improper things!
    Why, my Friend, does your mind utter improper things?
    The dream is important but very frightening,
    your lips are buzzing like flies.
    Though there is much fear, the dream is very important.
40   To the living the gods leave sorrow,
    to the living the dream leaves pain.
    I will pray, and beseech the Great Gods,
    I will seek . . . and appeal to your god.
            . . .
    What Enlil says . . . cannot go back,
45   What he has laid down cannot go back. . . ."

Just as dawn began to glow,
Enkidu raised his head and cried out to Shamash,
at the first gleam of the sun his tears poured forth.
    "I appeal to you, O Shamash, on behalf of my precious life,
50   because of that notorious trapper
    who did not let me attain the same as my friend.
    May the trapper not get enough to feed himself.
    May his profit be slashed, and his wages decrease! . . .

After he had cursed the trapper to his satisfaction,
55   his heart prompted him to curse the Harlot.
    "Come now, Harlot, I am going to decree your fate,
    a fate that will never come to an end for eternity!
    I will curse you with a Great Curse,
    may my curses overwhelm you suddenly, in an instant!
60   May you not be able to make a household,
    and not be able to love a child of your own! . . .
    May dregs of beer stain your beautiful lap,
    may a drunk soil your festal robe with vomit,
          . . .
    May you never acquire anything of bright alabaster, . . .
65   may shining silver, man's delight, not be cast into your house,
    may a gateway be where you take your pleasure,
    may a crossroad be your home,
    may a wasteland be your sleeping place,
    may the shadow of the city wall be your place to stand,
70   may the thorns and briars skin your feet,
    may both the drunk and the dry slap you on the cheek,
          . . .
    may the builder not seal the roof of your house,
    may owls nest in the cracks of your walls!"
          . . .
When Shamash heard what his mouth had uttered,
75   he suddenly called out to him from the sky:
    "Enkidu, why are you cursing the harlot, Shamhat,
    she who fed you bread fit for a god,
    she who gave you wine fit for a king,
    she who dressed you in grand garments,
80   and she who allowed you to make beautiful Gilgamesh your comrade?
    Now Gilgamesh is your beloved brother-friend!
    He will have you lie on a grand couch,
    will have you lie on a couch of honor.
    He will seat you in the seat of ease, the seat at his left,
85   so that the princes of the world kiss your feet.
    He will have the people of Uruk go into mourning and moaning over
        you,
    will fill the happy people with woe over you.
And after you he will let his body bear a filthy mat of hair,
will don the skin of a lion and roam the wilderness."

90   As soon as Enkidu heard the words of valiant Shamash,
        his agitated heart grew calm, his anger abated.
        Enkidu spoke to the harlot, saying:
            "Come, Shamhat, I will decree your fate for you.
            Let my mouth which has cursed you, now turn to bless you!
95   May governors and nobles love you,
            May he who is one league away bite his lip in anticipation,
            may he who is two leagues away shake out his locks in preparation!
            May the soldier not refuse you, but undo his buckle for you,
            may he give you rock crystal, lapis lazuli, and gold,
100   may his gift to you be earrings of filigree.
            May his supplies be heaped up. . . .
            May the wife, the mother of seven, be abandoned because of you!"

        Enkidu's innards were churning,
        lying there so alone.
105   He spoke everything he felt, saying to his friend:
            "Listen, my friend, to the dream that I had last night.
            The heavens cried out and the earth replied,
            and I was standing between them.
            There appeared a man of dark visage—
110   his face resembled the Anzu:°   *a lion-headed eagle*
            his hands were the paws of a lion,
            his nails the talons of an eagle!—
            he seized me by my hair and overpowered me.
            I struck him a blow, but he skipped about like a jump rope,
115   and then he struck me and capsized me like a raft,
            and trampled on me like a wild bull.
            He encircled my whole body in a clamp.
                'Help me, my friend!' I cried,
            but you did not rescue me, you were afraid and did not.
                                    . . . .
120   Then he turned me into a dove,
            so that my arms were feathered like a bird.
            Seizing me, he led me down to the House of Darkness, the dwelling of
                Irkalla,[6]
            to the House where those who enter do not come out,
            along the road of no return,
125   to the House where those who dwell do without light,
            where dirt is their drink, their food is of clay,
            where, like a bird, they wear garments of feathers,
            and light cannot be seen, they dwell in the dark,
            and upon the door and bolt lies dust.
130   On entering the House of Dust,
            everywhere I looked there were royal crowns gathered in heaps,
            everywhere I listened, it was the bearers of crowns who in the past had
                ruled the land,

---

6. This passage about the House of Dust has apparently been taken from *The Descent of Ishtar;* see page 99.

but who now served Anu and Enlil cooked meats,
served confections, and poured cool water from waterskins.

135   In the House of Dust that I entered
there sat the high priest and acolyte,
there sat the purification priest and ecstatic,
there sat the anointed priests of the Great Gods.
There sat Etana,[7] there sat Sumukan,

140   there sat Ereshkigal, the Queen of the Netherworld.
Beletseri, the Scribe of the Netherworld, knelt before her,
she was holding the tablet of destinies, and was reading it out to her.
She raised her head and when she saw me—
    'Who has taken this man?'[8]

                  . . .

145   I who went through every difficulty,
remember me and forget not all that I went through with you."
[Gilgamesh replied:]
    "My friend has had a dream that bodes ill."

Enkidu lies down a first day, a second day, . . .
a third day and fourth day, that Enkidu remains in his bed;

150   a fifth, a sixth, and seventh, that Enkidu remains in his bed;
an eighth, a ninth, a tenth, that Enkidu remains in his bed.
Enkidu's illness grew ever worse.
The eleventh and twelfth day his illness grew ever worse.
Enkidu drew up from his bed,

155   and called out to Gilgamesh.

[*Thirty fragmentary lines recount Enkidu's last words and his death.*]

Tablet 8

Just as day began to dawn
Gilgamesh addressed his friend, saying:
    "Enkidu, your mother, the gazelle,
and your father, the wild donkey, engendered you,

5   four wild asses raised you on their milk,
and the herds taught you all the grazing lands.
May the Roads of Enkidu to the Cedar Forest mourn you
and not fall silent night or day.
May the Elders of the broad city of Uruk-Haven mourn you.

10   May the peoples who gave their blessing after us mourn you.
May the men of the mountains and hills mourn you. . . .
May the pasture lands shriek in mourning as if it were your mother.
May the cypress and the cedar which we destroyed in our anger mourn you.
May the bear, hyena, panther, tiger, water buffalo, jackal, lion, wild bull,
    stag, ibex, all the creatures of the plains mourn you.

---

7. A famous ancient hero, subject of his own epic poem.   8. Fifty lines are missing. The text resumes with the conclusion of Enkidu's speech.

15   May the holy River Ulaja, along whose banks we grandly used to stroll,
          mourn you.
      May the pure Euphrates, to which we would offer water from our water
          skins, mourn you.
      May the men of Uruk-Haven, whom we saw in our battle when we killed
          the Bull of Heaven, mourn you.
      May the farmer, who extols your name in his sweet work song, mourn you.
      May the people of the broad city, who exalted your name, mourn you.
20   May the herder, who prepared butter and light beer for your mouth,
          mourn you.
      May . . . , who put ointments on your back, mourn you.
      May . . . , who prepared fine beer for your mouth, mourn you.
      May the harlot, with whom you rubbed yourself with oil and felt good,
          mourn you. . . .
      May the brothers go into mourning over you like sisters;
25   as for the lamentation priests, may their hair be shorn off on your behalf.
      Enkidu, your mother and your father are in the wastelands,
      I mourn you.
      Hear me, O Elders of Uruk, hear me, O men!
      I mourn for Enkidu, my friend,
30   I shriek in anguish like a mourner.
      You, axe at my side, so trusty at my hand—
      you, sword at my waist, shield in front of me,
      you, my festal garment, a sash over my loins—
      an evil demon appeared and took him away from me!
35   My friend, the swift mule, fleet wild ass of the mountain, panther of the
          wilderness,
      Enkidu, my friend, the swift mule, fleet wild ass of the mountain, panther
          of the wilderness,
      after we joined together and went up into the mountain,
      fought the Bull of Heaven and killed it,
      and overwhelmed Humbaba, who lived in the Cedar Forest,
40   now what is this sleep which has seized you?
      You have turned dark and do not hear me!"
      But Enkidu's eyes do not move,
      he touched his heart, but it beat no longer.
      He covered his friend's face like a bride,
45   swooping down over him like an eagle,
      and like a lioness deprived of her cubs
      he keeps pacing to and fro.
      He shears off his curls and heaps them onto the ground,
      ripping off his finery and casting it away as an abomination.

50   Just as day began to dawn, Gilgamesh arose
      and issued a call to the land:
          "You, blacksmith! You, lapidary!° You, coppersmith!   *gem carver*
          You, goldsmith! You, jeweler!
          Create 'My Friend,' fashion a statue of him."

55   . . . he fashioned a statue of his friend [and said]:
    "I had you recline on the great couch,
    indeed, on the couch of honor I let you recline,
    I had you sit in the position of ease, the seat at the left, so the princes of
        the world kissed your feet.
    I had the people of Uruk mourn and moan for you,
60   I filled happy people with woe over you,
    and after you died I let a filthy mat of hair grow over my body,
    and donned the skin of a lion and roamed the wilderness."

[*Some 160 lines are missing or fragmentary.*]

Tablet 9

Over his friend, Enkidu, Gilgamesh cried bitterly, roaming the wilderness.
    "I am going to die!—am I not like Enkidu?!
    Deep sadness penetrates my core,
    I fear death, and now roam the wilderness—
5   I will set out to the region of Utanapishtim, son of Ubartutu, and will go
        with utmost dispatch!
    When I arrived at mountain passes at nightfall,
    I saw lions, and I was terrified!
    I raised my head in prayer to Sin,
    to the Great Lady of the gods my supplications poured forth,
      'Save me from them!'"
10   He was sleeping in the night, but awoke with a start with a dream:
    A warrior enjoyed his life—
    he raised his axe in his hand,
    drew the dagger from his sheath,
    and fell into their midst like an arrow.
15   He struck and he scattered them.
        . . .
When he reached Mount Mashu,
    which daily guards the rising and setting of the Sun,
    above which only the dome of the heavens reaches,
    and whose flank reaches as far as the Netherworld below,
20   there were Scorpion-beings watching over its gate.
    Trembling terror they inspire, the sight of them is death,
    their frightening aura sweeps over the mountains.
    At the rising and setting they watch over the Sun.
    When Gilgamesh saw them, trembling terror blanketed his face,
25   but he pulled himself together and drew near to them.
    The scorpion-being called out to his female:
      "He who comes to us, his body is the flesh of gods!"
    The scorpion-being, his female, answered him:
      "Only two-thirds of him is a god, one-third is human."
30   The male scorpion-being called out, saying to the offspring of the gods:
      "Why have you traveled so distant a journey?

Why have you come here to me,
over rivers whose crossing is treacherous?"

[*Twenty-nine lines are only partially legible.*]

[Gilgamesh answered and said:]

35   "I have come on account of my ancestor Utanapishtim,
who joined the Assembly of the Gods, and was given eternal life.
About Death and Life I must ask him!"
The scorpion-being spoke to Gilgamesh, saying:
"Never has there been, Gilgamesh, a mortal man who could do that.

40   No one has crossed through the mountains,
for twelve leagues it is darkness throughout—
dense is the darkness, and light there is none."[9]

             . . .

Gilgamesh answered and said:
"Though it be in deep sadness and pain,

45   in cold or heat gasping after breath, I will go on!
Now! Open the Gate!"
The scorpion-being spoke to Gilgamesh, saying:
"Go on, Gilgamesh, fear not!
The Mashu mountains I give to you freely,

50   the mountains, the ranges, you may traverse.
In safety may your feet carry you. . . ."
As soon as Gilgamesh heard this
he heeded the utterances of the scorpion-being.
Along the Road of the Sun he journeyed—

55   one league he traveled . . . , dense was the darkness, light there was none.
Neither what lies ahead nor behind does it allow him to see.
Two leagues he traveled, dense was the darkness, light there was none,
neither what lies ahead nor behind does it allow him to see.
Three leagues he traveled, dense was the darkness, light there was none,

60   neither what lies ahead nor behind does it allow him to see.
Four leagues he traveled . . . , dense was the darkness, light there was none,
neither what lies ahead nor behind does it allow him to see.
Five leagues he traveled . . . , dense was the darkness, light there was none,
neither what lies ahead nor behind does it allow him to see.

65   Six leagues he traveled . . . , dense was the darkness, light there was none,
neither what lies ahead nor behind does it allow him to see.
Seven leagues he traveled . . . , dense was the darkness, light there was none,
neither what lies ahead nor behind does it allow him to see.
Eight leagues he traveled and cried out,

70   dense was the darkness, light there was none,
neither what lies ahead nor behind does it allow him to see.
Nine leagues he traveled, the North Wind licked at his face,
dense was the darkness, light there was none,

---

9. In 70 missing lines, Gilgamesh persuades the scorpion-men to let him through.

neither what lies ahead nor behind does it allow him to see.
75   Ten leagues he traveled; the end of the road is near. . . .
Eleven leagues he traveled and came out before the sunrise.
Twelve leagues he traveled and it grew brilliant.

Before him there were trees of precious stones,
and he went straight to look at them.
80   The tree bears carnelian° as its fruit,   *a red gemstone*
laden with clusters of jewels, dazzling to behold—
it bears lapis lazuli as foliage,
bearing fruit, a delight to look upon.

[*A long description of the jewelled garden here is too illegible to be tran-*
scribed.]

Tablet 10

The tavern-keeper Siduri who lives by the seashore, . . .
the pot-stand was made for her, the golden fermenting vat was made for her.
She is covered with a veil.
Gilgamesh was roving about, wearing a skin,
5   having the flesh of the gods in his body,
but sadness deep within him,
looking like one who has been traveling a long distance.
The tavern-keeper was gazing off into the distance,
puzzling to herself, she said,
10   wondering to herself:
    "That fellow is surely a murderer!
    Where is he heading?"
As soon as the tavern-keeper saw him, she bolted her door,
bolted her gate, bolted the lock.
15   But at her noise Gilgamesh pricked up his ears,
lifted his chin to look about and then laid his eyes on her.
Gilgamesh spoke to the tavern-keeper, saying:
    "Tavern-keeper, what have you seen that made you bolt your door,
    bolt your gate, bolt the lock?
20   If you do not let me in I will break your door, and smash the lock!
                              . . .
Gilgamesh said to the tavern-keeper:
    "I am Gilgamesh, I killed the Guardian!
    I destroyed Humbaba who lived in the Cedar Forest,
    I slew lions in the mountain passes!
25   I grappled with the Bull that came down from heaven, and killed him."
The tavern-keeper spoke to Gilgamesh, saying:
    "If you are Gilgamesh, who killed the Guardian,
    who destroyed Humbaba who lived in the Cedar Forest,
    who slew lions in the mountain passes,
30   who grappled with the Bull that came down from heaven, and killed him,
    why are your cheeks emaciated, your expression desolate?
    Why is your heart so wretched, your features so haggard?

Why is there such sadness deep within you?
Why do you look like one who has been traveling a long distance
35   so that ice and heat have seared your face?
Why do you roam the wilderness?"
Gilgamesh spoke to her, to the tavern-keeper he said:
"Tavern-keeper, should not my cheeks be emaciated?
Should my heart not be wretched, my features not haggard?
40   Should there not be sadness deep within me?
Should I not look like one who has been traveling a long distance,
and should ice and heat not have seared my face?
Should I not roam the wilderness?
My friend, the wild ass who chased the wild donkey, panther of the
        wilderness,
45   Enkidu, the wild ass who chased the wild donkey, panther of the
        wilderness,
we joined together, and went up into the mountain.
We grappled with and killed the Bull of Heaven,
we destroyed Humbaba who lived in the Cedar Forest,
we slew lions in the mountain passes!
50   My friend, whom I love deeply, who went through every hardship with me,
Enkidu, whom I love deeply, who went through every hardship with me,
the fate of mankind has overtaken him.
Six days and seven nights I mourned over him
and would not allow him to be buried
55   until a maggot fell out of his nose.
I was terrified by his appearance,
I began to fear death, and so roam the wilderness.
The issue of my friend oppresses me,
so I have been roaming long trails through the wilderness.
60   The issue of Enkidu, my friend, oppresses me,
so I have been roaming long roads through the wilderness.
How can I stay silent, how can I be still?
My friend whom I love has turned to clay.
Am I not like him? Will I lie down, never to get up again?"[1]
65 Gilgamesh spoke to the tavern-keeper, saying:
"So now, tavern-keeper, what is the way to Utanapishtim?
What are its markers? Give them to me! Give me the markers!
If possible, I will cross the sea;
if not, I will roam through the wilderness."
70 The tavern-keeper spoke to Gilgamesh, saying:
"There has never been, Gilgamesh, any passage whatever,
there has never been anyone since days of yore who crossed the sea.
The one who crosses the sea is valiant Shamash, except for him who can
        cross?
The crossing is difficult, its ways are treacherous—
75   and in between are the Waters of Death that bar its approaches!

---

1. The text omits a reply by the tavern-keeper. In the Old Babylonian version, she had urged Gilgamesh not to worry about death but to be content with the pleasures of life.

And even if, Gilgamesh, you should cross the sea,
when you reach the Waters of Death what would you do?
Gilgamesh, over there is Urshanabi, the ferryman of Utanapishtim.
'The stone things'° are with him,   *punting poles (?)*
    he is in the woods picking mint.

80   Go on, let him see your face.
If possible, cross with him;
    if not, you should turn back."

When Gilgamesh heard this
he raised the axe in his hand,
85   drew the dagger from his belt,
and slipped stealthily away after them.
Like an arrow he fell among the stone things.
From the middle of the woods their noise could be heard.
Urshanabi, the sharp-eyed, saw . . .
90   When he heard the axe, he ran toward it.
                      . . .
Gilgamesh spoke to Urshanabi, saying:
    "Now, Urshanabi! What is the way to Utanapishtim?
What are its markers? Give them to me! Give me the markers!
If possible, I will cross the sea;
95   if not, I will roam through the wilderness!"

Urshanabi spoke to Gilgamesh, saying:
    "It is your hands, Gilgamesh, that prevent the crossing!
You have smashed 'the stone things,' you have pulled out their retaining
    ropes.
'The stone things' have been smashed, their retaining ropes pulled out!
100   Gilgamesh, take the axe in your hand, go down into the woods,
and cut down 300 punting poles each 60 cubits in length.
    Strip them, attach caps, and bring them to the boat!"
When Gilgamesh heard this
he took up the axe in his hand, drew the dagger from his belt,
105   and went down into the woods,
and cut 300 punting poles each 60 cubits in length.
He stripped them and attached caps, and brought them to the boat.
Gilgamesh and Urshanabi boarded the boat,
Gilgamesh launched the boat and they sailed away.
110   By the third day they had traveled a stretch of a month and a half,
and Urshanabi arrived at the Waters of Death.
Urshanabi said to Gilgamesh:
    "Hold back, Gilgamesh, take a punting pole,
but your hand must not pass over the Waters of Death!
115   Take a second, Gilgamesh, a third, and a fourth pole,
take a fifth, Gilgamesh, a sixth, and a seventh pole,
take an eighth, Gilgamesh, a ninth, and a tenth pole,
take an eleventh, Gilgamesh, and a twelfth pole!"
In twice 60 rods Gilgamesh had used up the punting poles.
120   Then he loosened his waist-cloth for a sail;

Gilgamesh stripped off his garment
and held it up on the mast with his arms.

Utanapishtim was gazing off into the distance,
puzzling to himself he said, wondering to himself:
125   "Why are 'the stone things' of the boat smashed to pieces?
And why is someone not its master sailing on it?
The one who is coming is not a man of mine."

                                    . . .

[*Gilgamesh arrives and meets Utanapishtim.*]

Utanapishtim said to Gilgamesh:
"Why are your cheeks emaciated, your expression desolate?
130   Why is your heart so wretched, your features so haggard?
Why is there such sadness deep within you?
Why do you look like one who has been traveling a long distance
so that ice and heat have seared your face?
Why do you roam the wilderness?"
135   Gilgamesh spoke to Utanapishtim saying:
"Should not my cheeks be emaciated, my expression desolate?
Should my heart not be wretched, my features not haggard?
Should there not be sadness deep within me?
Should I not look like one who has been traveling a long distance,
140   and should ice and heat not have seared my face?
Should I not roam the wilderness?
My friend who chased wild asses in the mountain, the panther of the
     wilderness,
Enkidu, my friend, who chased wild asses in the mountain, the panther
     of the wilderness,
we joined together, and went up into the mountain.
145   We grappled with and killed the Bull of Heaven,
we destroyed Humbaba who dwelled in the Cedar Forest,
we slew lions in the mountain passes!
My friend, whom I love deeply, who went through every hardship with
     me,
Enkidu, my friend, whom I love deeply, who went through every hard
     ship with me,
150   the fate of mankind has overtaken him.
Six days and seven nights I mourned over him
and would not allow him to be buried
until a maggot fell out of his nose.
I was terrified by his appearance,
155   I began to fear death, and so roam the wilderness.
The issue of my friend oppresses me,
so I have been roaming long trails through the wilderness.
The issue of Enkidu, my friend, oppresses me,
so I have been roaming long roads through the wilderness.
160   How can I stay silent, how can I be still?
My friend whom I love has turned to clay;
Enkidu, my friend whom I love, has turned to clay!"

Am I not like him? Will I lie down never to get up again?"
Gilgamesh spoke to Utanapishtim, saying:

165   "That is why I must go on, to see Utanapishtim whom they call
      'The Faraway.'
I went circling through all the mountains,
I traversed treacherous mountains, and crossed all the seas—
that is why sweet sleep has not mellowed my face,
through sleepless striving I am strained,

170   my muscles are filled with pain.
I had not yet reached the tavern-keeper's area before my clothing gave out.
I killed bear, hyena, lion, panther, tiger, stag, red-stag, and beasts of the
      wilderness;
I ate their meat and wrapped their skins around me.
The gate of grief must be bolted shut, sealed with pitch and bitumen!"

175 Utanapishtim spoke to Gilgamesh, saying:
    "Why, Gilgamesh, do you feel such sadness?
You who were created from the flesh of gods and mankind!

[*Long but only partially legible passage follows.*]

You have toiled without cease, and what have you got?
Through toil you wear yourself out,

180   you fill your body with grief,
your long lifetime you are bringing near to a premature end!
Mankind, whose offshoot is snapped off like a reed in a canebreak,
      . . .
No one can see death,
no one can see the face of death,

185   no one can hear the voice of death,
yet there is savage death that snaps off mankind.
For how long do we build a household?
For how long do we seal a document?
For how long do brothers share the inheritance?

190   For how long is there to be jealousy in the land?
For how long has the river risen and brought the overflowing waters,
so that dragonflies drift down the river?
The face that could gaze upon the face of the Sun
has never existed ever.

195   How alike are the sleeping and the dead.
The image of Death cannot be depicted. . . .
After Enlil had pronounced the blessing,
the Anunnaki, the Great Gods, assembled.
Mammetum, she who fashions destiny, determined destiny with them.

200   They established Death and Life,
but they did not make known 'the days of death.'"

Tablet 11

Gilgamesh spoke to Utanapishtim, the Faraway:
    "I have been looking at you,

but your appearance is not strange—you are like me!
You yourself are not different—you are like me!
5   My mind was resolved to fight with you,
but instead my arm lies useless over you.
Tell me, how is it that you stand in the Assembly of the Gods,
  and have found life?"
Utanapishtim spoke to Gilgamesh, saying:
  "I will reveal to you, Gilgamesh, a thing that is hidden,
10   a secret of the gods I will tell you!
Shuruppak, a city that you surely know,
situated on the banks of the Euphrates,
that city was very old, and there were gods inside it.
The hearts of the Great Gods moved them to inflict the Flood.
15   Their Father Anu uttered the oath of secrecy,
Valiant Enlil was their Adviser,
Ninurta was their Chamberlain,
Ennugi was their Minister of Canals.
Ea, the Clever Prince, was under oath with them
20   so he repeated their talk to the reed house:
  'Reed house, reed house! Wall, wall!
  Hear, O reed house! Understand, O wall!
  O man of Shuruppak, son of Ubartutu:
  Tear down the house and build a boat!
25   Abandon wealth and seek living beings!
  Spurn possessions and keep alive living beings!
  Make all living beings go up into the boat.
  The boat which you are to build,
  its dimensions must measure equal to each other:
30   its length must correspond to its width.
  Roof it over like the Apsu.'°   *underworld sea*
I understood and spoke to my lord, Ea:
  'My lord, thus is the command which you have uttered
  I will heed and will do it.
35   But what shall I answer the city, the populace, and the Elders?'
Ea spoke, commanding me, his servant:
  'You, well then, this is what you must say to them:
    "It appears that Enlil is rejecting me
    so I cannot reside in your city,
40   nor set foot on Enlil's earth.
    I will go down to the Apsu to live with my lord, Ea,
    and upon you he will rain down abundance,
    a profusion of fowl, myriad fishes.
    He will bring to you a harvest of wealth,
45   in the morning he will let loaves of bread shower down,
    and in the evening a rain of wheat!"'
Just as dawn began to glow
the land assembled around me—
the carpenter carried his hatchet,
50   the reed worker carried his flattening stone,

the child carried the pitch,
the weak brought whatever else was needed.
On the fifth day I laid out her exterior.
It was a field in area,
55   its walls were each 10 times 12 cubits in height,
the sides of its top were of equal length, 10 times 12 cubits each.[2]
I laid out its interior structure and drew a picture of it.
I provided it with six decks,
thus dividing it into seven levels.
60   The inside of it I divided into nine compartments.
I drove plugs to keep out water in its middle part.
I saw to the punting poles and laid in what was necessary.
Three times 3,600 units of raw bitumen I poured into the bitumen kiln,
three times 3,600 units of pitch I put into it,
65   there were three times 3,600 porters of casks who carried vegetable oil,
apart from the 3,600 units of oil which they consumed
and two times 3,600 units of oil which the boatman stored away.
I butchered oxen for the meat,
and day upon day I slaughtered sheep.
70   I gave the workmen ale, beer, oil, and wine, as if it were river water,
so they could make a party like the New Year's Festival.
                                        . . .
The boat was finished by sunset.
The launching was very difficult.
They had to keep carrying a runway of poles front to back,
75   until two-thirds of it had gone into the water.
Whatever I had I loaded on it:
whatever silver I had I loaded on it,
whatever gold I had I loaded on it.
All the living beings that I had I loaded on it,
80   I had all my kith and kin go up into the boat,
all the beasts and animals of the field and the craftsmen I had go up.
Shamash had set a stated time:
     'In the morning I will let loaves of bread shower down,
        and in the evening a rain of wheat!
85   Go inside the boat, seal the entry!'
That stated time had arrived.
In the morning he let loaves of bread shower down,
and in the evening a rain of wheat.
I watched the appearance of the weather—
90   the weather was frightful to behold!
I went into the boat and sealed the entry.
For the caulking of the boat, to Puzuramurri, the boatman,
I gave the palace together with its contents.
Just as dawn began to glow
95   there arose from the horizon a black cloud.
Adad° rumbled inside of it,   *storm god*

2. The boat is described as a cube 80 feet on a side, making it a cross between a boat and a ziggurat, a pyramidal temple tower often with seven levels.

before him went Shullat and Hanish,
heralds going over mountain and land.
Erragal° pulled out the mooring poles,   *god of death*
100   forth went Ninurta° and made the dikes overflow.   *god of war*
The Anunnaki° lifted up the torches,   *underworld gods*
setting the land ablaze with their flare.
Stunned shock over Adad's deeds overtook the heavens,
and turned to blackness all that had been light.
105   The land shattered like a pot.
All day long the South Wind blew,
blowing fast, submerging the mountain in water,
overwhelming the people like an attack.
No one could see his fellow,
110   they could not recognize each other in the torrent.
The gods were frightened by the Flood,
and retreated, ascending to the heaven of Anu.
The gods were cowering like dogs, crouching by the outer wall.
Ishtar shrieked like a woman in childbirth,
115   the sweet-voiced Mistress of the Gods wailed:
      'The olden days have alas turned to clay,
      because I said evil things in the Assembly of the Gods!
      How could I say evil things in the Assembly of the Gods,
      ordering a catastrophe to destroy my people?
120   No sooner have I given birth to my dear people
      than they fill the sea like so many fish!'
The gods—those of the Anunnaki—were weeping with her,
the gods humbly sat weeping, sobbing with grief,
their lips burning, parched with thirst.
125   Six days and seven nights
came the wind and flood, the storm flattening the land.
When the seventh day arrived, the storm was pounding,
the flood was a war—struggling with itself like a woman writhing in labor.
The sea calmed, fell still, the whirlwind and flood stopped up.
130   I looked around all day long—quiet had set in
and all the human beings had turned to clay!
The terrain was as flat as a roof.
I opened a vent and fresh air fell upon the side of my nose.
I fell to my knees and sat weeping,
135   tears streaming down the side of my nose.
I looked around for coastlines in the expanse of the sea,
and at twelve leagues there emerged a region of land.
On Mt. Nimush³ the boat lodged firm,
Mt. Nimush held the boat, allowing no sway.
140   One day and a second Mt. Nimush held the boat, allowing no sway.
A third day, a fourth, Mt. Nimush held the boat, allowing no sway.
A fifth day, a sixth, Mt. Nimush held the boat, allowing no sway.

3. Likely a 9,000-foot mountain on the Persian border of northeastern Iraq.

When a seventh day arrived
I sent forth a dove and released it.
145   The dove went off, but came back to me;
no perch was visible so it circled back to me.
I sent forth a swallow and released it.
The swallow went off, but came back to me;
no perch was visible so it circled back to me.
150   I sent forth a raven and released it.
The raven went off, and saw the waters slither back.
It eats, it scratches, it bobs, but does not circle back to me.
Then I sent out everything in all directions and sacrificed a sheep.
I offered incense in front of the mountain-ziggurat.°   *stepped pyramid*
155   Seven and seven cult vessels I put in place,
and into their bowls I poured reeds, cedar, and myrtle.
The gods smelled the savor,
the gods smelled the sweet savor,
and collected like flies over a sacrifice.
160   Just then Beletili arrived.
She lifted up the large beads which Anu had made for his enjoyment:
    'You gods, as surely as I shall not forget this lapis lazuli around my
        neck,
    may I be mindful of these days, and never forget them!
    The gods may come to the incense offering,
165   but Enlil may not come to the incense offering,
    because without considering he brought about the Flood
    and consigned my people to annihilation.'
Just then Enlil arrived.
He saw the boat and became furious,
170   he was filled with rage at the Igigi:°   *sky gods*
    'Where did a living being escape?
    No man was to survive the annihilation!'
Ninurta spoke to Valiant Enlil, saying:
    'Who else but Ea could devise such a thing?
175   It is Ea who knows every machination!'
Ea spoke to Valiant Enlil, saying:
    'It is you, O Valiant One, who is the Sage of the Gods.
    How, how could you bring about a Flood without consideration?
    Charge the violation to the violator,
180   charge the offense to the offender,
    but be compassionate lest mankind be cut off,
    be patient lest they be killed.
    Instead of your bringing on the Flood,
    would that a lion had appeared to diminish the people!
185   Instead of your bringing on the Flood,
    would that a wolf had appeared to diminish the people!
    Instead of your bringing on the Flood,
    would that famine had occurred to slay the land!
    Instead of your bringing on the Flood,
190   would that Pestilent Erra had appeared to ravage the land!

It was not I who revealed the secret of the Great Gods,
I only made a dream appear to Atrahasis[4]
and thus he heard the secret of the gods.
Now then! The deliberation should be about him!'
Enlil went up inside the boat
195 and, grasping my hand, made me go up.
He had my wife go up and kneel by my side.
He touched our forehead and, standing between us, he blessed us:
 'Previously Utanapishtim was a human being.
But now let Utanapishtim and his wife become like us, the gods!
200 Let Utanapishtim reside far away, at the Mouth of the Rivers.'
They took us far away and settled us at the Mouth of the Rivers.
Now then, Gilgamesh, who will convene the gods on your behalf,
that you may find the life that you are seeking?
Wait! You must not lie down for six days and seven nights."

205 As soon as he sat down with his head between his legs
sleep, like a fog, blew upon him.
Utanapishtim said to his wife:
 "Look there! The man, the youth who wanted eternal life!
Sleep, like a fog, blew over him."
210 His wife said to Utanapishtim the Faraway:
 "Touch him, let the man awaken.
Let him return safely by the way he came.
Let him return to his land by the gate through which he left."
Utanapishtim said to his wife:
215 "Mankind is deceptive, and will deceive you.
Come, bake loaves for him and keep setting them by his head
and draw on the wall each day that he lay down."
She baked his loaves and placed them by his head
and marked on the wall the day that he lay down.
220 The first loaf was dessicated,
the second stale, the third moist, the fourth turned white, . . .
the fifth sprouted gray mold, the sixth is still fresh.
The seventh—suddenly he touched him and the man awoke.
Gilgamesh said to Utanapishtim:
225 "The very moment sleep was pouring over me
you touched me and alerted me!"
Utanapishtim spoke to Gilgamesh, saying:
 "Look over here, Gilgamesh, count your loaves!
You should be aware of what is marked on the wall!
230 Your first loaf is dessicated,
the second stale, the third moist, your fourth turned white, . . .
the fifth sprouted gray mold, the sixth is still fresh.
The seventh—at that instant you awoke!"
Gilgamesh said to Utanapishtim the Faraway:
235 "O woe! What shall I do, Utanapishtim, where shall I go?

---

4. "Exceedingly Wise," the hero of an earlier poem on the flood story, a source for this tablet; here written by mistake for "Utanapishtim" or else deliberately used as an alternate name.

The Snatcher has taken hold of my flesh,
in my bedroom Death dwells,
and wherever I set foot there too is Death!"

Utanapishtim said to Urshanabi, the ferryman:
240   "May the harbor reject you, may the ferry landing reject you!
May you who used to walk its shores be denied its shores!
The man in front of whom you walk, matted hair chains his body,
animal skins have ruined his beautiful skin.
Take him away, Urshanabi, bring him to the washing place.
245   Let him wash his matted hair in water.
Let him cast away his animal skin and have the sea carry it off,
let his body be moistened with fine oil,
let the wrap around his head be made new,
let him wear royal robes worthy of him!
250   Until he goes off to his city,
until he sets off on his way,
let his royal robe not become spotted, let it be perfectly new!"
Urshanabi took him away and brought him to the washing place.
He washed his matted hair with water. . . .
255   He cast off his animal skin and the sea carried it off.
He moistened his body with fine oil,
and made a new wrap for his head.
He put on a royal robe worthy of him.
Until he went away to his city,
260   until he set off on his way,
his royal robe remained unspotted, it was perfectly clean.
Gilgamesh and Urshanabi boarded the boat,
they cast off the boat, and sailed away.

The wife of Utanapishtim the Faraway said to him:
265   "Gilgamesh came here exhausted and worn out.
What can you give him so that he can return to his land with honor?"
Then Gilgamesh raised a punting pole
and drew the boat to shore.
Utanapishtim spoke to Gilgamesh, saying:
270   "Gilgamesh, you came here exhausted and worn out.
What can I give you so you can return to your land?
I will disclose to you a thing that is hidden, Gilgamesh,
a secret I will tell you.
There is a plant like a boxthorn,
275   whose thorns will prick your hand like a rose.
If your hands reach that plant you will become a young man again."
Hearing this, Gilgamesh opened a conduit to the Apsu°   *underworld sea*
and attached heavy stones to his feet.
They dragged him down, to the Apsu they pulled him.
280   He took the plant, though it pricked his hand,
and cut the heavy stones from his feet,
letting the waves throw him onto its shores.
Gilgamesh spoke to Urshanabi, the ferryman, saying:

"Urshanabi, this plant is a plant against decay
285   by which a man can attain his survival.
I will bring it to Uruk-Haven,
and have an old man eat the plant to test it.
The plant's name is 'The Old Man Becomes a Young Man.'[5]
Then I will eat it and return to the condition of my youth."
290   At twenty leagues they broke for some food,
at thirty leagues they stopped for the night.
Seeing a spring and how cool its waters were,
Gilgamesh went down and was bathing in the water.
A snake smelled the fragrance of the plant,
295   silently came up and carried off the plant.
While going back it sloughed off its casing.
At that point Gilgamesh sat down, weeping,
his tears streaming over the side of his nose.
"Counsel me, O ferryman Urshanabi!
300   For whom have my arms labored, Urshanabi?
For whom has my heart's blood roiled?
I have not secured any good deed for myself,
but done a good deed for the 'lion of the ground'!
Now the high waters are coursing twenty leagues distant,
305   as I was opening the conduit I turned my equipment over into it.
What can I find to serve as a marker for me?
I will turn back from the journey by sea and leave the boat by the shore!"

At twenty leagues they broke for some food,
at thirty leagues they stopped for the night.
310   They arrived in Uruk-Haven.
Gilgamesh said to Urshanabi, the ferryman:
"Go up, Urshanabi, onto the wall of Uruk and walk around.
Examine its foundation, inspect its brickwork thoroughly—
is not even the core of the brick structure of kiln-fired brick,
315   and did not the Seven Sages themselves lay out its plan?
One league city, one league palm gardens,
one league lowlands, the open area of the Ishtar Temple,
three leagues and the open area of Uruk the wall encloses."

---

5. This is probably the meaning of "Gilgamesh" in Sumerian.

≈✦ PERSPECTIVES ✦≈
Death and Immortality

Death was a constant presence in the ancient world. Infant mortality was high, and disease, warfare, and accidents could claim a life at any time. When Psalm 90 says that "the years of our life are threescore and ten, or even by reason of strength fourscore," the psalmist isn't giving an *average* life expectancy, as we may think of seventy or eighty years today, but the outer limit of what a fortunate person might hope to see. The same psalm describes humanity as like grass, flourishing in the morning, withered by evening. As the image of growing grass shows, the underworld had a double meaning: a place of death and burial, the earth was also the place of fertility and the growth of crops. Various ancient mythic tales probe this connection, as in *The Descent of Ishtar* given here, or later Greek tales of Ceres, goddess of grain, and her daughter Persephone, abducted by the underworld god Hades. The name "Hades" itself may come from an Akkadian term, *adeshu,* "underworld oath."

Near Eastern cultures responded in very different ways to the problem of death. Most people believed in some form of afterlife, but this could be envisioned either positively or negatively. As can be seen in Enkidu's frightened dreams in *The Epic of Gilgamesh,* the Mesopotamians often thought of the underworld as a grim place, "the House of Dust," where the deceased would live a reduced half-life: *The Descent of Ishtar* below gives the classic form of this view. Others, most notably the Egyptians, took a much more positive view, seeing the afterlife as a radiant paradise where the blessed soul could become one with the gods. Originally reserved for members of the royal family, over time the Egyptian afterlife became increasingly democratized, open to all who had lived virtuously and who could afford the elaborate incantations and rituals spelled out in the book known today as "the Book of the Dead."

The Bible shows a range of views. In some early references to the underworld realm, Sheol, it looks much like the Mesopotamian House of Dust, but normative Hebrew belief increasingly rejected any belief in a personal survival after death. God should be served and justice should be done for their own sake; the focus of future hope was on blessings for one's descendants rather than for oneself after death. In Genesis, paradise is a purely earthly garden ("paradise" comes from the Hebrew word for "garden"), a place to which Adam and Eve's descendants have no access. By New Testament times, however, a celestial paradise was increasingly in view, elaborately described in the Book of Revelation as "the new Jerusalem," made of gold, crystal, and precious jewels, an eternal city where God's chosen saints would dwell forever.

The problem of earthly evil was especially acute for those who didn't have a confident expectation of a glorious heavenly paradise. Much ancient wisdom literature sought to advise readers in the best ways to live so as to achieve divine favor on earth for oneself and one's descendants, while skeptical texts like the Book of Job probed the mysteries of undeserved suffering. The narrative poem *Erra and Ishum* sees the god of death as directly responsible for chaos and suffering in Babylon, unfolding very human motives of power politics among the gods to explain earthly events.

⟶ ≈✦≈ ⟵

The Descent of Ishtar to the Underworld
late 2nd millennium B.C.E.

This remarkable Babylonian poem gives a haunting picture of the underworld, the "House of Dust" where all ranks are made equal and the dead live a shadowy eternal half-life. The underworld is partly a version of the upper world with its pleasures muted or canceled out, but in this poem it also becomes the scene of an uncanny struggle for control between Ishtar, goddess of love, and her sister Ereshkigal, the queen of the underworld. Ereshkigal defeats Ishtar but spares her life on condition that she surrender her husband, Dumuzi, as a hostage; apparently he would be allowed to come back to life once a year. Based on an earlier Sumerian poem, *The Descent of Ishtar* was performed in the Assyrian capital of Nineveh during an annual ceremony that featured the anointing of a statue of Dumuzi, which was thought to guarantee the fertility of the crops. Such myths circulated widely around the ancient world; a similar explanation of seasonal renewal can be found in the Greek myth of Persephone. *The Epic of Gilgamesh* incorporated *The Descent of Ishtar*'s chilling description of the House of Dust, and built on its themes as well: Gilgamesh's journey to the immortal Utanapishtim is a kind of earthly rewriting of Ishtar's visit to her underworld sister.

PRONUNCIATIONS:
Dumuzi: dou-MOU-zee
Ereshkigal: air-ESH-key-gall
Sin: SEEN

The Descent of Ishtar to the Underworld[1]

To Kurnugi, Land of [No Return],
Ishtar daughter of Sin° was [determined] to go;   *the moon god*
The daughter of Sin was determined to go
To the dark house, dwelling of Erkalla's god,[2]
5   To the house which those who enter cannot leave,
On the road where travelling is one-way only,
To the house where those who enter are deprived of light,
Where dust is their food, clay their bread.
They see no light, they dwell in darkness,
10   They are clothed like birds, with feathers.
Over the door and the bolt, dust has settled.
Ishtar, when she arrived at the gate of Kurnugi,
Addressed her words to the keeper of the gate,
     "Here gatekeeper, open your gate for me,
15   Open your gate for me to come in!
If you do not open the gate for me to come in,
I shall smash the door and shatter the bolt,
I shall smash the doorpost and overturn the doors,
I shall raise up the dead and they shall eat the living:
20   The dead shall outnumber the living!"
The gatekeeper made his voice heard and spoke,
He said to great Ishtar,
     "Stop, lady, do not break it down!
Let me go and report your words to queen Ereshkigal."
25   The gatekeeper went in and spoke to [Ereshkigal],
     "Here she is, your sister Ishtar [. . .]
Who holds the great *keppū*-toy,°   *a spinning top (?)*
Stirs up the Apsu in Ea's presence [. . .]?"

1. Translated by Stephanie Dalley. Brackets indicate gaps in the cuneiform tablet.

2. Erkalla is the city of the dead, ruled by Ereshkigal and her consort Nergal or Erra, god of death.

When Ereshkigal heard this,
30 Her face grew livid as cut tamarisk,
    Her lips grew dark as the rim of a *kunīnu*-vessel.
        "What brings her to me? What has incited her against me?
        Surely not because I drink water with the Anunnaki,°   *underworld gods*
        I eat clay for bread, I drink muddy water for beer?
35   I have to weep for young men forced to abandon sweethearts.
        I have to weep for girls wrenched from their lovers' laps.
        For the infant child I have to weep, expelled before its time.
        Go, gatekeeper, open your gate to her.
        Treat her according to the ancient rites."
40 The gatekeeper went. He opened the gate to her.
        "Enter, my lady: may Kutha° give you joy,   *underworld city*
        May the palace of Kurnugi be glad to see you."
    He let her in through the first door, but stripped off and took away the great
        crown on her head.
        "Gatekeeper, why have you taken away the great crown on my head?"
45   "Go in, my lady. Such are the rites of the Mistress of Earth."
    He let her in through the second door, but stripped off and took away the
        rings in her ears.
        "Gatekeeper, why have you taken away the rings in my ears?"
        "Go in, my lady. Such are the rites of the Mistress of Earth."
    He let her in through the third door, but stripped off and took away the
        beads around her neck.
50   "Gatekeeper, why have you taken away the beads around my neck?"
        "Go in, my lady. Such are the rites of the Mistress of Earth."
    He let her in through the fourth door, but stripped off and took away the
        toggle-pins at her breast.
        "Gatekeeper, why have you taken away the toggle-pins at my breast?"
        "Go in, my lady. Such are the rites of the Mistress of Earth."
55 He let her in through the fifth door, but stripped off and took away the
        girdle of birthstones around her waist.
        "Gatekeeper, why have you taken away the girdle of birthstones around
            my waist?"
        "Go in, my lady. Such are the rites of the Mistress of Earth."
    He let her in through the sixth door, but stripped off and took away the
        bangles on her wrists and ankles.
        "Gatekeeper, why have you taken away the bangles from my wrists and
            ankles?"
60   "Go in, my lady. Such are the rites of the Mistress of Earth."
    He let her in through the seventh door, but stripped off and took away the
        proud garment of her body.
        "Gatekeeper, why have you taken away the proud garment of my body?"
        "Go in, my lady. Such are the rites of the Mistress of Earth."
    As soon as Ishtar went down to Kurnugi,
65 Ereshkigal looked at her and trembled before her.
    Ishtar did not deliberate, but leant over her.

Ereshkigal made her voice heard and spoke,
Addressed her words to Namtar her vizier,
   "Go, Namtar [   ] of my [   ]
70   Send out against her sixty diseases
    [   ] Ishtar:
    Disease of the eyes to her [eyes],
    Disease of the arms to her [arms],
    Disease of the feet to her [feet],
75   Disease of the heart to her [heart],
    Disease of the head [to her head],
    To every part of her and to [   ]."
After Ishtar the mistress of [. . . had gone down to Kurnugi],
No bull mounted a cow, [no donkey impregnated a jenny],
80   No young man impregnated a girl in [the street],
The young man slept in his private room,
The girl slept in the company of her friends.
Then Papsukkal, vizier of the great gods, hung his head,
    his face [became gloomy];
He wore mourning clothes, his hair was unkempt.
85   Dejected, he went and wept before Sin his father,
His tears flowed freely before king Ea.
    "Ishtar has gone down to the Earth and has not come up again.
    As soon as Ishtar went down to Kurnugi
    No bull mounted a cow, no donkey impregnated a jenny,
90   No young man impregnated a girl in the street,
    The young man slept in his private room,
    The girl slept in the company of her friends."
Ea, in the wisdom of his heart, created a person.
He created Good-looks the playboy.
95   "Come, Good-looks, set your face towards the gate of Kurnugi.
    The seven gates of Kurnugi shall be opened before you.
    Ereshkigal shall look at you and be glad to see you.
    When she is relaxed, her mood will lighten.
    Get her to swear the oath by the great gods.
100   Raise your head, pay attention to the waterskin,
    Saying, 'Hey, my lady, let them give me the waterskin,
      that I may drink water from it.'"
      (And so it happened. But)
When Ereshkigal heard this,
She struck her thigh and bit her finger.
105   "You have made a request of me that should not have been made!
    Come, Good-looks, I shall curse you with a great curse.
    I shall decree for you a fate that shall never be forgotten.
    Bread gleaned from the city's ploughs shall be your food,
    The city drains shall be your only drinking place,
110   The shade of a city wall your only standing place,
    Threshold steps your only sitting place,

The drunkard and the thirsty shall slap your cheek."
Ereshkigal made her voice heard and spoke;
She addressed her words to Namtar her vizier,

115   "Go, Namtar, knock at Egalgina,°   *underworld palace*
Decorate the threshold steps with coral,
Bring the Anunnaki out and seat them on golden thrones,
Sprinkle Ishtar with the waters of life and conduct her into my presence."
Namtar went, knocked at Egalgina,

120   Decorated the threshold steps with coral,
Brought out the Anunnaki, seated them on golden thrones,
Sprinkled Ishtar with the waters of life and brought her to her sister.
He let her out through the first door, and gave back to her the proud garment
    of her body.
He let her out through the second door, and gave back to her the bangles for
    her wrists and ankles.

125   He let her out through the third door, and gave back to her the girdle of birth
    stones around her waist.
He let her out through the fourth door, and gave back to her the toggle pins
    at her breast.
He let her out through the fifth door, and gave back to her the beads around
    her neck.
He let her out through the sixth door, and gave back to her the rings for her
    ears.
He let her out through the seventh door, and gave back to her the great
    crown for her head.

130   "Swear that she has paid you her ransom, and give her back in exchange
        for him,
    For Dumuzi, the lover of her youth.
    Wash him with pure water, anoint him with sweet oil,
    Clothe him in a red robe, let the lapis lazuli pipe play.
    Let party-girls raise a loud lament

135   Then Belili tore off her jewellery,
Her lap was filled with eyestones.
Belili heard the lament for her brother,
    she struck the jewellery [from her body],
The eyestones with which the front of the wild cow was filled.
    "You shall not rob me forever of my only brother!

140   On the day when Dumuzi comes back up,
    and the lapis lazuli pipe and the carnelian ring come up with him,
    When male and female mourners come up with him,
    The dead shall come up and smell the smoke offering."

from **The Book of the Dead**
2nd millennium B.C.E.

In early Egyptian belief, only the king was expected to achieve divine rebirth in the underworld; lesser mortals would have at most a kind of shadowy half-life beyond the grave. Over

From the *Book of the Dead*, Papyrus of Ani, Thebes, c. 1250 B.C.E. Anubis weighs a dead person's heart against the feather of Truth, as Thoth records the verdict beneath the watchful eyes of the underworld judges. Behind Thoth an underworld beast waits to snatch the deceased if he fails the test.

time, though, the king's otherworldly privileges extended to a wider and wider circle of court and temple officials and their families, who began to be buried equipped with papyrus scrolls containing elaborate series of spells to protect and aid them in the afterlife. Different scrolls varied in content and in length, partly depending on how many spells an individual chose to commission. Ready-made scrolls could also be purchased, with spaces left for the name of the deceased; in the selections below, this place-holder is indicated by "N."

In modern times called *The Book of the Dead*, these scrolls were originally titled *Sesh n peret m herew:* "The Book of Coming Forth by Day"—their real concern is not with death but with eternal life. They could be nearly two hundred chapters long, and were illustrated with scenes of the underworld. The illustration above shows the climactic judgment scene, in which the deceased person's heart is weighed against the feather of Truth, *maat* in Egyptian, often personified as a goddess. The underworld court, headed by Osiris, sits in judgment as the deceased makes a long series of negative claims—of sins he has not committed. If the heart of the deceased then proves lighter than the feather of truth, the successful soul becomes united with Osiris himself, guided every step of the way by spells that, as the book confidently asserts, are "effective a million times."

PRONUNCIATIONS:

Ennead: EN-nee-add

Maat: MAH-aht

Ptah: p'TAH

<h1>from The Book of the Dead[1]</h1>

<h2>[THE OPENING OF THE MOUTH]</h2>

Formula for opening N's mouth for him in the necropolis.[2] He shall say:

My mouth is opened by Ptah,°	*creator god*
My mouth's bonds are loosed by my city-god.	
Thoth° has come fully equipped with spells,	*god of writing*
He looses the bonds of Seth° from my mouth.	*slayer of Osiris*
5 Atum° has given me my hands,	*creator god*
They are placed as guardians.	

My mouth is given to me,	
My mouth is opened by Ptah	
With that chisel of metal	
10 With which he opened the mouth of the gods.	
I am Sakhmet-Wadjet° who dwells in the west of heaven,	*lion goddess*
I am Sahyt among the souls of On.	

As for any spells, any spells spoken against me,	
The gods shall rise up against them,	
15 The entire Ennead,° the entire Ennead!	*council of gods*

<h2>[THE HEART AS WITNESS]</h2>

Formula for not letting the heart of N oppose him in the necropolis. He shall
   say:

O my heart of my mother,	
O my heart of my mother,	
O my heart of my being!	
Do not rise up against me as witness,	
5 Do not oppose me in the tribunal,	
Do not rebel against me before the guardian of the scales!	

You are my *ka*° within my body,	*vital force*
The Khnum° who prospers my limbs.	*creator of life*
Go to the good place prepared for us,	
10 Do not make my name stink before them,	
The magistrates who put people in their places!	
If it's good for us it's good for the judge,	
It pleases him who renders judgment.	
Do not invent lies before the god,	
15 Before the great god, the lord of the west,	
Lo, your uprightness brings vindication!	

1. Translated by Miriam Lichtheim.
2. City of tombs outside Thebes. The "opening of the   mouth" was a ritual performed for mummies before burial, enabling them to communicate in the underworld.

[THE DECLARATION OF INNOCENCE]

To be said on reaching the Hall of the Two Truths so as to purge N of any
    sins committed and to see the face of every god:

Hail to you, great God, Lord of the Two Truths!
I have come to you, my Lord,
I was brought to see your beauty.
I know you, I know the names of the forty-two gods,
5   Who are with you in the Hall of the Two Truths,
Who live by warding off evildoers,
Who drink of their blood,
On that day of judging characters before Wennofer,°   *Osiris*
Lo, your name is "He-of-Two-Daughters,"
10   And "He-of-Maat's-Two-Eyes."
Lo, I come before you,
Bringing Maat° to you,   *Truth*
Having repelled evil for you.

I have not done crimes against people,
15   I have not mistreated cattle,
I have not sinned in the Place of Truth.
I have not known what should not be known,
I have not done any harm.
I did not begin a day by exacting more than my due,
20   My name did not reach the bark of the mighty ruler,
I have not blasphemed a god,
I have not robbed the poor.
I have not done what the god abhors,
I have not maligned a servant to his master.
25   I have not caused pain,
I have not caused tears.
I have not killed,
I have not ordered to kill,
I have not made anyone suffer.
30   I have not damaged the offerings in the temples,
I have not depleted the loaves of the gods,
I have not stolen the cakes of the dead.
I have not copulated nor defiled myself.
I have not increased nor reduced the measure,
35   I have not diminished the arura,°   *acreage*
I have not cheated in the fields.
I have not added to the weight of the balance,
I have not falsified the plummet of the scales.
I have not taken milk from the mouth of children,
40   I have not deprived cattle of their pasture.
I have not snared birds in the reeds of the gods,
I have not caught fish in their ponds.
I have not held back water in its season,

I have not dammed a flowing stream,
45   I have not quenched a needed fire.
I have not neglected the days of meat offerings,
I have not detained cattle belonging to the god,
I have not stopped a god in his procession.
I am pure, I am pure, I am pure, I am pure!
50   I am pure as is pure that great heron in Hnes.
I am truly the nose of the Lord of Breath,
Who sustains all the people,
On the day of completing the Eye in On,[3]
In the second month of winter, last day,
55   In the presence of the lord of this land.
I have seen the completion of the Eye in On!
No evil shall befall me in this land,
In this Hall of the Two Truths;
For I know the names of the gods in it,
60   The followers of the great God!

[THE FIRST INTERROGATION]

"Let him come," they say to me,
"Who are you?" they say to me,
"What is your name?" they say to me.
"I am the stalk of the papyrus,
5   He-who-is-in-the-moringa° is my name."   *Osiris*
"Where have you passed by?" they say to me,
"I have passed by the town north of the moringa."
"What have you seen there?"
"The Leg and the Thigh."
10   "What did you say to them?"
"I have witnessed the acclaim in the land of the Fenkhu."°   *Syria*
"What did they give you?"
"A firebrand and a faience column."
"What did you do with them?"
15   "I buried them on the shore of the pool Maaty,
At the time of the evening meal."
"What did you find there on the shore of the pool Maaty?"
"A scepter of flint whose name is 'Breath-giver'."
"What did you do to the firebrand and the faience column,
20   When you had buried them?"
"I lamented over them,
I took them up,
I extinguished the fire,
I broke the column,
25   Threw it in the pool."
"Come then, enter the gate of this Hall of the Two Truths,
For you know us."

---

3. City in the Nile delta, a center of the worship of the sun god.

[THE SECOND INTERROGATION]

"I shall not let you enter through me,"
Says the beam of this gate,
"Unless you tell my name."
"'Plummet-of-the-Place-of-Truth' is your name."
5   "I shall not let you enter through me,"
Says the right leaf of this gate,
"Unless you tell my name."
"'Scale-pan-that-carries-maat' is your name."
"I shall not let you enter through me,"
10   Says the left leaf of this gate,
"Unless you tell my name."
"'Scale-pan-of-wine' is your name."
"I shall not let you pass over me,"
Says the threshold of this gate,
15   "Unless you tell my name."
"'Ox-of-Geb'° is your name."   *earth god*
"I shall not open for you,"
Says the bolt of this gate,
"Unless you tell my name."
20   "'Toe-of-his-mother' is your name."
"I shall not open for you,"
Says the bolt-clasp of this gate,
"Unless you tell my name."
"'Eye-of-Sobk°-Lord-of-Bakhu' is your name."   *crocodile god*
25   "I shall not open for you,
I shall not let you enter by me,"
Says the keeper of this gate,
"Unless you tell my name."
"'Breast-of-Shu°-given-him-to-guard-Osiris' is your name."   *god of air*
30   "We shall not let you pass over us,"
Say the cross-timbers,
"Unless you tell our name."
"'Offspring-of-Renenutet'° is your name."   *goddess of fertility*
"You know us, pass over us."

35   "You shall not tread upon me,"
Says the floor of this hall.
"Why not, since I am pure?"
"Because we do not know your feet,
With which you tread on us;
40   Tell them to me."
"'Who-enters-before-Min'° is the name of my right foot,   *god of vegetation*
'Wnpt-of-Nephthys'4 is the name of my left foot."
"Tread upon us, since you know us."
"I shall not announce you,"

4. Sister of the goddess Isis. *Wnpt* is an unknown word.

45   Says the guard of the Hall,
       "Unless you tell my name."
       "'Knower-of-hearts Examiner-of-bellies' is your name."
       "To which god present shall I announce you?"
       "Tell it to the Interpreter of the Two Lands."
50   "Who is the Interpreter of the Two Lands?"
       "It is Thoth."

       "Come," says Thoth,
       "Why have you come?"
       "I have come here to report."
55   "What is your condition?"
       "I am free of all wrongdoing,
       I avoided the strife of those in their day,
       I am not one of them."
       "To whom shall I announce you?"
60   "To him whose roof is of fire,
       Whose walls are living cobras,
       The floor of whose house is in the flood."
       "Who is he?"
       "He is Osiris."
65   "Proceed, you are announced,
       The Eye is your bread,
       The Eye is your beer,
       The Eye is your offering on earth,"
       So says he to me.

[INSTRUCTIONS FOR USE]

This is the way to act toward the Hall of the Two Truths. A man says this speech when he is pure, clean, dressed in fresh clothes, shod in white sandals, painted with eye-paint, anointed with the finest oil of myrrh. One shall offer to him beef, fowl, incense, bread, beer, and herbs. And you make this image in drawing on a clean surface in red paint mixed with soil on which pigs and goats have not trodden.

He for whom this scroll is recited will prosper, and his children will prosper. He will be the friend of the king and his courtiers. He will receive bread, beer, and a big chunk of meat from the altar of the great god. He will not be held back at any gate of the west. He will be ushered in with the kings of Upper and Lower Egypt. He will be a follower of Osiris.

Effective a million times.

─── ⊰✦⊱ ───

Letters to the Dead
2nd to 1st millennia B.C.E.

The ancient Egyptians took great care of their dead, and they expected a good deal in return. Deceased relatives were supposed to intercede with the gods on behalf of the living, and they could influence earthly events for good or ill. Great believers in the power of the written word, the Egyptians didn't only pray to their dead but wrote letters to them as well, inscribing them on the bowls in which they left offerings at their tombs. The writers would remind the dead of all they had done for them while alive, even threatening their dearly departed if they should fail to meet their ongoing responsibilities. The letters given here show how fluid the Egyptians considered the boundary to be between the realms of the living and the dead.

Letters to the Dead[1]

[1: A LAWSUIT AGAINST A DECEASED WIFE]

To the excellent spirit Ankhere! What evil thing have I done to you, that I should be in this wretched state I am in? What have I done to you? What you have done is to lay hands on me, although I have done nothing evil to you. Since I lived with you as husband, and down to this day, what have I done that I must hide? What have I done to you? I must bring this accusation against you for what you have done. What have I done to you?

I will lodge a complaint against you with words of my mouth, in the presence of the Nine Gods of the West, and it shall be decided between you and me by means of this letter, which sets out our dispute in writing. What have I done to you? I made you a married woman when I was a youth. I was with you when I was performing all manner of offices: I was with you, and did not put you aside. I did not cause your heart to grieve. This was when I was a youth and when I was performing all manner of important offices for Pharaoh, without putting you aside but saying, "She must be with me"—so I said! And if people came to me before you, I did not receive them on your account, saying, "I will act according to your desire." But now, behold, you give my heart no rest. I will be judged against you, and wrong will be discerned from right.

* * * And when you became ill with your sickness, I hired a master physician, and he treated you, and he did everything you asked him to do. And when I followed after Pharaoh journeying to the south, and you had come into your present condition, I spent eight full months without eating or drinking like a man. When I returned to Memphis, I asked leave of Pharaoh, and I came to where you were, and I wept exceedingly together with my people in front of my street-quarter. And I gave linen clothes to wrap you, and I caused many clothes to be made, and I left no good thing undone for you,

And now, behold, I have passed three years living alone, without entering into a house, though it is not right that one like me should live like this. And behold, I have done it on your account. But behold, you do not know good from bad. It shall be decided between you and me. And behold, the sisters in the house, I have not gone in to any of them.

[2: AN INHERITANCE DISPUTE: LETTERS WRITTEN ON AN OFFERING BOWL]

[*Written on the inside of the bowl*]: It is Shepsi who speaks to his father Inkhenmet. This is a verbal reminder of your visit to the prison, to the place where Shon's son Hotpui was, when you brought the foreleg of an ox, and when this your son came with Newayof, and when you said, "Welcome to me, you two! Sit and eat meat!" Am

---

1. Translated by Alan H. Gardiner and Kurt Sethe.

I being injured in your presence by my brother, without this your son having done or said anything? Yet I buried him, I brought him from the town of I . . ., and I placed him among the fellow-owners of his desert tomb complex, even though he still owed me repayment of a loan worth 30 gallons of Upper Egyptian barley—1 *mnw*,[2] 6 gallons of Upper Egyptian barley, 6 flax, 1 *shn*, a *mht*-cup. So although I did for him what had never been done before, he has acted very wrongly against this your son, seeing that you had said to this your son, "All my property is vested in my son Shepsi." But see, my fields have been taken away by Sher's son Henu. Now my brother is with you in one city. Do you litigate with him, since your scribes are with you in one city. Joyful is one who does what is right, whereas wrongdoers are wretched!

[*Written on the outside of the bowl*]: It is Shepsi who speaks to his mother Iy. This is a verbal reminder of the fact that you said to this your son, "Bring me quails that I may eat them," and this your son brought you seven quails, and you did eat them. Am I being injured in your presence, the other children deeply angry with this your son? Who then will pour out water offerings for you? O that you might judge between me and Sebekhotep! I brought him from another town, and placed him in his town among the fellow-owners of his tomb complex, and gave him burial clothing. Why does he work against this your son, very wrongfully, without my having said or done anything? Wrongdoing is painful to the gods!

Kabti-ilani-Marduk
8th century B.C.E.

The afterlife can be seen as the negative image of life on earth or else as its glorious completion, but in times of trouble earthly life itself can seem to be "death's other Kingdom," in T. S. Eliot's phrase. The Babylonian poem *Erra and Ishum* imagines the consequences if Erra, god of pestilence and death, were to displace Babylon's ruling god, Marduk, and take the city over. This extraordinary poem was composed by a priest named Kabti-ilani-Marduk in the wake of a disastrous period of unrest and civil conflict that left Babylon open to invasion by nomads. The invaders sacked the city, even taking spoils from Marduk's own temple atop its magnificent ziggurat—famous in the Bible as "the tower of Babel." How could Marduk have allowed such shocking events to occur? Kabti-ilani-Marduk wants to show that Marduk wasn't defeated by the nomads' gods, nor did he personally order the destruction; in particular, the poet plainly wants to clear Marduk's priesthood from charges of neglect of their duties.

The poet frames his account by outlining the nature of responsible and irresponsible government, implicitly admonishing Babylon's human rulers through his story of the fatal consequences of power politics among the gods. Babylon's troubles begin when Erra persuades Marduk to journey away from Babylon and then usurps his place and wreaks havoc. He is moved to launch this plot at the urging of his seven disease demons. Normally mere henchmen, these demons are shown here as a kind of military-pestilential complex, fomenting a war so as to keep their own weapons and tactics in good order. They make a remarkably modern political argument as well, that a spectacular first strike against a weaker opponent will improve Erra's popularity at home.

---

2. A large container's worth.

For his part, Erra approves their plan because he realizes that he can use the ensuing disorder to dominate his fellow gods. His violence ends only when his chief lieutenant and counselor, Ishum, manages to calm him down. Ishum is a major focus of the poem. Though he is a loyal subordinate who must carry out his bloodthirsty master's orders, he desperately strives to cajole Erra into stopping the violence before the city and its people are utterly destroyed. With its dramatic dialogues and its moving descriptions of the war and its horrific effects, *Erra and Ishum* is a striking instance of mythic material used for acute social and political analysis. Kabti-ilani-Marduk's great poem so impressed his contemporaries that amulets were inscribed with the poem and hung in doorways to protect homes from the plague.

PRONUNCIATIONS:
Anunnaki: ah-nou-NAH-key
Erra: AIR-ah
Ishum: EESH-uhm
Kabti-ilani-Marduk: KAHB-tea-ill-AH-nee-MAR-duck

Erra and Ishum[1]

I sing of the son of the lord of the inhabited lands, creator of the universe,
of Hendursanga, Enlil's first-born son,[2] governor of the world,
bearer of the august scepter, guardian of the dark-headed ones,
    shepherd of humanity:
Ishum, glorious warrior whose hands are made to brandish his furious
    weapons,
5   at the flash of whose impetuous spear Erra himself,
    most valiant of the gods,
trembles on his throne!
When Erra's heart urges him on to battle,
he says to his weapons, "Spread on yourselves the poison of death!"
and to the Seven, heroes unequalled, "Strap your weapons on!"
10   To you, Ishum, he says, "I am ready to march;
you are the torch, we see by your light;
you are the herald, the gods follow your lead;
you are the blade, it is you who will slay."

"Then let us go, Erra!" Ishum replies. "To lay waste the lands,
15   how it refreshes your spirit, how it gladdens your heart!"
Yet Erra's arms are heavy, as of one who needs sleep.
He says to himself, "Should I arise? Should I lie down some more?"
He says to his weapons: "Remain in the corner!"
He says to the Seven, heroes unequalled, "Go back to your homes!"
20   Until you wake him, Ishum, he stays in his bed,
given over to pleasure with Mami, his wife.
O Engidudu,[3] lord who prowls at night, the prince's vigilant guardian,
he watches over the youths and the maidens and makes them shine like day.

But as for the Seven, heroes unequalled, their nature is different indeed.
25   Their origin is strange, they are replete with terrors,

1. Translated by David Damrosch from Luigi Cagni, *L'Epopea di Erra.*
2. Enlil is the chief Sumerian deity. Hendursanga is a name for his son Ishum, war leader of the gods, herald and adviser to Erra.
3. A name for Erra.

whoever sees them is horror-struck; their breath is fatal.
Mortals tremble, they dare not approach them;
Ishum is their bulwark, a door closed before them.
When Anu, king of the gods, impregnated the Earth,
30   she bore him seven gods, and he called them the Seven.
They stood before him, and he fixed their destinies.
He called the first to give him this order:
"Wherever you spread terror, may you have no rival!"
He said to the second, "Burn like fire, and scorch like flame!"
35   He said to the third, "Take the features of a lion:
          those who see you will return to nothingness!"
He said to the fourth, "When you raise your furious weapons,
          the mountains will crumble!"
He said to the fifth, "Howl like the wind,
          and search across the sphere of the universe!"
He ordered the sixth, "Go from the heights to the depths,
          and let no one be spared!"
He charged the seventh with viper's venom, saying, "Destroy the living!"
40   After Anu had fixed the destinies of all of the Seven,
          he gave them to Erra, champion of the gods, saying, "These will march at
              your side.
If the tumult of the inhabited lands becomes distressing to you,
and your heart is moved to wreak destruction,
to kill the dark-headed ones and slaughter the cattle of Shakkan,[4]
45   then let these be your furious weapons, may they march by your side!"

And now they brandish their arms in rage,
saying to Erra: "Get up! Go to it!
Why do you stay in the city, like a feeble old man,
why do you stay at home, like a weak little child?
50   Like those who do not take the field, should we eat women's bread?
As though we did not know battle, should we tremble, full of fear?
For young men, going to war is like going to a feast!
Even a prince who stays in town cannot eat his bread in peace;
he is mocked by his people, and his person is despised.
55   How can he measure up against those who take the field?
The one who stays in town, however great his strength,
in what can he prevail over one who takes the field?
City bread in plenty cannot compare to flat loaves baked in embers,
the sweetest beer cannot compare to water from a goatskin,
60   nor can a terraced palace be compared to a hut in the field.
Valiant Erra, go into the field, and let your arms resound!
Launch your battle-cry so strongly that all who hear will tremble;
that the Igigi,° hearing it, may magnify your name;   *heavenly gods*
that the Anunnaki,° hearing it, may tremble at your name;   *underworld gods*
65   that all the gods, hearing it, may bow beneath your yoke;
that kings, hearing it, may fall down at your feet;

4. God of cattle and herdsmen.

that the nations, hearing it, may bring their tribute to you;
that the demons, hearing it, may hide themselves away;
that the powerful, hearing it, may bite their lips in fear;
70   that the high mountains, hearing it, may shudder and bow their heads;
that the oceans, hearing it, may surge and drown all they produce;
that in the ancient forest, the tree-trunks may be shattered;
that in the densest cane-field, the reeds may all be broken;
that the humans may be filled with fear, and quiet their tumult down;
75   that the beasts be filled with panic, and all return to clay;
seeing all this, may the gods your fathers glorify your valor!
Valiant Erra, why have you shunned the field, to rest within the city?
Even the cattle of Shakkan and the other animals scorn us.
O valiant Erra, to you we speak, may our words not displease you!
80   Before the entire human land becomes too strong for us,
may you take our words to heart!
For the Anunnaki, who love silence, you should do a good deed—
the Anunnaki, troubled by the humans' noise, no longer can sleep.
The cattle are trampling down the pastures, the life of the land,
85   the laborer in his fields is weeping bitterly;
the lion and the wolf are carrying off the cattle of Shakkan,
and the shepherd, concerned for his flock, has no rest day or night:
    it is you he implores!
And we, who knew the mountain passes,
    have completely forgotten the way.
Across our weapons of war the spider has stretched her webs;
90   our trusty bow, rebelling, has become too strong for us,
the sharp edge of our arrow has been blunted,
and our sword is covered with rust instead of blood!"

The valiant Erra heard them;
the words of the Seven pleased him like fine oil.
95   He opened his mouth and said to Ishum,
"Why, having heard this, do you sit silent and still?
Open the way, I would take the path of war!
The Seven, heroes unequalled, are to accompany me;
let my valiant weapons march at my sides,
100   and as for you, march before me and behind me!"

When Ishum heard these words,
he opened his mouth and replied to valiant Erra,
"Lord Erra, why do you plan evil against the gods?
Why do you plan evil, to lay waste the lands and exterminate their people?"

105   Erra opened his mouth and spoke; to Ishum, his herald, he replied:
"Attend, Ishum, and hear what I have to say!
As for the inhabitants of the lands, whom you ask me to spare,
O herald of the gods, wise Ishum, whose counsel is good,
in heaven I am a wild bull, on earth I am a lion!
110   Among the nations I am the king, among the gods the ferocious one.
Among the Igigi I am the most valiant,
    among the Anunnaki the most powerful.

Among the cattle I am the butcher, among the mountains the wild ram.
In the cane-field, I am the fire; in the forest, the battle-axe.
On the path of war, I am the standard.

115 I howl like the wind, I thunder like Adad,°   *storm god*
like Shamash° I survey the entire sphere of the universe.   *sun god*
When I go into the field, I am at home like a wild sheep,
when I go up to heaven, I make my home there too.
All of the gods dread battle with me,

120 but the humans, the dark-headed ones, hold me in contempt!
And so I—since they fear my name no longer,
and since they follow their own inclination, rejecting Marduk's word—
I will stir lord Marduk to anger: I will cause him to leave his throne;
I will destroy the human race!"

125 Then valiant Erra turned his face toward Shuanna,[5]
     city of the king of the gods;
he entered Esagil,[6] palace of heaven and earth,
     and came before Marduk's presence.
He opened his mouth and spoke to the king of the gods:
"How could it be that your regalia, insignia of your sovereignty, are blem-
     ished,
though they should be full of splendor like the stars of heaven?

130 How could it be that the appearance of your royal crown is dimmed,
though it should illuminate the temple Ehalanki
     like your tower Etemenanki?"[7]

The king of the gods opened his mouth and spoke;
to Erra, champion of the gods, he returned these words:
"Valiant Erra, as for this task you urge me to undertake,

135 long ago I stirred myself to anger; I left my throne, and I brought about the
     Flood;
I left my throne, and the bonds of heaven and earth were untied,
And then the heavens trembled; the stars were shaken,
     and did not return to their place;
the underworld was stirred up, and the fruit of the furrows grew scarce:
     a tribute imposed forever.
When I had untied the bonds of heaven and earth, the deep waters dried up,
     and the floods ebbed away.

140 I returned and saw this: it was hard to bring the waters back!
The fertility of living things had diminished,
     and I could not return them to their former state,
until, like a farm laborer, I had taken their seed in my own hands,
and until I had built a house and installed myself within.
The appearance of my regalia, tarnished by the deluge, was darkened.

145 I assigned to Girru[8] the task of renewing the splendor of my features,
     and purifying my vestments.

---

5. A name for Babylon.   great ziggurat of Marduk.
6. Marduk's temple.   8. God of fire.
7. Ehalanki was a shrine in Babylon; Etemenanki was the

After he had restored the splendor of my regalia,
    and had completed this work for me,
and I had put back on the crown of my sovereignty
    and had resumed my place,
my features expressed haughtiness, and my look was awesome.
As for the humans who survived the flood and witnessed this work,
150   should I now wield my arms and destroy the rest?
As for the wise craftsmen, I had sent them into the Abyss,
    and I did not ordain their return.
And as for the materials, the rosewood and rock crystal,
    I had changed their location and revealed it to no one.
And so, for the work you propose, O valiant Erra,
where can be found the rosewood, flesh of the gods,
    insignia of the king of the universe?
155   It is the pure wood, the august youth, fitted for sovereignty,
whose root, reaching a hundred leagues into the waters of the great ocean,
    attains the foundations of the nether world;
whose root stretches up to the height of the heaven of Anu.
Where is the translucent sapphire, which I had set aside?
Where is Ninildu, great carpenter of my divinity,
160   who carries the golden adze, and who knows all timbers,
who makes his work shine like day, and who bows before me?
Where is Gushkinbanda, creator of god and of man, whose hands are pure?
Where is Ninagal, bearer of the hammer and anvil,
    who cuts hard copper as if it were leather, and who makes the needed tools?
165   Where are the precious stones to be found, product of the vast ocean,
    ornaments of my crown?
Where are now the Seven Sages of the Abyss, the holy carp,
filled like their father Ea with sublime understanding,
    adept at purifying my body?"[9]

Hearing him, valiant Erra stepped forward;
    he opened his mouth and spoke to lord Marduk.
"I, Marduk, I will retrieve the rock crystal that you desire,
170   I will bring back the pure rosewood that you desire."
Hearing this, Marduk opened his mouth and spoke to valiant Erra:
"If I should leave my throne again, the bonds of heaven and earth
    would be untied,
the waters would rise up and flood the land.
Bright day would change to darkness,
175   the tempest would arise and cover the stars;
the evil wind would blow and block the sight of mankind,
    the progeny of the living;
demons would ascend from the nether world,
    and death would seize the living;
until I had resumed my arms, who would repel them?"

---

9. Ea, god of fresh water and of wisdom, sent the Seven Sages in the form of fish to teach humanity the arts of civilization.

Hearing this, Erra opened his mouth and spoke to lord Marduk:

180　"O prince Marduk, until you have returned to your home,
　　　　vestments purified by Girru,
　　until you have returned to your place, until that very moment.
　　I myself will take your place,
　　　　and I will make fast the bonds of heaven and earth!
　　I will go up to heaven and give the Igigi their orders,
　　I will descend to the Abyss and assign the Anunnaki's tasks.
185　I will chase the savage demons to the Land of No Return;
　　I will unleash my furious weapons against them.
　　As for the evil wind, I will tie up its wings like a bird,
　　and at that house which you enter, O prince Marduk,
　　to the right and the left of your door, like guardian bulls,
190　I will cause the divine Anu and Enlil to lie!"
　　Lord Marduk heard him out; he was pleased by the words Erra said.
　　He arose from his inaccessible throne,
　　　　and turned his face toward the Anunnaki's dwelling.[1]

. . .

Erra entered Emeslam and occupied the throne.
　　He consulted with himself about what he should do,
　　but his heart was raging and gave him no reply.
270　To Ishum he repeated his commands:
　　"Make the way open: I wish to take the path of war!
　　The day is over, the term is at an end.
　　I say: Let the splendor of the rays of Shamash° be dimmed!　　　　*sun god*
　　I will cover the face of the Moon at night!
275　To Adad I will say: 'Hold back your well-springs,
　　withdraw your clouds, and stop the snow and the rain!'
　　To Marduk and to Ea I will carry this news:
　　The one who has flourished in times of abundance
　　　　will be buried in times of distress;
　　the one who has travelled on well-watered roads
　　　　will return on a pathway of dust!
280　To the king of the gods I will say: 'Reside in Esagil;
　　the words you have spoken will be carried out, your orders will be fulfilled,
　　but if the dark-headed ones cry out to you, do not grant their prayers!'
　　I will destroy the nations and reduce them to heaps of debris.
　　I will lay the cities low and reduce them all to desert.
285　I will shatter the mountains and slaughter the cattle on them;
　　I will stir up the oceans and destroy the things they produce;
　　I will devastate cane-field and forest, burning them up like fire;
　　I will slaughter the people, leaving no soul alive.
　　I will not spare a single one, that they could multiply;
290　I will not let the cattle of Shakkan or any animal escape.
　　I will take charge over one city after another:

---

1. Seventy-five fragmentary lines follow, describing the disasters that occur once Marduk leaves. Erra takes advantage of the chaos to seize power.

The son will no longer think of the health of his father,
  nor the father care for the son.
The mother will plot her daughter's misfortune
  in the midst of the joys of love.
Into the dwelling of the gods, forbidden to the wicked,
  I will cause the wicked to enter;
295 into the dwelling of princes I will introduce the scoundrel.
I will cause beasts to enter the city,
  and I will empty it of people.
I will cause them to strike at the hearts of the mountains;
  wherever they set their foot, I will devastate that place;
300 I will cause wild beasts of the steppe to roam about the city.
I will render omens evil; I will devastate the holy precincts.
Into the dwellings of the gods I will bring the demon Saghulhaga;
  the palace of kings I will bring to ruin.
I will silence the cry of humanity, and deprive them of every joy!"

305 Erra, in his rage, listens to no one;
  he ignores the counsel he is given,
  a lion in appearance and in voice.
Then to Ishum, who marches before him, he says these words:
  "I will change the sunlight into darkness!
310 I will take the wise man in his house, and I will cut short his days!
As for the just man, the good intercessor, I will cut off his life,
  and in his place I will put the wicked man, the cut-throat.
I will alter the human heart: the father will not heed his son,
  and the daughter will speak hatefully to her mother.
315 I will render their speech evil: they will forget their god,
  and against their goddess they will speak vile insults.
I will raise up brigands to block the roads,
  and within the cities, neighbors will steal each other's goods,
  while the lion and the wolf attack the cattle of Shakkan.
320 I will enrage the goddess of creation and she will put an end to childbirth;
I will deprive the wet-nurse of the crying of infants and of children.
I will disrupt the song of the workers in the fields;
  shepherd and herdsman will forget the shelter of their hut.
I will strip the clothing from the human body:
325 the young will creep naked through their cities,
  and I will make them, naked, descend to the nether world.
They will lack the sacrificial sheep to save their life;
  even for the prince the lamb needed for the oracles of Shamash will be rare,
  and one who is ill will long in vain for the roasted meat for his offering!"[2]
. . .
Ishum was filled with pity, and said to himself,
405 "Alas for my people, against whom Erra is enraged!
They have aroused the vengeance of valiant Nergal;
  now, as in days of combat,
  when he killed the conquered Asakku, his arms do not tire;

2. Several dozen fragmentary lines detail Erra's violence and the other gods' distress.

as if to bind the wicked Anzu, he stretches out his net!"[3]
Then Ishum opened his mouth and spoke;
    to valiant Erra he said these words:
410   "Why have you had evil thoughts against god and humankind?
Why these endless evil thoughts against the humans,
    the dark-headed ones?"

Erra opened his mouth and spoke; to Ishum, his herald, he said these words:
"You know the decrees of the Igigi, and the Anunnakis' counsel;
you give orders to humanity, the dark-headed ones,
    and open their understanding:
415   why then do you speak as one who knows nothing?
Why do you counsel me as though you did not know what Marduk has
    said?
The king of the gods has abandoned his throne—
how could the nations remain stable?
He has put aside the crown of his sovereignty:
420   kings and princes, like slaves, forget their duties.
He has loosened the buckle of his belt,
and the chain linking god and mortals is unfastened: it is hard to retie!
The terrible Girru has made Marduk's precious regalia shine like day,
    has raised up again his divine splendor.
His right hand has seized the mace, his great weapon,
425   and the glance of lord Marduk is fearsome.
O herald of the gods, wise Ishum, whose counsel is benevolent,
why do the words of Marduk displease you?"

Ishum opened his mouth and spoke to valiant Erra:
"Warrior Erra, you grasp the reins of heaven,
430   you are lord of all the earth, you are master of the nations;
you stir up the oceans, you lay the mountains low;
you govern humanity, you give the cattle pasture;
Esharra is at your disposal, Engurra is in your hands;
you control Shuanna, you give orders for Esagil;
435   you gather together all the sacred ordinances: the gods fear you,
the Igigi revere you, the Anunnaki tremble before you.
If you render a decision, even Anu heeds you,
even Enlil obeys you. Without you, would there be hostilities,
and without you, would there be battle?
440   A breastplate of battle is your robe!
And yet you say in your heart; 'They have despised me!'

"Valiant Erra, you have not feared the name of Marduk;
of the city of the king of the gods, Dimkurkurra, 'Bond of the Nations,'
    you have broken the bond.
You have altered your divine nature and taken the form of a man;
445   you have put on your weapons and entered inside the city;

---

3. The Asakku were a group of demons; Anzu was a fierce lion-headed eagle.

in Babylon, you have spoken as a master,
    like one who has conquered a city.
The people of Babylon, used to growing freely like the reeds of the canals,
    are all clustered around you.
The one who knew no weapons, has his sword unsheathed;
the one who knew no arrow, now his bow is bent;
450   he who knew no combat, his battle is engaged,
he who knew no haste, flies like a bird;
the slow one passes the swift, the feeble surpasses the strong.
Against the governor, provider of their holy city, great insults are spoken;
the gate of Babylon, canal of their abundance,
    the people themselves have blocked up;
455   they have put the sanctuary of Babylon to fire,
    as if they were their own conquerors!
And you, you marched before them as their herald!
You struck with an arrow the great wall Imgur-Enlil—
    'Ah, my heart!' it exclaimed.
The throne of Muhra, custodian of the entry,
    you drowned in children's blood.
The inhabitants of Babylon are birds, and you the decoy—
460   you led them into the net, to be captured and destroyed, O valiant Erra!
Then you left the city, and you went yet further:
You assumed the features of a lion and entered into the palace.
Seeing you, the troops put on their arms,
and the heart of the governor, Babylon's protector, became enraged.
465   He ordered his army to pillage like enemy looters,
and the captain of the guard he incited to evil:
'When I send you into the city, my brave one,
fear no god and dread no mortal;
young and old together, put them all to death,
470   do not spare a single babe or suckling!
Strip off Babylon's riches as your plunder!'
The king's army assembled and entered the city,
the arrow blazes, the sword is thrust!
The free man, protected by the holiness of Anu and of Dagan,
    you have called to arms;
475   you have spilled their blood like water down the city's drains,
you have opened their veins, and made the river flow in blood!

"The great lord Marduk has seen this and exclaimed 'Alas!'
His heart was seized, an inexpiable curse was on his lips.
He swore that he would never again drink the river's water;
480   he shunned their blood and refused to enter Esagil.
'Alas, Babylon,' he cried, 'whose head I ripened like a palm tree,
    now withered by the wind!
Alas, Babylon, which I filled with seeds like a pine-cone,
    whose fullness I cannot enjoy!
Alas, Babylon, which I planted like a lush garden,
    whose fruits I cannot taste!

Alas, Babylon, which like a crystal seal I set at the throat of Anu!
485   Alas, Babylon, which I held in my hands like the tablet of destiny,
        and entrusted to no one else!'
Thus spoke lord Marduk:
'Let the river routes dry up, till they are passable on foot!
May they need to haul the sailor's boat a hundred leagues to reach the
        waters of the sea!'

"As for Sippar, primeval city, which the Lord of the Lands did not let the
        Deluge drown, for it was dear in his sight,
490   against the will of Shamash you have destroyed its wall,
        you have felled its rampart.
And in Uruk, seat of Anu and of Ishtar—city of courtesans,
        of temple slaves and prostitutes,
all those whom Ishtar has deprived of husbands,
        devoting them to her service—
there the cries of Sutean men and women now ring out![4]
They rouse within Esagil eunuchs and transvestites,
495   whose masculinity Ishtar, to inspire the people with awe,
        had changed to femininity,
bearers of rapiers, of knives, of pruning knives and knives of flint,
those who, to rejoice the heart of Ishtar,
        give themselves over to abominations;
over these you have placed a cruel and pitiless governor,
who oppresses the people and transgresses their rites.
500   Ishtar herself, seized with rage, is angered at Uruk as well:
she raises an enemy who sweeps away the people
        like grain before onrushing water.
The citizens of Daksa lament without respite the loss of E'ugal,[5]
        committed to ruins.
The enemy you have raised up does not know when to stop!

"Ishtaran, god of Der, says these words:
505   'You have made a desert of my city;
you have broken those inside it like reeds,
and swept their cry away like foam upon the water!
Even me you have not left free: you have delivered me to the Suteans.
And so, on account of Der, my city,
510   no longer will I render judgments,
        I will not hand down decisions for the land,
I will give no more orders, not make my wishes known!'"
[Erra replies]:
"Since the people have forsaken equity, embracing violence instead,
since they have abandoned what is just and have turned to plotting evil,
therefore I have unleashed the seven winds against this single country!
515   Whoever does not die in battle will perish from the plague;
whoever does not die of plague, the enemy will plunder;

---

4. The Suteans were nomads, traditional enemies of the   5. A major temple of Enlil.
settled Akkadians.

whoever the enemy does not plunder will be robbed by the thief;
whoever the thief does not rob will be raked by the weapons of the king;
whoever is not raked by the weapons of the king will be struck down by the
    prince;
520   whoever the prince does not strike down, will be drowned by the storms of
    Adad;
whoever is not drowned by Adad, will be carried off by Shamash;
whoever escapes into the open will be smitten by the wind;
whoever goes into his own house will be struck down by a demon;
whoever climbs to a high place will perish of thirst;
525   whoever descends into a valley, will perish from the waters;
heights and valleys alike will all be fatal!
The governor of the city will speak to his mother thus:
'If only, on the day you bore me, I had been blocked within your womb!
If only you had died in childbirth, and our lives had ended then!
530   You delivered me into a city whose wall has collapsed;
its people become like cattle, and the butcher is their god!'
The net is tightly woven, there is none who can escape.
Whoever sires a son and exclaims: 'Behold my son,
whom I have raised: he will avenge me!'—
535   that son I will give over to death, and his father must inter him;
and then I will give the father to death,
      and there will be none to dig his grave.
Whoever has built a house, and exclaims: 'This is my dwelling,
this is what I have made, and within it I shall take my rest:
on the day my destiny claims my life, here I will find my resting-place'—
540   him will I give over to death, and I will have his dwelling plundered;
and once it has been sacked, I will give the house to another."

"O valiant Erra," (Ishum responded), "you have slain the just,
and you have slain the unjust alike!
You have slain the one who offended you,
545   and you have slain the one who has not offended you.
You have slain the priest zealous in bringing offerings to his god,
and you have slain the palace attendant, servant of his king.
You have slain the elders in their rooms,
and you have slain the young maiden in her bed.
550   Yet none of this has calmed you in the least!
You say within your heart: 'They have held me in contempt!'
As you say within your heart, O valiant Erra:
'I wish to fell the strong and terrify the weak;
I wish to kill the commander, and scatter his troops in flight;
555   I wish to shatter the chamber of the sanctuary and the parapet of the wall,
destroying the city's vital strength;
I wish to tear apart the mooring-post, that the current take the boat.
I wish to shatter the rudder, that the ship not be able to land;
I wish to shiver the mainmast, and tear its rigging off!
560   I wish to dry up the mother's breast, that her infant not survive;
I wish to dam the springs, that the rivers lose their water;

I wish to send earthquakes through the nether world,
    that even the heavens may shake;
I wish to extinguish the splendor of Shulpae's rays,[6] and cast aside the stars;
I wish to sever the roots of trees, that their buds may not unfold;
565   I wish to undermine the walls, that their pinnacles may totter,
and I will go to the throne of the king of the gods,
    that his counsel no longer hold!'"

When valiant Erra heard Ishum's words, they pleased him like fine oil.
Then valiant Erra spoke thus:
"The sea-folk, the sea-folk; the Subartean, the Subartean;
    the Assyrian, the Assyrian;
570   the Elamite, the Elamite; the Kassite, the Kassite;
the Sutean, the Sutean; the Gutean, the Gutean;
    the Lullubean, the Lullubean;[7]
one country, another country; one city, another city; one house, another
    house;
one man, another man; one brother, his brother, without mercy:
May they all kill each other!
575   Only then may Akkad arise again, destroy them all and rule over them!"

Then valiant Erra said these words to his herald Ishum:
"Go, Ishum! Satisfy the longing of your heart to do all that you've said!"
Ishum turned his face toward mount Hihi,[8]
the Seven, heroes unequalled, pressing on behind him.
580   The hero reached mount Hihi:
he raised his hand and destroyed the mountain,
razing mount Hihi to the ground,
and he uprooted the trunks of the forest of cypress.
Once the royal road was cleared, Erra followed after Ishum.
585   He annihilated the cities and reduced them all to desert,
he destroyed the mountains and slaughtered their cattle,
he stirred the oceans up and did not spare their produce,
he devastated cane and reed fields, and burned them up like fire,
he cursed the cattle and reduced them all to clay.

590   When Erra had calmed himself and returned to his throne,
all the gods looked toward his face.
Igigi and Anunnaki alike were full of fear.
Erra opened his mouth, and spoke to all the gods:
"Listen well, all of you! Pay attention to my words!
595   Truly, in this time of fault now past, I plotted wickedness;
my heart burned with rage, and I wished to slaughter the human race.
Like a mercenary shepherd, I stole the leader of the flock;
like one who knows no husbandry, I cut the orchard down;
like one who lays a country waste, I treated good and evil alike:
    I killed them all!

---

6. Shulpae was a Sumerian god, identified with the planet
Jupiter.

7. Erra names various groups in the region of Akkad in

southern Mesopotamia and to the north, east, and west.

8. A mythical mountain, birthplace of Anzu.

600   Yet one cannot pull a corpse from the mouth of a raging lion,
       and where one is in a rage, another cannot give counsel!
       Without Ishum, my herald, what more might have happened?
       Where would your temple supplies be, where would your high priest be?
       Where would your food offerings be? No longer would you smell incense!"

605   Ishum opened his mouth and spoke;
            to valiant Erra he addressed these words:
       "Valiant one, listen well! Pay attention to my words!
       Very well then, may you now be calm! We wish to be at your service;
       in the day of your wrath, who can affront you?"
       Erra heard this, and his visage cleared;
610   His radiant features shone like a sunlit day.
       He entered Emeslam and occupied his throne,
       while Ishum gave orders concerning the ruined people of Akkad:
       "Let the remnant of the people begin to multiply again!
       May little ones walk the roads with their elders once again.
615   May the weakened Akkadian overcome the mighty Sutean,
       may each of you lead seven in tow, as though they were sheep!
       May you reduce their cities to ruin, and their grazing lands to desert,
       and bring their massive booty into Shuanna!
       You will return the gods of your land, no longer angry,
            to their thrones in safety;
620   you will cause Shakkan and Nisaba[9] to descend to their land again.
       The steppe will again produce its riches, and the sea will provide its tribute;
       you will make the fields, laid waste, productive once again.
       The governors of all the cities will bear their massive tribute into Shuanna.
       May the temples now in ruins raise their heads like the rising sun,
625   may the Tigris and Euphrates flow with water in abundance;
       let all governors bring supplies to the providers for Esagil and for Babylon.
       For years without number, may you praise the great lord Nergal[1] and valiant
            Ishum:
       be it said that Erra, consumed with anger, planned to destroy the lands and
            their people,
       but Ishum, his counselor, calmed him down and saved a remnant!
630   To Kabti-ilani-Marduk, son of Dabibi, composer of these tablets,
       I revealed these verses at night; when he recited them in the morning,
       he did not omit a single line, nor did he add a line."

       Erra heard this and expressed his approbation;
       he was pleased with Ishum, his herald, and the gods all joined in his praise.
635   And then spoke valiant Erra thus:
       "As for the god who esteems this song, may his sanctuary grow in wealth,
       but the god who rejects it, may he never more smell incense!
       The king who magnifies my name will have lordship over the world,
       the prince who proclaims the praise of my valor, he will have no rival!

---

9. God of cattle and goddess of grain.   1. Chief god of the underworld, here identified with Erra.

640   The singer who chants this song will not perish from the plague,
      but his words will please both king and prince alike!
      The scribe who commits it to memory will escape the land of the enemy,
         and will be honored in his own land.
      In the sanctuary of the wise, where they will continually proclaim my name,
         I will give wisdom to them.
      In the house where these tablets are placed, should Erra become enraged,
         should the Seven turn murderous again,
645   the sword of destruction will not approach them,
         but safety will lie upon them.
      May this song endure forever, may it last throughout all time!
      May all the lands hear it and celebrate my valor,
      may all people come to know it, and magnify my name!"

[POSTSCRIPT TO THE COPY FROM ASSUR]

I, Ashurbanipal, great king, mighty king, king of the world, king of Assyria, son of Esarhaddon king of Assyria, son of Sennacherib king of Assyria, wrote, checked, and collated this tablet in the company of scholars in accordance with clay tablets and wooden writing boards, exemplars from Assyria, Sumer and Akkad, and put it in my palace for royal reading. Whoever erases my written name and writes his own name, may Nabu,[2] the scribe of all, erase his name.

✻ CROSSCURRENTS: DEATH AND IMMORTALITY ✻

- Ishtar's descent into the underworld has many later successors. Several ancient epic heroes in particular visit the underworld and meet family members at crucial moments. Compare the underworld landscape in Book 11 of Homer's *Odyssey* (page 384), in Book 6 of Virgil's *Aeneid* (page 1109), and in Dante's *Inferno* (Volume B). How do social and family relations in the afterlife compare in these works? What different perspectives on the world above are gained in the world below?

- *Erra and Ishum* is a remarkable exploration of the earthly consequences of struggles among the gods. How does this heavenly war on earth compare with the conflicts in Homer's *Iliad* (page 201), in the Sanskrit epics the *Mahabharata* (page 809) and the *Ramayana* (page 864), and in Milton's *Paradise Lost* (Volume C)?

- Erra's herald Ishum can be compared with Gilgamesh's companion Enkidu and with the friends who try to talk sense (as they see it) to Job (page 125). Ishum can also be seen as one of the first in a long line of literary confidants and more or less faithful sidekicks. How does his limited success in restraining Erra's insane rage compare with Sancho Panza's struggle to deal with his master's madness in *Don Quixote* (Volume C) and with Marlow's encounter with the doomed Mr. Kurtz in Conrad's *Heart of Darkness* (Volume F)?

⊨ END OF PERSPECTIVES: DEATH AND IMMORTALITY ⊨

2. God of writing.

The Book of Job

6th century B.C.E.

Why does God permit human suffering? Throughout the ancient Near East, a perennially popular kind of writing was wisdom literature, either in the form of proverbs or of moral tales, which instructed people on how to live a righteous life and achieve the god-given benefits of prosperity, progeny, and honor. Yet writers recognized that earthly happiness was not always granted according to merit. One response to this problem was to create a kind of *anti*-wisdom literature: works that explore problems of justice and knowledge in the face of the inscrutability of divine purposes and actions.

The Book of Job has direct predecessors in earlier pessimistic dialogues, notably "The Babylonian Theodicy," given here as a Resonance, whose hero insists that he hasn't done anything to deserve his mistreatment by the gods, rejecting his friend's suggestions that he must somehow be at fault for his own suffering. The Book of Job develops this theme more fully than ever before, perhaps because the problem of suffering was intensified with the coming of monotheism. In polytheistic systems, suffering could be caused by evil deities like Erra, god of pestilence and death, who could scheme to cause evil when good gods like Marduk weren't watching (as in *Erra and Ishum,* page 111). In Homer as well, human conflicts could be traced back to disputes among the gods of Olympus. Under Hebrew monotheism, however, the God of Israel was increasingly understood to be all-powerful, all-knowing, and entirely good: how could such a God allow the righteous to suffer?

The Book of Job was composed at a time of far more than individual suffering. It is thought to have been written in Babylon during the period of exile in the sixth century, at a time when the nation of Israel had been destroyed, seemingly forever. This great crisis led historical writers to rethink the history of Israel's monarchy in the books of Samuel and Kings, to try and understand what had gone wrong historically and politically. The author of the Book of Job took a different tack, revising an old folktale about a patient sufferer named Job in order to explore the trauma of loss and the struggle with God at an individual level. The old folk story is still present as a prose frame tale for the book as a whole (Chapters 1–2 and the latter part of Chapter 42). It is this old prose tale that has made "the patience of Job" proverbial, for Job refuses to complain or to desert God even when his children are killed and his whole household is ruined.

The poet who took up this old story inserted a series of moving dialogues that begin when Job's patience snaps and he curses the day of his birth. After Job's initial outcry, he rejects his wife's advice to "curse God and die." Instead, he demands to know why God has allowed so many misfortunes to pile upon him. His friends Eliphaz, Bildad, and Zophar come to comfort him; they make speeches trying to mollify Job or to justify God's actions, and Job replies to his friends in turn. After each friend has had his say, Job is still unpersuaded, and they try again in a second and then a third cycle of speeches. All the while, Job denies that he is at fault in any way, and demands an audience with God himself. Over the course of these three cycles of speeches, Job's friends show sympathy for Job's plight and then a growing irritation with his stubbornness. They are horrified when he seems to be verging on blasphemy, and yet they gradually begin to accept many of his arguments. Job in turn becomes increasingly ironic, often parodying commonplaces from wisdom literature and the Psalms (Resonances, page 140). Finally God suddenly appears in a whirlwind, silencing Job in a powerful speech; the book then closes with the end of the old prose tale.

In its complex dialogue form as in its themes, the Book of Job can be compared to later Greek tragedy as well as to earlier narratives of human-divine interaction like the *Epic of Gilgamesh.* Job's unrelenting quest for justice and his open accusations of God clearly disturbed the book's ancient editors, and the text as it appears in the Bible shows different attempts to soften the impact of Job's radical questioning, actually giving lines to Job that originally must have been his third friend's final speech (Chapter 28). A repetitive long speech (Chapters 32–37) was also added in, spoken by a new character named Elihu, who was abruptly introduced by an ancient editor who clearly felt that the original three friends hadn't done their job. Included here are extended passages from the three cycles of speeches, then God's dramatic, enigmatic response, which leaves the reader to decide whether Job finally bows before overwhelming force or achieves a direct communion with God beyond the limits of human understanding.

PRONUNCIATIONS:
> *Bildad:* BILL-dad
> *Eliphaz:* ELL-ih-phaz
> *Job:* JOHB
> *Leviathan:* leh-VAI-ah-than
> *Zophar:* ZOH-phar

from The Book of Job[1]

Chapter 1

There was a man in the land of Uz,[2] whose name was Job; and that man was blameless and upright, one who feared God, and turned away from evil. There were born to him seven sons and three daughters. He had seven thousand sheep, three thousand camels, five hundred yoke of oxen and five hundred she-asses, and very many servants; so that this man was the greatest of all the people of the east. His sons used to go and hold a feast in the house of each on his day; and they would send and invite their three sisters to eat and drink with them. And when the days of the feast had run their course, Job would send and sanctify them, and he would rise early in the morning and offer burnt offerings according to the number of them all; for Job said, "It may be that my sons have sinned, and cursed God in their hearts." Thus Job did continually.

Now there was a day when the sons of God came to present themselves before the LORD, and Satan[3] also came among them. The LORD said to Satan, "Whence have you come?" Satan answered the LORD, "From going to and fro on the earth, and from walking up and down on it." And the LORD said to Satan, "Have you considered my servant Job, that there is none like him on the earth, a blameless and upright man, who fears God and turns away from evil?" Then Satan answered the LORD, "Does Job fear God for nought? Hast thou not put a hedge about him and his house and all that he has, on every side? Thou hast blessed the work of his hands, and his possessions have increased in the land. But put forth thy hand now, and touch all that he has, and he will curse thee to thy face." And the LORD said to Satan, "Behold, all that he has is in your power; only upon himself do not put forth your hand." So Satan went forth from the presence of the LORD.

Now there was a day when his sons and daughters were eating and drinking wine in their eldest brother's house; and there came a messenger to Job, and said, "The oxen were plowing and the asses feeding beside them; and the Sabeans fell upon them and took them, and slew the servants with the edge of the sword; and I alone have escaped to tell you." While he was yet speaking, there came another, and said, "The fire of God fell from heaven and burned up the sheep and the servants, and consumed them; and I alone have escaped to tell you." While he was yet speaking, there came another, and said,

---

1. Revised Standard Version, so called because it revises the classic King James Version of 1611. These revisions correct the text in light of modern biblical scholarship and update phrasings that have become obscure since King James's time, so as to restore the immediacy the text has in Hebrew, while preserving the rhythmic eloquence of the King James version.
2. Probably Edom in southern Palestine. Interestingly, Job is not a Hebrew, though he calls on the God of Israel.
3. "The Accuser."

"The Chaldeans formed three companies, and made a raid upon the camels and took them, and slew the servants with the edge of the sword; and I alone have escaped to tell you." While he was yet speaking, there came another, and said, "Your sons and daughters were eating and drinking wine in their eldest brother's house; and behold, a great wind came across the wilderness, and struck the four corners of the house, and it fell upon the young people, and they are dead; and I alone have escaped to tell you."

Then Job arose, and rent his robe, and shaved his head, and fell upon the ground, and worshiped. And he said, "Naked I came from my mother's womb, and naked shall I return; the LORD gave, and the LORD has taken away; blessed be the name of the LORD." In all this Job did not sin or charge God with wrong.

Chapter 2

Again there was a day when the sons of God came to present themselves before the LORD, and Satan also came among them to present himself before the LORD. And the LORD said to Satan, "Whence have you come?" Satan answered the LORD, "From going to and fro on the earth, and from walking up and down on it." And the LORD said to Satan, "Have you considered my servant Job, that there is none like him on the earth, a blameless and upright man, who fears God and turns away from evil? He still holds fast his integrity, although you moved me against him, to destroy him without cause." Then Satan answered the LORD, "Skin for skin! All that a man has he will give for his life. But put forth thy hand now, and touch his bone and his flesh, and he will curse thee to thy face." And the LORD said to Satan, "Behold, he is in your power; only spare his life."

So Satan went forth from the presence of the LORD, and afflicted Job with loathsome sores from the sole of his foot to the crown of his head. And he took a potsherd with which to scrape himself, and sat among the ashes.

Then his wife said to him, "Do you still hold fast your integrity? Curse God, and die." But he said to her, "You speak as one of the foolish women would speak. Shall we receive good at the hand of God, and shall we not receive evil?" In all this Job did not sin with his lips.

Now when Job's three friends heard of all this evil that had come upon him, they came each from his own place, Eliphaz the Temanite, Bildad the Shuhite, and Zophar the Na'amathite.[4] They made an appointment together to come to condole with him and comfort him. And when they saw him from afar, they did not recognize him; and they raised their voices and wept; and they rent their robes and sprinkled dust upon their heads toward heaven. And they sat with him on the ground seven days and seven nights, and no one spoke a word to him, for they saw that his suffering was very great.

Chapter 3

After this Job opened his mouth and cursed the day of his birth.
And Job said:

> "Let the day perish wherein I was born,
>   and the night which said,
> 5   'A man-child is conceived.'
> Let that day be darkness!
> May God above not seek it,
>   nor light shine upon it.

---

4. Job's friends are from northwest Arabia.

Let gloom and deep darkness claim it.
10   Let clouds dwell upon it;
        let the blackness of the day terrify it.
That night—let thick darkness seize it!
        let it not rejoice among the days of the year,
        let it not come into the number of the months.
15   Yea, let that night be barren;
        let no joyful cry be heard in it.
Let those curse it who curse the day,
        who are skilled to rouse up Leviathan.[5]
Let the stars of its dawn be dark;
20   let it hope for light, but have none,
        nor see the eyelids of the morning;
because it did not shut the doors of my mother's womb,
        nor hide trouble from my eyes.

"Why did I not die at birth,
25   come forth from the womb and expire?
Why did the knees receive me?
        Or why the breasts, that I should suck?
For then I should have lain down and been quiet;
        I should have slept; then I should have been at rest,
30   with kings and counselors of the earth
        who rebuilt ruins for themselves,
or with princes who had gold,
        who filled their houses with silver.
Or why was I not as a hidden untimely birth,
35   as infants that never see the light?
There the wicked cease from troubling,
        and there the weary are at rest.
There the prisoners are at ease together;
        they hear not the voice of the taskmaster.
40   The small and the great are there,
        and the slave is free from his master.

"Why is light given to him that is in misery,
        and life to the bitter in soul,
who long for death, but it comes not,
45   and dig for it more than for hid treasures;
who rejoice exceedingly,
        and are glad, when they find the grave?
Why is light given to a man whose way is hid,
        whom God has hedged in?
50   For my sighing comes as my bread,
        and my groanings are poured out like water.
For the thing that I fear comes upon me,
        and what I dread befalls me.

5. A primeval sea monster.

I am not at ease, nor am I quiet;
55   I have no rest; but trouble comes."

Chapter 4

Then Eliphaz the Temanite answered:
"If one ventures a word with you, will you be offended?
    Yet who can keep from speaking?
Behold, you have instructed many,
5   and you have strengthened the weak hands.
Your words have upheld him who was stumbling,
    and you have made firm the feeble knees.
But now it has come to you, and you are impatient;
    it touches you, and you are dismayed.
10   Is not your fear of God your confidence,
    and the integrity of your ways your hope?

"Think now, who that was innocent ever perished?
    Or where were the upright cut off?
As I have seen, those who plow iniquity
15   and sow trouble reap the same.
By the breath of God they perish,
    and by the blast of his anger they are consumed.
The roar of the lion, the voice of the fierce lion,
    the teeth of the young lions, are broken.
20   The strong lion perishes for lack of prey,
    and the whelps of the lioness are scattered.

"Now a word was brought to me stealthily,
    my ear received the whisper of it.
Amid thoughts from visions of the night,
25   when deep sleep falls on men,
dread came upon me, and trembling,
    which made all my bones shake.
A spirit glided past my face;
    the hair of my flesh stood up.
30   It stood still,
    but I could not discern its appearance.
A form was before my eyes;
    there was silence, then I heard a voice:
'Can mortal man be righteous before God?
35   Can a man be pure before his Maker?
Even in his servants he puts no trust,
    and his angels he charges with error;
how much more those who dwell in houses of clay,
    whose foundation is in the dust,
40   who are crushed before the moth.
Between morning and evening they are destroyed;
    they perish for ever without any regarding it.
If their tent-cord is plucked up within them,
    do they not die, and that without wisdom?"

from Chapters 6–7

Then Job answered:
"O that my vexation were weighed,
    and all my calamity laid in the balances!
For then it would be heavier than the sand of the sea;
5   therefore my words have been rash.
For the arrows of the Almighty are in me;
    my spirit drinks their poison;
    the terrors of God are arrayed against me.
Does the wild ass bray when he has grass,
10   or the ox low over his fodder?
Can that which is tasteless be eaten without salt,
    or is there any taste in the slime of the purslane?°   *a weed*
My appetite refuses to touch them;
    they are as food that is loathsome to me.

15 "O that I might have my request,
    and that God would grant my desire;
that it would please God to crush me,
    that he would let loose his hand and cut me off!
This would be my consolation;
20   I would even exult in pain unsparing;
    for I have not denied the words of the Holy One.
What is my strength, that I should wait?
    And what is my end, that I should be patient?
Is my strength the strength of stones,
25   or is my flesh bronze?
In truth I have no help in me,
and any resource is driven from me.
                    * * *
"Therefore I will not restrain my mouth;
    I will speak in the anguish of my spirit;
30   I will complain in the bitterness of my soul.
Am I the sea, or a sea monster,
    that thou settest a guard over me?6
When I say, 'My bed will comfort me,
    my couch will ease my complaint,'
35 then thou dost scare me with dreams and terrify me with visions,
so that I would choose strangling and death rather than my bones.
I loathe my life; I would not live for ever.
    Let me alone, for my days are a breath.
What is man, that thou dost make so much of him,
40   and that thou dost set thy mind upon him,
dost visit him every morning,
    and test him every moment?7
How long wilt thou not look away from me,

6. Job ironically compares himself to the conquered Babylonian sea goddess Tiamat.
7. Here Job parodies Psalm 8, verses 4–5: "What is man that thou art mindful of him, and the son of man that thou dost care for him? / Yet thou hast made him little less than God, and dost crown him with glory and honor."

nor let me alone till I swallow my spittle?
45   If I sin, what do I do to thee, thou watcher of men?
      Why hast thou made me thy mark?
      Why have I become a burden to thee?
    Why dost thou not pardon my transgression
      and take away my iniquity?
50   For now I shall lie in the earth;
      thou wilt seek me, but I shall not be."

Chapter 22

Then Eliphaz the Temanite answered:
    "Can a man be profitable to God?
    Surely he who is wise is profitable to himself.
Is it any pleasure to the Almighty if you are righteous,
5   or is it gain to him if you make your ways blameless?
Is it for your fear of him that he reproves you,
      and enters into judgment with you?
Is not your wickedness great?
      There is no end to your iniquities.
10   For you have exacted pledges of your brothers for nothing,
      and stripped the naked of their clothing.
You have given no water to the weary to drink,
      and you have withheld bread from the hungry.
The man with power possessed the land,
15   and the favored man dwelt in it.
You have sent widows away empty,
      and the arms of the fatherless were crushed.
Therefore snares are round about you,
      and sudden terror overwhelms you;
20   your light is darkened, so that you cannot see,
      and a flood of water covers you.

"Is not God high in the heavens?
      See the highest stars, how lofty they are!
Therefore you say, 'What does God know?
25   Can he judge through the deep darkness?
Thick clouds enwrap him, so that he does not see,
      and he walks on the vault of heaven.'
Will you keep to the old way which wicked men have trod?
They were snatched away before their time;
30   their foundation was washed away.
They said to God, 'Depart from us,'
      and 'What can the Almighty do to us?'
Yet he filled their houses with good things—
      but the counsel of the wicked is far from me.
35   The righteous see it and are glad;
      the innocent laugh them to scorn,
saying, 'Surely our adversaries are cut off,
      and what they left the fire has consumed.'

40   "Agree with God, and be at peace;
       thereby good will come to you.
    Receive instruction from his mouth,
       and lay up his words in your heart.
    If you return to the Almighty and humble yourself,
       if you remove unrighteousness far from your tents,
45   if you lay gold in the dust,
       and gold of Ophir among the stones of the torrent bed,
    and if the Almighty is your gold,
       and your precious silver;
    then you will delight yourself in the Almighty,
50   and lift up your face to God.
    You will make your prayer to him,
       and he will hear you;
    and you will pay your vows.
    You will decide on a matter, and it will be established for you,
55   and light will shine on your ways.
    For God abases the proud,
       but he saves the lowly.
    He delivers the innocent man;
       you will be delivered through the cleanness of your hands."

Chapter 23

    Then Job answered:
    "Today also my complaint is bitter,
       his hand is heavy in spite of my groaning.
    Oh, that I knew where I might find him,
5   that I might come even to his seat!
    I would lay my case before him
       and fill my mouth with arguments.
    I would learn what he would answer me,
       and understand what he would say to me.
10   Would he contend with me in the greatness of his power?
       No; he would give heed to me.
    There an upright man could reason with him,
       and I should be acquitted for ever by my judge.

    "Behold, I go forward, but he is not there;
15   and backward, but I cannot perceive him;
    on the left hand I seek him, but I cannot behold him;
       I turn to the right hand, but I cannot see him.
    But he knows the way that I take;
       when he has tried me, I shall come forth as gold.
20   My foot has held fast to his steps;
       I have kept his way and have not turned aside.
    I have not departed from the commandment of his lips;
       I have treasured in my bosom the words of his mouth.
    But he is unchangeable and who can turn him?
25   What he desires, that he does.

For he will complete what he appoints for me;
    and many such things are in his mind.
Therefore I am terrified at his presence;
    when I consider, I am in dread of him.
30   God has made my heart faint;
    the Almighty has terrified me;
for I am hemmed in by darkness,
    and thick darkness covers my face.

Chapter 31

"I have made a covenant with my eyes;
    how then could I look upon a virgin?
What would be my portion from God above,
    and my heritage from the Almighty on high?
5   Does not calamity befall the unrighteous,
    and disaster the workers of iniquity?
Does not he see my ways,
    and number all my steps?

"If I have walked with falsehood,
10   and my foot has hastened to deceit;
(Let me be weighed in a just balance,
    and let God know my integrity!)[8]
if my step has turned aside from the way,
    and my heart has gone after my eyes,
15   and if any spot has cleaved to my hands;
then let me sow, and another eat;
    and let what grows for me be rooted out.

"If my heart has been enticed to a woman,
    and I have lain in wait at my neighbor's door;
20   then let my wife grind for another,
    and let others bow down upon her.
For that would be a heinous crime;
    that would be an iniquity to be punished by the judges;
for that would be a fire which consumes unto Abaddon,
25   and it would burn to the root all my increase.

"If I have rejected the cause of my manservant or my maidservant,
    when they brought a complaint against me;
what then shall I do when God rises up?
    When he makes inquiry, what shall I answer him?
30   Did not he who made me in the womb make him?
    And did not one fashion us in the womb?

"If I have withheld anything that the poor desired,
    or have caused the eyes of the widow to fail,

---

8. In his final speech in this chapter, Job makes an extended "negative confession" of the sins he has not committed, in terms resembling those found in the Egyptian Book of the Dead when the deceased person's heart is weighed against the feather of Truth; see page 105.

or have eaten my morsel alone,
35   and the fatherless has not eaten of it
(for from his youth I reared him as a father,
         and from his mother's womb I guided him);
if I have seen any one perish for lack of clothing,
         or a poor man without covering;
40   if his loins have not blessed me,
         and if he was not warmed with the fleece of my sheep;
if I have raised my hand against the fatherless,
         because I saw help in the gate;
then let my shoulder blade fall from my shoulder,
45   and let my arm be broken from its socket.
For I was in terror of calamity from God,
         and I could not have faced his majesty.

"If I have made gold my trust,
         or called fine gold my confidence;
50   if I have rejoiced because my wealth was great,
         or because my hand had gotten much;
if I have looked at the sun when it shone,
         or the moon moving in splendor,
and my heart has been secretly enticed,
55   and my mouth has kissed my hand;[9]
this also would be an iniquity to be punished by the judges,
         for I should have been false to God above.

"If I have rejoiced at the ruin of him that hated me,
         or exulted when evil overtook him
60   (I have not let my mouth sin
         by asking for his life with a curse);
if the men of my tent have not said,
         'Who is there that has not been filled with his meat?'
(the sojourner has not lodged in the street;
65   I have opened my doors to the wayfarer);
if I have concealed my transgressions from men,
         by hiding my iniquity in my bosom,
because I stood in great fear of the multitude,
         and the contempt of families terrified me,
70   so that I kept silence, and did not go out of doors—
Oh, that I had one to hear me!
         (Here is my signature! let the Almighty answer me!)
         Oh, that I had the indictment written by my adversary!
Surely I would carry it on my shoulder;
75   I would bind it on me as a crown;
I would give him an account of all my steps;
         like a prince I would approach him.

"If my land has cried out against me,
         and its furrows have wept together;

9. In worship of an idol.

80   if I have eaten its yield without payment,
            and caused the death of its owners;
        let thorns grow instead of wheat,
            and foul weeds instead of barley."

The words of Job are ended.

Chapter 38

Then the LORD answered Job out of the whirlwind:
"Who is this that darkens counsel by words without knowledge?
Gird up your loins like a man,
    I will question you, and you shall declare to me.

5   "Where were you when I laid the foundation of the earth?
            Tell me, if you have understanding.
        Who determined its measurements—surely you know!
            Or who stretched the line upon it?
        On what were its bases sunk,
10   or who laid its cornerstone,
        when the morning stars sang together,
            and all the sons of God shouted for joy?

        "Or who shut in the sea with doors,
            when it burst forth from the womb;
15   when I made clouds its garment,
            and thick darkness its swaddling band,
        and prescribed bounds for it,
            and set bars and doors,
        and said, 'Thus far shall you come, and no farther,
20   and here shall your proud waves be stayed'?

        "Have you commanded the morning since your days began,
            and caused the dawn to know its place,
        that it might take hold of the skirts of the earth,
            and the wicked be shaken out of it?
25   It is changed like clay under the seal,
            and it is dyed like a garment.
        From the wicked their light is withheld,
            and their uplifted arm is broken.

        "Have you entered into the springs of the sea,
30   or walked in the recesses of the deep?
        Have the gates of death been revealed to you,
            or have you seen the gates of deep darkness?
        Have you comprehended the expanse of the earth?
            Declare, if you know all this.

35   "Where is the way to the dwelling of light,
            and where is the place of darkness,
        that you may take it to its territory
            and that you may discern the paths to its home?
        You know, for you were born then,

40   and the number of your days is great!

"Have you entered the storehouses of the snow,
    or have you seen the storehouses of the hail,
which I have reserved for the time of trouble,
    for the day of battle and war?
45 What is the way to the place where the light is distributed,
    or where the east wind is scattered upon the earth?

"Who has cleft a channel for the torrents of rain,
    and a way for the thunderbolt,
to bring rain on a land where no man is,
50   on the desert in which there is no man;
to satisfy the waste and desolate land,
    and to make the ground put forth grass?

"Has the rain a father,
    or who has begotten the drops of dew?
55 From whose womb did the ice come forth,
    and who has given birth to the hoarfrost of heaven?
The waters become hard like stone,
    and the face of the deep is frozen.

"Can you bind the chains of the Pleiades,
60   or loose the cords of Orion?
Can you lead forth the Mazzaroth° in their season,   *another constellation*
    or can you guide the Bear with its children?
Do you know the ordinances of the heavens?
    Can you establish their rule on the earth?

65 "Can you lift up your voice to the clouds,
    that a flood of waters may cover you?
Can you send forth lightnings, that they may go
    and say to you, 'Here we are'?
Who has put wisdom in the clouds,
70   or given understanding to the mists?
Who can number the clouds by wisdom?
    Or who can tilt the waterskins of the heavens,
when the dust runs into a mass and the clods cleave fast together?

"Can you hunt the prey for the lion,
75   or satisfy the appetite of the young lions,
when they crouch in their dens,
    or lie in wait in their covert?
Who provides for the raven its prey,
    when its young ones cry to God,
80   and wander about for lack of food?"

Chapter 40

And the LORD said to Job:
    "Shall a faultfinder contend with the Almighty?

He who argues with God, let him answer it."

Then Job answered the LORD:

5   "Behold, I am of small account; what shall I answer thee?
      I lay my hand on my mouth.
I have spoken once, and I will not answer;
      twice, but I will proceed no further."

Then the LORD answered Job out of the whirlwind:

10   "Gird up your loins like a man;
      I will question you, and you declare to me.
Will you even put me in the wrong?
      Will you condemn me that you may be justified?
Have you an arm like God,

15   and can you thunder with a voice like his?

"Deck yourself with majesty and dignity;
      clothe yourself with glory and splendor.
Pour forth the overflowings of your anger,
      and look on every one that is proud, and abase him.

20   Look on every one that is proud, and bring him low;
      and tread down the wicked where they stand.
Hide them all in the dust together;
      bind their faces in the world below."
Then will I also acknowledge to you,

25   that your own right hand can give you victory.

"Behold, Behemoth,° which I made as I made you;   *hippopotamus*
      he eats grass like an ox.
Behold, his strength in his loins,
      and his power in the muscles of his belly.

30   He makes his tail stiff like a cedar;
      the sinews of his thighs are knit together.
His bones are tubes of bronze,
      his limbs like bars of iron.

"He is the first of the works of God;

35   let him who made him bring near his sword!
For the mountains yield food for him
      where all the wild beasts play.
Under the lotus plants he lies,
      in the covert of the reeds and in the marsh.

40   For his shade the lotus trees cover him;
      the willows of the brook surround him.
Behold, if the river is turbulent he is not frightened;
      he is confident though Jordan rushes against his mouth.
Can one take him with hooks,
      or pierce his nose with a snare?

Chapter 41

"Can you draw out Leviathan with a fishhook,
      or press down his tongue with a cord?

Can you put a rope in his nose,
　　or pierce his jaw with a hook?
5　Will he make many supplications to you?
　　Will he speak to you soft words?
Will he make a covenant with you
　　to take him for your servant for ever?
Will you play with him as with a bird,
10　　or will you put him on leash for your maidens?
Will traders bargain over him?
　　Will they divide him up among the merchants?
Can you fill his skin with harpoons,
　　or his head with fishing spears?
15　Lay hands on him;
　　think of the battle; you will not do it again!
Behold, the hope of a man is disappointed;
　　he is laid low even at the sight of him.
No one is so fierce that he dares to stir him up.
20　　Who then is he that can stand before me?
Who has given to me, that I should repay him?
　　Whatever is under the whole heaven is mine.

"I will not keep silence concerning his limbs,
　　or his mighty strength, or his goodly frame.
25　Who can strip off his outer garment?
　　Who can penetrate his double coat of mail?
Who can open the doors of his face?
　　Round about his teeth is terror.
His back is made of rows of shields,
30　　shut up closely as with a seal.
One is so near to another
　　that no air can come between them.
They are joined one to another;
　　they clasp each other and cannot be separated.
35　His sneezings flash forth light,
　　and his eyes are like the eyelids of the dawn.
Out of his mouth go flaming torches;
　　sparks of fire leap forth.
Out of his nostrils comes forth smoke,
40　　as from a boiling pot and burning rushes.
His breath kindles coals,
　　and a flame comes forth from his mouth.
In his neck abides strength,
　　and terror dances before him.
45　The folds of his flesh cleave together,
　　firmly cast upon him and immovable.
His heart is hard as a stone,
　　hard as the nether millstone.
When he raises himself up the mighty are afraid;
50　　at the crashing they are beside themselves.
Though the sword reaches him, it does not avail;

nor the spear, the dart, or the javelin.
He counts iron as straw,
    and bronze as rotten wood.
55   The arrow cannot make him flee;
    for him slingstones are turned to stubble.
Clubs are counted as stubble;
    he laughs at the rattle of javelins.
His underparts are like sharp potsherds;
60   he spreads himself like a threshing sledge on the mire.
He makes the deep boil like a pot;
    he makes the sea like a pot of ointment.
Behind him he leaves a shining wake;
    one would think the deep to be hoary.
65   Upon earth there is not his like,
    a creature without fear.
He beholds everything that is high;
    he is king over all the sons of pride.''

Chapter 42

Then Job answered the LORD:
    "I know that thou canst do all things,
and that no purpose of thine can be thwarted.
'Who is this that hides counsel without knowledge?'[1]
5   Therefore I have uttered what I did not understand,
    things too wonderful for me, which I did not know.
'Hear, and I will speak;
    I will question you, and you declare to me.'
I had heard of thee by the hearing of the ear,
10   but now my eye sees thee;
therefore I despise myself,
    and repent in dust and ashes.''

After the LORD had spoken these words to Job, the LORD said to Eliphaz the Temanite: "My wrath is kindled against you and against your two friends; for you have not spoken of me what is right, as my servant Job has. Now therefore take seven bulls and seven rams, and go to my servant Job, and offer up for yourselves a burnt offering; and my servant Job shall pray for you, for I will accept his prayer not to deal with you according to your folly; for you have not spoken of me what is right, as my servant Job has." So Eliphaz the Temanite and Bildad the Shuhite and Zophar the Na'amathite went and did what the LORD had told them; and the LORD accepted Job's prayer.

And the LORD restored the fortunes of Job, when he had prayed for his friends; and the LORD gave Job twice as much as he had before. Then came to him all his brothers and sisters and all who had known him before, and ate bread with him in his house; and they showed him sympathy and comforted him for all the evil that the LORD had brought upon him; and each of them gave him a piece of money and a ring of gold. And the LORD blessed the latter days of Job more than his beginning; and he had fourteen thousand sheep, six thousand camels, a thousand yoke of oxen, and a

---

1. Quoting the start of God's reply in Chapter 38.

thousand she-asses. He had also seven sons and three daughters. And he called the name of the first Jemimah; and the name of the second Keziah; and the name of the third Keren-happuch.[2] And in all the land there were no women so fair as Job's daughters; and their father gave them inheritance among their brothers. And after this Job lived a hundred and forty years, and saw his sons, and his sons' sons, four generations. And Job died, an old man, and full of days.

RESONANCES

from The Babylonian Theodicy[1]

[Sufferer]

O sage [. . .] come, [let] me tell you.

[. . . let] me inform you.

[. . .] . . . [. . .] . . . you,

5   I [. . .], who suffered greatly, will not cease to reverence you.

Where is the wise man of your caliber?

Where is the scholar who can rival you?

Where is the counsellor to whom I can relate my trouble?

I am finished. Anguish has come upon me.

10   When I was still a child, fate took my father;

My mother who bore me went to the Land of No Return.

My father and mother left me without anyone to be my guardian.

[Friend]

Respected friend, what you say is sad.

15   Dear friend, you have let your mind dwell on evil.

You have made your good sense like that of an imbecile,

You have changed your beaming face to scowls.

Our fathers do indeed give up and go the way of death.

It is an old saying that they cross the river Hubur.[2]

20   When you look upon all of mankind

. . . it is not . . . that has made the impoverished first-born rich.

Who prefers as a favorite the rich man?

He who looks to his god has a protective spirit;

The humble man who fears his goddess accumulates wealth.

* * *

25   [Sufferer]

Your mind is the north wind, a pleasant breeze for the people.

---

2. In this return to the folktale frame, Job's new daughters have names meaning Dove, Cinnamon, and Mascara.

1. The term "theodicy" (coined in 1710 by the philosopher Gottfried von Leibniz) means a justification of the purposes of God in a world marked by suffering and disorder. This poem, composed in Babylon in the early 1st millennium B.C.E., casts its justification into dialogue form, as its suffering hero questions the actions of the

gods and a friend responds, finally persuading him of the justice of divine ways. Both in content and in its dialogue form, this poem was likely a direct source for the Book of Job. The text is poorly preserved; brackets and ellipses indicate gaps in the text.

2. A river surrounding the underworld, like the Styx in Greek mythology.

Dearest friend, your advice is good.
Just one word would I put before you.
Those who do not seek the god go the way of prosperity,
30   While those who pray to the goddess become destitute and impoverished.
In my youth I tried to find the will of my god;
With prostration and prayer I sought my goddess.
But I was pulling a yoke in a useless corvée.°   *forced labor*
My god decreed poverty instead of wealth for me.
35   A cripple does better than I, a dullard keeps ahead of me.
The rogue has been promoted, but I have been brought low.

* * *

[Friend]
O wise one, O savant, who masters knowledge,
Your heart has become hardened and you accuse the god wrongly.
40   The mind of the god, like the center of the heavens, is remote;
Knowledge of it is very difficult; people cannot know it.
Among all the creatures whom Aruru° formed   *creator goddess*
Why should the oldest offspring be so[. . .]?
In the case of a cow, the first calf is a runt,
45   The later offspring is twice as big.
A first child is born a weakling,
But the second is called a mighty warrior.
Though it is possible to find out what the will of the god is, people do not
     know how to do it.

[Sufferer]
50   Pay attention, my friend, understand my clever ideas,
Heed my carefully chosen words.
People extol the word of a strong man who has learned to kill
But bring down the powerless who has done no wrong.
They confirm the wicked for whom an abomination is considered right
55   Yet drive off the honest man who heeds the will of his god.
They fill the storehouse of the oppressor with gold,
But empty the larder of the beggar of its provisions.
They support the powerful, whose [. . .] is guilt,
But destroy the weak and trample the powerless.
60   And as for me, an insignificant person, a prominent person persecutes me.

[Friend]
Narru, king of the gods, who created mankind,
And majestic Zulummar, who pinched off the clay for them,
And goddess Mami, the queen who fashioned them,
65   Gave twisted speech to the human race.
With lies, and not truth, they endowed them forever.
Solemnly they speak favorably of a rich man,
"He is a king," they say, "riches should be his,"
But they treat a poor man like a thief,
70   They have only bad to say of him and plot his murder,
Making him suffer every evil like a criminal, because he has no protection.

Terrifyingly they bring him to his end, and extinguish him like glowing
   coals.

[Sufferer]
You are kind, my friend; behold my trouble,
75   Help me; look on my distress; know it.
I, though humble, wise, and a suppliant,
Have not seen help or aid even for a moment.
I have gone about the square of my city unobtrusively,
My voice was not raised, my speech was kept low.
80   I did not raise my head, but looked at the ground,
I did not worship even as a slave in the company of my associates.
May the god who has abandoned me give help,
May the goddess who has forsaken me show mercy,
For the shepherd Shamash° guides the peoples as a god should.   *the sun god*

Psalm 22[1]

My God, my God, why hast thou forsaken me? why art thou so far from
   helping me, and from the words of my roaring?
O my God, I cry in the daytime, but thou hearest not; and in the night season, and am not silent.
But thou art holy, O thou that inhabitest the praises of Israel.
Our fathers trusted in thee: they trusted, and thou didst deliver them.
5   They cried unto thee, and were delivered: they trusted in thee, and were not
   confounded.
But I am a worm, and no man; a reproach of men, and despised of the people.
All they that see me laugh me to scorn: they shoot out the lip, they shake the
   head, saying:
He trusted in the LORD that he would deliver him: let him deliver him, see-
   ing he delighted in him.
But thou art he that took me out of the womb: thou didst make me hope
   when I was upon my mother's breasts.
10   I was cast upon thee from the womb: thou art my God from my mother's
   belly.
Be not far from me; for trouble is near; for there is none to help.
Many bulls have compassed me: strong bulls of Bashan have beset me
   round.
They gaped upon me with their mouths, as a ravening and a roaring lion.
I am poured out like water, and all my bones are out of joint: my heart is
   like wax; it is melted in the midst of my bowels.
15   My strength is dried up like a potsherd; and my tongue cleaveth to my jaws;
   and thou hast brought me into the dust of death.

---

1. King James Version. The Book of Psalms was Israel's hymnal. Traditionally attributed to King David, the 150 psalms
were likely composed by a variety of poets over the course of the centuries. The psalms are remarkable for their mixture of
intimacy and public address, and like the Book of Job they differ from most European poetry in using broad, powerful
rhythms and parallel variations of phrase, rather than a set meter or rhyme. The two psalms given here show how openly
the psalmists could, like Job, voice the anguish of defeat and loss, but unlike Job the speakers of these poems express an
unquestioning confidence in God's saving power.

For dogs have compassed me: the assembly of the wicked have inclosed
    me: they pierced my hands and my feet.

I may tell[2] all my bones: they look and stare upon me.

They part my garments among them, and cast lots upon my vesture.

But be not thou far from me, O LORD: O my strength, haste thee to help me.

20   Deliver my soul from the sword; my darling from the power of the dog.

Save me from the lion's mouth: for thou hast heard me from the horns of
    the unicorns.

I will declare thy name unto my brethren: in the midst of the congregation
    will I praise thee.

Ye that fear the LORD, praise him; all ye the seed of Jacob, glorify him; and
    fear him, all ye the seed of Israel.

For he hath not despised nor abhorred the affliction of the afflicted; neither
    hath he hid his face from him; but when he cried unto him, he heard.

25   My praise shall be of thee in the great congregation: I will pay my vows be-
    fore them that fear him.

The meek shall eat and be satisfied: they shall praise the LORD that seek
    him: your heart shall live for ever.

All the ends of the world shall remember and turn unto the LORD: and all
    the kindreds of the nations shall worship before thee.

For the kingdom is the LORD's: and he is the governor among the nations.

All they that be fat upon earth shall eat and worship: all they that go down
    to the dust shall bow before him: and none can keep alive his own soul.

30   A seed shall serve him: it shall be accounted to the Lord for a generation.

They shall come, and shall declare his righteousness unto a people that shall
    be born that he hath done this.

Psalm 102

Hear my prayer, O LORD, and let my cry come unto thee.

Hide not thy face from me in the day when I am in trouble; incline thine ear
    unto me: in the day when I call answer me speedily.

For my days are consumed like smoke, and my bones are burned as an
    hearth.

My heart is smitten, and withered like grass; so that I forget to eat my bread.

5   By reason of the voice of my groaning my bones cleave to my skin.

I am like a pelican of the wilderness: I am like an owl of the desert.

I watch, and am as a sparrow alone upon the house top.

Mine enemies reproach me all the day; and they that are mad against me are
    sworn against me.

For I have eaten ashes like bread, and mingled my drink with weeping,

10   Because of thine indignation and thy wrath: for thou hast lifted me up, and
    cast me down.

My days are like a shadow that declineth; and I am withered like grass.

But thou, O LORD, shalt endure for ever; and thy remembrance unto all gen-
    erations.

2. Count.

Thou shalt arise, and have mercy upon Zion:[3] for the time to favour her,
 yea, the set time, is come.

For thy servants take pleasure in her stones, and favour the dust thereof.

15 So the heathen shall fear the name of the LORD, and all the kings of the earth
 thy glory.

When the LORD shall build up Zion, he shall appear in his glory.

He will regard the prayer of the destitute, and not despise their prayer.

This shall be written for the generation to come: and the people which shall
 be created shall praise the LORD.

For he hath looked down from the height of his sanctuary; from heaven did
 the LORD behold the earth;

20 To hear the groaning of the prisoner; to loose those that are appointed to
 death;

To declare the name of the LORD in Zion, and his praise in Jerusalem;

When the people are gathered together, and the kingdoms, to serve the
 LORD.

He weakened my strength in the way; he shortened my days.

I said, O my God, take me not away in the midst of my days: thy years are
 throughout all generations.

25 Of old hast thou laid the foundation of the earth: and the heavens are the
 work of thy hands.

They shall perish, but thou shalt endure: yea, all of them shall wax old[4]
 like a garment; as a vesture shalt thou change them, and they shall be
 changed:

But thou art the same, and thy years shall have no end.

The children of thy servants shall continue, and their seed shall be established before thee.

---

3. A hill in Jerusalem on which the Temple was built;   4. Grow old.
metaphorically, Israel as a whole.

⇌✛ PERSPECTIVES ✛⇌
Strangers in a Strange Land

While many people in the ancient Near East would spend their entire lives within a few miles of their birthplace, individual and even mass migrations regularly occurred, as political upheaval or natural causes such as drought impelled people to forsake their homelands. It was no easy matter, though, to survive as "a stranger in a strange land," as Moses describes his life in Egypt, naming his first son "Gershom," from the term *ger,* "stranger, resident alien" (Exodus 2:22). Resident aliens had few rights and could be treated as virtual slaves. In societies built around the mutual support of extended families and clans, individual immigrants were in an especially difficult position. Even the most stable of all ancient societies, Egypt, experienced periods of political upheaval, and the first text below, the autobiographical "Story of Sinuhe," tells the life story of an Egyptian caught in a time of dynastic instability.

This real-life account is followed by a far more fanciful Egyptian story, "The Two Brothers," in which family discord leads the hero to abandon his home and exile himself to a mysterious, solitary region, a place of magic and eventual retribution against those who wronged him. This tale is also interesting because of the parallels it offers to the biblical story of Joseph. Like Joseph, the tale's hero is the object of a seduction attempt by a powerful woman who becomes furious when he rejects her advances; she then claims that he has actually tried to rape her. The Joseph story sets this event in the context of a far more realistic account of Israel's legendary prehistory—still a time of miraculous displays of God's power on behalf of his chosen servants. In Genesis and Exodus, the Hebrew people's sojourn in Egypt becomes a crucial time of testing and self-definition, a period of preparation for their eventual return northward to establish themselves as a nation. Centuries later, this material was reworked with different literary and theological emphases in the Qur'an, the holy book of Islam; see Volume B for the Joseph story in the Qur'an.

Finally, the biblical Book of Ruth portrays the particularly precarious situation of immigrant women, who were vulnerable to sexual abuse and to outright starvation if they lacked the protection of male relatives. The Book of Ruth movingly describes the devotion of Ruth, a Moabite woman who insists on staying with her mother-in-law, Naomi, even after their husbands die and Naomi decides to return to her homeland, Israel. Israel itself is a strange land to Ruth, a non-Israelite, yet she puts her faith in the God of Israel and is rewarded with a new life in a new land.

⊷ ⇌✛⇌ ⊷
The Story of Sinuhe
c. 1925 B.C.E.

Apparently an autobiography, "The Story of Sinuhe" was probably inscribed on its speaker's tomb, though the text survives only in later manuscript copies. It begins in 1961 B.C.E. with the death of Amenemhet I, the first king of Egypt's Twelfth Dynasty. Hearing of his pharaoh's death, the courtier Sinuhe flees Egypt, perhaps fearing that the new dynasty won't survive its founder's death, though Sinuhe expresses puzzlement at his own motives for leaving his beloved homeland. The ensuing story describes Sinuhe's survival and eventual prosperity in Syria and Palestine. He returns in old age to the court of Amenemhet's successor, Sesostris I, where he is received with honor and, best of all, is granted a lavish burial. Almost four thousand years old, "The Story of Sinuhe" is a masterpiece of realistic narration. It was immensely popular in ancient Egypt and survives in many fragmentary copies; modern scholars agree that it is the most accomplished prose work of Egypt's Middle Kingdom.

Hebrew captives being taken into exile. Detail of a relief from the palace of Sennacherib at Nineveh, showing the Assyrian conquest of the fortified Hebrew town of Lachish in 701 B.C.E. The animals' ribs are showing, indicating the exiles' weakness after the siege of their city, as they plod along with calm resignation to their new life in a strange land.

The Story of Sinuhe[1]

The Prince, Count, Governor of the domains of the sovereign in the lands of the Asiatics,[2] true and beloved Friend of the King, the Attendant Sinuhe, says:

I was an attendant who attended his lord, a servant of the royal harem, waiting on the Princess, the highly praised Royal Wife of King Sesostris in Khenemsut, the daughter of King Amenemhet in Kanefru, Nefru, the revered.

Year 30, third month of the inundation, day 7: the god ascended to his horizon. The King of Upper and Lower Egypt, Sehetepibre,[3] flew to heaven and united with the sun-disk, the divine body merging with its maker. Then the residence was hushed; hearts grieved; the great portals were shut; the courtiers were head-on-knee; the people moaned.

His majesty, however, had despatched an army to the land of the Tjemeh,[4] with his eldest son as its commander, the good god Sesostris. He had been sent to smite the foreign lands and to punish those of Tjehenu. Now he was returning, bringing captives of the Tjehenu and cattle of all kinds beyond number. The officials of the palace sent to the western border to let the king's son know the event that had occurred at the

---

1. Translated by Miriam Lichtheim.
2. Palestine.
3. A throne name of Amenemhet I; Sinuhe is an official of

Amenemhet's daughter, Princess Nefru, who was married to her brother, Sesostris I.
4. Libyans.

court. The messengers met him on the road, reaching him at night. Not a moment did he delay. The falcon flew with his attendants, without letting his army know it.

But the royal sons who had been with him on this expedition had also been sent for. One of them was summoned while I was standing there. I heard his voice, as he spoke, while I was in the near distance. My heart fluttered, my arms spread out, a trembling befell all my limbs. I removed myself in leaps, to seek a hiding place. I put myself between two bushes, so as to leave the road to its traveler.

I set out southward. I did not plan to go to the residence. I believed there would be turmoil and did not expect to survive it. I crossed Maaty near Sycamore; I reached Isle-of-Snefru. I spent the day there at the edge of the cultivation. Departing at dawn I encountered a man who stood on the road. He saluted me while I was afraid of him. At dinner time I reached "Cattle-Quay." I crossed in a barge without a rudder, by the force of the westwind. I passed to the east of the quarry, at the height of "Mistress of the Red Mountain." Then I made my way northward.[5] I reached the "Walls of the Ruler," which were made to repel the Asiatics and to crush the Sand-farers. I crouched in a bush for fear of being seen by the guard on duty upon the wall.

I set out at night. At dawn I reached Peten. I halted at "Isle-of-Kem-Wer." An attack of thirst overtook me; I was parched, my throat burned. I said, "This is the taste of death." I raised my heart and collected myself when I heard the lowing sound of cattle and saw Asiatics. One of their leaders, who had been in Egypt, recognized me. He gave me water and boiled milk for me. I went with him to his tribe. What they did for me was good.

Land gave me to land. I traveled to Byblos; I returned to Qedem. I spent a year and a half there. Then Ammunenshi, the ruler of Upper Retenu,[6] took me to him, saying to me: "You will be happy with me; you will hear the language of Egypt." He said this because he knew my character and had heard of my skill, Egyptians who were with him having borne witness for me. He said to me: "Why have you come here? Has something happened at the residence?" I said to him: "King Sehetepibre departed to the horizon, and one did not know the circumstances." But I spoke in half-truths: "When I returned from the expedition to the land of the Tjemeh, it was reported to me and my heart grew faint. It carried me away on the path of flight, though I had not been talked about; no one had spat in my face; I had not heard a reproach; my name had not been heard in the mouth of the herald. I do not know what brought me to this country; it is as if planned by god. As if a Delta-man saw himself in Yebu, a marshman in Nubia."[7]

Then he said to me: "How then is that land without that excellent god, fear of whom was throughout the lands like Sakhmet[8] in a year of plague?" I said to him in reply: "Of course his son has entered into the palace, having taken his father's heritage.

> He is a god without peer,
> No other comes before him;
> He is lord of knowledge, wise planner, skilled leader,
> One goes and comes by his will.

---

5. Sinuhe begins by traveling south and then turns northward after crossing the Nile.
6. In Syria and northern Palestine.

7. At the opposite end of the country.
8. Goddess of war.

He was the smiter of foreign lands,
While his father stayed in the palace,
He reported to him on commands carried out.

He is a champion who acts with his arm,
A fighter who has no equal,
When seen engaged in archery,
When joining the melee.

Horn-curber who makes hands turn weak,
His foes cannot close ranks;
Keen-sighted he smashes foreheads,
None can withstand his presence.

Wide-striding he smites the fleeing,
No retreat for him who turns his back;
Steadfast in time of attack,
He makes turn back and turns not his back.

Stouthearted when he sees the mass,
He lets not slackness fill his heart;
Eager at the sight of combat,
Joyful when he works his bow.

Clasping his shield he treads under foot,
No second blow needed to kill;
None can escape his arrow,
None turn aside his bow.

The Bowmen flee before him,
As before the might of the goddess;
As he fights he plans the goal,
Unconcerned about all else.

Lord of grace, rich in kindness,
He has conquered through affection;
His city loves him more than itself,
Acclaims him more than its own god.

Men outdo women in hailing him,
Now that he is king;
Victor while yet in the egg,
Set to be ruler since his birth.

Augmenter of those born with him,
He is unique, god-given;
Happy the land that he rules!

Enlarger of frontiers,
He will conquer southern lands,
While ignoring northern lands,
Though made to smite Asiatics and tread on Sand-farers!

"Send to him! Let him know your name as one who inquires while being far from his majesty. He will not fail to do good to a land that will be loyal to him."

He said to me: "Well then, Egypt is happy knowing that he is strong. But you are here. You shall stay with me. What I shall do for you is good."

He set me at the head of his children. He married me to his eldest daughter. He let me choose for myself of his land, of the best that was his, on his border with another land. It was a good land called Yaa. Figs were in it and grapes. It had more wine than water. Abundant was its honey, plentiful its oil. All kinds of fruit were on its trees. Barley was there and emmer, and no end of cattle of all kinds. Much also came to me because of the love of me; for he had made me chief of a tribe in the best part of his land. Loaves were made for me daily, and wine as daily fare, cooked meat, roast fowl, as well as desert game. For they snared for me and laid it before me, in addition to the catch of my hounds. Many sweets were made for me, and milk dishes of all kinds.

I passed many years, my children becoming strong men, each a master of his tribe. The envoy who came north or went south to the residence stayed with me. I let everyone stay with me. I gave water to the thirsty; I showed the way to him who had strayed; I rescued him who had been robbed. When Asiatics conspired to attack the Rulers of Hill-Countries, I opposed their movements. For this ruler of Retenu made me carry out numerous missions as commander of his troops. Every hill tribe against which I marched I vanquished, so that it was driven from the pasture of its wells. I plundered its cattle, carried off its families, seized their food, and killed people by my strong arm, by my bow, by my movements and my skillful plans. I won his heart and he loved me, for he recognized my valor. He set me at the head of his children, for he saw the strength of my arms.

> There came a hero of Retenu,
> To challenge me in my tent.
> A champion was he without peer,
> He had subdued it all.
> He said he would fight with me,
> He planned to plunder me,
> He meant to seize my cattle
> At the behest of his tribe.

The ruler conferred with me and I said: "I do not know him; I am not his ally, that I could walk about in his camp. Have I ever opened his back rooms or climbed over his fence? It is envy, because he sees me doing your commissions. I am indeed like a stray bull in a strange herd, whom the bull of the herd charges, whom the longhorn attacks. Is an inferior beloved when he becomes a superior? No Asiatic makes friends with a Delta-man. And what would make papyrus cleave to the mountain?[9] If a bull loves combat, should a champion bull retreat for fear of being equaled? If he wishes to fight, let him declare his wish. Is there a god who does not know what he has ordained, and a man who knows how it will be?"

At night I strung my bow, sorted my arrows, practiced with my dagger, polished my weapons. When it dawned Retenu came. It had assembled its tribes; it had gathered its neighboring peoples; it was intent on this combat.

He came toward me while I waited, having placed myself near him. Every heart burned for me; the women jabbered. All hearts ached for me thinking: "Is there another champion who could fight him?" He raised his battle-axe and shield, while his armful of missiles fell toward me. When I had made his weapons attack me, I let his arrows pass me by without effect, one following the other. Then, when he charged me, I shot him, my arrow sticking in his neck. He screamed; he fell on his nose; I slew

---

9. Papyrus grows in low-lying marshlands and would be out of place in the mountains.

him with his axe. I raised my war cry over his back, while every Asiatic shouted. I gave praise to Mont,[1] while his people mourned him. The ruler Ammunenshi took me in his arms.

Then I carried off his goods; I plundered his cattle. What he had meant to do to me I did to him. I took what was in his tent; I stripped his camp. Thus I became great, wealthy in goods, rich in herds. It was the god who acted, so as to show mercy to one with whom he had been angry, whom he had made stray abroad. For today his heart is appeased.

> A fugitive fled his surroundings—
>   I am famed at home.
> A laggard lagged from hunger—
>   I give bread to my neighbor.
> A man left his land in nakedness—
>   I have bright clothes, fine linen.
> A man ran for lack of one to send—
>   I am rich in servants.
> My house is fine, my dwelling spacious—
>   My thoughts are at the palace!

Whichever god decreed this flight, have mercy, bring me home! Surely you will let me see the place in which my heart dwells! What is more important than that my corpse be buried in the land in which I was born! Come to my aid! What if the happy event should occur! May god pity me! May he act so as to make happy the end of one whom he punished! May his heart ache for one whom he forced to live abroad! If he is truly appeased today, may he hearken to the prayer of one far away! May he return one whom he made roam the earth to the place from which he carried him off!

May Egypt's king have mercy on me, that I may live by his mercy! May I greet the mistress of the land who is in the palace! May I hear the commands of her children! Would that my body were young again! For old age has come; feebleness has overtaken me. My eyes are heavy, my arms weak; my legs fail to follow. The heart is weary; death is near. May I be conducted to the city of eternity! May I serve the Mistress of All. May she speak well of me to her children; may she spend eternity above me![2]

Now when the majesty of King Kheperkare was told of the condition in which I was, his majesty sent word to me with royal gifts, in order to gladden the heart of this servant like that of a foreign ruler. And the royal children who were in his palace sent me their messages. Copy of the decree brought to this servant concerning his return to Egypt:

Horus: Living in Births; the Two Ladies: Living in Births; the King of Upper and Lower Egypt: Kheperkare; the Son of Re: Sesostris, who lives forever. Royal decree to the Attendant Sinuhe:

This decree of the King is brought to you to let you know: That you circled the foreign countries, going from Qedem to Retenu, land giving you to land, was the counsel of your own heart. What had you done that one should act against you? You had not cursed, so that your speech would be reproved. You had not spoken against the counsel of the nobles, that your words should have been rejected. This matter—it

1. Patron god of warriors.   2. Sinuhe identifies the queen with the sky goddess, who shields souls in the underworld.

carried away your heart. It was not in my heart against you. This your heaven in the palace lives and prospers to this day. Her head is adorned with the kingship of the land; her children are in the palace. You will store riches which they give you; you will live on their bounty. Come back to Egypt! See the residence in which you lived! Kiss the ground at the great portals, mingle with the courtiers! For today you have begun to age. You have lost a man's strength. Think of the day of burial, the passing into reveredness.

A night is made for you with ointments and wrappings from the hand of Tait.[3] A funeral procession is made for you on the day of burial; the mummy case is of gold, its head of lapis lazuli. The sky is above you as you lie in the hearse, oxen drawing you, musicians going before you. The dance of the mourning-dancers is done at the door of your tomb; the offering-list is read to you; sacrifice is made before your offering-stone. Your tomb-pillars, made of white stone, are among those of the royal children. You shall not die abroad! Nor shall Asiatics inter you. You shall not be wrapped in the skin of a ram to serve as your coffin. Too long a roaming of the earth! Think of your corpse, come back!

This decree reached me while I was standing in the midst of my tribe. When it had been read to me, I threw myself on my belly. Having touched the soil, I spread it on my chest. I strode around my camp shouting: "What compares with this which is done to a servant whom his heart led astray to alien lands? Truly good is the kindness that saves me from death! Your ka[4] will grant me to reach my end, my body being at home!"

Copy of the reply to this decree:

The servant of the Palace, Sinuhe, says: In very good peace! Regarding the matter of this flight which this servant did in his ignorance. It is your ka, O good god, lord of the Two Lands, which Re loves and which Mont lord of Thebes favors; and Amun lord of Thrones-of-the-Two-Lands, and Sobk-Re lord of Sumenu, and Horus, Hathor, Atum with his Ennead, and Sopdu-Neferbau-Semseru the Eastern Horus, and the Lady of Yemet—may she enfold your head—and the conclave upon the flood, and Min-Horus of the hill-countries, and Wereret lady of Punt, Nut, Haroeris-Re, and all the gods of Egypt and the isles of the sea—may they give life and joy to your nostrils, may they endue you with their bounty, may they give you eternity without limit, infinity without bounds! May the fear of you resound in lowlands and highlands, for you have subdued all that the sun encircles! This is the prayer of this servant for his lord who saves from the West.

The lord of knowledge who knows people knew in the majesty of the palace that this servant was afraid to say it. It is like a thing too great to repeat. The great god, the peer of Re, knows the heart of one who has served him willingly. This servant is in the hand of one who thinks about him. He is placed under his care. Your Majesty is the conquering Horus; your arms vanquish all lands. May then your Majesty command to have brought to you the prince of Meki from Qedem, the mountain chiefs from Keshu, and the prince of Menus from the lands of the Fenkhu. They are rulers of renown who have grown up in the love of you. I do not mention Retenu—it belongs to you like your hounds.

Lo, this flight which the servant made—I did not plan it. It was not in my heart; I did not devise it. I do not know what removed me from my place. It was like a dream. As if a Delta-man saw himself in Yebu, a marsh-man in Nubia. I was not afraid; no one ran after me. I had not heard a reproach; my name was not heard in the mouth of

3. Goddess of weaving, including mummy wrappings.   4. Spirit, vital force.

the herald. Yet my flesh crept, my feet hurried, my heart drove me; the god who had willed this flight dragged me away. Nor am I a haughty man. He who knows his land respects men. Re has set the fear of you throughout the land, the dread of you in every foreign country. Whether I am at the residence, whether I am in this place, it is you who covers this horizon. The sun rises at your pleasure. The water in the river is drunk when you wish. The air of heaven is breathed at your bidding. This servant will hand over to the brood which this servant begot in this place. This servant has been sent for! Your Majesty will do as he wishes! One lives by the breath which you give. As Re, Horus, and Hathor love your august nose, may Mont lord of Thebes wish it to live forever![5]

I was allowed to spend one more day in Yaa, handing over my possessions to my children, my eldest son taking charge of my tribe; all my possessions became his— my serfs, my herds, my fruit, my fruit trees. This servant[6] departed southward. I halted at Horusways. The commander in charge of the garrison sent a message to the residence to let it be known. Then his majesty sent a trusted overseer of the royal domains with whom were loaded ships, bearing royal gifts for the Asiatics who had come with me to escort me to Horusways. I called each one by his name, while every butler was at his task. When I had started and set sail, there was kneading and straining beside me, until I reached the city of Itj-tawy.

When it dawned, very early, they came to summon me. Ten men came and ten men went to usher me into the palace. My forehead touched the ground between the sphinxes, and the royal children stood in the gateway to meet me. The courtiers who usher through the forecourt set me on the way to the audience-hall. I found his majesty on the great throne in a kiosk of gold. Stretched out on my belly, I did not know myself before him, while this god greeted me pleasantly. I was like a man seized by darkness. My *ba*[7] was gone, my limbs trembled; my heart was not in my body, I did not know life from death.

His majesty said to one of the courtiers: "Lift him up, let him speak to me." Then his majesty said: "Now you have come, after having roamed foreign lands. Flight has taken its toll of you. You have aged, have reached old age. It is no small matter that your corpse will be interred without being escorted by Bowmen. But don't act thus, don't act thus, speechless though your name was called!" Fearful of punishment I answered with the answer of a frightened man: "What has my lord said to me, that I might answer it? It is not disrespect to the god! It is the terror which is in my body, like that which caused the fateful flight! Here I am before you. Life is yours. May your Majesty do as he wishes!"

Then the royal daughters were brought in, and his majesty said to the queen: "Here is Sinuhe, come as an Asiatic, a product of nomads!" She uttered a very great cry, and the royal daughters shrieked all together. They said to his majesty: "Is it really he, O king, our lord?" Said his majesty: "It is really he!" Now having brought with them their necklaces, rattles, and sistra, they held them out to his majesty:

> Your hands upon the radiance, eternal king,
> Jewels of heaven's mistress!
> The Golden One gives life to your nostrils,
> The Lady of Stars enfolds you!
>
> Southcrown fared north, northcrown south,
> Joined, united by your majesty's word.

---

5. Associated with the breath of life, the nose was a center of sensation and emotion.

6. Sinuhe himself, emphasizing his loyalty to the king.
7. Soul.

While the Cobra decks your brow,
You deliver the poor from harm.
Peace to you from Re, Lord of Lands!
Hail to you and the Mistress of All!

Slacken your bow, lay down your arrow,
Give breath to him who gasps for breath!
Give us our good gift on this good day,
Grant us the son of northwind, Bowman born in Egypt!

He made the flight in fear of you,
He left the land in dread of you!
A face that sees you shall not pale,
Eyes that see you shall not fear!

His majesty said: "He shall not fear, he shall not dread!" He shall be a Companion among the nobles. He shall be among the courtiers. Proceed to the robing-room to wait on him!"

I left the audience-hall, the royal daughters giving me their hands. We went through the great portals, and I was put in the house of a prince. In it were luxuries: a bathroom and mirrors. In it were riches from the treasury; clothes of royal linen, myrrh, and the choice perfume of the king and of his favorite courtiers were in every room. Every servant was at his task. Years were removed from my body. I was shaved; my hair was combed. Thus was my squalor returned to the foreign land, my dress to the Sand-farers. I was clothed in fine linen; I was anointed with fine oil. I slept on a bed. I had returned the sand to those who dwell in it, the tree-oil to those who grease themselves with it.

I was given a house and garden that had belonged to a courtier. Many craftsmen rebuilt it, and all its woodwork was made anew. Meals were brought to me from the palace three times, four times a day, apart from what the royal children gave without a moment's pause. A stone pyramid was built for me in the midst of the pyramids. The masons who build tombs constructed it. A master draughtsman designed in it. A master sculptor carved in it. The overseers of construction in the necropolis busied themselves with it. All the equipment that is placed in a tomb-shaft was supplied. Mortuary priests were given me. A funerary domain was made for me. It had fields and a garden in the right place, as is done for a Companion of the first rank. My statue was overlaid with gold, its skirt with electrum.[8] It was his majesty who ordered it made. There is no commoner for whom the like has been done. I was in the favor of the king, until the day of landing came.[9]

Colophon: It is done from beginning to end as it was found in writing.

━━◆━━

The Two Brothers
c. 1200 B.C.E.

The protagonists of this powerful, mysterious tale have the names of two gods: Anubis was the god of the dead and embalming; Bata was a pastoral god, often pictured as a ram or as a bull—a form he takes at one point in the story. There was an old myth in which these two gods quarreled and then were reconciled, perhaps reflecting a conflict between two neighboring towns of

---

8. Gold and silver alloy.   9. Until he died.

which they were the patron gods. In this story, the old myth has been humanized; Anubis and Bata appear as human characters who share some traits with their divine namesakes. This story was found on a papyrus written by a scribe named Ennana, who lived around 1200 B.C.E., though we can't say whether Ennana was the tale's author, was copying an older work, or was writing down a popular tale told in the marketplace. In any case, the story mixes magical and earthly realism, with a highly developed presentation of familial tensions and psychological conflict.

The Two Brothers[1]

It is said, there were two brothers, of the same mother and the same father. Anubis was the name of the elder, and Bata the name of the younger. As for Anubis, he had a house and a wife; and his young brother was with him as if he were a son. He was the one who made clothes for him, and he went behind his cattle to the fields. He was the one who did the plowing, and he harvested for him. He was the one who did for him all kinds of labor in the fields. Indeed, his young brother was an excellent man. There was none like him in the whole land, for a god's strength was in him.

Now when many days had passed, his young brother [was tending] his cattle according to his daily custom. And he [returned] to his house in the evening, laden with all kinds of field plants, and with milk, with wood, and with every [good thing] of the field. He placed them before his [elder brother], as he was sitting with his wife. Then he drank and ate and [went to sleep in] his stable among his cattle.

Now when it had dawned and another day had come, [he took foods] that were cooked and placed them before his elder brother. Then he took bread for himself for the fields, and he drove his cattle to let them eat in the fields. He walked behind his cattle, and they would say to him: "The grass is good in such-and-such a place." And he heard all they said and took them to the place of good grass that they desired. Thus the cattle he tended became exceedingly fine, and they increased their offspring very much.

Now at plowing time his elder brother said to him: "Have a team of oxen made ready for us for plowing, for the soil has emerged and is right for plowing. Also, come to the field with seed, for we shall start plowing tomorrow." So he said to him. Then the young brother made all the preparations that his elder brother had told him.

Now when it had dawned and another day had come, they went to the field with their seed and began to plow. And their hearts were very pleased with this work they had undertaken. And many days later, when they were in the field, they had need of seed. Then he sent his young brother, saying: "Hurry, fetch us seed from the village." His young brother found the wife of his elder brother seated braiding her hair. He said to her: "Get up, give me seed, so that I may hurry to the field, for my elder brother is waiting for me. Don't delay." She said to him: "Go, open the storeroom and fetch what you want. Don't make me leave my hairdo unfinished."

Then the youth entered his stable and fetched a large vessel, for he wished to take a great quantity of seed. He loaded himself with barley and emmer[2] and came out with it. Thereupon she said to him: "How much is what you have on your shoulder?" He said to her: "Three sacks of emmer and two sacks of barley, five in all, are on my shoulder." So he said to her. Then she spoke to him saying: "There is great strength in

---

1. Translated by Miriam Lichtheim. Bracketed words indicate gaps in the text, with likely restorations.   2. A kind of wheat.

you. I see your vigor daily." And she desired to know him as a man. She got up, took hold of him, and said to him: "Come, let us spend an hour lying together. It will be good for you. And I will make fine clothes for you."

Then the youth became like a leopard in his anger over the wicked speech she had made to him; and she became very frightened. He rebuked her, saying: "Look, you are like a mother to me; and your husband is like a father to me. He who is older than I has raised me. What is this great wrong you said to me? Do not say it to me again! But I will not tell it to anyone. I will not let it come from my mouth to any man." He picked up his load; he went off to the field. He reached his elder brother, and they began to work at their task. When evening had come, his elder brother returned to his house. And his young brother tended his cattle, loaded himself with all things of the field, and drove his cattle before him to let them sleep in their stable in the village.

Now the wife of his elder brother was afraid on account of the speech she had made. So she took fat and grease and made herself appear as if she had been beaten, in order to tell her husband, "It was your young brother who beat me." Her husband returned in the evening according to his daily custom. He reached his house and found his wife lying down and seeming ill. She did not pour water over his hands in the usual manner; nor had she lit a fire for him. His house was in darkness, and she lay vomiting.

Her husband said to her: "Who has had words with you?" She said to him: "No one has had words with me except your young brother. When he came to take seed to you, he found me sitting alone. He said to me: 'Come, let us spend an hour lying together; loosen your braids.' So he said to me. But I would not listen to him. 'Am I not your mother? Is your elder brother not like a father to you?' So I said to him. He became frightened and he beat me, so as to prevent me from telling you. Now if you let him live, I shall die! Look, when he returns, do [not let him live]! For I am ill from this evil design which he was about to carry out in the morning."

Then his elder brother became like a leopard. He sharpened his spear and took it in his hand. Then he stood behind the door of his stable, in order to kill his young brother when he came in the evening to let his cattle enter the stable. Now when the sun had set he loaded himself with all the plants of the field according to his daily custom. He returned, and as the lead cow was about to enter the stable she said to her herdsman: "Here is your elder brother waiting for you with his spear in order to kill you. Run away from him." He heard what his lead cow said, and when another went in she said the same. He looked under the door of his stable and saw the feet of his elder brother as he stood behind the door with his spear in his hand. He set his load on the ground and took off at a run so as to flee. And his elder brother went after him with his spear.

Then his young brother prayed to Pre-Harakhti,[3] saying: "My good lord! It is you who judge between the wicked and the just!" And Pre heard all his plea; and Pre made a great body of water appear between him and his elder brother, and it was full of crocodiles. Thus one came to be on the one side, and the other on the other side. And his elder brother struck his own hand twice, because he had failed to kill him. Then his young brother called to him on this side, saying: "Wait here until dawn! When the Aten has risen, I shall contend with you before him; and he will hand over the wicked

3. A form of the sun god Re, who is also identified below with the Aten, the divine sun disk.

to the just! For I shall not be with you any more. I shall not be in the place in which you are. I shall go to the Valley of the Pine."

Now when it dawned and another day had come, and Pre-Harakhti had risen, one gazed at the other. Then the youth rebuked his elder brother, saying: "What is your coming after me to kill me wrongfully, without having listened to my words? For I am yet your young brother, and you are like a father to me, and your wife is like a mother to me. Is it not so that when I was sent to fetch seed for us your wife said to me: 'Come, let us spend an hour lying together'? But look, it has been turned about for you into another thing." Then he let him know all that had happened between him and his wife. And he swore by Pre-Harakhti, saying: "As to your coming to kill me wrongfully, you carried your spear on the testimony of a filthy whore!" Then he took a reed knife, cut off his phallus, and threw it into the water; and the catfish swallowed it. And he grew weak and became feeble. And his elder brother became very sick at heart and stood weeping for him loudly. He could not cross over to where his young brother was on account of the crocodiles.

Then his young brother called to him, saying: "If you recall something evil, will you not also recall something good, or something that I have done for you? Go back to your home and tend your cattle, for I shall not stay in the place where you are. I shall go to the Valley of the Pine. But what you shall do for me is to come and look after me, when you learn that something has happened to me. I shall take out my heart and place it on top of the blossom of the pine. If the pine is cut down and falls to the ground, you shall come to search for it. If you spend seven years searching for it, let your heart not be disgusted. And when you find it and place it in a bowl of cool water, I shall live to take revenge on him who wronged me. You will know that something has happened to me when one puts a jug of beer in your hand and it ferments. Do not delay at all when this happens to you."

Then he went away to the Valley of the Pine; and his elder brother went to his home, his hand on his head and smeared with dirt. When he reached his house, he killed his wife, cast her to the dogs, and sat mourning for his young brother.

Now many days after this, his young brother was in the Valley of the Pine. There was no one with him, and he spent the days hunting desert game. In the evening he returned to sleep under the pine on top of whose blossom his heart was. And after many days he built a mansion for himself with his own hand in the Valley of the Pine, filled with all good things, for he wanted to set up a household.

Coming out of his mansion, he encountered the Ennead[4] as they walked about administering the entire land. Then the Ennead addressed him in unison, saying: "O Bata, Bull of the Ennead, are you alone here, having left your town on account of the wife of Anubis, your elder brother? He has killed his wife and you are avenged of all the wrong done to you." And as they felt very sorry for him, Pre-Harakhti said to Khnum:[5] "Fashion a wife for Bata, that he not live alone!" Then Khnum made a companion for him who was more beautiful in body than any woman in the whole land, for [the fluid of] every god was in her. Then the seven Hathors[6] came to see her, and they said with one voice: "She will die by the knife."

He desired her very much. She sat in his house while he spent the day hunting desert game, bringing it and putting it before her. He said to her: "Do not go outdoors, lest the sea snatch you. I cannot rescue you from it, because I am a woman like you.

---

4. Council of nine chief gods.   6. Fates.
5. The potter god who shapes bodies.

And my heart lies on top of the blossom of the pine. But if another finds it, I shall fight with him." Then he revealed to her all his thoughts.

Now many days after this, when Bata had gone hunting according to his daily custom, the young girl went out to stroll under the pine which was next to her house. Then she saw the sea surging behind her, and she started to run before it and entered her house. Thereupon the sea called to the pine, saying: "Catch her for me!" And the pine took away a lock of her hair. Then the sea brought it to Egypt and laid it in the place of the washermen of Pharaoh. Thereafter the scent of the lock of hair got into the clothes of Pharaoh. And the king quarreled with the royal washermen, saying: "A scent of ointment is in the clothes of Pharaoh!" He quarreled with them every day, and they did not know what to do.

The chief of the royal washermen went to the shore, his heart very sore on account of the daily quarrel with him. Then he realized that he was standing on the shore opposite the lock of hair which was in the water. He had someone go down, and it was brought to him. Its scent was found to be very sweet, and he took it to Pharaoh.

Then the learned scribes of Pharaoh were summoned, and they said to Pharaoh: "As for this lock of hair, it belongs to a daughter of Pre-Harakhti in whom there is the fluid of every god. It is a greeting to you from another country. Let envoys go to every foreign land to search for her. As for the envoy who goes to the Valley of the Pine, let many men go with him to fetch her." His majesty said: "What you have said is very good." And they were sent.

Now many days after this, the men who had gone abroad returned to report to his majesty. But those who had gone to the Valley of the Pine did not return, for Bata had killed them, leaving only one of them to report to his majesty. Then his majesty sent many soldiers and charioteers to bring her back, and with them was a woman into whose hand one had given all kinds of beautiful ladies' jewelry. The woman returned to Egypt with her, and there was jubilation for her in the entire land. His majesty loved her very, very much, and he gave her the rank of Great Lady. He spoke with her in order to make her tell about her husband, and she said to his majesty: "Have the pine felled and cut up." The king sent soldiers with their tools to fell the pine. They reached the pine, they felled the blossom on which was Bata's heart, and he fell dead at that moment.

When it had dawned and the next day had come, and the pine had been felled, Anubis, the elder brother of Bata, entered his house. He sat down to wash his hands. He was given a jug of beer, and it fermented. He was given another of wine, and it turned bad. Then he took his staff and his sandals, as well as his clothes and his weapons, and he started to journey to the Valley of the Pine. He entered the mansion of his young brother and found his young brother lying dead on his bed. He wept when he saw his young brother lying dead. He went to search for the heart of his young brother beneath the pine under which his young brother had slept in the evening. He spent three years searching for it without finding it.

When he began the fourth year, his heart longed to return to Egypt, and he said: "I shall depart tomorrow." So he said in his heart. When it had dawned and another day had come, he went to walk under the pine and spent the day searching for it. When he turned back in the evening, he looked once again in search of it and he found a fruit. He came back with it, and it was the heart of his young brother! He fetched a bowl of cool water, placed it in it, and sat down according to his daily custom.

When night had come, his heart swallowed the water, and Bata twitched in all his body. He began to look at his elder brother while his heart was in the bowl. Then

Anubis, his elder brother, took the bowl of cool water in which was the heart of his young brother and let him drink it. Then his heart stood in its place, and he became as he had been. Thereupon they embraced each other, and they talked to one another.

Then Bata said to his elder brother: "Look, I shall change myself into a great bull of beautiful color, of a kind unknown to man, and you shall sit on my back. By the time the sun has risen, we shall be where my wife is, that I may avenge myself. You shall take me to where the king is, for he will do for you everything good. You shall be rewarded with silver and gold for taking me to Pharaoh. For I shall be a great marvel, and they will jubilate over me in the whole land. Then you shall depart to your village."

When it had dawned and the next day had come, Bata assumed the form which he had told his elder brother. Then Anubis, his elder brother, sat on his back. At dawn he reached the place where the king was. His majesty was informed about him; he saw him and rejoiced over him very much. He made a great offering for him, saying: "It is a great marvel." And there was jubilation over him in the entire land. Then the king rewarded his elder brother with silver and gold, and he dwelled in his village. The king gave him many people and many things, for Pharaoh loved him very much, more than anyone else in the whole land.

Now when many days had passed, he entered the kitchen, stood where the Lady was, and began to speak to her, saying: "Look, I am yet alive!" She said to him: "Who are you?" He said to her: "I am Bata. I know that when you had the pine felled for Pharaoh, it was on account of me, so that I should not live. Look, I am yet alive! I am a bull." The Lady became very frightened because of the speech her husband had made to her. Then he left the kitchen.

His majesty sat down to a day of feasting with her. She poured drink for his majesty, and he was very happy with her. Then she said to his majesty: "Swear to me by God, saying: 'Whatever she will say, I will listen to it!'" He listened to all that she said: "Let me eat of the liver of this bull; for he is good for nothing." So she said to him. He became very vexed over what she had said, and the heart of Pharaoh was very sore.

When it had dawned and another day had come, the king proclaimed a great offering, namely, the sacrifice of the bull. He sent one of the chief royal slaughterers to sacrifice the bull. And when he had been sacrificed and was carried on the shoulders of the men, he shook his neck and let fall two drops of blood beside the two doorposts of his majesty, one on the one side of the great portal of Pharaoh, and the other on the other side. They grew into two big Persea trees, each of them outstanding. Then one went to tell his majesty: "Two big Persea trees have grown this night—a great marvel for his majesty—beside the great portal of his majesty." There was jubilation over them in the whole land, and the king made an offering to them.

Many days after this, his majesty appeared at the audience window of lapis lazuli with a wreath of all kinds of flowers on his neck. Then he mounted a golden chariot and came out of the palace to view the Persea trees. Then the Lady came out on a team behind Pharaoh. His majesty sat down under one Persea tree and the Lady under the other. Then Bata spoke to his wife: "Ha, you false one! I am Bata! I am alive in spite of you. I know that when you had the pine felled for Pharaoh, it was on account of me. And when I became a bull, you had me killed."

Many days after this, the Lady stood pouring drink for his majesty, and he was happy with her. Then she said to his majesty: "Swear to me by God, saying: 'Whatever she will say, I will listen to it!' So you shall say." He listened to all that she said. She said: "Have the two Persea trees felled and made into fine furniture." The king listened to all that she said. After a short while his majesty sent skilled craftsmen. They felled the Persea trees of Pharaoh, and the Queen, the Lady, stood watching it. Then a splinter flew and entered the mouth of the Lady. She swallowed it, and in a moment she became pregnant. The king ordered made of them whatever she desired.

Many days after this, she gave birth to a son. One went to tell his majesty: "A son has been born to you." He was fetched, and a nurse and maids were assigned to him. And there was jubilation over him in the whole land. The king sat down to a feastday and held him on his lap. From that hour his majesty loved him very much, and he designated him as Viceroy of Kush. And many days after this, his majesty made him crown prince of the whole land.

Now many days after this, when he had spent [many years] as crown prince of the whole land, his majesty flew up to heaven.[7] Then the king said: "Let my great royal officials be brought to me, that I may let them know all that has happened to me." Then his wife was brought to him. He judged her in their presence, and they gave their assent. His elder brother was brought to him, and he made him crown prince of the whole land. He spent thirty years as king of Egypt. He departed from life; and his elder brother stood in his place on the day of death.

Colophon.—It has come to a good end under the scribe of the treasury, Kagab, and the scribes of the treasury, Hori and Meremope. Written by the scribe Ennana, the owner of this book. Whoever maligns this book, Thoth[8] will contend with him.

━━ ✦ ━━

The Joseph Story
1st millennium B.C.E.

The biblical story of Joseph gives a fascinating comparison to "The Story of Sinuhe" as Joseph is shown making the same migration in reverse, building a successful life in Egypt as Sinuhe does in Palestine. The Joseph story serves as a bridge between the history of the patriarchs and matriarchs of Israel (Genesis 12–36) and the story of Moses and the flight from Egypt in the Book of Exodus. It may have been written in the cosmopolitan court of Solomon in the late 900s B.C.E., or it may be of a later date. It looks back to a period sometime between 1700 and 1300 B.C.E. when Hebrew clans or tribes were periodically working in the Nile delta of northern Egypt—perhaps driven south, like Joseph and his family, by drought in Palestine—and where, according to the Book of Exodus, they gradually became slaves, before fleeing Egypt and making their way back to Palestine.

There is no evidence from Egypt that Joseph was a historical figure, but his story serves to encapsulate a broad migratory movement, as understood centuries after the fact. The story is developed with great psychological insight into the tensions in Joseph's family and their gradual resolution through the hidden guidance of God and through Joseph's own resourcefulness. The story makes sophisticated use of older story material, notably the theme of an older man's seductive wife found in the Egyptian tale "The Two Brothers." The three pairs of dreams that serve as turning points in Joseph's life can also be compared to the sets of dreams that punctuate the *Epic of Gilgamesh* (page 59). While they serve as a formal structuring device in

---

7. He died. Bata is now king.   8. The god of writing.

Gilgamesh, here they take on new meanings. Theologically, dreams reveal the hidden power of the God of Israel even in the foreign land of Egypt, and through Joseph's God-given skill in interpretation, he makes his fortune and gains for his starving family a haven of prosperity, allowing them to grow in numbers to become the eventual nation of Israel.

Equally important is the psychological weight given to the dreams' interpretations. Joseph begins the story rashly interpreting his own early dreams as signs of his dominance over his older brothers, thereby heightening sibling rivalries that lead to his being sold into slavery. Then as his later dream interpretations free him from prison and then elevate him to the high rank of Pharaoh's vizier, Joseph matures from a self-centered youth into a wise man of God and an effective administrator in a time of famine. The later scenes of the story movingly show Joseph's ambivalent response when his brothers appear in Egypt, years after they believe him dead, and beg him for grain—not realizing that the Egyptian vizier they are humbly addressing is in fact their long-lost brother. The story unfolds with rich dramatic ironies as Joseph's childhood dreams surprisingly come true. Family loves and hatreds, cross-cultural contacts and conflicts, and God's secret shaping design come together in a blend of sharp realism and folktale romance to create one of the masterpieces of ancient literature.

Genesis 37–50: The Joseph Story[1]

CHAPTER 37

This is the account of the family of Jacob.

Joseph, a young man of seventeen, was tending the flocks with his brothers, the sons of Bilhah and the sons of Zilpah, his father's wives, and he brought their father a bad report about them.

Now Israel[2] loved Joseph more than any of his other sons, because he had been born to him in his old age; and he made a richly ornamented robe for him. When his brothers saw that their father loved him more than any of them, they hated him and could not speak a kind word to him.

Joseph had a dream, and when he told it to his brothers, they hated him all the more. He said to them, "Listen to this dream I had. We were binding sheaves of grain out in the field when suddenly my sheaf rose and stood upright, while your sheaves gathered around mine and bowed down to it."

His brothers said to him, "Do you intend to reign over us? Will you actually rule us?" And they hated him all the more because of his dream and what he had said. Then he had another dream, and he told it to his brothers. "Listen," he said, "I had another dream, and this time the sun and moon and eleven stars were bowing down to me."

When he told his father as well as his brothers, his father rebuked him and said, "What is this dream you had? Will your mother and I and your brothers actually come and bow down to the ground before you?" His brothers were jealous of him, but his father kept the thing in mind.

Now his brothers had gone to graze their father's flocks near Shechem, and Israel said to Joseph, "As you know, your brothers are grazing the flocks near Shechem. Come, I am going to send you to them."

---

1. New International Version.
2. Jacob received the name "Israel" ("He who wrestles

with God") after struggling all night with an angel who tries to kill him (Genesis 32).

"Very well," he replied.

So he said to him, "Go and see if all is well with your brothers and with the flocks, and bring word back to me." So he sent him off from the Valley of Hebron.

When Joseph arrived at Shechem, a man found him wandering around in the fields and asked him, "What are you looking for?"

He replied, "I'm looking for my brothers. Can you tell me where they are grazing their flocks?"

"They have moved on from here," the man answered. "I heard them say, 'Let's go to Dothan.'"[3]

So Joseph went after his brothers and found them near Dothan. But they saw him in the distance, and before he reached them, they plotted to kill him.

"Here comes that dreamer!" they said to each other. "Come now, let's kill him and throw him into one of these cisterns and say that a ferocious animal devoured him. Then we'll see what comes of his dreams."

When Reuben[4] heard this, he tried to rescue him from their hands. "Let's not take his life," he said. "Don't shed any blood. Throw him into this cistern here in the desert, but don't lay a hand on him." Reuben said this to rescue him from them and take him back to his father.

So when Joseph came to his brothers, they stripped him of his robe—the richly ornamented robe he was wearing—and they took him and threw him into the cistern. Now the cistern was empty; there was no water in it.

As they sat down to eat their meal, they looked up and saw a caravan of Ishmaelites coming from Gilead. Their camels were loaded with spices, balm and myrrh, and they were on their way to take them down to Egypt.

Judah said to his brothers, "What will we gain if we kill our brother and cover up his blood? Come, let's sell him to the Ishmaelites and not lay our hands on him; after all, he is our brother, our own flesh and blood." His brothers agreed.

So when the Midianite merchants came by, his brothers pulled Joseph up out of the cistern and sold him for twenty shekels of silver to the Ishmaelites, who took him to Egypt.[5]

When Reuben returned to the cistern and saw that Joseph was not there, he tore his clothes. He went back to his brothers and said, "The boy isn't there! Where can I turn now?"

Then they got Joseph's robe, slaughtered a goat and dipped the robe in the blood. They took the ornamented robe back to their father and said, "We found this. Examine it to see whether it is your son's robe."

He recognized it and said, "It is my son's robe! Some ferocious animal has devoured him. Joseph has surely been torn to pieces."

Then Jacob tore his clothes, put on sackcloth and mourned for his son many days. All his sons and daughters came to comfort him, but he refused to be comforted. "No," he said, "in mourning will I go down to the grave to my son." So his father wept for him.

Meanwhile, the Midianites sold Joseph in Egypt to Potiphar, one of Pharaoh's officials, the captain of the guard.

3. A town on the trade route between Syria and Egypt.
4. Joseph's oldest brother.
5. Two different traditions are being combined here: in one version, Joseph is sold to Ishmaelites, but in another, Reuben finds that Joseph has been taken away from the pit by Midianites.

CHAPTER 38

At that time, Judah left his brothers and went down to stay with a man of Adullam named Hirah. There Judah met the daughter of a Canaanite man named Shua. He married her and lay with her; she became pregnant and gave birth to a son, who was named Er. She conceived again and gave birth to a son and named him Onan. She gave birth to still another son and named him Shelah. It was at Kezib that she gave birth to him.

Judah got a wife for Er, his firstborn, and her name was Tamar. But Er, Judah's firstborn, was wicked in the LORD's sight; so the LORD put him to death.

Then Judah said to Onan, "Lie with your brother's wife and fulfill your duty to her as a brother-in-law to produce offspring for your brother." But Onan knew that the offspring would not be his; so whenever he lay with his brother's wife, he spilled his seed on the ground to keep from producing offspring for his brother. What he did was wicked in the LORD's sight; so he put him to death also.

Judah then said to his daughter-in-law Tamar, "Live as a widow in your father's house until my son Shelah grows up." For he thought, "He may die too, just like his brothers." So Tamar went to live in her father's house.

After a long time Judah's wife, the daughter of Shua, died. When Judah had recovered from his grief, he went up to Timnah, to the men who were shearing his sheep, and his friend Hirah the Adullamite went with him.

When Tamar was told, "Your father-in-law is on his way to Timnah to shear his sheep," she took off her widow's clothes, covered herself with a veil to disguise herself, and then sat down at the entrance to Enaim, which is on the road to Timnah. For she saw that, though Shelah had now grown up, she had not been given to him as his wife.

When Judah saw her, he thought she was a prostitute, for she had covered her face. Not realizing that she was his daughter-in-law, he went over to her by the roadside and said, "Come now, let me sleep with you."

"And what will you give me to sleep with you?" she asked.

"I'll send you a young goat from my flock," he said.

"Will you give me something as a pledge until you send it?" she asked.

He said, "What pledge should I give you?"

"Your seal and its cord,[6] and the staff in your hand," she answered. So he gave them to her and slept with her, and she became pregnant by him. After she left, she took off her veil and put on her widow's clothes again.

Meanwhile Judah sent the young goat by his friend the Adullamite in order to get his pledge back from the woman, but he did not find her. He asked the men who lived there, "Where is the shrine prostitute who was beside the road at Enaim?"

"There hasn't been any shrine prostitute here," they said.

So he went back to Judah and said, "I didn't find her. Besides, the men who lived there said, 'There hasn't been any shrine prostitute here.'"

Then Judah said, "Let her keep what she has, or we will become a laughingstock. After all, I did send her this young goat, but you didn't find her."

About three months later Judah was told, "Your daughter-in-law Tamar is guilty of prostitution, and as a result she is now pregnant."

---

6. Documents would be signed with a seal bearing a distinctive design; Judah's seal is a small cylinder that is worn around the neck on a cord.

Judah said, "Bring her out and have her burned to death!"

As she was being brought out, she sent a message to her father-in-law. "I am pregnant by the man who owns these," she said. And she added, "See if you recognize whose seal and cord and staff these are."

Judah recognized them and said, "She is more righteous than I, since I wouldn't give her to my son Shelah." And he did not sleep with her again.

When the time came for her to give birth, there were twin boys in her womb. As she was giving birth, one of them put out his hand; so the midwife took a scarlet thread and tied it on his wrist and said, "This one came out first." But when he drew back his hand, his brother came out, and she said, "So this is how you have broken out!" And he was named Perez.[7] Then his brother, who had the scarlet thread on his wrist, came out and he was given the name Zerah.[8]

CHAPTER 39

Now Joseph had been taken down to Egypt. Potiphar, an Egyptian who was one of Pharaoh's officials, the captain of the guard, bought him from the Ishmaelites who had taken him there.

The LORD was with Joseph and he prospered, and he lived in the house of his Egyptian master. When his master saw that the LORD was with him and that the LORD gave him success in everything he did, Joseph found favor in his eyes and became his attendant. Potiphar put him in charge of his household, and he entrusted to his care everything he owned. From the time he put him in charge of his household and of all that he owned, the LORD blessed the household of the Egyptian because of Joseph. The blessing of the LORD was on everything Potiphar had, both in the house and in the field. So he left in Joseph's care everything he had; with Joseph in charge, he did not concern himself with anything except the food he ate.

Now Joseph was well-built and handsome, and after a while his master's wife took notice of Joseph and said, "Come to bed with me!"

But he refused. "With me in charge," he told her, "my master does not concern himself with anything in the house; everything he owns he has entrusted to my care. No one is greater in this house than I am. My master has withheld nothing from me except you, because you are his wife. How then could I do such a wicked thing and sin against God?" And though she spoke to Joseph day after day, he refused to go to bed with her or even be with her.

One day he went into the house to attend to his duties, and none of the household servants was inside. She caught him by his cloak and said, "Come to bed with me!" But he left his cloak in her hand and ran out of the house.

When she saw that he had left his cloak in her hand and had run out of the house, she called her household servants. "Look," she said to them, "this Hebrew has been brought to us to make sport of us! He came in here to sleep with me, but I screamed. When he heard me scream for help, he left his cloak beside me and ran out of the house."

She kept his cloak beside her until his master came home. Then she told him this story: "That Hebrew slave you brought us came to me to make sport of me. But as soon as I screamed for help, he left his cloak beside me and ran out of the house."

7. "Breaking out."　　　　　　8. "Scarlet."

When his master heard the story his wife told him, saying, "This is how your slave treated me," he burned with anger. Joseph's master took him and put him in prison, the place where the king's prisoners were confined.

But while Joseph was there in the prison, the LORD was with him; he showed him kindness and granted him favor in the eyes of the prison warden. So the warden put Joseph in charge of all those held in the prison, and he was made responsible for all that was done there. The warden paid no attention to anything under Joseph's care, because the LORD was with Joseph and gave him success in whatever he did.

CHAPTER 40

Some time later, the cupbearer and the baker of the king of Egypt offended their master, the king of Egypt. Pharaoh was angry with his two officials, the chief cupbearer and the chief baker, and put them in custody in the house of the captain of the guard, in the same prison where Joseph was confined. The captain of the guard assigned them to Joseph, and he attended them.

After they had been in custody for some time, each of the two men—the cupbearer and the baker of the king of Egypt, who were being held in prison—had a dream the same night, and each dream had a meaning of its own.

When Joseph came to them the next morning, he saw that they were dejected. So he asked Pharaoh's officials who were in custody with him in his master's house, "Why are your faces so sad today?"

"We both had dreams," they answered, "but there is no one to interpret them."

Then Joseph said to them, "Do not interpretations belong to God? Tell me your dreams."

So the chief cupbearer told Joseph his dream. He said to him, "In my dream I saw a vine in front of me, and on the vine were three branches. As soon as it budded, it blossomed, and its clusters ripened into grapes. Pharaoh's cup was in my hand, and I took the grapes, squeezed them into Pharaoh's cup and put the cup in his hand."

"This is what it means," Joseph said to him. "The three branches are three days. Within three days Pharaoh will lift up your head and restore you to your position, and you will put Pharaoh's cup in his hand, just as you used to do when you were his cupbearer. But when all goes well with you, remember me and show me kindness; mention me to Pharaoh and get me out of this prison. For I was forcibly carried off from the land of the Hebrews, and even here I have done nothing to deserve being put in a dungeon."

When the chief baker saw that Joseph had given a favorable interpretation, he said to Joseph, "I too had a dream: On my head were three baskets of bread. In the top basket were all kinds of baked goods for Pharaoh, but the birds were eating them out of the basket on my head."

"This is what it means," Joseph said. "The three baskets are three days. Within three days Pharaoh will lift off your head and hang you on a tree. And the birds will eat away your flesh."

Now the third day was Pharaoh's birthday, and he gave a feast for all his officials. He lifted up the heads of the chief cupbearer and the chief baker in the presence of his officials: He restored the chief cupbearer to his position, so that he once again put the cup into Pharaoh's hand, but he hanged the chief baker, just as Joseph had said to them in his interpretation.

The chief cupbearer, however, did not remember Joseph; he forgot him.

CHAPTER 41

When two full years had passed, Pharaoh had a dream: He was standing by the Nile, when out of the river there came up seven cows, sleek and fat, and they grazed among the reeds. After them, seven other cows, ugly and gaunt, came up out of the Nile and stood beside those on the riverbank. And the cows that were ugly and gaunt ate up the seven sleek, fat cows. Then Pharaoh woke up.

He fell asleep again and had a second dream: Seven heads of grain, healthy and good, were growing on a single stalk. After them, seven other heads of grain sprouted—thin and scorched by the east wind. The thin heads of grain swallowed up the seven healthy, full heads. Then Pharaoh woke up; it had been a dream.

In the morning his mind was troubled, so he sent for all the magicians and wise men of Egypt. Pharaoh told them his dreams, but no one could interpret them for him.

Then the chief cupbearer said to Pharaoh, "Today I am reminded of my shortcomings. Pharaoh was once angry with his servants, and he imprisoned me and the chief baker in the house of the captain of the guard. Each of us had a dream the same night, and each dream had a meaning of its own. Now a young Hebrew was there with us, a servant of the captain of the guard. We told him our dreams, and he interpreted them for us, giving each man the interpretation of his dream. And things turned out exactly as he interpreted them to us: I was restored to my position, and the other man was hanged."

So Pharaoh sent for Joseph, and he was quickly brought from the dungeon. When he had shaved and changed his clothes, he came before Pharaoh.

Pharaoh said to Joseph, "I had a dream, and no one can interpret it. But I have heard it said of you that when you hear a dream you can interpret it."

"I cannot do it," Joseph replied to Pharaoh, "but God will give Pharaoh the answer he desires."

Then Pharaoh said to Joseph, "In my dream I was standing on the bank of the Nile, when out of the river there came up seven cows, fat and sleek, and they grazed among the reeds. After them, seven other cows came up—scrawny and very ugly and lean. I had never seen such ugly cows in all the land of Egypt. The lean, ugly cows ate up the seven fat cows that came up first. But even after they ate them, no one could tell that they had done so; they looked just as ugly as before. Then I woke up.

"In my dreams I also saw seven heads of grain, full and good, growing on a single stalk. After them, seven other heads sprouted—withered and thin and scorched by the east wind. The thin heads of grain swallowed up the seven good heads. I told this to the magicians, but none could explain it to me."

Then Joseph said to Pharaoh, "The dreams of Pharaoh are one and the same. God has revealed to Pharaoh what he is about to do. The seven good cows are seven years, and the seven good heads of grain are seven years; it is one and the same dream. The seven lean, ugly cows that came up after they did are seven years, and so are the seven worthless heads of grain scorched by the east wind: They are seven years of famine.

"It is just as I said to Pharaoh: God has shown Pharaoh what he is about to do. Seven years of great abundance are coming throughout the land of Egypt, but seven years of famine will follow them. Then all the abundance in Egypt will be forgotten, and the famine will ravage the land. The abundance in the land will not be remembered, because the famine that follows it will be so severe. The reason the dream was given to Pharaoh in two forms is that the matter has been firmly decided by God, and God will do it soon.

"And now let Pharaoh look for a discerning and wise man and put him in charge of the land of Egypt. Let Pharaoh appoint commissioners over the land to take a fifth of the harvest of Egypt during the seven years of abundance. They should collect all the food of these good years that are coming and store up the grain under the authority of Pharaoh, to be kept in the cities for food. This food should be held in reserve for the country, to be used during the seven years of famine that will come upon Egypt, so that the country may not be ruined by the famine."

The plan seemed good to Pharaoh and to all his officials. So Pharaoh asked them, "Can we find anyone like this man, one in whom is the spirit of God?"[9]

Then Pharaoh said to Joseph, "Since God has made all this known to you, there is no one so discerning and wise as you. You shall be in charge of my palace, and all my people are to submit to your orders. Only with respect to the throne will I be greater than you."

So Pharaoh said to Joseph, "I hereby put you in charge of the whole land of Egypt." Then Pharaoh took his signet ring from his finger and put it on Joseph's finger. He dressed him in robes of fine linen and put a gold chain around his neck. He had him ride in a chariot as his second-in-command, and men shouted before him, "Make way!" Thus he put him in charge of the whole land of Egypt.

Then Pharaoh said to Joseph, "I am Pharaoh, but without your word no one will lift hand or foot in all Egypt." Pharaoh gave Joseph the name Zaphenath-Paneah and gave him Asenath daughter of Potiphera, priest of On, to be his wife.[1] And Joseph went throughout the land of Egypt.

Joseph was thirty years old when he entered the service of Pharaoh king of Egypt. And Joseph went out from Pharaoh's presence and traveled throughout Egypt. During the seven years of abundance the land produced plentifully. Joseph collected all the food produced in those seven years of abundance in Egypt and stored it in the cities. In each city he put the food grown in the fields surrounding it. Joseph stored up huge quantities of grain, like the sand of the sea; it was so much that he stopped keeping records because it was beyond measure.

Before the years of famine came, two sons were born to Joseph by Asenath daughter of Potiphera, priest of On. Joseph named his firstborn Manasseh[2] and said, "It is because God has made me forget all my trouble and all my father's household." The second son he named Ephraim[3] and said, "It is because God has made me fruitful in the land of my suffering."

The seven years of abundance in Egypt came to an end, and the seven years of famine began, just as Joseph had said. There was famine in all the other lands, but in the whole land of Egypt there was food. When all Egypt began to feel the famine, the people cried to Pharaoh for food. Then Pharaoh told all the Egyptians, "Go to Joseph and do what he tells you."

When the famine had spread over the whole country, Joseph opened the storehouses and sold grain to the Egyptians, for the famine was severe throughout Egypt. And all the countries came to Egypt to buy grain from Joseph, because the famine was severe in all the world.

---

9. "Elohim" in Hebrew—Pharaoh realizes that the foreigner's god has special powers.
1. Pharaoh gives Joseph an Egyptian name and marries

him into the priesthood of his own chief god, Re.
2. "Forgetfulness."
3. "Doubly fruitful."

CHAPTER 42

When Jacob learned that there was grain in Egypt, he said to his sons, "Why do you just keep looking at each other?" He continued, "I have heard that there is grain in Egypt. Go down there and buy some for us, so that we may live and not die."

Then ten of Joseph's brothers went down to buy grain from Egypt. But Jacob did not send Benjamin, Joseph's brother,[4] with the others, because he was afraid that harm might come to him. So Israel's sons were among those who went to buy grain, for the famine was in the land of Canaan also.

Now Joseph was the governor of the land, the one who sold grain to all its people. So when Joseph's brothers arrived, they bowed down to him with their faces to the ground. As soon as Joseph saw his brothers, he recognized them, but he pretended to be a stranger and spoke harshly to them. "Where do you come from?" he asked.

"From the land of Canaan," they replied, "to buy food."

Although Joseph recognized his brothers, they did not recognize him. Then he remembered his dreams about them and said to them, "You are spies! You have come to see where our land is unprotected."

"No, my lord," they answered. "Your servants have come to buy food. We are all the sons of one man. Your servants are honest men, not spies."

"No!" he said to them. "You have come to see where our land is unprotected."

But they replied, "Your servants were twelve brothers, the sons of one man, who lives in the land of Canaan. The youngest is now with our father, and one is no more."

Joseph said to them, "It is just as I told you: You are spies! And this is how you will be tested: As surely as Pharaoh lives, you will not leave this place unless your youngest brother comes here. Send one of your number to get your brother; the rest of you will be kept in prison, so that your words may be tested to see if you are telling the truth. If you are not, then as surely as Pharaoh lives, you are spies!" And he put them all in custody for three days.

On the third day, Joseph said to them, "Do this and you will live, for I fear God: If you are honest men, let one of your brothers stay here in prison, while the rest of you go and take grain back for your starving households. But you must bring your youngest brother to me, so that your words may be verified and that you may not die." This they proceeded to do.

They said to one another, "Surely we are being punished because of our brother. We saw how distressed he was when he pleaded with us for his life, but we would not listen; that's why this distress has come upon us."

Reuben replied, "Didn't I tell you not to sin against the boy? But you wouldn't listen! Now we must give an accounting for his blood." They did not realize that Joseph could understand them, since he was using an interpreter.

He turned away from them and began to weep, but then turned back and spoke to them again. He had Simeon taken from them and bound before their eyes.

Joseph gave orders to fill their bags with grain, to put each man's silver back in his sack, and to give them provisions for their journey. After this was done for them, they loaded their grain on their donkeys and left.

---

4. Benjamin, Jacob's youngest son, is Joseph's only full brother.

At the place where they stopped for the night one of them opened his sack to get feed for his donkey, and he saw his silver in the mouth of his sack. "My silver has been returned," he said to his brothers. "Here it is in my sack."

Their hearts sank and they turned to each other trembling and said, "What is this that God has done to us?"

When they came to their father Jacob in the land of Canaan, they told him all that had happened to them. They said, "The man who is lord over the land spoke harshly to us and treated us as though we were spying on the land. But we said to him, 'We are honest men; we are not spies. We were twelve brothers, sons of one father. One is no more, and the youngest is now with our father in Canaan.'

"Then the man who is lord over the land said to us, 'This is how I will know whether you are honest men: Leave one of your brothers here with me, and take food for your starving households and go. But bring your youngest brother to me so I will know that you are not spies but honest men. Then I will give your brother back to you, and you can trade in the land.'"

As they were emptying their sacks, there in each man's sack was his pouch of silver! When they and their father saw the money pouches, they were frightened. Their father Jacob said to them, "You have deprived me of my children. Joseph is no more and Simeon is no more, and now you want to take Benjamin. Everything is against me!"

Then Reuben said to his father, "You may put both of my sons to death if I do not bring him back to you. Entrust him to my care, and I will bring him back."

But Jacob said, "My son will not go down there with you; his brother is dead and he is the only one left. If harm comes to him on the journey you are taking, you will bring my gray head down to the grave in sorrow."

CHAPTER 43

Now the famine was still severe in the land. So when they had eaten all the grain they had brought from Egypt, their father said to them, "Go back and buy us a little more food."

But Judah said to him, "The man warned us solemnly, 'You will not see my face again unless your brother is with you.' If you will send our brother along with us, we will go down and buy food for you. But if you will not send him, we will not go down, because the man said to us, 'You will not see my face again unless your brother is with you.'"

Israel asked, "Why did you bring this trouble on me by telling the man you had another brother?"

They replied, "The man questioned us closely about ourselves and our family. 'Is your father still living?' he asked us. 'Do you have another brother?' We simply answered his questions. How were we to know he would say, 'Bring your brother down here'?"

Then Judah said to Israel his father, "Send the boy along with me and we will go at once, so that we and you and our children may live and not die. I myself will guarantee his safety; you can hold me personally responsible for him. If I do not bring him back to you and set him here before you, I will bear the blame before you all my life. As it is, if we had not delayed, we could have gone and returned twice."

Then their father Israel said to them, "If it must be, then do this: Put some of the best products of the land in your bags and take them down to the man as a gift—a little balm and a little honey, some spices and myrrh, some pistachio nuts and almonds.

Take double the amount of silver with you, for you must return the silver that was put back into the mouths of your sacks. Perhaps it was a mistake. Take your brother also and go back to the man at once. And may God Almighty grant you mercy before the man so that he will let your other brother and Benjamin come back with you. As for me, if I am bereaved, I am bereaved."

So the men took the gifts and double the amount of silver, and Benjamin also. They hurried down to Egypt and presented themselves to Joseph. When Joseph saw Benjamin with them, he said to the steward of his house, "Take these men to my house, slaughter an animal and prepare dinner; they are to eat with me at noon."

The man did as Joseph told him and took the men to Joseph's house. Now the men were frightened when they were taken to his house. They thought, "We were brought here because of the silver that was put back into our sacks the first time. He wants to attack us and overpower us and seize us as slaves and take our donkeys."

So they went up to Joseph's steward and spoke to him at the entrance to the house. "Please, sir," they said, "we came down here the first time to buy food. But at the place where we stopped for the night we opened our sacks and each of us found his silver—the exact weight—in the mouth of his sack. So we have brought it back with us. We have also brought additional silver with us to buy food. We don't know who put our silver in our sacks."

"It's all right," he said. "Don't be afraid. Your God and the God of your father has given you treasure in your sacks; I received your silver." Then he brought Simeon out to them.

The steward took the men into Joseph's house, gave them water to wash their feet and provided fodder for their donkeys. They prepared their gifts for Joseph's arrival at noon, because they had heard that they were to eat there.

When Joseph came home, they presented to him the gifts they had brought into the house, and they bowed down before him to the ground. He asked them how they were, and then he said, "How is your aged father you told me about? Is he still living?"

They replied, "Your servant our father is still alive and well." And they bowed low to pay him honor.

As he looked about and saw his brother Benjamin, his own mother's son, he asked, "Is this your youngest brother, the one you told me about?" And he said, "God be gracious to you, my son." Deeply moved at the sight of his brother, Joseph hurried out and looked for a place to weep. He went into his private room and wept there.

After he had washed his face, he came out and, controlling himself, said, "Serve the food."

They served him by himself, the brothers by themselves, and the Egyptians who ate with him by themselves, because Egyptians could not eat with Hebrews, for that is detestable to Egyptians. The men had been seated before him in the order of their ages, from the firstborn to the youngest; and they looked at each other in astonishment. When portions were served to them from Joseph's table, Benjamin's portion was five times as much as anyone else's. So they feasted and drank freely with him.

CHAPTER 44

Now Joseph gave these instructions to the steward of his house: "Fill the men's sacks with as much food as they can carry, and put each man's silver in the mouth of his sack. Then put my cup, the silver one, in the mouth of the youngest one's sack, along with the silver for his grain." And he did as Joseph said.

As morning dawned, the men were sent on their way with their donkeys. They had not gone far from the city when Joseph said to his steward, "Go after those men at once, and when you catch up with them, say to them, 'Why have you repaid good with evil? Isn't this the cup my master drinks from and also uses for divination? This is a wicked thing you have done.'"

When he caught up with them, he repeated these words to them. But they said to him, "Why does my lord say such things? Far be it from your servants to do anything like that! We even brought back to you from the land of Canaan the silver we found inside the mouths of our sacks. So why would we steal silver or gold from your master's house? If any of your servants is found to have it, he will die; and the rest of us will become my lord's slaves."

"Very well, then," he said, "let it be as you say. Whoever is found to have it will become my slave; the rest of you will be free from blame."

Each of them quickly lowered his sack to the ground and opened it. Then the steward proceeded to search, beginning with the oldest and ending with the youngest. And the cup was found in Benjamin's sack. At this, they tore their clothes. Then they all loaded their donkeys and returned to the city.

Joseph was still in the house when Judah and his brothers came in, and they threw themselves to the ground before him. Joseph said to them, "What is this you have done? Don't you know that a man like me can find things out by divination?"

"What can we say to my lord?" Judah replied. "What can we say? How can we prove our innocence? God has uncovered your servants' guilt. We are now my lord's slaves—we ourselves and the one who was found to have the cup."

But Joseph said, "Far be it from me to do such a thing! Only the man who was found to have the cup will become my slave. The rest of you, go back to your father in peace."

Then Judah went up to him and said: "Please, my lord, let your servant speak a word to my lord. Do not be angry with your servant, though you are equal to Pharaoh himself. My lord asked his servants, 'Do you have a father or a brother?' And we answered, 'We have an aged father, and there is a young son born to him in his old age. His brother is dead, and he is the only one of his mother's sons left, and his father loves him.'

"Then you said to your servants, 'Bring him down to me so I can see him for myself.' And we said to my lord, 'The boy cannot leave his father; if he leaves him, his father will die.' But you told your servants, 'Unless your youngest brother comes down with you, you will not see my face again.' When we went back to your servant my father, we told him what my lord had said.

"Then our father said, 'Go back and buy a little more food.' But we said, 'We cannot go down. Only if our youngest brother is with us will we go. We cannot see the man's face unless our youngest brother is with us.'

"Your servant my father said to us, 'You know that my wife bore me two sons. One of them went away from me, and I said, "He has surely been torn to pieces." And I have not seen him since. If you take this one from me too and harm comes to him, you will bring my gray head down to the grave in misery.'

"So now, if the boy is not with us when I go back to your servant my father and if my father, whose life is closely bound up with the boy's life, sees that the boy isn't there, he will die. Your servants will bring the gray head of our father down to the grave in sorrow. Your servant guaranteed the boy's safety to my father. I said, 'If I do not bring him back to you, I will bear the blame before you, my father, all my life!'

"Now then, please let your servant remain here as my lord's slave in place of the boy, and let the boy return with his brothers. How can I go back to my father if the boy is not with me? No! Do not let me see the misery that would come upon my father."

CHAPTER 45

Then Joseph could no longer control himself before all his attendants, and he cried out, "Have everyone leave my presence!" So there was no one with Joseph when he made himself known to his brothers. And he wept so loudly that the Egyptians heard him, and Pharaoh's household heard about it.

Joseph said to his brothers, "I am Joseph! Is my father still living?" But his brothers were not able to answer him, because they were terrified at his presence.

Then Joseph said to his brothers, "Come close to me." When they had done so, he said, "I am your brother Joseph, the one you sold into Egypt! And now, do not be distressed and do not be angry with yourselves for selling me here, because it was to save lives that God sent me ahead of you. For two years now there has been famine in the land, and for the next five years there will not be plowing and reaping. But God sent me ahead of you to preserve for you a remnant on earth and to save your lives by a great deliverance.

"So then, it was not you who sent me here, but God. He made me father to Pharaoh, lord of his entire household and ruler of all Egypt. Now hurry back to my father and say to him, 'This is what your son Joseph says: God has made me lord of all Egypt. Come down to me; don't delay. You shall live in the region of Goshen[5] and be near me—you, your children and grandchildren, your flocks and herds, and all you have. I will provide for you there, because five years of famine are still to come. Otherwise you and your household and all who belong to you will become destitute.'

"You can see for yourselves, and so can my brother Benjamin, that it is really I who am speaking to you. Tell my father about all the honor accorded me in Egypt and about everything you have seen. And bring my father down here quickly."

Then he threw his arms around his brother Benjamin and wept, and Benjamin embraced him, weeping. And he kissed all his brothers and wept over them. Afterward his brothers talked with him.

When the news reached Pharaoh's palace that Joseph's brothers had come, Pharaoh and all his officials were pleased. Pharaoh said to Joseph, "Tell your brothers, 'Do this: Load your animals and return to the land of Canaan, and bring your father and your families back to me. I will give you the best of the land of Egypt and you can enjoy the fat of the land.'

"You are also directed to tell them, 'Do this: Take some carts from Egypt for your children and your wives, and get your father and come. Never mind about your belongings, because the best of all Egypt will be yours.'"

So the sons of Israel did this. Joseph gave them carts, as Pharaoh had commanded, and he also gave them provisions for their journey. To each of them he gave new clothing, but to Benjamin he gave three hundred shekels of silver and five sets of clothes. And this is what he sent to his father: ten donkeys loaded with the best things

5. An area of grazing land in the Nile delta.

of Egypt, and ten female donkeys loaded with grain and bread and other provisions for his journey. Then he sent his brothers away, and as they were leaving he said to them, "Don't quarrel on the way!"

So they went up out of Egypt and came to their father Jacob in the land of Canaan. They told him, "Joseph is still alive! In fact, he is ruler of all Egypt." Jacob was stunned; he did not believe them. But when they told him everything Joseph had said to them, and when he saw the carts Joseph had sent to carry him back, the spirit of their father Jacob revived. And Israel said, "I'm convinced! My son Joseph is still alive. I will go and see him before I die."

CHAPTER 46

So Israel set out with all that was his, and when he reached Beersheba,[6] he offered sacrifices to the God of his father Isaac.

And God spoke to Israel in a vision at night and said, "Jacob! Jacob!"

"Here I am," he replied.

"I am God, the God of your father," he said. "Do not be afraid to go down to Egypt, for I will make you into a great nation there. I will go down to Egypt with you, and I will surely bring you back again. And Joseph's own hand will close your eyes."

Then Jacob left Beersheba, and Israel's sons took their father Jacob and their children and their wives in the carts that Pharaoh had sent to transport him. They also took with them their livestock and the possessions they had acquired in Canaan, and Jacob and all his offspring went to Egypt. He took with him to Egypt his sons and grandsons and his daughters and granddaughters—all his offspring.

These are the names of the Israelites (Jacob and his descendants) who went to Egypt:[7]

Reuben the firstborn of Jacob.

The sons of Reuben:

Hanoch, Pallu, Hezron and Carmi.

The sons of Simeon:

Jemuel, Jamin, Ohad, Jakin, Zohar and Shaul the son of a Canaanite woman.

The sons of Levi:

Gershon, Kohath and Merari.

The sons of Judah:

Er, Onan, Shelah, Perez and Zerah (but Er and Onan had died in the land of Canaan).

The sons of Perez:

Hezron and Hamul.

The sons of Issachar:

Tola, Puah, Jashub and Shimron.

The sons of Zebulun:

Sered, Elon and Jahleel.

These were the sons Leah bore to Jacob in Paddan Aram, besides his daughter Dinah. These sons and daughters of his were thirty-three in all.

---

6. An oasis in southern Palestine.
7. This listing gives the names of the legendary founders of the 12 tribes of Israel and symbolically makes the total number of migrants a full 70.

The sons of Gad:
    Zephon, Haggi, Shuni, Ezbon, Eri, Arodi and Areli.
The sons of Asher:
    Imnah, Ishvah, Ishvi and Beriah.
    Their sister was Serah.
The sons of Beriah:
    Heber and Malkiel.
These were the children born to Jacob by Zilpah, whom Laban had given to his daughter Leah—sixteen in all.

The sons of Jacob's wife Rachel:
    Joseph and Benjamin. In Egypt, Manasseh and Ephraim were born to Joseph by Asenath daughter of Potiphera, priest of On.
The sons of Benjamin:
    Bela, Beker, Ashbel, Gera, Naaman, Ehi, Rosh, Muppim, Huppim and Ard.
These were the sons of Rachel who were born to Jacob—fourteen in all.

The son of Dan:
    Hushim.
The sons of Naphtali:
    Jahziel, Guni, Jezer and Shillem.
These were the sons born to Jacob by Bilhah, whom Laban had given to his daughter Rachel—seven in all.

All those who went to Egypt with Jacob—those who were his direct descendants, not counting his sons' wives—numbered sixty-six persons. With the two sons who had been born to Joseph in Egypt, the members of Jacob's family, which went to Egypt, were seventy in all.

Now Jacob sent Judah ahead of him to Joseph to get directions to Goshen. When they arrived in the region of Goshen, Joseph had his chariot made ready and went to Goshen to meet his father Israel. As soon as Joseph appeared before him, he threw his arms around his father and wept for a long time.

Israel said to Joseph, "Now I am ready to die, since I have seen for myself that you are still alive."

Then Joseph said to his brothers and to his father's household, "I will go up and speak to Pharaoh and will say to him, 'My brothers and my father's household, who were living in the land of Canaan, have come to me. The men are shepherds; they tend livestock, and they have brought along their flocks and herds and everything they own.' When Pharaoh calls you in and asks, 'What is your occupation?' you should answer, 'Your servants have tended livestock from our boyhood on, just as our fathers did.' Then you will be allowed to settle in the region of Goshen, for all shepherds are detestable to the Egyptians."

CHAPTER 47

Joseph went and told Pharaoh, "My father and brothers, with their flocks and herds and everything they own, have come from the land of Canaan and are now in Goshen." He chose five of his brothers and presented them before Pharaoh.

Pharaoh asked the brothers, "What is your occupation?"

"Your servants are shepherds," they replied to Pharaoh, "just as our fathers were." They also said to him, "We have come to live here awhile, because the famine is severe in Canaan and your servants' flocks have no pasture. So now, please let your servants settle in Goshen."

Pharaoh said to Joseph, "Your father and your brothers have come to you, and the land of Egypt is before you; settle your father and your brothers in the best part of the land. Let them live in Goshen. And if you know of any among them with special ability, put them in charge of my own livestock."

Then Joseph brought his father Jacob in and presented him before Pharaoh. After Jacob blessed Pharaoh, Pharaoh asked him, "How old are you?"

And Jacob said to Pharaoh, "The years of my pilgrimage are a hundred and thirty. My years have been few and difficult, and they do not equal the years of the pilgrimage of my fathers." Then Jacob blessed Pharaoh and went out from his presence.

So Joseph settled his father and his brothers in Egypt and gave them property in the best part of the land, the district of Rameses, as Pharaoh directed. Joseph also provided his father and his brothers and all his father's household with food, according to the number of their children.

There was no food, however, in the whole region because the famine was severe; both Egypt and Canaan wasted away because of the famine. Joseph collected all the money that was to be found in Egypt and Canaan in payment for the grain they were buying, and he brought it to Pharaoh's palace. When the money of the people of Egypt and Canaan was gone, all Egypt came to Joseph and said, "Give us food. Why should we die before your eyes? Our money is used up."

"Then bring your livestock," said Joseph. "I will sell you food in exchange for your livestock, since your money is gone." So they brought their livestock to Joseph, and he gave them food in exchange for their horses, their sheep and goats, their cattle and donkeys. And he brought them through that year with food in exchange for all their livestock.

When that year was over, they came to him the following year and said, "We cannot hide from our lord the fact that since our money is gone and our livestock belongs to you, there is nothing left for our lord except our bodies and our land. Why should we perish before your eyes—we and our land as well? Buy us and our land in exchange for food, and we with our land will be in bondage to Pharaoh. Give us seed so that we may live and not die, and that the land may not become desolate."

So Joseph bought all the land in Egypt for Pharaoh. The Egyptians, one and all, sold their fields, because the famine was too severe for them. The land became Pharaoh's, and Joseph reduced the people to servitude, from one end of Egypt to the other. However, he did not buy the land of the priests, because they received a regular allotment from Pharaoh and had food enough from the allotment Pharaoh gave them. That is why they did not sell their land.[8]

Joseph said to the people, "Now that I have bought you and your land today for Pharaoh, here is seed for you so you can plant the ground. But when the crop comes in, give a fifth of it to Pharaoh. The other four-fifths you may keep as seed for the fields and as food for yourselves and your households and your children."

"You have saved our lives," they said. "May we find favor in the eyes of our lord; we will be in bondage to Pharaoh."

---

8. In this way the story accounts for the fact that the Egyptian priests and their lands were exempt from taxation and control by the king.

So Joseph established it as a law concerning land in Egypt—still in force today—that a fifth of the produce belongs to Pharaoh. It was only the land of the priests that did not become Pharaoh's.

Now the Israelites settled in Egypt in the region of Goshen. They acquired property there and were fruitful and increased greatly in number.

Jacob lived in Egypt seventeen years, and the years of his life were a hundred and forty-seven. When the time drew near for Israel to die, he called for his son Joseph and said to him, "If I have found favor in your eyes, put your hand under my thigh[9] and promise that you will show me kindness and faithfulness. Do not bury me in Egypt, but when I rest with my fathers, carry me out of Egypt and bury me where they are buried."

"I will do as you say," he said.

"Swear to me," he said. Then Joseph swore to him, and Israel sank back on the pillow.

CHAPTER 48

Some time later Joseph was told, "Your father is ill." So he took his two sons Manasseh and Ephraim along with him. When Jacob was told, "Your son Joseph has come to you," Israel rallied his strength and sat up on the bed.

Jacob said to Joseph, "God Almighty appeared to me at Luz in the land of Canaan, and there he blessed me and said to me, 'I am going to make you fruitful and will increase your numbers. I will make you a community of peoples, and I will give this land as an everlasting possession to your descendants after you.'

"Now then, your two sons born to you in Egypt before I came to you here will be reckoned as mine; Ephraim and Manasseh will be mine, just as Reuben and Simeon are mine. Any children born to you after them will be yours; in the territory they inherit they will be reckoned under the names of their brothers. As I was returning from Paddan, to my sorrow Rachel died in the land of Canaan while we were still on the way, a little distance from Ephrath. So I buried her there beside the road to Ephrath" (that is, Bethlehem).

When Israel saw the sons of Joseph, he asked, "Who are these?"

"They are the sons God has given me here," Joseph said to his father.

Then Israel said, "Bring them to me so I may bless them."

Now Israel's eyes were failing because of old age, and he could hardly see. So Joseph brought his sons close to him, and his father kissed them and embraced them.

Israel said to Joseph, "I never expected to see your face again, and now God has allowed me to see your children too."

Then Joseph removed them from Israel's knees and bowed down with his face to the ground. And Joseph took both of them, Ephraim on his right toward Israel's left hand and Manasseh on his left toward Israel's right hand, and brought them close to him. But Israel reached out his right hand and put it on Ephraim's head, though he was the younger, and crossing his arms, he put his left hand on Manasseh's head, even though Manasseh was the firstborn.[1]

Then he blessed Joseph and said,

---

9. A traditional gesture of submissive devotion.
1. As a young man, Jacob himself had tricked his blind fa- ther, Isaac, into giving him the blessing meant for his older brother Esau (Genesis 27).

> "May the God before whom my fathers
>   Abraham and Isaac walked,
> the God who has been my Shepherd
>   all my life to this day,
> the Angel who has delivered me from all harm
>   —may he bless these boys.
> May they be called by my name
>   and the names of my fathers
>   Abraham and Isaac,
> and may they increase greatly
>   upon the earth."

When Joseph saw his father placing his right hand on Ephraim's head he was displeased; so he took hold of his father's hand to move it from Ephraim's head to Manasseh's head. Joseph said to him, "No, my father, this one is the firstborn; put your right hand on his head."

But his father refused and said, "I know, my son, I know. He too will become a people, and he too will become great. Nevertheless, his younger brother will be greater than he, and his descendants will become a group of nations." He blessed them that day and said,

> "In your name will Israel pronounce this blessing:
> 'May God make you like Ephraim and Manasseh.'"

So he put Ephraim ahead of Manasseh.

Then Israel said to Joseph, "I am about to die, but God will be with you and take you back to the land of your fathers. And to you, as one who is over your brothers, I give the ridge of land I took from the Amorites with my sword and my bow."

CHAPTER 49[2]

* * * Then he gave them these instructions: "I am about to be gathered to my people. Bury me with my fathers in the cave in the field of Ephron the Hittite, the cave in the field of Machpelah, near Mamre in Canaan, which Abraham bought as a burial place from Ephron the Hittite, along with the field. There Abraham and his wife Sarah were buried, there Isaac and his wife Rebekah were buried, and there I buried Leah.[3] The field and the cave in it were bought from the Hittites."

When Jacob had finished giving instructions to his sons, he drew his feet up into the bed, breathed his last and was gathered to his people.

CHAPTER 50

Joseph threw himself upon his father and wept over him and kissed him. Then Joseph directed the physicians in his service to embalm his father Israel. So the physicians embalmed him, taking a full forty days, for that was the time required for embalming. And the Egyptians mourned for him seventy days.

---

2. The bulk of Chapter 49, omitted here, is a late addition to the story that gives Jacob's deathbed blessings and admonitions to his children.

3. Jacob's first wife, Rachel's older sister.

When the days of mourning had passed, Joseph said to Pharaoh's court, "If I have found favor in your eyes, speak to Pharaoh for me. Tell him, 'My father made me swear an oath and said, "I am about to die; bury me in the tomb I dug for myself in the land of Canaan." Now let me go up and bury my father; then I will return.'"

Pharaoh said, "Go up and bury your father, as he made you swear to do."

So Joseph went up to bury his father. All Pharaoh's officials accompanied him—the dignitaries of his court and all the dignitaries of Egypt—besides all the members of Joseph's household and his brothers and those belonging to his father's household. Only their children and their flocks and herds were left in Goshen. Chariots and horsemen also went up with him. It was a very large company.

When they reached the threshing floor of Atad, near the Jordan, they lamented loudly and bitterly; and there Joseph observed a seven-day period of mourning for his father. When the Canaanites who lived there saw the mourning at the threshing floor of Atad, they said, "The Egyptians are holding a solemn ceremony of mourning." That is why that place near the Jordan is called Abel Mizraim.[4]

So Jacob's sons did as he had commanded them: They carried him to the land of Canaan and buried him in the cave in the field of Machpelah, near Mamre, which Abraham had bought as a burial place from Ephron the Hittite, along with the field. After burying his father, Joseph returned to Egypt, together with his brothers and all the others who had gone with him to bury his father.

When Joseph's brothers saw that their father was dead, they said, "What if Joseph holds a grudge against us and pays us back for all the wrongs we did to him?" So they sent word to Joseph, saying, "Your father left these instructions before he died: 'This is what you are to say to Joseph: I ask you to forgive your brothers the sins and the wrongs they committed in treating you so badly.' Now please forgive the sins of the servants of the God of your father." When their message came to him, Joseph wept.

His brothers then came and threw themselves down before him. "We are your slaves," they said.

But Joseph said to them, "Don't be afraid. Am I in the place of God? You intended to harm me, but God intended it for good to accomplish what is now being done, the saving of many lives. So then, don't be afraid. I will provide for you and your children." And he reassured them and spoke kindly to them.

Joseph stayed in Egypt, along with all his father's family. He lived a hundred and ten years and saw the third generation of Ephraim's children. Also the children of Makir son of Manasseh were placed at birth on Joseph's knees.

Then Joseph said to his brothers, "I am about to die. But God will surely come to your aid and take you up out of this land to the land he promised on oath to Abraham, Isaac and Jacob." And Joseph made the sons of Israel swear an oath and said, "God will surely come to your aid, and then you must carry my bones up from this place."

So Joseph died at the age of a hundred and ten. And after they embalmed him, he was placed in a coffin in Egypt.

4. "The Egyptians' mourning."

The Book of Ruth
c. late 6th century B.C.E.

The Book of Ruth is set in the days of Judges, an era of widespread instability that preceded the establishment of the united Hebrew monarchy in the late eleventh century B.C.E. It was probably composed much later, though, after the Israelites returned from exile in Babylon around 538 B.C.E. The story is centrally concerned with issues of loss and return, and like the Joseph story it personalizes a broad social movement through a family history. The story concerns Naomi, a Hebrew woman from Bethlehem who has journeyed with her husband and two sons to the country of Moab during a time of famine. They settle there and their sons marry local women. Then Naomi's husband dies, as do their sons; left with no resources, she decides to return to her long-lost homeland and bids her daughters-in-law farewell.

To Naomi's surprise, one of her daughters-in-law, Ruth, insists on accompanying her, showing loyalty to her even at the price of leaving her own country. The relationship between Ruth and Naomi is one of the most beautiful in biblical literature, and together they make a new life back in Bethlehem in the household of Naomi's distant kinsman Boaz, in a powerful story of loyalty, struggle, and trust in God at a time of loss and dispossession.

The Book of Ruth[1]

CHAPTER 1

In the days when the judges ruled, there was a famine in the land, and a man from Bethlehem in Judah, together with his wife and two sons, went to live for a while in the country of Moab.[2] The man's name was Elimelech, his wife's name Naomi, and the names of his two sons were Mahlon and Kilion. They were Ephrathites from Bethlehem, Judah. And they went to Moab and lived there.

Now Elimelech, Naomi's husband, died, and she was left with her two sons. They married Moabite women, one named Orpah and the other Ruth. After they had lived there about ten years, both Mahlon and Kilion also died, and Naomi was left without her two sons and her husband.

When she heard in Moab that the LORD had come to the aid of his people by providing food for them, Naomi and her daughters-in-law prepared to return home from there. With her two daughters-in-law she left the place where she had been living and set out on the road that would take them back to the land of Judah.

Then Naomi said to her two daughters-in-law, "Go back, each of you, to your mother's home. May the LORD show kindness to you, as you have shown to your dead and to me. May the LORD grant that each of you will find rest in the home of another husband."

Then she kissed them and they wept aloud and said to her, "We will go back with you to your people."

But Naomi said, "Return home, my daughters. Why would you come with me? Am I going to have any more sons, who could become your husbands? Return home, my daughters; I am too old to have another husband. Even if I thought there was still hope for me—even if I had a husband tonight and then gave birth to sons—would you

---

1. New International Version.   2. The Moabites, east of the Dead Sea in southern Palestine, were often enemies of the Israelites.

wait until they grew up? Would you remain unmarried for them? No, my daughters. It is more bitter for me than for you, because the LORD's hand has gone out against me!"

At this they wept again. Then Orpah kissed her mother-in-law good-by, but Ruth clung to her.

"Look," said Naomi, "your sister-in-law is going back to her people and her gods. Go back with her."

But Ruth replied, "Don't urge me to leave you or to turn back from you. Where you go I will go, and where you stay I will stay. Your people will be my people and your God my God. Where you die I will die, and there I will be buried. May the LORD deal with me, be it ever so severely, if anything but death separates you and me." When Naomi realized that Ruth was determined to go with her, she stopped urging her.

So the two women went on until they came to Bethlehem. When they arrived in Bethlehem, the whole town was stirred because of them, and the women exclaimed, "Can this be Naomi?"

"Don't call me Naomi," she told them. "Call me Mara,[3] because the Almighty has made my life very bitter. I went away full, but the LORD has brought me back empty. Why call me Naomi?[4] The LORD has afflicted me; the Almighty has brought misfortune upon me."

So Naomi returned from Moab accompanied by Ruth the Moabitess, her daughter-in-law, arriving in Bethlehem as the barley harvest was beginning.

CHAPTER 2

Now Naomi had a relative on her husband's side, from the clan of Elimelech, a man of standing, whose name was Boaz.

And Ruth the Moabitess said to Naomi, "Let me go to the fields and pick up the leftover grain behind anyone in whose eyes I find favor."

Naomi said to her, "Go ahead, my daughter." So she went out and began to glean in the fields behind the harvesters. As it turned out, she found herself working in a field belonging to Boaz, who was from the clan of Elimelech.

Just then Boaz arrived from Bethlehem and greeted the harvesters, "The LORD be with you!"

"The LORD bless you!" they called back.

Boaz asked the foreman of his harvesters, "Whose young woman is that?"

The foreman replied, "She is the Moabitess who came back from Moab with Naomi. She said, 'Please let me glean and gather among the sheaves behind the harvesters.' She went into the field and has worked steadily from morning till now, except for a short rest in the shelter."

So Boaz said to Ruth, "My daughter, listen to me. Don't go and glean in another field and don't go away from here. Stay here with my servant girls. Watch the field where the men are harvesting, and follow along after the girls. I have told the men not to touch you. And whenever you are thirsty, go and get a drink from the water jars the men have filled."

At this, she bowed down with her face to the ground. She exclaimed, "Why have I found such favor in your eyes that you notice me—a foreigner?"

3. "Bitter."   4. "Pleasant."

Boaz replied, "I've been told all about what you have done for your mother-in-law since the death of your husband—how you left your father and mother and your homeland and came to live with a people you did not know before. May the LORD repay you for what you have done. May you be richly rewarded by the LORD, the God of Israel, under whose wings you have come to take refuge."

"May I continue to find favor in your eyes, my lord," she said. "You have given me comfort and have spoken kindly to your servant—though I do not have the standing of one of your servant girls."

At mealtime Boaz said to her, "Come over here. Have some bread and dip it in the wine vinegar."

When she sat down with the harvesters, he offered her some roasted grain. She ate all she wanted and had some left over. As she got up to glean, Boaz gave orders to his men, "Even if she gathers among the sheaves, don't embarrass her. Rather, pull out some stalks for her from the bundles and leave them for her to pick up, and don't rebuke her."

So Ruth gleaned in the field until evening. Then she threshed the barley she had gathered, and it amounted to about an ephah.[5] She carried it back to town, and her mother-in-law saw how much she had gathered. Ruth also brought out and gave her what she had left over after she had eaten enough.

Her mother-in-law asked her, "Where did you glean today? Where did you work? Blessed be the man who took notice of you!"

Then Ruth told her mother-in-law about the one at whose place she had been working. "The name of the man I worked with today is Boaz," she said.

"The LORD bless him!" Naomi said to her daughter-in-law. "The LORD has not stopped showing his kindness to the living and the dead." She added, "That man is our close relative; he is one of our kinsman-redeemers."[6]

Then Ruth the Moabitess said, "He even said to me, 'Stay with my workers until they finish harvesting all my grain.'"

Naomi said to Ruth her daughter-in-law, "It will be good for you, my daughter, to go with his girls, because in someone else's field you might be harmed."

So Ruth stayed close to the servant girls of Boaz to glean until the barley and wheat harvests were finished. And she lived with her mother-in-law.

CHAPTER 3

One day Naomi her mother-in-law said to her, "My daughter, should I not try to find a home for you, where you will be well provided for? Is not Boaz, with whose servant girls you have been, a kinsman of ours? Tonight he will be winnowing barley on the threshing floor. Wash and perfume yourself, and put on your best clothes. Then go down to the threshing floor, but don't let him know you are there until he has finished eating and drinking. When he lies down, note the place where he is lying. Then go and uncover his feet and lie down. He will tell you what to do."

"I will do whatever you say," Ruth answered. So she went down to the threshing floor and did everything her mother-in-law told her to do.

When Boaz had finished eating and drinking and was in good spirits, he went over to lie down at the far end of the grain pile. Ruth approached quietly, uncovered

---

5. A basketful.   6. The next of kin had the responsibility to maintain the
                                   property and honor of a deceased kinsman.

his feet and lay down. In the middle of the night something startled the man, and he turned and discovered a woman lying at his feet.

"Who are you?" he asked.

"I am your servant Ruth," she said. "Spread the corner of your garment over me,[7] since you are a kinsman-redeemer."

"The LORD bless you, my daughter," he replied. "This kindness is greater than that which you showed earlier: You have not run after the younger men, whether rich or poor. And now, my daughter, don't be afraid. I will do for you all you ask. All my fellow townsmen know that you are a woman of noble character. Although it is true that I am near of kin, there is a kinsman-redeemer nearer than I. Stay here for the night, and in the morning if he wants to redeem, good; let him redeem. But if he is not willing, I vow that, as surely as the LORD lives, I will do it. Lie here until morning."

So she lay at his feet until morning, but got up before anyone could be recognized; and he said, "Don't let it be known that a woman came to the threshing floor."

He also said, "Bring me the shawl you are wearing and hold it out." When she did so, he poured into it six measures of barley and put it on her. Then he went back to town.

When Ruth came to her mother-in-law, Naomi asked, "How did it go, my daughter?"

Then she told her everything Boaz had done for her and added, "He gave me these six measures of barley, saying, 'Don't go back to your mother-in-law empty-handed.'"

Then Naomi said, "Wait, my daughter, until you find out what happens. For the man will not rest until the matter is settled today."

CHAPTER 4

Meanwhile Boaz went up to the town gate and sat there. When the kinsman-redeemer he had mentioned came along, Boaz said, "Come over here, my friend, and sit down." So he went over and sat down.

Boaz took ten of the elders of the town and said, "Sit here," and they did so. Then he said to the kinsman-redeemer, "Naomi, who has come back from Moab, is selling the piece of land that belonged to our brother Elimelech. I thought I should bring the matter to your attention and suggest that you buy it in the presence of these seated here and in the presence of the elders of my people. If you will redeem it, do so. But if you will not, tell me, so I will know. For no one has the right to do it except you, and I am next in line."

"I will redeem it," he said.

Then Boaz said, "On the day you buy the land from Naomi and from Ruth the Moabitess, you acquire the dead man's widow, in order to maintain the name of the dead with his property."

At this, the kinsman-redeemer said, "Then I cannot redeem it because I might endanger my own estate. You redeem it yourself. I cannot do it."

(Now in earlier times in Israel, for the redemption and transfer of property to become final, one party took off his sandal and gave it to the other. This was the method of legalizing transactions in Israel.)

---

7. This would mean to accept her as his wife.

So the kinsman-redeemer said to Boaz, "Buy it yourself." And he removed his sandal.

Then Boaz announced to the elders and all the people, "Today you are witnesses that I have bought from Naomi all the property of Elimelech, Kilion and Mahlon. I have also acquired Ruth the Moabitess, Mahlon's widow, as my wife, in order to maintain the name of the dead with his property, so that his name will not disappear from among his family or from the town records. Today you are witnesses!"

Then the elders and all those at the gate said, "We are witnesses. May the LORD make the woman who is coming into your home like Rachel and Leah, who together built up the house of Israel. May you have standing in Ephratah and be famous in Bethlehem. Through the offspring the LORD gives you by this young woman, may your family be like that of Perez, whom Tamar bore to Judah."[8]

So Boaz took Ruth and she became his wife. And the LORD enabled her to conceive, and she gave birth to a son. The women said to Naomi: "Praise be to the LORD, who this day has not left you without a kinsman-redeemer. May he become famous throughout Israel! He will renew your life and sustain you in your old age. For your daughter-in-law, who loves you and who is better to you than seven sons, has given him birth."

Then Naomi took the child, laid him in her lap and cared for him. The women living there said, "Naomi has a son." And they named him Obed. He was the father of Jesse, the father of David.[9]

This, then, is the family line of Perez:

Perez was the father of Hezron,

Hezron the father of Ram,

Ram the father of Amminadab,

Amminadab the father of Nahshon,

Nahshon the father of Salmon,

Salmon the father of Boaz,

Boaz the father of Obed,

Obed the father of Jesse,

and Jesse the father of David.

CROSSCURRENTS: STRANGERS IN A STRANGE LAND

- Writers have always loved sending their heroes and heroines abroad, into distant lands filled with exciting possibilities. How do the travels of Sinuhe and Joseph compare with later adventures by real-life and fictional travelers? Among many possibilities, compare Odysseus's encounters with the foreign in the *Odyssey* (page 259), Marco Polo's and Ibn Battuta's globe-spanning travels (Volume B),

---

8. Rachel and Leah, wives of the patriarch Jacob, from whom the founders of the 12 tribes of Israel descended. Though conceived under unorthodox circumstances (see Genesis 38, page 162), Perez became the founder of a major lineage.
9. Naomi, Ruth, and Boaz thus become progenitors of Israel's greatest king.

Xuanzang's pilgrimage in Wu Cheng'en's *Journey to the West* (Volume C), Vasco da Gama's experiences in *The Lusiads* (Volume C), Candide's travels in Voltaire (Volume D), and Marlow's African journey in Conrad's *Heart of Darkness* (Volume F).

- The ancient Egyptians lived in a world where magical transformations were a constant possibility, and in works such as "The Two Brothers" metamorphosis becomes a central theme. Compare the use of metamorphosis, as a plot device and in symbolic terms, in Ovid's *Metamorphoses* (page 1208), in "The Tale of the Porter and the Young Girls" in *The Thousand and One Nights* (Volume B), and in Kafka's *Metamorphosis* (Volume F).

- Many literary works feature characters who are foreign, fundamentally out of place in their environment. How do Joseph, Ruth, and Naomi compare with Euripides' uncanny heroine Medea (page 729)? How do older biblical models of exile and restoration inflect Augustine's *Confessions* (page 1298)? How do the themes of exile and cultural border-crossing play out in *The Poem of the Cid* (Volume B)? In later periods, physical exile is often transformed into internal exile or alienation. How do these themes compare in Dostoevsky's *Notes from Underground* (Volume E), Beckett's *Endgame* (Volume F), and Chinua Achebe's *Things Fall Apart* (Volume F)?

END OF PERSPECTIVES: STRANGERS IN A STRANGE LAND

Statue of Zeus or Poseidon from Cape Artemision, Greece, c. 450 B.C.E.

Classical Greece

The ancient Greeks were both pioneering democrats and inveterate slaveholders; rational philosophers and followers of mystery cults marked by violence and drunken excess; they created a unique culture that would influence the Western world for millennia, yet were also deeply intertwined with the other Mediterranean and West Asian cultures around and before them. Surrounded to the east and the south by cultures very different from their own—empires governed by emperors and priests—the Greeks, scattered in many cities, developed a rich and complex set of writings that made them an important source for those who came after them. To call the writings of the ancient Greeks "literature" is perhaps to use a category foreign to their own culture. The works we inherit from the archaic and classical Greek worlds are religious, philosophical, mythological, and political all at once, created in a society of tiny yet powerful cities in which a separation between religion and politics, for example, had not yet been established.

To call the writings of the ancient Greeks "literature" is perhaps to use a category foreign to their own culture.

The Greeks lived in pockets in what is now mainland Greece, throughout the islands of the eastern Mediterranean, and along the shores of the Mediterranean Sea. Mycenaean civilization, named for the city of Mycenae, began developing in the late Bronze Age. (For a striking example of their art see Color Plate 3.) The Mycenaeans came into contact with the Minoan civilization of Crete and, through trade, with the eastern Mediterranean. Organizing their society around great palaces, they used writing to record lists of commodities including animals and people, numbers, and some syllabic signs. After a period of disruption, collapse, and decline, the Greeks began to recover, resettling mainland Greece and moving out into areas such as Ionia, the islands and coastal areas of the eastern Mediterrean. Some areas seem to have retained a few memories of Mycenaean splendor and connections with the east. The people spoke many different dialects of their common language, with different customs and religious practices as well, which they associated with tribal differences. The Dorian Spartans, for example, had habits the other Greeks thought strange: they organized their society as a military force, and their women exercised naked. "Greek society" was really a mosaic of many varied micro-cultures located in scores of cities sprinkled across Greece itself and in many more colonies that the Greeks founded as they expanded west, east, and south, to what is now France, North Africa, and Asia Minor.

The earliest writing in the Greek world dates from the Mycenaean period and was found in Mycenaean palaces and on the island of Crete. Like the writing of the ancient Near East, it was often written on clay tablets; it was used, so far as scholars know, to record the business of administering large bureacracies and gathering tribute for the palace culture of the ancient Minoans (the indigenous people of Crete) and the ancient Mycenaeans, the Greek speakers who conquered them and adopted their writing system to record the sounds of Greek. The Greeks later looked back on this period as a time of heroes and warriors, of men and women close to the many gods and goddesses

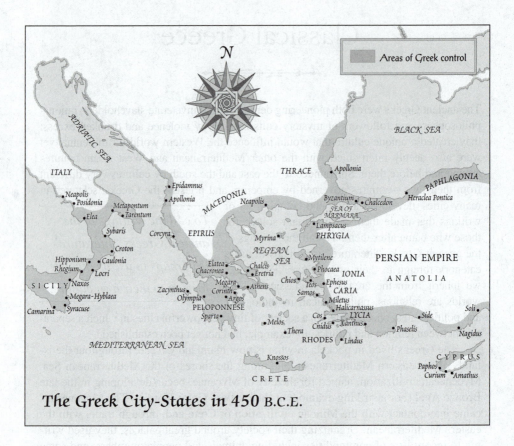

The Greek City-States in 450 B.C.E.

of the Greek pantheon. It was the time of Oedipus, the king who killed his father and married his mother, and of the expedition to Troy to retrieve the stolen Helen.

EPIC POETRY

Epic poetry is verse in hexameter meter and, in a more restricted sense, narrative poems that concern the works of gods and goddesses, heroes and heroines. The Greeks themselves placed epic poetry at the top of a hierarchy of ancient genres. The epic cycle began with the beginning of the world and extended to the end of the age of heroes. Many of these poems have been lost and are known only through plot summaries in works by ancient authors. There was, for example, a poem called the *Aethiopis,* or *Amazonia,* that told the story of the women warriors called the Amazons who helped the Trojans defend their city. The earliest surviving poems, the Homeric epics the *Iliad* and the *Odyssey,* record events of the Greeks' lost age and reflect on the distance between the audience of the poet's song and the period of lost splendor. In fact, there may have been a dark age, a time when writing was lost and when the stories of the heroes were passed on by word of mouth, to be recaptured in the eighth century B.C.E., when the many scattered communities of the Greeks regrouped and be-

Amazon combat, vase painting, 5th century B.C.E.

gan to grow and trade again after a period of devastation. They began to use an alphabet borrowed from the Phoenicians, adding vowels and making a supple and concise writing system that serves as the basis of our modern Roman alphabet. They seemed to have regarded writing with some suspicion. In the Homeric *Iliad,* the singer recalls the story of Bellerophon: a king named Proitos uses writing in an attempt to kill Bellerophon, whom Proitos's wife has falsely accused of trying to seduce her:

> He shrank from killing him, since his heart was awed by such action,
> but sent him away to Lykia, and handed him murderous symbols,
> which he inscribed in a folding tablet, enough to destroy life,
> and told him to show it to his wife's father, that he might perish.

Writing is often represented as something dangerous, used by tyrants over long distances to dominate and control. Yet it also fostered many of the most striking features of Greek culture: its democracy, which relied to some degree on written laws, accessible to all who could read; its dramatic works, tragedy and comedy; the first work of "historians," those who made inquiries in order to establish what had happened in the past; and philosophical dialogues questioning the assumptions of speakers engaged in intense, probing conversation.

The places named in the Homeric epic poems are the sites of Mycenaean culture and the cities and regions visited by the warriors in their journeys to Troy and back home again. The centuries between the singing of the epic songs and the classical democracy of the fifth and fourth centuries B.C.E., when writing was rediscovered or reinvented, was the time of the archaic lyric poets, who were representative of the dialects and cities of many regions of Greece and its colonies, and of philosophers, some of whom wrote in verse. Is their work literature? The poet-philosopher Parmenides, for example, questions the very nature of being itself and is greeted by a goddess who speaks in verse:

> Welcome, o youth, who comes to my abode in the chariot that bears you,
> Tended by immortal charioteers. It is no ill change, but right and justice,
> That has sent you forth to travel on this way.
> Far indeed does it lie from the tracks of men.
> Right it is that you should learn all things,
> As well the unshaken heart of well-rounded Truth,
> As the opinions of mortals in which is no true belief at all.

Poetry and philosophy are inseparable, written in verse that records a journey both like and unlike those of the epic heroes of Homer.

IMMORTALS

Much of the early writing of the Greeks celebrates the many gods of this society. Hesiod in his *Theogony* tells the story of the succession of gods, describing how Ouranos, "Sky," was castrated by his son Kronos, who ambushed his father and mutilated him with a sickle and then cast his member into the sea, where it mingled with the water to produce Aphrodite, goddess of the foam and sexual desire. The time of Kronos is described as a golden age:

> At first the immortals who dwell on Olympos
> created a golden race of mortal men.
> That was when Kronos was king of the sky,
> and they lived like gods, carefree in the hearts,
> shielded from pain and misery. Helpless old age
> did not exist, and with limbs of unsagging vigor
> they enjoyed the delights of feasts, out of evil's reach.
> A sleeplike death subdued them, and every good thing was theirs;
> the barley-giving earth asked for no toil to bring forth
> a rich and plentiful harvest.

This generation of golden mortals gives way to another of silver, which gives way to a third race of bronze. After the time of heroes come the mortals of the present day, men of iron: "All toiling humanity will be blighted by envy, / grim and strident envy that takes its joy in the ruin of others." Hesiod's myth of the declining generations of mortals, perhaps derived from ancient Iranian sources, records the Greeks' sense of time and of distance from a heroic past. The gods too suffer through change but finally achieve stability under the rule of Zeus. The battles of the generations of gods share themes and details as can be seen in the poems of ancient Mesopotamia, such as the *Babylonian Theogny* (page 24). In the Greek tales of succession, the original goddess, Gaia, or "Earth," who is equal to her mate, Ouranos, is replaced by many lesser female deities. The sky god is displaced first by the castrating Kronos, who swallows his children. One of these, Zeus, conquers his father and the earlier generations of gods, and establishes himself as the preeminent divinity of the Olympians.

Although Zeus has a sort of monarchic sovereignty over the host of quarreling, rivalrous, and amorous lesser gods, the Greeks worshiped all of them. Aphrodite stood for the domain of sexual desire, pleasure, and yearning, and Demeter stood for the reproductive powers of the citizen woman. Apollo, god of prophecy and the foundation of new cities, watched over philosophers and murderers. Travelers consulted

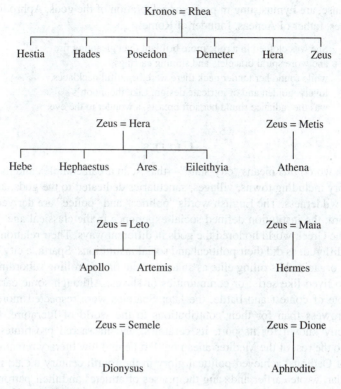

Lineage of the Olympian Gods

his oracle at Delphi, and the Pythian priestess there gave often enigmatic answers to their questions. Poseidon was the god of earthquakes, horses, and the sea, upon which many Greeks traveled great distances to lands known and unknown. Dionysos, god of wet things—wine, semen, milk, and honey—traveled from India with a band of ecstatic women, satyrs, and panthers and was celebrated with new wine and tragic performances. Hermes was the god of heralds and of traveling across boundaries—between cities, between properties, between life and death, between the underworld and the mortal world, and between Mount Olympus and earth. He was represented by herms, stone pillars with heads and erect phalluses. Worshipers at the mystery cult of Eleusis celebrated Demeter and her daughter Kore, or Persephone, who had been abducted by Hades, god of the underworld. Demeter, in despair at the loss of her child, brought famine to the earth. Because she ate from a pomegranate while in the land of the dead, Persephone, though allowed to join her mother again on earth, returned to spend part of each year with her husband in the underworld. Participants in the mystery cult honored mother and daughter and experienced the acting out of some sacred ritual that brought comfort in the face of human mortality.

Greek polytheism encompasses many gods and goddesses and many forms of worship, including animal sacrifice, ecstatic dancing, and ritualized sexual intercourse. Some of the most beautiful poems, before there were "poems" in a purely literary sense, are hymns sung in praise or celebration of the gods. Aphrodite appears to Anchises, father of Aeneas, founder of Rome:

> She was clothed in a robe more brilliant than gleaming fire
> and wore spiral bracelets and shining earrings,
> while round her tender neck there were beautiful necklaces,
> lovely, golden and of intricate design. Like the moon's
> was the radiance round her soft breasts, a wonder to the eye.

CITIES

The Greek word *polis* means "city-state"—that is, an urban complex and its surrounding territory including towns, villages, sanctuaries dedicated to the gods, agricultural land, and wilderness. The English words "politics" and "police" are derived from the Greek word; the institution defined social experience in the classical age. The many cities of the Greek world honored the gods in different ways. Their relationships with the gods differed, as did their political and social institutions. Sparta, a city of the Dorian tribe, organized its ruling elite as an army, bent on controlling subordinate inhabitants who lived like serfs, or communities of slaves. Although some early Spartan poets wrote of contest and battle, the later Spartans were respected more for their martial prowess than for their contributions to the world of literature. Corinth, a wealthy city known for its port, its ceramics, and its sacred prostitutes, sent out colonies to the rest of the Mediterranean but left behind few literary remains. Thebes, the city of Oedipus, achieved political glory in the fourth century B.C.E.; its greatest poet, Pindar, wrote earlier and sang the praises of athletes and their patrons, victorious in games like those held in Olympus in honor of Zeus and at Delphi, as a form of worship and celebration of the god Apollo. Although other cities have been excavated and explored in the modern period, we know most about ancient Athens, thanks to the rich record of writing left behind by the Athenians and recovered later throughout the ancient Mediterranean, from Egypt to Rome, where ancient people read the literary works of the ancient Athenians. In *Oedipus at Colonus,* the tragic poet Sophocles wrote of the environs of his city, Athens, at a time of war and great suffering:

> Here are the fairest homesteads of the world,
> here in this country, famed for its horses, stranger,
> where you have come:
> Here to Colonus, gleaming white,
> where the nightingale in constant trilling song
> cries from beneath the green leaves,
> where she lives in the wine dark ivy
> and the dark foliage of ten thousand berries,
> safe from the sun, safe from the wind
> of every storm, god's place, inviolable.

It is in the city of Athens, in Attica, that the most important literary contributions of the Greek classical age were written. The citizens of this city worshiped with particular devotion Athena, goddess of wisdom, who was born from Zeus's head.

Following the Mycenaean era, as the city-states grew they were governed by aristocracies, groups of nobles who often rivaled each other and engaged in repeated struggles for domination of their individual cities. Alkaios, for example, poet of Lesbos, records the conflict among different aristocratic families for domination over the city of Mytilene; supposedly the poet Sappho was exiled from Lesbos because of her involvement in these struggles. Some aristocrats eventually set themselves up as what the Greeks called "tyrants"—that is, usurpers of monarchic power. The tyrants, who only gradually became associated with cruelty and despotism, sometimes allied themselves with popular elements in the cities in order to rise over their fellow aristocrats; they frequently tried to establish dynasties in which their descendants would, like them, control their cities. Democracy, the form of government that characterized Athenian politics after the late sixth century B.C.E., evolved especially (though not only) in Athens. In the democracy, the free male citizens, understanding themselves to be equal in principle, ruled themselves by means of assemblies in which each citizen had a vote, and they usually chose their magistrates by lot. The development of the Greek institution of democracy, although it excluded women, slaves, and non-citizens from participation in government, appears especially remarkable given the theocracies, empires, and monarchies that governed the states surrounding the Greeks in the ancient world.

The Greeks seem to have thought urgently about temporal distance and the situation of the past in some stream of continuity with the present. The democracy of the fifth and fourth centuries B.C.E. represented a sharp break from the traditional forms of governance, ruling by aristocratic councils and nobles, which led the classical Greeks to try to understand the democratic experiment not as repetition but as difference. The writer of history

> *The Greeks seem to have thought urgently about . . . the past in some stream of continuity with the present.*

Herodotus came from his homeland in Asia Minor to democratic Athens, the great cultural center of the Greek-speaking world, and explored the pasts of the many Greek cities and traditions as he recorded legend, rumor, hearsay, and his own eyewitness experiences. After him the Athenian Thucydides sought to write a more accurate account of the great war among the Greeks, the Peloponnesian War of the fifth century B.C.E. Athenian democracy encouraged and supported the writing and performance of drama in festivals celebrated for another of the Greeks' many gods, Dionysos. And the questioning of received truths, first explored in the works of the pre-Socratics such as Parmenides, came to fruition in the circle of Socrates and his friends. Socrates' disciple Plato took the drama of the fifth-century city and transformed it into philosophical dialogues, the fictional record of conversations conducted to test knowledge and definition, the speakers' grasp of truth, and the proper conduct of life. The Platonic dialogues presented these sometimes heated discussions in dramatic form, with directly quoted speech that was often framed by a narrator; the author creates vividly realized characters who sometimes argue most artfully against art and poetry as mere imitations of a higher reality.

Plato and his student Aristotle began the long process of sorting out kinds of writing, in the earliest attempts at literary theory. As Plato wrote in the *Republic,*

> There is one kind of poetry and taletelling which works wholly through imitation, as you remarked, tragedy and comedy, and another which employs the recital of the poet himself, best exemplified, I presume, in the dithyramb, and there is again that which employs both, in epic poetry and in many other places. . . .

These early formulations went on to have a long history, as thinkers for centuries attempted to order the kinds of writing produced in many different cultures.

DRAMA

Greek drama grew up in the classical city. Dramatic festivals may have been instituted in Athens in the sixth century by the tyrant Peisistratos in festivals celebrated in honor of Dionysos, god of wine and of the release from cares, popular with the poor of the city who were Peisistratos's allies in the deposing of the aristocracy from domination over city life. Athens organized the dramatic festivals, and committees of citizens chose the plays to be performed and then awarded victory to the best. The theaters of various cities were situated in the open air, sometimes with a magnificent view (see Color Plate 5). The stone benches for the spectators rose in ranks above the thrones set in front for the priests of Dionysos; in front of them was the circular dance floor with a building façade called a "skene," a word originally meaning "tent," from which the actors emerged (the origin of our word "scene"). Some dramatists used a crane, ending plays with the appearance of a god or goddess on high, the *deus ex machina* or "god from the machine."

Tragedy was a crucial institution of the democratic city, one of the ways in which the city staged itself and made itself visible to its citizens. The celebration of Dionysos at the theater included, in addition to the dramatic performances, offerings to the gods and processions of war orphans. In contrast to comedy, tragedy was presented in song and dance, sung exchanges, and spoken dialogue, dramatizing the heroic myths of the Greeks from the epic cycles, and the legends of such heroes as Theseus and Herakles. Because we have only the written text of the tragedies, we miss a crucial part of their performance, the music and dance. Only early in the fifth century did tragedians present contemporary events on stage; in general the stories were drawn from the epic cycle and concerned the gods and goddesses and the heroes and heroines of the distant past. Nonetheless the tragedies touched on contemporary concerns and used the most advanced language—the developments of rhetoric, for example—for their vivid and intense productions. The plays that remain, just a handful of all those presented, were performed beyond Athens as well as in the city. The great playwright Aeschylus wrote a play in Sicily, and Euripides ended his life writing in Macedonia. In Athens, the tragedians presented their plays to a magistrate, who chose three tragedians' plays to be performed and a wealthy man to pay for the training of the actors and the choruses for each play, a form of philanthropy or taxation that benefited the city as a whole. The tragic performance had the agonistic quality, the focus on *agon,* or "contest," found in many institutions of the Greek city including the games, Olympian and others.

Tragedy was . . . one of the ways in which the city staged itself and made itself visible to its citizens.

The word "tragedy" means "goat song" and may have been used originally as a song sung at a goat sacrifice, connecting it perhaps with the part-animal satyrs who were Dionysos's companions. Tragedy as drama may have begun when the leaders of the "dithyramb," a choral hymn sung in honor of Dionysos, improvised and performed solos. As tragedy became more serious, diverging from goat songs and hymns to Dionysos, satyr plays were added as the last performance of the day in which three tragedies were presented, perhaps as a return to the satyric element now lost from the tragedies themselves. The plays staged confrontations between antagonists, with choral intervals of song and dance incorporating the meters and lyricism of archaic poetry. The speakers, always male actors like the members of the chorus, portrayed creatures of myth and legend from the archaic past and, paradoxically, spoke a language closer to that of the everyday life of the classical city, whereas the chorus, a collective being more like the assembly of citizens, sang in the elevated language of the archaic age. The greatest tragedies represented political conflict as well as mourning and loss, expressing much that the political discourses of the city, such as the speeches in the democratic assembly, could not contain. The form of tragedy enacted the engagement of the city with its own cultural and political history and attempted to bring to life some sort of synthesis of past and present and elite and democratic values, all the while recognizing the limits of the city's reach and the impossibility of political solutions to the inevitabilities of death and loss.

A *komos*—the likely root of the term "comedy"—was a group of festive singers. The comedies, also part of the city's dramatic festivals, may have had their origins in rituals, with the men's choruses dressed as animals, or in Dionysiac fertility processions, in which celebrants carried the *phallos,* a representation of an erect penis. The plays drew some of their verbal obscenity from the insulting iambic verse of earlier poets such as Arkhilokhos. The choruses of twenty-four members, probably dressed in elaborate costumes, made dancing entrances and exits. The actors, always male, wore padded bellies or buttocks, and phalluses for male roles, manipulating these props to comic effect at appropriate moments. The chorus of the comedy *Wasps,* Athenian jurymen, make much of their "stingers." In contrast to tragedy, which was based on heroic myth, the comedies had fantastic plots with such wildly imaginative narratives as the flight of a dung beetle to the home of the gods. The comedies included direct references to the situation of their audience, naming names and mocking and parodying prominent men in the city. Even the gods, especially Dionysos, could appear as cowardly and ignoble. Many of the jokes in comedy focused on sex, excrement, and politics.

A striking feature of the comic performance was the *parabasis,* a central moment during which the chorus leader, speaking in the voice of the playwright himself, directly addressed the audience and offered commentary on recent events, took political stances, and solicited votes for the prize that concluded the ritual festivities. Scholars continue to argue whether women were permitted to attend the dramatic performances. Both tragedy and comedy, the classical drama as a civic institution, were crucial political and religious institutions of the city, part of the worship of the gods and of the performance of citizenship, and served to explore urgent questions concerning the nature of hierarchy in the city, the role of the gods, will and responsibility in the law as it evolved, mortality and fate, heroism, the family and marriage, rhetoric, and other crucial concerns that emerged as the democracy consolidated itself, prospered, and engaged in war with barbarians and with other Greeks.

> *Both tragedy and comedy . . . were critical political and religious institutions of the city.*

GENDER

Although—perhaps because—the Greeks worshiped many powerful goddesses, and male actors depicted powerful women in tragedy, in the classical period women themselves had little place in the public life of the city. Daughters, wives, and mothers of citizens had no political rights themselves and couldn't vote in the assembly, hold political office, or even serve on juries. In legal matters they were represented by their fathers, husbands, or guardians. While there are examples of chastity and virtue in Greek tragedy displayed by women such as Alcestis, who is willing to die in her husband's place, others, such as Clytaemestra and Medea, kill their male relatives, husbands, and sons. In Euripides' *Hippolytus,* the hero, a worshiper of the virgin Artemis, goddess of the hunt, recoils from his stepmother's advances and expresses an extreme misogyny:

> Women! This coin which men find counterfeit!
> Why, why Lord Zeus, did you put them in the world,
> in the light of the sun? If you were so determined
> to breed the race of man, the source of it
> should not have been women. Men might have dedicated
> in your own temples images of gold,
> silver, or weight of bronze, and thus have bought
> the seed of progeny. . . .

This is an extreme view, and Hippolytus suffers a terrible death because he refuses to honor Aphrodite, goddess of sexual desire. Yet some have seen a consistent pattern of

. . . some have seen a consistent pattern of misogyny in ancient Greece . . .

misogyny in ancient Greece, especially in Athens, reflected in the representations of women in tragedy. There remains very little writing by women, except for the few fragments of Sappho's verse that remain from the earlier, aristocratic age.

Readers of Greek tragedy and myth have often remarked on the representations of powerful goddesses and even of heroines of the remote past, and contrasted their freedom and authority with the relatively closeted nature of Greek women's lives in the classical period. Virtuous women of the citizen class had some authority and power in their homes and played a crucial role in ritual life. Yet they were frequently seen as unruly by nature. Some attribute this paradox to a diminution of women's status in the democratic period, when all men were equal in principle, and all women—even the formerly powerful aristocrats—were subordinate. Others cite Greek patterns of child rearing, where women, frustrated and envious of their sons' imminent freedom, controlled the lives of small boys, who then developed fear and loathing of powerful females and perpetuated misogyny as adults.

Male virtue was strongly connected to military prowess; citizens served in their cities' armies, and initiation into the army marked a threshold of manhood and acceptance into the city. In a city such as Sparta, male bonding seems to have been a crucial element of military and civilian life; men dined together in messes, and the military unit seems to have been central to men's identities. Masculine existence focused on public life in the military and in politics. Male homosexuality, a locus for intimacy among men, was an important institution in civic life; young men, and some older men, courted boys before their beards had grown, and much of the erotic, or sexual, energy of the culture was focused on these relationships. The god Eros, son of Aphrodite, the goddess of sexual desire, personified the attraction of males to females, males to males, females to females.

BARBARIANS

The Greeks lived in Greece itself, but they also came in contact with others around the Black Sea and the Mediterranean, others they called "barbarians" because their language sounded to Greek ears like "bar-bar-bar": meaningless clumps of sound. Many of the barbarians familiar to the Greeks arrived as slaves, belonged to the free persons of the Greek cities, and worked as domestic servants, agricultural laborers, and artisans, sometimes alongside the free. Other barbarians were free, passing through Greece or settling there. Still others were enemies in war. The Greeks were fascinated with these others: their skills, their customs, their luxury goods, and their ways of organizing families, cities, and empires. From the beginning, in Homer, we see, for example, an interest in Asia Minor. When the hero Menelaus is wounded in the *Iliad,* the poet admires the skill of artisans from the east:

> As when some Maionian woman or Karian with purple
> colours ivory, to make it a cheek piece for horses;
> it lies away in an inner room, and many a rider
> longs to have it, but it is laid up to be a king's treasure,
> two things, to be the beauty of the horse, the pride of the horseman:
> so, Menelaos, your shapely thighs were stained with the colour
> of blood, and your legs also and the ankles beneath them.

The interest in the "barbarians" extends throughout the historical period of ancient Greece. Homer records contacts with non-Greek-speaking peoples, and Hesiod's work reflects the influence of Mesopotamian myth, religion, and poetry. The lyric poets of the Archaic period register trade with those surrounding the Greeks; Sappho sings: "A decorated slipper hid / her foot, a lovely piece of Lydian work." Herodotus wrote his history about the war between the Greeks and the Persians, interspersing it with elaborate accounts of the societies that made up the Persian empire and beyond. Curious about what he saw and diligent in interviewing people about what they had seen, he describes the Egyptian phoenix, Arabia's flying snakes, and the Arabians' harvesting of frankincense and cinnamon: "let me only add that the whole country exhales a more than earthly fragrance." He reports that the Indians live farthest to the east of Greece, and that beyond them is uninhabitable desert. (See the inside front cover of this volume for a map of the world as he knew it.) His interest in others, in the Greeks' neighbors, persists throughout Greek literature and makes the Greeks both proud of their innovations such as democracy and conscious of the alternatives that surround them.

> *. . . interest in the "barbarians" extends throughout the historical period of ancient Greece.*

ALEXANDER AND AFTER

After the Persian Wars, during which the Greek mainland was invaded by armies led by the Persian emperors, and after the Peloponnesian War, fought between the Spartans and the Athenians, struggles continued over which of the city-states would control Greece as a whole. This fighting came to an end with the victory of Philip of Macedon, who came from the north and defeated the alliance of Greek cities in 338 B.C.E. After his death, his kingdom was inherited by his son Alexander, said by some to be a son of Dionysos. During his short lifetime, Alexander not only conquered the Greeks but went deeply into the lands of the barbarians and overpowered army after army. He regretted that he had no Homer to immortalize his name, as Achilles had. Allegedly bent on avenging the Persians' invasion of Greece, Alexander swept through the Persian empire, conquering and dominating Egypt, where he was acclaimed as a god, and moving east, beyond the Persian capitals into what is now Afghanistan and beyond, to the Indus River. As he moved he founded cities, many named Alexandria in his honor.

When he died in Babylon in 323 B.C.E., Alexander left behind a contentious group of heirs, his generals, who fought over the fragile empire he had established and divided it. The rulers of these "Hellenistic" kingdoms tried to impose the Greek language, administrative policies, city planning, and architecture on the indigenous cultures. One of the cities that flourished was the Egyptian Alexandria, which became the intellectual capital of the Hellenistic world under the Ptolemies, Macedonians like Alexander who took the place of the Egyptian Pharoahs. They ruled over a burgeoning multi-ethnic city inhabited by Egyptians, Jews, Lebanese, Sudanese, Greeks, and Macedonians. The city welcomed an immense variety of religious practices and worship of the Hebrew Yahweh, the Egyptian Isis, and a new god named Serapis, invented to bring the heterogeneous population together. Alexandria was also the site of a monumental library that housed the greatest works of classical Greek antiquity. Poets such as Callimachus, Theokritos, and Apollonios Rhodios worked in Alexandria. Apollonios Rhodios made the journey of Jason and his Argonauts the subject of his late epic poem, with a portrait of the sorceress Medea that influenced the Roman poet Virgil's Carthaginian queen, Dido. Callimachus, a poet of exquisite, condensed, and esoteric poetry, who said "a big book is a big evil," was the model for some of Rome's greatest poets. Theokritos, who came from Sicily, virtually invented the genre of pastoral poetry, in which often sophisticated and brilliant shepherds and goatherds sang about country life, poetry, and erotic passions. The pastoral genre has had a long life, persisting through the works of Virgil and including such influential masterpieces as Milton's "Lycidas." Until the library in Alexandria burned, it was the inspiration for the first literary scholars, erudite men who pored especially over the works of Homer, attempting to identify obsolete words and lines that had been added after the time of Homer himself.

The poetry, literary criticism, science, and religious practices of Hellenistic Alexandria had great impact on the next conquering power, the Romans, who eventually brought Greece and the Hellenized East into their empire. Augustus Caesar defeated his rival, Marc Antony, and the Ptolemaic queen Cleopatra in a struggle recalled in Shakespeare's *Antony and Cleopatra,* and the vast wealth of Hellenized Egypt fell into Rome's hands. (See the cover of this volume for an illustration of the cultural mixing that ensued.) The intellectual legacy, rhetorical training, and literary examples of the Greeks also were assimilated into Roman culture, where they cohabited, sometimes uneasily, with traditional Roman genres and attitudes.

THE SPOILS

After the fall of the Roman empire and the tenuous preservation of Greek literature in the medieval European monasteries and libraries, Arab and Byzantine scholars helped to rekindle Western interest in Greek culture. In the European Renaissance, artists, scholars, and writers looked back to Greece for inspiration; the "re-naissance," re-birth, was seen as a new antiquity, and the thinkers and poets of classical Athens served as a source for writers as different as John Milton and Alexander Pope. Enlightenment thinkers including the founders of the American republic looked back to Greek democracy and the Roman republic as they debated the shape of the American polity. Greece itself eventually became part of the Ottoman Empire, and some of its greatest treasures were destroyed or carted off by Europeans newly interested in Greek civilization. In the nineteenth century Lord Elgin sawed off large portions of the frieze of the Parthenon and took what wasn't destroyed or sunk in a shipwreck back to London, where the fragments formed a key part of the collection that became the British Museum. The Romantics were stirred by the Greek struggle for independence from the Ottomans; Byron died at Missolonghi in central

. . . the founders of the American republic looked back to Greek democracy and the Roman republic as they debated the shape of the American polity.

Greece, having volunteered for the Greek war of liberation. Heinrich Schliemann, a wealthy German brewer, dug up the remains of preclassical civilization at Mycenae and at Troy, and the gold mask of Agamemnon (Color Plate 3) dazzled a world accustomed to the white marble of the Parthenon and Michelangelo's classicizing sculptures. With all their contradictions and in all their variety, the Greeks remain the still-potent ancestors of the Western tradition.

PRONUNCIATIONS:[1]

Achilles: a-KILL-eez
Aegisthus: eh-GIS-thus
Aeschylus: ESS-cue-luss
Agamemnon: agg-ah-MEM-nohn
Alcibiades: al-si-BYE-a-deez
Aristophanes: ar-ist-AW-fan-eez
Arkhilokhos: arkh-IH-lo-kuss
Clytaemestra: clie-teh-MES-tra
Dionysos: die-oh-NEE-sos
Euripides: you-RI-pid-eez
Eurycleia: you-ru-CLAY-uh
Herodotus: her-AW-do-tuss
Kassandra/Cassandra: kass-AND-ra
Laertes: lay-EHR-teez
Lysistrata: lus-is-STRAW-tuh
Medea: me-DEE-uh
Menelaos: men-eh-LAY-OHS
Orestes: oh-RES-teez
Penelope: pen-EL-lo-pee
Pericles: PER-ih-kleez
Plato: PLAY-toe
Sappho: SAF-foe
Sophocles: SOF-o-kleez
Telemachus: teh-LEH-ma-kuss
Thucydides: thoo-CID-i-deez

---

1. The transliteration of Greek names varies widely. Some scholars prefer to follow very closely, in our Roman alphabet, the Greek spelling in the Greek alphabet. For example, they call the great hero of the Greek army in the Trojan War "Akhilleus." Others call him by the name the Romans later gave him, "Achilles." Still others prefer the compromise: "Achilleus." Most translations combine these solutions, using the Latin versions of names for the most familiar and transliterating more closely the less familiar names. Remember, Achilleus is Akhilleus is Achilles. Greek Odysseus becomes "Ulysses" in Rome and in James Joyce's novel of the same name. Agamemnon's queen is "Klytaimestra," "Clytaemestra," and even "Clytemnestra."

Homer

8th century B.C.E.

The Greek word *homeros* means "hostage." Authorship of the great epic poems the *Iliad* and the *Odyssey* is attributed to someone bearing this name, but we don't know who or what he was. Several of the islands and cities of the eastern Mediterranean Sea claimed "Homer" as a native. What remains are the poems, amid passionate debates about when and where they were written down. Following research on the oral performance and composition of poetry in Serbia and Africa, scholars now believe that the poems represent the culmination of a long tradition of singers who assembled memories of a lost heroic age, vestiges of the story of the earliest Greeks' war against Troy in Asia Minor. The singers supplemented their oral tradition with more recent material and created two magnificent, long poems about the supposed ancestors, gods and men, of the aristocrats of the eighth century B.C.E.

Book 8 of the *Odyssey* shows us a scene of performance, where the singer Demodocus, blind as Homer was said to be, recounts part of the legend of Troy for feasting nobles:

> All reached out for the good things that lay at hand
> and when they'd put aside desire for food and drink,
> the Muse inspired the bard
> to sing the famous deeds of fighting heroes—
> the song whose fame had reached the skies those days:
> The Strife Between Odysseus and Achilles, Peleus' son . . .
> how once at the gods' flowing feast the captains clashed
> in a savage war of words, while Agamemnon, lord of armies,
> rejoiced at heart that Achaea's bravest men were battling so.

The Muse, a goddess, inspires the singer, who is seen as the channel through which memory and the divine pass to deliver these ancient stories, known to all the audience, drinking in the excellence of their retelling. Here the hero Odysseus, sitting disguised in the audience, is moved to tears.

The poems themselves preserve traces of the Mycenaean age (1500–1000 B.C.E.), hundreds of years before the date of their composition. Archaeologists have found, for example, an ivory figurine with a representation of a boar's tusk helmet like Odysseus's described in the *Iliad*. Both poems were composed in dactylic hexameter, that is, six feet based on a rhythm of a long syllable followed by two short syllables. The meter allowed the singers to retell and embellish the traditional stories of their people, while maintaining a steady flow of musical lines. Oral composition determined, with some flexibility, the "epithets," or qualifying terms used for the central figures of the poems; if Achilles, for example, is named in a certain position in a line, the words used to describe him, such as "swift-footed," must fit into the meter. If they don't, the song refers to him as the son of Peleus, or uses another qualifier that works rhythmically. Sometimes these epithets seem incongruous, or, some argue, ironic, where they fall:

> Aphrodite the sweetly laughing spoke . . .
> "Tydeus' son Diomedes, the too high-hearted, stabbed me
> as I was carrying my own beloved son out of the fighting . . . ."

Even in pain, the goddess of eros can be "sweetly laughing" if the meter requires it. Other features of oral composition include repetitions, for example, in the highly conventional, formulaic scenes of warriors putting on armor, and what is sometimes called "ring" form, a pattern of *abccba*, for example, in set scenes in the poems. The dactylic hexameter preserved, like flies in amber, ancient allusions to features of warfare and of everyday life no longer familiar to the audience. The poems provide a rich, complex, and stratified record of all the centuries between the early Mycenaean period and the people of the eighth century B.C.E., who were engaged in trade and colonization with a wide Mediterranean world, stretching from the Aegean and its many islands east to Asia Minor, to the lands north and east of the Black Sea, to the northern coast of Africa, and to the far western edges of the Mediterranean Sea, to what is now Italy and southern France.

Early in the twentieth century, the anthropologist Milman Parry, exploring storytelling in preliterate societies, discovered features of composition that explained mysteries found in Homer. Some readers had preferred such ancient poets as Virgil to Homer because, as Alexander Pope put it, Homer sometimes nods. That is, Homer forgets and repeats and skips. Parry and his followers found that Yugoslavian oral poetry sung in the twentieth century showed similar patterns; its singers sang thousands of lines of heroic poetry that they forged in the moment, without memorization or writing, using "formulae," set phrases to define particular characters and to fill out lines as required by meter. They had typical scenes, such as arming scenes, that they used as templates for various characters, and other techniques for keeping their stories pouring forth, as they benefited from the experience and innovations of generations of singers who had preceded them. The Resonance that follows the *Iliad* shows a modern oral poet using these ancient techniques.

The two Homeric poems share a language and a poetic tradition but tell very different stories. Both depend on the legend of a war with Troy, which the Greeks traced mythically to the abduction of the beautiful Helen of Sparta. The great god Zeus had raped her mother, Leda, appearing to her as a swan; Helen and her sister Clytemnestra were born from one egg, and their twin brothers, Castor and Pollux, later the Gemini in astrological lore, came from another. When Paris, son of King Priam of Troy, was promised the most beautiful woman in the world by the goddess of sexual love, Aphrodite, he came to the house of Menelaos in Sparta and stole away Menelaos's wife, Helen. Poets later differed on her willingness to be stolen. The Greeks' leaders, who had all courted Helen, had also pledged to get her back if she were ever taken from her husband; they set sail for Asia under the leadership of Menelaos's brother, Agamemnon, and fought for ten long years at Troy, finally winning the war through deception. The Greek army pretended to sail away from the battlefield, leaving an immense wooden horse as an offering. The Trojans pulled it inside the walls of their city, celebrated their victory, and in the night following, the Greeks, hidden inside the horse's belly, crept out and slaughtered and burned. The Greeks killed Priam, desecrated the altar of Athena, and killed children and enslaved the women of the city. The Trojan Aineias, whom the Romans called Aeneas, son of Venus, left burning Troy at the beginning of a long journey that culminated in the foundation of Rome. Because of sacrileges committed during the looting of Troy, the return of the Greek heroes to their homelands was often long and painful.

The singers of the Homeric tradition composed many poems recounting the events of this war and its aftermath. Most have been lost: poems that told of the giving of the prize, Helen, to Paris; of the arrival of the Amazons, women warriors, to help the Trojans on the battlefield; of the hero Achilles's falling in love with the queen of the Amazons, Penthesilea, even as he killed her with his spear; of the suicide of the hero Ajax; of the Trojan Horse and the sacking of Troy; and of the *nostoi*, or "returns," of the Greek heroes. The two Homeric poems that have come down to us focus vividly on two of the crucial stories contained within the greater epic tradition.

THE *ILIAD*

The *Iliad* recounts the story of Achilles: his wrath at being slighted by Agamemnon, his withdrawal from battle, and the Trojan hero Hektor's killing of Achilles' beloved companion, Patroklos, dressed in Achilles' armor. Achilles' mother, the goddess Thetis, has warned him that he would either live a long life without fame or die young and glorious in battle. He chooses finally to enter the battle, to fight and die, and she asks Hephaistos, the artisan god, to make him new armor. The poem describes the divine making of Achilles' shield in a scene that connects it to ancient Near Eastern and Egyptian myths in which the artisan god, a metalworker or potter, creates the world and peoples it. Achilles returns to battle in a great rage of mourning and slaughters many Trojans, including Hektor. In Book 20 the poem compares him to fire:

> As inhuman fire sweeps on in fury through the deep angles
> Of a drywood mountain and sets ablaze the depth of the timber
> And the blustering wind lashes the flame along, so Achilleus
> Swept everywhere with his spear like something more than a mortal
> Harrying them as they died, and the black earth ran blood.

The poem, which begins with a plague and the wrath of Achilles, ends with a scene of consolation between Priam, king of Troy, and his deadly enemy, Achilles, the warrior who killed his son.

Many of Homer's themes, characters, and even verbal patterns connect the epics with poems composed in the ancient Near East. The relationship between Achilles and the lost Patroklos echoes Gilgamesh's love for Enkidu in *The Epic of Gilgamesh* (see page 59), just as Homer's representation of Aphrodite recalls the ancient Near Eastern goddess Ishtar. The voyage of Odysseus to the land of the dead bears remarkable resemblances to the journey of Gilgamesh to visit his mentor, Utanapishtim, and scholars have linked such scenes as the Greek gods' assemblies with Sumerian, Akkadian, Ugaritic, Hittite, and Hebrew literature. While connecting with these earlier Eastern traditions, the Homeric poems began to elaborate crucial elements of the Greek civilization that followed them and were long used as the basis for classical education, as manuals for the proper conduct of a free citizen's life. Scholars have emphasized the ways in which classical Greek society posed all conflict in terms of the *agon,* the contest. The games, such as those held at Olympia every four years; the competition of the drama, in which the writers of tragedies and comedies were set against each other in a contest for a prize; even the law courts of the ancient Greek city-state repeated this shape of two or more antagonists, or combatants, who fought over a single prize, only one of whom left the contest as victor. The Trojan War and its battles defined the shape of conflict for Greek men in the centuries that followed.

THE ODYSSEY

The *Odyssey* differs radically from the *Iliad.* The *Iliad* in general confines its action to the battlefield around the walls of Troy, leaving the battlefield only to visit the world of the gods or to look outward through its similes, which compare the events of battle to natural phenomena and to the worlds of farmers, animals, and sailors on the "wine-dark sea." Although the goddesses play essential roles, as when Hera seduces her husband, Zeus, to distract him from the battlefield, the mortal women of the *Iliad* are taken like booty, or war prizes: traded, enslaved, and exchanged among the heroes. The women of the *Odyssey,* on the other hand, act: the poem begins with Odysseus's being held captive by the nymph Calypso, and it traces his long journey back to his waiting wife, Penelope, who both tantalizes and defends herself against a horde of suitors besieging her in their home on the island of Ithaca.

The *Odyssey* portrays a very different world from that of the battlefield around Troy; it presents a vast landscape of the Mediterranean that contains monsters, entrances to the underworld, and societies that test the Greeks' ideas of their own culture. This poem shows the noble household, with its dependent lordlings, slaves, farms, and palace, with all the tensions that grow out of such a hierarchical social arrangement. For a society that is about to form itself into many city-states and colonies overseas, the poem maps the imaginary geography of the Mediterranean and beyond, including societies of cannibals and one-eyed monsters, and explores the social hierarchies of class and gender and the border between the living and the dead. It bequeathes to the tradition a wily hero who lies when he needs to; who survives through endless ordeals to return home, kill his rivals, and then move on; and who visits the dead and manages to evade death through a cunning intelligence that the later Greeks both admired and despised. Both the *Iliad* and the *Odyssey* helped to define storytelling and the ideas of heroism, gender, and society for millennia. The poets of the *Aeneid* and the *Divine Comedy* knew the *Odyssey,* and the great poem of Odysseus's wandering had its impact on tales of Sindbad in Arabic, on romance, and on all prose fiction following Homer. The readings provided as Resonances for the *Odyssey* can suggest something of the ongoing life of Homeric epic among a wide range of twentieth-century writers.

PRONUNCIATIONS:

Achaians: ah-KAI-uns
Achilleus: ah-KILL-yuss
Agamemnon: agg-ah-MEM-nohn
Aias: EYE-ahs
Athene: ah-THEE-nay
Atreides: ah-TRAY-deez
Atreus: AY-tree-us
Briseis: bre-SEE-iss
Chryseis: cry-SEE-iss
Circe: SEER-say
Danaans: DAY-nay-uns
Hektor: HEK-tor
Hephaistos: heh-FYS-tohs
Hermes: HER-meez
Menelaus: men-eh-LAY-us
Nausicaa: now-SEE-kay-ah
Odysseus: oh-DISS-yuss
Patroklos: pah-TRO-klos
Peleus: PEAL-yuss
Penelope: pen-EL-oh-pee
Phaiacia: fie-AY-sha
Phoibus: fo-EE-bus
Polyphemos: poll-ee-FEE-mos
Priam: PRY-am
Telemakhos: tel-EH-ma-khos
Thetis: THEH-tis
Xanthus: ZAN-thus

from The Iliad[1]

Book 1

[THE WRATH OF ACHILLES]

Sing, goddess,[2] the anger of Peleus' son Achilleus
and its devastation, which put pains thousandfold upon the Achaians,[3]
hurled in their multitudes to the house of Hades strong souls
of heroes, but gave their bodies to be the delicate feasting

5   of dogs, of all birds, and the will of Zeus[4] was accomplished
since that time when first there stood in division of conflict

---

1. Translated by Richmond Lattimore.
2. The Muse, goddess of epic poetry.

3. The Greeks.
4. Greatest of the gods, son of Kronos.

Atreus' son the lord of men[5] and brilliant Achilleus.

What god was it then set them together in bitter collision?
Zeus' son and Leto's, Apollo,[6] who in anger at the king drove

10 the foul pestilence along the host, and the people perished,
since Atreus' son had dishonoured Chryses, priest of Apollo,
when he came beside the fast ships of the Achaians to ransom
back his daughter, carrying gifts beyond count and holding
in his hands wound on a staff of gold the ribbons of Apollo

15 who strikes from afar, and supplicated all the Achaians,
but above all Atreus' two sons, the marshals of the people:
"Sons of Atreus and you other strong-greaved Achaians,
to you may the gods grant who have their homes on Olympos[7]
Priam's city[8] to be plundered and a fair homecoming thereafter,

20 but may you give me back my own daughter and take the ransom,
giving honour to Zeus' son who strikes from afar, Apollo."

Then all the rest of the Achaians cried out in favour
that the priest be respected and the shining ransom be taken;
yet this pleased not the heart of Atreus' son Agamemnon,

25 but harshly he drove him away with a strong order upon him:
"Never let me find you again, old sir, near our hollow
ships, neither lingering now nor coming again hereafter,
for fear your staff and the god's ribbons help you no longer.
The girl I will not give back; sooner will old age come upon her

30 in my own house, in Argos, far from her own land, going
up and down by the loom and being in my bed as my companion.
So go now, do not make me angry; so you will be safer."

So he spoke, and the old man in terror obeyed him
and went silently away beside the murmuring sea beach.

35 Over and over the old man prayed as he walked in solitude
to King Apollo, whom Leto of the lovely hair bore: "Hear me,
lord of the silver bow who set your power about Chryse
and Killa the sacrosanct, who are lord in strength over Tenedos,
Smintheus, if ever it pleased your heart that I built your temple,

40 if ever it pleased you that I burned all the rich thigh pieces
of bulls, of goats, then bring to pass this wish I pray for:
let your arrows make the Danaans[9] pay for my tears shed."
So he spoke in prayer, and Phoibos Apollo heard him,
and strode down along the pinnacles of Olympos, angered

45 in his heart, carrying across his shoulders the bow and the hooded
quiver; and the shafts clashed on the shoulders of the god walking
angrily. He came as night comes down and knelt then
apart and opposite the ships and let go an arrow.
Terrible was the clash that rose from the bow of silver.

50 First he went after the mules and the circling hounds, then let go
a tearing arrow against the men themselves and struck them.

---

5. Agamemnon.
6. God of disease, healing, prophecy, music, and poetry.
7. Sacred mountain home of the gods.

8. Troy, also called Ilion, city of Priam and his 50 sons
and daughters, including Hektor, Paris, and Kassandra.
9. Like "Argives," another name for the Greeks.

The corpse fires burned everywhere and did not stop burning.
 Nine days up and down the host ranged the god's arrows,
but on the tenth Achilleus called the people to assembly;
55   a thing put into his mind by the goddess of the white arms, Hera,[1]
who had pity upon the Danaans when she saw them dying.
Now when they were all assembled in one place together,
Achilleus of the swift feet stood up among them and spoke forth:
"Son of Atreus, I believe now that straggling backwards
60   we must make our way home if we can even escape death,
if fighting now must crush the Achaians and the plague likewise.
No, come, let us ask some holy man, some prophet,
even an interpreter of dreams, since a dream also
comes from Zeus, who can tell why Phoibos Apollo is so angry,
65   if for the sake of some vow, some hecatomb he blames us,
if given the fragrant smoke of lambs, of he goats, somehow
he can be made willing to beat the bane aside from us."
 He spoke thus and sat down again, and among them stood up
Kalchas, Thestor's son, far the best of the bird interpreters,
70   who knew all things that were, the things to come and the things past,
who guided into the land of Ilion[2] the ships of the Achaians
through that seercraft of his own that Phoibos Apollo gave him.
He in kind intention toward all stood forth and addressed them:
"You have bidden me, Achilleus beloved of Zeus, to explain to
75   you this anger of Apollo the lord who strikes from afar. Then
I will speak; yet make me a promise and swear before me
readily by word and work of your hands to defend me,
since I believe I shall make a man angry who holds great kingship
over the men of Argos, and all the Achaians obey him.
80   For a king when he is angry with a man beneath him is too strong,
and suppose even for the day itself he swallow down his anger,
he still keeps bitterness that remains until its fulfilment
deep in his chest. Speak forth then, tell me if you will protect me."
 Then in answer again spoke Achilleus of the swift feet:
85   "Speak, interpreting whatever you know, and fear nothing.
In the name of Apollo beloved of Zeus to whom you, Kalchas,
make your prayers when you interpret the gods' will to the Danaans,
no man so long as I am alive above earth and see daylight
shall lay the weight of his hands on you beside the hollow ships,
90   not one of all the Danaans, even if you mean Agamemnon,
who now claims to be far the greatest of all the Achaians."
 At this the blameless seer took courage again and spoke forth:
"No, it is not for the sake of some vow or hecatomb[3] he blames us,
but for the sake of his priest whom Agamemnon dishonoured
95   and would not give him back his daughter nor accept the ransom.
Therefore the archer sent griefs against us and will send them
still, nor sooner thrust back the shameful plague from the Danaans

---

1. Goddess of marriage and the wife and sister of Zeus.   3. Animal sacrifice.
2. Troy.

until we give the glancing-eyed girl back to her father
without price, without ransom, and lead also a blessed hecatomb
100   to Chryse; thus we might propitiate and persuade him."
       He spoke thus and sat down again, and among them stood up
Atreus' son the hero wide-ruling Agamemnon
raging, the heart within filled black to the brim with anger
from beneath, but his two eyes showed like fire in their blazing.
105   First of all he eyed Kalchas bitterly and spoke to him:
"Seer of evil: never yet have you told me a good thing.
Always the evil things are dear to your heart to prophesy,
but nothing excellent have you said nor ever accomplished.
Now once more you make divination to the Danaans, argue
110   forth your reason why he who strikes from afar afflicts them,
because I for the sake of the girl Chryseis would not take
the shining ransom; and indeed I wish greatly to have her
in my own house; since I like her better than Klytaimestra
my own wife, for in truth she is no way inferior,
115   neither in build nor stature nor wit, not in accomplishment.
Still I am willing to give her back, if such is the best way.
I myself desire that my people be safe, not perish.
Find me then some prize that shall be my own, lest I only
among the Argives go without, since that were unfitting;
120   you are all witnesses to this thing, that my prize goes elsewhere."
       Then in answer again spoke brilliant swift-footed Achilleus:
"Son of Atreus, most lordly, greediest for gain of all men,
how shall the great-hearted Achaians give you a prize now?
There is no great store of things lying about I know of.
125   But what we took from the cities by storm has been distributed;
it is unbecoming for the people to call back things once given.
No, for the present give the girl back to the god; we Achaians
thrice and four times over will repay you, if ever Zeus gives
into our hands the strong-walled citadel of Troy to be plundered."
130   Then in answer again spoke powerful Agamemnon:
"Not that way, good fighter though you be, godlike Achilleus,
strive to cheat, for you will not deceive, you will not persuade me.
What do you want? To keep your own prize and have me sit here
lacking one? Are you ordering me to give this girl back?
135   Either the great-hearted Achaians shall give me a new prize
chosen according to my desire to atone for the girl lost,
or else if they will not give me one I myself shall take her,
your own prize, or that of Aias, or that of Odysseus,
going myself in person; and he whom I visit will be bitter.
140   Still, these are things we shall deliberate again hereafter.
Come, now, we must haul a black ship down to the bright sea,
and assemble rowers enough for it, and put on board it
the hecatomb, and the girl herself, Chryseis of the fair cheeks,
and let there be one responsible man in charge of her,
145   either Aias or Idomeneus or brilliant Odysseus,
or you yourself, son of Peleus, most terrifying of all men,

to reconcile by accomplishing sacrifice the archer."
    Then looking darkly at him Achilleus of the swift feet spoke:
"O wrapped in shamelessness, with your mind forever on profit,
150   how shall any one of the Achaians readily obey you
either to go on a journey or to fight men strongly in battle?
I for my part did not come here for the sake of the Trojan
spearmen to fight against them, since to me they have done nothing.
Never yet have they driven away my cattle or my horses,
155   never in Phthia where the soil is rich and men grow great did they
spoil my harvest, since indeed there is much that lies between us,
the shadowy mountains and the echoing sea; but for your sake,
o great shamelessness, we followed, to do you favour,
you with the dog's eyes, to win your honour and Menelaos'[4]
160   from the Trojans. You forget all this or else you care nothing.
And now my prize you threaten in person to strip from me,
for whom I laboured much, the gift of the sons of the Achaians.
Never, when the Achaians sack some well-founded citadel
of the Trojans, do I have a prize that is equal to your prize.
165   Always the greater part of the painful fighting is the work of
my hands; but when the time comes to distribute the booty
yours is far the greater reward, and I with some small thing
yet dear to me go back to my ships when I am weary with fighting.
Now I am returning to Phthia, since it is much better
170   to go home again with my curved ships, and I am minded no longer
to stay here dishonoured and pile up your wealth and your luxury."
    Then answered him in turn the lord of men Agamemnon:
"Run away by all means if your heart drives you. I will not
entreat you to stay here for my sake. There are others with me
175   who will do me honour, and above all Zeus of the counsels.
To me you are the most hateful of all the kings whom the gods love.
Forever quarrelling is dear to your heart, and wars and battles;
and if you are very strong indeed, that is a god's gift.
Go home then with your own ships and your own companions,
180   be king over the Myrmidons. I care nothing about you.
I take no account of your anger. But here is my threat to you.
Even as Phoibos Apollo is taking away my Chryseis,
I shall convey her back in my own ship, with my own
followers; but I shall take the fair-cheeked Briseis,
185   your prize, I myself going to your shelter, that you may learn well
how much greater I am than you, and another man may shrink back
from likening himself to me and contending against me."
    So he spoke. And the anger came on Peleus' son, and within
his shaggy breast the heart was divided two ways, pondering
190   whether to draw from beside his thigh the sharp sword, driving
away all those who stood between and kill the son of Atreus,
or else to check the spleen within and keep down his anger.

4. Agamemnon's brother and the husband of Helen.

Now as he weighed in mind and spirit these two courses
and was drawing from its scabbard the great sword, Athene descended
195   from the sky. For Hera the goddess of the white arms sent her,
who loved both men equally in her heart and cared for them.
The goddess standing behind Peleus' son caught him by the fair hair,
appearing to him only, for no man of the others saw her.
Achilleus in amazement turned about, and straightway
200   knew Pallas Athene and the terrible eyes shining.
He uttered winged words and addressed her: "Why have you come now,
o child of Zeus of the aegis, once more? Is it that you may see
the outrageousness of the son of Atreus Agamemnon?
Yet will I tell you this thing, and I think it shall be accomplished.
205   By such acts of arrogance he may even lose his own life."
      Then in answer the goddess grey-eyed Athene spoke to him:
"I have come down to stay your anger—but will you obey me?—
from the sky; and the goddess of the white arms Hera sent me,
who loves both of you equally in her heart and cares for you.
210   Come then, do not take your sword in your hand, keep clear of fighting,
though indeed with words you may abuse him, and it will be that way.
And this also will I tell you and it will be a thing accomplished.
Some day three times over such shining gifts shall be given you
by reason of this outrage. Hold your hand then, and obey us."
215   Then in answer again spoke Achilleus of the swift feet:
"Goddess, it is necessary that I obey the word of you two,
angry though I am in my heart. So it will be better.
If any man obeys the gods, they listen to him also."
He spoke, and laid his heavy hand on the silver sword hilt
220   and thrust the great blade back into the scabbard nor disobeyed
the word of Athene. And she went back again to Olympos
to the house of Zeus of the aegis with the other divinities.
      But Peleus' son once again in words of derision
spoke to Atreides, and did not yet let go of his anger:
225   "You wine sack, with a dog's eyes, with a deer's heart. Never
once have you taken courage in your heart to arm with your people
for battle, or go into ambuscade with the best of the Achaians.
No, for in such things you see death. Far better to your mind
is it, all along the widespread host of the Achaians
230   to take away the gifts of any man who speaks up against you.
King who feed on your people, since you rule nonentities;
otherwise, son of Atreus, this were your last outrage.
But I will tell you this and swear a great oath upon it:
in the name of this sceptre, which never again will bear leaf nor
235   branch, now that it has left behind the cut stump in the mountains,
nor shall it ever blossom again, since the bronze blade stripped
bark and leafage, and now at last the sons of the Achaians
carry it in their hands in state when they administer
the justice of Zeus. And this shall be a great oath before you:
240   some day longing for Achilleus will come to the sons of the Achaians,
all of them. Then stricken at heart though you be, you will be able

to do nothing, when in their numbers before man-slaughtering Hektor
they drop and die. And then you will eat out the heart within you
in sorrow, that you did no honour to the best of the Achaians."

245   Thus spoke Peleus' son and dashed to the ground the sceptre
studded with golden nails, and sat down again. But Atreides
raged still on the other side, and between them Nestor
the fair-spoken rose up, the lucid speaker of Pylos,
from whose lips the streams of words ran sweeter than honey.

250   In his time two generations of mortal men had perished,
those who had grown up with him and they who had been born to
these in sacred Pylos, and he was king in the third age.
He in kind intention toward both stood forth and addressed them:
"Oh, for shame. Great sorrow comes on the land of Achaia.

255   Now might Priam and the sons of Priam in truth be happy,
and all the rest of the Trojans be visited in their hearts with gladness,
were they to hear all this wherein you two are quarrelling,
you, who surpass all Danaans in council, in fighting.
Yet be persuaded. Both of you are younger than I am.

260   Yes, and in my time I have dealt with better men than
you are, and never once did they disregard me. Never
yet have I seen nor shall see again such men as these were,
men like Peirithoös, and Dryas, shepherd of the people,
Kaineus and Exadios, godlike Polyphemos,

265   or Theseus, Aigeus' son, in the likeness of the immortals.
These were the strongest generation of earth-born mortals,
the strongest, and they fought against the strongest, the beast men
living within the mountains, and terribly they destroyed them.
I was of the company of these men, coming from Pylos,

270   a long way from a distant land, since they had summoned me.
And I fought single-handed, yet against such men no one
of the mortals now alive upon earth could do battle. And also
these listened to the counsels I gave and heeded my bidding.
Do you also obey, since to be persuaded is better.

275   You, great man that you are, yet do not take the girl away
but let her be, a prize as the sons of the Achaians gave her
first. Nor, son of Peleus, think to match your strength with
the king, since never equal with the rest is the portion of honour
of the sceptred king to whom Zeus gives magnificence. Even

280   though you are the stronger man, and the mother who bore you was
        immortal,
yet is this man greater who is lord over more than you rule.
Son of Atreus, give up your anger; even I entreat you
to give over your bitterness against Achilleus, he who
stands as a great bulwark of battle over all the Achaians."

285   Then in answer again spoke powerful Agamemnon:
"Yes, old sir, all this you have said is fair and orderly.
Yet here is a man who wishes to be above all others,
who wishes to hold power over all, and to be lord of
all, and give them their orders, yet I think one will not obey him.

290 And if the everlasting gods have made him a spearman,
yet they have not given him the right to speak abusively."
     Then looking at him darkly brilliant Achilleus answered him:
"So must I be called of no account and a coward
if I must carry out every order you may happen to give me.
295 Tell other men to do these things, but give me no more
commands, since I for my part have no intention to obey you.
And put away in your thoughts this other thing I tell you.
With my hands I will not fight for the girl's sake, neither
with you nor any other man, since you take her away who gave her.
300 But of all the other things that are mine beside my fast black
ship, you shall take nothing away against my pleasure.
Come, then, only try it, that these others may see also;
instantly your own black blood will stain my spearpoint."
     So these two after battling in words of contention
305 stood up, and broke the assembly beside the ships of the Achaians.
Peleus' son went back to his balanced ships and his shelter
with Patroklos, Menoitios' son, and his own companions.
But the son of Atreus drew a fast ship down to the water
and allotted into it twenty rowers and put on board it
310 the hecatomb for the god and Chryseis of the fair cheeks
leading her by the hand. And in charge went crafty Odysseus.
     These then putting out went over the ways of the water
while Atreus' son told his people to wash off their defilement.
And they washed it away and threw the washings into the salt sea.
315 Then they accomplished perfect hecatombs to Apollo,
of bulls and goats along the beach of the barren salt sea.
The savour of the burning swept in circles up to the bright sky.
     Thus these were busy about the army. But Agamemnon
did not give up his anger and the first threat he made to Achilleus,
320 but to Talthybios he gave his orders and Eurybates
who were heralds and hard-working henchmen to him: "Go now
to the shelter of Peleus' son Achilleus, to bring back
Briseis of the fair cheeks leading her by the hand. And if he
will not give her, I must come in person to take her
325 with many men behind me, and it will be the worse for him."
     He spoke and sent them forth with this strong order upon them.
They went against their will beside the beach of the barren
salt sea, and came to the shelters and the ships of the Myrmidons.[5]
The man himself they found beside his shelter and his black ship
330 sitting. And Achilleus took no joy at all when he saw them.
These two terrified and in awe of the king stood waiting
quietly, and did not speak a word at all nor question him.
But he knew the whole matter in his own heart, and spoke first:
"Welcome, heralds, messengers of Zeus and of mortals.
335 Draw near. You are not to blame in my sight, but Agamemnon
who sent the two of you here for the sake of the girl Briseis.

5. Achilleus' men.

Go then, illustrious Patroklos, and bring the girl forth
and give her to these to be taken away. Yet let them be witnesses
in the sight of the blessed gods, in the sight of mortal
340   men, and of this cruel king, if ever hereafter
there shall be need of me to beat back the shameful destruction
from the rest. For surely in ruinous heart he makes sacrifice
and has not wit enough to look behind and before him
that the Achaians fighting beside their ships shall not perish."
345   So he spoke, and Patroklos obeyed his beloved companion.
He led forth from the hut Briseis of the fair cheeks and gave her
to be taken away; and they walked back beside the ships of the Achaians,
and the woman all unwilling went with them still. But Achilleus
weeping went and sat in sorrow apart from his companions
350   beside the beach of the grey sea looking out on the infinite water.
Many times stretching forth his hands he called on his mother:[6]
"Since, my mother, you bore me to be a man with a short life,
therefore Zeus of the loud thunder on Olympos should grant me
honour at least. But now he has given me not even a little.
355   Now the son of Atreus, powerful Agamemnon,
has dishonoured me, since he has taken away my prize and keeps it."
So he spoke in tears and the lady his mother heard him
as she sat in the depths of the sea at the side of her aged father,
and lightly she emerged like a mist from the grey water.
360   She came and sat beside him as he wept, and stroked him
with her hand and called him by name and spoke to him: "Why then,
child, do you lament? What sorrow has come to your heart now?
Tell me, do not hide it in your mind, and thus we shall both know."
Sighing heavily Achilleus of the swift feet answered her:
365   "You know; since you know why must I tell you all this?
We went against Thebe, the sacred city of Eëtion,
and the city we sacked, and carried everything back to this place,
and the sons of the Achaians made a fair distribution
and for Atreus' son they chose out Chryseis of the fair cheeks.
370   Then Chryses, priest of him who strikes from afar, Apollo,
came beside the fast ships of the bronze-armoured Achaians to ransom
back his daughter, carrying gifts beyond count and holding
in his hands wound on a staff of gold the ribbons of Apollo
who strikes from afar, and supplicated all the Achaians,
375   but above all Atreus' two sons, the marshals of the people.
Then all the rest of the Achaians cried out in favour
that the priest be respected and the shining ransom be taken;
yet this pleased not the heart of Atreus' son Agamemnon,
but harshly he sent him away with a strong order upon him.
380   The old man went back again in anger, but Apollo
listened to his prayer, since he was very dear to him, and let go
the wicked arrow against the Argives. And now the people
were dying one after another while the god's shafts ranged

---

6. The sea-nymph Thetis.

everywhere along the wide host of the Achaians, till the seer
385   knowing well the truth interpreted the designs of the archer.
It was I first of all urged then the god's appeasement;
and the anger took hold of Atreus' son, and in speed standing
he uttered his threat against me, and now it is a thing accomplished.
For the girl the glancing-eyed Achaians are taking to Chryse
390   in a fast ship, also carrying to the king presents. But even
now the heralds went away from my shelter leading
Briseus' daughter, whom the sons of the Achaians gave me.
You then, if you have power to, protect your own son, going
to Olympos and supplicating Zeus, if ever before now
395   either by word you comforted Zeus' heart or by action.
Since it is many times in my father's halls I have heard you
making claims, when you said you only among the immortals
beat aside shameful destruction from Kronos' son the dark-misted,[7]
that time when all the other Olympians sought to bind him,
400   Hera and Poseidon and Pallas Athene. Then you,
goddess, went and set him free from his shackles, summoning
in speed the creature of the hundred hands to tall Olympos,
that creature the gods name Briareus, but all men
Aigaios' son, but he is far greater in strength than his father.
405   He rejoicing in the glory of it sat down by Kronion,
and the rest of the blessed gods were frightened and gave up binding him.
Sit beside him and take his knees and remind him of these things
now, if perhaps he might be willing to help the Trojans,
and pin the Achaians back against the ships and the water,
410   dying, so that thus they may all have profit of their own king,
that Atreus' son wide-ruling Agamemnon may recognize
his madness, that he did no honour to the best of the Achaians."
   Thetis answered him then letting the tears fall: "Ah me,
my child. Your birth was bitterness. Why did I raise you?
415   If only you could sit by your ships untroubled, not weeping,
since indeed your lifetime is to be short, of no length.
Now it has befallen that your life must be brief and bitter
beyond all men's. To a bad destiny I bore you in my chambers.
But I will go to cloud-dark Olympos and ask this
420   thing of Zeus who delights in the thunder. Perhaps he will do it.
Do you therefore continuing to sit by your swift ships
be angry at the Achaians and stay away from all fighting.
For Zeus went to the blameless Aithiopians at the Ocean
yesterday to feast, and the rest of the gods went with him.
425   On the twelfth day he will be coming back to Olympos,
and then I will go for your sake to the house of Zeus, bronze-founded,
and take him by the knees and I think I can persuade him."
   So speaking she went away from that place and left him
sorrowing in his heart for the sake of the fair-girdled woman

7. Zeus.

430 whom they were taking by force against his will. But Odysseus
meanwhile drew near to Chryse conveying the sacred hecatomb.
These when they were inside the many-hollowed harbour
took down and gathered together the sails and stowed them in the black
    ship,
let down mast by the forestays, and settled it into the mast crutch
435 easily, and rowed her in with oars to the mooring.
They threw over the anchor stones and made fast the stern cables
and themselves stepped out on to the break of the sea beach,
and led forth the hecatomb to the archer Apollo,
and Chryseis herself stepped forth from the sea-going vessel.
440 Odysseus of the many designs guided her to the altar
and left her in her father's arms and spoke a word to him:
"Chryses, I was sent here by the lord of men Agamemnon
to lead back your daughter and accomplish a sacred hecatomb
to Apollo on behalf of the Danaans, that we may propitiate
445 the lord who has heaped unhappiness and tears on the Argives."

    He spoke, and left her in his arms. And he received gladly
his beloved child. And the men arranged the sacred hecatomb
for the god in orderly fashion around the strong-founded altar.
Next they washed their hands and took up the scattering barley.
450 Standing among them with lifted arms Chryses prayed in a great voice:
"Hear me, lord of the silver bow, who set your power about
Chryse and Killa the sacrosanct, who are lord in strength over
Tenedos; if once before you listened to my prayers
and did me honour and smote strongly the host of the Achaians,
455 so one more time bring to pass the wish that I pray for.
Beat aside at last the shameful plague from the Danaans."

    So he spoke in prayer, and Phoibos Apollo heard him.
And when all had made prayer and flung down the scattering barley
first they drew back the victims' heads and slaughtered them and skinned
    them,
460 and cut away the meat from the thighs and wrapped them in fat,
making a double fold, and laid shreds of flesh upon them.
The old man burned these on a cleft stick and poured the gleaming
wine over, while the young men with forks in their hands stood about him.
But when they had burned the thigh pieces and tasted the vitals,
465 they cut all the remainder into pieces and spitted them
and roasted all carefully and took off the pieces.
Then after they had finished the work and got the feast ready
they feasted, nor was any man's hunger denied a fair portion.
But when they had put away their desire for eating and drinking,
470 the young men filled the mixing bowls with pure wine, passing
a portion to all, when they had offered drink in the goblets.
All day long they propitiated the god with singing,
chanting a splendid hymn to Apollo, these young Achaians,
singing to the one who works from afar, who listened in gladness.
475   Afterwards when the sun went down and darkness came onward
they lay down and slept beside the ship's stern cables.

But when the young Dawn showed again with her rosy fingers,
they put forth to sea toward the wide camp of the Achaians.
And Apollo who works from afar sent them a favouring stern wind.
480   They set up the mast again and spread on it the white sails,
and the wind blew into the middle of the sail, and at the cutwater
a blue wave rose and sang strongly as the ship went onward.
She ran swiftly cutting across the swell her pathway.
But when they had come back to the wide camp of the Achaians
485   they hauled the black ship up on the mainland, high up
on the sand, and underneath her they fixed the long props.
Afterwards they scattered to their own ships and their shelters.
     But that other still sat in anger beside his swift ships,
Peleus' son divinely born, Achilleus of the swift feet.
490   Never now would he go to assemblies where men win glory,
never more into battle, but continued to waste his heart out
sitting there, though he longed always for the clamour and fighting.
     But when the twelfth dawn after this day appeared, the gods who
live forever came back to Olympos all in a body
495   and Zeus led them; nor did Thetis forget the entreaties
of her son, but she emerged from the sea's waves early
in the morning and went up to the tall sky and Olympos.
She found Kronos' broad-browed son apart from the others
sitting upon the highest peak of rugged Olympos.
500   She came and sat beside him with her left hand embracing
his knees, but took him underneath the chin with her right hand
and spoke in supplication to lord Zeus son of Kronos:
"Father Zeus, if ever before in word or action
I did you favour among the immortals, now grant what I ask for.
505   Now give honour to my son short-lived beyond all other
mortals. Since even now the lord of men Agamemnon
dishonours him, who has taken away his prize and keeps it.
Zeus of the counsels, lord of Olympos, now do him honour.
So long put strength into the Trojans, until the Achaians
510   give my son his rights, and his honour is increased among them."
     She spoke thus. But Zeus who gathers the clouds made no answer
but sat in silence a long time. And Thetis, as she had taken
his knees, clung fast to them and urged once more her question:
"Bend your head and promise me to accomplish this thing,
515   or else refuse it, you have nothing to fear, that I may know
by how much I am the most dishonoured of all gods."
     Deeply disturbed Zeus who gathers the clouds answered her:
"This is a disastrous matter when you set me in conflict
with Hera, and she troubles me with recriminations.
520   Since even as things are, forever among the immortals
she is at me and speaks of how I help the Trojans in battle.
Even so, go back again now, go away, for fear she
see us. I will look to these things that they be accomplished.
See then, I will bend my head that you may believe me.
525   For this among the immortal gods is the mightiest witness

I can give, and nothing I do shall be vain nor revocable
nor a thing unfulfilled when I bend my head in assent to it."

He spoke, the son of Kronos, and nodded his head with the dark brows,
and the immortally anointed hair of the great god
530   swept from his divine head, and all Olympos was shaken.
So these two who had made their plans separated, and Thetis
leapt down again from shining Olympos into the sea's depth,
but Zeus went back to his own house, and all the gods rose up
from their chairs to greet the coming of their father, not one had courage
535   to keep his place as the father advanced, but stood up to greet him.
Thus he took his place on the throne; yet Hera was not
ignorant, having seen how he had been plotting counsels
with Thetis the silver-footed, the daughter of the sea's ancient,
and at once she spoke revilingly to Zeus son of Kronos:
540   "Treacherous one, what god has been plotting counsels with you?
Always it is dear to your heart in my absence to think of
secret things and decide upon them. Never have you patience
frankly to speak forth to me the thing that you purpose."

Then to her the father of gods and men made answer:
545   "Hera, do not go on hoping that you will hear all my
thoughts, since these will be too hard for you, though you are my wife.
Any thought that it is right for you to listen to, no one
neither man nor any immortal shall hear it before you.
But anything that apart from the rest of the gods I wish to
550   plan, do not always question each detail nor probe me."

Then the goddess the ox-eyed lady Hera answered:
"Majesty, son of Kronos, what sort of thing have you spoken?
Truly too much in time past I have not questioned nor probed you,
but you are entirely free to think out whatever pleases you.
555   Now, though, I am terribly afraid you were won over
by Thetis the silver-footed, the daughter of the sea's ancient.
For early in the morning she sat beside you and took your
knees, and I think you bowed your head in assent to do honour
to Achilleus, and to destroy many beside the ships of the Achaians."

560   Then in return Zeus who gathers the clouds made answer:
"Dear lady, I never escape you, you are always full of suspicion.
Yet thus you can accomplish nothing surely, but be more
distant from my heart than ever, and it will be the worse for you.
If what you say is true, then that is the way I wish it.
565   But go then, sit down in silence, and do as I tell you,
for fear all the gods, as many as are on Olympos, can do nothing
if I come close and lay my unconquerable hands upon you."

He spoke, and the goddess the ox-eyed lady Hera was frightened
and went and sat down in silence wrenching her heart to obedience,
570   and all the Uranian gods in the house of Zeus were troubled.
Hephaistos the renowned smith rose up to speak among them,
to bring comfort to his beloved mother, Hera of the white arms:
"This will be a disastrous matter and not endurable
if you two are to quarrel thus for the sake of mortals

575 and bring brawling among the gods. There will be no pleasure
in the stately feast at all, since vile things will be uppermost.
And I entreat my mother, though she herself understands it,
to be ingratiating toward our father Zeus, that no longer
our father may scold her and break up the quiet of our feasting.
580 For if the Olympian who handles the lightning should be minded
to hurl us out of our places, he is far too strong for any.
Do you therefore approach him again with words made gentle,
and at once the Olympian will be gracious again to us."
       He spoke, and springing to his feet put a two-handled goblet
585 into his mother's hands and spoke again to her once more:
"Have patience, my mother, and endure it, though you be saddened,
for fear that, dear as you are, I see you before my own eyes
struck down, and then sorry though I be I shall not be able
to do anything. It is too hard to fight against the Olympian.
590 There was a time once before now I was minded to help you,
and he caught me by the foot and threw me from the magic threshold,
and all day long I dropped helpless, and about sunset
I landed in Lemnos, and there was not much life left in me.
After that fall it was the Sintian men who took care of me."
595   He spoke, and the goddess of the white arms Hera smiled at him,
and smiling she accepted the goblet out of her son's hand.
Thereafter beginning from the left he poured drinks for the other
gods, dipping up from the mixing bowl the sweet nectar.
But among the blessed immortals uncontrollable laughter
600 went up as they saw Hephaistos bustling about the palace.
       Thus thereafter the whole day long until the sun went under
they feasted, nor was anyone's hunger denied a fair portion,
nor denied the beautifully wrought lyre in the hands of Apollo
nor the antiphonal sweet sound of the Muses singing.
605   Afterwards when the light of the flaming sun went under
they went away each one to sleep in his home where
for each one the far-renowned strong-handed Hephaistos
had built a house by means of his craftsmanship and cunning.
Zeus the Olympian and lord of the lightning went to
610 his own bed, where always he lay when sweet sleep came on him.
Going up to the bed he slept and Hera of the gold throne beside him.

Book 18

[ACHILLES' SHIELD]

So these fought on in the likeness of blazing fire. Meanwhile,
Antilochos came, a swift-footed messenger, to Achilleus,
and found him sitting in front of the steep-horned ships, thinking
over in his heart of things which had now been accomplished.
5 Disturbed, Achilleus spoke to the spirit in his own great heart:
"Ah me, how is it that once again the flowing-haired Achaians
are driven out of the plain on their ships in fear and confusion?

May the gods not accomplish vile sorrows upon the heart in me
in the way my mother once made it clear to me, when she told me
10   how while I yet lived the bravest of all the Myrmidons
must leave the light of the sun beneath the hands of the Trojans.
Surely, then, the strong son of Menoitios has perished.
Unhappy! and yet I told him, once he had beaten the fierce fire
off, to come back to the ships, not fight in strength against Hektor."
15   Now as he was pondering this in his heart and his spirit,
meanwhile the son of stately Nestor was drawing near him
and wept warm tears, and gave Achilleus his sorrowful message:
"Ah me, son of valiant Peleus; you must hear from me
the ghastly message of a thing I wish never had happened.
20   Patroklos has fallen, and now they are fighting over his body
which is naked. Hektor of the shining helm has taken his armour."
       He spoke, and the black cloud of sorrow closed on Achilleus.
In both hands he caught up the grimy dust, and poured it
over his head and face, and fouled his handsome countenance,
25   and the black ashes were scattered over his immortal tunic.
And he himself, mightily in his might, in the dust lay
at length, and took and tore at his hair with his hands, and defiled it.
And the handmaidens Achilleus and Patroklos had taken
captive, stricken at heart cried out aloud, and came running
30   out of doors about valiant Achilleus, and all of them
beat their breasts with their hands, and the limbs went slack in each of them.
On the other side Antilochos mourned with him, letting the tears fall,
and held the hands of Achilleus as he grieved in his proud heart,
fearing Achilleus might cut his throat with the iron. He cried out
35   terribly, aloud, and the lady his mother heard him
as she sat in the depths of the sea at the side of her aged father,
and she cried shrill in turn, and the goddesses gathered about her,
all who along the depth of the sea were daughters of Nereus.
For Glauke was there, Kymodoke and Thaleia,
40   Nesaie and Speio and Thoë, and ox-eyed Halia;
Kymothoë was there, Aktaia and Limnoreia,
Melite and Iaira, Amphithoë and Agauë,
Doto and Proto, Dynamene and Pherousa,
Dexamene and Amphinome and Kallianeira;
45   Doris and Panope and glorious Galateia,
Nemertes and Apseudes and Kallianassa;
Klymene was there, Ianeira and Ianassa,
Maira and Oreithyia and lovely-haired Amatheia,
and the rest who along the depth of the sea were daughters of Nereus.
50   The silvery cave was filled with these, and together all of them
beat their breasts, and among them Thetis led out the threnody:
"Hear me, Nereids, my sisters; so you may all know
well all the sorrows that are in my heart, when you hear of them from me.
Ah me, my sorrow, the bitterness in this best of child-bearing,
55   since I gave birth to a son who was without fault and powerful,
conspicuous among heroes; and he shot up like a young tree,

and I nurtured him, like a tree grown in the pride of the orchard.
I sent him away with the curved ships into the land of Ilion
to fight with the Trojans; but I shall never again receive him

60   won home again to his country and into the house of Peleus.
Yet while I see him live and he looks on the sunlight, he has
sorrows, and though I go to him I can do nothing to help him.
Yet I shall go, to look on my dear son, and to listen
to the sorrow that has come to him as he stays back from the fighting."

65   So she spoke, and left the cave, and the others together
went with her in tears, and about them the wave of the water
was broken. Now these, when they came to the generous Troad,
followed each other out on the sea-shore, where close together
the ships of the Myrmidons were hauled up about swift Achilleus.

70   There as he sighed heavily the lady his mother stood by him
and cried out shrill and aloud, and took her son's head in her arms, then
sorrowing for him she spoke to him in winged words: "Why then,
child, do you lament? What sorrow has come to your heart now?
Speak out, do not hide it. These things are brought to accomplishment

75   through Zeus: in the way that you lifted your hands and prayed for,
that all the sons of the Achaians be pinned on their grounded vessels
by reason of your loss, and suffer things that are shameful."
Then sighing heavily Achilleus of the swift feet answered her:
"My mother, all these things the Olympian brought to accomplishment.

80   But what pleasure is this to me, since my dear companion has perished,
Patroklos, whom I loved beyond all other companions,
as well as my own life. I have lost him, and Hektor, who killed him,
has stripped away that gigantic armour, a wonder to look on
and splendid, which the gods gave Peleus, a glorious present,

85   on that day they drove you to the marriage bed of a mortal.
I wish you had gone on living then with the other goddesses
of the sea, and that Peleus had married some mortal woman.
As it is, there must be on your heart a numberless sorrow
for your son's death, since you can never again receive him

90   won home again to his country; since the spirit within does not drive me
to go on living and be among men, except on condition
that Hektor first be beaten down under my spear, lose his life
and pay the price for stripping Patroklos, the son of Menoitios."
Then in turn Thetis spoke to him, letting the tears fall:

95   "Then I must lose you soon, my child, by what you are saying,
since it is decreed your death must come soon after Hektor's."
Then deeply disturbed Achilleus of the swift feet answered her:
"I must die soon, then; since I was not to stand by my companion
when he was killed. And now, far away from the land of his fathers,

100 he has perished, and lacked my fighting strength to defend him.
Now, since I am not going back to the beloved land of my fathers,
since I was no light of safety to Patroklos, nor to my other
companions, who in their numbers went down before glorious Hektor,
but sit here beside my ships, a useless weight on the good land,

105 I, who am such as no other of the bronze-armoured Achaians

in battle, though there are others also better in council—
why, I wish that strife would vanish away from among gods and mortals,
and gall, which makes a man grow angry for all his great mind,
that gall of anger that swarms like smoke inside of a man's heart
110 and becomes a thing sweeter to him by far than the dripping of honey.
So it was here that the lord of men Agamemnon angered me.
Still, we will let all this be a thing of the past, and for all our
sorrow beat down by force the anger deeply within us.
Now I shall go, to overtake that killer of a dear life,
115 Hektor; then I will accept my own death, at whatever
time Zeus wishes to bring it about, and the other immortals.
For not even the strength of Herakles fled away from destruction,
although he was dearest of all to lord Zeus, son of Kronos,
but his fate beat him under, and the wearisome anger of Hera.
120 So I likewise, if such is the fate which has been wrought for me,
shall lie still, when I am dead. Now I must win excellent glory,
and drive some one of the women of Troy, or some deep-girdled
Dardanian woman, lifting up to her soft cheeks both hands
to wipe away the close bursts of tears in her lamentation,
125 and learn that I stayed too long out of the fighting. Do not
hold me back from the fight, though you love me. You will not persuade
    me."
      In turn the goddess Thetis of the silver feet answered him:
"Yes, it is true, my child, this is no cowardly action,
to beat aside sudden death from your afflicted companions.
130 Yet, see now, your splendid armour, glaring and brazen,
is held among the Trojans, and Hektor of the shining helmet
wears it on his own shoulders, and glories in it. Yet I think
he will not glory for long, since his death stands very close to him.
Therefore do not yet go into the grind of the war god,
135 not before with your own eyes you see me come back to you.
For I am coming to you at dawn and as the sun rises
bringing splendid armour to you from the lord Hephaistos."
      So she spoke, and turned, and went away from her son,
and turning now to her sisters of the sea she spoke to them:
140 "Do you now go back into the wide fold of the water
to visit the ancient of the sea and the house of our father,
and tell him everything. I am going to tall Olympos
and to Hephaistos, the glorious smith, if he might be willing
to give me for my son renowned and radiant armour."
145 She spoke, and they plunged back beneath the wave of the water,
while she the goddess Thetis of the silver feet went onward
to Olympos, to bring back to her son the glorious armour.
      So her feet carried her to Olympos; meanwhile the Achaians
with inhuman clamour before the attack of manslaughtering Hektor
150 fled until they were making for their own ships and the Hellespont;
nor could the strong-greaved Achaians have dragged the body
of Patroklos, henchman of Achilleus, from under the missiles,
for once again the men and the horses came over upon him,

and Hektor, Priam's son, who fought like a flame in his fury.

155 Three times from behind glorious Hektor caught him
by the feet, trying to drag him, and called aloud on the Trojans.
Three times the two Aiantes with their battle-fury upon them
beat him from the corpse, but he, steady in the confidence of his great
    strength,
kept making, now a rush into the crowd, or again at another time

160 stood fast, with his great cry, but gave not a bit of ground backward.
And as herdsmen who dwell in the fields are not able to frighten
a tawny lion in his great hunger away from a carcass,
so the two Aiantes, marshals of men, were not able
to scare Hektor, Priam's son, away from the body.

165 And now he would have dragged it away and won glory forever
had not swift wind-footed Iris come running from Olympos
with a message for Peleus' son to arm. She came secretly
from Zeus and the other gods, since it was Hera who sent her.
She came and stood close to him and addressed him in winged words:

170 "Rise up, son of Peleus, most terrifying of all men.
Defend Patroklos, for whose sake the terrible fighting
stands now in front of the ships. They are destroying each other;
the Achaians fight in defence over the fallen body
while the others, the Trojans, are rushing to drag the corpse off

175 to windy Ilion, and beyond all glorious Hektor
rages to haul it away, since the anger within him is urgent
to cut the head from the soft neck and set it on sharp stakes.
Up, then, lie here no longer; let shame come into your heart, lest
Patroklos become sport for the dogs of Troy to worry,

180 your shame, if the body goes from here with defilement upon it."
    Then in turn Achilleus of the swift feet answered her:
"Divine Iris, what god sent you to me with a message?"
    Then in turn swift wind-footed Iris spoke to him:
"Hera sent me, the honoured wife of Zeus; but the son of

185 Kronos, who sits on high, does not know this, nor any other
immortal, of all those who dwell by the snows of Olympos."
    Then in answer to her spoke Achilleus of the swift feet:
"How shall I go into the fighting? They have my armour.
And my beloved mother told me I must not be armoured,

190 not before with my own eyes I see her come back to me.
She promised she would bring magnificent arms from Hephaistos.
Nor do I know of another whose glorious armour I could wear
unless it were the great shield of Telamonian Aias.
But he himself wears it, I think, and goes in the foremost

195 of the spear-fight over the body of fallen Patroklos."
    Then in turn swift wind-footed Iris spoke to him:
"Yes, we also know well how they hold your glorious armour.
But go to the ditch, and show yourself as you are to the Trojans,
if perhaps the Trojans might be frightened, and give way

200 from their attack, and the fighting sons of the Achaians get wind
again after hard work. There is little breathing space in the fighting."

So speaking Iris of the swift feet went away from him;
but Achilleus, the beloved of Zeus, rose up, and Athene
swept about his powerful shoulders the fluttering aegis;
205 and she, the divine among goddesses, about his head circled
a golden cloud, and kindled from it a flame far-shining.
As when a flare goes up into the high air from a city
from an island far away, with enemies fighting about it
who all day long are in the hateful division of Ares
210 fighting from their own city, but as the sun goes down signal
fires blaze out one after another, so that the glare goes
pulsing high for men of the neighbouring islands to see it,
in case they might come over in ships to beat off the enemy;
so from the head of Achilleus the blaze shot into the bright air.
215 He went from the wall and stood by the ditch, nor mixed with the other
Achaians, since he followed the close command of his mother.
There he stood, and shouted, and from her place Pallas Athene
gave cry, and drove an endless terror upon the Trojans.
As loud as comes the voice that is screamed out by a trumpet
220 by murderous attackers who beleaguer a city,
so then high and clear went up the voice of Aiakides.[1]
But the Trojans, when they heard the brazen voice of Aiakides,
the heart was shaken in all, and the very floating-maned horses
turned their chariots about, since their hearts saw the coming afflictions.
225 The charioteers were dumbfounded as they saw the unwearied dangerous
fire that played above the head of great-hearted Peleion
blazing, and kindled by the goddess grey-eyed Athene.
Three times across the ditch brilliant Achilleus gave his great cry,
and three times the Trojans and their renowned companions were routed.
230 There at that time twelve of the best men among them perished
upon their own chariots and spears. Meanwhile the Achaians
gladly pulled Patroklos out from under the missiles
and set him upon a litter, and his own companions about him
stood mourning, and along with them swift-footed Achilleus
235 went, letting fall warm tears as he saw his steadfast companion
lying there on a carried litter and torn with the sharp bronze,
the man he had sent off before with horses and chariot
into the fighting; who never again came home to be welcomed.
Now the lady Hera of the ox eyes drove the unwilling
240 weariless sun god to sink in the depth of the Ocean,
and the sun went down, and the brilliant Achaians gave over
their strong fighting, and the doubtful collision of battle.
The Trojans on the other side moved from the strong encounter
in their turn, and unyoked their running horses from under the chariots,
245 and gathered into assembly before taking thought for their supper.
They stood on their feet in assembly, nor did any man have the patience
to sit down, but the terror was on them all, seeing that Achilleus

---

1. Achilleus, grandson of Aiakos, himself a son of Zeus.

had appeared, after he had stayed so long from the difficult fighting.
First to speak among them was the careful Poulydamas,

250   Panthoös' son, who alone of them looked before and behind him.
He was companion to Hektor, and born on the same night with him,
but he was better in words, the other with the spear far better.
He in kind intention toward all stood forth and addressed them:
"Now take careful thought, dear friends; for I myself urge you

255   to go back into the city and not wait for the divine dawn
in the plain beside the ships. We are too far from the wall now.
While this man was still angry with great Agamemnon,
for all that time the Achaians were easier men to fight with.
For I also used then to be one who was glad to sleep out

260   near their ships, and I hoped to capture the oarswept vessels.
But now I terribly dread the swift-footed son of Peleus.
So violent is the valour in him, he will not be willing
to stay here in the plain, where now Achaians and Trojans
from either side sunder between them the wrath of the war god.

265   With him, the fight will be for the sake of our city and women.
Let us go into the town; believe me; thus it will happen.
For this present, immortal night has stopped the swift-footed
son of Peleus, but if he catches us still in this place
tomorrow, and drives upon us in arms, a man will be well

270   aware of him, be glad to get back into sacred Ilion,
the man who escapes; there will be many Trojans the vultures
and dogs will feed on. But let such a word be out of my hearing!
If all of us will do as I say, though it hurts us to do it,
this night we will hold our strength in the market place, and the great walls

275   and the gateways, and the long, smooth-planed, close-joined gate timbers
that close to fit them shall defend our city. Then, early
in the morning, under dawn, we shall arm ourselves in our war gear
and take stations along the walls. The worse for him, if he endeavours
to come away from the ships and fight us here for our city.

280   Back he must go to his ships again, when he wears out the strong necks
of his horses, driving them at a gallop everywhere by the city.
His valour will not give him leave to burst in upon us
nor sack our town. Sooner the circling dogs will feed on him."
     Then looking darkly at him Hektor of the shining helm spoke:

285   "Poulydamas, these things that you argue please me no longer
when you tell us to go back again and be cooped in our city.
Have you not all had your glut of being fenced in our outworks?
There was a time when mortal men would speak of the city
of Priam as a place with much gold and much bronze. But now

290   the lovely treasures that lay away in our houses have vanished,
and many possessions have been sold and gone into Phrygia
and into Maionia the lovely, when great Zeus was angry.
But now, when the son of devious-devising Kronos has given
me the winning of glory by the ships, to pin the Achaians

295   on the sea, why, fool, no longer show these thoughts to our people.
Not one of the Trojans will obey you. I shall not allow it.

Come, then, do as I say and let us all be persuaded.
Now, take your supper by positions along the encampment,
and do not forget your watch, and let every man be wakeful.
300 And if any Trojan is strongly concerned about his possessions,
let him gather them and give them to the people, to use them in common.
It is better for one of us to enjoy them than for the Achaians.
In the morning, under dawn, we shall arm ourselves in our war gear
and waken the bitter god of war by the hollow vessels.
305 If it is true that brilliant Achilleus is risen beside their
ships, then the worse for him if he tries it, since I for my part
will not run from him out of the sorrowful battle, but rather
stand fast, to see if he wins the great glory, or if I can win it.
The war god is impartial. Before now he has killed the killer."
310   So spoke Hektor, and the Trojans thundered to hear him;
fools, since Pallas Athene had taken away the wits from them.
They gave their applause to Hektor in his counsel of evil,
but none to Poulydamas, who had spoken good sense before them.
They took their supper along the encampment. Meanwhile the Achaians
315 mourned all night in lamentation over Patroklos.
Peleus' son led the thronging chant of their lamentation,
and laid his manslaughtering hands over the chest of his dear friend
with outbursts of incessant grief. As some great bearded lion
when some man, a deer hunter, has stolen his cubs away from him
320 out of the close wood; the lion comes back too late, and is anguished,
and turns into many valleys quartering after the man's trail
on the chance of finding him, and taken with bitter anger;
so he, groaning heavily, spoke out to the Myrmidons:
"Ah me. It was an empty word I cast forth on that day
325 when in his halls I tried to comfort the hero Menoitios.
I told him I would bring back his son in glory to Opous
with Ilion sacked, and bringing his share of war spoils allotted.
But Zeus does not bring to accomplishment all thoughts in men's minds.
Thus it is destiny for us both to stain the same soil
330 here in Troy; since I shall never come home, and my father,
Peleus the aged rider, will not welcome me in his great house,
nor Thetis my mother, but in this place the earth will receive me.
But seeing that it is I, Patroklos, who follow you underground,
I will not bury you till I bring to this place the armour
335 and the head of Hektor, since he was your great-hearted murderer.
Before your burning pyre I shall behead twelve glorious
children of the Trojans, for my anger over your slaying.
Until then, you shall lie where you are in front of my curved ships
and beside you women of Troy and deep-girdled Dardanian women
340 shall sorrow for you night and day and shed tears for you, those whom
you and I worked hard to capture by force and the long spear
in days when we were storming the rich cities of mortals."
    So speaking brilliant Achilleus gave orders to his companions
to set a great cauldron across the fire, so that with all speed
345 they could wash away the clotted blood from Patroklos.

They set up over the blaze of the fire a bath-water cauldron
and poured water into it and put logs underneath and kindled them.
The fire worked on the swell of the cauldron, and the water heated.
But when the water had come to a boil in the shining bronze, then
350   they washed the body and anointed it softly with olive oil
and stopped the gashes in his body with stored-up unguents
and laid him on a bed, and shrouded him in a thin sheet
from head to foot, and covered that over with a white mantle.
        Then all night long, gathered about Achilleus of the swift feet,
355   the Myrmidons mourned for Patroklos and lamented over him.
But Zeus spoke to Hera, who was his wife and his sister:
"So you have acted, then, lady Hera of the ox eyes.
You have roused up Achilleus of the swift feet. It must be then
that the flowing-haired Achaians are born of your own generation."
360   Then the goddess the ox-eyed lady Hera answered him:
"Majesty, son of Kronos, what sort of thing have you spoken?
Even one who is mortal will try to accomplish his purpose
for another, though he be a man and knows not such wisdom as we do.
As for me then, who claim I am highest of all the goddesses,
365   both ways, since I am eldest born and am called your consort,
yours, and you in turn are lord over all the immortals,
how could I not weave sorrows for the men of Troy, when I hate them?"
        Now as these two were saying things like this to each other,
Thetis of the silver feet came to the house of Hephaistos,
370   imperishable, starry, and shining among the immortals,
built in bronze for himself by the god of the dragging footsteps.
She found him sweating as he turned here and there to his bellows
busily, since he was working on twenty tripods
which were to stand against the wall of his strong-founded dwelling.
375   And he had set golden wheels underneath the base of each one
so that of their own motion they could wheel into the immortal
gathering, and return to his house: a wonder to look at.
These were so far finished, but the elaborate ear handles
were not yet on. He was forging these, and beating the chains out.
380   As he was at work on this in his craftsmanship and his cunning
meanwhile the goddess Thetis the silver-footed drew near him.
Charis of the shining veil saw her as she came forward,
she, the lovely goddess the renowned strong-armed one had married.
She came, and caught her hand and called her by name and spoke to her:
385   "Why is it, Thetis of the light robes, you have come to our house now?
We honour you and love you; but you have not come much before this.
But come in with me, so I may put entertainment before you."
        She spoke, and, shining among divinities, led the way forward
and made Thetis sit down in a chair that was wrought elaborately
390   and splendid with silver nails, and under it was a footstool.
She called to Hephaistos the renowned smith and spoke a word to him:
"Hephaistos, come this way; here is Thetis, who has need of you."
        Hearing her the renowned smith of the strong arms answered her:
"Then there is a goddess we honour and respect in our house.

395   She saved me when I suffered much at the time of my great fall
      through the will of my own brazen-faced mother, who wanted
      to hide me, for being lame. Then my soul would have taken much suffering
      had not Eurynome and Thetis caught me and held me,
      Eurynome, daughter of Ocean, whose stream bends back in a circle.
400   With them I worked nine years as a smith, and wrought many intricate
      things; pins that bend back, curved clasps, cups, necklaces, working
      there in the hollow of the cave, and the stream of Ocean around us
      went on forever with its foam and its murmur. No other
      among the gods or among mortal men knew about us
405   except Eurynome and Thetis. They knew, since they saved me.
      Now she has come into our house; so I must by all means
      do everything to give recompense to lovely-haired Thetis
      for my life. Therefore set out before her fair entertainment
      while I am putting away my bellows and all my instruments."
410   He spoke, and took the huge blower off from the block of the anvil
      limping; and yet his shrunken legs moved lightly beneath him.
      He set the bellows away from the fire, and gathered and put away
      all the tools with which he worked in a silver strongbox.
      Then with a sponge he wiped clean his forehead, and both hands,
415   and his massive neck and hairy chest, and put on a tunic,
      and took up a heavy stick in his hand, and went to the doorway
      limping. And in support of their master moved his attendants.
      These are golden, and in appearance like living young women.
      There is intelligence in their hearts, and there is speech in them
420   and strength, and from the immortal gods they have learned how to do
          things.
      These stirred nimbly in support of their master, and moving
      near to where Thetis sat in her shining chair, Hephaistos
      caught her by the hand and called her by name and spoke a word to her:
      "Why is it, Thetis of the light robes, you have come to our house now?
425   We honour you and love you; but you have not come much before this.
      Speak forth what is in your mind. My heart is urgent to do it
      if I can, and if it is a thing that can be accomplished."
          Then in turn Thetis answered him, letting the tears fall:
      "Hephaistos, is there among all the goddesses on Olympos
430   one who in her heart has endured so many grim sorrows
      as the griefs Zeus, son of Kronos, has given me beyond others?
      Of all the other sisters of the sea he gave me to a mortal,
      to Peleus, Aiakos' son, and I had to endure mortal marriage
      though much against my will. And now he, broken by mournful
435   old age, lies away in his halls. Yet I have other troubles.
      For since he has given me a son to bear and to raise up
      conspicuous among heroes, and he shot up like a young tree,
      I nurtured him, like a tree grown in the pride of the orchard.
      I sent him away in the curved ships to the land of Ilion
440   to fight with the Trojans; but I shall never again receive him
      won home again to his country and into the house of Peleus.
      Yet while I see him live and he looks on the sunlight, he has

sorrows, and though I go to him I can do nothing to help him.
And the girl the sons of the Achaians chose out for his honour
445   powerful Agamemnon took her away again out of his hands.
For her his heart has been wasting in sorrow; but meanwhile the Trojans
pinned the Achaians against their grounded ships, and would not
let them win outside, and the elders of the Argives entreated
my son, and named the many glorious gifts they would give him.
450   But at that time he refused himself to fight the death from them;
nevertheless he put his own armour upon Patroklos
and sent him into the fighting, and gave many men to go with him.
All day they fought about the Skaian Gates, and on that day
they would have stormed the city, if only Phoibos Apollo
455   had not killed the fighting son of Menoitios there in the first ranks
after he had wrought much damage, and given the glory to Hektor.
Therefore now I come to your knees; so might you be willing
to give me for my short-lived son a shield and a helmet
and two beautiful greaves[2] fitted with clasps for the ankles
460   and a corselet. What he had was lost with his steadfast companion
when the Trojans killed him. Now my son lies on the ground, heart
    sorrowing."
    Hearing her the renowned smith of the strong arms answered her:
"Do not fear. Let not these things be a thought in your mind.
And I wish that I could hide him away from death and its sorrow
465   at that time when his hard fate comes upon him, as surely
as there shall be fine armour for him, such as another
man out of many men shall wonder at, when he looks on it."
    So he spoke, and left her there, and went to his bellows.
He turned these toward the fire and gave them their orders for working.
470   And the bellows, all twenty of them, blew on the crucibles,
from all directions blasting forth wind to blow the flames high
now as he hurried to be at this place and now at another,
wherever Hephaistos might wish them to blow, and the work went forward.
He cast on the fire bronze which is weariless, and tin with it
475   and valuable gold, and silver, and thereafter set forth
upon its standard the great anvil, and gripped in one hand
the ponderous hammer, while in the other he grasped the pincers.
    First of all he forged a shield that was huge and heavy,
elaborating it about, and threw around it a shining
480   triple rim that glittered, and the shield strap was cast of silver.
There were five folds composing the shield itself, and upon it
he elaborated many things in his skill and craftsmanship.
    He made the earth upon it, and the sky, and the sea's water,
and the tireless sun, and the moon waxing into her fullness,
485   and on it all the constellations that festoon the heavens,
the Pleiades and the Hyades and the strength of Orion
and the Bear, whom men give also the name of the Wagon,

2. Shin-guards.

who turns about in a fixed place and looks at Orion
and she alone is never plunged in the wash of the Ocean.
490   On it he wrought in all their beauty two cities of mortal
men. And there were marriages in one, and festivals.
They were leading the brides along the city from their maiden chambers
under the flaring of torches, and the loud bride song was arising.
The young men followed the circles of the dance, and among them
495   the flutes and lyres kept up their clamour as in the meantime
the women standing each at the door of her court admired them.
The people were assembled in the market place, where a quarrel
had arisen, and two men were disputing over the blood price
for a man who had been killed. One man promised full restitution
500   in a public statement, but the other refused and would accept nothing.
Both then made for an arbitrator, to have a decision;
and people were speaking up on either side, to help both men.
But the heralds kept the people in hand, as meanwhile the elders
were in session on benches of polished stone in the sacred circle
505   and held in their hands the staves of the heralds who lift their voices.
The two men rushed before these, and took turns speaking their cases,
and between them lay on the ground two talents of gold, to be given
to that judge who in this case spoke the straightest opinion.
    But around the other city were lying two forces of armed men
510   shining in their war gear. For one side counsel was divided
whether to storm and sack, or share between both sides the property
and all the possessions the lovely citadel held hard within it.
But the city's people were not giving way, and armed for an ambush.
Their beloved wives and their little children stood on the rampart
515   to hold it, and with them the men with age upon them, but meanwhile
the others went out. And Ares led them, and Pallas Athene.
These were gold, both, and golden raiment upon them, and they were
beautiful and huge in their armour, being divinities,
and conspicuous from afar, but the people around them were smaller.
520   These, when they were come to the place that was set for their ambush,
in a river, where there was a watering place for all animals,
there they sat down in place shrouding themselves in the bright bronze.
But apart from these were sitting two men to watch for the rest of them
and waiting until they could see the sheep and the shambling cattle,
525   who appeared presently, and two herdsmen went along with them
playing happily on pipes, and took no thought of the treachery.
Those others saw them, and made a rush, and quickly thereafter
cut off on both sides the herds of cattle and the beautiful
flocks of shining sheep, and killed the shepherds upon them.
530   But the other army, as soon as they heard the uproar arising
from the cattle, as they sat in their councils, suddenly mounted
behind their light-foot horses, and went after, and soon overtook them.
These stood their ground and fought a battle by the banks of the river,
and they were making casts at each other with their spears bronze-headed;
535   and Hate was there with Confusion among them, and Death the destructive;
she was holding a live man with a new wound, and another

one unhurt, and dragged a dead man by the feet through the carnage.
The clothing upon her shoulders showed strong red with the men's blood.
All closed together like living men and fought with each other
540   and dragged away from each other the corpses of those who had fallen.
    He made upon it a soft field, the pride of the tilled land,
wide and triple-ploughed, with many ploughmen upon it
who wheeled their teams at the turn and drove them in either direction.
And as these making their turn would reach the end-strip of the field,
545   a man would come up to them at this point and hand them a flagon
of honey-sweet wine, and they would turn again to the furrows
in their haste to come again to the end-strip of the deep field.
The earth darkened behind them and looked like earth that has been
    ploughed
though it was gold. Such was the wonder of the shield's forging.
550   He made on it the precinct of a king, where the labourers
were reaping, with the sharp reaping hooks in their hands. Of the cut
    swathes
some fell along the lines of reaping, one after another,
while the sheaf-binders caught up others and tied them with bind-ropes.
There were three sheaf-binders who stood by, and behind them
555   were children picking up the cut swathes, and filled their arms with them
and carried and gave them always; and by them the king in silence
and holding his staff stood near the line of the reapers, happily.
And apart and under a tree the heralds made a feast ready
and trimmed a great ox they had slaughtered. Meanwhile the women
560   scattered, for the workmen to eat, abundant white barley.
    He made on it a great vineyard heavy with clusters,
lovely and in gold, but the grapes upon it were darkened
and the vines themselves stood out through poles of silver. About them
he made a field-ditch of dark metal, and drove all around this
565   a fence of tin; and there was only one path to the vineyard,
and along it ran the grape-bearers for the vineyard's stripping.
Young girls and young men, in all their light-hearted innocence,
carried the kind, sweet fruit away in their woven baskets,
and in their midst a youth with a singing lyre played charmingly
570   upon it for them, and sang the beautiful song for Linos
in a light voice, and they followed him, and with singing and whistling
and light dance-steps of their feet kept time to the music.
    He made upon it a herd of horn-straight oxen. The cattle
were wrought of gold and of tin, and thronged in speed and with lowing
575   out of the dung of the farmyard to a pasturing place by a sounding
river, and beside the moving field of a reed bed.
The herdsmen were of gold who went along with the cattle,
four of them, and nine dogs shifting their feet followed them.
But among the foremost of the cattle two formidable lions
580   had caught hold of a bellowing bull, and he with loud lowings
was dragged away, as the dogs and the young men went in pursuit of him.
But the two lions, breaking open the hide of the great ox,
gulped the black blood and the inward guts, as meanwhile the herdsmen

were in the act of setting and urging the quick dogs on them.

585 But they, before they could get their teeth in, turned back from the lions,
but would come and take their stand very close, and bayed, and kept clear.

And the renowned smith of the strong arms made on it a meadow
large and in a lovely valley for the glimmering sheepflocks,
with dwelling places upon it, and covered shelters, and sheepfolds.

590 And the renowned smith of the strong arms made elaborate on it
a dancing floor, like that which once in the wide spaces of Knosos[3]
Daidalos[4] built for Ariadne of the lovely tresses.
And there were young men on it and young girls, sought for their beauty
with gifts of oxen, dancing, and holding hands at the wrist. These

595 wore, the maidens long light robes, but the men wore tunics
of finespun work and shining softly, touched with olive oil.
And the girls wore fair garlands on their heads, while the young men
carried golden knives that hung from sword-belts of silver.
At whiles on their understanding feet they would run very lightly,

600 as when a potter crouching makes trial of his wheel, holding
it close in his hands, to see if it will run smooth. At another
time they would form rows, and run, rows crossing each other.
And around the lovely chorus of dancers stood a great multitude
happily watching, while among the dancers two acrobats

605 led the measures of song and dance revolving among them.

He made on it the great strength of the Ocean River
which ran around the uttermost rim of the shield's strong structure.

Then after he had wrought this shield, which was huge and heavy,
he wrought for him a corselet brighter than fire in its shining,

610 and wrought him a helmet, massive and fitting close to his temples,
lovely and intricate work, and laid a gold top-ridge along it,
and out of pliable tin wrought him leg-armour. Thereafter
when the renowned smith of the strong arms had finished the armour
he lifted it and laid it before the mother of Achilleus.

615 And she like a hawk came sweeping down from the snows of Olympos
and carried with her the shining armour, the gift of Hephaistos.

Book 22

[THE DEATH OF HEKTOR]

So along the city the Trojans, who had run like fawns, dried
the sweat off from their bodies and drank and slaked their thirst, leaning
along the magnificent battlements. Meanwhile the Achaians
sloping their shields across their shoulders came close to the rampart.

5 But his deadly fate held Hektor shackled, so that he stood fast
in front of Ilion and the Skaian gates. Now Phoibos
Apollo spoke aloud to Peleion: "Why, son of Peleus,
do you keep after me in the speed of your feet, being mortal

3. Cretan city of King Minos, the father of Ariadne.   4. Mythic architect, artist, and inventor.

while I am an immortal god? Even yet you have not
10   seen that I am a god, but strain after me in your fury.
Now hard fighting with the Trojans whom you stampeded means nothing
to you. They are crowded in the city, but you bent away here.
You will never kill me. I am not one who is fated."
     Deeply vexed Achilleus of the swift feet spoke to him:
15   "You have balked me, striker from afar, most malignant of all gods,
when you turned me here away from the rampart, else many Trojans
would have caught the soil in their teeth before they got back into Ilion.
Now you have robbed me of great glory, and rescued these people
lightly, since you have no retribution to fear hereafter.
20   Else I would punish you, if only the strength were in me."
     He spoke, and stalked away against the city, with high thoughts
in mind, and in tearing speed, like a racehorse with his chariot
who runs lightly as he pulls the chariot over the flat land.
Such was the action of Achilleus in feet and quick knees.
25   The aged Priam was the first of all whose eyes saw him
as he swept across the flat land in full shining, like that star
which comes on in the autumn and whose conspicuous brightness
far outshines the stars that are numbered in the night's darkening,
the star they give the name of Orion's Dog, which is brightest
30   among the stars, and yet is wrought as a sign of evil
and brings on the great fever for unfortunate mortals.
Such was the flare of the bronze that girt his chest in his running.
The old man groaned aloud and with both hands high uplifted
beat his head, and groaned amain, and spoke supplicating
35   his beloved son, who there still in front of the gateway
stood fast in determined fury to fight with Achilleus.
The old man stretching his hands out called pitifully to him:
"Hektor, beloved child, do not wait the attack of this man
alone, away from the others. You might encounter your destiny
40   beaten down by Peleion, since he is far stronger than you are.
A hard man: I wish he were as beloved of the immortal
as loved by me. Soon he would lie dead, and the dogs and the vultures
would eat him, and bitter sorrow so be taken from my heart.
He has made me desolate of my sons, who were brave and many.
45   He killed them, or sold them away among the far-lying islands.
Even now there are two sons, Lykaon and Polydoros,
whom I cannot see among the Trojans pent up in the city,
sons Laothoë a princess among women bore to me.
But if these are alive somewhere in the army, then I can
50   set them free for bronze and gold; it is there inside, since
Altes the aged and renowned gave much with his daughter.
But if they are dead already and gone down to the house of Hades,
it is sorrow to our hearts, who bore them, myself and their mother,
but to the rest of the people a sorrow that will be fleeting
55   beside their sorrow for you, if you go down before Achilleus.
Come then inside the wall, my child, so that you can rescue
the Trojans and the women of Troy, neither win the high glory

for Peleus' son, and yourself be robbed of your very life. Oh, take
pity on me, the unfortunate still alive, still sentient
60 but ill-starred, whom the father, Kronos' son, on the threshold of old age
will blast with hard fate, after I have looked upon evils
and seen my sons destroyed and my daughters dragged away captive
and the chambers of marriage wrecked and the innocent children taken
and dashed to the ground in the hatefulness of war, and the wives
65 of my sons dragged off by the accursed hands of the Achaians.
And myself last of all, my dogs in front of my doorway
will rip me raw, after some man with stroke of the sharp bronze
spear, or with spearcast, has torn the life out of my body;
those dogs I raised in my halls to be at my table, to guard my
70 gates, who will lap my blood in the savagery of their anger
and then lie down in my courts. For a young man all is decorous
when he is cut down in battle and torn with the sharp bronze, and lies there
dead, and though dead still all that shows about him is beautiful;
but when an old man is dead and down, and the dogs mutilate
75 the grey head and the grey beard and the parts that are secret,
this, for all sad mortality, is the sight most pitiful."
    So the old man spoke, and in his hands seizing the grey hairs
tore them from his head, but could not move the spirit in Hektor.
And side by side with him his mother in tears was mourning
80 and laid the fold of her bosom bare and with one hand held out
a breast, and wept her tears for him and called to him in winged words:
"Hektor, my child, look upon these and obey, and take pity
on me, if ever I gave you the breast to quiet your sorrow.
Remember all these things, dear child, and from inside the wall
85 beat off this grim man. Do not go out as champion against him,
o hard one; for if he kills you I can no longer
mourn you on the death-bed, sweet branch, o child of my bearing,
nor can your generous wife mourn you, but a big way from us
beside the ships of the Argives the running dogs will feed on you."
90   So these two in tears and with much supplication called out
to their dear son, but could not move the spirit in Hektor,
but he awaited Achilleus as he came on, gigantic.
But as a snake waits for a man by his hole, in the mountains,
glutted with evil poisons, and the fell venom has got inside him,
95 and coiled about the hole he stares malignant, so Hektor
would not give ground but kept unquenched the fury within him
and sloped his shining shield against the jut of the bastion.
Deeply troubled he spoke to his own great-hearted spirit:
"Ah me! If I go now inside the wall and the gateway,
100 Poulydamas will be first to put a reproach upon me,
since he tried to make me lead the Trojans inside the city
on that accursed night when brilliant Achilleus rose up,
and I would not obey him, but that would have been far better.
Now, since by my own recklessness I have ruined my people,
105 I feel shame before the Trojans and the Trojan women with trailing
robes, that someone who is less of a man than I will say of me:

'Hektor believed in his own strength and ruined his people.'
Thus they will speak; and as for me, it would be much better
at that time, to go against Achilleus, and slay him, and come back,

110   or else be killed by him in glory in front of the city.
Or if again I set down my shield massive in the middle
and my ponderous helm, and lean my spear up against the rampart
and go out as I am to meet Achilleus the blameless
and promise to give back Helen, and with her all her possessions,

115   all those things that once in the hollow ships Alexandros[1]
brought back to Troy, and these were the beginning of the quarrel;
to give these to Atreus' sons to take away, and for the Achaians
also to divide up all that is hidden within the city,
and take an oath thereafter for the Trojans in conclave

120   not to hide anything away, but distribute all of it,
as much as the lovely citadel keeps guarded within it;
yet still, why does the heart within me debate on these things?
I might go up to him, and he take no pity upon me
nor respect my position, but kill me naked so, as if I were

125   a woman, once I stripped my armour from me. There is no
way any more from a tree or a rock to talk to him gently
whispering like a young man and a young girl, in the way
a young man and a young maiden whisper together.
Better to bring on the fight with him as soon as it may be.

130   We shall see to which one the Olympian grants the glory."
        So he pondered, waiting, but Achilleus was closing upon him
in the likeness of the lord of battles, the helm-shining warrior,
and shaking from above his shoulder the dangerous Pelian
ash spear, while the bronze that closed about him was shining

135   like the flare of blazing fire or the sun in its rising.
And the shivers took hold of Hektor when he saw him, and he could no
        longer
stand his ground there, but left the gates behind, and fled, frightened,
and Peleus' son went after him in the confidence of his quick feet.
As when a hawk in the mountains who moves lightest of things flying

140   makes his effortless swoop for a trembling dove, but she slips away
from beneath and flies and he shrill screaming close after her
plunges for her again and again, heart furious to take her;
so Achilleus went straight for him in fury, but Hektor
fled away under the Trojan wall and moved his knees rapidly.

145   They raced along by the watching point and the windy fig tree
always away from under the wall and along the wagon-way
and came to the two sweet-running well springs. There there are double
springs of water that jet up, the springs of whirling Skamandros.
One of these runs hot water and the steam on all sides

150   of it rises as if from a fire that was burning inside it.
But the other in the summer-time runs water that is like hail

1. Paris.

or chill snow or ice that forms from water. Beside these
in this place, and close to them, are the washing-hollows
of stone, and magnificent, where the wives of the Trojans and their lovely
155 daughters washed the clothes to shining, in the old days
when there was peace, before the coming of the sons of the Achaians.
They ran beside these, one escaping, the other after him.
It was a great man who fled, but far better he who pursued him
rapidly, since here was no festal beast, no ox-hide
160 they strove for, for these are prizes that are given men for their running.
No, they ran for the life of Hektor, breaker of horses.
As when about the turnposts racing single-foot horses
run at full speed, when a great prize is laid up for their winning,
a tripod or a woman, in games for a man's funeral,
165 so these two swept whirling about the city of Priam
in the speed of their feet, while all the gods were looking upon them.
First to speak among them was the father of gods and mortals:
"Ah me, this is a man beloved whom now my eyes watch
being chased around the wall; my heart is mourning for Hektor
170 who has burned in my honour many thigh pieces of oxen
on the peaks of Ida with all her folds, or again on the uttermost
part of the citadel, but now the brilliant Achilleus
drives him in speed of his feet around the city of Priam.
Come then, you immortals, take thought and take counsel, whether
175 to rescue this man or whether to make him, for all his valour,
go down under the hands of Achilleus, the son of Peleus."
    Then in answer the goddess grey-eyed Athene spoke to him:
"Father of the shining bolt, dark misted, what is this you said?
Do you wish to bring back a man who is mortal, one long since
180 doomed by his destiny, from ill-sounding death and release him?
Do it, then; but not all the rest of us gods shall approve you."
    Then Zeus the gatherer of the clouds spoke to her in answer:
"Tritogeneia, dear daughter, do not lose heart; for I say this
not in outright anger, and my meaning toward you is kindly.
185 Act as your purpose would have you do, and hold back no longer."
    So he spoke, and stirred on Athene, who was eager before this,
and she went in a flash of speed down the pinnacles of Olympos.
    But swift Achilleus kept unremittingly after Hektor,
chasing him, as a dog in the mountains who has flushed from his covert
190 a deer's fawn follows him through the folding ways and the valleys,
and though the fawn crouched down under a bush and be hidden
he keeps running and noses him out until he comes on him;
so Hektor could not lose himself from swift-footed Peleion.
If ever he made a dash right on for the gates of Dardanos
195 to get quickly under the strong-built bastions, endeavouring
that they from above with missiles thrown might somehow defend him,
each time Achilleus would get in front and force him to turn back
into the plain, and himself kept his flying course next the city.
As in a dream a man is not able to follow one who runs
200 from him, nor can the runner escape, nor the other pursue him,

so he could not run him down in his speed, nor the other get clear.
How then could Hektor have escaped the death spirits, had not
Apollo, for this last and uttermost time, stood by him
close, and driven strength into him, and made his knees light?

205 But brilliant Achilleus kept shaking his head at his own people
and would not let them throw their bitter projectiles at Hektor
for fear the thrower might win the glory, and himself come second.
But when for the fourth time they had come around to the well springs
then the Father balanced his golden scales, and in them

210 he set two fateful portions of death, which lays men prostrate,
one for Achilleus, and one for Hektor, breaker of horses,
and balanced it by the middle; and Hektor's death-day was heavier
and dragged downward toward death, and Phoibos Apollo forsook him.
But the goddess grey-eyed Athene came now to Peleion

215 and stood close beside him and addressed him in winged words: "Beloved
of Zeus, shining Achilleus, I am hopeful now that you and I
will take back great glory to the ships of the Achaians, after
we have killed Hektor, for all his slakeless fury for battle.
Now there is no way for him to get clear away from us,

220 not though Apollo who strikes from afar should be willing to undergo
much, and wallow before our father Zeus of the aegis."
Stand you here then and get your wind again, while I go
to this man and persuade him to stand up to you in combat."

So spoke Athene, and he was glad at heart, and obeyed her,
225 and stopped, and stood leaning on his bronze-barbed ash spear. Meanwhile
Athene left him there, and caught up with brilliant Hektor,
and likened herself in form and weariless voice to Deïphobos.
She came now and stood close to him and addressed him in winged words:
"Dear brother, indeed swift-footed Achilleus is using you roughly

230 and chasing you on swift feet around the city of Priam.
Come on, then; let us stand fast against him and beat him back from us."

Then tall Hektor of the shining helm answered her: "Deïphobos,
before now you were dearest to me by far of my brothers,
of all those who were sons of Priam and Hekabe, and now

235 I am minded all the more within my heart to honour you,
you who dared for my sake, when your eyes saw me, to come forth
from the fortifications, while the others stand fast inside them."

Then in turn the goddess grey-eyed Athene answered him:
"My brother, it is true our father and the lady our mother, taking

240 my knees in turn, and my companions about me, entreated
that I stay within, such was the terror upon all of them.
But the heart within me was worn away by hard sorrow for you.
But now let us go straight on and fight hard, let there be no sparing
of our spears, so that we can find out whether Achilleus

245 will kill us both and carry our bloody war spoils back
to the hollow ships, or will himself go down under your spear."

So Athene spoke and led him on by beguilement.
Now as the two in their advance were come close together,
first of the two to speak was tall helm-glittering Hektor:

250   "Son of Peleus, I will no longer run from you, as before this
I fled three times around the great city of Priam, and dared not
stand to your onfall. But now my spirit in turn has driven me
to stand and face you. I must take you now, or I must be taken.
Come then, shall we swear before the gods? For these are the highest
255   who shall be witnesses and watch over our agreements.
Brutal as you are I will not defile you, if Zeus grants
to me that I can wear you out, and take the life from you.
But after I have stripped your glorious armour, Achilleus,
I will give your corpse back to the Achaians. Do you do likewise."
260   Then looking darkly at him swift-footed Achilleus answered:
"Hektor, argue me no agreements. I cannot forgive you.
As there are no trustworthy oaths between men and lions,
nor wolves and lambs have spirit that can be brought to agreement
but forever these hold feelings of hate for each other,
265   so there can be no love between you and me, nor shall there be
oaths between us, but one or the other must fall before then
to glut with his blood Ares the god who fights under the shield's guard.
Remember every valour of yours, for now the need comes
hardest upon you to be a spearman and a bold warrior.
270   There shall be no more escape for you, but Pallas Athene
will kill you soon by my spear. You will pay in a lump for all those
sorrows of my companions you killed in your spear's fury."
    So he spoke, and balanced the spear far shadowed, and threw it;
but glorious Hektor kept his eyes on him, and avoided it,
275   for he dropped, watchful, to his knee, and the bronze spear flew over his
        shoulder
and stuck in the ground, but Pallas Athene snatched it, and gave it
back to Achilleus, unseen by Hektor shepherd of the people.
But now Hektor spoke out to the blameless son of Peleus:
"You missed; and it was not, o Achilleus like the immortals,
280   from Zeus that you knew my destiny; but you thought so; or rather
you are someone clever in speech and spoke to swindle me,
to make me afraid of you and forget my valour and war strength.
You will not stick your spear in my back as I run away from you
but drive it into my chest as I storm straight in against you;
285   if the god gives you that; and now look out for my brazen
spear. I wish it might be taken full length in your body.
And indeed the war would be a lighter thing for the Trojans
if you were dead, seeing that you are their greatest affliction."
    So he spoke, and balanced the spear far shadowed, and threw it,
290   and struck the middle of Peleïdes' shield, nor missed it,
but the spear was driven far back from the shield, and Hektor was angered
because his swift weapon had been loosed from his hand in a vain cast.
He stood discouraged, and had no other ash spear; but lifting
his voice he called aloud on Deïphobos of the pale shield,
295   and asked him for a long spear, but Deïphobos was not near him.
And Hektor knew the truth inside his heart, and spoke aloud:
"No use. Here at last the gods have summoned me deathward.

I thought Deïphobos the hero was here close beside me,
but he is behind the wall and it was Athene cheating me,
and now evil death is close to me, and no longer far away,
and there is no way out. So it must long since have been pleasing
to Zeus, and Zeus' son who strikes from afar, this way; though before this
they defended me gladly. But now my death is upon me.
Let me at least not die without a struggle, inglorious,
but do some big thing first, that men to come shall know of it."
  So he spoke, and pulling out the sharp sword that was slung
at the hollow of his side, huge and heavy, and gathering
himself together, he made his swoop, like a high-flown eagle
who launches himself out of the murk of the clouds on the flat land
to catch away a tender lamb or a shivering hare; so
Hektor made his swoop, swinging his sharp sword, and Achilleus
charged, the heart within him loaded with savage fury.
In front of his chest the beautiful elaborate great shield
covered him, and with the glittering helm with four horns
he nodded; the lovely golden fringes were shaken about it
which Hephaistos had driven close along the horn of the helmet.
And as a star moves among stars in the night's darkening,
Hesper, who is the fairest star who stands in the sky, such
was the shining from the pointed spear Achilleus was shaking
in his right hand with evil intention toward brilliant Hektor.
He was eyeing Hektor's splendid body, to see where it might best
give way, but all the rest of the skin was held in the armour,
brazen and splendid, he stripped when he cut down the strength of
    Patroklos;
yet showed where the collar-bones hold the neck from the shoulders,
the throat, where death of the soul comes most swiftly; in this place
brilliant Achilleus drove the spear as he came on in fury,
and clean through the soft part of the neck the spearpoint was driven.
Yet the ash spear heavy with bronze did not sever the windpipe,
so that Hektor could still make exchange of words spoken.
But he dropped in the dust, and brilliant Achilleus vaunted above him:
"Hektor, surely you thought as you killed Patroklos you would be
safe, and since I was far away you thought nothing of me,
o fool, for an avenger was left, far greater than he was,
behind him and away by the hollow ships. And it was I;
and I have broken your strength; on you the dogs and the vultures
shall feed and foully rip you; the Achaians will bury Patroklos."
  In his weakness Hektor of the shining helm spoke to him:
"I entreat you, by your life, by your knees, by your parents,
do not let the dogs feed on me by the ships of the Achaians,
but take yourself the bronze and gold that are there in abundance,
those gifts that my father and the lady my mother will give you,
and give my body to be taken home again, so that the Trojans
and the wives of the Trojans may give me in death my rite of burning."
  But looking darkly at him swift-footed Achilleus answered:
"No more entreating of me, you dog, by knees or parents.

I wish only that my spirit and fury would drive me
to hack your meat away and eat it raw for the things that
you have done to me. So there is no one who can hold the dogs off
from your head, not if they bring here and set before me ten times
350 and twenty times the ransom, and promise more in addition,
not if Priam son of Dardanos should offer to weigh out
your bulk in gold; not even so shall the lady your mother
who herself bore you lay you on the death-bed and mourn you:
no, but the dogs and the birds will have you all for their feasting."
355   Then, dying, Hektor of the shining helmet spoke to him:
"I know you well as I look upon you, I know that I could not
persuade you, since indeed in your breast is a heart of iron.
Be careful now; for I might be made into the gods' curse
upon you, on that day when Paris and Phoibos Apollo
360 destroy you in the Skaian gates, for all your valour."
     He spoke, and as he spoke the end of death closed in upon him,
and the soul fluttering free of the limbs went down into Death's house
mourning her destiny, leaving youth and manhood behind her.
Now though he was a dead man brilliant Achilleus spoke to him:
365 "Die: and I will take my own death at whatever time
Zeus and the rest of the immortals choose to accomplish it."
     He spoke, and pulled the brazen spear from the body, and laid it
on one side, and stripped away from the shoulders the bloody
armour. And the other sons of the Achaians came running about him,
370 and gazed upon the stature and on the imposing beauty
of Hektor; and none stood beside him who did not stab him;
and thus they would speak one to another, each looking at his neighbour:
"See now, Hektor is much softer to handle than he was
when he set the ships ablaze with the burning firebrand."
375   So as they stood beside him they would speak, and stab him.
But now, when he had despoiled the body, swift-footed brilliant
Achilleus stood among the Achaians and addressed them in winged words:
"Friends, who are leaders of the Argives and keep their counsel:
since the gods have granted me the killing of this man
380 who has done us much damage, such as not all the others together
have done, come, let us go in armour about the city
to see if we can find out what purpose is in the Trojans,
whether they will abandon their high city, now that this man
has fallen, or are minded to stay, though Hektor lives no longer.
385 Yet still, why does the heart within me debate on these things?
There is a dead man who lies by the ships, unwept, unburied:
Patroklos: and I will not forget him, never so long as
I remain among the living and my knees have their spring beneath me.
And though the dead forget the dead in the house of Hades,
390 even there I shall still remember my beloved companion.
But now, you young men of the Achaians, let us go back, singing
a victory song, to our hollow ships; and take this with us.
We have won ourselves enormous fame; we have killed the great Hektor
whom the Trojans glorified as if he were a god in their city."

395   He spoke, and now thought of shameful treatment for glorious Hektor.
In both of his feet at the back he made holes by the tendons
in the space between ankle and heel, and drew thongs of ox-hide through
      them,
and fastened them to the chariot so as to let the head drag,
and mounted the chariot, and lifted the glorious armour inside it,
400   then whipped the horses to a run, and they winged their way unreluctant.
A cloud of dust rose where Hektor was dragged, his dark hair was falling
about him, and all that head that was once so handsome was tumbled
in the dust; since by this time Zeus had given him over
to his enemies, to be defiled in the land of his fathers.
405   So all his head was dragged in the dust; and now his mother
tore out her hair, and threw the shining veil far from her
and raised a great wail as she looked upon her son; and his father
beloved groaned pitifully, and all his people about him
were taken with wailing and lamentation all through the city.
410   It was most like what would have happened, if all lowering
Ilion had been burning top to bottom in fire.
His people could scarcely keep the old man in his impatience
from storming out of the Dardanian gates; he implored them
all, and wallowed in the muck before them calling on each man
415   and naming him by his name: "Give way, dear friends,
and let me alone though you care for me, leave me to go out
from the city and make my way to the ships of the Achaians.
I must be suppliant to this man, who is harsh and violent,
and he might have respect for my age and take pity upon it
420   since I am old, and his father also is old, as I am,
Peleus, who begot and reared him to be an affliction
on the Trojans. He has given us most sorrow, beyond all others,
such is the number of my flowering sons he has cut down.
But for all of these I mourn not so much, in spite of my sorrow,
425   as for one, Hektor, and the sharp grief for him will carry me downward
into Death's house. I wish he had died in my arms, for that way
we two, I myself and his mother who bore him unhappy,
might so have glutted ourselves with weeping for him and mourning."
So he spoke, in tears, and beside him mourned the citizens.
430   But for the women of Troy Hekabe[2] led out the thronging
chant of sorrow: "Child, I am wretched. What shall my life be
in my sorrows, now you are dead, who by day and in the night
were my glory in the town, and to all of the Trojans
and the women of Troy a blessing throughout their city. They adored you
435   as if you were a god, since in truth you were their high honour
while you lived. Now death and fate have closed in upon you."
So she spoke in tears but the wife of Hektor had not yet
heard: for no sure messenger had come to her and told her
how her husband had held his ground there outside the gates;

2. Hektor's mother.

440 but she was weaving a web in the inner room of the high house,
a red folding robe, and inworking elaborate figures.
She called out through the house to her lovely-haired handmaidens
to set a great cauldron over the fire, so that there would be
hot water for Hektor's bath as he came back out of the fighting;
445 poor innocent, nor knew how, far from waters for bathing,
Pallas Athene had cut him down at the hands of Achilleus.
She heard from the great bastion the noise of mourning and sorrow.
Her limbs spun, and the shuttle dropped from her hand to the ground. Then
she called aloud to her lovely-haired handmaidens: "Come here.
450 Two of you come with me, so I can see what has happened.
I heard the voice of Hektor's honoured mother; within me
my own heart rising beats in my mouth, my limbs under me
are frozen. Surely some evil is near for the children of Priam.
May what I say come never close to my ear; yet dreadfully
455 I fear that great Achilleus might have cut off bold Hektor
alone, away from the city, and be driving him into the flat land,
might put an end to that bitter pride of courage, that always
was on him, since he would never stay back where the men were in
     numbers
but break far out in front, and give way in his fury to no man."
460 So she spoke, and ran out of the house like a raving woman
with pulsing heart, and her two handmaidens went along with her.
But when she came to the bastion and where the men were gathered
she stopped, staring, on the wall; and she saw him
being dragged in front of the city, and the running horses
465 dragged him at random toward the hollow ships of the Achaians.
The darkness of night misted over the eyes of Andromache.
She fell backward, and gasped the life breath from her, and far off
threw from her head the shining gear that ordered her headdress,
the diadem and the cap, and the holding-band woven together,
470 and the circlet, which Aphrodite the golden once had given her
on that day when Hektor of the shining helmet led her forth
from the house of Eëtion, and gave numberless gifts to win her.
And about her stood thronging her husband's sisters and the wives of his
     brothers
and these, in her despair for death, held her up among them.
475 But she, when she breathed again and the life was gathered back into her,
lifted her voice among the women of Troy in mourning:
"Hektor, I grieve for you. You and I were born to a single
destiny, you in Troy in the house of Priam, and I
in Thebe, underneath the timbered mountain of Plakos
480 in the house of Eëtion, who cared for me when I was little,
ill-fated he, I ill-starred. I wish he had never begotten me.
Now you go down to the house of Death in the secret places
of the earth, and left me here behind in the sorrow of mourning,
a widow in your house, and the boy is only a baby
485 who was born to you and me, the unfortunate. You cannot help him,
Hektor, any more, since you are dead. Nor can he help you.

Though he escape the attack of the Achaians with all its sorrows,
yet all his days for your sake there will be hard work for him
and sorrows, for others will take his lands away from him. The day
490 of bereavement leaves a child with no agemates to befriend him.
He bows his head before every man, his cheeks are bewept, he
goes, needy, a boy among his father's companions,
and tugs at this man by the mantle, that man by the tunic,
and they pity him, and one gives him a tiny drink from a goblet,
495 enough to moisten his lips, not enough to moisten his palate.
But one whose parents are living beats him out of the banquet
hitting him with his fists and in words also abuses him:
"Get out, you! Your father is not dining among us."
And the boy goes away in tears to his widowed mother,
500 Astyanax, who in days before on the knees of his father
would eat only the marrow or the flesh of sheep that was fattest.
And when sleep would come upon him and he was done with his playing,
he would go to sleep in a bed, in the arms of his nurse, in a soft
bed, with his heart given all its fill of luxury.
505 Now, with his dear father gone, he has much to suffer:
he, whom the Trojans have called Astyanax, lord of the city,
since it was you alone who defended the gates and the long walls.
But now, beside the curving ships, far away from your parents,
the writhing worms will feed, when the dogs have had enough of you,
510 on your naked corpse, though in your house there is clothing laid up
that is fine-textured and pleasant, wrought by the hands of women.
But all of these I will burn up in the fire's blazing,
no use to you, since you will never be laid away in them;
but in your honour, from the men of Troy and the Trojan women."
515   So she spoke, in tears; and the women joined in her mourning.

Book 24

[ACHILLES AND PRIAM]

And the games broke up, and the people scattered to go away, each man
to his fast-running ship, and the rest of them took thought of their dinner
and of sweet sleep and its enjoyment; only Achilleus
wept still as he remembered his beloved companion, nor did sleep
5   who subdues all come over him, but he tossed from one side to the other
in longing for Patroklos, for his manhood and his great strength
and all the actions he had seen to the end with him, and the hardships
he had suffered; the wars of men; hard crossing of the big waters.
Remembering all these things he let fall the swelling tears, lying
10   sometimes along his side, sometimes on his back, and now again
prone on his face; then he would stand upright, and pace turning
in distraction along the beach of the sea, nor did dawn rising
escape him as she brightened across the sea and the beaches.
Then, when he had yoked running horses under the chariot
15   he would fasten Hektor behind the chariot, so as to drag him,

and draw him three times around the tomb of Menoitios' fallen
son, then rest again in his shelter, and throw down the dead man
and leave him to lie sprawled on his face in the dust. But Apollo
had pity on him, though he was only a dead man, and guarded
20   the body from all ugliness, and hid all of it under the golden
aegis, so that it might not be torn when Achilleus dragged it.
    So Achilleus in his standing fury outraged great Hektor.
The blessed gods as they looked upon him were filled with compassion
and kept urging clear-sighted Argeïphontes[1] to steal the body.
25   There this was pleasing to all the others, but never to Hera
nor Poseidon, nor the girl of the grey eyes,[2] who kept still
their hatred for sacred Ilion as in the beginning,
and for Priam and his people, because of the delusion of Paris
who insulted the goddesses when they came to him in his courtyard
30   and favoured her who supplied the lust that led to disaster.
But now, as it was the twelfth dawn after the death of Hektor,
Phoibos Apollo spoke his word out among the immortals:
"You are hard, you gods, and destructive. Now did not Hektor
burn thigh pieces of oxen and unblemished goats in your honour?
35   Now you cannot bring yourselves to save him, though he is only
a corpse, for his wife to look upon, his child and his mother
and Priam his father, and his people, who presently thereafter
would burn his body in the fire and give him his rites of burial.
No, you gods; your desire is to help this cursed Achilleus
40   within whose breast there are no feelings of justice, nor can
his mind be bent, but his purposes are fierce, like a lion
who when he has given way to his own great strength and his haughty
spirit, goes among the flocks of men, to devour them.
So Achilleus has destroyed pity, and there is not in him
45   any shame; which does much harm to men but profits them also.
For a man must some day lose one who was even closer
than this; a brother from the same womb, or a son. And yet
he weeps for him, and sorrows for him, and then it is over,
for the Destinies put in mortal men the heart of endurance.
50   But this man, now he has torn the heart of life from great Hektor,
ties him to his horses and drags him around his beloved companion's
tomb; and nothing is gained thereby for his good, or his honour.
Great as he is, let him take care not to make us angry;
for see, he does dishonour to the dumb earth in his fury."
55   Then bitterly Hera of the white arms answered him, saying:
"What you have said could be true, lord of the silver bow, only
if you give Hektor such pride of place as you give to Achilleus.
But Hektor was mortal, and suckled at the breast of a woman,
while Achilleus is the child of a goddess, one whom I myself
60   nourished and brought up and gave her as bride to her husband
Peleus, one dear to the hearts of the immortals, for you all
went, you gods, to the wedding; and you too feasted among them

---

1. Hermes.   2. Athene.

and held your lyre, o friend of the evil, faithless forever."

In turn Zeus who gathers the clouds spoke to her in answer:
65 "Hera, be not utterly angry with the gods, for there shall not
be the same pride of place given both. Yet Hektor also
was loved by the gods, best of all the mortals in Ilion.
I loved him too. He never failed of gifts to my liking.
Never yet has my altar gone without fair sacrifice,
70 the smoke and the savour of it, since that is our portion of honour.
The stealing of him we will dismiss, for it is not possible
to take bold Hektor secretly from Achilleus, since always
his mother is near him night and day; but it would be better
if one of the gods would summon Thetis here to my presence
75 so that I can say a close word to her, and see that Achilleus
is given gifts by Priam and gives back the body of Hektor."

He spoke, and Iris storm-footed sprang away with the message,
and at a point between Samos and Imbros of the high cliffs
plunged in the dark water, and the sea crashed moaning about her.
80 She plummeted to the sea floor like a lead weight which, mounted
along the horn of an ox who ranges the fields, goes downward
and takes death with it to the raw-ravening fish. She found Thetis
inside the hollow of her cave, and gathered about her
sat the rest of the sea goddesses, and she in their midst
85 was mourning the death of her blameless son, who so soon was destined
to die in Troy of the rich soil, far from the land of his fathers.
Iris the swift-foot came close beside her and spoke to her:
"Rise, Thetis. Zeus whose purposes are infinite calls you."

In turn Thetis the goddess, the silver-footed, answered her:
90 "What does he, the great god, want with me? I feel shamefast
to mingle with the immortals, and my heart is confused with sorrows.
But I will go. No word shall be in vain, if he says it."

So she spoke, and shining among the divinities took up
her black veil, and there is no darker garment. She went
95 on her way, and in front of her rapid wind-footed Iris
guided her, and the wave of the water opened about them.
They stepped out on the dry land and swept to the sky. There they found
the son of Kronos of the wide brows, and gathered about him
sat all the rest of the gods, the blessed, who live forever.
100 She sat down beside Zeus father, and Athene made a place for her.
Hera put into her hand a beautiful golden goblet
and spoke to her to comfort her, and Thetis accepting drank from it.
The father of gods and men began the discourse among them:
"You have come to Olympos, divine Thetis, for all your sorrow,
105 with an unforgotten grief in your heart. I myself know this.
But even so I will tell you why I summoned you hither.
For nine days there has risen a quarrel among the immortals
over the body of Hektor, and Achilleus, stormer of cities.
They keep urging clear-sighted Argeïphontes to steal the body,
110 but I still put upon Achilleus the honour that he has, guarding
your reverence and your love for me into time afterwards. Go then

in all speed to the encampment and give to your son this message:
tell him that the gods frown upon him, that beyond all other
immortals I myself am angered that in his heart's madness
115   he holds Hektor beside the curved ships and did not give him
back. Perhaps in fear of me he will give back Hektor.
Then I will send Iris to Priam of the great heart, with an order
to ransom his dear son, going down to the ships of the Achaians
and bringing gifts to Achilleus which might soften his anger."
120   He spoke and the goddess silver-foot Thetis did not disobey him
but descended in a flash of speed from the peaks of Olympos
and made her way to the shelter of her son, and there found him
in close lamentation, and his beloved companions about him
were busy at their work and made ready the morning meal, and there
125   stood a great fleecy sheep being sacrificed in the shelter.
His honoured mother came close to him and sat down beside him,
and stroked him with her hand and called him by name and spoke to him:
"My child, how long will you go on eating your heart out in sorrow
and lamentation, and remember neither your food nor going
130   to bed? It is a good thing even to lie with a woman
in love. For you will not be with me long, but already
death and powerful destiny stand closely above you.
But listen hard to me, for I come from Zeus with a message.
He says that the gods frown upon you, that beyond all other
135   immortals he himself is angered that in your heart's madness
you hold Hektor beside the curved ships and did not redeem him.
Come, then, give him up and accept ransom for the body."
Then in turn Achilleus of the swift feet answered her:
"So be it. He can bring the ransom and take off the body,
140   if the Olympian himself so urgently bids it."
So, where the ships were drawn together, the son and his mother
conversed at long length in winged words. But the son of Kronos
stirred Iris to go down to sacred Ilion, saying:
"Go forth, Iris the swift, leaving your place on Olympos,
145   and go to Priam of the great heart within Ilion, tell him
to ransom his dear son, going down to the ships of the Achaians
and bringing gifts to Achilleus which might soften his anger:
alone, let no other man of the Trojans go with him, but only
let one elder herald attend him, one who can manage
150   the mules and the easily running wagon, so he can carry
the dead man, whom great Achilleus slew, back to the city.
Let death not be a thought in his heart, let him have no fear;
such an escort shall I send to guide him, Argeïphontes
who shall lead him until he brings him to Achilleus. And after
155   he has brought him inside the shelter of Achilleus, neither
will the man himself kill him, but will hold back all the others,
for he is no witless man nor unwatchful, nor is he wicked,
but will in all kindness spare one who comes to him as a suppliant."
He spoke, and storm-footed Iris swept away with the message
160   and came to the house of Priam. There she found outcry and mourning.

The sons sitting around their father inside the courtyard
made their clothes sodden with their tears, and among them the old man
sat veiled, beaten into his mantle. Dung lay thick
on the head and neck of the aged man, for he had been rolling
165 in it, he had gathered and smeared it on with his hands. And his daughters
all up and down the house and the wives of his sons were mourning
as they remembered all those men in their numbers and valour
who lay dead, their lives perished at the hands of the Argives.
The messenger of Zeus stood beside Priam and spoke to him
170 in a small voice, and yet the shivers took hold of his body:
"Take heart, Priam, son of Dardanos, do not be frightened.
I come to you not eyeing you with evil intention
but with the purpose of good toward you. I am a messenger
of Zeus, who far away cares much for you and is pitiful.
175 The Olympian orders you to ransom Hektor the brilliant,
to bring gifts to Achilleus which may soften his anger:
alone, let no other man of the Trojans go with you, but only
let one elder herald attend you, one who can manage
the mules and the easily running wagon, so he can carry
180 the dead man, whom great Achilleus slew, back to the city.
Let death not be a thought in your heart, you need have no fear,
such an escort shall go with you to guide you, Argeïphontes
who will lead you till he brings you to Achilleus. And after
he has brought you inside the shelter of Achilleus, neither
185 will the man himself kill you but will hold back all the others;
for he is no witless man nor unwatchful, nor is he wicked
but will in all kindness spare one who comes to him as a suppliant."
    So Iris the swift-footed spoke and went away from him.
Thereupon he ordered his sons to make ready the easily rolling
190 mule wagon, and to fasten upon it the carrying basket.
He himself went into the storeroom, which was fragrant
and of cedar, and high-ceilinged, with many bright treasures inside it.
He called out to Hekabe his wife, and said to her:
"Dear wife, a messenger came to me from Zeus on Olympos,
195 that I must go to the ships of the Achaians and ransom my dear son,
bringing gifts to Achilleus which may soften his anger.
Come then, tell me. What does it seem best to your own mind
for me to do? My heart, my strength are terribly urgent
that I go there to the ships within the wide army of the Achaians."
200   So he spoke, and his wife cried out aloud, and answered him:
"Ah me, where has that wisdom gone for which you were famous
in time before, among outlanders and those you rule over?
How can you wish to go alone to the ships of the Achaians
before the eyes of a man who has slaughtered in such numbers
205 such brave sons of yours? The heart in you is iron. For if
he has you within his grasp and lays eyes upon you, that man
who is savage and not to be trusted will not take pity upon you
nor have respect for your rights. Let us sit apart in our palace
now, and weep for Hektor, and the way at the first strong Destiny

210   spun with his life line when he was born, when I gave birth to him,
that the dogs with their shifting feet should feed on him, far from his
        parents,
gone down before a stronger man; I wish I could set teeth
in the middle of his liver and eat it. That would be vengeance
for what he did to my son; for he slew him when he was no coward
215   but standing before the men of Troy and the deep-girdled women
of Troy, with no thought in his mind of flight or withdrawal."
       In turn the aged Priam, the godlike, answered her saying:
"Do not hold me back when I would be going, neither yourself be
a bird of bad omen in my palace. You will not persuade me.
220   If it had been some other who ordered me, one of the mortals,
one of those who are soothsayers, or priests, or diviners,
I might have called it a lie and we might rather have rejected it.
But now, for I myself heard the god and looked straight upon her,
I am going, and this word shall not be in vain. If it is my destiny
225   to die there by the ships of the bronze-armoured Achaians,
then I wish that. Achilleus can slay me at once, with my own son
caught in my arms, once I have my fill of mourning above him."
       He spoke, and lifted back the fair covering of his clothes-chest
and from inside took out twelve robes surpassingly lovely
230   and twelve mantles to be worn single, as many blankets,
as many great white cloaks, also the same number of tunics.
He weighed and carried out ten full talents of gold, and brought forth
two shining tripods, and four cauldrons, and brought out a goblet
of surpassing loveliness that the men of Thrace had given him
235   when he went to them with a message, but now the old man spared not
even this in his halls, so much was it his heart's desire
to ransom back his beloved son. But he drove off the Trojans
all from his cloister walks, scolding them with words of revilement:
"Get out, you failures, you disgraces. Have you not also
240   mourning of your own at home that you come to me with your sorrows?
Is it not enough that Zeus, son of Kronos, has given me sorrow
in losing the best of my sons? You also shall be aware of this
since you will be all the easier for the Achaians to slaughter
now he is dead. But, for myself, before my eyes look
245   upon this city as it is destroyed and its people are slaughtered,
my wish is to go sooner down to the house of the death god."
       He spoke, and went after the men with a stick, and they fled outside
before the fury of the old man. He was scolding his children
and cursing Helenos, and Paris, Agathon the brilliant,
250   Pammon and Antiphonos, Polites of the great war cry,
Deïphobos and Hippothoös and proud Dios. There were nine
sons to whom now the old man gave orders and spoke to them roughly:
"Make haste, wicked children, my disgraces. I wish all of you
had been killed beside the running ships in the place of Hektor.
255   Ah me, for my evil destiny. I have had the noblest
of sons in Troy, but I say not one of them is left to me,
Mestor like a god and Troilos whose delight was in horses,

and Hektor, who was a god among men, for he did not seem like
one who was child of a mortal man, but of a god. All these
260   Ares has killed, and all that are left me are the disgraces,
the liars and the dancers, champions of the chorus, the plunderers
of their own people in their land of lambs and kids. Well then,
will you not get my wagon ready and be quick about it,
and put all these things on it, so we can get on with our journey?"
265   So he spoke, and they in terror at the old man's scolding
hauled out the easily running wagon for mules, a fine thing
new-fabricated, and fastened the carrying basket upon it.
They took away from its peg the mule yoke made of boxwood
with its massive knob, well fitted with guiding rings, and brought forth
270   the yoke lashing (together with the yoke itself) of nine cubits
and snugged it well into place upon the smooth-polished wagon-pole
at the foot of the beam, then slipped the ring over the peg, and lashed it
with three turns on either side to the knob, and afterwards
fastened it all in order and secured it under a hooked guard.
275   Then they carried out and piled into the smooth-polished mule wagon
all the unnumbered spoils to be given for the head of Hektor,
then yoked the powerful-footed mules who pulled in the harness
and whom the Mysians gave once as glorious presents to Priam;
but for Priam they led under the yoke those horses the old man
280   himself had kept, and cared for them at his polished manger.
Now in the high house the yoking was done for the herald
and Priam, men both with close counsels in their minds. And now came
Hekabe with sorrowful heart and stood close beside them
carrying in her right hand the kind, sweet wine in a golden
285   goblet, so that before they went they might pour a drink-offering.
She stood in front of the horses, called Priam by name and spoke to him:
"Here, pour a libation to Zeus father, and pray you may come back
home again from those who hate you, since it seems the spirit
within you drives you upon the ships, though I would not have it.
290   Make your prayer then to the dark-misted, the son of Kronos
on Ida, who looks out on all the Troad, and ask him
for a bird of omen, a rapid messenger, which to his own mind
is dearest of all birds and his strength is the biggest, one seen
on the right, so that once your eyes have rested upon him
295   you can trust in him and go to the ships of the fast-mounted Danaans.
But if Zeus of the wide brows will not grant you his own messenger,
then I, for one, would never urge you on nor advise you
to go to the Argive ships, for all your passion to do it."
Then in answer to her again spoke Priam the godlike:
300   "My lady, I will not disregard this wherein you urge me.
It is well to lift hands to Zeus and ask if he will have mercy."
The old man spoke, and told the housekeeper who attended them
to pour unstained water over his hands. She standing beside them
and serving them held the washing-bowl in her hands, and a pitcher.
305   He washed his hands and took the cup from his wife. He stood up
in the middle of the enclosure, and prayed, and poured the wine out

looking up into the sky, and gave utterance and spoke, saying:
"Father Zeus, watching over us from Ida, most high, most honoured:
grant that I come to Achilleus for love and pity; but send me
310 a bird of omen, a rapid messenger which to your own mind
is dearest of all birds and his strength is biggest, one seen
on the right, so that once my eyes have rested upon him
I may trust in him and go to the ships of the fast-mounted Danaans."
So he spoke in prayer, and Zeus of the counsels heard him.
315 Straightway he sent down the most lordly of birds, an eagle,
the dark one, the marauder, called as well the black eagle.
And as big as is the build of the door to a towering chamber
in the house of a rich man, strongly fitted with bars, of such size
was the spread of his wings on either side. He swept through the city
320 appearing on the right hand, and the people looking upon him
were uplifted and the hearts made glad in the breasts of all of them.
Now in urgent haste the old man mounted into his chariot
and drove out through the forecourt and the thundering close. Before him
the mules hauled the wagon on its four wheels, Idaios
325 the sober-minded driving them, and behind him the horses
came on as the old man laid the lash upon them and urged them
rapidly through the town, and all his kinsmen were following
much lamenting, as if he went to his death. When the two men
had gone down through the city, and out, and come to the flat land,
330 the rest of them turned back to go to Ilion, the sons
and the sons-in-law. And Zeus of the wide brows failed not to notice
the two as they showed in the plain. He saw the old man and took pity
upon him, and spoke directly to his beloved son, Hermes:
"Hermes, for to you beyond all other gods it is dearest
335 to be man's companion, and you listen to whom you will, go now
on your way, and so guide Priam inside the hollow ships
of the Achaians, that no man shall see him, none be aware of him,
of the other Danaans, till he has come to the son of Peleus."
He spoke, nor disobeyed him the courier, Argeïphontes.
340 Immediately he bound upon his feet the fair sandals
golden and immortal, that carried him over the water
as over the dry land of the main abreast of the wind's blast.
He caught up the staff, with which he mazes the eyes of those mortals
whose eyes he would maze, or wakes again the sleepers. Holding
345 this in his hands, strong Argeïphontes winged his way onward
until he came suddenly to Troy and the Hellespont, and there
walked on, and there took the likeness of a young man, a noble,
with beard new grown, which is the most graceful time of young manhood.
Now when the two had driven past the great tomb of Ilos
350 they stayed their mules and horses to water them in the river,
for by this time darkness had descended on the land; and the herald
made out Hermes, who was coming toward them at a short distance.
He lifted his voice and spoke aloud to Priam: "Take thought,
son of Dardanos. Here is work for a mind that is careful.
355 I see a man; I think he will presently tear us to pieces.

Come then, let us run away with our horses, or if not, then
clasp his knees and entreat him to have mercy upon us."
    So he spoke, and the old man's mind was confused, he was badly
frightened, and the hairs stood up all over his gnarled body
360 and he stood staring, but the kindly god himself coming closer
took the old man's hand, and spoke to him and asked him a question:
"Where, my father, are you thus guiding your mules and horses
through the immortal night while other mortals are sleeping?
Have you no fear of the Achaians whose wind is fury,
365 who hate you, who are your enemies, and are near? For if one
of these were to see you, how you are conveying so many
treasures through the swift black night, what then could you think of?
You are not young yourself, and he who attends you is aged
for beating off any man who might pick a quarrel with you.
370 But I will do you no harm myself, I will even keep off
another who would. You seem to me like a beloved father."
    In answer to him again spoke aged Priam the godlike:
"Yes, in truth, dear child, all this is much as you tell me;
yet still there is some god who has held his hand above me,
375 who sent such a wayfarer as you to meet me, an omen
of good, for such you are by your form, your admired beauty
and the wisdom in your mind. Your parents are fortunate in you."
    Then in turn answered him the courier Argeïphontes:
"Yes, old sir, all this that you said is fair and orderly.
380 But come, tell me this thing and recite it to me accurately.
Can it be you convey these treasures in all their numbers and beauty
to outland men, so that they can be still kept safe for you?
Or are all of you by now abandoning sacred Ilion
in fear, such a one was he who died, the best man among you,
385 your son; who was never wanting when you fought against the Achaians."
    In answer to him again spoke aged Priam the godlike:
"But who are you, o best of men, and who are your parents?
Since you spoke of my ill-starred son's death, and with honour."
    Then in turn answered him the courier Argeïphontes:
390 "You try me out, aged sir. You ask me of glorious Hektor
whom many a time my eyes have seen in the fighting where men win
glory, as also on that time when he drove back the Argives
on their ships and kept killing them with the stroke of the sharp bronze,
and we stood by and wondered at him; for then Achilleus
395 would not let us fight by reason of his anger at Agamemnon.
For I am Achilleus' henchman, and the same strong-wrought vessel
brought us here; and I am a Myrmidon, and my father
is Polyktor; a man of substance, but aged, as you are.
He has six sons beside, and I am the seventh, and I shook
400 lots with the others, and it was my lot to come on this venture.
But now I have come to the plain away from the ships, for at daybreak
the glancing-eyed Achaians will do battle around the city.
They chafe from sitting here too long, nor have the Achaians'
kings the strength to hold them back as they break for the fighting."

405   In answer to him again spoke aged Priam the godlike:
"If then you are henchman to Peleïd Achilleus,
come, tell me the entire truth, and whether my son lies
still beside the ships, or whether by now he has been hewn
limb from limb and thrown before the dogs by Achilleus."
410   Then in turn answered him the courier Argeïphontes:
"Aged sir, neither have any dogs eaten him, nor have
the birds, but he lies yet beside the ship of Achilleus
at the shelters, and as he was; now here is the twelfth dawn
he has lain there, nor does his flesh decay, nor do worms feed
415 on him, they who devour men who have fallen in battle.
It is true, Achilleus drags him at random around his beloved
companion's tomb, as dawn on dawn appears, yet he cannot
mutilate him; you yourself can see when you go there
how fresh with dew he lies, and the blood is all washed from him,
420 nor is there any corruption, and all the wounds have been closed up
where he was struck, since many drove the bronze in his body.
So it is that the blessed immortals care for your son, though
he is nothing but a dead man; because in their hearts they loved him."
He spoke, and the old man was made joyful and answered him, saying:
425 "My child, surely it is good to give the immortals
their due gifts; because my own son, if ever I had one,
never forgot in his halls the gods who live on Olympos.
Therefore they remembered him even in death's stage. Come, then,
accept at my hands this beautiful drinking-cup, and give me
430 protection for my body, and with the gods' grace be my escort
until I make my way to the shelter of the son of Peleus."
In turn answered him the courier Argeïphontes:
"You try me out, aged sir, for I am young, but you will not
persuade me, telling me to accept your gifts when Achilleus
435 does not know. I fear him at heart and have too much reverence
to rob him. Such a thing might be to my sorrow hereafter.
But I would be your escort and take good care of you, even
till I came to glorious Argos in a fast ship or following
on foot, and none would fight you because he despised your escort."
440   The kind god spoke, and sprang up behind the horses and into
the chariot, and rapidly caught in his hands the lash and the guide reins,
and breathed great strength into the mules and horses. Now after
they had got to the fortifications about the ships, and the ditch, there
were sentries, who had just begun to make ready their dinner,
445 but about these the courier Argeïphontes drifted
sleep, on all, and quickly opened the gate, and shoved back
the door-bars, and brought in Priam and the glorious gifts on the wagon.
But when they had got to the shelter of Peleus' son: a towering
shelter the Myrmidons had built for their king, hewing
450 the timbers of pine, and they made a roof of thatch above it
shaggy with grass that they had gathered out of the meadows;
and around it made a great courtyard for their king, with hedgepoles
set close together; the gate was secured by a single door-piece

of pine, and three Achaians could ram it home in its socket
455 and three could pull back and open the huge door-bar; three other
Achaians, that is, but Achilleus all by himself could close it.
At this time Hermes, the kind god, opened the gate for the old man
and brought in the glorious gifts for Peleus' son, the swift-footed,
and dismounted to the ground from behind the horses, and spoke forth:
460 "Aged sir, I who came to you am a god immortal,
Hermes. My father sent me down to guide and go with you.
But now I am going back again, and I will not go in
before the eyes of Achilleus, for it would make others angry
for an immortal god so to face mortal men with favour.
465 But go you in yourself and clasp the knees of Peleion
and entreat him in the name of his father, the name of his mother
of the lovely hair, and his child, and so move the spirit within him."

So Hermes spoke, and went away to the height of Olympos,
but Priam vaulted down to the ground from behind the horses
470 and left Idaios where he was, for he stayed behind, holding
in hand the horses and mules. The old man made straight for the dwelling
where Achilleus the beloved of Zeus was sitting. He found him
inside, and his companions were sitting apart, as two only,
Automedon the hero and Alkimos, scion of Ares,
475 were busy beside him. He had just now got through with his dinner,
with eating and drinking, and the table still stood by. Tall Priam
came in unseen by the other men and stood close beside him
and caught the knees of Achilleus in his arms, and kissed the hands
that were dangerous and manslaughtering and had killed so many
480 of his sons. As when dense disaster closes on one who has murdered
a man in his own land, and he comes to the country of others,
to a man of substance, and wonder seizes on those who behold him,
so Achilleus wondered as he looked on Priam, a godlike
man, and the rest of them wondered also, and looked at each other.
485 But now Priam spoke to him in the words of a suppliant:
"Achilleus like the gods, remember your father, one who
is of years like mine, and on the door-sill of sorrowful old age.
And they who dwell nearby encompass him and afflict him,
nor is there any to defend him against the wrath, the destruction.
490 Yet surely he, when he hears of you and that you are still living,
is gladdened within his heart and all his days he is hopeful
that he will see his beloved son come home from the Troad.
But for me, my destiny was evil. I have had the noblest
of sons in Troy, but I say not one of them is left to me.
495 Fifty were my sons, when the sons of the Achaians came here.
Nineteen were born to me from the womb of a single mother,
and other women bore the rest in my palace; and of these
violent Ares broke the strength in the knees of most of them,
but one was left me who guarded my city and people, that one
500 you killed a few days since as he fought in defence of his country,
Hektor; for whose sake I come now to the ships of the Achaians
to win him back from you, and I bring you gifts beyond number.

Honour then the gods, Achilleus, and take pity upon me
remembering your father, yet I am still more pitiful;
505   I have gone through what no other mortal on earth has gone through;
I put my lips to the hands of the man who has killed my children."
    So he spoke, and stirred in the other a passion of grieving
for his own father. He took the old man's hand and pushed him
gently away, and the two remembered, as Priam sat huddled
510   at the feet of Achilleus and wept close for manslaughtering Hektor
and Achilleus wept now for his own father, now again
for Patroklos. The sound of their mourning moved in the house. Then
when great Achilleus had taken full satisfaction in sorrow
and the passion for it had gone from his mind and body, thereafter
515   he rose from his chair, and took the old man by the hand, and set him
on his feet again, in pity for the grey head and the grey beard,
and spoke to him and addressed him in winged words: "Ah, unlucky,
surely you have had much evil to endure in your spirit.
How could you dare to come alone to the ships of the Achaians
520   and before my eyes, when I am one who have killed in such numbers
such brave sons of yours? The heart in you is iron. Come, then,
and sit down upon this chair, and you and I will even let
our sorrows lie still in the heart for all our grieving. There is not
any advantage to be won from grim lamentation.
525   Such is the way the gods spun life for unfortunate mortals,
that we live in unhappiness, but the gods themselves have no sorrows.
There are two urns that stand on the door-sill of Zeus. They are unlike
for the gifts they bestow: an urn of evils, an urn of blessings.
If Zeus who delights in thunder mingles these and bestows them
530   on man, he shifts, and moves now in evil, again in good fortune.
But when Zeus bestows from the urn of sorrows, he makes a failure
of man, and the evil hunger drives him over the shining
earth, and he wanders respected neither of gods nor mortals.
Such were the shining gifts given by the gods to Peleus
535   from his birth, who outshone all men beside for his riches
and pride of possession, and was lord over the Myrmidons. Thereto
the gods bestowed an immortal wife on him, who was mortal.
But even on him the god piled evil also. There was not
any generation of strong sons born to him in his great house
540   but a single all-untimely child he had, and I give him
no care as he grows old, since far from the land of my fathers
I sit here in Troy, and bring nothing but sorrow to you and your children.
And you, old sir, we are told you prospered once; for as much
as Lesbos, Makar's hold, confines to the north above it
545   and Phrygia from the north confines, and enormous Hellespont,
of these, old sir, you were lord once in your wealth and your children.
But now the Uranian gods brought us, an affliction upon you,
forever there is fighting about your city, and men killed.
But bear up, nor mourn endlessly in your heart, for there is not
550   anything to be gained from grief for your son; you will never
bring him back; sooner you must go through yet another sorrow."

In answer to him again spoke aged Priam the godlike:
"Do not, beloved of Zeus, make me sit on a chair while Hektor
lies yet forlorn among the shelters; rather with all speed
555   give him back, so my eyes may behold him, and accept the ransom
we bring you, which is great. You may have joy of it, and go back
to the land of your own fathers, since once you have permitted me
to go on living myself and continue to look on the sunlight."
      Then looking darkly at him spoke swift-footed Achilleus:
560   "No longer stir me up, old sir. I myself am minded
to give Hektor back to you. A messenger came to me from Zeus,
my mother, she who bore me, the daughter of the sea's ancient.
I know you, Priam, in my heart, and it does not escape me
that some god led you to the running ships of the Achaians.
565   For no mortal would dare come to our encampment, not even
one strong in youth. He could not get by the pickets, he could not
lightly unbar the bolt that secures our gateway. Therefore
you must not further make my spirit move in my sorrows,
for fear, old sir, I might not let you alone in my shelter,
570   suppliant as you are; and be guilty before the god's orders."
      He spoke, and the old man was frightened and did as he told him.
The son of Peleus bounded to the door of the house like a lion,
nor went alone, but the two henchmen followed attending,
the hero Automedon and Alkimos, those whom Achilleus
575   honoured beyond all companions after Patroklos dead. These two
now set free from under the yoke the mules and the horses,
and led inside the herald, the old king's crier, and gave him
a chair to sit in, then from the smooth-polished mule wagon
lifted out the innumerable spoils for the head of Hektor,
580   but left inside it two great cloaks and a finespun tunic
to shroud the corpse in when they carried him home. Then Achilleus
called out to his serving-maids to wash the body and anoint it
all over; but take it first aside, since otherwise Priam
might see his son and in the heart's sorrow not hold in his anger
585   at the sight, and the deep heart in Achilleus be shaken to anger;
that he might not kill Priam and be guilty before the god's orders.
Then when the serving-maids had washed the corpse and anointed it
with olive oil, they threw a fair great cloak and a tunic
about him, and Achilleus himself lifted him and laid him
590   on a litter, and his friends helped him lift it to the smooth-polished
mule wagon. He groaned then, and called by name on his beloved
      companion:
"Be not angry with me, Patroklos, if you discover,
though you be in the house of Hades, that I gave back great Hektor
to his loved father, for the ransom he gave me was not unworthy.
595   I will give you your share of the spoils, as much as is fitting."
      So spoke great Achilleus and went back into the shelter
and sat down on the elaborate couch from which he had risen,
against the inward wall, and now spoke his word to Priam:
"Your son is given back to you, aged sir, as you asked it.

600 He lies on a bier. When dawn shows you yourself shall see him
as you take him away. Now you and I must remember our supper.
For even Niobe, she of the lovely tresses, remembered
to eat, whose twelve children were destroyed in her palace,
six daughters, and six sons in the pride of their youth, whom Apollo
605 killed with arrows from his silver bow, being angered
with Niobe, and shaft-showering Artemis killed the daughters;
because Niobe likened herself to Leto of the fair colouring
and said Leto had borne only two, she herself had borne many;
but the two, though they were only two, destroyed all those others.
610 Nine days long they lay in their blood, nor was there anyone
to bury them, for the son of Kronos made stones out of
the people; but on the tenth day the Uranian gods buried them.
But she remembered to eat when she was worn out with weeping.
And now somewhere among the rocks, in the lonely mountains,
615 in Sipylos, where they say is the resting place of the goddesses
who are nymphs, and dance beside the waters of Acheloios,
there, stone still, she broods on the sorrows that the gods gave her.
Come then, we also, aged magnificent sir, must remember
to eat, and afterwards you may take your beloved son back
620 to Ilion, and mourn for him; and he will be much lamented."
    So spoke fleet Achilleus and sprang to his feet and slaughtered
a gleaming sheep, and his friends skinned it and butchered it fairly,
and cut up the meat expertly into small pieces, and spitted them,
and roasted all carefully and took off the pieces.
625 Automedon took the bread and set it out on the table
in fair baskets, while Achilleus served the meats. And thereon
they put their hands to the good things that lay ready before them.
But when they had put aside their desire for eating and drinking,
Priam, son of Dardanos, gazed upon Achilleus, wondering
630 at his size and beauty, for he seemed like an outright vision
of gods. Achilleus in turn gazed on Dardanian Priam
and wondered, as he saw his brave looks and listened to him talking.
But when they had taken their fill of gazing one on the other,
first of the two to speak was the aged man, Priam the godlike:
635 "Give me, beloved of Zeus, a place to sleep presently, so that
we may even go to bed and take the pleasure of sweet sleep.
For my eyes have not closed underneath my lids since that time
when my son lost his life beneath your hands, but always
I have been grieving and brooding over my numberless sorrows
640 and wallowed in the muck about my courtyard's enclosure.
Now I have tasted food again and have let the gleaming
wine go down my throat. Before, I had tasted nothing."
    He spoke, and Achilleus ordered his serving-maids and companions
to make a bed in the porch's shelter and to lay upon it
645 fine underbedding of purple, and spread blankets above it
and fleecy robes to be an over-all covering. The maid-servants
went forth from the main house, and in their hands held torches,
and set to work, and presently had two beds made. Achilleus

of the swift feet now looked at Priam and said, sarcastic:
650 "Sleep outside, aged sir and good friend, for fear some Achaian
might come in here on a matter of counsel, since they keep coming
and sitting by me and making plans; as they are supposed to.
But if one of these come through the fleeting black night should notice you,
he would go straight and tell Agamemnon, shepherd of the people,
655 and there would be delay in the ransoming of the body.
But come, tell me this and count off for me exactly
how many days you intend for the burial of great Hektor.
Tell me, so I myself shall stay still and hold back the people."
    In answer to him again spoke aged Priam the godlike:
660 "If you are willing that we accomplish a complete funeral
for great Hektor, this, Achilleus, is what you could do and give
me pleasure. For you know surely how we are penned in our city,
and wood is far to bring in from the hills, and the Trojans are frightened
badly. Nine days we would keep him in our palace and mourn him,
665 and bury him on the tenth day, and the people feast by him,
and on the eleventh day we would make the grave-barrow for him,
and on the twelfth day fight again; if so we must do."
    Then in turn swift-footed brilliant Achilleus answered him:
"Then all this, aged Priam, shall be done as you ask it.
670 I will hold off our attack for as much time as you bid me."
    So he spoke, and took the aged king by the right hand
at the wrist, so that his heart might have no fear. Then these two,
Priam and the herald who were both men of close counsel,
slept in the place outside the house, in the porch's shelter;
675 but Achilleus slept in the inward corner of the strong-built shelter,
and at his side lay Briseis of the fair colouring.
    Now the rest of the gods and men who were lords of chariots
slept nightlong, with the easy bondage of slumber upon them,
only sleep had not caught Hermes the kind god, who pondered
680 now in his heart the problem of how to escort King Priam
from the ships and not be seen by the devoted gate-wardens.
He stood above his head and spoke a word to him, saying:
"Aged sir, you can have no thought of evil from the way
you sleep still among your enemies now Achilleus has left you
685 unharmed. You have ransomed now your dear son and given much for him.
But the sons you left behind would give three times as much ransom
for you, who are alive, were Atreus' son Agamemnon
to recognize you, and all the other Achaians learn of you."
    He spoke, and the old man was afraid, and wakened his herald,
690 and lightly Hermes harnessed for them the mules and the horses
and himself drove them through the encampment. And no man knew of
    them.
    But when they came to the crossing-place of the fair-running river,
of whirling Xanthos, a stream whose father was Zeus the immortal,
there Hermes left them and went away to the height of Olympos,
695 and dawn, she of the yellow robe, scattered over all earth,
and they drove their horses on to the city with lamentation

and clamour, while the mules drew the body. Nor was any other
aware of them at the first, no man, no fair-girdled woman,
only Kassandra, a girl like Aphrodite the golden,
700 who had gone up to the height of the Pergamos. She saw
her dear father standing in the chariot, his herald and crier
with him. She saw Hektor drawn by the mules on a litter.
She cried out then in sorrow and spoke to the entire city:
"Come, men of Troy and Trojan women; look upon Hektor
705 if ever before you were joyful when you saw him come back living
from battle; for he was a great joy to his city, and all his people."

She spoke, and there was no man left there in all the city
nor woman, but all were held in sorrow passing endurance.
They met Priam beside the gates as he brought the dead in.
710 First among them were Hektor's wife and his honoured mother
who tore their hair, and ran up beside the smooth-rolling wagon,
and touched his head. And the multitude, wailing, stood there about them.
And now and there in front of the gates they would have lamented
all day till the sun went down and let fall their tears for Hektor,
715 except that the old man spoke from the chariot to his people:
"Give me way to get through with my mules; then afterwards
you may sate yourselves with mourning, when I have him inside the
    palace."

So he spoke, and they stood apart and made way for the wagon.
And when they had brought him inside the renowned house, they laid him
720 then on a carved bed, and seated beside him the singers
who were to lead the melody in the dirge, and the singers
chanted the song of sorrow, and the women were mourning beside them.
Andromache of the white arms led the lamentation
of the women, and held in her arms the head of manslaughtering Hektor:
725 "My husband, you were lost young from life, and have left me
a widow in your house, and the boy is only a baby
who was born to you and me, the unhappy. I think he will never
come of age, for before then head to heel this city
will be sacked, for you, its defender, are gone, you who guarded
730 the city, and the grave wives, and the innocent children,
wives who before long must go away in the hollow ships,
and among them I shall also go, and you, my child, follow
where I go, and there do much hard work that is unworthy
of you, drudgery for a hard master; or else some Achaian
735 will take you by hand and hurl you from the tower into horrible
death, in anger because Hektor once killed his brother,
or his father, or his son; there were so many Achaians
whose teeth bit the vast earth, beaten down by the hands of Hektor.
Your father was no merciful man in the horror of battle.
740 Therefore your people are grieving for you all through their city,
Hektor, and you left for your parents mourning and sorrow
beyond words, but for me passing all others is left the bitterness
and the pain, for you did not die in bed, and stretch your arms to me,
nor tell me some last intimate word that I could remember

745   always, all the nights and days of my weeping for you."
        So she spoke in tears, and the women were mourning about her.
        Now Hekabe led out the thronging chant of their sorrow:
        "Hektor, of all my sons the dearest by far to my spirit;
        while you still lived for me you were dear to the gods, and even
750   in the stage of death they cared about you still. There were others
        of my sons whom at times swift-footed Achilleus captured,
        and he would sell them as slaves far across the unresting salt water
        into Samos, and Imbros, and Lemnos in the gloom of the mists. You,
        when he had taken your life with the thin edge of the bronze sword,
755   he dragged again and again around his beloved companion's
        tomb, Patroklos', whom you killed, but even so did not
        bring him back to life. Now you lie in the palace, handsome
        and fresh with dew, in the likeness of one whom he of the silver
        bow, Apollo, has attacked and killed with his gentle arrows."
760   So she spoke, in tears, and wakened the endless mourning.
        Third and last Helen led the song of sorrow among them:
        "Hektor, of all my lord's brothers dearest by far to my spirit:
        my husband is Alexandros, like an immortal, who brought me
        here to Troy; and I should have died before I came with him;
765   and here now is the twentieth year upon me since I came
        from the place where I was, forsaking the land of my fathers. In this time
        I have never heard a harsh saying from you, nor an insult.
        No, but when another, one of my lord's brothers or sisters, a fair-robed
        wife of some brother, would say a harsh word to me in the palace,
770   or my lord's mother—but his father was gentle always, a father
        indeed—then you would speak and put them off and restrain them
        by your own gentleness of heart and your gentle words. Therefore
        I mourn for you in sorrow of heart and mourn myself also
        and my ill luck. There was no other in all the wide Troad
775   who was kind to me, and my friend; all others shrank when they saw me."
        So she spoke in tears, and the vast populace grieved with her.
        Now Priam the aged king spoke forth his word to his people:
        "Now, men of Troy, bring timber into the city, and let not
        your hearts fear a close ambush of the Argives. Achilleus
780   promised me, as he sent me on my way from the black ships,
        that none should do us injury until the twelfth dawn comes."
        He spoke, and they harnessed to the wagons their mules and their oxen
        and presently were gathered in front of the city. Nine days
        they spent bringing in an endless supply of timber. But when
785   the tenth dawn had shone forth with her light upon mortals,
        they carried out bold Hektor, weeping, and set the body
        aloft a towering pyre for burning. And set fire to it.
        But when the young dawn showed again with her rosy fingers,
        the people gathered around the pyre of illustrious Hektor.
790   But when all were gathered to one place and assembled together,
        first with gleaming wine they put out the pyre that was burning,
        all where the fury of the fire still was in force, and thereafter
        the brothers and companions of Hektor gathered the white bones

up, mourning, as the tears swelled and ran down their cheeks. Then
795   they laid what they had gathered up in a golden casket
and wrapped this about with soft robes of purple, and presently
put it away in the hollow of the grave, and over it
piled huge stones laid close together. Lightly and quickly
they piled up the grave-barrow, and on all sides were set watchmen
800   for fear the strong-greaved Achaians might too soon set upon them.
They piled up the grave-barrow and went away, and thereafter
assembled in a fair gathering and held a glorious
feast within the house of Priam, king under God's hand.
   Such was their burial of Hektor, breaker of horses.

❧

RESONANCE

Filip Višnjić: The Death of Kraljević Marko[1]

Kraljević Marko arose early
On a Sunday before the bright sun,
On Mount Urvina beside the sea.
While Marko was on Urvina,
5   Šarac° began to stumble,   *his horse*
To stumble and to shed tears.
Marko was very troubled over this,
And Marko spoke to Šarac:
"Alas, Šarac, my dear stalwart!
10   It's been one hundred sixty years
Since I took up with you,
And you never tripped anywhere;
Now today you begin to stumble,
To stumble and to shed tears:
15   God knows this does not bode well!
It will sometime be on our heads,
On either mine or yours!"
As Marko was speaking these words,
A vila° from Mount Urvina hailed him,   *peasant*
20   And called out to Kraljević Marko:

---

1. Translated by John Miles Foley. For many centuries, illiterate Serbian bards such as Filip Višnjić (c. 1760–1830) maintained a major tradition of oral epic poetry concerning the heroic deeds of their ancestors. It was studying these poets' practices in the early 20th century that gave Milman Parry his pathbreaking insight into the oral composition of the Homeric epics 300 miles to the south. Given here is a scene from Višnjić's epic account of the life and death of Prince Marko, a 14th-century warrior who came to embody the long Serbian struggle for independence from Turkish rule. The poem was transcribed in 1815 by Vuk Karadžić, a founder of modern Serbian literature and a collector of old traditions.
   This scene uses oral techniques of repetition and the filling out of lines by stock phrases, and its themes echo moments of the *Iliad* as well: the address to the faithful horse, the arming scene in which the hero arms himself for battle (here, reversed as a disarming scene), and the scene of burial and mourning. The abbot who buries Marko prudently leaves his grave unmarked, to protect it from being despoiled by his enemies: the poem itself is the living monument to its hero's life.

"Blood-brother, Kraljević Marko,
Do you know, brother, why your horse stumbled?—
Šarac is mourning you, his master,
Because you two will soon be parted."
25   But Marko announced to the vila:
"White vila, curse your throat!
How should I part from Šarac,
Since I have passed through the land and towns,
And gone from east to west,
30   And there is no better horse than Šarac,
Nor any better hero than I!
I do not expect to be parted from Šarac
While my head is on my shoulders."
But the white vila responded to him:
35   "Blood-brother, Kraljević Marko,
No one will take Šarac from you,
Nor are you fated to die, Marko,
By means of a hero or a sharp saber,
By means of a mace or a war-lance:
40   You need fear no hero on earth;
But, wretched Marko, you shall die
At the hand of God, the old executioner.
If you do not believe me,
When you go to the top of the mountain,
45   You will look around from left to right,
Catch sight of two slim fir-trees
Which tower over the entire mountain,
Draping the peak in a green tapestry:
Between them is a spring of water,
50   You will direct Šarac to that place,
Dismount the horse, tie him to the fir,
Bend down over the spring, over the water,
And you will be looking at your own face;
Then you will see when you will die."
55   Marko took the vila's advice:
When he came to the top of the mountain,
He looked around from left to right,
Caught sight of two slim fir-trees
Which towered over the entire mountain,
60   Draping the peak in a green tapestry:
Then Marko directed Šarac to that place,
Dismounted the horse, tied him to the fir;
He bent down over the spring, over the water,
In the water he was looking at his own face:
65   And when Marko looked at his own face,
Marko saw when he would die;
He shed tears, then he spoke:
"O false world, my beautiful flower!

Beautiful you were, and I have walked but little,
70   But little, just three hundred years!
The time has come for me to change worlds."
Then Kraljević Marko drew it out,
Drew out his saber from his belt,
And he went to his horse Šarac,
75   Cut off Šarac's head with the saber,
So that Šarac would not fall into Turkish hands,
Not perform service for the Turks,
Not carry water or copper vessels.
And when Marko had beheaded Šarac,
80   He buried his horse Šarac,
Šarac better than his brother Andrija;
He broke his sharp saber in four pieces,
So the saber would not fall into Turkish hands,
So the Turks could not cherish it
85   Because it was left to them by Marko,
So that the Christians would not curse Marko.
And when Marko had broken the sharp saber,
He smashed his war-lance into seven pieces,
Then he threw it among the fir-branches;
90   Marko took his spiked mace,
He took it in his right hand,
Then he cast it from Mount Urvina
And into the blue, into the deep sea.
Then Marko called after the mace:
95   "When my mace issues forth from the sea,
Then let another such hero be born!"
When Marko had destroyed his arms,
He pulled a writing-box from his belt,
And from his pocket a clean sheet of paper;
100   Kraljević Marko wrote a letter:
"Whoever comes to Mount Urvina
To the cold spring between the fir-trees,
And there finds the hero Marko,
Let him know that Marko is dead!
105   Alongside Marko are three belts of riches,
Such riches, all golden ducats!
One belt I shall bestow on him
If he will bury my body;
Let the second belt adorn the churches;
110   The third belt to the lame and the blind:
Let the blind walk through the world,
Let them sing about and celebrate Marko!"[2]
When Marko had decorated the letter,

---

2. As in ancient Greece, Serbian bards were often blind men—including Filip Višnjić, the singer of this poem.

He tied the letter on a fir-branch,
115   Where it could be seen from the road;
He cast the gold writing-box into the spring;
Marko took off his green cloak,
Laid it on the grass under the fir-tree,
Made the sign of the cross, sat on the cloak,
120   Pulled his sable cap down over his eyes;
He lay down, he did not get back up.
The dead Marko was near the spring
From one day to the next for a week of days:
Whoever passed by on the wide road,
125   And caught sight of Kraljević Marko,
Thought to a man that Marko was sleeping there,
And so veered far around him,
For fear that he would be roused
Where there is fortune, there is also misfortune;
130   Where misfortune, also fortune:
And now all good fortune brought—
The abbot Vaso from Mount Athos,[3]
From the white church of Vilindar,
With his novice Isaiah.
135   When the abbot caught sight of Marko,
He reached for the deacon with his right hand:
"More softly, son, don't rouse him!—
For Marko is ill-tempered waking from a dream,
And he may kill us both."
140   Looking on while Marko slept, the monk
Caught sight of the letter above Marko,
He studied the letter in front of him:—
The letter said that this was Marko, dead.
Then the monk dismounted from his horse,
145   And took hold of the hero Marko,
But Marko had long since passed away.
Abbot Vaso shed tears,
For he sorrowed deeply over Marko;
He unbuckled the three belts of riches,
150   Unbuckled them, and buckled them on himself.
Abbot Vaso thought and thought
Where he might bury the dead Marko;
He thought and thought, then he made his decision:
He tied the dead Marko on his horse,
155   Then he bore him to the sea's shore,
Sat beside the dead Marko on a galley,
Took him straight to Mount Athos,
Took him to the church below Vilindar,
Bore him into the church at Vilindar;

---

3. A center of Eastern Orthodox monastic culture in northern Greece.

160   He read for Marko a service for the dead,
Sang a requiem for his body on earth
In the midst of the white church at Vilindar;
And then the old man buried Marko,
But he fixed no sign above him,
165   So that Marko's grave would not be known,
So that his enemies would not take revenge.

❧

The Odyssey[1]

BOOK 1. ATHENA INSPIRES THE PRINCE

Sing to me of the man, Muse,[2] the man of twists and turns
driven time and again off course, once he had plundered
the hallowed heights of Troy.
Many cities of men he saw and learned their minds,
5   many pains he suffered, heartsick on the open sea,
fighting to save his life and bring his comrades home.
But he could not save them from disaster, hard as he strove—
the recklessness of their own ways destroyed them all,
the blind fools, they devoured the cattle of the Sun
10   and the Sungod wiped from sight the day of their return.
Launch out on his story, Muse, daughter of Zeus,
start from where you will—sing for our time too.

                                 By now,
all the survivors, all who avoided headlong death
were safe at home, escaped the wars and waves.
15   But one man alone . . .
his heart set on his wife and his return—Calypso,
the bewitching nymph, the lustrous goddess, held him back,
deep in her arching caverns, craving him for a husband.
But then, when the wheeling seasons brought the year around,
20   that year spun out by the gods when he should reach his home,
Ithaca—though not even there would he be free of trials,
even among his loved ones—then every god took pity,
all except Poseidon.[3] He raged on, seething against
the great Odysseus till he reached his native land.

                                  But now
25   Poseidon had gone to visit the Ethiopians worlds away,
Ethiopians off at the farthest limits of mankind,
a people split in two, one part where the Sungod sets
and part where the Sungod rises. There Poseidon went
to receive an offering, bulls and rams by the hundred—

---

1. Translated by Robert Fagles.
2. Goddess of epic poetry, one of several Muses.
3. God of the sea, of earthquakes, and of horses.

30   far away at the feast the Sea-lord sat and took his pleasure.
      But the other gods, at home in Olympian Zeus's halls,
      met for full assembly there, and among them now
      the father of men and gods was first to speak,
      sorely troubled, remembering handsome Aegisthus,
35   the man Agamemnon's son, renowned Orestes, killed.
      Recalling Aegisthus, Zeus harangued the immortal powers:
      "Ah how shameless—the way these mortals blame the gods.
      From us alone, they say, come all their miseries, yes,
      but they themselves, with their own reckless ways,
40   compound their pains beyond their proper share.
      Look at Aegisthus now . . .
      above and beyond *his* share he stole Atrides'[4] wife,
      he murdered the warlord coming home from Troy
      though he knew it meant his own total ruin.
45   Far in advance we told him so ourselves,
      dispatching the guide, the giant-killer Hermes.[5]
      'Don't murder the man,' he said, 'don't court his wife.
      Beware, revenge will come from Orestes, Agamemnon's son,
      that day he comes of age and longs for his native land.'
50   So Hermes warned, with all the good will in the world,
      but would Aegisthus' hardened heart give way?
      Now he pays the price—all at a single stroke."

          And sparkling-eyed Athena drove the matter home:
      "Father, son of Cronus, our high and mighty king,
55   surely he goes down to a death he earned in full!
      Let them all die so, all who do such things.
      But my heart breaks for Odysseus,
      that seasoned veteran cursed by fate so long—
      far from his loved ones still, he suffers torments
60   off on a wave-washed island rising at the center of the seas.
      A dark wooded island, and there a goddess makes her home,
      a daughter of Atlas, wicked Titan who sounds the deep
      in all its depths, whose shoulders lift on high
      the colossal pillars thrusting earth and sky apart.
65   Atlas' daughter it is who holds Odysseus captive,
      luckless man—despite his tears, forever trying
      to spellbind his heart with suave, seductive words
      and wipe all thought of Ithaca from his mind.
      But he, straining for no more than a glimpse
70   of hearth-smoke drifting up from his own land,
      Odysseus longs to die . . .
                                  Olympian Zeus,
      have you no care for *him* in your lofty heart?
      Did he never win your favor with sacrifices
      burned beside the ships on the broad plain of Troy?

---

4. "Son of Atreus," Agamemnon.   5. Messenger god.

75   Why, Zeus, why so dead set against Odysseus?"

        "My child," Zeus who marshals the thunderheads replied,
        "what nonsense you let slip through your teeth. Now,
        how on earth could I forget Odysseus? Great Odysseus
        who excels all men in wisdom, excels in offerings too
80   he gives the immortal gods who rule the vaulting skies?
        No, it's the Earth-Shaker, Poseidon, unappeased,
        forever fuming against him for the Cyclops
        whose giant eye he blinded: godlike Polyphemus,
        towering over all the Cyclops' clans in power.
85   The nymph Thoosa bore him, daughter of Phorcys,
        lord of the barren salt sea—she met Poseidon
        once in his vaulted caves and they made love.
        And now for his blinded son the earthquake god—
        though he won't quite kill Odysseus—
90   drives him far off course from native land.
        But come, all of us here put heads together now,
        work out his journey home so Odysseus can return.
        Lord Poseidon, I trust, will let his anger go.
        How can he stand his ground against the will
95   of all the gods at once—one god alone?"

        Athena, her eyes flashing bright, exulted,
        "Father, son of Cronus, our high and mighty king!
        If now it really pleases the blissful gods
        that wise Odysseus shall return—home at last—
100   let us dispatch the guide and giant-killer Hermes
        down to Ogygia Island, down to announce at once
        to the nymph with lovely braids our fixed decree:
        Odysseus journeys home—the exile must return!
        While I myself go down to Ithaca, rouse his son
105   to a braver pitch, inspire his heart with courage
        to summon the flowing-haired Achaeans to full assembly,
        speak his mind to all those suitors, slaughtering on and on
        his droves of sheep and shambling longhorn cattle.
        Next I will send him off to Sparta and sandy Pylos,
110   there to learn of his dear father's journey home.
        Perhaps he will hear some news and make his name
        throughout the mortal world."
                                    So Athena vowed
        and under her feet she fastened the supple sandals,
        ever-glowing gold, that wing her over the waves
115   and boundless earth with the rush of gusting winds.
        She seized the rugged spear tipped with a bronze point—
        weighted, heavy, the massive shaft she wields to break the lines
        of heroes the mighty Father's daughter storms against.
        And down she swept from Olympus' craggy peaks
120   and lit on Ithaca, standing tall at Odysseus' gates,
        the threshold of his court. Gripping her bronze spear,

she looked for all the world like a stranger now,
like Mentes, lord of the Taphians.
There she found the swaggering suitors, just then
125 amusing themselves with rolling dice before the doors,
lounging on hides of oxen they had killed themselves.
While heralds and brisk attendants bustled round them,
some at the mixing-bowls, mulling wine and water,
others wiping the tables down with sopping sponges,
130 setting them out in place, still other servants
jointed and carved the great sides of meat.

First by far to see her was Prince Telemachus,
sitting among the suitors, heart obsessed with grief.
He could almost see his magnificent father, here . . .
135 in the mind's eye—if only *he* might drop from the clouds
and drive these suitors all in a rout throughout the halls
and regain his pride of place and rule his own domains!
Daydreaming so as he sat among the suitors,
he glimpsed Athena now
140 and straight to the porch he went, mortified
that a guest might still be standing at the doors.
Pausing beside her there, he clasped her right hand
and relieving her at once of her long bronze spear,
met her with winged words: "Greetings, stranger!
145 Here in our house you'll find a royal welcome.
Have supper first, then tell us what you need."

He led the way and Pallas Athena followed.
Once in the high-roofed hall, he took her lance
and fixed it firm in a burnished rack against
150 a sturdy pillar, there where row on row of spears,
embattled Odysseus' spears, stood stacked and waiting.
Then he escorted her to a high, elaborate chair of honor,
over it draped a cloth, and here he placed his guest
with a stool to rest her feet. But for himself
155 he drew up a low reclining chair beside her,
richly painted, clear of the press of suitors,
concerned his guest, offended by their uproar,
might shrink from food in the midst of such a mob.
He hoped, what's more, to ask her about his long-lost father.
160 A maid brought water soon in a graceful golden pitcher
and over a silver basin tipped it out
so they might rinse their hands,
then pulled a gleaming table to their side.
A staid housekeeper brought on bread to serve them,
165 appetizers aplenty too, lavish with her bounty.
A carver lifted platters of meat toward them,
meats of every sort, and set beside them golden cups
and time and again a page came round and poured them wine.

　　　But now the suitors trooped in with all their swagger
170　and took their seats on low and high-backed chairs.
　　　Heralds poured water over their hands for rinsing,
　　　serving maids brought bread heaped high in trays
　　　and the young men brimmed the mixing-bowls with wine.
　　　They reached out for the good things that lay at hand,
175　and when they'd put aside desire for food and drink
　　　the suitors set their minds on other pleasures,
　　　song and dancing, all that crowns a feast.
　　　A herald placed an ornate lyre in Phemius' hands,
　　　the bard who always performed among them there;
180　they forced the man to sing.
　　　　　　　　　　　　　　　A rippling prelude—
　　　and no sooner had he struck up his rousing song
　　　than Telemachus, head close to Athena's sparkling eyes,
　　　spoke low to his guest so no one else could hear:
　　　"Dear stranger, would you be shocked by what I say?
185　Look at them over there. Not a care in the world,
　　　just lyres and tunes! It's easy for them, all right,
　　　they feed on another's goods and go scot-free—
　　　a man whose white bones lie strewn in the rain somewhere,
　　　rotting away on land or rolling down the ocean's salty swells.
190　But that man—if they caught sight of him home in Ithaca,
　　　by god, they'd all pray to be faster on their feet
　　　than richer in bars of gold and heavy robes.
　　　But now, no use, he's died a wretched death.
　　　No comfort's left for us . . . not even if
195　someone, somewhere, says he's coming home.
　　　The day of his return will never dawn.
　　　　　　　　　　　　　　　　　　Enough.
　　　Tell me about yourself now, clearly, point by point.
　　　Who are you? where are you from? your city? your parents?
　　　What sort of vessel brought you? Why did the sailors
200　land you here in Ithaca? Who did they say they are?
　　　I hardly think you came this way on foot!
　　　And tell me this for a fact—I need to know—
　　　is this your first time here? Or are you a friend of father's,
　　　a guest from the old days? Once, crowds of other men
205　would come to our house on visits—visitor that he was,
　　　when he walked among the living."
　　　　　　　　　　　　　　　　　Her eyes glinting,
　　　goddess Athena answered, "My whole story, of course,
　　　I'll tell it point by point. Wise old Anchialus
　　　was my father. My own name is Mentes,
210　lord of the Taphian men who love their oars.
　　　And here I've come, just now, with ship and crew,
　　　sailing the wine-dark sea to foreign ports of call,
　　　to Temese, out for bronze—our cargo gleaming iron.

Our ship lies moored off farmlands far from town,
215   riding in Rithron Cove, beneath Mount Nion's woods.
        As for the ties between your father and myself,
        we've been friends forever, I'm proud to say,
        and he would bear me out
        if you went and questioned old lord Laertes.[6]
220   He, I gather, no longer ventures into town
        but lives a life of hardship, all to himself,
        off on his farmstead with an aged serving-woman
        who tends him well, who gives him food and drink
        when weariness has taken hold of his withered limbs
225   from hauling himself along his vineyard's steep slopes.
        And now I've come—and why? I heard that he was back . . .
        your father, that is. But no, the gods thwart his passage.
        Yet I tell you great Odysseus is not dead. He's still alive,
        somewhere in this wide world, held captive, out at sea
230   on a wave-washed island, and hard men, savages,
        somehow hold him back against his will.
                                                Wait,
        I'll make you a prophecy, one the immortal gods
        have planted in my mind—it will come true, I think,
        though I am hardly a seer or know the flights of birds.
235   He won't be gone long from the native land he loves,
        not even if iron shackles bind your father down.
        He's plotting a way to journey home at last;
        he's never at a loss.
                            But come, please,
        tell me about yourself now, point by point.
240   You're truly Odysseus' son? You've sprung up so!
        Uncanny resemblance . . . the head, and the fine eyes—
        I see him now. How often we used to meet in the old days
        before he embarked for Troy, where other Argive captains,
        all the best men, sailed in the long curved ships.
245   From then to this very day
        I've not set eyes on Odysseus or he on me."

        And young Telemachus cautiously replied,
        "I'll try, my friend, to give you a frank answer.
        Mother has always told me I'm his son, it's true,
250   but I am not so certain. Who, on his own,
        has ever really known who gave him life?
        Would to god I'd been the son of a happy man
        whom old age overtook in the midst of his possessions!
        Now, think of the most unlucky mortal ever born—
255   since you ask me, yes, they say I am his son."

---

6. Odysseus's father.

"Still," the clear-eyed goddess reassured him,
"trust me, the gods have not marked out your house
for such an unsung future,
not if Penelope has borne a son like you.

260   But tell me about all this and spare me nothing.
What's this banqueting, this crowd carousing here?
And what part do you play yourself? Some wedding-feast,
some festival? Hardly a potluck supper, I would say.
How obscenely they lounge and swagger here, look,

265   gorging in your house. Why, any man of sense
who chanced among them would be outraged,
seeing such behavior."
                                      Ready Telemachus
took her up at once: "Well, my friend,
seeing you want to probe and press the question,

270   once this house was rich, no doubt, beyond reproach
when the man you mentioned still lived here, at home.
Now the gods have reversed our fortunes with a vengeance—
wiped that man from the earth like no one else before.
I would never have grieved so much about his death

275   if he'd gone down with comrades off in Troy
or died in the arms of loved ones,
once he had wound down the long coil of war.
Then all united Achaea would have raised his tomb
and he'd have won his son great fame for years to come.

280   But now the whirlwinds have ripped him away, no fame for him!
He's lost and gone now—out of sight, out of mind—and I . . .
he's left me tears and grief. Nor do I rack my heart
and grieve for him alone. No longer. Now the gods
have invented other miseries to plague me.
                                                        Listen.

285   All the nobles who rule the islands round about,
Dulichion, and Same, and wooded Zacynthus too,
and all who lord it in rocky Ithaca as well—
down to the last man they court my mother,
they lay waste my house! And mother . . .

290   she neither rejects a marriage she despises
nor can she bear to bring the courting to an end—
while they continue to bleed my household white.
Soon—you wait—they'll grind *me* down as well."
                                                        "Shameful!"—
brimming with indignation, Pallas Athena broke out.

295   "Oh how much you need Odysseus, gone so long—
how *he*'d lay hands on all these brazen suitors!
If only he would appear, now,
at his house's outer gates and take his stand,
armed with his helmet, shield and pair of spears,

300   as strong as the man I glimpsed that first time

in our own house, drinking wine and reveling there . . .
just come in from Ephyra, visiting Ilus, Mermerus' son.
Odysseus sailed that way, you see, in his swift trim ship,
hunting deadly poison to smear on his arrows' bronze heads.
305   Ilus refused—he feared the wrath of the everlasting gods—
but father, so fond of him, gave him all he wanted.
If only *that* Odysseus sported with these suitors,
a blood wedding, a quick death would take the lot!
True, but all lies in the lap of the great gods,
310   whether or not he'll come and pay them back,
here, in his own house.
                But you, I urge you,
think how to drive these suitors from your halls.
Come now, listen closely. Take my words to heart.
At daybreak summon the island's lords to full assembly,
315   give your orders to all and call the gods to witness:
tell the suitors to scatter, each to his own place.
As for your mother, if the spirit moves her to marry,
let her go back to her father's house, a man of power.
Her kin will arrange the wedding, provide the gifts,
320   the array that goes with a daughter dearly loved.
                         For you,
I have some good advice, if only you will accept it.
Fit out a ship with twenty oars, the best in sight,
sail in quest of news of your long-lost father.
Someone may tell you something
325   or you may catch a rumor straight from Zeus,
rumor that carries news to men like nothing else.
First go down to Pylos, question old King Nestor,
then cross over to Sparta, to red-haired Menelaus,
of all the bronze-armored Achaeans the last man back.
330   Now, if you hear your father's alive and heading home,
hard-pressed as you are, brave out one more year.
If you hear he's dead, no longer among the living,
then back you come to the native land you love,
raise his grave-mound, build his honors high
335   with the full funeral rites that he deserves—
and give your mother to another husband.
                      Then,
once you've sealed those matters, seen them through,
think hard, reach down deep in your heart and soul
for a way to kill these suitors in your house,
340   by stealth or in open combat.
You must not cling to your boyhood any longer—
it's time you were a man. Haven't you heard
what glory Prince Orestes won throughout the world
when he killed that cunning, murderous Aegisthus,
345   who'd killed his famous father?
                    And you, my friend—

how tall and handsome I see you now—be brave, you too,
so men to come will sing your praises down the years.
But now I must go back to my swift trim ship
and all my shipmates, chafing there, I'm sure,
350 waiting for my return. It all rests with you.
Take my words to heart."
                                "Oh stranger,"
heedful Telemachus replied, "indeed I will.
You've counseled me with so much kindness now,
like a father to a son. I won't forget a word.
355 But come, stay longer, keen as you are to sail,
so you can bathe and rest and lift your spirits,
then go back to your ship, delighted with a gift,
a prize of honor, something rare and fine
as a keepsake from myself. The kind of gift
360 a host will give a stranger, friend to friend."

      Her eyes glinting, Pallas declined in haste:
"Not now. Don't hold me here. I long to be on my way.
As for the gift—whatever you'd give in kindness—
save it for my return so I can take it home.
365 Choose something rare and fine, and a good reward
that gift is going to bring you."
                                With that promise,
off and away Athena the bright-eyed goddess flew
like a bird in soaring flight
but left his spirit filled with nerve and courage,
370 charged with his father's memory more than ever now.
He felt his senses quicken, overwhelmed with wonder—
this was a god, he knew it well and made at once
for the suitors, a man like a god himself.
                                Amidst them still
the famous bard sang on, and they sat in silence, listening
375 as he performed The Achaeans' Journey Home from Troy:
all the blows Athena doomed them to endure.
                                And now,
from high above in her room and deep in thought,
she caught his inspired strains . . .
Icarius' daughter Penelope, wary and reserved,
380 and down the steep stair from her chamber she descended,
not alone: two of her women followed close behind.
That radiant woman, once she reached her suitors,
drawing her glistening veil across her cheeks,
paused now where a column propped the sturdy roof,
385 with one of her loyal handmaids stationed either side.
Suddenly, dissolving in tears and bursting through
the bard's inspired voice, she cried out, "Phemius!
So many other songs you know to hold us spellbound,
works of the gods and men that singers celebrate.

390 Sing one of those as you sit beside them here
and they drink their wine in silence.
                              But break off this song—
the unendurable song that always rends the heart inside me . . .
the unforgettable grief, it wounds me most of all!
How I long for my husband—alive in memory, always,
395 that great man whose fame resounds through Hellas
right to the depths of Argos!"
                              "Why, mother,"
poised Telemachus put in sharply, "why deny
our devoted bard the chance to entertain us
any way the spirit stirs him on?
400 Bards are not to blame—
Zeus is to blame. He deals to each and every
laborer on this earth whatever doom he pleases.
Why fault the bard if he sings the Argives' harsh fate?
It's always the latest song, the one that echoes last
405 in the listeners' ears, that people praise the most.
Courage, mother. Harden your heart, and listen.
Odysseus was scarcely the only one, you know,
whose journey home was blotted out at Troy.
Others, so many others, died there too.
                              So, mother,
410 go back to your quarters. Tend to your own tasks,
the distaff and the loom, and keep the women
working hard as well. As for giving orders,
men will see to that, but I most of all:
I hold the reins of power in this house."
                              Astonished,
415 she withdrew to her own room. She took to heart
the clear good sense in what her son had said.
Climbing up to the lofty chamber with her women,
she fell to weeping for Odysseus, her beloved husband,
till watchful Athena sealed her eyes with welcome sleep.

420   But the suitors broke into uproar through the shadowed halls,
all of them lifting prayers to lie beside her, share her bed,
until discreet Telemachus took command: "You suitors
who plague my mother, you, you insolent, overweening . . .
for this evening let us dine and take our pleasure,
425 no more shouting now. What a fine thing it is
to listen to such a bard as we have here—
the man sings like a god.
                              But at first light
we all march forth to assembly, take our seats
so I can give my orders and say to you straight out:
430 You must leave my palace! See to your feasting elsewhere,
devour your own possessions, house to house by turns.
But if you decide the fare is better, richer here,
destroying one man's goods and going scot-free,

all right then, carve away!
435 But I'll cry out to the everlasting gods in hopes
that Zeus will pay you back with a vengeance—all of you
destroyed in my house while I go scot-free myself!"

So Telemachus declared. And they all bit their lips,
amazed the prince could speak with so much daring.

440 Eupithes' son Antinous broke their silence:
"Well, Telemachus, only the gods could teach you
to sound so high and mighty! Such brave talk.
I pray that Zeus will never make *you* king of Ithaca,
though your father's crown is no doubt yours by birth."

445 But cool-headed Telemachus countered firmly:
"Antinous, even though my words may offend you,
I'd be happy to take the crown if Zeus presents it.
You think that nothing worse could befall a man?
It's really not so bad to be a king. All at once
450 your palace grows in wealth, your honors grow as well.
But there are hosts of other Achaean princes, look—
young and old, crowds of them on our island here—
and any one of the lot might hold the throne,
now great Odysseus is dead . . .
455 But I'll be lord of my own house and servants,
all that King Odysseus won for me by force."

And now Eurymachus, Polybus' son, stepped in:
"Surely this must lie in the gods' lap, Telemachus—
which Achaean will lord it over seagirt Ithaca.
460 Do hold on to your own possessions, rule your house.
God forbid that anyone tear your holdings from your hands
while men still live in Ithaca.
                              But about your guest,
dear boy, I have some questions. Where does he come from?
Where's his country, his birth, his father's old estates?
465 Did he bring some news of your father, his return?
Or did he come on business of his own?
How he leapt to his feet and off he went!
No waiting around for proper introductions.
And no mean man, not by the looks of him, I'd say."

470 "Eurymachus," Telemachus answered shrewdly,
"clearly my father's journey home is lost forever.
I no longer trust in rumors—rumors from the blue—
nor bother with any prophecy, when mother calls
some wizard into the house to ask him questions.
475 As for the stranger, though,
the man's an old family friend, from Taphos,
wise Anchialus' son. He says his name is Mentes,
lord of the Taphian men who love their oars."
                                        So he said

but deep in his mind he knew the immortal goddess.
480 Now the suitors turned to dance and song,
to the lovely beat and sway,
waiting for dusk to come upon them there . . .
and the dark night came upon them, lost in pleasure.
Finally, to bed. Each to his own house.
                                                    Telemachus,
485 off to his bedroom built in the fine courtyard—
a commanding, lofty room set well apart—
retired too, his spirit swarming with misgivings.
His devoted nurse attended him, bearing a glowing torch,
Eurycleia the daughter of Ops, Pisenor's son.
490 Laertes had paid a price for the woman years ago,
still in the bloom of youth. He traded twenty oxen,
honored her on a par with his own loyal wife at home
but fearing the queen's anger, never shared her bed.
She was his grandson's escort now and bore a torch,
495 for she was the one of all the maids who loved
the prince the most—she'd nursed him as a baby.
He spread the doors of his snug, well-made room,
sat down on the bed and pulled his soft shirt off,
tossed it into the old woman's conscientious hands,
500 and after folding it neatly, patting it smooth,
she hung it up on a peg beside his corded bed,
then padded from the bedroom,
drawing the door shut with the silver hook,
sliding the doorbolt home with its rawhide strap.
505 There all night long, wrapped in a sheep's warm fleece,
he weighed in his mind the course Athena charted.

Book 2. Telemachus Sets Sail

When young Dawn with her rose-red fingers shone once more
the true son of Odysseus sprang from bed and dressed,
over his shoulder he slung his well-honed sword,
fastened rawhide sandals under his smooth feet
5 and stepped from his bedroom, handsome as a god.
At once he ordered heralds to cry out loud and clear
and summon the flowing-haired Achaeans to full assembly.
Their cries rang out. The people filed in quickly.
When they'd grouped, crowding the meeting grounds,
10 Telemachus strode in too, a bronze spear in his grip
and not alone: two sleek hounds went trotting at his heels.
And Athena lavished a marvelous splendor on the prince
so the people all gazed in wonder as he came forward,
the elders making way as he took his father's seat.
15 The first to speak was an old lord, Aegyptius,
stooped with age, who knew the world by heart.

For one dear son had sailed with King Odysseus,
bound in the hollow ships to the stallion-land of Troy—
the spearman Antiphus—but the brutal Cyclops killed him,
20   trapped in his vaulted cave, the last man the monster ate.
Three other sons he had: one who mixed with the suitors,
Eurynomus, and two kept working their father's farms.
Still, he never forgot the soldier, desolate in his grief.
In tears for the son he lost, he rose and said among them,
25   "Hear me, men of Ithaca. Hear what I have to say.
Not once have we held assembly, met in session
since King Odysseus sailed away in the hollow ships.
Who has summoned us now—one of the young men,
one of the old-timers? What crisis spurs him on?
30   Some news he's heard of an army on the march,
word he's caught firsthand so he can warn us now?
Or some other public matter he'll disclose and argue?
He's a brave man, I'd say. God be with him, too!
May Zeus speed him on to a happy end,
35   whatever his heart desires!"
                                        Winning words
with a lucky ring. Odysseus' son rejoiced;
the boy could sit no longer—fired up to speak,
he took his stand among the gathered men.
The herald Pisenor, skilled in custom's ways,
40   put the staff in his hand, and then the prince,
addressing old Aegyptius first, led off with, "Sir,
that man is not far off—you'll soon see for yourself—
I was the one who called us all together.
Something wounds me deeply . . .
45   not news I've heard of an army on the march,
word I've caught firsthand so I can warn you now,
or some other public matter I'll disclose and argue.
No, the crisis is my own. Trouble has struck my house—
a double blow. First, I have lost my noble father
50   who ruled among you years ago, each of you here,
and kindly as a father to his children.
                                        But now this,
a worse disaster that soon will grind my house down,
ruin it all, and all my worldly goods in the bargain.
Suitors plague my mother—against her will—
55   sons of the very men who are your finest here!
They'd sooner die than approach her father's house
so Icarius himself might see to his daughter's bridal,
hand her to whom he likes, whoever meets his fancy.
Not they—they infest our palace day and night,
60   they butcher our cattle, our sheep, our fat goats,
feasting themselves sick, swilling our glowing wine
as if there's no tomorrow—all of it, squandered.

Now we have no man like Odysseus in command
to drive this curse from the house. We ourselves?
65   We're hardly the ones to fight them off. All we'd do
is parade our wretched weakness. A boy inept at battle.
Oh I'd swing to attack if I had the power in me.
By god, it's intolerable, what they do—disgrace,
my house a shambles!
                         You should be ashamed yourselves,
70   mortified in the face of neighbors living round about!
Fear the gods' wrath—before they wheel in outrage
and make these crimes recoil on your heads.
I beg you by Olympian Zeus, by Themis[1] too,
who sets assemblies free and calls us into session—
75   stop, my friends! Leave me alone to pine away in anguish . . .
Unless, of course, you think my noble father Odysseus
did the Achaean army damage, deliberate harm,
and to pay me back you'd do me harm, deliberately
setting these parasites against me. Better for me
80   if *you* were devouring all my treasure, all my cattle—
if you were the ones, we'd make amends in no time.
We'd approach you for reparations round the town,
demanding our goods till you'd returned the lot.
But now, look, you load my heart with grief—
85   there's nothing I can do!"
                                   Filled with anger,
down on the ground he dashed the speaker's scepter—
bursting into tears. Pity seized the assembly.
All just sat there, silent . . .
no one had the heart to reply with harshness.
90   Only Antinous, who found it in himself to say,
"So high and mighty, Telemachus—such unbridled rage!
Well now, fling your accusations at *us*?
Think to pin the blame on *us*? You think again.
It's not the suitors here who deserve the blame,
95   it's your own dear mother, the matchless queen of cunning.
Look here. For three years now, getting on to four,
she's played it fast and loose with all our hearts,
building each man's hopes—
dangling promises, dropping hints to each—
100   but all the while with something else in mind.
This was her latest masterpiece of guile:
she set up a great loom in the royal halls
and she began to weave, and the weaving finespun,
the yarns endless, and she would lead us on: 'Young men,
105   my suitors, now that King Odysseus is no more,
go slowly, keen as you are to marry me, until
I can finish off this web . . .

---

1. Goddess of justice, right, and law.

so my weaving won't all fray and come to nothing.
This is a shroud for old lord Laertes, for that day
110   when the deadly fate that lays us out at last will take him down.
I dread the shame my countrywomen would heap upon me,
yes, if a man of such wealth should lie in state
without a shroud for cover.'
                                              Her very words,
and despite our pride and passion we believed her.
115   So by day she'd weave at her great and growing web—
by night, by the light of torches set beside her,
she would unravel all she'd done. Three whole years
she deceived us blind, seduced us with this scheme . . .
Then, when the wheeling seasons brought the fourth year on,
120   one of her women, in on the queen's secret, told the truth
and we caught her in the act—unweaving her gorgeous web.
So she finished it off. Against her will. We forced her.

      Now Telemachus, here is how the suitors answer *you*—
you burn it in your mind, you and all our people:
125   send your mother back! Direct her to marry
whomever her father picks, whoever pleases her.
So long as she persists in tormenting us,
quick to exploit the gifts Athena gave her—
a skilled hand for elegant work, a fine mind
130   and subtle wiles too—we've never heard the like,
not even in old stories sung of all Achaea's
well-coifed queens who graced the years gone by:
Mycenae crowned with garlands, Tyro and Alcmena . . .
Not one could equal Penelope for intrigue
135   but in this case she intrigued beyond all limits.
So, we will devour your worldly goods and wealth
as long as *she* holds out, holds to that course
the gods have charted deep inside her heart.
Great renown she wins for herself, no doubt,
140   great loss for you in treasure. We'll not go back
to our old estates or leave for other parts,
not till she weds the Argive man she fancies."

      But with calm good sense Telemachus replied:
"Antinous, how can I drive my mother from our house
145   against her will, the one who bore me, reared me too?
My father is worlds away, dead or alive, who knows?
Imagine the high price I'd have to pay Icarius
if all on my own I send my mother home.
Oh what I would suffer from her father—
150   and some dark god would hurt me even more
when mother, leaving her own house behind,
calls down her withering Furies[2] on my head,

---

2. Earth goddesses who avenge crimes against family members.

and our people's cries of shame would hound my heels.
I will never issue that ultimatum to my mother.

155 And you, if you have any shame in your own hearts,
you must leave my palace! See to your feasting elsewhere,
devour your own possessions, house to house by turns.
But if you decide the fare is better, richer here,
destroying one man's goods and going scot-free,

160 all right then, carve away!
But I'll cry out to the everlasting gods in hopes
that Zeus will pay you back with a vengeance—all of you
destroyed in my house while I go scot-free myself!"

And to seal his prayer, farseeing Zeus sent down a sign.

165 He launched two eagles soaring high from a mountain ridge
and down they glided, borne on the wind's draft a moment,
wing to wingtip, pinions straining taut till just
above the assembly's throbbing hum they whirled,
suddenly, wings thrashing, wild onslaught of wings

170 and banking down at the crowd's heads—a glaring, fatal sign—
talons slashing each other, tearing cheeks and throats
they swooped away on the right through homes and city.
All were dumbstruck, watching the eagles trail from sight,
people brooding, deeply, what might come to pass . . .

175 Until the old warrior Halitherses,
Mastor's son, broke the silence for them—
the one who outperformed all men of his time
at reading bird-signs, sounding out the omens,
rose and spoke, distraught for each man there:

180 "Hear me, men of Ithaca! Hear what I have to say,
though my revelations strike the suitors first of all—
a great disaster is rolling like a breaker toward their heads.
Clearly Odysseus won't be far from loved ones any longer—
now, right now, he's somewhere near, I tell you,

185 breeding bloody death for all these suitors here,
pains aplenty too for the rest of us who live
in Ithaca's sunlit air.
                              Long before that,
we must put heads together, find some way
to stop these men, or let them stop themselves.

190 Better for them that way, by far. I myself
am no stranger to prophecy—I can see it now!
Odysseus . . . all is working out for him, I say,
just as I said it would that day the Argives sailed
for Troy and the mastermind of battle boarded with them.

195 I said then: after many blows, and all his shipmates lost,
after twenty years had wheeled by, he would come home,
unrecognized by all . . .
and now, look, it all comes to pass!"

                              "Stop, old man!"

Eurymachus, Polybus' son, rose up to take him on.
200   "Go home and babble your omens to your children—
save *them* from some catastrophe coming soon.
I'm a better hand than you at reading portents.
Flocks of birds go fluttering under the sun's rays,
not all are fraught with meaning. Odysseus?
205   He's dead now, far from home—
would to god that you'd died with him too.
We'd have escaped your droning prophecies then
and the way you've loosed the dogs of this boy's anger—
your eyes peeled for a house-gift he might give you.
210   Here's *my* prophecy, bound to come to pass.
If you, you old codger, wise as the ages,
talk him round, incite the boy to riot,
he'll be the first to suffer, let me tell you.
And you, old man, we'll clap some fine on you
215   you'll weep to pay, a fine to crush your spirit!
                                                    Telemachus?
Here in front of you all, here's my advice for him.
Let him urge his mother back to her father's house—
her kin will arrange the wedding, provide the gifts,
the array that goes with a daughter dearly loved.
220   Not till then, I'd say, will the island princes quit
their taxing courtship. Who's there to fear? I ask you.
Surely not Telemachus, with all his tiresome threats.
Nor do we balk, old man, at the prophecies you mouth—
they'll come to grief, they'll make us hate you more.
225   The prince's wealth will be devoured as always,
mercilessly—no reparations, ever . . . not
while the queen drags out our hopes to wed her,
waiting, day after day, all of us striving hard
to win one matchless beauty. Never courting others,
230   bevies of brides who'd suit each noble here."

        Telemachus answered, firm in his resolve:
"Eurymachus—the rest of you fine, brazen suitors—
I have done with appeals to you about these matters.
I'll say no more. The gods know how things stand
235   and so do all the Achaeans. And now all I ask
is a good swift ship and a crew of twenty men
to speed me through my passage out and back.
I'm sailing off to Sparta, sandy Pylos too,
for news of my long-lost father's journey home.
240   Someone may tell me something
or I may catch a rumor straight from Zeus,
rumor that carries news to men like nothing else.
Now, if I hear my father's alive and heading home,
hard-pressed as I am, I'll brave out one more year.
245   If I hear he's dead, no longer among the living,

then back I'll come to the native land I love,
raise his grave-mound, build his honors high
with the full funeral rites that he deserves—
and give my mother to another husband."
                                   A declaration,
250 and the prince sat down as Mentor took the floor,
Odysseus' friend-in-arms to whom the king,
sailing off to Troy, committed his household,
ordering one and all to obey the old man
and he would keep things steadfast and secure.
255 With deep concern for the realm, he rose and warned,
"Hear me, men of Ithaca. Hear what I have to say.
Never let any sceptered king be kind and gentle now,
not with all his heart, or set his mind on justice—
no, let him be cruel and always practice outrage.
260 Think: not one of the people whom he ruled
remembers Odysseus now, that godlike man,
and kindly as a father to his children!
I don't grudge these arrogant suitors for a moment,
weaving their violent work with all their wicked hearts—
265 they lay their lives on the line when they consume
Odysseus' worldly goods, blind in their violence,
telling themselves that he'll come home no more.
But all the rest of you, how you rouse my fury!
Sitting here in silence . . .
270 never a word put forth to curb these suitors,
paltry few as they are and you so many."
                                   "Mentor!"
Euenor's son Leocritus rounded on him, shouting,
"Rabble-rousing fool, now what's this talk?
Goading them on to try and hold us back!
275 It's uphill work, I warn you,
fighting a force like ours—for just a meal.
Even if Odysseus of Ithaca did arrive in person,
to find us well-bred suitors feasting in his halls,
and the man were hell-bent on routing us from the palace—
280 little joy would his wife derive from his return,
for all her yearning. Here on the spot he'd meet
a humiliating end if he fought against such odds.
You're talking nonsense—idiocy.
                                   No more. Come,
dissolve the assembly. Each man return to his holdings.
285 Mentor and Halitherses can speed our young prince on,
his father's doddering friends since time began.
He'll sit tight a good long while, I trust,
scrabbling for news right here in Ithaca—
he'll never make that trip."
290   This broke up the assembly, keen to leave.
The people scattered quickly, each to his own house,

while the suitors strolled back to King Odysseus' palace.

Telemachus, walking the beach now, far from others,
washed his hands in the foaming surf and prayed to Pallas:[3]
295   "Dear god, hear me! Yesterday you came to my house,
you told me to ship out on the misty sea and learn
if father, gone so long, is ever coming home . . .
Look how my countrymen—the suitors most of all,
the pernicious bullies—foil each move I make."

300   Athena came to his prayer from close at hand,
for all the world with Mentor's build and voice,
and she urged him on with winging words: "Telemachus,
you'll lack neither courage nor sense from this day on,
not if your father's spirit courses through your veins—
305   now there was a man, I'd say, in words and action both!
So how can your journey end in shipwreck or defeat?
Only if you were not his stock, Penelope's too,
then I'd fear your hopes might come to grief.
Few sons are the equals of their fathers;
310   most fall short, all too few surpass them.
But you, brave and adept from this day on—
Odysseus' cunning has hardly given out in you—
there's every hope that you will reach your goal.
Put them out of your mind, these suitors' schemes and plots.
315   They're madmen. Not a shred of sense or decency in the crowd.
Nor can they glimpse the death and black doom hovering
just at their heads to crush them all in one short day.
But you, the journey that stirs you now is not far off,
not with the likes of me, your father's friend and yours,
320   to rig you a swift ship and be your shipmate too.
Now home you go and mix with the suitors there.
But get your rations ready,
pack them all in vessels, the wine in jars,
and barley-meal—the marrow of men's bones—
325   in durable skins, while I make rounds in town
and quickly enlist your crew of volunteers.
Lots of ships in seagirt Ithaca, old and new.
I'll look them over, choose the best in sight,
we'll fit her out and launch her into the sea at once!"

330   And so Athena, daughter of Zeus, assured him.
No lingering now—he heard the goddess' voice—
but back he went to his house with aching heart
and there at the palace found the brazen suitors
skinning goats in the courtyard, singeing pigs for roasting.
335   Antinous, smiling warmly, sauntered up to the prince,
grasped his hand and coaxed him, savoring his name:

---

3. Athena, virgin and masculine goddess and protector of Odysseus.

"Telemachus, my high and mighty, fierce young friend,
no more nursing those violent words and actions now.
Come, eat and drink with us, just like the old days.
340   Whatever you want our people will provide. A ship
and a picked crew to speed you to holy Pylos,
out for the news about your noble father."

    But self-possessed Telemachus drew the line:
"Antinous, now how could I dine with you in peace
345   and take my pleasure? You ruffians carousing here!
Isn't it quite enough that you, my mother's suitors,
have ravaged it all, my very best, these many years,
while I was still a boy? But now that I'm full-grown
and can hear the truth from others, absorb it too—
350   now, yes, that the anger seethes inside me . . .
I'll stop at nothing to hurl destruction at your heads,
whether I go to Pylos or sit tight here at home.
But the trip I speak of will not end in failure.
Go I will, as a passenger, nothing more,
355   since I don't seem to command my own crew.
That, I'm sure, is the way that suits you best."

                                      With this
he nonchalantly drew his hand from Antinous' hand
while the suitors, busy feasting in the halls,
mocked and taunted him, flinging insults now.
360   "God help us," one young buck kept shouting,
"he wants to slaughter us all!
He's off to sandy Pylos to hire cutthroats,
even Sparta perhaps, so hot to have our heads.
Why, he'd rove as far as Ephyra's dark rich soil
365   and run back home with lethal poison, slip it
into the bowl and wipe us out with drink!"

    "Who knows?" another young blade up and ventured.
"Off in that hollow ship of his, he just might drown,
far from his friends, a drifter like his father.
370   What a bore! He'd double our work for us,
splitting up his goods, parceling out his house
to his mother and the man who weds the queen."

                                    So they scoffed
but Telemachus headed down to his father's storeroom,
broad and vaulted, piled high with gold and bronze,
375   chests packed with clothing, vats of redolent oil.
And there, standing in close ranks against the wall,
were jars of seasoned, mellow wine, holding the drink
unmixed inside them, fit for a god, waiting the day
Odysseus, worn by hardship, might come home again.
380   Doors, snugly fitted, doubly hung, were bolted shut
and a housekeeper was in charge by night and day—
her care, her vigilance, guarding all those treasures—

Eurycleia the daughter of Ops, Pisenor's son.
Telemachus called her into the storeroom: "Come, nurse,
385   draw me off some wine in smaller traveling jars,
mellow, the finest vintage you've been keeping,
next to what you reserve for our unlucky king—
in case Odysseus might drop in from the blue
and cheat the deadly spirits, make it home.
390   Fill me an even dozen, seal them tightly.
Pour me barley in well-stitched leather bags,
twenty measures of meal, your stone-ground best.
But no one else must know. These rations now,
put them all together. I'll pick them up myself,
395   toward evening, just about the time that mother
climbs to her room and thinks of turning in.
I'm sailing off to Sparta, sandy Pylos too,
for news of my dear father's journey home.
Perhaps I'll catch some rumor."
                          A wail of grief—
400   and his fond old nurse burst out in protest, sobbing:
"Why, dear child, what craziness got into your head?
Why bent on rambling over the face of the earth?—
a darling only son! Your father's worlds away,
god's own Odysseus, dead in some strange land.
405   And these brutes here, just wait, the moment you're gone
they'll all be scheming against you. Kill you by guile,
they will, and carve your birthright up in pieces.
No, sit tight here, guard your own things here.
Don't go roving over the barren salt sea—
410   no need to suffer so!"
                        "Courage, old woman,"
thoughtful Telemachus tried to reassure her,
"there's a god who made this plan.
But swear you won't say anything to my mother.
Not till ten or a dozen days have passed
415   or she misses me herself and learns I'm gone.
She mustn't mar her lovely face with tears."

    The old one swore a solemn oath to the gods
and vowing she would never breathe a word,
quickly drew off wine in two-eared jars
420   and poured barley in well-stitched leather bags.
Telemachus returned to the hall and joined the suitors.

    Then bright-eyed Pallas thought of one more step.
Disguised as the prince, the goddess roamed through town,
pausing beside each likely crewman, giving orders:
425   "Gather beside our ship at nightfall—be there."
She asked Noëmon, Phronius' generous son,
to lend her a swift ship. He gladly volunteered.

The sun sank and the roads of the world grew dark.
Now the goddess hauled the swift ship down to the water,
430   stowed in her all the tackle well-rigged vessels carry,
moored her well away at the harbor's very mouth
and once the crew had gathered, rallying round,
she heartened every man.

Then bright-eyed Pallas thought of one last thing.
435   Back she went to King Odysseus' halls and there
she showered sweet oblivion over the suitors,
dazing them as they drank, knocking cups from hands.
No more loitering now, their eyes weighed down with sleep,
they rose and groped through town to find their beds.
440   But calling the prince outside his timbered halls,
taking the build and voice of Mentor once again,
flashing-eyed Athena urged him on: "Telemachus,
your comrades-at-arms are ready at the oars,
waiting for your command to launch. So come,
445   on with our voyage now, we're wasting time."

And Pallas Athena sped away in the lead
as he followed in her footsteps, man and goddess.
Once they reached the ship at the water's edge
they found their long-haired shipmates on the beach.
450   The prince, inspired, gave his first commands:
"Come, friends, get the rations aboard!
They're piled in the palace now.
My mother knows nothing of this. No servants either.
Only one has heard our plan."
He led them back
455   and the men fell in and fetched down all the stores
and stowed them briskly, deep in the well-ribbed holds
as Odysseus' son directed. Telemachus climbed aboard.
Athena led the way, assuming the pilot's seat
reserved astern, and he sat close beside her.
460   Cables cast off, the crew swung to the oarlocks.
Bright-eyed Athena sent them a stiff following wind
rippling out of the west, ruffling over the wine-dark sea
as Telemachus shouted out commands to all his shipmates:
"All lay hands to tackle!" They sprang to orders,
465   hoisting the pinewood mast, they stepped it firm
in its block amidships, lashed it fast with stays
and with braided rawhide halyards hauled the white sail high.
Suddenly wind hit full and the canvas bellied out
and a dark blue wave, foaming up at the bow,
470   sang out loud and strong as the ship made way,
skimming the whitecaps, cutting toward her goal.
All running gear secure in the swift black craft,
they set up bowls and brimmed them high with wine
and poured libations out to the everlasting gods

475   who never die—to Athena first of all,
the daughter of Zeus with flashing sea-gray eyes—
and the ship went plunging all night long and through the dawn.

Book 3. King Nestor Remembers

As the sun sprang up, leaving the brilliant waters in its wake,
climbing the bronze sky to shower light on immortal gods
and mortal men across the plowlands ripe with grain—
the ship pulled into Pylos, Neleus' storied citadel,
5   where the people lined the beaches,
sacrificing sleek black bulls to Poseidon,
god of the sea-blue mane who shakes the earth.
They sat in nine divisions, each five hundred strong,
each division offering up nine bulls, and while the people
10   tasted the innards, burned the thighbones for the god,
the craft and crew came heading straight to shore.
Striking sail, furling it in the balanced ship,
they moored her well and men swung down on land.
Telemachus climbed out last, with Athena far in front
15   and the bright-eyed goddess urged the prince along:
"Telemachus, no more shyness, this is not the time!
We sailed the seas for this, for news of your father—
where does he lie buried? what fate did he meet?
So go right up to Nestor, breaker of horses.
20   We'll make him yield the secrets of his heart.
Press him yourself to tell the whole truth:
he'll never lie—the man is far too wise."

    The prince replied, wise in his own way too,
"How can I greet him, Mentor, even approach the king?
25   I'm hardly adept at subtle conversation.
Someone my age *might* feel shy, what's more,
interrogating an older man."
                                    "Telemachus,"
the bright-eyed goddess Athena reassured him,
"some of the words you'll find within yourself,
30   the rest some power will inspire you to say.
You least of all—I know—
were born and reared without the gods' good will."

    And Pallas Athena sped away in the lead
as he followed in her footsteps—man and goddess
35   gained the place where the Pylians met and massed.
There sat Nestor among his sons as friends around them
decked the banquet, roasted meats and skewered strips for broiling.
As soon as they saw the strangers, all came crowding down,
waving them on in welcome, urging them to sit.
40   Nestor's son Pisistratus, first to reach them,

grasped their hands and sat them down at the feast
on fleecy throws spread out along the sandbanks,
flanking his brother Thrasymedes and his father.
He gave them a share of innards, poured some wine
45   in a golden cup and, lifting it warmly toward Athena,
daughter of Zeus whose shield is storm and thunder,
greeted the goddess now with an invitation:
"Say a prayer to lord Poseidon, stranger,
his is the feast you've found on your arrival.
50   But once you've made your libation and your prayer—
all according to ancient custom—hand this cup
of hearty, seasoned wine to your comrade here
so he can pour forth too. He too, I think,
should pray to the deathless ones himself.
55   All men need the gods . . .
but the man is younger, just about my age.
That's why I give the gold cup first to you."
                                                With that
Pisistratus placed in her hand the cup of mellow wine
and Pallas rejoiced at the prince's sense of tact
60   in giving the golden winecup first to her.
At once she prayed intensely to Poseidon:
"Hear me, Sea-lord, you who embrace the earth—
don't deny our wishes, bring our prayers to pass!
First, then, to Nestor and all his sons grant glory.
65   Then to all these Pylians, for their splendid rites
grant a reward that warms their gracious hearts.
And last, Poseidon, grant Telemachus and myself
safe passage home, the mission accomplished
that sped us here in our rapid black ship."

70   So she prayed, and brought it all to pass.
She offered the rich two-handled cup to Telemachus,
Odysseus' son, who echoed back her prayer word for word.
They roasted the prime cuts, pulled them off the spits
and sharing out the portions, fell to the royal feast.
75   Once they'd put aside desire for food and drink,
old Nestor the noble charioteer began, at last:
"Now's the time, now they've enjoyed their meal,
to probe our guests and find out who they are.
Strangers—friends, who are you?
80   Where did you sail from, over the running sea-lanes?
Out on a trading spree or roving the waves like pirates,
sea-wolves raiding at will, who risk their lives
to plunder other men?"
                                    Poised Telemachus answered,
filled with heart, the heart Athena herself inspired,
85   to ask for the news about his father, gone so long,
and make his name throughout the mortal world.

"Nestor, son of Neleus, Achaea's pride and glory—
where are we from, you ask? I will tell you all.
We hail from Ithaca, under the heights of Nion.

90   Our mission here is personal, nothing public now.
I am on the trail of my father's widespread fame,
you see, searching the earth to catch some news
of great-hearted King Odysseus who, they say,
fought with you to demolish Troy some years ago.

95   About all the rest who fought the Trojans there,
we know where each one died his wretched death,
but father . . . even his death—
the son of Cronus shrouds it all in mystery.
No one can say for certain where he died,

100 whether he went down on land at enemy hands
or out on the open sea in Amphitrite's breakers.
That's why I've come to plead before you now,
if you can tell me about his cruel death:
perhaps you saw him die with your own eyes

105 or heard the wanderer's end from someone else.
More than all other men, that man was born for pain.
Don't soften a thing, from pity, respect for me—
tell me, clearly, all your eyes have witnessed.
I beg you—if ever my father, lord Odysseus,

110 pledged you his word and made it good in action
once on the fields of Troy where you Achaeans suffered,
remember his story now, tell *me* the truth."

     Nestor the noble charioteer replied at length:
"Ah dear boy, since you call back such memories,

115 such living hell we endured in distant Troy—
we headstrong fighting forces of Achaea—
so many raids from shipboard down the foggy sea,
cruising for plunder, wherever Achilles led the way;
so many battles round King Priam's walls we fought,

120 so many gone, our best and bravest fell.
There Ajax lies, the great man of war.
There lies Achilles too.
There Patroclus, skilled as the gods in counsel.
And there my own dear son, both strong and staunch,

125 Antilochus—lightning on his feet and every inch a fighter!
But so many other things we suffered, past that count—
what mortal in this wide world could tell it all?
Not if you sat and probed his memory, five, six years,
delving for all the pains our brave Achaeans bore there.

130 Your patience would fray, you'd soon head for home . . .

     Nine years we wove a web of disaster for those Trojans,
pressing them hard with every tactic known to man,
and only after we slaved did Zeus award us victory.

And no one there could hope to rival Odysseus,
135 not for sheer cunning—
at every twist of strategy he excelled us all.
Your father, yes, if you are in fact his son . . .
I look at you and a sense of wonder takes me.
Your way with words—it's just like his—I'd swear
140 no youngster could ever speak like you, so apt, so telling.
As long as I and great Odysseus soldiered there,
why, never once did we speak out at odds,
neither in open muster nor in royal council:
forever one in mind, in judgment balanced, shrewd,
145 we mapped our armies' plans so things might turn out best.
But then, once we'd sacked King Priam's craggy city,
Zeus contrived in his heart a fatal homeward run
for all the Achaeans who were fools, at least,
dishonest too, so many met a disastrous end,
150 thanks to the lethal rage
of the mighty Father's daughter. Eyes afire,
Athena set them feuding, Atreus' two sons[1] . . .
They summoned all the Achaean ranks to muster,
rashly, just at sunset—no hour to rally troops—
155 and in they straggled, sodden with wine, our heroes.
The brothers harangued them, told them why they'd met:
a crisis—Menelaus urging the men to fix their minds
on the voyage home across the sea's broad back,
but it brought no joy to Agamemnon, not at all.
160 He meant to detain us there and offer victims,
anything to appease Athena's dreadful wrath—
poor fool, he never dreamed Athena would not comply.
The minds of the everlasting gods don't change so quickly.
So the two of them stood there, wrangling, back and forth
165 till the armies sprang up, their armor clashing, ungodly uproar—
the two plans split the ranks. That night we barely slept,
seething with hard feelings against our own comrades,
for Zeus was brooding over us, poised to seal our doom . . .
At dawn, half of us hauled our vessels down to sea,
170 we stowed our plunder, our sashed and lovely women.
But half the men held back, camped on the beach,
waiting it out for Agamemnon's next commands
while our contingent embarked—
we pushed off and sailed at a fast clip
175 as a god smoothed out the huge troughing swells.
We reached Tenedos quickly, sacrificed to the gods,
the crews keen for home, but a quick return was not
in Zeus's plans, not yet: that cruel power
loosed a cursed feud on us once again.

1. Agamemnon and Menelaus.

180 Some swung their rolling warships hard about—
Odysseus sailed them back, the flexible, wily king,
veering over to Agamemnon now to shore his fortunes up.
But not I. Massing the ships that came in my flotilla,
I sped away as the god's mischief kept on brewing,
185 dawning on me now. And Tydeus' fighting son
Diomedes fled too, rousing all his comrades.
Late in the day the red-haired Menelaus joined us,
overtook us at Lesbos, debating the long route home:
whether to head north, over the top of rocky Chios,
190 skirting Psyrie, keeping that island off to port
or run south of Chios, by Mimas' gusty cape.
We asked the god for a sign. He showed us one,
he urged us to cut out on the middle passage,
straight to Euboea now,
195 escape a catastrophe, fast as we could sail!
A shrilling wind came up, stiff, driving us on
and on we raced, over the sea-lanes rife with fish
and we made Geraestus Point in the dead of night.
Many thighs of bulls we offered Poseidon there—
200 thank god we'd crossed that endless reach of sea.
Then on the fourth day out the crews of Diomedes,
breaker of horses, moored their balanced ships
at Argos port, but I held course for Pylos, yes,
and never once did the good strong wind go limp
205 from the first day the god unleashed its blast.

     And so, dear boy, I made it home from Troy,
in total ignorance, knowing nothing of their fates,
the ones who stayed behind:
who escaped with their lives and who went down.
210 But still, all I've gathered by hearsay, sitting here
in my own house—that you'll learn, it's only right,
I'll hide nothing now.
                              They say the Myrmidons,
those savage spearmen led by the shining son
of lionhearted Achilles, traveled home unharmed.
215 Philoctetes the gallant son of Poias, safe as well.
Idomeneus brought his whole contingent back to Crete,
all who'd escaped the war—the sea snatched none from him.
But Atreus' son Agamemnon . . . you yourselves, even
in far-off Ithaca, must have heard how he returned,
220 how Aegisthus hatched the king's horrendous death.
But what a price he paid, in blood, in suffering.
Ah how fine it is, when a man is brought down,
to leave a son behind! Orestes took revenge,
he killed that cunning, murderous Aegisthus,
225 who'd killed his famous father.
                              And you, my friend—

how tall and handsome I see you now—be brave, you too,
so men to come will sing your praises down the years."

    Telemachus, weighing the challenge closely, answered,
"Oh Nestor, son of Neleus, Achaea's pride and glory,
230   what a stroke of revenge that was! All Achaeans
will spread Orestes' fame across the world,
a song for those to come.
If only the gods would arm me in such power
I'd take revenge on the lawless, brazen suitors
235   riding roughshod over me, plotting reckless outrage.
But for me the gods have spun out no such joy,
for my father or myself. I must bear up,
that's all."
                And the old charioteer replied,
"Now that you mention it, dear boy, I do recall
240   a mob of suitors, they say, besets your mother
there in your own house, against your will,
and plots your ruin. Tell me, though, do you
let yourself be so abused, or do people round about,
stirred up by the prompting of some god, despise you now?
245   Who knows if he will return someday to take revenge
on all their violence? Single-handed perhaps
or with an Argive army at his back? If only
the bright-eyed goddess chose to love you just
as she lavished care on brave Odysseus, years ago
250   in the land of Troy where we Achaeans struggled!
I've never seen the immortals show so much affection
as Pallas openly showed *him,* standing by your father—
if only she'd favor you, tend you with all her heart,
many a suitor then would lose all thought of marriage,
255   blotted out forever."
                      "Never, your majesty,"
Telemachus countered gravely, "that will never
come to pass, I know. What you say dumbfounds me,
staggers imagination! Hope, hope as I will,
that day will never dawn . . .
260   not even if the gods should will it so."
                          "Telemachus!"
Pallas Athena broke in sharply, her eyes afire—
"What's this nonsense slipping through your teeth?
It's light work for a willing god to save a mortal
even half the world away. Myself, I'd rather
265   sail through years of trouble and labor home
and see that blessed day, than hurry home
to die at my own hearth like Agamemnon,
killed by Aegisthus' cunning—by his own wife.
But the great leveler, Death: not even the gods
270   can defend a man, not even one they love, that day

when fate takes hold and lays him out at last."

                                "Mentor,"
wise Telemachus said, "distraught as we are for him,
let's speak of this no more. My father's return?
It's inconceivable now. Long ago the undying gods

275   have sealed his death, his black doom. But now
there's another question I would put to Nestor:
Nestor excels all men for sense and justice,
his knowledge of the world.
Three generations he has ruled, they say,

280   and to my young eyes he seems a deathless god!
Nestor, son of Neleus, tell me the whole story—
how did the great king Agamemnon meet his death?
Where was Menelaus? What fatal trap did he set,
that treacherous Aegisthus, to bring down a man

285   far stronger than himself? Was Menelaus gone
from Achaean Argos, roving the world somewhere,
so the coward found the nerve to kill the king?"

    And old Nestor the noble charioteer replied:
"Gladly, my boy, I'll tell you the story first to last . . .

290   Right you are, you guess what would have happened
if red-haired Menelaus, arriving back from Troy,
had found Aegisthus alive in Agamemnon's palace.
No barrow piled high on the earth for *his* dead body,
no, the dogs and birds would have feasted on his corpse,

295   sprawled on the plain outside the city gates, and no one,
no woman in all Achaea, would have wept a moment,
such a monstrous crime the man contrived!
But there we were, camped at Troy, battling out
the long hard campaign while he at his ease at home,

300   in the depths of Argos, stallion-country—he lay siege
to the wife of Agamemnon, luring, enticing her with talk.
At first, true, she spurned the idea of such an outrage,
Clytemnestra the queen, her will was faithful still.
And there was a man, what's more, a bard close by,

305   to whom Agamemnon, setting sail for Troy,
gave strict commands to guard his wife. But then,
that day the doom of the gods had bound her to surrender,
Aegisthus shipped the bard away to a desert island,
marooned him there, sweet prize for the birds of prey,

310   and swept her off to his own house, lover lusting for lover.
And many thighbones he burned on the gods' holy altars,
many gifts he hung on the temple walls—gold, brocades—
in thanks for a conquest past his maddest hopes.
                                  Now we,
you see, were sailing home from Troy in the same squadron,

315   Menelaus and I, comrades-in-arms from years of war.
But as we rounded holy Sounion, Athens' headland,

lord Apollo[2] attacked Atrides' helmsman, aye,
with his gentle shafts he shot the man to death—
an iron grip on the tiller, the craft scudding fast—
320 Phrontis, Onetor's son, who excelled all men alive
at steering ships when gales bore down in fury.
So Menelaus, straining to sail on, was held back
till he could bury his mate with fitting rites.
But once he'd got off too, plowing the wine-dark sea
325 in his ribbed ships, and made a run to Malea's beetling cape,
farseeing Zeus decided to give the man rough sailing,
poured a hurricane down upon him, shrilling winds,
giant, rearing whitecaps, monstrous, mountains high.
There at a stroke he cut the fleet in half and drove
330 one wing to Crete, where Cydonians make their homes
along the Iardanus River. Now, there's a sheer cliff
plunging steep to the surf at the farthest edge of Gortyn,
out on the mist-bound sea, where the South Wind piles breakers,
huge breakers, left of the headland's horn, toward Phaestos,
335 with only a low reef to block the crushing tides.
In they sailed, and barely escaped their death—
the ships' crews, that is—
the rollers smashed their hulls against the rocks.
But as for the other five with pitch-black prows,
340 the wind and current swept them on toward Egypt.

     So Menelaus, amassing a hoard of stores and gold,
was off cruising his ships to foreign ports of call
while Aegisthus hatched his vicious work at home.
Seven years he lorded over Mycenae rich in gold,
345 once he'd killed Agamemnon—he ground the people down.
But the eighth year ushered in his ruin, Prince Orestes
home from Athens, yes, he cut him down, that cunning,
murderous Aegisthus, who'd killed his famous father.
Vengeance done, he held a feast for the Argives,
350 to bury his hated mother, craven Aegisthus too,
the very day Menelaus arrived, lord of the warcry,
freighted with all the wealth his ships could carry.
                                                    So you,
dear boy, take care. Don't rove from home too long,
too far, leaving your own holdings unprotected—
355 crowds in your palace so brazen
they'll carve up all your wealth, devour it all,
and then your journey here will come to nothing.
Still I advise you, urge you to visit Menelaus.
He's back from abroad at last, from people so removed
360 you might abandon hope of ever returning home,

---

2. Archer god of prophecy, disease, healing, poetry, and music.

once the winds had driven you that far off course,
into a sea so vast not even cranes could wing their way
in one year's flight—so vast it is, so awesome . . .

So, off you go with your ships and shipmates now.
365   Or if you'd rather go by land, there's team and chariot,
my sons at your service too, and they'll escort you
to sunny Lacedaemon,[3] home of the red-haired king.
Press him yourself to tell the whole truth:
he'll never lie—the man is far too wise."

                     So he closed
370   as the sun set and darkness swept across the earth
and the bright-eyed goddess Pallas spoke for all:
"There was a tale, old soldier, so well told.
Come, cut out the victims' tongues and mix the wine,
so once we've poured libations out to the Sea-lord
375   and every other god, we'll think of sleep. High time—
the light's already sunk in the western shadows.
It's wrong to linger long at the gods' feast;
we must be on our way."

                     Zeus's daughter—
they all hung closely on every word she said.
380   Heralds sprinkled water over their hands for rinsing,
the young men brimmed the mixing bowls with wine,
they tipped first drops for the god in every cup
then poured full rounds for all. They rose and flung
the victims' tongues on the fire and poured libations out.
385   When they'd poured, and drunk to their hearts' content,
Athena and Prince Telemachus both started up
to head for their ship at once.
But Nestor held them there, objecting strongly:
"Zeus forbid—and the other deathless gods as well—
390   that you resort to your ship and put my house behind
like a rank pauper's without a stitch of clothing,
no piles of rugs, no blankets in his place
for host and guests to slumber soft in comfort.
Why, I've plenty of fine rugs and blankets here.
395   No, by god, the true son of my good friend Odysseus
won't bed down on a ship's deck, not while I'm alive
or my sons are left at home to host our guests,
whoever comes to our palace, newfound friends."

                     "Dear old man,
you're right," Athena exclaimed, her eyes brightening now.
400   "Telemachus should oblige you. Much the better way.
Let him follow you now, sleep in your halls,
but I'll go back to our trim black ship,

hearten the crew and give each man his orders.
I'm the only veteran in their ranks, I tell you.
405   All the rest, of an age with brave Telemachus,
are younger men who sailed with him as friends.
I'll bed down there by the dark hull tonight,
at dawn push off for the proud Cauconians.
Those people owe me a debt long overdue,
410   and no mean sum, believe me.
But you, seeing my friend is now your guest,
speed him on his way with a chariot and your son
and give him the finest horses that you have,
bred for stamina, trained to race the wind."

415   With that the bright-eyed goddess winged away
in an eagle's form and flight.
Amazement fell on all the Achaeans there.
The old king, astonished by what he'd seen,
grasped Telemachus' hand and cried out to the prince,
420   "Dear boy—never fear you'll be a coward or defenseless,
not if at your young age the gods will guard you so.
Of all who dwell on Olympus, this was none but she,
Zeus's daughter, the glorious one, his third born,
who prized your gallant father among the Argives.
425   Now, O Queen, be gracious! Give us high renown,
myself, my children, my loyal wife and queen.
And I will make you a sacrifice, a yearling heifer
broad in the brow, unbroken, never yoked by men.
I'll offer it up to you—I'll sheathe its horns in gold."

430   So he prayed, and Pallas Athena heard his prayer.
And Nestor the noble chariot-driver led them on,
his sons and sons-in-law, back to his regal palace.
Once they reached the storied halls of the aged king
they sat on rows of low and high-backed chairs.
435   As they arrived the old man mixed them all a bowl,
stirring the hearty wine, seasoned eleven years
before a servant broached it, loosed its seal.
Mulling it in the bowl, old Nestor poured
a libation out, praying hard to Pallas Athena,
440   daughter of Zeus whose shield is storm and thunder.

        Once they had poured their offerings, drunk their fill,
the Pylians went to rest, each in his own house.
But the noble chariot-driver let Telemachus,
King Odysseus' son, sleep at the palace now,
445   on a corded bed inside the echoing colonnade,
with Prince Pisistratus close beside him there,
the young spearman, already captain of armies,
though the last son still unwed within the halls.
The king retired to chambers deep in his lofty house

450   where the queen his wife arranged and shared their bed.

         When young Dawn with her rose-red fingers shone once more
         old Nestor the noble chariot-driver climbed from bed,
         went out and took his seat on the polished stones,
         a bench glistening white, rubbed with glossy oil,
455   placed for the king before his looming doors.
         There Neleus held his sessions years ago,
         a match for the gods in counsel,
         but his fate had long since forced him down to Death.
         Now royal Nestor in turn, Achaea's watch and ward,
460   sat there holding the scepter while his sons,
         coming out of their chambers, clustered round him,
         hovering near: Echephron, Stratius, Perseus
         and Aretus, Thrasymedes like a god, and sixth,
         young lord Pisistratus came to join their ranks.
465   They escorted Prince Telemachus in to sit beside them.
         Nestor, noble charioteer, began the celebration:
         "Quickly, my children, carry out my wishes now
         so I may please the gods, Athena first of all—
         she came to me at Poseidon's flowing feast,
470   Athena in all her glory!
         Now someone go to the fields to fetch a heifer,
         lead her here at once—a herdsman drive her in.
         Someone hurry down to Prince Telemachus' black ship
         and bring up all his crewmen, leave just two behind.
475   And another tell our goldsmith, skilled Laerces,
         to come and sheathe the heifer's horns in gold.
         The rest stay here together. Tell the maids
         inside the hall to prepare a sumptuous feast—
         bring seats and firewood, bring pure water too."

480   They all pitched in to carry out his orders.
         The heifer came from the fields, the crewmen came
         from brave Telemachus' ship, and the smith came in
         with all his gear in hand, the tools of his trade,
         the anvil, hammer and well-wrought tongs he used
485   for working gold. And Athena came as well
         to attend her sacred rites.
         The old horseman passed the gold to the smith,
         and twining the foil, he sheathed the heifer's horns
         so the goddess' eyes might dazzle, delighted with the gift.
490   Next Stratius and Echephron led the beast by the horns.
         Aretus, coming up from the storeroom, brought them
         lustral water filling a flower-braided bowl,
         in his other hand, the barley in a basket.
         Thrasymedes, staunch in combat, stood ready,
495   whetted ax in his grasp to cut the heifer down,
         and Perseus held the basin for the blood.

Now Nestor the old charioteer began the rite.
Pouring the lustral water, scattering barley-meal,
he lifted up his ardent prayers to Pallas Athena,
500   launching the sacrifice, flinging onto the fire
the first tufts of hair from the victim's head.

Prayers said, the scattering barley strewn,
suddenly Nestor's son impetuous Thrasymedes
strode up close and struck—the ax chopped
505   the neck tendons through—
                          and the blow stunned
the heifer's strength—
                     The women shrilled their cry,
Nestor's daughters, sons' wives and his own loyal wife
Eurydice, Clymenus' eldest daughter. Then, hoisting up
the victim's head from the trampled earth, they held her fast
510   as the captain of men Pisistratus slashed her throat.
Dark blood gushed forth, life ebbed from her limbs—
they quartered her quickly, cut the thighbones out
and all according to custom wrapped them round in fat,
a double fold sliced clean and topped with strips of flesh.
515   And the old king burned these over dried split wood
and over the fire poured out glistening wine
while young men at his side held five-pronged forks.
Once they'd burned the bones and tasted the organs,
they sliced the rest into pieces, spitted them on skewers
520   and raising points to the fire, broiled all the meats.

During the ritual lovely Polycaste, youngest daughter
of Nestor, Neleus' son, had bathed Telemachus.
Rinsing him off now, rubbing him down with oil,
she drew a shirt and handsome cape around him.
525   Out of his bath he stepped, glistening like a god,
strode in and sat by the old commander Nestor.

They roasted the prime cuts, pulled them off the spits
and sat down to the feast while ready stewards saw
to rounds of wine and kept the gold cups flowing.
530   When they'd put aside desire for food and drink,
Nestor the noble chariot-driver issued orders:
"Hurry, my boys! Bring Telemachus horses,
a good full-maned team—
hitch them to a chariot—he must be off at once."

535   They listened closely, snapped to his commands
and hitched a rapid team to a chariot's yoke in haste.
A housekeeper stowed some bread and wine aboard
and meats too, food fit for the sons of kings.
Telemachus vaulted onto the splendid chariot—
540   right beside him Nestor's son Pisistratus,
captain of armies, boarded, seized the reins,

whipped the team to a run and on the horses flew,
holding nothing back, out into open country,
leaving the heights of Pylos fading in their trail,
545   shaking the yoke across their shoulders all day long.

   The sun sank and the roads of the world grew dark
as they reached Phera, pulling up to Diocles' halls,
the son of Ortilochus, son of the Alpheus River.
He gave them a royal welcome; there they slept the night.

550   When young Dawn with her rose-red fingers shone once more
they yoked their pair again, mounted the blazoned car
and out through the gates and echoing colonnade
they whipped the team to a run and on they flew,
holding nothing back—and the princes reached
555   the wheatlands, straining now for journey's end,
so fast those purebred stallions raced them on
as the sun sank and the roads of the world grew dark.

BOOK 4. THE KING AND QUEEN OF SPARTA

At last they gained the ravines of Lacedaemon ringed by hills
and drove up to the halls of Menelaus in his glory.
They found the king inside his palace, celebrating
with throngs of kinsmen a double wedding-feast
5   for his son and lovely daughter. The princess
he was sending on to the son of great Achilles,
breaker of armies. Years ago Menelaus vowed,
he nodded assent at Troy and pledged her hand
and now the gods were sealing firm the marriage.
10   So he was sending her on her way with team and chariot,
north to the Myrmidons' famous city governed by her groom.
From Sparta he brought Alector's daughter as the bride
for his own full-grown son, the hardy Megapenthes,
born to him by a slave. To Helen the gods had granted
15   no more offspring once she had borne her first child,
the breathtaking Hermione,
a luminous beauty gold as Aphrodite.
                                        So now
they feasted within the grand, high-roofed palace,
all the kin and clansmen of Menelaus in his glory,
20   reveling warmly here as in their midst
an inspired bard sang out and struck his lyre—
and through them a pair of tumblers dashed and sprang,
whirling in leaping handsprings, leading on the dance.

   The travelers, Nestor's shining son and Prince Telemachus,
25   had brought themselves and their horses to a standstill
just outside the court when good lord Eteoneus,
passing through the gates now, saw them there,

and the ready aide-in-arms of Menelaus
took the message through his sovereign's halls
30   and stepping close to his master broke the news:
"Strangers have just arrived, your majesty, Menelaus.
Two men, but they look like kin of mighty Zeus himself.
Tell me, should we unhitch their team for them
or send them to someone free to host them well?"

35   The red-haired king took great offense at that:
"Never a fool before, Eteoneus, son of Boëthous,
now I see you're babbling like a child!
Just think of all the hospitality *we* enjoyed
at the hands of other men before we made it home,
40   and god save us from such hard treks in years to come.
Quick, unhitch their team. And bring them in,
strangers, guests, to share our flowing feast."

        Back through the halls he hurried, calling out
to other brisk attendants to follow quickly.
45   They loosed the sweating team from under the yoke,
tethered them fast by reins inside the horse-stalls,
tossing feed at their hoofs, white barley mixed with wheat,
and canted the chariot up against the polished walls,
shimmering in the sun, then ushered in their guests,
50   into that magnificent place. Both struck by the sight,
they marveled up and down the house of the warlord dear to Zeus—
a radiance strong as the moon or rising sun came flooding
through the high-roofed halls of illustrious Menelaus.
Once they'd feasted their eyes with gazing at it all,
55   into the burnished tubs they climbed and bathed.
When women had washed them, rubbed them down with oil
and drawn warm fleece and shirts around their shoulders,
they took up seats of honor next to Atrides Menelaus.
A maid brought water soon in a graceful golden pitcher
60   and over a silver basin tipped it out
so they might rinse their hands,
then pulled a gleaming table to their side.
A staid housekeeper brought on bread to serve them,
appetizers aplenty too, lavish with her bounty.
65   As a carver lifted platters of meat toward them,
meats of every sort, and set before them golden cups,
the red-haired king Menelaus greeted both guests warmly:
"Help yourselves to food, and welcome! Once you've dined
we'll ask you who you are. But your parents' blood
70   is hardly lost in you. You must be born of kings,
bred by the gods to wield the royal scepter.
No mean men could sire sons like you."
                                        With those words
he passed them a fat rich loin with his own hands,
the choicest part, that he'd been served himself.

75   They reached for the good things that lay outspread
         and when they'd put aside desire for food and drink,
         Telemachus, leaning his head close to Nestor's son,
         spoke low to the prince so no one else could hear:
         "Look, Pisistratus—joy of my heart, my friend—
80   the sheen of bronze, the blaze of gold and amber,
         silver, ivory too, through all this echoing mansion!
         Surely Zeus's court on Olympus must be just like this,
         the boundless glory of all this wealth inside!
         My eyes dazzle . . . I am struck with wonder."

85   But the red-haired warlord overheard his guest
         and cut in quickly with winged words for both:
         "No man alive could rival Zeus, dear boys,
         with his everlasting palace and possessions.
         But among men, I must say, few if any
90   could rival *me* in riches. Believe me,
         much I suffered, many a mile I roved to haul
         such treasures home in my ships. Eight years out,
         wandering off as far as Cyprus, Phoenicia,[1] even Egypt,
         I reached the Ethiopians, Sidonians, Erembians—Libya too,
95   where lambs no sooner spring from the womb than they grow horns.
         Three times in the circling year the ewes give birth.
         So no one, neither king nor shepherd could want
         for cheese or mutton, or sweet milk either,
         udders swell for the sucklings round the year.

100   But while I roamed those lands, amassing a fortune,
         a stranger killed my brother, blind to the danger, duped blind—
         thanks to the cunning of his cursed, murderous queen!
         So I rule all this wealth with no great joy.
         You must have heard my story from your fathers,
105   whoever they are—what hardships I endured,
         how I lost this handsome palace built for the ages,
         filled to its depths with hoards of gorgeous things.
         Well, would to god I'd stayed right here in my own house
         with a third of all that wealth and they were still alive,
110   all who died on the wide plain of Troy those years ago,
         far from the stallion-land of Argos.
                                           And still,
         much as I weep for all my men, grieving sorely,
         time and again, sitting here in the royal halls,
         now indulging myself in tears, now brushing tears away—
115   the grief that numbs the spirit gluts us quickly—
         for none of all those comrades, pained as I am,
         do I grieve as much for one . . .
         that man who makes sleep hateful, even food,
         as I pore over his memory. No one, no Achaean

---

1. Modern Syria, Lebanon, and Galilee.

120　　labored hard as Odysseus labored or achieved so much.
　　　And how did his struggles end? In suffering for that man;
　　　for me, in relentless, heartbreaking grief for him,
　　　lost and gone so long now—dead or alive, who knows?
　　　How they must mourn him too, Laertes, the old man,
125　　and self-possessed Penelope. Telemachus as well,
　　　the boy he left a babe in arms at home."
　　　　　　　　　　　　　　　　　　　Such memories
　　　stirred in the young prince a deep desire to grieve
　　　for Odysseus. Tears streamed down his cheeks
　　　and wet the ground when he heard his father's name,
130　　both hands clutching his purple robe before his eyes.
　　　Menelaus recognized him at once but pondered
　　　whether to let him state his father's name
　　　or probe him first and prompt him step by step.

　　　　　While he debated all this now within himself,
135　　Helen emerged from her scented, lofty chamber—
　　　striking as Artemis with her golden shafts—
　　　and a train of women followed . . .
　　　Adreste drew up her carved reclining-chair,
　　　Alcippe brought a carpet of soft-piled fleece,
140　　Phylo carried her silver basket given by Alcandre,
　　　King Polybus' wife, who made his home in Egyptian Thebes
　　　where the houses overflow with the greatest troves of treasure.
　　　The king gave Menelaus a pair of bathing-tubs in silver,
　　　two tripods, ten bars of gold, and apart from these
145　　his wife presented Helen her own precious gifts:
　　　a golden spindle, a basket that ran on casters,
　　　solid silver polished off with rims of gold.
　　　Now Phylo her servant rolled it in beside her,
　　　heaped to the brim with yarn prepared for weaving;
150　　the spindle swathed in violet wool lay tipped across it.
　　　Helen leaned back in her chair, a stool beneath her feet,
　　　and pressed her husband at once for each detail:
　　　"Do we know, my lord Menelaus, who our visitors
　　　claim to be, our welcome new arrivals?
155　　Right or wrong, what can I say? My heart tells me
　　　to come right out and say I've never seen such a likeness,
　　　neither in man nor woman—I'm amazed at the sight.
　　　To the life he's like the son of great Odysseus,
　　　surely he's Telemachus! The boy that hero left
160　　a babe in arms at home when all you Achaeans
　　　fought at Troy, launching your headlong battles
　　　just for *my* sake, shameless whore that I was."

　　　　　"My dear, my dear," the red-haired king assured her,
　　　"now that you mention it, I see the likeness too . . .
165　　Odysseus' feet were like the boy's, his hands as well,
　　　his glancing eyes, his head, and the fine shock of hair.

Yes, and just now, as I was talking about Odysseus,
remembering how he struggled, suffered, all for me,
a flood of tears came streaming down his face
170 and he clutched his purple robe before his eyes."

"Right you are"—Pisistratus stepped in quickly—
"son of Atreus, King Menelaus, captain of armies:
here is the son of that great hero, as you say.
But the man is modest, he would be ashamed
175 to make a show of himself, his first time here,
and interrupt you. We delight in your voice
as if some god were speaking!
The noble horseman Nestor sent me along
to be his escort. Telemachus yearned to see you,
180 so you could give him some advice or urge some action.
When a father's gone, his son takes much abuse
in a house where no one comes to his defense.
So with Telemachus now. His father's gone.
No men at home will shield him from the worst."

185 "Wonderful!" the red-haired king cried out.
"The son of my dearest friend, here in my own house!
That man who performed a hundred feats of arms for me.
And I swore that when he came I'd give him a hero's welcome,
him above all my comrades—if only Olympian Zeus,
190 farseeing Zeus, had granted us both safe passage
home across the sea in our swift trim ships.
Why, I'd have settled a city in Argos for him,
built him a palace, shipped him over from Ithaca,
him and all his wealth, his son, his people too—
195 emptied one of the cities nestling round about us,
one I rule myself. Both fellow-countrymen then,
how often we'd have mingled side-by-side!
Nothing could have parted us,
bound by love for each other, mutual delight . . .
200 till death's dark cloud came shrouding round us both.
But god himself, jealous of all this, no doubt,
robbed that unlucky man, him and him alone,
of the day of his return."
                                         So Menelaus mused
and stirred in them all a deep desire to grieve.
205 Helen of Argos, daughter of Zeus, dissolved in tears,
Telemachus wept too, and so did Atreus' son Menelaus.
Nor could Nestor's son Pisistratus stay dry-eyed,
remembering now his gallant brother Antilochus,
cut down by Memnon,[2] splendid son of the Morning.
210 Thinking of him, the young prince broke out:

2. King of Ethiopia.

"Old Nestor always spoke of you, son of Atreus,
as the wisest man of all the men he knew,
whenever we talked about you there at home,
questioning back and forth. So now, please,
215   if it isn't out of place, indulge me, won't you?
Myself, I take no joy in weeping over supper.
Morning will soon bring time enough for that.
Not that I'd grudge a tear
for any man gone down to meet his fate.
220   What other tribute can we pay to wretched men
than to cut a lock, let tears roll down our cheeks?
And I have a brother of my own among the dead,
and hardly the poorest soldier in our ranks.
You probably knew him. I never met him, never
225   saw him myself. But they say he outdid our best,
Antilochus—lightning on his feet and every inch a fighter!"

        "Well said, my friend," the red-haired king replied.
"Not even an older man could speak and do as well.
Your father's son you are—your words have all his wisdom.
230   It's easy to spot the breed of a man whom Zeus
has marked for joy in birth and marriage both.
Take great King Nestor now:
Zeus has blessed him, all his livelong days,
growing rich and sleek in his old age at home,
235   his sons expert with spears and full of sense.
Well, so much for the tears that caught us just now;
let's think again of supper. Come, rinse our hands.
Tomorrow, at dawn, will offer me and Telemachus
time to talk and trade our thoughts in full."

240   Asphalion quickly rinsed their hands with water,
another of King Menelaus' ready aides-in-arms.
Again they reached for the good things set before them.

        Then Zeus's daughter Helen thought of something else.
Into the mixing-bowl from which they drank their wine
245   she slipped a drug, heart's-ease, dissolving anger,
magic to make us all forget our pains . . .
No one who drank it deeply, mulled in wine,
could let a tear roll down his cheeks that day,
not even if his mother should die, his father die,
250   not even if right before his eyes some enemy brought down
a brother or darling son with a sharp bronze blade.
So cunning the drugs that Zeus's daughter plied,
potent gifts from Polydamna the wife of Thon,
a woman of Egypt, land where the teeming soil
255   bears the richest yield of herbs in all the world:
many health itself when mixed in the wine,
and many deadly poison.

Every man is a healer there, more skilled
than any other men on earth—Egyptians born
260   of the healing god himself. So now Helen, once
she had drugged the wine and ordered winecups filled,
resuming the conversation, entertained the group:
"My royal king Menelaus—welcome guests here,
sons of the great as well! Zeus can present us
265   times of joy and times of grief in turn:
all lies within his power.
So come, let's sit back in the palace now,
dine and warm our hearts with the old stories.
I will tell something perfect for the occasion.
270   Surely I can't describe or even list them all,
the exploits crowding fearless Odysseus' record,
but what a feat that hero dared and carried off
in the land of Troy where you Achaeans suffered!
Scarring his own body with mortifying strokes,
275   throwing filthy rags on his back like any slave,
he slipped into the enemy's city, roamed its streets—
all disguised, a totally different man, a beggar,
hardly the figure he cut among Achaea's ships.
That's how Odysseus infiltrated Troy,
280   and no one knew him at all . . .
I alone, I spotted him for the man he was,
kept questioning him—the crafty one kept dodging.
But after I'd bathed him, rubbed him down with oil,
given him clothes to wear and sworn a binding oath
285   not to reveal him as Odysseus to the Trojans, not
till he was back at his swift ships and shelters,
then at last he revealed to me, step by step,
the whole Achaean strategy. And once he'd cut
a troop of Trojans down with his long bronze sword,
290   back he went to his comrades, filled with information.
The rest of the Trojan women shrilled their grief. Not I:
my heart leapt up—
                              my heart had changed by now—
                                                        I yearned
to sail back home again! I grieved too late for the madness
Aphrodite[3] sent me, luring me there, far from my dear land,
295   forsaking my own child, my bridal bed, my husband too,
a man who lacked for neither brains nor beauty."

    And the red-haired Menelaus answered Helen:
"There was a tale, my lady. So well told.
Now then, I have studied, in my time,
300   the plans and minds of great ones by the score.

---

3. Goddess of physical love.

And I have traveled over a good part of the world
but never once have I laid eyes on a man like him—
what a heart that fearless Odysseus had inside him!
What a piece of work the hero dared and carried off
305   in the wooden horse where all our best encamped,
our champions armed with bloody death for Troy . . .
when along you came, Helen—roused, no doubt,
by a dark power bent on giving Troy some glory,
and dashing Prince Deiphobus squired your every step.
310   Three times you sauntered round our hollow ambush,
feeling, stroking its flanks,
challenging all our fighters, calling each by name—
yours was the voice of all our long-lost wives!
And Diomedes and I, crouched tight in the midst
315   with great Odysseus, hearing you singing out,
were both keen to spring up and sally forth
or give you a sudden answer from inside,
but Odysseus damped our ardor, reined us back.
Then all the rest of the troops kept stock-still,
320   all but Anticlus. He was hot to salute you now
but Odysseus clamped his great hands on the man's mouth
and shut it, brutally—yes, he saved us all,
holding on grim-set till Pallas Athena
lured you off at last."

325   But clear-sighted Telemachus ventured,
"Son of Atreus, King Menelaus, captain of armies,
so much the worse, for not one bit of that
saved *him* from grisly death . . .
not even a heart of iron could have helped.
330   But come, send us off to bed. It's time to rest,
time to enjoy the sweet relief of sleep."

         And Helen briskly told her serving-women
to make beds in the porch's shelter, lay down
some heavy purple throws for the beds themselves,
335   and over them spread some blankets, thick woolly robes,
a warm covering laid on top. Torches in hand,
they left the hall and made up beds at once.
The herald led the two guests on and so they slept
outside the palace under the forecourt's colonnade,
340   young Prince Telemachus and Nestor's shining son.
Menelaus retired to chambers deep in his lofty house
with Helen the pearl of women loosely gowned beside him.

         When young Dawn with her rose-red fingers shone once more
the lord of the warcry climbed from bed and dressed,
345   over his shoulder he slung his well-honed sword,
fastened rawhide sandals under his smooth feet,
stepped from his bedroom, handsome as a god,
and sat beside Telemachus, asking, kindly,

"Now, my young prince, tell me what brings you here
350 to sunny Lacedaemon, sailing over the sea's broad back.
A public matter or private? Tell me the truth now."

And with all the poise he had, Telemachus replied,
"Son of Atreus, King Menelaus, captain of armies,
I came in the hope that you can tell me now
355 some news about my father.
My house is being devoured, my rich farms destroyed,
my palace crammed with enemies, slaughtering on and on
my droves of sheep and shambling longhorn cattle.
Suitors plague my mother—the insolent, overweening . . .
360 That's why I've come to plead before you now,
if you can tell me about his cruel death:
perhaps you saw him die with your own eyes
or heard the wanderer's end from someone else.
More than all other men, that man was born for pain.
365 Don't soften a thing, from pity, respect for me—
tell me, clearly, all your eyes have witnessed.
I beg you—if ever my father, lord Odysseus,
pledged you his word and made it good in action
once on the fields of Troy where you Achaeans suffered,
370 remember his story now, tell *me* the truth."

                                        "How shameful!"
the red-haired king burst out in anger. "That's the bed
of a brave man of war they'd like to crawl inside,
those spineless, craven cowards!
Weak as the doe that beds down her fawns
375 in a mighty lion's den—her newborn sucklings—
then trails off to the mountain spurs and grassy bends
to graze her fill, but back the lion comes to his own lair
and the master deals both fawns a ghastly bloody death,
just what Odysseus will deal that mob—ghastly death.
380 Ah if only—Father Zeus, Athena and lord Apollo—
that man who years ago in the games at Lesbos
rose to Philomelides' challenge, wrestled him,
pinned him down with one tremendous throw
and the Argives roared with joy . . .
385 if only *that* Odysseus sported with those suitors,
a blood wedding, a quick death would take the lot!
But about the things you've asked me, so intently,
I'll skew and sidestep nothing, not deceive you, ever.
Of all he told me—the Old Man of the Sea who never lies—
390 I'll hide or hold back nothing, not a single word.

It was in Egypt, where the gods still marooned me,
eager as I was to voyage home . . . I'd failed,
you see, to render them full, flawless victims,
and gods are always keen to see their rules obeyed.
395 Now, there's an island out in the ocean's heavy surge,

well off the Egyptian coast—they call it Pharos—
far as a deep-sea ship can go in one day's sail
with a whistling wind astern to drive her on.
There's a snug harbor there, good landing beach
400   where crews pull in, draw water up from the dark wells
then push their vessels off for passage out.
But here the gods becalmed me twenty days . . .
not a breath of the breezes ruffling out to sea
that speed a ship across the ocean's broad back.
405   Now our rations would all have been consumed,
our crews' stamina too, if one of the gods
had not felt sorry for me, shown me mercy,
Eidothea, a daughter of Proteus,
that great power, the Old Man of the Sea.
410   My troubles must have moved her to the heart
when she met me trudging by myself without my men.
They kept roaming around the beach, day in, day out,
fishing with twisted hooks, their bellies racked by hunger.
Well, she came right up to me, filled with questions:
415   'Are you a fool, stranger—soft in the head and lazy too?
Or do you let things slide because you *like* your pain?
Here you are, cooped up on an island far too long,
with no way out of it, none that you can find,
while all your shipmates' spirit ebbs away.'

420   So she prodded and I replied at once,
'Let me tell you, goddess—whoever you are—
I'm hardly landlocked here of my own free will.
So I must have angered one of the deathless gods
who rule the skies up there. But you tell *me*—
425   you immortals know it all—which one of you
blocks my way here, keeps me from my voyage?
How can I cross the swarming sea and reach home at last?'

    And the glistening goddess reassured me warmly,
'Of course, my friend, I'll answer all your questions.
430   Who haunts these parts? Proteus of Egypt does,
the immortal Old Man of the Sea who never lies,
who sounds the deep in all its depths, Poseidon's servant.
He's my father, they say, he gave me life. And he,
if only you ambush him somehow and pin him down,
435   will tell you the way to go, the stages of your voyage,
how you can cross the swarming sea and reach home at last.
And he can tell you too, if you want to press him—
you are a king, it seems—
all that's occurred within your palace, good and bad,
440   while you've been gone your long and painful way.'

    'Then you are the one'—I quickly took her up.
'Show me the trick to trap this ancient power,

or he'll see or sense me first and slip away.
It's hard for a mortal man to force a god.'

445   'True, my friend,' the glistening one agreed,
'and again I'll tell you all you need to know.
When the sun stands striding at high noon,
then up from the waves he comes—
the Old Man of the Sea who never lies—
450   under a West Wind's gust that shrouds him round
in shuddering dark swells, and once he's out on land
he heads for his bed of rest in deep hollow caves
and around him droves of seals—sleek pups bred
by his lovely ocean-lady—bed down too
455   in a huddle, flopping up from the gray surf,
giving off the sour reek of the salty ocean depths.
I'll lead you there myself at the break of day
and couch you all for attack, side-by-side.
Choose three men from your crew, choose well,
460   the best you've got aboard the good decked hulls.
Now I will tell you all the old wizard's tricks . . .
First he will make his rounds and count the seals
and once he's checked their number, reviewed them all,
down in their midst he'll lie, like a shepherd with his flock.
465   That's your moment. Soon as you see him bedded down,
muster your heart and strength and hold him fast,
wildly as he writhes and fights you to escape.
He'll try all kinds of escape—twist and turn
into every beast that moves across the earth,
470   transforming himself into water, superhuman fire,
but you hold on for dear life, hug him all the harder!
And when, at last, he begins to ask you questions—
back in the shape you saw him sleep at first—
relax your grip and set the old god free
475   and ask him outright, hero,
which of the gods is up in arms against you?
How can you cross the swarming sea and reach home at last?'

So she urged and under the breaking surf she dove
as I went back to our squadron beached in sand,
480   my heart a heaving storm at every step . . .
Once I reached my ship hauled up on shore
we made our meal and the godsent night came down
and then we slept at the sea's smooth shelving edge.
When young Dawn with her rose-red fingers shone once more
485   I set out down the coast of the wide-ranging sea,
praying hard to the gods for all their help,
taking with me the three men I trusted most
on every kind of mission.
                              Eidothea, now,

had slipped beneath the sea's engulfing folds
490   but back from the waves she came with four sealskins,
all freshly stripped, to deceive her father blind.
She scooped out lurking-places deep in the sand
and sat there waiting as we approached her post,
then couching us side-by-side she flung a sealskin
495   over each man's back. Now there was an ambush
that would have overpowered us all—overpowering,
true, the awful reek of all those sea-fed brutes!
Who'd dream of bedding down with a monster of the deep?
But the goddess sped to our rescue, found the cure
500   with ambrosia,[4] daubing it under each man's nose—
that lovely scent, it drowned the creatures' stench.
So all morning we lay there waiting, spirits steeled,
while seals came crowding, jostling out of the sea
and flopped down in rows, basking along the surf.
505   At high noon the old man emerged from the waves
and found his fat-fed seals and made his rounds,
counting them off, counting *us* the first four,
but he had no inkling of all the fraud afoot.
Then down he lay and slept, but we with a battle-cry,
510   we rushed him, flung our arms around him—he'd lost nothing,
the old rascal, none of his cunning quick techniques!
First he shifted into a great bearded lion
and then a serpent—
                a panther—
                        a ramping wild boar—
a torrent of water—
                    a tree with soaring branchtops—
515   but we held on for dear life, braving it out
until, at last, that quick-change artist,
the old wizard, began to weary of all this
and burst out into rapid-fire questions:
'Which god, Menelaus, conspired with you
520   to trap me in ambush? seize me against my will?
What on earth do you want?'
                        'You know, old man,'
I countered now. 'Why put me off with questions?
Here I am, cooped up on an island far too long,
with no way out of it, none that I can find,
525   while my spirit ebbs away. But you tell *me*—
you immortals know it all—which one of you
blocks my way here, keeps me from my voyage?
How can I cross the swarming sea and reach home at last?'

    'How wrong you were!' the seer shot back at once.
530   'You should have offered Zeus and the other gods

4. Food of the immortals.

a handsome sacrifice, *then* embarked, if you ever hoped
for a rapid journey home across the wine-dark sea.
It's not your destiny yet to see your loved ones,
reach your own grand house, your native land at last,
535   not till you sail back through Egyptian waters—
the great Nile swelled by the rains of Zeus—
and make a splendid rite to the deathless gods
who rule the vaulting skies. Then, only then
will the gods grant you the voyage you desire.'

540   So he urged, and broke the heart inside me,
having to double back on the mist-bound seas,
back to Egypt, that, that long and painful way . . .
Nevertheless I caught my breath and answered,
'That I will do, old man, as you command.
545   But tell me this as well, and leave out nothing:
Did all the Achaeans reach home in the ships unharmed,
all we left behind, Nestor and I, en route from Troy?
Or did any die some cruel death by shipwreck
or die in the arms of loved ones,
550   once they'd wound down the long coil of war?'

       And he lost no time in saying, 'Son of Atreus,
why do you ask me that? Why do you need to know?
Why probe my mind? You won't stay dry-eyed long,
I warn you, once you have heard the whole story.
555   Many of them were killed, many survived as well,
but only two who captained your bronze-armored units
died on the way home—you know who died in the fighting,
you were there yourself.
                   And one is still alive,
held captive, somewhere, off in the endless seas . . .
560   Ajax, now, went down with his long-oared fleet.
First Poseidon drove him onto the cliffs of Gyrae,
looming cliffs, then saved him from the breakers—
he'd have escaped his doom, too, despite Athena's hate,
if he hadn't flung that brazen boast, the mad blind fool.
565   "In the teeth of the gods," he bragged, "I have escaped
the ocean's sheer abyss!" Poseidon heard that frantic vaunt
and the god grasped his trident in both his massive hands
and struck the Gyraean headland, hacked the rock in two,
and the giant stump stood fast but the jagged spur
570   where Ajax perched at first, the raving madman—
toppling into the sea, it plunged him down, down
in the vast, seething depths. And so he died,
having drunk his fill of brine.
                   Your brother?
He somehow escaped that fate; Agamemnon got away

575   in his beaked ships. Queen Hera[5] pulled him through.
    But just as he came abreast of Malea's beetling cape
    a hurricane snatched him up and swept him way off course—
    groaning, desperate—driving him over the fish-infested sea
    to the wild borderland where Thyestes made his home
580   in the days of old and his son Aegisthus lived now.
    But even from there a safe return seemed likely,
    yes, the immortals swung the wind around to fair
    and the victors sailed home. How he rejoiced,
    Atrides setting foot on his fatherland once more—
585   he took that native earth in his hands and kissed it,
    hot tears flooding his eyes, so thrilled to see his land!
    But a watchman saw him too—from a lookout high above—
    a spy that cunning Aegisthus stationed there,
    luring the man with two gold bars in payment.
590   One whole year he'd watched . . .
    so the great king would not get past unseen,
    his fighting power intact for self-defense.
    The spy ran the news to his master's halls
    and Aegisthus quickly set his stealthy trap.
595   Picking the twenty best recruits from town
    he packed them in ambush at one end of the house,
    at the other he ordered a banquet dressed and spread
    and went to welcome the conquering hero, Agamemnon,
    went with team and chariot, and a mind aswarm with evil.
600   Up from the shore he led the king, he ushered him in—
    suspecting nothing of all his doom—he feasted him well
    then cut him down as a man cuts down some ox at the trough!
    Not one of your brother's men-at-arms was left alive,
    none of Aegisthus' either. All, killed in the palace.'

605   So Proteus said, and his story crushed my heart.
    I knelt down in the sand and wept. I'd no desire
    to go on living and see the rising light of day.
    But once I'd had my fill of tears and writhing there,
    the Old Man of the Sea who never lies continued,
610   'No more now, Menelaus. How long must you weep?
    Withering tears, what good can come of tears?
    None I know of. Strive instead to return
    to your native country—hurry home at once!
    Either you'll find the murderer still alive
615   or Orestes will have beaten you to the kill.
    You'll be in time to share the funeral feast.'

    So he pressed, and I felt my heart, my old pride,
    for all my grieving, glow once more in my chest
    and I asked the seer in a rush of winging words,

---

5. Wife and sister of Zeus, the greatest of the gods.

620 'Those two I know now. Tell me the third man's name.
     Who is still alive, held captive off in the endless seas?
     Unless he's dead by now. I want to know the truth
     though it grieves me all the more.'
                                        'Odysseus'—
     the old prophet named the third at once—
625 'Laertes' son, who makes his home in Ithaca . . .
     I saw him once on an island, weeping live warm tears
     in the nymph Calypso's house—she holds him there by force.
     He has no way to voyage home to his own native land,
     no trim ships in reach, no crew to ply the oars
630 and send him scudding over the sea's broad back.
     But about your own destiny, Menelaus,
     dear to Zeus, it's not for you to die
     and meet your fate in the stallion-land of Argos,
     no, the deathless ones will sweep you off to the world's end,
635 the Elysian Fields, where gold-haired Rhadamanthys waits,
     where life glides on in immortal ease for mortal man;
     no snow, no winter onslaught, never a downpour there
     but night and day the Ocean River sends up breezes,
     singing winds of the West refreshing all mankind.
640 All this because you are Helen's husband now—
     the gods count *you* the son-in-law of Zeus.'

        So he divined and down the breaking surf he dove
     as I went back to the ships with my brave men,
     my heart a rising tide at every step.
645 Once I reached my craft hauled up on shore
     we made our meal and the godsent night came down
     and then we slept at the sea's smooth shelving edge.
     When young Dawn with her rose-red fingers shone once more
     we hauled the vessels down to the sunlit breakers first
650 then stepped the masts amidships, canvas brailed—
     the crews swung aboard, they sat to the oars in ranks
     and in rhythm churned the water white with stroke on stroke.
     Back we went to the Nile swelled by the rains of Zeus,
     I moored the ships and sacrificed in a splendid rite,
655 and once I'd slaked the wrath of the everlasting gods
     I raised a mound for Agamemnon, his undying glory.
     All this done, I set sail and the gods sent me
     a stiff following wind that sped me home,
     home to the native land I love.
                                      But come,
660 my boy, stay on in my palace now with me,
     at least till ten or a dozen days have passed.
     Then I'll give you a princely send-off—shining gifts,
     three stallions and a chariot burnished bright—
     and I'll add a gorgeous cup so you can pour
665 libations out to the deathless gods on high

and remember Menelaus all your days."
                                    Telemachus,
summoning up his newfound tact, replied,
"Please, Menelaus, don't keep me quite so long.
True, I'd gladly sit beside you one whole year
670   without a twinge of longing for home or parents.
It's wonderful how you tell your stories, all you say—
I delight to listen! Yes, but now, I'm afraid,
my comrades must be restless in sacred Pylos,
and here you'd hold me just a little longer.
675   As for the gift you give me, let it be a keepsake.
Those horses I really cannot take to Ithaca;
better to leave them here to be your glory.
You rule a wide level plain
where the fields of clover roll and galingale
680   and wheat and oats and glistening full-grain barley.
No running-room for mares in Ithaca, though, no meadows.
Goat, not stallion, land, yet it means the world to me.
None of the rugged islands slanting down to sea
is good for pasture or good for bridle paths,
685   but Ithaca, best of islands, crowns them all!"

    So he declared. The lord of the warcry smiled,
patted him with his hand and praised his guest, concluding,
"Good blood runs in you, dear boy, your words are proof.
Certainly I'll exchange the gifts. The power's mine.
690   Of all the treasures lying heaped in my palace
you shall have the finest, most esteemed. Why,
I'll give you a mixing-bowl, forged to perfection—
it's solid silver finished off with a lip of gold.
Hephaestus[6] made it himself. And a royal friend,
695   Phaedimus, king of Sidon, lavished it on me
when his palace welcomed me on passage home.
How pleased I'd be if you took it as a gift!"

    And now as the two confided in each other,
banqueters arrived at the great king's palace,
700   leading their own sheep, bearing their hearty wine,
and their wives in lovely headbands sent along the food.
And so they bustled about the halls preparing dinner . . .
But all the while the suitors, before Odysseus' palace,
amused themselves with discus and long throwing spears,
705   out on the leveled grounds, free and easy as always,
full of swagger. But lord Antinous sat apart,
dashing Eurymachus beside him, ringleaders,
head and shoulders the strongest of the lot.
Phronius' son Noëmon approached them now,
710   quick to press Antinous with a question:

6. Crippled god of fire, smiths, and artisans, husband of Aphrodite.

"Antinous, have we any notion or not
when Telemachus will return from sandy Pylos?
He sailed in a ship of mine and now I need her back
to cross over to Elis Plain where I keep a dozen horses,
715   brood-mares suckling some heavy-duty mules, unbroken.
I'd like to drive one home and break him in."

    That dumbfounded them both. They never dreamed
the prince had gone to Pylos, Neleus' city—
certain the boy was still nearby somewhere,
720   out on his farm with flocks or with the swineherd.

    "Tell me the truth!" Antinous wheeled on Noëmon.
"When did he go? And what young crew went with him?
Ithaca's best? Or his own slaves and servants?
Surely he has enough to man a ship.
725   Tell me this—be clear—I've got to know:
did he commandeer your ship against your will
or did you volunteer it once he'd won you over?"

    "I volunteered it, of course," Noëmon said.
"What else could anyone do, when such a man,
730   a prince weighed down with troubles,
asked a favor? Hard to deny him anything.
And the young crew that formed his escort? Well,
they're the finest men on the island, next to us.
And Mentor took command—I saw him climb aboard—
735   or a god who looked like Mentor head to foot,
and that's what I find strange. I saw good Mentor
yesterday, just at sunup, here. But clearly
he boarded ship for Pylos days ago."

    With that he headed back to his father's house,
740   leaving the two lords stiff with indignation.
They made the suitors sit down in a group
and stop their games at once. Eupithes' son
Antinous rose up in their midst to speak,
his dark heart filled with fury,
745   blazing with anger—eyes like searing fire:
"By god, what a fine piece of work he's carried off!
Telemachus—what insolence—and we thought his little jaunt
would come to grief. But in spite of us all, look,
the young cub slips away, just like that—
750   picks the best crew in the land and off he sails.
And this is just the start of the trouble he can make.
Zeus kill that brazen boy before he hits his prime!
Quick, fetch me a swift ship and twenty men—
I'll waylay him from ambush, board him coming back
755   in the straits between Ithaca and rocky Same.
This gallant voyage of his to find his father
will find *him* wrecked at last!"

They all roared approval, urged him on,
rose at once and retired to Odysseus' palace.

760   But not for long was Penelope unaware
of the grim plots her suitors planned in secret.
The herald Medon told her. He'd overheard their schemes,
listening in outside the court while they wove on within.
He rushed the news through the halls to tell the queen

765   who greeted him as he crossed her chamber's threshold:
"Herald, why have the young blades sent you now?
To order King Odysseus' serving-women
to stop their work and slave to fix their feast?
I hate their courting, their running riot here—

770   would to god that this meal, here and now,
were their last meal on earth!
                                        Day after day,
all of you swarming, draining our life's blood,
my wary son's estate. What, didn't you listen
to your fathers—when you were children, years ago—

775   telling you how Odysseus treated them, your parents?
Never an unfair word, never an unfair action
among his people here, though that's the way
of our god-appointed kings,
hating one man, loving the next, with luck.

780   Not Odysseus. Never an outrage done to any man alive.
But you, you and your ugly outbursts, shameful acts,
they're plain to see. Look at the thanks he gets
for all past acts of kindness!"
                                        Medon replied,
sure of his own discretion, "Ah my queen,

785   if only *that* were the worst of all you face.
Now your suitors are plotting something worse,
harsher, crueler. God forbid they bring it off!
They're poised to cut Telemachus down with bronze swords
on his way back home. He's sailed off, you see . . .

790   for news of his father—to sacred Pylos first,
then out to the sunny hills of Lacedaemon."

Her knees gave way on the spot, her heart too.
She stood there speechless a while, struck dumb,
tears filling her eyes, her warm voice choked.

795   At last she found some words to make reply:
"Oh herald, why has my child gone and left me?
No need in the world for him to board the ships,
those chariots of the sea that sweep men on,
driving across the ocean's endless wastes . . .

800   Does he want his very name wiped off the earth?"

Medon, the soul of thoughtfulness, responded,
"I don't know if a god inspired your son
or the boy's own impulse led him down to Pylos,

but he went to learn of his father's journey home,
805   or whatever fate he's met."

          Back through King Odysseus' house he went
     but a cloud of heartbreak overwhelmed the queen.
     She could bear no longer sitting on a chair
     though her room had chairs aplenty.
810 Down she sank on her well-built chamber's floor,
     weeping, pitifully, as the women whimpered round her,
     all the women, young and old, who served her house.
     Penelope, sobbing uncontrollably, cried out to them,
     "Hear me, dear ones! Zeus has given me torment—
815 me above all the others born and bred in *my* day.
     My lionhearted husband, lost, long years ago,
     who excelled the Argives all in every strength—
     that great man whose fame resounds through Hellas
     right to the depths of Argos!
                              But now my son,
820 my darling boy—the whirlwinds have ripped him
     out of the halls without a trace! I never heard
     he'd gone—not even from you, you hard, heartless . . .
     not one of you even thought to rouse me from my bed,
     though well you knew when he boarded that black ship.
825 Oh if only I had learned he was planning such a journey,
     he would have stayed, by god, keen as he was to sail—
     or left me dead right here within our palace.
     Go, someone, quickly! Call old Dolius now,
     the servant my father gave me when I came,
830 the man who tends my orchard green with trees,
     so he can run to Laertes, sit beside him,
     tell him the whole story, point by point.
     Perhaps—who knows?—he'll weave some plan,
     he'll come out of hiding, plead with all these people
835 mad to destroy his line, his son's line of kings!"

          "Oh dear girl," Eurycleia the fond old nurse replied,
     "kill me then with a bronze knife—no mercy—or let me live,
     here in the palace—I'll hide nothing from you now!
     I knew it all, I gave him all he asked for,
840 bread and mellow wine, but he made me take
     a binding oath that I, I wouldn't tell you,
     no, not till ten or a dozen days had passed
     or you missed the lad yourself and learned he'd gone,
     so tears would never mar your lovely face . . .
845 Come, bathe now, put on some fresh clothes,
     climb to the upper rooms with all your women
     and pray to Pallas, daughter of storming Zeus—
     she may save Telemachus yet, even at death's door.
     Don't worry an old man, worried enough by now.
850 I can't believe the blessed gods so hate

the heirs of King Arcesius, through and through.
One will still live on—I know it—born to rule
this lofty house and the green fields far and wide."
                                                    With that
she lulled Penelope's grief and dried her eyes of tears.

855   And the queen bathed and put fresh clothing on,
climbed to the upper rooms with all her women
and sifting barley into a basket, prayed to Pallas,
"Hear me, daughter of Zeus whose shield is thunder—
tireless one, Athena! If ever, here in his halls,

860   resourceful King Odysseus
burned rich thighs of sheep or oxen in your honor,
oh remember it now for *my* sake, save my darling son,
defend him from these outrageous, overbearing suitors!"

      She shrilled a high cry and the goddess heard her prayer

865   as the suitors burst into uproar through the shadowed halls
and one of the lusty young men began to brag, "Listen,
our long-courted queen's preparing us all a marriage—
with no glimmer at all
how the murder of her son has been decreed."
                                             Boasting so,

870   with no glimmer at all of what had been decreed.
But Antinous took the floor and issued orders:
"Stupid fools! Muzzle your bragging now—
before someone slips inside and reports us.
Up now, not a sound, drive home our plan—

875   it suits us well, we approved it one and all."

      With that he picked out twenty first-rate men
and down they went to the swift ship at the sea's edge.
First they hauled the craft into deeper water,
stepped the mast amidships, canvas brailed,

880   made oars fast in the leather oarlock straps
while zealous aides-in-arms brought weapons on.
They moored her well out in the channel, disembarked
and took their meal on shore, waiting for dusk to fall.

      But there in her upper rooms she lay, Penelope

885   lost in thought, fasting, shunning food and drink,
brooding now . . . would her fine son escape his death
or go down at her overweening suitors' hands?
Her mind in torment, wheeling
like some lion at bay, dreading gangs of hunters

890   closing their cunning ring around him for the finish.
Harried so she was, when a deep kind sleep overcame her,
back she sank and slept, her limbs fell limp and still.

      And again the bright-eyed goddess Pallas thought
of one more way to help. She made a phantom now,

895   its build like a woman's build, Iphthime's, yes,

another daughter of generous Lord Icarius,
Eumelus' bride, who made her home in Pherae.
Athena sped her on to King Odysseus' house
to spare Penelope, worn with pain and sobbing,
900   further spells of grief and storms of tears.
The phantom entered her bedroom,
passing quickly in through the doorbolt slit
and hovering at her head she rose and spoke now:
"Sleeping, Penelope, your heart so wrung with sorrow?
905   No need, I tell you, no, the gods who live at ease
can't bear to let you weep and rack your spirit.
Your son will still come home—it is decreed.
He's never wronged the gods in any way."

And Penelope murmured back, still cautious,
910   drifting softly now at the gate of dreams,
"Why have you come, my sister?
Your visits all too rare in the past,
for you make your home so very far away.
You tell me to lay to rest the grief and tears
915   that overwhelm me now, torment me, heart and soul?
With my lionhearted husband lost long years ago,
who excelled the Argives all in every strength?
That great man whose fame resounds through Hellas
right to the depths of Argos . . .
                                    And now my darling boy,
920   he's off and gone in a hollow ship! Just a youngster,
still untrained for war or stiff debate.
Him I mourn even more than I do my husband—
I quake in terror for all that he might suffer
either on open sea or shores he goes to visit.
925   Hordes of enemies scheme against him now,
keen to kill him off
before he can reach his native land again."

"Courage!" the shadowy phantom reassured her.
"Don't be overwhelmed by all your direst fears.
930   He travels with such an escort, one that others
would pray to stand beside them. She has power—
Pallas Athena. She pities you in your tears.
She wings me here to tell you all these things."

But the circumspect Penelope replied,
935   "If you *are* a god and have heard a god's own voice,
come, tell me about that luckless man as well.
Is he still alive? does he see the light of day?
Or is he dead already, lost in the House of Death?"

"About that man," the shadowy phantom answered,
940   "I cannot tell you the story start to finish,
whether he's dead or alive.

It's wrong to lead you on with idle words."
At that
she glided off by the doorpost past the bolt—
gone on a lifting breeze. Icarius' daughter
945   started up from sleep, her spirit warmed now
that a dream so clear had come to her in darkest night.

But the suitors boarded now and sailed the sea-lanes,
plotting in their hearts Telemachus' plunge to death.
Off in the middle channel lies a rocky island,
950   just between Ithaca and Same's rugged cliffs—
Asteris—not large, but it has a cove,
a harbor with two mouths where ships can hide.
Here the Achaeans lurked in ambush for the prince.

Book 5. Odysseus—Nymph and Shipwreck

As Dawn rose up from bed by her lordly mate Tithonus,
bringing light to immortal gods and mortal men,
the gods sat down in council, circling Zeus
the thunder king whose power rules the world.
5   Athena began, recalling Odysseus to their thoughts,
the goddess deeply moved by the man's long ordeal,
held captive still in the nymph Calypso's house:
"Father Zeus—you other happy gods who never die—
never let any sceptered king be kind and gentle now,
10   not with all his heart, or set his mind on justice—
no, let him be cruel and always practice outrage.
Think: not one of the people whom he ruled
remembers Odysseus now, that godlike man,
and kindly as a father to his children.
Now
15   he's left to pine on an island, racked with grief
in the nymph Calypso's house—she holds him there by force.
He has no way to voyage home to his own native land,
no trim ships in reach, no crew to ply the oars
and send him scudding over the sea's broad back.
20   And now his dear son . . . they plot to kill the boy
on his way back home. Yes, he has sailed off
for news of his father, to holy Pylos first,
then out to the sunny hills of Lacedaemon."

"My child," Zeus who marshals the thunderheads replied,
25   "what nonsense you let slip through your teeth. Come now,
wasn't the plan your own? You conceived it yourself:
Odysseus shall return and pay the traitors back.
Telemachus? Sail him home with all your skill—
the power is yours, no doubt—
30   home to his native country all unharmed
while the suitors limp to port, defeated, baffled men."

With those words, Zeus turned to his own son Hermes.
"You are our messenger, Hermes, sent on all our missions.
Announce to the nymph with lovely braids our fixed decree:
35   Odysseus journeys home—the exile must return.
But not in the convoy of the gods or mortal men.
No, on a lashed, makeshift raft and wrung with pains,
on the twentieth day he will make his landfall, fertile Scheria,
the land of Phaeacians, close kin to the gods themselves,
40   who with all their hearts will prize him like a god
and send him off in a ship to his own beloved land,
giving him bronze and hoards of gold and robes—
more plunder than he could ever have won from Troy
if Odysseus had returned intact with his fair share.
45   So his destiny ordains. He shall see his loved ones,
reach his high-roofed house, his native land at last."

So Zeus decreed and the giant-killing guide obeyed at once.
Quickly under his feet he fastened the supple sandals,
ever-glowing gold, that wing him over the waves
50   and boundless earth with the rush of gusting winds.
He seized the wand that enchants the eyes of men
whenever Hermes wants, or wakes us up from sleep.
That wand in his grip, the powerful giant-killer,
swooping down from Pieria, down the high clear air,
55   plunged to the sea and skimmed the waves like a tern
that down the deadly gulfs of the barren salt swells
glides and dives for fish,
dipping its beating wings in bursts of spray—
so Hermes skimmed the crests on endless crests.
60   But once he gained that island worlds apart,
up from the deep-blue sea he climbed to dry land
and strode on till he reached the spacious cave
where the nymph with lovely braids had made her home,
and he found her there inside . . .
                                                  A great fire
65   blazed on the hearth and the smell of cedar
cleanly split and sweetwood burning bright
wafted a cloud of fragrance down the island.
Deep inside she sang, the goddess Calypso, lifting
her breathtaking voice as she glided back and forth
70   before her loom, her golden shuttle weaving.
Thick, luxuriant woods grew round the cave,
alders and black poplars, pungent cypress too,
and there birds roosted, folding their long wings,
owls and hawks and the spread-beaked ravens of the sea,
75   black skimmers who make their living off the waves.
And round the mouth of the cavern trailed a vine
laden with clusters, bursting with ripe grapes.
Four springs in a row, bubbling clear and cold,

running side-by-side, took channels left and right.
80   Soft meadows spreading round were starred with violets,
lush with beds of parsley. Why, even a deathless god
who came upon that place would gaze in wonder,
heart entranced with pleasure. Hermes the guide,
the mighty giant-killer, stood there, spellbound . . .
85   But once he'd had his fill of marveling at it all
he briskly entered the deep vaulted cavern.
Calypso, lustrous goddess, knew him at once,
as soon as she saw his features face-to-face.
Immortals are never strangers to each other,
90   no matter how distant one may make her home.
But as for great Odysseus—
Hermes could not find him within the cave.
Off he sat on a headland, weeping there as always,
wrenching his heart with sobs and groans and anguish,
95   gazing out over the barren sea through blinding tears.
But Calypso, lustrous goddess, questioned Hermes,
seating him on a glistening, polished chair.
"God of the golden wand, why have you come?
A beloved, honored friend,
100   but it's been so long, your visits much too rare.
Tell me what's on your mind. I'm eager to do it,
whatever I _can_ do . . . whatever can be done."

    And the goddess drew a table up beside him,
heaped with ambrosia, mixed him deep-red nectar.[1]
105   Hermes the guide and giant-killer ate and drank.
Once he had dined and fortified himself with food
he launched right in, replying to her questions:
"As one god to another, you ask me why I've come.
I'll tell you the whole story, mince no words—
110   your wish is my command.
It was Zeus who made me come, no choice of mine.
Who would willingly roam across a salty waste so vast,
so endless? Think: no city of men in sight, and not a soul
to offer the gods a sacrifice and burn the fattest victims.
115   But there is no way, you know, for another god to thwart
the will of storming Zeus and make it come to nothing.
Zeus claims you keep beside you a most unlucky man,
most harried of all who fought for Priam's Troy
nine years, sacking the city in the tenth,
120   and then set sail for home.
But voyaging back they outraged Queen Athena
who loosed the gales and pounding seas against them.
There all the rest of his loyal shipmates died
but the wind drove him on, the current bore him here.
125   Now Zeus commands you to send him off with all good speed:

1. Drink of the gods.

it is not his fate to die here, far from his own people.
Destiny still ordains that he shall see his loved ones,
reach his high-roofed house, his native land at last."

      But lustrous Calypso shuddered at those words
130 and burst into a flight of indignation. "Hard-hearted
you are, you gods! You unrivaled lords of jealousy—
scandalized when goddesses sleep with mortals,
openly, even when one has made the man her husband.
So when Dawn with her rose-red fingers took Orion,
135 you gods in your everlasting ease were horrified
till chaste Artemis[2] throned in gold attacked him,
out on Delos, shot him to death with gentle shafts.
And so when Demeter[3] the graceful one with lovely braids
gave way to her passion and made love with Iasion,
140 bedding down in a furrow plowed three times—
Zeus got wind of it soon enough, I'd say,
and blasted the man to death with flashing bolts.
So now at last, you gods, you train your spite on *me*
for keeping a mortal man beside me. The man I saved,
145 riding astride his keel-board, all alone, when Zeus
with one hurl of a white-hot bolt had crushed
his racing warship down the wine-dark sea.
There all the rest of his loyal shipmates died
but the wind drove him on, the current bore him here.
150 And I welcomed him warmly, cherished him, even vowed
to make the man immortal, ageless, all his days . . .
But since there is no way for another god to thwart
the will of storming Zeus and make it come to nothing,
let the man go—if the Almighty insists, commands—
155 and destroy himself on the barren salt sea!
I'll send him off, but not with any escort.
I have no ships in reach, no crew to ply the oars
and send him scudding over the sea's broad back.
But I will gladly advise him—I'll hide nothing—
160 so he can reach his native country all unharmed."

      And the guide and giant-killer reinforced her words:
"Release him at once, just so. Steer clear of the rage of Zeus!
Or down the years he'll fume and make your life a hell."

      With that the powerful giant-killer sped away.
165 The queenly nymph sought out the great Odysseus—
the commands of Zeus still ringing in her ears—
and found him there on the headland, sitting, still,
weeping, his eyes never dry, his sweet life flowing away
with the tears he wept for his foiled journey home,
170 since the nymph no longer pleased. In the nights, true,

2. Virgin goddess of wilderness and the hunt.   3. Goddess of grain.

he'd sleep with her in the arching cave—he had no choice—
unwilling lover alongside lover all too willing . . .
But all his days he'd sit on the rocks and beaches,
wrenching his heart with sobs and groans and anguish,
175   gazing out over the barren sea through blinding tears.
So coming up to him now, the lustrous goddess ventured,
"No need, my unlucky one, to grieve here any longer,
no, don't waste your life away. Now I am willing,
heart and soul, to send you off at last. Come,
180   take bronze tools, cut your lengthy timbers,
make them into a broad-beamed raft
and top it off with a half-deck high enough
to sweep you free and clear on the misty seas.
And I myself will stock her with food and water,
185   ruddy wine to your taste—all to stave off hunger—
give you clothing, send you a stiff following wind
so you can reach your native country all unharmed.
If only the gods are willing. They rule the vaulting skies.
They're stronger than I to plan and drive things home."

190   Long-enduring Odysseus shuddered at that
and broke out in a sharp flight of protest.
"Passage home? Never. Surely you're plotting
something else, goddess, urging me—in a raft—
to cross the ocean's mighty gulfs. So vast, so full
190   of danger not even deep-sea ships can make it through,
swift as they are and buoyed up by the winds of Zeus himself.
I won't set foot on a raft until you show good faith,
until you consent to swear, goddess, a binding oath
you'll never plot some new intrigue to harm me!"

200   He was so intense the lustrous goddess smiled,
stroked him with her hand, savored his name and chided,
"Ah what a wicked man you are, and never at a loss.
What a thing to imagine, what a thing to say!
Earth be my witness now, the vaulting Sky above
205   and the dark cascading waters of the Styx[4]—I swear
by the greatest, grimmest oath that binds the happy gods:
I will never plot some new intrigue to harm you.
Never. All I have in mind and devise for *you*
are the very plans I'd fashion for myself
210   if I were in your straits. My every impulse
bends to what is right. Not iron, trust me,
the heart within *my* breast. I am all compassion."

And lustrous Calypso quickly led the way
as he followed in the footsteps of the goddess.

4. Underworld river and the goddess who guaranteed the gods' oaths.

215   They reached the arching cavern, man and god as one,
        and Odysseus took the seat that Hermes just left,
        while the nymph set out before him every kind
        of food and drink that mortal men will take.
        Calypso sat down face-to-face with the king
220   and the women served her nectar and ambrosia.
        They reached out for the good things that lay at hand
        and when they'd had their fill of food and drink
        the lustrous one took up a new approach. "So then,
        royal son of Laertes, Odysseus, man of exploits,
225   still eager to leave at once and hurry back
        to your own home, your beloved native land?
        Good luck to you, even so. Farewell!
        But if you only knew, down deep, what pains
        are fated to fill your cup before you reach that shore,
230   you'd stay right here, preside in our house with me
        and be immortal. Much as you long to see your wife,
        the one you pine for all your days . . . and yet
        I just might claim to be nothing less than she,
        neither in face nor figure. Hardly right, is it,
235   for mortal woman to rival immortal goddess?
        How, in build? in beauty?"
                                    "Ah great goddess,"
        worldly Odysseus answered, "don't be angry with me,
        please. All that you say is true, how well I know.
        Look at my wise Penelope. She falls far short of you,
240   your beauty, stature. She is mortal after all
        and you, you never age or die . . .
        Nevertheless I long—I pine, all my days—
        to travel home and see the dawn of my return.
        And if a god will wreck me yet again on the wine-dark sea,
245   I can bear that too, with a spirit tempered to endure.
        Much have I suffered, labored long and hard by now
        in the waves and wars. Add this to the total—
        bring the trial on!"
                            Even as he spoke
        the sun set and the darkness swept the earth.
250   And now, withdrawing into the cavern's deep recesses,
        long in each other's arms they lost themselves in love.

        When young Dawn with her rose-red fingers shone once more
        Odysseus quickly dressed himself in cloak and shirt
        while the nymph slipped on a loose, glistening robe,
255   filmy, a joy to the eye, and round her waist
        she ran a brocaded golden belt
        and over her head a scarf to shield her brow,
        then turned to plan the great man's voyage home.
        She gave him a heavy bronze ax that fit his grip,
260   both blades well-honed, with a fine olive haft
        lashed firm to its head. She gave him a polished

smoothing-adze as well and then she led the way
to the island's outer edge where trees grew tall,
alders, black poplars and firs that shot sky-high,
265   seasoned, drying for years, ideal for easy floating.
Once she'd shown her guest where the tall timber stood,
Calypso the lustrous goddess headed home again.
He set to cutting trunks—the work was done in no time.
Twenty in all he felled, he trimmed them clean with his ax
270   and split them deftly, trued them straight to the line.
Meanwhile the radiant goddess brought him drills—
he bored through all his planks and wedged them snugly,
knocking them home together, locked with pegs and joints.
Broad in the beam and bottom flat as a merchantman
275   when a master shipwright turns out her hull,
so broad the craft Odysseus made himself.
Working away at speed
he put up half-decks pinned to close-set ribs
and a sweep of gunwales rounded off the sides.
280   He fashioned the mast next and sank its yard in deep
and added a steering-oar to hold her right on course,
then he fenced her stem to stern with twigs and wicker,
bulwark against the sea-surge, floored with heaps of brush.
And lustrous Calypso came again, now with bolts of cloth
285   to make the sail, and he finished that off too, expertly.
Braces, sheets and brails—he rigged all fast on board,
then eased her down with levers into the sunlit sea.

    That was the fourth day and all his work was done.
On the fifth, the lovely goddess launched him from her island,
290   once she had bathed and decked him out in fragrant clothes.
And Calypso stowed two skins aboard—dark wine in one,
the larger one held water—added a sack of rations,
filled with her choicest meats to build his strength,
and summoned a wind to bear him onward, fair and warm.
295   The wind lifting his spirits high, royal Odysseus
spread sail—gripping the tiller, seated astern—
and now the master mariner steered his craft,
sleep never closing his eyes, forever scanning
the stars, the Pleiades and the Plowman late to set
300   and the Great Bear that mankind also calls the Wagon:
she wheels on her axis always fixed, watching the Hunter,
and she alone is denied a plunge in the Ocean's baths.
Hers were the stars the lustrous goddess told him
to keep hard to port as he cut across the sea.
305   And seventeen days he sailed, making headway well;
on the eighteenth, shadowy mountains slowly loomed . . .
the Phaeacians' island reaching toward him now,
over the misty breakers, rising like a shield.

But now Poseidon, god of the earthquake, saw him—
310   just returning home from his Ethiopian friends,
from miles away on the Solymi mountain-range
he spied Odysseus sailing down the sea
and it made his fury boil even more.
He shook his head and rumbled to himself,
315   "Outrageous! Look how the gods have changed their minds
about Odysseus—while I was off with my Ethiopians.
Just look at him there, nearing Phaeacia's shores
where he's fated to escape his noose of pain
that's held him until now. Still my hopes ride high—
320   I'll give that man his swamping fill of trouble!"

    With that he rammed the clouds together—both hands
clutching his trident—churned the waves into chaos, whipping
all the gales from every quarter, shrouding over in thunderheads
the earth and sea at once—and night swept down from the sky—
325   East and South Winds clashed and the raging West and North,
sprung from the heavens, roiled heaving breakers up—
and Odysseus' knees quaked, his spirit too;
numb with fear he spoke to his own great heart:
"Wretched man—what becomes of me now, at last?
330   I fear the nymph foretold it all too well—
on the high seas, she said, before I can reach
my native land I'll fill my cup of pain! And now,
look, it all comes to pass. What monstrous clouds—
King Zeus crowning the whole wide heaven black—
335   churning the seas in chaos, gales blasting,
raging around my head from every quarter—
my death-plunge in a flash, it's certain now!
Three, four times blessed, my friends-in-arms
who died on the plains of Troy those years ago,
340   serving the sons of Atreus to the end. Would to god
I'd died there too and met my fate that day the Trojans,
swarms of them, hurled at *me* with bronze spears,
fighting over the corpse of proud Achilles!
A hero's funeral then, my glory spread by comrades—
345   now what a wretched death I'm doomed to die!"

    At that a massive wave came crashing down on his head,
a terrific onslaught spinning his craft round and round—
he was thrown clear of the decks—

                      the steering-oar wrenched
from his grasp—

                and in one lightning attack the brawling
350   galewinds struck full-force, snapping the mast mid-shaft
and hurling the sail and sailyard far across the sea.
He went under a good long while, no fast way out,
no struggling up from under the giant wave's assault,

his clothing dragged him down—divine Calypso's gifts—
355   but at last he fought his way to the surface spewing
bitter brine, streams of it pouring down his head.
But half-drowned as he was, he'd not forget his craft—
he lunged after her through the breakers, laying hold
and huddling amidships, fled the stroke of death.
360   Pell-mell the rollers tossed her along down-current,
wild as the North Wind tossing thistle along the fields
at high harvest—dry stalks clutching each other tightly—
so the galewinds tumbled her down the sea, this way, that way,
now the South Wind flinging her over to North to sport with,
365   now the East Wind giving her up to West to harry on and on.

But someone saw him—Cadmus' daughter with lovely ankles,
Ino, a mortal woman once with human voice and called
Leucothea now she lives in the sea's salt depths,
esteemed by all the gods as she deserves.
370   She pitied Odysseus, tossed, tormented so—
she broke from the waves like a shearwater on the wing,
lit on the wreck and asked him kindly, "Ah poor man,
why is the god of earthquakes so dead set against you?
Strewing your way with such a crop of troubles!
375   But he can't destroy you, not for all his anger.
Just do as I say. You seem no fool to me.
Strip off those clothes and leave your craft
for the winds to hurl, and swim for it now, you must,
strike out with your arms for landfall there,
380   Phaeacian land where destined safety waits.
Here, take this scarf,
tie it around your waist—it is immortal.
Nothing to fear now, neither pain nor death.
But once you grasp the mainland with your hands
385   untie it quickly, throw it into the wine-dark sea,
far from the shore, but you, you turn your head away!"

With that the goddess handed him the scarf
and slipped back in the heavy breaking seas
like a shearwater once again
390   and a dark heaving billow closed above her.
But battle-weary Odysseus weighed two courses,
deeply torn, probing his fighting spirit: "Oh no—
I fear another immortal weaves a snare to trap me,
urging me to abandon ship! I won't. Not yet.
395   That shore's too far away—
I glimpsed it myself—where she says refuge waits.
No, here's what I'll do, it's what seems best to *me*.
As long as the timbers cling and joints stand fast,
I'll hold out aboard her and take a whipping—
400   once the breakers smash my craft to pieces,
then I'll swim—no better plan for now."

But just as great Odysseus thrashed things out,
Poseidon god of the earthquake launched a colossal wave,
terrible, murderous, arching over him, pounding down on him,
405   hard as a windstorm blasting piles of dry parched chaff,
scattering flying husks—so the long planks of his boat
were scattered far and wide. But Odysseus leapt aboard
one timber and riding it like a plunging racehorse
stripped away his clothes, divine Calypso's gifts,
410   and quickly tying the scarf around his waist
he dove headfirst in the sea,
stretched his arms and stroked for life itself.
But again the mighty god of earthquakes spied him,
shook his head and grumbled deep in his spirit, "Go, go,
415   after all you've suffered—rove your miles of sea—
till you fall in the arms of people loved by Zeus.
Even so I can hardly think you'll find
your punishments too light!"
                        With that threat
he lashed his team with their long flowing manes,
420   gaining Aegae port where his famous palace stands.

But Zeus's daughter Athena countered him at once.
The rest of the winds she stopped right in their tracks,
commanding them all to hush now, go to sleep.
All but the boisterous North—she whipped him up
425   and the goddess beat the breakers flat before Odysseus,
dear to Zeus, so he could reach the Phaeacians,
mingle with men who love their long oars
and escape his death at last.
                        Yes, but now,
adrift on the heaving swells two nights, two days—
430   quite lost—again and again the man foresaw his death.
Then when Dawn with her lovely locks brought on
the third day, the wind fell in an instant,
all glazed to a dead calm, and Odysseus,
scanning sharply, raised high by a groundswell,
435   looked up and saw it—landfall, just ahead.
Joy . . . warm as the joy that children feel
when they see their father's life dawn again,
one who's lain on a sickbed racked with torment,
wasting away, slowly, under some angry power's onslaught—
440   then what joy when the gods deliver him from his pains!
So warm, Odysseus' joy when he saw that shore, those trees,
as he swam on, anxious to plant his feet on solid ground again.
But just offshore, as far as a man's shout can carry,
he caught the boom of a heavy surf on jagged reefs—
445   roaring breakers crashing down on an ironbound coast,
exploding in fury—
                        the whole sea shrouded—
                                    sheets of spray—

no harbors to hold ships, no roadstead where they'd ride,
nothing but jutting headlands, riptooth reefs, cliffs.
Odysseus' knees quaked and the heart inside him sank;
450 he spoke to his fighting spirit, desperate: "Worse and worse!
Now that Zeus has granted a glimpse of land beyond my hopes,
now I've crossed this waste of water, the end in sight,
there's no way out of the boiling surf—I see no way!
Rugged reefs offshore, around them breakers roaring,
455 above them a smooth rock face, rising steeply, look,
and the surge too deep inshore, no spot to stand
on my own two legs and battle free of death.
If I clamber out, some big comber will hoist me,
dash me against that cliff—my struggles all a waste!
460 If I keep on swimming down the coast, trying to find
a seabeach shelving against the waves, a sheltered cove—
I dread it—another gale will snatch me up and haul me
back to the fish-infested sea, retching in despair.
Or a dark power will loose some monster at me,
465 rearing out of the waves—one of the thousands
Amphitrite's[5] breakers teem with. Well I know
the famous god of earthquakes hates my very name!"

        Just as that fear went churning through his mind
a tremendous roller swept him toward the rocky coast
470 where he'd have been flayed alive, his bones crushed
if the bright-eyed goddess Pallas had not inspired him now.
He lunged for a reef, he seized it with both hands and clung
for dear life, groaning until the giant wave surged past
and so he escaped its force, but the breaker's backwash
475 charged into him full fury and hurled him out to sea.
Like pebbles stuck in the suckers of some octopus
dragged from its lair—so strips of skin torn
from his clawing hands stuck to the rock face.
A heavy sea covered him over, then and there
480 unlucky Odysseus would have met his death—
against the will of Fate—
but the bright-eyed one inspired him yet again.
Fighting out from the breakers pounding toward the coast,
out of danger he swam on, scanning the land, trying to find
485 a seabeach shelving against the waves, a sheltered cove,
and stroking hard he came abreast of a river's mouth,
running calmly, the perfect spot, he thought . . .
free of rocks, with a windbreak from the gales.
As the current flowed he felt the river's god and
490 prayed to him in spirit: "Hear me, lord, whoever you are,
I've come to you, the answer to all my prayers—
rescue me from the sea, the Sea-lord's curse!

5. Goddess, queen of the sea.

Even immortal gods will show a man respect,
whatever wanderer seeks their help—like me—
495   I throw myself on your mercy, on your current now—
I have suffered greatly. Pity me, lord,
your suppliant cries for help!"
                                                    So the man prayed
and the god stemmed his current, held his surge at once
and smoothing out the swells before Odysseus now,
500   drew him safe to shore at the river's mouth.
His knees buckled, massive arms fell limp,
the sea had beaten down his striving heart.
His whole body swollen, brine aplenty gushing
out of his mouth and nostrils—breathless, speechless,
505   there he lay, with only a little strength left in him,
deathly waves of exhaustion overwhelmed him now . . .
But once he regained his breath and rallied back to life,
at last he loosed the goddess' scarf from his body,
dropped it into the river flowing out to sea
510   and a swift current bore it far downstream
and suddenly Ino caught it in her hands.
Struggling up from the banks, he flung himself
in the deep reeds, he kissed the good green earth
and addressed his fighting spirit, desperate still:
515   "Man of misery, what next? Is this the end?
If I wait out a long tense night by the banks,
I fear the sharp frost and the soaking dew together
will do me in—I'm bone-weary, about to breathe my last,
and a cold wind blows from a river on toward morning.
520   But what if I climb that slope, go for the dark woods
and bed down in the thick brush? What if I'm spared
the chill, fatigue, and a sweet sleep comes my way?
I fear wild beasts will drag me off as quarry."

        But this was the better course, it struck him now.
525   He set out for the woods and not far from the water
found a grove with a clearing all around and crawled
beneath two bushy olives sprung from the same root,
one olive wild, the other well-bred stock.
No sodden gusty winds could ever pierce them,
530   nor could the sun's sharp rays invade their depths,
nor could a downpour drench them through and through,
so dense they grew together, tangling side-by-side.
Odysseus crept beneath them, scraping up at once
a good wide bed for himself with both hands.
535   A fine litter of dead leaves had drifted in,
enough to cover two men over, even three,
in the wildest kind of winter known to man.
Long-enduring great Odysseus, overjoyed at the sight,
bedded down in the midst and heaped the leaves around him.

540 As a man will bury his glowing brand in black ashes,
off on a lonely farmstead, no neighbors near,
to keep a spark alive—no need to kindle fire
from somewhere else—so great Odysseus buried
himself in leaves and Athena showered sleep
545 upon his eyes . . . sleep in a swift wave
delivering him from all his pains and labors,
blessed sleep that sealed his eyes at last.

BOOK 6. THE PRINCESS AND THE STRANGER

So there he lay at rest, the storm-tossed great Odysseus,
borne down by his hard labors first and now deep sleep
as Athena traveled through the countryside
and reached the Phaeacians' city. Years ago
5 they lived in a land of spacious dancing-circles,
Hyperia, all too close to the overbearing Cyclops,
stronger, violent brutes who harried them without end.
So their godlike king, Nausithous, led the people off
in a vast migration, settled them in Scheria,
10 far from the men who toil on this earth—
he flung up walls around the city, built the houses,
raised the gods' temples and shared the land for plowing.
But his fate had long since forced him down to Death
and now Alcinous ruled, and the gods made him wise.
15 Straight to his house the clear-eyed Pallas went,
full of plans for great Odysseus' journey home.
She made her way to the gaily painted room
where a young girl lay asleep . . .
a match for the deathless gods in build and beauty,
20 Nausicaa, the daughter of generous King Alcinous.
Two handmaids fair as the Graces slept beside her,
flanking the two posts, with the gleaming doors closed.
But the goddess drifted through like a breath of fresh air,
rushed to the girl's bed and hovering close she spoke,
25 in face and form like the shipman Dymas' daughter,
a girl the princess' age, and dearest to her heart.
Disguised, the bright-eyed goddess chided, "Nausicaa,
how could your mother bear a careless girl like you?
Look at your fine clothes, lying here neglected—
30 with your marriage not far off,
the day you should be decked in all your glory
and offer elegant dress to those who form your escort.
That's how a bride's good name goes out across the world
and it brings her father and queenly mother joy. Come,
35 let's go wash these clothes at the break of day—
I'll help you, lend a hand, and the work will fly!
You won't stay unwed long. The noblest men

in the country court you now, all Phaeacians
just like you, Phaeacia-born and raised. So come,
40   the first thing in the morning press your kingly father
to harness the mules and wagon for you, all to carry
your sashes, dresses, glossy spreads for your bed.
It's so much nicer for you to ride than go on foot.
The washing-pools are just too far from town."
                                                              With that
45   the bright-eyed goddess sped away to Olympus, where,
they say, the gods' eternal mansion stands unmoved,
never rocked by galewinds, never drenched by rains,
nor do the drifting snows assail it, no, the clear air
stretches away without a cloud, and a great radiance
50   plays across that world where the blithe gods
live all their days in bliss. There Athena went,
once the bright-eyed one had urged the princess on.

      Dawn soon rose on her splendid throne and woke
Nausicaa finely gowned. Still beguiled by her dream,
55   down she went through the house to tell her parents now,
her beloved father and mother. She found them both inside.
Her mother sat at the hearth with several waiting-women,
spinning yarn on a spindle, lustrous sea-blue wool.
Her father she met as he left to join the lords
60   at a council island nobles asked him to attend.
She stepped up close to him, confiding, "Daddy dear,
I wonder, won't you have them harness a wagon for me,
the tall one with the good smooth wheels . . . so I
can take our clothes to the river for a washing?
65   Lovely things, but lying before me all soiled.
And you yourself, sitting among the princes,
debating points at your council,
you really should be wearing spotless linen.
Then you have five sons, full-grown in the palace,
70   two of them married, but three are lusty bachelors
always demanding crisp shirts fresh from the wash
when they go out to dance. Look at my duties—
that all rests on me."
                                          So she coaxed, too shy
to touch on her hopes for marriage, young warm hopes,
75   in her father's presence. But he saw through it all
and answered quickly, "I won't deny you the mules,
my darling girl . . . I won't deny you anything.
Off you go, and the men will harness a wagon,
the tall one with the good smooth wheels,
80   fitted out with a cradle on the top."
                                                              With that
he called to the stablemen and they complied.
They trundled the wagon out now, rolling smoothly,

backed the mule-team into the traces, hitched them up,
while the princess brought her finery from the room
85   and piled it into the wagon's polished cradle.
Her mother packed a hamper—treats of all kinds,
favorite things to refresh her daughter's spirits—
poured wine in a skin, and as Nausicaa climbed aboard,
the queen gave her a golden flask of suppling olive oil
90   for her and her maids to smooth on after bathing.
Then, taking the whip in hand and glistening reins,
she touched the mules to a start and out they clattered,
trotting on at a clip, bearing the princess and her clothes
and not alone: her maids went with her, stepping briskly too.

95   Once they reached the banks of the river flowing strong
where the pools would never fail, with plenty of water
cool and clear, bubbling up and rushing through
to scour the darkest stains—they loosed the mules,
out from under the wagon yoke, and chased them down
100   the river's rippling banks to graze on luscious clover.
Down from the cradle they lifted clothes by the armload,
plunged them into the dark pools and stamped them down
in the hollows, one girl racing the next to finish first
until they'd scoured and rinsed off all the grime,
105   then they spread them out in a line along the beach
where the surf had washed a pebbly scree ashore.
And once they'd bathed and smoothed their skin with oil,
they took their picnic, sitting along the river's banks
and waiting for all the clothes to dry in the hot noon sun.
110   Now fed to their hearts' content, the princess and her retinue
threw their veils to the wind, struck up a game of ball.
White-armed Nausicaa led their singing, dancing beat . . .
as lithe as Artemis with her arrows striding down
from a high peak—Taygetus' towering ridge or Erymanthus—
115   thrilled to race with the wild boar or bounding deer,
and nymphs of the hills race with her,
daughters of Zeus whose shield is storm and thunder,
ranging the hills in sport, and Leto's heart exults
as head and shoulders over the rest her daughter rises,
120   unmistakable—she outshines them all, though all are lovely.
So Nausicaa shone among her maids, a virgin, still unwed.

    But now, as she was about to fold her clothes
and yoke the mules and turn for home again,
now clear-eyed Pallas thought of what came next,
125   to make Odysseus wake and see this young beauty
and she would lead him to the Phaeacians' town.
The ball—
                the princess suddenly tossed it to a maid
but it missed the girl, it splashed in a deep swirling pool

and they all shouted out—
and that woke great Odysseus.
130 He sat up with a start, puzzling, his heart pounding:
"Man of misery, whose land have I lit on now?
What *are* they here—violent, savage, lawless?
or friendly to strangers, god-fearing men?
Listen: shouting, echoing round me—women, girls—
135 or the nymphs who haunt the rugged mountaintops
and the river springs and meadows lush with grass!
Or am I really close to people who speak my language?
Up with you, see how the land lies, see for yourself now . . ."

  Muttering so, great Odysseus crept out of the bushes,
140 stripping off with his massive hand a leafy branch
from the tangled olive growth to shield his body,
hide his private parts. And out he stalked
as a mountain lion exultant in his power
strides through wind and rain and his eyes blaze
145 and he charges sheep or oxen or chases wild deer
but his hunger drives him on to go for flocks,
even to raid the best-defended homestead.
So Odysseus moved out . . .
about to mingle with all those lovely girls,
150 naked now as he was, for the need drove him on,
a terrible sight, all crusted, caked with brine—
they scattered in panic down the jutting beaches.
Only Alcinous' daughter held fast, for Athena planted
courage within her heart, dissolved the trembling in her limbs,
155 and she firmly stood her ground and faced Odysseus, torn now—
Should he fling his arms around her knees, the young beauty,
plead for help, or stand back, plead with a winning word,
beg her to lead him to the town and lend him clothing?
This was the better way, he thought. Plead now
160 with a subtle, winning word and stand well back,
don't clasp her knees, the girl might bridle, yes.
He launched in at once, endearing, sly and suave:
"Here I am at your mercy, princess—
are you a goddess or a mortal? If one of the gods
165 who rule the skies up there, you're Artemis to the life,
the daughter of mighty Zeus—I see her now—just look
at your build, your bearing, your lithe flowing grace . . .
But if you're one of the mortals living here on earth,
three times blest are your father, your queenly mother,
170 three times over your brothers too. How often their hearts
must warm with joy to see you striding into the dances—
such a bloom of beauty. True, but he is the one
more blest than all other men alive, that man
who sways you with gifts and leads you home, his bride!
175 I have never laid eyes on anyone like you,

neither man nor woman . . .
I look at you and a sense of wonder takes me.
                                        Wait,
once I saw the like—in Delos,[1] beside Apollo's altar—
the young slip of a palm-tree springing into the light.
180   There I'd sailed, you see, with a great army in my wake,
out on the long campaign that doomed my life to hardship.
That vision! Just as I stood there gazing, rapt, for hours . . .
no shaft like that had ever risen up from the earth—
so now I marvel at *you,* my lady: rapt, enthralled,
185   too struck with awe to grasp you by the knees
though pain has ground me down.
                                        Only yesterday,
the twentieth day, did I escape the wine-dark sea.
Till then the waves and the rushing gales had swept me on
from the island of Ogygia. Now some power has tossed me here,
190   doubtless to suffer still more torments on your shores.
I can't believe they'll stop. Long before that
the gods will give me more, still more.
                                        Compassion—
princess, please! You, after all that I have suffered,
you are the first I've come to. I know no one else,
195   none in your city, no one in your land.
Show me the way to town, give me a rag for cover,
just some cloth, some wrapper you carried with you here.
And may the good gods give you all your heart desires:
husband, and house, and lasting harmony too.
200   No finer, greater gift in the world than that . . .
when man and woman possess their home, two minds,
two hearts that work as one. Despair to their enemies,
a joy to all their friends. Their own best claim to glory."

      "Stranger," the white-armed princess answered staunchly,
205   "friend, you're hardly a wicked man, and no fool, I'd say—
it's Olympian Zeus himself who hands our fortunes out,
to each of us in turn, to the good and bad,
however Zeus prefers . . .
He gave you pain, it seems. You simply have to bear it.
210   But now, seeing you've reached our city and our land,
you'll never lack for clothing or any other gift,
the right of worn-out suppliants come our way.
I'll show you our town, tell you our people's name.
Phaeacians we are, who hold this city and this land,
215   and I am the daughter of generous King Alcinous.
All our people's power stems from him."

      She called out to her girls with lovely braids:
"Stop, my friends! Why run when you see a man?

---

1. Island between Greece and Asia Minor that was sacred to Apollo.

Surely you don't think *him* an enemy, do you?
220 There's no one alive, there never will be one,
who'd reach Phaeacian soil and lay it waste.
The immortals love us far too much for that.
We live too far apart, out in the surging sea,
off at the world's end—
225 no other mortals come to mingle with us.
But here's an unlucky wanderer strayed our way
and we must tend him well. Every stranger and beggar
comes from Zeus, and whatever scrap we give him
he'll be glad to get. So, quick, my girls,
230 give our newfound friend some food and drink
and bathe the man in the river,
wherever you find some shelter from the wind."

At that
they came to a halt and teased each other on
and led Odysseus down to a sheltered spot
235 where he could find a seat,
just as great Alcinous' daughter told them.
They laid out cloak and shirt for him to wear,
they gave him the golden flask of suppling olive oil
and pressed him to bathe himself in the river's stream.
240 Then thoughtful Odysseus reassured the handmaids,
"Stand where you are, dear girls, a good way off,
so I can rinse the brine from my shoulders now
and rub myself with oil . . .
how long it's been since oil touched my skin!
245 But I won't bathe in front of you. I would be embarrassed—
stark naked before young girls with lovely braids."

    The handmaids scurried off to tell their mistress.
Great Odysseus bathed in the river, scrubbed his body
clean of brine that clung to his back and broad shoulders,
250 scoured away the brackish scurf that caked his head.
And then, once he had bathed all over, rubbed in oil
and donned the clothes the virgin princess gave him,
Zeus's daughter Athena made him taller to all eyes,
his build more massive now, and down from his brow
255 she ran his curls like thick hyacinth clusters
full of blooms. As a master craftsman washes
gold over beaten silver—a man the god of fire
and Queen Athena trained in every fine technique—
and finishes off his latest effort, handsome work,
260 so she lavished splendor over his head and shoulders now.
And down to the beach he walked and sat apart,
glistening in his glory, breathtaking, yes,
and the princess gazed in wonder . . .
then turned to her maids with lovely braided hair:
265 "Listen, my white-armed girls, to what I tell you.
The gods of Olympus can't be all against this man

who's come to mingle among our noble people.
At first he seemed appalling, I must say—
now he seems like a god who rules the skies up there!
270   Ah, if only a man like *that* were called my husband,
lived right here, pleased to stay forever . . .
                                        Enough.
Give the stranger food and drink, my girls."
They hung on her words and did her will at once,
set before Odysseus food and drink, and he ate and drank,
275   the great Odysseus, long deprived, so ravenous now—
it seemed like years since he had tasted food.

    The white-armed princess thought of one last thing.
Folding the clothes, she packed them into her painted wagon,
hitched the sharp-hoofed mules, and climbing up herself,
280   Nausicaa urged Odysseus, warmly urged her guest,
"Up with you now, my friend, and off to town we go.
I'll see you into my wise father's palace where,
I promise you, you'll meet all the best Phaeacians.
Wait, let's do it this way. You seem no fool to me.
285   While we're passing along the fields and plowlands,
you follow the mules and wagon, stepping briskly
with all my maids. I'll lead the way myself.
But once we reach our city, ringed by walls
and strong high towers too, with a fine harbor either side . . .
290   and the causeway in is narrow; along the road the rolling ships
are all hauled up, with a slipway cleared for every vessel.
There's our assembly, round Poseidon's royal precinct,
built of quarried slabs planted deep in the earth.
Here the sailors tend their black ships' tackle,
295   cables and sails, and plane their oarblades down.
Phaeacians, you see, care nothing for bow or quiver,
only for masts and oars and good trim ships themselves—
we glory in our ships, crossing the foaming seas!
But I shrink from all our sea-dogs' nasty gossip.
300   Some old salt might mock us behind our backs—
we have our share of insolent types in town
and one of the coarser sort, spying us, might say,
'Now who's that tall, handsome stranger Nausicaa has in tow?
Where'd she light on *him?* Her husband-to-be, just wait!
305   But who—some shipwrecked stray she's taken up with,
some alien from abroad? Since nobody lives nearby.
Unless it's really a god come down from the blue
to answer all her prayers, and to have her all his days.
Good riddance! Let the girl go roving to find herself
310   a man from foreign parts. She only spurns her own—
countless Phaeacians round about who court her,
nothing but our best.'
                        So they'll scoff . . .

just think of the scandal that would face me then.
I'd find fault with a girl who carried on that way,
315 flouting her parents' wishes—father, mother, still alive—
consorting with men before she'd tied the knot in public.
No, stranger, listen closely to what I say, the sooner
to win your swift voyage home at my father's hands.
Now, you'll find a splendid grove along the road—
320 poplars, sacred to Pallas—
a bubbling spring's inside and meadows run around it.
There lies my father's estate, his blossoming orchard too,
as far from town as a man's strong shout can carry.
Take a seat there, wait a while, and give us time
325 to make it into town and reach my father's house.
Then, when you think we're home, walk on yourself
to the city, ask the way to my father's palace,
generous King Alcinous. You cannot miss it,
even an innocent child could guide you there.
330 No other Phaeacian's house is built like that:
so grand, the palace of Alcinous, our great hero.
Once the mansion and courtyard have enclosed you, go,
quickly, across the hall until you reach my mother.
Beside the hearth she sits in the fire's glare,
335 spinning yarn on a spindle, sea-blue wool—
a stirring sight, you'll see . . .
she leans against a pillar, her ladies sit behind.
And my father's throne is drawn up close beside her;
there he sits and takes his wine, a mortal like a god.
340 Go past him, grasp my mother's knees—if you want
to see the day of your return, rejoicing, soon,
even if your home's a world away.
If only the queen will take you to her heart,
then there's hope that you will see your loved ones,
345 reach your own grand house, your native land at last."

At that she touched the mules with her shining whip
and they quickly left the running stream behind.
The team trotted on, their hoofs wove in and out.
She drove them back with care so all the rest,
350 maids and Odysseus, could keep the pace on foot,
and she used the whip discreetly.
The sun sank as they reached the hallowed grove,
sacred to Athena, where Odysseus stopped and sat
and said a prayer at once to mighty Zeus's daughter:
355 "Hear me, daughter of Zeus whose shield is thunder—
tireless one, Athena! Now hear my prayer at last,
for you never heard me then, when I was shattered,
when the famous god of earthquakes wrecked my craft.
Grant that here among the Phaeacian people
360 I may find some mercy and some love!"

So he prayed and Athena heard his prayer
but would not yet appear to him undisguised.
She stood in awe of her Father's brother, lord of the sea
who still seethed on, still churning with rage against
365   the great Odysseus till he reached his native land.

BOOK 7. PHAEACIA'S HALLS AND GARDENS

Now as Odysseus, long an exile, prayed in Athena's grove,
the hardy mule-team drew the princess toward the city.
Reaching her father's splendid halls, she reined in,
just at the gates—her brothers clustering round her,
5   men like gods, released the mules from the yoke
and brought the clothes indoors
as Nausicaa made her way toward her bedroom.
There her chambermaid lit a fire for her—
Eurymedusa, the old woman who'd come from Apiraea
10   years ago, when the rolling ships had sailed her in
and the country picked her out as King Alcinous' prize,
for he ruled all the Phaeacians, they obeyed him like a god.
Once, she had nursed the white-armed princess in the palace.
Now she lit a fire and made her supper in the room.

15   At the same time, Odysseus set off toward the city.
Pallas Athena, harboring kindness for the hero,
drifted a heavy mist around him, shielding him
from any swaggering islander who'd cross his path,
provoke him with taunts and search out who he was.
20   Instead, as he was about to enter the welcome city,
the bright-eyed goddess herself came up to greet him there,
for all the world like a young girl, holding a pitcher,
standing face-to-face with the visitor, who asked,
"Little girl, now wouldn't you be my guide
25   to the palace of the one they call Alcinous?
The king who rules the people of these parts.
I am a stranger, you see, weighed down with troubles,
come this way from a distant, far-off shore.
So I know no one here, none at all
30   in your city and the farmlands round about."

"Oh yes, sir,
good old stranger," the bright-eyed goddess said,
"I'll show you the very palace that you're after—
the king lives right beside my noble father.
Come, quietly too, and I will lead the way.
35   Now not a glance at anyone, not a question.
The men here never suffer strangers gladly,
have no love for hosting a man from foreign lands.
All they really trust are their fast, flying ships
that cross the mighty ocean. Gifts of Poseidon,

40   ah what ships they are—
       quick as a bird, quick as a darting thought!"

         And Pallas Athena sped away in the lead
       as he followed in her footsteps, man and goddess.
       But the famed Phaeacian sailors never saw him,
45   right in their midst, striding down their streets.
       Athena the one with lovely braids would not permit it,
       the awesome goddess poured an enchanted mist around him,
       harboring kindness for Odysseus in her heart.
       And he marveled now at the balanced ships and havens,
50   the meeting grounds of the great lords and the long ramparts
       looming, coped and crowned with palisades of stakes—
       an amazing sight to see . . .
       And once they reached the king's resplendent halls
       the bright-eyed goddess cried out, "Good old stranger,
55   here, here is the very palace that you're after—
       I've guided you all the way. Here you'll find
       our princes dear to the gods, busy feasting.
       You go on inside. Be bold, nothing to fear.
       In every venture the bold man comes off best,
60   even the wanderer, bound from distant shores.
       The queen is the first you'll light on in the halls.
       Arete,[1] she is called, and earns the name:
       she answers all our prayers. She comes, in fact,
       from the same stock that bred our King Alcinous.
65   First came Nausithous, son of the earthquake god
       Poseidon and Periboea, the lovely, matchless beauty,
       the youngest daughter of iron-willed Eurymedon,
       king of the overweening Giants years ago.
       He led that reckless clan to its own ruin,
70   killed himself in the bargain, but the Sea-lord
       lay in love with Periboea and she produced a son,
       Nausithous, that lionheart who ruled Phaeacia well.
       Now, Nausithous had two sons, Rhexenor and Alcinous,
       but the lord of the silver bow, Apollo, shot Rhexenor down—
75   married, true, yet still without a son in the halls,
       he left one child behind, a daughter named Arete.
       Alcinous made the girl his wife and honors her
       as no woman is honored on this earth, of all the wives
       now keeping households under their husbands' sway.
80   Such is her pride of place, and always will be so:
       dear to her loving children, to Alcinous himself
       and all our people. They gaze on her as a god,
       saluting her warmly on her walks through town.
       She lacks nothing in good sense and judgment—
85   she can dissolve quarrels, even among men,

---

1. Connected to the verb "pray."

whoever wins her sympathies.
If only our queen will take you to her heart,
then there's hope that you will see your loved ones,
reach your high-roofed house, your native land at last."

90   And with that vow the bright-eyed goddess sped away,
over the barren sea, leaving welcome Scheria far behind,
and reaching Marathon and the spacious streets of Athens,
entered Erechtheus' sturdy halls, Athena's stronghold.
Now as Odysseus approached Alcinous' famous house
95   a rush of feelings stirred within his heart,
bringing him to a standstill,
even before he crossed the bronze threshold . . .
A radiance strong as the moon or rising sun came flooding
through the high-roofed halls of generous King Alcinous.
100   Walls plated in bronze, crowned with a circling frieze
glazed as blue as lapis, ran to left and right
from outer gates to the deepest court recess,
and solid golden doors enclosed the palace.
Up from the bronze threshold silver doorposts rose
105   with silver lintel above, and golden handles too.
And dogs of gold and silver were stationed either side,
forged by the god of fire with all his cunning craft
to keep watch on generous King Alcinous' palace,
his immortal guard-dogs, ageless, all their days.
110   Inside to left and right, in a long unbroken row
from farthest outer gate to the inmost chamber,
thrones stood backed against the wall, each draped
with a finely spun brocade, women's handsome work.
Here the Phaeacian lords would sit enthroned,
115   dining, drinking—the feast flowed on forever.
And young boys, molded of gold, set on pedestals
standing firm, were lifting torches high in their hands
to flare through the nights and light the feasters down the hall.
And Alcinous has some fifty serving-women in his house:
120   some, turning the handmill, grind the apple-yellow grain,
some weave at their webs or sit and spin their yarn,
fingers flickering quick as aspen leaves in the wind
and the densely woven woolens dripping oil droplets.
Just as Phaeacian men excel the world at sailing,
125   driving their swift ships on the open seas,
so the women excel at all the arts of weaving.
That is Athena's gift to them beyond all others—
a genius for lovely work, and a fine mind too.

        Outside the courtyard, fronting the high gates,
130   a magnificent orchard stretches four acres deep
with a strong fence running round it side-to-side.
Here luxuriant trees are always in their prime,
pomegranates and pears, and apples glowing red,

succulent figs and olives swelling sleek and dark.
135 And the yield of all these trees will never flag or die,
neither in winter nor in summer, a harvest all year round
for the West Wind always breathing through will bring
some fruits to the bud and others warm to ripeness—
pear mellowing ripe on pear, apple on apple,
140 cluster of grapes on cluster, fig crowding fig.
And here is a teeming vineyard planted for the kings,
beyond it an open level bank where the vintage grapes
lie baking to raisins in the sun while pickers gather others;
some they trample down in vats, and here in the front rows
145 bunches of unripe grapes have hardly shed their blooms
while others under the sunlight slowly darken purple.
And there by the last rows are beds of greens,
bordered and plotted, greens of every kind,
glistening fresh, year in, year out. And last,
150 there are two springs, one rippling in channels
over the whole orchard—the other, flanking it,
rushes under the palace gates
to bubble up in front of the lofty roofs
where the city people come and draw their water.
                                                    Such
155 were the gifts, the glories showered down by the gods
on King Alcinous' realm.
                              And there Odysseus stood,
gazing at all this bounty, a man who'd borne so much . . .
Once he'd had his fill of marveling at it all,
he crossed the threshold quickly,
160 strode inside the palace. Here he found
the Phaeacian lords and captains tipping out
libations now to the guide and giant-killer Hermes,
the god to whom they would always pour the final cup
before they sought their beds. Odysseus went on
165 striding down the hall, the man of many struggles
shrouded still in the mist Athena drifted round him,
till he reached Arete and Alcinous the king. And then,
the moment he flung his arms around Arete's knees,
the godsent mist rolled back to reveal the great man.
170 And silence seized the feasters all along the hall—
seeing him right before their eyes, they marveled,
gazing on him now as Odysseus pleaded, "Queen,
Arete, daughter of godlike King Rhexenor!
Here after many trials I come to beg for mercy,
175 your husband's, yours, and all these feasters' here.
May the gods endow them with fortune all their lives,
may each hand down to his sons the riches in his house
and the pride of place the realm has granted *him.*
But as for myself, grant me a rapid convoy home
180 to my own native land. How far away I've been

from all my loved ones—how long I have suffered!"

    Pleading so, the man sank down in the ashes,
just at the hearth beside the blazing fire,
while all the rest stayed hushed, stock-still.
185   At last the old revered Echeneus broke the spell,
the eldest lord in Phaeacia, finest speaker too,
a past master at all the island's ancient ways.
Impelled by kindness now, he rose and said,
"This is no way, Alcinous. How indecent, look,
190   our guest on the ground, in the ashes by the fire!
Your people are holding back, waiting for your signal.
Come, raise him up and seat the stranger now,
in a silver-studded chair,
and tell the heralds to mix more wine for all
195   so we can pour out cups to Zeus who loves the lightning,
champion of suppliants—suppliants' rights are sacred.
And let the housekeeper give our guest his supper,
unstinting with her stores."
                        Hearing that,
Alcinous, poised in all his majesty, took the hand
200   of the seasoned, worldly-wise Odysseus, raised him up
from the hearth and sat him down in a burnished chair,
displacing his own son, the courtly Lord Laodamas
who had sat beside him, the son he loved the most.
A maid brought water soon in a graceful golden pitcher
205   and over a silver basin tipped it out
so the guest might rinse his hands,
then pulled a gleaming table to his side.
A staid housekeeper brought on bread to serve him,
appetizers aplenty too, lavish with her bounty.
210   As long-suffering great Odysseus ate and drank,
the hallowed King Alcinous called his herald:
"Come, Pontonous! Mix the wine in the bowl,
pour rounds to all our banqueters in the house
so we can pour out cups to Zeus who loves the lightning,
215   champion of suppliants—suppliants' rights are sacred."

    At that Pontonous mixed the heady, honeyed wine
and tipped first drops for the god in every cup,
then poured full rounds for all. And once they'd poured
libations out and drunk to their hearts' content,
220   Alcinous rose and addressed his island people:
"Hear me, lords and captains of Phaeacia,
hear what the heart inside me has to say.
Now, our feast finished, home you go to sleep.
But at dawn we call the elders in to full assembly,
225   host our guest in the palace, sacrifice to the gods
and then we turn our minds to his passage home,
so under our convoy our new friend can travel back

to his own land—no toil, no troubles—soon,
rejoicing, even if his home's a world away.
230 And on the way no pain or hardship suffered,
not till he sets foot on native ground again.
There in the future he must suffer all that Fate
and the overbearing Spinners spun out on his life line
the very day his mother gave him birth . . . But if
235 he's one of the deathless powers, out of the blue,
the gods are working now in strange, new ways.
Always, up to now, they came to us face-to-face
whenever we'd give them grand, glorious sacrifices—
they always sat beside us here and shared our feasts.
240 Even when some lonely traveler meets them on the roads,
they never disguise themselves. We're too close kin for that,
close as the wild Giants are, the Cyclops too."
                                        "Alcinous!"
wary Odysseus countered, "cross that thought from your mind.
I'm nothing like the immortal gods who rule the skies,
245 either in build or breeding. I'm just a mortal man.
Whom do you know most saddled down with sorrow?
They are the ones I'd equal, grief for grief.
And I could tell a tale of still more hardship,
all I've suffered, thanks to the gods' will.
250 But despite my misery, let me finish dinner.
The belly's a shameless dog, there's nothing worse.
Always insisting, pressing, it never lets us forget—
destroyed as I am, my heart racked with sadness,
sick with anguish, still it keeps demanding,
255 'Eat, drink!' It blots out all the memory
of my pain, commanding, 'Fill me up!'
                                        But you,
at the first light of day, hurry, please,
to set your unlucky guest on his own home soil.
How much I have suffered . . . Oh just let me see
260 my lands, my serving-men and the grand high-roofed house—
then I can die in peace."
                                        All burst into applause,
urging passage home for their newfound friend,
his pleading rang so true. And once they'd poured
libations out and drunk to their hearts' content,
265 each one made his way to rest in his own house.
But King Odysseus still remained at hall,
seated beside the royal Alcinous and Arete
as servants cleared the cups and plates away.
The white-armed Queen Arete took the lead;
270 she'd spotted the cape and shirt Odysseus wore,
fine clothes she'd made herself with all her women,
so now her words flew brusquely, sharply: "Stranger,
I'll be the first to question you—myself.

Who are you? Where are you from?
275   Who gave you the clothes you're wearing now?
Didn't you say you reached us roving on the sea?"

   "What hard labor, queen," the man of craft replied,
"to tell you the story of my troubles start to finish.
The gods on high have given me my share.
280   Still, this much I will tell you . . .
seeing you probe and press me so intently.
There is an island, Ogygia, lying far at sea,
where the daughter of Atlas, Calypso, has her home,
the seductive nymph with lovely braids—a danger too,
285   and no one, god or mortal, dares approach her there. But I,
cursed as I am, some power brought me to her hearth,
alone, when Zeus with a white-hot bolt had crushed
my racing warship down the wine-dark sea.
There all the rest of my loyal shipmates died
290   but I, locking my arms around my good ship's keel,
drifted along nine days. On the tenth, at dead of night,
the gods cast me up on Ogygia, Calypso's island,
home of the dangerous nymph with glossy braids,
and the goddess took me in in all her kindness,
295   welcomed me warmly, cherished me, even vowed
to make me immortal, ageless, all my days—
but she never won the heart inside me, never.
Seven endless years I remained there, always drenching
with my tears the immortal clothes Calypso gave me.
300   Then, at last, when the eighth came wheeling round,
she insisted that I sail—inspired by warnings sent
from Zeus, perhaps, or her own mind had changed.
She saw me on my way in a solid craft,
tight and trim, and gave me full provisions,
305   food and mellow wine, immortal clothes to wear
and summoned a wind to bear me onward, fair and warm.
And seventeen days I sailed, making headway well;
on the eighteenth, shadowy mountains slowly loomed . . .
your land! My heart leapt up, unlucky as I am,
310   doomed to be comrade still to many hardships.
Many pains the god of earthquakes piled upon me,
loosing the winds against me, blocking passage through,
heaving up a terrific sea, beyond belief—nor did the whitecaps
let me cling to my craft, for all my desperate groaning.
315   No, the squalls shattered her stem to stern, but I,
I swam hard, I plowed my way through those dark gulfs
till at last the wind and current bore me to your shores.
But here, had I tried to land, the breakers would have hurled me,
smashed me against the jagged cliffs of that grim coast,
320   so I pulled away, swam back till I reached a river,
the perfect spot at last, or so it struck me,

free of rocks, with a windbreak from the gales.
So, fighting for life, I flung myself ashore
and the godsent, bracing night came on at once.
325   Clambering up from the river, big with Zeus's rains,
I bedded down in the brush, my body heaped with leaves,
and a god poured down a boundless sleep upon me, yes,
and there in the leaves, exhausted, sick at heart,
I slept the whole night through
330   and on to the break of day and on into high noon
and the sun was wheeling down when sweet sleep set me free.
And I looked up, and there were your daughter's maids
at play on the beach, and she, she moved among them
like a deathless goddess! I begged her for help
335   and not once did her sense of tact desert her;
she behaved as you'd never hope to find
in one so young, not in a random meeting—
time and again the youngsters prove so flighty.
Not she. She gave me food aplenty and shining wine,
340   a bath in the river too, and gave me all this clothing.
That's my whole story. Wrenching to tell, but true."

     "Ah, but in one regard, my friend," the king replied,
"her good sense missed the mark, this daughter of mine.
She never escorted you to our house with all her maids
345   but she was the first you asked for care and shelter."

     "Your majesty," diplomatic Odysseus answered,
"don't find fault with a flawless daughter now,
not for my sake, please.
She urged me herself to follow with her maids.
350   I chose not to, fearing embarrassment in fact—
what if you took offense, seeing us both together?
Suspicious we are, we men who walk the earth."

     "Oh no, my friend," Alcinous stated flatly,
"I'm hardly a man for reckless, idle anger.
355   Balance is best in all things.
Father Zeus, Athena and lord Apollo! if only—
seeing the man you are, seeing we think as one—
you could wed my daughter and be my son-in-law
and stay right here with us. I'd give you a house
360   and great wealth—if you chose to stay, that is.
No Phaeacian would hold you back by force.
The curse of Father Zeus on such a thing!
And about your convoy home, you rest assured:
I have chosen the day and I decree it is tomorrow.
365   And all that voyage long you'll lie in a deep sleep
while my people sail you on through calm and gentle tides
till you reach your land and house, or any place you please.
True, even if landfall lies more distant than Euboea,

off at the edge of the world . . .

370   So say our crews, at least, who saw it once,
that time they carried the gold-haired Rhadamanthys
out to visit Tityus, son of Mother Earth. Imagine,
there they sailed and back they came in the same day,
they finished the homeward run with no strain at all.
375   You'll see for yourself how far they top the best—
my ships and their young shipmates
tossing up the whitecaps with their oars!"
                                        So he vowed
and the long-enduring great Odysseus glowed with joy
and raised a prayer and called the god by name:
380   "Father Zeus on high—
may the king fulfill his promises one and all!
Then his fame would ring through the fertile earth
and never die—and I should reach my native land at last!"

    And now as the two men exchanged their hopes,
385   the white-armed queen instructed her palace maids
to make a bed in the porch's shelter, lay down
some heavy purple throws for the bed itself,
and over it spread some blankets, thick woolly robes,
a warm covering laid on top. Torches in hand,
390   they left the hall and fell to work at once,
briskly prepared a good snug resting-place
and then returned to Odysseus, urged the guest,
"Up, friend, time for sleep. Your bed is made."
How welcome the thought of sleep to that man now . . .
395   So there after many trials Odysseus lay at rest
on a corded bed inside the echoing colonnade.
Alcinous slept in chambers deep in his lofty house
where the queen his wife arranged and shared their bed.

BOOK 8. A DAY FOR SONGS AND CONTESTS

When young Dawn with her rose-red fingers shone once more
royal Alcinous, hallowed island king, rose from bed
and great Odysseus, raider of cities, rose too.
Poised in his majesty, Alcinous led the way
5   to Phaeacia's meeting grounds, built for all
beside the harbored ships. Both men sat down
on the polished stone benches side-by-side
as Athena started roaming up and down the town,
in build and voice the wise Alcinous' herald,
10   furthering plans for Odysseus' journey home,
and stopped beside each citizen, urged them all,
"Come this way, you lords and captains of Phaeacia,
come to the meeting grounds and learn about the stranger!
A new arrival! Here at our wise king's palace now,
15   he's here from roving the ocean, driven far off course—

he looks like a deathless god!"
                                        Rousing their zeal,
their curiosity, each and every man, and soon enough
the assembly seats were filled with people thronging,
gazing in wonder at the seasoned man of war . . .
20   Over Odysseus' head and shoulders now
Athena lavished a marvelous splendor, yes,
making him taller, more massive to all eyes,
so Phaeacians might regard the man with kindness,
awe and respect as well, and he might win through
25   the many trials they'd pose to test the hero's strength.
Once they'd grouped, crowding the meeting grounds,
Alcinous rose and addressed his island people:
"Hear me, lords and captains of Phaeacia,
hear what the heart inside me has to say.
30   This stranger here, our guest—
I don't know who he is, or whether he comes
from sunrise lands or the western lands of evening,
but he has come in his wanderings to my palace;
he pleads for passage, he begs we guarantee it.
35   So now, as in years gone by, let us press on
and grant him escort. No one, I tell you, no one
who comes to *my* house will languish long here,
heartsick for convoy home.
                                        Come, my people!
Haul a black ship down to the bright sea,
40   rigged for her maiden voyage—
enlist a crew of fifty-two young sailors,
the best in town, who've proved their strength before.
Let all hands lash their oars to the thwarts then disembark,
come to my house and fall in for a banquet, quickly.
45   I'll lay on a princely feast for all. So then,
these are the orders I issue to our crews.
For the rest, you sceptered princes here,
you come to my royal halls so we can give
this stranger a hero's welcome in our palace—
50   no one here refuse. Call in the inspired bard
Demodocus. God has given the man the gift of song,
to him beyond all others, the power to please,
however the spirit stirs him on to sing."

     With those commands Alcinous led the way
55   and a file of sceptered princes took his lead
while the herald went to find the gifted bard.
And the fifty-two young sailors, duly chosen,
briskly following orders,
went down to the shore of the barren salt sea.
60   And once they reached the ship at the surf's edge,
first they hauled the craft into deeper water,
stepped the mast amidships, canvas brailed,

they made oars fast in the leather oarlock straps,
moored her riding high on the swell, then disembarked
65   and made their way to wise Alcinous' high-roofed halls.
There colonnades and courts and rooms were overflowing
with crowds, a mounting host of people young and old.
The king slaughtered a dozen sheep to feed his guests,
eight boars with shining tusks and a pair of shambling oxen.
70   These they skinned and dressed, and then laid out a feast
to fill the heart with savor.
                                                In came the herald now,
leading along the faithful bard the Muse adored
above all others, true, but her gifts were mixed
with good and evil both: she stripped him of sight
75   but gave the man the power of stirring, rapturous song.
Pontonous brought the bard a silver-studded chair,
right amid the feasters, leaning it up against
a central column—hung his high clear lyre
on a peg above his head and showed him how
80   to reach up with his hands and lift it down.
And the herald placed a table by his side
with a basket full of bread and cup of wine
for him to sip when his spirit craved refreshment.
All reached out for the good things that lay at hand
85   and when they'd put aside desire for food and drink,
the Muse inspired the bard
to sing the famous deeds of fighting heroes—
the song whose fame had reached the skies those days:
The Strife Between Odysseus and Achilles, Peleus' Son . . .
90   how once at the gods' lavish feast the captains clashed
in a savage war of words, while Agamemnon, lord of armies,
rejoiced at heart that Achaea's bravest men were battling so.
For this was the victory sign that Apollo prophesied
at his shrine in Pytho[1] when Agamemnon strode across
95   the rocky threshold, asking the oracle for advice—
the start of the tidal waves of ruin tumbling down
on Troy's and Achaea's forces, both at once,
thanks to the will of Zeus who rules the world.

        That was the song the famous harper sang
100   but Odysseus, clutching his flaring sea-blue cape
in both powerful hands, drew it over his head
and buried his handsome face,
ashamed his hosts might see him shedding tears.
Whenever the rapt bard would pause in the song,
105   he'd lift the cape from his head, wipe off his tears
and hoisting his double-handled cup, pour it out to the gods.
But soon as the bard would start again, impelled to sing

1. Delphi.

by Phaeacia's lords, who reveled in his tale,
again Odysseus hid his face and wept.
110 His weeping went unmarked by all the others;
only Alcinous, sitting close beside him,
noticed his guest's tears,
heard the groan in the man's labored breathing
and said at once to the master mariners around him,
115 "Hear me, my lords and captains of Phaeacia!
By now we've had our fill of food well-shared
and the lyre too, our loyal friend at banquets.
Now out we go again and test ourselves in contests,
games of every kind—so our guest can tell his friends,
120 when he reaches home, how far we excel the world
at boxing, wrestling, jumping, speed of foot."

He forged ahead and the rest fell in behind.
The herald hung the ringing lyre back on its peg
and taking Demodocus by the hand, led him from the palace,
125 guiding him down the same path the island lords
had just pursued, keen to watch the contests.
They reached the meeting grounds
with throngs of people streaming in their trail
as a press of young champions rose for competition.
130 Topsail and Riptide rose, the helmsman Rowhard too
and Seaman and Sternman, Surf-at-the-Beach and Stroke-Oar,
Breaker and Bowsprit, Racing-the-Wind and Swing-Aboard
and Seagirt the son of Greatfleet, Shipwrightson
and the son of Launcher, Broadsea, rose up too,
135 a match for murderous Ares,[2] death to men—
in looks and build the best of all Phaeacians
after gallant Laodamas, the Captain of the People.
Laodamas rose with two more sons of great Alcinous,
Halius bred to the sea and Clytoneus famed for ships.
140 And now the games began, the first event a footrace . . .
They toed the line—
                    and broke flat out from the start
with a fast pack flying down the field in a whirl of dust
and Clytoneus the prince outstripped them all by far,
flashing ahead the length two mules will plow a furrow
145 before he turned for home, leaving the pack behind
and raced to reach the crowds.
                              Next the wrestling,
grueling sport. They grappled, locked, and Broadsea,
pinning the strongest champions, won the bouts.
Next, in the jumping, Seagirt leapt and beat the field.
150 In the discus Rowhard up and outhurled them all by far.
And the king's good son Laodamas boxed them to their knees.

2. God of war.

When all had enjoyed the games to their hearts' content
Alcinous' son Laodamas spurred them: "Come, my friends,
let's ask our guest if he knows the ropes of any sport.
155   He's no mean man, not with a build like that . . .
Look at his thighs, his legs, and what a pair of arms—
his massive neck, his big, rippling strength!
Nor is he past his prime,
just beaten down by one too many blows.
160   Nothing worse than the sea, I always say,
to crush a man, the strongest man alive."

       And Broadsea put in quickly,
"Well said, Laodamas, right to the point.
Go up to the fellow, challenge him yourself."

165   On that cue, the noble prince strode up
before Odysseus, front and center, asking,
"Come, stranger, sir, won't you try your hand
at our contests now? If you have skill in any.
It's fit and proper for you to know your sports.
170   What greater glory attends a man, while he's alive,
than what he wins with his racing feet and striving hands?
Come and compete then, throw your cares to the wind!
It won't be long, your journey's not far off—
your ship's already hauled down to the sea,
175   your crew is set to sail."
                              "Laodamas,"
quick to the mark Odysseus countered sharply,
"why do you taunt me so with such a challenge?
Pains weigh on my spirit now, not your sports—
I've suffered much already, struggled hard.
180   But here I sit amid your assembly still,
starved for passage home, begging your king,
begging all your people."
                          "Oh I knew it!"
Broadsea broke in, mocking him to his face.
"I never took you for someone skilled in games,
185   the kind that real men play throughout the world.
Not a chance. You're some skipper of profiteers,
roving the high seas in his scudding craft,
reckoning up his freight with a keen eye out
for home-cargo, grabbing the gold he can!
190   You're no athlete. I see that."
                                    With a dark glance
wily Odysseus shot back, "Indecent talk, my friend.
You, you're a reckless fool—I see *that*. So,
the gods don't hand out all their gifts at once,
not build and brains and flowing speech to all.
195   One man may fail to impress us with his looks

but a god can crown his words with beauty, charm,
and men look on with delight when he speaks out.
Never faltering, filled with winning self-control,
he shines forth at assembly grounds and people gaze
200 at him like a god when he walks through the streets.
Another man may look like a deathless one on high
but there's not a bit of grace to crown his words.
Just like you, my fine, handsome friend. Not even
a god could improve those lovely looks of yours
205 but the mind inside is worthless.
Your slander fans the anger in my heart!
I'm no stranger to sports—for all your taunts—
I've held my place in the front ranks, I tell you,
long as I could trust to my youth and striving hands.
210 But now I'm wrestled down by pain and hardship, look,
I've borne my share of struggles, cleaving my way
through wars of men and pounding waves at sea.
Nevertheless, despite so many blows,
I'll compete in your games, just watch. Your insults
215 cut to the quick—you rouse my fighting blood!"

Up he sprang, cloak and all, and seized a discus,
huge and heavy, more weighty by far than those
the Phaeacians used to hurl and test each other.
Wheeling round, he let loose with his great hand
220 and the stone whirred on—and down to ground they went,
those lords of the long oars and master mariners cringing
under the rock's onrush, soaring lightly out of his grip,
flying away past all the other marks, and Queen Athena,
built like a man, staked out the spot and cried
225 with a voice of triumph, "Even a blind man,
friend, could find your mark by groping round—
it's not mixed up in the crowd, it's far in front!
There's nothing to fear in *this* event—
no one can touch you, much less beat your distance!"

230 At that the heart of the long-suffering hero laughed,
so glad to find a ready friend in the crowd that,
lighter in mood, he challenged all Phaeacia's best:
"Now go match *that,* you young pups, and straightaway
I'll hurl you another just as far, I swear, or even farther!
235 All the rest of you, anyone with the spine and spirit,
step right up and try me—you've incensed me so—
at boxing, wrestling, racing; nothing daunts me.
Any Phaeacian here except Laodamas himself.
The man's my host. Who would fight his friend?
240 He'd have to be good-for-nothing, senseless, yes,
to challenge his host and come to grips in games,
in a far-off land at that. He'd cut his own legs short.

But there are no others I'd deny or think beneath me—
I'll take on all contenders, gladly, test them head-to-head!
245 I'm no disgrace in the world of games where men compete.
Well I know how to handle a fine polished bow,
the first to hit my man in a mass of enemies,
even with rows of comrades pressing near me,
taking aim with our shafts to hit our targets.
250 Philoctetes alone outshot me there at Troy
when ranks of Achaean archers bent their bows.
Of the rest I'd say that I outclass them all—
men still alive, who eat their bread on earth.
But I'd never vie with the men of days gone by,
255 not Heracles, not Eurytus of Oechalia—archers
who rivaled immortal powers with their bows.
That's why noble Eurytus died a sudden death:
no old age, creeping upon him in his halls . . .
Apollo shot him down, enraged that the man
260 had challenged *him,* the Archer God.
                                        As for spears,
I can fling a spear as far as the next man wings an arrow!
Only at sprinting I fear you'd leave me in the dust.
I've taken a shameful beating out on heavy seas,
no conditioning there on shipboard day by day.
265 My legs have lost their spring."

    He finished. All stood quiet, hushed.
Only Alcinous found a way to answer. "Stranger,
friend—nothing you say among us seems ungracious.
You simply want to display the gifts you're born with,
270 stung that a youngster marched up to you in the games,
mocking, ridiculing your prowess as no one would
who had some sense of fit and proper speech.
But come now, hear me out,
so you can tell our story to other lords
275 as you sit and feast in your own halls someday,
your own wife and your children by your side,
remembering there our island prowess here:
what skills great Zeus has given *us* as well,
down all the years from our fathers' days till now.
280 We're hardly world-class boxers or wrestlers, I admit,
but we can race like the wind, we're champion sailors too,
and always dear to our hearts, the feast, the lyre and dance
and changes of fresh clothes, our warm baths and beds.
So come—all you Phaeacian masters of the dance—
285 now dance away! So our guest can tell his friends,
when he reaches home, how far we excel the world
in sailing, nimble footwork, dance and song.
                                        Go, someone,
quickly, fetch Demodocus now his ringing lyre.

It must be hanging somewhere in the palace.''

290   At the king's word the herald sprang to his feet
and ran to fetch the vibrant lyre from the house.
And stewards rose, nine in all, picked from the realm
to set the stage for contests: masters-at-arms who
leveled the dancing-floor to make a fine broad ring.
295   The herald returned and placed the ringing lyre now
in Demodocus' hands, and the bard moved toward the center,
flanked by boys in the flush of youth, skilled dancers
who stamped the ground with marvelous pulsing steps
as Odysseus gazed at their flying, flashing feet,
300   his heart aglow with wonder.
                                                    A rippling prelude—
now the bard struck up an irresistible song:
The Love of Ares and Aphrodite Crowned with Flowers . . .
how the two had first made love in Hephaestus' mansion,
all in secret. Ares had showered her with gifts
305   and showered Hephaestus' marriage bed with shame
but a messenger ran to tell the god of fire—
Helios, lord of the sun, who'd spied the couple
lost in each other's arms and making love.
Hephaestus, hearing the heart-wounding story,
310   bustled toward his forge, brooding on his revenge—
planted the huge anvil on its block and beat out chains,
not to be slipped or broken, all to pin the lovers on the spot.
This snare the Firegod forged, ablaze with his rage at War,
then limped to the room where the bed of love stood firm
315   and round the posts he poured the chains in a sweeping net
with streams of others flowing down from the roofbeam,
gossamer-fine as spider webs no man could see,
not even a blissful god—
the Smith had forged a masterwork of guile.
320   Once he'd spun that cunning trap around his bed
he feigned a trip to the well-built town of Lemnos,
dearest to him by far of all the towns on earth.
But the god of battle kept no blind man's watch.
As soon as he saw the Master Craftsman leave
325   he plied his golden reins and arrived at once
and entered the famous god of fire's mansion,
chafing with lust for Aphrodite crowned with flowers.
She'd just returned from her father's palace, mighty Zeus,
and now she sat in her rooms as Ares strode right in
330   and grasped her hand with a warm, seductive urging:
"Quick, my darling, come, let's go to bed
and lose ourselves in love! Your husband's away—
by now he must be off in the wilds of Lemnos,
consorting with his raucous Sintian friends.''
                                                    So he pressed

335   and her heart raced with joy to sleep with War
        and off they went to bed and down they lay—
        and down around them came those cunning chains
        of the crafty god of fire, showering down now
        till the couple could not move a limb or lift a finger—
340   then they knew at last: there was no way out, not now.
        But now the glorious crippled Smith was drawing near . . .
        he'd turned around, miles short of the Lemnos coast,
        for the Sungod kept *his* watch and told Hephaestus all,
        so back he rushed to his house, his heart consumed with anguish.
345   Halting there at the gates, seized with savage rage
        he howled a terrible cry, imploring all the gods,
        "Father Zeus, look here—
        the rest of you happy gods who live forever—
        here is a sight to make you laugh, revolt you too!
350   Just because I am crippled, Zeus's daughter Aphrodite
        will always spurn me and love that devastating Ares,
        just because of his striking looks and racer's legs
        while I am a weakling, lame from birth, and who's to blame?
        Both my parents—who else? If only they'd never bred me!
355   Just look at the two lovers . . . crawled inside my bed,
        locked in each other's arms—the sight makes me burn!
        But I doubt they'll want to lie that way much longer,
        not a moment more—mad as they are for each other.
        No, they'll soon tire of bedding down together,
360   but then my cunning chains will bind them fast
        till our Father pays my bride-gifts back in full,
        all I handed *him* for that shameless bitch his daughter,
        irresistible beauty—all unbridled too!"
                                        So Hephaestus wailed
        as the gods came crowding up to his bronze-floored house.
365   Poseidon god of the earthquake came, and Hermes came,
        the running god of luck, and the Archer, lord Apollo,
        while modesty kept each goddess to her mansion.
        The immortals, givers of all good things, stood at the gates,
        and uncontrollable laughter burst from the happy gods
370   when they saw the god of fire's subtle, cunning work.
        One would glance at his neighbor, laughing out,
        "A bad day for adultery! Slow outstrips the Swift."

            "Look how limping Hephaestus conquers War,
        the quickest of all the gods who rule Olympus!"

375   "The cripple wins by craft."
                                        "The adulterer,
        he will pay the price!"
                                        So the gods would banter
        among themselves but lord Apollo goaded Hermes on:
        "Tell me, Quicksilver, giver of all good things—
        even with those unwieldy shackles wrapped around you,

380   how would you like to bed the golden Aphrodite?"

"Oh Apollo, if only!" the giant-killer cried.
"Archer, bind me down with triple those endless chains!
Let all you gods look on, and all you goddesses too—
how I'd love to bed that golden Aphrodite!"

385   A peal of laughter broke from the deathless ones
but not Poseidon, not a smile from him; he kept on
begging the famous Smith to loose the god of war,
pleading, his words flying, "Let him go!
I guarantee you Ares will pay the price,
390   whatever you ask, Hephaestus,
whatever's right in the eyes of all the gods."

But the famous crippled Smith appealed in turn,
"God of the earthquake, please don't urge this on me.
A pledge for a worthless man is a worthless pledge indeed.
395   What if he slips out of his chains—his debts as well?
How could I shackle *you* while all the gods look on?"

But the god of earthquakes reassured the Smith,
"Look, Hephaestus, if Ares scuttles off and away,
squirming out of his debt, I'll pay the fine myself."

400   And the famous crippled Smith complied at last:
"Now *there*'s an offer I really can't refuse!"

With all his force the god of fire loosed the chains
and the two lovers, free of the bonds that overwhelmed them so,
sprang up and away at once, and the Wargod sped to Thrace
405   while Love with her telltale laughter sped to Paphos,
Cyprus Isle, where her grove and scented altar stand.
There the Graces bathed and anointed her with oil,
ambrosial oil, the bloom that clings to the gods
who never die, and swathed her round in gowns
410   to stop the heart . . . an ecstasy—a vision.

That was the song the famous harper sang
and Odysseus relished every note as the islanders,
the lords of the long oars and master mariners rejoiced.

Next the king asked Halius and Laodamas to dance,
415   the two alone, since none could match that pair.
So taking in hand a gleaming sea-blue ball
made by the craftsman Polybus—arching back,
one prince would hurl it toward the shadowy clouds
as the other leaping high into the air would catch it
420   quickly, nimbly, before his feet hit ground again.
Once they'd vied at throwing the ball straight up,
they tossed it back and forth in a blur of hands
as they danced across the earth that feeds us all,
while boys around the ring stamped out the beat

425   and a splendid rhythmic drumming sound arose
       and good Odysseus looked at his host, exclaiming,
       "King Alcinous, shining among your island people,
       you boasted Phaeacia's dancers are the best—
       they prove your point—I watch and I'm amazed!"

430   His praises cheered the hallowed island king
       who spoke at once to the master mariners around him:
       "Hear me, my lords and captains of Phaeacia,
       our guest is a man of real taste, I'd say. Come,
       let's give him the parting gifts a guest deserves.
435   There are twelve peers of the realm who rule our land,
       thirteen, counting myself. Let each of us contribute
       a fresh cloak and shirt and a bar of precious gold.
       Gather the gifts together, hurry, so our guest
       can have them all in hand when he goes to dine,
440   his spirit filled with joy.
       As for Broadsea, let him make amends,
       man-to-man, with his words as well as gifts.
       His first remarks were hardly fit to hear."

           All assented and gave their own commands,
445   each noble sent a page to fetch his gifts.
       And Broadsea volunteered in turn, obliging:
       "Great Alcinous, shining among our island people,
       of course I'll make amends to our newfound friend
       as you request. I'll give the man this sword.
450   It's solid bronze and the hilt has silver studs,
       the sheath around it ivory freshly carved.
       Here's a gift our guest will value highly."

           He placed the silver-studded sword in Odysseus' hands
       with a burst of warm words: "Farewell, stranger, sir—
455   if any remark of mine gave you offense,
       may stormwinds snatch it up and sweep it off!
       May the gods grant *you* safe passage home to see your wife—
       you've been so far from loved ones, suffered so!"

           Tactful Odysseus answered him in kind:
460   "And a warm farewell to you, too, my friend.
       May the gods grant *you* good fortune—
       may you never miss this sword, this gift you give
       with such salutes. You've made amends in full."
                                                    With that
       he slung the silver-studded sword across his shoulder.
465   As the sun sank, his glittering gifts arrived
       and proud heralds bore them into the hall
       where sons of King Alcinous took them over,
       spread them out before their noble mother's feet—
       a grand array of gifts. The king in all his majesty
470   led the rest of his peers inside, following in a file

and down they sat on rows of high-backed chairs.
The king turned to the queen and urged her, "Come,
my dear, bring in an elegant chest, the best you have,
and lay inside it a fresh cloak and shirt, your own gifts.
475   Then heat a bronze cauldron over the fire, boil water,
so once our guest has bathed and reviewed his gifts—
all neatly stacked for sailing,
gifts our Phaeacian lords have brought him now—
he'll feast in peace and hear the harper's songs.
480   And I will give him this gorgeous golden cup of mine,
so he'll remember Alcinous all his days to come
when he pours libations out in his own house
to Father Zeus and the other gods on high."

     And at that Arete told her serving-women,
485   "Set a great three-legged cauldron over the fire—
do it right away!"
                        And hoisting over the blaze
a cauldron, filling it brimful with bathing water,
they piled fresh logs beneath and lit them quickly.
The fire lapped at the vessel's belly, the water warmed.
490   Meanwhile the queen had a polished chest brought forth
from an inner room and laid the priceless gifts inside,
the clothes and gold the Phaeacian lords had brought,
and added her own gifts, a cloak and a fine shirt,
and gave her guest instructions quick and clear:
495   "Now look to the lid yourself and bind it fast
with a good tight knot, so no one can rob you
on your voyage—drifting into a sweet sleep
as the black ship sails you home."
                       Hearing that,
the storm-tossed man secured the lid straightway,
500   he battened it fast with a swift, intricate knot
the lady Circe had taught him long ago.
And the housekeeper invited him at once
to climb into a waiting tub and bathe—
a hot, steaming bath . . .
505   what a welcome sight to Odysseus' eyes!
He'd been a stranger to comforts such as these
since he left the lovely-haired Calypso's house,
yet all those years he enjoyed such comforts there,
never-ending, as if he were a god . . . And now,
510   when maids had washed him, rubbed him down with oil
and drawn warm fleece and a shirt around his shoulders,
he stepped from the bath to join the nobles at their wine.
And there stood Nausicaa as he passed. Beside a column
that propped the sturdy roof she paused, endowed
515   by the gods with all her beauty, gazing at
Odysseus right before her eyes. Wonderstruck,

she hailed her guest with a winning flight of words:
"Farewell, my friend! And when you are at home,
home in your own land, remember me at times.
520   Mainly to me you owe the gift of life."

Odysseus rose to the moment deftly, gently:
"Nausicaa, daughter of generous King Alcinous,
may Zeus the Thunderer, Hera's husband, grant it so—
that I travel home and see the dawn of my return.
525   Even at home I'll pray to you as a deathless goddess
all my days to come. You saved my life, dear girl."

And he went and took his seat beside the king.
By now they were serving out the portions, mixing wine,
and the herald soon approached, leading the faithful bard
530   Demodocus, prized by all the people—seated him in a chair
amid the feasters, leaning it against a central column.
At once alert Odysseus carved a strip of loin,
rich and crisp with fat, from the white-tusked boar
that still had much meat left, and called the herald over:
535   "Here, herald, take this choice cut to Demodocus
so he can eat his fill—with warm regards
from a man who knows what suffering is . . .
From all who walk the earth our bards deserve
esteem and awe, for the Muse herself has taught them
540   paths of song. She loves the breed of harpers."

The herald placed the gift in Demodocus' hands
and the famous blind bard received it, overjoyed.
They reached for the good things that lay outspread
and when they'd put aside desire for food and drink,
545   Odysseus, master of many exploits, praised the singer:
"I respect you, Demodocus, more than any man alive—
surely the Muse has taught you, Zeus's daughter,
or god Apollo himself. How true to life,
all too true . . . you sing the Achaeans' fate,
550   all they did and suffered, all they soldiered through,
as if you were there yourself or heard from one who was.
But come now, shift your ground. Sing of the wooden horse
Epeus built with Athena's help, the cunning trap that
good Odysseus brought one day to the heights of Troy,
555   filled with fighting men who laid the city waste.
Sing that for me—true to life as it deserves—
and I will tell the world at once how freely
the Muse gave *you* the gods' own gift of song."

Stirred now by the Muse, the bard launched out
560   in a fine blaze of song, starting at just the point
where the main Achaean force, setting their camps afire,
had boarded the oarswept ships and sailed for home
but famed Odysseus' men already crouched in hiding—

	in the heart of Troy's assembly—dark in that horse
565	the Trojans dragged themselves to the city heights.
	Now it stood there, looming . . .
	and round its bulk the Trojans sat debating,
	clashing, days on end. Three plans split their ranks:
	either to hack open the hollow vault with ruthless bronze
570	or haul it up to the highest ridge and pitch it down the cliffs
	or let it stand—a glorious offering made to pacify the gods—
	and that, that final plan, was bound to win the day.
	For Troy was fated to perish once the city lodged
	inside her walls the monstrous wooden horse
575	where the prime of Argive power lay in wait
	with death and slaughter bearing down on Troy.
	And he sang how troops of Achaeans broke from cover,
	streaming out of the horse's hollow flanks to plunder Troy—
	he sang how left and right they ravaged the steep city,
580	sang how Odysseus marched right up to Deiphobus' house
	like the god of war on attack with diehard Menelaus.
	There, he sang, Odysseus fought the grimmest fight
	he had ever braved but he won through at last,
	thanks to Athena's superhuman power.

585	That was the song the famous harper sang
	but great Odysseus melted into tears,
	running down from his eyes to wet his cheeks . . .
	as a woman weeps, her arms flung round her darling husband,
	a man who fell in battle, fighting for town and townsmen,
590	trying to beat the day of doom from home and children.
	Seeing the man go down, dying, gasping for breath,
	she clings for dear life, screams and shrills—
	but the victors, just behind her,
	digging spear-butts into her back and shoulders,
595	drag her off in bondage, yoked to hard labor, pain,
	and the most heartbreaking torment wastes her cheeks.
	So from Odysseus' eyes ran tears of heartbreak now.
	But his weeping went unmarked by all the others;
	only Alcinous, sitting close beside him,
600	noticed his guest's tears,
	heard the groan in the man's labored breathing
	and said at once to the master mariners around him,
	"Hear me, my lords and captains of Phaeacia!
	Let Demodocus rest his ringing lyre now—
605	this song he sings can hardly please us all.
	Ever since our meal began and the stirring bard
	launched his song, our guest has never paused
	in his tears and throbbing sorrow.
	Clearly grief has overpowered his heart.
610	Break off this song! Let us all enjoy ourselves,
	the hosts and guest together. Much the warmer way.

All these things are performed for him, our honored guest,
the royal send-off here and gifts we give in love.
Treat your guest and suppliant like a brother:
615   anyone with a touch of sense knows that.
So don't be crafty now, my friend, don't hide
the truth I'm after. Fair is fair, speak out!
Come, tell us the name they call you there at home—
your mother, father, townsmen, neighbors round about.
620   Surely no man in the world is nameless, all told.
Born high, born low, as soon as he sees the light
his parents always name him, once he's born.
And tell me your land, your people, your city too,
so our ships can sail you home—their wits will speed them there.
625   For we have no steersmen here among Phaeacia's crews
or steering-oars that guide your common craft.
Our ships know in a flash their mates' intentions,
know all ports of call and all the rich green fields.
With wings of the wind they cross the sea's huge gulfs,
630   shrouded in mist and cloud—no fear in the world of foundering,
fatal shipwreck.
              True, there's an old tale I heard
my father telling once. Nausithous used to say
that lord Poseidon was vexed with us because
we escorted all mankind and never came to grief.
635   He said that one day, as a well-built ship of ours
sailed home on the misty sea from such a convoy,
the god would crush it, yes,
and pile a huge mountain round about our port.
So the old king foretold . . . And as for the god, well,
640   he can do his worst or leave it quite undone,
whatever warms his heart.
                  But come, my friend,
tell us your own story now, and tell it truly.
Where have your rovings forced you?
What lands of men have you seen, what sturdy towns,
645   what men themselves? Who were wild, savage, lawless?
Who were friendly to strangers, god-fearing men? Tell me,
why do you weep and grieve so sorely when you hear
the fate of the Argives, hear the fall of Troy?
That is the gods' work, spinning threads of death
650   through the lives of mortal men,
and all to make a song for those to come . . .
Did one of your kinsmen die before the walls of Troy,
some brave man—a son by marriage? father by marriage?
Next to our own blood kin, our nearest, dearest ties.
655   Or a friend perhaps, someone close to your heart,
staunch and loyal? No less dear than a brother,
the brother-in-arms who shares our inmost thoughts."

BOOK 9. IN THE ONE-EYED GIANT'S CAVE

Odysseus, the great teller of tales, launched out on his story:
"Alcinous, majesty, shining among your island people,
what a fine thing it is to listen to such a bard
as we have here—the man sings like a god.
5 The crown of life, I'd say. There's nothing better
than when deep joy holds sway throughout the realm
and banqueters up and down the palace sit in ranks,
enthralled to hear the bard, and before them all, the tables
heaped with bread and meats, and drawing wine from a mixing-bowl
10 the steward makes his rounds and keeps the winecups flowing.
This, to my mind, is the best that life can offer.
          But now
you're set on probing the bitter pains I've borne,
so I'm to weep and grieve, it seems, still more.
Well then, what shall I go through first,
15 what shall I save for last?
What pains—the gods have given me my share.
Now let me begin by telling you my name . . .
so you may know it well and I in times to come,
if I can escape the fatal day, will be your host,
20 your sworn friend, though my home is far from here.
I am Odysseus, son of Laertes, known to the world
for every kind of craft—my fame has reached the skies.
Sunny Ithaca is my home. Atop her stands our seamark,
Mount Neriton's leafy ridges shimmering in the wind.
25 Around her a ring of islands circle side-by-side,
Dulichion, Same, wooded Zacynthus too, but mine
lies low and away, the farthest out to sea,
rearing into the western dusk
while the others face the east and breaking day.
30 Mine is a rugged land but good for raising sons—
and I myself, I know no sweeter sight on earth
than a man's own native country.
         True enough,
Calypso the lustrous goddess tried to hold me back,
deep in her arching caverns, craving me for a husband.
35 So did Circe, holding me just as warmly in her halls,
the bewitching queen of Aeaea keen to have me too.
But they never won the heart inside me, never.
So nothing is as sweet as a man's own country,
his own parents, even though he's settled down
40 in some luxurious house, off in a foreign land
and far from those who bore him.
        No more. Come,
let me tell you about the voyage fraught with hardship
Zeus inflicted on me, homeward bound from Troy . . .

　　　　The wind drove me out of Ilium on to Ismarus,
45　　the Cicones'[1] stronghold. There I sacked the city,
　　　　killed the men, but as for the wives and plunder,
　　　　that rich haul we dragged away from the place—
　　　　we shared it round so no one, not on my account,
　　　　would go deprived of his fair share of spoils.
50　　Then I urged them to cut and run, set sail,
　　　　but would they listen? Not those mutinous fools;
　　　　there was too much wine to swill, too many sheep to slaughter
　　　　down along the beach, and shambling longhorn cattle.
　　　　And all the while the Cicones sought out other Cicones,
55　　called for help from their neighbors living inland:
　　　　a larger force, and stronger soldiers too,
　　　　skilled hands at fighting men from chariots,
　　　　skilled, when a crisis broke, to fight on foot.
　　　　Out of the morning mist they came against us—
60　　packed as the leaves and spears that flower forth in spring—
　　　　and Zeus presented us with disaster, me and my comrades
　　　　doomed to suffer blow on mortal blow. Lining up,
　　　　both armies battled it out against our swift ships,
　　　　both raked each other with hurtling bronze lances.
65　　Long as morning rose and the blessed day grew stronger
　　　　we stood and fought them off, massed as they were, but then,
　　　　when the sun wheeled past the hour for unyoking oxen,
　　　　the Cicones broke our lines and beat us down at last.
　　　　Out of each ship, six men-at-arms were killed;
70　　the rest of us rowed away from certain doom.

　　　　　From there we sailed on, glad to escape our death
　　　　yet sick at heart for the dear companions we had lost.
　　　　But I would not let our rolling ships set sail until the crews
　　　　had raised the triple cry, saluting each poor comrade
75　　cut down by the fierce Cicones on that plain.
　　　　Now Zeus who masses the stormclouds hit the fleet
　　　　with the North Wind—
　　　　　　　　　　　　　a howling, demonic gale, shrouding over
　　　　in thunderheads the earth and sea at once—
　　　　　　　　　　　　　　　　　　　and night swept down
　　　　from the sky and the ships went plunging headlong on,
80　　our sails slashed to rags by the hurricane's blast!
　　　　We struck them—cringing at death we rowed our ships
　　　　to the nearest shoreline, pulled with all our power.
　　　　There, for two nights, two days, we lay by, no letup,
　　　　eating our hearts out, bent with pain and bone-tired.
85　　When Dawn with her lovely locks brought on the third day,
　　　　then stepping the masts and hoisting white sails high,

---

1. In Thrace, across the opening of the Black Sea from Troy.

we lounged at the oarlocks, letting wind and helmsmen
keep us true on course . . .
                              And now, at long last,
I might have reached my native land unscathed,
90   but just as I doubled Malea's cape, a tide-rip
and the North Wind drove me way off course
careering past Cythera.
                              Nine whole days
I was borne along by rough, deadly winds
on the fish-infested sea. Then on the tenth
95   our squadron reached the land of the Lotus-eaters,
people who eat the lotus, mellow fruit and flower.
We disembarked on the coast, drew water there
and crewmen snatched a meal by the swift ships.
Once we'd had our fill of food and drink I sent
100 a detail ahead, two picked men and a third, a runner,
to scout out who might live there—men like us perhaps,
who live on bread? So off they went and soon enough
they mingled among the natives, Lotus-eaters, Lotus-eaters
who had no notion of killing my companions, not at all,
105 they simply gave them the lotus to taste instead . . .
Any crewmen who ate the lotus, the honey-sweet fruit,
lost all desire to send a message back, much less return,
their only wish to linger there with the Lotus-eaters,
grazing on lotus, all memory of the journey home
110 dissolved forever. But *I* brought them back, back
to the hollow ships, and streaming tears—I forced them,
hauled them under the rowing benches, lashed them fast
and shouted out commands to my other, steady comrades:
'Quick, no time to lose, embark in the racing ships!'—
115 so none could eat the lotus, forget the voyage home.
They swung aboard at once, they sat to the oars in ranks
and in rhythm churned the water white with stroke on stroke.

    From there we sailed on, our spirits now at a low ebb,
and reached the land of the high and mighty Cyclops,
120 lawless brutes, who trust so to the everlasting gods
they never plant with their own hands or plow the soil.
Unsown, unplowed, the earth teems with all they need,
wheat, barley and vines, swelled by the rains of Zeus
to yield a big full-bodied wine from clustered grapes.
125 They have no meeting place for council, no laws either,
no, up on the mountain peaks they live in arching caverns—
each a law to himself, ruling his wives and children,
not a care in the world for any neighbor.
                                           Now,
a level island stretches flat across the harbor,
130 not close inshore to the Cyclops' coast, not too far out,
thick with woods where the wild goats breed by hundreds.

No trampling of men to start them from their lairs,
no hunters roughing it out on the woody ridges,
stalking quarry, ever raid their haven.
135   No flocks browse, no plowlands roll with wheat;
unplowed, unsown forever—empty of humankind—
the island just feeds droves of bleating goats.
For the Cyclops have no ships with crimson prows,
no shipwrights there to build them good trim craft
140   that could sail them out to foreign ports of call
as most men risk the seas to trade with other men.
Such artisans would have made this island too
a decent place to live in . . . No mean spot,
it could bear you any crop you like in season.
145   The water-meadows along the low foaming shore
run soft and moist, and your vines would never flag.
The land's clear for plowing. Harvest on harvest,
a man could reap a healthy stand of grain—
the subsoil's dark and rich.
150   There's a snug deep-water harbor there, what's more,
no need for mooring-gear, no anchor-stones to heave,
no cables to make fast. Just beach your keels, ride out
the days till your shipmates' spirit stirs for open sea
and a fair wind blows. And last, at the harbor's head
155   there's a spring that rushes fresh from beneath a cave
and black poplars flourish round its mouth.
                                                    Well,
here we landed, and surely a god steered us in
through the pitch-black night.
Not that he ever showed himself, with thick fog
160   swirling around the ships, the moon wrapped in clouds
and not a glimmer stealing through that gloom.
Not one of us glimpsed the island—scanning hard—
or the long combers rolling us slowly toward the coast,
not till our ships had run their keels ashore.
165   Beaching our vessels smoothly, striking sail,
the crews swung out on the low shelving sand
and there we fell asleep, awaiting Dawn's first light.

      When young Dawn with her rose-red fingers shone once more
we all turned out, intrigued to tour the island.
170   The local nymphs, the daughters of Zeus himself,
flushed mountain-goats so the crews could make their meal.
Quickly we fetched our curved bows and hunting spears
from the ships and, splitting up into three bands,
we started shooting, and soon enough some god
175   had sent us bags of game to warm our hearts.
A dozen vessels sailed in my command
and to each crew nine goats were shared out
and mine alone took ten. Then all day long

till the sun went down we sat and feasted well
180   on sides of meat and rounds of heady wine.
The good red stock in our vessels' holds
had not run out, there was still plenty left;
the men had carried off a generous store in jars
when we stormed and sacked the Cicones' holy city.
185   Now we stared across at the Cyclops' shore, so near
we could even see their smoke, hear their voices,
their bleating sheep and goats . . .
And then when the sun had set and night came on
we lay down and slept at the water's shelving edge.
190   When young Dawn with her rose-red fingers shone once more
I called a muster briskly, commanding all the hands,
'The rest of you stay here, my friends-in-arms.
I'll go across with my own ship and crew
and probe the natives living over there.
195   What *are* they—violent, savage, lawless?
or friendly to strangers, god-fearing men?'

        With that I boarded ship and told the crew
to embark at once and cast off cables quickly.
They swung aboard, they sat to the oars in ranks
200   and in rhythm churned the water white with stroke on stroke.
But as soon as we reached the coast I mentioned—no long trip—
we spied a cavern just at the shore, gaping above the surf,
towering, overgrown with laurel. And here big flocks,
sheep and goats, were stalled to spend the nights,
205   and around its mouth a yard was walled up
with quarried boulders sunk deep in the earth
and enormous pines and oak-trees looming darkly . . .
Here was a giant's lair, in fact, who always pastured
his sheepflocks far afield and never mixed with others.
210   A grim loner, dead set in his own lawless ways.
Here was a piece of work, by god, a monster
built like no mortal who ever supped on bread,
no, like a shaggy peak, I'd say—a man-mountain
rearing head and shoulders over the world.
                                    Now then,
215   I told most of my good trusty crew to wait,
to sit tight by the ship and guard her well
while I picked out my dozen finest fighters
and off I went. But I took a skin of wine along,
the ruddy, irresistible wine that Maron gave me once,
220   Euanthes' son, a priest of Apollo, lord of Ismarus,
because we'd rescued him, his wife and children,
reverent as we were;
he lived, you see, in Apollo's holy grove.
And so in return he gave me splendid gifts,
225   he handed me seven bars of well-wrought gold,

a mixing-bowl of solid silver, then this wine . . .
He drew it off in generous wine-jars, twelve in all,
all unmixed—and such a bouquet, a drink fit for the gods!
No maid or man of his household knew that secret store,
230   only himself, his loving wife and a single servant.
Whenever they'd drink the deep-red mellow vintage,
twenty cups of water he'd stir in one of wine
and what an aroma wafted from the bowl—
what magic, what a godsend—
235   no joy in holding back when *that* was poured!
Filling a great goatskin now, I took this wine,
provisions too in a leather sack. A sudden foreboding
told my fighting spirit I'd soon come up against
some giant clad in power like armor-plate—
240   a savage deaf to justice, blind to law.

Our party quickly made its way to his cave
but we failed to find our host himself inside;
he was off in his pasture, ranging his sleek flocks.
So we explored his den, gazing wide-eyed at it all,
245   the large flat racks loaded with drying cheeses,
the folds crowded with young lambs and kids,
split into three groups—here the spring-born,
here mid-yearlings, here the fresh sucklings
off to the side—each sort was penned apart.
250   And all his vessels, pails and hammered buckets
he used for milking, were brimming full with whey.
From the start my comrades pressed me, pleading hard,
'Let's make away with the cheeses, then come back—
hurry, drive the lambs and kids from the pens
255   to our swift ship, put out to sea at once!'
But I would not give way—
and how much better it would have been—
not till I saw him, saw what gifts he'd give.
But he proved no lovely sight to my companions.

260   There we built a fire, set our hands on the cheeses,
offered some to the gods and ate the bulk ourselves
and settled down inside, awaiting his return . . .
And back he came from pasture, late in the day,
herding his flocks home, and lugging a huge load
265   of good dry logs to fuel his fire at supper.
He flung them down in the cave—a jolting crash—
we scuttled in panic into the deepest dark recess.
And next he drove his sleek flocks into the open vault,
all he'd milk at least, but he left the males outside,
270   rams and billy goats out in the high-walled yard.
Then to close his door he hoisted overhead
a tremendous, massive slab—
no twenty-two wagons, rugged and four-wheeled,

could budge that boulder off the ground, I tell you,
275 such an immense stone the monster wedged to block his cave!
Then down he squatted to milk his sheep and bleating goats,
each in order, and put a suckling underneath each dam.
And half of the fresh white milk he curdled quickly,
set it aside in wicker racks to press for cheese,
280 the other half let stand in pails and buckets,
ready at hand to wash his supper down.
As soon as he'd briskly finished all his chores
he lit his fire and spied us in the blaze and
'Strangers!' he thundered out, 'now who are you?
285 Where did you sail from, over the running sea-lanes?
Out on a trading spree or roving the waves like pirates,
sea-wolves raiding at will, who risk their lives
to plunder other men?'
                                          The hearts inside us shook,
terrified by his rumbling voice and monstrous hulk.
290 Nevertheless I found the nerve to answer, firmly,
'Men of Achaea we are and bound now from Troy!
Driven far off course by the warring winds,
over the vast gulf of the sea—battling home
on a strange tack, a route that's off the map,
295 and so we've come to you . . .
so it must please King Zeus's plotting heart.
We're glad to say we're men of Atrides Agamemnon,
whose fame is the proudest thing on earth these days,
so great a city he sacked, such multitudes he killed!
300 But since we've chanced on you, we're at your knees
in hopes of a warm welcome, even a guest-gift,
the sort that hosts give strangers. That's the custom.
Respect the gods, my friend. We're suppliants—at your mercy!
Zeus of the Strangers guards all guests and suppliants:
305 strangers are sacred—Zeus will avenge their rights!'

    'Stranger,' he grumbled back from his brutal heart,
'you must be a fool, stranger, or come from nowhere,
telling *me* to fear the gods or avoid their wrath!
We Cyclops never blink at Zeus and Zeus's shield
310 of storm and thunder, or any other blessed god—
we've got more force by far.
I'd never spare you in fear of Zeus's hatred,
you or your comrades here, unless I had the urge.
But tell me, where did you moor your sturdy ship
315 when you arrived? Up the coast or close in?
I'd just like to know.'
                                  So he laid his trap
but he never caught me, no, wise to the world
I shot back in my crafty way, 'My ship?
Poseidon god of the earthquake smashed my ship,

320   he drove it against the rocks at your island's far cape,
     he dashed it against a cliff as the winds rode us in.
     I and the men you see escaped a sudden death.'

       Not a word in reply to that, the ruthless brute.
     Lurching up, he lunged out with his hands toward my men
325   and snatching two at once, rapping them on the ground
     he knocked them dead like pups—
     their brains gushed out all over, soaked the floor—
     and ripping them limb from limb to fix his meal
     he bolted them down like a mountain-lion, left no scrap,
330   devoured entrails, flesh and bones, marrow and all!
     We flung our arms to Zeus, we wept and cried aloud,
     looking on at his grisly work—paralyzed, appalled.
     But once the Cyclops had stuffed his enormous gut
     with human flesh, washing it down with raw milk,
335   he slept in his cave, stretched out along his flocks.
     And I with my fighting heart, I thought at first
     to steal up to him, draw the sharp sword at my hip
     and stab his chest where the midriff packs the liver—
     I groped for the fatal spot but a fresh thought held me back.
340   There at a stroke we'd finish off ourselves as well—
     how could *we* with our bare hands heave back
     that slab he set to block his cavern's gaping maw?
     So we lay there groaning, waiting Dawn's first light.

       When young Dawn with her rose-red fingers shone once more
345   the monster relit his fire and milked his handsome ewes,
     each in order, putting a suckling underneath each dam,
     and as soon as he'd briskly finished all his chores
     he snatched up two more men and fixed his meal.
     Well-fed, he drove his fat sheep from the cave,
350   lightly lifting the huge doorslab up and away,
     then slipped it back in place
     as a hunter flips the lid of his quiver shut.
     Piercing whistles—turning his flocks to the hills
     he left me there, the heart inside me brooding on revenge:
355   how could I pay him back? would Athena give me glory?
     Here was the plan that struck my mind as best . . .
     the Cyclops' great club: there it lay by the pens,
     olivewood, full of sap. He'd lopped it off to brandish
     once it dried. Looking it over, we judged it big enough
360   to be the mast of a pitch-black ship with her twenty oars,
     a freighter broad in the beam that plows through miles of sea—
     so long, so thick it bulked before our eyes. Well,
     flanking it now, I chopped off a fathom's length,
     rolled it to comrades, told them to plane it down,
365   and they made the club smooth as I bent and shaved
     the tip to a stabbing point. I turned it over
     the blazing fire to char it good and hard,

then hid it well, buried deep under the dung
that littered the cavern's floor in thick wet clumps.
370   And now I ordered my shipmates all to cast lots—
who'd brave it out with me
to hoist our stake and grind it into his eye
when sleep had overcome him? Luck of the draw:
I got the very ones I would have picked myself,
375   four good men, and I in the lead made five . . .

    Nightfall brought him back, herding his woolly sheep
and he quickly drove the sleek flock into the vaulted cavern,
rams and all—none left outside in the walled yard—
his own idea, perhaps, or a god led him on.
380   Then he hoisted the huge slab to block the door
and squatted to milk his sheep and bleating goats,
each in order, putting a suckling underneath each dam,
and as soon as he'd briskly finished all his chores
he snatched up two more men and fixed his meal.
385   But this time I lifted a carved wooden bowl,
brimful of my ruddy wine,
and went right up to the Cyclops, enticing,
'Here, Cyclops, try this wine—to top off
the banquet of human flesh you've bolted down!
390   Judge for yourself what stock our ship had stored.
I brought it here to make you a fine libation,
hoping you would pity me, Cyclops, send me home,
but your rages are insufferable. You barbarian—
how can any man on earth come visit you after *this?*
395   What you've done outrages all that's right!'

    At that he seized the bowl and tossed it off
and the heady wine pleased him immensely—'More'—
he demanded a second bowl—'a hearty helping!
And tell me your name now, quickly,
400   so I can hand my guest a gift to warm *his* heart.
Our soil yields the Cyclops powerful, full-bodied wine
and the rains from Zeus build its strength. But this,
this is nectar, ambrosia—this flows from heaven!'

    So he declared. I poured him another fiery bowl—
405   three bowls I brimmed and three he drank to the last drop,
the fool, and then, when the wine was swirling round his brain,
I approached my host with a cordial, winning word:
'So, you ask me the name I'm known by, Cyclops?
I will tell you. But you must give me a guest-gift
410   as you've promised. Nobody—that's my name. Nobody—
so my mother and father call me, all my friends.'

    But he boomed back at me from his ruthless heart,
'*Nobody?* I'll eat Nobody last of all his friends—

I'll eat the others first! That's my gift to *you!*'
                                        With that
415   he toppled over, sprawled full-length, flat on his back
      and lay there, his massive neck slumping to one side,
      and sleep that conquers all overwhelmed him now
      as wine came spurting, flooding up from his gullet
      with chunks of human flesh—he vomited, blind drunk.
420   Now, at last, I thrust our stake in a bed of embers
      to get it red-hot and rallied all my comrades:
      'Courage—no panic, no one hang back now!'
      And green as it was, just as the olive stake
      was about to catch fire—the glow terrific, yes—
425   I dragged it from the flames, my men clustering round
      as some god breathed enormous courage through us all.
      Hoisting high that olive stake with its stabbing point,
      straight into the monster's eye they rammed it hard—
      I drove my weight on it from above and bored it home
430   as a shipwright bores his beam with a shipwright's drill
      that men below, whipping the strap back and forth, whirl
      and the drill keeps twisting faster, never stopping—
      So we seized our stake with its fiery tip
      and bored it round and round in the giant's eye
435   till blood came boiling up around that smoking shaft
      and the hot blast singed his brow and eyelids round the core
      and the broiling eyeball burst—
                              its crackling roots blazed
      and hissed—
                        as a blacksmith plunges a glowing ax or adze
      in an ice-cold bath and the metal screeches steam
440   and its temper hardens—that's the iron's strength—
      so the eye of the Cyclops sizzled round that stake!
      He loosed a hideous roar, the rock walls echoed round
      and we scuttled back in terror. The monster wrenched the spike
      from his eye and out it came with a red geyser of blood—
445   he flung it aside with frantic hands, and mad with pain
      he bellowed out for help from his neighbor Cyclops
      living round about in caves on windswept crags.
      Hearing his cries, they lumbered up from every side
      and hulking round his cavern, asked what ailed him:
450   'What, Polyphemus, what in the world's the trouble?
      Roaring out in the godsent night to rob us of our sleep.
      Surely no one's rustling your flocks against your will—
      surely no one's trying to kill you now by fraud or force!'

        '*Nobody,* friends'—Polyphemus bellowed back from his cave—
455   'Nobody's killing me now by fraud and not by force!'
      'If you're alone,' his friends boomed back at once,
      'and nobody's trying to overpower you now—look,
      it must be a plague sent here by mighty Zeus

and there's no escape from *that*.
460   You'd better pray to your father, Lord Poseidon.'

          They lumbered off, but laughter filled my heart
to think how nobody's name—my great cunning stroke—
had duped them one and all. But the Cyclops there,
still groaning, racked with agony, groped around
465   for the huge slab, and heaving it from the doorway,
down he sat in the cave's mouth, his arms spread wide,
hoping to catch a comrade stealing out with sheep—
such a blithering fool he took me for!
But I was already plotting . . .
470   what was the best way out? how could I find
escape from death for my crew, myself as well?
My wits kept weaving, weaving cunning schemes—
life at stake, monstrous death staring us in the face—
till this plan struck my mind as best. That flock,
475   those well-fed rams with their splendid thick fleece,
sturdy, handsome beasts sporting their dark weight of wool:
I lashed them abreast, quietly, twisting the willow-twigs
the Cyclops slept on—giant, lawless brute—I took them
three by three; each ram in the middle bore a man
480   while the two rams either side would shield him well.
So three beasts to bear each man, but as for myself?
There was one bellwether ram, the prize of all the flock,
and clutching him by his back, tucked up under
his shaggy belly, there I hung, face upward,
485   both hands locked in his marvelous deep fleece,
clinging for dear life, my spirit steeled, enduring . . .
So we held on, desperate, waiting Dawn's first light.
                                                    As soon
as young Dawn with her rose-red fingers shone once more
the rams went rumbling out of the cave toward pasture,
490   the ewes kept bleating round the pens, unmilked,
their udders about to burst. Their master now,
heaving in torment, felt the back of each animal
halting before him here, but the idiot never sensed
my men were trussed up under their thick fleecy ribs.
495   And last of them all came my great ram now, striding out,
weighed down with his dense wool and my deep plots.
Stroking him gently, powerful Polyphemus murmured,
'Dear old ram, why last of the flock to quit the cave?
In the good old days you'd never lag behind the rest—
500   you with your long marching strides, first by far
of the flock to graze the fresh young grasses,
first by far to reach the rippling streams,
first to turn back home, keen for your fold
when night comes on—but now you're last of all.
505   And why? Sick at heart for your master's eye

that coward gouged out with his wicked crew?—
only after he'd stunned my wits with wine—
that, that Nobody . . .
who's not escaped his death, I swear, not yet.
510   Oh if only you thought like *me,* had words like *me*
to tell me where that scoundrel is cringing from my rage!
I'd smash him against the ground, I'd spill his brains—
flooding across my cave—and that would ease my heart
of the pains that good-for-nothing Nobody made me suffer!'

515   And with that threat he let my ram go free outside.
But soon as we'd got one foot past cave and courtyard,
first I loosed myself from the ram, then loosed my men,
then quickly, glancing back again and again we drove
our flock, good plump beasts with their long shanks,
520   straight to the ship, and a welcome sight we were
to loyal comrades—we who'd escaped our deaths—
but for all the rest they broke down and wailed.
I cut it short, I stopped each shipmate's cries,
my head tossing, brows frowning, silent signals
525   to hurry, tumble our fleecy herd on board,
launch out on the open sea!
They swung aboard, they sat to the oars in ranks
and in rhythm churned the water white with stroke on stroke.
But once offshore as far as a man's shout can carry,
530   I called back to the Cyclops, stinging taunts:
'So, Cyclops, no weak coward it was whose crew
you bent to devour there in your vaulted cave—
you with your brute force! Your filthy crimes
came down on your own head, you shameless cannibal,
535   daring to eat your guests in your own house—
so Zeus and the other gods have paid you back!'

       That made the rage of the monster boil over.
Ripping off the peak of a towering crag, he heaved it
so hard the boulder landed just in front of our dark prow
540   and a huge swell reared up as the rock went plunging under—
a tidal wave from the open sea. The sudden backwash
drove us landward again, forcing us close inshore
but grabbing a long pole, I thrust us off and away,
tossing my head for dear life, signaling crews
545   to put their backs in the oars, escape grim death.
They threw themselves in the labor, rowed on fast
but once we'd plowed the breakers twice as far,
again I began to taunt the Cyclops—men around me
trying to check me, calm me, left and right:
550   'So headstrong—why? Why rile the beast again?'

       'That rock he flung in the sea just now, hurling our ship
to shore once more—we thought we'd die on the spot!'

'If he'd caught a sound from one of us, just a moan,
he would have crushed our heads and ship timbers
555   with one heave of another flashing, jagged rock!'

'Good god, the brute can throw!'
                              So they begged
but they could not bring my fighting spirit round.
I called back with another burst of anger, 'Cyclops—
if any man on the face of the earth should ask you
560   who blinded you, shamed you so—say Odysseus,
raider of cities, *he* gouged out your eye,
Laertes' son who makes his home in Ithaca!'

     So I vaunted and he groaned back in answer,
'Oh no, no—that prophecy years ago . . .
565   it all comes home to me with a vengeance now!
We once had a prophet here, a great tall man,
Telemus, Eurymus' son, a master at reading signs,
who grew old in his trade among his fellow-Cyclops.
All this, he warned me, would come to pass someday—
570   that I'd be blinded here at the hands of one Odysseus.
But I always looked for a handsome giant man to cross my path,
some fighter clad in power like armor-plate, but now,
look what a dwarf, a spineless good-for-nothing,
stuns me with wine, then gouges out my eye!
575   Come here, Odysseus, let me give you a guest-gift
and urge Poseidon the earthquake god to speed you home.
I am his son and he claims to be my father, true,
and he himself will heal me if he pleases—
no other blessed god, no man can do the work!'
                                'Heal you!'—
580   here was my parting shot—'Would to god I could strip you
of life and breath and ship you down to the House of Death
as surely as no one will ever heal your eye,
not even your earthquake god himself!'

     But at that he bellowed out to lord Poseidon,
585   thrusting his arms to the starry skies, and prayed, 'Hear me—
Poseidon, god of the sea-blue mane who rocks the earth!
If I really am your son and you claim to be my father—
come, grant that Odysseus, raider of cities,
Laertes' son who makes his home in Ithaca,
590   never reaches home. Or if he's fated to see
his people once again and reach his well-built house
and his own native country, let him come home late
and come a broken man—all shipmates lost,
alone in a stranger's ship—
595   and let him find a world of pain at home!'
                              So he prayed
and the god of the sea-blue mane, Poseidon, heard his prayer.
The monster suddenly hoisted a boulder—far larger—

wheeled and heaved it, putting his weight behind it,
massive strength, and the boulder crashed close,
600 landing just in the wake of our dark stern,
just failing to graze the rudder's bladed edge.
A huge swell reared up as the rock went plunging under,
yes, and the tidal breaker drove us out to our island's
far shore where all my well-decked ships lay moored,
605 clustered, waiting, and huddled round them, crewmen
sat in anguish, waiting, chafing for our return.
We beached our vessel hard ashore on the sand,
we swung out in the frothing surf ourselves,
and herding Cyclops' sheep from our deep holds
610 we shared them round so no one, not on my account,
would go deprived of his fair share of spoils.
But the splendid ram—as we meted out the flocks
my friends-in-arms made him my prize of honor,
mine alone, and I slaughtered him on the beach
615 and burnt his thighs to Cronus' mighty son,
Zeus of the thundercloud who rules the world.
But my sacrifices failed to move the god:
Zeus was still obsessed with plans to destroy
my entire oarswept fleet and loyal crew of comrades.
620 Now all day long till the sun went down we sat
and feasted on sides of meat and heady wine.
Then when the sun had set and night came on
we lay down and slept at the water's shelving edge.
When young Dawn with her rose-red fingers shone once more
625 I roused the men straightway, ordering all crews
to man the ships and cast off cables quickly.
They swung aboard at once, they sat to the oars in ranks
and in rhythm churned the water white with stroke on stroke.
And from there we sailed on, glad to escape our death
630 yet sick at heart for the comrades we had lost."

BOOK 10. THE BEWITCHING QUEEN OF AEAEA

"We reached the Aeolian island next, the home of Aeolus,
Hippotas' son, beloved by the gods who never die—
a great floating island it was, and round it all
huge ramparts rise of indestructible bronze
5   and sheer rock cliffs shoot up from sea to sky.
The king had sired twelve children within his halls,
six daughters and six sons in the lusty prime of youth,
so he gave his daughters as wives to his six sons.
Seated beside their dear father and doting mother,
10 with delicacies aplenty spread before them,
they feast on forever . . . All day long
the halls breathe the savor of roasted meats

and echo round to the low moan of blowing pipes,
and all night long, each one by his faithful mate,
15   they sleep under soft-piled rugs on corded bedsteads.
To this city of theirs we came, their splendid palace,
and Aeolus hosted me one entire month, he pressed me for news
of Troy and the Argive ships and how we sailed for home,
and I told him the whole long story, first to last.
20   And then, when I begged him to send me on my way,
he denied me nothing, he went about my passage.
He gave me a sack, the skin of a full-grown ox,
binding inside the winds that howl from every quarter,
for Zeus had made that king the master of all the winds,
25   with power to calm them down or rouse them as he pleased.
Aeolus stowed the sack inside my holds, lashed so fast
with a burnished silver cord
not even a slight puff could slip past that knot.
Yet he set the West Wind free to blow us on our way
30   and waft our squadron home. But his plan was bound to fail,
yes, our own reckless folly swept us on to ruin . . .

    Nine whole days we sailed, nine nights, nonstop.
On the tenth our own land hove into sight at last—
we were so close we could see men tending fires.
35   But now an enticing sleep came on me, bone-weary
from working the vessel's sheet myself, no letup,
never trusting the ropes to any other mate,
the faster to journey back to native land.
But the crews began to mutter among themselves,
40   sure I was hauling troves of gold and silver home,
the gifts of open-hearted Aeolus, Hippotas' son.
'The old story!' One man glanced at another, grumbling.
'Look at our captain's luck—so loved by the world,
so prized at every landfall, every port of call.'

45   'Heaps of lovely plunder he hauls home from Troy,
while we who went through slogging just as hard,
we go home empty-handed.'
                            'Now this Aeolus loads him
down with treasure. Favoritism, friend to friend!'

    'Hurry, let's see what loot is in that sack,
50   how much gold and silver. Break it open—now!'

    A fatal plan, but it won my shipmates over.
They loosed the sack and all the winds burst out
and a sudden squall struck and swept us back to sea,
wailing, in tears, far from our own native land.
55   And I woke up with a start, my spirit churning—
should I leap over the side and drown at once or
grit my teeth and bear it, stay among the living?

I bore it all, held firm, hiding my face,
clinging tight to the decks

60 while heavy squalls blasted our squadron back
again to Aeolus' island, shipmates groaning hard.

    We disembarked on the coast, drew water there
and crewmen snatched a meal by the swift ships.
Once we'd had our fill of food and drink

65 I took a shipmate along with me, a herald too,
and approached King Aeolus' famous halls and here
we found him feasting beside his wife and many children.
Reaching the doorposts at the threshold, down we sat
but our hosts, amazed to see us, only shouted questions:

70 'Back again, Odysseus—why? Some blustering god attacked you?
Surely we launched you well, we sped you on your way
to your own land and house, or any place you pleased.'

    So they taunted, and I replied in deep despair,
'A mutinous crew undid me—that and a cruel sleep.

75 Set it to rights, my friends. You have the power!'

    So I pleaded—gentle, humble appeals—
but our hosts turned silent, hushed . . .
and the father broke forth with an ultimatum:
'Away from my island—fast—most cursed man alive!

80 It's a crime to host a man or speed him on his way
when the blessed deathless gods despise him so.
Crawling back like this—
it proves the immortals hate you! Out—get out!'

    Groan as I did, his curses drove me from his halls

85 and from there we pulled away with heavy hearts,
with the crews' spirit broken under the oars' labor,
thanks to our own folly . . . no favoring wind in sight.

    Six whole days we rowed, six nights, nonstop.
On the seventh day we raised the Laestrygonian land,

90 Telepylus heights where the craggy fort of Lamus rises.
Where shepherd calls to shepherd as one drives in his flocks
and the other drives his out and he calls back in answer,
where a man who never sleeps could rake in double wages,
one for herding cattle, one for pasturing fleecy sheep,

95 the nightfall and the sunrise march so close together.
We entered a fine harbor there, all walled around
by a great unbroken sweep of sky-scraping cliff
and two steep headlands, fronting each other, close
around the mouth so the passage in is cramped.

100 Here the rest of my rolling squadron steered,
right into the gaping cove and moored tightly,
prow by prow. Never a swell there, big or small;
a milk-white calm spreads all around the place.

But I alone anchored my black ship outside,
105   well clear of the harbor's jaws
I tied her fast to a cliffside with a cable.
I scaled its rock face to a lookout on its crest
but glimpsed no trace of the work of man or beast from there;
all I spied was a plume of smoke, drifting off the land.
110   So I sent some crew ahead to learn who lived there—
men like us perhaps, who live on bread?
Two good mates I chose and a third to run the news.
They disembarked and set out on a beaten trail
the wagons used for hauling timber down to town
115   from the mountain heights above . . . .
and before the walls they met a girl, drawing water,
Antiphates' strapping daughter—king of the Laestrygonians.
She'd come down to a clear running spring, Artacia,
where the local people came to fill their pails.
120   My shipmates clustered round her, asking questions:
who was king of the realm? who ruled the natives here?
She waved at once to her father's high-roofed halls.
They entered the sumptuous palace, found his wife inside—
a woman huge as a mountain crag who filled them all with horror.
125   Straightaway she summoned royal Antiphates from assembly,
her husband, who prepared my crew a barbarous welcome.
Snatching one of my men, he tore him up for dinner—
the other two sprang free and reached the ships.
But the king let loose a howling through the town
130   that brought tremendous Laestrygonians swarming up
from every side—hundreds, not like men, like Giants!
Down from the cliffs they flung great rocks a man could hardly hoist
and a ghastly shattering din rose up from all the ships—
men in their death-cries, hulls smashed to splinters—
135   They speared the crews like fish
and whisked them home to make their grisly meal.
But while they killed them off in the harbor depths
I pulled the sword from beside my hip and hacked away
at the ropes that moored my blue-prowed ship of war
140   and shouted rapid orders at my shipmates:
'Put your backs in the oars—now row or die!'
In terror of death they ripped the swells—all as one—
and what a joy as we darted out toward open sea,
clear of those beetling cliffs . . . my ship alone.
145   But the rest went down en masse. Our squadron sank.

    From there we sailed on, glad to escape our death
yet sick at heart for the dear companions we had lost.
We reached the Aeaean island next, the home of Circe
the nymph with lovely braids, an awesome power too
150   who can speak with human voice,
the true sister of murderous-minded Aeetes.

Both were bred by the Sun who lights our lives;
their mother was Perse, a child the Ocean bore.
We brought our ship to port without a sound
155   as a god eased her into a harbor safe and snug,
and for two days and two nights we lay by there,
eating our hearts out, bent with pain and bone-tired.
When Dawn with her lovely locks brought on the third day,
at last I took my spear and my sharp sword again,
160   rushed up from the ship to find a lookout point,
hoping to glimpse some sign of human labor,
catch some human voices . . .
I scaled a commanding crag and, scanning hard,
I could just make out some smoke from Circe's halls,
165   drifting up from the broad terrain through brush and woods.
Mulling it over, I thought I'd scout the ground—
that fire aglow in the smoke, I saw it, true,
but soon enough this seemed the better plan:
I'd go back to shore and the swift ship first,
170   feed the men, then send *them* out for scouting.
I was well on my way down, nearing our ship
when a god took pity on me, wandering all alone;
he sent me a big stag with high branching antlers,
right across my path—the sun's heat forced him down
175   from his forest range to drink at a river's banks—
just bounding out of the timber when I hit him
square in the backbone, halfway down the spine
and my bronze spear went punching clean through—
he dropped in the dust, groaning, gasping out his breath.
180   Treading on him, I wrenched my bronze spear from the wound,
left it there on the ground, and snapping off some twigs
and creepers, twisted a rope about a fathom long,
I braided it tight, hand over hand, then lashed
the four hocks of that magnificent beast.
185   Loaded round my neck I lugged him toward the ship,
trudging, propped on my spear—no way to sling him
over a shoulder, steadying him with one free arm—
the kill was so immense!
I flung him down by the hull and roused the men,
190   going up to them all with a word to lift their spirits:
'Listen to me, my comrades, brothers in hardship—
we won't go down to the House of Death, not yet,
not till our day arrives. Up with you, look,
there's still some meat and drink in our good ship.
195   Put our minds on food—why die of hunger here?'

   My hardy urging brought them round at once.
Heads came up from cloaks and there by the barren sea
they gazed at the stag, their eyes wide—my noble trophy.
But once they'd looked their fill and warmed their hearts,

200   they washed their hands and prepared a splendid meal.
        Now all day long till the sun went down we sat
        and feasted on sides of meat and seasoned wine.
        Then when the sun had set and night came on
        we lay down and slept at the water's shelving edge.
205   When young Dawn with her rose-red fingers shone once more
        I called a muster quickly, informing all the crew,
        'Listen to me, my comrades, brothers in hardship,
        we can't tell east from west, the dawn from the dusk,
        nor where the sun that lights our lives goes under earth
210   nor where it rises. We must think of a plan at once,
        some cunning stroke. I doubt there's one still left.
        I scaled a commanding crag and from that height
        surveyed an entire island
        ringed like a crown by endless wastes of sea.
215   But the land itself lies low, and I did see smoke
        drifting up from its heart through thick brush and woods.'

        My message broke their spirit as they recalled
        the gruesome work of the Laestrygonian king Antiphates
        and the hearty cannibal Cyclops thirsting for our blood.
220   They burst into cries, wailing, streaming live tears
        that gained us nothing—what good can come of grief?

        And so, numbering off my band of men-at-arms
        into two platoons, I assigned them each a leader:
        I took one and lord Eurylochus the other.
225   We quickly shook lots in a bronze helmet—
        the lot of brave Eurylochus leapt out first.
        So he moved off with his two and twenty comrades,
        weeping, leaving us behind in tears as well . . .
        Deep in the wooded glens they came on Circe's palace
230   built of dressed stone on a cleared rise of land.
        Mountain wolves and lions were roaming round the grounds—
        she'd bewitched them herself, she gave them magic drugs.
        But they wouldn't attack my men; they just came pawing
        up around them, fawning, swishing their long tails—
235   eager as hounds that fawn around their master,
        coming home from a feast,
        who always brings back scraps to calm them down.
        So they came nuzzling round my men—lions, wolves
        with big powerful claws—and the men cringed in fear
240   at the sight of those strange, ferocious beasts . . .But still
        they paused at her doors, the nymph with lovely braids,
        Circe—and deep inside they heard her singing, lifting
        her spellbinding voice as she glided back and forth
        at her great immortal loom, her enchanting web
245   a shimmering glory only goddesses can weave.
        Polites, captain of armies, took command,

the closest, most devoted man I had: 'Friends,
there's someone inside, plying a great loom,
and how she sings—enthralling!
250   The whole house is echoing to her song.
Goddess or woman—let's call out to her now!'

    So he urged and the men called out and hailed her.
She opened her gleaming doors at once and stepped forth,
inviting them all in, and in they went, all innocence.
255   Only Eurylochus stayed behind—he sensed a trap . . .
She ushered them in to sit on high-backed chairs,
then she mixed them a potion—cheese, barley
and pale honey mulled in Pramnian wine—
but into the brew she stirred her wicked drugs
260   to wipe from their memories any thought of home.
Once they'd drained the bowls she filled, suddenly
she struck with her wand, drove them into her pigsties,
all of them bristling into swine—with grunts,
snouts—even their bodies, yes, and only
265   the men's minds stayed steadfast as before.
So off they went to their pens, sobbing, squealing
as Circe flung them acorns, cornel nuts and mast,
common fodder for hogs that root and roll in mud.

    Back Eurylochus ran to our swift black ship
270   to tell the disaster our poor friends had faced.
But try as he might, he couldn't get a word out.
Numbing sorrow had stunned the man to silence—
tears welled in his eyes, his heart possessed by grief.
We assailed him with questions—all at our wits' end—
275   till at last he could recount the fate our friends had met:
'Off we went through the brush, captain, as you commanded.
Deep in the wooded glens we came on Circe's palace
built of dressed stone on a cleared rise of land.
Someone inside was plying a great loom,
280   and how she sang—in a high clear voice!
Goddess or woman—we called out and hailed her . . .
She opened her gleaming doors at once and stepped forth,
inviting us all in, and in we went, all innocence.
But *I* stayed behind—I sensed a trap. Suddenly
285   all vanished—blotted out—not one face showed again,
though I sat there keeping watch a good long time.'

    At that report I slung the hefty bronze blade
of my silver-studded sword around my shoulder,
slung my bow on too and told our comrade,
290   'Lead me back by the same way that you came.'
But he flung both arms around my knees and pleaded,
begging me with his tears and winging words:

'Don't force me back there, captain, king—
leave me here on the spot.
295   You will never return yourself, I swear,
you'll never bring back a single man alive.
Quick, cut and run with the rest of us here—
we can still escape the fatal day!'

    But I shot back, 'Eurylochus, stay right here,
300   eating, drinking, safe by the black ship.
I must be off. Necessity drives me on.'

    Leaving the ship and shore, I headed inland,
clambering up through hushed, entrancing glades until,
as I was nearing the halls of Circe skilled in spells,
305   approaching her palace—Hermes god of the golden wand
crossed my path, and he looked for all the world
like a young man sporting his first beard,
just in the prime and warm pride of youth,
and grasped me by the hand and asked me kindly,
310   'Where are you going now, my unlucky friend—
trekking over the hills alone in unfamiliar country?
And your men are all in there, in Circe's palace,
cooped like swine, hock by jowl in the sties.
Have you come to set them free?
315   Well, I warn you, you won't get home yourself,
you'll stay right there, trapped with all the rest.
But wait, I can save you, free you from that great danger.
Look, here is a potent drug. Take it to Circe's halls—
its power alone will shield you from the fatal day.
320   Let me tell you of all the witch's subtle craft . . .
She'll mix you a potion, lace the brew with drugs
but she'll be powerless to bewitch you, even so—
this magic herb I give will fight her spells.
Now here's your plan of action, step by step.
325   The moment Circe strikes with her long thin wand,
you draw your sharp sword sheathed at your hip
and rush her fast as if to run her through!
She'll cower in fear and coax you to her bed—
but don't refuse the goddess' bed, not then, not if
330   she's to release your friends and treat you well yourself.
But have her swear the binding oath of the blessed gods
she'll never plot some new intrigue to harm you,
once you lie there naked—
never unman you, strip away your courage!'
                                 With that
335   the giant-killer handed over the magic herb,
pulling it from the earth,
and Hermes showed me all its name and nature.
Its root is black and its flower white as milk

and the gods call it moly. Dangerous for a mortal man
340   to pluck from the soil but not for deathless gods.
All lies within their power.
                                        Now Hermes went his way
to the steep heights of Olympus, over the island's woods
while I, just approaching the halls of Circe,
my heart a heaving storm at every step,
345   paused at her doors, the nymph with lovely braids—
I stood and shouted to her there. She heard my voice,
she opened her gleaming doors at once and stepped forth,
inviting me in, and in I went, all anguish now . . .
She led me in to sit on a silver-studded chair,
350   ornately carved, with a stool to rest my feet.
In a golden bowl she mixed a potion for me to drink,
stirring her poison in, her heart aswirl with evil.
And then she passed it on, I drank it down
but it never worked its spell—
355   she struck with her wand and 'Now,' she cried,
'off to your sty, you swine, and wallow with your friends!'
But I, I drew my sharp sword sheathed at my hip
and rushed her fast as if to run her through—
She screamed, slid under my blade, hugged my knees
360   with a flood of warm tears and a burst of winging words:
'Who are you? where are you from? your city? your parents?
I'm wonderstruck—you drank my drugs, you're not bewitched!
Never has any other man withstood my potion, never,
once it's past his lips and he has drunk it down.
365   You have a mind in *you* no magic can enchant!
You must be Odysseus, man of twists and turns—
Hermes the giant-killer, god of the golden wand,
he always said you'd come,
homeward bound from Troy in your swift black ship.
370   Come, sheathe your sword, let's go to bed together,
mount my bed and mix in the magic work of love—
we'll breed deep trust between us.'
                                        So she enticed
but I fought back, still wary. 'Circe, Circe,
how dare you tell me to treat you with any warmth?
375   You who turned my men to swine in your own house and now
you hold me here as well—teeming with treachery
you lure me to your room to mount your bed,
so once I lie there naked
you'll unman me, strip away my courage!
380   Mount your bed? Not for all the world. Not
until you consent to swear, goddess, a binding oath
you'll never plot some new intrigue to harm me!'
                                        Straightaway
she began to swear the oath that I required—never,
she'd never do me harm—and when she'd finished,

385   then, at last, I mounted Circe's gorgeous bed . . .

      At the same time her handmaids bustled through the halls,
four in all who perform the goddess' household tasks:
nymphs, daughters born of the springs and groves
and the sacred rivers running down to open sea.
390   One draped the chairs with fine crimson covers
over the seats she'd spread with linen cloths below.
A second drew up silver tables before the chairs
and laid out golden trays to hold the bread.
A third mulled heady, heart-warming wine
395   in a silver bowl and set out golden cups.
A fourth brought water and lit a blazing fire
beneath a massive cauldron. The water heated soon,
and once it reached the boil in the glowing bronze
she eased me into a tub and bathed me from the cauldron,
400   mixing the hot and cold to suit my taste, showering
head and shoulders down until she'd washed away
the spirit-numbing exhaustion from my body.
The bathing finished, rubbing me sleek with oil,
throwing warm fleece and a shirt around my shoulders,
405   she led me in to sit on a silver-studded chair,
ornately carved, with a stool to rest my feet.
A maid brought water soon in a graceful golden pitcher
and over a silver basin tipped it out
so I might rinse my hands,
410   then pulled a gleaming table to my side.
A staid housekeeper brought on bread to serve me,
appetizers aplenty too, lavish with her bounty.
She pressed me to eat. I had no taste for food.
I just sat there, mind wandering, far away . . .
415   lost in grim forebodings.
                     As soon as Circe saw me,
huddled, not touching my food, immersed in sorrow,
she sidled near with a coaxing, winged word:
'Odysseus, why just sit there, struck dumb,
eating your heart out, not touching food or drink?
420   Suspect me of still more treachery? Nothing to fear.
Haven't I just sworn my solemn, binding oath?'

      So she asked, but I protested, 'Circe—
how could any man in his right mind endure
the taste of food and drink before he'd freed
425   his comrades-in-arms and looked them in the eyes?
If you, you really want me to eat and drink,
set them free, all my beloved comrades—
let me feast my eyes.'
                So I demanded.
Circe strode on through the halls and out,
430   her wand held high in hand and, flinging open the pens,

drove forth my men, who looked like full-grown swine.
Facing her, there they stood as she went along the ranks,
anointing them one by one with some new magic oil—
and look, the bristles grown by the first wicked drug

435   that Circe gave them slipped away from their limbs
and they turned men again: younger than ever,
taller by far, more handsome to the eye, and yes,
they knew me at once and each man grasped my hands
and a painful longing for tears overcame us all,

440   a terrible sobbing echoed through the house . . .
The goddess herself was moved and, standing by me,
warmly urged me on—a lustrous goddess now:
'Royal son of Laertes, Odysseus, tried and true,
go at once to your ship at the water's edge,

445   haul her straight up on the shore first
and stow your cargo and running gear in caves,
then back you come and bring your trusty crew.'

    Her urging won my stubborn spirit over.
Down I went to the swift ship at the water's edge,

450   and there on the decks I found my loyal crew
consumed with grief and weeping live warm tears.
But now, as calves in stalls when cows come home,
droves of them herded back from field to farmyard
once they've grazed their fill—as all their young calves

455   come frisking out to meet them, bucking out of their pens,
lowing nonstop, jostling, rushing round their mothers—
so my shipmates there at the sight of my return
came pressing round me now, streaming tears,
so deeply moved in their hearts they felt as if

460   they'd made it back to their own land, their city,
Ithaca's rocky soil where they were bred and reared.
And through their tears their words went winging home:
'You're back again, my king! How thrilled we are—
as if we'd reached our country, Ithaca, at last!

465   But come, tell us about the fate our comrades met.'

    Still I replied with a timely word of comfort:
'Let's haul our ship straight up on the shore first
and stow our cargo and running gear in caves.
Then hurry, all of you, come along with me

470   to see our friends in the magic halls of Circe,
eating and drinking—the feast flows on forever.'

    So I said and they jumped to do my bidding.
Only Eurylochus tried to hold my shipmates back,
his mutinous outburst aimed at one and all:

475   'Poor fools, where are we running now?
Why are we tempting fate?—
why stumble blindly down to Circe's halls?

She'll turn us all into pigs or wolves or lions
made to guard that palace of hers—by force, I tell you—
480   just as the Cyclops trapped our comrades in his lair
with hotheaded Odysseus right beside them all—
thanks to this man's rashness they died too!'

So he declared and I had half a mind
to draw the sharp sword from beside my hip
485   and slice his head off, tumbling down in the dust,
close kin that he was. But comrades checked me,
each man trying to calm me, left and right:
'Captain, we'll leave him here if you command,
just where he is, to sit and guard the ship.
490   Lead us on to the magic halls of Circe.'
                                    With that,
up from the ship and shore they headed inland.
Nor did Eurylochus malinger by the hull;
he straggled behind the rest,
dreading the sharp blast of my rebuke.
                                    All the while
495   Circe had bathed my other comrades in her palace,
caring and kindly, rubbed them sleek with oil
and decked them out in fleecy cloaks and shirts.
We found them all together, feasting in her halls.
Once we had recognized each other, gazing face-to-face,
500   we all broke down and wept—and the house resounded now
and Circe the lustrous one came toward me, pleading,
'Royal son of Laertes, Odysseus, man of action,
no more tears now, calm these tides of sorrow.
Well I know what pains you bore on the swarming sea,
505   what punishment you endured from hostile men on land.
But come now, eat your food and drink your wine
till the same courage fills your chests, now as then,
when you first set sail from native land, from rocky Ithaca!
Now you are burnt-out husks, your spirits haggard, sere,
510   always brooding over your wanderings long and hard,
your hearts never lifting with any joy—
you've suffered far too much.'
                                    So she enticed
and won our battle-hardened spirits over.
And there we sat at ease,
515   day in, day out, till a year had run its course,
feasting on sides of meat and drafts of heady wine . . .
But then, when the year was gone and the seasons wheeled by
and the months waned and the long days came round again,
my loyal comrades took me aside and prodded,
520   'Captain, this is madness!
High time you thought of your own home at last,
if it really is your fate to make it back alive

and reach your well-built house and native land.'

  Their urging brought my stubborn spirit round.
525 So all that day till the sun went down we sat
and feasted on sides of meat and heady wine.
Then when the sun had set and night came on
the men lay down to sleep in the shadowed halls
but I went up to that luxurious bed of Circe's,
530 hugged her by the knees
and the goddess heard my winging supplication:
'Circe, now make good a promise you gave me once—
it's time to help me home. My heart longs to be home,
my comrades' hearts as well. They wear me down,
535 pleading with me whenever you're away.'
         So I pressed
and the lustrous goddess answered me in turn:
'Royal son of Laertes, Odysseus, old campaigner,
stay on no more in my house against your will.
But first another journey calls. You must travel down
540 to the House of Death and the awesome one, Persephone,[1]
there to consult the ghost of Tiresias, seer of Thebes,
the great blind prophet whose mind remains unshaken.
Even in death—Persephone has given him wisdom,
everlasting vision to him and him alone . . .
545 the rest of the dead are empty, flitting shades.'

  So she said and crushed the heart inside me.
I knelt in her bed and wept. I'd no desire
to go on living and see the rising light of day.
But once I'd had my fill of tears and writhing there,
550 at last I found the words to venture, 'Circe, Circe,
who can pilot us on that journey? Who has ever
reached the House of Death in a black ship?'

  The lustrous goddess answered, never pausing,
'Royal son of Laertes, Odysseus, born for exploits,
555 let no lack of a pilot at the helm concern you, no,
just step your mast and spread your white sail wide—
sit back and the North Wind will speed you on your way.
But once your vessel has cut across the Ocean River
you will raise a desolate coast and Persephone's Grove,
560 her tall black poplars, willows whose fruit dies young.
Beach your vessel hard by the Ocean's churning shore
and make your own way down to the moldering House of Death.
And there into Acheron, the Flood of Grief, two rivers flow,
the torrent River of Fire, the wailing River of Tears
565 that branches off from Styx, the Stream of Hate,
and a stark crag looms
where the two rivers thunder down and meet.

1. Divine queen of the underworld, wife of Hades, and daughter of Demeter.

Once there, go forward, hero. Do as I say now.
Dig a trench of about a forearm's depth and length
570 and around it pour libations out to all the dead—
first with milk and honey, and then with mellow wine,
then water third and last, and sprinkle glistening barley
over it all, and vow again and again to all the dead,
to the drifting, listless spirits of their ghosts,
575 that once you return to Ithaca you will slaughter
a barren heifer in your halls, the best you have,
and load a pyre with treasures—and to Tiresias,
alone, apart, you will offer a sleek black ram,
the pride of all your herds. And once your prayers
580 have invoked the nations of the dead in their dim glory,
slaughter a ram and a black ewe, turning both their heads
toward Erebus,[2] but turn your head away, looking toward
the Ocean River. Suddenly then the countless shades
of the dead and gone will surge around you there.
585 But order your men at once to flay the sheep
that lie before you, killed by your ruthless blade,
and burn them both, and then say prayers to the gods,
to the almighty god of death and dread Persephone.
But you—draw your sharp sword from beside your hip,
590 sit down on alert there, and never let the ghosts
of the shambling, shiftless dead come near that blood
till you have questioned Tiresias yourself. Soon, soon
the great seer will appear before you, captain of armies:
he will tell you the way to go, the stages of your voyage,
595 how you can cross the swarming sea and reach home at last.'

      And with those words Dawn rose on her golden throne
and Circe dressed me quickly in sea-cloak and shirt
while the queen slipped on a loose, glistening robe,
filmy, a joy to the eye, and round her waist
600 she ran a brocaded golden belt
and over her head a scarf to shield her brow.
And I strode on through the halls to stir my men,
hovering over each with a winning word: 'Up now!
No more lazing away in sleep, we must set sail—
605 Queen Circe has shown the way.'
                              I brought them round,
my hardy friends-in-arms, but not even from there
could I get them safely off without a loss . . .
There was a man, Elpenor, the youngest in our ranks,
none too brave in battle, none too sound in mind.
610 He'd strayed from his mates in Circe's magic halls
and keen for the cool night air,
sodden with wine he'd bedded down on her roofs.
But roused by the shouts and tread of marching men,

2. The dark underworld.

he leapt up with a start at dawn but still so dazed
615 he forgot to climb back down again by the long ladder—
headfirst from the roof he plunged, his neck snapped
from the backbone, his soul flew down to Death.

Once on our way, I gave the men their orders:
'You think we are headed home, our own dear land?
620 Well, Circe sets us a rather different course . . .
down to the House of Death and the awesome one, Persephone,
there to consult the ghost of Tiresias, seer of Thebes.'

So I said, and it broke my shipmates' hearts.
They sank down on the ground, moaning, tore their hair.
625 But it gained us nothing—what good can come of grief?

Back to the swift ship at the water's edge we went,
our spirits deep in anguish, faces wet with tears.
But Circe got to the dark hull before us,
tethered a ram and black ewe close by—
630 slipping past unseen. Who can glimpse a god
who wants to be invisible gliding here and there?"

BOOK 11. THE KINGDOM OF THE DEAD

"Now down we came to the ship at the water's edge,
we hauled and launched her into the sunlit breakers first,
stepped the mast in the black craft and set our sail
and loaded the sheep aboard, the ram and ewe,
5   then we ourselves embarked, streaming tears,
our hearts weighed down with anguish . . .
But Circe, the awesome nymph with lovely braids
who speaks with human voice, sent us a hardy shipmate,
yes, a fresh following wind ruffling up in our wake,
10   bellying out our sail to drive our blue prow on as we,
securing the running gear from stem to stern, sat back
while the wind and helmsman kept her true on course.
The sail stretched taut as she cut the sea all day
and the sun sank and the roads of the world grew dark.

15   And she made the outer limits, the Ocean River's bounds
where Cimmerian people have their homes—their realm and city
shrouded in mist and cloud. The eye of the Sun can never
flash his rays through the dark and bring them light,
not when he climbs the starry skies or when he wheels
20   back down from the heights to touch the earth once more—
an endless, deadly night overhangs those wretched men.
There, gaining that point, we beached our craft
and herding out the sheep, we picked our way
by the Ocean's banks until we gained the place
25   that Circe made our goal.
                    Here at the spot

Perimedes and Eurylochus held the victims fast,
and I, drawing my sharp sword from beside my hip,
dug a trench of about a forearm's depth and length
and around it poured libations out to all the dead,
30   first with milk and honey, and then with mellow wine,
then water third and last, and sprinkled glistening barley
over it all, and time and again I vowed to all the dead,
to the drifting, listless spirits of their ghosts,
that once I returned to Ithaca I would slaughter
35   a barren heifer in my halls, the best I had,
and load a pyre with treasures—and to Tiresias,
alone, apart, I would offer a sleek black ram,
the pride of all my herds. And once my vows
and prayers had invoked the nations of the dead,
40   I took the victims, over the trench I cut their throats
and the dark blood flowed in—and up out of Erebus they came,
flocking toward me now, the ghosts of the dead and gone . . .
Brides and unwed youths and old men who had suffered much
and girls with their tender hearts freshly scarred by sorrow
45   and great armies of battle dead, stabbed by bronze spears,
men of war still wrapped in bloody armor—thousands
swarming around the trench from every side—
unearthly cries—blanching terror gripped me!
I ordered the men at once to flay the sheep
50   that lay before us, killed by my ruthless blade,
and burn them both, and then say prayers to the gods,
to the almighty god of death and dread Persephone.
But I, the sharp sword drawn from beside my hip,
sat down on alert there and never let the ghosts
55   of the shambling, shiftless dead come near that blood
till I had questioned Tiresias myself.
                                    But first
the ghost of Elpenor, my companion, came toward me.
He'd not been buried under the wide ways of earth,
not yet, we'd left his body in Circe's house,
60   unwept, unburied—this other labor pressed us.
But I wept to see him now, pity touched my heart
and I called out a winged word to him there: 'Elpenor,
how did you travel down to the world of darkness?
Faster on foot, I see, than I in my black ship.'

65   My comrade groaned as he offered me an answer:
'Royal son of Laertes, Odysseus, old campaigner,
the doom of an angry god, and god knows how much wine—
they were my ruin, captain . . . I'd bedded down
on the roof of Circe's house but never thought
70   to climb back down again by the long ladder—
headfirst from the roof I plunged, my neck snapped
from the backbone, my soul flew down to Death. Now,

I beg you by those you left behind, so far from here,
your wife, your father who bred and reared you as a boy,
75   and Telemachus, left at home in your halls, your only son.
Well I know when you leave this lodging of the dead
that you and your ship will put ashore again
at the island of Aeaea—then and there,
my lord, remember me, I beg you! Don't sail off
80   and desert me, left behind unwept, unburied, don't,
or my curse may draw god's fury on your head.
No, burn me in full armor, all my harness,
heap my mound by the churning gray surf—
a man whose luck ran out—
85   so even men to come will learn my story.
Perform my rites, and plant on my tomb that oar
I swung with mates when I rowed among the living.'

    'All this, my unlucky friend,' I reassured him,
'I will do for you. I won't forget a thing.'
                       So we sat
90   and faced each other, trading our bleak parting words,
I on my side, holding my sword above the blood,
he across from me there, my comrade's phantom
dragging out his story.
                    But look, the ghost
of my mother came! My mother, dead and gone now . . .
95   Anticleia—daughter of that great heart Autolycus—
whom I had left alive when I sailed for sacred Troy.
I broke into tears to see her here, but filled with pity,
even throbbing with grief, I would not let her ghost
approach the blood till I had questioned Tiresias myself.

100   At last he came. The shade of the famous Theban prophet,
holding a golden scepter, knew me at once and hailed me:
'Royal son of Laertes, Odysseus, master of exploits,
man of pain, what now, what brings you here,
forsaking the light of day
105   to see this joyless kingdom of the dead?
Stand back from the trench—put up your sharp sword
so I can drink the blood and tell you all the truth.'

    Moving back, I thrust my silver-studded sword
deep in its sheath, and once he had drunk the dark blood
110   the words came ringing from the prophet in his power:
'A sweet smooth journey home, renowned Odysseus,
that is what you seek
but a god will make it hard for you—I know—
you will never escape the one who shakes the earth,
115   quaking with anger at you still, still enraged
because you blinded the Cyclops, his dear son.
Even so, you and your crew may still reach home,

suffering all the way, if you only have the power
to curb their wild desire and curb your own, what's more,
120   from the day your good trim vessel first puts in
at Thrinacia Island, flees the cruel blue sea.
There you will find them grazing,
herds and fat flocks, the cattle of Helios,
god of the sun who sees all, hears all things.
125   Leave the beasts unharmed, your mind set on home,
and you all may still reach Ithaca—bent with hardship,
true—but harm them in any way, and I can see it now:
your ship destroyed, your men destroyed as well.
And even if *you* escape, you'll come home late
130   and come a broken man—all shipmates lost,
alone in a stranger's ship—
and you will find a world of pain at home,
crude, arrogant men devouring all your goods,
courting your noble wife, offering gifts to win her.
135   No doubt you will pay them back in blood when you come home!
But once you have killed those suitors in your halls—
by stealth or in open fight with slashing bronze—
go forth once more, you must . . .
carry your well-planed oar until you come
140   to a race of people who know nothing of the sea,
whose food is never seasoned with salt, strangers all
to ships with their crimson prows and long slim oars,
wings that make ships fly. And here is your sign—
unmistakable, clear, so clear you cannot miss it:
145   When another traveler falls in with you and calls
that weight across your shoulder a fan to winnow grain,
then plant your bladed, balanced oar in the earth
and sacrifice fine beasts to the lord god of the sea,
Poseidon—a ram, a bull and a ramping wild boar—
150   then journey home and render noble offerings up
to the deathless gods who rule the vaulting skies,
to all the gods in order.
And at last your own death will steal upon you . . .
a gentle, painless death, far from the sea it comes
155   to take you down, borne down with the years in ripe old age
with all your people there in blessed peace around you.
All that I have told you will come true.'
                    'Oh Tiresias,'
I replied as the prophet finished, 'surely the gods
have spun this out as fate, the gods themselves.
160   But tell me one thing more, and tell me clearly.
I see the ghost of my long-lost mother here before me.
Dead, crouching close to the blood in silence,
she cannot bear to look me in the eyes—
her own son—or speak a word to me. How,
165   lord, can I make her know me for the man I am?'

'One rule there is,' the famous seer explained,
'and simple for me to say and you to learn.
Any one of the ghosts you let approach the blood
will speak the truth to you. Anyone you refuse

170   will turn and fade away.'
                                          And with those words,
now that his prophecies had closed, the awesome shade
of lord Tiresias strode back to the House of Death.
But I kept watch there, steadfast till my mother
approached and drank the dark, clouding blood.

175   She knew me at once and wailed out in grief
and her words came winging toward me, flying home:
'Oh my son—what brings you down to the world
of death and darkness? You are still alive!
It's hard for the living to catch a glimpse of this . . .

180   Great rivers flow between us, terrible waters,
the Ocean first of all—no one could ever ford
that stream on foot, only aboard some sturdy craft.
Have you just come from Troy, wandering long years
with your men and ship? Not yet returned to Ithaca?

185   You've still not seen your wife inside your halls?'
                                                      'Mother,'
I replied, 'I had to venture down to the House of Death,
to consult the shade of Tiresias, seer of Thebes.
Never yet have I neared Achaea, never once
set foot on native ground,

190   always wandering—endless hardship from that day
I first set sail with King Agamemnon bound for Troy,
the stallion-land, to fight the Trojans there.
But tell me about yourself and spare me nothing.
What form of death overcame you, what laid you low,

195   some long slow illness? Or did Artemis showering arrows
come with her painless shafts and bring you down?
Tell me of father, tell of the son I left behind:
do my royal rights still lie in their safekeeping?
Or does some stranger hold the throne by now

200   because men think that I'll come home no more?
Please, tell me about my wife, her turn of mind,
her thoughts . . . still standing fast beside our son,
still guarding our great estates, secure as ever now?
Or has she wed some other countryman at last,

205   the finest prince among them?'
                                          'Surely, surely,'
my noble mother answered quickly, 'she's still waiting
there in your halls, poor woman, suffering so,
her life an endless hardship like your own . . .
wasting away the nights, weeping away the days.

210   No one has taken over your royal rights, not yet.
Telemachus still holds your great estates in peace,

he attends the public banquets shared with all,
the feasts a man of justice should enjoy,
for every lord invites him. As for your father,
215   he keeps to his own farm—he never goes to town—
with no bed for him there, no blankets, glossy throws;
all winter long he sleeps in the lodge with servants,
in the ashes by the fire, his body wrapped in rags.
But when summer comes and the bumper crops of harvest,
220   any spot on the rising ground of his vineyard rows
he makes his bed, heaped high with fallen leaves,
and there he lies in anguish . . .
with his old age bearing hard upon him, too,
and his grief grows as he longs for your return.
225   And I with the same grief, I died and met my fate.
No sharp-eyed Huntress showering arrows through the halls
approached and brought me down with painless shafts,
nor did some hateful illness strike me, that so often
devastates the body, drains our limbs of power.
230   No, it was my longing for *you,* my shining Odysseus—
you and your quickness, you and your gentle ways—
that tore away my life that had been sweet.'

And I, my mind in turmoil, how I longed
to embrace my mother's spirit, dead as she was!
235   Three times I rushed toward her, desperate to hold her,
three times she fluttered through my fingers, sifting away
like a shadow, dissolving like a dream, and each time
the grief cut to the heart, sharper, yes, and I,
I cried out to her, words winging into the darkness:
240   'Mother—why not wait for me? How I long to hold you!—
so even here, in the House of Death, we can fling
our loving arms around each other, take some joy
in the tears that numb the heart. Or is this just
some wraith that great Persephone sends my way
245   to make me ache with sorrow all the more?'

My noble mother answered me at once:
'My son, my son, the unluckiest man alive!
This is no deception sent by Queen Persephone,
this is just the way of mortals when we die.
250   Sinews no longer bind the flesh and bones together—
the fire in all its fury burns the body down to ashes
once life slips from the white bones, and the spirit,
rustling, flitters away . . . flown like a dream.
But you must long for the daylight. Go, quickly.
255   Remember all these things
so one day you can tell them to your wife.'

And so we both confided, trading parting words,
and there slowly came a grand array of women,

all sent before me now by august Persephone,
260   and all were wives and daughters once of princes.
They swarmed in a flock around the dark blood
while I searched for a way to question each alone,
and the more I thought, the more this seemed the best:
Drawing forth the long sharp sword from beside my hip,
265   I would not let them drink the dark blood, all in a rush,
and so they waited, coming forward one after another.
Each declared her lineage, and I explored them all.

    And the first I saw there? Tyro, born of kings,
who said her father was that great lord Salmoneus,
270   said that she was the wife of Cretheus, Aeolus' son.
And once she fell in love with the river god, Enipeus,
far the clearest river flowing across the earth,
and so she'd haunt Enipeus' glinting streams,
till taking his shape one day
275   the god who girds the earth and makes it tremble
bedded her where the swirling river rushes out to sea,
and a surging wave reared up, high as a mountain, dark,
arching over to hide the god and mortal girl together.
Loosing her virgin belt, he lapped her round in sleep
280   and when the god had consummated his work of love
he took her by the hand and hailed her warmly:
'Rejoice in our love, my lady! And when this year
has run its course you will give birth to glorious children—
bedding down with the gods is never barren, futile—
285   and you must tend them, breed and rear them well.
Now home you go, and restrain yourself, I say,
never breathe your lover's name but know—
I am Poseidon, god who rocks the earth!'

    With that he dove back in the heaving waves
290   and she conceived for the god and bore him Pelias, Neleus,
and both grew up to be stalwart aides of Zeus almighty,
both men alike. Pelias lived on the plains of Iolcos,
rich in sheepflocks, Neleus lived in sandy Pylos.
And the noble queen bore sons to Cretheus too:
295   Aeson, Pheres and Amythaon, exultant charioteer.

    And after Tyro I saw Asopus' daughter Antiope,
proud she'd spent a night in the arms of Zeus himself
and borne the god twin sons, Amphion and Zethus,
the first to build the footings of seven-gated Thebes,
300   her bastions too, for lacking ramparts none could live
in a place so vast, so open—strong as both men were.

    And I saw Alcmena next, Amphitryon's wife,
who slept in the clasp of Zeus and merged in love
and brought forth Heracles, rugged will and lion heart.
305   And I saw Megara too, magnanimous Creon's daughter

wed to the stalwart Heracles, the hero never daunted.

    And I saw the mother of Oedipus, beautiful Epicaste.
What a monstrous thing she did, in all innocence—
she married her own son . . .
310   who'd killed his father, then he married *her!*
But the gods soon made it known to all mankind.
So he in growing pain ruled on in beloved Thebes,
lording Cadmus' people—thanks to the gods' brutal plan—
while she went down to Death who guards the massive gates.
315   Lashing a noose to a steep rafter, there she hanged aloft,
strangling in all her anguish, leaving her son to bear
the world of horror a mother's Furies bring to life.

    And I saw magnificent Chloris, the one whom Neleus
wooed and won with a hoard of splendid gifts,
320   so dazzled by her beauty years ago . . .
the youngest daughter of Iasus' son Amphion,
the great Minyan king who ruled Orchomenos once.
She was his queen in Pylos, she bore him shining sons,
Nestor and Chromius, Periclymenus too, good prince.
325   And after her sons she bore a daughter, majestic Pero,
the marvel of her time, courted by all the young lords
round about. But Neleus would not give her to any suitor,
none but the man who might drive home the herds
that powerful Iphiclus had stolen. Lurching,
330   broad in the brow, those longhorned beasts,
and no small task to round them up from Phylace.
Only the valiant seer Melampus volunteered—
he would drive them home—
but a god's iron sentence bound him fast:
335   barbarous herdsmen dragged him off in chains.
Yet when the months and days had run their course
and the year wheeled round and the seasons came again,
then mighty Iphiclus loosed the prophet's shackles,
once he had told him all the gods' decrees.
340   And so the will of Zeus was done at last.

    And I saw Leda next, Tyndareus' wife,
who'd borne the king two sons, intrepid twins,
Castor, breaker of horses, and the hardy boxer Polydeuces,
both buried now in the life-giving earth though still alive.
345   Even under the earth Zeus grants them that distinction:
one day alive, the next day dead, each twin by turns,
they both hold honors equal to the gods'.

    And I saw Iphimedeia next, Aloeus' wife,
who claimed she lay in the Sea-lord's loving waves
350   and gave the god two sons, but they did not live long,
Otus staunch as a god and far-famed Ephialtes.
They were the tallest men the fertile earth has borne,

the handsomest too, by far, aside from renowned Orion.
Nine yards across they measured, even at nine years old,
355   nine fathoms tall they towered. They even threatened
the deathless gods they'd storm Olympus' heights
with the pounding rush and grinding shock of battle.
They were wild to pile Ossa upon Olympus, then on Ossa
Pelion dense with timber—their toeholds up the heavens.
360   And they'd have won the day if they had reached peak strength
but Apollo the son of Zeus, whom sleek-haired Leto bore,
laid both giants low before their beards had sprouted,
covering cheek and chin with a fresh crop of down.

      Phaedra and Procris too I saw, and lovely Ariadne,
365   daughter of Minos, that harsh king. One day Theseus tried
to spirit her off from Crete to Athens' sacred heights
but he got no joy from her. Artemis killed her first
on wave-washed Dia's shores, accused by Dionysus.

      And I saw Clymene, Maera and loathsome Eriphyle—
370   bribed with a golden necklace
to lure her lawful husband to his death . . .
But the whole cortege I could never tally, never name,
not all the daughters and wives of great men I saw there.
Long before that, the godsent night would ebb away.
375   But the time has come for sleep, either with friends
aboard your swift ship or here in your own house.
My passage home will rest with the gods and you."

      Odysseus paused . . . They all fell silent, hushed,
his story holding them spellbound down the shadowed halls
380   till the white-armed queen Arete suddenly burst out,
"Phaeacians! How does this man impress you now,
his looks, his build, the balanced mind inside him?
The stranger is my guest
but each of you princes shares the honor here.
385   So let's not be too hasty to send him on his way,
and don't scrimp on his gifts. His need is great,
great as the riches piled up in your houses,
thanks to the gods' good will."
                 Following her,
the old revered Echeneus added his support,
390   the eldest lord on the island of Phaeacia:
"Friends, the words of our considerate queen—
they never miss the mark or fail our expectations.
So do as Arete says, though on Alcinous here
depend all words and action."
                 "And so it will be"—
395   Alcinous stepped in grandly—"sure as I am alive
and rule our island men who love their oars!
Our guest, much as he longs for passage home,
must stay and wait it out here till tomorrow,

till I can collect his whole array of parting gifts.
400 His send-off rests with every noble here
but with me most of all:
I hold the reins of power in the realm."

Odysseus, deft and tactful, echoed back,
"Alcinous, majesty, shining among your island people,
405 if you would urge me now to stay here one whole year
then speed me home weighed down with lordly gifts,
I'd gladly have it so. Better by far, that way.
The fuller my arms on landing there at home,
the more respected, well received I'd be
410 by all who saw me sailing back to Ithaca."

"Ah Odysseus," Alcinous replied, "one look at you
and we know that you are no one who would cheat us—
no fraud, such as the dark soil breeds and spreads
across the face of the earth these days. Crowds of vagabonds
415 frame their lies so tightly none can test them. But you,
what grace you give your words, and what good sense within!
You have told your story with all a singer's skill,
the miseries you endured, your great Achaeans too.
But come now, tell me truly: your godlike comrades—
420 did you see any heroes down in the House of Death,
any who sailed with you and met their doom at Troy?
The night's still young, I'd say the night is endless.
For us in the palace now, it's hardly time for sleep.
Keep telling us your adventures—they are wonderful.
425 I could hold out here till Dawn's first light
if only you could bear, here in our halls,
to tell the tale of all the pains you suffered."

So the man of countless exploits carried on:
"Alcinous, majesty, shining among your island people,
430 there is a time for many words, a time for sleep as well.
But if you insist on hearing more, I'd never stint
on telling my own tale and those more painful still,
the griefs of my comrades, dead in the war's wake,
who escaped the battle-cries of Trojan armies
435 only to die in blood at journey's end—
thanks to a vicious woman's will.
                                Now then,
no sooner had Queen Persephone driven off
the ghosts of lovely women, scattering left and right,
than forward marched the shade of Atreus' son Agamemnon,
440 fraught with grief and flanked by all his comrades,
troops of his men-at-arms who died beside him,
who met their fate in lord Aegisthus' halls.
He knew me at once, as soon as he drank the blood,
and wailed out, shrilly; tears sprang to his eyes,
445 he thrust his arms toward me, keen to embrace me there—

no use—the great force was gone, the strength lost forever,
now, that filled his rippling limbs in the old days.
I wept at the sight, my heart went out to the man,
my words too, in a winging flight of pity:
450 'Famous Atrides, lord of men Agamemnon!
What fatal stroke of destiny brought you down?
Wrecked in the ships when lord Poseidon roused
some punishing blast of stormwinds, gust on gust?
Or did ranks of enemies mow you down on land
455 as you tried to raid and cut off herds and flocks
or fought to win their city, take their women?'

    The field marshal's ghost replied at once:
'Royal son of Laertes, Odysseus, mastermind of war,
I was not wrecked in the ships when lord Poseidon
460 roused some punishing blast of stormwinds, gust on gust,
nor did ranks of enemies mow me down on land—
Aegisthus hatched my doom and my destruction,
he killed me, he with my own accursed wife . . .
he invited me to his palace, sat me down to feast
465 then cut me down as a man cuts down some ox at the trough!
So I died—a wretched, ignominious death—and round me
all my comrades killed, no mercy, one after another,
just like white-tusked boars
butchered in some rich lord of power's halls
470 for a wedding, banquet or groaning public feast.
You in your day have witnessed hundreds slaughtered,
killed in single combat or killed in pitched battle, true,
but if you'd laid eyes on this it would have wrenched your heart—
how we sprawled by the mixing-bowl and loaded tables there,
475 throughout the palace, the whole floor awash with blood.
But the death-cry of Cassandra,[1] Priam's daughter—
the most pitiful thing I heard! My treacherous queen,
Clytemnestra, killed her over my body, yes, and I,
lifting my fists, beat them down on the ground,
480 dying, dying, writhing around the sword.
But she, that whore, she turned her back on me,
well on my way to Death—she even lacked the heart
to seal my eyes with her hand or close my jaws.
                                        So,
there's nothing more deadly, bestial than a woman
485 set on works like these—what a monstrous thing
she plotted, slaughtered her own lawful husband!
Why, I expected, at least, some welcome home
from all my children, all my household slaves
when I came sailing back again . . . But she—

---

1. Trojan princess and Agamemnon's war prize.

490 the queen hell-bent on outrage—bathes in shame
not only herself but the whole breed of womankind,
even the honest ones to come, forever down the years!'

So he declared and I cried out, 'How terrible!
Zeus from the very start, the thunder king
495 has hated the race of Atreus with a vengeance—
his trustiest weapon women's twisted wiles.
What armies of us died for the sake of Helen . . .
Clytemnestra schemed your death while you were worlds away!'

'True, true,' Agamemnon's ghost kept pressing on,
500 'so even your own wife—never indulge her too far.
Never reveal the whole truth, whatever you may know;
just tell her a part of it, be sure to hide the rest.
Not that you, Odysseus, will be murdered by your wife.
She's much too steady, her feelings run too deep,
505 Icarius' daughter Penelope, that wise woman.
She was a young bride, I well remember . . .
we left her behind when we went off to war,
with an infant boy she nestled at her breast.
That boy must sit and be counted with the men now—
510 happy man! His beloved father will come sailing home
and see his son, and he will embrace his father,
that is only right. But *my* wife—she never
even let me feast my eyes on my own son;
she killed me first, his father!
515 I tell you this—bear it in mind, you must—
when you reach your homeland steer your ship
into port in secret, never out in the open . . .
the time for trusting women's gone forever!

Enough. Come, tell me this, and be precise.
520 Have you heard news of my son? Where's he living now?
Perhaps in Orchomenos, perhaps in sandy Pylos
or off in the Spartan plains with Menelaus?
He's not dead yet, my Prince Orestes, no,
he's somewhere on the earth.'
                                    So he probed
525 but I cut it short: 'Atrides, why ask me that?
I know nothing, whether he's dead or alive.
It's wrong to lead you on with idle words.'

So we stood there, trading heartsick stories,
deep in grief, as the tears streamed down our faces.
530 But now there came the ghosts of Peleus' son Achilles,
Patroclus,[2] fearless Antilochus—and Great Ajax too,

2. Achilles' companion.

the first in stature, first in build and bearing
of all the Argives after Peleus' matchless son.
The ghost of the splendid runner knew me at once
535   and hailed me with a flight of mournful questions:
'Royal son of Laertes, Odysseus, man of tactics,
reckless friend, what next?
What greater feat can that cunning head contrive?
What daring brought you down to the House of Death?—
540   where the senseless, burnt-out wraiths of mortals make their home.'

    The voice of his spirit paused, and I was quick to answer:
'Achilles, son of Peleus, greatest of the Achaeans,
I had to consult Tiresias, driven here by hopes
he would help me journey home to rocky Ithaca.
545   Never yet have I neared Achaea, never once
set foot on native ground . . .
my life is endless trouble.
                  But you, Achilles,
there's not a man in the world more blest than you—
there never has been, never will be one.
550   Time was, when you were alive, we Argives
honored you as a god, and now down here, I see,
you lord it over the dead in all your power.
So grieve no more at dying, great Achilles.'

    I reassured the ghost, but he broke out, protesting,
555   'No winning words about death to *me*, shining Odysseus!
By god, I'd rather slave on earth for another man—
some dirt-poor tenant farmer who scrapes to keep alive—
than rule down here over all the breathless dead.
But come, tell me the news about my gallant son.
560   Did he make his way to the wars,
did the boy become a champion—yes or no?
Tell me of noble Peleus, any word you've heard—
still holding pride of place among his Myrmidon hordes,
or do they despise the man in Hellas and in Phthia
565   because old age has lamed his arms and legs?
For I no longer stand in the light of day—
the man I was—comrade-in-arms to help my father
as once I helped our armies, killing the best fighters
Troy could field in the wide world up there . . .
570   Oh to arrive at father's house—the man I was,
for one brief day—I'd make my fury and my hands,
invincible hands, a thing of terror to all those men
who abuse the king with force and wrest away his honor!'

    So he grieved but I tried to lend him heart:
575   'About noble Peleus I can tell you nothing,
but about your own dear son, Neoptolemus,
I can report the whole story, as you wish.

I myself, in my trim ship, I brought him
out of Scyros to join the Argives under arms.
580 And dug in around Troy, debating battle-tactics,
he always spoke up first, and always on the mark—
godlike Nestor and I alone excelled the boy. Yes,
and when our armies fought on the plain of Troy
he'd never hang back with the main force of men—
585 he'd always charge ahead,
giving ground to no one in his fury,
and scores of men he killed in bloody combat.
How could I list them all, name them all, now,
the fighting ranks he leveled, battling for the Argives?
590 But what a soldier he laid low with a bronze sword:
the hero Eurypylus, Telephus' son, and round him
troops of his own Cetean comrades slaughtered,
lured to war by the bribe his mother took.
The only man I saw to put Eurypylus
595 in the shade was Memnon, son of the Morning.
Again, when our champions climbed inside the horse
that Epeus built with labor, and I held full command
to spring our packed ambush open or keep it sealed,
all our lords and captains were wiping off their tears,
600 knees shaking beneath each man—but not your son.
Never once did I see his glowing skin go pale;
he never flicked a tear from his cheeks, no,
he kept on begging me there to let him burst
from the horse, kept gripping his hilted sword,
605 his heavy bronze-tipped javelin, keen to loose
his fighting fury against the Trojans. Then,
once we'd sacked King Priam's craggy city,
laden with his fair share and princely prize
he boarded his own ship, his body all unscarred.
610 Not a wound from a flying spear or a sharp sword,
cut-and-thrust close up—the common marks of war.
Random, raging Ares plays no favorites.'
                         So I said and
off he went, the ghost of the great runner, Aeacus' grandson
loping with long strides across the fields of asphodel,
615 triumphant in all I had told him of his son,
his gallant, glorious son.

     Now the rest of the ghosts, the dead and gone
came swarming up around me—deep in sorrow there,
each asking about the grief that touched him most.
620 Only the ghost of Great Ajax, son of Telamon,
kept his distance, blazing with anger at me still
for the victory I had won by the ships that time
I pressed my claim for the arms of Prince Achilles.
His queenly mother had set them up as prizes,

625   Pallas and captive Trojans served as judges.
        Would to god I'd never won such trophies!
        All for them the earth closed over Ajax,
        that proud hero Ajax . . .
        greatest in build, greatest in works of war
630   of all the Argives after Peleus' matchless son.
        I cried out to him now, I tried to win him over:
        'Ajax, son of noble Telamon, still determined,
        even in death, not once to forget that rage
        you train on me for those accursed arms?
635   The gods set up that prize to plague the Achaeans—
        so great a tower of strength we lost when you went down!
        For *your* death we grieved as we did for Achilles' death—
        we grieved incessantly, true, and none's to blame
        but Zeus, who hated Achaea's fighting spearmen
640   so intensely, Zeus sealed your doom.
        Come closer, king, and listen to my story.
        Conquer your rage, your blazing, headstrong pride!'

        So I cried out but Ajax answered not a word.
        He stalked off toward Erebus, into the dark
645   to join the other lost, departed dead.
        Yet now, despite his anger,
        he might have spoken to me, or I to him,
        but the heart inside me stirred with some desire
        to see the ghosts of others dead and gone.

650   And I saw Minos there, illustrious son of Zeus,
        firmly enthroned, holding his golden scepter,
        judging all the dead . . .
        Some on their feet, some seated, all clustering
        round the king of justice, pleading for his verdicts
655   reached in the House of Death with its all-embracing gates.

        I next caught sight of Orion, that huge hunter,
        rounding up on the fields of asphodel those wild beasts
        the man in life cut down on the lonely mountain-slopes,
        brandishing in his hands the bronze-studded club
660   that time can never shatter.

                      I saw Tityus too,
        son of the mighty goddess Earth—sprawling there
        on the ground, spread over nine acres—two vultures
        hunched on either side of him, digging into his liver,
        beaking deep in the blood-sac, and he with his frantic hands
665   could never beat them off, for he had once dragged off
        the famous consort of Zeus in all her glory,
        Leto, threading her way toward Pytho's ridge,
        over the lovely dancing-rings of Panopeus.

        And I saw Tantalus too, bearing endless torture.

670 He stood erect in a pool as the water lapped his chin—
     parched, he tried to drink, but he could not reach the surface,
     no, time and again the old man stooped, craving a sip,
     time and again the water vanished, swallowed down,
     laying bare the caked black earth at his feet—
675 some spirit drank it dry. And over his head
     leafy trees dangled their fruit from high aloft,
     pomegranates and pears, and apples glowing red,
     succulent figs and olives swelling sleek and dark,
     but as soon as the old man would strain to clutch them fast
680 a gust would toss them up to the lowering dark clouds.

         And I saw Sisyphus too, bound to his own torture,
     grappling his monstrous boulder with both arms working,
     heaving, hands struggling, legs driving, he kept on
     thrusting the rock uphill toward the brink, but just
685 as it teetered, set to topple over—
                                     time and again
     the immense weight of the thing would wheel it back and
     the ruthless boulder would bound and tumble down to the plain again—
     so once again he would heave, would struggle to thrust it up,
690 sweat drenching his body, dust swirling above his head.

         And next I caught a glimpse of powerful Heracles—
     his ghost, I mean: the man himself delights
     in the grand feasts of the deathless gods on high,
     wed to Hebe, famed for her lithe, alluring ankles,
     the daughter of mighty Zeus and Hera shod in gold.
695 Around him cries of the dead rang out like cries of birds,
     scattering left and right in horror as on he came like night,
     naked bow in his grip, an arrow grooved on the bowstring,
     glaring round him fiercely, forever poised to shoot.
     A terror too, that sword-belt sweeping across his chest,
700 a baldric of solid gold emblazoned with awesome work . . .
     bears and ramping boars and lions with wild, fiery eyes,
     and wars, routs and battles, massacres, butchered men.
     May the craftsman who forged that masterpiece—
     whose skills could conjure up a belt like that—
705 never forge another!
     Heracles knew me at once, at first glance,
     and hailed me with a winging burst of pity:
     'Royal son of Laertes, Odysseus famed for exploits,
     luckless man, you too? Braving out a fate as harsh
710 as the fate I bore, alive in the light of day?
     Son of Zeus that I was, my torments never ended,
     forced to slave for a man not half the man I was:
     he saddled me with the worst heartbreaking labors.
     Why, he sent me down here once, to retrieve the hound
715 that guards the dead—no harder task for me, he thought—
     but I dragged the great beast up from the underworld to earth

and Hermes and gleaming-eyed Athena blazed the way!'

　　With that he turned and back he went to the House of Death
but I held fast in place, hoping that others might still come,
720　shades of famous heroes, men who died in the old days
and ghosts of an even older age I longed to see,
Theseus and Pirithous, the gods' own radiant sons.
But before I could, the dead came surging round me,
hordes of them, thousands raising unearthly cries,
725　and blanching terror gripped me—panicked now
that Queen Persephone might send up from Death
some monstrous head, some Gorgon's staring face!
I rushed back to my ship, commanded all hands
to take to the decks and cast off cables quickly.
730　They swung aboard at once, they sat to the oars in ranks
and a strong tide of the Ocean River swept her on downstream,
sped by our rowing first, then by a fresh fair wind."

BOOK 12. THE CATTLE OF THE SUN

"Now when our ship had left the Ocean River rolling in her wake
and launched out into open sea with its long swells to reach
the island of Aeaea—east where the Dawn forever young
has home and dancing-rings and the Sun his risings—
5　heading in we beached our craft on the sands,
the crews swung out on the low sloping shore
and there we fell asleep, awaiting Dawn's first light.

　　As soon as Dawn with her rose-red fingers shone again
I dispatched some men to Circe's halls to bring
10　the dead Elpenor's body. We cut logs in haste
and out on the island's sharpest jutting headland
held his funeral rites in sorrow, streaming tears.
Once we'd burned the dead man and the dead man's armor,
heaping his grave-mound, hauling a stone that coped it well,
15　we planted his balanced oar aloft to crown his tomb.

　　And so we saw to his rites, each step in turn.
Nor did our coming back from Death escape Circe—
she hurried toward us, decked in rich regalia,
handmaids following close with trays of bread
20　and meats galore and glinting ruddy wine.
And the lustrous goddess, standing in our midst,
hailed us warmly: 'Ah my daring, reckless friends!
You who ventured down to the House of Death alive,
doomed to die twice over—others die just once.
25　Come, take some food and drink some wine,
rest here the livelong day
and then, tomorrow at daybreak, you must sail.
But I will set you a course and chart each seamark,
so neither on sea nor land will some new trap

30   ensnare you in trouble, make you suffer more.'

Her foresight won our fighting spirits over.
So all that day till the sun went down we sat
and feasted on sides of meat and heady wine,
and then when the sun had set and night came on
35   the men lay down to sleep by the ship's stern-cables.
But Circe, taking me by the hand, drew me away
from all my shipmates there and sat me down
and lying beside me probed me for details.
I told her the whole story, start to finish,
40   then the queenly goddess laid my course:
'Your descent to the dead is over, true,
but listen closely to what I tell you now
and god himself will bring it back to mind.
First you will raise the island of the Sirens,
45   those creatures who spellbind any man alive,
whoever comes their way. Whoever draws too close,
off guard, and catches the Sirens' voices in the air—
no sailing home for him, no wife rising to meet him,
no happy children beaming up at their father's face.
50   The high, thrilling song of the Sirens will transfix him,
lolling there in their meadow, round them heaps of corpses
rotting away, rags of skin shriveling on their bones . . . .
Race straight past that coast! Soften some beeswax
and stop your shipmates' ears so none can hear,
55   none of the crew, but if you are bent on hearing,
have them tie you hand and foot in the swift ship,
erect at the mast-block, lashed by ropes to the mast
so you can hear the Sirens' song to your heart's content.
But if you plead, commanding your men to set you free,
60   then they must lash you faster, rope on rope.

But once your crew has rowed you past the Sirens
a choice of routes is yours. I cannot advise you
which to take, or lead you through it all—
you must decide for yourself—
65   but I can tell you the ways of either course.
On one side beetling cliffs shoot up, and against them
pound the huge roaring breakers of blue-eyed Amphitrite—
the Clashing Rocks they're called by all the blissful gods.
Not even birds can escape them, no, not even the doves
70   that veer and fly ambrosia home to Father Zeus:
even of those the sheer Rocks always pick off one
and Father wings one more to keep the number up.
No ship of men has ever approached and slipped past—
always some disaster—big timbers and sailors' corpses
75   whirled away by the waves and lethal blasts of fire.
One ship alone, one deep-sea craft sailed clear,
the *Argo,* sung by the world, when heading home

from Aeetes' shores. And *she* would have crashed
against those giant rocks and sunk at once if Hera,
80   for love of Jason, had not sped her through.

    On the other side loom two enormous crags . . .
One thrusts into the vaulting sky its jagged peak,
hooded round with a dark cloud that never leaves—
no clear bright air can ever bathe its crown,
85   not even in summer's heat or harvest-time.
No man on earth could scale it, mount its crest,
not even with twenty hands and twenty feet for climbing,
the rock's so smooth, like dressed and burnished stone.
And halfway up that cliffside stands a fog-bound cavern
90   gaping west toward Erebus, realm of death and darkness—
past it, great Odysseus, you should steer your ship.
No rugged young archer could hit that yawning cave
with a winged arrow shot from off the decks.
Scylla lurks inside it—the yelping horror,
95   yelping, no louder than any suckling pup
but she's a grisly monster, I assure you.
No one could look on her with any joy,
not even a god who meets her face-to-face . . .
She has twelve legs, all writhing, dangling down
100   and six long swaying necks, a hideous head on each,
each head barbed with a triple row of fangs, thickset,
packed tight—and armed to the hilt with black death!
Holed up in the cavern's bowels from her waist down
she shoots out her heads, out of that terrifying pit,
105   angling right from her nest, wildly sweeping the reefs
for dolphins, dogfish or any bigger quarry she can drag
from the thousands Amphitrite spawns in groaning seas.
No mariners yet can boast they've raced their ship
past Scylla's lair without some mortal blow—
110   with each of her six heads she snatches up
a man from the dark-prowed craft and whisks him off.

    The other crag is lower—you will see, Odysseus—
though both lie side-by-side, an arrow-shot apart.
Atop it a great fig-tree rises, shaggy with leaves,
115   beneath it awesome Charybdis gulps the dark water down.
Three times a day she vomits it up, three times she gulps it down,
that terror! Don't be there when the whirlpool swallows down—
not even the earthquake god could save you from disaster.
No, hug Scylla's crag—sail on past her—top speed!
120   Better by far to lose six men and keep your ship
than lose your entire crew.'
               'Yes, yes,
but tell me the truth now, goddess,' I protested.
'Deadly Charybdis—can't I possibly cut and run from *her*
and still fight Scylla off when Scylla strikes my men?'

125 'So stubborn!' the lovely goddess countered.
     'Hell-bent yet again on battle and feats of arms?
     Can't you bow to the deathless gods themselves?
     Scylla's no mortal, she's an immortal devastation,
     terrible, savage, wild, no fighting her, no defense—
130 just flee the creature, that's the only way.
     Waste any time, arming for battle beside her rock,
     I fear she'll lunge out again with all of her six heads
     and seize as many men. No, row for your lives,
     invoke Brute Force, I tell you, Scylla's mother—
135 she spawned her to scourge mankind,
     she can stop the monster's next attack!

     Then you will make the island of Thrinacia . . .
     where herds of the Sungod's cattle graze, and fat sheep
     and seven herds of oxen, as many sheepflocks, rich and woolly,
140 fifty head in each. No breeding swells their number,
     nor do they ever die. And goddesses herd them on,
     nymphs with glinting hair, Phäethusa, Lampetie,
     born to the Sungod Helios by radiant Neaera.
     Their queenly mother bred and reared them both
145 then settled them on the island of Thrinacia—
     their homeland seas away—
     to guard their father's sheep and longhorn cattle.
     Leave the beasts unharmed, your mind set on home,
     and you all may still reach Ithaca—bent with hardship,
150 true—but harm them in any way, and I can see it now:
     your ship destroyed, your men destroyed as well!
     And even if *you* escape, you'll come home late,
     all shipmates lost, and come a broken man.'

     At those words Dawn rose on her golden throne
155 and lustrous Circe made her way back up the island.
     I went straight to my ship, commanding all hands
     to take to the decks and cast off cables quickly.
     They swung aboard at once, they sat to the oars in ranks
     and in rhythm churned the water white with stroke on stroke.
160 And Circe the nymph with glossy braids, the awesome one
     who speaks with human voice, sent us a hardy shipmate,
     yes, a fresh following wind ruffling up in our wake,
     bellying out our sail to drive our blue prow on as we,
     securing the running gear from stem to stern, sat back
165 while the wind and helmsman kept her true on course.
     At last, and sore at heart, I told my shipmates,
     'Friends . . . it's wrong for only one or two
     to know the revelations that lovely Circe
     made to me alone. I'll tell you all,
170 so we can die with our eyes wide open now
     or escape our fate and certain death together.
     First, she warns, we must steer clear of the Sirens,

Odysseus and the Sirens, Etruscan red-figure amphora, c. 500 B.C.E.

their enchanting song, their meadow starred with flowers.
I alone was to hear their voices, so she said,
175   but you must bind me with tight chafing ropes
so I cannot move a muscle, bound to the spot,
erect at the mast-block, lashed by ropes to the mast.
And if I plead, commanding you to set me free,
then lash me faster, rope on pressing rope.'

180   So I informed my shipmates point by point,
all the while our trim ship was speeding toward
the Sirens' island, driven on by the brisk wind.
But then—the wind fell in an instant,
all glazed to a dead calm . . .
185   a mysterious power hushed the heaving swells.
The oarsmen leapt to their feet, struck the sail,
stowed it deep in the hold and sat to the oarlocks,
thrashing with polished oars, frothing the water white.
Now with a sharp sword I sliced an ample wheel of beeswax
190   down into pieces, kneaded them in my two strong hands
and the wax soon grew soft, worked by my strength
and Helios' burning rays, the sun at high noon,
and I stopped the ears of my comrades one by one.

They bound me hand and foot in the tight ship—
195   erect at the mast-block, lashed by ropes to the mast—
and rowed and churned the whitecaps stroke on stroke.
We were just offshore as far as a man's shout can carry,
scudding close, when the Sirens sensed at once a ship
was racing past and burst into their high, thrilling song:
200   'Come closer, famous Odysseus—Achaea's pride and glory—
moor your ship on our coast so you can hear our song!
Never has any sailor passed our shores in his black craft
until he has heard the honeyed voices pouring from our lips,
and once he hears to his heart's content sails on, a wiser man.
205   We know all the pains that the Greeks and Trojans once endured
on the spreading plain of Troy when the gods willed it so—
all that comes to pass on the fertile earth, we know it all!'

    So they sent their ravishing voices out across the air
and the heart inside me throbbed to listen longer.
210   I signaled the crew with frowns to set me free—
they flung themselves at the oars and rowed on harder,
Perimedes and Eurylochus springing up at once
to bind me faster with rope on chafing rope.
But once we'd left the Sirens fading in our wake,
215   once we could hear their song no more, their urgent call—
my steadfast crew was quick to remove the wax I'd used
to seal their ears and loosed the bonds that lashed me.

    We'd scarcely put that island astern when suddenly
I saw smoke and heavy breakers, heard their booming thunder.
220   The men were terrified—oarblades flew from their grip,
clattering down to splash in the vessel's wash.
She lay there, dead in the water . . .
no hands to tug the blades that drove her on.
But I strode down the decks to rouse my crewmen,
225   halting beside each one with a bracing, winning word:
'Friends, we're hardly strangers at meeting danger—
and this danger is no worse than what we faced
when Cyclops penned us up in his vaulted cave
with crushing force! But even from there my courage,
230   my presence of mind and tactics saved us all,
and we will live to remember *this* someday,
I have no doubt. Up now, follow my orders,
all of us work as one! You men at the thwarts—
lay on with your oars and strike the heaving swells,
235   trusting that Zeus will pull us through these straits alive.
You, helmsman, here's your order—burn it in your mind—
the steering-oar of our rolling ship is in your hands.
Keep her clear of that smoke and surging breakers,
head for those crags or she'll catch you off guard,
240   she'll yaw over there—you'll plunge us all in ruin!'

So I shouted. They snapped to each command.
No mention of Scylla—how to fight that nightmare?—
for fear the men would panic, desert their oars
and huddle down and stow themselves away.
245   But now I cleared my mind of Circe's orders—
cramping my style, urging me not to arm at all.
I donned my heroic armor, seized long spears
in both my hands and marched out on the half-deck,
forward, hoping from there to catch the first glimpse
250   of Scylla, ghoul of the cliffs, swooping to kill my men.
But nowhere could I make her out—and my eyes ached,
scanning that mist-bound rock face top to bottom.

    Now wailing in fear, we rowed on up those straits,
Scylla to starboard, dreaded Charybdis off to port,
255   her horrible whirlpool gulping the sea-surge down, down
but when she spewed it up—like a cauldron over a raging fire—
all her churning depths would seethe and heave—exploding spray
showering down to splatter the peaks of both crags at once!
But when she swallowed the sea-surge down her gaping maw
260   the whole abyss lay bare and the rocks around her roared,
terrible, deafening—
                    bedrock showed down deep, boiling
black with sand—
               and ashen terror gripped the men.
But now, fearing death, all eyes fixed on Charybdis—
now Scylla snatched six men from our hollow ship,
265   the toughest, strongest hands I had, and glancing
backward over the decks, searching for my crew
I could see their hands and feet already hoisted,
flailing, high, higher, over my head, look—
wailing down at me, comrades riven in agony,
270   shrieking out my name for one last time!
Just as an angler poised on a jutting rock
flings his treacherous bait in the offshore swell,
whips his long rod—hook sheathed in an oxhorn lure—
and whisks up little fish he flips on the beach-break,
275   writhing, gasping out their lives . . . so now they writhed,
gasping as Scylla swung them up her cliff and there
at her cavern's mouth she bolted them down raw—
screaming out, flinging their arms toward me,
lost in that mortal struggle . . .
280   Of all the pitiful things I've had to witness,
suffering, searching out the pathways of the sea,
this wrenched my heart the most.
                        But now, at last,
putting the Rocks, Scylla and dread Charybdis far astern,
we quickly reached the good green island of the Sun
285   where Helios, lord Hyperion, keeps his fine cattle,
broad in the brow, and flocks of purebred sheep.

Still aboard my black ship in the open sea
I could hear the lowing cattle driven home,
the bleating sheep. And I was struck once more
290   by the words of the blind Theban prophet, Tiresias,
and Aeaean Circe too: time and again they told me
to shun this island of the Sun, the joy of man.
So I warned my shipmates gravely, sick at heart,
'Listen to me, my comrades, brothers in hardship,
295   let me tell you the dire prophecies of Tiresias
and Aeaean Circe too: time and again they told me
to shun this island of the Sun, the joy of man.
Here, they warned, the worst disaster awaits us.
Row straight past these shores—race our black ship on!'

300   So I said, and the warnings broke their hearts.
But Eurylochus waded in at once—with mutiny on his mind:
'You're a hard man, Odysseus. Your fighting spirit's
stronger than ours, your stamina never fails.
You must be made of iron head to foot. Look,
305   your crew's half-dead with labor, starved for sleep,
and you forbid us to set foot on land, this island here,
washed by the waves, where we might catch a decent meal again.
Drained as we are, night falling fast, you'd have us desert
this haven and blunder off, into the mist-bound seas?
310   Out of the night come winds that shatter vessels—
how can a man escape his headlong death
if suddenly, out of nowhere, a cyclone hits,
bred by the South or stormy West Wind? They're the gales
that tear a ship to splinters—the gods, our masters,
315   willing or not, it seems. No, let's give way
to the dark night, set out our supper here.
Sit tight by our swift ship and then at daybreak
board and launch her, make for open sea!'

    So Eurylochus urged, and shipmates cheered.
320   Then I knew some power was brewing trouble for us,
so I let fly with an anxious plea: 'Eurylochus,
I'm one against all—the upper hand is yours.
But swear me a binding oath, all here, that if
we come on a herd of cattle or fine flock of sheep,
325   not one man among us—blind in his reckless ways—
will slaughter an ox or ram. Just eat in peace,
content with the food immortal Circe gave us.'

    They quickly swore the oath that I required
and once they had vowed they'd never harm the herds,
330   they moored our sturdy ship in the deep narrow harbor,
close to a fresh spring, and all hands disembarked
and adeptly set about the evening meal.
Once they'd put aside desire for food and drink,
they recalled our dear companions, wept for the men

335   that Scylla plucked from the hollow ship and ate alive,
      and a welcome sleep came on them in their tears.
                                          But then,
      at the night's third watch, the stars just wheeling down,
      Zeus who marshals the stormclouds loosed a ripping wind,
      a howling, demonic gale, shrouding over in thunderheads
340   the earth and sea at once—and night swept down from the sky.
      When young Dawn with her rose-red fingers shone once more
      we hauled our craft ashore, securing her in a vaulted cave
      where nymphs have lovely dancing-rings and hold their sessions.
      There I called a muster, warning my shipmates yet again,
345   'Friends, we've food and drink aplenty aboard the ship—
      keep your hands off all these herds or we will pay the price!
      The cattle, the sleek flocks, belong to an awesome master,
      Helios, god of the sun who sees all, hears all things.'

          So I warned, and my headstrong men complied.
350   But for one whole month the South Wind blew nonstop,
      no other wind came up, none but the South-southeast.
      As long as our food and ruddy wine held out, the crew,
      eager to save their lives, kept hands off the herds.
      But then, when supplies aboard had all run dry,
355   when the men turned to hunting, forced to range
      for quarry with twisted hooks: for fish, birds,
      anything they could lay their hands on—
      hunger racked their bellies—I struck inland,
      up the island, there to pray to the gods.
360   If only one might show me some way home!
      Crossing into the heartland, clear of the crew,
      I rinsed my hands in a sheltered spot, a windbreak,
      but soon as I'd prayed to all the gods who rule Olympus,
      down on my eyes they poured a sweet, sound sleep . . .
365   as Eurylochus opened up his fatal plan to friends:
      'Listen to me, my comrades, brothers in hardship.
      All ways of dying are hateful to us poor mortals,
      true, but to die of hunger, starve to death—
      that's the worst of all. So up with you now,
370   let's drive off the pick of Helios' sleek herds,
      slaughter them to the gods who rule the skies up there.
      If we ever make it home to Ithaca, native ground,
      erect at once a glorious temple to the Sungod,
      line the walls with hoards of dazzling gifts!
375   But if the Sun, inflamed for his longhorn cattle,
      means to wreck our ship and the other gods pitch in—
      I'd rather die at sea, with one deep gulp of death,
      than die by inches on this desolate island here!'

          So he urged, and shipmates cheered again.
380   At once they drove off the Sungod's finest cattle—
      close at hand, not far from the blue-prowed ship they grazed,

those splendid beasts with their broad brows and curving horns.
Surrounding them in a ring, they lifted prayers to the gods,
plucking fresh green leaves from a tall oak for the rite,
385   since white strewing-barley was long gone in the ship.
Once they'd prayed, slaughtered and skinned the cattle,
they cut the thighbones out, they wrapped them round in fat,
a double fold sliced clean and topped with strips of flesh.
And since they had no wine to anoint the glowing victims,
390   they made libations with water, broiling all the innards,
and once they'd burned the bones and tasted the organs—
hacked the rest into pieces, piercing them with spits.

That moment soothing slumber fell from my eyes
and down I went to our ship at the water's edge
395   but on my way, nearing the long beaked craft,
the smoky savor of roasts came floating up around me . . .
I groaned in anguish, crying out to the deathless gods:
'Father Zeus! the rest of you blissful gods who never die—
you with your fatal sleep, you lulled me into disaster.
400   Left on their own, look what a monstrous thing
my crew concocted!'
                  Quick as a flash
with her flaring robes Lampetie sped the news
to the Sun on high that we had killed his herds
and Helios burst out in rage to all the immortals:
405   'Father Zeus! the rest of you blissful gods who never die—
punish them all, that crew of Laertes' son Odysseus—
what an outrage! They, they killed my cattle,
the great joy of my heart . . . day in, day out,
when I climbed the starry skies and when I wheeled
410   back down from the heights to touch the earth once more.
Unless they pay me back in blood for the butchery of my herds,
down I go to the House of Death and blaze among the dead!'

But Zeus who marshals the thunderheads insisted,
'Sun, you keep on shining among the deathless gods
415   and mortal men across the good green earth.
And as for the guilty ones, why, soon enough
on the wine-dark sea I'll hit their racing ship
with a white-hot bolt, I'll tear it into splinters.'

—Or so I heard from the lovely nymph Calypso,
420   who heard it herself, she said, from Hermes, god of guides.

As soon as I reached our ship at the water's edge
I took the men to task, upbraiding each in turn,
but how to set things right? We couldn't find a way.
The cattle were dead already . . .
425   and the gods soon showed us all some fateful signs—
the hides began to crawl, the meat, both raw and roasted,
bellowed out on the spits, and we heard a noise

like the moan of lowing oxen.
                                          Yet six more days
my eager companions feasted on the cattle of the Sun,
430   the pick of the herds they'd driven off, but then,
when Cronian Zeus brought on the seventh day,
the wind in its ceaseless raging dropped at last,
and stepping the mast at once, hoisting the white sail
we boarded ship and launched her, made for open sea.

435   But once we'd left that island in our wake—
no land at all in sight, nothing but sea and sky—
then Zeus the son of Cronus mounted a thunderhead
above our hollow ship and the deep went black beneath it.
Nor did the craft scud on much longer. All of a sudden
440   killer-squalls attacked us, screaming out of the west,
a murderous blast shearing the two forestays off
so the mast toppled backward, its running tackle spilling
into the bilge. The mast itself went crashing into the stern,
it struck the helmsman's head and crushed his skull to pulp
445   and down from his deck the man flipped like a diver—
his hardy life spirit left his bones behind.
Then, then in the same breath Zeus hit the craft
with a lightning-bolt and thunder. Round she spun,
reeling under the impact, filled with reeking brimstone,
450   shipmates pitching out of her, bobbing round like seahawks
swept along by the whitecaps past the trim black hull—
and the god cut short their journey home forever.

But I went lurching along our battered hulk
till the sea-surge ripped the plankings from the keel
455   and the waves swirled it away, stripped bare, and snapped
the mast from the decks—but a backstay made of bull's-hide
still held fast, and with this I lashed the mast and keel
together, made them one, riding my makeshift raft
as the wretched galewinds bore me on and on.

460   At last the West Wind quit its wild rage
but the South came on at once to hound me even more,
making me double back my route toward cruel Charybdis.
All night long I was rushed back and then at break of day
I reached the crag of Scylla and dire Charybdis' vortex
465   right when the dreadful whirlpool gulped the salt sea down.
But heaving myself aloft to clutch at the fig-tree's height,
like a bat I clung to its trunk for dear life—not a chance
for a good firm foothold there, no clambering up it either,
the roots too far to reach, the boughs too high overhead,
470   huge swaying branches that overshadowed Charybdis.
But I held on, dead set . . . waiting for her
to vomit my mast and keel back up again—
Oh how I ached for both! and back they came,

late but at last, at just the hour a judge at court,
475 who's settled the countless suits of brash young claimants,
rises, the day's work done, and turns home for supper—
that's when the timbers reared back up from Charybdis.
I let go—I plunged with my hands and feet flailing,
crashing into the waves beside those great beams
480 and scrambling aboard them fast
I rowed hard with my hands right through the straits . . .
And the father of men and gods did not let Scylla see me,
else I'd have died on the spot—no escape from death.

I drifted along nine days. On the tenth, at night,
485 the gods cast me up on Ogygia, Calypso's island,
home of the dangerous nymph with glossy braids
who speaks with human voice, and she took me in,
she loved me . . . Why cover the same ground again?
Just yesterday, here at hall, I told you all the rest,
490 you and your gracious wife. It goes against my grain
to repeat a tale told once, and told so clearly."

BOOK 13. ITHACA AT LAST

His tale was over now. The Phaeacians all fell silent, hushed,
his story holding them spellbound down the shadowed halls
until Alcinous found the poise to say, "Odysseus,
now that you have come to my bronze-floored house,
5 my vaulted roofs, I know you won't be driven
off your course, nothing can hold you back—
however much you've suffered, you'll sail home.
Here, friends, here's a command for one and all,
you who frequent my palace day and night and drink
10 the shining wine of kings and enjoy the harper's songs.
The robes and hammered gold and a haul of other gifts
you lords of our island council brought our guest—
all lie packed in his polished sea-chest now. Come,
each of us add a sumptuous tripod, add a cauldron!

15 Then recover our costs with levies on the people:
it's hard to afford such bounty man by man."

The king's instructions met with warm applause
and home they went to sleep, each in his own house.
When young Dawn with her rose-red fingers shone once more
20 they hurried down to the ship with handsome bronze gifts,
and striding along the decks, the ardent King Alcinous
stowed them under the benches, shipshape, so nothing
could foul the crewmen tugging at their oars.
Then back the party went to Alcinous' house
25 and shared a royal feast.
                                    The majestic king

slaughtered an ox for them to Cronus' mighty son,
Zeus of the thundercloud, whose power rules the world.
They burned the thighs and fell to the lordly banquet,
reveling there, while in their midst the inspired bard
30   struck up a song, Demodocus, prized by all the people.
True, but time and again Odysseus turned his face
toward the radiant sun, anxious for it to set,
yearning now to be gone and home once more . . .
As a man aches for his evening meal when all day long
35   his brace of wine-dark oxen have dragged the bolted plowshare
down a fallow field—how welcome the setting sun to him,
the going home to supper, yes, though his knees buckle,
struggling home at last. So welcome now to Odysseus
the setting light of day, and he lost no time
40   as he pressed Phaeacia's men who love their oars,
addressing his host, Alcinous, first and foremost:
"Alcinous, majesty, shining among your island people,
make your libations, launch me safely on my way—
to one and all, farewell!
45   All is now made good, my heart's desire,
your convoy home, your precious, loving gifts,
and may the gods of Olympus bless them for me!
May I find an unswerving wife when I reach home,
and loved ones hale, unharmed! And you, my friends
50   remaining here in your kingdom now, may you delight
in your loyal wives and children! May the gods
rain down all kinds of fortune on your lives,
misfortune never harbor in your homeland!"

All burst into applause, urging passage home
55   for their parting guest, his farewell rang so true.
Hallowed King Alcinous briskly called his herald:
"Come, Pontonous! Mix the wine in the bowl,
pour rounds to all our banqueters in the house,
so we, with a prayer to mighty Zeus the Father,
60   can sail our new friend home to native land."

Pontonous mixed the heady, honeyed wine
and hovering closely, poured full rounds for all.
And from where they sat they tipped libations out
to the happy gods who rule the vaulting skies.
65   Then King Odysseus rose up from his seat
and placing his two-eared cup in Arete's hands,
addressed the queen with parting wishes on the wing:
"Your health, my queen, through all your days to come—
until old age and death, that visit all mankind,
70   pay you a visit too. Now I am on my way
but you, may you take joy in this house of yours,
in your children, your people, in Alcinous the king!"

With that the great Odysseus strode across the threshold.
And King Alcinous sent the herald off with the guest
75 to lead him down to the swift ship and foaming surf.
And Arete sent her serving-women, one to carry
a sea-cloak, washed and fresh, a shirt as well,
another assigned to bear the sturdy chest
and a third to take the bread and ruddy wine.

80   When they reached the ship at the water's edge
the royal escorts took charge of the gifts at once
and stores of food and wine, stowed them deep in the holds,
and then for their guest they spread out rug and sheets
on the half-deck, clear astern on the ship's hull
85 so he might sleep there soundly, undisturbed.
And last, Odysseus climbed aboard himself
and down he lay, all quiet
as crewmen sat to the oarlocks, each in line.
They slipped the cable free of the drilled stone post
90 and soon as they swung back and the blades tossed up the spray
an irresistible sleep fell deeply on his eyes, the sweetest,
soundest oblivion, still as the sleep of death itself . . .
And the ship like a four-horse team careering down the plain,
all breaking as one with the whiplash cracking smartly,
95 leaping with hoofs high to run the course in no time—
so the stern hove high and plunged with the seething rollers
crashing dark in her wake as on she surged unwavering,
never flagging, no, not even a darting hawk,
the quickest thing on wings, could keep her pace
100 as on she ran, cutting the swells at top speed,
bearing a man endowed with the gods' own wisdom,
one who had suffered twenty years of torment, sick at heart,
cleaving his way through wars of men and pounding waves at sea
but now he slept in peace, the memory of his struggles
105 laid to rest.
                    And then, that hour the star rose up,
the clearest, brightest star, that always heralds
the newborn light of day, the deep-sea-going ship
made landfall on the island . . . Ithaca, at last.

     There on the coast a haven lies, named for Phorcys,
110 the old god of the deep—with two jutting headlands,
sheared off at the seaward side but shelving toward the bay,
that break the great waves whipped by the gales outside
so within the harbor ships can ride unmoored
whenever they come in mooring range of shore.
115 At the harbor's head a branching olive stands
with a welcome cave nearby it, dank with sea-mist,
sacred to nymphs of the springs we call the Naiads.
There are mixing-bowls inside and double-handled jars,

crafted of stone, and bees store up their honey in the hollows.
120 There are long stone looms as well, where the nymphs weave out
their webs from clouds of sea-blue wool—a marvelous sight—
and a wellspring flows forever. The cave has two ways in,
one facing the North Wind, a pathway down for mortals;
the other, facing the South, belongs to the gods,
125 no man may go that way . . .
it is the path for all the deathless powers.

Here at this bay the Phaeacian crew put in—
they'd known it long before—driving the ship so hard
she ran up onto the beach for a good half her length,
130 such way the oarsmen's brawny arms had made.
Up from the benches, swinging down to land,
first they lifted Odysseus off the decks—
linen and lustrous carpet too—and laid him
down on the sand asleep, still dead to the world,
135 then hoisted out the treasures proud Phaeacians,
urged by open-hearted Pallas, had lavished on him,
setting out for home. They heaped them all
by the olive's trunk, in a neat pile, clear
of the road for fear some passerby might spot
140 and steal Odysseus' hoard before he could awaken.
Then pushing off, they pulled for home themselves.

But now Poseidon, god of the earthquake, never once
forgetting the first threats he leveled at the hero,
probed almighty Zeus to learn his plans in full:
145 "Zeus, Father, I will lose all my honor now
among the immortals, now there are mortal men
who show me no respect—Phaeacians, too,
born of my own loins! I said myself
that Odysseus would suffer long and hard
150 before he made it home, but I never dreamed
of blocking his return, not absolutely at least,
once *you* had pledged your word and bowed your head.
But now they've swept him across the sea in their swift ship,
they've set him down in Ithaca, sound asleep, and loaded the man
155 with boundless gifts—bronze and hoards of gold and robes—
aye, more plunder than he could ever have won from Troy
if Odysseus had returned intact with his fair share!"

"Incredible," Zeus who marshals the thunderheads replied.
"Earth-shaker, you with your massive power, why moaning so?
160 The gods don't disrespect you. What a stir there'd be
if they flung abuse at the oldest, noblest of them all.
Those mortals? If any man, so lost in his strength
and prowess, pays you no respect—just pay him back.
The power is always yours.
165 Do what you like. Whatever warms your heart."

"King of the dark cloud," the earthquake god agreed,
"I'd like to avenge myself at once, as you advise,
but I've always feared your wrath and shied away.
But now I'll crush that fine Phaeacian cutter
170 out on the misty sea, now on her homeward run
from the latest convoy. They will learn at last
to cease and desist from escorting every man alive—
I'll pile a huge mountain round about their port!"

"Wait, dear brother," Zeus who collects the clouds
175 had second thoughts. "Here's what seems best to *me*.
As the people all lean down from the city heights
to watch her speeding home, strike her into a rock
that looks like a racing vessel, just offshore—
amaze all men with a marvel for the ages.
180 Then pile your huge mountain round about their port."

Hearing that from Zeus, the god of the earthquake
sped to Scheria now, the Phaeacians' island home,
and waited there till the ship came sweeping in,
scudding lightly along—and surging close abreast,
185 the earthquake god with one flat stroke of his hand
struck her to stone, rooted her to the ocean floor
and made for open sea.
                              The Phaeacians, aghast,
those lords of the long oars, the master mariners
traded startled glances, sudden outcries:
190 "Look—who's pinned our swift ship to the sea?"

"Just racing for home!"
                              "Just hove into plain view!"

They might well wonder, blind to what had happened,
till Alcinous rose and made things all too clear:
"Oh no—my father's prophecy years ago . . .
195 it all comes home to me with a vengeance now!
He used to say Poseidon was vexed with us because
we escorted all mankind and never came to grief.
He said that one day, as a well-built ship of ours
sailed home on the misty sea from such a convoy,
200 the god would crush it, yes,
and pile a huge mountain round about our port.
So the old king foretold. Now, look, it all comes true!
Hurry, friends, do as I say, let us all comply:
stop our convoys home for every castaway
205 chancing on our city! As for Poseidon,
sacrifice twelve bulls to the god at once—
the pick of the herds. Perhaps he'll pity us,
pile no looming mountain ridge around our port."

The people, terrified, prepared the bulls at once.

210 So all of Phaeacia's island lords and captains,
     milling round the altar, lifted prayers
     to Poseidon, master of the sea . . .
                                    That very moment
     great Odysseus woke from sleep on native ground at last—
     he'd been away for years—but failed to know the land
215 for the goddess Pallas Athena, Zeus's daughter,
     showered mist over all, so under cover
     she might change his appearance head to foot
     as she told him every peril he'd meet at home—
     keep him from being known by wife, townsmen, friends,
220 till the suitors paid the price for all their outrage.
     And so to the king himself all Ithaca looked strange . . .
     the winding beaten paths, the coves where ships can ride,
     the steep rock face of the cliffs and the tall leafy trees.
     He sprang to his feet and, scanning his own native country,
225 groaned, slapped his thighs with his flat palms
     and Odysseus cried in anguish:
     "Man of misery, whose land have I lit on now?
     What *are* they here—violent, savage, lawless?
     or friendly to strangers, god-fearing men?
230 Where can I take this heap of treasure now
     and where in the world do I wander off myself?
     If only the trove had stayed among the Phaeacians there
     and I had made my way to some other mighty king
     who would have hosted me well and sent me home!
235 But now I don't know where to stow all this,
     and I can't leave it here, inviting any bandit
     to rob me blind.
                    So damn those lords and captains,
     those Phaeacians! Not entirely honest or upright, were they?
     Sweeping me off to this, this no-man's-land, and they,
240 they swore they'd sail me home to sunny Ithaca—well,
     they never kept their word. Zeus of the Suppliants
     pay them back—he keeps an eye on the world of men
     and punishes all transgressors!
                                    Come, quickly,
     I'll inspect my treasure and count it up myself.
245 Did they make off with anything in their ship?"

     With that he counted up the gorgeous tripods,
     cauldrons, bars of gold and the lovely woven robes.
     Not a stitch was missing from the lot. But still
     he wept for his native country, trailing down the shore
250 where the wash of sea on shingle ebbs and flows,
     his homesick heart in turmoil.
     But now Athena appeared and came toward him.
     She looked like a young man . . . a shepherd boy
     yet elegant too, with all the gifts that grace the sons of kings,

255   with a well-cut cloak falling in folds across her shoulders,
sandals under her shining feet, a hunting spear in hand.
Odysseus, overjoyed at the sight, went up to meet her,
joining her now with salutations on the wing:
"Greetings, friend! Since you are the first

260   I've come on in this harbor, treat me kindly—
no cruelty, please. Save these treasures,
save me too. I pray to you like a god,
I fall before your knees and ask your mercy!
And tell me this for a fact—I need to know—

265   where on earth am I? what land? who lives here?
Is it one of the sunny islands or some jutting shore
of the good green mainland slanting down to sea?"

    Athena answered, her eyes brightening now,
"You must be a fool, stranger, or come from nowhere,

270   if you really have to ask what land this is.
Trust me, it's not so nameless after all.
It's known the world around,
to all who live to the east and rising sun
and to all who face the western mists and darkness.

275   It's a rugged land, too cramped for driving horses,
but though it's far from broad, it's hardly poor.
There's plenty of grain for bread, grapes for wine,
the rains never fail and the dewfall's healthy.
Good country for goats, good for cattle too—

280   there's stand on stand of timber
and water runs in streambeds through the year.
                         So,
stranger, the name of Ithaca's reached as far as Troy,
and Troy, they say, is a long hard sail from Greece."

    Ithaca . . . Heart racing, Odysseus that great exile

285   filled with joy to hear Athena, daughter of storming Zeus,
pronounce that name. He stood on native ground at last
and he replied with a winging word to Pallas,
not with a word of truth—he choked it back,
always invoking the cunning in his heart:

290   "Ithaca . . . yes, I seem to have heard of Ithaca,
even on Crete's broad island far across the sea,
and now I've reached it myself, with all this loot,
but I left behind an equal measure for my children.
I'm a fugitive now, you see. I killed Idomeneus' son,

295   Orsilochus, lightning on his legs, a man who beat
all runners alive on that long island—what a racer!
He tried to rob me of all the spoil I'd won at Troy,
the plunder I went to hell and back to capture, true,
cleaving my way through wars of men and waves at sea—

300   and just because I refused to please his father,
serve under *him* at Troy. I led my own command.

So now with a friend I lay in wait by the road,
I killed him just loping in from the fields—
with one quick stroke of my bronze spear
305 in the dead of night, the heavens pitch-black . . .
no one could see us, spot me tearing out his life
with a weapon honed for action. Once I'd cut him down
I made for a ship and begged the Phoenician crew for mercy,
paying those decent hands a hearty share of plunder—
310 asked them to take me on and land me down in Pylos,
there or lovely Elis, where Epeans rule in power.
But a heavy galewind blew them way off course,
much against their will—
they'd no desire to cheat me. Driven afar,
315 we reached this island here at the midnight hour,
rowing for dear life, we made it into your harbor—
not a thought of supper, much as we all craved food,
we dropped from the decks and lay down, just like that!
A welcome sleep came over my weary bones at once,
320 while the crew hoisted up my loot from the holds
and set it down on the sand near where I slept.
They reembarked, now homeward bound for Sidon,
their own noble city, leaving me here behind,
homesick in my heart . . ."
                                        As his story ended,
325 goddess Athena, gray eyes gleaming, broke into a smile
and stroked him with her hand, and now she appeared a woman,
beautiful, tall and skilled at weaving lovely things.
Her words went flying straight toward Odysseus:
"Any man—any god who met you—would have to be
330 some champion lying cheat to get past *you*
for all-round craft and guile! You terrible man,
foxy, ingenious, never tired of twists and tricks—
so, not even here, on native soil, would you give up
those wily tales that warm the cockles of your heart!
335 Come, enough of this now. We're both old hands
at the arts of intrigue. Here among mortal men
you're far the best at tactics, spinning yarns,
and I am famous among the gods for wisdom,
cunning wiles, too.
340 Ah, but you never recognized me, did you?
Pallas Athena, daughter of Zeus—who always
stands beside you, shields you in every exploit:
thanks to me the Phaeacians all embraced you warmly.
And now I am here once more, to weave a scheme with you
345 and to hide the treasure-trove Phaeacia's nobles
lavished on you then—I willed it, planned it so
when you set out for home—and to tell you all
the trials you must suffer in your palace . . .
Endure them all. You must. You have no choice.

350   And to no one—no man, no woman, not a soul—
        reveal that you are the wanderer home at last.
        No, in silence you must bear a world of pain,
        subject yourself to the cruel abuse of men."

         "Ah goddess," the cool tactician countered,
355   "you're so hard for a mortal man to know on sight,
        however shrewd he is—the shapes you take are endless!
        But I do know this: you were kind to me in the war years,
        so long as we men of Achaea soldiered on at Troy.
        But once we'd sacked King Priam's craggy city,
360   boarded ship, and a god dispersed the fleet,
        from then on, daughter of Zeus, I never saw you,
        never glimpsed you striding along my decks
        to ward off some disaster. No, I wandered on,
        my heart forever torn to pieces inside my chest
365   till the gods released me from my miseries at last,
        that day in the fertile kingdom of Phaeacia when
        you cheered me with words, in person, led me to their city.
        But now I beg you by your almighty Father's name . . .
        for I can't believe I've reached my sunny Ithaca,
370   I must be roaming around one more exotic land—
        you're mocking me, I know it, telling me tales
        to make me lose my way. Tell me the truth now,
        have I really reached the land I love?"

         "Always the same, your wary turn of mind,"
375   Athena exclaimed, her glances flashing warmly.
        "That's why I can't forsake you in your troubles—
        you are so winning, so worldly-wise, so self-possessed!
        Anyone else, come back from wandering long and hard,
        would have hurried home at once, delighted to see
380   his children and his wife. Oh, but not you,
        it's not your pleasure to probe for news of them—
        you must put your wife to the proof yourself!
        But she, she waits in your halls, as always,
        her life an endless hardship . . .
385   wasting away the nights, weeping away the days.
        I never had doubts myself, no, I knew down deep
        that you would return at last, with all your shipmates lost.
        But I could not bring myself to fight my Father's brother,
        Poseidon, quaking with anger at you, still enraged
390   because you blinded the Cyclops, his dear son.
        But come, let me show you Ithaca's setting,
        I'll convince you. This haven—look around—
        it's named for Phorcys, the old god of the deep,
        and here at the harbor's head the branching olive stands
395   with the welcome cave nearby it, dank with sea-mist,
        sacred to nymphs of the springs we call the Naiads.
        Here, under its arching vault, time and again

you'd offer the nymphs a generous sacrifice
to bring success! And the slopes above you, look,
400   Mount Neriton decked in forests!"
                                    At those words
the goddess scattered the mist and the country stood out clear
and the great man who had borne so much rejoiced at last,
thrilled to see his Ithaca—he kissed the good green earth
and raised his hands to the nymphs and prayed at once,
405   "Nymphs of the springs, Naiads, daughters of Zeus,
I never dreamed I would see you yet again . . .
Now rejoice in my loving prayers—and later,
just like the old days, I will give you gifts
if Athena, Zeus's daughter, Queen of Armies
410   comes to my rescue, grants this fighter life
and brings my son to manhood!"
                                    "Courage!"—
goddess Athena answered, eyes afire—
"Free your mind of all that anguish now.
Come, quick, let's bury your treasures here
415   in some recess of this haunted hallowed cave
where they'll be safe and sound,
then we'll make plans so we can win the day."
                                    With that
the goddess swept into the cavern's shadowed vault,
searching for hiding-places far inside its depths
420   while Odysseus hauled his treasures closer up,
the gold, durable bronze and finespun robes,
the Phaeacians' parting gifts.
Once he'd stowed them well away, the goddess,
Pallas Athena, daughter of storming Zeus,
425   sealed the mouth of the cavern with a stone.

    Then down they sat by the sacred olive's trunk
to plot the death of the high and mighty suitors.
The bright-eyed goddess Athena led the way:
"Royal son of Laertes, Odysseus, old campaigner,
430   think how to lay your hands on all those brazen suitors,
lording it over your house now, three whole years,
courting your noble wife, offering gifts to win her.
But she, forever broken-hearted for your return,
builds up each man's hopes—
435   dangling promises, dropping hints to each—
but all the while with something else in mind."

    "God help me!" the man of intrigue broke out:
"Clearly I might have died the same ignoble death
as Agamemnon, bled white in my own house too,
440   if you had never revealed this to me now,
goddess, point by point.
Come, weave us a scheme so I can pay them back!

Stand beside me, Athena, fire me with daring, fierce
as the day we ripped Troy's glittering crown of towers down.
445　Stand by me—furious now as then, my bright-eyed one—
and I would fight three hundred men, great goddess,
with you to brace me, comrade-in-arms in battle!"

　　Gray eyes ablaze, the goddess urged him on:
"Surely I'll stand beside you, not forget you,
450　not when the day arrives for us to do our work.
Those men who court your wife and waste your goods?
I have a feeling some will splatter your ample floors
with all their blood and brains. Up now, quickly.
First I will transform you—no one must know you.
455　I will shrivel the supple skin on your lithe limbs,
strip the russet curls from your head and deck you out
in rags you'd hate to see some other mortal wear;
I'll dim the fire in your eyes, so shining once—
until you seem appalling to all those suitors,
460　even your wife and son you left behind at home.
But you, you make your way to the swineherd first,
in charge of your pigs, and true to you as always,
loyal friend to your son, to Penelope, so self-possessed.
You'll find him posted beside his swine, grubbing round
465　by Raven's Rock and the spring called Arethusa,
rooting for feed that makes pigs sleek and fat,
the nuts they love, the dark pools they drink.
Wait there, sit with him, ask him all he knows.
I'm off to Sparta, where the women are a wonder,
470　to call Telemachus home, your own dear son, Odysseus.
He's journeyed to Lacedaemon's rolling hills
to see Menelaus, searching for news of you,
hoping to learn if you are still alive."

　　Shrewd Odysseus answered her at once:
475　"Why not tell him the truth? You know it all.
Or is *he* too—like father, like son—condemned
to hardship, roving over the barren salt sea
while strangers devour our livelihood right here?"

　　But the bright-eyed goddess reassured him firmly:
480　"No need for anguish, trust me, not for him—
I escorted your son myself
so he might make his name by sailing there.
Nor is he saddled down with any troubles now.
He sits at ease in the halls of Menelaus,
485　bathed in endless bounty . . . True enough,
some young lords in a black cutter lurk in ambush,
poised to kill the prince before he reaches home,
but I have my doubts they will. Sooner the earth
will swallow down a few of those young gallants

490   who eat you out of house and home these days!"

    No more words, not now—
Athena stroked Odysseus with her wand.
She shriveled the supple skin on his lithe limbs,
stripped the russet curls from his head, covered his body
495   top to toe with the wrinkled hide of an old man
and dimmed the fire in his eyes, so shining once.
She turned his shirt and cloak into squalid rags,
ripped and filthy, smeared with grime and soot.
She flung over this the long pelt of a bounding deer,
500   rubbed bare, and gave him a staff and beggar's sack,
torn and tattered, slung from a fraying rope.
                   All plans made,
they went their separate ways—Athena setting off
to bring Telemachus home from hallowed Lacedaemon.

BOOK 14. THE LOYAL SWINEHERD

So up from the haven now Odysseus climbed a rugged path
through timber along high ground—Athena had shown the way—
to reach the swineherd's place, that fine loyal man
who of all the household hands Odysseus ever had
5   cared the most for his master's worldly goods.

    Sitting at the door of his lodge he found him,
there in his farmstead, high-walled, broad and large,
with its long view on its cleared rise of ground . . .
The swineherd made those walls with his own hands
10   to enclose the pigs of his master gone for years.
Alone, apart from his queen or old Laertes,
he'd built them up of quarried blocks of stone
and coped them well with a fence of wild pear.

    Outside he'd driven stakes in a long-line stockade,
15   a ring of thickset palings split from an oak's dark heart.
Within the yard he'd built twelve sties, side-by-side,
to bed his pigs, and in each one fifty brood-sows
slept aground, penned and kept for breeding.
The boars slept outside, but far fewer of them,
20   thanks to the lordly suitors' feasts that kept on
thinning the herd and kept the swineherd stepping,
sending to town each day the best fat hog in sight.
By now they were down to three hundred and sixty head.
But guarding them all the time were dogs like savage beasts,
25   a pack of four, reared by the swineherd, foreman of men.
The man himself was fitting sandals to his feet,
carving away at an oxhide, dark and supple.
As for his men, three were off with their pigs,
herding them here or there. Under orders he'd sent
30   a fourth to town, with hog in tow for the gorging suitors

to slaughter off and glut themselves with pork.

   Suddenly—those snarling dogs spotted Odysseus,
charged him fast—a shatter of barks—but Odysseus
sank to the ground at once, he knew the trick:
35   the staff dropped from his hand but here and now,
on his own farm, he might have taken a shameful mauling.
Yes, but the swineherd, quick to move, dashed for the gate,
flinging his oxhide down, rushed the dogs with curses,
scattered them left and right with flying rocks
40   and warned his master, "Lucky to be alive, old man—
a moment more, my pack would have torn you limb from limb!
Then you'd have covered me with shame. As if the gods
had never given me blows and groans aplenty . . .
Here I sit, my heart aching, broken for *him,*
45   my master, my great king—fattening up
his own hogs for other men to eat, while he,
starving for food, I wager, wanders the earth,
a beggar adrift in strangers' cities, foreign-speaking lands,
if he's still alive, that is, still sees the rising sun.
50   Come, follow me into my place, old man, so you,
at least, can eat your fill of bread and wine.
Then you can tell me where you're from
and all the pains you've weathered."
                                        On that note
the loyal swineherd led the way to his shelter,
55   showed his guest inside and sat Odysseus down
on brush and twigs he piled up for the visitor,
flinging over these the skin of a shaggy wild goat,
broad and soft, the swineherd's own good bedding.
The king, delighted to be so well received,
60   thanked the man at once: "My host—may Zeus
and the other gods give *you* your heart's desire
for the royal welcome you have shown me here!"

   And you replied, Eumaeus, loyal swineherd,
"It's wrong, my friend, to send any stranger packing—
65   even one who arrives in worse shape than you.
Every stranger and beggar comes from Zeus
and whatever scrap they get from the likes of us,
they'll find it welcome. That's the best we can do,
we servants, always cowed by our high and mighty masters,
70   especially our young lords . . . But my old king?
The gods, they must have blocked his journey home.
He'd have treated me well, he would, with a house,
a plot of land and a wife you'd gladly prize.
Goods that a kind lord will give a household hand
75   who labors for him, hard, whose work the gods have sped,
just as they speed the work I labor at all day.
My master, I tell you, would have repaid me well

if he'd grown old right here. But now he's dead . . .
If only Helen and all her kind had died out too,
80   brought to her knees, just as she cut the legs
from under troops of men! My king among them,
he went off to the stallion-land of Troy
to fight the Trojans, save Agamemnon's honor!"

Enough—

he brusquely cinched his belt around his shirt,
85   strode out to the pens, crammed with droves of pigs,
picked out two, bundled them in and slaughtered both,
singed them, sliced them down, skewered them through
and roasting all to a turn, set them before Odysseus,
sizzling hot on the spits.
90   Then coating the meat with white barley groats
and mixing honeyed wine in a carved wooden bowl,
he sat down across from his guest, inviting warmly,
"Eat up now, my friend. It's all we slaves have got,
scrawny pork, while the suitors eat the fatted hogs—
95   no fear of the gods in their hard hearts, no mercy!
Trust me, the blessed gods have no love for crime.
They honor justice, honor the decent acts of men.
Even cutthroat bandits who raid foreign parts—
and Zeus grants them a healthy share of plunder,
100   ships filled to the brim, and back they head for home—
even their dark hearts are stalked by the dread of vengeance.
But the suitors know, they've caught some godsent rumor
of master's grisly death! That's why they have no mind
to do their courting fairly or go back home in peace.
105   No, at their royal ease they devour all his goods,
those brazen rascals never spare a scrap!
Not a day or a night goes by, sent down by Zeus,
but they butcher victims, never stopping at one or two,
and drain his wine as if there's no tomorrow—
110   swilling the last drop . . .
Believe me, my master's wealth was vast!
No other prince on earth could match his riches,
not on the loamy mainland or here at home in Ithaca—
no twenty men in the world could equal his great treasures!
115   Let me count them off for you. A dozen herds of cattle
back on the mainland, just as many head of sheep,
as many droves of pigs and goatflocks ranging free;
hired hands or his own herdsmen keep them grazing there.
Here in Ithaca, goatflocks, eleven in all, scatter
120   to graze the island, out at the wild end,
and trusty goatherds watch their every move.
And each herdsman, day after day, it never ends,
drives in a beast for the suitors—best in sight,
a sheep or well-fed goat. While I tend to these pigs,
125   I guard them, pick the best for those carousers

and send it to the slaughter!"
His voice rose
while the stranger ate his meat and drank his wine,
ravenous, bolting it all down in silence . . .
brooding on ways to serve the suitors right.
130 But once he'd supped and refreshed himself with food,
he filled the wooden bowl he'd been drinking from,
brimmed it with wine and passed it to his host
who received the offer gladly, spirit cheered
as the stranger probed him now with winging words:
135 "Friend, who was the man who bought you with his goods,
the master of such vast riches, powerful as you say?
You tell me he died defending Agamemnon's honor?
What's his name? I just might know such a man . . .
Zeus would know, and the other deathless gods,
140 if I ever saw him, if I bring you any news.
I've roamed the whole earth over."

    And the good swineherd answered, foreman of men,
"Old friend, no wanderer landing here with news of *him*
is likely to win his wife and dear son over.
145 Random drifters, hungry for bed and board,
lie through their teeth and swallow back the truth.
Why, any tramp washed up on Ithaca's shores
scurries right to my mistress, babbling lies,
and she ushers him in, kindly, pressing for details,
150 and the warm tears of grief come trickling down her cheeks,
the loyal wife's way when her husband's died abroad.
Even you, old codger, could rig up some fine tale—
and soon enough, I'd say,
if they gave you shirt and clothing for your pains.
155 My master? Well, no doubt the dogs and wheeling birds
have ripped the skin from his ribs by now, his life is through—
or fish have picked him clean at sea, and the man's bones
lie piled up on the mainland, buried deep in sand . . .
he's dead and gone. Aye, leaving a broken heart
160 for loved ones left behind, for *me* most of all.
Never another master kind as he!
I'll never find one—no matter where I go,
not even if I went back to mother and father,
the house where I was born and my parents reared me once.
165 Ah, but much as I grieve for them, much as I long
to lay my eyes on them, set foot on the old soil,
it's longing for him, him that wrings my heart—
Odysseus, lost and gone!
That man, old friend, far away as he is . . .
170 I can scarcely bear to say his name aloud,
so deeply he loved me, cared for me, so deeply.
Worlds away as he is, I call him Master, Brother!"

"My friend," the great Odysseus, long in exile, answered,
"since you are dead certain, since you still insist
175   he's never coming back, still the soul of denial,
I won't simply say it—on my oath I swear
Odysseus is on his way!
Reward for such good news? Let me have it
the moment he sets foot in his own house,
180   dress me in shirt and cloak, in handsome clothes.
Before then, poor as I am, I wouldn't take a thing.
I hate that man like the very Gates of Death who,
ground down by poverty, stoops to peddling lies.
I swear by Zeus, the first of all the gods,
185   by this table of hospitality here, my host,
by Odysseus' hearth where I have come for help:
all will come to pass, I swear, exactly as I say.
True, this very month—just as the old moon dies
and the new moon rises into life—Odysseus will return!
190   He will come home and take revenge on any man
who offends his wedded wife and princely son!"

"Good news," you replied, Eumaeus, loyal swineherd,
"but I will never pay a reward for *that,* old friend—
Odysseus, he'll never come home again. Never . . .
195   Drink your wine, sit back, let's talk of other things.
Don't remind me of all this. The heart inside me
breaks when anyone mentions my dear master.
That oath of yours, we'll let it pass—
                                        Odysseus,
oh come back!—
                        just as *I* wish, I and Penelope,
200   old Laertes too, Telemachus too, the godlike boy.
How I grieve for *him* now, I can't stop—Odysseus' son,
Telemachus. The gods reared him up like a fine young tree
and I often said, 'In the ranks of men he'll match his father,
his own dear father—amazing in build and looks, that boy!'
205   But all of a sudden a god wrecks his sense of balance—
god or man, no matter—off he's gone to catch
some news of his father, down to holy Pylos.
And now those gallant suitors lie in wait for him,
sailing home, to tear the royal line of Arcesius
210   out of Ithaca, root and branch, good name and all!
Enough. Let *him* pass too—whether he's trapped
or the hand of Zeus will pull him through alive.
                                                    Come,
old soldier, tell me the story of your troubles,
tell me truly, too, I'd like to know it well . . .
215   Who are you? where are you from? your city? your parents?
What sort of vessel brought you? Why did the sailors
land you here in Ithaca? Who did they say they are?
I hardly think you came this way on foot."

     The great teller of tales returned at length,
220 "My story—the whole truth—I'm glad to tell it all.
     If only the two of us had food and mellow wine
     to last us long, here in your shelter now,
     for us to sup on, undisturbed,
     while others take the work of the world in hand,
225 I could easily spend all year and never reach the end
     of my endless story, all the heartbreaking trials
     I struggled through. The gods willed it so . . .

     I hail from Crete's broad land, I'm proud to say,
     and I am a rich man's son. And many other sons
230 he brought up in his palace, born in wedlock,
     sprung of his lawful wife. Unlike my mother.
     She was a slave, a concubine he'd purchased, yes,
     but he treated me on a par with all his true-born sons—
     Castor, Hylax' son. I'm proud to boast his blood, that man
235 revered like a god throughout all Crete those days,
     for wealth, power and all his glorious offspring.
     But the deadly spirits soon swept him down
     to the House of Death, and his high and mighty sons
     carved up his lands and then cast lots for the parts
240 and gave me just a pittance, a paltry house as well.
     But I won myself a wife from wealthy, landed people,
     thanks to my own strong points. I was no fool
     and never shirked a fight.
                              But now my heyday's gone—
     I've had my share of blows. Yet look hard at the husk
245 and you'll still see, I think, the grain that gave it life.
     By heaven, Ares gave me courage, Athena too, to break
     the ranks of men wide open, once, in the old days,
     whenever I picked my troops and formed an ambush,
     plotting attacks to spring against our foes—
250 no hint of death could daunt my fighting spirit!
     Far out of the front I'd charge and spear my man,
     I'd cut down any enemy soldier backing off.
     Such was I in battle, true, but I had no love
     for working the land, the chores of households either,
255 the labor that raises crops of shining children. No,
     it was always oarswept ships that thrilled my heart,
     and wars, and the long polished spears and arrows,
     dreadful gear that makes the next man cringe.
     I loved them all—god planted that love inside me.
260 Each man delights in the work that suits him best.
     Why, long before we Achaeans ever camped at Troy,
     nine commands I led in our deep-sea-going ships,
     raiding foreign men, and a fine haul reached my hands.
     I helped myself to the lion's share and still more spoils
265 came by lot. And my house grew by leaps and bounds,
     I walked among the Cretans, honored, feared as well.

But then, when thundering Zeus contrived that expedition—
that disaster that brought so many fighters to their knees—
and men kept pressing me and renowned Idomeneus
270   to head a fleet to Troy,
there was no way out, no denying them then,
the voice of the people bore down much too hard.
So nine whole years we Achaeans soldiered on at Troy,
in the tenth we sacked King Priam's city, then embarked
275   for home in the long ships, and a god dispersed the fleet.
Unlucky me. Shrewd old Zeus was plotting still more pain.
No more than a month I stayed at home, taking joy
in my children, loyal wife and lovely plunder.
But a spirit in me urged, 'Set sail for Egypt—
280   fit out ships, take crews of seasoned heroes!'
Nine I fitted out, the men joined up at once
and then six days my shipmates feasted well,
while I provided a flock of sheep to offer up
to the gods and keep the feasters' table groaning.
285   On the seventh we launched out from the plains of Crete
with a stiff North Wind fair astern—smooth sailing,
aye, like coasting on downstream . . .
And not one craft in our squadron foundered;
all shipshape, and all hands sound, we sat back
290   while the wind and helmsmen kept us true on course.

Five days out and we raised the great river Nile
and there in the Nile delta moored our ships of war.
God knows I ordered my trusty crews to stand by,
just where they were, and guard the anchored fleet
295   and I sent a patrol to scout things out from higher ground.
But swept away by their own reckless fury, the crew went berserk—
they promptly began to plunder the lush Egyptian farms,
dragged off the women and children, killed the men.
Outcries reached the city in no time—stirred by shouts
300   the entire town came streaming down at the break of day,
filling the river plain with chariots, ranks of infantry
and the gleam of bronze. Zeus who loves the lightning
flung down murderous panic on all my men-at-arms—
no one dared to stand his ground and fight,
305   disaster ringed us round from every quarter.
Droves of my men they hacked down with swords,
led off the rest alive, to labor for them as slaves.
And I? Zeus flashed an inspiration through my mind,
though I wish I'd died a soldier down in Egypt then!
310   A world of pain, you see, still lay in wait for me . . .
Quickly I wrenched the skullcap helmet off my head,
I tore the shield from my back and dropped my spear
and ran right into the path of the king's chariot,
hugged and kissed his knees. He pitied me, spared me,

315   hoisted me onto his war-car, took me home in tears.
        Troops of his men came rushing after, shaking javelins,
        mad to kill me—their fighting blood at the boil—
        but their master drove them off.
        He feared the wrath of Zeus, the god of guests,
320   the first of the gods to pay back acts of outrage.
                                            So,
        there I lingered for seven years, amassing a fortune
        from all the Egyptian people loading me with gifts.
        Then, at last, when the eighth had come full turn,
        along comes this Phoenician one fine day . . .
325   a scoundrel, swindler, an old hand at lies
        who'd already done the world a lot of damage.
        Well, he smoothly talked me round and off we sailed,
        Phoenicia-bound, where his house and holdings lay.
        There in his care I stayed till the year was out.
330   Then, when the months and days had run their course
        and the year wheeled round and the seasons came again,
        he conned me aboard his freighter bound for Libya,
        pretending I'd help him ship a cargo there for sale
        but in fact he'd sell *me* there and make a killing!
335   I suspected as much, of course, but had no choice,
        so I boarded with him, yes, and the ship ran on
        with a good strong North Wind gusting—
        fast on the middle passage clear of Crete—
        but Zeus was brewing mischief for that crew . . .
340   Once we'd left the island in our wake—
        no land at all in sight, nothing but sea and sky—
        then Zeus the son of Cronus mounted a thunderhead
        above our hollow ship and the deep went black beneath it.
        Then, then in the same breath Zeus hit the craft
345   with a lightning-bolt and thunder. Round she spun,
        reeling under the impact, filled with reeking brimstone,
        shipmates pitching out of her, bobbing round like seahawks
        swept along by the breakers past the trim black hull—
        and the god cut short their journey home forever.
                                         Not mine.
350   Zeus himself—when I was just at the final gasp—
        thrust the huge mast of my dark-prowed vessel
        right into my arms so I might flee disaster
        one more time. Wrapping myself around it,
        I was borne along by the wretched galewinds,
355   rushed along nine days—on the tenth, at dead of night,
        a shouldering breaker rolled me up along Thesprotia's beaches.[1]
        There the king of Thesprotia, Phidon, my salvation,
        treated me kindly, asked for no reward at all.

---

1. In northwestern Greece.

His own good son had found me, half-dead
360   from exhaustion and the cold. He raised me up
by the hand and led me home to his father's house
and dressed me in cloak and shirt and decent clothes.
That's where I first got wind of *him*—Odysseus . . .
The king told me he'd hosted the man in style,
365   befriended him on his way home to native land,
and showed me all the treasure Odysseus had amassed.
Bronze and gold and plenty of hard wrought iron,
enough to last a man and ten generations of his heirs—
so great the wealth stored up for *him* in the king's vaults!
370   But Odysseus, he made clear, was off at Dodona then
to hear the will of Zeus that rustles forth
from the god's tall leafy oak: how should he return,
after all the years away, to his own green land of Ithaca—
openly or in secret? Phidon swore to me, what's more,
375   as the princely man poured out libations in his house,
'The ship's hauled down and the crew set to sail,
to take Odysseus home to native land.'
                                        But I . . .
he shipped me off before. A Thesprotian cutter
chanced to be heading for Dulichion rich in wheat,
380   so he told the crew to take me to the king, Acastus,
treat me kindly, too, but it pleased them more
to scheme foul play against me,
sink me into the very depths of pain. As soon
as the ship was far off land, scudding in mid-sea,
385   they sprang their trap—my day of slavery then and there!
They stripped from my back the shirt and cloak I wore,
decked me out in a new suit of clothes, all rags,
ripped and filthy—the rags you see right now.
But then, once they'd gained the fields of Ithaca,
390   still clear in the evening light, they lashed me fast
to the rowing-benches, twisting a cable round me;
all hands went ashore
and rushed to catch their supper on the beach.
But the gods themselves unhitched my knots at once
395   with the gods' own ease. I wrapped my head in rags,
slid down the gangplank polished smooth, slipped my body
into the water, not a splash, chest-high, then quick,
launched out with both my arms and swam away—
out of the surf in no time, clear of the crew.
400   I clambered upland, into a flowery, fragrant brush
and crouched there, huddling low. They raised a hue and cry,
wildly beat the bushes, but when it seemed no use
to pursue the hunt, back they trudged again and
boarded their empty ship.
                            The gods hid me themselves—
405   it's light work for them—and brought me here,

the homestead of a man who knows the world.
So it seems to be my lot that I'll live on."

    And you replied, Eumaeus, loyal swineherd,
"So much misery, friend! You've moved my heart,
410   deeply, with your long tale . . . such blows, such roving.
But one part's off the mark, I know—you'll never persuade me—
what you say about Odysseus. A man in your condition,
who are *you*, I ask you, to lie for no good reason?
Well I know the truth of my good lord's return,
415   how the gods detested him, with a vengeance—
never letting him go under, fighting Trojans,
or die in the arms of loved ones,
once he'd wound down the long coil of war.
Then all united Achaea would have raised his tomb
420   and he'd have won his son great fame for years to come.
But now the whirlwinds have ripped him away—no fame for him!
And I live here, cut off from the world, with all my pigs.
I never go into town unless, perhaps, wise Penelope
calls me back, when news drops in from nowhere.
425   There they crowd the messenger, cross-examine him,
heartsick for their long-lost lord or all too glad
to eat him out of house and home, scot-free.
But I've no love for all that probing, prying,
not since some Aetolian fooled me with his yarn.
430   He'd killed a man, wandered over the face of the earth,
stumbled onto my hut, and I received him warmly.
He told me he'd seen Odysseus
lodged with King Idomeneus down in Crete—
refitting his ships, hard-hit by the gales,
435   but he'd be home, he said, by summer or harvest-time,
his hulls freighted with treasure, manned by fighting crews.
So you, old misery, seeing a god has led you here to me,
don't try to charm me now, don't spellbind me with lies!
Never for *that* will I respect you, treat you kindly;
440   no, it's my fear of Zeus, the god of guests,
and because I pity you . . ."

    "Good god," the crafty man pressed on,
"what a dark, suspicious heart you have inside you!
Not even my oath can win you over, make you see the light.
445   Come, strike a bargain—all the gods of Olympus
witness now our pact!
If your master returns, here to your house,
dress me in shirt and cloak and send me off
to Dulichion at once, the place I long to be.
450   But if your master doesn't return as I predict,
set your men on me—fling me off some rocky crag
so the next beggar here may just think twice
before he peddles lies."

"Surely, friend!"—
the swineherd shook his head—"and just think
455   of the praise and fame I'd win among mankind,
now and for all time to come, if first I took you
under my roof, I treated you kindly as my guest
then cut you down and robbed you of your life—
how keen I'd be to say my prayers to Zeus!
460   But it's high time for a meal.
I hope the men will be home at any moment
so we can fix a tasty supper in the lodge."

As host and guest confided back and forth
the herdsmen came in, driving their hogs up close,
465   penning sows in their proper sties for the night,
squealing for all they're worth, shut inside their yard,
and the good swineherd shouted to his men,
"Bring in your fattest hog!
I'll slaughter it for our guest from far abroad.
470   We'll savor it ourselves. All too long we've sweated
over these white-tusked boars—our wretched labor—
while others wolf our work down free of charge!"
Calling out
as he split up kindling now with a good sharp ax
and his men hauled in a tusker five years old,
475   rippling fat, and stood him steady by the hearth.
The swineherd, soul of virtue, did not forget the gods.
He began the rite by plucking tufts from the porker's head,
threw them into the fire and prayed to all the powers,
"Bring him home, our wise Odysseus, home at last!"
480   Then raising himself full-length, with an oak log
he'd left unsplit he clubbed and stunned the beast
and it gasped out its life . . .
The men slashed its throat, singed the carcass,
quickly quartered it all, and then the swineherd,
485   cutting first strips for the gods from every limb,
spread them across the thighs, wrapped in sleek fat,
and sprinkling barley over them, flung them on the fire.
They sliced the rest into pieces, pierced them with skewers,
broiled them all to a turn and, pulling them off the spits,
490   piled the platters high. The swineherd, standing up
to share the meat—his sense of fairness perfect—
carved it all out into seven equal portions.
One he set aside, lifting up a prayer
to the forest nymphs and Hermes, Maia's son,
495   and the rest he handed on to each man in turn.
But to Odysseus he presented the boar's long loin
and the cut of honor cheered his master's heart.
The man for all occasions thanked his host:
"I pray, Eumaeus, you'll be as dear to Father Zeus
500   as you are to me—a man in my condition—

you honor me by giving me your best."

    You replied in kind, Eumaeus, swineherd:
"Eat, my strange new friend . . . enjoy it now,
it's all we have to offer. As for Father Zeus,
505 one thing he will give and another he'll hold back,
whatever his pleasure. All things are in his power."

    He burned choice parts for the gods who never die
and pouring glistening wine in a full libation,
placed the cup in his guest's hands—Odysseus,
510 raider of cities—and down he sat to his own share.
Mesaulius served them bread, a man the swineherd
purchased for himself in his master's absence—
alone, apart from his queen or old Laertes—
bought him from Taphians, bartered his own goods.
515 They reached out for the spread that lay at hand
and when they'd put aside desire for food and drink,
Mesaulius cleared the things away. And now, content
with bread and meat, they made for bed at once.

    A foul night came on—the dark of the moon—and Zeus
520 rained from dusk to dawn and a sodden West Wind raged.
Odysseus spoke up now, keen to test the swineherd.
Would he take his cloak off, hand it to his guest
or at least tell one of his men to do the same?
He cared for the stranger so, who ventured now,
525 "Listen, Eumaeus, and all you comrades here,
allow me to sing my praises for a moment.
Say it's the wine that leads me on, the wild wine
that sets the wisest man to sing at the top of his lungs,
laugh like a fool—it drives the man to dancing . . . it even
530 tempts him to blurt out stories better never told.
But now that I'm sounding off, I can't hold back.
Oh make me young again, and the strength inside me
steady as a rock! Just as I was that day
we sprang a sudden ambush against the Trojans.
535 Odysseus led the raid with Atreus' son Menelaus.
I was third in command—they'd chosen me themselves.
Once we'd edged up under the city's steep ramparts,
crowding the walls but sinking into the thick brake,
the reeds and marshy flats, huddling under our armor
540 there we lay, and a foul night came on, the North Wind struck,
freezing cold, and down from the skies the snow fell like frost,
packed hard—the rims of our shields armored round with ice.
There all the rest of the men wore shirts and cloaks and,
hunching shields over their shoulders, slept at ease.
545 Not I. I'd left my cloak at camp when I set out—
idiot—never thinking it might turn cold,
so I joined in with just the shield on my back
and a shining waist-guard . . . But then at last,

the night's third watch, the stars just wheeling down—
550   I muttered into his ear, Odysseus, right beside me,
nudging him with an elbow—he perked up at once—
'Royal son of Laertes, Odysseus, full of tactics,
I'm not long for the living. The cold will do me in.
See, I've got no cloak. Some spirit's fooled me—
555   I came out half-dressed. Now there's no escape!'
I hadn't finished—a thought flashed in his mind;
no one could touch the man at plots or battles.
'Shhh!' he hissed back—Odysseus had a plan—
'One of our fighters over there might hear you.'
560   Then he propped his head on his forearm, calling out,
'Friends, wake up. I slept and a god sent down a dream.
It warned that we're too far from the ships, exposed.
Go, someone, tell Agamemnon, our field marshal—
he might rush reinforcements from the beach.'
565   Thoas, son of Andraemon, sprang up at once,
flung off his purple cloak and ran to the ships
while I, bundling into his wrap, was glad at heart
till Dawn rose on her golden throne once more.
Oh make me young again
570   and the strength inside me steady as a rock!
One of the swineherds here would lend a wrap
for love of a good soldier, respect as well.
Now they spurn me, dressed in filthy rags."

        And you replied, Eumaeus, loyal swineherd,
575   "Now that was a fine yarn you told, old-timer,
not without point, not without profit either.
You won't want for clothes or whatever else
is due a worn-out traveler come for help—
not for tonight at least. Tomorrow morning
580   you'll have to flap around in rags again.
Here we've got no store of shirts and cloaks,
no changes. Just one wrap per man, that's all.
But just you wait till Odysseus' dear son comes back—
that boy will deck you out in a cloak and shirt
585   and send you off, wherever your heart desires!"
                                                    With that
he rose to his feet and laid out a bed by the fire,
throwing over it skins of sheep and goats and
down Odysseus lay. Eumaeus flung on his guest
the heavy flaring cloak he kept in reserve
590   to wear when winter brought some wild storm.
                                                    So here
Odysseus slept and the young hands slept beside him.
Not the swineherd. Not his style to bed indoors,
apart from his pigs. He geared up to go outside
and it warmed Odysseus' heart,
595   Eumaeus cared so much for his absent master's goods.

First, over his broad shoulders he slung a whetted sword,
wrapped himself in a cloak stitched tight to block the wind,
and adding a cape, the pelt of a shaggy well-fed goat,
he took a good sharp lance to fight off men and dogs.
600   Then out he went to sleep where his white-tusked boars
had settled down for the night . . . just under
a jutting crag that broke the North Wind's blast.

BOOK 15. THE PRINCE SETS SAIL FOR HOME

Now south through the spacious dancing-rings of Lacedaemon
Athena went to remind the hero's princely son
of his journey home and spur him on his way.
She found him there with Nestor's gallant son,
5   bedded down in the porch of illustrious Menelaus—
Pisistratus, at least, overcome with deep sound sleep,
but not Telemachus. Welcome sleep could not hold him.
All through the godsent night he lay awake . . .
tossing with anxious thoughts about his father.
10   Hovering over him, eyes ablaze, Athena said,
"It's wrong, Telemachus, wrong to rove so far,
so long from home, leaving your own holdings
unprotected—crowds in your palace so brazen
they'll carve up all your wealth, devour it all,
15   and then your journey here will come to nothing.
Quickly, press Menelaus, lord of the warcry,
to speed you home at once, if you want to find
your irreproachable mother still inside your house.
Even now her father and brothers urge Penelope
20   to marry Eurymachus, who excels all other suitors
at giving gifts and drives the bride-price higher.
She must not carry anything off against your will!
You know how the heart of a woman always works:
she likes to build the wealth of her new groom—
25   of the sons she bore, of her dear, departed husband,
not a memory of the dead, no questions asked.
So sail for home, I say!
With your own hands turn over all your goods
to the one serving-woman you can trust the most,
30   till the gods bring to light your own noble bride.

And another thing. Take it to heart, I tell you.
Picked men of the suitors lie in ambush, grim-set
in the straits between Ithaca and rocky Same,
poised to kill you before you can reach home,
35   but I have my doubts they will. Sooner the earth
will swallow down a few of those young gallants
who eat you out of house and home these days!
Just give the channel islands a wide berth,
push on in your trim ship, sail night and day,

40   and the deathless god who guards and pulls you through
    will send you a fresh fair wind from hard astern.
    At your first landfall, Ithaca's outer banks,
    speed ship and shipmates round to the city side.
    But you—you make your way to the swineherd first,
45   in charge of your pigs, and true to you as always.
    Sleep the night there, send him to town at once
    to tell the news to your mother, wise Penelope—
    you've made it back from Pylos safe and sound."

      Mission accomplished, back she went to Olympus' heights
50   as Telemachus woke Nestor's son from his sweet sleep;
    he dug a heel in his ribs and roused him briskly:
    "Up, Pisistratus. Hitch the team to the chariot—
    let's head for home at once!"
                          "No, Telemachus,"
    Nestor's son objected, "much as we long to go,
55   we cannot drive a team in the dead of night.
    Morning will soon be here. So wait, I say,
    wait till he loads our chariot down with gifts—
    the hero Atrides, Menelaus, the great spearman—
    and gives us warm salutes and sees off like princes.
60   That's the man a guest will remember all his days:
    the lavish host who showers him with kindness."

      At those words Dawn rose on her golden throne
    and Menelaus, lord of the warcry, rising up from bed
    by the side of Helen with her loose and lovely hair,
65   walked toward his guests. As soon as he saw him,
    Telemachus rushed to pull a shimmering tunic on,
    over his broad shoulders threw his flaring cape
    and the young prince, son of King Odysseus,
    strode out to meet his host: "Menelaus,
70   royal son of Atreus, captain of armies,
    let me go back to my own country now.
    The heart inside me longs for home at last."

      The lord of the warcry reassured the prince,
    "I'd never detain you here too long, Telemachus,
75   not if your heart is set on going home.
    I'd find fault with another host, I'm sure,
    too warm to his guests, too pressing or too cold.
    Balance is best in all things. It's bad either way,
    spurring the stranger home who wants to linger,
80   holding the one who longs to leave—you know,
    'Welcome the coming, speed the parting guest!'
    But wait till I load your chariot down with gifts—
    fine ones, too, you'll see with your own eyes—
    and tell the maids to serve a meal at hall.
85   We have god's plenty here.
    It's honor and glory to us, a help to you as well

if you dine in style first, then leave to see the world.
And if you're keen for the grand tour of all Hellas,
right to the depths of Argos, I'll escort you myself,
90   harness the horses, guide you through the towns.
And no host will turn us away with empty hands,
each will give us at least one gift to prize—
a handsome tripod, cauldron forged in bronze,
a brace of mules or a solid golden cup."

95   Firmly resolved, Telemachus replied,
"Menelaus, royal Atrides, captain of armies,
I must go back to my own home at once.
When I started out I left no one behind
to guard my own possessions. God forbid,
100   searching for my great father, I lose my life
or lose some priceless treasure from my house!"

As soon as the lord of the warcry heard *that,*
he told his wife and serving-women to lay out a meal
in the hall at once. They'd stores aplenty there.
105   Eteoneus, son of Boëthous, came to join them—
fresh from bed, he lived close by the palace.
The warlord Menelaus told him to build a fire
and broil some meat. He quickly did his bidding.
Down Atrides walked to a storeroom filled with scent,
110   and not alone: Helen and Megapenthes went along.
Reaching the spot where all the heirlooms lay,
Menelaus chose a generous two-handled cup;
he told his son Megapenthes to take a mixing-bowl,
solid silver, while Helen lingered beside the chests,
115   and there they were, brocaded, beautiful robes
her own hands had woven. Queenly Helen,
radiance of women, lifted one from the lot,
the largest, loveliest robe, and richly worked
and like a star it glistened, deep beneath the others.
120   Then all three went up and on through the halls until
they found Telemachus. The red-haired king spoke out:
"Oh my boy, may Zeus the Thunderer, Hera's lord,
grant you the journey home your heart desires!
Of all the treasures lying heaped in my palace
125   you shall have the finest, most esteemed. Look,
I'll give you this mixing-bowl, forged to perfection—
it's solid silver finished off with a lip of gold.
Hephaestus made it himself. And a royal friend,
Phaedimus, king of Sidon, lavished it on *me*
130   when his palace welcomed me on passage home.
How pleased I'd be if you took it as a gift!"

And the warlord placed the two-eared cup
in his hands while stalwart Megapenthes carried in
the glittering silver bowl and set it down before him.

135   Helen, her cheeks flushed with beauty, moved beside him,
holding the robe in her arms, and offered, warmly,
"Here, dear boy, I too have a gift to give you,
a keepsake of Helen—I wove it with my hands—
for your own bride to wear

140   when the blissful day of marriage dawns . . .
Until then, let it rest in your mother's room.
And may you return in joy—my parting wish—
to your own grand house, your native land at last."
                                    With that
she laid the robe in his arms, and he received it gladly.

145   Prince Pisistratus, taking the gifts, stowed them deep
in the chariot cradle, viewed them all with wonder.
The red-haired warlord led them back to his house
and the guests took seats on low and high-backed chairs.
A maid brought water soon in a graceful golden pitcher

150   and over a silver basin tipped it out
so they might rinse their hands,
then pulled a gleaming table to their side.
A staid housekeeper brought on bread to serve them,
appetizers aplenty too, lavish with her bounty.

155   Ready Eteoneus carved and passed the meat,
the son of illustrious Menelaus poured their wine.
They reached out for the good things that lay at hand
and once they'd put aside desire for food and drink,
Prince Telemachus and the gallant son of Nestor

160   yoked their team, mounted the blazoned car
and drove through the gates and echoing colonnade.
The red-haired King Menelaus followed both boys out,
his right hand holding a golden cup of honeyed wine
so the two might pour libations forth at parting.

165   Just in front of the straining team he strode,
lifting his cup and pledging both his guests:
"Farewell, my princes! Give my warm greetings
to Nestor, the great commander,
always kind to me as a father, long ago

170   when we young men of Achaea fought at Troy."

    And tactful Telemachus replied at once,
"Surely, my royal host, we'll tell him all,
as soon as we reach old Nestor—all you say.
I wish I were just as sure I'd find Odysseus

175   waiting there at home when I reach Ithaca.
I'd tell him I come from you,
treated with so much kindness at your hands,
loaded down with all these priceless gifts!"

    At his last words a bird flew past on the right,

180   an eagle clutching a huge white goose in its talons,
plucked from the household yards. And all rushed after,

shouting, men and women, and swooping toward the chariot now
the bird veered off to the right again before the horses.
All looked up, overjoyed—people's spirits lifted.
185 Nestor's son Pisistratus spoke out first:
"Look there! King Menelaus, captain of armies,
what, did the god send down that sign for you
or the two of us?"
                              The warlord fell to thinking—
how to read the omen rightly, how to reply? . . .
190 But long-robed Helen stepped in well before him:
"Listen to me and I will be your prophet,
sure as the gods have flashed it in my mind
and it will come to pass, I know it will.
Just as the eagle swooped down from the crags
195 where it was born and bred, just as it snatched
that goose fattened up for the kill inside the house,
just so, after many trials and roving long and hard,
Odysseus will descend on his house and take revenge—
unless he's home already, sowing seeds of ruin
200 for that whole crowd of suitors!"
                              "Oh if only,"
pensive Telemachus burst out in thanks to Helen,
"Zeus the thundering lord of Hera makes it so—
even at home I'll pray to you as a deathless goddess!"

      He cracked the lash and the horses broke quickly,
205 careering through the city out into open country,
shaking the yoke across their shoulders all day long.

      The sun sank and the roads of the world grew dark
as they reached Phera, pulling up to Diocles' halls,
the son of Ortilochus, son of the Alpheus River.
210 He gave them a royal welcome; there they slept the night.

      When young Dawn with her rose-red fingers shone once more
they yoked their pair again, mounted the blazoned car
and out through the gates and echoing colonnade
they whipped the team to a run and on they flew,
215 holding nothing back, approaching Pylos soon,
the craggy citadel. That was when Telemachus
turned to Pisistratus, saying, "Son of Nestor,
won't you do as I ask you, see it through?
We're friends for all our days now, so we claim,
220 thanks to our fathers' friendship. We're the same age as well
and this tour of ours has made us more like brothers.
Prince, don't drive me past my vessel, drop me there.
Your father's old, in love with his hospitality;
I fear he'll hold me, chafing in his palace—
225 I must hurry home!"
                              The son of Nestor pondered . . .

how to do it properly, see it through?
Pausing a moment, then this way seemed best.
Swerving his team, he drove down to the ship
tied up on shore and loaded into her stern

230   the splendid gifts, the robes and gold Menelaus gave,
and sped his friend with a flight of winging words:
"Climb aboard now—fast! Muster all your men
before I get home and break the news to father.
With that man's overbearing spirit—I know it,

235   know it all too well—he'll never let you go,
he'll come down here and summon you himself.
He won't return without you, believe me—
in any case he'll fly into a rage."

       With that warning he whipped his sleek horses
240   back to Pylos city and reached his house in no time.
Telemachus shouted out commands to all his shipmates:
"Stow our gear, my comrades, deep in the holds
and board at once—we must be on our way!"

       His shipmates snapped to orders,
245   swung aboard and sat to the oars in ranks.
But just as Telemachus prepared to launch,
praying, sacrificing to Pallas by the stern,
a man from a far-off country came toward him now,
a fugitive out of Argos: he had killed a man . . .

250   He was a prophet, sprung of Melampus' line of seers,
Melampus who lived in Pylos, mother of flocks, some years ago,
rich among his Pylians, at home in his great high house.
But then he was made to go abroad to foreign parts,
fleeing his native land and hot-blooded Neleus—

255   most imperious man alive—who'd commandeered
his vast estate and held it down by force
for one entire year. That year Melampus,
bound by cruel chains in the halls of Phylacus,
suffered agonies—all for Neleus' daughter Pero,

260   that and the mad spell a Fury, murderous spirit,
cast upon his mind. But the seer worked free of death
and drove the lusty, bellowing cattle out of Phylace,
back to Pylos. There he avenged himself on Neleus
for the shameful thing the king had done to him,

265   and escorted Pero home as his brother's bride.
But he himself went off to a distant country,
Argos, land of stallions—his destined home
where he would live and rule the Argive nation.
Here he married a wife and built a high-roofed house

270   and sired Antiphates and Mantius, two staunch sons.
Antiphates fathered Oicles, gallant heart,
Oicles fathered Amphiaraus, driver of armies,
whom storming Zeus and Apollo loved intensely,

showering him with every form of kindness.
275   But he never reached the threshold of old age,
he died at Thebes—undone by a bribe his wife accepted—
leaving behind his two sons, Alcmaeon and Amphilochus.
On his side Mantius sired Polyphides and Clitus both
but Dawn of the golden throne whisked Clitus away,
280   overwhelmed by his beauty,
so the boy would live among the deathless gods.
Yet Apollo made magnanimous Polyphides a prophet—
after Amphiaraus' death—the greatest seer on earth.
But a feud with his father drove him off to Hyperesia
285   where he made his home and prophesied to the world . . . .

This prophet's son it was—Theoclymenus his name—
who approached Telemachus now and found him pouring
wine to a god and saying prayers beside his ship.
"Friend," he said in a winging supplication,
290   "since I find you burning offerings here,
I beg you by these rites and the god you pray to,
then by your own life and the lives of all the men
who travel with you—tell me truly, don't hold back,
who are you? where are you from? your city? your parents?"

295   "Of course, stranger," the forthright prince responded,
"I will tell you everything, clearly as I can.
Ithaca is my country. Odysseus is my father—
there was a man, or was he all a dream? . . .
but he's surely died a wretched death by now.
300   Yet here I've come with my crew and black ship,
out for news of my father, lost and gone so long."

And the godlike seer Theoclymenus replied,
"Just like you, I too have left my land—
I because I killed a man of my own tribe.
305   But he has many brothers and kin in Argos,
stallion-land, who rule the plains in force.
Fleeing death at their hands, a dismal fate,
I am a fugitive now,
doomed to wander across this mortal world.
310   So take me aboard, hear a fugitive's prayer:
don't let them kill me—they're after me, well I know!"

"So desperate!" thoughtful Telemachus exclaimed.
"How could I drive you from my ship? Come sail with us,
we'll tend you at home, with all we can provide."

315   And he took the prophet's honed bronze spear,
laid it down full-length on the rolling deck,
swung aboard the deep-sea craft himself,
assuming the pilot's seat reserved astern
and put the seer beside him. Cables cast off,

320   Telemachus shouted out commands to all his shipmates:
    "All lay hands to tackle!" They sprang to orders,
    hoisting the pinewood mast, they stepped it firm
    in its block amidships, lashed it fast with stays
    and with braided rawhide halyards hauled the white sail high.
325   Now bright-eyed Athena sent them a stiff following wind
    blustering out of a clear sky, gusting on so the ship
    might run its course through the salt sea at top speed—
    and past the Springs she raced and the Chalcis' rushing stream
    as the sun sank and the roads of the world grew dark and
330   on she pressed for Pheae, driven on by a wind from Zeus
    and flew past lovely Elis, where Epeans rule in power,
    and then Telemachus veered for the Jagged Islands,
    wondering all the way—
    would he sweep clear of death or be cut down?

335   The king and loyal swineherd, just that night,
    were supping with other fieldhands in the lodge.
    And once they'd put aside desire for food and drink,
    Odysseus spoke up, eager to test the swineherd,
    see if he'd stretch out his warm welcome now,
340   invite him to stay on in the farmstead here
    or send him off to town. "Listen, Eumaeus,
    all you comrades here—at the crack of dawn
    I mean to go to town and do my begging,
    not be a drain on you and all your men.
345   But advise me well, give me a trusty guide
    to see me there. And then I'm on my own
    to roam the streets—I must, I have no choice—
    hoping to find a handout, just a crust or cupful.
    I'd really like to go to the house of King Odysseus
350   and give my news to his cautious queen, Penelope.
    Why, I'd even mix with those overweening suitors—
    would they spare me a plateful? Look at all they have!
    I'd do good work for them, promptly, anything they want.
    Let me tell you, listen closely, catch my drift . . .
355   Thanks to Hermes the guide, who gives all work
    of our hands the grace and fame that it deserves,
    no one alive can match me at household chores:
    building a good fire, splitting kindling neatly,
    carving, roasting meat and pouring rounds of wine . . .
360   anything menials do to serve their noble masters."

       "God's sake, my friend!" you broke in now,
    Eumaeus, loyal swineherd, deeply troubled.
    "What's got into your head, what crazy plan?
    You must be hell-bent on destruction, on the spot,
365   if you're keen to mingle with that mob of suitors—
    their pride and violence hit the iron skies!
    They're a far cry from you,

the men who do their bidding. Young bucks,
all rigged out in their fine robes and shirts,
370 hair sleeked down with oil, faces always beaming,
the ones who slave for *them!* The tables polished,
sagging under the bread and meat and wine.
No, stay here. No one finds you a burden,
surely not I, nor any comrade here.
375 You wait till Odysseus' dear son comes back—
that boy will deck you out in a cloak and shirt
and send you off, wherever your heart desires!"

   "If only, Eumaeus," the wayworn exile said,
"you were as dear to Father Zeus as you are to me!
380 You who stopped my pain, my endless, homesick roving.
Tramping about the world—there's nothing worse for a man.
But the fact is that men put up with misery
to stuff their cursed bellies.
But seeing you hold me here, urging me now
385 to wait for *him,* the prince who's on his way,
tell me about the mother of King Odysseus, please,
the father he left as well—on the threshold of old age—
when he sailed off to war. Are they still alive,
perhaps, still looking into the light of day?
390 Or dead by now, and down in Death's long house?"

                              "Friend,"
the swineherd, foreman of men, assured his guest,
"I'll tell you the whole story, point by point.
Laertes is still alive, but night and day
he prays to Zeus, waiting there in his house,
395 for the life breath to slip away and leave his body.
His heart's so racked for his son, lost and gone these years,
for his wife so fine, so wise—*her* death is the worst blow
he's had to suffer—it made him old before his time.
She died of grief for her boy, her glorious boy,
400 it wore her down, a wretched way to go.
I pray that no one I love dies such a death,
no island neighbor of mine who treats me kindly!
While she was still alive, heartsick as she was,
it always moved me to ask about her, learn the news.
405 She'd reared me herself, and right beside her daughter,
Ctimene, graceful girl with her long light gown,
the youngest one she'd borne . . .
Just the two of us, growing up together,
the woman tending me almost like her child,
410 till we both reached the lovely flush of youth
and then her parents gave her away in marriage, yes,
to a Samian man, and a haul of gifts they got.
But her mother decked me out in cloak and shirt,
good clothing she wrapped about me—gave me sandals,

415   sent me here, this farm. She loved me from the heart.
Oh how I miss her kindness now! The happy gods
speed the work that I labor at, that gives me
food and drink to spare for the ones I value.
But from Queen Penelope I never get a thing,
420   never a winning word, no friendly gesture,
not since this, this plague has hit the house—
these high and mighty suitors. Servants miss it,
terribly, gossiping back and forth with the mistress,
gathering scraps of news, a snack and a cup or two,
425   then taking home to the fields some little gift.
It never fails to cheer a servant's heart."

      "Imagine that," his canny master said,
"you must have been just a little fellow, Eumaeus,
when you were swept so far from home and parents.
430   Come, tell me the whole story, truly too.
Was your city sacked?—
some city filled with people and wide streets
where your father and your mother made their home?
Or were you all alone, herding your sheep and cattle,
435   when pirates kidnapped, shipped and sold you off
to this man's house, who paid a healthy price?"

      "My friend," the swineherd answered, foreman of men,
"you really want my story? So many questions—well,
listen in quiet, then, and take your ease, sit back
440   and drink your wine. The nights are endless now.
We've plenty of time to sleep or savor a long tale.
No need, you know, to turn in before the hour.
Even too much sleep can be a bore.
But anyone else who feels the urge
445   can go to bed and then, at the crack of dawn,
break bread, turn out and tend our master's pigs.
We two will keep to the shelter here, eat and drink
and take some joy in each other's heartbreaking sorrows,
sharing each other's memories. Over the years, you know,
450   a man finds solace even in old sorrows, true, a man
who's weathered many blows and wandered many miles.
My own story? This will answer all your questions . . .

      There's an island, Syrie—you may have heard of it—
off above Ortygia, out where the sun wheels around.
455   Not so packed with people, still a good place, though,
fine for sheep and cattle, rich in wine and wheat.
Hunger never attacks the land, no sickness either,
that always stalks the lives of us poor men.
No, as each generation grows old on the island,
460   down Apollo comes with his silver bow, with Artemis,
and they shoot them all to death with gentle arrows.
Two cities there are, that split the land in half,

and over them both my father ruled in force—
Ormenus' son Ctesius, a man like a deathless god.
                                                    One day
465 a band of Phoenicians landed there. The famous sea-dogs,
sharp bargainers too, the holds of their black ship
brimful with a hoard of flashy baubles. Now,
my father kept a Phoenician woman in his house,
beautiful, tall and skilled at weaving lovely things,
470 and her rascal countrymen lusted to seduce her, yes,
and lost no time—she was washing clothes when one of them
waylaid her beside their ship, in a long deep embrace
that can break a woman's will, even the best alive.
And then he asked her questions . . .
475 her name, who was she, where did she come from?
She waved at once to my father's high-roofed house—
'But I'm proud to hail from Sidon paved in bronze,' she said,
'and Arybas was my father, a man who rolled in wealth.
I was heading home from the fields when Taphian pirates
480 snatched me away, and they shipped and sold me here
to this man's house. He paid a good stiff price!'

   The sailor, her secret lover, lured her on:
'Well then, why don't you sail back home with us?—
see your own high house, your father and mother there.
485 They're still alive, and people say they're rich!'

   'Now there's a tempting offer,' she said in haste,
'if only you sailors here would swear an oath
you'll land me safe at home without a scratch.'

   Those were her terms, and once they vowed to keep them,
490 swore their oaths they'd never do her harm,
the woman hatched a plan: 'Now not a word!
Let none of your shipmates say a thing to me,
meeting me on the street or at the springs.
Someone might go running off to the house
495 and tell the old king—he'd think the worst,
clap me in cruel chains and find a way to kill you.
So keep it a secret, down deep, get on with buying
your home cargo, quickly. But once your holds
are loaded up with goods, then fast as you can
500 you send the word to me over there at the palace.
I'll bring you all the gold I can lay my hands on
and something else I'll give you in the bargain,
fare for passage home . . .
I'm nurse to my master's son in the palace now—
505 such a precious toddler, scampering round outside,
always at my heels. I'll bring him aboard as well.
Wherever you sell him off, whatever foreign parts,
he'll fetch you quite a price!'
                                        Bargain struck,

back the woman went to our lofty halls
510   and the rovers stayed on with us one whole year,
bartering, piling up big hoards in their hollow ship,
and once their holds were loaded full for sailing
they sent a messenger, fast, to alert the woman.
This crafty bandit came to my father's house,
515   dangling a golden choker linked with amber beads,
and while the maids at hall and my noble mother
kept on fondling it—dazzled, feasting their eyes
and making bids—he gave a quiet nod to my nurse,
he gave her the nod and slunk back to his ship.
520   Grabbing my hand, she swept me through the house
and there in the porch she came on cups and tables
left by the latest feasters, father's men of council
just gone off to the meeting grounds for full debate—
and quick as a flash she snatched up three goblets,
525   tucked them into her bosom, whisked them off
and I tagged along, lost in all my innocence!
The sun sank, the roads of the world grew dark
and both on the run, we reached the bay at once
where the swift Phoenician ship lay set to sail.
530   Handing us up on board, the crewmen launched out
on the foaming lanes and Zeus sent wind astern.
Six whole days we sailed, six nights, nonstop
and then, when the god brought on the seventh day,
Artemis showering arrows came and shot the woman—
535   headfirst into the bilge she splashed like a diving tern
and the crewmen heaved her body over, a nice treat
for the seals and fish, but left me all alone,
cowering, sick at heart . . .
                                    Until, at last,
the wind and current bore us on to Ithaca,
540   here where Laertes bought me with his wealth.
And so I first laid eyes on this good land."

    And royal King Odysseus answered warmly,
"Eumaeus, so much misery! You've moved my heart,
deeply, with your long tale—such pain, such sorrow.
545   True, but look at the good fortune Zeus sends you,
hand-in-hand with the bad. After all your toil
you reached the house of a decent, kindly man
who gives you all you need in meat and drink—
he's seen to that, I'd say—
550   it's a fine life you lead! Better than mine . . .
I've been drifting through cities up and down the earth
and now I've landed here."
                                    So guest and host
confided through the night until they slept,
a little at least, not long.
555   Dawn soon rose and took her golden throne.

                                        That hour
Telemachus and his shipmates raised the coasts of home,
they struck sail and lowered the mast, smartly,
rowed her into a mooring under oars.
Out went the bow-stones, cables fast astern,
560   the crew themselves swung out in the breaking surf,
they got a meal together and mixed some ruddy wine.
And once they'd put aside desire for food and drink,
clear-headed Telemachus gave the men commands:
"Pull our black ship round to the city now—
565   I'm off to my herdsmen and my farms. By nightfall,
once I've seen to my holdings, I'll be down in town.
In the morning I'll give you wages for the voyage,
a handsome feast of meat and hearty wine."

       The seer Theoclymenus broke in quickly,
570   "Where shall I go, dear boy? Of all the lords
in rocky Ithaca, whose house shall I head for now?
Or do I go straight to your mother's house and yours?"

       "Surely in better times," discreet Telemachus replied,
"I would invite you home. Our hospitality never fails
575   but now, I fear, it could only serve you poorly.
I'll be away, and mother would never see you.
She rarely appears these days,
what with those suitors milling in the hall;
she keeps to her upper story, weaving at her loom.
580   But I'll mention someone else you might just visit:
Eurymachus, wise Polybus' fine, upstanding son.
He's the man of the hour! Our island people
look on him like a god—the prince of suitors,
hottest to wed my mother, seize my father's powers.
585   But god knows—Zeus up there in his bright Olympus—
whether or not before that wedding day arrives
he'll bring the day of death on all their heads!"

       At his last words a bird flew past on the right,
a hawk, Apollo's wind-swift herald—tight in his claws
590   a struggling dove, and he ripped its feathers out
and they drifted down to earth between the ship
and the young prince himself . . .
The prophet called him aside, clear of his men,
and grasped his hand, exclaiming, "Look, Telemachus,
595   the will of god just winged that bird on your right!
Why, the moment I saw it, here before my eyes,
I knew it was a sign. No line more kingly than yours
in all of Ithaca—yours will reign forever!"

                                        "If only, friend,"
alert Telemachus answered, "all you say comes true!
600   You'd soon know my affection, know my gifts.
Any man you meet would call you blest."

He turned to a trusted friend and said, "Piraeus,
son of Clytius, you are the one who's done my bidding,
more than all other friends who sailed with me to Pylos.
605   Please, take this guest of mine to your own house,
treat him kindly, host him with all good will
till I can come myself."
                        "Of course, Telemachus,"
Piraeus the gallant spearman offered warmly:
"Stay up-country just as long as you like.
610   I'll tend the man, he'll never lack a lodging."

Piraeus boarded ship and told the crew
to embark at once and cast off cables quickly—
they swung aboard and sat to the oars in ranks.
Telemachus fastened rawhide sandals on his feet
615   and took from the decks his rugged bronze-tipped spear.
The men cast off, pushed out and pulled for town
as Telemachus ordered, King Odysseus' son.
The prince strode out briskly,
legs speeding him on till he reached the farm
620   where his great droves of pigs crowded their pens
and the loyal swineherd often slept beside them,
always the man to serve his masters well.

BOOK 16. FATHER AND SON

As dawn came into the lodge, the king and loyal swineherd
set out breakfast, once they had raked the fire up
and got the herdsmen off with droves of pigs.
And now Telemachus . . .
5   the howling dogs went nuzzling up around him,
not a growl as he approached. From inside
Odysseus noticed the pack's quiet welcome,
noticed the light tread of footsteps too
and turned to Eumaeus quickly, winged a word:
10   "Eumaeus, here comes a friend of yours, I'd say.
Someone you know, at least. The pack's not barking,
must be fawning around him. I can hear his footfall."

The words were still on his lips when his own son
stood in the doorway, there. The swineherd started up,
15   amazed, he dropped the bowls with a clatter—he'd been busy
mixing ruddy wine. Straight to the prince he rushed
and kissed his face and kissed his shining eyes,
both hands, as the tears rolled down his cheeks.
As a father, brimming with love, welcomes home
20   his darling only son in a warm embrace—
what pain he's borne for him and him alone!—
home now, in the tenth year from far abroad,

so the loyal swineherd hugged the beaming prince,
he clung for dear life, covering him with kisses, yes,
25   like one escaped from death. Eumaeus wept and sobbed,
his words flew from the heart: "You're home, Telemachus,
sweet light of my eyes! I never thought I'd see you again,
once you'd shipped to Pylos! Quick, dear boy, come in,
let me look at you, look to my heart's content—
30   under my own roof, the rover home at last.
You rarely visit the farm and men these days,
always keeping to town, as if it *cheered* you
to see them there, that infernal crowd of suitors!"

        "Have it your way," thoughtful Telemachus replied.
35   "Dear old man, it's all for you that I've come,
to see you for myself and learn the news—
whether mother still holds out in the halls
or some other man has married her at last,
and Odysseus' bed, I suppose, is lying empty,
40   blanketed now with filthy cobwebs."
                              "Surely,"
the foreman of men responded, "she's still waiting
there in your halls, poor woman, suffering so,
her life an endless hardship . . .
wasting away the nights, weeping away the days."
                                        With that
45   he took the bronze spear from the boy, and Telemachus,
crossing the stone doorsill, went inside the lodge.
As he approached, his father, Odysseus, rose
to yield his seat, but the son on his part
waved him back: "Stay where you are, stranger.
50   I know we can find another seat somewhere,
here on our farm, and here's the man to fetch it."

        So Odysseus, moving back, sat down once more,
and now for the prince the swineherd strewed a bundle
of fresh green brushwood, topped it off with sheepskin
55   and there the true son of Odysseus took his place.
Eumaeus set before them platters of roast meat
left from the meal he'd had the day before;
he promptly served them bread, heaped in baskets,
mixed their hearty wine in a wooden bowl
60   and then sat down himself to face the king.
They reached for the good things that lay at hand,
and when they'd put aside desire for food and drink
Telemachus asked his loyal serving-man at last,
"Old friend, where does this stranger come from?
65   Why did the sailors land him here in Ithaca?
Who did they say they are?
I hardly think he came this way on foot."

You answered him, Eumaeus, loyal swineherd,
"Here, my boy, I'll tell you the whole true story.
He hails from Crete's broad land, he's proud to say,
but he claims he's drifted round through countless towns of men,
roaming the earth . . . and so a god's spun out his fate.
He just now broke away from some Thesprotian ship
and came to my farm. I'll put him in *your* hands,
you tend to him as you like.
He counts on you, he says, for care and shelter."

    "Shelter? Oh Eumaeus," Telemachus replied,
"that word of yours, it cuts me to the quick!
How can I lend the stranger refuge in my house?
I'm young myself. I can hardly trust my hands
to fight off any man who rises up against me.
Then my mother's wavering, always torn two ways:
whether to stay with me and care for the household,
true to her husband's bed, the people's voice as well,
or leave at long last with the best man in Achaea
who courts her in the halls, who offers her the most.
But our new guest, since he's arrived at your house,
I'll give him a shirt and cloak to wear, good clothing,
give him a two-edged sword and sandals for his feet
and send him off, wherever his heart desires.
Or if you'd rather, keep him here at the farmstead,
tend to him here, and I'll send up the clothes
and full rations to keep the man in food;
he'll be no drain on you and all your men.
But I can't let him go down and join the suitors.
They're far too abusive, reckless, know no limits:
they'll make a mockery of him—that would break my heart.
It's hard for a man to win his way against a mob,
even a man of iron. They are much too strong."

    "Friend"—the long-enduring Odysseus stepped in—
"surely it's right for *me* to say a word at this point.
My heart, by god, is torn to pieces hearing this,
both of you telling how these reckless suitors,
there in your own house, against your will,
plot your ruin—a fine young prince like you.
Tell me, though, do you let yourself be so abused
or do people round about, stirred up by the prompting
of some god, despise you? Or are your brothers at fault?
Brothers a man can trust to fight beside him, true,
no matter what deadly blood-feud rages on.
Would I were young as you, to match my spirit now,
or I were the son of great Odysseus, or the king himself
returned from all his roving—there's still room for hope!
Then let some foreigner lop my head off if I failed
to march right into Odysseus' royal halls

and kill them all. And what if I went down,
crushed by their numbers—I, fighting alone?
I'd rather die, cut down in my own house
than have to look on at their outrage day by day.
120 Guests treated to blows, men dragging the serving-women
through the noble house, exploiting them all, no shame,
and the gushing wine swilled, the food squandered—
gorging for gorging's sake—
and the courting game goes on, no end in sight!"

125   "You're right, my friend," sober Telemachus agreed.
"Now let me tell you the whole story, first to last.
It's not that all our people have turned against me,
keen for a showdown. Nor have I any brothers at fault,
brothers a man can trust to fight beside him, true,
130 no matter what deadly blood-feud rages on . . .
Zeus made our line a line of only sons.
Arcesius had only one son, Laertes,
and Laertes had only one son, Odysseus,
and I am Odysseus' only son. He fathered me,
135 he left me behind at home, and from me he got no joy.
So now our house is plagued by swarms of enemies.
All the nobles who rule the islands round about,
Dulichion, and Same, and wooded Zacynthus too,
and all who lord it in rocky Ithaca as well—
140 down to the last man they court my mother,
they lay waste my house! And mother . . .
she neither rejects a marriage she despises
nor can she bear to bring the courting to an end—
while they continue to bleed my household white.
145 Soon—you wait—they'll grind *me* down as well!
But all lies in the lap of the great gods.
                              Eumaeus,
good old friend, go, quickly, to wise Penelope.
Tell her I'm home from Pylos safe and sound.
I'll stay on right here. But you come back
150 as soon as you've told the news to her alone.
No other Achaean must hear—
all too many plot to take my life."
                              "I know,"
you assured your prince, Eumaeus, loyal swineherd.
"I see your point—there's sense in this old head.
155 One thing more, and make your orders clear.
On the same trip do I go and give the news
to King Laertes too? For many years, poor man,
heartsick for his son, he'd always keep an eye
on the farm and take his meals with the hired hands
160 whenever he felt the urge to. Now, from the day
you sailed away to Pylos, not a sip or a bite

he's touched, they say, not as he did before,
and his eyes are shut to all the farmyard labors.
Huddled over, groaning in grief and tears,
165 he wastes away—the man's all skin and bones."

       "So much the worse," Telemachus answered firmly.
"Leave him alone; though it hurts us now, we must.
If men could have all they want, free for the taking,
I'd take first my father's journey home. So,
170 you go and give the message, then come back,
no roaming over the fields to find Laertes.
Tell my mother to send her housekeeper,
fast as she can, in secret—
she can give the poor old man the news."

175   That roused Eumaeus. The swineherd grasped his sandals,
strapped them onto his feet and made for town.
His exit did not escape Athena's notice . . .
Approaching, closer, now she appeared a woman,
beautiful, tall and skilled at weaving lovely things.
180 Just at the shelter's door she stopped, visible to Odysseus
but Telemachus could not see her, sense her there—
the gods don't show themselves to every man alive.
Odysseus saw her, so did the dogs; no barking now,
they whimpered, cringing away in terror through the yard.
185 She gave a sign with her brows, Odysseus caught it,
out of the lodge he went and past the high stockade
and stood before the goddess. Athena urged him on:
"Royal son of Laertes, Odysseus, old campaigner,
now is the time, now tell your son the truth.
190 Hold nothing back, so the two of you can plot
the suitors' doom and then set out for town.
I myself won't lag behind you long—
I'm blazing for a battle!"

       Athena stroked him with her golden wand.
195 First she made the cloak and shirt on his body
fresh and clean, then made him taller, supple, young,
his ruddy tan came back, the cut of his jawline firmed
and the dark beard clustered black around his chin.
Her work complete, she went her way once more
200 and Odysseus returned to the lodge. His own son
gazed at him, wonderstruck, terrified too, turning
his eyes away, suddenly—
                            this must be some god—
and he let fly with a burst of exclamations:
"Friend, you're a new man—not what I saw before!
205 Your clothes, they've changed, even your skin has changed—
surely you are some god who rules the vaulting skies!
Oh be kind, and we will give you offerings,
gifts of hammered gold to warm your heart—

spare us, please, I beg you!"
                                    "No, I am not a god,"
210 the long-enduring, great Odysseus returned.
"Why confuse me with one who never dies?
No, I am your father—
the Odysseus you wept for all your days,
you bore a world of pain, the cruel abuse of men."

215   And with those words Odysseus kissed his son
and the tears streamed down his cheeks and wet the ground,
though before he'd always reined his emotions back.
But still not convinced that it was his father,
Telemachus broke out, wild with disbelief,
220 "No, you're not Odysseus! Not my father!
Just some spirit spellbinding me now—
to make me ache with sorrow all the more.
Impossible for a mortal to work such marvels,
not with his own devices, not unless some god
225 comes down in person, eager to make that mortal
young or old—like that! Why, just now
you were old, and wrapped in rags, but *now,* look,
you seem like a god who rules the skies up there!"

     "Telemachus," Odysseus, man of exploits, urged his son,
230 "it's wrong to marvel, carried away in wonder so
to see your father here before your eyes.
No other Odysseus will ever return to you.
That man and I are one, the man you see . . .
here after many hardships,
235 endless wanderings, after twenty years
I have come home to native ground at last.
My changing so? Athena's work, the Fighter's Queen—
she has that power, she makes me look as she likes,
now like a beggar, the next moment a young man,
240 decked out in handsome clothes about my body.
It's light work for the gods who rule the skies
to exalt a mortal man or bring him low."
                                    At that
Odysseus sat down again, and Telemachus threw his arms
around his great father, sobbing uncontrollably
245 as the deep desire for tears welled up in both.
They cried out, shrilling cries, pulsing sharper
than birds of prey—eagles, vultures with hooked claws—
when farmers plunder their nest of young too young to fly.
Both men so filled with compassion, eyes streaming tears,
250 that now the sunlight would have set upon their cries
if Telemachus had not asked his father, all at once,
"What sort of ship, dear father, brought you here?—
Ithaca, at last. Who did the sailors say they are?
I hardly think you came back home on foot!"

255   So long an exile, great Odysseus replied,
"Surely, my son, I'll tell you the whole story now.
Phaeacians brought me here, the famous sailors
who ferry home all men who reach their shores.
They sailed me across the sea in their swift ship,
260   they set me down in Ithaca, sound asleep, and gave me
glittering gifts—bronze and hoards of gold and robes.
All lie stowed in a cave, thanks to the gods' help,
and Athena's inspiration spurred me here, now,
so we could plan the slaughter of our foes.
265   Come, give me the full tally of these suitors—
I must know their numbers, gauge their strength.
Then I'll deploy this old tactician's wits,
decide if the two of us can take them on,
alone, without allies,
270   or we should hunt reserves to back us up."
                                        "Father,"
clear-headed Telemachus countered quickly,
"all my life I've heard of your great fame—
a brave man in war and a deep mind in counsel—
but what you say dumbfounds me, staggers imagination!
275   How on earth could two men fight so many and so strong?
These suitors are not just ten or twenty, they're far more—
you count them up for yourself now, take a moment . . .
From Dulichion, fifty-two of them, picked young men,
six servants in their troop; from Same, twenty-four,
280   from Zacynthus, twenty Achaeans, nobles all,
and the twelve best lords from Ithaca itself.
Medon the herald's with them, a gifted bard,
and two henchmen, skilled to carve their meat.
If we pit ourselves against all these in the house,
285   I fear the revenge you come back home to take
will recoil on our heads—a bitter, deadly blow.
Think: can you come up with a friend-in-arms?
Some man to fight beside us, some brave heart?"

        "Let me tell you," the old soldier said,
290   "bear it in mind now, listen to me closely.
Think: will Athena flanked by Father Zeus
do for the two of us?
Or shall I rack my brains for another champion?"

        Telemachus answered shrewdly, full of poise,
295   "Two great champions, those you name, it's true.
Off in the clouds they sit
and they lord it over gods and mortal men."

        "Trust me," his seasoned father reassured him,
"they won't hold off long from the cries and clash of battle,
300   not when we and the suitors put our fighting strength

to proof in my own halls! But now, with daybreak,
home you go and mix with that overbearing crowd.
The swineherd will lead me into the city later,
looking old and broken, a beggar once again.
305 If they abuse me in the palace, steel yourself,
no matter what outrage I must suffer, even
if they drag me through our house by the heels
and throw me out or pelt me with things they hurl—
you just look on, endure it. Prompt them to quit
310 their wild reckless ways, try to win them over
with friendly words. Those men will never listen,
now the day of doom is hovering at their heads.
One more thing. Take it to heart, I urge you.
When Athena, Queen of Tactics, tells me it is time,
315 I'll give you a nod, and when you catch that signal
round up all the deadly weapons kept in the hall,
stow them away upstairs in a storeroom's deep recess—
all the arms and armor—and when the suitors miss them
and ask you questions, put them off with a winning story:
320 'I stowed them away, clear of the smoke. A far cry
from the arms Odysseus left when he went to Troy,
fire-damaged equipment, black with reeking fumes.
And a god reminded me of something darker too.
When you're in your cups a quarrel might break out,
325 you'd wound each other, shame your feasting here
and cast a pall on your courting.
Iron has powers to draw a man to ruin.'
                                    Just you leave
a pair of swords for the two of us, a pair of spears
and a pair of oxhide bucklers right at hand so we
330 can break for the weapons, seize them! Then Athena,
Zeus in his wisdom—they will daze the suitors' wits.
Now one last thing. Bear it in mind. You must.
If you are my own true son, born of my blood,
let no one hear that Odysseus has come home.
335 Don't let Laertes know, not Eumaeus either,
none in the household, not Penelope herself.
You and I alone will assess the women's mood
and we might test a few of the serving-men as well:
where are the ones who still respect us both,
340 who hold us in awe? And who shirk their duties?—
slighting you because you are so young."

    "Soon enough, father," his gallant son replied,
"you'll sense the courage inside me, that I know—
I'm hardly a flighty, weak-willed boy these days.
345 But I think your last plan would gain us nothing.
Reconsider, I urge you.
You'll waste time, roaming around our holdings,

probing the fieldhands man by man, while the suitors
sit at ease in our house, devouring all our goods—
350   those brazen rascals never spare a scrap!
But I do advise you to sound the women out:
who are disloyal to you, who are guiltless?
The men—I say no to testing them farm by farm.
That's work for later, if you have really seen
355   a sign from Zeus whose shield is storm and thunder."

    Now as father and son conspired, shaping plans,
the ship that brought the prince and shipmates back
from Pylos was just approaching Ithaca, home port.
As soon as they put in to the harbor's deep bay
360   they hauled the black vessel up onto dry land
and eager deckhands bore away their gear
and rushed the priceless gifts to Clytius' house.
But they sent a herald on to Odysseus' halls at once
to give the news to thoughtful, cautious Penelope
365   that Telemachus was home—just up-country now
but he'd told his mates to sail across to port—
so the noble queen would not be seized with fright
and break down in tears. And now those two men met,
herald and swineherd, both out on the same errand,
370   to give the queen the news. But once they reached
the house of the royal king the herald strode up,
into the serving-women's midst, and burst out,
"Your beloved son, my queen, is home at last!"
Eumaeus though, bending close to Penelope,
375   whispered every word that her dear son
entrusted him to say. Message told in full,
he left the halls and precincts, heading for his pigs.

    But the news shook the suitors, dashed their spirits.
Out of the halls they crowded, past the high-walled court
380   and there before the gates they sat in council.
Polybus' son Eurymachus opened up among them:
"Friends, what a fine piece of work he's carried off!
Telemachus—what insolence—and we thought his little jaunt
would come to grief! Up now, launch a black ship,
385   the best we can find—muster a crew of oarsmen,
row the news to our friends in ambush, fast,
bring them back at once."
                              And just then—
he'd not quite finished when Amphinomus,
wheeling round in his seat,
390   saw their vessel moored in the deep harbor,
their comrades striking sail and hoisting oars.
He broke into heady laughter, called his friends:
"No need for a message now. They're home, look there!
Some god gave them the news, or they saw the prince's ship

395   go sailing past and failed to overtake her."

Rising, all trooped down to the water's edge
as the crew hauled the vessel up onto dry land
and the hot-blooded hands bore off their gear.
Then in a pack they went to the meeting grounds,
400   suffering no one else, young or old, to sit among them.
Eupithes' son Antinous rose and harangued them all:
"What a blow! See how the gods have saved this boy
from bloody death? And our lookouts all day long,
stationed atop the windy heights, kept watch,
405   shift on shift; and once the sun went down
we'd never sleep the night ashore, never,
always aboard our swift ship, cruising till dawn,
patrolling to catch Telemachus, kill him on the spot,
410   and all the while some spirit whisked him home!
So here at home we'll plot his certain death:
he must never slip through our hands again,
that boy—while he still lives,
I swear we'll never bring our venture off.
The clever little schemer, he does have his skills,
415   and the crowds no longer show us favor, not at all.
So act! before he can gather his people in assembly.
He'll never give in an inch, I know, he'll rise
and rage away, shouting out to them all how we,
we schemed his sudden death but never caught him.
420   Hearing of our foul play, they'll hardly sing our praises.
Why, they might do us damage, run us off our lands,
drive us abroad to hunt for strangers' shores.
Strike first, I say, and kill him!—
clear of town, in the fields or on the road.
425   Then we'll seize his estates and worldly goods,
carve them up between us, share and share alike.
But as for his palace, let his mother keep it,
she and the man she weds.
                                            There's my plan.
If you find it offensive, if you want him
430   living on—in full command of his patrimony—
gather here no more then, living the life of kings,
consuming all his wealth. Each from his own house
must try to win her, showering her with gifts.
Then she can marry the one who offers most,
435   the man marked out by fate to be her husband."

That brought them all to a hushed, stunned silence
till Amphinomus rose to have his say among them—
the noted son of Nisus, King Aretias' grandson,
the chief who led the suitors from Dulichion,
440   land of grass and grains,
and the man who pleased Penelope the most,

thanks to his timely words and good clear sense.
Concerned for their welfare now, he stood and argued:
"Friends, I've no desire to kill Telemachus, not I—
445   it's a terrible thing to shed the blood of kings.
Wait, sound out the will of the gods—that first.
If the decrees of mighty Zeus commend the work,
I'll kill the prince myself and spur on all the rest.
If the gods are against it, then I say hold back!"

450   So Amphinomus urged, and won them over.
They rose at once, returned to Odysseus' palace,
entered and took their seats on burnished chairs.

But now an inspiration took the discreet Penelope
to face her suitors, brutal, reckless men.
455   The queen had heard it all . . .
how they plotted inside the house to kill her son.
The herald Medon told her—he'd overheard their schemes.
And so, flanked by her ladies, she descended to the hall.
That luster of women, once she reached her suitors,
460   drawing her glistening veil across her cheeks,
paused now where a column propped the sturdy roof
and rounding on Antinous, cried out against him:
"You, Antinous! Violent, vicious, scheming—
you, they say, are the best man your age in Ithaca,
465   best for eloquence, counsel. You're nothing of the sort!
Madman, why do you weave destruction for Telemachus?—
show no pity to those who need it?—those over whom
almighty Zeus stands guard. It's wrong, unholy, yes,
weaving death for those who deserve your mercy!
470   Don't you know how your father fled here once?
A fugitive, terrified of the people, up in arms
against him because he'd joined some Taphian pirates
out to attack Thesprotians, sworn allies of ours.
The mobs were set to destroy him, rip his life out,
475   devour his vast wealth to their heart's content,
but Odysseus held them back, he kept their fury down.
And this is the man whose house you waste, scot-free,
whose wife you court, whose son you mean to kill—
you make my life an agony! Stop, I tell you,
480   stop all this, and make the rest stop too!"

But Polybus' son Eurymachus tried to calm her:
"Wise Penelope, daughter of Icarius, courage!
Disabuse yourself of all these worries now.
That man is not alive—
485   he never will be, he never can be born—
who'll lift a hand against Telemachus, your son,
not while I walk the land and I can see the light.
I tell you this—so help me, it will all come true—

in an instant that man's blood will spurt around my spear!
490 *My* spear, since time and again Odysseus dandled me
on his knees, the great raider of cities fed me
roasted meat and held the red wine to my lips.
So to *me* your son is the dearest man alive,
and I urge the boy to have no fear of death,
495 not from the suitors at least.
What comes from the gods—there's no escaping that.'"

Encouraging, all the way, but all the while
plotting the prince's murder in his mind . . .
The queen, going up to her lofty well-lit room,
500 fell to weeping for Odysseus, her beloved husband,
till watchful Athena sealed her eyes with welcome sleep.

Returning just at dusk to Odysseus and his son,
the loyal swineherd found they'd killed a yearling pig
and standing over it now were busy cooking supper.
505 But Athena had approached Laertes' son Odysseus,
tapped him with her wand and made him old again.
She dressed him in filthy rags too, for fear Eumaeus,
recognizing his master face-to-face, might hurry
back to shrewd Penelope, blurting out the news
510 and never hide the secret in his heart.

Telemachus was the first to greet the swineherd:
"Welcome home, my friend! What's the talk in town?
Are the swaggering suitors back from ambush yet—
or still waiting to catch me coming home?"

515 You answered the prince, Eumaeus, loyal swineherd,
"I had no time to go roaming all through town,
digging round for that. My heart raced me on
to get my message told and rush back here.
But I met up with a fast runner there,
520 sent by your crew, a herald,
first to tell your mother all the news.
And this I know, I saw with my own eyes—
I was just above the city, heading home,
clambering over Hermes' Ridge, when I caught sight
525 of a trim ship pulling into the harbor, loaded down
with a crowd aboard her, shields and two-edged spears.
I *think* they're the men you're after—I'm not sure."

At that the young prince Telemachus smiled,
glancing toward his father, avoiding Eumaeus' eyes.
And now,
530 with the roasting done, the meal set out, they ate well
and no one's hunger lacked a proper share of supper.
When they'd put aside desire for food and drink,
they remembered bed and took the gift of sleep.

BOOK 17. STRANGER AT THE GATES

When young Dawn with her rose-red fingers shone once more
Telemachus strapped his rawhide sandals to his feet
and the young prince, the son of King Odysseus,
picked up the rugged spear that fit his grip
5   and striking out for the city, told his swineherd,
"I'm off to town, old friend, to present myself to mother.
She'll never stop her bitter tears and mourning,
well I know, till she sees me face-to-face.
And for you I have some orders—
10   take this luckless stranger to town, so he can beg
his supper there, and whoever wants can give the man
some crumbs and a cup to drink. How can *I* put up with
every passerby? My mind's weighed down with troubles.
If the stranger resents it, all the worse for him.
15   I like to tell the truth and tell it plainly."

                                        "My friend,
subtle Odysseus broke in, "I've no desire, myself,
to linger here. Better that beggars cadge their meals
in town than in the fields. Some willing soul
will see to my needs. I'm hardly fit, at my age,
20   to keep to a farm and jump to a foreman's every order.
Go on then. This man will take me, as you've told him,
once I'm warm from the fire and the sun's good and strong.
Look at the clothing on my back—all rags and tatters.
I'm afraid the frost at dawn could do me in,
25   and town, you say, is a long hard way from here."

     At that Telemachus strode down through the farm
in quick, firm strides, brooding death for the suitors.
And once he reached his well-constructed palace,
propping his spear against a sturdy pillar
30   and crossing the stone threshold, in he went.

     His old nurse was the first to see him, Eurycleia,
just spreading fleeces over the carved, inlaid chairs.
Tears sprang to her eyes, she rushed straight to the prince
as the other maids of great Odysseus flocked around him,
35   hugged him warmly, kissed his head and shoulders.

     Now down from her chamber came discreet Penelope,
looking for all the world like Artemis or golden Aphrodite—
bursting into tears as she flung her arms around her darling son
and kissed his face and kissed his shining eyes and sobbed,
40   "You're home, Telemachus!"—words flew from her heart—
"sweet light of my eyes! I never thought I'd see you again,
once you shipped to Pylos—against my will, so secret,
out for news of your dear father. Quick tell me,

did you catch sight of the man—meet him—what?"

45   "Please, mother," steady Telemachus replied,
"don't move me to tears, don't stir the heart inside me.
I've just escaped from death. Sudden death.
No. Bathe now, put on some fresh clothes,
go up to your own room with your serving-women,
50   pray, and promise the gods a generous sacrifice
to bring success, if Zeus will ever grant us
the hour of our revenge. I myself am off
to the meeting grounds to summon up a guest
who came with me from abroad when I sailed home.
55   I sent him on ahead with my trusted crew.
I told Piraeus to take him to his house,
treat him well, host him with all good will
till I could come myself."
                                            Words to the mark
that left his mother silent . . .
60   She bathed now, put on some fresh clothes,
prayed, and promised the gods a generous sacrifice
to bring success, if Zeus would ever grant
the hour of their revenge.
                                            Spear in hand,
Telemachus strode on through the hall and out,
65   and a pair of sleek hounds went trotting at his heels.
And Athena lavished a marvelous splendor on the prince
so the people all gazed in wonder as he came forward.
The swaggering suitors clustered, milling round him,
welcome words on their lips, and murder in their hearts.
70   But he gave them a wide berth as they came crowding in
and there where Mentor sat, Antiphus, Halitherses too—
his father's loyal friends from days gone by—
he took his seat as they pressed him with their questions.
And just then Piraeus the gallant spearman approached,
75   leading the stranger through the town and out onto
the meeting grounds. Telemachus, not hanging back,
went right up to greet Theoclymenus, his guest,
but Piraeus spoke out first: "Quickly now,
Telemachus, send some women to my house
80   to retrieve the gifts that Menelaus gave you."

"Wait, Piraeus," wary Telemachus cautioned,
"we've no idea how all of this will go.
If the brazen suitors cut me down in the palace—
off guard—and carve apart my father's whole estate,
85   I'd rather you yourself, or one of his friends here,
keep those gifts and get some pleasure from them.
But if I can bring down slaughter on that crew,
you send the gifts to my house—we'll share the joy."

Their plans made, he led the wayworn stranger home
90   and once they reached the well-constructed palace,
spreading out their cloaks on a chair or bench,
into the burnished tubs they climbed and bathed.
When women had washed them, rubbed them down with oil
and drawn warm fleece and shirts around their shoulders,
95   out of the baths they stepped and sat on high-backed chairs.
A maid brought water soon in a graceful golden pitcher
and over a silver basin tipped it out
so they might rinse their hands,
then pulled a gleaming table to their side.
100   A staid housekeeper brought on bread to serve them,
appetizers aplenty too, lavish with her bounty.
Penelope sat across from her son, beside a pillar,
leaning back on a low chair and winding finespun yarn.
They reached out for the good things that lay at hand
105   and when they'd put aside desire for food and drink,
the queen, for all her composure, said at last,
"Telemachus, I'm going back to my room upstairs
and lie down on my bed . . .
that bed of pain my tears have streaked, year in,
110   year out, from the day Odysseus sailed away to Troy
with Atreus' two sons.
                          But you, you never had the heart—
before those insolent suitors crowd back to the house—
to tell me clearly about your father's journey home,
if you've heard any news."
                          "Of course, mother,"
115   thoughtful Telemachus reassured her quickly,
"I will tell you the whole true story now.
We sailed to Pylos, to Nestor, the great king,
and he received me there in his lofty palace,
treated me well and warmly, yes, as a father treats
120   a long-lost son just home from voyaging, years abroad:
such care he showered on me, he and his noble sons.
But of strong, enduring Odysseus, dead or alive,
he's heard no news, he said, from any man on earth.
He sent me on to the famous spearman Atrides Menelaus,
125   on with a team of horses drawing a bolted chariot.
And there I saw her, Helen of Argos—all for her
Achaeans and Trojans suffered so much hardship,
thanks to the gods' decree . . .
The lord of the warcry, Menelaus, asked at once
130   what pressing need had brought me to lovely Lacedaemon,
and when I told him the whole story, first to last,
the king burst out, 'How shameful! That's the bed
of a brave man of war they'd like to crawl inside,
those spineless, craven cowards!
135   Weak as the doe that beds down her fawns

in a mighty lion's den—her newborn sucklings—
then trails off to the mountain spurs and grassy bends
to graze her fill, but back the lion comes to his own lair
and the master deals both fawns a ghastly bloody death,
140 just what Odysseus will deal that mob—ghastly death.
Ah if only—Father Zeus, Athena and lord Apollo—
that man who years ago in the games at Lesbos
rose to Philomelides' challenge, wrestled him,
pinned him down with one tremendous throw
145 and the Argives roared with joy . . .
if only *that* Odysseus sported with those suitors,
a blood wedding, a quick death would take the lot!
But about the things you've asked me, so intently,
I'll skew and sidestep nothing, not deceive you, ever.
150 Of all he told me—the Old Man of the Sea who never lies—
I'll hide or hold back nothing, not a single word.
He said he'd seen Odysseus on an island,
ground down in misery, off in a goddess' house,
the nymph Calypso, who holds him there by force.
155 He has no way to voyage home to his own native land,
no trim ships in reach, no crew to ply the oars
and send him scudding over the sea's broad back.'

So Menelaus, the famous spearman, told me.
My mission accomplished, back I came at once,
160 and the gods sent me a stiff following wind
that sped me home to the native land I love."

His reassurance stirred the queen to her depths
and the godlike seer Theoclymenus added firmly,
"Noble lady, wife of Laertes' son, Odysseus,
165 Menelaus can have no perfect revelations;
mark *my* words—I will make you a prophecy,
quite precise, and *I'*ll hold nothing back.
I swear by Zeus, the first of all the gods,
by this table of hospitality here, my host,
170 by Odysseus' hearth where I have come for help—
I swear Odysseus *is* on native soil, here and now!
Poised or on the prowl, learning of these rank crimes
he's sowing seeds of ruin for all your suitors.
So clear, so true, that bird-sign I saw
175 as I sat on the benched ship
and sounded out the future to the prince!"

"If only, my friend," reserved Penelope exclaimed,
"everything you say would come to pass!
You'd soon know my affection, know my gifts.
180 Any man you meet would call you blest."

And so the three confided in the halls
while all the suitors, before Odysseus' palace,

185
amused themselves with discus and long throwing spears,
out on the leveled grounds, free and easy as always,
full of swagger. When the dinner-hour approached
and sheep came home from pastures near and far,
driven in by familiar drovers,
Medon called them all, their favorite herald,
always present at their meals: "My young lords,

190
now you've played your games to your hearts' content,
come back to the halls so we can fix your supper.
Nothing's better than dining well on time!"

They came at his summons, rising from the games
and now, bustling into the well-constructed palace,

195
flinging down their cloaks on a chair or bench,
they butchered hulking sheep and fatted goats,
full-grown hogs and a young cow from the herd,
preparing for their feast.
                                    At the same time
the king and his loyal swineherd geared to leave

200
the country for the town. Eumaeus, foreman of men,
set things in motion: "Friend, I know you're keen
on going down to town today, just as my master bid,
though I'd rather you stay here to guard the farm.
But I prize the boy, I fear he'll blame me later—

205
a dressing-down from your master's hard to bear.
So off we go now. The shank of the day is past.
You'll find it colder with nightfall coming on."

"I know, I see your point," the crafty man replied.
"There's sense in this old head. So let's be off.

210
And from now on, you lead me all the way.
Just give me a stick to lean on,
if you have one ready-cut. You say the road
is treacherous, full of slips and slides."
                                                    With that
he flung his beggar's sack across his shoulders—

215
torn and tattered, slung from a fraying rope.
Eumaeus gave him a staff that met his needs.
Then the two moved out, leaving behind them
dogs and herdsmen to stay and guard the farm.
And so the servant led his master toward the city,

220
looking for all the world like an old and broken beggar
hunched on a stick, his body wrapped in shameful rags . . .

Down over the rugged road they went till hard by town
they reached the stone-rimmed fountain running clear
where the city people came and drew their water.

225
Ithacus built it once, with Neritus and Polyctor.
Round it a stand of poplar thrived on the dank soil,
all in a nestling ring, and down from a rock-ledge overhead

the cold water splashed, and crowning the fountain
rose an altar-stone erected to the nymphs,
230   where every traveler paused and left an offering.
Here Dolius' son, Melanthius, crossed their path,
herding his goats with a pair of drovers' help,
the pick of his flocks to make the suitors' meal.
As soon as he saw them there he broke into a flood
235   of brutal, foul abuse that made Odysseus' blood boil.
"Look!"—he sneered—"one scum nosing another scum along,
dirt finds dirt by the will of god—it never fails!
Wretched pig-boy, where do you take your filthy swine,
this sickening beggar who licks the pots at feasts?
240   Hanging round the doorposts, rubbing his back,
scavenging after scraps,
no hero's swords and cauldrons, not for *him*.
Hand him over to me—I'll teach him to work a farm,
muck out my stalls, pitch feed to the young goats;
245   whey to drink will put some muscle on his hams!
Oh no, he's learned his lazy ways too well,
he's got no itch to stick to good hard work,
he'd rather go scrounging round the countryside,
begging for crusts to stuff his greedy gut!
250   Let me tell you—so help me it's the truth—
if he sets foot in King Odysseus' royal palace,
salvos of footstools flung at his head by all the lords
will crack his ribs as he runs the line of fire through the house!"

Wild, reckless taunts—and just as he passed Odysseus
255   the idiot lurched out with a heel and kicked his hip
but he couldn't knock the beggar off the path,
he stood his ground so staunchly. Odysseus was torn . . .
should he wheel with his staff and beat the scoundrel senseless?—
or hoist him by the midriff, split his skull on the rocks?
260   He steeled himself instead, his mind in full control.
But Eumaeus glared at the goatherd, cursed him to his face,
then lifted up his hands and prayed his heart out:
"O nymphs of the fountain, daughters of Zeus—
if Odysseus ever burned you the long thighs
265   of lambs or kids, covered with rich fat,
now bring my prayer to pass!
Let that man come back—some god guide him now!
He'd toss to the winds the flashy show you make,
Melanthius, so cocksure—always strutting round the town
270   while worthless fieldhands leave your flocks a shambles!"

"Listen to him!" the goatherd shouted back.
"All bark and no bite from the vicious mutt!
One fine day I'll ship him out in a black lugger,
miles from Ithaca—sell him off for a good stiff price!

275   Just let Apollo shoot Telemachus down with his silver bow,
       today in the halls, or the suitors snuff his life out—
       as sure as I know the day of the king's return
       is blotted out, the king is worlds away!"

       With his parting shot he left them trudging on
280   and went and reached the royal house in no time.
       Slipping in, he took his seat among the suitors,
       facing Eurymachus, who favored him the most.
       The carvers set before him his plate of meat,
       a staid housekeeper brought the man his bread.

285   And now at last the king and loyal swineherd,
       drawing near the palace, halted just outside
       as the lyre's rippling music drifted round them—
       Phemius, striking up a song for assembled guests—
       and the master seized his servant's hand, exclaiming,
290   "Friend, what a noble house! Odysseus' house, it must be!
       No mistaking it—you could tell it among a townful, look.
       One building linked to the next, and the courtyard wall
       is finished off with a fine coping, the double doors
       are battle-proof—no man could break them down!
295   I can tell a crowd is feasting there in force—
       smell the savor of roasts . . . the ringing lyre, listen,
       the lyre that god has made the friend of feasts."

           "An easy guess," you said, Eumaeus, swineherd,
       "for a man as keen as you at every turn.
300   Put heads together. What do we do next?
       Either you're the first one into the palace—
       mix with the suitors, leave me where I am.
       Or if you like, stay put, and I'll go first myself.
       Don't linger long. Someone might spot you here outside,
305   knock you down or pelt you. Mark my words. Take care."

           The man who'd borne long years abroad replied,
       "Well I know. Remember? There's sense in this old head.
       You go in, you first, while I stay here behind.
       Stones and blows and I are hardly strangers.
310   My heart is steeled by now,
       I've had my share of pain in the waves and wars.
       Add this to the total. Bring the trial on.
       But there's no way to hide the belly's hungers—
       what a curse, what mischief it brews in all our lives!
315   Just for hunger we rig and ride our long benched ships
       on the barren salt sea, speeding death to enemies."

           Now, as they talked on, a dog that lay there
       lifted up his muzzle, pricked his ears . . .
       It was Argos, long-enduring Odysseus' dog
320   he trained as a puppy once, but little joy he got

since all too soon he shipped to sacred Troy.
In the old days young hunters loved to set him
coursing after the wild goats and deer and hares.
But now with his master gone he lay there, castaway,
325 on piles of dung from mules and cattle, heaps collecting
out before the gates till Odysseus' serving-men
could cart it off to manure the king's estates.
Infested with ticks, half-dead from neglect,
here lay the hound, old Argos.
330 But the moment he sensed Odysseus standing by
he thumped his tail, nuzzling low, and his ears dropped,
though he had no strength to drag himself an inch
toward his master. Odysseus glanced to the side
and flicked away a tear, hiding it from Eumaeus,
335 diverting his friend in a hasty, offhand way:
"Strange, Eumaeus, look, a dog like this,
lying here on a dung-hill . . .
what handsome lines! But I can't say for sure
if he had the running speed to match his looks
340 or he was only the sort that gentry spoil at table,
show-dogs masters pamper for their points."

    You told the stranger, Eumaeus, loyal swineherd,
"Here—it's all too true—here's the dog of a man
who died in foreign parts. But if he had now
345 the form and flair he had in his glory days—
as Odysseus left him, sailing off to Troy—
you'd be amazed to see such speed, such strength.
No quarry he chased in the deepest, darkest woods
could ever slip this hound. A champion tracker too!
350 Ah, but he's run out of luck now, poor fellow . . .
his master's dead and gone, so far from home,
and the heartless women tend him not at all. Slaves,
with their lords no longer there to crack the whip,
lose all zest to perform their duties well. Zeus,
355 the Old Thunderer, robs a man of half his virtue
the day the yoke clamps down around his neck."

    With that he entered the well-constructed palace,
strode through the halls and joined the proud suitors.
But the dark shadow of death closed down on Argos' eyes
360 the instant he saw Odysseus, twenty years away.

    Now Prince Telemachus, first by far to note
the swineherd coming down the hall, nodded briskly,
called and waved him on. Eumaeus, glancing about,
picked up a handy stool where the carver always sat,
365 slicing meat for the suitors feasting through the house.
He took and put it beside the prince's table, facing him,
straddled it himself as a steward set a plate of meat

before the man and served him bread from trays.

370   Right behind him came Odysseus, into his own house,
looking for all the world like an old and broken beggar
hunched on a stick, his body wrapped in shameful rags.
Just in the doorway, just at the ashwood threshold,
there he settled down . . .
leaning against the cypress post a master joiner
375   planed smooth and hung with a plumb line years ago.
Telemachus motioned the swineherd over now,
and choosing a whole loaf from a fine wicker tray
and as much meat as his outstretched hands could hold,
he said, "Now take these to the stranger, tell him too
380   to make the rounds of the suitors, beg from one and all.
Bashfulness, for a man in need, is no great friend."

And Eumaeus did his bidding, went straight up
to the guest and winged a greeting: "Here, stranger,
Prince Telemachus sends you these, and tells you too
385   to make the rounds of the suitors, beg from one and all.
Bashfulness for a beggar, he says, is no great friend."

"Powerful Zeus!" the crafty king responded,
"grant that your prince be blest among mankind—
and all his heart's desires come to pass!"

390   Taking the food in both hands, setting it down,
spread out on his filthy sack before his feet,
the beggar fell to his meal
as the singer raised a song throughout the house.
Once he'd supped and the stirring bard had closed,
395   the suitors broke into uproar down along the hall.
And now Athena came to the side of Laertes' royal son
and urged him, "Go now, gather crusts from all the suitors,
test them, so we can tell the innocent from the guilty."
But not even so would Athena save one man from death.
400   Still, off he went, begging from each in turn,
circling left to right, reaching out his hand
like a beggar from the day that he was born.
They pitied him, gave him scraps, were puzzled too,
asking each other, "Who is this?" "Where's he from?"
405   Till the goatherd Melanthius shouted out in their midst,
"Listen to me, you lords who court our noble queen—
I'll tell you about the stranger. I've seen him before.
I know for a fact the swineherd led him in,
though I have no idea who the fellow is
410   or where he thinks he comes from."

At that
Antinous wheeled on Eumaeus, lashing out at him:
"Your highness, swineherd—why drag *this* to town?
Haven't we got our share of vagabonds to deal with,

disgusting beggars who lick the feasters' plates?
415 Isn't it quite enough, these swarming crowds
consuming your master's bounty—
must you invite this rascal in the bargain?"
                                    "Antinous,
highborn as you are," you told the man, Eumaeus,
"that was a mean low speech!
420 Now who'd go out, who on his own hook—
not I—and ask a stranger in from nowhere
unless he had some skills to serve the house?
A prophet, a healer who cures disease, a worker in wood
or even a god-inspired bard whose singing warms the heart—
425 they're the ones asked in around the world. A beggar?
Who'd invite a beggar to bleed his household white?
You, you of all the suitors are always roughest
on the servants of our king, on me most of all.
Not that I care, no, so long as his queen,
430 his wise queen, is still alive in the palace,
Prince Telemachus too."
                                    "Stop, Eumaeus,"
poised Telemachus broke in quickly now,
"don't waste so much breath on Antinous here.
It's just his habit to bait a man with abuse
435 and spur the rest as well."
                                    He wheeled on the suitor,
letting loose: "How kind you are to me, Antinous,
kind as a father to his son! Encouraging me
to send this stranger packing from my house
with a harsh command! I'd never do it. God forbid.
440 Take and give to the beggar. I don't grudge it—
I'd even urge you on. No scruples now,
never fear your gifts will upset my mother
or any servant in King Odysseus' royal house.
But no such qualm could enter that head of yours,
445 bent on feeding your own face, not feeding strangers!"

    Antinous countered the young prince in kind:
"So high and mighty, Telemachus—such unbridled rage!
If all the suitors gave him the sort of gift I'll give,
the house would be rid of *him* for three whole months!"
450 With that, from under his table he seized the stool
that propped his smooth feet as he reveled on—
just lifting it into view . . .
                                    But as for the rest,
all gave to the beggar, filled his sack with handouts,
bread and meat. And Odysseus seemed at the point
455 of getting back to his doorsill,
done with testing suitors, home free himself
when he stopped beside Antinous, begging face-to-face:

"Give me a morsel, friend. You're hardly the worst
Achaean here, it seems. The noblest one, in fact.
460   You look like a king to me!
So you should give a bigger crust than the rest
and I will sing your praises all across the earth.
I too once lived in a lofty house that men admired;
rolling in wealth, I'd often give to a vagabond like myself,
465   whoever he was, whatever need had brought him to my door.
And crowds of servants I had, and lots of all it takes
to live the life of ease, to make men call you rich.
But Zeus ruined it all—god's will, no doubt—
when he shipped me off with a roving band of pirates
470   bound for Egypt, a long hard sail, to wreck my life.
There in the Nile delta I moored our ships of war.
God knows I ordered my trusty crews to stand by,
just where they were, and guard the anchored fleet
and I sent a patrol to scout things out from higher ground.
475   But swept away by their own reckless fury, the crew went berserk—
they promptly began to plunder the lush Egyptian farms,
dragged off the women and children, killed the men.
Outcries reached the city in no time—stirred by shouts
the entire town came streaming down at the break of day,
480   filling the river plain with chariots, ranks of infantry
and the gleam of bronze. Zeus who loves the lightning
flung down murderous panic on all my men-at-arms—
no one dared to stand his ground and fight,
disaster ringed us round from every quarter.
485   Droves of my men they hacked down with swords,
led off the rest alive, to labor for them as slaves.
Myself? They passed me on to a stranger come their way,
to ship me to Cyprus—Iasus' son Dmetor it was,
who ruled Cyprus then with an iron fist.
490   And from there I sailed to Ithaca,
just as you see me now, ground down by pain and sorrow—"

     "Good god almighty!" Antinous cut the beggar short.
"What spirit brought this pest to plague our feast?
Back off! Into the open, clear of my table, or you,
495   you'll soon land in an Egypt, Cyprus, to break your heart!
What a brazen, shameless beggar! Scrounging food
from each man in turn, and look at their handouts,
reckless, never a qualm, no holding back, not
when making free with the next man's goods—
500   each one's got plenty here."
                         "Pity, pity,"
the wry Odysseus countered, drawing away.
"No sense in your head to match your handsome looks.
You'd grudge your servant a pinch of salt from your own larder,
you who lounge at the next man's board but lack the heart
505   to tear a crust of bread and hand it on to me,

though there's god's plenty here."
                                          Boiling over
Antinous gave him a scathing look and let fly,
"*Now* you won't get out of the hall unscarred, I swear,
not after such a filthy string of insults!"
                                          With that
510   he seized the stool and hurled it—
                                          Square in the back
it struck Odysseus, just under the right shoulder
but he stood up against it—steady as a rock,
unstaggered by Antinous' blow—just shook his head,
silent, his mind churning with thoughts of bloody work.
515   Back he went to the doorsill, crouched, and setting down
his sack about to burst, he faced the suitors, saying,
"Hear me out, you lords who court the noble queen,
I must say what the heart inside me urges.
There's nothing to groan about, no hurt, when a man
520   takes a blow as he fights to save his own possessions,
cattle or shining flocks. But Antinous struck me
all because of my good-for-nothing belly—that,
that curse that makes such pain for us poor men.
But if beggars have their gods and Furies too,
525   let Antinous meet his death before he meets his bride!"

       "Enough, stranger!" Antinous volleyed back.
"Sit there and eat in peace—or go get lost! Or else,
for the way you talk, these young men will hale you
up and down the halls by your hands or feet
530   until you're skinned alive!"
                                          Naked threats—
but the rest were outraged, even those brash suitors.
One would say to another, "Look, Antinous,
that was a crime, to strike the luckless beggar!"

       "Your fate is sealed if he's some god from the blue."

535   "And the gods do take on the look of strangers
dropping in from abroad—"
                                          "Disguised in every way
as they roam and haunt our cities, watching over us—"

       "All our foul play, all our fair play too!"

So they warned, but Antinous paid no heed.
540   And the anguish welled up in Telemachus' breast
for the blow his father took, yet he let no tears
go rolling down his face—he just shook his head,
silent, his mind churning with thoughts of bloody work.

       But then, when cautious Queen Penelope heard
545   how Antinous struck the stranger, there in the halls,
she cried out, with her serving-women round her,

"May Apollo the Archer strike you just as hard!"
And her housekeeper Eurynome added quickly,
"If only our prayers were granted—

550   then not one of the lot would live to see
Dawn climb her throne tomorrow!"
                                    "Dear old woman,"
alert Penelope replied, "they're all hateful,
plotting their vicious plots. But Antinous
is the worst of all—he's black death itself.

555   Here's this luckless stranger, wandering down
the halls and begging scraps—hard-pressed by need—
and the rest all give the man his fill of food
but that one gives him a footstool
hurled at his right shoulder, hits his back!"

560   While she exclaimed among her household women,
sitting there in her room, Odysseus bent to supper.
Penelope called the swineherd in and gave instructions:
"Go, good Eumaeus, tell the stranger to come at once.
I'd like to give him a warm welcome, ask the man

565   if he's heard some news about my gallant husband
or seen him in the flesh . . .
He seems like one who's roved around the world."

           "My queen," you answered, Eumaeus, loyal swineherd,
"if only the lords would hold their peace a moment!

570   Such stories he tells—he'd charm you to your depths.
Three nights, three days I kept him in my shelter;
I was the first the fellow stumbled onto,
fleeing from some ship. But not even so
could he bring his tale of troubles to an end.

575   You know how you can stare at a bard in wonder—
trained by the gods to sing and hold men spellbound—
how you can long to sit there, listening, all your life
when the man begins to sing. So he charmed my heart,
I tell you, huddling there beside me at my fire.

580   He and Odysseus' father go way back, he says,
sworn friends, and the stranger hails from Crete
where the stock of old King Minos still lives on,
and from Crete he made his way, racked by hardship,
tumbling on like a rolling stone until he turned up here.

585   He swears he's heard of Odysseus—just in reach,
in rich Thesprotian country—still alive,
laden with treasure, heading home at last!"
                                    "Go,"
the cautious queen responded, "call him here
so he can tell me his own tale face-to-face.

590   Our friends can sit at the gates or down the halls
and play their games, debauched to their hearts' content.
Why not? Their own stores, their bread and seasoned wine,

lie intact at home; food for their serving-men alone.
But they, they infest our palace day and night,
595 they butcher our cattle, our sheep, our fat goats,
feasting themselves sick, swilling our glowing wine
as if there's no tomorrow—all of it, squandered.
No, there is no man like Odysseus in command
to drive this curse from the house. Dear god,
600 if only Odysseus came back home to native soil now,
he and his son would avenge the outrage of these men—like that!"

At her last words Telemachus shook with a lusty sneeze[1]
like a thunderclap resounding up and down the halls.
The queen was seized with laughter, calling out
605 to Eumaeus winged words: "Quickly, go!
Bring me this stranger now, face-to-face!
You hear how my son sealed all I said with a sneeze?
So let death come down with grim finality on these suitors—
one and all—not a single man escape his sudden doom!
610 And another thing. Mark my words, I tell you.
If I'm convinced that all he says is true,
I'll dress him in shirt and cloak, in handsome clothes."

Off the swineherd went, following her instructions,
made his way to the stranger's side and winged a word:
615 "Old friend—our queen, wise Penelope, summons you,
the prince's mother! The spirit moves her now,
heartsick as she is,
to ask a question or two about her husband.
And if she's convinced that all you say is true,
620 she'll dress you in shirt and cloak. That's what you need,
that most of all now. Bread you can always beg
around the country, fill your belly well—
they'll give you food, whoever has a mind to."

"Gladly, Eumaeus," the patient man replied,
625 "I'll tell her the whole truth and nothing but,
Icarius' daughter, your wise queen Penelope.
I know all about that man . . .
it's been my lot to suffer what he's suffered.
But I fear the mob's abuse, those rough young bucks,
630 their pride and violence hit the iron skies!
Just now that scoundrel—as I went down the halls,
harming no one—up and dealt me a jolting blow,
and who would raise a hand to save me? Telemachus?
Anyone else? No one. So tell Penelope now,
635 anxious as she may be, to wait in the halls
until the sun goes down. Then she can ask me
all she likes about her husband's journey home.

---

1. A sign from the gods.

But let her give me a seat close by the fire.
The clothes on my back are tatters. Well you know—
640   you are the first I begged for care and shelter."

    Back the swineherd went, following his instructions.
Penelope, just as he crossed her threshold, broke out,
"Didn't you bring him? What's in the vagrant's mind?
Fear of someone? Embarrassed by something else,
645   here in the house? Is the fellow bashful?
A bashful man will make a sorry beggar."

    You answered your queen, Eumaeus, loyal swineherd,
"He talks to the point—he thinks as the next man would
who wants to dodge their blows, that brutal crew.
650   He tells you to wait here till the sun goes down.
It's better for you, my queen. Then you can talk
with the man in private, hear the stranger's news."

    "Nobody's fool, that stranger," wise Penelope said,
"he sees how things could go. Surely no men on earth
655   can match that gang for reckless, deadly schemes."

    So she agreed, and now, mission accomplished,
back the loyal swineherd went to mix with the suitors.
Moving next to the prince, he whispered a parting word,
their heads close together so no one else could hear.
660   "Dear boy, I must be off, to see to the pigs
and the whole farm—your living, mine as well.
You're the one to tend to all things here.
Look out for your own skin first,
do take care, you mustn't come to grief.
665   Crowds of your own countrymen plot your death—
let Zeus wipe out the lot before they kill us all!"

    "Right you are, old friend," the canny prince replied.
"Now off you go, once you've had your supper.
But come back bright and early,
670   bring some good sound boars for slaughter. Yes,
I'll tend to all things here, I and the deathless gods."

    And the swineherd sat down again on his polished stool
and once he'd supped and drunk to his heart's content,
back he went to his pigs, leaving the royal precincts
675   still filled with feasters, all indulging now
in the joys of dance and song.
The day was over. Dusk was falling fast.

BOOK 18. THE BEGGAR-KING OF ITHACA

Now along came this tramp, this public nuisance
who used to scrounge a living round the streets of Ithaca—
notorious for his belly, a ravenous, bottomless pit

for food and drink, but he had no pith, no brawn,
5   despite the looming hulk that met your eyes.
Arnaeus was his name,
so his worthy mother called him at birth,
but all the young men called him Irus for short
because he'd hustle messages at any beck and call.[1]
10 Well *he* came by to rout the king from his own house
and met Odysseus now with a rough, abusive burst:
"Get off the porch, you old goat, before I haul you
off by the leg! Can't you see them give me the wink,
all of them here, to drag you out—and so I would
15 but I've got some pangs of conscience. Up with you, man,
or before you know it, we'll be trading blows!"

A killing look,
and the wily old soldier countered, "Out of your mind?
What damage have I done *you?* What have I said?
I don't grudge you anything,
20 not if the next man up and gives you plenty.
This doorsill is big enough for the both of us—
you've got no call to grudge me what's not yours.
You're another vagrant, just like me, I'd say,
and it lies with the gods to make us rich or poor. So,
25 keep your fists to yourself, don't press your luck, don't rile me,
or old as I am, I'll bloody your lip, splatter your chest
and buy myself some peace and quiet for tomorrow.
I doubt you'll ever come lumbering back again
to the halls of Laertes' royal son Odysseus."

30   "Look who's talking!" the beggar rumbled in anger.
"How this pot-bellied pig runs off at the mouth—
like an old crone at her oven!
Well *I*'ve got a knock-out blow in store for *him*—
I'll batter the tramp with both fists, crack every tooth
35 from his jaws, I'll litter the ground with teeth
like a rogue sow's, punished for rooting corn!
Belt up—so the lords can see us fight it out.
How can you beat a champion half your age?"

Tongue-lashing each other, tempers flaring,
40 there on the polished sill before the lofty doors.
And Antinous, that grand prince, hearing them wrangle,
broke into gloating laughter, calling out to the suitors,
"Friends, nothing like this has come our way before—
what sport some god has brought the palace now!
45 The stranger and Irus, look,
they'd battle it out together, fists flying.
Come, let's pit them against each other—fast!"

---

1. His name resembles that of Iris, messenger of the gods.

All leapt from their seats with whoops of laughter,
clustering round the pair of ragged beggars there
50   as Eupithes' son Antinous planned the contest.
"Quiet, my fine friends. Here's what I propose.
These goat sausages sizzling here in the fire—
we packed them with fat and blood to have for supper.
Now, whoever wins this bout and proves the stronger,
55   let that man step up and take his pick of the lot!
What's more, from this day on he feasts among us—
no other beggar will we allow inside
to cadge his meals from us!"
                                    They all cheered
but Odysseus, foxy veteran, plotted on . . .
60   "Friends, how can an old man, worn down with pain,
stand up to a young buck? It's just this belly of mine,
this trouble-maker, tempts me to take a licking.
So first, all of you swear me a binding oath:
come, not one of you steps in for Irus here,
65   strikes me a foul blow to pull him through
and lays me in the dust."
                                    And at that
they all mouthed the oath that he required,
and once they vowed they'd never interfere,
Prince Telemachus drove the matter home:
70   "Stranger, if your spine and fighting pride
prompt you to go against this fellow now,
have no fear of any suitor in the pack—
whoever fouls you will have to face a crowd.
Count on *me,* your host. And two lords back me up,
75   Antinous and Eurymachus—both are men of sense."

    They all shouted approval of the prince
as Odysseus belted up, roping his rags around his loins,
baring his big rippling thighs—his boxer's broad shoulders,
his massive chest and burly arms on full display
80   as Athena stood beside him,
fleshing out the limbs of the great commander . . .
Despite their swagger, the suitors were amazed,
gaping at one another, trading forecasts:
"Irus will soon be ironed out for good!"

85   "He's in for the beating he begged for all along."

    "Look at the hams on that old-timer—"

                                    "Just under his rags!"

    Each outcry jolted Irus to the core—too late.
The servants trussed his clothes up, dragged him on,
the flesh on his body quaking now with terror.
90   Antinous rounded on him, flinging insults:
"You, you clumsy ox, you're better off dead

or never born at all, if you cringe at *him,*
paralyzed with fear of an old, broken hulk,
ground down by the pains that hound his steps.
95   Mark my word—so help me I'll make it good—
if that old relic whips you and wins the day,
I'll toss you into a black ship and sail you off
to Echetus, the mainland king who wrecks all men alive!
He'll lop your nose and ears with his ruthless blade,
100   he'll rip your privates out by the roots, he will,
and serve them up to his dogs to bolt down raw!"

    That threat shook his knees with a stronger fit
but they hauled him into the ring. Both men put up their fists—
with the seasoned fighter Odysseus deeply torn now . . .
105   should he knock him senseless, leave him dead where he dropped
or just stretch him out on the ground with a light jab?
As he mulled things over, that way seemed the best:
a glancing blow, the suitors would not detect him.
The two men squared off—
                   and Irus hurled a fist
110   at Odysseus' right shoulder as *he* came through
with a hook below the ear, pounding Irus' neck,
smashing the bones inside—
                suddenly red blood
came spurting out of his mouth, and headlong down
he pitched in the dust, howling, teeth locked in a grin,
115   feet beating the ground—
                 and the princely suitors,
flinging their hands in the air, died laughing.
Grabbing him by the leg, Odysseus hauled him
through the porch, across the yard to the outer gate,
heaped him against the courtyard wall, sitting slumped,
120   stuck his stick in his hand and gave him a parting shot:
"Now hold your post—play the scarecrow to all the pigs and dogs!
But no more lording it over strangers, no more playing
the beggar-king for you, you loathsome fool,
or you'll bring down something worse around your neck!"

125   He threw his beggar's sack across his shoulders—
torn and tattered, slung from a fraying rope—
then back he went to the sill and took his seat.
The suitors ambled back as well, laughing jauntily,
toasting the beggar warmly now, those proud young blades,
130   one man egging the other on: "Stranger, friend, may Zeus
and the other deathless gods fill up your sack with blessings!"

    "All your heart desires!"
                    "You've knocked him out of action,
that insatiable tramp—"
                   "That parasite on the land!"

"Ship him off to Echetus, fast—the mainland king
135   who wrecks all men alive!"
                                                    Welcome words
and a lucky omen too—Odysseus' heart leapt up.
Antinous laid before him a generous goat sausage,
bubbling fat and blood. Amphinomus took two loaves
from the wicker tray and set them down beside him,
140   drank his health in a golden cup and said,
"Cheers, old friend, old father,
saddled now as you are with so much trouble—
here's to your luck, great days from this day on!"

        And the one who knew the world replied at length,
145   "Amphinomus, you seem like a man of good sense to me.
Just like your father—at least I've heard his praises,
Nisus of Dulichion, a righteous man, and rich.
You're his son, they say, you seem well-spoken, too.
So I will tell you something. Listen. Listen closely.
150   Of all that breathes and crawls across the earth,
our mother earth breeds nothing feebler than a man.
So long as the gods grant him power, spring in his knees,
he thinks he will never suffer affliction down the years.
But then, when the happy gods bring on the long hard times,
155   bear them he must, against his will, and steel his heart.
Our lives, our mood and mind as we pass across the earth,
turn as the days turn . . .
as the father of men and gods makes each day dawn.
I too seemed destined to be a man of fortune once
160   and a wild wicked swath I cut, indulged my lust for violence,
staking all on my father and my brothers.
                                                    Look at me now.
And so, I say, let no man ever be lawless all his life,
just take in peace what gifts the gods will send.
                                                    True,
but here I see you suitors plotting your reckless work,
165   carving away at the wealth, affronting the loyal wife
of a man who won't be gone from kin and country long.
I say he's right at hand—and may some power save you,
spirit you home before you meet him face-to-face
the moment he returns to native ground!
170   Once under his own roof, he and your friends,
believe you me, won't part till blood has flowed."
                                                    With that
he poured out honeyed wine to the gods and drank deeply,
then restored the cup to the young prince's hands.
Amphinomus made his way back through the hall,
175   his heart sick with anguish, shaking his head,
fraught with grave forebodings . . .
but not even so could he escape his fate.
Even then Athena had bound him fast to death

at the hands of Prince Telemachus and his spear.
180   Now back he went to the seat that he'd left empty.

    But now the goddess Athena with her glinting eyes
inspired Penelope, Icarius' daughter, wary, poised,
to display herself to her suitors, fan their hearts,
inflame them more, and make her even more esteemed
185   by her husband and her son than she had been before.
Forcing a laugh, she called her maid: "Eurynome,
my spirit longs—though it never did till now—
to appear before my suitors, loathe them as I do.
I'd say a word to my son too, for his own good,
190   not to mix so much with that pernicious crowd,
so glib with their friendly talk
but plotting wicked plots they'll hatch tomorrow."

    "Well said, my child," the old woman answered,
"all to the point. Go to the boy and warn him now,
195   hold nothing back. But first you should bathe yourself,
give a gloss to your face. Don't go down like that—
your eyes dimmed, your cheeks streaked with tears.
It makes things worse, this grieving on and on.
Your son's now come of age—your fondest prayer
200   to the deathless gods, to see him wear a beard."

    "Eurynome," discreet Penelope objected,
"don't try to coax me, care for me as you do,
to bathe myself, refresh my face with oils.
Whatever glow I had died long ago . . .
205   the gods of Olympus snuffed it out that day
my husband sailed away in the hollow ships.
But please, have Autonoë and Hippodameia come
and support me in the hall. I'll never brave
those men alone. I'd be too embarrassed."

210   Now as the old nurse bustled through the house
to give the women orders, call them to the queen,
the bright-eyed goddess thought of one more thing.
She drifted a sound slumber over Icarius' daughter,
back she sank and slept, her limbs fell limp and still,
215   reclining there on her couch, all the while Athena,
luminous goddess, lavished immortal gifts on her
to make her suitors lose themselves in wonder . . .
The divine unguent first. She cleansed her cheeks,
her brow and fine eyes with ambrosia smooth as the oils
220   the goddess Love applies, donning her crown of flowers
whenever she joins the Graces' captivating dances.
She made her taller, fuller in form to all men's eyes,
her skin whiter than ivory freshly carved, and now,
Athena's mission accomplished, off the bright one went
225   as bare-armed maids came in from their own quarters,

chattering all the way, and sleep released the queen.
She woke, touched her cheek with a hand, and mused,
"Ah, what a marvelous gentle sleep, enfolding me
in the midst of all my anguish! Now if only
230 blessed Artemis sent me a death as gentle, now,
this instant—no more wasting away my life,
my heart broken in longing for my husband . . .
He had every strength,
rising over his countrymen, head and shoulders."

235   Then, leaving her well-lit chamber, she descended,
not alone: two of her women followed close behind.
That radiant woman, once she reached her suitors,
drawing her glistening veil across her cheeks,
paused now where a column propped the sturdy roof,
240 with one of her loyal handmaids stationed either side.
The suitors' knees went slack, their hearts dissolved in lust—
all of them lifted prayers to lie beside her, share her bed.
But turning toward her son, she warned, "Telemachus,
your sense of balance is not what it used to be.
245 When you were a boy you had much better judgment.
Now that you've grown and reached your young prime
and any stranger, seeing how tall and handsome you are,
would think you the son of some great man of wealth—
now your sense of fairness seems to fail you.
250 Consider the dreadful thing just done in our halls—
how you let the stranger be so abused! Why,
suppose our guest, sitting here at peace,
here in our own house,
were hauled and badly hurt by such cruel treatment?
255 You'd be shamed, disgraced in all men's eyes!"

    "Mother . . ." Telemachus paused, then answered.
"I cannot fault your anger at all this.
My heart takes note of everything, feels it, too,
both the good and the bad—the boy you knew is gone.
260 But how can I plan my world in a sane, thoughtful way?
These men drive me mad, hedging me round, right and left,
plotting their lethal plots, and no one takes my side.
Still, this battle between the stranger and Irus
hardly went as the suitors might have hoped:
265 the stranger beat him down!
If only—Father Zeus, Athena and lord Apollo—
these gallants, now, this moment, here in our house,
were battered senseless, heads lolling, knees unstrung,
some sprawled in the courtyard, some sprawled outside!
270 Slumped like Irus down at the front gates now,
whipped, and his head rolling like some drunk.
He can't stand up on his feet and stagger home,
whatever home he's got—the man's demolished."

So Penelope and her son exchanged their hopes
275 as Eurymachus stepped in to praise the queen.
"Ah, daughter of Icarius, wise Penelope,
if all the princes in Ionian Argos saw you now!
What a troop of suitors would banquet in your halls
tomorrow at sunrise! You surpass all women
280 in build and beauty, refined and steady mind."

"Oh no, Eurymachus," wise Penelope demurred,
"whatever form and feature I had, what praise I'd won,
the deathless gods destroyed that day the Achaeans
sailed away to Troy, my husband in their ships,
285 Odysseus—if *he* could return to tend my life
the renown I had would only grow in glory.
Now my life is torment . . .
look at the griefs some god has loosed against me!
I'll never forget the day he left this land of ours;
290 he caught my right hand by the wrist and said, gently,
'Dear woman, I doubt that every Achaean under arms
will make it home from Troy, all safe and sound.
The Trojans, they say, are fine soldiers too,
hurling javelins, shooting flights of arrows,
295 charioteers who can turn the tide—like that!—
when the great leveler, War, brings on some deadlock.
So I cannot tell if the gods will sail me home again
or I'll go down out there, on the fields of Troy,
but all things here must rest in your control.
300 Watch over my father and mother in the palace,
just as now, or perhaps a little more,
when I am far from home.
But once you see the beard on the boy's cheek,
you wed the man you like, and leave your house behind.'
305 So my husband advised me then. Now it all comes true . . .
a night will come when a hateful marriage falls my lot—
this cursed life of mine! Zeus has torn away my joy.
But there's something else that mortifies me now.
Your way is a far cry from the time-honored way
310 of suitors locked in rivalry, striving to win
some noble woman, a wealthy man's daughter.
They bring in their own calves and lambs
to feast the friends of the bride-to-be, yes,
and shower her with gleaming gifts as well.
315 They don't devour the woman's goods scot-free."

Staunch Odysseus glowed with joy to hear all this—
his wife's trickery luring gifts from her suitors now,
enchanting their hearts with suave seductive words
but all the while with something else in mind.
"Gifts?"
320 Eupithes' son Antinous took her point at once.

"Daughter of Icarius, sensible Penelope,
whatever gifts your suitors would like to bring,
accept them. How ungracious to turn those gifts away!
We won't go back to our own estates, or anywhere else,
325   till you have wed the man you find the best."

    So he proposed, and all the rest agreed.
Each suitor sent a page to go and get a gift.
Antinous' man brought in a grand, resplendent robe,
stiff with embroidery, clasped with twelve gold brooches,
330   long pins that clipped into sheathing loops with ease.
Eurymachus' man brought in a necklace richly wrought,
gilded, strung with amber and glowing like the sun.
Eurydamas' two men came with a pair of earrings,
mulberry clusters dangling in triple drops
335   with a glint to catch the heart.
From the halls of lord Pisander, Polyctor's son,
a servant brought a choker, a fine, gleaming treasure.
And so each suitor in turn laid on a handsome gift.
Then the noble queen withdrew to her upper room,
340   her file of waiting ladies close behind her,
bearing the gorgeous presents in their arms.

    Now the suitors turned to dance and song,
to the lovely beat and sway,
waiting for dusk to come upon them there . . .
345   and the dark night came upon them, lost in pleasure.
They rushed to set up three braziers along the walls
to give them light, piled them high with kindling,
sere, well-seasoned, just split with an ax,
and mixed in chips to keep the torches flaring.
350   The maids of Odysseus, steady man, took turns
to keep the fires up, but the king himself,
dear to the gods and cunning to the core,
gave them orders brusquely: "Maids of Odysseus,
your master gone so long—quick now, off you go
355   to the room where your queen and mistress waits.
Sit with her there and try to lift her spirits,
combing wool in your hands or spinning yarn.
But I will trim the torches for all her suitors,
even if they would like to revel on till Morning
360   mounts her throne. They'll never wear me down.
I have a name for lasting out the worst."
                         At that
the women burst into laughter, glancing back and forth.
Flushed with beauty, Melantho mocked him shamelessly—
Dolius was her father but Penelope brought her up;
365   she treated her like her own child and gave her toys
to cheer her heart. But despite that, her heart
felt nothing for all her mistress' anguish now.

She was Eurymachus' lover, always slept with him.
She was the one who mocked her king and taunted,
370   "Cock of the walk, did someone beat your brains out?
Why not go bed down at the blacksmith's cozy forge?
Or a public place where tramps collect? Why here—
blithering on, nonstop,
bold as brass in the face of all these lords?
375   No fear in your heart? Wine's got to your wits?—
or do you always play the fool and babble nonsense?
Lost your head, have you, because you drubbed that hobo Irus?
You wait—a better man than Irus will take you on,
he'll box both sides of your skull with heavy fists
380   and cart you from the palace gushing blood!"
                                    "*You* wait,
you bitch"—the hardened veteran flashed a killing look.
"I'll go straight to the prince with your foul talk.
The prince will chop you to pieces here and now!"

        His fury sent the women fluttering off, scattering
385   down the hall with panic shaking every limb—
they knew he spoke the truth.
But he took up his post by the flaring braziers,
tending the fires closely, looking after them all,
though the heart inside him stirred with other things,
390   ranging ahead, now, to all that must be done . . .

        But Athena had no mind to let the brazen suitors
hold back now from their heart-rending insults—
she meant to make the anguish cut still deeper
into the core of Laertes' son Odysseus.
395   Polybus' son Eurymachus launched in first,
baiting the king to give his friends a laugh:
"Listen to me, you lords who court our noble queen!
I simply have to say what's on my mind. Look,
surely the gods have fetched this beggar here
400   to Odysseus' house. At least our torchlight *seems*
to come from the sheen of the man's own head—
there's not a hair on his bald pate, not a wisp!"

        Then he wheeled on Odysseus, raider of cities:
"Stranger, how would you like to work for me
405   if I took you on—I'd give you decent wages—
picking the stones to lay a tight dry wall
or planting tall trees on the edge of my estate?
I'd give you rations to last you year-round,
clothes for your body, sandals for your feet.
410   Oh no, you've learned your lazy ways too well,
you've got no itch to stick to good hard work,
you'd rather go scrounging round the countryside,
begging for crusts to stuff your greedy gut!"

"Ah, Eurymachus," Odysseus, master of many exploits,
415   answered firmly, "if only the two of us *could* go
man-to-man in the labors of the field . . .
In the late spring, when the long days come round,
out in the meadow, I swinging a well-curved scythe
and you swinging yours—we'd test our strength for work,
420   fasting right till dusk with lots of hay to mow.
Or give us a team of oxen to drive, purebreds,
hulking, ruddy beasts, both lusty with fodder,
paired for age and pulling-power that never flags—
with four acres to work, the loam churning under the plow—
425   you'd see what a straight unbroken furrow I could cut you then.
Or if Zeus would bring some battle on—out of the blue,
this very day—and give me a shield and two spears
and a bronze helmet to fit this soldier's temples,
then you'd see me fight where front ranks clash—
430   no more mocking this belly of mine, not then.
Enough. You're sick with pride, you brutal fool.
No doubt you count yourself a great, powerful man
because you sport with a puny crowd, ill-bred to boot.
If only Odysseus came back home and stood right here,
435   in a flash you'd find those doors—broad as they are—
too cramped for your race to safety through the porch!"

That made Eurymachus' fury seethe and burst—
he gave the beggar a dark look and let fly, "You,
you odious—I'll make you pay for your ugly rant!
440   Bold as brass in the face of all these lords?
No fear in your heart? Wine's got to your wits?—
or do you always play the fool and babble nonsense?
Lost your head, have you, because you drubbed that hobo Irus?"

As he shouted out he seized a stool, but Odysseus,
445   fearing the blow, crouched at Amphinomus' knees
as Eurymachus hurled and hit the wine-steward,
clipping his right hand—
his cup dropped, clattered along the floor
and flat on his back he went, groaning in the dust.
450   The suitors broke into uproar through the shadowed halls,
glancing at one another, trading angry outcries:
"Would to god this drifter had dropped dead—"

"Anywhere else before he landed here!"

"Then he'd never have loosed such pandemonium."

455   "Now we're squabbling over *beggars!*"
                                        "No more joy
in the sumptuous feast . . ."
                        "Now riot rules the day!"

But now Prince Telemachus dressed them down:

"Fools, you're out of your minds! No hiding it,
food and wine have gone to your heads. Some god
460 has got your blood up. Come, now you've eaten well
go home to bed—when the spirit moves, that is.
I, for one, I'll drive no guest away."

    So he declared. And they all bit their lips,
amazed the prince could speak with so much daring.
465 At last Amphinomus rose to take the floor,
the noted son of Nisus, King Aretias' grandson.
"Fair enough, my friends; when a man speaks well
we have no grounds for wrangling, no cause for abuse.
Hands off the stranger! And any other servant
470 in King Odysseus' palace. Come, steward,
pour first drops for the god in every cup;
let's make libations, then go home to bed.
The stranger? Leave him here in Odysseus' halls
and have his host, Telemachus, tend him well—
475 it's the prince's royal house the man has reached."

    So he said. His proposal pleased them all.
And gallant Mulius, a herald of Dulichion,
a friend-in-arms of lord Amphinomus too,
mixed the men a bowl and, hovering closely,
480 poured full rounds for all. They tipped cups
to the blissful gods and then, libations made,
they drank the heady wine to their hearts' content
and went their ways to bed, each suitor to his house.

BOOK 19. PENELOPE AND HER GUEST

That left the great Odysseus waiting in his hall
as Athena helped him plot the slaughter of the suitors.
He turned at once to Telemachus, brisk with orders:
"Now we must stow the weapons out of reach, my boy,
5 all the arms and armor—and when the suitors miss them
and ask you questions, put them off with a winning story:
'I stowed them away, clear of the smoke. A far cry
from the arms Odysseus left when he went to Troy,
fire-damaged equipment, black with reeking fumes.
10 And a god reminded me of something darker too.
When you're in your cups a quarrel might break out,
you'd wound each other, shame your feasting here
and cast a pall on your courting.
Iron has powers to draw a man to ruin.'"

15   Telemachus did his father's will at once,
calling out to his old nurse Eurycleia: "Quick,
dear one, close the women up in their own quarters,
till I can stow my father's weapons in the storeroom.
Splendid gear, lying about, neglected, black with soot

20   since father sailed away. I was only a boy then.
      Now I must safeguard them from the smoke."

         "High time, child," the loving nurse replied.
      "If only you'd bother to tend your whole house
      and safeguard *all* your treasures. Tell me,
25   who's to fetch and carry the torch for you?
      You won't let out the maids who'd light your way."

         "Our friend here will," Telemachus answered coolly.
      "I won't put up with a man who shirks his work,
      not if he takes his ration from my stores,
30   even if he's miles away from home."

         That silenced the old nurse.
      She barred the doors that led from the long hall—
      and up they sprang, Odysseus and his princely son,
      and began to carry off the helmets, studded shields
35   and pointed spears, and Pallas Athena strode before them,
      lifting a golden lamp that cast a dazzling radiance round about.
      "Father," Telemachus suddenly burst out to Odysseus,
      "oh what a marvel fills my eyes! Look, look there—
      all the sides of the hall, the handsome crossbeams,
40   pinewood rafters, the tall columns towering—
      all glow in my eyes like flaming fire!
      Surely a god is here—
      one of those who rule the vaulting skies!"

         "Quiet," his father, the old soldier, warned him.
45   "Get a grip on yourself. No more questions now.
      It's just the way of the gods who rule Olympus.
      Off you go to bed. I'll stay here behind
      to test the women, test your mother too.
      She in her grief will ask me everything I know."

50   Under the flaring torchlight, through the hall
      Telemachus made his way to his own bedroom now,
      where he always went when welcome sleep came on him.
      There he lay tonight as well, till Dawn's first light.
      That left the great king still waiting in his hall
55   as Athena helped him plot the slaughter of the suitors . . .

         Now down from her chamber came reserved Penelope,
      looking for all the world like Artemis or golden Aphrodite.
      Close to the fire her women drew her favorite chair
      with its whorls of silver and ivory, inlaid rings.
60   The craftsman who made it years ago, Icmalius,
      added a footrest under the seat itself,
      mortised into the frame,
      and over it all was draped a heavy fleece.
      Here Penelope took her place, discreet, observant.
65   The women, arms bared, pressing in from their quarters,

cleared away the tables, the heaped remains of the feast
and the cups from which the raucous lords had drunk.
Raking embers from the braziers onto the ground,
they piled them high again with seasoned wood,
70   providing light and warmth.
                        And yet again
Melantho lashed out at Odysseus: "You still here?—
you pest, slinking around the house all night,
leering up at the women?
Get out, you tramp—be glad of the food you got—
75   or we'll sling a torch at you, rout you out at once!"

    A killing glance, and the old trooper countered,
"What's possessed you, woman? Why lay into me? Such abuse!
Just because I'm filthy, because I wear such rags,
roving round the country, living hand-to-mouth.
80   But it's fate that drives me on:
that's the lot of beggars, homeless drifters.
I too once lived in a lofty house that men admired;
rolling in wealth, I'd often give to a vagabond like myself,
whoever he was, whatever need had brought him to my door.
85   And crowds of servants I had, and lots of all it takes
to live the life of ease, to make men call you rich.
But Zeus ruined it all—god's will, no doubt.
So beware, woman, or one day you may lose it all,
all your glitter that puts your work-mates in the shade.
90   Or your mistress may just fly in a rage and dress you down
or Odysseus may return—there's still room for hope!
Or if he's dead as you think and never coming home,
well there's his son, Telemachus . . .
like father, like son—thanks to god Apollo.
95   No women's wildness here in the house escapes
the prince's eye. He's come of age at last."

    So he warned, and alert Penelope heard him,
wheeled on the maid and tongue-lashed her smartly:
"Make no mistake, you brazen, shameless bitch,
100   none of your ugly work escapes me either—
you will pay for it with your life, you will!
How well you knew—you heard from my own lips—
that I meant to probe this stranger in our house
and ask about my husband . . . my heart breaks for him."

105   She turned to her housekeeper Eurynome and said,
"Now bring us a chair and spread it soft with fleece,
so our guest can sit and tell me his whole story
and hear me out as well.
I'd like to ask him questions, point by point."

110   Eurynome bustled off to fetch a polished chair
and set it down and spread it soft with fleece.

Here Odysseus sat, the man of many trials,
as cautious Penelope began the conversation:
"Stranger, let me start our questioning myself . . .
115   Who are you? where are you from? your city? your parents?"

    "My good woman," Odysseus, master of craft, replied,
"no man on the face of the earth could find fault with *you*.
Your fame, believe me, has reached the vaulting skies.
Fame like a flawless king's who dreads the gods,
120   who governs a kingdom vast, proud and strong—
who upholds justice, true, and the black earth
bears wheat and barley, trees bow down with fruit
and the sheep drop lambs and never fail and the sea
teems with fish—thanks to his decent, upright rule,
125   and under his sovereign sway the people flourish.
So then, here in your house, ask me anything else
but don't, please, search out my birth, my land,
or you'll fill my heart to overflowing even more
as I bring back the past . . .
130   I am a man who's had his share of sorrows.
It's wrong for me, in someone else's house,
to sit here moaning and groaning, sobbing so—
it makes things worse, this grieving on and on.
One of your maids, or you yourself, might scold me,
135   think it's just the wine that had doused my wits
and made me drown in tears."

    "No, no, stranger," wise Penelope demurred,
"whatever form and feature I had, what praise I'd won,
the deathless gods destroyed that day the Achaeans
140   sailed away to Troy, my husband in their ships,
Odysseus—if *he* could return to tend my life
the renown I had would only grow in glory.
Now my life is torment . . .
look at the griefs some god has loosed against me!
145   All the nobles who rule the islands round about,
Dulichion, Same, and wooded Zacynthus too,
and all who lord it in sunny Ithaca itself—
they court me against my will, they lay waste my house.
So I pay no heed to strangers, suppliants at my door,
150   not even heralds out on their public errands here—
I yearn for Odysseus, always, my heart pines away.
They rush the marriage on, and I spin out my wiles.
A god from the blue it was inspired me first
to set up a great loom in our royal halls
155   and I began to weave, and the weaving finespun,
the yarns endless, and I would lead them on: 'Young men,
my suitors, now that King Odysseus is no more,
go slowly, keen as you are to marry me, until
I can finish off this web . . .

160 so my weaving won't all fray and come to nothing.
This is a shroud for old lord Laertes, for that day
when the deadly fate that lays us out at last will take him down.
I dread the shame my countrywomen would heap upon me,
yes, if a man of such wealth should lie in state
165 without a shroud for cover.'
                                        My very words,
and despite their pride and passion they believed me.
So by day I'd weave at my great and growing web—
by night, by the light of torches set beside me,
I would unravel all I'd done. Three whole years
170 I deceived them blind, seduced them with this scheme.
Then, when the wheeling seasons brought the fourth year on
and the months waned and the long days came round once more,
then, thanks to my maids—the shameless, reckless creatures—
the suitors caught me in the act, denounced me harshly.
175 So I finished it off. Against my will. They forced me.
And now I cannot escape a marriage, nor can I contrive
a deft way out. My parents urge me to tie the knot
and my son is galled as they squander his estate—
he sees it all. He's a grown man by now, equipped
180 to tend to his own royal house and tend it well:
Zeus grants my son that honor . . .
But for all that—now tell me who you are.
Where do you come from? You've hardly sprung
from a rock or oak like some old man of legend."

185   The master improviser answered, slowly,
"My lady . . . wife of Laertes' son, Odysseus,
will your questions about my family never end?
All right then. Here's my story. Even though
it plunges me into deeper grief than I feel now.
190 But that's the way of the world, when one has been
so far from home, so long away as I, roving over
many cities of men, enduring many hardships.
                                        Still,
my story will tell you all you need to know.

     There is a land called Crete . . .
195 ringed by the wine-dark sea with rolling whitecaps—
handsome country, fertile, thronged with people
well past counting—boasting ninety cities,
language mixing with language side-by-side.
First come the Achaeans, then the native Cretans,
200 hardy, gallant in action, then Cydonian clansmen,
Dorians living in three tribes, and proud Pelasgians last.
Central to all their cities is magnificent Cnossos,
the site where Minos ruled and each ninth year
conferred with almighty Zeus himself. Minos,
205 father of my father, Deucalion, that bold heart.

Besides myself Deucalion sired Prince Idomeneus,
who set sail for Troy in his beaked ships of war,
escorting Atreus' sons. My own name is Aethon.
I am the younger-born;
210   my older brother's a better man than I am.
Now, it was there in Cnossos that I saw him . . .
Odysseus—and we traded gifts of friendship.
A heavy gale had landed him on our coast,
driven him way off course, rounding Malea's cape
215   when he was bound for Troy. He anchored in Amnisus,
hard by the goddess' cave of childbirth and labor,
that rough harbor—barely riding out the storm.
He came into town at once, asking for Idomeneus,
claiming to be my brother's close, respected friend.
220   Too late. Ten or eleven days had already passed
since he set sail for Troy in his beaked ships.
So I took Odysseus back to my own house,
gave him a hero's welcome, treated him in style—
stores in our palace made for princely entertainment.
225   As for his comrades, all who'd shipped with him,
I dipped into public stock to give them barley,
ruddy wine and fine cattle for slaughter,
beef to their hearts' content. A dozen days
they stayed with me there, those brave Achaeans,
230   penned up by a North Wind so stiff that a man,
even on dry land, could never keep his feet—
some angry spirit raised that blast, I'd say.
Then on the thirteenth day the wind died down
and they set sail for Troy."
                    Falsehoods all,
235   but he gave his falsehoods all the ring of truth.
As she listened on, her tears flowed and soaked her cheeks
as the heavy snow melts down from the high mountain ridges,
snow the West Wind piles there and the warm East Wind thaws
and the snow, melting, swells the rivers to overflow their banks—
240   so she dissolved in tears, streaming down her lovely cheeks,
weeping for him, her husband, sitting there beside her.
Odysseus' heart went out to his grief-stricken wife
but under his lids his eyes remained stock-still—
they might have been horn or iron—
245   his guile fought back his tears. And she,
once she'd had her fill of grief and weeping,
turned again to her guest with this reply:
"Now, stranger, I think I'll test you, just to see
if there in your house, with all his friends-in-arms,
250   you actually entertained my husband as you say.
Come, tell me what sort of clothing he wore,
what cut of man was he?

What of the men who followed in his train?"
                                        "Ah good woman,"
       Odysseus, the great master of subtlety, returned,
255   "how hard it is to speak, after so much time
       apart . . . why, some twenty years have passed
       since he left my house and put my land behind him.
       Even so, imagine the man as I portray him—
       I can see him now.
                          King Odysseus . . .
260   he was wearing a heavy woolen cape, sea-purple
       in double folds, with a golden brooch to clasp it,
       twin sheaths for the pins, on the face a work of art:
       a hound clenching a dappled fawn in its front paws,
       slashing it as it writhed. All marveled to see it,
265   solid gold as it was, the hound slashing, throttling
       the fawn in its death-throes, hoofs flailing to break free.
       I noticed his glossy tunic too, clinging to his skin
       like the thin glistening skin of a dried onion,
       silky, soft, the glint of the sun itself.
270   Women galore would gaze on it with relish.
       And this too. Bear it in mind, won't you?
       I've no idea if Odysseus wore these things at home
       or a comrade gave him them as he boarded ship,
       or a host perhaps—the man was loved by many.
275   There were few Achaeans to equal him . . . and I?
       I gave him a bronze sword myself, a lined cloak,
       elegant, deep red, and a fringed shirt as well,
       and I saw him off in his long benched ship of war
       in lordly style.
                         Something else. He kept a herald
280   beside him, a man a little older than himself.
       I'll try to describe him to you, best I can.
       Round-shouldered he was, swarthy, curly-haired.
       His name? Eurybates. And Odysseus prized him
       most of all his men. Their minds worked as one."

285   His words renewed her deep desire to weep,
       recognizing the strong clear signs Odysseus offered.
       But as soon as she'd had her fill of tears and grief,
       Penelope turned again to her guest and said,
       "Now, stranger, much as I pitied you before,
290   now in my house you'll be my special friend,
       my honored guest. I am the one, myself,
       who gave him the very clothes that you describe.
       I brought them up from the storeroom, folded them neatly,
       fastened the golden brooch to adorn my husband,
295   Odysseus—never again will I embrace him,
       striding home to his own native land.

A black day it was
when he took ship to see that cursed city . . .
Destroy, I call it—I hate to say its name!"

300   "Ah my queen," the man of craft assured her,
"noble wife of Laertes' son, Odysseus,
ravage no more your lovely face with tears
or consume your heart with grieving for your husband.
Not that I'd blame you, ever. Any woman will mourn
305   the bridegroom she has lost, lain with in love
and borne his children too. Even though he
was no Odysseus—a man like a god, they say.
But dry your tears and take my words to heart.
I will tell you the whole truth and hide nothing:
310   I have heard that Odysseus now, at last, is on his way,
he's just in reach, in rich Thesprotian country—
the man is still alive
and he's bringing home a royal hoard of treasure,
gifts he won from the people of those parts.
315   His crew? He's lost his crew and hollow ship
on the wine-dark waters off Thrinacia Island.
Zeus and Helios raged, dead set against Odysseus
for his men-at-arms had killed the cattle of the Sun,
so down to the last hand they drowned in crashing seas.
320   But not Odysseus, clinging tight to his ship's keel—
the breakers flung him out onto dry land, on Scheria,
the land of Phaeacians, close kin to the gods themselves,
and with all their hearts they prized him like a god,
showered the man with gifts, and they'd have gladly
325   sailed him home unscathed. In fact Odysseus
would have been here beside you long ago
but he thought it the better, shrewder course
to recoup his fortunes roving through the world.
At sly profit-turning there's not a man alive
330   to touch Odysseus. He's got no rival there.
So I learned from Phidon, king of Thesprotia,
who swore to me as he poured libations in his house,
'The ship's hauled down and the shipmates set to sail,
to take Odysseus home to native land.'
                                        But I . . .
335   he shipped me off before. A Thesprotian cutter
chanced to be heading for Dulichion rich in wheat.
But he showed me all the treasure Odysseus had amassed,
enough to last a man and ten generations of his heirs—
so great the wealth stored up for *him* in the king's vaults!
340   But Odysseus, he made clear, was off at Dodona then
to hear the will of Zeus that rustles forth
from the god's tall leafy oak: how should he return,
after all the years away, to his own beloved Ithaca,

openly or in secret?
                              And so the man is safe,
345   as you can see, and he's coming home, soon,
      he's close, close at hand—
      he won't be severed long from kin and country,
      no, not now. I give you my solemn, binding oath.
      I swear by Zeus, the first, the greatest god—
350   by Odysseus' hearth, where I have come for help:
      all will come to pass, I swear, exactly as I say.
      True, this very month—just as the old moon dies
      and the new moon rises into life—Odysseus will return!"

      "If only, my friend," reserved Penelope exclaimed,
355   "everything you say would come to pass!
      You'd soon know my affection, know my gifts.
      Any man you meet would call you blest.
      But my heart can sense the way it all will go.
      Odysseus, I tell you, is never coming back,
360   nor will you ever gain your passage home,
      for we have no masters in our house like him
      at welcoming in or sending off an honored guest.
      Odysseus. There was a man, or was he all a dream?
      But come, women, wash the stranger and make his bed,
365   with bedding, blankets and lustrous spreads to keep him warm
      till Dawn comes up and takes her golden throne.
      Then, tomorrow at daybreak, bathe him well
      and rub him down with oil, so he can sit beside
      Telemachus in the hall, enjoy his breakfast there.
370   And anyone who offends our guest beyond endurance—
      he defeats himself; he's doomed to failure here,
      no matter how raucously he raves and blusters on.
      For how can you know, my friend, if I surpass
      all women in thoughtfulness and shrewd good sense,
375   if I'd allow you to take your meals at hall
      so weatherbeaten, clad in rags and tatters?
      Our lives are much too brief . . .
      If a man is cruel by nature, cruel in action,
      the mortal world will call down curses on his head
380   while he is alive, and all will mock his memory after death.
      But then if a man is kind by nature, kind in action,
      his guests will carry his fame across the earth
      and people all will praise him from the heart."

      "Wait, my queen," the crafty man objected,
385   "noble wife of Laertes' son, Odysseus—
      blankets and glossy spreads? They're not my style.
      Not from the day I launched out in my long-oared ship
      and the snowy peaks of Crete went fading far astern.
      I'll lie as I've done through sleepless nights before.
390   Many a night I've spent on rugged beds afield,

waiting for Dawn to mount her lovely throne.
Nor do I pine for any footbaths either.
Of all the women who serve your household here,
not one will touch my feet. Unless, perhaps,
395   there is some old retainer, the soul of trust,
someone who's borne as much as I have borne . . .
I wouldn't mind if she would touch my feet."

"Dear friend,"
the discreet Penelope replied, "never has any man
so thoughtful—of all the guests in my palace
400   come from foreign parts—been as welcome as you . . .
so sensible, so apt, is every word you say.
I have just such an old woman, seasoned, wise,
who carefully tended my unlucky husband, reared him,
took him into her arms the day his mother bore him—
405   frail as the woman is, she'll wash your feet.
Up with you now, my good old Eurycleia,
come and wash your master's . . . equal in years.
Odysseus must have feet and hands like his by now—
hardship can age a person overnight."

At that name
410   the old retainer buried her face in both hands,
burst into warm tears and wailed out in grief,
"Oh my child, how helpless I am to help you now!
How Zeus despised you, more than all other men,
god-fearing man that you were . . .
415   Never did any mortal burn the Old Thunderer
such rich thighbones—offerings charred and choice—
never as many as *you* did, praying always to reach
a ripe old age and raise a son to glory. Now,
you alone he's robbed of your home-coming day!
420   Just so, the women must have mocked my king,
far away, when he'd stopped at some fine house—
just as all these bitches, stranger, mock you here.
And because you shrink from their taunts, their wicked barbs,
you will not let them wash you. The work is mine—
425   Icarius' daughter, wise Penelope, bids me now
and I am all too glad. I will wash your feet,
both for my own dear queen and for yourself—
your sorrows wring my heart . . . and why?
Listen to me closely, mark my words.
430   Many a wayworn guest has landed here
but never, I swear, has one so struck my eyes—
your build, your voice, your feet—you're like Odysseus . . .
to the life!"

"Old woman," wily Odysseus countered,
"that's what they all say who've seen us both.
435   We bear a striking resemblance to each other,
as you have had the wit to say yourself."

　　　　The old woman took up a burnished basin
　　　　she used for washing feet and poured in bowls
　　　　of fresh cold water before she stirred in hot.
440　　Odysseus, sitting full in the firelight, suddenly
　　　　swerved round to the dark, gripped by a quick misgiving—
　　　　soon as she touched him she might spot the scar!
　　　　The truth would all come out.
　　　　　　　　　　　　　　　　　　Bending closer
　　　　she started to bathe her master . . . then,
445　　in a flash, she knew the scar—
　　　　　　　　　　　　　　　that old wound
　　　　made years ago by a boar's white tusk when Odysseus
　　　　went to Parnassus, out to see Autolycus and his sons.
　　　　The man was his mother's noble father, one who excelled
　　　　the world at thievery, that and subtle, shifty oaths.
450　　Hermes gave him the gift, overjoyed by the thighs
　　　　of lambs and kids he burned in the god's honor—
　　　　Hermes the ready partner in his crimes. Now,
　　　　Autolycus once visited Ithaca's fertile land,
　　　　to find his daughter's son had just been born.
455　　Eurycleia set him down on the old man's knees
　　　　as he finished dinner, urging him, "Autolycus,
　　　　you must find a name for your daughter's darling son.
　　　　The baby comes as the answer to her prayers."
　　　　　　　　　　　　　　　　　　　　　　"You,
　　　　my daughter, and you, my son-in-law," Autolycus replied,
460　　"give the boy the name I tell you now. Just as I
　　　　have come from afar, creating pain for many—
　　　　men and women across the good green earth—
　　　　so let his name be *Odysseus* . . .
　　　　the Son of Pain, a name he'll earn in full.[1]
465　　And when he has come of age and pays his visit
　　　　to Parnassus—the great estate of his mother's line
　　　　where all my treasures lie—I will give him enough
　　　　to cheer his heart, then speed him home to you."
　　　　　　　　　　　　　　　　　　　　　　　And so,
　　　　in time, Odysseus went to collect the splendid gifts.
470　　Autolycus and the sons of Autolycus warmed him in
　　　　with eager handclasps, hearty words of welcome.
　　　　His mother's mother, Amphithea, hugged the boy
　　　　and kissed his face and kissed his shining eyes.
　　　　Autolycus told his well-bred sons to prepare
475　　a princely feast. They followed orders gladly,
　　　　herded an ox inside at once, five years old,
　　　　skinned it and split the carcass into quarters,
　　　　deftly cut it in pieces, skewered these on spits,
　　　　roasted all to a turn and served the portions out.

1. The name suggests Greek words for rage and pain.

480   So all day long till the sun went down they feasted,
       consuming equal shares to their hearts' content.
       Then when the sun had set and night came on
       they turned to bed and took the gift of sleep.
                                           As soon
       as young Dawn with her rose-red fingers shone once more
485   they all moved out for the hunt, hounds in the lead,
       Autolycus' sons and Prince Odysseus in their ranks.
       Climbing Parnassus' ridges, thick with timber,
       they quickly reached the mountain's windy folds
       and just as the sun began to strike the plowlands,
490   rising out of the deep calm flow of the Ocean River,
       the beaters came to a wooded glen, the hounds broke,
       hot on a trail, and right behind the pack they came,
       Autolycus' sons—Odysseus out in front now,
       pressing the dogs, brandishing high his spear
495   with its long shadow waving. Then and there
       a great boar lay in wait, in a thicket lair so dense
       that the sodden gusty winds could never pierce it,
       nor could the sun's sharp rays invade its depths
       nor a downpour drench it through and through,
500   so dense, so dark, and piled with fallen leaves.
       Here, as the hunters closed in for the kill,
       crowding the hounds, the tramp of men and dogs
       came drumming round the boar—he crashed from his lair,
       his razor back bristling, his eyes flashing fire
505   and charging up to the hunt he stopped, at bay—
       and Odysseus rushed him first,
       shaking his long spear in a sturdy hand,
       wild to strike but the boar struck faster,
       lunging in on the slant, a tusk thrusting up
510   over the boy's knee, gouging a deep strip of flesh
       but it never hit the bone—
                                  Odysseus thrust and struck,
       stabbing the beast's right shoulder—
                                           a glint of bronze—
       the point ripped clean through and down in the dust he dropped,
       grunting out his breath as his life winged away.
515   The sons of Autolycus, working over Odysseus,
       skillfully binding up his open wound—
       the gallant, godlike prince—
       chanted an old spell that stanched the blood
       and quickly bore him home to their father's palace.
520   There, in no time, Autolycus and the sons of Autolycus
       healed him well and, showering him with splendid gifts,
       sped Odysseus back to his native land, to Ithaca,
       a young man filled with joy. His happy parents,
       his father and noble mother, welcomed him home
525   and asked him of all his exploits, blow-by-blow:

how did he get that wound? He told his tale with style,
how the white tusk of a wild boar had gashed his leg,
hunting on Parnassus with Autolycus and his sons . . .
                                              That scar—
as the old nurse cradled his leg and her hands passed down
530 she felt it, knew it, suddenly let his foot fall—
down it dropped in the basin—the bronze clanged,
tipping over, spilling water across the floor.
Joy and torment gripped her heart at once,
tears rushed to her eyes—voice choked in her throat
535 she reached for Odysseus' chin and whispered quickly,
"Yes, yes! you are *Odysseus*—oh dear boy—
I couldn't know you before . . .
not till I touched the body of my king!"

      She glanced at Penelope, keen to signal her
540 that here was her own dear husband, here and now,
but she could not catch the glance, she took no heed,
Athena turned her attention elsewhere. But Odysseus—
his right hand shot out, clutching the nurse's throat,
with his left he hugged her to himself and muttered,
545 "Nurse, you want to kill me? You suckled me yourself
at your own breast—and now I'm home, at last,
after bearing twenty years of brutal hardship,
home, on native ground. But now you know,
now that a god has flashed it in your mind,
550 quiet! not a word to anyone in the house.
Or else, I warn you—and I mean business too—
if a god beats down these brazen suitors at my hands,
I will not spare you—my old nurse that you are—
when I kill the other women in my house."

555   "Child," shrewd old Eurycleia protested,
"what nonsense you let slip through your teeth!
You know *me*—I'm stubborn, never give an inch—
I'll keep still as solid rock or iron.
One more thing. Take it to heart, I tell you.
560 If a god beats down these brazen suitors at your hands,
I'll report in full on the women in your house:
who are disloyal to you, who are guiltless."

      "Nurse," the cool tactician Odysseus said,
"why bother to count them off? A waste of breath.
565 I'll observe them, judge each one myself.
Just be quiet. Keep your tales to yourself.
Leave the rest to the gods."
                                    Hushed so,
the old nurse went padding along the halls
to fetch more water—her basin had all spilled—
570 and once she'd bathed and rubbed him down with oil,

Odysseus drew his chair up near the fire again,
trying to keep warm,
but he hid his scar beneath his beggar's rags
as cautious Penelope resumed their conversation:

575   "My friend, I have only one more question for you,
something slight, now the hour draws on for welcome sleep—
for those who can yield to sweet repose, that is,
heartsick as they are. As for myself, though,
some god has sent me pain that knows no bounds.

580   All day long I indulge myself in sighs and tears
as I see to my tasks, direct the household women.
When night falls and the world lies lost in sleep,
I take to my bed, my heart throbbing, about to break,
anxieties swarming, piercing—I may go mad with grief.

585   Like Pandareus' daughter, the nightingale in the green woods
lifting her lovely song at the first warm rush of spring,
perched in the treetops' rustling leaves and pouring forth
her music shifting, trilling and sinking, rippling high to burst
in grief for Itylus, her beloved boy, King Zethus' son

590   whom she in innocence once cut down with bronze[2] . . .
so my wavering heart goes shuttling, back and forth:
Do I stay beside my son and keep all things secure—
my lands, my serving-women, the grand high-roofed house—
true to my husband's bed, the people's voice as well?

595   Or do I follow, at last, the best man who courts me
here in the halls, who gives the greatest gifts?
My son—when he was a boy and lighthearted—
urged me not to marry and leave my husband's house.
But now he has grown and reached his young prime,

600   he begs me to leave our palace, travel home.
Telemachus, so obsessed with his own estate,
the wealth my princely suitors bleed away.
                                        But please,
read this dream for me, won't you? Listen closely . . .
I keep twenty geese in the house, from the water trough

605   they come and peck their wheat—I love to watch them all.
But down from a mountain swooped this great hook-beaked eagle,
yes, and he snapped their necks and killed them one and all
and they lay in heaps throughout the halls while he,
back to the clear blue sky he soared at once.

610   But I wept and wailed—only a dream, of course—
and our well-groomed ladies came and clustered round me,
sobbing, stricken: the eagle killed my geese. But down
he swooped again and settling onto a jutting rafter
called out in a human voice that dried my tears,

615   'Courage, daughter of famous King Icarius!
This is no dream but a happy waking vision,

---

2. Aedon accidentally killed her own son and prayed to be changed into a nightingale.

real as day, that will come true for you.
The geese were your suitors—I was once the eagle
but now I am your husband, back again at last,
620   about to launch a terrible fate against them all!'
So he vowed, and the soothing sleep released me.
I peered around and saw my geese in the house,
pecking at their wheat, at the same trough
where they always took their meal."

                                       "Dear woman,"
625   quick Odysseus answered, "twist it however you like,
your dream can only mean one thing. Odysseus
told you himself—he'll make it come to pass.
Destruction is clear for each and every suitor;
not a soul escapes his death and doom."

630   "Ah my friend," seasoned Penelope dissented,
"dreams are hard to unravel, wayward, drifting things—
not all we glimpse in them will come to pass . . .
Two gates there are for our evanescent dreams,
one is made of ivory, the other made of horn.
635   Those that pass through the ivory cleanly carved
are will-o'-the-wisps, their message bears no fruit.
The dreams that pass through the gates of polished horn
are fraught with truth, for the dreamer who can see them.
But I can't believe my strange dream has come that way,
640   much as my son and I would love to have it so.
One more thing I'll tell you—weigh it well.
The day that dawns today, this cursed day,
will cut me off from Odysseus' house. Now,
I mean to announce a contest with those axes,
645   the ones he would often line up here inside the hall,
twelve in a straight unbroken row like blocks to shore a keel,
then stand well back and whip an arrow through the lot.
Now I will bring them on as a trial for my suitors.
The hand that can string the bow with greatest ease,
650   that shoots an arrow clean through all twelve axes—
he's the man I follow, yes, forsaking this house
where I was once a bride, this gracious house
so filled with the best that life can offer—
I shall always remember it, that I know . . .
655   even in my dreams."

                        "Oh my queen,"
Odysseus, man of exploits, urged her on,
"royal wife of Laertes' son, Odysseus, now,
don't put off this test in the halls a moment.
Before that crew can handle the polished bow,
660   string it taut and shoot through all those axes—
Odysseus, man of exploits, will be home with you!"

"If only, my friend," the wise Penelope replied,
"you were willing to sit beside me in the house,
indulging me in the comfort of your presence,
665   sleep would never drift across my eyes.
But one can't go without one's sleep forever.
The immortals give each thing its proper place
in our mortal lives throughout the good green earth.
So now I'm going back to my room upstairs
670   and lie down on my bed,
that bed of pain my tears have streaked, year in,
year out, from the day Odysseus sailed away to see . . .
Destroy, I call it—I hate to say its name!
There I'll rest, while you lie here in the hall,
675   spreading your blankets somewhere on the floor,
or the women will prepare a decent bed."
                                With that
the queen went up to her lofty well-lit room
and not alone: her women followed close behind.
Penelope, once they reached the upper story,
680   fell to weeping for Odysseus, her beloved husband,
till watchful Athena sealed her eyes with welcome sleep.

BOOK 20. PORTENTS GATHER

Off in the entrance-hall the great king made his bed,
spreading out on the ground the raw hide of an ox,
heaping over it fleece from sheep the suitors
butchered day and night, then Eurynome threw
5   a blanket over him, once he'd nestled down.
And there Odysseus lay . . .
plotting within himself the suitors' death—
awake, alert, as the women slipped from the house,
the maids who whored in the suitors' beds each night,
10   tittering, linking arms and frisking as before.
The master's anger rose inside his chest,
torn in thought, debating, head and heart—
should he up and rush them, kill them one and all
or let them rut with their lovers one last time?
15   The heart inside him growled low with rage,
as a bitch mounting over her weak, defenseless puppies
growls, facing a stranger, bristling for a showdown—
so he growled from his depths, hackles rising at their outrage.
But he struck his chest and curbed his fighting heart:
20   "Bear up, old heart! You've borne worse, far worse,
that day when the Cyclops, man-mountain, bolted
your hardy comrades down. But you held fast—
Nobody but your cunning pulled you through
the monster's cave you thought would be your death."

25   So he forced his spirit into submission,
        the rage in his breast reined back—unswerving,
        all endurance. But he himself kept tossing, turning,
        intent as a cook before some white-hot blazing fire
        who rolls his sizzling sausage back and forth,
30   packed with fat and blood—keen to broil it quickly,
        tossing, turning it, this way, that way—so he cast about:
        how could he get these shameless suitors in his clutches,
        one man facing a mob? . . . when close to his side she came,
        Athena sweeping down from the sky in a woman's build
35   and hovering at his head, the goddess spoke:
        "Why still awake? The unluckiest man alive!
        Here is your house, your wife at home, your son,
        as fine a boy as one could hope to have."
                                    "True,"
        the wily fighter replied, "how right you are, goddess,
40   but still this worry haunts me, heart and soul—
        how can I get these shameless suitors in my clutches?
        Single-handed, braving an army always camped inside.
        There's another worry, that haunts me even more.
        What if I kill them—thanks to you and Zeus—
45   how do I run from under their avengers?
        Show me the way, I ask you."
                                    "Impossible man!"
        Athena bantered, the goddess' eyes ablaze.
        "Others are quick to trust a weaker comrade,
        some poor mortal, far less cunning than I.
50   But I am a goddess, look, the very one who
        guards you in all your trials to the last.
        I tell you this straight out:
        even if fifty bands of mortal fighters
        closed around us, hot to kill us off in battle,
55   still you could drive away their herds and sleek flocks!
        So, surrender to sleep at last. What a misery,
        keeping watch through the night, wide awake—
        you'll soon come up from under all your troubles."

        With that she showered sleep across his eyes
60   and back to Olympus went the lustrous goddess.
        As soon as sleep came on him, loosing his limbs,
        slipping the toils of anguish from his mind,
        his devoted wife awoke and,
        sitting up in her soft bed, returned to tears.
65   When the queen had wept to her heart's content
        she prayed to the Huntress, Artemis, first of all:
        "Artemis—goddess, noble daughter of Zeus, if only
        you'd whip an arrow through my breast and tear my life out,
        now, at once! Or let some whirlwind pluck me up
70   and sweep me away along those murky paths and
        fling me down where the Ocean River running

round the world rolls back upon itself!
                                        Quick
as the whirlwinds swept away Pandareus' daughters—
years ago, when the gods destroyed their parents,
75   leaving the young girls orphans in their house.
But radiant Aphrodite nursed them well
on cheese and luscious honey and heady wine,
and Hera gave them beauty and sound good sense,
more than all other women—virgin Artemis made them tall
80   and Athena honed their skills to fashion lovely work.
But then, when Aphrodite approached Olympus' peaks
to ask for the girls their crowning day as brides
from Zeus who loves the lightning—Zeus who knows all,
all that's fated, all not fated, for mortal man—
85   then the storm spirits snatched them away
and passed them on to the hateful Furies,
yes, for all their loving care.
                                        Just so
may the gods who rule Olympus blot me out!
Artemis with your glossy braids, come shoot me dead—
90   so I can plunge beneath this loathsome earth
with the image of Odysseus vivid in my mind.
Never let me warm the heart of a weaker man!
Even grief is bearable, true, when someone weeps
through the days, sobbing, heart convulsed with pain
95   yet embraced by sleep all night—sweet oblivion, sleep
dissolving all, the good and the bad, once it seals our eyes—
but even my dreams torment me, sent by wicked spirits.
Again—just this night—someone lay beside me . . .
like Odysseus to the life, when he embarked
100   with his men-at-arms. My heart raced with joy.
No dream, I thought, the waking truth at last!"
                                        At those words
Dawn rose on her golden throne in a sudden gleam of light.
And great Odysseus caught the sound of his wife's cry
and began to daydream—deep in his heart it seemed
105   she stood beside him, knew him, now, at last . . .
Gathering up the fleece and blankets where he'd slept,
he laid them on a chair in the hall, he took the oxhide out
and spread it down, lifted his hands and prayed to Zeus:
"Father Zeus, if you really willed it so—to bring me
110   home over land and sea-lanes, home to native ground
after all the pain you brought me—show me a sign,
a good omen voiced by someone awake indoors,
another sign, outside, from Zeus himself!"

        And Zeus in all his wisdom heard that prayer.
115   He thundered at once, out of his clear blue heavens
high above the clouds, and Odysseus' spirit lifted.
Then from within the halls a woman grinding grain

let fly a lucky word. Close at hand she was,
where the good commander set the handmills once
120 and now twelve women in all performed their tasks,
grinding the wheat and barley, marrow of men's bones.
The rest were abed by now—they'd milled their stint—
this one alone, the frailest of all, kept working on.
Stopping her mill, she spoke an omen for her master:
125 "Zeus, Father! King of gods and men, now *there*
was a crack of thunder out of the starry sky—
and not a cloud in sight!
Sure it's a sign you're showing someone now.
So, poor as I am, grant *me* my prayer as well:
130 let this day be the last, the last these suitors
bolt their groaning feasts in King Odysseus' house!
These brutes who break my knees—heart-wrenching labor,
grinding their grain—now let them eat their last!"

  A lucky omen, linked with Zeus's thunder.
135 Odysseus' heart leapt up, the man convinced
he'd grind the scoundrels' lives out in revenge.
                                    By now
the other maids were gathering in Odysseus' royal palace,
raking up on the hearth the fire still going strong.
Telemachus climbed from bed and dressed at once,
140 brisk as a young god—
over his shoulder he slung his well-honed sword,
he fastened rawhide sandals under his smooth feet,
he seized his tough spear tipped with a bronze point
and took his stand at the threshold, calling Eurycleia:
145 "Dear nurse, how did you treat the stranger in our house?
With bed and board? Or leave him to lie untended?
That would be mother's way—sensible as she is—
all impulse, doting over some worthless stranger,
turning a good man out to face the worst."

150   "Please, child," his calm old nurse replied,
"don't blame *her*—your mother's blameless this time.
He sat and drank his wine till he'd had his fill.
Food? He'd lost his hunger. But she asked him.
And when it was time to think of turning in,
155 she told the maids to spread a decent bed, but he—
so down-and-out, poor soul, so dogged by fate—
said no to snuggling into a bed, between covers.
No sir, the man lay down in the entrance-hall,
on the raw hide of an ox and sheep's fleece,
160 and we threw a blanket over him, so we did."
                                    Hearing that,
Telemachus strode out through the palace, spear in hand,
and a pair of sleek hounds went trotting at his heels.
He made for the meeting grounds to join the island lords

while Eurycleia the daughter of Ops, Pisenor's son,
165   that best of women, gave the maids their orders:
"Quick now, look alive, sweep out the house,
wet down the floors!
                            You, those purple coverlets,
fling them over the fancy chairs!
                                              All those tables,
sponge them down—scour the winebowls, burnished cups!
170   The rest—now off you go to the spring and fetch some water,
fast as your legs can run!
Our young gallants won't be long from the palace,
they'll be bright and early—today's a public feast."

They hung on her words and ran to do her bidding.
175   Full twenty scurried off to the spring's dark water,
others bent to the housework, all good hands.
Then in they trooped, the strutting serving-men,
who split the firewood cleanly now as the women
bustled in from the spring, the swineherd at their heels,
180   driving three fat porkers, the best of all his herds.
And leaving them to root in the broad courtyard,
up he went to Odysseus, hailed him warmly:
"Friend, do the suitors show you more respect
or treat you like the dregs of the earth as always?"

185   "Good Eumaeus," the crafty man replied,
"if only the gods would pay back their outrage!
Wild and reckless young cubs, conniving here
in another's house. They've got no sense of shame."

And now as the two confided in each other,
190   the goatherd Melanthius sauntered toward them,
herding his goats with a pair of drovers' help,
the pick of his flocks to make the suitors' meal.
Under the echoing porch he tethered these, then turned
on Odysseus once again with cutting insults: "Still alive?
195   Still hounding your betters, begging round the house?
Why don't you cart yourself away? Get out!
We'll never part, I swear,
till we taste each other's fists. Riffraff,
you and your begging make us sick! Get out—
200   we're hardly the only banquet on the island."

No reply. The wily one just shook his head,
silent, his mind churning with thoughts of bloody work . . .

Third to arrive was Philoetius, that good cowherd,
prodding in for the crowd a heifer and fat goats.
205   Boatmen had brought them over from the mainland,
crews who ferry across all travelers too,
whoever comes for passage.

Under the echoing porch he tethered all heads well
and then approached the swineherd, full of questions:
210 "Who's this stranger, Eumaeus, just come to the house?
What roots does the man claim—who are his people?
Where are his blood kin? his father's fields?
Poor beggar. But what a build—a royal king's!
Ah, once the gods weave trouble into our lives
215 they drive us across the earth, they drown us all in pain,
even kings of the realm."
                                        And with that thought
he walked up to Odysseus, gave him his right hand
and winged a greeting: "Cheers, old friend, old father,
here's to your luck, great days from this day on—
220 saddled now as you are with so much trouble.
Father Zeus, no god's more deadly than you!
No mercy for men, you give them life yourself
then plunge them into misery, brutal hardship.
I broke into sweat, my friend, when I first saw you—
225 see, my eyes still brim with tears, remembering *him,*
Odysseus . . . He must wear such rags, I know it,
knocking about, drifting through the world
if he's still alive and sees the light of day.
If he's dead already, lost in the House of Death,
230 my heart aches for Odysseus, my great lord and master.
He set me in charge of his herds, in Cephallenian country,
when I was just a youngster. How they've grown by now,
past counting! No mortal on earth could breed
a finer stock of oxen—broad in the brow,
235 they thrive like ears of corn. But just look,
these interlopers tell me to drive them in
for their own private feasts. Not a thought
for the young prince in the house, they never flinch—
no regard for the gods' wrath—in their mad rush
240 to carve up his goods, my master gone so long!
I'm tossed from horn to horn in my own mind . . .
What a traitor I'd be, with the prince still alive,
if I'd run off to some other country, herds and all,
to a new set of strangers. Ah, but isn't it worse
245 to hold out here, tending the herds for upstarts,
not their owners—suffering all the pains of hell?
I could have fled, ages ago, to some great king
who'd give me shelter. It's unbearable here.
True, but I still dream of my old master,
250 unlucky man—if only *he*'d drop in from the blue
and drive these suitors all in a rout throughout the halls!"

    "Cowherd," the cool tactician Odysseus answered,
"you're no coward, and nobody's fool, I'd say.
Even I can see there's sense in that old head.

255 So I tell you this on my solemn, binding oath:
     I swear by Zeus, the first of all the gods—
     by the table of hospitality waiting for us,
     by Odysseus' hearth where I have come for help,
     Odysseus will come home while you're still here.
260 You'll see with your own eyes, if you have the heart,
     these suitors who lord it here cut down in blood."

        "Stranger, if only," the cowherd cried aloud,
     "if only Zeus would make that oath come true—
     you'd see my power, my fighting arms in action!"

265 Eumaeus echoed his prayer to all the gods
     that their wise king would soon come home again.

        Now as they spoke and urged each other on,
     and once more the suitors were plotting certain doom
     for the young prince—suddenly, banking high on the left
270 an omen flew past, an eagle clutching a trembling dove.
     And Amphinomus rose in haste to warn them all,
     "My friends, we'll never carry off this plot
     to kill the prince. Let's concentrate on feasting."

        His timely invitation pleased them all.
275 The suitors ambled into Odysseus' royal house
     and flinging down their cloaks on a chair or bench,
     they butchered hulking sheep and fatted goats,
     full-grown hogs and a young cow from the herd.
     They roasted all the innards, served them round
280 and filled the bowls with wine and mixed it well.
     Eumaeus passed out cups; Philoetius, trusty herdsman,
     brought on loaves of bread in ample wicker trays;
     Melanthius poured the wine. The whole company
     reached out for the good things that lay at hand.

285   Telemachus, maneuvering shrewdly, sat his father down
     on the stone threshold, just inside the timbered hall,
     and set a rickety stool and cramped table there.
     He gave him a share of innards, poured his wine
     in a golden cup and added a bracing invitation:
290 "Now sit right there. Drink your wine with the crowd.
     I'll defend you from all their taunts and blows,
     these young bucks. This is no public place,
     this is *Odysseus'* house—
     my father won it for me, so it's mine.
295 You suitors, control yourselves. No insults now,
     no brawling, no, or it's war between us all."

        So he declared. And they all bit their lips,
     amazed the prince could speak with so much daring.
     Only Eupithes' son Antinous ventured,
300 "Fighting words, but do let's knuckle under—

to our *prince*. Such abuse, such naked threats!
But clearly Zeus has foiled us. Or long before
we would have shut his mouth for him in the halls,
fluent and flowing as he is."

                                        So he mocked.
305   Telemachus paid no heed.

                            And now through the streets
the heralds passed, leading the beasts marked out
for sacrifice on Apollo's grand festal day,
and the islanders with their long hair were filing
into the god's shady grove—the distant deadly Archer.

310   Those in the palace, once they'd roasted the prime cuts,
pulled them off the spits and, sharing out the portions,
fell to the royal feast . . .
The men who served them gave Odysseus his share,
as fair as the helping they received themselves.
315   So Telemachus ordered, the king's own son.

        But Athena had no mind to let the brazen suitors
hold back now from their heart-rending insults—
she meant to make the anguish cut still deeper
into the core of Laertes' son Odysseus.
320   There was one among them, a lawless boor—
Ctesippus was his name, he made his home in Same,
a fellow so impressed with his own astounding wealth
he courted the wife of Odysseus, gone for years.
Now the man harangued his swaggering comrades:
325   "Listen to me, my fine friends, here's what I say!
From the start our guest has had his fair share—
it's only right, you know.
How impolite it would be, how wrong to scant
whatever guest Telemachus welcomes to his house.
330   Look here, I'll give him a proper guest-gift too,
a prize he can hand the crone who bathes his feet
or a tip for another slave who haunts the halls
of our great king Odysseus!"

                                On that note,
grabbing an oxhoof out of a basket where it lay,
335   with a brawny hand he flung it straight at the king—
but Odysseus ducked his head a little, dodging the blow,
and seething just as the oxhoof hit the solid wall
he clenched his teeth in a wry sardonic grin.
Telemachus dressed Ctesippus down at once:
340   "Ctesippus, you can thank your lucky stars
you missed our guest—he ducked your blow, by god!
Else I would have planted my sharp spear in your bowels—
your father would have been busy with your funeral,
not your wedding here. Enough.
345   Don't let me see more offenses in my house,

not from anyone! I'm alive to it all, now,
the good and the bad—the boy you knew is gone.
But I still must bear with this, this lovely sight . . .
sheepflocks butchered, wine swilled, food squandered—
how can a man fight off so many single-handed?
But no more of your crimes against me, please!
Unless you're bent on cutting me down, now,
and I'd rather die, yes, better that by far
than have to look on at your outrage day by day:
guests treated to blows, men dragging the serving-women
through our noble house, exploiting them all, no shame!"

    Dead quiet. The suitors all fell silent, hushed.
At last Damastor's son Agelaus rose and said,
"Fair enough, my friends; when a man speaks well
we have no grounds for wrangling, no cause for abuse.
Hands off this stranger! Or any other servant
in King Odysseus' palace. But now a word
of friendly advice for Telemachus and his mother—
here's hoping it proves congenial to them both.
So long as your hearts still kept a spark alive
that Odysseus would return—that great, deep man—
who could blame you, playing the waiting game at home
and holding off the suitors? The better course, it's true.
What if Odysseus had returned, had made it home at last?
But now it's clear as day—the man will come no more.
So go, Telemachus, sit with your mother, coax her
to wed the best man here, the one who offers most,
so you can have and hold your father's estate,
eating and drinking here, your mind at peace
while mother plays the wife in another's house."

    The young prince, keeping his poise, replied,
"I swear by Zeus, Agelaus, by all my father suffered—
dead, no doubt, or wandering far from Ithaca these days—
I don't delay my mother's marriage, not a moment,
I press her to wed the man who takes her heart.
I'll shower her myself with boundless gifts.
But I shrink from driving mother from our house,
issuing harsh commands against her will.
God forbid it ever comes to that!"
                                    So he vowed
and Athena set off uncontrollable laughter in the suitors,
crazed them out of their minds—mad, hysterical laughter
seemed to break from the jaws of strangers, not their own,
and the meat they were eating oozed red with blood—
tears flooded their eyes, hearts possessed by grief.
The inspired seer Theoclymenus wailed out in their midst,
"Poor men, what terror is this that overwhelms you so?
Night shrouds your heads, your faces, down to your knees—

cries of mourning are bursting into fire—cheeks rivering tears—
the walls and the handsome crossbeams dripping dank with blood!
395   Ghosts, look, thronging the entrance, thronging the court,
go trooping down to the world of death and darkness!
The sun is blotted out of the sky—look there—
a lethal mist spreads all across the earth!"

                                 At that
they all broke into peals of laughter aimed at the seer—
400   Polybus' son Eurymachus braying first and foremost,
"Our guest just in from abroad, the man is raving!
Quick, my boys, hustle him out of the house,
into the meeting grounds, the light of day—
everything *here* he thinks is dark as night!"

405   "Eurymachus," the inspired prophet countered,
"when I want your escort, I'll ask for it myself.
I have eyes and ears, and both my feet, still,
and a head that's fairly sound,
nothing to be ashamed of. These will do
410   to take me past those doors . . .
                         Oh I can see it now—
the disaster closing on you all! There's no escaping it,
no way out—not for a single one of you suitors,
wild reckless fools, plotting outrage here,
the halls of Odysseus, great and strong as a god!"

415   With that he marched out of the sturdy house
and went home to Piraeus, the host who warmed him in.
Now all the suitors, trading their snide glances, started
heckling Telemachus, made a mockery of his guests.
One or another brash young gallant scoffed,
420   "Telemachus, no one's more unlucky with his guests!"

   "Look what your man dragged in—this mangy tramp
scraping for bread and wine!"
                      "Not fit for good hard work,
the bag of bones—"
                  "A useless dead weight on the land!"

   "And then this charlatan up and apes the prophet."

425   "Take it from me—you'll be better off by far—
toss your friends in a slave-ship—"
                     "Pack them off
to Sicily, fast—they'll fetch you one sweet price!"

   So they jeered, but the prince paid no attention . . .
silent, eyes riveted on his father, always waiting
430   the moment he'd lay hands on that outrageous mob.

   And all the while Icarius' daughter, wise Penelope,
had placed her carved chair within earshot, at the door,

so she could catch each word they uttered in the hall.
Laughing rowdily, men prepared their noonday meal,
435 succulent, rich—they'd butchered quite a herd.
But as for supper, what could be less enticing
than what a goddess and a powerful man
would spread before them soon? A groaning feast—
for they'd been first to plot their vicious crimes.

BOOK 21. ODYSSEUS STRINGS HIS BOW

The time had come. The goddess Athena with her blazing eyes
inspired Penelope, Icarius' daughter, wary, poised,
to set the bow and the gleaming iron axes out
before her suitors waiting in Odysseus' hall—
5 to test their skill and bring their slaughter on.
Up the steep stairs to her room she climbed
and grasped in a steady hand the curved key—
fine bronze, with ivory haft attached—
and then with her chamber-women made her way
10 to a hidden storeroom, far in the palace depths,
and there they lay, the royal master's treasures:
bronze, gold and a wealth of hard wrought iron
and there it lay as well . . . his backsprung bow
with its quiver bristling arrows, shafts of pain.
15 Gifts from the old days, from a friend he'd met
in Lacedaemon—Iphitus, Eurytus' gallant son.
Once in Messene the two struck up together,
in sly Ortilochus' house, that time Odysseus
went to collect a debt the whole realm owed him,
20 for Messenian raiders had lifted flocks from Ithaca,
three hundred head in their oarswept ships, the herdsmen too.
So his father and island elders sent Odysseus off,
a young boy on a mission,
a distant embassy made to right that wrong.
25 Iphitus went there hunting the stock that *he* had lost,
a dozen mares still nursing their hardy suckling mules.
The same mares that would prove his certain death
when he reached the son of Zeus, that iron heart,
Heracles—the past master of monstrous works—
30 who killed the man, a guest in his own house.
Brutal. Not a care for the wrathful eyes of god
or rites of hospitality he had spread before him,
no, he dined him, then he murdered him, commandeered
those hard-hoofed mares for the hero's own grange.
35 Still on the trail of these when he met Odysseus,
Iphitus gave him the bow his father, mighty Eurytus,
used to wield as a young man, but when he died
in his lofty house he left it to his son.
In turn, Odysseus gave his friend a sharp sword

40   and a rugged spear to mark the start of friendship,
       treasured ties that bind. But before they got to know
       the warmth of each other's board, the son of Zeus
       had murdered Iphitus, Eurytus' magnificent son
       who gave the prince the bow.
                            That great weapon—
45   King Odysseus never took it abroad with him
       when he sailed off to war in his long black ships.
       He kept it stored away in his stately house,
       guarding the memory of a cherished friend,
       and only took that bow on hunts at home.
                                 Now,
50   the lustrous queen soon reached the hidden vault
       and stopped at the oaken doorsill, work an expert
       sanded smooth and trued to the line some years ago,
       planting the doorjambs snugly, hanging shining doors.
       At once she loosed the thong from around its hook,
55   inserted the key and aiming straight and true,
       shot back the bolts—and the rasping doors groaned
       as loud as a bull will bellow, champing grass at pasture.
       So as the key went home those handsome double doors
       rang out now and sprang wide before her.
60   She stepped onto a plank where chests stood tall,
       brimming with clothing scented sweet with cedar.
       Reaching, tiptoe, lifting the bow down off its peg,
       still secure in the burnished case that held it,
       down she sank, laying the case across her knees,
65   and dissolved in tears with a high thin wail
       as she drew her husband's weapon from its sheath . . . .
       Then, having wept and sobbed to her heart's content,
       off she went to the hall to meet her proud admirers,
       cradling her husband's backsprung bow in her arms,
70   its quiver bristling arrows, shafts of pain.
       Her women followed, bringing a chest that held
       the bronze and the iron axes, trophies won by the master.
       That radiant woman, once she reached her suitors,
       drawing her glistening veil across her cheeks,
75   paused now where a column propped the sturdy roof,
       with one of her loyal handmaids stationed either side,
       and delivered an ultimatum to her suitors:
       "Listen to me, my overbearing friends!
       You who plague this palace night and day,
80   drinking, eating us out of house and home
       with the lord and master absent, gone so long—
       the only excuse that you can offer is your zest
       to win me as your bride. So, to arms, my gallants!
       Here is the prize at issue, right before you, look—
85   I set before you the great bow of King Odysseus now!
       The hand that can string this bow with greatest ease,

that shoots an arrow clean through all twelve axes—
he is the man I follow, yes, forsaking this house
where I was once a bride, this gracious house
90   so filled with the best that life can offer—
I shall always remember it, that I know . . .
even in my dreams."
                              She turned to Eumaeus,
ordered the good swineherd now to set the bow
and the gleaming iron axes out before the suitors.
95   He broke into tears as he received them, laid them down.
The cowherd wept too, when he saw his master's bow.
But Antinous wheeled on both and let them have it:
"Yokels, fools—you can't tell night from day!
You mawkish idiots, why are you sniveling here?
100   You're stirring up your mistress! Isn't she drowned
in grief already? She's lost her darling husband.
Sit down. Eat in peace, or take your snuffling
out of doors! But leave that bow right here—
our crucial test that makes or breaks us all.
105   No easy game, I wager, to string *his* polished bow.
Not a soul in the crowd can match Odysseus—
what a man he was . . .
I saw him once, remember him to this day,
though I was young and foolish way back then."
                                          Smooth talk,
110   but deep in the suitor's heart his hopes were bent
on stringing the bow and shooting through the axes.
Antinous—fated to be the first man to taste
an arrow whipped from great Odysseus' hands,
the king he mocked, at ease in the king's house,
115   egging comrades on to mock him too.
                                    "Amazing!"
Prince Telemachus waded in with a laugh:
"Zeus up there has robbed me of my wits.
My own dear mother, sensible as she is,
says she'll marry again, forsake our house,
120   and look at *me*—laughing for all I'm worth,
giggling like some fool. Step up, my friends!
Here is the prize at issue, right before you, look—
a woman who has no equal now in all Achaean country,
neither in holy Pylos, nor in Argos or Mycenae,
125   not even Ithaca itself or the loamy mainland.
You know it well. Why sing my mother's praises?
Come, let the games begin! No dodges, no delays,
no turning back from the stringing of the bow—
we'll see who wins, we will.
130   I'd even take a crack at the bow myself . . .
If I string it and shoot through all the axes,
I'd worry less if my noble mother left our house

with another man and left me here behind—man enough
at last to win my father's splendid prizes!"

                                        With that
135 he leapt to his feet and dropped his bright-red cloak,
slipping the sword and sword-belt off his shoulders.
First he planted the axes, digging a long trench,
one for all, and trued them all to a line
then tamped the earth to bed them. Wonder took
140 the revelers looking on: his work so firm, precise,
though he'd never seen the axes ranged before.
He stood at the threshold, poised to try the bow . . .
Three times he made it shudder, straining to bend it,
three times his power flagged—but his hopes ran high
145 he'd string his father's bow and shoot through every iron
and now, struggling with all his might for the fourth time,
he would have strung the bow, but Odysseus shook his head
and stopped him short despite his tensing zeal.
"God help me," the inspired prince cried out,
150 "must I be a weakling, a failure all my life?
Unless I'm just too young to trust my hands
to fight off any man who rises up against me.
Come, my betters, so much stronger than I am—
try the bow and finish off the contest."

155   He propped his father's weapon on the ground,
tilting it up against the polished well-hung doors
and resting a shaft aslant the bow's fine horn,
then back he went to the seat that he had left.
"Up, friends!" Antinous called, taking over.
160 "One man after another, left to right,
starting from where the steward pours the wine."

       So Antinous urged and all agreed.
The first man up was Leodes, Oenops' son,
a seer who could see their futures in the smoke,
165 who always sat by the glowing winebowl, well back,
the one man in the group who loathed their reckless ways,
appalled by all their outrage. His turn first . . .
Picking up the weapon now and the swift arrow,
he stood at the threshold, poised to try the bow
170 but failed to bend it. As soon as he tugged the string
his hands went slack, his soft, uncallused hands,
and he called back to the suitors, "Friends,
I can't bend it. Take it, someone—try.
Here is a bow to rob our best of life and breath,
175 all our best contenders! Still, better be dead
than live on here, never winning the prize
that tempts us all—forever in pursuit,
burning with expectation every day.
If there's still a suitor here who hopes,

180   who aches to marry Penelope, Odysseus' wife,
       just let him try the bow; he'll see the truth!
       He'll soon lay siege to another Argive woman
       trailing her long robes, and shower her with gifts—
       and then our queen can marry the one who offers most,
185   the man marked out by fate to be her husband."

       With those words he thrust the bow aside,
       tilting it up against the polished well-hung doors
       and resting a shaft aslant the bow's fine horn,
       then back he went to the seat that he had left.
190   But Antinous turned on the seer, abuses flying:
       "Leodes! what are you saying? what's got past your lips?
       What awful, grisly nonsense—it shocks me to hear it—
       'here is a bow to rob our best of life and breath!'
       Just because *you* can't string it, you're so weak?
195   Clearly your genteel mother never bred her boy
       for the work of bending bows and shooting arrows.
       We have champions in our ranks to string it quickly.
       Hop to it, Melanthius!"—he barked at the goatherd—
       "Rake the fire in the hall, pull up a big stool,
200   heap it with fleece and fetch that hefty ball
       of lard from the stores inside. So we young lords
       can heat and limber the bow and rub it down with grease
       before we try again and finish off the contest!"

       The goatherd bustled about to rake the fire
205   still going strong. He pulled up a big stool,
       heaped it with fleece and fetched the hefty ball
       of lard from the stores inside. And the young men
       limbered the bow, rubbing it down with hot grease,
       then struggled to bend it back but failed. No use—
210   they fell far short of the strength the bow required.
       Antinous still held off, dashing Eurymachus too,
       the ringleaders of all the suitors,
       head and shoulders the strongest of the lot.
                                                    But now
       the king's two men, the cowherd and the swineherd,
215   had slipped out of the palace side-by-side
       and great Odysseus left the house to join them.
       Once they were past the courtyard and the gates
       he probed them deftly, surely: "Cowherd, swineherd,
       what, shall I blurt this out or keep it to myself?
220   No, speak out. The heart inside me says so.
       How far would you go to fight beside Odysseus?
       Say he dropped like *that* from a clear blue sky
       and a god brought him back—
       would you fight for the suitors or your king?
225   Tell me how you feel inside your hearts."

"Father Zeus," the trusty cowherd shouted,
"bring my prayer to pass! Let the master come—
some god guide him now! You'd see my power,
my fighting arms in action!"

230 Eumaeus echoed his prayer to all the gods
that their wise king would soon come home again.
Certain at least these two were loyal to the death,
Odysseus reassured them quickly: "I'm right here,
here in the flesh—myself—and home at last,
235 after bearing twenty years of brutal hardship.
Now I know that of all my men you two alone
longed for my return. From the rest I've heard
not one real prayer that I come back again.
So now I'll tell you what's in store for *you.*
240 If a god beats down the lofty suitors at my hands,
I'll find you wives, both of you, grant you property,
sturdy houses beside my own, and in my eyes you'll be
comrades to Prince Telemachus, brothers from then on.
Come, I'll show you something—living proof—
245 know me for certain, put your minds at rest.
        This scar,
look, where a boar's white tusk gored me, years ago,
hunting on Parnassus, Autolycus' sons and I."
           With that,
pushing back his rags, he revealed the great scar . . .
And the men gazed at it, scanned it, knew it well,
250 broke into tears and threw their arms around their master—
lost in affection, kissing his head and shoulders,
and so Odysseus kissed their heads and hands.
Now the sun would have set upon their tears
if Odysseus had not called a halt himself.
255 "No more weeping. Coming out of the house
a man might see us, tell the men inside.
Let's slip back in—singly, not in a pack.
I'll go first. You're next. Here's our signal.
When all the rest in there, our lordly friends,
260 are dead against my having the bow and quiver,
good Eumaeus, carry the weapon down the hall
and put it in my hands. Then tell the serving-women
to lock the snugly fitted doors to their own rooms.
If anyone hears from there the jolting blows
265 and groans of men, caught in our huge net,
not one of them show her face—
sit tight, keep to her weaving, not a sound.
You, my good Philoetius, here are your orders.
Shoot the bolt of the courtyard's outer gate,
270 lock it, lash it fast."
       With that command
the master entered his well-constructed house

and back he went to the stool that he had left.
The king's two men, in turn, slipped in as well.

275 Just now Eurymachus held the bow in his hands,
turning it over, tip to tip, before the blazing fire
to heat the weapon. But he failed to bend it even so
and the suitor's high heart groaned to bursting.
"A black day," he exclaimed in wounded pride,
"a blow to myself, a blow to each man here!
280 It's less the marriage that mortifies me now—
that's galling too, but lots of women are left,
some in seagirt Ithaca, some in other cities.
What breaks my heart is the fact we fall so short
of great Odysseus' strength we cannot string his bow.
285 A disgrace to ring in the ears of men to come."

"Eurymachus," Eupithes' son Antinous countered,
"it will never come to that, as you well know.
Today is a feast-day up and down the island
in honor of the Archer God. Who flexes bows today?
290 Set it aside. Rest easy now. And all the axes,
let's just leave them planted where they are.
Trust me, no one's about to crash the gates
of Laertes' son and carry off these trophies.
Steward, pour some drops for the god in every cup,
295 we'll tip the wine, then put the bow to bed.
And first thing in the morning have Melanthius
bring the pick of his goats from all his herds
so we can burn the thighs to Apollo, god of archers—
then try the bow and finish off the contest."

300 Welcome advice. And again they all agreed.
Heralds sprinkled water over their hands for rinsing,
the young men brimmed the mixing bowls with wine,
they tipped first drops for the god in every cup,
then poured full rounds for all. And now, once
305 they'd tipped libations out and drunk their fill,
the king of craft, Odysseus, said with all his cunning,
"Listen to me, you lords who court the noble queen.
I have to say what the heart inside me urges.
I appeal especially to Eurymachus, and you,
310 brilliant Antinous, who spoke so shrewdly now.
Give the bow a rest for today, leave it to the gods—
at dawn the Archer God will grant a victory
to the man he favors most.
                                For the moment,
give me the polished bow now, won't you? So,
315 to amuse you all, I can try my hand, my strength . . .
is the old force still alive inside these gnarled limbs?
Or has a life of roaming, years of rough neglect,
destroyed it long ago?"

                              Modest words
            that sent them all into hot, indignant rage,
320   fearing he just might string the polished bow.
            So Antinous rounded on him, dressed him down:
            "Not a shred of sense in your head, you filthy drifter!
            Not content to feast at your ease with us, the island's pride?
            Never denied your full share of the banquet, never,
325   you can listen in on our secrets. No one else
            can eavesdrop on our talk, no tramp, no beggar.
            The wine has overpowered you, heady wine—
            the ruin of many another man, whoever
            gulps it down and drinks beyond his limit.
330   Wine—it drove the Centaur,[1] famous Eurytion,
            mad in the halls of lionhearted Pirithous.
            There to visit the Lapiths, crazed with wine
            the headlong Centaur bent to his ugly work
            in the prince's own house! His hosts sprang up,
335   seized with fury, dragged him across the forecourt,
            flung him out of doors, hacking his nose and ears off
            with their knives, no mercy. The creature reeled away,
            still blind with drink, his heart like a wild storm,
            loaded with all the frenzy in his mind!
                                                  And so
340   the feud between mortal men and Centaurs had its start.
            But the drunk was first to bring disaster on himself
            by drowning in his cups. You too, I promise you
            no end of trouble if you should string that bow.
            You'll meet no kindness in our part of the world—
345   we'll sail you off in a black ship to Echetus,
            the mainland king who wrecks all men alive.
            Nothing can save you from his royal grip!
            So drink, but hold your peace,
            don't take on the younger, stronger men."

350   "Antinous," watchful Penelope stepped in,
            "how impolite it would be, how wrong, to scant
            whatever guest Telemachus welcomes to his house.
            You really think—if the stranger trusts so to his hands
            and strength that he strings Odysseus' great bow—
355   he'll take me home and claim me as his bride?
            He never dreamed of such a thing, I'm sure.
            Don't let that ruin the feast for any reveler here.
            Unthinkable—nothing, nothing could be worse."

               Polybus' son Eurymachus had an answer:
360   "Wise Penelope, daughter of Icarius, do we really
            expect the man to wed you? Unthinkable, I know.
            But we do recoil at the talk of men and women.

---

1. Half-man, half-horse.

One of the island's meaner sort will mutter,
'Look at the riffraff courting a king's wife.
365   Weaklings, look, they can't even string his bow.
But along came this beggar, drifting out of the blue—
strung his bow with ease and shot through all the axes!'
Gossip will fly. We'll hang our heads in shame."

        "Shame?" alert Penelope protested—
370   "How can you hope for any public fame at all?
You who disgrace, devour a great man's house and home!
Why hang your heads in shame over next to nothing?
Our friend here is a strapping, well-built man
and claims to be the son of a noble father.
375   Come, hand him the bow now, let's just see . . .
I tell you this—and I'll make good my word—
if he strings the bow and Apollo grants him glory,
I'll dress him in shirt and cloak, in handsome clothes,
I'll give him a good sharp lance to fight off men and dogs,
380   give him a two-edged sword and sandals for his feet
and send him off, wherever his heart desires."

                                        "Mother,"
poised Telemachus broke in now, "my father's bow—
no Achaean on earth has more right than I
to give it or withhold it, as I please.
385   Of all the lords in Ithaca's rocky heights
or the islands facing Elis grazed by horses,
not a single one will force or thwart my will,
even if I decide to give our guest this bow—
a gift outright—to carry off himself.

                                        So, mother,
390   go back to your quarters. Tend to your own tasks,
the distaff and the loom, and keep the women
working hard as well. As for the bow now,
men will see to that, but I most of all:
I hold the reins of power in this house."

                                        Astonished,
395   she withdrew to her own room. She took to heart
the clear good sense in what her son had said.
Climbing up to the lofty chamber with her women,
she fell to weeping for Odysseus, her beloved husband,
till watchful Athena sealed her eyes with welcome sleep.

400   And now the loyal swineherd had lifted up the bow,
was taking it toward the king, when all the suitors
burst out in an ugly uproar through the palace—
brash young bullies, this or that one heckling,
"Where on earth are you going with that bow?"

405   "You, you grubby swineherd, are you crazy?"

"The speedy dogs you reared will eat your corpse—"

"Out there with your pigs, out in the cold, alone!"

"If only Apollo and all the gods shine down on us!"

Eumaeus froze in his tracks, put down the bow,
410   panicked by every outcry in the hall.
Telemachus shouted too, from the other side,
and full of threats: "Carry on with the bow, old boy!
If you serve too many masters, you'll soon suffer.
Look sharp, or I'll pelt you back to your farm
415   with flying rocks. I may be younger than you
but I'm much stronger. If only I had that edge
in fists and brawn over all this courting crowd,
I'd soon dispatch them—licking their wounds at last—
clear of our palace where they plot their vicious plots!"

420   His outburst sent them all into gales of laughter,
blithe and oblivious, that dissolved their pique
against the prince. The swineherd took the bow,
carried it down the hall to his ready, waiting king
and standing by him, placed it in his hands,
425   then he called the nurse aside and whispered,
"Good Eurycleia—Telemachus commands you now
to lock the snugly fitted doors to your own rooms.
If anyone hears from there the jolting blows
and groans of men, caught in our huge net,
430   not one of you show your face—
sit tight, keep to your weaving, not a sound."

That silenced the old nurse—
she barred the doors that led from the long hall.
The cowherd quietly bounded out of the house
435   to lock the gates of the high-stockaded court.
Under the portico lay a cable, ship's tough gear:
he lashed the gates with this, then slipped back in
and ran and sat on the stool that he'd just left,
eyes riveted on Odysseus.
                Now *he* held the bow
440   in his own hands, turning it over, tip to tip,
testing it, this way, that way . . . fearing worms
had bored through the weapon's horn with the master gone abroad.
A suitor would glance at his neighbor, jeering, taunting,
"Look at our connoisseur of bows!"
                         "Sly old fox—
445   maybe he's got bows like it, stored in *his* house."

"That or he's bent on making one himself."

"Look how he twists and turns it in his hands!"

"The clever tramp means trouble—"

"I wish him luck," some cocksure lord chimed in,

450   "as good as his luck in bending back that weapon!"

         So they mocked, but Odysseus, mastermind in action,
         once he'd handled the great bow and scanned every inch,
         then, like an expert singer skilled at lyre and song—
         who strains a string to a new peg with ease,
455   making the pliant sheep-gut fast at either end—
         so with his virtuoso ease Odysseus strung his mighty bow.
         Quickly his right hand plucked the string to test its pitch
         and under his touch it sang out clear and sharp as a swallow's cry.
         Horror swept through the suitors, faces blanching white,
460   and Zeus cracked the sky with a bolt, his blazing sign,
         and the great man who had borne so much rejoiced at last
         that the son of cunning Cronus flung that omen down for *him*.
         He snatched a winged arrow lying bare on the board—
         the rest still bristled deep inside the quiver,
465   soon to be tasted by all the feasters there.
         Setting shaft on the handgrip, drawing the notch
         and bowstring back, back . . . right from his stool,
         just as he sat but aiming straight and true, he let fly—
         and never missing an ax from the first ax-handle
470   clean on through to the last and out
         the shaft with its weighted brazen head shot free!
                                                           "Telemachus,"
         Odysseus looked to his son and said, "your guest,
         sitting here in your house, has not disgraced you.
         No missing the mark, look, and no long labor spent
475   to string the bow. My strength's not broken yet,
         not quite so frail as the mocking suitors thought.
         But the hour has come to serve our masters right—
         supper in broad daylight—then to other revels,
         song and dancing, all that crowns a feast."

480   He paused with a warning nod, and at that sign
         Prince Telemachus, son of King Odysseus,
         girding his sharp sword on, clamping hand to spear,
         took his stand by a chair that flanked his father—
         his bronze spearpoint glinting now like fire . . . .

BOOK 22. SLAUGHTER IN THE HALL

Now stripping back his rags Odysseus master of craft and battle
vaulted onto the great threshold, gripping his bow and quiver
bristling arrows, and poured his flashing shafts before him,
loose at his feet, and thundered out to all the suitors:
5   "Look—your crucial test is finished, now, at last!
But another target's left that no one's hit before—
we'll see if *I* can hit it—Apollo give me glory!"

With that he trained a stabbing arrow on Antinous . . .
just lifting a gorgeous golden loving-cup in his hands,
10   just tilting the two-handled goblet back to his lips,
about to drain the wine—and slaughter the last thing
on the suitor's mind: who could dream that one foe
in that crowd of feasters, however great his power,
would bring down death on himself, and black doom?
15   But Odysseus aimed and shot Antinous square in the throat
and the point went stabbing clean through the soft neck and out—
and off to the side he pitched, the cup dropped from his grasp
as the shaft sank home, and the man's life-blood came spurting
from his nostrils—
                thick red jets—
                                a sudden thrust of his foot—
20   he kicked away the table—
                            food showered across the floor,
the bread and meats soaked in a swirl of bloody filth.
The suitors burst into uproar all throughout the house
when they saw their leader down. They leapt from their seats,
milling about, desperate, scanning the stone walls—
25   not a shield in sight, no rugged spear to seize.
They wheeled on Odysseus, lashing out in fury:
"Stranger, shooting at men will cost your life!"

    "Your game is over—you, you've shot your last!"

    "You'll never escape your own headlong death!"

30   "You killed the best in Ithaca—our fine prince!"

    "Vultures will eat your corpse!"
                              Groping, frantic—
each one persuading himself the guest had killed
the man by chance. Poor fools, blind to the fact
that all their necks were in the noose, their doom sealed.
35   With a dark look, the wily fighter Odysseus shouted back,
"You dogs! you never imagined I'd return from Troy—
so cocksure that you bled my house to death,
ravished my serving-women—wooed my wife
behind my back while I was still alive!
40   No fear of the gods who rule the skies up there,
no fear that men's revenge might arrive someday—
now all your necks are in the noose—your doom is sealed!"

    Terror gripped them all, blanched their faces white,
each man glancing wildly—how to escape his instant death?
45   Only Eurymachus had the breath to venture, "If you,
you're truly Odysseus of Ithaca, home at last,
you're right to accuse these men of what they've done—
so much reckless outrage here in your palace,

so much on your lands. But here he lies,
50   quite dead, and he incited it all—Antinous—
look, the man who drove us all to crime!
Not that he needed marriage, craved it so;
he'd bigger game in mind—though Zeus barred his way—
he'd lord it over Ithaca's handsome country, king himself,
55   once he'd lain in wait for your son and cut him down!
But now he's received the death that he deserved.
So spare your own people! Later we'll recoup
your costs with a tax laid down upon the land,
covering all we ate and drank inside your halls,
60   and each of us here will pay full measure too—
twenty oxen in value, bronze and gold we'll give
until we melt your heart. Before we've settled,
who on earth could blame you for your rage?"

       But the battle-master kept on glaring, seething.
65   "No, Eurymachus! Not if you paid me all your father's wealth—
all you possess now, and all that could pour in from the world's end—
no, not even then would I stay my hands from slaughter
till all you suitors had paid for all your crimes!
Now life or death—your choice—fight me or flee
70   if you hope to escape your sudden bloody doom!
I doubt one man in the lot will save his skin!"

       His menace shook their knees, their hearts too
but Eurymachus spoke again, now to the suitors: "Friends!
This man will never restrain his hands, invincible hands—
75   now that he's seized that polished bow and quiver, look,
he'll shoot from the sill until he's killed us all!
So fight—call up the joy of battle! Swords out!
Tables lifted—block his arrows winging death!
Charge him, charge in a pack—
80   try to rout the man from the sill, the doors,
race through town and sound an alarm at once—
our friend would soon see he's shot his bolt!"
                                          Brave talk—
he drew his two-edged sword, bronze, honed for the kill
and hurled himself at the king with a raw savage cry
85   in the same breath that Odysseus loosed an arrow
ripping his breast beside the nipple so hard
it lodged in the man's liver—
out of his grasp the sword dropped to the ground—
over his table, head over heels he tumbled, doubled up,
90   flinging his food and his two-handled cup across the floor—
he smashed the ground with his forehead, writhing in pain,
both feet flailing out, and his high seat tottered—
the mist of death came swirling down his eyes.

Amphinomus rushed the king in all his glory,
95   charging him face-to-face, a slashing sword drawn—
if only he could force him clear of the doorway, now,
but Telemachus—too quick—stabbed the man from behind,
plunging his bronze spear between the suitor's shoulders
and straight on through his chest the point came jutting out—
100   down he went with a thud, his forehead slammed the ground.
Telemachus swerved aside, leaving his long spearshaft
lodged in Amphinomus—fearing some suitor just might
lunge in from behind as he tugged the shaft,
impale him with a sword or hack him down,
105   crouching over the corpse.
He went on the run, reached his father at once
and halting right beside him, let fly, "Father—
now I'll get you a shield and a pair of spears,
a helmet of solid bronze to fit your temples!
110   I'll arm myself on the way back and hand out
arms to the swineherd, arm the cowherd too—
we'd better fight equipped!"
                   "Run, fetch them,"
the wily captain urged, "while I've got arrows left
to defend me—or they'll force me from the doors
115   while I fight on alone!"

    Telemachus moved to his father's orders smartly.
Off he ran to the room where the famous arms lay stored,
took up four shields, eight spears, four bronze helmets
ridged with horsehair crests and, loaded with these,
120   ran back to reach his father's side in no time.
The prince was first to case himself in bronze
and his servants followed suit—both harnessed up
and all three flanked Odysseus, mastermind of war,
and he, as long as he'd arrows left to defend himself,
125   kept picking suitors off in the palace, one by one
and down they went, corpse on corpse in droves.
Then, when the royal archer's shafts ran out,
he leaned his bow on a post of the massive doors—
where walls of the hallway catch the light—and armed:
130   across his shoulder he slung a buckler four plies thick,
over his powerful head he set a well-forged helmet,
the horsehair crest atop it tossing, bristling terror,
and grasped two rugged lances tipped with fiery bronze.

    Now a side-door was fitted into the main wall—
135   right at the edge of the great hall's stone sill—
and led to a passage always shut by good tight boards.
But Odysseus gave the swineherd strict commands
to stand hard by the side-door, guard it well—
the only way the suitors might break out.

140 Agelaus called to his comrades with a plan:
"Friends, can't someone climb through the hatch?—
tell men outside to sound the alarm, be quick—
our guest would soon see he'd shot his last!"

The goatherd Melanthius answered, "Not a chance,
145 my lord—the door to the courtyard's much too near,
dangerous too, the mouth of the passage cramped.
One strong man could block us, one and all!
No, I'll fetch you some armor to harness on,
out of the storeroom—there, nowhere else, I'm sure,
150 the king and his gallant son have stowed their arms!"

With that the goatherd clambered up through smoke-ducts
high on the wall and scurried into Odysseus' storeroom,
bundled a dozen shields, as many spears and helmets
ridged with horsehair crests and, loaded with these,
155 rushed back down to the suitors, quickly issued arms.
Odysseus' knees shook, his heart too, when he saw them
buckling on their armor, brandishing long spears—
here was a battle looming, well he knew.
He turned at once to Telemachus, warnings flying:
160 "A bad break in the fight, my boy! One of the women's
tipped the odds against us—or could it be the goatherd?"

"My fault, father," the cool clear prince replied,
"the blame's all mine. That snug door to the vault,
I left it ajar—they've kept a better watch than I.
165 Go, Eumaeus, shut the door to the storeroom,
check and see if it's one of the women's tricks
or Dolius' son Melanthius. He's our man, I'd say."

And even as they conspired, back the goatherd
climbed to the room to fetch more burnished arms,
170 but Eumaeus spotted him, quickly told his king
who stood close by: "Odysseus, wily captain,
there he goes again, the infernal nuisance—
just as we suspected—back to the storeroom.
Give me a clear command!
175 Do I kill the man—if I can take him down—
or drag him back to you, here, to pay in full
for the vicious work he's plotted in your house?"

Odysseus, master of tactics, answered briskly,
"I and the prince will keep these brazen suitors
180 crammed in the hall, for all their battle-fury.
You two wrench Melanthius' arms and legs behind him,
fling him down in the storeroom—lash his back to a plank
and strap a twisted cable fast to the scoundrel's body,
hoist him up a column until he hits the rafters—
185 let him dangle in agony, still alive,
for a good long time!"

They hung on his orders, keen to do his will.
Off they ran to the storeroom, unseen by him inside—
Melanthius, rummaging after arms, deep in a dark recess
190   as the two men took their stand, either side of the doorposts,
poised till the goatherd tried to cross the doorsill . . .
one hand clutching a crested helmet, the other
an ample old buckler blotched with mildew,
the shield Laertes bore as a young soldier once
195   but there it lay for ages, seams on the handstraps split—
Quick, they rushed him, seized him, haled him back by the hair,
flung him down on the floor, writhing with terror, bound him
hand and foot with a chafing cord, wrenched his limbs
back, back till the joints locked tight—
200   just as Laertes' cunning son commanded—
they strapped a twisted cable round his body,
hoisted him up a column until he hit the rafters,
then you mocked him, Eumaeus, my good swineherd:
"Now stand guard through the whole night, Melanthius—
205   stretched out on a soft bed fit for *you,* your highness!
You're bound to see the Morning rising up from the Ocean,
mounting her golden throne—at just the hour you always
drive in goats to feast the suitors in the hall!"

So they left him, trussed in his agonizing sling;
210   they clapped on armor again, shut the gleaming doors
and ran to rejoin Odysseus, mastermind of war.
And now as the ranks squared off, breathing fury—
four at the sill confronting a larger, stronger force
arrayed inside the hall—now Zeus's daughter Athena,
215   taking the build and voice of Mentor, swept in
and Odysseus, thrilled to see her, cried out,
"Rescue us, Mentor, now it's life or death!
Remember your old comrade—all the service
I offered you! We were boys together!"
So he cried
220   yet knew in his bones it was Athena, Driver of Armies.
But across the hall the suitors brayed against her,
Agelaus first, his outburst full of threats:
"Mentor, never let Odysseus trick you into
siding with *him* to fight against the suitors.
225   Here's our plan of action, and we will see it through!
Once we've killed them both, the father and the son,
we'll kill you too, for all you're bent on doing
here in the halls—you'll pay with your own head!
And once our swords have stopped your violence cold—
230   all your property, all in your house, your fields,
we'll lump it all with Odysseus' rich estate
and never let your sons live on in your halls
or free your wife and daughters to walk through town!"

Naked threats—and Athena hit new heights of rage,
235 she lashed out at Odysseus now with blazing accusations:
"Where's it gone, Odysseus—your power, your fighting heart?
The great soldier who fought for famous white-armed Helen,
battling Trojans nine long years—nonstop, no mercy,
mowing their armies down in grueling battle—
240 you who seized the broad streets of Troy
with your fine strategic stroke! How can you—
now you've returned to your own house, your own wealth—
bewail the loss of your combat strength in a war with *suitors?*
Come, old friend, stand by me! You'll see action now,
245 see how Mentor the son of Alcimus, that brave fighter,
kills your enemies, pays you back for service!"
                                        Rousing words—
but she gave no all-out turning of the tide, not yet,
she kept on testing Odysseus and his gallant son,
putting their force and fighting heart to proof.
250 For all the world like a swallow in their sight
she flew on high to perch
on the great hall's central roofbeam black with smoke.

But the suitors closed ranks, commanded now by Damastor's son
Agelaus, flanked by Eurynomus, Demoptolemus and Amphimedon,
255 Pisander, Polyctor's son, and Polybus ready, waiting—
head and shoulders the best and bravest of the lot
still left to fight for their lives,
now that the pelting shafts had killed the rest.
Agelaus spurred his comrades on with battle-plans:
260 "Friends, at last the man's invincible hands are useless!
Mentor has mouthed some empty boasts and flitted off—
just four are left to fight at the front doors. So now,
no wasting your long spears—all at a single hurl,
just six of us launch out in the first wave!
265 If Zeus is willing, we may hit Odysseus,
carry off the glory! The rest are nothing
once the captain's down!"
                                At his command,
concentrating their shots, all six hurled as one
but Athena sent the whole salvo wide of the mark—
270 one of them hit the jamb of the great hall's doors,
another the massive door itself, and the heavy bronze point
of a third ashen javelin crashed against the wall.
Seeing his men untouched by the suitors' flurry,
steady Odysseus leapt to take command:
275 "Friends! now it's for *us* to hurl at them, I say,
into this ruck of suitors! Topping all their crimes
they're mad to strip the armor off our bodies!"

Taking aim at the ranks, all four let fly as one
and the lances struck home—Odysseus killed Demoptolemus,

280 Telemachus killed Euryades—the swineherd, Elatus—
     and the cowherd cut Pisander down in blood.
     They bit the dust of the broad floor, all as one.
     Back to the great hall's far recess the others shrank
     as the four rushed in and plucked up spears from corpses.

285   And again the suitors hurled their whetted shafts
     but Athena sent the better part of the salvo wide—
     one of them hit the jamb of the great hall's doors,
     another the massive door itself, and the heavy bronze point
     of a third ashen javelin crashed against the wall.
290 True, Amphimedon nicked Telemachus on the wrist—
     the glancing blade just barely broke his skin.
     Ctesippus sent a long spear sailing over
     Eumaeus' buckler, grazing his shoulder blade
     but the weapon skittered off and hit the ground.
295 And again those led by the brilliant battle-master
     hurled their razor spears at the suitors' ranks—
     and now Odysseus raider of cities hit Eurydamas,
     Telemachus hit Amphimedon—Eumaeus, Polybus—
     and the cowherd stabbed Ctesippus
300 right in the man's chest and triumphed over his body:
     "Love your mockery, do you? Son of that blowhard Polytherses!
     No more shooting off your mouth, you idiot, such big talk—
     leave the last word to the gods—they're much stronger!
     Take this spear, this guest-gift, for the cow's hoof
305 you once gave King Odysseus begging in his house!"

         So the master of longhorn cattle had his say—
     as Odysseus, fighting at close quarters, ran Agelaus
     through with a long lance—Telemachus speared Leocritus
     so deep in the groin the bronze came punching out his back
310 and the man crashed headfirst, slamming the ground full-face.
     And now Athena, looming out of the rafters high above them,
     brandished her man-destroying shield of thunder, terrifying
     the suitors out of their minds, and down the hall they panicked—
     wild, like herds stampeding, driven mad as the darting gadfly
315 strikes in the late spring when the long days come round.
     The attackers struck like eagles, crook-clawed, hook-beaked,
     swooping down from a mountain ridge to harry smaller birds
     that skim across the flatland, cringing under the clouds
     but the eagles plunge in fury, rip their lives out—hopeless,
320 never a chance of flight or rescue—and people love the sport—
     so the attackers routed suitors headlong down the hall,
     wheeling into the slaughter, slashing left and right
     and grisly screams broke from skulls cracked open—
     the whole floor awash with blood.
                                      Leodes now—
325 he flung himself at Odysseus, clutched his knees,
     crying out to the king with a sudden, winging prayer:

"I hug your knees, Odysseus—mercy! spare my life!
Never, I swear, did I harass any woman in your house—
never a word, a gesture—nothing, no, I tried
330   to restrain the suitors, whoever did such things.
They wouldn't listen, keep their hands to themselves—
so reckless, so they earn their shameful fate.
But I was just their prophet—
my hands are clean—and I'm to die their death!
335   Look at the thanks I get for years of service!"

    A killing look, and the wry soldier answered,
"Only a priest, a prophet for this mob, you say?
How hard you must have prayed in my own house
that the heady day of my return would never dawn—
340   my dear wife would be yours, would bear your children!
For that there's no escape from grueling death—you die!"

    And snatching up in one powerful hand a sword
left on the ground—Agelaus dropped it when he fell—
Odysseus hacked the prophet square across the neck
345   and the praying head went tumbling in the dust.
                                        Now one was left,
trying still to escape black death. Phemius, Terpis' son,
the bard who always performed among the suitors—
they forced the man to sing . . .
There he stood, backing into the side-door,
350   still clutching his ringing lyre in his hands,
his mind in turmoil, torn—what should he do?
Steal from the hall and crouch at the altar-stone
of Zeus who Guards the Court, where time and again
Odysseus and Laertes burned the long thighs of oxen?
355   Or throw himself on the master's mercy, clasp his knees?
That was the better way—or so it struck him, yes,
grasp the knees of Laertes' royal son. And so,
cradling his hollow lyre, he laid it on the ground
between the mixing-bowl and the silver-studded throne,
360   then rushed up to Odysseus, yes, and clutched his knees,
singing out to his king with a stirring, winged prayer:
"I hug your knees, Odysseus—mercy! spare my life!
What a grief it will be to you for all the years to come
if you kill the singer now, who sings for gods and men.
365   I taught myself the craft, but a god has planted
deep in my spirit all the paths of song—
songs I'm fit to sing for you as for a god.
Calm your bloodlust now—don't take my head!
He'd bear me out, your own dear son Telemachus—
370   never of *my* own will, never for any gain did I
perform in your house, singing after the suitors
had their feasts. They were too strong, too many—
they forced me to come and sing—I had no choice!"

The inspired Prince Telemachus heard his pleas
375   and quickly said to his father close beside him,
"Stop, don't cut him down! This one's innocent.
So is the herald Medon—the one who always
tended me in the house when I was little—
spare him too. Unless he's dead by now,
380   killed by Philoetius or Eumaeus here—
or ran into *you* rampaging through the halls."

The herald pricked up his anxious ears at that . . .
cautious soul, he cowered, trembling, under a chair—
wrapped in an oxhide freshly stripped—to dodge black death.
385   He jumped in a flash from there, threw off the smelly hide
and scuttling up to Telemachus, clutching his knees,
the herald begged for life in words that fluttered:
"Here I am, dear boy—spare me! Tell your father,
flushed with victory, not to kill me with his sword—
390   enraged as he is with these young lords who bled
his palace white and showed you no respect,
the reckless fools!"
                                 Breaking into a smile
the canny Odysseus reassured him, "Courage!
The prince has pulled you through, he's saved you now
395   so you can take it to heart and tell the next man too:
clearly doing good puts doing bad to shame.
Now leave the palace, go and sit outside—
out in the courtyard, clear of the slaughter—
you and the bard with all his many songs.
400   Wait till I've done some household chores
that call for my attention."

The two men scurried out of the house at once
and crouched at the altar-stone of mighty Zeus—
glancing left and right,
405   fearing death would strike at any moment.

Odysseus scanned his house to see if any man
still skulked alive, still hoped to avoid black death.
But he found them one and all in blood and dust . . .
great hauls of them down and out like fish that fishermen
410   drag from the churning gray surf in looped and coiling nets
and fling ashore on a sweeping hook of beach—some noble catch
heaped on the sand, twitching, lusting for fresh salt sea
but the Sungod hammers down and burns their lives out . . .
so the suitors lay in heaps, corpse covering corpse.
415   At last the seasoned fighter turned to his son:
"Telemachus, go, call the old nurse here—
I must tell her all that's on my mind."

Telemachus ran to do his father's bidding,
shook the women's doors, calling Eurycleia:

420   "Come out now! Up with you, good old woman!
You who watch over all the household hands—
quick, my father wants you, needs to have a word!"

    Crisp command that left the old nurse hushed—
she spread the doors to the well-constructed hall,
425   slipped out in haste, and the prince led her on . . .
She found Odysseus in the thick of slaughtered corpses,
splattered with bloody filth like a lion that's devoured
some ox of the field and lopes home, covered with blood,
his chest streaked, both jaws glistening, dripping red—
430   a sight to strike terror. So Odysseus looked now,
splattered with gore, his thighs, his fighting hands,
and she, when she saw the corpses, all the pooling blood,
was about to lift a cry of triumph—here was a great exploit,
look—but the soldier held her back and checked her zeal
435   with warnings winging home: "Rejoice in your heart,
old woman—peace! No cries of triumph now.
It's unholy to glory over the bodies of the dead.
These men the doom of the gods has brought low,
and their own indecent acts. They'd no regard
440   for any man on earth—good or bad—
who chanced to come their way. And so, thanks
to their reckless work, they met this shameful fate.
Quick, report in full on the women in my halls—
who are disloyal to me, who are guiltless?"

                                "Surely, child,"
445   his fond old nurse replied, "now here's the truth.
Fifty women you have inside your house,
women we've trained to do their duties well,
to card the wool and bear the yoke of service.
Some dozen in all went tramping to their shame,
450   thumbing their noses at me, at the queen herself!
And Telemachus, just now come of age—his mother
would never let the boy take charge of the maids.
But let me climb to her well-lit room upstairs
and tell your wife the news—
455   some god has put the woman fast asleep."

    "Don't wake her yet," the crafty man returned,
"you tell those women to hurry here at once—
just the ones who've shamed us all along."

    Away the old nurse bustled through the house
460   to give the women orders, rush them to the king.
Odysseus called Telemachus over, both herdsmen too,
with strict commands: "Start clearing away the bodies.
Make the women pitch in too. Chairs and tables—
scrub them down with sponges, rinse them clean.
465   And once you've put the entire house in order,

march the women out of the great hall—between
the roundhouse and the courtyard's strong stockade—
and hack them with your swords, slash out all their lives—
blot out of their minds the joys of love they relished
470   under the suitors' bodies, rutting on the sly!"

    The women crowded in, huddling all together . . .
wailing convulsively, streaming live warm tears.
First they carried out the bodies of the dead
and propped them under the courtyard colonnade,
475   standing them one against another. Odysseus
shouted commands himself, moving things along
and they kept bearing out the bodies—they were forced.
Next they scrubbed down the elegant chairs and tables,
washed them with sopping sponges, rinsed them clean.
480   Then Telemachus and the herdsmen scraped smooth
the packed earth floor of the royal house with spades
as the women gathered up the filth and piled it outside.
And then, at last, once the entire house was put in order,
they marched the women out of the great hall—between
485   the roundhouse and the courtyard's strong stockade—
crammed them into a dead end, no way out from there,
and stern Telemachus gave the men their orders:
"No clean death for the likes of them, by god!
Not from me—they showered abuse on my head,
490   my mother's too!
                 You sluts—the suitors' whores!"

    With that, taking a cable used on a dark-prowed ship
he coiled it over the roundhouse, lashed it fast to a tall column,
hoisting it up so high no toes could touch the ground.
Then, as doves or thrushes beating their spread wings
495   against some snare rigged up in thickets—flying in
for a cozy nest but a grisly bed receives them—
so the women's heads were trapped in a line,
nooses yanking their necks up, one by one
so all might die a pitiful, ghastly death . . .
500   they kicked up heels for a little—not for long.
                            Melanthius?
They hauled him out through the doorway, into the court,
lopped his nose and ears with a ruthless knife,
tore his genitals out for the dogs to eat raw
and in manic fury hacked off hands and feet.
                         Then,
505   once they'd washed their own hands and feet,
they went inside again to join Odysseus.
Their work was done with now.
But the king turned to devoted Eurycleia, saying,
"Bring sulfur, nurse, to scour all this pollution—
510   bring me fire too, so I can fumigate the house.

And call Penelope here with all her women—
tell all the maids to come back in at once."

    "Well said, my boy," his old nurse replied,
"right to the point. But wait,

515   let me fetch you a shirt and cloak to wrap you.
No more dawdling round the palace, nothing but rags
to cover those broad shoulders—it's a scandal!"

    "Fire first," the good soldier answered.
"Light me a fire to purify this house."

520   The devoted nurse snapped to his command,
brought her master fire and brimstone. Odysseus
purged his palace, halls and court, with cleansing fumes.

    Then back through the royal house the old nurse went
to tell the women the news and bring them in at once.

525   They came crowding out of their quarters, torch in hand,
flung their arms around Odysseus, hugged him, home at last,
and kissed his head and shoulders, seized his hands, and he,
overcome by a lovely longing, broke down and wept . . .
deep in his heart he knew them one and all.

Book 23. The Great Rooted Bed

Up to the rooms the old nurse clambered, chuckling all the way,
to tell the queen her husband was here now, home at last.
Her knees bustling, feet shuffling over each other,
till hovering at her mistress' head she spoke:

5   "Penelope—child—wake up and see for yourself,
with your own eyes, all you dreamed of, all your days!
He's here—Odysseus—he's come home, at long last!
He's killed the suitors, swaggering young brutes
who plagued his house, wolfed his cattle down,

10   rode roughshod over his son!"

    "Dear old nurse," wary Penelope replied,
"the gods have made you mad. They have that power,
putting lunacy into the clearest head around
or setting a half-wit on the path to sense.

15   They've unhinged you, and you were once so sane.
Why do you mock me?—haven't I wept enough?—
telling such wild stories, interrupting my sleep,
sweet sleep that held me, sealed my eyes just now.
Not once have I slept so soundly since the day

20   Odysseus sailed away to see that cursed city . . .
Destroy, I call it—I hate to say its name!
Now down you go. Back to your own quarters.
If any other woman of mine had come to me,
rousing me out of sleep with such a tale,

25   I'd have her bundled back to her room in pain.
It's only your old gray head that spares you that!"

    "Never"—the fond old nurse kept pressing on—
"dear child, I'd never mock you! No, it's all true,
he's here—Odysseus—he's come home, just as I tell you!
30   He's the stranger they all manhandled in the hall.
Telemachus knew he was here, for days and days,
but he knew enough to hide his father's plans
so *he* could pay those vipers back in kind!"

    Penelope's heart burst in joy, she leapt from bed,
35   her eyes streaming tears, she hugged the old nurse
and cried out with an eager, winging word,
"Please, dear one, give me the whole story.
If he's really home again, just as you tell me,
how did he get those shameless suitors in his clutches?—
40   single-handed, braving an army always camped inside."

    "I have no idea," the devoted nurse replied.
"I didn't see it, I didn't ask—all I heard
was the choking groans of men cut down in blood.
We crouched in terror—a dark nook of our quarters—
45   all of us locked tight behind those snug doors
till your boy Telemachus came and called me out—
his father rushed him there to do just that. And then
I found Odysseus in the thick of slaughtered corpses;
there he stood and all around him, over the beaten floor,
50   the bodies sprawled in heaps, lying one on another . . .
How it would have thrilled your heart to see him—
splattered with bloody filth, a lion with his kill!
And now they're all stacked at the courtyard gates—
he's lit a roaring fire,
55   he's purifying the house with cleansing fumes
and he's sent me here to bring you back to him.
Follow me down! So now, after all the years of grief,
you two can embark, loving hearts, along the road to joy.
Look, your dreams, put off so long, come true at last—
60   he's back alive, home at his hearth, and found you,
found his son still here. And all those suitors
who did him wrong, he's paid them back, he has,
right in his own house!"
                   "Hush, dear woman,"
guarded Penelope cautioned her at once.
65   "Don't laugh, don't cry in triumph—not yet.
You know how welcome the sight of him would be
to all in the house, and to me most of all
and the son we bore together.
But the story can't be true, not as you tell it,
70   no, it must be a god who's killed our brazen friends—

up in arms at their outrage, heartbreaking crimes.
They'd no regard for any man on earth—
good or bad—who chanced to come their way. So,
thanks to their reckless work they die their deaths.
75   Odysseus? Far from Achaea now, he's lost all hope
of coming home . . . he's lost and gone himself."

    "Child," the devoted old nurse protested,
"what nonsense you let slip through your teeth.
Here's your husband, warming his hands at his own hearth,
80   here—and you, you say he'll never come home again,
always the soul of trust! All right, this too—
I'll give you a sign, a proof that's plain as day.
That scar, made years ago by a boar's white tusk—
I spotted the scar myself, when I washed his feet,
85   and I tried to tell you, ah, but he, the crafty rascal,
clamped his hand on my mouth—I couldn't say a word.
Follow me down now. I'll stake my life on it:
if I am lying to *you*—
kill me with a thousand knives of pain!"

90   "Dear old nurse," composed Penelope responded,
"deep as you are, my friend, you'll find it hard
to plumb the plans of the everlasting gods.
All the same, let's go and join my son
so I can see the suitors lying dead
95   and see . . . the one who killed them."

                              With that thought
Penelope started down from her lofty room, her heart
in turmoil, torn . . . should she keep her distance,
probe her husband? Or rush up to the man at once
and kiss his head and cling to both his hands?
100   As soon as she stepped across the stone threshold,
slipping in, she took a seat at the closest wall
and radiant in the firelight, faced Odysseus now.
There he sat, leaning against the great central column,
eyes fixed on the ground, waiting, poised for whatever words
105   his hardy wife might say when she caught sight of him.
A long while she sat in silence . . . numbing wonder
filled her heart as her eyes explored his face.
One moment he seemed . . . Odysseus, to the life—
the next, no, he was not the man she knew,
110   a huddled mass of rags was all she saw.

    "Oh mother," Telemachus reproached her,
"cruel mother, you with your hard heart!
Why do you spurn my father so—why don't you
sit beside him, engage him, ask him questions?
115   What other wife could have a spirit so unbending?
Holding back from her husband, home at last for *her*
after bearing twenty years of brutal struggle—

your heart was always harder than a rock!"
                              "My child,"
Penelope, well-aware, explained, "I'm stunned with wonder,
120 powerless. Cannot speak to him, ask him questions,
look him in the eyes . . . But if he is truly
Odysseus, home at last, make no mistake:
we two will know each other, even better—
we two have secret signs,
125 known to us both but hidden from the world."

     Odysseus, long-enduring, broke into a smile
and turned to his son with pointed, winging words:
"Leave your mother here in the hall to test me
as she will. She soon will know me better.
130 Now because I am filthy, wear such grimy rags,
she spurns me—your mother still can't bring herself
to believe I am her husband.
                         But you and I,
put heads together. What's our best defense?
When someone kills a lone man in the realm
135 who leaves behind him no great band of avengers,
still the killer flees, goodbye to kin and country.
But *we* brought down the best of the island's princes,
the pillars of Ithaca. Weigh it well, I urge you."

     "Look to it all yourself now, father," his son
140 deferred at once. "You are the best on earth,
they say, when it comes to mapping tactics.
No one, no mortal man, can touch you there.
But we're behind you, hearts intent on battle,
nor do I think you'll find us short on courage,
145 long as our strength will last."
                              "Then here's our plan,"
the master of tactics said. "I think it's best.
First go and wash, and pull fresh tunics on
and tell the maids in the hall to dress well too.
And let the inspired bard take up his ringing lyre
150 and lead off for us all a dance so full of heart
that whoever hears the strains outside the gates—
a passerby on the road, a neighbor round about—
will think it's a wedding-feast that's under way.
No news of the suitors' death must spread through town
155 till we have slipped away to our own estates,
our orchard green with trees. There we'll see
what winning strategy Zeus will hand us then."

     They hung on his words and moved to orders smartly.
First they washed and pulled fresh tunics on,
160 the women arrayed themselves—the inspired bard
struck up his resounding lyre and stirred in all
a desire for dance and song, the lovely lilting beat,

till the great house echoed round to the measured tread
of dancing men in motion, women sashed and lithe.
165   And whoever heard the strains outside would say,
"A miracle—someone's married the queen at last!"

 "One of her hundred suitors."
     "That callous woman,
too faithless to keep her lord and master's house
to the bitter end—"
     "Till he came sailing home."

170   So they'd say, blind to what had happened:
the great-hearted Odysseus was home again at last.
The maid Eurynome bathed him, rubbed him down with oil
and drew around him a royal cape and choice tunic too.
And Athena crowned the man with beauty, head to foot,
175   made him taller to all eyes, his build more massive,
yes, and down from his brow the great goddess
ran his curls like thick hyacinth clusters
full of blooms. As a master craftsman washes
gold over beaten silver—a man the god of fire
180   and Queen Athena trained in every fine technique—
and finishes off his latest effort, handsome work . . .
so she lavished splendor over his head and shoulders now.
He stepped from his bath, glistening like a god,
and back he went to the seat that he had left
185   and facing his wife, declared,
"Strange woman! So hard—the gods of Olympus
made you harder than any other woman in the world!
What other wife could have a spirit so unbending?
Holding back from her husband, home at last for *her*
190   after bearing twenty years of brutal struggle.
Come, nurse, make me a bed, I'll sleep alone.
She has a heart of iron in her breast."
     "Strange *man*,"
wary Penelope said. "I'm not so proud, so scornful,
nor am I overwhelmed by your quick change . . .
195   You look—how well I know—the way he looked,
setting sail from Ithaca years ago
aboard the long-oared ship.
    Come, Eurycleia,
move the sturdy bedstead out of our bridal chamber—
that room the master built with his own hands.
200   Take it out now, sturdy bed that it is,
and spread it deep with fleece,
blankets and lustrous throws to keep him warm."

Putting her husband to the proof—but Odysseus
blazed up in fury, lashing out at his loyal wife:
205   "Woman—your words, they cut me to the core!

Who could move my bed? Impossible task,
even for some skilled craftsman—unless a god
came down in person, quick to lend a hand,
lifted it out with ease and moved it elsewhere.
210   Not a man on earth, not even at peak strength,
would find it easy to prise it up and shift it, no,
a great sign, a hallmark lies in its construction.
I know, I built it myself—no one else . . .
There was a branching olive-tree inside our court,
215   grown to its full prime, the bole like a column, thickset.
Around it I built my bedroom, finished off the walls
with good tight stonework, roofed it over soundly
and added doors, hung well and snugly wedged.
Then I lopped the leafy crown of the olive,
220   clean-cutting the stump bare from roots up,
planing it round with a bronze smoothing-adze—
I had the skill—I shaped it plumb to the line to make
my bedpost, bored the holes it needed with an auger.
Working from there I built my bed, start to finish,
225   I gave it ivory inlays, gold and silver fittings,
wove the straps across it, oxhide gleaming red.
There's our secret sign, I tell you, our life story!
Does the bed, my lady, still stand planted firm?—
I don't know—or has someone chopped away
230   that olive-trunk and hauled our bedstead off?"

                                        Living proof—
Penelope felt her knees go slack, her heart surrender,
recognizing the strong clear signs Odysseus offered.
She dissolved in tears, rushed to Odysseus, flung her arms
around his neck and kissed his head and cried out,
235   "Odysseus—don't flare up at me now, not you,
always the most understanding man alive!
The gods, it was the gods who sent us sorrow—
they grudged us both a life in each other's arms
from the heady zest of youth to the stoop of old age.
240   But don't fault me, angry with me now because I failed,
at the first glimpse, to greet you, hold you, so . . .
In my heart of hearts I always cringed with fear
some fraud might come, beguile me with his talk;
the world is full of the sort,
245   cunning ones who plot their own dark ends.
Remember Helen of Argos, Zeus's daughter—
would *she* have sported so in a stranger's bed
if she had dreamed that Achaea's sons were doomed
to fight and die to bring her home again?
250   Some god spurred her to do her shameless work.
Not till then did her mind conceive that madness,
blinding madness that caused her anguish, ours as well.
But now, since you have revealed such overwhelming proof—

the secret sign of our bed, which no one's ever seen
255   but you and I and a single handmaid, Actoris,
the servant my father gave me when I came,
who kept the doors of our room you built so well . . .
you've conquered my heart, my hard heart, at last!"

The more she spoke, the more a deep desire for tears
260   welled up inside his breast—he wept as he held the wife
he loved, the soul of loyalty, in his arms at last.
Joy, warm as the joy that shipwrecked sailors feel
when they catch sight of land—Poseidon has struck
their well-rigged ship on the open sea with gale winds
265   and crushing walls of waves, and only a few escape, swimming,
struggling out of the frothing surf to reach the shore,
their bodies crusted with salt but buoyed up with joy
as they plant their feet on solid ground again,
spared a deadly fate. So joyous now to her
270   the sight of her husband, vivid in her gaze,
that her white arms, embracing his neck
would never for a moment let him go . . .
Dawn with her rose-red fingers might have shone
upon their tears, if with her glinting eyes
275   Athena had not thought of one more thing.
She held back the night, and night lingered long
at the western edge of the earth, while in the east
she reined in Dawn of the golden throne at Ocean's banks,
commanding her not to yoke the windswift team that brings men light,
280   Blaze and Aurora, the young colts that race the Morning on.
Yet now Odysseus, seasoned veteran, said to his wife,
"Dear woman . . . we have still not reached the end
of all our trials. One more labor lies in store—
boundless, laden with danger, great and long,
285   and I must brave it out from start to finish.
So the ghost of Tiresias prophesied to me,
the day that I went down to the House of Death
to learn our best route home, my comrades' and my own.
But come, let's go to bed, dear woman—at long last
290   delight in sleep, delight in each other, come!"

"If it's bed you want," reserved Penelope replied,
"it's bed you'll have, whenever the spirit moves you,
now that the gods have brought you home again
to native land, your grand and gracious house.
295   But since you've alluded to it,
since a god has put it in your mind,
please, tell me about this trial still to come.
I'm bound to learn of it later, I am sure—
what's the harm if I hear of it tonight?"

                                        "Still so strange,"

300 Odysseus, the old master of stories, answered.
"Why again, why force me to tell you all?
Well, tell I shall. I'll hide nothing now.
But little joy it will bring you, I'm afraid,
as little joy for me.   The prophet said
305 that I must rove through towns on towns of men,
that I must carry a well-planed oar until
I come to a people who know nothing of the sea,
whose food is never seasoned with salt, strangers all
to ships with their crimson prows and long slim oars,
310 wings that make ships fly. And here is my sign,
he told me, clear, so clear I cannot miss it,
and I will share it with you now . . .
When another traveler falls in with me and calls
that weight across my shoulder a fan to winnow grain,
315 then, he told me, I must plant my oar in the earth
and sacrifice fine beasts to the lord god of the sea,
Poseidon—a ram, a bull and a ramping wild boar—
then journey home and render noble offerings up
to the deathless gods who rule the vaulting skies,
320 to all the gods in order.
And at last my own death will steal upon me . . .
a gentle, painless death, far from the sea it comes
to take me down, borne down with the years in ripe old age
with all my people here in blessed peace around me.
325 All this, the prophet said, will come to pass."

"And so," Penelope said, in her great wisdom,
"if the gods will really grant a happier old age,
there's hope that we'll escape our trials at last."

So husband and wife confided in each other,
330 while nurse and Eurynome, under the flaring brands,
were making up the bed with coverings deep and soft.
And working briskly, soon as they'd made it snug,
back to her room the old nurse went to sleep
as Eurynome, their attendant, torch in hand,
335 lighted the royal couple's way to bed and,
leading them to their chamber, slipped away.
Rejoicing in each other, they returned to their bed,
the old familiar place they loved so well.

Now Telemachus, the cowherd and the swineherd
340 rested their dancing feet and had the women do the same,
and across the shadowed hall the men lay down to sleep.

But the royal couple, once they'd reveled in all
the longed-for joys of love, reveled in each other's stories,
the radiant woman telling of all she'd borne at home,

345   watching them there, the infernal crowd of suitors
    slaughtering herds of cattle and good fat sheep—
    while keen to win her hand—
    draining the broached vats dry of vintage wine.
    And great Odysseus told his wife of all the pains
350   he had dealt out to other men and all the hardships
    he'd endured himself—his story first to last—
    and she listened on, enchanted . . .
    Sleep never sealed her eyes till all was told.

      He launched in with how he fought the Cicones down,
355   then how he came to the Lotus-eaters' lush green land.
    Then all the crimes of the Cyclops and how he paid him back
    for the gallant men the monster ate without a qualm—
    then how he visited Aeolus, who gave him a hero's welcome
    then he sent him off, but the homeward run was not his fate,
360   not yet—some sudden squalls snatched him away once more
    and drove him over the swarming sea, groaning in despair.
    Then how he moored at Telepylus, where Laestrygonians
    wrecked his fleet and killed his men-at-arms.
    He told her of Circe's cunning magic wiles
365   and how he voyaged down in his long benched ship
    to the moldering House of Death, to consult Tiresias,
    ghostly seer of Thebes, and he saw old comrades there
    and he saw his mother, who bore and reared him as a child.
    He told how he caught the Sirens' voices throbbing in the wind
370   and how he had scudded past the Clashing Rocks, past grim Charybdis,
    past Scylla—whom no rover had ever coasted by, home free—
    and how his shipmates slaughtered the cattle of the Sun
    and Zeus the king of thunder split his racing ship
    with a reeking bolt and killed his hardy comrades,
375   all his fighting men at a stroke, but he alone
    escaped their death at sea. He told how he reached
    Ogygia's shores and the nymph Calypso held him back,
    deep in her arching caverns, craving him for a husband—
    cherished him, vowed to make him immortal, ageless, all his days,
380   yes, but she never won the heart inside him, never . . .
    then how he reached the Phaeacians—heavy sailing there—
    who with all their hearts had prized him like a god
    and sent him off in a ship to his own beloved land,
    giving him bronze and hoards of gold and robes . . .
385   and that was the last he told her, just as sleep
    overcame him . . . sleep loosing his limbs,
    slipping the toils of anguish from his mind.

      Athena, her eyes afire, had fresh plans.
    Once she thought he'd had his heart's content
390   of love and sleep at his wife's side, straightaway
    she roused young Dawn from Ocean's banks to her golden throne
    to bring men light and roused Odysseus too, who rose

from his soft bed and advised his wife in parting,
"Dear woman, we both have had our fill of trials.
395   You in our house, weeping over my journey home,
fraught with storms and torment, true, and I,
pinned down in pain by Zeus and other gods,
for all my desire, blocked from reaching home.
But now that we've arrived at our bed together—
400   the reunion that we yearned for all those years—
look after the things still left me in our house.
But as for the flocks those brazen suitors plundered,
much I'll recoup myself, making many raids;
the rest our fellow-Ithacans will supply
405   till all my folds are full of sheep again.
But now I must be off to the upland farm,
our orchard green with trees, to see my father,
good old man weighed down with so much grief for me.
And you, dear woman, sensible as you are,
410   I would advise you, still . . .
quick as the rising sun the news will spread
of the suitors that I killed inside the house.
So climb to your lofty chamber with your women.
Sit tight there. See no one. Question no one."

415   He strapped his burnished armor round his shoulders,
roused Telemachus, the cowherd and the swineherd,
and told them to take up weapons honed for battle.
They snapped to commands, harnessed up in bronze,
opened the doors and strode out, Odysseus in the lead.
420   By now the daylight covered the land, but Pallas,
shrouding them all in darkness,
quickly led the four men out of town.

BOOK 24. PEACE

Now Cyllenian Hermes called away the suitors' ghosts,
holding firm in his hand the wand of fine pure gold
that enchants the eyes of men whenever Hermes wants
or wakes us up from sleep.
5   With a wave of this he stirred and led them on
and the ghosts trailed after with high thin cries
as bats cry in the depths of a dark haunted cavern,
shrilling, flittering, wild when one drops from the chain—
slipped from the rock face, while the rest cling tight . . .
10   So with their high thin cries the ghosts flocked now
and Hermes the Healer led them on, and down the dank
moldering paths and past the Ocean's streams they went
and past the White Rock and the Sun's Western Gates and past
the Land of Dreams, and they soon reached the fields of asphodel
15   where the dead, the burnt-out wraiths of mortals, make their home.

       There they found the ghosts of Peleus' son Achilles,
Patroclus, fearless Antilochus—and Great Ajax too,
the first in stature, first in build and bearing
of all the Argives after Peleus' matchless son.
20   They had grouped around Achilles' ghost, and now
the shade of Atreus' son Agamemnon marched toward them—
fraught with grief and flanked by all his comrades,
troops of his men-at-arms who died beside him,
who met their fate in lord Aegisthus' halls.
25   Achilles' ghost was first to greet him: "Agamemnon,
you were the one, we thought, of all our fighting princes
Zeus who loves the lightning favored most, all your days,
because you commanded such a powerful host of men
on the fields of Troy where we Achaeans suffered.
30   But you were doomed to encounter fate so early,
you too, yet no one born escapes its deadly force.
If only you had died your death in the full flush
of the glory you had mastered—died on Trojan soil!
Then all united Achaea would have raised your tomb
35   and you'd have won your son great fame for years to come.
Not so. You were fated to die a wretched death."

       And the ghost of Atrides Agamemnon answered,
"Son of Peleus, great godlike Achilles! Happy man,
you died on the fields of Troy, a world away from home,
40   and the best of Trojan and Argive champions died around you,
fighting for your corpse. And you . . . there you lay
in the whirling dust, overpowered in all your power
and wiped from memory all your horseman's skills.
That whole day we fought, we'd never have stopped
45   if Zeus had not stopped us with sudden gales.
Then we bore you out of the fighting, onto the ships,
we laid you down on a litter, cleansed your handsome flesh
with warm water and soothing oils, and round your body
troops of Danaans wept hot tears and cut their locks.
50   Hearing the news, your mother, Thetis, rose from the sea,
immortal sea-nymphs in her wake, and a strange unearthly cry
came throbbing over the ocean. Terror gripped Achaea's armies,
they would have leapt in panic, boarded the long hollow ships
if one man, deep in his age-old wisdom, had not checked them:
55   Nestor—from the first his counsel always seemed the best,
and now, concerned for the ranks, he rose and shouted,
'Hold fast, Argives! Sons of Achaea, don't run now!
This is Achilles' mother rising from the sea
with all her immortal sea-nymphs—
60   she longs to join her son who died in battle!'
That stopped our panicked forces in their tracks
as the Old Man of the Sea's daughters gathered round you—
wailing, heartsick—dressed you in ambrosial, deathless robes
and the Muses, nine in all, voice-to-voice in choirs,

65   their vibrant music rising, raised your dirge.
      Not one soldier would you have seen dry-eyed,
      the Muses' song so pierced us to the heart.
      For seventeen days unbroken, days and nights
      we mourned you—immortal gods and mortal men.
70   At the eighteenth dawn we gave you to the flames
      and slaughtered around your body droves of fat sheep
      and shambling longhorn cattle, and you were burned
      in the garments of the gods and laved with soothing oils
      and honey running sweet, and a long cortege of Argive heroes
75   paraded in review, in battle armor round your blazing pyre,
      men in chariots, men on foot—a resounding roar went up.
      And once the god of fire had burned your corpse to ash,
      at first light we gathered your white bones, Achilles,
      cured them in strong neat wine and seasoned oils.
80   Your mother gave us a gold two-handled urn,
      a gift from Dionysus, she said,
      a masterwork of the famous Smith, the god of fire.
      Your white bones rest in that, my brilliant Achilles,
      mixed with the bones of dead Patroclus, Menoetius' son,
85   apart from those of Antilochus, whom you treasured
      more than all other comrades once Patroclus died.
      Over your bones we reared a grand, noble tomb—
      devoted veterans all, Achaea's combat forces—
      high on its jutting headland over the Hellespont's[1]
90   broad reach, a landmark glimpsed from far out at sea
      by men of our own day and men of days to come.
                                            And then
      your mother, begging the gods for priceless trophies,
      set them out in the ring for all our champions.
      You in your day have witnessed funeral games
95   for many heroes, games to honor the death of kings,
      when young men cinch their belts, tense to win some prize—
      but if you'd laid eyes on these it would have thrilled your heart,
      magnificent trophies the goddess, glistening-footed Thetis,
      held out in your honor. You were dear to the gods,
100   so even in death your name will never die . . .
      Great glory is yours, Achilles,
      for all time, in the eyes of all mankind!
                                            But I?
      What joy for *me* when the coil of war had wound down?
      For my return Zeus hatched a pitiful death
105   at the hands of Aegisthus—and my accursed wife."

          As they exchanged the stories of their fates,
      Hermes the guide and giant-killer drew up close to both,
      leading down the ghosts of the suitors King Odysseus killed.
      Struck by the sight, the two went up to them right away

1. Strait between Europe and Asia, the modern Dardanelles.

110   and the ghost of Atreus' son Agamemnon recognized
       the noted prince Amphimedon, Melaneus' dear son
       who received him once in Ithaca, at his home,
       and Atrides' ghost called out to his old friend now,
       "Amphimedon, what disaster brings you down to the dark world?
115   All of you, good picked men, and all in your prime—
       no captain out to recruit the best in any city
       could have chosen better. What laid you low?
       Wrecked in the ships when lord Poseidon roused
       some punishing blast of gales and heavy breakers?
120   Or did ranks of enemies mow you down on land
       as you tried to raid and cut off herds and flocks
       or fought to win their city, take their women?
       Answer me, tell me. I was once your guest.
       Don't you recall the day I came to visit
125   your house in Ithaca—King Menelaus came too—
       to urge Odysseus to sail with us in the ships
       on our campaign to Troy? And the long slow voyage,
       crossing wastes of ocean, cost us one whole month.
       That's how hard it was to bring him round,
130   Odysseus, raider of cities."
                                    "Famous Atrides!"
       Amphimedon's ghost called back. "Lord of men, Agamemnon,
       I remember it all, your majesty, as you say,
       and I will tell you, start to finish now,
       the story of our death,
135   the brutal end contrived to take us off.
       We were courting the wife of Odysseus, gone so long.
       She neither spurned nor embraced a marriage she despised,
       no, she simply planned our death, our black doom!
       This was her latest masterpiece of guile:
140   she set up a great loom in the royal halls
       and she began to weave, and the weaving finespun,
       the yarns endless, and she would lead us on: 'Young men,
       my suitors, now that King Odysseus is no more,
       go slowly, keen as you are to marry me, until
145   I can finish off this web . . .
       so my weaving won't all fray and come to nothing.
       This is a shroud for old lord Laertes, for that day
       when the deadly fate that lays us out at last will take him down.
       I dread the shame my countrywomen would heap upon me,
150   yes, if a man of such wealth should lie in state
       without a shroud for cover.'
                                    Her very words,
       and despite our pride and passion we believed her.
       So by day she'd weave at her great and growing web—
       by night, by the light of torches set beside her,
155   she would unravel all she'd done. Three whole years

she deceived us blind, seduced us with this scheme . . .
Then, when the wheeling seasons brought the fourth year on
and the months waned and the long days came round once more,
one of her women, in on the queen's secret, told the truth
160 and we caught her in the act—unweaving her gorgeous web.
So she finished it off. Against her will. We forced her.
But just as she bound off that great shroud and washed it,
spread it out—glistening like the sunlight or the moon—
just then some wicked spirit brought Odysseus back,
165 from god knows where, to the edge of his estate
where the swineherd kept his pigs. And back too,
to the same place, came Odysseus' own dear son,
scudding home in his black ship from sandy Pylos.
The pair of them schemed our doom, our deathtrap,
170 then lit out for town—
Telemachus first in fact, Odysseus followed,
later, led by the swineherd, and clad in tatters,
looking for all the world like an old and broken beggar
hunched on a stick, his body wrapped in shameful rags.
175 Disguised so none of us, not even the older ones,
could spot that tramp for the man he really was,
bursting in on us there, out of the blue. No,
we attacked him, blows and insults flying fast,
and he took it all for a time, in his own house,
180 all the taunts and blows—he had a heart of iron.
But once the will of thundering Zeus had roused his blood,
he and Telemachus bore the burnished weapons off
and stowed them deep in a storeroom, shot the bolts
and he—the soul of cunning—told his wife to set
185 the great bow and the gleaming iron axes out
before the suitors—all of us doomed now—
to test our skill and bring our slaughter on . . .
Not one of us had the strength to string that powerful weapon,
all of us fell far short of what it took. But then,
190 when the bow was coming round to Odysseus' hands,
we raised a hue and cry—he must not have it,
no matter how he begged! Only Telemachus
urged him to take it up, and once he got it
in his clutches, long-suffering great Odysseus
195 strung his bow with ease and shot through all the axes,
then, vaulting onto the threshold, stood there poised, and pouring
his flashing arrows out before him, glaring for the kill,
he cut Antinous down, then shot his painful arrows
into the rest of us, aiming straight and true,
200 and down we went, corpse on corpse in droves.
Clearly a god was driving him and all his henchmen,
routing us headlong in their fury down the hall,
wheeling into the slaughter, slashing left and right

and grisly screams broke from skulls cracked open—
205   the whole floor awash with blood.

So we died,
Agamemnon . . . our bodies lie untended even now,
strewn in Odysseus' palace. They know nothing yet,
the kin in our houses who might wash our wounds
of clotted gore and lay us out and mourn us.
210   These are the solemn honors owed the dead."

"Happy Odysseus!"
Agamemnon's ghost cried out. "Son of old Laertes—
mastermind—what a fine, faithful wife you won!
What good sense resided in your Penelope—
how well Icarius' daughter remembered you,
215   Odysseus, the man she married once!
The fame of her great virtue will never die.
The immortal gods will lift a song for all mankind,
a glorious song in praise of self-possessed Penelope.
A far cry from the daughter of Tyndareus, Clytemnestra—
220   what outrage she committed, killing the man *she* married once!—
yes, and the song men sing of her will ring with loathing.
She brands with a foul name the breed of womankind,
even the honest ones to come!"

So they traded stories,
the two ghosts standing there in the House of Death,
225   far in the hidden depths below the earth.

Odysseus and his men had stridden down from town
and quickly reached Laertes' large, well-tended farm
that the old king himself had wrested from the wilds,
years ago, laboring long and hard. His lodge was here
230   and around it stretched a row of sheds where fieldhands,
bondsmen who did his bidding, sat and ate and slept.
And an old Sicilian woman was in charge,
who faithfully looked after her aged master
out on his good estate remote from town.
235   Odysseus told his servants and his son,
"Into the timbered lodge now, go, quickly,
kill us the fattest porker, fix our meal.
And I will put my father to the test,
see if the old man knows me now, on sight,
240   or fails to, after twenty years apart."

With that he passed his armor to his men
and in they went at once, his son as well. Odysseus
wandered off, approaching the thriving vineyard, searching,
picking his way down to the great orchard, searching,
245   but found neither Dolius nor his sons nor any hand.
They'd just gone off, old Dolius in the lead,
to gather stones for a dry retaining wall
to shore the vineyard up. But he did find

his father, alone, on that well-worked plot,
250 spading round a sapling—clad in filthy rags,
in a patched, unseemly shirt, and round his shins
he had some oxhide leggings strapped, patched too,
to keep from getting scraped, and gloves on his hands
to fight against the thorns, and on his head
255 he wore a goatskin skullcap
to cultivate his misery that much more . . .
Long-enduring Odysseus, catching sight of him now—
a man worn down with years, his heart racked with sorrow—
halted under a branching pear-tree, paused and wept.
260 Debating, head and heart, what should he do now?
Kiss and embrace his father, pour out the long tale—
how he had made the journey home to native land—
or probe him first and test him every way?
Torn, mulling it over, this seemed better:
265 test the old man first,
reproach him with words that cut him to the core.
Convinced, Odysseus went right up to his father.
Laertes was digging round the sapling, head bent low
as his famous offspring hovered over him and began,
270 "You want no skill, old man, at tending a garden.
All's well-kept here; not one thing in the plot,
no plant, no fig, no pear, no olive, no vine,
not a vegetable, lacks your tender, loving care.
But I must say—and don't be offended now—
275 your plants are doing better than yourself.
Enough to be stooped with age
but look how squalid you are, those shabby rags.
Surely it's not for sloth your master lets you go to seed.
There's nothing of slave about your build or bearing.
280 I have eyes: you look like a king to me. The sort
entitled to bathe, sup well, then sleep in a soft bed.
That's the right and pride of you old-timers.
Come now, tell me—in no uncertain terms—
whose slave are you? whose orchard are you tending?
285 And tell me this—I must be absolutely sure—
this place I've reached, is it truly Ithaca?
Just as that fellow told me, just now . . .
I fell in with him on the road here. Clumsy,
none too friendly, couldn't trouble himself
290 to hear me out or give me a decent answer
when I asked about a long-lost friend of mine,
whether he's still alive, somewhere in Ithaca,
or dead and gone already, lost in the House of Death.
Do you want to hear his story? Listen. Catch my drift.
295 I once played host to a man in my own country;
he'd come to my door, the most welcome guest
from foreign parts I ever entertained.

He claimed he came of good Ithacan stock,
said his father was Arcesius' son, Laertes.
300 So I took the new arrival under my own roof,
I gave him a hero's welcome, treated him in style—
stores in our palace made for princely entertainment.
And I gave my friend some gifts to fit his station,
handed him seven bars of well-wrought gold,
305 a mixing-bowl of solid silver, etched with flowers,
a dozen cloaks, unlined and light, a dozen rugs
and as many full-cut capes and shirts as well,
and to top it off, four women, perfect beauties
skilled in crafts—he could pick them out himself."

310   "Stranger," his father answered, weeping softly,
"the land you've reached is the very one you're after,
true, but it's in the grip of reckless, lawless men.
And as for the gifts you showered on your guest,
you gave them all for nothing.
315 But if you'd found him alive, here in Ithaca,
he would have replied in kind, with gift for gift,
and entertained you warmly before he sent you off.
That's the old custom, when one has led the way.
But tell me, please—in no uncertain terms—
320 how many years ago did you host the man,
that unfortunate guest of yours, my son . . .
there was a son, or was he all a dream?
That most unlucky man, whom now, I fear,
far from his own soil and those he loves,
325 the fish have swallowed down on the high seas
or birds and beasts on land have made their meal.
Nor could the ones who bore him—mother, father—
wrap his corpse in a shroud and mourn him deeply.
Nor could his warm, generous wife, so self-possessed,
330 Penelope, ever keen for her husband on his deathbed,
the fit and proper way, or close his eyes at last.
These are the solemn honors owed the dead.
But tell me your own story—that I'd like to know:
Who are you? where are you from? your city? your parents?
335 Where does the ship lie moored that brought you here,
your hardy shipmates too? Or did you arrive
as a passenger aboard some stranger's craft
and men who put you ashore have pulled away?"

                                                "The whole tale,"
his crafty son replied, "I'll tell you start to finish.
340 I come from Roamer-Town, my home's a famous place,
my father's Unsparing, son of old King Pain,
and my name's Man of Strife . . .
I sailed from Sicily, aye, but some ill wind
blew me here, off course—much against my will—

345   and my ship lies moored off farmlands far from town.
       As for Odysseus, well, five years have passed
       since he left my house and put my land behind him,
       luckless man! But the birds were good as he launched out,
       all on the right, and I rejoiced as I sent him off
350   and he rejoiced in sailing. We had high hopes
       we'd meet again as guests, as old friends,
       and trade some shining gifts."
                                    At those words
       a black cloud of grief came shrouding over Laertes.
       Both hands clawing the ground for dirt and grime,
355   he poured it over his grizzled head, sobbing, in spasms.
       Odysseus' heart shuddered, a sudden twinge went shooting up
       through his nostrils, watching his dear father struggle . . .
       He sprang toward him, kissed him, hugged him, crying,
       "Father—I am your son—myself, the man you're seeking,
360   home after twenty years, on native ground at last!
       Hold back your tears, your grief.
       Let me tell you the news, but we must hurry—
       I've cut the suitors down in our own house,
       I've paid them back their outrage, vicious crimes!"
                                              "Odysseus . . ."
365   Laertes, catching his breath, found words to answer.
       "You—you're truly my son, Odysseus, home at last?
       Give me a sign, some proof—I must be sure."
                                         "This scar first,"
       quick to the mark, his son said, "look at this—
       the wound I took from the boar's white tusk
370   on Mount Parnassus. There you'd sent me, you
       and mother, to see her fond old father, Autolycus,
       and collect the gifts he vowed to give me, once,
       when he came to see us here.
                                 Or these, these trees—
       let me tell you the trees you gave me years ago,
375   here on this well-worked plot . . .
       I begged you for everything I saw, a little boy
       trailing you through the orchard, picking our way
       among these trees, and you named them one by one.
       You gave me thirteen pear, ten apple trees
380   and forty figs—and promised to give me, look,
       fifty vinerows, bearing hard on each other's heels,
       clusters of grapes year-round at every grade of ripeness,
       mellowed as Zeus's seasons weigh them down."
                                            Living proof—
       and Laertes' knees went slack, his heart surrendered,
385   recognizing the strong clear signs Odysseus offered.
       He threw his arms around his own dear son, fainting
       as hardy great Odysseus hugged him to his heart
       until he regained his breath, came back to life

and cried out, "Father Zeus—
390   you gods of Olympus, you still rule on high
if those suitors have truly paid in blood
for all their reckless outrage! Oh, but now
my heart quakes with fear that all the Ithacans
will come down on us in a pack, at any time,
395   and rush the alarm through every island town!"

    "There's nothing to fear," his canny son replied,
"put it from your mind. Let's make for your lodge
beside the orchard here. I sent Telemachus on ahead,
the cowherd, swineherd too, to fix a hasty meal."

400   So the two went home, confiding all the way
and arriving at the ample, timbered lodge,
they found Telemachus with the two herdsmen
carving sides of meat and mixing ruddy wine.
Before they ate, the Sicilian serving-woman
405   bathed her master, Laertes—his spirits high
in his own room—and rubbed him down with oil
and round his shoulders drew a fresh new cloak.
And Athena stood beside him, fleshing out the limbs
of the old commander, made him taller to all eyes,
410   his build more massive, stepping from his bath,
so his own son gazed at him, wonderstruck—
face-to-face he seemed a deathless god . . .
"Father"—Odysseus' words had wings—"surely
one of the everlasting gods has made you
415   taller, stronger, shining in my eyes!"

    Facing his son, the wise old man returned,
"If only—Father Zeus, Athena and lord Apollo—
I were the man I was, king of the Cephallenians
when I sacked the city of Nericus, sturdy fortress
420   out on its jutting cape! If I'd been young in arms
last night in our house with harness on my back,
standing beside you, fighting off the suitors,
how many I would have cut the knees from under—
the heart inside you would have leapt for joy!"

425   So father and son confirmed each other's spirits.
And then, with the roasting done, the meal set out,
the others took their seats on chairs and stools,
were just putting their hands to bread and meat
when old Dolius trudged in with his sons,
430   worn out from the fieldwork.
The old Sicilian had gone and fetched them home,
the mother who reared the boys and tended Dolius well,
now that the years had ground the old man down . . .
When they saw Odysseus—knew him in their bones—
435   they stopped in their tracks, staring, struck dumb,

but the king waved them on with a warm and easy air:
"Sit down to your food, old friend. Snap out of your wonder.
We've been cooling our heels here long enough,
eager to get our hands on all this pork,
440   hoping you'd all troop in at any moment."

       Spreading his arms, Dolius rushed up to him,
clutched Odysseus by the wrist and kissed his hand,
greeting his king now with a burst of winging words:
"Dear master, you're back—the answer to our prayers!
445   We'd lost all hope but the gods have brought you home!
Welcome—health! The skies rain blessings on you!
But tell me the truth now—this I'd like to know—
shrewd Penelope, has she heard you're home?
Or should we send a messenger?"
                                    "She knows by now,
450   old man," his wily master answered brusquely.
"Why busy yourself with that?"

       So Dolius went back to his sanded stool.
His sons too, pressing around the famous king,
greeted Odysseus warmly, grasped him by the hand
455   then took their seats in order by their father.

       But now, as they fell to supper in the lodge,
Rumor the herald sped like wildfire through the city,
crying out the news of the suitors' bloody death and doom,
and massing from every quarter as they listened, kinsmen milled
460   with wails and moans of grief before Odysseus' palace.
And then they carried out the bodies, every family
buried their own, and the dead from other towns
they loaded onto the rapid ships for crews
to ferry back again, each to his own home . . .
465   Then in a long, mourning file they moved to assembly
where, once they'd grouped, crowding the meeting grounds,
old lord Eupithes rose in their midst to speak out.
Unforgettable sorrow wrung his heart for his son,
Antinous, the first that great Odysseus killed.
470   In tears for the one he lost, he stood and cried,
"My friends, what a mortal blow this man has dealt
to all our island people! Those fighters, many and brave,
he led away in his curved ships—he lost the ships
and he lost the men and back he comes again
475   to kill the best of our Cephallenian princes.
Quick, after him! Before he flees to Pylos
or holy Elis, where Epeans rule in power—
up, attack! Or we'll hang our heads forever,
all disgraced, even by generations down the years,
480   if we don't punish the murderers of our brothers and our sons!
Why, life would lose its relish—for me, at least—

I'd rather die at once and go among the dead.
Attack!—before the assassins cross the sea
and leave us in their wake."
                                    He closed in tears
485   and compassion ran through every Achaean there.
Suddenly Medon and the inspired bard approached them,
fresh from Odysseus' house, where they had just awakened.
They strode into the crowds; amazement took each man
but the herald Medon spoke in all his wisdom:
490   "Hear me, men of Ithaca. Not without the hand
of the deathless gods did Odysseus do these things!
Myself, I saw an immortal fighting at his side—
like Mentor to the life. I saw the same god,
now in front of Odysseus, spurring him on,
495   now stampeding the suitors through the hall,
crazed with fear, and down they went in droves!"

    Terror gripped them all, their faces ashen white.
At last the old warrior Halitherses, Mastor's son—
who alone could see the days behind and days ahead—
500   rose up and spoke, distraught for each man there:
"Hear me, men of Ithaca. Hear what I have to say.
Thanks to your own craven hearts these things were done!
You never listened to me or the good commander Mentor,
you never put a stop to your sons' senseless folly.
505   What fine work they did, so blind, so reckless,
carving away the wealth, affronting the wife
of a great and famous man, telling themselves
that he'd return no more! So let things rest now.
Listen to me for once—I say don't attack!
510   Else some will draw the lightning on their necks."
                                    So he urged
and some held fast to their seats, but more than half
sprang up with warcries now. They had no taste
for the prophet's sane plan—winning Eupithes
quickly won them over. They ran for armor
515   and once they'd harnessed up in burnished bronze
they grouped in ranks before the terraced city.
Eupithes led them on in their foolish, mad campaign,
certain he would avenge the slaughter of his son
but the father was not destined to return—
520   he'd meet his death in battle then and there.

    Athena at this point made appeals to Zeus:
"Father, son of Cronus, our high and mighty king,
now let me ask you a question . . .
tell me the secrets hidden in your mind.
525   Will you prolong the pain, the cruel fighting here
or hand down pacts of peace between both sides?"

    "My child," Zeus who marshals the thunderheads replied,

"why do you pry and probe me so intently? Come now,
wasn't the plan your own? You conceived it yourself:
530   Odysseus should return and pay the traitors back.
Do as your heart desires—
but let me tell you how it should be done.
Now that royal Odysseus has taken his revenge,
let both sides seal their pacts that he shall reign for life,
535   and let us purge their memories of the bloody slaughter
of their brothers and their sons. Let them be friends,
devoted as in the old days. Let peace and wealth
come cresting through the land."
                                                So Zeus decreed
and launched Athena already poised for action—
540   down she swept from Olympus' craggy peaks.

     By then Odysseus' men had had their fill
of hearty fare, and the seasoned captain said,
"One of you go outside—see if they're closing in."
A son of Dolius snapped to his command,
545   ran to the door and saw them all too close
and shouted back to Odysseus,
"They're on top of us! To arms—and fast!"
Up they sprang and strapped themselves in armor,
the three men with Odysseus, Dolius' six sons
550   and Dolius and Laertes clapped on armor too,
gray as they were, but they would fight if forced.
Once they had all harnessed up in burnished bronze
they opened the doors and strode out, Odysseus in the lead.

     And now, taking the build and voice of Mentor,
555   Zeus's daughter Athena marched right in.
The good soldier Odysseus thrilled to see her,
turned to his son and said in haste, "Telemachus,
you'll learn soon enough—as you move up to fight
where champions strive to prove themselves the best—
560   not to disgrace your father's line a moment.
In battle prowess we've excelled for ages
all across the world."
                                        Telemachus reassured him,
"Now you'll see, if you care to watch, father,
now I'm fired up. Disgrace, you say?
565   I won't disgrace your line!"

          Laertes called out in deep delight,
"What a day for me, dear gods! What joy—
my son and my grandson vying over courage!"
                                                        "Laertes!"
Goddess Athena rushed beside him, eyes ablaze:
570   "Son of Arcesius, dearest of all my comrades,
say a prayer to the bright-eyed girl and Father Zeus,
then brandish your long spear and wing it fast!"

Athena breathed enormous strength in the old man.
He lifted a prayer to mighty Zeus's daughter,
575 brandished his spear a moment, winged it fast
and hit Eupithes, pierced his bronze-sided helmet
that failed to block the bronze point tearing through—
down Eupithes crashed, his armor clanging against his chest.
Odysseus and his gallant son charged straight at the front lines,
580 slashing away with swords, with two-edged spears and now
they would have killed them all, cut them off from home
if Athena, daughter of storming Zeus, had not cried out
in a piercing voice that stopped all fighters cold,
"Hold back, you men of Ithaca, back from brutal war!
585 Break off—shed no more blood—make peace at once!"

So Athena commanded. Terror blanched their faces,
they went limp with fear, weapons slipped from their hands
and strewed the ground at the goddess' ringing voice.
They spun in flight to the city, wild to save their lives,
590 but loosing a savage cry, the long-enduring great Odysseus,
gathering all his force, swooped like a soaring eagle—
just as the son of Cronus hurled a reeking bolt
that fell at her feet, the mighty Father's daughter,
and blazing-eyed Athena wheeled on Odysseus, crying,
595 "Royal son of Laertes, Odysseus, master of exploits,
hold back now! Call a halt to the great leveler, War—
don't court the rage of Zeus who rules the world!"

So she commanded. He obeyed her, glad at heart.
And Athena handed down her pacts of peace
600 between both sides for all the years to come—
the daughter of Zeus whose shield is storm and thunder,
yes, but the goddess still kept Mentor's build and voice.

❧

RESONANCES

Franz Kafka: The Silence of the Sirens[1]

Proof that inadequate, even childish measures may serve to rescue one from peril:

To protect himself from the Sirens Ulysses stopped his ears with wax and had
himself bound to the mast of his ship. Naturally any and every traveler before him
could have done the same, except those whom the Sirens allured even from a great
distance; but it was known to all the world that such things were of no help whatever.
The song of the Sirens could pierce through everything, and the longing of those they
seduced would have broken far stronger bonds than chains and masts. But Ulysses did

---

1. Translated by Willa and Edwin Muir. The great modernist writer Franz Kafka (1883–1924) was born and raised in the
German-Jewish section of Prague, at that time part of the Austro-Hungarian Empire. Both drawn to and estranged from the
cultures around him—Czech, German, and Jewish—Kafka wrote enigmatic parables, stories, and novels such as *The Trial*
and *The Metamorphosis* (see Volume F) probing the absurdities of existence. A self-doubting perfectionist, he published
little before his early death from tuberculosis. In the short parable given here, Kafka revisits the famous scene of the Sirens
(page 405) to create an image of a man—or an artist—struggling against silence rather than seductive song.

not think of that, although he had probably heard of it. He trusted absolutely to his handful of wax and his fathom of chain, and in innocent elation over his little stratagem sailed out to meet the Sirens.

Now the Sirens have a still more fatal weapon than their song, namely their silence. And though admittedly such a thing has never happened, still it is conceivable that someone might possibly have escaped from their singing; but from their silence certainly never. Against the feeling of having triumphed over them by one's own strength, and the consequent exaltation that bears down everything before it, no earthly powers can resist.

And when Ulysses approached them the potent songstresses actually did not sing, whether because they thought that this enemy could be vanquished only by their silence, or because the look of bliss on the face of Ulysses, who was thinking of nothing but his wax and his chains, made them forget their singing.

But Ulysses, if one may so express it, did not hear their silence; he thought they were singing and that he alone did not hear them. For a fleeting moment he saw their throats rising and falling, their breasts lifting, their eyes filled with tears, their lips half-parted, but believed that these were accompaniments to the airs which died unheard around him. Soon, however, all this faded from his sight as he fixed his gaze on the distance, the Sirens literally vanished before his resolution, and at the very moment when they were nearest to him he knew of them no longer.

But they—lovelier than ever—stretched their necks and turned, let their awesome hair flutter free in the wind, and freely stretched their claws on the rocks. They no longer had any desire to allure; all that they wanted was to hold as long as they could the radiance that fell from Ulysses' great eyes.

If the Sirens had possessed consciousness they would have been annihilated at that moment. But they remained as they had been; all that had happened was that Ulysses had escaped them.

A codicil[2] to the foregoing has also been handed down. Ulysses, it is said, was so full of guile, was such a fox, that not even the goddess of fate could pierce his armor. Perhaps he had really noticed, although here the human understanding is beyond its depths, that the Sirens were silent, and held up to them and to the gods the aforementioned pretense merely as a sort of shield.

George Seferis: Upon a Foreign Verse[1]

For Elli, Christmas 1931

Fortunate he who's made the voyage of Odysseus.
Fortunate if on setting out he's felt the rigging of a love strong in his body,
    spreading there like veins where the blood throbs.

2. A clause added at the end of a legal document.
1. Translated by Edmund Keeley and Philip Sherrard. The modern Greek poet George Seferis (1900–1971) studied law in Paris and then joined the Greek diplomatic service; he was ambassador to England at the end of his career. He wrote all the while, publishing a dozen books of verse, essays, diaries, and fiction, mostly written while abroad. His verse achieved international acclaim, and he won the No-

bel Prize in literature in 1963. Influenced by French Symbolist poetry, T. S. Eliot, and Ezra Pound, Seferis became the first major modernist poet in Greece. At the same time, his work is filled with references to classical literature, particularly to the wanderings of Odysseus, as in this 1940 poem, which sees Homer's epic both as a living presence and as deeply foreign, despite the apparent closeness of ancient and modern Greek.

A love of indissoluble rhythm, unconquerable like music and endless
because it was born when we were born and when it dies, if it does die,
   neither we know nor does anyone else.

5   I ask God to help me say, at some moment of great happiness, what that
   love is;
sometimes when I sit surrounded by exile I hear its distant murmur like the
   sound of sea struck by an inexplicable hurricane.

And again and again the shade of Odysseus appears before me, his eyes red
   from the waves' salt,
from his ripe longing to see once more the smoke ascending from his warm
   hearth and the dog grown old waiting by the door.

A large man, whispering through his whitened beard words in our language
   spoken as it was three thousand years ago.
10 He extends a palm calloused by the ropes and the tiller, his skin weathered
   by the dry north wind, by heat and snow.

It's as if he wants to expel from among us the superhuman one-eyed
   Cyclops, the Sirens who make you forget with their song, Scylla and
   Charybdis:
so many complex monsters that prevent us from remembering that he too
   was a man struggling in the world with soul and body.

He is the mighty Odysseus: he who proposed the wooden horse with which
   the Achaeans captured Troy.
I imagine he's coming to tell me how I too may build a wooden horse to
   capture my own Troy.

15 Because he speaks humbly and calmly, without effort, as though he were
   my father
or certain old sailors of my childhood who, leaning on their nets with winter
   coming on and the wind angering,

used to recite, with tears in their eyes, the song of Erotocritos;[2]
it was then I would shudder in my sleep at the unjust fate of Aretousa descending the marble steps.

He tells me of the harsh pain you feel when the ship's sails swell with memory and your soul becomes a rudder;
20 of being alone, dark in the night, and helpless as chaff on the threshing
   floor;

of the bitterness of seeing your companions one by one pulled down into the
   elements and scattered;
and of how strangely you gain strength conversing with the dead when the
   living who remain are no longer enough.

He speaks . . . I still see his hands that knew how to judge the carving of the
   mermaid at the prow
presenting me the waveless blue sea in the heart of winter.

---

2. A 17th-century epic from Crete by Vizentzos Kornaros, telling of the love between the valiant knight Erotokritos and the king's daughter, Aretousa.

Derek Walcott: *from* Omeros[1]

Seven Seas rose in the half-dark to make coffee.
Sunrise was heating the ring of the horizon
and clouds were rising like loaves. By the heat of the

glowing iron rose he slid the saucepan's base on-
5   to the ring and anchored it there. The saucepan shook
from the weight of water in it, then it settled.

* * *

The dog scratched at the kitchen door for him to open
35   but he made it wait. He drummed the kitchen table
with his fingers. Two blackbirds quarrelled at breakfast.

Except for one hand he sat as still as marble,
with his egg-white eyes, fingers recounting the past
of another sea, measured by the stroking oars.

40   O open this day with the conch's moan, Omeros,
as you did in my boyhood, when I was a noun
gently exhaled from the palate of the sunrise.

A lizard on the sea-wall darted its question
at the waking sea, and a net of golden moss
45   brightened the reef, which the sails of their far canoes

avoided. Only in you, across centuries
of the sea's parchment atlas, can I catch the noise
of the surf lines wandering like the shambling fleece

of the lighthouse's flock, that Cyclops whose blind eye
50   shut from the sunlight. Then the canoes were galleys
over which a frigate sawed its scythed wings slowly.

In you the seeds of grey almonds guessed a tree's shape,
and the grape leaves rusted like serrated islands,
and the blind lighthouse, sensing the edge of a cape,

55   paused like a giant, a marble cloud in its hands,
to hurl its boulder that splashed into phosphorous
stars; then a black fisherman, his stubbled chin coarse

as a dry sea-urchin's, hoisted his flour-sack
sail on its bamboo spar, and scanned the opening line
60   of our epic horizon; now I can look back

1. Born in 1930 on St. Lucia in the Caribbean island chain known as the Antilles, Derek Walcott received a British colonial education there, then went to college in Jamaica. He then settled in Trinidad and wrote poetry and plays. For many years he split his time between Trinidad and a teaching post at Boston University, while writing 15 volumes of poetry and a dozen plays. Long recognized as one of the greatest poets writing in English, he received the Nobel Prize in literature in 1992, two years after the publication of his epic verse novel *Omeros*. See Volume F for more of Walcott's poetry.

    Written in three-line stanzas based on the form of Dante's *Divine Comedy,* Walcott's poem tells of the rivalry of two St. Lucian fishermen, Achille and Hector, for the love of a local woman, Helen. They are observed by various other characters, including a blind fisherman nicknamed Seven Seas who may be a reincarnation of Homer. Walcott himself also appears in the poem as an Odysseus-like voyager; in the scene given here, which takes place early in the poem, he visits the Boston studio of a young Greek sculptor, Antigone, who has become his lover, and he meditates on Homer's persistent presence, connecting the islands of Greece and the Caribbean.

to rocks that see their own feet when light nets the waves,
as the dugouts set out with ebony captains,
since it was your light that startled our sunlit wharves

where schooners swayed idly, moored to their cold capstans.
65   A wind turns the harbour's pages back to the voice
that hummed in the vase of a girl's throat: "Omeros."

"O-meros," she laughed. "That's what we call him in Greek,"
stroking the small bust with its boxer's broken nose,
and I thought of Seven Seas sitting near the reek

70   of drying fishnets, listening to the shallows' noise.
I said: "Homer and Virg are New England farmers,
and the winged horse guards their gas-station, you're right."[2]

I felt the foam head watching as I stroked an arm, as
cold as its marble, then the shoulders in winter light
75   in the studio attic. I said, "Omeros,"

and O was the conch-shell's invocation, *mer* was
both mother and sea in our Antillean patois,°   *dialect*
os, a grey bone, and the white surf as it crashes

and spreads its sibilant collar on a lace shore.
80   Omeros was the crunch of dry leaves, and the washes
that echoed from a cave-mouth when the tide has ebbed.

The name stayed in my mouth. I saw how light was webbed
on her Asian cheeks, defined her eyes with a black
almond's outline, as Antigone turned and said:

85   "I'm tired of America, it's time for me to go back
to Greece. I miss my islands." I write, it returns—
the way she turned and shook out the black gust of hair.

I saw how the surf printed its lace in patterns
on the shore of her neck, then the lowering shallows
90   of silk swirled at her ankles, like surf without noise,

and felt that another cold bust, not hers, but yours
saw this with stone almonds for eyes, its broken nose
turning away, as the rustling silk agrees.

But if it could read between the lines of her floor
95   like a white-hot deck uncaulked by Antillean heat,
to the shadows in its hold, its nostrils might flare

at the stench from manacled ankles, the coffled feet°   *roped in line*
scraping like leaves, and perhaps the inculpable marble
would have turned its white seeds away, to widen

---

2. In the 1950s and 1960s, an American chain of gas stations had a winged Pegasus as its symbol.

100   the bow of its mouth at the horror under her table,
          from the lyre of her armchair draped with its white chiton,°   *Greek tunic*
          to do what the past always does: suffer, and stare.

          She lay calm as a port, and a cloud covered her
          with my shadow; then a prow with painted eyes
105   slowly emerged from the fragrant rain of black hair.

          And I heard a hollow moan exhaled from a vase,
          not for kings floundering in lances of rain; the prose
          of abrupt fishermen cursing over canoes.

❧

ARCHAIC LYRIC POETRY

Lyric poetry exists alongside epic poetry, may even precede it in time, and offers an alternative to the bloody terrain of the Homeric battlefield. Sung by a single singer or a chorus of voices, these poems emerge in the world of aristocratic palaces, tyrants' courts, and the early city-states. Many different voices compose this body of work, which they performed in a variety of settings, some celebrating aristocratic bonding, others expressing discontent with the social order and its values, and still others participating in the rituals of worship that bound citizens into communities.

The singers of these poems, whether individuals or choruses, performed them to music, to the sound of stringed instruments such as the lyre, from which the word "lyric" comes. Every line of the Homeric poems was composed in one meter, or verse pattern, but the lyrics vary widely in their meters and in the moods and energies that different rhythms convey. Homer mentions lyric poetry and the choruses, music, and dance of the early forms, but it isn't until the seventh century B.C.E. that the names of individual lyric singers begin to be noted. These names are connected with particular city-states in the vast Greek world, stretching from Asia Minor to Africa to what is now France, and the poems themselves often mark specific occasions rather than retelling the well-known, often-told, and beloved stories of a tradition, as do the epic poems. If Homer understands himself to be a conduit for the Muses—the goddesses of music, poetry, and dance and the daughters of the goddess Memory—these lyric singers begin to speak and sing as individuals, with names and voices that set them apart from the epic tradition, even as they use this tradition for their own purposes.

These poems stand in contrast to earlier Sumerian and Egyptian poetry such as the "poetry of love and devotion" (page 41) sung in the voice of an individual who is not particularized. At the same time, the Near Eastern poems already present much of the image repertoire available to the ancient Greek lyric poets. In Greece, stories were told about individual poets such as Simonides, said to be stingy and greedy for money, as poets began to be rewarded more openly for their labors. These poets sang victory odes, praise poems, poems of insult and blame, songs in honor of the gods, many varieties of love poetry (of women desiring each other and men desiring girls and boys, slave and free), songs for symposia (drinking parties), witty epigrams, and solemn epitaphs composed to mark tombs. Those who could afford to—including the newly rich, athletes, and tyrants—commissioned poems. The archaic lyric poets span the period from Homer to the invention of democracy in Athens and reveal new, contradictory strains in ancient society. And they establish the bases for future lyric poetry, from Catullus and Horace in ancient Rome to the early modern English poets Shakespeare and Donne to twentieth-century poets such as H. D. and William Butler Yeats.

Arkhilokhos

7th century B.C.E.

Arkhilokhos used violent, abusive, and sexual language to humiliate his enemies. The Greeks said that his poetry caused a certain Lycambes and his daughters to hang themselves in shame after Arkhilokhos described in detail the sexual experiences he claimed to have shared with the girls. He belongs to a tradition of verbal abuse called the *iambos,* which may have begun with ritual insults and obscenities performed in honor of Demeter, goddess of grain, and Dionysos, god of wine. He stands firmly against the heroic, aristocratic, idealizing strain of the Homeric epic, boasting that he threw away his shield in battle to lighten his load and run rather than die with honor like Achilles. He came from the Greek island of Paros and may have served as a mercenary soldier, observing the politics of his day and surviving battles and shipwrecks. His reference to animal fables connects him to popular traditions such as that of Aesop, the freed slave who was said to have invented the fable. The Greeks probably learned many such stories from the East, from Mesopotamia, and in turn influenced Indian and later fable traditions with their potent stories in which animals talk.

PRONUNCIATION:
  Arkhilokhos: ar-KHIL-oh-khos

Encounter in a Meadow[1]

      . . . No, my dear friend,
      I'm overcome by crippling desire.
      " . . . holding entirely off . . .

      If you can't wait and your desire is urgent,
5   there's somebody else at our house
      now longing for a man,

      a lovely slender girl, there's nothing wrong
      (if I'm any judge) with her looks.
      Why not make friends with her?"

10   That's what she said, and here's how I replied:
      "Daughter of Amphimedo,
      that lady fine and true

      whom now the mouldy earth has taken in,
      the love-goddess offers young men
15   a range of joys besides

      the sacrament, and one of them will serve.
      We'll talk of all this, you and I,
      at leisure, when . . .

            . . . grows dark, and may God be our aid.
20   I'll do it all just as you say.

---

1. Translated by M. L. West. As with many of the lyric poets, Arkhilokhos's verses survived in partially fragmentary form, as shown by ellipses.

But please, my dear, don't grudge it if I go
under the arch, through the gates;
I'll dock at the grass borders,

be sure of that. Now as for Neoboule,
25   someone else have her. Dear me,
she's past ripe, twice your age;

her girlhood's flower has shed its petals, lost
all the enchantment it had.
She never got enough;

30   she's proved her . . .'s measure, crazy woman.
Keep her away—for the crows!
I pray no friend of mine

would have me marry somebody like her
and give all the neighbours a laugh.
35   No, you're the one I want.

You're not untrustworthy, you're not two-faced,
but she's so precipitate, she
makes friends with crowds of men.

I don't want babies blind and premature,
40   like the proverbial bitch,
from showing too much haste."

That's what I said; and then I took the girl,
and laying her down in the flowers,
with my soft-textured cloak

45   I covered her; my arm cradled her neck,
while she in her fear like a fawn
gave up the attempt to run.

Gently I touched her breasts, where the young flesh
peeped from the edge of her dress,
50   her ripeness newly come,

and then, caressing all her lovely form,
I shot my hot energy off,
just brushing golden hairs.

The Fox and the Hedgehog

The fox knows lots of tricks,
the hedgehog only one—but it's a winner.

Elegies

I am a servant of the lord god of war,
and one versed in the Muses' lovely gifts.

On my spear's my daily bread,
   on my spear my wine
from Ismaros; and drinking it,
   it's on my spear I recline.

5   There won't be many bows drawn, nor much slingshot,
when on the plain the War-god brings the fight
together; it will be an agony
of swords—that is the warfare that the doughty
barons of Euboea are expert at . . .

10   But come now, take the cup and pass along
the clipper's benches, open up the casks
and draw the red wine off the lees—we too
shall need some drink to get us through this watch.

Some Saian[1] sports my splendid shield:
15   I had to leave it in a wood,
but saved my skin. Well, I don't care—
   I'll get another just as good.

Sappho

early 7th century B.C.E.

The Greeks so valued Sappho's poetry that they called her the tenth Muse. Born to an aristocratic family on the island of Lesbos, she wrote poems reflecting a world of luxury, strongly marked by her island's proximity to the Asian coast and its wealthy cities. The fragmentary remains of her poetry reveal an aristocratic taste for adornments, flowers, perfumed oils, and erotic pleasures. Her poems include songs of sexual pursuit and remembrances of beloved women, sometimes framed as hymns to the goddess of *eros,* Aphrodite. Sappho was known for her verse celebrating same-sex desire, giving rise to the modern term "lesbian," which at root means simply "a native of Lesbos." Sappho also wrote wedding poems, poems of insult, and poems that refer to the heroic legends of the Trojan War. Her aesthetic oftens evokes what the Greeks called *pothos,* "yearning," a recollecting of scenes of pleasure or festival or the arrival among women of the immortal goddess. She belongs to the aristocratic world of the Archaic period, secure in its privileges and possibly even committed to preserving its way of life against tyrannical ambitions, since she was said to have been exiled in the turmoil of Lesbian politics during her lifetime. Although her poetry is fragmentary, it is the most substantial body of work by a woman that remains from classical antiquity.

PRONUNCIATION:
   Sappho: SAF-fo

Rich-throned immortal Aphrodite[1]

Rich-throned immortal Aphrodite,
scheming daughter of Zeus, I pray you,

---

1. From Thrace, in northern Greece.   1. Translated by M. L. West.

Sappho and Alkaios, red-figure
vase, c. 500 B.C.E.

with pain and sickness, Queen, crush not my heart,

    but come, if ever in the past you
5   heard my voice from afar and hearkened,
and left your father's halls and came, with gold

    chariot yoked; and pretty sparrows
    brought you swiftly across the dark earth
fluttering wings from heaven through the air.

10   Soon they were here, and you, Blest Goddess,
       smiling with your immortal features,
asked why I'd called, what was the matter now,

    what was my heart insanely craving:
    "Who is it this time I must cozen
15   to love you, Sappho? Who's unfair to you?

"For though she flee, soon she'll be chasing;
   though she refuse gifts, she'll be giving;
though she love not, she'll love despite herself."

20

Yes, come once more, from sore obsession
   free me; all that my heart desires
fulfilled, fulfil—help me to victory!

Come, goddess

Come, goddess, to your holy shrine,
   where your delightful apple grove
awaits, and altars smoke with frankincense.

5

A cool brook sounds through apple boughs,
   and all's with roses overhung;
from shimmering leaves a trancelike sleep takes hold.

Here is a flowery meadow, too,
   where horses graze, and gentle blow
the breezes . . .

10

Here, then, Love-goddess much in mind,
   infuse our feast in gracious style
with nectar poured in cups that turn to gold.

Some think a fleet

Some think a fleet, a troop of horse
   or soldiery the finest sight
in all the world; but I say, what one loves.

5

Easy it is to make this plain
   to anyone. She the most fair
of mortals, Helen, having a man of the best,

deserted him, and sailed to Troy,
   without a thought for her dear child
or parents, led astray by [love's power.]

10

[For though the heart be pr]oud [and strong,]
   [Love] quickly [bends it to his will.—]
That makes me think of Anactoria.

I'd sooner see her lovely walk
   and the bright sparkling of her face
15   than all the horse and arms of Lydia.[1]

_____

1. Wealthy kingdom near Lesbos in Asia Minor.

He looks to me to be in heaven

He looks to me to be in heaven,
   that man who sits across from you
and listens near you to your soft speaking,

   your laughing lovely: that, I vow,
5   makes the heart leap in my breast;
for watching you a moment, speech fails me,

   my tongue is paralysed, at once
   a light fire runs beneath my skin,
my eyes are blinded, and my ears drumming,

10   the sweat pours down me, and I shake
   all over, sallower than grass:
I feel as if I'm not far off dying.

   But no thing is too hard to bear;
   for [God can make] the poor man [rich,
15 or bring to nothing heaven-high fortune.]

Love shakes my heart

Love
shakes my heart like the wind rushing down on
   the mountain oaks.

Honestly, I wish I were dead

Honestly, I wish I were dead.
She was covered in tears as she went away,

   left me, saying "Oh, it's too bad!
   How unlucky we are! I swear,
5 Sappho, I don't want to be leaving you."

   This is what I replied to her:
   "Go, be happy, and think of me.
You remember how we looked after you;

   or if not, then let me remind
     . . . . .
10 all the lovely and beautiful times we had,

   all the garlands of violets
   and of roses and . . .
and . . . that you've put on in my company,

   all the delicate chains of flowers
15   that encircled your tender neck
     . . . . .
     . . . . .
and the costly unguent with which

you anointed yourself, and the royal myrrh.

On soft couches . . .
Tender . . .
20 you assuaged your longing . . .

There was never a . . .
or a shrine or a . . .
. . . that we were not present at,

no grove . . . no festive dance . . .

. . . she worshipped you

. . . she worshipped you
and always in your singing she most delighted.

But now among the women of Lydia
she shines, as after the sun has set
5   the rosy-fingered moon will appear, surpassing

all the stars, bestowing her light alike
upon the waves of the briny sea
and on the fields that sparkle with countless flowers.

Everything is bathed in the lovely dew:
10 roses take their nourishment, and
soft chervil, and the blossoming honey-lotus.

Often, as she moves on her daily round,
she'll be eating her tender heart
when she thinks of her love for gentle Atthis.

15 And for us to go there . . .
. . . it's not possible . . .
with the wedding-song (?) ringing loud between us.

Like the sweet-apple

Like the sweet-apple that's gleaming red on the topmost bough,
right at the very end, that the apple-pickers forgot,
or rather didn't forget, but were just unable to reach.

Like the hyacinth on the hills that the passing shepherds
5   trample under their feet, and the purple bloom on the ground . . .

The doorman's feet

The doorman's feet are size 90:
five cowhides went into his sandals,
and it took ten cobblers to make them!

High must be the chamber—
5   Hymenaeum!
Make it high, you builders!

A bridegroom's coming—
    Hymenaeum!
like the War-god himself, the tallest of the tall!

RESONANCE

Alejandra Pizarnik: Poems[1]

Poem

You choose the place of the wound
where we speak our silence.
You make of my life
this ceremony excessively pure.

Lovers

a flower
        not far from the night
        my mute body
    opens
to the delicate urgency of dew

Recognition

You make the silence of lilacs fluttering
in the tragedy of wind in my heart.
You make of my life a child's story
where shipwrecks and deaths
are pretexts for adorable ceremonies.

Meaning of His Absence

    if I dare
    to look or to speak
    it is due to his shadow
    united so gently
5   to my name
    far away
    in the rain
    in my memory

---

1. Translated by Frank Graziano, Maria Rosa Fort, and Suzanne Levine. A student of philosophy and painting in Buenos Aires, Alejandra Pizarnik (1936–1972) also studied religion and French literature at the Sorbonne. She lived in Paris for several years and translated into Spanish works by experimental French and Francophone writers such as Antonin Artaud and Aimé Césaire. She committed suicide at age 36 through a barbiturate overdose. Melancholy, obsessive, and given to states of ecstasy and depression, she explored in her poetry the whole gamut of mental states that range from the sublime to the obscene, from lyrical tenderness to sadomasochism.

Pizarnik's poetry has earned her a devout following among readers of 20th-century Latin American poetry. In the decade before her death, she moved progressively into a world of language and poetry, speculating about suicide and the ecstasies of Sapphic love. In the end, her poetic language became disembodied and deliberately chaotic; in the poems given here, she plays both on Sappho's themes and on the fragmentary quality of Sappho's surviving verses.

10   due to his face
that burning in my poem
beautifully disperses
a perfume
to the loved face disappeared

Dawn

Nude dreaming a solar night.
I have lain down animal days.
The wind and rain erased me
like a flame, like a poem
written on a wall.

Falling

Never again the hope
in a coming and going
of names, of figures.
Someone dreamed very badly,
by mistake someone used up
the forgotten distances.

◦—◦═◈═◦—◦

Alkaios

7th–6th centuries B.C.E.

From Lesbos like his contemporary Sappho, Alkaios too was implicated in the aristocratic intrigues of the island. The surviving fragments of his work record an intense engagement with the troubled politics of Lesbos in the seventh and sixth centuries B.C.E. The aristocratic men of Archaic society intensified their bonds in *symposia* (drinking parties), attended by slaves and entertained with lyrics. Alkaios sings against a political rival, calling him "Pot-belly"; in verses reminiscent of the iambics of Arkhilokhos, Alkaios found material for his elite attitudes in the Homeric poems, condemned Helen of Troy, and was famous for his drinking songs, such as the fragment "Slave-boy, trickle the scent over my long-suffering head for me . . . and my chest with its gray hairs, . . . while we're drinking." Alkaios may have fought the Athenians over land in Asia Minor, traveled to Egypt, and been exiled, as was Sappho. His poems celebrating the armory and comparing the city-state to a ship at sea vividly convey the sense of Archaic society's aristocratic fraternity and its vulnerability to chaotic power struggles.

and fluttered Argive Helen's heart[1]

and fluttered Argive Helen's heart
within her breast. She, crazy for
the Trojan cheat-host, sailed away with him,

---

1. Translated by M. L. West.

abandoning her daughter dear
5   and her rich husband's bed: the child
of Zeus and Leda heard the call of love.

[Now Paris has his due.] The earth
full many of his brothers keeps,
felled in the Trojan plain because of her.

10   Many the chariots that hit
the dust, many the bright-eyed lads
trampled, as prince Achilles gleed in blood.

They tell that Priam and his sons

They tell that Priam and his sons
found yours a bitter marriage-bond,
Helen, that sank fair Ilios° in flames.   *Troy*

How different was the graceful bride
5   Aeacus' son[1] from Nereus' deeps
brought home to Chiron's cave, with all the gods

guests at the wedding! He undid
her virgin waistband: love grew well
for Peleus and the flower of Nereids.[2]

10   In time she bore a hero son
to drive his tawny steeds in pride
while Troy and Trojans paid for Helen's sin.

The high hall is agleam

The high hall is agleam
with bronze; the roof is all arrayed
    with shining helms, and white
horse-plumes to ornament men's heads
5   nod from their crests. Bright greaves
of bronze to keep strong arrows off
    cover the unseen pegs,
and corselets of new linen, and
    a pile of convex shields.
10   Chalcidian swords are there,
and belts in plenty, tunics too.
    We can't forget this store
now that we've taken on this task.

I can't make out the lie of the winds

I can't make out the lie of the winds.
One wave rolls up from one side, one

---

1. Peleus, father of Achilles.   2. The sea nymph Thetis.

from t'other; we between them toss
in our dark vessel, struggling against

a furious storm. We've water shipped
above the mast-box; you can see
all through the sail, it's torn across,
the stays are working slack, the rudder's gone.

. . . . .
. . . . .
. . . Both legs
stay tangled in the ropes—it's only this

keeps me from being washed away:
the cargo, walloped off the deck,
floats overhead . . .

—◦—≒◆≒—◦—

Pindar

518–438 B.C.E.

The poems of the Theban aristocrat Pindar celebrate athletes, gods, other aristocrats, and wealthy men, praising the victors in pan-Hellenic festivals such as the Olympic Games, in which Greeks gathered every four years to compete in a pentathlon, footraces in armor, chariot racing, wrestling, and boxing, all in honor of Zeus, the father of the gods. The victors won prizes, crowns of olive, and fame for the wealthy men who had sponsored their training. And these patrons in turn commissioned odes, songs performed to commemorate the victories. In dense, discontinuous verse, Pindar sings of the myths of the aristocratic families of the far-flung Greek world including such colonies as Syracuse in Sicily and Cyrene in Africa. His verses touch on the cities' foundations and on the contact between the legendary founders, their heroic ancestors, and the many gods the Greeks worshiped. Pindar focuses on the intense, radiant moment of victory and on the electrifying contact between gods and men. He links the older world of aristocratic domination to the emergent city-states with their many conflicts and factions, where the practice of payment for songs might be seen to conflict with aristocratic ideas of fraternity and gift giving.

First Olympian Ode[1]

Turn 1

Water is preeminent and gold, like a fire
burning in the night, outshines
all possessions that magnify men's pride.
But if, my soul, you yearn

5
to celebrate great games,
look no further
for another star
shining through the deserted ether

---

1. Translated by Frank J. Nisetich. A chorus would sing this ode as it danced, its moves indicated by "Turns" and "Counterturns."

brighter than the sun, or for a contest

10   mightier than Olympia—

          where the song

has taken its coronal

design of glory, plaited

in the minds of poets

as they come, calling on Zeus' name,

15   to the rich radiant hall of Hieron

Counterturn 1   who wields the scepter of justice in Sicily,

reaping the prime of every distinction.

And he delights in the flare of music,

the brightness of song circling

20   his table from man to man.

Then take the Dorian lyre

down from its peg

if the beauty of Pisa[2]

and of Pherenikos[3]

25   somehow

          cast your mind

under a gracious spell,

when by the stream

of Alpheos, keeping his flanks

ungrazed by the spur, he sped

30   and put his lord in the embrace of power—

Stand 1   Syracusan knight and king, blazoned

with glory in the land of Pelops:[4]

Pelops, whom earth-cradling Poseidon loved,

since Klotho had taken him

35   out of the pure cauldron, his ivory shoulder

gleaming in the hearth-light.

Yes! marvels are many, stories

starting from mortals somehow

stretch truth to deception

40   woven cunningly on the loom of lies.

Turn 2   Grace, the very one who fashions every delight

for mortal men, by lending her sheen

to what is unbelievable, often makes it believed.

But the days to come

45   are the wisest witness.

It is proper for a man

to speak well of the gods—

the blame will be less.

Pelops, I will tell your story

---

2. District of Olympia, site of a pan-Hellenic sanctuary of Zeus and of the Olympic Games.

3. Victorious horse owned by Hieron of Syracuse in Sicily.

4. The Peloponnesus, site of Olympia, was a peninsula forming the southern part of mainland Greece, called "the island of Pelops." Pelops was said by some to have been fed to the gods by his father, Tantalus; his shoulder, which was consumed, was replaced by one of ivory.

50   differently from the men of old.
                                    Your father Tantalos[5]
            had invited the gods to banquet
            in his beloved Sipylos, providing
            a stately feast in return
            for the feast they had given him.
55   It was then Poseidon seized you,

Counterturn 2   overwhelmed in his mind with desire, and swept you
            on golden mares to Zeus' glorious palace
            on Olympos, where, at another time, Ganymede[6] came also
            for the same passion in Zeus.
60   But after you had disappeared
            and searchers
            again and again
            returned to your mother
            without you, then one of the neighbors,
65   invidious, whispered
                                    that the gods had sliced you
            limb by limb into the fury
            of boiling water,
            and then they passed
            morsels of your flesh
70   around the table, and ate them.

Stand 2   No! I cannot call any of the blessed gods
            a savage: I stand apart.
            Disaster has often claimed the slanderer.
            If ever the watchlords of Olympos
75   honored a man, this was Tantalos.
            But he could not digest
            his great bliss—in his fullness he earned the doom
            that the father poised above him, the looming
            boulder which, in eternal
80   distraction, he strains to heave from his brow.

Turn 3   Such is the misery upon him, a fourth affliction
            among three others, because he robbed
            the immortals—their nektar and ambrosia,
            which had made him deathless,
85   he stole and gave
            to his drinking companions.
            But a man who hopes
            to hide his doings from the gods
            is deluded.
90   For this they hurled his son Pelops
                                    back among the short-lived

---

5. Son of Zeus, punished in the underworld (see *Odyssey*,
Book 11, page 384).

6. Beautiful son of Priam, king of Troy, immortalized as
Zeus's cupbearer.

generations of men.
But when he grew
toward the time of bloom
and black down curled on his cheeks,

95   he thought of a marriage there for his seeking—

Counterturn 3   to win from her Pisan father the girl Hippodameia.
Going down by the dim sea,
alone in the dark, he called on the god
of the trident, loud pounding

100   Poseidon, who appeared
and stood close by.
"If in any way,"
Pelops said to him,
"the gifts of Aphrodite

105   count in my favor,
                        shackle the bronze spear of Oinomaos,[7]
bring me on the swiftest chariot
to Elis, and put me
within the reach
of power, for he has slain

110   thirteen suitors now, and so he delays

Stand 3   his daughter's marriage. Great danger
does not come upon
the spineless man, and yet, if we must die,
why squat in the shadows, coddling a bland

115   old age, with no nobility, for nothing?
As for me, I will undertake this exploit.
And you—I beseech you: let me achieve it."
He spoke, and his words found fulfillment:
the god made him glow with gifts—

120   a golden chariot and winged horses never weary.

Turn 4   He tore the strength from Oinomaos and took
the maiden to his bed.
She bore him six sons, leaders of the people,
intent on prowess.

125   Now in the bright blood rituals
Pelops has his share, reclining
by the ford of Alpheos.
Men gather at his tomb, near the crowded altar.
The glory of the Olympiads

130   shoots its rays afar
                        in his races, where speed
and strength are matched
in the bruise of toil.
But the victor,

---

7. Father of Hippodameia, who pursued her suitors in a chariot race and killed them.

for the rest of his life,

135   enjoys days of contentment,

Counterturn 4   as far as contests can assure them.
A single day's blessing
is the highest good a mortal knows.
I must crown him now

140   to the horseman's tune,
in Aiolian rhythms,[8]
for I believe
the shimmering folds of my song
shall never embrace

145   a host more lordly in power
                    or perception of beauty.
Hieron, a god is overseer
to your ambitions, keeping watch,
cherishing them as his own.
If he does not abandon you soon,

150   still sweeter the triumph I hope

Stand 4   will fall to your speeding chariot,
and may I be the one to praise it,
riding up the sunny Hill of Kronos![9]
The Muse is tempering her mightiest arrow for me.

155   Men are great in various ways, but in kingship
the ultimate crest is attained.
Peer no farther into the beyond.
For the time we have, may you continue to walk on high,
and may I for as long consort with victors,

160   conspicuous for my skill among Greeks everywhere.

RESONANCES

John Keats: Ode on a Grecian Urn[1]

1

Thou still unravish'd bride of quietness,
   Thou foster-child of silence and slow time,
Sylvan° historian, who canst thus express   *forest*
   A flow'ry tale more sweetly than our rhyme:

5   What leaf-fring'd legend° haunts about thy shape   *caption*
   Of deities or mortals, or of both,

8. Dialect of Sappho and Alkaios of Lesbos.
9. At Olympia.
1. Pindar's odes had enormous influence on later poetry. The British Romantic poet John Keats (1795–1821) wrote a series of odes in 1819, two years before his early death from tuberculosis. Son of a stable keeper, Keats had little formal education, yet he was always fascinated by classical culture, which he encountered largely in translation. In his "Ode on a Grecian Urn," Keats describes three scenes on an imaginary Greek vase: first, an image of feasting and sexual pursuit; second, a musician playing panpipes; third, a religious rite outside a rustic town. Keats builds on the mixture of divine serenity and barely suppressed violence seen in Pindar and reflects on the mysterious beauty of an ancient relic of the past.

In Tempe or the dales of Arcady?[2]
What men or gods are these? What maidens loth?
What mad pursuit? What struggle to escape?
10   What pipes and timbrels?° What wild ecstasy?   *tambourines*

2

Heard melodies are sweet, but those unheard
Are sweeter; therefore, ye soft pipes, play on;
Not to the sensual° ear, but, more endear'd,   *physical*
Pipe to the spirit ditties of no tone:
15   Fair youth, beneath the trees, thou canst not leave
Thy song, nor ever can those trees be bare;
Bold Lover, never, never canst thou kiss,
Though winning near the goal—yet, do not grieve;
She cannot fade, though thou hast not thy bliss,
20   Forever wilt thou love, and she be fair!

3

Ah, happy, happy boughs! that cannot shed
Your leaves, nor ever bid the Spring adieu;
And, happy melodist, unwearièd,
Forever piping songs forever new;
25   More happy love! more happy, happy love!
Forever warm and still to be enjoy'd,
Forever panting, and forever young;
All breathing human passion far above,
That leaves a heart high-sorrowful and cloy'd,
30   A burning forehead, and a parching tongue.

4

Who are these coming to the sacrifice?
To what green altar, O mysterious priest,[3]
Lead'st thou that heifer lowing at the skies,
And all her silken flanks with garlands dressed?
35   What little town by river or sea shore,
Or mountain-built with peaceful citadel,
Is emptied of this folk, this pious morn?
And, little town, thy streets for evermore
Will silent be; and not a soul to tell
40   Why thou art desolate, can e'er return.

5

O Attic shape![4] Fair attitude!° with brede°   *pose / design*
Of marble men and maidens overwrought,°   *overlaid*
With forest branches and the trodden weed;
Thou, silent form, dost tease us out of thought
45   As doth eternity: Cold Pastoral!°   *poem of shepherds*
When old age shall this generation waste,
Thou shalt remain, in midst of other woe

---

2. Beautiful regions of Greece where the gods loved to descend to earth.

3. Priest of religious rites or "mysteries."

4. From Attica, the region where Athens is located.

Than ours, a friend to man, to whom thou say'st,
  "Beauty is truth, truth beauty,"—that is all
50   Ye know on earth, and all ye need to know.

Rainer Maria Rilke: Archaic Torso of Apollo[1]

We have no inkling of the fabled head
Wherein the eyeballs ripened. Even so
His trunk still sends a candelabrum glow
By which his gaze, with just its wick set low,

5   Persists and gleams. Else could the torso's curve
Not so bedazzle you, nor with the shifting
Of loins could then a vagrant smile be drifting
Toward that center point, begetting's nerve.

Else would this boulder stand, defaced and squat,
10   Beneath the shoulders' lucent° fall, and not   *shining*
Ashimmer like the coat of some wild beast;

Nor would it then through every margin knife
Forth like a star: for there is not the least
Of parts but sees you. You must change your life.

[END OF ARCHAIC POETRY]

Aeschylus
525–456 B.C.E.

The first great Athenian tragedian, Aeschylus fought at the battle of Marathon and wanted this fact recorded on his gravestone, which read:

> Under this monument lies Aeschylus the Athenian,
>   Euphorion's son, who died in the wheatlands of Gela. The grove
> of Marathon with its glories can speak of his valor in battle.
>   The long-haired Persian remembers and can speak of it too.

Aeschylus met the great invasion of the Persians from the east and with his fellow citizen-soldiers struggled to preserve the independence of the Hellenes and of his city, Athens. This experience seems to have marked him forever; he was a patriot who knew other cities of the Greek world, including those of distant Sicily, where he wrote a play to celebrate the foundation of the new city of Aetna and where he died. Yet Aeschylus is remembered as a man who remained passionately attached to the newly democratic city of Athens.

---

1. Translated by Walter Arndt. The German poet Rainer Maria Rilke (1875–1926) was a modernist experimenter who often turned to classical forms and themes. Like Keats's ode, this sonnet describes a work of Greek art, in this case a torso of Apollo, god of light and patron of music, who has often been taken as an emblem of Greek order and reason. Whereas Keats emphasizes the timeless perfection of his Grecian urn, Rilke reflects on the enduring power of an artwork that has lost what ought to have been its key feature, its head, but that nonetheless seems to see the modern viewer and speak in terms of challenge and inspiration.

Aeschylus wrote more than seventy plays, of which only seven have survived: *The Suppliants; The Persians; The Seven Against Thebes; Prometheus Bound* (whose authorship is disputed); and a trilogy called the *Oresteia,* a series of three plays all performed on the same day: *Agamemnon, The Libation Bearers,* and *The Eumenides.* Aeschylus was the first of the great tragedians of Athens whose work survives to the present, and his innovations helped establish the definitive form of classical tragedy. The earliest tragedians, including Aeschylus, experimented with subjects from contemporary events; the older Phrynichus wrote a play about the fall of Miletus, a city in Asia Minor linked through tribal ties to the Athenians and conquered by the Persians. The audience was so distressed by the spectacle that after this performance, tragedians, with the exception of Aeschylus, did not show episodes from the present on stage. Aeschylus's *Persians* (first performed in 472 B.C.E.) exceptionally depicts the catastrophe of Persian defeat by the Greeks at the battle of Salamis in 480, in which Aeschylus may have fought, and represents the Persian emperor Xerxes with great nobility and compassion. The dead emperor Darius, who rises from the grave, pronounces words of wisdom that are meant to chasten the listening Persians—and to remind the Athenian audience itself of its mortality:

> And corpses, piled up like sand, shall witness
> Mute, even to the century to come,
> Before the eyes of men, that never, being
> Mortal, ought we cast our thoughts too high.
> Insolence, once blossoming, bears
> Its fruit, a tasseled field of doom, from which
> A weeping harvest's reaped, all tears.

In *The Suppliants,* the fifty daughters of Danaus arrive in Argos, pursued by their Egyptian suitors. The king at first does not recognize them as Greeks, descended from Io:

> You speak beyond my credence, strangers, claiming
> Argive birth: more like Libyans you seem
> Than like to women native here; or the Nile may foster
> Such a likeness; or the images
> Of Cyprus, carved by native craftsmen;
> And of the camel-backed nomads I've heard,
> Neighbors to the Ethiopian;
> I should have thought you were the unwed
> Barbarous Amazons, were you armed with bows.

The king of Argos exhibits a distinctly cosmopolitan knowledge of the inhabitants of the southern Mediterranean.

Aeschylus is said to focus more on action and on dramatic events than on the development of character, a feature of Sophoclean tragedy. Perhaps because he was closer in the history of tragedy to its evolution from the chorus, he also uses the chorus with great effectiveness, so that rather than merely commenting on the action of the characters, they emerge as characters in their own right, sometimes recalling as if in a dream state such events as the sacrifice of Iphigeneia in *Agamemnon,* and then behaving as ineffectual elders as they hear of the slaughter of Agamemnon and Cassandra by Clytaemestra. He uses vivid, archaic language, sometimes borrowed from the epic vocabulary, painting dramatic scenes such as the sacrifice of Agamemnon and Clytaemestra's daughter:

> Pouring then to the ground her saffron mantle
> she struck the sacrifiers with
> the eyes' arrows of pity,
> lovely as in a painted scene. . . .

Aeschylus takes advantage of visual effects such as the purple cloth on which Agamemnon steps as he goes to his death, and some say the dawn over the open-air theater acted as the leaping beacons of fire that announced the fall of Troy, "plunging skyward to arch the shoulders of the sea."

Agamemnon is the first play of the *Oresteia,* centered on the troubles of the house of Agamemnon. This trilogy develops the theme of the *nostos,* the return, as do *The Odyssey* and other lost poems of the epic cycle; in contrast to Clytaemestra, Odysseus's wife Penelope waited faithfully for him and preserved his house. The second play of the trilogy presents Orestes, son of Agamemnon and Clytaemestra, who himself returns from exile to avenge his father's murder and kills his mother and her lover, Aegisthus. For his crime against his mother, the Furies, earthy goddesses of blood right, pursue him as he flees from Argos. *The Eumenides,* or the Kindly Ones, shows Orestes seeking sanctuary at the oracle of Apollo at Delphi and then being tried before the first Athenian homicide court, presided over by Athena herself. She ends by declaring him innocent of crime, since

> The mother is no parent of that which is called
> her child, but only nurse of the new-planted seed
> that grows. The parent is he who mounts. A stranger she
> preserves a stranger's seed, if no god interferes.

The Furies are persuaded to bless, not curse, the city of Athens and are led beneath the earth, as the beneficent Eumenides. A satyr play, *Proteus,* now lost, followed the set of tragedies.

The trilogy as a whole lays out the ways in which learning comes through suffering. From terrible errors—adultery, cannibalism, human sacrifice, and murder—spreads disaster, but the great institutions of democracy and the system of trial by jury follow. Each individual drama in the trilogy can stand alone, but they are bound together by a magnificent pattern of images and themes. Light comes after darkness; the image of the net recurs. In *Agamemnon,* the chorus recalls Zeus's plan for the destruction of Troy:

> O Zeus our lord and Night beloved,
> bestower of power and beauty,
> you slung above the bastions of Troy
> the binding net, that none, neither great
> nor young, might outleap
> the gigantic toils
> of enslavement and final disaster.

Agamemnon says of Troy that he and his soldiers "fenced within our toils / of wrath the city. . . ." Then Clytaemestra takes her revenge:

> That he might not escape nor beat aside his death,
> as fishermen cast their huge circling nets, I spread
> deadly abundance of rich robes, and caught him fast.

Orestes displays "this net that caught a man" in *The Libation Bearers,* and the language of the ensnaring echoes throughout the trilogy.

Aeschylus was an intensely political writer. Some critics think the *Oresteia* celebrates democratic limitations of the traditional authority of the aristocrats, who had ruled in the centuries before the installation of democracy. This poet knew war, its violence, and its boredom; the herald in *Agamemnon* recalls the battleground: "the meadow dews came out / to soak our clothes and fill our hair with lice." Aeschylus desired peace for his city. He expressed a complex and muted hope for that democracy in his vision of the buried Furies, and although they wait beneath the surface of the city, they cast a spell on the city Aeschylus loved, as Athena commands them to:

Let it come out of the ground, out of the sea's water,
and from the high air make the waft of gentle gales
wash over the country in full sunlight, and the seed
and stream of the soil's yield and of the grazing beasts
be strong and never fail our people as time goes,
and make the human seed be kept alive. Make more
the issue of those who worship more your ways, for as
the gardener works in love, so love I best of all
the unblighted generation of these upright men.

PRONUNCIATIONS:
Aegisthus: ay-GIS-thus
Aeschylus: ES-kyou-lus
Clytaemestra: clue-ty-MES-tra
Eumenides: you-MEN-ih-deez
Oresteia: or-est-AY-ah

Agamemnon[1]

Characters

WATCHMAN

CLYTAEMESTRA

HERALD

AGAMEMNON

CASSANDRA

AEGISTHUS

CHORUS OF ARGIVE ELDERS

ATTENDANTS OF CLYTAEMESTRA, OF AGAMEMNON, BODYGUARD OF AEGISTHUS

(*ALL SILENT PARTS*)

[*Time, directly after the fall of Troy.*]

Scene: *Argos, before the palace of King Agamemnon. The Watchman, who speaks the opening lines, is posted on the roof of the palace. Clytaemestra's entrances are made from a door in the center of the stage; all others, from the wings.*

[*The Watchman, alone.*]

I ask the gods some respite from the weariness
of this watchtime measured by years I lie awake
elbowed upon the Atreidae's[2] roof dogwise to mark
the grand processionals of all the stars of night

5 burdened with winter and again with heat for men,
dynasties in their shining blazoned on the air,
these stars, upon their wane and when the rest arise.

I wait; to read the meaning in that beacon light,

---

1. Translated by Richmond Lattimore.   2. Menelaus and Agamemnon, the sons of Atreus.

a blaze of fire to carry out of Troy the rumor
10   and outcry of its capture; to such end a lady's
male strength of heart in its high confidence ordains.
Now as this bed stricken with night and drenched with dew
I keep, nor ever with kind dreams for company:
since fear in sleep's place stands forever at my head
15   against strong closure of my eyes, or any rest:
I mince such medicine against sleep failed: I sing,
only to weep again the pity of this house
no longer, as once, administered in the grand way.
Now let there be again redemption from distress,
20   the flare burning from the blackness in good augury.

[*A light shows in the distance.*]

Oh hail, blaze of the darkness, harbinger of day's
shining, and of processionals and dance and choirs
of multitudes in Argos for this day of grace.
Ahoy!
25   I cry the news aloud to Agamemnon's queen,
that she may rise up from her bed of state with speed
to raise the rumor of gladness welcoming this beacon,
and singing rise, if truly the citadel of Ilium[3]
has fallen, as the shining of this flare proclaims.
30   I also, I, will make my choral prelude, since
my lord's dice cast aright are counted as my own,
and mine the tripled sixes of this torchlit throw.

May it only happen. May my king come home, and I
take up within this hand the hand I love. The rest
35   I leave to silence; for an ox stands huge upon
my tongue. The house itself, could it take voice, might speak
aloud and plain. I speak to those who understand,
but if they fail, I have forgotten everything.

[*Exit. The Chorus enters, speaking.*]

Ten years since the great contestants
40   of Priam's[4] right,
Menelaus and Agamemnon, my lord,
twin throned, twin sceptered, in twofold power
of kings from God, the Atreidae,
put forth from this shore
45   the thousand ships of the Argives,
the strength and the armies.
Their cry of war went shrill from the heart,
as eagles stricken in agony
for young perished, high from the nest
50   eddy and circle

---

3. Troy, in the northwest corner of Asia Minor.   4. King of Troy.

to bend and sweep of the wings' stroke,
lost far below
the fledgelings, the nest, and the tendance.
Yet someone hears in the air, a god,
55   Apollo, Pan, or Zeus, the high
thin wail of these sky-guests, and drives
late to its mark
the Fury upon the transgressors.

So drives Zeus the great guest god
60   the Atreidae against Alexander:[5]
for one woman's promiscuous sake
the struggling masses, legs tired,
knees grinding in dust,
spears broken in the onset.
65   Danaans and Trojans
they have it alike. It goes as it goes
now. The end will be destiny.
You cannot burn flesh or pour unguents,
not innocent cool tears,
70   that will soften the gods' stiff anger.

But we; dishonored, old in our bones,
cast off even then from the gathering horde,
stay here, to prop up
on staves the strength of a baby.
75   Since the young vigor that urges
inward to the heart
is frail as age, no warcraft yet perfect,
while beyond age, leaf
withered, man goes three footed
80   no stronger than a child is,
a dream that falters in daylight.

[*Clytaemestra enters quietly. The Chorus continues to speak.*]

But you, lady,
daughter of Tyndareus, Clytaemestra, our queen:
What is there to be done? What new thing have you heard?
85   In persuasion of what
report do you order such sacrifice?
To all the gods of the city,
the high and the deep spirits,
to them of the sky and the market places,
90   the altars blaze with oblations.
The staggered flame goes sky high
one place, then another,
drugged by the simple soft

5. Son of Priam and Hecuba, better known as Paris, who took Helen from her husband, Menelaus.

persuasion of sacred unguents,

95   the deep stored oil of the kings.
Of these things what can be told
openly, speak.
Be healer to this perplexity
that grows now into darkness of thought,

100   while again sweet hope shining from the flames
beats back the pitiless pondering
of sorrow that eats my heart.

I have mastery yet to chant the wonder at the wayside
given to kings. Still by God's grace there surges within me

105   singing magic
grown to my life and power,
how the wild bird portent
hurled forth the Achaeans'
twin-stemmed power single hearted,

110   lords of the youth of Hellas,
with spear and hand of strength
to the land of Teucrus.[6]
Kings of birds to the kings of the ships,
one black, one blazed with silver,

115   clear seen by the royal house
on the right, the spear hand,
they lighted, watched by all
tore a hare, ripe, bursting with young unborn yet,
stayed from her last fleet running.

120   Sing sorrow, sorrow: but good win out in the end.

Then the grave seer of the host saw through to the hearts divided,
knew the fighting sons of Atreus feeding on the hare
with the host, their people.
Seeing beyond, he spoke:

125   "With time, this foray
shall stalk the castle of Priam.
Before then, under
the walls, Fate shall spoil
in violence the rich herds of the people.

130   Only let no doom of the gods darken
upon this huge iron forged to curb Troy—
from inward. Artemis the undefiled[7]
is angered with pity
at the flying hounds of her father

135   eating the unborn young in the hare and the shivering mother.
She is sick at the eagles' feasting.
Sing sorrow, sorrow: but good win out in the end.

Lovely you are and kind

---

6. Troy.   7. Goddess of virgins and the hunt.

to the tender young of ravening lions.

140   For sucklings of all the savage
      beasts that lurk in the lonely places you have sympathy.
      Grant meaning to these appearances
      good, yet not without evil.
      Healer Apollo,[8] I pray you

145   let her not with cross winds
      bind the ships of the Danaans
      to time-long anchorage
      forcing a second sacrifice unholy, untasted,
      working bitterness in the blood

150   and faith lost. For the terror returns like sickness to lurk in the house;
      the secret anger remembers the child that shall be avenged."
      Such, with great good things beside, rang out in the voice of Calchas,
      these fatal signs from the birds by the way to the house of the princes,
      wherewith in sympathy

155   sing sorrow, sorrow: but good win out in the end.

      Zeus:[9] whatever he may be, if this name
      pleases him in invocation,
      thus I call upon him.
      I have pondered everything

160   yet I cannot find a way,
      only Zeus, to cast this dead weight of ignorance
      finally from out my brain.

      He who in time long ago was great,
      throbbing with gigantic strength,

165   shall be as if he never were, unspoken.
      He who followed him has found
      his master, and is gone.
      Cry aloud without fear the victory of Zeus,
      you will not have failed the truth:

170   Zeus, who guided men to think,
      who has laid it down that wisdom
      comes alone through suffering.
      Still there drips in sleep against the heart
      grief of memory; against

175   our pleasure we are temperate.
      From the gods who sit in grandeur
      grace comes somehow violent.

      On that day the elder king
      of the Achaean ships, no more

180   strict against the prophet's word,
      turned with the crosswinds of fortune,
      when no ship sailed, no pail was full,

8. Brother of Artemis and god of healing, music, murder,   9. Greatest of the Olympian gods.
purification, and prophecy at the Pythian oracle in Delphi.

and the Achaean people sulked
fast against the shore at Aulis
185   facing Chalcis, where the tides ebb and surge:

and winds blew from the Strymon, bearing
sick idleness, ships tied fast, and hunger,
distraction of the mind, carelessness
for hull and cable;
190   with time's length bent to double measure
by delay crumbled the flower and pride
of Argos. Then against the bitter wind
the seer's voice clashed out
another medicine
195   more hateful yet, and spoke of Artemis,[1] so that the kings
dashed their staves to the ground and could not hold their tears.

The elder lord spoke aloud before them:
"My fate is angry if I disobey these,
but angry if I slaughter
200   this child, the beauty of my house,
with maiden blood shed staining
these father's hands beside the altar.
What of these things goes now without disaster?
How shall I fail my ships
205   and lose my faith of battle?
For them to urge such sacrifice of innocent blood
angrily, for their wrath is great—it is right. May all be well yet."

But when necessity's yoke was put upon him
he changed, and from the heart the breath came bitter
210   and sacrilegious, utterly infidel,
to warp a will now to be stopped at nothing.
The sickening in men's minds, tough,
reckless in fresh cruelty brings daring. He endured then
to sacrifice his daughter
215   to stay the strength of war waged for a woman,
first offering for the ships' sake.

Her supplications and her cries of father
were nothing, nor the child's lamentation
to kings passioned for battle.
220   The father prayed, called to his men to lift her
with strength of hand swept in her robes aloft
and prone above the altar, as you might lift
a goat for sacrifice, with guards
against the lips' sweet edge, to check
225   the curse cried on the house of Atreus
by force of bit and speech drowned in strength.

---

1. The Greeks (also called "Achaeans," "Danaans," and "Argives") had offended Artemis, who demanded the sacrifice of Iphigeneia, daughter of Agamemnon and Clytaemestra.

Pouring then to the ground her saffron mantle
she struck the sacrificers with
the eyes' arrows of pity,
230   lovely as in a painted scene, and striving
to speak—as many times
at the kind festive table of her father
she had sung, and in the clear voice of a stainless maiden
with love had graced the song
235   of worship when the third cup was poured.

What happened next I saw not, neither speak it.
The crafts of Calchas fail not of outcome.
Justice so moves that those only learn
who suffer; and the future
240   you shall know when it has come; before then, forget it.
It is grief too soon given.
All will come clear in the next dawn's sunlight.
Let good fortune follow these things as
she who is here desires,
245   our Apian land's singlehearted protectress.

[*The Chorus now turns toward Clytaemestra, and the leader speaks to her.*]

I have come in reverence, Clytaemestra, of your power.
For when the man is gone and the throne void, his right
falls to the prince's lady, and honor must be given.
Is it some grace—or otherwise—that you have heard
250   to make you sacrifice at messages of good hope?
I should be glad to hear, but must not blame your silence.
CLYTAEMESTRA: As it was said of old, may the dawn child be born
to be an angel of blessing from the kindly night.
You shall know joy beyond all you ever hoped to hear.
255   The men of Argos have taken Priam's citadel.
CHORUS: What have you said? Your words escaped my unbelief.
CLYTAEMESTRA: The Achaeans are in Troy. Is that not clear enough?
CHORUS: This slow delight steals over me to bring forth tears.
CLYTAEMESTRA: Yes, for your eyes betray the loyal heart within.
CHORUS: Yet how can I be certain? Is there some evidence?
CLYTAEMESTRA: There is, there must be; unless a god has lied to me.
CHORUS: Is it dream visions, easy to believe, you credit?
CLYTAEMESTRA: I accept nothing from a brain that is dull with sleep.
CHORUS: The charm, then, of some rumor, that made rich your hope?
CLYTAEMESTRA: Am I some young girl, that you find my thoughts so silly?
CHORUS: How long, then, is it since the citadel was stormed?
CLYTAEMESTRA: It is the night, the mother of this dawn I hailed.
CHORUS: What kind of messenger could come in speed like this?
CLYTAEMESTRA: Hephaestus, who cast forth the shining blaze from Ida.
270   And beacon after beacon picking up the flare
carried it here; Ida to the Hermaean horn
of Lemnos, where it shone above the isle, and next
the sheer rock face of Zeus on Athos caught it up;

and plunging skyward to arch the shoulders of the sea
275   the strength of the running flare in exultation,
pine timbers flaming into gold, like the sunrise,
brought the bright message to Macistus' sentinel cliffs,
who, never slow nor in the carelessness of sleep
caught up, sent on his relay in the courier chain,
280   and far across Euripus' streams the beacon flare
carried to signal watchmen on Messapion.
These took it again in turn, and heaping high a pile
of silvery brush flamed it to throw the message on.
And the flare sickened never, but grown stronger yet
285   outleapt the river valley of Asopus like
the very moon for shining, to Cithaeron's scaur°   *cliff*
to waken the next station of the flaming post.
These watchers, not contemptuous of the far-thrown blaze,
kindled another beacon vaster than commanded.
290   The light leaned high above Gorgopis' staring marsh,
and striking Aegyplanctus' mountain top, drove on
yet one more relay, lest the flare die down in speed.
Kindled once more with stintless heaping force, they send
the beard of flame to hugeness, passing far beyond
295   the promontory that gazes on the Saronic strait
and flaming far, until it plunged at last to strike
the steep rock of Arachnus near at hand, our watchtower.
And thence there fell upon this house of Atreus' sons
the flare whose fathers mount to the Idaean beacon.
300   These are the changes on my torchlight messengers,
one from another running out the laps assigned.
The first and the last sprinters have the victory.
By such proof and such symbol I announce to you
my lord at Troy has sent his messengers to me.
CHORUS: The gods, lady, shall have my prayers and thanks straightway.
And yet to hear your story till all wonder fades
would be my wish, could you but tell it once again.
CLYTAEMESTRA: The Achaeans have got Troy, upon this very day.
I think the city echoes with a clash of cries.
310   Pour vinegar and oil into the selfsame bowl,
you could not say they mix in friendship, but fight on.
Thus variant sound the voices of the conquerors
and conquered, from the opposition of their fates.
Trojans are stooping now to gather in their arms
315   their dead, husbands and brothers; children lean to clasp
the aged who begot them, crying upon the death
of those most dear, from lips that never will be free.
The Achaeans have their midnight work after the fighting
that sets them down to feed on all the city has,
320   ravenous, headlong, by no rank and file assigned,
but as each man has drawn his shaken lot by chance.
And in the Trojan houses that their spears have taken

they settle now, free of the open sky, the frosts
and dampness of the evening; without sentinels set
325 they sleep the sleep of happiness the whole night through.
And if they reverence the gods who hold the city
and all the holy temples of the captured land,
they, the despoilers, might not be despoiled in turn.
Let not their passion overwhelm them; let no lust
330 seize on these men to violate what they must not.
The run to safety and home is yet to make; they must turn
the pole, and run the backstretch of the double course.
Yet, though the host come home without offence to high
gods, even so the anger of these slaughtered men
335 may never sleep. Oh, let there be no fresh wrong done!

Such are the thoughts you hear from me, a woman merely.
Yet may the best win through, that none may fail to see.
Of all good things to wish this is my dearest choice.
CHORUS: My lady, no grave man could speak with better grace.
340 I have listened to the proofs of your tale, and I believe,
and go to make my glad thanksgivings to the gods.
This pleasure is not unworthy of the grief that gave it.
O Zeus our lord and Night beloved,
bestower of power and beauty,
345 you slung above the bastions of Troy
the binding net, that none, neither great
nor young, might outleap
the gigantic toils
of enslavement and final disaster.
350 I gaze in awe on Zeus of the guests
who wrung from Alexander such payment.
He bent the bow with slow care, that neither
the shaft might hurdle the stars, nor fall
spent to the earth, short driven.

355 They have the stroke of Zeus to tell of.
This thing is clear and you may trace it.
He acted as he had decreed. A man thought
the gods deigned not to punish mortals
who trampled down the delicacy of things
360 inviolable. That man was wicked.
The curse on great daring
shines clear; it wrings atonement
from those high hearts that drive to evil,
from houses blossoming to pride
365 and peril. Let there be
wealth without tears; enough for
the wise man who will ask no further.
There is not any armor
in gold against perdition
370 for him who spurns the high altar

of Justice down to the darkness.

Persuasion the persistent overwhelms him,
she, strong daughter of designing Ruin.
And every medicine is vain; the sin
375   smolders not, but burns to evil beauty.
As cheap bronze tortured
at the touchstone relapses
to blackness and grime, so this man
tested shows vain
380   as a child that strives to catch the bird flying
and wins shame that shall bring down his city.
No god will hear such a man's entreaty,
but whoso turns to these ways
they strike him down in his wickedness.
385   This was Paris: he came
to the house of the sons of Atreus,
stole the woman away, and shamed
the guest's right of the board shared.

She left among her people the stir and clamor
390   of shields and of spearheads,
the ships to sail and the armor.
She took to Ilium her dowry, death.
She stepped forth lightly between the gates
daring beyond all daring. And the prophets
395   about the great house wept aloud and spoke:
"Alas, alas for the house and for the champions,
alas for the bed signed with their love together.
Here now is silence, scorned, unreproachful.
The agony of his loss is clear before us.
400   Longing for her who lies beyond the sea
he shall see a phantom queen in his household.
Her images in their beauty
are bitterness to her lord now
where in the emptiness of eyes
405   all passion has faded."

Shining in dreams the sorrowful
memories pass; they bring him
vain delight only.
It is vain, to dream and to see splendors,
410   and the image slipping from the arms' embrace
escapes, not to return again,
on wings drifting down the ways of sleep.
Such have the sorrows been in the house by the hearthside;
such have there been, and yet there are worse than these.
415   In all Hellas, for those who swarmed to the host
the heartbreaking misery
shows in the house of each.
Many are they who are touched at the heart by these things.

Those they sent forth they knew;
420   now, in place of the young men
urns and ashes are carried home
to the houses of the fighters.

The god of war, money changer of dead bodies,
held the balance of his spear in the fighting,
425   and from the corpse-fires at Ilium
sent to their dearest the dust
heavy and bitter with tears shed
packing smooth the urns with
ashes that once were men.
430   They praise them through their tears, how this man
knew well the craft of battle, how another
went down splendid in the slaughter:
and all for some strange woman.
Thus they mutter in secrecy,
435   and the slow anger creeps below their grief
at Atreus' sons and their quarrels.
There by the walls of Ilium
the young men in their beauty keep
graves deep in the alien soil
440   they hated and they conquered.

The citizens speak: their voice is dull with hatred.
The curse of the people must be paid for.
There lurks for me in the hooded night
terror of what may be told me.
445   The gods fail not to mark
those who have killed many.
The black Furies stalking the man
fortunate beyond all right
wrench back again the set of his life
450   and drop him to darkness. There among
the ciphers there is no more comfort
in power. And the vaunt of high glory
is bitterness; for God's thunderbolts
crash on the towering mountains.
455   Let me attain no envied wealth,
let me not plunder cities,
neither be taken in turn, and face
life in the power of another.

[*Various members of the Chorus, speaking severally.*]

From the beacon's bright message
460   the fleet rumor runs
through the city. If this be real
who knows? Perhaps the gods have sent some lie to us.

Who of us is so childish or so reft of wit
that by the beacon's messages

465   his heart flamed must despond again
        when the tale changes in the end?

        It is like a woman indeed
        to take the rapture before the fact has shown for true.

        They believe too easily, are too quick to shift
470   from ground to ground; and swift indeed
        the rumor voiced by a woman dies again.

        Now we shall understand these torches and their shining,
        the beacons, and the interchange of flame and flame.
        They may be real; yet bright and dreamwise ecstasy
475   in light's appearance might have charmed our hearts awry.
        I see a herald coming from the beach, his brows
        shaded with sprigs of olive; and upon his feet
        the dust, dry sister of the mire, makes plain to me
        that he will find a voice, not merely kindle flame
480   from mountain timber, and make signals from the smoke,
        but tell us outright, whether to be happy, or—
        but I shrink back from naming the alternative.
        That which appeared was good; may yet more good be given.

        And any man who prays that different things befall
485   the city, may he reap the crime of his own heart.

        [*The Herald enters, and speaks.*]

        Soil of my fathers, Argive earth I tread upon,
        in daylight of the tenth year I have come back to you.
        All my hopes broke but one, and this I have at last.
        I never could have dared to dream that I might die
490   in Argos, and be buried in this beloved soil.
        Hail to the Argive land and to its sunlight, hail
        to its high sovereign, Zeus, and to the Pythian king.
        May you no longer shower your arrows on our heads.
        Beside Scamandrus you were grim; be satisfied
495   and turn to savior now and healer of our hurts,
        my lord Apollo. Gods of the market place assembled,
        I greet you all, and my own patron deity
        Hermes, beloved herald, in whose right all heralds
        are sacred; and you heroes that sent forth the host,
500   propitiously take back all that the spear has left.
        O great hall of the kings and house beloved; seats
        of sanctity; divinities that face the sun:
        if ever before, look now with kind and glowing eyes
        to greet our king in state after so long a time.
505   He comes, lord Agamemnon, bearing light in gloom
        to you, and to all that are assembled here.
        Salute him with good favor, as he well deserves,
        the man who has wrecked Ilium with the spade of Zeus
        vindictive, whereby all their plain has been laid waste.

510   Gone are their altars, the sacred places of the gods
        are gone, and scattered all the seed within the ground.
        With such a yoke as this gripped to the neck of Troy
        he comes, the king, Atreus' elder son, a man
        fortunate to be honored far above all men
515   alive; not Paris nor the city tied to him
        can boast he did more than was done him in return.
        Guilty of rape and theft, condemned, he lost the prize
        captured, and broke to sheer destruction all the house
        of his fathers, with the very ground whereon it stood.
520   Twice over the sons of Priam have atoned their sins.

CHORUS: Hail and be glad, herald of the Achaean host.

HERALD: I am happy; I no longer ask the gods for death.

CHORUS: Did passion for your country so strip bare your heart?

HERALD: So that the tears broke in my eyes, for happiness.

CHORUS: You were taken with that sickness, then, that brings delight.

HERALD: How? I cannot deal with such words until I understand.

CHORUS: Struck with desire of those who loved as much again.

HERALD: You mean our country longed for us, as we for home?

CHORUS: So that I sighed, out of the darkness of my heart.

HERALD: Whence came this black thought to afflict the mind with fear?

CHORUS: Long since it was my silence kept disaster off.

HERALD: But how? There were some you feared when the kings went away?

CHORUS: So much that as you said now, even death were grace.

HERALD: Well: the end has been good. And in the length of time
535   part of our fortune you could say held favorable,
        but part we cursed again. And who, except the gods,
        can live time through forever without any pain?
        Were I to tell you of the hard work done, the nights
        exposed, the cramped sea-quarters, the foul beds—what part
540   of day's disposal did we not cry out loud?
        Ashore, the horror stayed with us and grew. We lay
        against the ramparts of our enemies, and from
        the sky, and from the ground, the meadow dews came out
        to soak our clothes and fill our hair with lice. And if
545   I were to tell of winter time, when all birds died,
        the snows of Ida past endurance she sent down,
        or summer heat, when in the lazy noon the sea
        fell level and asleep under a windless sky—
        but why live such grief over again? That time is gone
550   for us, and gone for those who died. Never again
        need they rise up, nor care again for anything.
        Why must a live man count the numbers of the slain,
        why grieve at fortune's wrath that fades to break once more?
        I call a long farewell to all our unhappiness.
555   For us, survivors of the Argive armament,
        the pleasure wins, pain casts no weight in the opposite scale.
        And here, in this sun's shining, we can boast aloud,
        whose fame has gone with wings across the land and sea:

"Upon a time the Argive host took Troy, and on
560   the houses of the gods who live in Hellas nailed
the spoils, to be the glory of days long ago."
And they who hear such things shall call this city blest
and the leaders of the host; and high the grace of God
shall be exalted, that did this. You have the story.

CHORUS: I must give way; your story shows that I was wrong.
Old men are always young enough to learn, with profit.
But Clytaemestra and her house must hear, above
others, this news that makes luxurious my life.

[Clytaemestra comes forward and speaks.]

I raised my cry of joy, and it was long ago
570   when the first beacon flare of message came by night
to speak of capture and of Ilium's overthrow.
But there was one who laughed at me, who said: "You trust
in beacons so, and you believe that Troy has fallen?
How like a woman, for the heart to lift so light."
575   Men spoke like that; they thought I wandered in my wits;
yet I made sacrifice, and in the womanish strain
voice after voice caught up the cry along the city
to echo in the temples of the gods and bless
and still the fragrant flame that melts the sacrifice.

580   Why should you tell me then the whole long tale at large
when from my lord himself I shall hear all the story?
But now, how best to speed my preparation to
receive my honored lord come home again—what else
is light more sweet for woman to behold than this,
585   to spread the gates before her husband home from war
and saved by God's hand?—take this message to the king:
Come, and with speed, back to the city that longs for him,
and may he find a wife within his house as true
as on the day he left her, watchdog of the house
590   gentle to him alone, fierce to his enemies,
and such a woman in all her ways as this, who has
not broken the seal upon her in the length of days.
With no man else have I known delight, nor any shame
of evil speech, more than I know how to temper bronze.

[Clytaemestra goes to the back of the stage.]

HERALD: A vaunt like this, so loaded as it is with truth,
it well becomes a highborn lady to proclaim.
CHORUS: Thus has she spoken to you, and well you understand,
words that impress interpreters whose thought is clear.
But tell me, herald; I would learn of Menelaus,
600   that power beloved in this land. Has he survived
also, and come with you back to his home again?
HERALD: I know no way to lie and make my tale so fair
that friends could reap joy of it for any length of time.

CHORUS: Is there no means to speak us fair, and yet tell the truth?
605   It will not hide, when truth and good are torn asunder.
HERALD: He is gone out of the sight of the Achaean host,
     vessel and man alike. I speak no falsehood there.
CHORUS: Was it when he had put out from Ilium in your sight,
     or did a storm that struck you both whirl him away?
HERALD: How like a master bowman you have hit the mark
     and in your speech cut a long sorrow to brief stature.
CHORUS: But then the rumor in the host that sailed beside,
     was it that he had perished, or might yet be living?
HERALD: No man knows. There is none could tell us that for sure
615   except the Sun, from whom this earth has life and increase.
CHORUS: How did this storm, by wrath of the divinities,
     strike on our multitude at sea? How did it end?
HERALD: It is not well to stain the blessing of this day
     with speech of evil weight. Such gods are honored apart.
620   And when the messenger of a shaken host, sad faced,
     brings to his city news it prayed never to hear,
     this scores one wound upon the body of the people;
     and that from many houses many men are slain
     by the two-lashed whip dear to the War God's hand, this turns
625   disaster double-bladed, bloodily made two.
     The messenger so freighted with a charge of tears
     should make his song of triumph at the Furies' door.
     But, carrying the fair message of our hopes' salvation,
     come home to a glad city's hospitality,
630   how shall I mix my gracious news with foul, and tell
     of the storm on the Achaeans by God's anger sent?
     For they, of old the deepest enemies, sea and fire,
     made a conspiracy and gave the oath of hand
     to blast in ruin our unhappy Argive army.
635   At night the sea began to rise in waves of death.
     Ship against ship the Thracian stormwind shattered us,
     and gored and split, our vessels, swept in violence
     of storm and whirlwind, beaten by the breaking rain,
     drove on in darkness, spun by the wicked shepherd's hand.
640   But when the sun came up again to light the dawn,
     we saw the Aegaean Sea blossoming with dead men,
     the men of Achaea, and the wreckage of their ships.
     For us, and for our ship, some god, no man, by guile
     or by entreaty's force prevailing, laid his hand
645   upon the helm and brought us through with hull unscarred.
     Life-giving fortune deigned to take our ship in charge
     that neither riding in deep water she took the surf
     nor drove to shoal and break upon some rocky shore.
     But then, delivered from death at sea, in the pale day,
650   incredulous of our own luck, we shepherded
     in our sad thoughts the fresh disaster of the fleet
     so pitifully torn and shaken by the storm.

Now of these others, if there are any left alive
they speak of us as men who perished, must they not?
655 Even as we, who fear that they are gone. But may
it all come well in the end. For Menelaus: be sure
if any of them come back that he will be the first.
If he is still where some sun's gleam can track him down,
alive and open-eyed, by blessed hand of God
660 who willed that not yet should his seed be utterly gone,
there is some hope that he will still come home again.
You have heard all; and be sure, you have heard the truth.

   [*The Herald goes out.*]

CHORUS: Who is he that named you so
fatally in every way?
665 Could it be some mind unseen
in divination of your destiny
shaping to the lips that name
for the bride of spears and blood,
Helen, which is death? Appropriately
670 death of ships, death of men and cities
from the bower's soft curtained
and secluded luxury she sailed then,
driven on the giant west wind,
and armored men in their thousands came,
675 huntsmen down the oar blade's fading footprint
to struggle in blood with those
who by the banks of Simoeis
beached their hulls where the leaves break.

And on Ilium in truth
680 in the likeness of the name
the sure purpose of the Wrath drove
marriage with death: for the guest board
shamed, and Zeus kindly to strangers,
the vengeance wrought on those men
685 who graced in too loud voice the bride-song
fallen to their lot to sing,
the kinsmen and the brothers.
And changing its song's measure
the ancient city of Priam
690 chants in high strain of lamentation,
calling Paris him of the fatal marriage;
for it endured its life's end
in desolation and tears
and the piteous blood of its people.

695 Once a man fostered in his house
a lion cub, from the mother's milk
torn, craving the breast given.
In the first steps of its young life

700 mild, it played with children
and delighted the old.
Caught in the arm's cradle
they pampered it like a newborn child,
shining eyed and broken to the hand
to stay the stress of its hunger.

705 But it grew with time, and the lion
in the blood strain came out; it paid
grace to those who had fostered it
in blood and death for the sheep flocks,
a grim feast forbidden.
710 The house reeked with blood run
nor could its people beat down the bane,
the giant murderer's onslaught.
This thing they raised in their house was blessed
by God to be priest of destruction.

715 And that which first came to the city of Ilium,
call it a dream of calm
and the wind dying,
the loveliness and luxury of much gold,
the melting shafts of the eyes' glances,
720 the blossom that breaks the heart with longing.
But she turned in mid-step of her course to make
bitter the consummation,
whirling on Priam's people
to blight with her touch and nearness.
725 Zeus hospitable sent her,
a vengeance to make brides weep.

It has been made long since and grown old among men,
this saying: human wealth
grown to fulness of stature
730 breeds again nor dies without issue.
From high good fortune in the blood
blossoms the quenchless agony.
Far from others I hold my own
mind; only the act of evil
735 breeds others to follow,
young sins in its own likeness.
Houses clear in their right are given
children in all loveliness.

But Pride aging is made
740 in men's dark actions
ripe with the young pride
late or soon when the dawn of destiny
comes and birth is given
to the spirit none may fight nor beat down,
745 sinful Daring; and in those halls

the black visaged Disasters stamped
in the likeness of their fathers.

And Righteousness is a shining in
the smoke of mean houses.
750   Her blessing is on the just man.
From high halls starred with gold by reeking hands
she turns back
with eyes that glance away to the simple in heart,
spurning the strength of gold
755   stamped false with flattery.
And all things she steers to fulfilment.

[*Agamemnon enters in a chariot, with Cassandra beside him. The Chorus speaks to him.*]

Behold, my king: sacker of Troy's citadel,
own issue of Atreus.
How shall I hail you? How give honor
760   not crossing too high nor yet bending short
of this time's graces?
For many among men are they who set high
the show of honor, yet break justice.
If one be unhappy, all else are fain
765   to grieve with him: yet the teeth of sorrow
come nowise near to the heart's edge.
And in joy likewise they show joy's semblance,
and torture the face to the false smile.
Yet the good shepherd, who knows his flock,
770   the eyes of men cannot lie to him,
that with water of feigned
love seem to smile from the true heart.
But I: when you marshalled this armament
for Helen's sake, I will not hide it,
775   in ugly style you were written in my heart
for steering aslant the mind's course
to bring home by blood
sacrifice and dead men that wild spirit.
But now, in love drawn up from the deep heart,
780   not skimmed at the edge, we hail you.
You have won, your labor is made gladness.
Ask all men: you will learn in time
which of your citizens have been just
in the city's sway, which were reckless.

AGAMEMNON: To Argos first, and to the gods within the land,
I must give due greeting; they have worked with me to bring
me home; they helped me in the vengeance I have wrought
on Priam's city. Not from the lips of men the gods
heard justice, but in one firm cast they laid their votes
790   within the urn of blood that Ilium must die
and all her people; while above the opposite vase

the hand hovered and there was hope, but no vote fell.
The stormclouds of their ruin live; the ash that dies
upon them gushes still in smoke their pride of wealth.
795 For all this we must thank the gods with grace of much
high praise and memory, we who fenced within our toils
of wrath the city; and, because one woman strayed,
the beast of Argos broke them, the fierce young within
the horse, the armored people who marked out their leap
800 against the setting of the Pleiades. A wild
and bloody lion swarmed above the towers of Troy
to glut its hunger lapping at the blood of kings.

This to the gods, a prelude strung to length of words.
But, for the thought you spoke, I heard and I remember
805 and stand behind you. For I say that it is true.
In few men is it part of nature to respect
a friend's prosperity without begrudging him,
as envy's wicked poison settling to the heart
piles up the pain in one sick with unhappiness,
810 who, staggered under sufferings that are all his own,
winces again to the vision of a neighbor's bliss.
And I can speak, for I have seen, I know it well,
this mirror of companionship, this shadow's ghost,
these men who seemed my friends in all sincerity.
815 One man of them all, Odysseus, he who sailed unwilling,
once yoked to me carried his harness, nor went slack.
Dead though he be or living, I can say it still.

Now in the business of the city and the gods
we must ordain full conclave of all citizens
820 and take our counsel. We shall see what element
is strong, and plan that it shall keep its virtue still.
But that which must be healed—we must use medicine,
or burn, or amputate, with kind intention, take
all means at hand that might beat down corruption's pain.
825 So to the King's house and the home about the hearth
I take my way, with greeting to the gods within
who sent me forth, and who have brought me home once more.
My prize was conquest; may it never fail again.

[*Clytaemestra comes forward and speaks.*]

Grave gentlemen of Argolis assembled here,
830 I take no shame to speak aloud before you all
the love I bear my husband. In the lapse of time
modesty fades; it is human.
                                        What I tell you now
I learned not from another; this is my own sad life
all the long years this man was gone at Ilium.
835 It is evil and a thing of terror when a wife
sits in the house forlorn with no man by, and hears

rumors that like a fever die to break again,
and men come in with news of fear, and on their heels
another messenger, with worse news to cry aloud

840   here in this house. Had Agamemnon taken all
the wounds the tale whereof was carried home to me,
he had been cut full of gashes like a fishing net.
If he had died each time that rumor told his death,
he must have been some triple-bodied Geryon[2]

845   back from the dead with threefold cloak of earth upon
his body, and killed once for every shape assumed.
Because such tales broke out forever on my rest,
many a time they cut me down and freed my throat
from the noose overslung where I had caught it fast.

850   And therefore is your son, in whom my love and yours
are sealed and pledged, not here to stand with us today,
Orestes. It were right; yet do not be amazed.
Strophius of Phocis, comrade in arms and faithful friend
to you, is keeping him. He spoke to me of peril

855   on two counts; of your danger under Ilium,
and here, of revolution and the clamorous people
who might cast down the council—since it lies in men's
nature to trample on the fighter already down.
Such my excuse to you, and without subterfuge.

860   For me: the rippling springs that were my tears have dried
utterly up, nor left one drop within. I keep
the pain upon my eyes where late at night I wept
over the beacons long ago set for your sake,
untended left forever. In the midst of dreams

865   the whisper that a gnat's thin wings could winnow broke
my sleep apart. I thought I saw you suffer wounds
more than the time that slept with me could ever hold.

Now all my suffering is past, with griefless heart
I hail this man, the watchdog of the fold and hall;

870   the stay that keeps the ship alive; the post to grip
groundward the towering roof; a father's single child;
land seen by sailors after all their hope was gone;
splendor of daybreak shining from the night of storm;
the running spring a parched wayfarer strays upon.

875   Oh, it is sweet to escape from all necessity!

Such is my greeting to him, that he well deserves.
Let none bear malice; for the harm that went before
I took, and it was great.
                                    Now, my beloved one,
step from your chariot; yet let not your foot, my lord,

880   sacker of Ilium, touch the earth. My maidens there!

2. A mythical giant.

Why this delay? Your task has been appointed you,
to strew the ground before his feet with tapestries.
Let there spring up into the house he never hoped
to see, where Justice leads him in, a crimson path.

885   In all things else, my heart's unsleeping care shall act
with the gods' aid to set aright what fate ordained.

[*Clytaemestra's handmaidens spread a bright carpet between the chariot and the door.*]

AGAMEMNON: Daughter of Leda, you who kept my house for me,
there is one way your welcome matched my absence well.
You strained it to great length. Yet properly to praise
890   me thus belongs by right to other lips, not yours.
And all this—do not try in woman's ways to make
me delicate, nor, as if I were some Asiatic
bow down to earth and with wide mouth cry out to me,
nor cross my path with jealousy by strewing the ground
895   with robes. Such state becomes the gods, and none beside.
I am a mortal, a man; I cannot trample upon
these tinted splendors without fear thrown in my path.
I tell you, as a man, not god, to reverence me.
Discordant is the murmur at such treading down
900   of lovely things; while God's most lordly gift to man
is decency of mind. Call that man only blest
who has in sweet tranquillity brought his life to close.
If I could only act as such, my hope is good.
CLYTAEMESTRA: Yet tell me this one thing, and do not cross my will.
AGAMEMMON: My will is mine. I shall not make it soft for you.
CLYTAEMESTRA: It was in fear surely that you vowed this course to God.
AGAMEMNON: No man has spoken knowing better what he said.
CLYTAEMESTRA: If Priam had won as you have, what would he have done?
AGAMEMNON: I well believe he might have walked on tapestries.
CLYTAEMESTRA: Be not ashamed before the bitterness of men.
AGAMEMNON: The people murmur, and their voice is great in strength.
CLYTAEMESTRA: Yet he who goes unenvied shall not be admired.
AGAMEMNON: Surely this lust for conflict is not womanlike?
CLYTAEMESTRA: Yet for the mighty even to give way is grace.
AGAMEMNON: Does such a victory as this mean so much to you?
CLYTAEMESTRA: Oh yield! The power is yours. Give way of your free will.
AGAMEMNON: Since you must have it—here, let someone with all speed
take off these sandals, slaves for my feet to tread upon.
And as I crush these garments stained from the rich sea
920   let no god's eyes of hatred strike me from afar.
Great the extravagance, and great the shame I feel
to spoil such treasure and such silver's worth of webs.

So much for all this. Take this stranger girl within
now, and be kind. The conqueror who uses softly
925   his power, is watched from far in the kind eyes of God,

and this slave's yoke is one no man will wear from choice.
Gift of the host to me, and flower exquisite
from all my many treasures, she attends me here.

Now since my will was bent to listen to you in this
930   my feet crush purple as I pass within the hall.
CLYTAEMESTRA: The sea is there, and who shall drain its yield? It breeds
precious as silver, ever of itself renewed,
the purple ooze wherein our garments shall be dipped.
And by God's grace this house keeps full sufficiency
935   of all. Poverty is a thing beyond its thought.
I could have vowed to trample many splendors down
had such decree been ordained from the oracles
those days when all my study was to bring home your life.
For when the root lives yet the leaves will come again
940   to fence the house with shade against the Dog Star's heat,
and now you have come home to keep your hearth and house
you bring with you the symbol of our winter's warmth;
but when Zeus ripens the green clusters into wine
there shall be coolness in the house upon those days
945   because the master ranges his own halls once more.

Zeus, Zeus accomplisher, accomplish these my prayers.
Let your mind bring these things to pass. It is your will.

[*Agamemnon and Clytaemestra enter the house. Cassandra remains in the
chariot. The Chorus speaks.*]

Why must this persistent fear
beat its wings so ceaselessly
950   and so close against my mantic heart?
Why this strain unwanted, unrepaid, thus prophetic?
Nor can valor of good hope
seated near the chambered depth
of the spirit cast it out
955   as dreams of dark fancy; and yet time
has buried in the mounding sand
the sea cables since that day
when against Ilium
the army and the ships put to sea.

960   Yet I have seen with these eyes
Agamemnon home again.
Still the spirit sings, drawing deep
from within this unlyric threnody of the Fury.
Hope is gone utterly,
965   the sweet strength is far away.
Surely this is not fantasy.
Surely it is real, this whirl of drifts
that spin the stricken heart.
Still I pray; may all this

970   expectation fade as vanity
         into unfulfilment, and not be.

         Yet it is true: the high strength of men
         knows no content with limitation. Sickness
         chambered beside it beats at the wall between.
975   Man's fate that sets a true
         course yet may strike upon
         the blind and sudden reefs of disaster.
         But if before such time, fear
         throw overboard some precious thing
980   of the cargo, with deliberate cast,
         not all the house, laboring
         with weight of ruin, shall go down,
         nor sink the hull deep within the sea.
         And great and affluent the gift of Zeus
985   in yield of ploughed acres year on year
         makes void again sick starvation.

         But when the black and mortal blood of man
         has fallen to the ground before his feet, who then
         can sing spells to call it back again?
990   Did Zeus not warn us once
         when he struck to impotence
         that one who could in truth charm back the dead men?[3]
         Had the gods not so ordained
         that fate should stand against fate
995   to check any man's excess,
         my heart now would have outrun speech
         to break forth the water of its grief.
         But this is so; I murmur deep in darkness
         sore at heart; my hope is gone now
1000   ever again to unwind some crucial good
         from the flames about my heart.

   [Clytaemestra comes out from the house again and speaks to Cassandra.]

         Cassandra, you may go within the house as well,
         since Zeus in no unkindness has ordained that you
         must share our lustral water, stand with the great throng
1005   of slaves that flock to the altar of our household god.
         Step from this chariot, then, and do not be so proud.
         And think—they say that long ago Alcmena's son[4]
         was sold in bondage and endured the bread of slaves.
         But if constraint of fact forces you to such fate,
1010   be glad indeed for masters ancient in their wealth.
         They who have reaped success beyond their dreams of hope
         are savage above need and standard toward their slaves.

---

3. The physician Asclepius.   4. Herakles (Hercules).

From us you shall have all you have the right to ask.

CHORUS: What she has spoken is for you, and clear enough.

1015   Fenced in these fatal nets wherein you find yourself
you should obey her if you can; perhaps you can not.

CLYTAEMESTRA: Unless she uses speech incomprehensible,
barbarian, wild as the swallow's song, I speak
within her understanding, and she must obey.

CHORUS: Go with her. What she bids is best in circumstance
that rings you now. Obey, and leave this carriage seat.

CLYTAEMESTRA: I have no leisure to stand outside the house and waste
time on this woman. At the central altarstone
the flocks are standing, ready for the sacrifice

1025   we make to this glad day we never hoped to see.
You: if you are obeying my commands at all, be quick.
But if in ignorance you fail to comprehend,
speak not, but make with your barbarian hand some sign.

CHORUS: I think this stranger girl needs some interpreter

1030   who understands. She is like some captive animal.

CLYTAEMESTRA: No, she is in the passion of her own wild thoughts.
Leaving her captured city she has come to us
untrained to take the curb, and will not understand
until her rage and strength have foamed away in blood.

1035   I shall throw down no more commands for her contempt.

[*Clytaemestra goes back into the house.*]

CHORUS: I, though, shall not be angry, for I pity her.
Come down, poor creature, leave the empty car. Give way
to compulsion and take up the yoke that shall be yours.

[*Cassandra descends from the chariot and cries out loud.*]

Oh shame upon the earth!

1040   Apollo, Apollo!

CHORUS: You cry on Loxias in agony? He is not
of those immortals the unhappy supplicate.

CASSANDRA: Oh shame upon the earth!
Apollo, Apollo!

CHORUS: Now once again in bitter voice she calls upon
this god, who has not part in any lamentation.

CASSANDRA: Apollo, Apollo!
Lord of the ways, my ruin.
You have undone me once again, and utterly.

CHORUS: I think she will be prophetic of her own disaster.
Even in the slave's heart the gift divine lives on.

CASSANDRA: Apollo, Apollo!
Lord of the ways, my ruin.
Where have you led me now at last? What house is this?

CHORUS: The house of the Atreidae. If you understand
not that, I can tell you; and so much at least is true.

CASSANDRA: No, but a house that God hates, guilty within

of kindred blood shed, torture of its own,
the shambles for men's butchery, the dripping floor.

CHORUS: The stranger is keen scented like some hound upon
the trail of blood that leads her to discovered death.

CASSANDRA: Behold there the witnesses to my faith.
The small children wail for their own death
and the flesh roasted that their father fed upon.[5]

CHORUS: We had been told before of this prophetic fame
of yours: we want no prophets in this place at all.

CASSANDRA: Ah, for shame, what can she purpose now?
What is this new and huge
stroke of atrocity she plans within the house
1070   to beat down the beloved beyond hope of healing?
Rescue is far away.

CHORUS: I can make nothing of these prophecies. The rest
I understood; the city is full of the sound of them.

CASSANDRA: So cruel then, that you can do this thing?
1075   The husband of your own bed
to bathe bright with water—how shall I speak the end?
This thing shall be done with speed. The hand gropes now,
and the other hand follows in turn.

CHORUS: No, I am lost. After the darkness of her speech
1080   I go bewildered in a mist of prophecies.

CASSANDRA: No, no, see there! What is that thing that shows?
Is it some net of death?
Or is the trap the woman there, the murderess?
Let now the slakeless fury in the race
1085   rear up to howl aloud over this monstrous death.

CHORUS: Upon what demon in the house do you call, to raise
the cry of triumph? All your speech makes dark my hope.
And to the heart below trickles the pale drop
as in the hour of death
1090   timed to our sunset and the mortal radiance.
Ruin is near, and swift.

CASSANDRA: See there, see there! Keep from his mate the bull.
Caught in the folded web's
entanglement she pinions him and with the black horn
1095   strikes. And he crumples in the watered bath.
Guile, I tell you, and death there in the caldron wrought.

CHORUS: I am not proud in skill to guess at prophecies,
yet even I can see the evil in this thing.
From divination what good ever has come to men?
1100   Art, and multiplication of words
drifting through tangled evil bring
terror to them that hear.

---

5. Atreus fed to him the flesh of his brother Thyestes's children, as vengeance for adultery with Atreus's wife Aerope, mother of Agamemnon and Menelaus. Of Thyestes's children, only Aegisthus survived.

CASSANDRA: Alas, alas for the wretchedness of my ill-starred life.
          This pain flooding the song of sorrow is mine alone.
1105   Why have you brought me here in all unhappiness?
          Why, why? Except to die with him? What else could be?
CHORUS: You are possessed of God, mazed at heart
          to sing your own death
          song, the wild lyric as
1110   in clamor for Itys, Itys over and over again
          her long life of tears weeping forever grieves
          the brown nightingale.[6]
CASSANDRA: Oh for the nightingale's pure song and a fate like hers.
          With fashion of beating wings the gods clothed her about
1115   and a sweet life gave her and without lamentation.
          But mine is the sheer edge of the tearing iron.
CHORUS: Whence come, beat upon beat, driven of God,
          vain passions of tears?
          Whence your cries, terrified, clashing in horror,
1120   in wrought melody and the singing speech?
          Whence take you the marks to this path of prophecy
          and speech of terror?
CASSANDRA: Oh marriage of Paris, death to the men beloved!
          Alas, Scamandrus, water my fathers drank.
1125   There was a time I too at your springs
          drank and grew strong. Ah me,
          for now beside the deadly rivers, Cocytus
          and Acheron, I must cry out my prophecies.
CHORUS: What is this word, too clear, you have uttered now?
1130   A child could understand.
          And deep within goes the stroke of the dripping fang
          as mortal pain at the trebled song of your agony
          shivers the heart to hear.
CASSANDRA: O sorrow, sorrow of my city dragged to uttermost death.
1135   O sacrifices my father made at the wall.
          Flocks of the pastured sheep slaughtered there.
          And no use at all
          to save our city from its pain inflicted now.
          And I too, with brain ablaze in fever, shall go down.
CHORUS: This follows the run of your song.
          Is it, in cruel force of weight,
          some divinity kneeling upon you brings
          the death song of your passionate suffering?
          I can not see the end.
CASSANDRA: No longer shall my prophecies like some young girl
          new-married glance from under veils, but bright and strong
          as winds blow into morning and the sun's uprise
          shall wax along the swell like some great wave, to burst
          at last upon the shining of this agony.

6. Tereus, husband of Procne, raped his sister-in-law and cut out her tongue. Procne killed her own and Tereus's son Itys and was transformed into a nightingale.

1150   Now I will tell you plainly and from no cryptic speech;
         bear me then witness, running at my heels upon
         the scent of these old brutal things done long ago.
         There is a choir that sings as one, that shall not again
         leave this house ever; the song thereof breaks harsh with menace.
1155   And drugged to double fury on the wine of men's
         blood shed, there lurks forever here a drunken rout
         of ingrown vengeful spirits never to be cast forth.
         Hanging above the hall they chant their song of hate
         and the old sin; and taking up the strain in turn
1160   spit curses on that man who spoiled his brother's bed.
         Did I go wide, or hit, like a real archer? Am I
         some swindling seer who hawks his lies from door to door?
         Upon your oath, bear witness that I know by heart
         the legend of ancient wickedness within this house.
CHORUS: And how could an oath, though cast in rigid honesty,
         do any good? And still we stand amazed at you,
         reared in an alien city far beyond the sea,
         how can you strike, as if you had been there, the truth.
CASSANDRA: Apollo was the seer who set me to this work.
CHORUS: Struck with some passion for you, and himself a god?
CASSANDRA: There was a time I blushed to speak about these things.
CHORUS: True; they who prosper take on airs of vanity.
CASSANDRA: Yes, then; he wrestled with me, and he breathed delight.
CHORUS: Did you come to the getting of children then, as people do?
CASSANDRA: I promised that to Loxias, but I broke my word.
CHORUS: Were you already ecstatic in the skills of God?
CASSANDRA: Yes; even then I read my city's destinies.
CHORUS: So Loxias' wrath did you no harm? How could that be?
CASSANDRA: For this my trespass, none believed me ever again.
CHORUS: But we do; all that you foretell seems true to us.
CASSANDRA: But this is evil, see!
         Now once again the pain of grim, true prophecy
         shivers my whirling brain in a storm of things foreseen.
         Look there, see what is hovering above the house,
1185   so small and young, imaged as in the shadow of dreams,
         like children almost, killed by those most dear to them,
         and their hands filled with their own flesh, as food to eat.
         I see them holding out the inward parts, the vitals,
         oh pitiful, that meat their father tasted of. . . .
1190   I tell you: There is one that plots vengeance for this,
         the strengthless lion rolling in his master's bed,
         who keeps, ah me, the house against his lord's return;
         my lord too, now that I wear the slave's yoke on my neck.
         King of the ships, who tore up Ilium by the roots,
1195   what does he know of this accursed bitch, who licks
         his hand, who fawns on him with lifted ears, who like
         a secret death shall strike the coward's stroke, nor fail?
         No, this is daring when the female shall strike down

the male. What can I call her and be right? What beast
1200   of loathing? Viper double-fanged, or Scylla witch
holed in the rocks and bane of men that range the sea;
smoldering mother of death to smoke relentless hate
on those most dear. How she stood up and howled aloud
and unashamed, as at the breaking point of battle,
1205   in feigned gladness for his salvation from the sea!
What does it matter now if men believe or no?
What is to come will come. And soon you too will stand
beside, to murmur in pity that my words were true.

CHORUS: Thyestes' feast upon the flesh of his own children
1210   I understand in terror at the thought, and fear
is on me hearing truth and no tale fabricated.
The rest: I heard it, but wander still far from the course.

CASSANDRA: I tell you, you shall look on Agamemnon dead.

CHORUS: Peace, peace, poor woman; put those bitter lips to sleep.

CASSANDRA: Useless; there is no god of healing in this story.

CHORUS: Not if it must be; may it somehow fail to come.

CASSANDRA: Prayers, yes; they do not pray; they plan to strike, and kill.

CHORUS: What man is it who moves this beastly thing to be?

CASSANDRA: What man? You did mistake my divination then.

CHORUS: It may be; I could not follow through the schemer's plan.

CASSANDRA: Yet I know Greek; I think I know it far too well.

CHORUS: And Pythian oracles are Greek, yet hard to read.

CASSANDRA: Oh, flame and pain that sweeps me once again! My lord,
Apollo, King of Light, the pain, aye me, the pain!
1225   This is the woman-lioness, who goes to bed
with the wolf, when her proud lion ranges far away,
and she will cut me down; as a wife mixing drugs
she wills to shred the virtue of my punishment
into her bowl of wrath as she makes sharp the blade
1230   against her man, death that he brought a mistress home.
Why do I wear these mockeries upon my body,
this staff of prophecy, these flowers at my throat?
At least I will spoil you before I die. Out, down,
break, damn you! This for all that you have done to me.
1235   Make someone else, not me, luxurious in disaster. . . .
Lo now, this is Apollo who has stripped me here
of my prophetic robes. He watched me all the time
wearing this glory, mocked of all, my dearest ones
who hated me with all their hearts, so vain, so wrong;
1240   called like some gypsy wandering from door to door
beggar, corrupt, half-starved, and I endured it all.
And now the seer has done with me, his prophetess,
and led me into such a place as this, to die.
Lost are my father's altars, but the block is there
1245   to reek with sacrificial blood, my own. We two
must die, yet die not vengeless by the gods. For there
shall come one to avenge us also, born to slay

his mother, and to wreak death for his father's blood.
Outlaw and wanderer, driven far from his own land,
1250   he will come back to cope these stones of inward hate.
For this is a strong oath and sworn by the high gods,
that he shall cast men headlong for his father felled.
Why am I then so pitiful? Why must I weep?
Since once I saw the citadel of Ilium
1255   die as it died, and those who broke the city, doomed
by the gods, fare as they have fared accordingly,
I will go through with it. I too will take my fate.
I call as on the gates of death upon these gates
to pray only for this thing, that the stroke be true,
1260   and that with no convulsion, with a rush of blood
in painless death, I may close up these eyes, and rest.

CHORUS: O woman much enduring and so greatly wise,
you have said much. But if this thing you know be true,
this death that comes upon you, how can you, serene,
1265   walk to the altar like a driven ox of God?

CASSANDRA: Friends, there is no escape for any longer time.

CHORUS: Yet longest left in time is to be honored still.

CASSANDRA: The day is here and now; I can not win by flight.

CHORUS: Woman, be sure your heart is brave; you can take much.

CASSANDRA: None but the unhappy people ever hear such praise.

CHORUS: Yet there is a grace on mortals who so nobly die.

CASSANDRA: Alas for you, father, and for your lordly sons.
        Ah!

CHORUS: What now? What terror whirls you backward from the door?

CASSANDRA: Foul, foul!

CHORUS: What foulness then, unless some horror in the mind?

CASSANDRA: That room within reeks with blood like a slaughter house.

CHORUS: What then? Only these victims butchered at the hearth.

CASSANDRA: There is a breath about it like an open grave.

CHORUS: This is no Syrian pride of frankincense you mean.

CASSANDRA: So. I am going in, and mourning as I go
my death and Agamemnon's. Let my life be done.
Ah friends,
truly this is no wild bird fluttering at a bush,
1285   nor vain my speech. Bear witness to me when I die,
when falls for me, a woman slain, another woman,
and when a man dies for this wickedly mated man.
Here in my death I claim this stranger's grace of you.

CHORUS: Poor wretch, I pity you the fate you see so clear.

CASSANDRA: Yet once more will I speak, and not this time my own
death's threnody. I call upon the Sun in prayer
against that ultimate shining when the avengers strike
these monsters down in blood, that they avenge as well
one simple slave who died, a small thing, lightly killed.
1295   Alas, poor men, their destiny. When all goes well
a shadow will overthrow it. If it be unkind

one stroke of a wet sponge wipes all the picture out;
and that is far the most unhappy thing of all.

[*Cassandra goes slowly into the house.*]

CHORUS: High fortune is a thing slakeless
1300   for mortals. There is no man who shall point
            his finger to drive it back from the door
            and speak the words: "Come no longer."
            Now to this man the blessed ones have given
            Priam's city to be captured
1305   and return in the gods' honor.
            Must he give blood for generations gone,
            die for those slain and in death pile up
            more death to come for the blood shed,
            what mortal else who hears shall claim
1310   he was born clear of the dark angel?

[*Agamemnon, inside the house.*]

        Ah, I am struck a deadly blow and deep within!
CHORUS: Silence: who cried out that he was stabbed to death within the house?
AGAMEMNON: Ah me, again, they struck again. I am wounded twice.
CHORUS: How the king cried out aloud to us! I believe the thing is done.
1315   Come, let us put our heads together, try to find some safe way out.

[*The members of the Chorus go about distractedly, each one speaking in turn.*]

        Listen, let me tell you what I think is best to do.
        Let the herald call all citizens to rally here.

        No, better to burst in upon them now, at once,
        and take them with the blood still running from their blades.

1320   I am with this man and I cast my vote to him.
            Act now. This is the perilous and instant time.

        Anyone can see it, by these first steps they have taken,
        they purpose to be tyrants here upon our city.

        Yes, for we waste time, while they trample to the ground
1325   deliberation's honor, and their hands sleep not.

        I can not tell which counsel of yours to call my own.
        It is the man of action who can plan as well.

        I feel as he does; nor can I see how by words
        we shall set the dead man back upon his feet again.

1330   Do you mean, to drag our lives out long, that we must yield
            to the house shamed, and leadership of such as these?

        No, we can never endure that; better to be killed.
        Death is a softer thing by far than tyranny.

        Shall we, by no more proof than that he cried in pain,
1335   be sure, as by divination, that our lord is dead?

Yes, we should know what is true before we break our rage.
Here is sheer guessing and far different from sure knowledge.

From all sides the voices multiply to make me choose
this course; to learn first how it stands with Agamemnon.

[*The doors of the palace open, disclosing the bodies of Agamemnon and Cassandra, with Clytaemestra standing over them.*]

CLYTAEMESTRA: Much have I said before to serve necessity,
but I will take no shame now to unsay it all.
How else could I, arming hate against hateful men
disguised in seeming tenderness, fence high the nets
of ruin beyond overleaping? Thus to me
1345   the conflict born of ancient bitterness is not
a thing new thought upon, but pondered deep in time.
I stand now where I struck him down. The thing is done.
Thus have I wrought, and I will not deny it now.
That he might not escape nor beat aside his death,
1350   as fishermen cast their huge circling nets, I spread
deadly abundance of rich robes, and caught him fast.
I struck him twice. In two great cries of agony
he buckled at the knees and fell. When he was down
I struck him the third blow, in thanks and reverence
1355   to Zeus the lord of dead men underneath the ground.
Thus he went down, and the life struggled out of him;
and as he died he spattered me with the dark red
and violent driven rain of bitter savored blood
to make me glad, as gardens stand among the showers
1360   of God in glory at the birthtime of the buds.

These being the facts, elders of Argos assembled here,
be glad, if it be your pleasure; but for me, I glory.
Were it religion to pour wine above the slain,
this man deserved, more than deserved, such sacrament.
1365   He filled our cup with evil things unspeakable
and now himself come home has drunk it to the dregs.
CHORUS: We stand here stunned. How can you speak this way, with mouth
so arrogant, to vaunt above your fallen lord?
CLYTAEMESTRA: You try me out as if I were a woman and vain;
1370   but my heart is not fluttered as I speak before you.
You know it. You can praise or blame me as you wish;
it is all one to me. That man is Agamemnon,
my husband; he is dead; the work of this right hand
that struck in strength of righteousness. And that is that.
CHORUS: Woman, what evil thing planted upon the earth
or dragged from the running salt sea could you have tasted now
to wear such brutality and walk in the people's hate?
You have cast away, you have cut away. You shall go homeless now,
crushed with men's bitterness.
CLYTAEMESTRA: Now it is I you doom to be cast out from my city
with men's hate heaped and curses roaring in my ears.

Yet look upon this dead man; you would not cross him once
when with no thought more than as if a beast had died,
when his ranged pastures swarmed with the deep fleece of flocks,
1385   he slaughtered like a victim his own child, my pain
grown into love, to charm away the winds of Thrace.
Were you not bound to hunt him then clear of this soil
for the guilt stained upon him? Yet you hear what I
have done, and lo, you are a stern judge. But I say to you:
1390   go on and threaten me, but know that I am ready,
if fairly you can beat me down beneath your hand,
for you to rule; but if the god grant otherwise,
you shall be taught—too late, for sure—to keep your place.
CHORUS: Great your design, your speech is a clamor of pride.
1395   Swung to the red act drives the fury within your brain
signed clear in the splash of blood over your eyes.
Yet to come is stroke given for stroke
vengeless, forlorn of friends.
CLYTAEMESTRA: Now hear you this, the right behind my sacrament:
1400   By my child's Justice driven to fulfilment, by
her Wrath and Fury, to whom I sacrificed this man,
the hope that walks my chambers is not traced with fear
while yet Aegisthus makes the fire shine on my hearth,
my good friend, now as always, who shall be for us
1405   the shield of our defiance, no weak thing; while he,
this other, is fallen, stained with this woman you behold,
plaything of all the golden girls at Ilium;
and here lies she, the captive of his spear, who saw
wonders, who shared his bed, the wise in revelations
1410   and loving mistress, who yet knew the feel as well
of the men's rowing benches. Their reward is not
unworthy. He lies there; and she who swanlike cried
aloud her lyric mortal lamentation out
is laid against his fond heart, and to me has given
1415   a delicate excitement to my bed's delight.
CHORUS: O that in speed, without pain
and the slow bed of sickness
death could come to us now, death that forever
carries sleep without ending, now that our lord is down,
1420   our shield, kindest of men,
who for a woman's grace suffered so much,
struck down at last by a woman.

Alas, Helen, wild heart
for the multitudes, for the thousand lives
1425   you killed under Troy's shadow,
you alone, to shine in man's memory
as blood flower never to be washed out. Surely a demon then
of death walked in the house, men's agony.
CLYTAEMESTRA: No, be not so heavy, nor yet draw down
1430   in prayer death's ending,

neither turn all wrath against Helen
for men dead, that she alone killed
all those Danaan lives, to work
the grief that is past all healing.

CHORUS: Divinity that kneel on this house and the two
strains of the blood of Tantalus,[7]
in the hands and hearts of women you steer
the strength tearing my heart.
Standing above the corpse, obscene

1440 as some carrion crow she sings
the crippled song and is proud.

CLYTAEMESTRA: Thus have you set the speech of your lips
straight, calling by name
the spirit thrice glutted that lives in this race.

1445 From him deep in the nerve is given
the love and the blood drunk, that before
the old wound dries, it bleeds again.

CHORUS: Surely it is a huge
and heavy spirit bending the house you cry;

1450 alas, the bitter glory
of a doom that shall never be done with;
and all through Zeus, Zeus,
first cause, prime mover.
For what thing without Zeus is done among mortals?

1455 What here is without God's blessing?

O king, my king
how shall I weep for you?
What can I say out of my heart of pity?
Caught in this spider's web you lie,

1460 Your life gasped out in indecent death,
struck prone to this shameful bed
by your lady's hand of treachery
and the stroke twin edged of the iron.

CLYTAEMESTRA: Can you claim I have done this?

1465 Speak of me never
more as the wife of Agamemnon.
In the shadow of this corpse's queen
the old stark avenger
of Atreus for his revel of hate

1470 struck down this man,
last blood for the slaughtered children.

CHORUS: What man shall testify
your hands are clean of this murder?
How? How? Yet from his father's blood

1475 might swarm some fiend to guide you.
The black ruin that shoulders

---

7. Ancestor of Atreus. He fed his son Pelops to the gods and was eternally "tantalized" with unreachable food and drink as punishment in the underworld.

through the streaming blood of brothers
strides at last where he shall win requital
for the children who were eaten.

1480   O king, my king
how shall I weep for you?
What can I say out of my heart of pity?
Caught in this spider's web you lie,
your life gasped out in indecent death,
1485   struck prone to this shameful bed
by your lady's hand of treachery
and the stroke twin edged of the iron.

CLYTAEMESTRA: No shame, I think, in the death given
this man. And did he not
1490   first of all in this house wreak death
by treachery?
The flower of this man's love and mine,
Iphigeneia of the tears
he dealt with even as he has suffered.
1495   Let his speech in death's house be not loud.
With the sword he struck,
with the sword he paid for his own act.

CHORUS: My thoughts are swept away and I go bewildered.
Where shall I turn the brain's
1500   activity in speed when the house is falling?
There is fear in the beat of the blood rain breaking
wall and tower. The drops come thicker.
Still fate grinds on yet more stones the blade
for more acts of terror.

1505   Earth, my earth, why did you not fold me under
before ever I saw this man lie dead
fenced by the tub in silver?
Who shall bury him? Who shall mourn him?
Shall you dare this who have killed
1510   your lord? Make lamentation,
render the graceless grace to his soul
for huge things done in wickedness?
Who over this great man's grave shall lay
the blessing of tears
1515   worked soberly from a true heart?

CLYTAEMESTRA: Not for you to speak of such tendance.
Through us he fell,
by us he died; we shall bury.
There will be no tears in this house for him.
1520   It must be Iphigeneia
his child, who else,
shall greet her father by the whirling stream
and the ferry of tears
to close him in her arms and kiss him.

CHORUS: Here is anger for anger. Between them

who shall judge lightly?
The spoiler is robbed; he killed, he has paid.
The truth stands ever beside God's throne
eternal: he who has wrought shall pay; that is law.
1530   Then who shall tear the curse from their blood?
The seed is stiffened to ruin.
CLYTAEMESTRA: You see truth in the future
at last. Yet I wish
to seal my oath with the Spirit
1535   in the house: I will endure all things as they stand
now, hard though it be. Hereafter
let him go forth to make bleed with death
and guilt the houses of others.
I will take some small
1540   measure of our riches, and be content
that I swept from these halls
the murder, the sin, and the fury.

[*Aegisthus enters, followed at a little distance by his armed bodyguard.*]

AEGISTHUS: O splendor and exaltation of this day of doom!
Now I can say once more that the high gods look down
1545   on mortal crimes to vindicate the right at last,
now that I see this man—sweet sight—before me here
sprawled in the tangling nets of fury, to atone
the calculated evil of his father's hand.
For Atreus, this man's father, King of Argolis—
1550   I tell you the clear story—drove my father forth,
Thyestes, his own brother, who had challenged him
in his king's right—forth from his city and his home.
Yet sad Thyestes came again to supplicate
the hearth, and win some grace, in that he was not slain
1555   nor soiled the doorstone of his fathers with blood spilled.
Not his own blood. But Atreus, this man's godless sire,
angrily hospitable set a feast for him,
in seeming a glad day of fresh meat slain and good
cheer; then served my father his own children's flesh
1560   to feed on. For he carved away the extremities,
hands, feet, and cut the flesh apart, and covered them
served in a dish to my father at his table apart,
who with no thought for the featureless meal before him ate
that ghastly food whose curse works now before your eyes.
1565   But when he knew the terrible thing that he had done,
he spat the dead meat from him with a cry, and reeled
spurning the table back to heel with strength the curse:
"Thus crash in ruin all the seed of Pleisthenes."
Out of such acts you see this dead man stricken here,
1570   and it was I, in my right, who wrought this murder, I
third born to my unhappy father, and with him
driven, a helpless baby in arms, to banishment.
Yet I grew up, and justice brought me home again,

till from afar I laid my hands upon this man,

1575   since it was I who pieced together the fell plot.

Now I can die in honor again, if die I must,

having seen him caught in the cords of his just punishment.

CHORUS: Aegisthus, this strong vaunting in distress is vile.

You claim that you deliberately killed the king,

1580   you, and you only, wrought the pity of this death.

I tell you then: There shall be no escape, your head

shall face the stones of anger from the people's hands.

AEGISTHUS: So loud from you, stooped to the meanest rowing bench

with the ship's masters lordly on the deck above?

1585   You are old men; well, you shall learn how hard it is

at your age, to be taught how to behave yourselves.

But there are chains, there is starvation with its pain,

excellent teachers of good manners to old men,

wise surgeons and exemplars. Look! Can you not see it?

1590   Lash not at the goads for fear you hit them, and be hurt.

CHORUS: So then you, like a woman, waited the war out

here in the house, shaming the master's bed with lust,

and planned against the lord of war this treacherous death?

AEGISTHUS: It is just such words as these will make you cry in pain.

1595   Not yours the lips of Orpheus, no, quite otherwise,

whose voice of rapture dragged all creatures in his train.

You shall be dragged, for baby whimperings sobbed out

in rage. Once broken, you will be easier to deal with.

CHORUS: How shall you be lord of the men of Argos, you

1600   who planned the murder of this man, yet could not dare

to act it out, and cut him down with your own hand?

AEGISTHUS: No, clearly the deception was the woman's part,

and I was suspect, that had hated him so long.

Still with his money I shall endeavor to control

1605   the citizens. The mutinous man shall feel the yoke

drag at his neck, no cornfed racing colt that runs

free traced; but hunger, grim companion of the dark

dungeon shall see him broken to the hand at last.

CHORUS: But why, why then, you coward, could you not have slain

1610   your man yourself? Why must it be his wife who killed,

to curse the country and the gods within the ground?

Oh, can Orestes live, be somewhere in sunlight still?

Shall fate grown gracious ever bring him back again

in strength of hand to overwhelm these murderers?

AEGISTHUS: You shall learn then, since you stick to stubbornness of mouth and hand.

Up now from your cover, my henchmen: here is work for you to do.

CHORUS: Look, they come! Let every man clap fist upon his hilted sword.

AEGISTHUS: I too am sword-handed against you; I am not afraid of death.

CHORUS: Death you said and death it shall be; we take up the word of fate.

CLYTAEMESTRA: No, my dearest, dearest of all men, we have done enough.

No more violence. Here is a monstrous harvest and a bitter reaping

time. There is pain enough already. Let us not be bloody now.

> Honored gentlemen of Argos, go to your homes now and give way
> to the stress of fate and season. We could not do otherwise
> 1625   than we did. If this is the end of suffering, we can be content
> broken as we are by the brute heel of angry destiny.
> Thus a woman speaks among you. Shall men deign to understand?
>
> AEGISTHUS: Yes, but think of these foolish lips that blossom into leering gibes,
> think of the taunts they spit against me daring destiny and power,
> 1630   sober opinion lost in insults hurled against my majesty.
>
> CHORUS: It was never the Argive way to grovel at a vile man's feet.
>
> AEGISTHUS: I shall not forget this; in the days to come I shall be there.
>
> CHORUS: Nevermore, if God's hand guiding brings Orestes home again.
>
> AEGISTHUS: Exiles feed on empty dreams of hope. I know it. I was one.
>
> CHORUS: Have your way, gorge and grow fat, soil justice, while the power is yours.
>
> AEGISTHUS: You shall pay, make no mistake, for this misguided insolence.
>
> CHORUS: Crow and strut, brave cockerel by your hen; you have no threats to fear.
>
> CLYTAEMESTRA: These are howls of impotent rage; forget them, dearest; you and I
> have the power; we two shall bring good order to our house at least.

[They enter the house. The doors close. All persons leave the stage.]

RESONANCE

William Butler Yeats: Leda and the Swan[1]

A sudden blow: the great wings beating still
Above the staggering girl, her thighs caressed
By the dark webs, her nape caught in his bill,
He holds her helpless breast upon his breast.

5   How can those terrified vague fingers push
The feathered glory from her loosening thighs?
And how can body, laid in that white rush,
But feel the strange heart beating where it lies?

A shudder in the loins engenders there
10   The broken wall, the burning roof and tower
And Agamemnon dead.
                        Being so caught up,
So mastered by the brute blood of the air,
Did she put on his knowledge with his power
Before the indifferent beak could let her drop?

---

1. The Irish poet and dramatist W. B. Yeats (1865–1939) constantly infused his modern poetry with ancient myths—Greek, Celtic, and Indian, among others. He developed an elaborate private mythology in which the world's history moves in 2,000-year cycles, hinging upon charged moments of divine-human interaction. Jesus' birth was one such moment; Zeus's rape of Leda 2,000 years earlier (as Yeats dated it) signaled the violent birth of classical culture. The children born of this rape were Helen of Troy and Agamemnon's wife, Clytaemnestra. At the end of his 1924 sonnet, Yeats alludes to them and to the epic and dramatic traditions of Homer and Aeschylus. Like his classical predecessors, Yeats sees the ancient myth as having an ongoing, uncanny power, which his intensely visualized poem seeks to bring out in fresh, even shocking terms.

Sophocles

c. 496–406 B.C.E.

A citizen of Athens and its radical, innovative democracy, Sophocles won many victories in the drama festivals of his native city. His great predecessor in the writing of tragedy, Aeschylus, wrote the *Oresteia,* a trilogy consisting of three linked plays that celebrate the founding of one of the city's important legal institutions and express a tenuous optimism about the democratic experiment. Sophocles was a more conservative thinker, and he feared for his fellow citizens and for their city.

An ancient story records the piety of Sophocles. When the worship of Asclepius the healing god was introduced into the city of Athens in 420 B.C.E., Sophocles invited the god's representative, a snake, to live in his house until a suitable sanctuary was erected. Sophocles' piety was not at all otherworldly; he shared his fellow citizens' susceptibility to eros and the beauty of boys, and said at the end of his long life that he was glad no longer to be tormented by the goddess of sexuality, Aphrodite. Throughout his tragedies, one of the themes that concerns him is reverence for the gods, and he feared that democratic Athens, having turned away from the elite aristocratic form of government of earlier centuries, now risked abandoning the gods in a proud burst of wealth, confidence, and sometimes arrogant domination of its former allies in an Athenian empire. Among the Athenians of his day were intellectuals proud of their accomplishments in the development of logic, rhetoric, political theory, and philosophy. Radical thinkers such as the sophists insisted that human beings were the "measure of all things," rather than urging the traditional practices of worshiping the gods. Sophocles' tragedies intervene in the intense social, political, and religious debates of the fifth century B.C.E., when Athens participated in the victory over the huge Persian Empire's invasion at the beginning of the century, flourished in an atmosphere of risk and daring at midcentury, and went down to devastating defeat by the Spartans in the Peloponnesian War at the century's end.

In his long career, Sophocles wrote more than 120 tragedies, of which only a handful remain. His career began in 468 and ended with his death, just after the death of Euripides, the third of the great fifth-century tragedians. Sophocles lived in Athens at the time of Pericles, the brilliant aristocratic statesman of the classical age, which was also the time of Socrates, a founder of Greek philosophy, and of Aristophanes, the obscene, wild comic dramatist. This was also the period of Athens' great building program, when the treasures from the Athenians' empire were spent on embellishing the city with such magnificent buildings as the Parthenon, the temple of Athena, the patron goddess of Athens. Sophocles' plays take on some of the powerful myths the Greeks told themselves, seeking to reconcile the ideology of the democratic city, in which all men were said to be equal, with the myths of the pre-eminent heroes and gods they inherited from the Archaic age. Sophocles' *Electra* focuses on the unhappy family of Atreus, representing the daughter of the house as a wretched victim of her parent's enmity. His *Philoktetes* goes back to the myths of Homer and the Trojan War and shows the now-ruthless and rhetorically skilled Odysseus in conflict with the values of the past. *The Women of Trachis* portrays the great hero Herakles as he returns home from battle with a captive slave bride; his wife, having waited at home, tries to win him back to her with what she believes to be a love potion, but that is in fact a deadly poison that destroys him. In the *Ajax,* Sophocles portrays the great Homeric warrior driven mad by Athena, slaughtering his wife and children in a world he can no longer understand. In all of these plays, Sophocles engages questions of time and eternity and the conflict between the human values of the democratic city and the old Homeric virtues and devotion to the gods. In interrogating received stories and myths, he engages in a prolonged meditation on the relationship between civilization and its limits—nature, the gods, madness, death—all that cannot be known through the civilized discourses of human beings.

THE MYTH OF THEBES

The myth of the Greek city of Thebes engaged Sophocles throughout his life as a tragedian, and in plays such as *Oedipus the King* and *Antigone,* he gave a searching development to stark old stories that his audience would have known well. Thebes was said to have been founded by Kadmos, a prince from Tyre in Asia Minor; his sister Europa was one day playing on the beach with her friends when a lovely white bull took her off. This was Zeus in one of the many forms he assumed to seduce mortal women and boys. He took Europa to Crete, and she gave the continent of Europe her name. Kadmos journeyed to the mainland and after consulting with the oracle, came to the land of Thebes, where he had been instructed to kill the dragon guarding a spring. He took the dragon's teeth, sowed them in the ground, and warriors sprang up who fought to the death until only five survived. These were the Spartoi, the founding aristocratic families of Thebes. Kadmos founded the ruling dynasty, which suffered many troubles. One of the kings refused to worship Dionysos, even though the god was the son of Zeus and a Theban princess; he was dismembered and perhaps eaten alive by his own mother in a Dionysiac ecstasy. Another offspring of the house of Thebes was Aktaion, who while hunting one day came upon the virgin goddess Artemis bathing naked; enraged, she turned him into a stag to be eaten by his own dogs. The family also included Laios (or Laius), who in exile as a young man carried off his host's son, which, according to some legends, began the Greek practice of pederasty, the amorous, erotic relationship between men and young or adolescent boys. Laius returned to Thebes but was warned never to have children with his wife, Jocasta. When a son was born, they pierced the boy's ankles and gave him to a slave to expose on Mount Parnassos above the city of Thebes. He instead gave the child to a shepherd, who delivered him to the childless ruling family of Corinth.

This deliverance only plunged the child into new troubles. The boy, in Greek *Oidipous,* "Swollen-foot," was taunted as he grew up, and he went to visit the oracle of Apollo at Delphi, where he was told that he would kill his father and marry his mother. Seeking to avoid this fate, he traveled to Thebes, not Corinth, which he believed to be his home, and on the way killed a man on the road. When he arrived in Thebes, it was besieged by an uncanny monster called the Sphinx, who killed those who could not answer her riddle: What goes on four feet in the morning, two feet at noon, three at dusk? Only Oedipus knew the answer: the human being, who crawls as an infant, walks upright as an adult, and uses a stick in old age. He won both the city and its queen, Jocasta, and had children with her. Set after these events, Sophocles' play *Oedipus the King* portrays his anguished discovery of who he is.

The myth goes beyond the episodes portrayed in the tragedy: Oedipus cursed his sons just before the end of his life in Colonus, near Athens, where he blessed a shrine to protect the city of the Athenians from harm. Oedipus, who had known his mother's body twice (once as her child, once as her husband) with all his sufferings bestowed the benefit only a monster could give. His sons killed one another over the right to rule the city of Thebes; their sister, Antigone, went to her death defending her right to bury her despised brother, cast outside the city to be eaten by birds and dogs. Each of the great tragedians of classical Athens represented episodes from the Theban story of incest and horror for their audiences.

As presented in Athenian tragedy, archaic, mythic Thebes stands as a sort of anti-Athens, a place where repetition, terrible contact with the gods, sterility, dismemberment, incest, and filial hatred present a negative mirror for Athens, of all that Athens wishes not to bring forth as a *polis,* all that it fears as a dark side of its optimism. Sophocles returned to the myth of Thebes again and again, telling the story over many years. He probably first wrote *Antigone,* producing *Oedipus the King* some time after, and late in life gave the city *Oedipus at Colonus* at the end of the horrors of the Peloponnesian War, the great war among the Greeks. The tragedy *Oedipus the King* was probably first performed in a period of great trouble for the Athenians. Some have argued that in the tragedy, Oedipus stands as a figure for the city of Athens itself, as a model of intellectual confidence and seeking, exemplifying all the skills of rhetoric, science, mathematics, philosophy, and medicine on which the democratic city prided itself and on which it based its claims to the right to govern other cities in an empire. Others see Oedipus as a figure for the human being as such, existing between the gods and the animals, aspiring to godhood, brought down to the level of the beasts for that very aspiration, in an exemplary spectacle. The Athenians practiced both ostracism—the expulsion of dangerously powerful men from their midst—and a *pharmakos* ritual, like the scapegoating of the Hebrew Bible, expelling the lowest of their members. The Theban king, once compared to a god, becomes a blinded, wandering beast. Oedipus, whether an allegory for Athens itself or an exemplary human being, citizen of the city, has haunted the imagination of the West from Sophocles to Freud and beyond.

ANTIGONE

Sophocles' first play to draw on the myth of Thebes also sums up the fatal history of the royal family. By identifying herself as "the last" of the "great growing family of the dead," Antigone powerfully recalls her grandfather's murder and her mother's suicide (the subject of *Oedipus the King*) and her father's death (the subject of *Oedipus at Colonus*), and her brothers' deaths at each other's hands. Antigone further suggests that her family is cursed, because the relationships that should bring life have instead caused death and ruin. In ancient Greek society, she reminds us, death was considered natural rather than tragic: in the normal course of events, a husband or a child could be replaced, the pain of loss assuaged by the proper burial rites, the lost spirit embraced when met again in the underworld, realm of the goddess Persephone. Indeed, the event that causes the play's action to spin out of control into tragedy is a family drama with broad social repercussions: Antigone's betrothal to Creon's son Haemon, meant to regenerate the fortunes of her dying house and consolidate the dynasty, instead cuts it off at the roots when Haemon kills himself over Antigone's body and Creon's wife Eurydice hangs herself in despair over the loss of her son. The most frequently staged in modern dress of Sophocles' Theban plays, *Antigone* is perhaps the one that speaks most directly to the ethical conflicts, gender divisions, and tragic consequences of the impossible decisions endemic to civil strife both then and now.

PRONUNCIATIONS:

> *Antigone:* an-TI-go-nee
> *Creon:* KREE-on
> *Eurydice:* you-RID-uh-see
> *Haemon:* HI-moan
> *Jocasta:* jo-KAS-ta
> *Oedipus:* EE-di-pus
> *Teiresias:* ty-REE-see-as

Oedipus the King[1]

Characters

OEDIPUS, *king of Thebes*
JOCASTA, *his wife*
CREON, *his brother-in-law*
TEIRESIAS, *an old blind prophet*
A PRIEST

FIRST MESSENGER
SECOND MESSENGER
A HERDSMAN
A CHORUS OF OLD MEN OF THEBES

Scene: In front of the palace of Oedipus at Thebes. To the right of the stage near the altar stands the Priest with a crowd of children. Oedipus emerges from the central door.

OEDIPUS: Children, young sons and daughters of old Cadmus,[2]
    why do you sit here with your suppliant crowns?

---

1. Translated by David Grene.   2. Founder of Thebes.

The town is heavy with a mingled burden
of sounds and smells, of groans and hymns and incense;
5   I did not think it fit that I should hear
of this from messengers but came myself,—
I Oedipus whom all men call the Great.

[*He turns to the Priest.*]

You're old and they are young; come, speak for them.
What do you fear or want, that you sit here
10   suppliant? Indeed I'm willing to give all
that you may need; I would be very hard
should I not pity suppliants like these.

PRIEST: O ruler of my country, Oedipus,
you see our company around the altar;
15   you see our ages; some of us, like these,
who cannot yet fly far, and some of us
heavy with age; these children are the chosen
among the young, and I the priest of Zeus.
Within the market place sit others crowned
20   with suppliant garlands, at the double shrine
of Pallas and the temple where Ismenus
gives oracles by fire. King, you yourself
have seen our city reeling like a wreck
already; it can scarcely lift its prow
25   out of the depths, out of the bloody surf.
A blight is on the fruitful plants of the earth,
a blight is on the cattle in the fields,
a blight is on our women that no children
are born to them; a God that carries fire,
30   a deadly pestilence, is on our town,
strikes us and spares not, and the house of Cadmus
is emptied of its people while black Death
grows rich in groaning and in lamentation.
We have not come as suppliants to this altar
35   because we thought of you as of a God,
but rather judging you the first of men
in all the chances of this life and when
we mortals have to do with more than man.
You came and by your coming saved our city,
40   freed us from tribute which we paid of old
to the Sphinx, cruel singer. This you did
in virtue of no knowledge we could give you,
in virtue of no teaching; it was God
that aided you, men say, and you are held
45   with God's assistance to have saved our lives.
Now Oedipus, Greatest in all men's eyes,
here falling at your feet we all entreat you,
find us some strength for rescue.

Perhaps you'll hear a wise word from some God,
50   perhaps you will learn something from a man
        (for I have seen that for the skilled of practice
        the outcome of their counsels live the most).
        Noblest of men, go, and raise up our city,
        go,—and give heed. For now this land of ours
55   calls you its savior since you saved it once.
        So, let us never speak about your reign
        as of a time when first our feet were set
        secure on high, but later fell to ruin.
        Raise up our city, save it and raise it up.
60   Once you have brought us luck with happy omen;
        be no less now in fortune.
        If you will rule this land, as now you rule it,
        better to rule it full of men than empty.
        For neither tower nor ship is anything
65   when empty, and none live in it together.
OEDIPUS: I pity you, children. You have come full of longing,
        but I have known the story before you told it
        only too well. I know you are all sick,
        yet there is not one of you, sick though you are,
70   that is as sick as I myself.
        Your several sorrows each have single scope
        and touch but one of you. My spirit groans
        for city and myself and you at once.
        You have not roused me like a man from sleep;
75   know that I have given many tears to this,
        gone many ways wandering in thought,
        but as I thought I found only one remedy
        and that I took. I sent Menoeceus' son
        Creon, Jocasta's brother, to Apollo,
80   to his Pythian temple,
        that he might learn there by what act or word
        I could save this city. As I count the days,
        it vexes me what ails him; he is gone
        far longer than he needed for the journey.
85   But when he comes, then, may I prove a villain,
        if I shall not do all the God commands.
PRIEST: Thanks for your gracious words. Your servants here
        signal that Creon is this moment coming.
OEDIPUS: His face is bright. O holy Lord Apollo,
90   grant that his news too may be bright for us
        and bring us safety.
PRIEST: It is happy news,
        I think, for else his head would not be crowned
        with sprigs of fruitful laurel.
OEDIPUS: We will know soon,
95   he's within hail. Lord Creon, my good brother,
        what is the word you bring us from the God?

[*Creon enters.*]

CREON: A good word,—for things hard to bear themselves
         if in the final issue all is well
         I count complete good fortune.

OEDIPUS: What do you mean?
100   What you have said so far
         leaves me uncertain whether to trust or fear.

CREON: If you will hear my news before these others
         I am ready to speak, or else to go within.

OEDIPUS: Speak it to all;
105   the grief I bear, I bear it more for these
         than for my own heart.

CREON: I will tell you, then,
         what I heard, from the God.
         King Phoebus[3] in plain words commanded us
         to drive out a pollution from our land,
110   pollution grown ingrained within the land;
         drive it out, said the God, not cherish it,
         till it's past cure.

OEDIPUS: What is the rite
         of purification? How shall it be done?

CREON: By banishing a man, or expiation
115   of blood by blood, since it is murder guilt
         which holds our city in this destroying storm.

OEDIPUS: Who is this man whose fate the God pronounces?

CREON: My Lord, before you piloted the state
         we had a king called Laius.

OEDIPUS: I know of him by hearsay. I have not seen him.

CREON: The God commanded clearly: let some one
         punish with force this dead man's murderers.

OEDIPUS: Where are they in the world? Where would a trace
         of this old crime be found? It would be hard
         to guess where.

CREON: The clue is in this land;
         that which is sought is found;
         the unheeded thing escapes:
         so said the God.

OEDIPUS: Was it at home,
         or in the country that death came upon him,
130   or in another country travelling?

CREON: He went, he said himself, upon an embassy,
         but never returned when he set out from home.

OEDIPUS: Was there no messenger, no fellow traveller
         who knew what happened? Such a one might tell
135   something of use.

CREON: They were all killed save one. He fled in terror
         and he could tell us nothing in clear terms

---

3. Apollo, god of the Pythian oracle at Delphi.

of what he knew, nothing, but one thing only.

OEDIPUS: What was it?

140   If we could even find a slim beginning
        in which to hope, we might discover much.

CREON: This man said that the robbers they encountered
        were many and the hands that did the murder
        were many; it was no man's single power.

OEDIPUS: How could a robber dare a deed like this
        were he not helped with money from the city,
        money and treachery?

CREON: That indeed was thought.
        But Laius was dead and in our trouble
        there was none to help.

OEDIPUS: What trouble was so great to hinder you
        inquiring out the murder of your king?

CREON: The riddling Sphinx induced us to neglect
        mysterious crimes and rather seek solution
        of troubles at our feet.

OEDIPUS: I will bring this to light again. King Phoebus
        fittingly took this care about the dead,
        and you too fittingly.
        And justly you will see in me an ally,
        a champion of my country and the God.

160   For when I drive pollution from the land
        I will not serve a distant friend's advantage,
        but act in my own interest. Whoever
        he was that killed the king may readily
        wish to dispatch me with his murderous hand;

165   so helping the dead king I help myself.

        Come, children, take your suppliant boughs and go;
        up from the altars now. Call the assembly
        and let it meet upon the understanding
        that I'll do everything. God will decide

170   whether we prosper or remain in sorrow.

PRIEST: Rise, children—it was this we came to seek,
        which of himself the king now offers us.
        May Phoebus who gave us the oracle
        come to our rescue and stay the plague.

[*Exeunt all but the Chorus.*]

Strophe[4]

CHORUS: What is the sweet spoken word of God from the shrine of Pytho rich in gold
        that has come to glorious Thebes?
        I am stretched on the rack of doubt, and terror and trembling hold
        my heart, O Delian Healer, and I worship full of fears
        for what doom you will bring to pass, new or renewed in the revolving years.

---

4. Strophe ("turn") and Antistrophe ("counterturn") refer to the moves the chorus would make, dancing as it sang.

180 Speak to me, immortal voice,
child of golden Hope.

Antistrophe

First I call on you, Athene, deathless daughter of Zeus,
and Artemis, Earth Upholder,
who sits in the midst of the market place in the throne which men call Fame,
185 and Phoebus, the Far Shooter, three averters of Fate,
come to us now, if ever before, when ruin rushed upon the state,
you drove destruction's flame away
out of our land.

Strophe

Our sorrows defy number;
190 all the ship's timbers are rotten;
taking of thought is no spear for the driving away of the plague.
There are no growing children in this famous land;
there are no women bearing the pangs of childbirth.
You may see them one with another, like birds swift on the wing,
195 quicker than fire unmastered,
speeding away to the coast of the Western God.[5]

Antistrophe

In the unnumbered deaths
of its people the city dies;
those children that are born lie dead on the naked earth
200 unpitied, spreading contagion of death; and grey haired mothers and wives
everywhere stand at the altar's edge, suppliant, moaning;
the hymn to the healing God rings out but with it the wailing voices are
blended.
From these our sufferings grant us, O golden Daughter of Zeus,
glad-faced deliverance.

Strophe

205 There is no clash of brazen shields but our fight is with the War God,
a War God ringed with the cries of men, a savage God who burns us;
grant that he turn in racing course backwards out of our country's bounds
to the great palace of Amphitrite or where the waves of the Thracian sea
deny the stranger safe anchorage.
210 Whatsoever escapes the night
at last the light of day revisits;
so smite the War God, Father Zeus,
beneath your thunderbolt,
for you are the Lord of the lightning, the lightning that carries fire.

---

5. Hades or death.

Antistrophe

215   And your unconquered arrow shafts, winged by the golden corded bow,
       Lycean King, I beg to be at our side for help;
       and the gleaming torches of Artemis with which she scours the Lycean hills,
       and I call on the God with the turban of gold, who gave his name to this
               country of ours,
       the Bacchic God with the wind flushed face,[6]

220   Evian One, who travel
       with the Maenad company,
       combat the God that burns us
       with your torch of pine;
       for the God that is our enemy is a God unhonoured among the Gods.

       [*Oedipus returns.*]

OEDIPUS: For what you ask me—if you will hear my words,
       and hearing welcome them and fight the plague,
       you will find strength and lightening of your load.

       Hark to me; what I say to you, I say
       as one that is a stranger to the story
230   as stranger to the deed. For I would not
       be far upon the track if I alone
       were tracing it without a clue. But now,
       since after all was finished, I became
       a citizen among you, citizens—
235   now I proclaim to all the men of Thebes:
       who so among you knows the murderer
       by whose hand Laius, son of Labdacus,
       died—I command him to tell everything
       to me,—yes, though he fears himself to take the blame
240   on his own head; for bitter punishment
       he shall have none, but leave this land unharmed.
       Or if he knows the murderer, another,
       a foreigner, still let him speak the truth.
       For I will pay him and be grateful, too.
245   But if you shall keep silence, if perhaps
       some one of you, to shield a guilty friend,
       or for his own sake shall reject my words—
       hear what I shall do then:
       I forbid that man, whoever he be, my land,
250   my land where I hold sovereignty and throne;
       and I forbid any to welcome him
       or cry him greeting or make him a sharer
       in sacrifice or offering to the Gods,
       or give him water for his hands to wash.
255   I command all to drive him from their homes,

---

6. Dionysus, who traveled with frenzied female devotees, the Maemads.

since he is our pollution, as the oracle
of Pytho's God proclaimed him now to me.
So I stand forth a champion of the God
and of the man who died.

260 Upon the murderer I invoke this curse—
whether he is one man and all unknown,
or one of many—may he wear out his life
in misery to miserable doom!
If with my knowledge he lives at my hearth

265 I pray that I myself may feel my curse.
On you I lay my charge to fulfill all this
for me, for the God, and for this land of ours
destroyed and blighted, by the God forsaken.

Even were this no matter of God's ordinance
270 it would not fit you so to leave it lie,
unpurified, since a good man is dead
and one that was a king. Search it out.
Since I am now the holder of his office,
and have his bed and wife that once was his,
275 and had his line not been unfortunate
we would have common children—[fortune leaped
upon his head]—because of all these things,
I fight in his defence as for my father,
and I shall try all means to take the murderer
280 of Laius the son of Labdacus
the son of Polydorus and before him
of Cadmus and before him of Agenor.
Those who do not obey me, may the Gods
grant no crops springing from the ground they plough
285 nor children to their women! May a fate
like this, or one still worse than this consume them!
For you whom these words please, the other Thebans,
may Justice as your ally and all the Gods
live with you, blessing you now and for ever!
CHORUS: As you have held me to my oath, I speak:
I neither killed the king nor can declare
the killer; but since Phoebus set the quest
it is his part to tell who the man is.
OEDIPUS: Right; but to put compulsion on the Gods
295 against their will—no man can do that.
CHORUS: May I then say what I think second best?
OEDIPUS: If there's a third best, too, spare not to tell it.
CHORUS: I know that what the Lord Teiresias
sees, is most often what the Lord Apollo
300 sees. If you should inquire of this from him
you might find out most clearly.
OEDIPUS: Even in this my actions have not been sluggard.
On Creon's word I have sent two messengers

and why the prophet is not here already
305   I have been wondering.

CHORUS: His skill apart
there is besides only an old faint story.

OEDIPUS: What is it?
I look at every story.

CHORUS: It was said
that he was killed by certain wayfarers.

OEDIPUS: I heard that, too, but no one saw the killer.

CHORUS: Yet if he has a share of fear at all,
his courage will not stand firm, hearing your curse.

OEDIPUS: The man who in the doing did not shrink
will fear no word.

CHORUS: Here comes his prosecutor:
315   led by your men the godly prophet comes
in whom alone of mankind truth is native.

[Enter Teiresias, led by a little boy.]

OEDIPUS: Teiresias, you are versed in everything,
things teachable and things not to be spoken,
things of the heaven and earth-creeping things.
320   You have no eyes but in your mind you know
with what a plague our city is afflicted.
My lord, in you alone we find a champion,
in you alone one that can rescue us.
Perhaps you have not heard the messengers,
325   but Phoebus sent in answer to our sending
an oracle declaring that our freedom
from this disease would only come when we
should learn the names of those who killed King Laius,
and kill them or expel from our country.
330   Do not begrudge us oracles from birds,
or any other way of prophecy
within your skill; save yourself and the city,
save me; redeem the debt of our pollution
that lies on us because of this dead man.
335   We are in your hands; pains are most nobly taken
to help another when you have means and power.

TEIRESIAS: Alas, how terrible is wisdom when
it brings no profit to the man that's wise!
This I knew well, but had forgotten it,
340   else I would not have come here.

OEDIPUS: What is this?
How sad you are now you have come!

TEIRESIAS: Let me
go home. It will be easiest for us both
to bear our several destinies to the end
if you will follow my advice.

OEDIPUS: You'd rob us

345   of this your gift of prophecy? You talk
      as one who had no care for law nor love
      for Thebes who reared you.
TEIRESIAS: Yes, but I see that even your own words
      miss the mark; therefore I must fear for mine.
OEDIPUS: For God's sake if you know of anything,
      do not turn from us; all of us kneel to you,
      all of us here, your suppliants.
TEIRESIAS: All of you here know nothing. I will not
      bring to the light of day my troubles, mine—
355   rather than call them yours.
OEDIPUS: What do you mean?
      You know of something but refuse to speak.
      Would you betray us and destroy the city?
TEIRESIAS: I will not bring this pain upon us both,
      neither on you nor on myself. Why is it
360   you question me and waste your labour? I
      will tell you nothing.
OEDIPUS: You would provoke a stone! Tell us, you villain,
      tell us, and do not stand there quietly
      unmoved and balking at the issue.
TEIRESIAS: You blame my temper but you do not see
      your own that lives within you; it is me
      you chide.
OEDIPUS: Who would not feel his temper rise
      at words like these with which you shame our city?
TEIRESIAS: Of themselves things will come, although I hide them
      and breathe no word of them.
OEDIPUS: Since they will come
      tell them to me.
TEIRESIAS: I will say nothing further.
      Against this answer let your temper rage
      as wildly as you will.
OEDIPUS: Indeed I am
375   so angry I shall not hold back a jot
      of what I think. For I would have you know
      I think you were complotter of the deed
      and doer of the deed save in so far
      as for the actual killing. Had you had eyes
380   I would have said alone you murdered him.
TEIRESIAS: Yes? Then I warn you faithfully to keep
      the letter of your proclamation and
      from this day forth to speak no word of greeting
      to these nor me; you are the land's pollution.
OEDIPUS: How shamelessly you started up this taunt!
      How do you think you will escape?
TEIRESIAS: I have.
      I have escaped; the truth is what I cherish
      and that's my strength.

OEDIPUS: And who has taught you truth?
        Not your profession surely!
TEIRESIAS: You have taught me,
390   for you have made me speak against my will.
OEDIPUS: Speak what? Tell me again that I may learn it better.
TEIRESIAS: Did you not understand before or would you
        provoke me into speaking?
OEDIPUS: I did not grasp it,
        not so to call it known. Say it again.
TEIRESIAS: I say you are the murderer of the king
        whose murderer you seek.
OEDIPUS: Not twice you shall
        say calumnies like this and stay unpunished.
TEIRESIAS: Shall I say more to tempt your anger more?
OEDIPUS: As much as you desire; it will be said
400   in vain.
TEIRESIAS: I say that with those you love best
        you live in foulest shame unconsciously
        and do not see where you are in calamity.
OEDIPUS: Do you imagine you can always talk
        like this, and live to laugh at it hereafter?
TEIRESIAS: Yes, if the truth has anything of strength.
OEDIPUS: It has, but not for you; it has no strength
        for you because you are blind in mind and ears
        as well as in your eyes.
TEIRESIAS: You are a poor wretch
        to taunt me with the very insults which
410   every one soon will heap upon yourself.
OEDIPUS: Your life is one long night so that you cannot
        hurt me or any other who sees the light.
TEIRESIAS: It is not fate that I should be your ruin,
        Apollo is enough; it is his care
        to work this out.
OEDIPUS: Was this your own design
        or Creon's?
TEIRESIAS: Creon is no hurt to you,
        but you are to yourself.
OEDIPUS: Wealth, sovereignty and skill outmatching skill
        for the contrivance of an envied life!
420   Great store of jealousy fill your treasury chests,
        if my friend Creon, friend from the first and loyal,
        thus secretly attacks me, secretly
        desires to drive me out and secretly
        suborns this juggling, trick devising quack,
425   this wily beggar who has only eyes
        for his own gains, but blindness in his skill.
        For, tell me, where have you seen clear, Teiresias,
        with your prophetic eyes? When the dark singer,

the sphinx, was in your country, did you speak
430   word of deliverance to its citizens?
And yet the riddle's answer was not the province
of a chance comer. It was a prophet's task
and plainly you had no such gift of prophecy
from birds nor otherwise from any God
435   to glean a word of knowledge. But I came,
Oedipus, who knew nothing, and I stopped her.
I solved the riddle by my wit alone.
Mine was no knowledge got from birds. And now
you would expel me,
440   because you think that you will find a place
by Creon's throne. I think you will be sorry,
both you and your accomplice, for your plot
to drive me out. And did I not regard you
as an old man, some suffering would have taught you
445   that what was in your heart was treason.
CHORUS: We look at this man's words and yours, my king,
and we find both have spoken them in anger.
We need no angry words but only thought
how we may best hit the God's meaning for us.
TEIRESIAS: If you are king, at least I have the right
no less to speak in my defence against you.
Of that much I am master. I am no slave
of yours, but Loxias',[7] and so I shall not
enroll myself with Creon for my patron.
455   Since you have taunted me with being blind,
here is my word for you.
You have your eyes but see not where you are
in sin, nor where you live, nor whom you live with.
Do you know who your parents are? Unknowing
460   you are an enemy to kith and kin
in death, beneath the earth, and in this life.
A deadly footed, double striking curse,
from father and mother both, shall drive you forth
out of this land, with darkness on your eyes,
465   that now have such straight vision. Shall there be
a place will not be harbour to your cries,
a corner of Cithaeron will not ring
in echo to your cries, soon, soon,—
when you shall learn the secret of your marriage,
470   which steered you to a haven in this house,—
haven no haven, after lucky voyage?
And of the multitude of other evils
establishing a grim equality
between you and your children, you know nothing.

7. Apollo's.

475   So, muddy with contempt my words and Creon's!
       Misery shall grind no man as it will you.
OEDIPUS: Is it endurable that I should hear
       such words from him? Go and a curse go with you!
       Quick, home with you! Out of my house at once!
TEIRESIAS: I would not have come either had you not called me.
OEDIPUS: I did not know then you would talk like a fool—
       or it would have been long before I called you.
TEIRESIAS: I am a fool then, as it seems to you—
       but to the parents who have bred you, wise.
OEDIPUS: What parents? Stop! Who are they of all the world?
TEIRESIAS: This day will show your birth and will destroy you.
OEDIPUS: How needlessly your riddles darken everything.
TEIRESIAS: But it's in riddle answering you are strongest.
OEDIPUS: Yes. Taunt me where you will find me great.
TEIRESIAS: It is this very luck that has destroyed you.
OEDIPUS: I do not care, if it has saved this city.
TEIRESIAS: Well, I will go. Come, boy, lead me away.
OEDIPUS: Yes, lead him off. So long as you are here,
       you'll be a stumbling block and a vexation;
495   once gone, you will not trouble me again.
TEIRESIAS: I have said
       what I came here to say not fearing your
       countenance: there is no way you can hurt me.
       I tell you, king, this man, this murderer
       (whom you have long declared you are in search of,
500   indicting him in threatening proclamation
       as murderer of Laius)—he is here.
       In name he is a stranger among citizens
       but soon he will be shown to be a citizen
       true native Theban, and he'll have no joy
505   of the discovery: blindness for sight
       and beggary for riches his exchange,
       he shall go journeying to a foreign country
       tapping his way before him with a stick.
       He shall be proved father and brother both
510   to his own children in his house; to her
       that gave him birth, a son and husband both;
       a fellow sower in his father's bed
       with that same father that he murdered.
       Go within, reckon that out, and if you find me
515   mistaken, say I have no skill in prophecy.

       [*Exeunt separately Teiresias and Oedipus.*]

                                        Strophe
CHORUS: Who is the man proclaimed
       by Delphi's prophetic rock
       as the bloody handed murderer,

the doer of deeds that none dare name?
520 Now is the time for him to run
with a stronger foot
than Pegasus
for the child of Zeus leaps in arms upon him
with fire and the lightning bolt,
525 and terribly close on his heels
are the Fates that never miss.

Antistrophe

Lately from snowy Parnassus
clearly the voice flashed forth,
bidding each Theban track him down,
530 the unknown murderer.
In the savage forests he lurks and in
the caverns like
the mountain bull.
He is sad and lonely, and lonely his feet
535 that carry him far from the navel of earth;
but its prophecies, ever living,
flutter around his head.

Strophe

The augur has spread confusion,
terrible confusion;
540 I do not approve what was said
nor can I deny it.
I do not know what to say;
I am in a flutter of foreboding;
I never heard in the present
545 nor past of a quarrel between
the sons of Labdacus and Polybus,
that I might bring as proof
in attacking the popular fame
of Oedipus, seeking
550 to take vengeance for undiscovered
death in the line of Labdacus.

Antistrophe

Truly Zeus and Apollo are wise
and in human things all knowing;
but amongst men there is no
555 distinct judgment, between the prophet
and me—which of us is right.
One man may pass another in wisdom
but I would never agree
with those that find fault with the king
560 till I should see the word
proved right beyond doubt. For once

in visible form the Sphinx
came on him and all of us
saw his wisdom and in that test
565   he saved the city. So he will not be condemned by my mind.

[*Enter Creon.*]

CREON: Citizens, I have come because I heard
deadly words spread about me, that the king
accuses me. I cannot take that from him.
If he believes that in these present troubles
570   he has been wronged by me in word or deed
I do not want to live on with the burden
of such a scandal on me. The report
injures me doubly and most vitally—
for I'll be called a traitor to my city
575   and traitor also to my friends and you.
CHORUS: Perhaps it was a sudden gust of anger
that forced that insult from him, and no judgment.
CREON: But did he say that it was in compliance
with schemes of mine that the seer told him lies?
CHORUS: Yes, he said that, but why, I do not know.
CREON: Were his eyes straight in his head? Was his mind right
when he accused me in this fashion?
CHORUS: I do not know; I have no eyes to see
what princes do. Here comes the king himself.

[*Enter Oedipus.*]

OEDIPUS: You, sir, how is it you come here? Have you so much
brazen-faced daring that you venture in
my house although you are proved manifestly
the murderer of that man, and though you tried,
openly, highway robbery of my crown?
590   For God's sake, tell me what you saw in me,
what cowardice or what stupidity,
that made you lay a plot like this against me?
Did you imagine I should not observe
the crafty scheme that stole upon me or
595   seeing it, take no means to counter it?
Was it not stupid of you to make the attempt,
to try to hunt down royal power without
the people at your back or friends? For only
with the people at your back or money can
600   the hunt end in the capture of a crown.
CREON: Do you know what you're doing? Will you listen
to words to answer yours, and then pass judgment?
OEDIPUS: You're quick to speak, but I am slow to grasp you,
for I have found you dangerous,—and my foe.
CREON: First of all hear what I shall say to that.
OEDIPUS: At least don't tell me that you are not guilty.

CREON: If you think obstinacy without wisdom
    a valuable possession, you are wrong.

OEDIPUS: And you are wrong if you believe that one,
610   a criminal, will not be punished only
    because he is my kinsman.

CREON: This is but just—
    but tell me, then, of what offense I'm guilty?

OEDIPUS: Did you or did you not urge me to send
    to this prophetic mumbler?

CREON: I did indeed,
615   and I shall stand by what I told you.

OEDIPUS: How long ago is it since Laius. . . .

CREON: What about Laius? I don't understand.

OEDIPUS: Vanished—died—was murdered?

CREON: It is long,
    a long, long time to reckon.

OEDIPUS: Was this prophet
620   in the profession then?

CREON: He was, and honoured
    as highly as he is today.

OEDIPUS: At that time did he say a word about me?

CREON: Never, at least when I was near him.

OEDIPUS: You never made a search for the dead man?

CREON: We searched, indeed, but never learned of anything.

OEDIPUS: Why did our wise old friend not say this then?

CREON: I don't know; and when I know nothing, I
    usually hold my tongue.

OEDIPUS: You know this much,
    and can declare this much if you are loyal.

CREON: What is it? If I know, I'll not deny it.

OEDIPUS: That he would not have said that I killed Laius
    had he not met you first.

CREON: You know yourself
    whether he said this, but I demand that I
    should hear as much from you as you from me.

OEDIPUS: Then hear,—I'll not be proved a murderer.

CREON: Well, then. You're married to my sister.

OEDIPUS: Yes,
    that I am not disposed to deny.

CREON: You rule
    this country giving her an equal share
    in the government?

OEDIPUS: Yes, everything she wants
640   she has from me.

CREON: And I, as thirdsman to you,
    am rated as the equal of you two?

OEDIPUS: Yes, and it's there you've proved yourself false friend.

CREON: Not if you will reflect on it as I do.
    Consider, first, if you think any one

645   would choose to rule and fear rather than rule
       and sleep untroubled by a fear if power
       were equal in both cases. I, at least,
       I was not born with such a frantic yearning
       to be a king—but to do what kings do.
650   And so it is with every one who has learned
       wisdom and self-control. As it stands now,
       the prizes are all mine—and without fear.
       But if I were the king myself, I must
       do much that went against the grain.
655   How should despotic rule seem sweeter to me
       than painless power and an assured authority?
       I am not so besotted yet that I
       want other honours than those that come with profit.
       Now every man's my pleasure; every man greets me;
660   now those who are your suitors fawn on me,—
       success for them depends upon my favour.
       Why should I let all this go to win that?
       My mind would not be traitor if it's wise;
       I am no treason lover, of my nature,
665   nor would I ever dare to join a plot.
       Prove what I say. Go to the oracle
       at Pytho and inquire about the answers,
       if they are as I told you. For the rest,
       if you discover I laid any plot
670   together with the seer, kill me, I say,
       not only by your vote but by my own.
       But do not charge me on obscure opinion
       without some proof to back it. It's not just
       lightly to count your knaves as honest men,
675   nor honest men as knaves. To throw away
       an honest friend is, as it were, to throw
       your life away, which a man loves the best.
       In time you will know all with certainty;
       time is the only test of honest men,
680   one day is space enough to know a rogue.
CHORUS: His words are wise, king, if one fears to fall.
       Those who are quick of temper are not safe.
OEDIPUS: When he that plots against me secretly
       moves quickly, I must quickly counterplot.
685   If I wait taking no decisive measure
       his business will be done, and mine be spoiled.
CREON: What do you want to do then? Banish me?
OEDIPUS: No, certainly; kill you, not banish you.
CREON: I do not think that you've your wits about you.
OEDIPUS: For my own interests, yes.
CREON: But for mine, too,
       you should think equally.
OEDIPUS: You are a rogue.

CREON: Suppose you do not understand?
OEDIPUS: But yet
I must be ruler.
CREON: Not if you rule badly.
OEDIPUS: O, city, city!
CREON: I too have some share
695   in the city; it is not yours alone.
CHORUS: Stop, my lords! Here—and in the nick of time
I see Jocasta coming from the house;
with her help lay the quarrel that now stirs you.

[*Enter Jocasta.*]

JOCASTA: For shame! Why have you raised this foolish squabbling
700   brawl? Are you not ashamed to air your private
griefs when the country's sick? Go in, you, Oedipus,
and you, too, Creon, into the house. Don't magnify
your nothing troubles.
CREON: Sister, Oedipus,
your husband, thinks he has the right to do
705   terrible wrongs—he has but to choose between
two terrors: banishing or killing me.
OEDIPUS: He's right, Jocasta; for I find him plotting
with knavish tricks against my person.
CREON: That God may never bless me! May I die
710   accursed, if I have been guilty of
one tittle of the charge you bring against me!
JOCASTA: I beg you, Oedipus, trust him in this,
spare him for the sake of this his oath to God,
for my sake, and the sake of those who stand here.
CHORUS: Be gracious, be merciful,
we beg of you.
OEDIPUS: In what would you have me yield?
CHORUS: He has been no silly child in the past.
He is strong in his oath now.
720   Spare him.
OEDIPUS: Do you know what you ask?
CHORUS: Yes.
OEDIPUS: Tell me then.

CHORUS: He has been your friend before all men's eyes; do not cast him
725   away dishonoured on an obscure conjecture.

OEDIPUS: I would have you know that this request of yours
really requests my death or banishment.

CHORUS: May the Sun God, king of Gods, forbid! May I die without God's
blessing, without friends' help, if I had any such thought. But my
730   spirit is broken by my unhappiness for my wasting country; and
this would but add troubles amongst ourselves to the other troubles.

OEDIPUS: Well, let him go then—if I must die ten times for it,

or be sent out dishonoured into exile.
It is your lips that prayed for him I pitied,
735   not his; wherever he is, I shall hate him.

CREON: I see you sulk in yielding and you're dangerous
when you are out of temper; natures like yours
are justly heaviest for themselves to bear.

OEDIPUS: Leave me alone! Take yourself off, I tell you.

CREON: I'll go, you have not known me, but they have,
and they have known my innocence.

[*Exit.*]

CHORUS: Won't you take him inside, lady?

JOCASTA: Yes, when I've found out what was the matter.

CHORUS: There was some misconceived suspicion of a story, and on the other
side the sting of injustice.

JOCASTA: So, on both sides?

CHORUS: Yes.

JOCASTA: What was the story?

CHORUS: I think it best, in the interests of the country, to leave it where
it ended.

OEDIPUS: You see where you have ended, straight of judgment
although you are, by softening my anger.

CHORUS: Sir, I have said before and I say again—be sure that I would have
been proved a madman, bankrupt in sane council, if I should put
you away, you who steered the country I love safely when she
was crazed with troubles. God grant that now, too, you may
prove a fortunate guide for us.

JOCASTA: Tell me, my lord, I beg of you, what was it
that roused your anger so?

OEDIPUS: Yes, I will tell you.
760   I honour you more than I honour them.
It was Creon and the plots he laid against me.

JOCASTA: Tell me—if you can clearly tell the quarrel—

OEDIPUS: Creon says
that I'm the murderer of Laius.

JOCASTA: Of his own knowledge or on information?

OEDIPUS: He sent this rascal prophet to me, since
he keeps his own mouth clean of any guilt.

JOCASTA: Do not concern yourself about this matter;
listen to me and learn that human beings
have no part in the craft of prophecy.
770   Of that I'll show you a short proof.
There was an oracle once that came to Laius,—
I will not say that it was Phoebus' own,
but it was from his servants—and it told him
that it was fate that he should die a victim
775   at the hands of his own son, a son to be born

of Laius and me. But, see now, he,
the king, was killed by foreign highway robbers
at a place where three roads meet—so goes the story;
and for the son—before three days were out
780   after his birth King Laius pierced his ankles
and by the hands of others cast him forth
upon a pathless hillside. So Apollo
failed to fulfill his oracle to the son,
that he should kill his father, and to Laius
785   also proved false in that the thing he feared,
death at his son's hands, never came to pass.
So clear in this case were the oracles,
so clear and false. Give them no heed, I say;
what God discovers need of, easily
790   he shows to us himself.
OEDIPUS: O dear Jocasta,
as I hear this from you, there comes upon me
a wandering of the soul—I could run mad.
JOCASTA: What trouble is it, that you turn again
and speak like this?
OEDIPUS: I thought I heard you say
795   that Laius was killed at a crossroads.
JOCASTA: Yes, that was how the story went and still
that word goes round.
OEDIPUS: Where is this place, Jocasta,
where he was murdered?
JOCASTA: Phocis is the country
and the road splits there, one of two roads from Delphi,
800   another comes from Daulia.
OEDIPUS: How long ago is this?
JOCASTA: The news came to the city just before
you became king and all men's eyes looked to you.
What is it, Oedipus, that's in your mind?
OEDIPUS: What have you designed, O Zeus, to do with me?
JOCASTA: What is the thought that troubles your heart?
OEDIPUS: Don't ask me yet—tell me of Laius—
How did he look? How old or young was he?
JOCASTA: He was a tall man and his hair was grizzled
already—nearly white—and in his form
810   not unlike you.
OEDIPUS: O God, I think I have
called curses on myself in ignorance.
JOCASTA: What do you mean? I am terrified
when I look at you.
OEDIPUS: I have a deadly fear
that the old seer had eyes. You'll show me more
815   if you can tell me one more thing.
JOCASTA: I will.
I'm frightened,—but if I can understand,

I'll tell you all you ask.

OEDIPUS: How was his company?
Had he few with him when he went this journey,
or many servants, as would suit a prince?

JOCASTA: In all there were but five, and among them
a herald; and one carriage for the king.

OEDIPUS: It's plain—it's plain—who was it told you this?

JOCASTA: The only servant that escaped safe home.

OEDIPUS: Is he at home now?

JOCASTA: No, when he came home again

825   and saw you king and Laius was dead,
he came to me and touched my hand and begged
that I should send him to the fields to be
my shepherd and so he might see the city
as far off as he might. So I

830   sent him away. He was an honest man,
as slaves go, and was worthy of far more
than what he asked of me.

OEDIPUS: O, how I wish that he could come back quickly!

JOCASTA: He can. Why is your heart so set on this?

OEDIPUS: O dear Jocasta, I am full of fears
that I have spoken far too much; and therefore
I wish to see this shepherd.

JOCASTA: He will come;
but, Oedipus, I think I'm worthy too
to know what it is that disquiets you.

OEDIPUS: It shall not be kept from you, since my mind
has gone so far with its forebodings. Whom
should I confide in rather than you, who is there
of more importance to me who have passed
through such a fortune?

845   Polybus was my father, king of Corinth,
and Merope, the Dorian, my mother.
I was held greatest of the citizens
in Corinth till a curious chance befell me
as I shall tell you—curious, indeed,

850   but hardly worth the store I set upon it.
There was a dinner and at it a man,
a drunken man, accused me in his drink
of being bastard. I was furious
but held my temper under for that day.

855   Next day I went and taxed my parents with it;
they took the insult very ill from him,
the drunken fellow who had uttered it.
So I was comforted for their part, but
still this thing rankled always, for the story

860   crept about widely. And I went at last
to Pytho, though my parents did not know.
But Phoebus sent me home again unhonoured

in what I came to learn, but he foretold
other and desperate horrors to befall me,
865   that I was fated to lie with my mother,
and show to daylight an accursed breed
which men would not endure, and I was doomed
to be murderer of the father that begot me.
When I heard this I fled, and in the days
870   that followed I would measure from the stars
the whereabouts of Corinth—yes, I fled
to somewhere where I should not see fulfilled
the infamies told in that dreadful oracle.
And as I journeyed I came to the place
875   where, as you say, this king met with his death.
Jocasta, I will tell you the whole truth.
When I was near the branching of the crossroads,
going on foot, I was encountered by
a herald and a carriage with a man in it,
880   just as you tell me. He that led the way
and the old man himself wanted to thrust me
out of the road by force. I became angry
and struck the coachman who was pushing me.
When the old man saw this he watched his moment,
885   and as I passed he struck me from his carriage,
full on the head with his two pointed goad.
But he was paid in full and presently
my stick had struck him backwards from the car
and he rolled out of it. And then I killed them
890   all. If it happened there was any tie
of kinship twixt this man and Laius,
who is then now more miserable than I,
what man on earth so hated by the Gods,
since neither citizen nor foreigner
895   may welcome me at home or even greet me,
but drive me out of doors? And it is I,
I and no other have so cursed myself.
And I pollute the bed of him I killed
by the hands that killed him. Was I not born evil?
900   Am I not utterly unclean? I had to fly
and in my banishment not even see
my kindred nor set foot in my own country,
or otherwise my fate was to be yoked
in marriage with my mother and kill my father,
905   Polybus who begot me and had reared me.
Would not one rightly judge and say that on me
these things were sent by some malignant God?
O no, no, no—O holy majesty
of God on high, may I not see that day!
910   May I be gone out of men's sight before
I see the deadly taint of this disaster

come upon me.

CHORUS: Sir, we too fear these things. But until you see this man face to
face and hear his story, hope.

OEDIPUS: Yes, I have just this much of hope—to wait until the herdsman comes.

JOCASTA: And when he comes, what do you want with him?

OEDIPUS: I'll tell you; if I find that his story is the same as yours, I at least
will be clear of this guilt.

JOCASTA: Why what so particularly did you learn from my story?

OEDIPUS: You said that he spoke of highway *robbers* who killed Laius. Now
if he uses the same number, it was not I who killed him. One man
cannot be the same as many. But if he speaks of a man travelling
alone, then clearly the burden of the guilt inclines towards me.

JOCASTA: Be sure, at least, that this was how he told the story. He cannot
unsay it now, for every one in the city heard it—not I alone. But,
Oedipus, even if he diverges from what he said then, he shall
never prove that the murder of Laius squares rightly with the
prophecy—for Loxias declared that the king should be killed by
his own son. And that poor creature did not kill him surely,—
for he died himself first. So as far as prophecy goes, henceforward
I shall not look to the right hand or the left.

OEDIPUS: Right. But yet, send some one for the peasant to bring him here;
do not neglect it.

JOCASTA: I will send quickly. Now let me go indoors. I will do nothing
except what pleases you.

[*Exeunt.*]

Strophe

CHORUS: May destiny ever find me
pious in word and deed
prescribed by the laws that live on high:
940   laws begotten in the clear air of heaven,
whose only father is Olympus;[8]
no mortal nature brought them to birth,
no forgetfulness shall lull them to sleep;
for God is great in them and grows not old.

Antistrophe

945   Insolence breeds the tyrant, insolence
if it is glutted with a surfeit, unseasonable, unprofitable,
climbs to the roof-top and plunges
sheer down to the ruin that must be,
and there its feet are no service.
950   But I pray that the God may never
abolish the eager ambition that profits the state.
For I shall never cease to hold the God as our protector.

8. Mountain throne of Zeus and home of the gods.

Strophe

If a man walks with haughtiness
of hand or word and gives no heed
955 to Justice and the shrines of Gods
despises—may an evil doom
smite him for his ill-starred pride of heart!—
if he reaps gains without justice
and will not hold from impiety
960 and his fingers itch for untouchable things.
When such things are done, what man shall contrive
to shield his soul from the shafts of the God?
When such deeds are held in honour,
why should I honour the Gods in the dance?

Antistrophe

965 No longer to the holy place,
to the navel of earth I'll go
to worship, nor to Abae
nor to Olympia,
unless the oracles are proved to fit,
970 for all men's hands to point at.
O Zeus, if you are rightly called
the sovereign lord, all-mastering,
let this not escape you nor your ever-living power!
The oracles concerning Laius
975 are old and dim and men regard them not.
Apollo is nowhere clear in honour; God's service perishes.

[*Enter Jocasta, carrying garlands.*]

JOCASTA: Princes of the land, I have had the thought to go
to the Gods' temples, bringing in my hand
garlands and gifts of incense, as you see.
980 For Oedipus excites himself too much
at every sort of trouble, not conjecturing,
like a man of sense, what will be from what was,
but he is always at the speaker's mercy,
when he speaks terrors. I can do no good
985 by my advice, and so I came as suppliant
to you, Lycaean Apollo, who are nearest.
These are the symbols of my prayer and this
my prayer: grant us escape free of the curse.
Now when we look to him we are all afraid;
990 he's pilot of our ship and he is frightened.

[*Enter Messenger.*]

MESSENGER: Might I learn from you, sirs, where is the house of Oedipus?
Or best of all, if you know, where is the king himself?
CHORUS: This is his house and he is within doors. This lady is his wife and

mother of his children.

MESSENGER: God bless you, lady, and God bless your household! God bless
Oedipus' noble wife!

JOCASTA: God bless you, sir, for your kind greeting! What do you want
of us that you have come here? What have you to tell us?

MESSENGER: Good news, lady. Good for your house and for your husband.

JOCASTA: What is your news? Who sent you to us?

MESSENGER: I come from Corinth and the news I bring will give you pleasure.
Perhaps a little pain too.

JOCASTA: What is this news of double meaning?

MESSENGER: The people of the Isthmus will choose Oedipus to be their king.
1005   That is the rumour there.

JOCASTA: But isn't their king still old Polybus?

MESSENGER: No. He is in his grave. Death has got him.

JOCASTA: Is that the truth? Is Oedipus' father dead?

MESSENGER: May I die myself if it be otherwise!

JOCASTA [to a servant]: Be quick and run to the King with the news! O oracles of the
Gods, where are you now? It was from this man Oedipus fled, lest
he should be his murderer! And now he is dead, in the course of
nature, and not killed by Oedipus.

[Enter Oedipus.]

OEDIPUS: Dearest Jocasta, why have you sent for me?

JOCASTA: Listen to this man and when you hear reflect what is the outcome
of the holy oracles of the Gods.

OEDIPUS: Who is he? What is his message for me?

JOCASTA: He is from Corinth and he tells us that your father Polybus is
dead and gone.

OEDIPUS: What's this you say, sir? Tell me yourself.

MESSENGER: Since this is the first matter you want clearly told: Polybus has
gone down to death. You may be sure of it.

OEDIPUS: By treachery or sickness?

MESSENGER: A small thing will put old bodies asleep.

OEDIPUS: So he died of sickness, it seems,—poor old man!

MESSENGER: Yes, and of age—the long years he had measured.

OEDIPUS: Ha! Ha! O dear Jocasta, why should one
look to the Pythian hearth? Why should one look
to the birds screaming overhead? They prophesied
1030   that I should kill my father! But he's dead,
and hidden deep in earth, and I stand here
who never laid a hand on spear against him,—
unless perhaps he died of longing for me,
and thus I am his murderer. But they,
1035   the oracles, as they stand—he's taken them
away with him, they're dead as he himself is,
and worthless.

JOCASTA: That I told you before now.

OEDIPUS: You did, but I was misled by my fear.

JOCASTA: Then lay no more of them to heart, not one.

OEDIPUS: But surely I must fear my mother's bed?

JOCASTA: Why should man fear since chance is all in all
  for him, and he can clearly foreknow nothing?
  Best to live lightly, as one can, unthinkingly.
  As to your mother's marriage bed,—don't fear it.

1045 Before this, in dreams too, as well as oracles,
  many a man has lain with his own mother.
  But he to whom such things are nothing bears
  his life most easily.

OEDIPUS: All that you say would be said perfectly

1050 if she were dead; but since she lives I must
  still fear, although you talk so well, Jocasta.

JOCASTA: Still in your father's death there's light of comfort?

OEDIPUS: Great light of comfort; but I fear the living.

MESSENGER: Who is the woman that makes you afraid?

OEDIPUS: Merope, old man, Polybus' wife.

MESSENGER: What about her frightens the queen and you?

OEDIPUS: A terrible oracle, stranger, from the Gods.

MESSENGER: Can it be told? Or does the sacred law
  forbid another to have knowledge of it?

OEDIPUS: O no! Once on a time Loxias said
  that I should lie with my own mother and
  take on my hands the blood of my own father.
  And so for these long years I've lived away
  from Corinth; it has been to my great happiness;

1065 but yet it's sweet to see the face of parents.

MESSENGER: This was the fear which drove you out of Corinth?

OEDIPUS: Old man, I did not wish to kill my father.

MESSENGER: Why should I not free you from this fear, sir,
  since I have come to you in all goodwill?

OEDIPUS: You would not find me thankless if you did.

MESSENGER: Why, it was just for this I brought the news,—
  to earn your thanks when you had come safe home.

OEDIPUS: No, I will never come near my parents.

MESSENGER: Son,
  it's very plain you don't know what you're doing.

OEDIPUS: What do you mean, old man? For God's sake, tell me.

MESSENGER: If your homecoming is checked by fears like these.

OEDIPUS: Yes, I'm afraid that Phoebus may prove right.

MESSENGER: The murder and the incest?

OEDIPUS: Yes, old man;
  that is my constant terror.

MESSENGER: Do you know

1080 that all your fears are empty?

OEDIPUS: How is that,
  if they are father and mother and I their son?

MESSENGER: Because Polybus was no kin to you in blood.

OEDIPUS: What, was not Polybus my father?

MESSENGER: No more than I but just so much.

OEDIPUS: How can
1085   my father be my father as much as one
         that's nothing to me?

MESSENGER: Neither he nor I
         begat you.

OEDIPUS: Why then did he call me son?

MESSENGER: A gift he took you from these hands of mine.

OEDIPUS: Did he love so much what he took from another's hand?

MESSENGER: His childlessness before persuaded him.

OEDIPUS: Was I a child you bought or found when I
         was given to him?

MESSENGER: On Cithaeron's slopes
         in the twisting thickets you were found.

OEDIPUS: And why
         were you a traveller in those parts?

MESSENGER: I was
1095   in charge of mountain flocks.

OEDIPUS: You were a shepherd?
         A hireling vagrant?

MESSENGER: Yes, but at least at that time
         the man that saved your life, son.

OEDIPUS: What ailed me when you took me in your arms?

MESSENGER: In that your ankles should be witnesses.

OEDIPUS: Why do you speak of that old pain?

MESSENGER: I loosed you;
         the tendons of your feet were pierced and fettered,—

OEDIPUS: My swaddling clothes brought me a rare disgrace.

MESSENGER: So that from this you're called your present name.

OEDIPUS: Was this my father's doing or my mother's?
1105   For God's sake, tell me.

MESSENGER: I don't know, but he
         who gave you to me has more knowledge than I.

OEDIPUS: You yourself did not find me then? You took me
         from someone else?

MESSENGER: Yes, from another shepherd.

OEDIPUS: Who was he? Do you know him well enough
1110   to tell?

MESSENGER: He was called Laius' man.

OEDIPUS: You mean the king who reigned here in the old days?

MESSENGER: Yes, he was that man's shepherd.

OEDIPUS: Is he alive
         still, so that I could see him?

MESSENGER: You who live here
         would know that best.

OEDIPUS: Do any of you here
1115   know of this shepherd whom he speaks about
         in town or in the fields? Tell me. It's time

that this was found out once for all.

CHORUS: I think he is none other than the peasant
whom you have sought to see already; but
1120   Jocasta here can tell us best of that.

OEDIPUS: Jocasta, do you know about this man
whom we have sent for? Is he the man he mentions?

JOCASTA: Why ask of whom he spoke? Don't give it heed;
nor try to keep in mind what has been said.
1125   It will be wasted labour.

OEDIPUS: With such clues
I could not fail to bring my birth to light.

JOCASTA: I beg you—do not hunt this out—I beg you,
if you have any care for your own life.
What I am suffering is enough.

OEDIPUS: Keep up
1130   your heart, Jocasta. Though I'm proved a slave,
thrice slave, and though my mother is thrice slave,
you'll not be shown to be of lowly lineage.

JOCASTA: O be persuaded by me, I entreat you;
do not do this.

OEDIPUS: I will not be persuaded to let be
the chance of finding out the whole thing clearly.

JOCASTA: It is because I wish you well that I
give you this counsel—and it's the best counsel.

OEDIPUS: Then the best counsel vexes me, and has
1140   for some while since.

JOCASTA: O Oedipus, God help you!
God keep you from the knowledge of who you are!

OEDIPUS: Here, some one, go and fetch the shepherd for me;
and let her find her joy in her rich family!

JOCASTA: O Oedipus, unhappy Oedipus!
1145   that is all I can call you, and the last thing
that I shall ever call you.

[*Exit.*]

CHORUS: Why has the queen gone, Oedipus, in wild
grief rushing from us? I am afraid that trouble
will break out of this silence.

OEDIPUS: Break out what will! I at least shall be
willing to see my ancestry, though humble.
Perhaps she is ashamed of my low birth,
for she has all a woman's high-flown pride.
But I account myself a child of Fortune,
1155   beneficent Fortune, and I shall not be
dishonoured. She's the mother from whom I spring;
the months, my brothers, marked me, now as small,
and now again as mighty. Such is my breeding,
and I shall never prove so false to it,

1160   as not to find the secret of my birth.
CHORUS:

Strophe

If I am a prophet and wise of heart
you shall not fail, Cithaeron,
by the limitless sky, you shall not!—
to know at tomorrow's full moon
1165   that Oedipus honours you,
as native to him and mother and nurse at once;
and that you are honoured in dancing by us, as finding favour in
sight of our king.
Apollo, to whom we cry, find these things pleasing!

Antistrophe

1170   Who was it bore you, child? One of
the long-lived nymphs who lay with Pan—
the father who treads the hills?
Or was she a bride of Loxias, your mother? The grassy slopes
are all of them dear to him. Or perhaps Cyllene's king
1175   or the Bacchants' God that lives on the tops
of the hills received you a gift from some
one of the Helicon Nymphs, with whom he mostly plays?

[*Enter an old man, led by Oedipus' servants.*]

OEDIPUS: If some one like myself who never met him
may make a guess,—I think this is the herdsman,
1180   whom we were seeking. His old age is consonant
with the other. And besides, the men who bring him
I recognize as my own servants. You
perhaps may better me in knowledge since
you've seen the man before.
CHORUS: You can be sure
1185   I recognize him. For if Laius
had ever an honest shepherd, this was he.
OEDIPUS: You, sir, from Corinth, I must ask you first,
is this the man you spoke of?
MESSENGER: This is he
before your eyes.
OEDIPUS: Old man, look here at me
1190   and tell me what I ask you. Were you ever
a servant of King Laius?
HERDSMAN: I was,—
no slave he bought but reared in his own house.
OEDIPUS: What did you do as work? How did you live?
HERDSMAN: Most of my life was spent among the flocks.
OEDIPUS: In what part of the country did you live?
HERDSMAN: Cithaeron and the places near to it.
OEDIPUS: And somewhere there perhaps you knew this man?
HERDSMAN: What was his occupation? Who?

OEDIPUS: This man here,
    have you had any dealings with him?
HERDSMAN: No—
1200   not such that I can quickly call to mind.

MESSENGER: That is no wonder, master. But I'll make him remember what he
    does not know. For I know, that he well knows the country of
    Cithaeron, how he with two flocks, I with one kept company for
    three years—each year half a year—from spring till autumn time
1205   and then when winter came I drove my flocks to our fold home
    again and he to Laius' steadings. Well—am I right or not in what
    I said we did?

HERDSMAN: You're right—although it's a long time ago.
MESSENGER: Do you remember giving me a child
1210   to bring up as my foster child?
HERDSMAN: What's this?
    Why do you ask this question?
MESSENGER: Look old man,
    here he is—here's the man who was that child!
HERDSMAN: Death take you! Won't you hold your tongue?
OEDIPUS: No, no,
    do not find fault with him, old man. Your words
1215   are more at fault than his.
HERDSMAN: O best of masters,
    how do I give offense?
OEDIPUS: When you refuse
    to speak about the child of whom he asks you.
HERDSMAN: He speaks out of his ignorance, without meaning.
OEDIPUS: If you'll not talk to gratify me, you
1220   will talk with pain to urge you.
HERDSMAN: O please, sir,
    don't hurt an old man, sir.
OEDIPUS [to the servants]:   Here, one of you,
    twist his hands behind him.
HERDSMAN: Why, God help me, why?
    What do you want to know?
OEDIPUS: You gave a child
    to him,—the child he asked you of?
HERDSMAN: I did.
1225   I wish I'd died the day I did.
OEDIPUS: You will
    unless you tell me truly.
HERDSMAN: And I'll die
    far worse if I should tell you.
OEDIPUS: This fellow
    is bent on more delays, as it would seem.
HERDSMAN: O no, no! I have told you that I gave it.
OEDIPUS: Where did you get this child from? Was it your own or did you
    get it from another?

HERDSMAN: Not
          my own at all; I had it from some one.
OEDIPUS: One of these citizens? or from what house?
HERDSMAN: O master, please—I beg you, master, please
1235   don't ask me more.
OEDIPUS: You're a dead man if I
          ask you again.
HERDSMAN: It was one of the children
          of Laius.
OEDIPUS: A slave? Or born in wedlock?
HERDSMAN: O God, I am on the brink of frightful speech.
OEDIPUS: And I of frightful hearing. But I must hear.
HERDSMAN: The child was called his child; but she within,
          your wife would tell you best how all this was.
OEDIPUS: *She* gave it to you?
HERDSMAN: Yes, she did, my lord.
OEDIPUS: To do what with it?
HERDSMAN: Make away with it.
OEDIPUS: She was so hard—its mother?
HERDSMAN: Aye, through fear
1245   of evil oracles.
OEDIPUS: Which?
HERDSMAN: They said that he
          should kill his parents.
OEDIPUS: How was it that you
          gave it away to this old man?
HERDSMAN: O master,
          I pitied it, and thought that I could send it
          off to another country and this man
1250   was from another country. But he saved it
          for the most terrible troubles. If you are
          the man he says you are, you're bred to misery.
OEDIPUS: O, O, O, they will all come,
          all come out clearly! Light of the sun, let me
1255   look upon you no more after today!
          I who first saw the light bred of a match
          accursed, and accursed in my living
          with them I lived with, cursed in my killing.

          [*Exeunt all but the Chorus.*]

CHORUS:
                              Strophe
          O generations of men, how I
1260   count you as equal with those who live
          not at all!
          What man, what man on earth wins more
          of happiness than a seeming
          and after that turning away?
1265   Oedipus, you are my pattern of this,

Oedipus, you and your fate!
Luckless Oedipus, whom of all men
I envy not at all.

Antistrophe

In as much as he shot his bolt
1270 beyond the others and won the prize
of happiness complete—
O Zeus—and killed and reduced to nought
the hooked taloned maid of the riddling speech,
standing a tower against death for my land:
1275 hence he was called my king and hence
was honoured the highest of all
honours; and hence he ruled
in the great city of Thebes.

Strophe

But now whose tale is more miserable?
1280 Who is there lives with a savager fate?
Whose troubles so reverse his life as his?

O Oedipus, the famous prince
for whom a great haven
the same both as father and son
1285 sufficed for generation,
how, O how, have the furrows ploughed
by your father endured to bear you, poor wretch,
and hold their peace so long?

Antistrophe

Time who sees all has found you out
1290 against your will; judges your marriage accursed,
begetter and begot at one in it.

O child of Laius,
would I had never seen you.
I weep for you and cry
1295 a dirge of lamentation.

To speak directly, I drew my breath
from you at the first and so now I lull
my mouth to sleep with your name.

[*Enter a second messenger.*]

SECOND MESSENGER: O Princes always honoured by our country,
1300 what deeds you'll hear of and what horrors see,
what grief you'll feel, if you as true born Thebans
care for the house of Labdacus's sons.
Phasis nor Ister cannot purge this house,
I think, with all their streams, such things

1305   it hides, such evils shortly will bring forth
      into the light, whether they will or not;
      and troubles hurt the most
      when they prove self-inflicted.

CHORUS: What we had known before did not fall short
1310   of bitter groaning's worth; what's more to tell?

SECOND MESSENGER: Shortest to hear and tell—our glorious queen
      Jocasta's dead.

CHORUS: Unhappy woman! How?

SECOND MESSENGER: By her own hand. The worst of what was done
      you cannot know. You did not see the sight.
1315   Yet in so far as I remember it
      you'll hear the end of our unlucky queen.
      When she came raging into the house she went
      straight to her marriage bed, tearing her hair
      with both her hands, and crying upon Laius
1320   long dead—Do you remember, Laius,
      that night long past which bred a child for us
      to send you to your death and leave
      a mother making children with her son?
      And then she groaned and cursed the bed in which
1325   she brought forth husband by her husband, children
      by her own child, an infamous double bond.
      How after that she died I do not know,—
      for Oedipus distracted us from seeing.
      He burst upon us shouting and we looked
1330   to him as he paced frantically around,
      begging us always: Give me a sword, I say,
      to find this wife no wife, this mother's womb,
      this field of double sowing whence I sprang
      and where I sowed my children! As he raved
1335   some god showed him the way—none of us there.
      Bellowing terribly and led by some
      invisible guide he rushed on the two doors,—
      wrenching the hollow bolts out of their sockets,
      he charged inside. There, there, we saw his wife
1340   hanging, the twisted rope around her neck.
      When he saw her, he cried out fearfully
      and cut the dangling noose. Then, as she lay,
      poor woman, on the ground, what happened after,
      was terrible to see. He tore the brooches—
1345   the gold chased brooches fastening her robe—
      away from her and lifting them up high
      dashed them on his own eyeballs, shrieking out
      such things as: they will never see the crime
      I have committed or had done upon me!
1350   Dark eyes, now in the days to come look on
      forbidden faces, do not recognize
      those whom you long for—with such imprecations

he struck his eyes again and yet again
with the brooches. And the bleeding eyeballs gushed
1355　and stained his beard—no sluggish oozing drops
but a black rain and bloody hail poured down.

So it has broken—and not on one head
but troubles mixed for husband and for wife.
The fortune of the days gone by was true
1360　good fortune—but today groans and destruction
and death and shame—of all ills can be named
not one is missing.
CHORUS: Is he now in any ease from pain?
SECOND MESSENGER:　　　　　　　　　　　He shouts
for some one to unbar the doors and show him
1365　to all the men of Thebes, his father's killer,
his mother's—no I cannot say the word,
it is unholy—for he'll cast himself,
out of the land, he says, and not remain
to bring a curse upon his house, the curse
1370　he called upon it in his proclamation. But
he wants for strength, aye, and some one to guide him;
his sickness is too great to bear. You, too,
will be shown that. The bolts are opening.
Soon you will see a sight to waken pity
1375　even in the horror of it.

　　　[*Enter the blinded Oedipus.*]

CHORUS: This is a terrible sight for men to see!
I never found a worse!
Poor wretch, what madness came upon you!
What evil spirit leaped upon your life
1380　to your ill-luck—a leap beyond man's strength!
Indeed I pity you, but I cannot
look at you, though there's much I want to ask
and much to learn and much to see.
I shudder at the sight of you.
OEDIPUS: O, O,
where am I going? Where is my voice
borne on the wind to and fro?
Spirit, how far have you sprung?
CHORUS: To a terrible place whereof men's ears
1390　may not hear, nor their eyes behold it.
OEDIPUS: Darkness!
Horror of darkness enfolding, resistless, unspeakable visitant
　　　sped by an ill wind in haste!
madness and stabbing pain and memory
of evil deeds I have done!
CHORUS: In such misfortunes it's no wonder
if double weighs the burden of your grief.

OEDIPUS: My friend,
>you are the only one steadfast, the only one that attends on me;
>you still stay nursing the blind man.
1400   Your care is not unnoticed. I can know
>your voice, although this darkness is my world.
CHORUS: Doer of dreadful deeds, how did you dare
>so far to do despite to your own eyes?
>what spirit urged you to it?
OEDIPUS: It was Apollo, friends, Apollo,
>that brought this bitter bitterness, my sorrows to completion.
>But the hand that struck me
>was none but my own.
>Why should I see
1410   whose vision showed me nothing sweet to see?
CHORUS: These things are as you say.
OEDIPUS: What can I see to love?
>What greeting can touch my ears with joy?
>Take me away, and haste—to a place out of the way!
1415   Take me away, my friends, the greatly miserable,
>the most accursed, whom God too hates
>above all men on earth!
CHORUS: Unhappy in your mind and your misfortune,
>would I had never known you!
OEDIPUS: Curse on the man who took
>the cruel bonds from off my legs, as I lay in the field.
>He stole me from death and saved me,
>no kindly service.
>Had I died then
1425   I would not be so burdensome to friends.
CHORUS: I, too, could have wished it had been so.
OEDIPUS: Then I would not have come
>to kill my father and marry my mother infamously.
>Now I am godless and child of impurity,
1430   begetter in the same seed that created my wretched self.
>If there is any ill worse than ill,
>that is the lot of Oedipus.
CHORUS: I cannot say your remedy was good;
>you would be better dead than blind and living.
OEDIPUS: What I have done here was best done—don't tell me
>otherwise, do not give me further counsel.
>I do not know with what eyes I could look
>upon my father when I die and go
>under the earth, nor yet my wretched mother—
1440   those two to whom I have done things deserving
>worse punishment than hanging. Would the sight
>of children, bred as mine are, gladden me?
>No, not these eyes, never. And my city,
>its towers and sacred places of the Gods,
1445   of these I robbed my miserable self

when I commanded all to drive *him* out,
the criminal since proved by God impure
and of the race of Laius.
To this guilt I bore witness against myself—
1450   with what eyes shall I look upon my people?
No. If there were a means to choke the fountain
of hearing I would not have stayed my hand
from locking up my miserable carcase,
seeing and hearing nothing; it is sweet
1455   to keep our thoughts out of the range of hurt.

Cithaeron, why did you receive me? Why
having received me did you not kill me straight?
And so I had not shown to men my birth.

O Polybus and Corinth and the house,
1460   the old house that I used to call my father's—
what fairness you were nurse to, and what foulness
festered beneath! Now I am found to be
a sinner and a son of sinners. Crossroads,
and hidden glade, oak and the narrow way
1465   at the crossroads, that drank my father's blood
offered you by my hands, do you remember
still what I did as you looked on, and what
I did when I came here? O marriage, marriage!
you bred me and again when you had bred
1470   bred children of your child and showed to men
brides, wives and mothers and the foulest deeds
that can be in this world of ours.

Come—it's unfit to say what is unfit
to do.—I beg of you in God's name hide me
1475   somewhere outside your country, yes, or kill me,
or throw me into the sea, to be forever
out of your sight. Approach and deign to touch me
for all my wretchedness, and do not fear.
No man but I can bear my evil doom.
CHORUS: Here Creon comes in fit time to perform
or give advice in what you ask of us.
Creon is left sole ruler in your stead.
OEDIPUS: Creon! Creon! What shall I say to him?
How can I justly hope that he will trust me?
1485   In what is past I have been proved towards him
an utter liar.

  [*Enter Creon.*]

CREON: Oedipus, I've come
not so that I might laugh at you nor taunt you
with evil of the past. But if you still
are without shame before the face of men

1490   reverence at least the flame that gives all life,
        our Lord the Sun, and do not show unveiled
        to him pollution such that neither land
        nor holy rain nor light of day can welcome.

[*To a servant.*]

        Be quick and take him in. It is most decent
1495   that only kin should see and hear the troubles
        of kin.

OEDIPUS: I beg you, since you've torn me from
        my dreadful expectations and have come
        in a most noble spirit to a man
        that has used you vilely—do a thing for me.
1500   I shall speak for your own good, not for my own.

CREON: What do you need that you would ask of me?

OEDIPUS: Drive me from here with all the speed you can
        to where I may not hear a human voice.

CREON: Be sure, I would have done this had not I
1505   wished first of all to learn from the God the course
        of action I should follow.

OEDIPUS: But his word
        has been quite clear to let the parricide,
        the sinner, die.

CREON: Yes, that indeed was said.
        But in the present need we had best discover
1510   what we should do.

OEDIPUS: And will you ask about
        a man so wretched?

CREON: Now even you will trust
        the God.

OEDIPUS: So. I command you—and will beseech you—
        to her that lies inside that house give burial
        as you would have it; she is yours and rightly
1515   you will perform the rites for her. For me—
        never let this my father's city have me
        living a dweller in it. Leave me live
        in the mountains where Cithaeron is, that's called
        my mountain, which my mother and my father
1520   while they were living would have made my tomb.
        So I may die by their decree who sought
        indeed to kill me. Yet I know this much:
        no sickness and no other thing will kill me.
        I would not have been saved from death if not
1525   for some strange evil fate. Well, let my fate
        go where it will.

                    Creon, you need not care
        about my sons; they're men and so wherever
        they are, they will not lack a livelihood.
        But my two girls—so sad and pitiful—

1530 whose table never stood apart from mine,
and everything I touched they always shared—
O Creon, have a thought for them! And most
I wish that you might suffer me to touch them
and sorrow with them.

[*Enter Antigone and Ismene, Oedipus' two daughters.*]

1535 O my lord! O true noble Creon! Can I
really be touching them, as when I saw?
What shall I say?
Yes, I can hear them sobbing—my two darlings!
and Creon has had pity and has sent me
1540 what I loved most?
Am I right?
CREON: You're right: it was I gave you this
because I knew from old days how you loved them
as I see now.
OEDIPUS: God bless you for it, Creon,
1545 and may God guard you better on your road
than he did me!
                    O children,
where are you? Come here, come to my hands,
a brother's hands which turned your father's eyes,
those bright eyes you knew once, to what you see,
1550 a father seeing nothing, knowing nothing,
begetting you from his own source of life.
I weep for you—I cannot see your faces—
I weep when I think of the bitterness
there will be in your lives, how you must live
1555 before the world. At what assemblages
of citizens will you make one? to what
gay company will you go and not come home
in tears instead of sharing in the holiday?
And when you're ripe for marriage, who will he be;
1560 the man who'll risk to take such infamy
as shall cling to my children, to bring hurt
on them and those that marry with them? What
curse is not there? "Your father killed his father
and sowed the seed where he had sprung himself
1565 and begot you out of the womb that held him."
These insults you will hear. Then who will marry you?
No one, my children; clearly you are doomed
to waste away in barrenness unmarried.
Son of Menoeceus, since you are all the father
1570 left these two girls, and we, their parents, both
are dead to them—do not allow them wander
like beggars, poor and husbandless.
They are of your own blood.
And do not make them equal with myself

1575   in wretchedness; for you can see them now
        so young, so utterly alone, save for you only.
        Touch my hand, noble Creon, and say yes.
        If you were older, children, and were wiser,
        there's much advice I'd give you. But as it is,
1580   let this be what you pray: give me a life
        wherever there is opportunity
        to live, and better life than was my father's.

CREON: Your tears have had enough of scope; now go within the house.

OEDIPUS: I must obey, though bitter of heart.

CREON: In season, all is good.

OEDIPUS: Do you know on what conditions I obey?

CREON: You tell me them,
          and I shall know them when I hear.

OEDIPUS: That you shall send me out
          to live away from Thebes.

CREON: That gift you must ask of the God.

OEDIPUS: But I'm now hated by the Gods.

CREON: So quickly you'll obtain your prayer.

OEDIPUS: You consent then?

CREON: What I do not mean, I do not use to say.

OEDIPUS: Now lead me away from here.

CREON: Let go the children, then, and come.

OEDIPUS: Do not take them from me.

CREON: Do not seek to be master in everything,
          for the things you mastered did not follow you throughout your life.

          [*As Creon and Oedipus go out.*]

CHORUS: You that live in my ancestral Thebes, behold this Oedipus,—
1595   him who knew the famous riddles and was a man most masterful;
          not a citizen who did not look with envy on his lot—
          see him now and see the breakers of misfortune swallow him!
          Look upon that last day always. Count no mortal happy till
          he has passed the final limit of his life secure from pain.

Antigone[1]

Characters

ANTIGONE, *daughter of Oedipus and Jocasta*
ISMENE, *sister of Antigone*
A CHORUS, *of old Theban citizens and their Leader*
CREON, *king of Thebes, uncle of Antigone and Ismene*
A SENTRY
HAEMON, *son of Creon and Eurydice*
TIRESIAS, *a blind prophet*
A MESSENGER
EURYDICE, *wife of Creon*
GUARDS, ATTENDANTS, AND A BOY

1. Translated by Robert Fagles.

Time and Scene: The royal house of Thebes. It is still night, and the invading armies of Argos have just been driven from the city. Fighting on opposite sides, the sons of Oedipus, Eteocles and Polynices, have killed each other in combat. Their uncle, Creon, is now king of Thebes.

Enter Antigone, slipping through the central doors of the palace. She motions to her sister, Ismene, who follows her cautiously toward an altar at the center of the stage.

ANTIGONE: My own flesh and blood—dear sister, dear Ismene,
　　　　how many griefs our father Oedipus handed down!
　　　　Do you know one, I ask you, one grief
　　　　that Zeus will not perfect for the two of us
5　　　　while we still live and breathe! There's nothing,
　　　　no pain—our lives are pain—no private shame,
　　　　no public disgrace, nothing I haven't seen
　　　　in your griefs and mine. And now this:
　　　　an emergency decree, they say, the Commander
10　　　has just declared for all of Thebes.
　　　　What, haven't you heard? Don't you see?
　　　　The doom reserved for enemies
　　　　marches on the ones we love the most.

ISMENE: Not I, I haven't heard a word, Antigone.
15　　　Nothing of loved ones,
　　　　no joy or pain has come my way, not since
　　　　the two of us were robbed of our two brothers,
　　　　both gone in a day, a double blow—
　　　　not since the armies of Argos vanished,
20　　　just this very night. I know nothing more,
　　　　whether our luck's improved or ruin's still to come.

ANTIGONE: I thought so. That's why I brought you out here,
　　　　past the gates, so you could hear in private.

ISMENE: What's the matter? Trouble, clearly . . .
25　　　you sound so dark, so grim.

ANTIGONE: Why not? Our own brothers' burial!
　　　　Hasn't Creon graced one with all the rites,
　　　　disgraced the other? Eteocles, they say,
　　　　has been given full military honors,
30　　　rightly so—Creon's laid him in the earth
　　　　and he goes with glory down among the dead.
　　　　But the body of Polynices, who died miserably—
　　　　why, a city-wide proclamation, rumor has it,
　　　　forbids anyone to bury him, even mourn him.
35　　　He's to be left unwept, unburied, a lovely treasure
　　　　for birds that scan the field and feast to their heart's content.

　　　　Such, I hear, is the martial law our good Creon
　　　　lays down for you and me—yes, me, I tell you—
　　　　and he's coming here to alert the uninformed
40　　　in no uncertain terms,
　　　　and he won't treat the matter lightly. Whoever
　　　　disobeys in the least will die, his doom is sealed:

stoning to death inside the city walls!

	There you have it. You'll soon show what you are,
45	worth your breeding, Ismene, or a coward—
	for all your royal blood.

ISMENE: My poor sister, if things have come to this,
who am I to make or mend them, tell me,
what good am I to you?

ANTIGONE: Decide.

50   Will you share the labor, share the work?

ISMENE: What work, what's the risk? What do you mean?

ANTIGONE: [*Raising her hands.*] Will you lift up his body with these bare hands
and lower it with me?

ISMENE: What? You'd bury him—
when a law forbids the city?

ANTIGONE: Yes!

55   He is my brother and—deny it as you will—
your brother too.
No one will ever convict me for a traitor.

ISMENE: So desperate, and Creon has expressly—

ANTIGONE: No,
he has no right to keep me from my own.

ISMENE: Oh my sister, think—
think how our own father died, hated,
his reputation in ruins, driven on
by the crimes he brought to light himself
to gouge out his eyes with his own hands—

65   then mother . . . his mother and wife, both in one,
mutilating her life in the twisted noose—
and last, our two brothers dead in a single day,
both shedding their own blood, poor suffering boys,
battling out their common destiny hand-to-hand.

70   Now look at the two of us, left so alone . . .
think what a death we'll die, the worst of all
if we violate the laws and override
the fixed decree of the throne, its power—
we must be sensible. Remember we are women,

75   we're not born to contend with men. Then too,
we're underlings, ruled by much stronger hands,
so we must submit in this, and things still worse.

I, for one, I'll beg the dead to forgive me—
I'm forced, I have no choice—I must obey

80   the ones who stand in power. Why rush to extremes?
It's madness, madness.

ANTIGONE: I won't insist,
no, even if you should have a change of heart,
I'd never welcome you in the labor, not with me.
So, do as you like, whatever suits you best—

85   I'll bury him myself.

And even if I die in the act, that death will be a glory.
I'll lie with the one I love and loved by him—
an outrage sacred to the gods! I have longer
to please the dead than please the living here:
90   in the kingdom down below I'll lie forever.
Do as you like, dishonor the laws
the gods hold in honor.

ISMENE: I'd do them no dishonor . . .
but defy the city? I have no strength for that.

ANTIGONE: You have your excuses. I am on my way,
95   I'll raise a mound for him, for my dear brother.

ISMENE: Oh Antigone, you're so rash—I'm so afraid for you!

ANTIGONE: Don't fear for me. Set your own life in order.

ISMENE: Then don't, at least, blurt this out to anyone.
Keep it a secret. I'll join you in that, I promise.

ANTIGONE: Dear god, shout it from the rooftops. I'll hate you
all the more for silence—tell the world!

ISMENE: So fiery—and it ought to chill your heart.

ANTIGONE: I know I please where I must please the most.

ISMENE: Yes, if you can, but you're in love with impossibility.

ANTIGONE: Very well then, once my strength gives out
I will be done at last.

ISMENE: You're wrong from the start,
you're off on a hopeless quest.

ANTIGONE: If you say so, you will make me hate you,
and the hatred of the dead, by all rights,
110   will haunt you night and day.
But leave me to my own absurdity, leave me
to suffer this—dreadful thing. I'll suffer
nothing as great as death without glory.   *[Exit to the side.]*

ISMENE: Then go if you must, but rest assured,
115   wild, irrational as you are, my sister,
you are truly dear to the ones who love you.

*[Withdrawing to the palace. Enter a Chorus, the old citizens of Thebes,
chanting as the sun begins to rise.]*

CHORUS: Glory!—great beam of sun, brightest of all
that ever rose on the seven gates of Thebes,
you burn through night at last!
120   Great eye of the golden day,
mounting the Dirce's banks[2] you throw him back—
the enemy out of Argos, the white shield, the man of bronze—
he's flying headlong now
the bridle of fate stampeding him with pain!

125   And he had driven against our borders,
launched by the warring claims of Polynices—
like an eagle screaming, winging havoc

2. A river near Thebes.

over the land, wings of armor
shielded white as snow,
130   a huge army massing,
crested helmets bristling for assault.

He hovered above our roofs, his vast maw gaping
closing down around our seven gates,
his spears thirsting for the kill
135   but now he's gone, look,
before he could glut his jaws with Theban blood
or the god of fire put our crown of towers to the torch.
He grappled the Dragon none can master—Thebes—
the clang of our arms like thunder at his back!

140   Zeus hates with a vengeance all bravado,
the mighty boasts of men. He watched them
coming on in a rising flood, the pride
of their golden armor ringing shrill—
and brandishing his lightning
145   blasted the fighter just at the goal,
rushing to shout his triumph from our walls.

Down from the heights he crashed, pounding down on the earth!
And a moment ago, blazing torch in hand—
mad for attack, ecstatic
150   he breathed his rage, the storm
of his fury hurling at our heads!
But now his high hopes have laid him low
and down the enemy ranks the iron god of war
deals his rewards, his stunning blows—Ares
155   rapture of battle, our right arm in the crisis.

Seven captains marshaled at seven gates
seven against their equals, gave
their brazen trophies up to Zeus,
god of the breaking rout of battle,
160   all but two: those blood brothers,
one father, one mother—matched in rage,
spears matched for the twin conquest—
clashed and won the common prize of death.

But now for Victory! Glorious in the morning,
165   joy in her eyes to meet our joy
she is winging down to Thebes,
our fleets of chariots wheeling in her wake—
Now let us win oblivion from the wars,
thronging the temples of the gods
170   in singing, dancing choirs through the night!
Lord Dionysus, god of the dance
that shakes the land of Thebes, now lead the way!

[*Enter Creon from the palace, attended by his guard.*]

But look, the king of the realm is coming,
Creon, the new man for the new day,
175 whatever the gods are sending now . . .
what new plan will he launch?
Why this, this special session?
Why this sudden call to the old men
summoned at one command?

CREON: My countrymen,
180 the ship of state is safe. The gods who rocked her,
after a long, merciless pounding in the storm,
have righted her once more.

                                   Out of the whole city
I have called you here alone. Well I know,
first, your undeviating respect
185 for the throne and royal power of King Laius.
Next, while Oedipus steered the land of Thebes,
and even after he died, your loyalty was unshakable,
you still stood by their children. Now then,
since the two sons are dead—two blows of fate
190 in the same day, cut down by each other's hands,
both killers, both brothers stained with blood—
as I am next in kin to the dead,
I now possess the throne and all its powers.

Of course you cannot know a man completely,
195 his character, his principles, sense of judgment,
not till he's shown his colors, ruling the people,
making laws. Experience, there's the test.
As I see it, whoever assumes the task,
the awesome task of setting the city's course,
200 and refuses to adopt the soundest policies
but fearing someone, keeps his lips locked tight,
he's utterly worthless. So I rate him now,
I always have. And whoever places a friend
above the good of his own country, he is nothing:
205 I have no use for him. Zeus my witness,
Zeus who sees all things, always—
I could never stand by silent, watching destruction
march against our city, putting safety to rout,
nor could I ever make that man a friend of mine
210 who menaces our country. Remember this:
our country is our safety.
Only while she voyages true on course
can we establish friendships, truer than blood itself.
Such are my standards. They make our city great.
215 Closely akin to them I have proclaimed,
just now, the following decree to our people
concerning the two sons of Oedipus.
Eteocles, who died fighting for Thebes,
excelling all in arms: he shall be buried,

220   crowned with a hero's honors, the cups we pour
       to soak the earth and reach the famous dead.

       But as for his blood brother, Polynices,
       who returned from exile, home to his father-city
       and the gods of his race, consumed with one desire—
225   to burn them roof to roots—who thirsted to drink
       his kinsmen's blood and sell the rest to slavery:
       that man—a proclamation has forbidden the city
       to dignify him with burial, mourn him at all.
       No, he must be left unburied, his corpse
230   carrion for the birds and dogs to tear,
       an obscenity for the citizens to behold!

       These are my principles. Never at my hands
       will the traitor be honored above the patriot.
       But whoever proves his loyalty to the state:
235   I'll prize that man in death as well as life.
LEADER: If this is your pleasure, Creon, treating
       our city's enemy and our friend this way . . .
       The power is yours, I suppose, to enforce it
       with the laws, both for the dead and all of us,
       the living.
CREON: Follow my orders closely then,
       be on your guard.
LEADER: We're too old.
       Lay that burden on younger shoulders.
CREON: No, no,
       I don't mean the body—I've posted guards already.
LEADER: What commands for us then? What other service?
CREON: See that you never side with those who break my orders.
LEADER: Never. Only a fool could be in love with death.
CREON: Death is the price—you're right. But all too often
       the mere hope of money has ruined many men.

       [*A Sentry enters from the side.*]

SENTRY: My lord,
       I can't say I'm winded from running, or set out
250   with any spring in my legs either—no sir,
       I was lost in thought, and it made me stop, often,
       dead in my tracks, wheeling, turning back,
       and all the time a voice inside me muttering,
       "Idiot, why? You're going straight to your death."
255   Then muttering, "Stopped again, poor fool?
       If somebody gets the news to Creon first,
       what's to save your neck?"
                                  And so,
       mulling it over, on I trudged, dragging my feet,
       you can make a short road take forever . . .
260   but at last, look, common sense won out,

I'm here, and I'm all yours,
and even though I come empty-handed
I'll tell my story just the same, because
I've come with a good grip on one hope,
265   what will come will come, whatever fate—
CREON: Come to the point!
    What's wrong—why so afraid?
SENTRY: First, myself, I've got to tell you,
    I didn't do it, didn't see who did—
270   Be fair, don't take it out on me.
CREON: You're playing it safe, soldier,
    barricading yourself from any trouble.
    It's obvious, you've something strange to tell.
SENTRY: Dangerous too, and danger makes you delay
275   for all you're worth.
CREON: Out with it—then dismiss!
SENTRY: All right, here it comes. The body—
    someone's just buried it, then run off . . .
    sprinkled some dry dust on the flesh,
    given it proper rites.
CREON: What?
    What man alive would dare—
SENTRY: I've no idea, I swear it.
    There was no mark of a spade, no pickaxe there,
    no earth turned up, the ground packed hard and dry,
    unbroken, no tracks, no wheelruts, nothing,
285   the workman left no trace. Just at sunup
    the first watch of the day points it out—
    it was a wonder! We were stunned . . .
    a terrific burden too, for all of us, listen:
    you can't see the corpse, not that it's buried,
290   really, just a light cover of road-dust on it,
    as if someone meant to lay the dead to rest
    and keep from getting cursed.
    Not a sign in sight that dogs or wild beasts
    had worried the body, even torn the skin.

295   But what came next! Rough talk flew thick and fast,
    guard grilling guard—we'd have come to blows
    at last, nothing to stop it; each man for himself
    and each the culprit, no one caught red-handed,
    all of us pleading ignorance, dodging the charges,
300   ready to take up red-hot iron in our fists,
    go through fire, swear oaths to the gods—
    "I didn't do it, I had no hand in it either,
    not in the plotting, not in the work itself!"

    Finally, after all this wrangling came to nothing,
305   one man spoke out and made us stare at the ground,
    hanging our heads in fear. No way to counter him,

no way to take his advice and come through
safe and sound. Here's what he said:
"Look, we've got to report the facts to Creon,
310 we can't keep this hidden." Well, that won out,
and the lot fell on me, condemned me,
unlucky as ever, I got the prize. So here I am,
against my will and yours too, well I know—
no one wants the man who brings bad news.

LEADER: My king,
315 ever since he began I've been debating in my mind,
could this possibly be the work of the gods?

CREON: Stop—
before you make me choke with anger—the gods!
You, you're senile, must you be insane?
You say—why it's intolerable—say the gods
320 could have the slightest concern for that corpse?
Tell me, was it for meritorious service
they proceeded to bury him, prized him so? The hero
who came to burn their temples ringed with pillars,
their golden treasures—scorch their hallowed earth
325 and fling their laws to the winds.
Exactly when did you last see the gods
celebrating traitors? Inconceivable!

No, from the first there were certain citizens
who could hardly stand the spirit of my regime,
330 grumbling against me in the dark, heads together,
tossing wildly, never keeping their necks beneath
the yoke, loyally submitting to their king.
These are the instigators, I'm convinced—
they've perverted my own guard, bribed them
to do their work.
335   Money! Nothing worse
in our lives, so current, rampant, so corrupting.
Money—you demolish cities, root men from their homes,
you train and twist good minds and set them on
to the most atrocious schemes. No limit,
340 you make them adept at every kind of outrage,
every godless crime—money!
                        Everyone—
the whole crew bribed to commit this crime,
they've made one thing sure at least:
sooner or later they will pay the price.

[Wheeling on the Sentry.]
                       You—
345 I swear to Zeus as I still believe in Zeus,
if you don't find the man who buried that corpse,
the very man, and produce him before my eyes,
simple death won't be enough for you,

not till we string you up alive
350   and wring the immortality out of you.
Then you can steal the rest of your days,
better informed about where to make a killing.
You'll have learned, at last, it doesn't pay
to itch for rewards from every hand that beckons.
355   Filthy profits wreck most men, you'll see—
they'll never save your life.

SENTRY: Please,
may I say a word or two, or just turn and go?

CREON: Can't you tell? Everything you say offends me.

SENTRY: Where does it hurt you, in the ears or in the heart?

CREON: And who are you to pinpoint my displeasure?

SENTRY: The culprit grates on your feelings,
I just annoy your ears.

CREON: Still talking?
You talk too much! A born nuisance—

SENTRY: Maybe so,
but I never did this thing, so help me!

CREON: Yes you did—
365   what's more, you squandered your life for silver!

SENTRY: Oh it's terrible when the one who does the judging
judges things all wrong.

CREON: Well now,
you just be clever about your judgments—
if you fail to produce the criminals for me,
370   you'll swear your dirty money brought you pain.

[*Turning sharply, reentering the palace.*]

SENTRY: I hope he's found. Best thing by far.
But caught or not, that's in the lap of fortune;
I'll never come back, you've seen the last of me.
I'm saved, even now, and I never thought,
375   I never hoped—
dear gods, I owe you all my thanks!   [*Rushing out.*]

CHORUS: Numberless wonders
terrible wonders walk the world but none the match for man—
that great wonder crossing the heaving gray sea,
driven on by the blast of winter
380   on through breakers crashing left and right,
holds his steady course
and the oldest of the gods he wears away—
the Earth, the immortal, the inexhaustible—
as his plows go back and forth, year in, year out
385   with the breed of stallions turning up the furrows.

And the blithe, lightheaded race of birds he snares,
the tribes of savage beasts, the life that swarms the depths—
with one fling of his nets
woven and coiled tight, he takes them all,

390   man the skilled, the brilliant!
        He conquers all, taming with his techniques
        the prey that roams the cliffs and wild lairs,
        training the stallion, clamping the yoke across
            his shaggy neck, and the tireless mountain bull.

395   And speech and thought, quick as the wind
        and the mood and mind for law that rules the city—
            all these he has taught himself
        and shelter from the arrows of the frost
        when there's rough lodging under the cold clear sky
400   and the shafts of lashing rain—
                    ready, resourceful man!
                        Never without resources
        never an impasse as he marches on the future—
        only Death, from Death alone he will find no rescue
405   but from desperate plagues he has plotted his escapes.

        Man the master, ingenious past all measure
        past all dreams, the skills within his grasp—
            he forges on, now to destruction
        now again to greatness. When he weaves in
410   the laws of the land, and the justice of the gods
        that binds his oaths together
                    he and his city rise high—
                        but the city casts out
        that man who weds himself to inhumanity
415   thanks to reckless daring. Never share my hearth
        never think my thoughts, whoever does such things.

        [Enter Antigone from the side, accompanied by the Sentry.]

        Here is a dark sign from the gods—
        what to make of this? I know her,
        how can I deny it? That young girl's Antigone!
420   Wretched, child of a wretched father,
        Oedipus. Look, is it possible?
        They bring you in like a prisoner—
        why? did you break the king's laws?
        Did they take you in some act of mad defiance?
SENTRY: She's the one, she did it single-handed—
        we caught her burying the body. Where's Creon?

        [Enter Creon from the palace.]

LEADER: Back again, just in time when you need him.
CREON: In time for what? What is it?
SENTRY: My king,
        there's nothing you can swear you'll never do—
430   second thoughts make liars of us all.
        I could have sworn I wouldn't hurry back
        (what with your threats, the buffeting I just took),
        but a stroke of luck beyond our wildest hopes,

what a joy, there's nothing like it. So,
435   back I've come, breaking my oath, who cares?
I'm bringing in our prisoner—this young girl—
we took her giving the dead the last rites.
But no casting lots this time, this is *my* luck,
my prize, no one else's.
                                Now, my lord,
440   here she is. Take her, question her,
cross-examine her to your heart's content.
But set me free, it's only right—
I'm rid of this dreadful business once for all.

CREON: Prisoner! Her? You took her—where, doing what?

SENTRY: Burying the man. That's the whole story.

CREON: What?
You mean what you say, you're telling me the truth?

SENTRY: She's the one. With my own eyes I saw her
bury the body, just what you've forbidden.
There. Is that plain and clear?

CREON: What did you see? Did you catch her in the act?

SENTRY: Here's what happened. We went back to our post,
those threats of yours breathing down our necks—
we brushed the corpse clean of the dust that covered it,
stripped it bare . . . it was slimy, going soft,
455   and we took to high ground, backs to the wind
so the stink of him couldn't hit us;
jostling, baiting each other to keep awake,
shouting back and forth—no napping on the job,
not this time. And so the hours dragged by
460   until the sun stood dead above our heads,
a huge white ball in the noon sky, beating,
blazing down, and then it happened—
suddenly, a whirlwind!
Twisting a great dust-storm up from the earth,
465   a black plague of the heavens, filling the plain,
ripping the leaves off every tree in sight,
choking the air and sky. We squinted hard
and took our whipping from the gods.

And after the storm passed—it seemed endless—
470   there, we saw the girl!
And she cried out a sharp, piercing cry,
like a bird come back to an empty nest,
peering into its bed, and all the babies gone . . .
Just so, when she sees the corpse bare
475   she bursts into a long, shattering wail
and calls down withering curses on the heads
of all who did the work. And she scoops up dry dust,
handfuls, quickly, and lifting a fine bronze urn,
lifting it high and pouring, she crowns the dead
with three full libations.

480   Soon as we saw
        we rushed her, closed on the kill like hunters,
        and she, she didn't flinch. We interrogated her,
        charging her with offenses past and present—
        she stood up to it all, denied nothing. I tell you,
485   it made me ache and laugh in the same breath.
        It's pure joy to escape the worst yourself,
        it hurts a man to bring down his friends.
        But all that, I'm afraid, means less to me
        than my own skin. That's the way I'm made.

CREON [*wheeling on Antigone*]:   You,
490   with your eyes fixed on the ground—speak up.
        Do you deny you did this, yes or no?

ANTIGONE: I did it. I don't deny a thing.

CREON [*to the Sentry*]: You, get out, wherever you please—
        you're clear of a very heavy charge.

        [*He leaves; Creon turns back to Antigone.*]

495   You, tell me briefly, no long speeches—
        were you aware a decree had forbidden this?

ANTIGONE: Well aware. How could I avoid it? It was public.

CREON: And still you had the gall to break this law?

ANTIGONE: Of course I did. It wasn't Zeus, not in the least,
500   who made this proclamation—not to me.
        Nor did that Justice, dwelling with the gods
        beneath the earth, ordain such laws for men.
        Nor did I think your edict had such force
        that you, a mere mortal, could override the gods,
505   the great unwritten, unshakable traditions.
        They are alive, not just today or yesterday:
        they live forever, from the first of time,
        and no one knows when they first saw the light.

        These laws—I was not about to break them,
510   not out of fear of some man's wounded pride,
        and face the retribution of the gods.
        Die I must, I've known it all my life—
        how could I keep from knowing?—even without
        your death-sentence ringing in my ears.
515   And if I am to die before my time
        I consider that a gain. Who on earth,
        alive in the midst of so much grief as I,
        could fail to find his death a rich reward?
        So for me, at least, to meet this doom of yours
520   is precious little pain. But if I had allowed
        my own mother's son to rot, an unburied corpse—
        that would have been an agony! This is nothing.
        And if my present actions strike you as foolish,
        let's just say I've been accused of folly
        by a fool.

LEADER: Like father like daughter,
 passionate, wild . . .
 she hasn't learned to bend before adversity.
CREON: No? Believe me, the stiffest stubborn wills
 fall the hardest; the toughest iron,
530 tempered strong in the white-hot fire,
 you'll see it crack and shatter first of all.
 And I've known spirited horses you can break
 with a light bit—proud, rebellious horses.
 There's no room for pride, not in a slave
535 not with the lord and master standing by.

 This girl was an old hand at insolence
 when she overrode the edicts we made public.
 But once she'd done it—the insolence,
 twice over—to glory in it, laughing,
540 mocking us to our face with what she'd done.
 I'm not the man, not now: she is the man
 if this victory goes to her and she goes free.

 Never! Sister's child or closer in blood
 than all my family clustered at my altar
545 worshiping Guardian Zeus—she'll never escape,
 she and her blood sister, the most barbaric death.
 Yes, I accuse her sister of an equal part
 in scheming this, this burial.

 [To his Attendants.]

                                    Bring her here!
 I just saw her inside, hysterical, gone to pieces.
550 It never fails: the mind convicts itself
 in advance, when scoundrels are up to no good,
 plotting in the dark. Oh but I hate it more
 when a traitor, caught red-handed,
 tries to glorify his crimes.
ANTIGONE: Creon, what more do you want
 than my arrest and execution?
CREON: Nothing. Then I have it all.
ANTIGONE: Then why delay? Your moralizing repels me,
 every word you say—pray god it always will.
 So naturally all I say repels you too.
560   Enough.
 Give me glory! What greater glory could I win
 than to give my own brother decent burial?
 These citizens here would all agree,

 [To the Chorus.]

 they'd praise me too
565 if their lips weren't locked in fear.

 [Pointing to Creon.]

Lucky tyrants—the perquisites of power!
Ruthless power to do and say whatever pleases *them*.

CREON: You alone, of all the people in Thebes,
see things that way.

ANTIGONE: They see it just that way
570   but defer to you and keep their tongues in leash.

CREON: And you, aren't you ashamed to differ so from them?
So disloyal!

ANTIGONE: Not ashamed for a moment,
not to honor my brother, my own flesh and blood.

CREON: Wasn't Eteocles a brother too—cut down, facing him?

ANTIGONE: Brother, yes, by the same mother, the same father.

CREON: Then how can you render his enemy such honors,
such impieties in his eyes?

ANTIGONE: He'll never testify to that,
Eteocles dead and buried.

CREON: He will—
580   if you honor the traitor just as much as him.

ANTIGONE: But it was his brother, not some slave that died—

CREON: Ravaging our country!—
but Eteocles died fighting in our behalf.

ANTIGONE: No matter—Death longs for the same rites for all.

CREON: Never the same for the patriot and the traitor.

ANTIGONE: Who, Creon, who on earth can say the ones below
don't find this pure and uncorrupt?

CREON: Never. Once an enemy, never a friend,
not even after death.

ANTIGONE: I was born to join in love, not hate—
that is my nature.

CREON: Go down below and love,
if love you must—love the dead! While I'm alive,
no woman is going to lord it over me.

[*Enter Ismene from the palace, under guard.*]

CHORUS: Look,
Ismene's coming, weeping a sister's tears,
595   loving sister, under a cloud . . .
her face is flushed, her cheeks streaming.
Sorrow puts her lovely radiance in the dark.

CREON: You—
in my house, you viper, slinking undetected,
sucking my life-blood! I never knew
600   I was breeding twin disasters, the two of you
rising up against my throne. Come, tell me,
will you confess your part in the crime or not?
Answer me. Swear to me.

ISMENE: I did it, yes—
if only she consents—I share the guilt,
the consequences too.

ANTIGONE: No,
          Justice will never suffer that—not you,
          you were unwilling. I never brought you in.
ISMENE: But now you face such dangers . . . I'm not ashamed
          to sail through trouble with you,
          make your troubles mine.
ANTIGONE: Who did the work?
          Let the dead and the god of death bear witness!
          I've no love for a friend who loves in words alone.
ISMENE: Oh no, my sister, don't reject me, please,
          let me die beside you, consecrating
          the dead together.
ANTIGONE: Never share my dying,
          don't lay claim to what you never touched.
          My death will be enough.
ISMENE: What do I care for life, cut off from you?
ANTIGONE: Ask Creon. Your concern is all for him.
ISMENE: Why abuse me so? It doesn't help you now.
ANTIGONE: You're right—
          if I mock you, I get no pleasure from it,
          only pain.
ISMENE: Tell me, dear one,
          what can I do to help you, even now?
ANTIGONE: Save yourself. I don't grudge you your survival.
ISMENE: Oh no, no, denied my portion in your death?
ANTIGONE: You chose to live, I chose to die.
ISMENE: Not, at least,
          without every kind of caution I could voice.
ANTIGONE: Your wisdom appealed to one world—mine, another.
ISMENE: But look, we're both guilty, both condemned to death.
ANTIGONE: Courage! Live your life. I gave myself to death,
          long ago, so I might serve the dead.
CREON: They're both mad, I tell you, the two of them.
          One's just shown it, the other's been that way
          since she was born.
ISMENE: True, my king,
635   the sense we were born with cannot last forever . . .
          commit cruelty on a person long enough
          and the mind begins to go.
CREON: Yours did,
          when you chose to commit your crimes with her.
ISMENE: How can I live alone, without her?
CREON: Her?
640   Don't even mention her—she no longer exists.
ISMENE: What? You'd kill your own son's bride?
CREON: Absolutely:
          there are other fields for him to plow.
ISMENE: Perhaps,
          but never as true, as close a bond as theirs.

CREON: A worthless woman for my son? It repels me.
ISMENE: Dearest Haemon, your father wrongs you so!
CREON: Enough, enough—you and your talk of marriage!
ISMENE: Creon—you're really going to rob your son of Antigone?
CREON: Death will do it for me—break their marriage off.
LEADER: So, it's settled then? Antigone must die?
CREON: Settled, yes—we both know that.

[*To the Guards.*]

Stop wasting time. Take them in.
From now on they'll act like women.
Tie them up, no more running loose;
even the bravest will cut and run,
655   once they see Death coming for their lives.

[*The Guards escort Antigone and Ismene into the palace. Creon remains while the old citizens form their chorus.*]

CHORUS: Blest, they are truly blest who all their lives
have never tasted devastation. For others, once
the gods have rocked a house to its foundations
     the ruin will never cease, cresting on and on
655   from one generation on throughout the race—
like a great mounting tide
driven on by savage northern gales,
          surging over the dead black depths
roiling up from the bottom dark heaves of sand
665   and the headlands, taking the storm's onslaught full-force,
roar, and the low moaning
                    echoes on and on
                              and now
as in ancient times I see the sorrows of the house,
the living heirs of the old ancestral kings,
piling on the sorrows of the dead
670   and one generation cannot free the next—
some god will bring them crashing down,
the race finds no release.
And now the light, the hope
          springing up from the late last root
675   in the house of Oedipus, that hope's cut down in turn
by the long, bloody knife swung by the gods of death
by a senseless word
                    by fury at the heart.
                              Zeus,
yours is the power, Zeus, what man on earth
can override it, who can hold it back?
680   Power that neither Sleep, the all-ensnaring
          no, nor the tireless months of heaven
can ever overmaster—young through all time,
mighty lord of power, you hold fast
          the dazzling crystal mansions of Olympus.

685   And throughout the future, late and soon
      as through the past, your law prevails:
      no towering form of greatness
            enters into the lives of mortals
                        free and clear of ruin.
                                          True,
690   our dreams, our high hopes voyaging far and wide
      bring sheer delight to many, to many others
            delusion, blithe, mindless lusts
      and the fraud steals on one slowly . . . unaware
      till he trips and puts his foot into the fire.
695   He was a wise old man who coined
      the famous saying: "Sooner or later
      foul is fair, fair is foul
      to the man the gods will ruin"—
            He goes his way for a moment only
700   free of blinding ruin.

      [*Enter Haemon from the palace.*]

      Here's Haemon now, the last of all your sons.
      Does he come in tears for his bride,
      his doomed bride, Antigone—
      bitter at being cheated of their marriage?
CREON: We'll soon know, better than seers could tell us.

      [*Turning to Haemon.*]

      Son, you've heard the final verdict on your bride?
      Are you coming now, raving against your father?
      Or do you love me, no matter what I do?
HAEMON: Father, I'm your *son* . . . you in your wisdom
710   set my bearings for me—I obey you.
      No marriage could ever mean more to me than you,
      whatever good direction you may offer.
CREON: Fine, Haemon.
      That's how you ought to feel within your heart,
      subordinate to your father's will in every way.
715   That's what a man prays for: to produce good sons—
      households full of them, dutiful and attentive,
      so they can pay his enemy back with interest
      and match the respect their father shows his friend.
      But the man who rears a brood of useless children,
720   what has he brought into the world, I ask you?
      Nothing but trouble for himself, and mockery
      from his enemies laughing in his face.
                              Oh Haemon,
      never lose your sense of judgment over a woman.
      The warmth, the rush of pleasure, it all goes cold
725   in your arms, I warn you . . . a worthless woman
      in your house, a misery in your bed.
      What wound cuts deeper than a loved one

turned against you? Spit her out,
like a mortal enemy—let the girl go.
730   Let her find a husband down among the dead.

Imagine it: I caught her in naked rebellion,
the traitor, the only one in the whole city.
I'm not about to prove myself a liar,
not to my people, no, I'm going to kill her!
735   That's right—so let her cry for mercy, sing her hymns
to Zeus who defends all bonds of kindred blood.
Why, if I bring up my own kin to be rebels,
think what I'd suffer from the world at large.
Show me the man who rules his household well:
740   I'll show you someone fit to rule the state.
That good man, my son,
I have every confidence he and he alone
can give commands and take them too. Staunch
in the storm of spears he'll stand his ground,
745   a loyal, unflinching comrade at your side.

But whoever steps out of line, violates the laws
or presumes to hand out orders to his superiors,
he'll win no praise from me. But that man
the city places in authority, his orders
750   must be obeyed, large and small,
right and wrong.
                    Anarchy—
show me a greater crime in all the earth!
She, she destroys cities, rips up houses,
breaks the ranks of spearmen into headlong rout.
755   But the ones who last it out, the great mass of them
owe their lives to discipline. Therefore
we must defend the men who live by law,
never let some woman triumph over us.
Better to fall from power, if fall we must,
760   at the hands of a man—never be rated
inferior to a woman, never.

LEADER: To us,
unless old age has robbed us of our wits,
you seem to say what you have to say with sense.

HAEMON: Father, only the gods endow a man with reason,
765   the finest of all their gifts, a treasure.
Far be it from me—I haven't the skill,
and certainly no desire, to tell you when,
if ever, you make a slip in speech . . . though
someone else might have a good suggestion.

770   Of course it's not for you,
in the normal run of things, to watch
whatever men say or do, or find to criticize.
The man in the street, you know, dreads your glance,

he'd never say anything displeasing to your face.
775 But it's for me to catch the murmurs in the dark,
the way the city mourns for this young girl.
"No woman," they say, "ever deserved death less,
and such a brutal death for such a glorious action.
She, with her own dear brother lying in his blood—
780 she couldn't bear to leave him dead, unburied,
food for the wild dogs or wheeling vultures.
Death? She deserves a glowing crown of gold!"
So they say, and the rumor spreads in secret,
darkly . . .
    I rejoice in your success, father—
785 nothing more precious to me in the world.
What medal of honor brighter to his children
than a father's growing glory? Or a child's
to his proud father? Now don't, please,
be quite so single-minded, self-involved,
790 or assume the world is wrong and you are right.
Whoever thinks that he alone possesses intelligence,
the gift of eloquence, he and no one else,
and character too . . . such men, I tell you,
spread them open—you will find them empty.
           No,
795 it's no disgrace for a man, even a wise man,
to learn many things and not to be too rigid.
You've seen trees by a raging winter torrent,
how many sway with the flood and salvage every twig,
but not the stubborn—they're ripped out, roots and all.
800 Bend or break. The same when a man is sailing:
haul your sheets too taut, never give an inch,
you'll capsize, go the rest of the voyage
keel up and the rowing-benches under.

 Oh give way. Relax your anger—change!
805 I'm young, I know, but let me offer this:
it would be best by far, I admit,
if a man were born infallible, right by nature.
If not—and things don't often go that way,
it's best to learn from those with good advice.

LEADER: You'd do well, my lord, if he's speaking to the point,
to learn from him.

 [*Turning to Haemon.*]
       and you, my boy, from him.
You both are talking sense.

CREON: So,
men our age, we're to be lectured, are we?—
schooled by a boy his age?

HAEMON: Only in what is right. But if I seem young,
look less to my years and more to what I do.

CREON: Do? Is admiring rebels an achievement?

HAEMON: I'd never suggest that you admire treason.

CREON: Oh?—
        isn't that just the sickness that's attacked her?

HAEMON: The whole city of Thebes denies it, to a man.

CREON: And is Thebes about to tell me how to rule?

HAEMON: Now, you see? Who's talking like a child?

CREON: Am I to rule this land for others—or myself?

HAEMON: It's no city at all, owned by one man alone.

CREON: What? The city *is* the king's—that's the law!

HAEMON: What a splendid king you'd make of a desert island—
        you and you alone.

CREON [*to the Chorus*]: This boy, I do believe,
        is fighting on her side, the woman's side.

HAEMON: If you are a woman, yes;
830   my concern is all for you.

CREON: Why, you degenerate—bandying accusations,
        threatening me with justice, your own father!

HAEMON: I see my father offending justice—wrong.

CREON: Wrong?
        To protect my royal rights?

HAEMON: Protect your rights?
835   When you trample down the honors of the gods?

CREON: You, you soul of corruption, rotten through—
        woman's accomplice!

HAEMON: That may be,
        but you'll never find me accomplice to a criminal.

CREON: That's what *she* is,
840   and every word you say is a blatant appeal for her—

HAEMON: And you, and me, and the gods beneath the earth.

CREON: You'll never marry her, not while she's alive.

HAEMON: Then she'll die . . . but her death will kill another.

CREON: What, brazen threats? You go too far!

HAEMON: What threat?
845   Combating your empty, mindless judgments with a word?

CREON: You'll suffer for your sermons, you and your empty wisdom!

HAEMON: If you weren't my father, I'd say you were insane.

CREON: Don't flatter me with Father—you woman's slave!

HAEMON: You really expect to fling abuse at me
        and not receive the same?

CREON: Is that so!
        Now, by heaven, I promise you, you'll pay—
        taunting, insulting me! Bring her out,
        that hateful—she'll die now, here,
        in front of his eyes, beside her groom!

HAEMON: No, no, she will never die beside me—
        don't delude yourself. And you will never
        see me, never set eyes on my face again.
        Rage your heart out, rage with friends
        who can stand the sight of you.   [*Rushing out.*]

LEADER: Gone, my king, in a burst of anger.
　　　　A temper young as his . . . hurt him once,
　　　　he may do something violent.
CREON:　　　　　　　　　　Let him do—
　　　　dream up something desperate, past all human limit!
　　　　Good riddance. Rest assured,
865　　　he'll never save those two young girls from death.
LEADER: Both of them, you really intend to kill them both?
CREON: No, not her, the one whose hands are clean;
　　　　you're quite right.
LEADER:　　　　　　　　But Antigone—
　　　　what sort of death do you have in mind for her?
CREON: I'll take her down some wild, desolate path
　　　　never trod by men, and wall her up alive
　　　　in a rocky vault, and set out short rations,
　　　　just a gesture of piety
　　　　to keep the entire city free of defilement.
875　　　There let her pray to the one god she worships:
　　　　Death—who knows?—may just reprieve her from death.
　　　　Or she may learn at last, better late than never,
　　　　what a waste of breath it is to worship Death.

　　　　[Exit to the palace.]

CHORUS: Love, never conquered in battle
880　　　Love the plunderer laying waste the rich!
　　　　Love standing the night-watch
　　　　　　　　　　guarding a girl's soft cheek,
　　　　you range the seas, the shepherds' steadings off in the wilds—
　　　　not even the deathless gods can flee your onset,
885　　　nothing human born for a day—
　　　　whoever feels your grip is driven mad.
　　　　　　　　　　　　Love
　　　　you wrench the minds of the righteous into outrage,
　　　　swerve them to their ruin—you have ignited this,
　　　　this kindred strife, father and son at war
890　　　　　　　　　　and Love alone the victor—
　　　　warm glance of the bride triumphant, burning with desire!
　　　　Throned in power, side-by-side with the mighty laws!
　　　　Irresistible Aphrodite, never conquered—
　　　　Love, you mock us for your sport.

　　　　[Antigone is brought from the palace under guard.]

895　　　　　　But now, even I'd rebel against the king,
　　　　　　I'd break all bounds when I see this—
　　　　　　I fill with tears, can't hold them back,
　　　　　　not any more . . . I see Antigone make her way
　　　　　　to the bridal vault where all are laid to rest.
ANTIGONE: Look at me, men of my fatherland,
　　　　　　setting out on the last road
　　　　looking into the last light of day

the last I'll ever see . . .
the god of death who puts us all to bed

905   takes me down to the banks of Acheron³ alive—
denied my part in the wedding-songs,
no wedding-song in the dusk has crowned my marriage—
I go to wed the lord of the dark waters.

CHORUS: Not crowned with glory, crowned with a dirge,
910   you leave for the deep pit of the dead.
No withering illness laid you low,
no strokes of the sword—a law to yourself,
alone, no mortal like you, ever, you go down
to the halls of Death alive and breathing.

ANTIGONE: But think of Niobe⁴—well I know her story—
think what a living death she died,
Tantalus' daughter, stranger queen from the east:
there on the mountain heights, growing stone
binding as ivy, slowly walled her round
920   and the rains will never cease, the legends say
the snows will never leave her . . .
wasting away, under her brows the tears
showering down her breasting ridge and slopes—
a rocky death like hers puts me to sleep.

CHORUS: But she was a god, born of gods,
and we are only mortals born to die.
And yet, of course, it's a great thing
for a dying girl to hear, just hear
she shares a destiny equal to the gods,
during life and later, once she's dead.

ANTIGONE: O you mock me!
Why, in the name of all my fathers' gods
why can't you wait till I am gone—
must you abuse me to my face?
O my city, all your fine rich sons!
935   And you, you springs of the Dirce,
holy grove of Thebes where the chariots gather,
you at least, you'll bear me witness, look,
unmourned by friends and forced by such crude laws
I go to my rockbound prison, strange new tomb—
940   always a stranger, O dear god,
I have no home on earth and none below,
not with the living, not with the breathless dead.

CHORUS: You went too far, the last limits of daring—
smashing against the high throne of Justice!
945   Your life's in ruins, child—I wonder . . .
do you pay for your father's terrible ordeal?

ANTIGONE: There—at last you've touched it, the worst pain

---

3. A river of the underworld.   4. A queen of Thebes punished by the gods for boasting
of her twelve children; Apollo and Artemis slew them
and Niobe turned to stone in her grief.

the worst anguish! Raking up the grief for father
    three times over, for all the doom

950   that's struck us down, the brilliant house of Laius.
O mother, your marriage-bed
the coiling horrors, the coupling there—
    you with your own son, my father—doomstruck mother!
Such, such were my parents, and I their wretched child.

955   I go to them now, cursed, unwed, to share their home—
    I am a stranger! O dear brother, doomed
    in your marriage—your marriage murders mine,
      your dying drags me down to death alive!

    [Enter Creon.]

CHORUS: Reverence asks some reverence in return—
960   but attacks on power never go unchecked,
    not by the man who holds the reins of power.
Your own blind will, your passion has destroyed you.

ANTIGONE: No one to weep for me, my friends,
    no wedding-song—they take me away
965   in all my pain . . . the road lies open, waiting.
Never again, the law forbids me to see
the sacred eye of day. I am agony!
No tears for the destiny that's mine,
no loved one mourns my death.

CREON: Can't you see?
970   If a man could wail his own dirge before he dies,
he'd never finish.

    [To the Guards.]

                   Take her away, quickly!
Wall her up in the tomb, you have your orders.
Abandon her there, alone, and let her choose—
death or a buried life with a good roof for shelter.

975   As for myself, my hands are clean. This young girl—
dead or alive, she will be stripped of her rights,
her stranger's rights, here in the world above.

ANTIGONE: O tomb, my bridal-bed—my house, my prison
cut in the hollow rock, my everlasting watch!
980   I'll soon be there, soon embrace my own,
the great growing family of our dead
Persephone has received among her ghosts.

                          I,
the last of them all, the most reviled by far,
go down before my destined time's run out.

985   But still I go, cherishing one good hope:
my arrival may be dear to father,
dear to you, my mother,
dear to you, my loving brother, Eteocles—
When you died I washed you with my hands,
990   I dressed you all, I poured the cups

across your tombs. But now, Polynices,
because I laid your body out as well,
this, this is my reward. Nevertheless
I honored you—the decent will admit it—
well and wisely too.

995   Never, I tell you,
if I had been the mother of children
or if my husband died, exposed and rotting—
I'd never have taken this ordeal upon myself,
never defied our people's will. What law,
1000   you ask, do I satisfy with what I say?
A husband dead, there might have been another.
A child by another too, if I had lost the first.
But mother and father both lost in the halls of Death,
no brother could ever spring to light again.

1005   For this law alone I held you first in honor.
For this, Creon, the king, judges me a criminal
guilty of dreadful outrage, my dear brother!
And now he leads me off, a captive in his hands,
with no part in the bridal-song, the bridal-bed,
1010   denied all joy of marriage, raising children—
deserted so by loved ones, struck by fate,
I descend alive to the caverns of the dead.
What law of the mighty gods have I transgressed?
Why look to the heavens any more, tormented as I am?
1015   Whom to call, what comrades now? Just think,
my reverence only brands me for irreverence!
Very well: if this is the pleasure of the gods,
once I suffer I will know that I was wrong.
But if these men are wrong, let them suffer
1020   nothing worse than they mete out to me—
these masters of injustice!
LEADER: Still the same rough winds, the wild passion
raging through the girl.
CREON [to the Guards]: Take her away.
You're wasting time—you'll pay for it too.
ANTIGONE: Oh god, the voice of death. It's come, it's here.
CREON: True. Not a word of hope—your doom is sealed.
ANTIGONE: Land of Thebes, city of all my fathers—
O you gods, the first gods of the race!
They drag me away, now, no more delay.
1030   Look on me, you noble sons of Thebes—
the last of a great line of kings,
I alone, see what I suffer now
at the hands of what breed of men—
all for reverence, my reverence for the gods!

[She leaves under guard; the Chorus gathers.]

CHORUS: Danaë,[5] Danaë—
                even she endured a fate like yours,
                    in all her lovely strength she traded
                the light of day for the bolted brazen vault—
                buried within her tomb, her bridal-chamber,
1040   wed to the yoke and broken.
                    But she was of glorious birth
                                        my child, my child
            and treasured the seed of Zeus within her womb,
            the cloudburst streaming gold!

1045   The power of fate is a wonder,
                    dark, terrible wonder—
                neither wealth nor armies
                towered walls nor ships
                black hulls lashed by the salt
1050   can save us from that force.

            The yoke tamed him too
                    young Lycurgus[6] flaming in anger
            king of Edonia, all for his mad taunts
            Dionysus clamped him down, encased
1055   in the chain-mail of rock
                    and there his rage
                                his terrible flowering rage burst—
            sobbing, dying away . . . at last that madman
            came to know his god—
1060   the power he mocked, the power
                he taunted in all his frenzy
                trying to stamp out
                the women strong with the god—
                the torch, the raving sacred cries—
1065   enraging the Muses who adore the flute.

            And far north where the Black Rocks
                    cut the sea in half
            and murderous straits
            split the coast of Thrace
1070   a forbidding city stands
            where once, hard by the walls
            the savage Ares thrilled to watch
            a king's new queen, a Fury rearing in rage
                    against his two royal sons—
1075   her bloody hands, her dagger-shuttle
            stabbing out their eyes—cursed, blinding wounds—
            their eyes blind sockets screaming for revenge!

            They wailed in agony, cries echoing cries
                    the princes doomed at birth . . .

---

5. Danaë was locked in a vault by her father because of a prophecy that the son she bore would kill him. Zeus impregnated her in the form of a golden shower; their son was the hero Perseus.

6. Dionysos punished Lycurgus for banning the god's cult by making him insane. The Thracian king first slew his own son, then was killed by his own people.

1080   and their mother doomed to chains,
       walled off in a tomb of stone—
            but she traced her own birth back
       to a proud Athenian line and the high gods
       and off in caverns half the world away,
1085   born of the wild North Wind
            she sprang on her father's gales,
                 racing stallions up the leaping cliffs—
       child of the heavens. But even on her the Fates
       the gray everlasting Fates rode hard
       my child, my child.

[*Enter Tiresias, the blind prophet, led by a Boy.*]

TIRESIAS: Lords of Thebes,
       I and the boy have come together,
       hand in hand. Two see with the eyes of one . . .
       so the blind must go, with a guide to lead the way.
CREON: What is it, old Tiresias? What news now?
TIRESIAS: I will teach you. And you obey the seer.
CREON: I will,
       I've never wavered from your advice before.
TIRESIAS: And so you kept the city straight on course.
CREON: I owe you a great deal, I swear to that.
TIRESIAS: Then reflect, my son: you are poised,
1100   once more, on the razor-edge of fate.
CREON: What is it? I shudder to hear you.
TIRESIAS: You will learn
       when you listen to the warnings of my craft.
       As I sat in the ancient seat of augury,
       in the sanctuary where every bird I know
1105   will hover at my hands—suddenly I heard it,
       a strange voice in the wingbeats, unintelligible,
       barbaric, a mad scream! Talons flashing, ripping,
       they were killing each other—that much I knew—
       the murderous fury whirring in those wings
       made that much clear!
1110   I was afraid,
       I turned quickly, tested the burnt-sacrifice,
       ignited the altar at all points—but no fire,
       the god in the fire never blazed.
       Not from those offerings . . . over the embers
1115   slid a heavy ooze from the long thighbones,
       smoking, sputtering out, and the bladder
       puffed and burst—spraying gall into the air—
       and the fat wrapping the bones slithered off
       and left them glistening white. No fire!
1120   The rites failed that might have blazed the future
       with a sign. So I learned from the boy here;
       he is my guide, as I am guide to others.

And it's you—
your high resolve that sets this plague on Thebes.
The public altars and sacred hearths are fouled,
1125   one and all, by the birds and dogs with carrion
torn from the corpse, the doomstruck son of Oedipus!
And so the gods are deaf to our prayers, they spurn
the offerings in our hands, the flame of holy flesh.
No birds cry out an omen clear and true—
1130   they're gorged with the murdered victim's blood and fat.
Take these things to heart, my son, I warn you.
All men make mistakes, it is only human.
But once the wrong is done, a man
can turn his back on folly, misfortune too,
1135   if he tries to make amends, however low he's fallen,
and stops his bullnecked ways. Stubbornness
brands you for stupidity—pride is a crime.
No, yield to the dead!
Never stab the fighter when he's down.
1140   Where's the glory, killing the dead twice over?

I mean you well. I give you sound advice.
It's best to learn from a good adviser
when he speaks for your own good:
it's pure gain.
CREON: Old man—all of you! So,
1145   you shoot your arrows at my head like archers at the target—
I even have *him* loosed on me, this fortune-teller.
Oh his ilk has tried to sell me short
and ship me off for years. Well,
drive your bargains, traffic—much as you like—
1150   in the gold of India, silver-gold of Sardis.
You'll never bury that body in the grave,
not even if Zeus's eagles rip the corpse
and wing their rotten pickings off to the throne of god!
Never, not even in fear of such defilement
1155   will I tolerate his burial, that traitor.
Well I know, we can't defile the gods—
no mortal has the power.
                    No,
reverend old Tiresias, all men fall,
it's only human, but the wisest fall obscenely
1160   when they glorify obscene advice with rhetoric—
all for their own gain.
TIRESIAS: Oh god, is there a man alive
who knows, who actually believes . . .
CREON: What now?
What earth-shattering truth are you about to utter?
TIRESIAS: . . . just how much a sense of judgment, wisdom
is the greatest gift we have?

CREON: Just as much, I'd say,
          as a twisted mind is the worst affliction going.
TIRESIAS: You are the one who's sick, Creon, sick to death.
CREON: I am in no mood to trade insults with a seer.
TIRESIAS: You have already, calling my prophecies a lie.
CREON: Why not?
          You and the whole breed of seers are mad for money!
TIRESIAS: And the whole race of tyrants lusts to rake it in.
CREON: This slander of yours—
          are you aware you're speaking to the king?
TIRESIAS: Well aware. Who helped you save the city?
CREON: You—
          you have your skills, old seer, but you lust for injustice!
TIRESIAS: You will drive me to utter the dreadful secret in my heart.
CREON: Spit it out! Just don't speak it out for profit.
TIRESIAS: Profit? No, not a bit of profit, not for you.
CREON: Know full well, you'll never buy off my resolve.
TIRESIAS: Then know this too, learn this by heart!
          The chariot of the sun will not race through
          so many circuits more, before you have surrendered
          one born of your own loins, your own flesh and blood,
1185   a corpse for corpses given in return, since you have thrust
          to the world below a child sprung from the world above,
          ruthlessly lodged a living soul within the grave—
          then you've robbed the gods below the earth,
          keeping a dead body here in the bright air,
1190   unburied, unsung, unhallowed by the rites.

          You, you have no business with the dead,
          nor do the gods above—this is violence
          you have forced upon the heavens.
          And so the avengers, the dark destroyers late
1195   but true to the mark, now lie in wait for you,
          the Furies sent by the gods and the god of death
          to strike you down with the pains that you perfected!

          There. Reflect on that, tell me I've been bribed.
          The day comes soon, no long test of time, not now,
1200   that wakes the wails for men and women in your halls.
          Great hatred rises against you—
          cities in tumult, all whose mutilated sons
          the dogs have graced with burial, or the wild beasts,
          some wheeling crow that wings the ungodly stench of carrion
1205   back to each city, each warrior's heart and home.

          These arrows for your heart! Since you've raked me
          I loose them like an archer in my anger,
          arrows deadly true. You'll never escape
          their burning, searing force.

          [*Motioning to his escort.*]

1210   Come, boy, take me home.
        So he can vent his rage on younger men,
        and learn to keep a gentler tongue in his head
        and better sense than what he carries now.

        [*Exit to the side.*]

LEADER: The old man's gone, my king—
1215   terrible prophecies. Well I know,
        since the hair on his old head went gray,
        he's never lied to Thebes.
CREON: I know it myself—I'm shaken, torn.
        It's a dreadful thing to yield . . . but resist now?
1220   Lay my pride bare to the blows of ruin?
        That's dreadful too.
LEADER: But good advice,
        Creon, take it now, you must.
CREON: What should I do? Tell me . . . I'll obey.
LEADER: Go! Free the girl from the rocky vault
1225   and raise a mound for the body you exposed.
CREON: That's your advice? You think I should give in?
LEADER: Yes, my king, quickly. Disasters sent by the gods
        cut short our follies in a flash.
CREON: Oh it's hard.
        giving up the heart's desire . . . but I will do it—
1230   no more fighting a losing battle with necessity.
LEADER: Do it now, go, don't leave it to others.
CREON: Now—I'm on my way! Come, each of you,
        take up axes, make for the high ground,
        over there, quickly! I and my better judgment
1235   have come round to this—I shackled her,
        I'll set her free myself. I am afraid . . .
        it's best to keep the established laws
        to the very day we die.

        [*Rushing out, followed by his entourage. The Chorus clusters around
        the altar.*]

CHORUS: God of a hundred names!
                            Great Dionysus—
1240   Son and glory of Semele! Pride of Thebes—
        Child of Zeus whose thunder rocks the clouds—
        Lord of the famous lands of evening—
        King of the Mysteries!
                            King of Eleusis, Demeter's plain[7]
        her breasting hills that welcome in the world—
        Great Dionysus!
1245   Bacchus,[8] living in Thebes
        the mother-city of all your frenzied women—
                                            Bacchus

---

7. Eleusis, near Athens, was a major site for the worship   8. Dionysos.
of Demeter, goddess of grain and fertility.

living along the Ismenus'⁹ rippling waters
standing over the field sown with the Dragons' teeth¹

You—we have seen you through the flaring smoky fires,
1250   your torches blazing over the twin peaks
where nymphs of the hallowed cave climb onward
                        fired with you, your sacred rage—
we have seen you at Castalia's running spring²
and down from the heights of Nysa³ crowned with ivy
1255   the greening shore rioting vines and grapes
                down you come in your storm of wild women
ecstatic, mystic cries—
                    Dionysus—
down to watch and ward the roads of Thebes!
First of all cities, Thebes you honor first
1260   you and your mother, bride of the lightning—
come, Dionysus! now your people lie
in the iron grip of plague,
come in your racing, healing stride
                        down Parnassus'⁴ slopes
or across the moaning straits.
1265   Lord of the dancing—
dance, dance the constellations breathing fire!
Great master of the voices of the night!
Child of Zeus, God's offspring, come, come forth!
Lord, king, dance with your nymphs, swirling, raving
1270   arm-in-arm in frenzy through the night
they dance you, Iacchus⁵—
                    Dance, Dionysus
giver of all good things!

[Enter a Messenger from the side.]

MESSENGER: Neighbors,
friends of the house of Cadmus and the kings,
there's not a thing in this life of ours
1275   I'd praise or blame as settled once for all.
Fortune lifts and Fortune fells the lucky
and unlucky every day. No prophet on earth
can tell a man his fate. Take Creon:
there was a man to rouse your envy once,
1280   as I see it. He saved the realm from enemies;
taking power, he alone, the lord of the fatherland,
he set us true on course—flourished like a tree
with the noble line of sons he bred and reared . . .
and now it's lost, all gone. Believe me,

9. A river near Thebes.
1. Thebes was founded by Cadmus when men emerged
from the dragon's teeth he sowed.
2. Sacred spring of the oracle of Apollo at Delphi; later
dedicated to the Muses.

3. Mountain sacred to Dionysos.
4. Mountain sacred to Dionysos; also home to the Muses
and scared to Apollo.
5. Dionysos.

1285   when a man has squandered his true joys,
        he's good as dead, I tell you, a living corpse.
        Pile up riches in your house, as much as you like—
        live like a king with a huge show of pomp,
        but if real delight is missing from the lot,
1290   I wouldn't give you a wisp of smoke for it,
        not compared with joy.
LEADER: What now?
        What new grief do you bring the house of kings?
MESSENGER: Dead, dead—and the living are guilty of their death!
LEADER: Who's the murderer? Who is dead? Tell us.
MESSENGER: Haemon's gone, his blood spilled by the very hand—
LEADER: His father's or his own?
MESSENGER: His own . . .
        raging mad with his father for the death—
LEADER: Oh great seer,
        you saw it all, you brought your word to birth!
MESSENGER: Those are the facts. Deal with them as you will.

        [As he turns to go, Eurydice enters from the palace.]

LEADER: Look, Eurydice. Poor woman, Creon's wife,
        so close at hand. By chance perhaps,
        unless she's heard the news about her son.
EURYDICE: My countrymen,
        all of you—I caught the sound of your words
        as I was leaving to do my part,
1305   to appeal to queen Athena with my prayers.
        I was just loosing the bolts, opening the doors,
        when a voice filled with sorrow, family sorrow,
        struck my ears, and I fell back, terrified,
        into the women's arms—everything went black.
1310   Tell me the news, again, whatever it is . . .
        sorrow and I are hardly strangers;
        I can bear the worst.
MESSENGER: I—dear lady,
        I'll speak as an eye-witness. I was there.
        And I won't pass over one word of the truth.
1315   Why should I try to soothe you with a story,
        only to prove a liar in a moment?
        Truth is always best.
                        So,
        I escorted your lord, I guided him
        to the edge of the plain where the body lay,
1320   Polynices, torn by the dogs and still unmourned.
        And saying a prayer to Hecate of the Crossroads,
        Pluto[6] too, to hold their anger and be kind,
        we washed the dead in a bath of holy water

6. Underworld deities.

and plucking some fresh branches, gathering . . .
1325   what was left of him, we burned them all together
and raised a high mound of native earth, and then
we turned and made for that rocky vault of hers,
the hollow, empty bed of the bride of Death.
And far off, one of us heard a voice,
1330   a long wail rising, echoing
out of that unhallowed wedding-chamber;
he ran to alert the master and Creon pressed on,
closer—the strange, inscrutable cry came sharper,
throbbing around him now, and he let loose
1335   a cry of his own, enough to wrench the heart,
"Oh god, am I the prophet now? going down
the darkest road I've ever gone? My son—
it's *his* dear voice, he greets me! Go, men,
closer, quickly! Go through the gap,
1340   the rocks are dragged back—
right to the tomb's very mouth—and look,
see if it's Haemon's voice I think I hear,
or the gods have robbed me of my senses."

The king was shattered. We took his orders,
1345   went and searched, and there in the deepest,
dark recesses of the tomb we found her . . .
hanged by the neck in a fine linen noose,
strangled in her veils—and the boy,
his arms flung around her waist,
1350   clinging to her, wailing for his bride,
dead and down below, for his father's crimes
and the bed of his marriage blighted by misfortune.
When Creon saw him, he gave a deep sob,
he ran in, shouting, crying out to him,
1355   "Oh my child—what have you done? what seized you,
what insanity? what disaster drove you mad?
Come out, my son! I beg you on my knees!"
But the boy gave him a wild burning glance,
spat in his face, not a word in reply,
1360   he drew his sword—his father rushed out,
running as Haemon lunged and missed!—
and then, doomed, desperate with himself,
suddenly leaning his full weight on the blade,
he buried it in his body, halfway to the hilt.
1365   And still in his senses, pouring his arms around her,
he embraced the girl and breathing hard,
released a quick rush of blood,
bright red on her cheek glistening white.
And there he lies, body enfolding body . . .
1370   he has won his bride at last, poor boy,
not here but in the houses of the dead.

Creon shows the world that of all the ills
afflicting men the worst is lack of judgment.

[*Eurydice turns and reenters the palace.*]

LEADER: What do you make of that? The lady's gone,
without a word, good or bad.

MESSENGER: I'm alarmed too
but here's my hope—faced with her son's death,
she finds it unbecoming to mourn in public.
Inside, under her roof, she'll set her women
to the task and wail the sorrow of the house.

1380 She's too discreet. She won't do something rash.

LEADER: I'm not so sure. To me, at least,
a long heavy silence promises danger,
just as much as a lot of empty outcries.

MESSENGER: We'll see if she's holding something back,

1385 hiding some passion in her heart.
I'm going in. You may be right—who knows?
Even too much silence has its dangers.

[*Exit to the palace. Enter Creon from the side, escorted by attendants
carrying Haemon's body on a bier.*]

LEADER: The king himself! Coming toward us,
look, holding the boy's head in his hands.

1390 Clear, damning proof, if it's right to say so—
proof of his own madness, no one else's,
    no, his own blind wrongs.

CREON: Ohhh,
so senseless, so insane . . . my crimes,
my stubborn, deadly—

1395 Look at us, the killer, the killed,
father and son, the same blood—the misery!
My plans, my mad fanatic heart,
my son, cut off so young!
Ai, dead, lost to the world,
not through your stupidity, no, my own.

LEADER: Too late,
too late, you see what justice means.

CREON: Oh I've learned
through blood and tears! Then, it was then,
when the god came down and struck me—a great weight
shattering, driving me down that wild savage path,

1405 ruining, trampling down my joy. Oh the agony,
the heartbreaking agonies of our lives.

[*Enter the Messenger from the palace.*]

MESSENGER: Master,
what a hoard of grief you have, and you'll have more.
The grief that lies to hand you've brought yourself—

[*Pointing to Haemon's body.*]

the rest, in the house, you'll see it all too soon.

CREON: What now? What's worse than this?

MESSENGER: The queen is dead.
The mother of this dead boy . . . mother to the end—
poor thing, her wounds are fresh.

CREON: No, no,
harbor of Death, so choked, so hard to cleanse!—
why me? why are you killing me?

1415   Herald of pain, more words, more grief?
I died once, you kill me again and again!
What's the report, boy . . . some news for me?
My wife dead? O dear god!
Slaughter heaped on slaughter?

[*The doors open; the body of Eurydice is brought out on her bier.*]

MESSENGER: See for yourself:
now they bring her body from the palace.

CREON: Oh no,
another, a second loss to break the heart.
What next, what fate still waits for me?
I just held my son in my arms and now,
look, a new corpse rising before my eyes—

1425   wretched, helpless mother—O my son!

MESSENGER: She stabbed herself at the altar,
then her eyes went dark, after she'd raised
a cry for the noble fate of Megareus,[7] the hero
killed in the first assault, then for Haemon,

1430   then with her dying breath she called down
torments on your head—you killed her sons.

CREON: Oh the dread,
I shudder with dread! Why not kill me too?—
run me through with a good sharp sword?
Oh god, the misery, anguish—

1435   I, I'm churning with it, going under.

MESSENGER: Yes, and the dead, the woman lying there,
piles the guilt of all their deaths on you.

CREON: How did she end her life, what bloody stroke?

MESSENGER: She drove home to the heart with her own hand,

1440   once she learned her son was dead . . . that agony.

CREON: And the guilt is all mine—
can never be fixed on another man,
no escape for me. I killed you,
I, god help me, I admit it all!

[*To his Attendants.*]

1445   Take me away, quickly, out of sight.
I don't even exist—I'm no one. Nothing.

7. Elder son of Creon and Eurydice.

LEADER: Good advice, if there's any good in suffering.
             Quickest is best when troubles block the way.
CREON:

[*Kneeling in prayer.*]

             Come, let it come!—that best of fates for me
1450   that brings the final day, best fate of all.
             Oh quickly, now—
             so I never have to see another sunrise.
LEADER: That will come when it comes;
             we must deal with all that lies before us.
1455   The future rests with the ones who tend the future.
CREON: That prayer—I poured my heart into that prayer!
LEADER: No more prayers now. For mortal men
             there is no escape from the doom we must endure.
CREON: Take me away, I beg you, out of sight.
1460   A rash, indiscriminate fool!
             I murdered you, my son, against my will—
             you too, my wife . . .
                                    Wailing wreck of a man,
             whom to look to? where to lean for support?

[*Desperately turning from Haemon to Eurydice on their biers.*]

             Whatever I touch goes wrong—once more
1465   a crushing fate's come down upon my head.

[*The Messenger and attendants lead Creon into the palace.*]

CHORUS: Wisdom is by far the greatest part of joy,
             and reverence toward the gods must be safeguarded.
             The mighty words of the proud are paid in full
             with mighty blows of fate, and at long last
1470   those blows will teach us wisdom.

[*The old citizens exit to the side.*]

⸏⟡⸎

RESONANCE

Aristotle: from Poetics[1]

Tragedy, then, is a representation of an action that is worth serious attention, complete in itself, and of some amplitude; in language enriched by a variety of artistic

1. Translated by T. S. Dorsch. The philosopher Aristotle wrote the *Poetics* in the 4th century B.C.E., the century after the flowering of Athenian tragedy in the hands of Aeschylus, Sophocles, and Euripides. The *Poetics* falls into a group of practical manuals, among the many treatises of Aristotle, and explains how to make poetry. Part of it has been lost; the part that remains discusses the writing of tragedies. Unlike Plato, who dismissed tragedy from his ideal city because it aroused weakness and unseemly emotion in its spectators, Aristotle valued it as fiction and as spectacle, arguing that it inspires feelings of pity and fear in its audience and provides a *katharsis*, a cleansing or purgation, of these emotions. In the properly written play, the tragic hero should fall from greatness because of some *hamartia*—not a tragic "flaw," as it is often mistakenly translated, but a "missing of the mark," an error. Arguing that poetry is more philosophical than historical accounts, since it represents human universals rather than actual events, Aristotle praises Sophocles' *Oedipus the King* as an exemplary tragedy, with its dramatic reversal of fortune and terrible passage from ignorance to knowledge.

devices appropriate to the several parts of the play; presented in the form of action, not narration; by means of pity and fear bringing about the purgation of such emotions. By language that is enriched I refer to language possessing rhythm, and music or song; and by artistic devices appropriate to the several parts I mean that some are produced by the medium of verse alone, and others again with the help of song.

Now since the representation is carried out by men performing the actions, it follows, in the first place, that spectacle is an essential part of tragedy, and secondly that there must be song and diction, these being the medium of representation. By diction I mean here the arrangement of the verses; song is a term whose sense is obvious to everyone.

In tragedy it is action that is imitated, and this action is brought about by agents who necessarily display certain distinctive qualities both of character and of thought, according to which we also define the nature of the actions. Thought and character are, then, the two natural causes of actions, and it is on them that all men depend for success or failure. The representation of the action is the plot of the tragedy; for the ordered arrangement of the incidents is what I mean by plot. Character, on the other hand, is that which enables us to define the nature of the participants, and thought comes out in what they say when they are proving a point or expressing an opinion.

Necessarily, then, every tragedy has six constituents, which will determine its quality. They are plot, character, diction, thought, spectacle, and song. Of these, two represent the media in which the action is represented, one involves the manner of representation, and three are connected with the objects of the representation; beyond them nothing further is required. These, it may be said, are the dramatic elements that have been used by practically all playwrights; for all plays alike possess spectacle, character, plot, diction, song, and thought.

***

A plot does not possess unity, as some people suppose, merely because it is about one man. Many things, countless things indeed, may happen to one man, and some of them will not contribute to any kind of unity; and similarly he may carry out many actions from which no single unified action will emerge. It seems, therefore, that all those poets have been on the wrong track who have written a *Heracleid,* or a *Theseid,* or some other poem of this kind, in the belief that, Heracles being a single person, his story must necessarily possess unity. Homer, exceptional in this as in all other respects, seems, whether by art or by instinct, to have been well aware of what was required. In writing his *Odyssey* he did not put in everything that happened to Odysseus, that he was wounded on Mount Parnassus, for example, or that he feigned madness at the time of the call to arms, for it was not a matter of necessity or probability that either of these incidents should have led to the other; on the contrary, he constructed the *Odyssey* round a single action of the kind I have spoken of, and he did this with the *Iliad* too. Thus, just as in the other imitative arts each individual representation is the representation of a single object, so too the plot of a play, being the representation of an action, must present it as a unified whole; and its various incidents must be so arranged that if any one of them is differently placed or taken away the effect of wholeness will be seriously disrupted. For if the presence or absence of something makes no apparent difference, it is no real part of the whole.

It will be clear from what I have said that it is not the poet's function to describe what has actually happened, but the kinds of thing that might happen, that is, that could happen because they are, in the circumstances, either probable or necessary.

The difference between the historian and the poet is not that the one writes in prose and the other in verse; the work of Herodotus might be put into verse, and in this metrical form it would be no less a kind of history than it is without metre. The difference is that the one tells of what has happened, the other of the kinds of things that might happen. For this reason poetry is something more philosophical and more worthy of serious attention than history; for while poetry is concerned with universal truths, history treats of particular facts.

By universal truths are to be understood the kinds of thing a certain type of person will probably or necessarily say or do in a given situation; and this is the aim of poetry, although it gives individual names to its characters. The particular facts of the historian are what, say, Alcibiades did, or what happened to him. By now this distinction has become clear where comedy is concerned, for comic poets build up their plots out of probable occurrences, and then add any names that occur to them; they do not, like the iambic poets, write about actual people. In tragedy, on the other hand, the authors keep to the names of real people, the reason being that what is possible is credible. Whereas we cannot be certain of the possibility of something that has not happened, what has happened is obviously possible, for it would not have happened if this had not been so. Nevertheless, even in some tragedies only one or two of the names are well known, and the rest are fictitious; and indeed there are some in which nothing is familiar, Agathon's *Antheus,* for example, in which both the incidents and the names are fictitious, and the play is none the less well liked for that. It is not necessary, therefore, to keep entirely to the traditional stories which form the subjects of our tragedies. Indeed it would be absurd to do so, since even the familiar stories are familiar only to a few, and yet they please everybody.

What I have said makes it obvious that the poet must be a maker of plots rather than of verses, since he is a poet by virtue of his representation, and what he represents is actions. And even if he writes about things that have actually happened, that does not make him any the less a poet, for there is nothing to prevent some of the things that have happened from being in accordance with the laws of possibility and probability, and thus he will be a poet in writing about them.

Of simple plots and actions those that are episodic are the worst. By an episodic plot I mean one in which the sequence of the episodes is neither probable nor necessary. Plays of this kind are written by bad poets because they cannot help it, and by good poets because of the actors; writing for the dramatic competitions, they often strain a plot beyond the bounds of possibility, and are thus obliged to dislocate the continuity of events.

However, tragedy is the representation not only of a complete action, but also of incidents that awaken fear and pity, and effects of this kind are heightened when things happen unexpectedly as well as logically, for then they will be more remarkable than if they seem merely mechanical or accidental. Indeed, even chance occurrences seem most remarkable when they have the appearance of having been brought about by design—when, for example, the statue of Mitys at Argos killed the man who had caused Mitys's death by falling down on him at a public entertainment. Things like this do not seem mere chance occurrences. Thus plots of this type are necessarily better than others.

⟞⟝ PERSPECTIVES ⟞⟝
Tyranny and Democracy

The Greek word "tyrant" means a ruler—such as Oedipus—who has gained power by unconventional means but suggests nothing about the nature of his rule. Tyrants often came from the ranks of the aristocracy and seized control of the city-states with the support of the previously powerless *demos,* or "people." In Athens, the relatively benign tyrant Peisistratos won power after faking an assassination attempt and asking for bodyguards, later parading into town with a tall, armed woman he claimed was the goddess Athena, who'd come to offer support for his rule. He broke the back of aristocratic domination in the city, perhaps instituting such reforms as the drama festivals in honor of Dionysos, and ruled for thirty-six years, dying in 527 B.C.E. The tyrant slayers Harmodios and Aristogeiton, who were lovers, assassinated one of Peisistratos's sons in an erotic intrigue; the other son, deposed and in exile, aided the Persians in their invasion of Greece. More notorious tyrants in other cities included Periander of Corinth; when his wife died, he had sex with her corpse and then stripped all the women of his city naked and burned their clothes to warm her in the underworld. Another had a hollow brass bull made to torture and roast his opponents in, then inserted its maker as the bull's first victim.

In Athens, democracy, "rule by the people," followed the rule of the tyrants. The *demos* was the body of citizens: those who were free, male, and Athenian by descent but not women, slaves, barbarians, or Greeks from other cities. In a one-man, one-vote assembly, the citizens met, argued, often furiously, and then decided on the city's course of action. The Athenians prided themselves on their freedom and eloquently contrasted their form of government with the empires of Asia and Africa and the oligarchies, aristocracies, and tyrannies of the rest of Greece. The Athenians chose to spend their wealth on a fleet, paying a wage to the rowers, who were the city's poorest citizens, rather than slaves as elsewhere; they lavished funds as well on the magnificent buildings of the *agora,* the marketplace, and the Acropolis, site of the Parthenon, the great temple of Athena. Eventually, the city paid its jurors in a sort of welfare system for its older citizens and even paid for the audience to attend the performances of the drama festivals. The city also zealously restricted the privileges of citizenship to those descended from other citizens. The following selections point out the differences the Greeks saw between their own forms of governance and those under which the Persians lived; they illustrate Greek views of the proper eloquence of their leaders, the great lawgiver Solon, a renowned poet, the noble Perikles, who celebrates the greatness of Athens in a time of mourning, urging its citizens to fall in love with their city and their martyr, the philosopher Socrates, executed on charges of impiety. Much modern political thought derives from the pathbreaking and highly literary reflections given here.

⟞⟝⟞⟝

Solon
c. 640–558 B.C.E.

In a time of struggle between rich aristocrats and poor citizens, when the poor were being sold into slavery by the rich, Solon the lawgiver averted revolution. At the request of the Athenians, he changed the city's laws, paving the way for democracy. He made it illegal to enslave citizens, changed the hierarchy in the city to reflect degrees of wealth rather than noble birth, and altered the severe laws regarding homicide established by an earlier lawgiver, Drako (from whom our word "draconian" derives). His compromises seem to have fully satisfied neither rich nor poor. He then left the city for ten years, to avoid having to alter his new laws, and traveled around the Mediterranean, visiting Egypt, Cyprus, and Asia Minor. He was said to have met the rich Croesus, king of Lydia, who asked him who was the happiest man on earth, hoping to be so named by the wise man from Athens. Solon instead named modest men of Greece who had died heroically, telling Croesus: look to the end, and count no man happy until he has died happily. Solon's wisdom was later proved when Croesus was placed alive on a funeral pyre by the conquering Persian emperor (only by calling out Solon's name and appealing to Apollo, to whom he had given many gifts, did Croesus save himself from the fire). Solon then returned to Athens. His poems celebrate and defend the laws he made for the Athenians.

Our state will never fall[1]

Our state will never fall by Zeus's ordinance
    or the immortal blessed gods' intent:
such a stout-hearted guardian, she of the mighty sire,
    Pallas Athene, holds her hand above:
5   but by their foolishness the citizens themselves
    seek to destroy its pride, from avarice,
with the unprincipled mob-leaders, who are set
    to suffer badly for their great misdeeds.
They know not how to prosper modestly, enjoy
10   in festive peace the happiness they have.

    . . . . .

    and they grow wealthy by unrighteousness.
[When wicked men . . .]
    and, sparing neither sacred property
nor public, seize by plunder, each one what he can,
15   careless of Righteousness's august shrine—
the silent one, who knows what is and has been done,
    and comes at last to claim the payment due—
this aims a sure blow at the whole community,
    and soon it comes to wretched slavery
20   which rouses war from sleep, and strife within the clan,
    and sunders many from their lovely youth.
For if men injure their own people, they soon find
    their lovely city scarred and faction-torn.
Among the populace these evils roam at large,
25   and many of the poor folk find themselves
in foreign lands, sold into slavery and bound
    in shameful bonds . . .
And so the public ill comes home to every man:
    the yard doors are no more disposed to hold;
30   it leaps the high wall, and it finds him out for sure,
    though he take refuge in his inmost room.
This lesson I desire to teach the Athenians:
    Lawlessness brings the city countless ills,

1. Translated by M. L. West.

while Lawfulness sets all in order as is due;
35   many a criminal it puts in irons.
It makes the rough smooth, curbs excess, effaces wrong,
        and shrivels up the budding flowers of sin;
it straightens out distorted judgements, pacifies
        the violent, brings discord to an end,
40   brings to an end ill-tempered quarrelling. It makes
        all men's affairs correct and rational.

The commons I have granted

The commons I have granted privilege enough,
        not lessening their estate nor giving more;
the influential, who were envied for their wealth,
        I have saved them from all mistreatment too.
5   I took my stand with strong shield covering both sides,
        allowing neither unjust dominance.
Thus would the commons and its leaders best accord,
        not given too free a rein, nor pushed too hard.
Surplus breeds arrogance, when too much wealth attends
10   such men as have no soundness of intent.
Hard to please everyone in politics.

Those aims for which I called the public meeting

Those aims for which I called the public meeting—
which of them, when I stopped, was still to achieve?
I call as witness in the court of Time
the mighty mother of the Olympian gods,
5   dark Earth, from whom I lifted boundary-stones[1]
that did beset her—slave before, now free.
And many to Athena's holy land
I brought back, sold abroad illegally
or legally, and others whom their debts
10   had forced to leave, their speech no longer Attic,
so great their wanderings; and others here
in ugly serfdom at their masters' mercy
I set free. These things I did in power,
blending strength with justice, carried out
15   all that I promised. I wrote laws for all,
for high and low alike, made straight and just.
But if another man had got the goad,
someone imprudent or acquisitive,
he'd not have checked the mob. If I'd agreed
20   to what the opposition favoured then,

---

1. Markers on debtors' land.

and then to what the other party thought,
this city would be mourning many dead.
Therefore I turned to guard my every side,
a wolf at bay amid a pack of hounds.

━━ ⊰◈⊱ ━━

Thucydides
c. 460–400 B.C.E.

The fifth century B.C.E. began with the Persian Wars, fought between the Greeks and the barbarians, recounted by Herodotus; it ended with the war among the Greeks, the Peloponnesian War, set down by his intellectual heir and rival, the Athenian Thucydides. A soldier and general himself, Thucydides records the thirty-year struggle between the Athenians and their allies against the Spartans and their allies, who fought to contain Athens' ambitions. Implicitly critical of earlier historians' storytelling, Thucydides adopts a method of strict judgment and commitment to accuracy. He presents vivid portraits of the political figures of his day including Perikles, who led Athens in the period of its greatest prosperity and who celebrated the city in his famous funeral oration. Thucydides offers many such elaborate speeches, either delivered by his protagonists and recorded by his attentive ear, or else imaginatively reconstructed. These orations embody the intense rhetorical training and persuasive techniques of the fifth-century democratic assembly. Like most Greek intellectuals critical of democracy, Thucydides portrays the Athenian people as swayed by flattering rhetoric, their virtue gradually eroded and drawn into a disastrous imperialist invasion of Sicily by the charismatic Alcibiades, who was the object of women's and men's desire and who lived a wild and dissolute life while conducting brilliant military campaigns that endeared him to the Athenians. The invasion ended with its generals murdered and the Athenians imprisoned and dying in the quarries of Syracuse, enslaved, or sold for ransom; according to some accounts, only those who could recite lines from the tragedies of Euripides were spared.

Thucydides' Athens counted among its residents the pre-Socratics—early physicists, political theorists, and anthropologists—as well as the philosophers Socrates and Plato. Thucydides the historian shared their critical, questioning spirit and sought to distinguish rigorously between truth and falsehood, myth and reason, and cant and integrity in recording the events of his day. Critics in antiquity and after have admired Thucydides' brilliant style, characterized by a poetic vocabulary, a great variety of rhetorical figures, roughness in the joints of his prose, and the speed with which he conveys his meanings. Democratic Athens exiled Thucydides for a military failure; he returned after twenty years, when the war had ended, only to die with his history unfinished.

PRONUNCIATION:
  Thucydides: thu-SIH-dih-deez

from The Peloponnesian War[1]

from Book 1

[HISTORICAL METHOD]

Thucydides, an Athenian, recorded the war between the Peloponnesians and the Athenians, writing how they waged it against each other and beginning his work as soon as

---

1. Translated by Steven Lattimore.

the war broke out in expectation that it would be a major one and notable beyond all previous wars, basing this assumption on the fact that both sides came into it flourishing in overall preparedness and on seeing that the rest of the Hellenes were aligning themselves with one or the other, some immediately and others at least intending to. This was certainly the greatest disturbance to effect the Hellenes and a considerable number of barbarians—one might say the majority of mankind.

While it was impossible, because of the amount of time elapsed, to discover clearly what happened in the previous era or the still more remote past, I believe— using the evidence I have come to trust by investigating as far back as possible—that these events were not on a large scale either regarding warfare or in other respects. For it is clear that what is now called Hellas was not a land securely settled long ago, but that there were migrations in former times and each group readily abandoned its territory under pressure from anyone more numerous at the time. In the absence of commerce (they didn't associate with one another on either land or sea with any confidence), utilizing their native resources to the level of a bare living without possessing surplus goods and without planting crops (since it was uncertain when someone else would come and take these from people who also had no fortifications) and supposing that they could obtain the minimal daily subsistence anywhere, they each emigrated without hesitation and accordingly were strong neither in the size of their cities nor in the rest of their preparation. It was especially the finest land that constantly changed population: what is now called Thessaly, Boiotia, most of the Peloponnesos except Arkadia, and the best parts elsewhere in Hellas. For on account of the fertility of the land, there were individual gains bringing about factional strife that ruined the people living there, and it also made them all the more the object of plots from outside. Attica, in any case, was without faction from remotest times because of its poor soil, and the same people always occupied it. And here is not the worst evidence for arguing that the failure of other parts of Hellas to grow in the same way as Attica was due to migrations. For of the people driven from the rest of Hellas by war or faction, the most capable took refuge among the Athenians, considering it secure, and because from the start they immediately became citizens, they made the city's population even larger, so that later, with Attica insufficient, the Athenians also sent out colonies to Ionia.

And the following also shows me clearly the weakness of early societies: before the Trojan War, the Hellenes are not known to have accomplished anything in common. Nor, it seems to me, did they share the name Hellas yet; rather, in the days before Hellen, the son of Deukalion, this title in fact did not even exist, and the various tribes, most extensively the Pelasgian, gave their names to the areas, but when Hellen and his sons became powerful in Phthiotis and were called in to help other cities, each tended now to be called Hellenes through the association, although it was a long process for this to prevail for all. And Homer is the best evidence; born long after even the Trojan War, he never uses this term collectively nor for any except Achilles' followers from Phthiotis (precisely the first Hellenes) but refers in his poems to Danaans, Argives, and Achaians. He does not even speak of barbarians, in my opinion because the Hellenes had not yet been comparably distinguished by a single name. The Hellenes, then, as they increasingly came to be called, both city by city (all speaking the same language) and later as a whole, accomplished nothing together before the Trojan War on account of weakness and lack of contact with one another. But it was only when they were becoming more experienced in seafaring that they united even for this expedition.

Minos was the earliest known in our tradition to acquire a navy, and he controlled most of the sea now called Hellenic, ruled the Cyclades, and in most cases was also their first colonizer, driving out the Karians and installing his sons as governors. He also naturally cleared the seas of piracy as far as possible to direct revenues toward himself instead. For the Hellenes in early times, as well as the barbarians along the coast and all who were islanders, turned to piracy as soon as they increased their contacts by sea, some of the most powerful men leading the way for their own profit and to support the needy. Falling on unwalled cities consisting of villages, they plundered them and made their main living from this, the practice not yet bringing disgrace but even conferring a certain prestige; witness those mainlanders even of the present who glory in successful raiding, also the request everywhere in early poetry that men arriving by sea say whether they were pirates, as though those questioned would not deny the practice nor would those who wanted to know blame them. They also raided each other on land. Much of Hellas still lives in the old way up to the present, Ozolian Lokris, Aitolia, Akarnania, that part of the mainland generally, and for these mainlanders the habit of carrying weapons has survived as a result of the old-style plundering. For all Hellas used to carry weapons because their settlements were unprotected and their routes unsafe, and they spent their ordinary daily life under arms, like barbarians.

Those parts of Hellas that still live in this way are an indication of what was also the former way of life for all alike. The Athenians were the first to put weapons aside and make their lives more sumptuous as well as more relaxed, and the elder of their rich men only recently gave up the indulgence of wearing linen tunics and tying up their hair in a knot fastened with gold grasshoppers; from the influence of kinship, the same fashion lasted for a long time among Ionian elders. By contrast, it was the Lacedaemonians[2] who first dressed simply in the present style, and in general their wealthy men began to live most like common people. They were also the first to strip publicly for athletics and anoint themselves with oil afterward; the old way was for athletes to compete with their genitals covered, even in the Olympic games, and this ended quite recently. Even now, there are some barbarians, especially Asians, who hold boxing and wrestling contests and do it wearing loincloths. And one might point to many other ways in which early Hellenic life resembled that of barbarians today.

As for cities, those built later in a time of increased seafaring and with more abundant wealth were fortified establishments right on the coast and occupied the isthmuses for trade as well as defense against their neighbors. The old cities, however, on account of the long survival of piracy, were usually built away from the sea, whether on the islands or the mainland (for the pirates raided both one another and the nonseafaring populations of the coast), and are inland settlements to this day. Islanders were the most active pirates, both Karians and Phoenicians. These settled most of the islands, and here is proof: when Delos was purified by the Athenians in this war and all the burials on the island removed, more than half proved to be Karian, recognizable by the weaponry used as grave furnishings and by the method of burial which is still in use. When the navy of Minos was established, communication by sea improved, since his colonization of most of the islands involved expelling the lawless elements, and coastal populations now increasingly proceeded to acquire wealth and live more securely, some even building city walls as a reflection of their

2. The Spartans, who lived in the Peloponnesus and led the opponents of the Athenians.

new prosperity. Love of profit caused the weaker to submit to the domination of the strong and the more powerful, with their abundant wealth, to make the smaller cities subject to them. It was after they had already entered this stage that they later campaigned against Troy.

And Agamemnon, as I see it, assembled his force more by surpassing his contemporaries in power than by leading suitors bound by the oaths to Tyndareus. Those Peloponnesians who have received the clearest account through ancestral tradition say that first Pelops acquired power through the enormous wealth he brought with him among a poor population when he came from Asia and gave his name to the land, even though he was an immigrant, and that later the position of his descendants was even greater when Eurystheus was killed in Attica by the Herakleidai after entrusting his kingdom to his maternal uncle Atreus (banished by his father, as it happened, because of the death of Chrysippos) at the start of his campaign on account of their kinship, and when Eurystheus never came back, Atreus with the consent of the Mycenaeans, since they feared the Herakleidai, and he was considered powerful and had also cultivated the common people, succeeded as king of Mycenae and all Eurystheus' other holdings, and the descendants of Pelops became greater than the descendants of Perseus. I think that Agamemnon, combining this inheritance with greater naval strength than anyone else, assembled and launched the expedition less because of good will than because he was feared. For he obviously brought with him the greatest number of ships and in addition supplied the Arkadians, as Homer, if he is good enough evidence, has stated clearly. And he says further, in the "Transmission of the Scepter," that "he was lord over many islands and all Argos"; now as a mainlander he wouldn't have ruled any but offshore islands (and these wouldn't be "many") unless he had possessed a navy. It is this campaign that must be used to gauge what earlier ones were like.

And the fact that Mycenae was a small place or that some other town of that period does not seem impressive now is not a reliable basis for anyone to doubt that the expedition was fully as large as the poets have said and tradition maintains. For if the city of the Lacedaemonians were deserted and the shrines and foundations of buildings preserved, I think that after the passage of considerable time there would eventually be wide-spread doubt that their power measured up to their reputation (and yet they occupy two-fifths of the Peloponnesos and preside over the whole of it as well as numerous allies beyond; nevertheless, since the city is not unified nor furnished with elaborate shrines or public buildings but settled in villages in the old Hellenic way, it would look inferior), but that if the Athenians were to suffer the same fate their power would be estimated, from the city's pure appearance, as twice what it is.

It is therefore reasonable to avoid the skepticism that comes from looking at the appearance of cities rather than their military resources and to believe that the Trojan expedition was greater than previous ones—yet fell short of those of the present, again if it is right to trust Homer's poetry here as well, where he probably embellished with exaggerations, being a poet; even if we do trust him, it is still obvious that the expedition was not very strong. For out of twelve hundred ships he puts those of the Boiotians at a hundred and twenty men and those of Philoktetes at fifty, in my opinion indicating the largest and the smallest crews; at any rate, he does not mention other sizes in the "Catalogue of Ships." That the rowers were also fighters he has made clear regarding Philoktetes' ships, since he says all the oarsmen were archers. It is not probable that many except kings and those of the highest rank sailed as passengers, especially since they had to cross the sea with military equipment, moreover using boats that had no decks but were built in the old piratical style. Now if one takes an average from the largest and the smallest ships, those who sailed do not seem numerous considering that they were sent out by Hellas as a whole.

The reason was not so much shortage of men as shortage of money. On account of low supplies, they led an army limited to the size they considered capable of living off the land while campaigning, and even after winning a battle when they arrived (as they clearly did, or they could not have built a wall for their camp), they apparently did not use their whole force but turned to cultivating the Chersonesos and to plundering— because of low supplies. And with their army divided in this way, the Trojans were the more able to hold out for ten years of active warfare, since they were a match for whatever forces were left to face them. If they had come with abundant supplies and carried on the war in unison and continuously without plundering or cultivating land, they would easily have conquered in battle and captured the city, since they actually held their own without using all their forces but only the detachment on hand at any time; if they had settled down and pressed the siege, they would have taken Troy with less time and effort. Instead, because of lack of funds, not only were previous efforts feeble, but even this very one which became so renowned in comparison is actually revealed by the facts as less significant than its reputation and the idea about it, which now prevails on account of the poets.

Even after the Trojan War, of course, Hellas was still going through migrations and incursions that prevented its untroubled development. The delayed return of the Hellenes from Troy caused much turmoil, and there was widespread faction in the cities, creating refugees who established new ones. The present-day Boiotians, sixty years after the capture of Troy, were driven from Arne by the Thessalians and settled the land now called Boiotia, formerly Kadmeis (there was also a contingent in this land earlier, including some who campaigned against Ilion). And in the eightieth year after the fall of Troy, the Dorians and the Herakleidai took over the Peloponnesos. After a long period of difficulty, Hellas was securely pacified, without further population changes, and sent out colonies; the Athenians colonized most of Ionia and the islands, whereas the Peloponnesians sent out most of the colonies in Italy and Sicily as well as some elsewhere in Hellas.

All these settlements were after the Trojan War. When Hellas became stronger and placed even more emphasis on acquiring wealth, tyrannies were set up in most of the cities as a result of increased revenues (previously, there were hereditary monarchies with formally restricted powers), and the Hellenes equipped navies and were more active at sea. The Corinthians are said to have been the first to develop ships almost like today's, and Corinth was the first place in Hellas where triremes were built. And Ameinokles, a Corinthian shipwright, evidently built four ships for the Samians; it is about three hundred years from the end of this war since he went to Samos. The earliest sea battle we know of involved Corinthians against Corcyreans; this was about two hundred and sixty years before the same date. For the Corinthians, with their city situated on the isthmus, were always engaged in commerce from the earliest times, since making them pay tribute but by taking great pains to have them governed through oligarchies, the Athenians by taking over the fleets of the allied cities, Chios and Lesbos excepted, in the course of time and assigning amounts of money for each to pay. So both as a result had greater preparedness for this war individually than the strongest power they ever enjoyed with their alliance intact.

Such, then, I found to be the nature of early events, although with difficulty in trusting every piece of evidence. For men accept one another's accounts of the past, even about their native countries, with a uniform lack of examination. For example, the Athenians commonly believe that Hipparchos was a tyrant when he was killed by Harmodios and Aristogeiton and do not know that Hippias as the eldest son of Peisistratos was the ruler, Hipparchos and Thessalos being his brothers, but Harmodios and Aristogeiton, suspecting at the last minute on that very day that Hippias had received some information from their fellow conspirators, kept away from him as forewarned, but since they could accept their danger only if they actually accomplished something before being arrested, when they found Hipparchos by the sanctuary called the Leokoreion organizing the Panathenaic procession they killed him. And there is a great deal more, from the present as well as the dimly remembered past, that the other Hellenes too are wrong about, such as that each king of the Lacedaemonians casts two votes instead of one, or that they have a Pitanate army division, which never existed. So devoid of effort is most people's search for the truth, and they would rather turn toward what is readily available. In light of the evidence I have cited, however, no one would go wrong in supposing that the early events I have related happened much in that way: not believing that the past was more like what the poets have sung, embellishing with their exaggerations, or the prose chroniclers have composed, in versions that cannot be checked and for the most part have forfeited credibility over time by winning victories as patriotic fiction, but regarding my discoveries from the clearest possible evidence as adequate for what concerns antiquity. And this war—even though men always consider the war on hand the most important while they are fighting but once they have ended it are more impressed by ancient ones—will nevertheless stand out clearly as greater than the others for anyone who examines it from the facts themselves.

Insofar as these facts involve what the various participants said both before and during the actual conflict, recalling the exact words was difficult for me regarding speeches I heard myself and for my informants about speeches made elsewhere; in the way I thought each would have said what was especially required in the given situation, I have stated accordingly, with the closest possible fidelity on my part to the overall sense of what was actually said. About the actions of the war, however, I considered it my responsibility to write neither as I learned from the chance informant nor according to my own opinion, but after examining what I witnessed myself and what I learned from others, with the utmost possible accuracy in each case. Finding out the facts involved great effort, because eye-witnesses did not report the same specific events in the same way, but according to individual partisanship or ability to remember. And the results, by avoiding patriotic storytelling, will perhaps seem the less enjoyable for listening. Yet if they are judged useful by any who wish to look at the plain truth about both past events and those that at some future time, in accordance with human nature, will recur in similar or comparable ways, that will suffice. It is a possession for all time, not a competition piece to be heard for the moment, that has been composed.

The Persian War was the greatest action of the past, yet it had a quick resolution in two battles on sea and two on land. But this war not only was great by its extended length but also was accompanied by such sufferings as never afflicted Hellas in any comparable period of time. For never had there been so many cities captured or left desolate, some by barbarians and others by the Hellenes as they fought each other (and some cities even changed population after they were taken), nor were there so many men exiled or slaughtered, both in the war itself and because of faction. And things formerly known from hearsay accounts, less often from factual confirmation, could now be believed, such as earthquakes, since these came without parallel in their wide distribution as well as severity, along with eclipses of the sun, which occurred more frequently than in any memories of the past, also droughts in some parts and the famines caused by them, and the disease that did the most damage and destroyed a large number: the plague. All these descended in conjunction with this war.

The Athenians and the Peloponnesians began it by breaking the Thirty-Year Peace that they made after the capture of Euboia. As to why they broke the peace, I have first written an account of the complaints and disputes so that no one may ever search for the reasons that so great a war broke out among the Hellenes. For I consider the truest cause the one least openly expressed, that increasing Athenian greatness and the resulting fear among the Lacedaemonians made going to war inevitable.

from **Book 2**

[PERIKLES' FUNERAL ORATION]

In this winter, following their traditional custom, the Athenians held burial rites at public expense for the first to die in this war, in the following manner. They lay out the bones of the dead two days beforehand, after setting up a tent, and each person brings whatever offerings he wishes to his own relatives. When the procession takes place, wagons carry cypress coffins, one for each tribe, and within are the bones of each man, according to tribe. One empty bier, fully decorated, is brought for the missing, all who were not found and recovered. Any man who wishes, citizen or foreigner, joins the procession, and female relatives are present at the grave as mourners. They bury them in the public tomb, which is in the most beautiful suburb of the city and in which they always bury those killed in war, except of course for the men who fought at Marathon; judging their virtue outstanding, they gave them burial right there. After they cover them with earth, a man chosen by the state, known for wise judgment and of high reputation, makes an appropriate speech of praise, and after this they depart. This is their burial practice, and throughout the whole war, whenever there was occasion, they followed the custom. Now for these first casualties, Perikles son of Xanthippos was chosen to speak. And when the moment arrived, coming forward from the tomb to a platform that had been elevated so that he could be heard by as much of the crowd as possible, he spoke as follows:

"Most of those who have already spoken here praise the man who made this speech part of the custom, saying that for this address to be made at the burial of those lost in war is a fine thing. I myself would have thought it sufficient that the honors for those who proved good in deed be bestowed by deed as well, just as you now see carried out at public expense for this burial, rather than that the virtues of many men depend for their credibility on whether a single man speaks well or badly. To speak in due proportion is difficult where grasp of the truth itself is hardly assured. For the man listening with understanding and good will may well consider what is set forth in some way inferior, measured against both his wishes and his knowledge, yet the one listening in ignorance may consider some things exaggerated, out of envy when he hears anything going beyond his natural endowments. Praise spoken of others can only be endured as long as each believes himself capable of doing something of what he hears about; toward what goes further, men feel envy and then actual disbelief. But since it was so judged by those of long ago, that this speech is a fine thing, I too must follow the custom and try to conform with the wishes and opinions of each one of you as far as is possible.

"First of all, I will begin with our ancestors, since it is right and also appropriate on such an occasion as the present that the honor of this remembrance should be given to them. For it is the same men, always occupying the land through the succession of generations, who have handed it down in freedom until the present time because of their bravery. They are worthy of praise, and our fathers still more. In addition to what they received, they acquired through great effort the whole of the empire we now rule and left it to us in the present generation. Those of us here now who are still somewhere in the prime of life have expanded most areas of it and in all respects provided the city with the fullest resources for both war and peace. I will pass over the deeds in war that led to each of our acquisitions and every instance of stout resistance we or our fathers made against attacking enemies, whether barbarian or Hellene, since I do not wish to recount them at length among those who know of them. But I will turn to praise of the dead after I have first set forth the principles by which we came into this position and the form of government from which its greatness resulted, since I believe that these are not inappropriate to mention in the present circumstances and are advantageous for the whole gathering, both citizens and foreigners, to hear about.

"We have a form of government that does not emulate the practices of our neighbors, setting an example to some rather than imitating others. In name it is called a democracy on account of being administered in the interest not of the few but the many, yet even though there are equal rights for all in private disputes in accordance with the laws, wherever each man has earned recognition he is singled out for public service in accordance with the claims of distinction, not by rotation but by merit, nor when it comes to poverty, if a man has real ability to benefit the city, is he prevented by obscure renown. In public life we conduct ourselves with freedom and also, regarding that suspicion of others because of their everyday habits, without getting angry at a neighbor if he does something so as to suit himself, and without wearing expressions of vexation, that inflict no punishment yet cause distress. But while we associate in private without undue pressure, in public we are especially law abiding because of fear, in our obedience both to anyone holding office and to the laws, above all those established to aid people who are wronged and those which, although unwritten, bring down acknowledged shame. Furthermore, we have provided for the spirit the most plentiful respites from labor by providing games and festivals throughout the year as well as attractive surroundings for private life, a source of daily delight, which drives away cares. Because of the importance of the city, everything is brought in from every land, and it is our fortune to enjoy good things from other people with as much familiarity as what comes from here.

"In our approach to warfare, we also differ from our opponents, in the following ways. We leave our city accessible to all and do not, by xenelasia,[3] prevent anyone from either listening or observing, although some enemy might benefit by seeing what we do not hide, because we do not put more trust in contrivance and deception than in the courageous readiness for action, which comes from within. As for education, starting as children they pursue manhood with laborious training, but with our more relaxed way of life we are no less willing to take on equivalent dangers. Here is proof: the Lacedaemonians do not invade our land alone but with all their allies, and we attack other lands by ourselves, and fighting in hostile territory against men defending their own possessions, we usually win easily. And no enemy has yet encountered our united forces, on account of our simultaneously maintaining the fleet and

---

3. Expulsion of foreigners, practiced in Sparta.

dispatching our own men to many points on land, but wherever our enemies meet a detachment, they flatter themselves that they have repelled all of us if they beat some of us and that they were defeated by all if they lose. And if we are willing to face danger with a mind at ease rather than with the habit of stress, with bravery owing no more to law than to character, surely it is our gain that we are not afflicted by hardships before they occur, that when we do encounter them we prove no less daring than those who are constantly straining, and that our city deserves admiration for these reasons and still others.

"For we love beauty while practicing economy and we love wisdom without being enervated. We use wealth for opportune action rather than boastful speech, and there is no disgrace for one to admit poverty but much more in not avoiding it through activity. And it is within the capacity of some of us to manage private right along with public business and of the rest, while concentrating on their own occupations, to have no inferior understanding of public affairs; we are unique in considering the man who takes no part in these to be not apolitical but useless, and we ourselves either ratify or even propound successful policies, finding harm not in the effect of speeches on action but in failing to get instruction by speech before proceeding to what must be done. For in that we are both especially daring and especially thorough in calculating what we attempt, we can truly be distinguished from other men, for whom ignorance is boldness but calculation brings hesitancy. Rightly would they be judged strongest in spirit who recognize both dangers and pleasures with utmost clarity and are on neither count deterred from risks. In matters of goodness, we also contrast with most people, since we acquire friends by conferring rather than by receiving benefits. The giver is the more secure, through preserving the feeling of gratitude by good will toward the recipient, who is less fulfilled because he knows that he will repay the goodness not to inspire gratitude but to return an obligation. We are unique in being benefactors not out of calculation of advantage but with the fearless confidence of our freedom.

"In summary I claim that our city as a whole is an education for Hellas, and that it is among us as individuals, in my opinion, that a single man would represent an individual self-sufficient for the most varied forms of conduct, and with the most attractive qualities. And that this is not boastful speaking for the occasion but factual truth our city's very power, which we acquired because of these characteristics, proclaims clearly. For she alone of existing cities surpasses her reputation when put to the test, and only she brings neither chagrin to the attacking enemy as to the sort of men by whom he has been worsted nor reproach to the subject that he is ruled by the unworthy. Through great proofs, and by exhibiting power in no way unwitnessed, we will be admired by this and future generations, thus requiring no Homer to sing our praises nor any other whose verses will charm for the moment and whose claims the factual truth will destroy, since we have compelled every sea and land to become open to our daring and populated every region with lasting monuments of our acts of harm and good. It is for such a city, then, that these men nobly died in battle, thinking it right not to be deprived of her, just as each of their survivors should be willing to toil for her sake.

"This above all is the reason I have lengthened my speech about the city, to explain why our efforts have no equivalent among people who do not share these values, and at the same time to give evidence for the glory of those whom I am now eulogizing. The most important part of the eulogy has been said. For it is their virtues, and those of men like them, that have given honor to the qualities I have praised in the city, and for few other Hellenes would it be manifest, as it is for them, that reputation is equal to the deeds. It seems to me that this conclusion of these men's lives is what reveals a man's virtue, whether as the first indication or final confirmation. Even for those who were worse in other ways it is right that first place be given to valor against enemies on behalf of country; by effacing evil with good, they became public benefactors rather than individual malefactors. None of these men turned coward from preferring the further enjoyment of wealth, nor did any, from the poor man's hope that he might still escape poverty and grow rich, contrive a way to postpone the danger. Thinking defeat of the enemy more desirable than prosperity, just as they considered this the fairest of risks, they were willing to vanquish him at that risk and long for the rest, leaving to hope the uncertainty of prospering in the future but resolving to rely on their own actions in what confronted them now, and recognizing that it meant resisting and dying rather than surviving by submission, they fled disgrace in word but stood up to the deed with their lives and through the fortune of the briefest critical moment, at the height of glory rather than fear, departed.

"So fared these men, worthy of their city; you their survivors must pray to meet the enemy at lesser cost but resolve to do so just as unflinchingly, not calculating the benefits by words alone—although one might recite at length to you who know them just as well all the rewards of resisting the enemy—but wondering at the city's power as you actually see it each day and becoming her lovers, reflecting whenever her fame appears great to you that men who were daring, who realized their duty, and who honored it in their actions acquired this, men who even when they failed in some attempt did not on that account think it right to deprive the city of their virtue, but to offer it to her as their finest contribution. For in giving their lives in common cause, they individually gained imperishable praise and the most distinctive tomb, not the one where they are buried but the one where on every occasion for word and deed their glory is left after them eternally. The whole earth is the tomb of famous men, and not only inscriptions set up in their own country mark it but even in foreign lands an unwritten memorial, present not in monument but in mind, abides within each man. Emulate them now, judge that happiness is freedom and freedom courage, and do not stand aside from the dangers of war. For failures, men bereft of good expectations, have no more reason to be unstinting of their lives than those for whom reversal is always a threat as long as they live, and in whose sight the most important things are at stake if they come to grief. Indeed, for a man of pride, misfortune associated with cowardice is more painful than death coming imperceptibly in the midst of vigor along with shared hopes.

"It is for this reason that I offer comfort, not pity, to all those present as parents of these men. You know that you were reared among ever-changing fortunes. It is happiness whenever men find the most glorious end, just like these men, even while you find sorrow, and for those whose success in life has been measured out to the same limit as their mortality. I know that it is difficult to persuade you in that you will often have reminders of them through the happiness of others, which you once enjoyed as well; for sorrow is not felt over the deprivation of good things one has not experienced, but over the removal of what one was used to. But those still of age to have children must take strength from hopes of other sons. On the personal level, those who come later will be a means of forgetting those who are no more, and the city will benefit doubly, both in not being left short and in security; for it is not possible for men to counsel anything fair or just if they are not at risk by staking their sons equally. All of you who have passed beyond this, however, consider that the greater portion of your life, in which you were fortunate, is a gain, that this part will be short, and that your heart will be lightened by the fame of these men. For a love of honor is the only thing that has no old age, and it is not profit, as some claim, but honor that brings delight in the period of uselessness.

"For all those present who are sons or brothers of these men, however, I see that the effort will be a great one, since everyone tends to praise those who are no longer, and it will be difficult for you to be judged not equal, because of their surpassing merit, but only slightly inferior. For the living incur the envy for a rival, but those who no longer offer opposition receive honor with a good will lacking in competitiveness. And if I should make any mention of the virtue of women, regarding all who will now be widows, I will express all of it in brief advice. Your renown is great through keeping up to the standard of your basic nature, and if your reputation has the least circulation among men, whether for virtue or in blame.

"In words, as much as I in my turn could say suitably in accordance with the custom has been said, and in deed, these have been honored in burial now, and from this time the city will rear their sons at public expense until they are of age, conferring on both the dead and their survivors a beneficial crown for such contests as these. For it is among those who establish the greatest prizes for courage that men are the best citizens. And now, after each of you has made full lament for his own, you must depart."

Such was the funeral that occurred in this winter, and when the winter was over, the first year of this war ended.

from **Book 3**

[REVOLUTION IN CORCYRA]

The Corcyreans butchered those fellow-citizens they regarded as enemies, charging them with putting down the democracy, but some also died because of personal hatred and others at the hands of those who owed them money. Every form of death prevailed, and whatever is likely in such situations happened—and still worse. Fathers killed sons, men were dragged from the sanctuaries and killed beside them, and some were even walled up in the sanctuary of Dionysos and died there.

With this savagery, the civil war progressed, and it seemed all the more savage because it was the first, while later the rest of Hellas, almost without exception, was also in turmoil, with rival efforts everywhere by the popular leaders to bring in the Athenians and the oligarchs, the Lacedaemonians. In peacetime they had neither the pretext nor the willingness to call them in, but during war, with alliances available to both factions for damaging their opponents and at the same time strengthening themselves, occasions for bringing in outsiders were readily found by those wishing to make any change in government. And during the civil wars the cities suffered many cruelties that occur and will always occur as long as men have the same nature, sometimes more terribly and sometimes less, varying in their forms as each change of fortune dictates. For in peace and good circumstances, both states and individuals have better inclinations through not falling into involuntary necessities; but war, stripping away the easy access to daily needs, is a violent teacher and brings most men's passions into line with the present situations.

So the condition of the cities was civil war, and where it came later, awareness of earlier events pushed to extremes the revolution in thinking, both in extraordinarily ingenious attempts to seize power and in outlandish retaliations. And in self-justification men inverted the usual verbal evaluations of actions. Irrational recklessness was now considered courageous commitment, hesitation while looking to the future was high-styled cowardice, moderation was a cover for lack of manhood, and circumspection meant inaction, while senseless anger now helped to define a true man, and deliberation for security was a specious excuse for dereliction. The man of violent temper was always credible, anyone opposing him was suspect. The intriguer who succeeded was intelligent, anyone who detected a plot was still more clever, but a man who made provisions to avoid both alternatives was undermining his party and letting the opposition terrorize him. Quite simply, one was praised for outracing everyone else to commit a crime—and for encouraging a crime by someone who had never before considered one.

Kinship became alien compared with party affiliation, because the latter led to drastic action with less hesitation. For party meetings did not take place to use the benefits of existing laws, but to find any advantage in breaking them. They strengthened their trust in one another less by religious law than by association in committing some illegal act. Men responded to reasonable words from their opponents with defensive actions, if they had the advantage, and not with magnanimity. Revenge mattered more than not being harmed in the first place. And if there were actually reconciliations under oath, they occurred because of both sides' lack of alternatives and lasted only as long as neither found some other source of power. The one who first recovered his confidence at the right moment, when he saw the other off guard, enjoyed vengeance more in a situation of trust than if accomplished openly; the element of safety was an asset, and because of prevailing through deception he also won the prize for intelligence. As a rule, men are more easily called clever when they are scoundrels than virtuous when ignorant—and are as ashamed of the second description as they are exultant in the first.

All this was caused by leadership based on greed and ambition and led in turn to fanaticism once men were committed to the power struggle. For the leading men in the cities, through their emphasis on an attractive slogan for each side—political equality for the masses, the moderation of aristocracy—treated as their prize the public interest to which they paid lip service and, competing by every means to get the better of one another, boldly committed atrocities and proceeded to still worse acts of revenge, stopping at limits set by neither justice nor the city's interest but by the gratification of their parties at every stage, and whether by condemnations through unjust voting or by acquiring superiority in brute force, both sides were ready to satisfy to the utmost their immediate hopes of victory. And so neither side acted with piety, but those who managed to accomplish something hateful by using honorable arguments were more highly regarded. The citizens in the middle, either because they had not taken sides or because begrudged their survival, were destroyed by both factions.

In this way, every form of viciousness was established in the Hellenic world on account of the civil wars, and the simplicity that is especially found in noble natures disappeared because it became ridiculous. The division into distrustful groups opposed in their thinking was very extensive. To reconcile them, there was no secure principle, no oath that was feared, but those who were stronger, in contemplation of the impossibility of security, all took measures to avoid suffering rather than allowing themselves to feel trust. The weaker in intellect were more often the survivors; out of fear of their own deficiency and their enemies' craft, lest they be defeated in debate and become the first victims of plots as a result of the others' resourceful intellects, they went straight into action. And those who contemptuously supposed that they would know all in advance, and that there was no need to seize by force what would come to them through intellect, were instead caught off guard and destroyed.

In Corcyra, then, most of these atrocities were first committed: all that men do in resisting those who, after ruling them abusively rather than moderately, provide opportunity for revenge; all that men resolve unjustly when, wishing to escape their

usual poverty—especially if pressed by disaster—they desire their neighbors' possessions; all that others, attacking not for gain but on clearly equal terms, impelled most
by raw fury, carry out savagely and without mercy. With public life confused to the
critical point, human nature, always ready to act unjustly even in violation of laws,
overthrew the laws themselves and gladly showed itself powerless over passion but
stronger than justice and hostile to any kind of superiority. For men would not have
placed revenge above pity, gain above justice, if not for the destructive power of
envy. And the universal laws about such things, laws that offer hope of salvation to all
in adversity, men see fit to do away with at the outset in taking revenge instead of letting them stand until they actually run into danger and find need of them.

<hr />

Plato
c. 429–347 B.C.E.

The Athenians executed Socrates, Plato's beloved teacher, in 399 B.C.E., in the aftermath of
their defeat in the Peloponnesian War, condemning him on charges of impiety and for the corruption of young men. Socrates, who wrote nothing, left behind Plato, who wrote the founding
texts of Western philosophy. His dialogues recorded or invented conversations among
Socrates, his circle, and other men. Though Plato himself isn't a character in these dialogues,
he used them as his vehicle for setting out defining issues for the Western traditions of ethics,
political theory, logic, linguistics, theory of knowledge, rhetoric, and metaphysics. Plato was
brought to remarkably sophisticated considerations of definition and knowledge by his dissatis-
factions with the teachings of earlier thinkers including the pre-Socratics, the first physicists;
the sophists, traveling teachers of rhetoric; and the politics of the city of his day. He portrays
Socrates and his friends seeking to clarify such questions as the difference between opinion and
true knowledge, the relationship between rhetoric and philosophy, the nature of language, the
place of the gods in ethical life, and the role of poetry in society. What are often seen as earlier
dialogues conclude with the participants' mutual recognition of ignorance. Later conversations
explore such matters as the ideal society and its laws. In the course of Plato's writings, philosophy itself, "the love of wisdom," emerges for the first time as a distinct enterprise. Plato's dialogues combine highly rhetorical prose with dramatic techniques in order to explore the limits
of knowledge and human existence, sometimes offering vivid portraits of men in flirtatious or
passionate debate. Plato demonstrates an enduring suspicion of democracy, which allowed all
citizen men to engage in politics, a task he believed should be conducted by experts—the
guardian class he proposed to govern his ideal city, described in *The Republic*. *The Apology* is
presented as the speech Socrates offers in his defense when put on trial by his enemies in
Athens, written by Plato after Socrates was executed by being forced to drink hemlock, dying a
martyr's death. In Plato's moving presentation, Socrates's trial becomes nothing less than a
struggle for the soul of the Athenian polity.

Apology[1]

How you, O Athenians, have been affected by my accusers, I cannot tell; but I know
that they almost made me forget who I was—so persuasively did they speak; and yet
they have hardly uttered a word of truth. But of the many falsehoods told by them,
there was one which quite amazed me;—I mean when they said that you should be
upon your guard and not allow yourselves to be deceived by the force of my

1. Translated by Benjamin Jowett.

eloquence. To say this, when they were certain to be detected as soon as I opened my lips and proved myself to be anything but a great speaker, did indeed appear to me most shameless—unless by the force of eloquence they mean the force of truth; for if such is their meaning, I admit that I am eloquent. But in how different a way from theirs!

Well, as I was saying, they have scarcely spoken the truth at all; but from me you shall hear the whole truth; not, however, delivered after their manner in a set oration duly ornamented with words and phrases. No, by heaven! but I shall use the words and arguments which occur to me at the moment; for I am confident in the justice of my cause: at my time of life I ought not to be appearing before you, O men of Athens, in the character of a juvenile orator—let no one expect it of me. And I must beg of you to grant me a favour:—If I defend myself in my accustomed manner, and you hear me using the words which I have been in the habit of using in the agora,[2] at the tables of the money-changers, or anywhere else, I would ask you not to be surprised, and not to interrupt me on this account. For I am more than seventy years of age, and appearing now for the first time in a court of law, I am quite a stranger to the language of the place; and therefore I would have you regard me as if I were really a stranger, whom you would excuse if he spoke in his native tongue, and after the fashion of his country:—Am I making an unfair request of you? Never mind the manner, which may or may not be good; but think only of the truth of my words, and give heed to that: let the speaker speak truly and the judge decide justly.

And first, I have to reply to the older charges and to my first accusers, and then I will go on to the later ones. For of old I have had many accusers, who have accused me falsely to you during many years; and I am more afraid of them than of Anytus and his associates, who are dangerous, too, in their own way. But far more dangerous are the others, who began when you were children, and took possession of your minds with their falsehoods, telling of one Socrates, a wise man, who speculated about the heaven above, and searched into the earth beneath, and made the worse appear the better cause. The disseminators of this tale are the accusers whom I dread; for their hearers are apt to fancy that such enquirers do not believe in the existence of the gods. And they are many, and their charges against me are of ancient date, and they were made by them in the days when you were more impressible than you are now—in childhood, or it may have been in youth—and the cause when heard went by default, for there was none to answer. And hardest of all, I do not know and cannot tell the names of my accusers; unless in the chance case of a Comic poet. All who from envy and malice have persuaded you—some of them having first convinced themselves—all this class of men are most difficult to deal with; for I cannot have them up here, and cross-examine them, and therefore I must simply fight with shadows in my own defence, and argue when there is no one who answers. I will ask you then to assume with me, as I was saying, that my opponents are of two kinds; one recent, the other ancient: and I hope that you will see the propriety of my answering the latter first, for these accusations you heard long before the others, and much oftener.

Well, then, I must make my defence, and endeavor to clear away in a short time, a slander which has lasted a long time. May I succeed, if to succeed be for my good and yours, or likely to avail me in my cause! The task is not an easy one; I quite understand the nature of it. And so leaving the event with God, in obedience to the law I will now make my defence.

---

2. Place of assembly, a marketplace.

I will begin at the beginning, and ask what is the accusation which has given rise to the slander of me, and in fact has encouraged Meletus to prefer this charge against me. Well, what do the slanderers say? They shall be my prosecutors, and I will sum up their words in an affidavit: "Socrates is an evil-doer, and a curious person, who searches into things under the earth and in heaven, and he makes the worse appear the better cause; and he teaches the aforesaid doctrines to others." Such is the nature of the accusation: it is just what you have yourselves seen in the comedy of Aristophanes, who has introduced a man whom he calls Socrates, going about and saying that he walks in air, and talking a deal of nonsense concerning matters of which I do not pretend to know either much or little[3]—not that I mean to speak disparagingly of any one who is a student of natural philosophy. I should be very sorry if Meletus could bring so grave a charge against me. But the simple truth is, O Athenians, that I have nothing to do with physical speculations. Very many of those here present are witnesses to the truth of this, and to them I appeal. Speak then, you who have heard me, and tell your neighbours whether any of you have ever known me hold forth in few words or in many upon such matters. . . . You hear their answer. And from what they say of this part of the charge you will be able to judge of the truth of the rest.

As little foundation is there for the report that I am a teacher, and take money; this accusation has no more truth in it than the other.[4] Although, if a man were really able to instruct mankind, to receive money for giving instruction would, in my opinion, be an honour to him. There is Gorgias of Leontium, and Prodicus of Ceos, and Hippias of Elis, who go the round of the cities, and are able to persuade the young men to leave their own citizens by whom they might be taught for nothing, and come to them whom they not only pay, but are thankful if they may be allowed to pay them. There is at this time a Parian philosopher residing in Athens, of whom I have heard; and I came to hear of him in this way:—I came across a man who has spent a world of money on the Sophists, Callias, the son of Hipponicus, and knowing that he had sons, I asked him: "Callias," I said "if your two sons were foals or calves, there would be no difficulty in finding some one to put over them; we should hire a trainer of horses, or a farmer probably, who would improve and perfect them in their own proper virtue and excellence; but as they are human beings, whom are you thinking of placing over them? Is there any one who understands human and political virtue? You must have thought about the matter, for you have sons; is there any one?" "There is," he said. "Who is he?" said I; "and of what country? and what does he charge?" "Evenus the Parian," he replied; "he is the man, and his charge is five minae." Happy is Evenus, I said to myself, if he really has this wisdom, and teaches at such a moderate charge. Had I the same, I should have been very proud and conceited; but the truth is that I have no knowledge of the kind.

I dare say, Athenians, that some one among you will reply, "Yes, Socrates, but what is the origin of these accusations which are brought against you; there must have been something strange which you have been doing? All these rumours and this talk about you would never have arisen if you had been like other men: tell us, then, what is the cause of them, for we should be sorry to judge hastily of you." Now I regard this as a fair challenge, and I will endeavour to explain to you the reason why I am called wise and have such an evil fame. Please to attend then. And although some of you may think that I am joking, I declare that I will tell you the entire truth. Men

3. In Aristophanes' *Clouds*, which attacks Socrates as a ridiculous master of false reasoning.

4. Protagoras and other popular teachers of rhetoric made fortunes by their teaching.

of Athens, this reputation of mine has come of a certain sort of wisdom which I possess. If you ask me what kind of wisdom, I reply, wisdom such as may perhaps be attained by man, for to that extent I am inclined to believe that I am wise; whereas the persons of whom I was speaking have a superhuman wisdom, which I may fail to describe, because I have it not myself; and he who says that I have, speaks falsely, and is taking away my character. And here, O men of Athens, I must beg you not to interrupt me, even if I seem to say something extravagant. For the word which I will speak is not mine. I will refer you to a witness who is worthy of credit; that witness shall be the God of Delphi[5]—he will tell you about my wisdom, if I have any, and of what sort it is. You must have known Chaerephon; he was early a friend of mine, and also a friend of yours, for he shared in the recent exile of the people, and returned with you. Well, Chaerephon, as you know, was very impetuous in all his doings, and he went to Delphi and boldly asked the oracle to tell him whether—as I was saying, I must beg you not to interrupt—he asked the oracle to tell him whether any one was wiser than I was, and the Pythian prophetess answered, that there was no man wiser. Chaerephon is dead himself; but his brother, who is in court, will confirm the truth of what I am saying.

Why do I mention this? Because I am going to explain to you why I have such an evil name. When I heard the answer, I said to myself, What can the god mean? and what is the interpretation of his riddle? for I know that I have no wisdom, small or great. What then can he mean when he says that I am the wisest of men? And yet he is a god, and cannot lie; that would be against his nature. After long consideration, I thought of a method of trying the question. I reflected that if I could only find a man wiser than myself, then I might go to the god with a refutation in my hand. I should say to him, "Here is a man who is wiser than I am; but you said that I was the wisest." Accordingly I went to one who had the reputation of wisdom, and observed him—his name I need not mention; he was a politician whom I selected for examination—and the result was as follows: When I began to talk with him, I could not help thinking that he was not really wise, although he was thought wise by many, and still wiser by himself; and thereupon I tried to explain to him that he thought himself wise, but was not really wise; and the consequence was that he hated me, and his enmity was shared by several who were present and heard me. So I left him, saying to myself, as I went away: Well, although I do not suppose that either of us knows anything really beautiful and good, I am better off than he is,—for he knows nothing, and thinks that he knows; I neither know nor think that I know. In this latter particular, then, I seem to have slightly the advantage of him. Then I went to another who had still higher pretensions to wisdom, and my conclusion was exactly the same. Whereupon I made another enemy of him, and of many others besides him.

Then I went to one man after another, being not unconscious of the enmity which I provoked, and I lamented and feared this: But necessity was laid upon me,—the word of God, I thought, ought to be considered first. And I said to myself, Go I must to all who appear to know, and find out the meaning of the oracle. And I swear to you, Athenians, by the dog I swear!—for I must tell you the truth—the result of my mission was just this: I found that the men most in repute were all but the most foolish; and that others less esteemed were really wiser and better. I will tell you the tale of my wanderings and of the "Herculean" labours, as I may call them, which I endured only to find at last the oracle irrefutable.

5. Apollo.

After the politicians, I went to the poets; tragic, dithyrambic, and all sorts. And there, I said to myself, you will be instantly detected; now you will find out that you are more ignorant than they are. Accordingly, I took them some of the most elaborate passages in their own writings, and asked what was the meaning of them—thinking that they would teach me something. Will you believe me? I am almost ashamed to confess the truth, but I must say that there is hardly a person present who would not have talked better about their poetry than they did themselves. Then I knew that not by wisdom do poets write poetry, but by a sort of genius and inspiration; they are like diviners or soothsayers who also say many fine things, but do not understand the meaning of them. The poets appeared to me to be much in the same case; and I further observed that upon the strength of their poetry they believed themselves to be the wisest of men in other things in which they were not wise. So I departed, conceiving myself to be superior to them for the same reason that I was superior to the politicians.

At last I went to the artisans, for I was conscious that I knew nothing at all, as I may say; and I was sure that they knew many fine things; and here I was not mistaken, for they did know many things of which I was ignorant, and in this they certainly were wiser than I was. But I observed that even the good artisans fell into the same error as the poets;—because they were good workmen they thought that they also knew all sorts of high matters, and this defect in them overshadowed their wisdom; and therefore I asked myself on behalf of the oracle, whether I would like to be as I was, neither having their knowledge nor their ignorance, or like them in both; and I made answer to myself and to the oracle that I was better off as I was.

This inquisition has led to my having many enemies of the worst and most dangerous kind, and has given occasion also to many calumnies. And I am called wise, for my hearers always imagine that I myself possess the wisdom which I find wanting in others: but the truth is, O men of Athens, that God only is wise; and by his answer he intends to show that the wisdom of men is worth little or nothing; he is not speaking of Socrates, he is only using my name by way of illustration, as if he said, He, O men, is the wisest, who, like Socrates, knows that his wisdom is in truth worth nothing. And so I go about the world, obedient to the god, and search and make enquiry into the wisdom of any one, whether citizen or stranger, who appears to be wise; and if he is not wise, then in vindication of the oracle I show him that he is not wise; and my occupation quite absorbs me, and I have no time to give either to any public matter of interest or to any concern of my own, but I am in utter poverty by reason of my devotion to the god.

There is another thing:—young men of the richer classes, who have not much to do, come about me of their own accord; they like to hear the pretenders examined, and they often imitate me, and proceed to examine others; there are plenty of persons, as they quickly discover, who think that they know something, but really know little or nothing; and then those who are examined by them instead of being angry with themselves are angry with me: This confounded Socrates, they say; this villainous misleader of youth!—and then if somebody asks them, Why, what evil does he practise or teach? they do not know, and cannot tell; but in order that they may not appear to be at a loss, they repeat the ready-made charges which are used against all philosophers about teaching things up in the clouds and under the earth, and having no gods, and making the worse appear the better cause; for they do not like to confess that their pretence of knowledge has been detected—which is the truth; and as they are numerous and ambitious and energetic, and are drawn up in battle array and have persuasive tongues, they have filled your ears with their loud and inveterate calumnies. And this is the reason why my three accusers, Meletus and Anytus and Lycon, have set upon me; Meletus, who has a quarrel with me on behalf of the poets; Anytus, on behalf of the craftsmen and politicians; Lycon, on behalf of the rhetoricians: and as I said at the beginning, I cannot expect to get rid of such a mass of calumny all in a moment. And this, O men of Athens, is the truth and the whole truth; I have concealed nothing, I have dissembled nothing. And yet, I know that my plainness of speech makes them hate me, and what is their hatred but a proof that I am speaking the truth?——Hence has arisen the prejudice against me; and this is the reason of it, as you will find out either in this or in any future enquiry.

I have said enough in my defence against the first class of my accusers; I turn to the second class. They are headed by Meletus, that good man and true lover of his country, as he calls himself. Against these, too, I must try to make a defence:——Let their affidavit be read: it contains something of this kind: It says that Socrates is a doer of evil, who corrupts the youth; and who does not believe in the gods of the state, but has other new divinities of his own. Such is the charge; and now let us examine the particular counts. He says that I am a doer of evil, and corrupt the youth; but I say, O men of Athens, that Meletus is a doer of evil, in that he pretends to be in earnest when he is only in jest, and is so eager to bring men to trial from a pretended zeal and interest about matters in which he really never had the smallest interest. And the truth of this I will endeavour to prove to you.

Come hither, Meletus, and let me ask a question of you. You think a great deal about the improvement of youth?

Yes, I do.

Tell the judges, then, who is their improver; for you must know, as you have taken the pains to discover their corrupter, and are citing and accusing me before them. Speak, then, and tell the judges who their improver is.——Observe, Meletus, that you are silent, and have nothing to say. But is not this rather disgraceful, and a very considerable proof of what I was saying, that you have no interest in the matter? Speak up, friend, and tell us who their improver is.

The laws.

But that, my good sir, is not my meaning. I want to know who the person is, who, in the first place, knows the laws.

The judges,[6] Socrates, who are present in court.

What, do you mean to say, Meletus, that they are able to instruct and improve youth?

Certainly they are.

What, all of them, or some only and not others?

All of them.

By the goddess Hera, that is good news! There are plenty of improvers, then. And what do you say of the audience,—do they improve them?

Yes, they do.

And the senators?

Yes, the senators improve them.

But perhaps the members of the assembly corrupt them?—or do they too improve them?

They improve them.

Then every Athenian improves and elevates them; all with the exception of myself; and I alone am their corrupter? Is that what you affirm?

6. Or jury; cases were judged by panels of as many as 500 fellow citizens.

That is what I stoutly affirm.

I am very unfortunate if you are right. But suppose I ask you a question: How about horses? Does one man do them harm and all the world good? Is not the exact opposite the truth? One man is able to do them good, or at least not many;—the trainer of horses, that is to say, does them good, and others who have to do with them rather injure them? Is not that true, Meletus, of horses, or of any other animals? Most assuredly it is; whether you and Anytus say yes or no. Happy indeed would be the condition of youth if they had one corrupter only, and all the rest of the world were their improvers. But you, Meletus, have sufficiently shown that you never had a thought about the young: your carelessness is seen in your not caring about the very things which you bring against me.

And now, Meletus, I will ask you another question—by Zeus I will: Which is better, to live among bad citizens, or among good ones? Answer, friend, I say; the question is one which may be easily answered. Do not the good do their neighbours good, and the bad do them evil?

Certainly.

And is there any one who would rather be injured than benefited by those who live with him? Answer, my good friend, the law requires you to answer—does any one like to be injured?

Certainly not.

And when you accuse me of corrupting and deteriorating the youth, do you allege that I corrupt them intentionally or unintentionally?

Intentionally, I say.

But you have just admitted that the good do their neighbours good, and evil do them evil. Now, is that a truth which your superior wisdom has recognized thus early in life, and am I, at my age, in such darkness and ignorance as not to know that if a man with whom I have to live is corrupted by me, I am very likely to be harmed by him; and yet I corrupt him, and intentionally, too—so you say, although neither I nor any other human being is ever likely to be convinced by you. But either I do not corrupt them, or I corrupt them unintentionally; and on either view of the case you lie. If my offense is unintentional, the law has no cognizance of unintentional offences: you ought to have taken me privately, and warned and admonished me; for if I had been better advised, I should have left off doing what I only did unintentionally—no doubt I should; but you would have nothing to say to me and refused to teach me. And now you bring me up in this court, which is a place not of instruction, but of punishment.

It will be very clear to you, Athenians, as I was saying, that Meletus has no care at all, great or small, about the matter. But still I should like to know, Meletus, in what I am affirmed to corrupt the young. I suppose you mean, as I infer from your indictment, that I teach them not to acknowledge the gods which the state acknowledges, but some other new divinities or spiritual agencies in their stead. These are the lessons by which I corrupt the youth, as you say.

Yes, that I say emphatically.

Then, by the gods, Meletus, of whom we are speaking, tell me and the court, in somewhat plainer terms, what you mean! for I do not as yet understand whether you affirm that I teach other men to acknowledge some gods, and therefore that I do believe in gods, and am not an entire atheist—this you do not lay to my charge,—but only you say that they are not the same gods which the city recognizes—the charge is that they are different gods. Or, do you mean that I am an atheist simply, and a teacher of atheism?

I mean the latter—that you are a complete atheist.

What an extraordinary statement! Why do you think so, Meletus? Do you mean that I do not believe in the godhead of the sun or moon, like other men?

I assure you, judges, that he does not: for he says that the sun is stone, and the moon earth.

Friend Meletus, you think that you are accusing Anaxagoras:[7] and you have but a bad opinion of the judges, if you fancy them illiterate to such a degree as not to know that these doctrines are found in the books of Anaxagoras the Clazomenian, which are full of them. And so, forsooth, the youth are said to be taught them by Socrates, when there are not unfrequently exhibitions of them at the theatre (price of admission one drachma at the most); and they might pay their money, and laugh at Socrates if he pretends to father these extraordinary views. And so, Meletus, you really think that I do not believe in any god?

I swear by Zeus that you believe absolutely in none at all.

Nobody will believe you, Meletus, and I am pretty sure that you do not believe yourself. I cannot help thinking, men of Athens, that Meletus is reckless and impudent, and that he has written this indictment in a spirit of mere wantonness and youthful bravado. Has he not compounded a riddle, thinking to try me? He said to himself:—I shall see whether the wise Socrates will discover my facetious contradiction, or whether I shall be able to deceive him and the rest of them. For he certainly does appear to me to contradict himself in the indictment as much as if he said that Socrates is guilty of not believing in the gods, and yet of believing in them—but this is not like a person who is in earnest.

I should like you, O men of Athens, to join me in examining what I conceive to be his inconsistency; and do you, Meletus, answer. And I must remind the audience of my request that they would not make a disturbance if I speak in my accustomed manner:

Did ever man, Meletus, believe in the existence of human things, and not of human beings? . . . I wish, men of Athens, that he would answer, and not be always trying to get up, an interruption. Did ever any man believe in horsemanship, and not in horses? or in flute-playing, and not in flute-players? No, my friend; I will answer to you and to the court, as you refuse to answer for yourself. There is no man who ever did. But now please to answer the next question: Can a man believe in spiritual and divine agencies, and not in spirits or demigods?

He cannot.

How lucky I am to have extracted that answer, by the assistance of the court! But then you swear in the indictment that I teach and believe in divine or spiritual agencies (new or old, no matter for that); at any rate, I believe in spiritual agencies,—so you say and swear in the affidavit; and yet if I believe in divine beings, how can I help believing in spirits or demigods;—must I not? To be sure I must; and therefore I may assume that your silence gives consent. Now what are spirits or demigods? are they not either gods or the sons of gods?

Certainly they are.

But this is what I call the facetious riddle invented by you: the demigods or spirits are gods, and you say first that I do not believe in gods, and then again that I do believe in gods; that is, if I believe in demigods. For if the demigods are the illegitimate

---

7. A philosopher tried for impiety.

sons of gods, whether by the nymphs or by any other mothers, of whom they are said to be the sons—what human being will ever believe that there are no gods if they are the sons of gods? You might as well affirm the existence of mules, and deny that of horses and asses. Such nonsense, Meletus, could only have been intended by you to make trial of me. You have put this into the indictment because you had nothing real of which to accuse me. But no one who has a particle of understanding will ever be convinced by you that the same men can believe in divine and superhuman things, and yet not believe that there are gods and demigods and heroes.

I have said enough in answer to the charge of Meletus: any elaborate defence is unnecessary; but I know only too well how many are the enmities which I have incurred, and this is what will be my destruction if I am destroyed;—not Meletus, nor yet Anytus, but the envy and detraction of the world, which has been the death of many good men, and will probably be the death of many more; there is no danger of my being the last of them.

Someone will say: And are you not ashamed, Socrates, of a course of life which is likely to bring you to an untimely end? To him I may fairly answer: There you are mistaken: a man who is good for anything ought not to calculate the chance of living or dying; he ought only to consider whether in doing anything he is doing right or wrong—acting the part of a good man or of a bad. Whereas, upon your view, the heroes who fell at Troy were not good for much, and the son of Thetis[8] above all, who altogether despised danger in comparison with disgrace; and when he was so eager to slay Hector, his goddess mother said to him, that if he avenged his companion Patroclus, and slew Hector, he would die himself—"Fate," she said, in these or the like words, "waits for you next after Hector"; he, receiving this warning, utterly despised danger and death, and instead of fearing them, feared rather to live in dishonour, and not to avenge his friend. "Let me die forthwith," he replies, "and be avenged of my enemy, rather than abide here by the beaked ships, a laughing-stock and a burden of the earth." Had Achilles any thought of death and danger? For wherever a man's place is, whether the place which he has chosen or that in which he has been placed by a commander, there he ought to remain in the hour of danger; he should not think of death or of anything but of disgrace. And this, O men of Athens, is a true saying.

Strange, indeed, would be my conduct, O men of Athens, if I who, when I was ordered by the generals whom you chose to command me at Potidaea and Amphipolis and Delium,[9] remained where they placed me, like any other man, facing death—if now, when, as I conceive and imagine, God orders me to fulfil the philosopher's mission of searching into myself and other men, I were to desert my post through fear of death, or any other fear; that would indeed be strange, and I might justly be arraigned in court for denying the existence of the gods, if I disobeyed the oracle because I was afraid of death, fancying that I was wise when I was not wise. For the fear of death is indeed the pretence of wisdom, and not real wisdom, being a pretence of knowing the unknown; and no one knows whether death, which men in their fear apprehend to be the greatest evil, may not be the greatest good. Is not this ignorance of a disgraceful sort, the ignorance which is the conceit that man knows what he does not know? And in this respect only I believe myself to differ from men in general, and may perhaps claim to be wiser than they are:—that whereas I know but little of the world below, I do not suppose that I know: but I do know that injustice and disobedience to a better,

8. Achilles.

9. As a younger man, Socrates had been a foot soldier in these battles during the Peloponnesian War.

whether God or man, is evil and dishonourable, and I will never fear or avoid a possible good rather than a certain evil.

And therefore if you let me go now, and are not convinced by Anytus, who said that since I had been prosecuted I must be put to death (or if not that I ought never to have been prosecuted at all); and that if I escape now, your sons will all be utterly ruined by listening to my words—if you say to me, Socrates, this time we will not mind Anytus, and you shall be let off, but upon one condition, that you are not to enquire and speculate in this way any more, and that if you are caught doing so again you shall die;—if this was the condition on which you let me go, I should reply: Men of Athens, I honour and love you; but I shall obey God rather than you, and while I have life and strength I shall never cease from the practice and teaching of philosophy, exhorting any one whom I meet and saying to him after my manner: You, my friend,—a citizen of the great and mighty and wise city of Athens,—are you not ashamed of heaping up the greatest amount of money and honour and reputation, and caring so little about wisdom and truth and the greatest improvement of the soul, which you never regard or heed at all? And if the person with whom I am arguing, says: Yes, but I do care; then I do not leave him or let him go at once; but I proceed to interrogate and examine and cross-examine him, and if I think that he has no virtue in him, but only says that he has, I reproach him with undervaluing the greater, and over-valuing the less. And I shall repeat the same words to every one whom I meet, young and old, citizen and alien, but especially to the citizens, inasmuch as they are my brethren.

For know that this is the command of God; and I believe that no greater good has ever happened in the state than my service to the God. For I do nothing but go about persuading you all, old and young alike, not to take thought for your persons or your properties, but first and chiefly to care about the greatest improvement of the soul. I tell you that virtue is not given by money, but that from virtue comes money and every other good of man, public as well as private. This is my teaching, and if this is the doctrine which corrupts the youth, I am a mischievous person. But if any one says that this is not my teaching, he is speaking an untruth. Wherefore, O men of Athens, I say to you, do as Anytus bids or not as Anytus bids, and either acquit me or not; but whichever you do, understand that I shall never alter my ways, not even if I have to die many times.

Men of Athens, do not interrupt, but hear me; there was an understanding between us that you should hear me to the end: I have something more to say, at which you may be inclined to cry out; but I believe that to hear me will be good for you, and therefore I beg that you will not cry out. I would have you know, that if you kill such a one as I am, you will injure yourselves more than you will injure me. Nothing will injure me, not Meletus nor yet Anytus—they cannot, for a bad man is not permitted to injure a better than himself. I do not deny that Anytus may, perhaps, kill him, or drive him into exile, or deprive him of civil rights; and he may imagine, and others may imagine, that he is inflicting a great injury upon him: but there I do not agree. For the evil of doing as he is doing—the evil of unjustly taking away the life of another—is greater far.

And now, Athenians, I am not going to argue for my own sake, as you may think, but for yours, that you may not sin against the God by condemning me, who am his gift to you. For if you kill me you will not easily find a successor to me, who, if I may use such a ludicrous figure of speech, am a sort of gadfly,[1] given to the state by God;

---

1. Horsefly.

and the state is a great and noble steed who is tardy in his motions owing to his very size, and requires to be stirred into life. I am that gadfly which God has attached to the state, and all day long and in all places am always fastening upon you, arousing and persuading and reproaching you. You will not easily find another like me, and therefore I would advise you to spare me. I dare say that you may feel out of temper (like a person who is suddenly awakened from sleep), and you think that you might easily strike me dead as Anytus advises, and then you would sleep on for the remainder of your lives, unless God in his care of you sent you another gadfly. When I say that I am given to you by God, the proof of my mission is this:—if I had been like other men, I should not have neglected all my own concerns or patiently seen the neglect of them during all these years, and have been doing yours, coming to you individually like a father or elder brother, exhorting you to regard virtue; such conduct, I say, would be unlike human nature. If I had gained anything, or if my exhortations had been paid, there would have been some sense in my doing so; but now, as you will perceive, not even the impudence of my accusers dares to say that I have ever exacted or sought pay of any one; of that they have no witness. And I have a sufficient witness to the truth of what I say—my poverty.

Some one may wonder why I go about in private giving advice and busying myself with the concerns of others, but do not venture to come forward in public and advise the state. I will tell you why. You have heard me speak at sundry times and in divers places of an oracle or sign which comes to me, and is the divinity which Meletus ridicules in the indictment. This sign, which is a kind of voice, first began to come to me when I was a child; it always forbids but never commands me to do anything which I am going to do. This is what deters me from being a politician. And rightly, as I think. For I am certain, O men of Athens, that if I had engaged in politics, I should have perished long ago, and done no good either to you or to myself. And do not be offended at my telling you the truth: for the truth is, that no man who goes to war with you or any other multitude, honestly striving against the many lawless and unrighteous deeds which are done in a state, will save his life; he who will fight for the right, if he would live even for a brief space, must have a private station and not a public one.

I can give you convincing evidence of what I say, not words only, but what you value far more—actions. Let me relate to you a passage of my own life which will prove to you that I should never have yielded to injustice from any fear of death, and that "as I should have refused to yield" I must have died at once. I will tell you a tale of the courts, not very interesting perhaps, but nevertheless true. The only office of state which I ever held, O men of Athens, was that of senator: the tribe Antiochis, which is my tribe, had the presidency at the trial of the generals who had not taken up the bodies of the slain after the battle of Arginusae;[2] and you proposed to try them in a body, contrary to law, as you all thought afterwards; but at the time I was the only one of the Prytanes who was opposed to the illegality, and I gave my vote against you; and when the orators threatened to impeach and arrest me, and you called and shouted, I made up my mind that I would run the risk, having law and justice with me, rather than take part in your injustice because I feared imprisonment and death. This happened in the days of the democracy. But when the oligarchy of the Thirty[3] was in power, they sent for me and four others into the rotunda, and bade us bring Leon the

Salaminian from Salamis, as they wanted to put him to death. This was a specimen of the sort of commands which they were always giving with the view of implicating as many as possible in their crimes; and then I showed, not in word only but in deed, that, if I may be allowed to use such an expression, I cared not a straw for death, and that my great and only care was lest I should do an unrighteous or unholy thing. For the strong arm of that oppressive power did not frighten me into doing wrong; and when we came out of the rotunda the other four went to Salamis and fetched Leon, but I went quietly home. For which I might have lost my life, had not the power of the Thirty shortly afterwards come to an end. And many will witness to my words.

Now do you really imagine that I could have survived all these years, if I had led a public life, supposing that like a good man I had always maintained the right and had made justice, as I ought, the first thing? No indeed, men of Athens, neither I nor any other man. But I have been always the same in all my actions, public as well as private, and never have I yielded any base compliance to those who are slanderously termed my disciples, or to any other. Not that I have any regular disciples. But if any-one likes to come and hear me while I am pursuing my mission, whether he be young or old, he is not excluded. Nor do I converse only with those who pay; but anyone, whether he be rich or poor, may ask and answer me and listen to my words; and whether he turns out to be a bad man or a good one, neither result can be justly im-puted to me; for I never taught or professed to teach him anything. And if anyone says that he has ever learned or heard anything from me in private which all the world has not heard, let me tell you that he is lying.

But I shall be asked, Why do people delight in continually conversing with you? I have told you already, Athenians, the whole truth about this matter: they like to hear the cross-examination of the pretenders to wisdom; there is amusement in it. Now this duty of cross-examining other men has been imposed upon me by God; and has been signified to me by oracles, visions, and in every way in which the will of divine power was ever intimated to any one. This is true, O Athenians; or, if not true, would be soon refuted. If I am or have been corrupting the youth, those of them who are now grown up and become sensible that I gave them bad advice in the days of their youth should come forward as accusers, and take their revenge; or if they do not like to come themselves, some of their relatives, fathers, brothers, or other kinsmen, should say what evil their families have suffered at my hands.

Now is their time. Many of them I see in the court. There is Crito, who is of the same age and of the same deme with myself, and there is Critobulus his son, whom I also see. Then again there is Lysanias of Sphettus, who is the father of Aeschines—he is present; and also there is Antiphon of Cephisus, who is the father of Epigenes; and there are the brothers of several who have associated with me. There is Nicostra-tus the son of Theosdotides, and the brother of Theodotus (now Theodotus himself is dead, and therefore he, at any rate, will not seek to stop him); and there is Paralus the son of Demodocus, who had a brother Theages; and Adeimantus the son of Ariston, whose brother Plato is present; and Aeantodorus, who is the brother of Apollodorus, whom I also see. I might mention a great many others, some of whom Meletus should have produced as witnesses in the course of his speech; and let him still pro-duce them, if he has forgotten—I will make way for him. And let him say, if he has any testimony of the sort which he can produce. Nay, Athenians, the very opposite is the truth. For all these are ready to witness on behalf of the corrupter, of the injurer of their kindred, as Meletus and Anytus call me; not the corrupted youth only—there might have been a motive for that—but their uncorrupted elder relatives. Why should they too support me with their testimony? Why, indeed, except for the sake of truth and justice, and because they know that I am speaking the truth, and that Meletus is a liar.

Well, Athenians, this and the like of this is all the defence which I have to offer. Yet a word more. Perhaps there may be some one who is offended at me, when he calls to mind how he himself on a similar, or even a less serious occasion, prayed and entreated the judges with many tears, and how he produced his children in court, which was a moving spectacle, together with a host of relations and friends; whereas I, who am probably in danger of my life, will do none of these things. The contrast may occur to his mind, and he may be set against me, and vote in anger because he is displeased at me on this account. Now if there be such a person among you,—mind, I do not say that there is,—to him I may fairly reply: My friend, I am a man, and like other men, a creature of flesh and blood, and not "of wood or stone," as Homer says;[4] and I have a family, yes, and sons, O Athenians, three in number, one almost a man, and two others who are still young; and yet I will not bring any of them hither in order to petition you for an acquittal. And why not? Not from any self-assertion or want of respect for you. Whether I am or am not afraid of death is another question, of which I will not now speak. But, having regard to public opinion, I feel that such conduct would be discreditable to myself, and to you, and to the whole state. One who has reached my years, and who has a name for wisdom, ought not to demean himself.

Whether this opinion of me be deserved or not, at any rate the world has decided that Socrates is in some way superior to other men. And if those among you who are said to be superior in wisdom and courage, and any other virtue, demean themselves in this way, how shameful is their conduct! I have seen men of reputation, when they have been condemned, behaving in the strangest manner: they seemed to fancy that they were going to suffer something dreadful if they died, and that they could be immortal if you only allowed them to live; and I think that such are a dishonour to the state, and that any stranger coming in would have said of them that the most eminent men of Athens, to whom the Athenians themselves give honour and command, are no better than women. And I say that these things ought not to be done by those of us who have a reputation; and if they are done, you ought not to permit them; you ought rather to show that you are far more disposed to condemn the man who gets up a doleful scene and makes the city ridiculous, than him who holds his peace.

But, setting aside the question of public opinion, there seems to be something wrong in asking a favour of a judge, and thus procuring an acquittal, instead of informing and convincing him. For his duty is, not to make a present of justice, but to give judgment; and he has sworn that he will judge according to the laws, and not according to his own good pleasure; and we ought not to encourage you, nor should you allow yourself to be encouraged, in this habit of perjury—there can be no piety in that. Do not then require me to do what I consider dishonourable and impious and wrong, especially now, when I am being tried for impiety on the indictment of Meletus. For if, O men of Athens, by force of persuasion and entreaty I could overpower your oaths, then I should be teaching you to believe that there are no gods, and in defending should simply convict myself of the charge of not believing in them. But that is not so—far otherwise. For I do believe that there are gods, and in a sense higher than that in which any of my accusers believe in them. And to you and to God I commit my cause, to be determined by you as is best for you and me.

4. In the *Odyssey,* Book 19, line 184.

There are many reasons why I am not grieved, O men of Athens, at the vote of condemnation. I expected it, and am only surprised that the votes are so nearly equal; for I had thought that the majority against me would have been far larger; but now, had thirty votes gone over to the other side, I should have been acquitted. And I may say, I think, that I have escaped Meletus. I may say more; for without the assistance of Anytus and Lycon, anyone may see that he would not have had a fifth part of the votes, as the law requires, in which case he would have incurred a fine of a thousand drachmae.

And so he proposes death as the penalty. And what shall I propose on my part, O men of Athens? Clearly that which is my due. And what is my due? What return shall be made to the man who has never had the wit to be idle during his whole life; but has been careless of what the many care for—wealth, and family interests, and military offices, and speaking in the assembly, and magistracies, and plots, and parties. Reflecting that I was really too honest a man to be a politician and live, I did not go where I could do no good to you or to myself; but where I could do the greatest good privately to every one of you, thither I went, and sought to persuade every man among you that he must look to himself, and seek virtue and wisdom before he looks to his private interests, and look to the state before he looks to the interests of the state; and that this should be the order which he observes in all his actions. What shall be done to such a one? Doubtless some good thing, O men of Athens, if he has his reward; and the good should be of a kind suitable to him. What would be a reward suitable to a poor man who is your benefactor, and who desires leisure that he may instruct you? There can be no reward so fitting as maintenance in the Prytaneum,[5] O men of Athens, a reward which he deserves far more than the citizen who has won the prize at Olympia in the horse or chariot race, whether the chariots were drawn by two horses or by many. For I am in want, and he has enough; and he only gives you the appearance of happiness, and I give you the reality. And if I am to estimate the penalty fairly, I should say that maintenance in the Prytaneum is the just return.

Perhaps you think that I am defying you in what I am saying now, as in what I said before about the tears and prayers. But this is not so. I speak rather because I am convinced that I never intentionally wronged any one, although I cannot convince you—the time has been too short; if there were a law at Athens, as there is in other cities, that a capital cause should not be decided in one day, then I believe that I should have convinced you. But I cannot in a moment refute great slanders; and, as I am convinced that I never wronged another, I will assuredly not wrong myself. I will not say of myself that I deserve any evil, or propose any penalty. Why should I? Because I am afraid of the penalty of death which Meletus proposes? When I do not know whether death is a good or an evil, why should I propose a penalty which would certainly be an evil? Shall I say imprisonment? And why should I live in prison, and be the slave of the magistrates of the year—of the Eleven? Or shall the penalty be a fine, and imprisonment until the fine is paid? There is the same objection. I should have to lie in prison, for money I have none, and cannot pay. And if I say exile (and this may possibly be the penalty which you will affix), I must indeed be blinded by the love of life, if I am so irrational as to expect that when you, who are my own citizens, cannot endure my discourses and words, and have found them so grievous and odious that you will have no more of them, others are likely to endure me. No indeed, men of Athens, that is not very likely. And what a life should I lead, at my age, wandering from city to city, ever changing my place of exile, and always being driven

---

5. Building where officials dined at the democratic city's expense.

out! For I am quite sure that wherever I go, there, as here, the young men will flock to me; and if I drive them away, their elders will drive me out at their request; and if I let them come, their fathers and friends will drive me out for their sakes.

Some one will say: Yes, Socrates, but cannot you hold your tongue, and then you may go into a foreign city, and no one will interfere with you? Now I have great difficulty in making you understand my answer to this. For if I tell you that to do as you say would be a disobedience to the God, and therefore that I cannot hold my tongue, you will not believe that I am serious; and if I say again that daily to discourse about virtue, and of those other things about which you hear me examining myself and others, is the greatest good of man, and that the unexamined life is not worth living, you are still less likely to believe me. Yet I say what is true, although a thing of which it is hard for me to persuade you. Also, I have never been accustomed to think that I deserve to suffer any harm. Had I money I might have estimated the offence at what I was able to pay, and not have been much the worse. But I have none, and therefore I must ask you to proportion the fine to my means. Well, perhaps I could afford a mina,[6] and therefore I propose that penalty: Plato, Crito, Critobulus, and Apollodorus, my friends here, bid me say thirty minae, and they will be the sureties. Let thirty minae be the penalty; for which sum they will be ample security to you.

Not much time will be gained, O Athenians, in return for the evil name which you will get from the detractors of the city, who will say that you killed Socrates, a wise man; for they will call me wise, even although I am not wise, when they want to reproach you. If you had waited a little while, your desire would have been fulfilled in the course of nature. For I am far advanced in years, as you may perceive, and not far from death. I am speaking now not to all of you, but only to those who have condemned me to death. And I have another thing to say to them: You think that I was convicted because I had no words of the sort which would have procured my acquittal—I mean, if I had thought fit to leave nothing undone or unsaid. Not so; the deficiency which led to my conviction was not of words—certainly not. But I had not the boldness or impudence or inclination to address you as you would have liked me to do, weeping and wailing and lamenting, and saying and doing many things which you have been accustomed to hear from others, and which, as I maintain, are unworthy of me.

I thought at the time that I ought not to do anything common or mean when in danger: nor do I now repent of the style of my defence; I would rather die having spoken after my manner, than speak in your manner and live. For neither in war nor yet at law ought I or any man to use every way of escaping death. Often in battle there can be no doubt that if a man will throw away his arms, and fall on his knees before his pursuers, he may escape death; and in other dangers there are other ways of escaping death, if a man is willing to say and do anything. The difficulty, my friends, is not to avoid death, but to avoid unrighteousness; for that runs faster than death. I am old and move slowly, and the slower runner has overtaken me, and my accusers are keen and quick, and the faster runner, who is unrighteousness, has overtaken them. And now I depart hence condemned by you to suffer the penalty of death,—they too go their ways condemned by the truth to suffer the penalty of villainy and wrong; and I must abide by my award—let them abide by

---

6. According to Xenophon, this modest sum was a fifth of Socrates' possessions.

theirs. I suppose that these things may be regarded as fated,—and I think that they are well.

And now, O men who have condemned me, I would like to prophesy to you; for I am about to die, and in the hour of death men are gifted with prophetic power. And I prophesy to you who are my murderers, that immediately after my departure punishment far heavier than you have inflicted on me will surely await you. Me you have killed because you wanted to escape the accuser, and not to give an account of your lives. But that will not be as you suppose: far otherwise. For I say that there will be more accusers of you than there are now; accusers whom hitherto I have restrained: and as they are younger they will be more inconsiderate with you, and you will be more offended at them. If you think that by killing men you can prevent some one from censuring your evil lives, you are mistaken; that is not a way of escape which is either possible or honourable; the easiest and the noblest way is not to be disabling others, but to be improving yourselves. This is the prophecy which I utter before my departure to the judges who have condemned me.

Friends, who would have acquitted me, I would like also to talk with you about the thing which has come to pass, while the magistrates are busy, and before I go to the place at which I must die. Stay then a little, for we may as well talk with one another while there is time. You are my friends, and I should like to show you the meaning of this event which has happened to me. O my judges—for you I may truly call judges—I should like to tell you of a wonderful circumstance. Hitherto the divine faculty of which the internal oracle is the source has constantly been in the habit of opposing me even about trifles, if I was going to make a slip or error in any matter; and now as you see there has come upon me that which may be thought, and is generally believed to be, the last and worst evil. But the oracle made no sign of opposition, either when I was leaving my house in the morning, or when I was on my way to the court, or while I was speaking, at anything which I was going to say; and yet I have often been stopped in the middle of a speech, but now in nothing I either said or did touching the matter in hand has the oracle opposed me. What do I take to be the explanation of this silence? I will tell you. It is an intimation that what has happened to me is a good, and that those of us who think that death is an evil are in error. For the customary sign would surely have opposed me had I been going to evil and not to good.

Let us reflect in another way, and we shall see that there is great reason to hope that death is a good; for one of two things—either death is a state of nothingness and utter unconsciousness, or, as men say, there is a change and migration of the soul from this world to another. Now if you suppose that there is no consciousness, but a sleep like the sleep of him who is undisturbed even by dreams, death will be an unspeakable gain. For if a person were to select the night in which his sleep was undisturbed even by dreams, and were to compare with this the other days and nights of his life, and then were to tell us how many days and nights he had passed in the course of his life better and more pleasantly than this one, I think that any man, I will not say a private man, but even the great king[7] will not find many such days or nights, when compared with the others. Now if death be of such a nature, I say that to die is gain; for eternity is then only a single night.

But if death is the journey to another place, and there, as men say, all the dead abide, what good, O my friends and judges, can be greater than this? If indeed when

---

7. The Persian emperor.

the pilgrim arrives in the world below, he is delivered from the professors of justice in this world, and finds the true judges who are said to give judgment there, Minos and Rhadamanthus and Aeacus and Triptolemus, and other sons of God who were righteous in their own life, that pilgrimage will be worth making. What would not a man give if he might converse with Orpheus and Musaeus and Hesiod and Homer?[8] Nay, if this be true, let me die again and again. I myself, too, shall have a wonderful interest in there meeting and conversing with Palamedes, and Ajax the son of Telamon, and any other ancient hero who has suffered death through an unjust judgment; and there will be no small pleasure, as I think, in comparing my own sufferings with theirs. Above all, I shall then be able to continue my search into true and false knowledge; as in this world, so also in the next; and I shall find out who is wise, and who pretends to be wise, and is not. What would not a man give, O judges, to be able to examine the leader of the great Trojan expedition; or Odysseus or Sisyphus, or numberless others, men and women too! What infinite delight would there be in conversing with them and asking them questions! In another world they do not put a man to death for asking questions: assuredly not. For besides being happier than we are, they will be immortal, if what is said is true.

Wherefore, O judges, be of good cheer about death, and know of a certainty, that no evil can happen to a good man, either in life or after death. He and his are not neglected by the gods; nor has my own approaching end happened by mere chance. But I see clearly that the time had arrived when it was better for me to die and be released from trouble; wherefore the oracle gave no sign. For which reason, also, I am not angry with my condemners, or with my accusers; they have done me no harm, although they did not mean to do me any good; and for this I may gently blame them.

Still I have a favour to ask of them. When my sons are grown up, I would ask you, O my friends, to punish them; and I would have you trouble them, as I have troubled you, if they seem to care about riches, or anything, more than about virtue; or if they pretend to be something when they are really nothing,—then reprove them, as I have reproved you, for not caring about that for which they ought to care, and thinking that they are something when they are really nothing. And if you do this, both I and my sons will have received justice at your hands.

The hour of departure has arrived, and we go our ways—I to die, and you to live. Which is better God only knows.

❦ CROSSCURRENTS: TYRANNY AND DEMOCRACY ❦

- The tragedies of fifth-century B.C.E. Athens used the context of the legendary past and the format of drama to raise questions regarding the limits of individual power and the relationship between individuals and the state. In what ways does the political organization of Athens during this period manifest itself within the predemocratic settings of plays such as Aeschylus's *Agamemnon* (page 579) and Sophocles's *Oedipus the King* (page 618) and *Antigone* (page 656)?

- The ancient South Asian epics *The Ramayana* (page 864) and *The Mahabharata* (page 809) approach the question of the meaning and extent of power within the context of kingly rule. How does the presence or absence of a political conception of democracy affect the presentation and meaning of power?

8. The four legendary founders of poetry.

- Perhaps the most famous meditation on power in Western literature is Niccolò Machiavelli's *The Prince* (Volume C). How does Machiavelli's portrayal of politics in the city-state of Florence compare with the conceptions discussed here regarding fifth-century B.C.E. Athens?

- The concept of "nation" was essential to nineteenth-century political theory. The Perspectives section "The National Poet" (Volume E) presents a selection of literary meditations on what it means to be part of a nation. How do these different conceptions of nation compare with the ideas about democracy in classical Greece?

⇥⊰ END OF PERSPECTIVES: TYRANNY AND DEMOCRACY ⊱⇤

Euripides

c. 480–405 B.C.E.

The Greeks found Euripides peculiar. His tragedies featured talking slaves, extravagantly demonstrative women, and rhetorical excesses previously unheard in the works of his predecessors. He was said to be the son of a lettuce monger, to compose his tragedies in isolation in a cave, and even to own a library full of books, a great oddity in a world of limited literacy. In the drama contests organized by the city to honor the god Dionysos, in which Euripides' plays were performed, he often lost. Yet we have more of his tragedies than of any other Greek playwright, nineteen of the ninety he wrote.

In his tragedies, Euripides represents a complex mixture of the ordinary, the everyday, and the radically deviant, calling attention to the deep strangeness of tragedy, a genre that crosses the world of heroic legend with the daily life of the citizen audience. Maidservants scheme calmly about adultery. The deposed queen of Troy, Hecuba, who after the city's fall is a slave, murders her enemy's children; it is predicted in the tragedy named for her that she will end her life changed to a dog, "a bitch with blazing eyes."

Euripides' gods exhibit cruelty and petty selfishness and torment human beings for their own amusement. The goddesses Artemis and Aphrodite fight over the sexual fate of the chaste misogynist Hippolytus, entangled in the desire of his stepmother, Phaedra; accused of seduction, he dies a battered wreck in the arms of his father. The god Dionysos, in the *Bacchae,* seduces Thebes' king, Pentheus, into dressing as a woman so that he can spy on the maenads, the maddened women worshipers of the god. Dionysos provokes his devotees, including Pentheus's own mother, into a frenzy in which the king is torn to pieces, his head brought home as a trophy by his mother; in a devastating recognition scene, she slowly realizes what she carries.

Euripides takes seriously the human status of women, children, slaves, barbarians, foreigners, and prisoners of war and gives them voices in his tragedies, decentering the focus on the free Greek male citizen typical of the ancient city. He demonstrates a special fascination for women, their psychology, their motivations, and their fates. Several of his tragedies focus on idealistic young women who choose to sacrifice themselves for their idealism and are exploited by older characters of great cynicism; Iphigeneia, for example, dies at the hands of her father, Agamemnon, who sacrifices her so that the Greek fleet can sail to Troy from Aulis, where the fleet has been stalled for an offense committed against the goddess Artemis. In *Alcestis,* a husband allows his wife to die in his place and then, immediately after promising never to replace

A Maenad cup by the Brygos Painter, mid-first millennium B.C.E. The maenad carries her thyrsus (a staff crowned with pine cones, symbol of Dionysos) and a small leopard she has just slain, probably to make another fur stole like the one she wears around her neck, identifying with the leopard's wild, foreign power.

her, receives into his household what he believes to be another woman. In other plays, the choruses are made up of enslaved women who lament their losses of loved ones and of freedom, as in *The Trojan Women:*

> Beside their altars the Trojans
> died in their blood. Desolate now,
> men murdered, our sleeping rooms gave up
> their brides' beauty
> to breed sons for Greek men,
> sorrow for our own country.

Such lines speak to the audience of slaveholders and touch on both their status as the possessors of other human beings and their vulnerability to enslavement themselves, in a world of war where the killing of men and the enslaving of women in conquered cities was often a matter of course. It may be that radical thinkers of this period were questioning whether slaves were slaves "by nature." In one dramatic scene in the *Ion,* a slave pronounces what may have seemed to some like a heretical idea: "A slave bears only this / Disgrace: the name. In every other way / An honest slave is equal to the free." Euripides returns several times to the aftermath of the fall of Troy, the paradigmatic city whose conquest stood for the loss of civilization itself. Rather than showing the scenes of warriors in the long battle that preceded the Greeks' victory, he concentrates on the Trojan victims, the humiliation and sexual slavery of the former free inhabitants, royal princesses taken to the lands of their conquerors and forced into new masters' beds.

In his own time Euripides was the object of mockery for his questioning of the status quo and for his peculiarities. The comic playwright Aristophanes ridicules him frequently, presenting in *The Women at the Thesmophoria* the case that the women of the city are furious at Euripides for his misogyny and want to destroy him. In his play *The Frogs,* first performed in 405 B.C.E., Aristophanes sends the god Dionysos, portrayed as a coward and a fool, and his slave Xanthias into the underworld to bring the recently deceased Euripides back from the dead. The comedy engages in a merciless and hilarious attack on Euripides, who is seen ultimately, after a drama contest between him and Aeschylus, as precisely not what the world above needs.

Euripides' plays call into question the heroism of traditional heroes such as Jason, husband of Medea, or Admetus, Alcestis' mate. They expose the all-too-human motives of the gods. They deploy the highly wrought argumentation of the contemporary rhetoricians and the sophists. They put into play new forms of music and almost operatic lyricism. The plays partake of the critical, questioning spirit of the later fifth century B.C.E., a world of exhausting war, with the Athenian democracy rocked by power struggles between manipulative orators, soon to be overwhelmed in defeat by the Spartans and their allies. The intellectual climate favored questioning everything—received ideas about the gods, forms of government and political hierarchies, the divine or noble origin of the Athenians, differences among Greeks and between Greeks and barbarians, the ambiguous power of rhetorical speech, the nature of slavery, and gender roles and relations. And Euripides, without committing himself definitively, presents the contradictory difficulties for his audiences.

THE MEDEA

One of the plays that most dramatically embodies these contradictions, *The Medea,* was produced in 431 B.C.E., at the time when the Peloponnesian War between the Athenians and the Spartans began and when the Athenians suffered a devastating plague that eventually carried off the great statesman Perikles. The play shares many of the concerns of other Euripidean dramas: a focus on women, with a servant taking an important role; rhetoric influenced by philosophical developments of the latter half of the fifth century; a questioning of traditional morality; and a central role for an outsider, in this case a barbarian woman, Medea, brought into the heart of Greece by her husband, Jason. The play fastens on her difference—her exotic origins and her history as a sorceress, her murder of her own brother and the fatal boiling of an old man in a fake effort of rejuvenation. It places this barbarian witch in the heart of the household and gives her a speech in which she laments the fate of the Greek woman. She stands apart by virtue of her foreign birth, yet expresses the common dismay of a wife whose man can seek comfort elsewhere while she is confined to the house. Medea says she would prefer military combat to childbirth.

Greek brides, often half the age of husbands they had barely met by their wedding day, were taken from their fathers' houses and moved into the houses of their husbands' fathers as strangers in the midst of an unfamiliar domestic life. Like the mythical women warriors called the Amazons, or the women of the island of Lemnos, who killed their husbands and administered their island themselves, Medea represents the danger at the center of the Greek household, the female brought inside, a potential source of discontent and even violence. Euripides shows Medea first as dangerously jealous, then scheming, and then violent, vengeful, and destructive, escaping from the city of Corinth only to flee to Athens, to the site of the play's first performance. Euripides cunningly twists his portrait of Medea in the course of the play. She may begin as an object of sympathy, suffering like any wife at the prospect of her husband's new alliance. As the play continues, her bestial, barbaric nature comes into the foreground, and she becomes an exemplar of the ruthless, violent, and strange. Her extreme violence may exceed the incipient sympathy of the audience and send it away from the theater in horror and revulsion. Some scholars see Euripides representing Medea throughout as the object of sympathy and identification; others argue, however, that Euripides seems to understand her, along with other women, as vulnerable, as the canary in the mine, liable to break down in situations of extremity and, victims themselves, to turn toward acts of passionate despair and hatred that bring down the world.

PRONUNCIATIONS:
> *Aegeus:* ay-GEE-us
> *Euripides:* you-RIP-pid-eez
> *Medea:* meh-DEE-ah

The Medea[1]

Characters

MEDEA, *princess of Colchis and wife of*
JASON, *son of Aeson, king of Iolcus*
TWO CHILDREN OF MEDEA AND JASON
CREON, *king of Corinth*
AEGEUS, *king of Athens*
NURSE TO MEDEA
TUTOR TO MEDEA'S CHILDREN
MESSENGER
CHORUS OF CORINTHIAN WOMEN

In front of Medea's house in Corinth. Enter from the house Medea's nurse.

NURSE: How I wish the Argo[2] never had reached the land
Of Colchis,[3] skimming through the blue Symplegades,[4]
Nor ever had fallen in the glades of Pelion
The smitten fir-tree to furnish oars for the hands
5   Of heroes who in Pelias' name attempted
The Golden Fleece! For then my mistress Medea
Would not have sailed for the towers of the land of Iolcus,[5]
Her heart on fire with passionate love for Jason;
Nor would she have persuaded the daughters of Pelias
10   To kill their father, and now be living here
In Corinth with her husband and children. She gave
Pleasure to the people of her land of exile,
And she herself helped Jason in every way.
This is indeed the greatest salvation of all—
15   For the wife not to stand apart from the husband.
But now there's hatred everywhere, Love is diseased.
For, deserting his own children and my mistress,
Jason has taken a royal wife to his bed,
The daughter of the ruler of this land, Creon.
20   And poor Medea is slighted, and cries aloud on the
Vows they made to each other, the right hands clasped
In eternal promise. She calls upon the gods to witness
What sort of return Jason has made to her love.
She lies without food and gives herself up to suffering,
25   Wasting away every moment of the day in tears.

---

1. Translated by Rex Warner.
2. Ship of Jason and the Argonauts.
3. On the east coast of the Black Sea.

4. The "Clashing Rocks" at the entrance to the Black Sea.
5. In northern Greece.

So it has gone since she knew herself slighted by him.
Not stirring an eye, not moving her face from the ground,
No more than either a rock or surging sea water
She listens when she is given friendly advice.
30   Except that sometimes she twists back her white neck and
Moans to herself, calling out on her father's name,
And her land, and her home betrayed when she came away with
A man who now is determined to dishonor her.
Poor creature, she has discovered by her sufferings
35   What it means to one not to have lost one's own country.
She has turned from the children and does not like to see them.
I am afraid she may think of some dreadful thing,
For her heart is violent. She will never put up with
The treatment she is getting. I know and fear her
40   Lest she may sharpen a sword and thrust to the heart,
Stealing into the palace where the bed is made,
Or even kill the king and the new-wedded groom,
And thus bring a greater misfortune on herself.
She's a strange woman. I know it won't be easy
45   To make an enemy of her and come off best.
But here the children come. They have finished playing.
They have no thought at all of their mother's trouble.
Indeed it is not usual for the young to grieve.

[*Enter from the right the slave who is the tutor to Medea's two small children. The children follow him.*]

TUTOR: You old retainer of my mistress' household,
50   Why are you standing here all alone in front of the
Gates and moaning to yourself over your misfortune?
Medea could not wish you to leave her alone.

NURSE: Old man, and guardian of the children of Jason,
If one is a good servant, it's a terrible thing
55   When one's master's luck is out; it goes to one's heart.
So I myself have got into such a state of grief
That a longing stole over me to come outside here
And tell the earth and air of my mistress' sorrows.

TUTOR: Has the poor lady not yet given up her crying?

NURSE: Given up? She's at the start, not halfway through her tears.

TUTOR: Poor fool—if I may call my mistress such a name—
How ignorant she is of trouble more to come.

NURSE: What do you mean, old man? You needn't fear to speak.

TUTOR: Nothing. I take back the words which I used just now.

NURSE: Don't, by your beard, hide this from me, your fellow-servant.
If need be, I'll keep quiet about what you tell me.

TUTOR: I heard a person saying, while I myself seemed
Not to be paying attention, when I was at the place
Where the old draught-players sit, by the holy fountain,
70   That Creon, ruler of the land, intends to drive
These children and their mother in exile from Corinth.

But whether what he said is really true or not
I do not know. I pray that it may not be true.

NURSE: And will Jason put up with it that his children
75   Should suffer so, though he's no friend to their mother?

TUTOR: Old ties give place to new ones. As for Jason, he
No longer has a feeling for this house of ours.

NURSE: It's black indeed for us, when we add new to old
Sorrows before even the present sky has cleared.

TUTOR: But you be silent, and keep all this to yourself.
It is not the right time to tell our mistress of it.

NURSE: Do you hear, children, what a father he is to you?
I wish he were dead—but no, he is still my master.
Yet certainly he has proved unkind to his dear ones.

TUTOR: What's strange in that? Have you only just discovered
That everyone loves himself more than his neighbor?
Some have good reason, others get something out of it.
So Jason neglects his children for the new bride.

NURSE: Go indoors, children. That will be the best thing.
90   And you, keep them to themselves as much as possible.
Don't bring them near their mother in her angry mood.
For I've seen her already blazing her eyes at them
As though she meant some mischief and I am sure that
She'll not stop raging until she has struck at someone.
95   May it be an enemy and not a friend she hurts!

[Medea is heard inside the house.]

MEDEA: Ah, wretch! Ah, lost in my sufferings,
I wish, I wish I might die.

NURSE: What did I say, dear children? Your mother
Frets her heart and frets it to anger.
100   Run away quickly into the house,
And keep well out of her sight.
Don't go anywhere near, but be careful
Of the wildness and bitter nature
Of that proud mind.
105   Go now! Run quickly indoors.
It is clear that she soon will put lightning
In that cloud of her cries that is rising
With a passion increasing. O, what will she do,
Proud-hearted and not to be checked on her course,
110   A soul bitten into with wrong?

[The Tutor takes the children into the house.]

MEDEA: Ah, I have suffered
What should be wept for bitterly. I hate you,
Children of a hateful mother. I curse you
And your father. Let the whole house crash.

NURSE: Ah, I pity you, you poor creature.
How can your children share in their father's

Wickedness? Why do you hate them? Oh children,
How much I fear that something may happen!
Great people's tempers are terrible, always
120   Having their own way, seldom checked,
Dangerous they shift from mood to mood.
How much better to have been accustomed
To live on equal terms with one's neighbors.
I would like to be safe and grow old in a
125   Humble way. What is moderate sounds best,
Also in practice *is* best for everyone.
Greatness brings no profit to people.
God indeed, when in anger, brings
Greater ruin to great men's houses.

[*Enter, on the right, a Chorus of Corinthian Women. They have come to inquire about Medea and to attempt to console her.*]

CHORUS: I heard the voice, I heard the cry
Of Colchis' wretched daughter.
Tell me, mother, is she not yet
At rest? Within the double gates
Of the court I heard her cry. I am sorry
135   For the sorrow of this home. O, say, what has happened?
NURSE: There is no home. It's over and done with.
Her husband holds fast to his royal wedding,
While she, my mistress, cries out her eyes
There in her room, and takes no warmth from
140   Any word of any friend.
MEDEA: Oh, I wish
That lightning from heaven would split my head open.
Oh, what use have I now for life?
I would find my release in death
145   And leave hateful existence behind me.
CHORUS: O God and Earth and Heaven!
Did you hear what a cry was that
Which the sad wife sings?
Poor foolish one, why should you long
150   For that appalling rest?
The final end of death comes fast.
No need to pray for that.
Suppose your man gives honor
To another woman's bed.
155   It often happens. Don't be hurt.
God will be your friend in this.
You must not waste away
Grieving too much for him who shared your bed.
MEDEA: Great Themis, lady Artemis,[6] behold

_____

6. Goddess of justice, virgins, and the hunt.

160   The things I suffer, though I made him promise,
         My hateful husband. I pray that I may see him,
         Him and his bride and all their palace shattered
         For the wrong they dare to do me without cause.
         Oh, my father! Oh, my country! In what dishonor
165   I left you, killing my own brother for it.
NURSE: Do you hear what she says, and how she cries
         On Themis, the goddess of Promises, and on Zeus,
         Whom we believe to be the Keeper of Oaths?
         Of this I am sure, that no small thing
170   Will appease my mistress' anger.
CHORUS: Will she come into our presence?
         Will she listen when we are speaking
         To the words we say?
         I wish she might relax her rage
175   And temper of her heart.
         My willingness to help will never
         Be wanting to my friends.
         But go inside and bring her
         Out of the house to us,
180   And speak kindly to her: hurry,
         Before she wrongs her own.
         This passion of hers moves to something great.
NURSE: I will, but I doubt if I'll manage
         To win my mistress over.
185   But still I'll attempt it to please you.
         Such a look she will flash on her servants
         If any comes near with a message,
         Like a lioness guarding her cubs.
         It is right, I think, to consider
190   Both stupid and lacking in foresight
         Those poets of old who wrote songs
         For revels and dinners and banquets,
         Pleasant sounds for men living at ease;
         But none of them all has discovered
195   How to put to an end with their singing
         Or musical instruments grief,
         Bitter grief, from which death and disaster
         Cheat the hopes of a house. Yet how good
         If music could cure men of this! But why raise
200   To no purpose the voice at a banquet? For *there* is
         Already abundance of pleasure for men
         With a joy of its own.

    [*The Nurse goes into the house.*]

CHORUS: I heard a shriek that is laden with sorrow.
         Shrilling out her hard grief she cries out
205   Upon him who betrayed both her bed and her marriage.
         Wronged, she calls on the gods,

On the justice of Zeus, the oath sworn,
Which brought her away
To the opposite shore of the Greeks
210   Through the gloomy salt straits to the gateway
Of the salty unlimited sea.

[*Medea, attended by servants, comes out of the house.*]

MEDEA: Women of Corinth, I have come outside to you
Lest you should be indignant with me; for I know
That many people are overproud, some when alone,
215   And others when in company. And those who live
Quietly, as I do, get a bad reputation.
For a just judgment is not evident in the eyes
When a man at first sight hates another, before
Learning his character, being in no way injured;
220   And a foreigner especially must adapt himself.
I'd not approve of even a fellow-countryman
Who by pride and want of manners offends his neighbors.
But on me this thing has fallen so unexpectedly,
It has broken my heart. I am finished. I let go
225   All my life's joy. My friends, I only want to die.
It was everything to me to think well of one man,
And he, my own husband, has turned out wholly vile.
Of all things which are living and can form a judgment
We women are the most unfortunate creatures.
230   Firstly, with an excess of wealth it is required
For us to buy a husband and take for our bodies
A master; for not to take one is even worse.
And now the question is serious whether we take
A good or bad one; for there is no easy escape
235   For a woman, nor can she say no to her marriage.
She arrives among new modes of behavior and manners,
And needs prophetic power, unless she has learned at home,
How best to manage him who shares the bed with her.
And if we work out all this well and carefully,
240   And the husband lives with us and lightly bears his yoke,
Then life is enviable. If not, I'd rather die.
A man, when he's tired of the company in his home,
Goes out of the house and puts an end to his boredom
And turns to a friend or companion of his own age.
245   But we are forced to keep our eyes on one alone.
What they say of us is that we have a peaceful time
Living at home, while they do the fighting in war.
How wrong they are! I would very much rather stand
Three times in the front of battle than bear one child.
250   Yet what applies to me does not apply to you.
You have a country. Your family home is here.
You enjoy life and the company of your friends.
But I am deserted, a refugee, thought nothing of

By my husband—something he won in a foreign land.
255 I have no mother or brother, nor any relation
With whom I can take refuge in this sea of woe.
This much then is the service I would beg from you:
If I can find the means or devise any scheme
To pay my husband back for what he has done to me—
260 Him and his father-in-law and the girl who married him—
Just to keep silent. For in other ways a woman
Is full of fear, defenseless, dreads the sight of cold
Steel; but, when once she is wronged in the matter of love,
No other soul can hold so many thoughts of blood.
CHORUS: This I will promise. You are in the right, Medea,
In paying your husband back. I am not surprised at you
For being sad.
            But look! I see our King Creon
Approaching. He will tell us of some new plan.

[*Enter, from the right, Creon, with attendants.*]

CREON: You, with that angry look, so set against your husband,
270 Medea, I order you to leave my territories
An exile, and take along with you your two children,
And not to waste time doing it. It is my decree,
And I will see it done. I will not return home
Until you are cast from the boundaries of my land.
MEDEA: Oh, this is the end for me. I am utterly lost.
Now I am in the full force of the storm of hate
And have no harbor from ruin to reach easily.
Yet still, in spite of it all, I'll ask the question:
What is your reason, Creon, for banishing me?
CREON: I am afraid of you—why should I dissemble it?—
Afraid that you may injure my daughter mortally.
Many things accumulate to support my feeling.
You are a clever woman, versed in evil arts,
And are angry at having lost your husband's love.
285 I hear that you are threatening, so they tell me,
To do something against my daughter and Jason
And me, too. I shall take my precautions first.
I tell you, I prefer to earn your hatred now
Than to be soft-hearted and afterward regret it.
MEDEA: This is not the first time, Creon. Often previously
Through being considered clever I have suffered much
A person of sense ought never to have his children
Brought up to be more clever than the average.
For, apart from cleverness bringing them no profit,
295 It will make them objects of envy and ill-will.
If you put new ideas before the eyes of fools
They'll think you foolish and worthless into the bargain;
And if you are thought superior to those who have
Some reputation for learning, you will become hated.

300 I have some knowledge myself of how this happens;
For being clever, I find that some will envy me,
Others object to me. Yet all my cleverness
Is not so much.
Well, then, are you frightened, Creon,
That I should harm you? There is no need. It is not
305 My way to transgress the authority of a king.
How have you injured me? You gave your daughter away
To the man you wanted. Oh, certainly I hate
My husband, but you, I think, have acted wisely;
Nor do I grudge it you that your affairs go well.
310 May the marriage be a lucky one! Only let me
Live in this land. For even though I have been wronged,
I will not raise my voice, but submit to my betters.
CREON: What you say sounds gentle enough. Still in my heart
I greatly dread that you are plotting some evil,
315 And therefore I trust you even less than before.
A sharp-tempered woman, or, for that matter, a man,
Is easier to deal with than the clever type
Who holds her tongue. No. You must go. No need for more
Speeches. The thing is fixed. By no manner of means
320 Shall you, an enemy of mine, stay in my country.
MEDEA: I beg you. By your knees, by your new-wedded girl.
CREON: Your words are wasted. You will never persuade me.
MEDEA: Will you drive me out, and give no heed to my prayers?
CREON: I will, for I love my family more than you.
MEDEA: O my country! How bitterly now I remember you!
CREON: I love my country too—next after my children.
MEDEA: Oh what an evil to men is passionate love!
CREON: That would depend on the luck that goes along with it.
MEDEA: O God, do not forget who is the cause of this!
CREON: Go. It is no use. Spare me the pain of forcing you.
MEDEA: I'm spared no pain. I lack no pain to be spared me.
CREON: Then you'll be removed by force by one of my men.
MEDEA: No, Creon, not that! But do listen, I beg you.
CREON: Woman, you seem to want to create a disturbance.
MEDEA: I *will* go into exile. *This* is not what I beg for.
CREON: Why then this violence and clinging to my hand?
MEDEA: Allow me to remain here just for this one day,
So I may consider where to live in my exile,
And look for support for my children, since their father
340 Chooses to make no kind of provision for them.
Have pity on them! You have children of your own.
It is natural for you to look kindly on them.
For myself I do not mind if I go into exile.
It is the children being in trouble that I mind.
CREON: There is nothing tyrannical about my nature,
And by showing mercy I have often been the loser.
Even now I know that I am making a mistake.

All the same you shall have your will. But this I tell you,
That if the light of heaven tomorrow shall see you,
350   You and your children in the confines of my land,
You die. This word I have spoken is firmly fixed.
But now, if you must stay, stay for this day alone.
For in it you can do none of the things I fear.

[*Exit Creon with his attendants.*]

CHORUS: Oh, unfortunate one! Oh, cruel!
355   Where will you turn? Who will help you?
What house or what land to preserve you
From ill can you find?
Medea, a god has thrown suffering
Upon you in waves of despair.

MEDEA: Things have gone badly every way. No doubt of that
But not these things this far, and don't imagine so.
There are still trials to come for the new-wedded pair,
And for their relations pain that will mean something.
Do you think that I would ever have fawned on that man
365   Unless I had some end to gain or profit in it?
I would not even have spoken or touched him with my hands.
But he has got to such a pitch of foolishness
That, though he could have made nothing of all my plans
By exiling me, he has given me this one day
370   To stay here, and in this I will make dead bodies
Of three of my enemies—father, the girl, and my husband.
I have many ways of death which I might suit to them,
And do not know, friends, which one to take in hand;
Whether to set fire underneath their bridal mansion,
375   Or sharpen a sword and thrust it to the heart,
Stealing into the palace where the bed is made.
There is just one obstacle to this. If I am caught
Breaking into the house and scheming against it,
I shall die, and give my enemies cause for laughter.
380   It is best to go by the straight road, the one in which
I am most skilled, and make away with them by poison.
So be it then.
And now suppose them dead. What town will receive me?
What friend will offer me a refuge in his land,
385   Or the guaranty of his house and save my own life?
There is none. So I must wait a little time yet,
And if some sure defense should then appear for me,
In craft and silence I will set about this murder.
But if my fate should drive me on without help,
390   Even though death is certain, I will take the sword
Myself and kill, and steadfastly advance to crime.
It shall not be—I swear it by her, my mistress,
Whom most I honor and have chosen as partner,

Hecate,[7] who dwells in the recesses of my hearth—
395   That any man shall be glad to have injured me.
Bitter I will make their marriage for them and mournful,
Bitter the alliance and the driving me out of the land.
Ah, come, Medea, in your plotting and scheming
Leave nothing untried of all those things which you know.
400   Go forward to the dreadful act. The test has come
For resolution. You see how you are treated. Never
Shall you be mocked by Jason's Corinthian wedding,
Whose father was noble, whose grandfather Helius.[8]
You have the skill. What is more, you were born a woman,
405   And women, though most helpless in doing good deeds,
Are of every evil the cleverest of contrivers.

CHORUS: Flow backward to your sources, sacred rivers,
And let the world's great order be reversed.
It is the thoughts of *men* that are deceitful,
410   *Their* pledges that are loose.
Story shall now turn my condition to a fair one,
Women are paid their due.
No more shall evil-sounding fame be theirs.

Cease now, you muses of the ancient singers,
415   To tell the tale of my unfaithfulness;
For not on us did Phoebus, lord of music,[9]
Bestow the lyre's divine
Power, for otherwise I should have sung an answer
To the other sex. Long time
420   Has much to tell of us, and much of them.

You sailed away from your father's home,
With a heart on fire you passed
The double rocks of the sea.
And now in a foreign country
425   You have lost your rest in a widowed bed,
And are driven forth, a refugee
In dishonor from the land.

Good faith has gone, and no more remains
In great Greece a sense of shame.
430   It has flown away to the sky.
No father's house for a haven
Is at hand for you now, and another queen
Of your bed has dispossessed you and
Is mistress of your home.

[*Enter Jason, with attendants.*]

7. Goddess associated with witchcraft.   9. The god Apollo.
8. God of the sun.

JASON: This is not the first occasion that I have noticed
        How hopeless it is to deal with a stubborn temper.
        For, with reasonable submission to our ruler's will,
        You might have lived in this land and kept your home.
        As it is you are going to be exiled for your loose speaking.
440   Not that I mind myself. You are free to continue
        Telling everyone that Jason is a worthless man.
        But as to your talk about the king, consider
        Yourself most lucky that exile is your punishment.
        I, for my part, have always tried to calm down
445   The anger of the king, and wished you to remain.
        But you will not give up your folly, continually
        Speaking ill of him, and so you are going to be banished.
        All the same, and in spite of your conduct, I'll not desert
        My friends, but have come to make some provision for you,
450   So that you and the children may not be penniless
        Or in need of anything in exile. Certainly
        Exile brings many troubles with it. And even
        If you hate me, I cannot think badly of you.
MEDEA: O coward in every way—that is what I call you,
455   With bitterest reproach for your lack of manliness,
        You have come, you, my worst enemy, have come to me!
        It is not an example of overconfidence
        Or of boldness thus to look your friends in the face,
        Friends you have injured—no, it is the worst of all
460   Human diseases, shamelessness. But you did well
        To come, for I can speak ill of you and lighten
        My heart, and you will suffer while you are listening.
        And first I will begin from what happened first.
        I saved your life, and every Greek knows I saved it,
465   Who was a shipmate of yours aboard the Argo,
        When you were sent to control the bulls that breathed fire
        And yoke them, and when you would sow that deadly field.
        Also that snake, who encircled with his many folds
        The Golden Fleece and guarded it and never slept,
470   I killed, and so gave you the safety of the light.
        And I myself betrayed my father and my home,
        And came with you to Pelias' land of Iolcus.
        And then, showing more willingness to help than wisdom,
        I killed him, Pelias, with a most dreadful death
475   At his own daughters' hands,[1] and took away your fear.
        This is how I behaved to you, you wretched man,
        And you forsook me, took another bride to bed,
        Though you had children; for, if that had not been,
        You would have had an excuse for another wedding.
480   Faith in your word has gone. Indeed, I cannot tell

---

1. Convinced by Medea that they would rejuvenate him, his daughters boiled Pelias.

Whether you think the gods whose names you swore by then
Have ceased to rule and that new standards are set up,
Since you must know you have broken your word to me.
O my right hand, and the knees which you often clasped
485   In supplication, how senselessly I am treated
By this bad man, and how my hopes have missed their mark!
Come, I will share my thoughts as though you were a friend—
You! Can I think that you would ever treat me well?
But I will do it, and these questions will make you
490   Appear the baser. Where am I to go? To my father's?
Him I betrayed and his land when I came with you.
To Pelias' wretched daughters? What a fine welcome
They would prepare for me who murdered their father!
For this is my position—hated by my friends
495   At home, I have, in kindness to you, made enemies
Of others whom there was no need to have injured.
And how happy among Greek women you have made me
On your side for all this! A distinguished husband
I have—for breaking promises. When in misery
500   I am cast out of the land and go into exile,
Quite without friends and all alone with my children,
That will be a fine shame for the new-wedded groom,
For his children to wander as beggars and she who saved him.
O God, you have given to mortals a sure method
505   Of telling the gold that is pure from the counterfeit;
Why is there no mark engraved upon men's bodies,
By which we could know the true ones from the false ones?

CHORUS: It is a strange form of anger, difficult to cure,
When two friends turn upon each other in hatred.

JASON: As for me, it seems I must be no bad speaker.
But, like a man who has a good grip of the tiller,
Reef up his sail, and so run away from under
This mouthing tempest, woman, of your bitter tongue.
Since you insist on building up your kindness to me,
515   My view is that Cypris[2] was alone responsible
Of men and gods for the preserving of my life.
You are clever enough—but really I need not enter
Into the story of how it was love's inescapable
Power that compelled you to keep my person safe.
520   On this I will not go into too much detail.
In so far as you helped me, you did well enough.
But on this question of saving me, I can prove
You have certainly got from me more than you gave.
Firstly, instead of living among barbarians,
525   You inhabit a Greek land and understand our ways,

2. Aphrodite, goddess of sexual desire.

How to live by law instead of the sweet will of force.
And all the Greeks considered you a clever woman.
You were honored for it; while, if you were living at
The ends of the earth, nobody would have heard of you.
530   For my part, rather than stores of gold in my house
Or power to sing even sweeter songs than Orpheus,
I'd choose the fate that made me a distinguished man.
There is my reply to your story of my labors.
Remember it was you who started the argument.
535   Next for your attack on my wedding with the princess:
Here I will prove that, first, it was a clever move,
Secondly, a wise one, and, finally, that I made it
In your best interests and the children's. Please keep calm.
When I arrived here from the land of Iolcus,
540   Involved, as I was, in every kind of difficulty,
What luckier chance could I have come across than this,
An exile to marry the daughter of the king?
It was not—the point that seems to upset you—that I
Grew tired of your bed and felt the need of a new bride;
545   Nor with any wish to outdo your number of children.
We have enough already. I am quite content.
But—this was the main reason—that we might live well,
And not be short of anything. I know that all
A man's friends leave him stone-cold if he becomes poor.
550   Also that I might bring my children up worthily
Of my position, and, by producing more of them
To be brothers of yours, we would draw the families
Together and all be happy. You need no children.
And it pays me to do good to those I have now
555   By having others. Do you think this a bad plan?
You wouldn't if the love question hadn't upset you.
But you women have got into such a state of mind
That, if your life at night is good, you think you have
Everything; but, if in that quarter things go wrong,
560   You will consider your best and truest interests
Most hateful. It would have been better far for men
To have got their children in some other way, and women
Not to have existed. Then life would have been good.
CHORUS: Jason, though you have made this speech of yours look well,
565   Still I think, even though others do not agree,
You have betrayed your wife and are acting badly.
MEDEA: Surely in many ways I hold different views
From others, for I think that the plausible speaker
Who is a villain deserves the greatest punishment.
570   Confident in his tongue's power to adorn evil,
He stops at nothing. Yet he is not really wise.
As in your case. There is no need to put on the airs
Of a clever speaker, for one word will lay you flat.
If you were not a coward, you would not have married

575		Behind my back, but discussed it with me first.
	JASON:	And you, no doubt, would have furthered the proposal,
		If I had told you of it, you who even now
		Are incapable of controlling your bitter temper.
	MEDEA:	It was not that. No, you thought it was not respectable
580		As you got on in years to have a foreign wife.
	JASON:	Make sure of this: it was not because of a woman
		I made the royal alliance in which I now live,
		But, as I said before, I wished to preserve you
		And breed a royal progeny to be brothers
585		To the children I have now, a sure defense to us.
	MEDEA:	Let me have no happy fortune that brings pain with it,
		Or prosperity which is upsetting to the mind!
	JASON:	Change your ideas of what you want, and show more sense.
		Do not consider painful what is good for you,
590		Nor, when you are lucky, think yourself unfortunate.
	MEDEA:	You can insult me. You have somewhere to turn to.
		But I shall go from this land into exile, friendless.
	JASON:	It was what you chose yourself. Don't blame others for it.
	MEDEA:	And how did I choose it? Did I betray my husband?
	JASON:	You called down wicked curses on the king's family.
	MEDEA:	A curse, that is what I am become to your house too.
	JASON:	I do not propose to go into all the rest of it;
		But, if you wish for the children or for yourself
		In exile to have some of my money to help you,
600		Say so, for I am prepared to give with open hand,
		Or to provide you with introductions to my friends
		Who will treat you well. You are a fool if you do not
		Accept this. Cease your anger and you will profit.
	MEDEA:	I shall never accept the favors of friends of yours,
605		Nor take a thing from you, so you need not offer it.
		There is no benefit in the gifts of a bad man.
	JASON:	Then, in any case, I call the gods to witness that
		I wish to help you and the children in every way,
		But you refuse what is good for you. Obstinately
610		You push away your friends. You are sure to suffer for it.
	MEDEA:	Go! No doubt you hanker for your virginal bride,
		And are guilty of lingering too long out of her house.
		Enjoy your wedding. But perhaps—with the help of God—
		You will make the kind of marriage that you will regret.

[*Jason goes out with his attendants.*]

	CHORUS:	When love is in excess
		It brings a man no honor
		Nor any worthiness.
		But if in moderation Cypris comes,
		There is no other power at all so gracious.
620		O goddess, never on me let loose the unerring
		Shaft of your bow in the poison of desire.

Let my heart be wise.
It is the gods' best gift.
On me let mighty Cypris
625   Inflict no wordy wars or restless anger
To urge my passion to a different love.
But with discernment may she guide women's weddings,
Honoring most what is peaceful in the bed.

O country and home,
630   Never, never may I be without you,
Living the hopeless life,
Hard to pass through and painful,
Most pitiable of all.
Let death first lay me low and death
635   Free me from this daylight.
There is no sorrow above
The loss of a native land.

I have seen it myself,
Do not tell of a secondhand story.
640   Neither city nor friend
Pitied you when you suffered
The worst of sufferings.
O let him die ungraced whose heart
Will not reward his friends,
645   Who cannot open an honest mind
No friend will he be of mine.

[*Enter Aegeus, king of Athens, an old friend of Medea.*]

AEGEUS: Medea, greeting! This is the best introduction
Of which men know for conversation between friends.
MEDEA: Greeting to you too, Aegeus, son of King Pandion.
650   Where have you come from to visit this country's soil?
AEGEUS: I have just left the ancient oracle of Phoebus.
MEDEA: And why did you go to earth's prophetic center?
AEGEUS: I went to inquire how children might be born to me.
MEDEA: Is it so? Your life still up to this point is childless?
AEGEUS: Yes. By the fate of some power we have no children.
MEDEA: Have you a wife, or is there none to share your bed?
AEGEUS: There is. Yes, I am joined to my wife in marriage.
MEDEA: And what did Phoebus say to you about children?
AEGEUS: Words too wise for a mere man to guess their meaning.
MEDEA: It is proper for me to be told the god's reply?
AEGEUS: It is. For sure what is needed is cleverness.
MEDEA: Then what was his message? Tell me, if I may hear.
AEGEUS: I am not to loosen the hanging foot of the wine-skin . . .
MEDEA: Until you have done something, or reached some country?
AEGEUS: Until I return again to my hearth and house.
MEDEA: And for what purpose have you journeyed to this land?
AEGEUS: There is a man called Pittheus, king of Troezen.

MEDEA:	A son of Pelops, they say, a most righteous man.
AEGEUS:	With him I wish to discuss the reply of the god.
MEDEA:	Yes. He is wise and experienced in such matters.
AEGEUS:	And to me also the dearest of all my spear-friends.
MEDEA:	Well, I hope you have good luck, and achieve your will.
AEGEUS:	But why this downcast eye of yours, and this pale cheek?
MEDEA:	O Aegeus, my husband has been the worst of all to me.
AEGEUS:	What do you mean? Say clearly what has caused this grief.
MEDEA:	Jason wrongs me, though I have never injured him.
AEGEUS:	What has he done? Tell me about it in clearer words.
MEDEA:	He has taken a wife to his house, supplanting me.
AEGEUS:	Surely he would not dare to do a thing like that.
MEDEA:	Be sure he has. Once dear, I now am slighted by him.
AEGEUS:	Did he fall in love? Or is he tired of your love?
MEDEA:	He was greatly in love, this traitor to his friends.
AEGEUS:	Then let him go, if, as you say, he is so bad.
MEDEA:	A passionate love—for an alliance with the king.
AEGEUS:	And who gave him his wife? Tell me the rest of it.
MEDEA:	It was Creon, he who rules this land of Corinth.
AEGEUS:	Indeed, Medea, your grief was understandable.
MEDEA:	I am ruined. And there is more to come: I am banished.
AEGEUS:	Banished? By whom? Here you tell me of a new wrong.
MEDEA:	Creon drives me an exile from the land of Corinth.
AEGEUS:	Does Jason consent? I cannot approve of this.
MEDEA:	He pretends not to, but he will put up with it.

MEDEA:

Ah, Aegeus, I beg and beseech you, by your beard
And by your knees I am making myself your suppliant,
695   Have pity on me, have pity on your poor friend,
And do not let me go into exile desolate,
But receive me in your land and at your very hearth.
So may your love, with God's help, lead to the bearing
Of children, and so may you yourself die happy.
700   You do not know what a chance you have come on here.
I will end your childlessness, and I will make you able
To beget children. The drugs I know can do this.

AEGEUS: For many reasons, woman, I am anxious to do
This favor for you. First, for the sake of the gods,
705   And then for the birth of children which you promise,
For in that respect I am entirely at my wits' end.
But this is my position: if you reach my land,
I, being in my rights, will try to befriend you.
But this much I must warn you of beforehand:
710   I shall not agree to take you out of this country;
But if you by yourself can reach my house, then you
Shall stay there safely. To none will I give you up
But from this land you must make your escape yourself,
For I do not wish to incur blame from my friends.

MEDEA: It shall be so. But, if I might have a pledge from you
For this, then I would have from you all I desire.

AEGEUS: Do you not trust me? What is it rankles with you?
MEDEA: I trust you, yes. But the house of Pelias hates me,
         And so does Creon. If you are bound by this oath,
720   When they try to drag me from your land, you will not
         Abandon me; but if our pact is only words,
         With no oath to the gods, you will be lightly armed,
         Unable to resist their summons. I am weak,
         While they have wealth to help them and a royal house.
AEGEUS: You show much foresight for such negotiations.
         Well, if you will have it so, I will not refuse.
         For, both on my side this will be the safest way
         To have some excuse to put forward to your enemies,
         And for you it is more certain. You may name the gods.
MEDEA: Swear by the plain of Earth, and Helius, father
         Of my father, and name together all the gods . . .
AEGEUS: That I will act or not act in what way? Speak.
MEDEA: That you yourself will never cast me from your land,
         Nor, if any of my enemies should demand me,
735   Will you, in your life, willingly hand me over.
AEGEUS: I swear by the Earth, by the holy light of Helius,
         By all the gods, I will abide by this you say.
MEDEA: Enough. And, if you fail, what shall happen to you?
AEGEUS: What comes to those who have no regard for heaven.
MEDEA: Go on your way. Farewell. For I am satisfied.
         And I will reach your city as soon as I can,
         Having done the deed I have to do and gained my end.

     [*Aegeus goes out.*]

CHORUS: May Hermes, god of travelers,
         Escort you, Aegeus, to your home!
745   And may you have the things you wish
         So eagerly; for you
         Appear to me to be a generous man.
MEDEA: God, and God's daughter, justice, and light of Helius!
         Now, friends, has come the time of my triumph over
750   My enemies, and now my foot is on the road.
         Now I am confident they will pay the penalty.
         For this man, Aegeus, has been like a harbor to me
         In all my plans just where I was most distressed.
         To him I can fasten the cable of my safety
755   When I have reached the town and fortress of Pallas.[3]
         And now I shall tell to you the whole of my plan.
         Listen to these words that are not spoken idly.
         I shall send one of my servants to find Jason
         And request him to come once more into my sight.
760   And when he comes, the words I'll say will be soft ones.

---

3. Athena, goddess of Athens.

I'll say that I agree with him, that I approve
The royal wedding he has made, betraying me.
I'll say it was profitable, an excellent idea.
But I shall beg that my children may remain here:
765   Not that I would leave in a country that hates me
Children of mine to feel their enemies' insults,
But that by a trick I may kill the king's daughter.
For I will send the children with gifts in their hands
To carry to the bride, so as not to be banished—
770   A finely woven dress and a golden diadem.
And if she takes them and wears them upon her skin
She and all who touch the girl will die in agony;
Such poison will I lay upon the gifts I send.
But there, however, I must leave that account paid.
775   I weep to think of what a deed I have to do
Next after that; for I shall kill my own children.
My children, there is none who can give them safety.
And when I have ruined the whole of Jason's house,
I shall leave the land and flee from the murder of my
780   Dear children, and I shall have done a dreadful deed.
For it is not bearable to be mocked by enemies.
So it must happen. What profit have I in life?
I have no land, no home, no refuge from my pain.
My mistake was made the time I left behind me
785   My father's house, and trusted the words of a Greek,
Who, with heaven's help, will pay me the price for that.
For those children he had from me he will never
See alive again, nor will he on his new bride
Beget another child, for she is to be forced
790   To die a most terrible death by these my poisons.
Let no one think me a weak one, feeble-spirited,
A stay-at-home, but rather just the opposite,
One who can hurt my enemies and help my friends;
For the lives of such persons are most remembered.
CHORUS: Since you have shared the knowledge of your plan with us,
I both wish to help you and support the normal
Ways of mankind, and tell you not to do this thing.
MEDEA: I can do no other thing. It is understandable
For you to speak thus. You have not suffered as I have.
CHORUS: But can you have the heart to kill your flesh and blood?
MEDEA: Yes, for this is the best way to wound my husband.
CHORUS: And you, too. Of women you will be most unhappy.
MEDEA: So it must be. No compromise is possible.

[*She turns to the Nurse.*]

Go, you, at once, and tell Jason to come to me.
805   You I employ on all affairs of greatest trust.
Say nothing of these decisions which I have made,
If you love your mistress, if you were born a woman.

CHORUS: From of old the children of Erechtheus are
       Splendid, the sons of blessed gods. They dwell
810   In Athens' holy and unconquered land,
       Where famous Wisdom feeds them and they pass gaily
       Always through that most brilliant air where once, they say,
       That golden Harmony gave birth to the nine
       Pure Muses of Pieria.

815   And beside the sweet flow of Cephisus' stream,
       Where Cypris sailed, they say, to draw the water,
       And mild soft breezes breathed along her path,
       And on her hair were flung the sweet-smelling garlands
       Of flowers of roses by the Lovers, the companions
820   Of Wisdom, her escort, the helpers of men
       In every kind of excellence.

       How then can these holy rivers
       Or this holy land love you,
       Or the city find you a home,
825   You, who will kill your children,
       You, not pure with the rest?
       O think of the blow at your children
       And think of the blood that you shed.
       O, over and over I beg you,
830   By your knees I beg you do not
       Be the murderess of your babes!

       O where will you find the courage
       Or the skill of hand and heart,
       When you set yourself to attempt
835   A deed so dreadful to do?
       How, when you look upon them,
       Can you tearlessly hold the decision
       For murder? You will not be able,
       When your children fall down and implore you,
840   You will not be able to dip
       Steadfast your hand in their blood.

    [*Enter Jason with attendants.*]

JASON: I have come at your request. Indeed, although you are
       Bitter against me, this you shall have: I will listen
       To what new thing you want, woman, to get from me.
MEDEA: Jason, I beg you to be forgiving toward me
       For what I said. It is natural for you to bear with
       My temper, since we have had much love together.
       I have talked with myself about this and I have
       Reproached myself. "Fool" I said, "why am I so mad?
850   Why am I set against those who have planned wisely?
       Why make myself an enemy of the authorities
       And of my husband, who does the best thing for me
       By marrying royalty and having children who

Will be as brothers to my own? What is wrong with me?
855   Let me give up anger, for the gods are kind to me.
Have I not children, and do I not know that we
In exile from our country must be short of friends?"
When I considered this I saw that I had shown
Great lack of sense, and that my anger was foolish.
860   Now I agree with you. I think that you are wise
In having this other wife as well as me, and I
Was mad. I should have helped you in these plans of yours,
Have joined in the wedding, stood by the marriage bed,
Have taken pleasure in attendance on your bride.
865   But we women are what we are—perhaps a little
Worthless; and you men must not be like us in this,
Nor be foolish in return when we are foolish.
Now, I give in, and admit that then I was wrong.
I have come to a better understanding now.

[*She turns toward the house.*]

870   Children, come here, my children, come outdoors to us!
Welcome your father with me, and say goodbye to him,
And with your mother, who just now was his enemy,
Join again in making friends with him who loves us.

[*Enter the children, attended by the Tutor.*]

We have made peace, and all our anger is over.
875   Take hold of his right hand—O God, I am thinking
Of something which may happen in the secret future.
O children, will you just so, after a long life,
Hold out your loving arms at the grave? O children,
How ready to cry I am, how full of foreboding!
880   I am ending at last this quarrel with your father,
And, look my soft eyes have suddenly filled with tears.
CHORUS: And the pale tears have started also in my eyes.
O may the trouble not grow worse than now it is!
JASON: I approve of what you say. And I cannot blame you
885   Even for what you said before. It is natural
For a woman to be wild with her husband when he
Goes in for secret love. But now your mind has turned
To better reasoning. In the end you have come to
The right decision, like the clever woman you are.
890   And of you, children, your father is taking care.
He has made, with God's help, ample provision for you.
For I think that a time will come when you will be
The leading people in Corinth with your brothers.
You must grow up. As to the future, your father
895   And those of the gods who love him will deal with that.
I want to see you, when you have become young men,
Healthy and strong, better men than my enemies.
Medea, why are your eyes all wet with pale tears?

Why is your cheek so white and turned away from me?

900   Are not these words of mine pleasing for you to hear?

MEDEA: It is nothing. I was thinking about these children.

JASON: You must be cheerful. I shall look after them well.

MEDEA: I will be. It is not that I distrust your words,
    But a woman is a frail thing, prone to crying.

JASON: But why then should you grieve so much for these children?

MEDEA: I am their mother. When you prayed that they might live
    I felt unhappy to think that these things will be.
    But come, I have said something of the things I meant
    To say to you, and now I will tell you the rest.

910   Since it is the king's will to banish me from here—
    And for me, too, I know that this is the best thing,
    Not to be in your way by living here or in
    The king's way, since they think me ill-disposed to them—
    I then am going into exile from this land;

915   But do you, so that you may have the care of them,
    Beg Creon that the children may not be banished.

JASON: I doubt if I'll succeed, but still I'll attempt it.

MEDEA: Then you must tell your wife to beg from her father
    That the children may be reprieved from banishment.

JASON: I will, and with her I shall certainly succeed.

MEDEA: If she is like the rest of us women, you will.
    And I, too, will take a hand with you in this business,
    For I will send her some gifts which are far fairer,
    I am sure of it, than those which now are in fashion,

925   A finely woven dress and a golden diadem,
    And the children shall present them. Quick, let one of you
    Servants bring here to me that beautiful dress.

[One of her attendants goes into the house.]

She will be happy not in one way, but in a hundred,
    Having so fine a man as you to share her bed,

930   And with this beautiful dress which Helius of old,
    My father's father, bestowed on his descendants.

[Enter attendant carrying the poisoned dress and diadem.]

There, children, take these wedding presents in your hands.
    Take them to the royal princess, the happy bride,
    And give them to her. She will not think little of them.

JASON: No, don't be foolish, and empty your hands of these.
    Do you think the palace is short of dresses to wear?
    Do you think there is no gold there? Keep them, don't give them
    Away. If my wife considers me of any value,
    She will think more of me than money, I am sure of it.

MEDEA: No, let me have my way. They say the gods themselves
    Are moved by gifts, and gold does more with men than words.
    Hers is the luck, her fortune that which god blesses;
    She is young and a princess; but for my children's reprieve

I would give my very life, and not gold only.
945   Go children, go together to that rich palace,
Be suppliants to the new wife of your father,
My lady, beg her not to let you be banished.
And give her the dress—for this is of great importance,
That she should take the gift into her hand from yours.
950   Go, quick as you can. And bring your mother good news
By your success of those things which she longs to gain.

[*Jason goes out with his attendants, followed by the Tutor and the children carrying the poisoned gifts.*]

CHORUS: Now there is no hope left for the children's lives.
Now there is none. They are walking already to murder.
The bride, poor bride, will accept the curse of the gold,
955   Will accept the bright diadem.
Around her yellow hair she will set that dress
Of death with her own hands.

The grace and the perfume and glow of the golden robe
Will charm her to put them upon her and wear the wreath,
960   And now her wedding will be with the dead below,
Into such a trap she will fall,
Poor thing, into such a fate of death and never
Escape from under that curse.
You, too, O wretched bridegroom, making your match with kings,
965   You do not see that you bring
Destruction on your children and on her,
Your wife, a fearful death.
Poor soul, what a fall is yours!

In your grief, too, I weep, mother of little children,
970   You who will murder your own,
In vengeance for the loss of married love
Which Jason has betrayed
As he lives with another wife.

[*Enter the Tutor with the children.*]

TUTOR: Mistress, I tell you that these children are reprieved,
975   And the royal bride has been pleased to take in her hands
Your gifts. In that quarter the children are secure.
But come,
Why do you stand confused when you are fortunate?
Why have you turned round with your cheek away from me?
980   Are not these words of mine pleasing for you to hear?
MEDEA: Oh! I am lost!
TUTOR: That word is not in harmony with my tidings.
MEDEA: I am lost, I am lost!
TUTOR: Am I in ignorance telling you
Of some disaster, and not the good news I thought?
MEDEA: You have told what you have told. I do not blame you.

TUTOR: Why then this downcast eye, and this weeping of tears?
MEDEA: Oh, I am forced to weep, old man. The gods and I,
         I in a kind of madness, have contrived all this.
TUTOR: Courage! You, too, will be brought home by your children.
MEDEA: Ah, before that happens I shall bring others home.
TUTOR: Others before you have been parted from their children.
         Mortals must bear in resignation their ill luck.
MEDEA: That is what I shall do. But go inside the house,
         And do for the children your usual daily work.

[*The Tutor goes into the house. Medea turns to her children.*]

995   O children, O my children, you have a city,
         You have a home, and you can leave me behind you,
         And without your mother you may live there forever.
         But I am going in exile to another land
         Before I have seen you happy and taken pleasure in you,
1000   Before I have dressed your brides and made your marriage beds
         And held up the torch at the ceremony of wedding.
         Oh, what a wretch I am in this my self-willed thought!
         What was the purpose, children, for which I reared you?
         For all my travail and wearing myself away?
1005   They were sterile, those pains I had in the bearing of you.
         Oh surely once the hopes in you I had, poor me,
         Were high ones: you would look after me in old age,
         And when I died would deck me well with your own hands;
         A thing which all would have done. Oh but now it is gone,
1010   That lovely thought. For, once I am left without you,
         Sad will be the life I'll lead and sorrowful for me.
         And you will never see your mother again with
         Your dear eyes, gone to another mode of living.
         Why, children, do you look upon me with your eyes?
1015   Why do you smile so sweetly that last smile of all?
         Oh, Oh, what can I do? My spirit has gone from me,
         Friends, when I saw that bright look in the children's eyes.
         I cannot bear to do it. I renounce my plans
         I had before. I'll take my children away from
1020   This land. Why should I hurt their father with the pain
         They feel, and suffer twice as much of pain myself?
         No, no, I will not do it. I renounce my plans.
         Ah, what is wrong with me? Do I want to let go
         My enemies unhurt and be laughed at for it?
1025   I must face this thing. Oh, but what a weak woman
         Even to admit to my mind these soft arguments.
         Children, go into the house. And he whom law forbids
         To stand in attendance at my sacrifices,
         Let him see to it. I shall not mar my handiwork.
1030   Oh! Oh!
         Do not, O my heart, you must not do these things!
         Poor heart, let them go, have pity upon the children.

If they live with you in Athens they will cheer you.
No! By Hell's avenging furies it shall not be—
1035   This shall never be, that I should suffer my children
To be the prey of my enemies' insolence.
Every way is it fixed. The bride will not escape.
No, the diadem is now upon her head, and she,
The royal princess, is dying in the dress, I know it.
1040   But—for it is the most dreadful of roads for me
To tread, and them I shall send on a more dreadful still—
I wish to speak to the children.

[*She calls the children to her.*]

Come, children, give
Me your hands, give your mother your hands to kiss them.
Oh the dear hands, and O how dear are these lips to me,
1045   And the generous eyes and the bearing of my children!
I wish you happiness, but not here in this world.
What is here your father took. Oh how good to hold you!
How delicate the skin, how sweet the breath of children!
Go, go! I am no longer able, no longer
1050   To look upon you. I am overcome by sorrow.

[*The children go into the house.*]

I know indeed what evil I intend to do,
But stronger than all my afterthoughts is my fury,
Fury that brings upon mortals the greatest evils.

[*She goes out to the right, toward the royal palace.*]

CHORUS: Often before
1055   I have gone through more subtle reasons,
And have come upon questionings greater
Than a woman should strive to search out.
But we too have a goddess to help us
And accompany us into wisdom.
1060   Not all of us. Still you will find
Among many women a few,
And our sex is not without learning.
This I say, that those who have never
Had children, who know nothing of it,
1065   In happiness have the advantage
Over those who are parents.
The childless, who never discover
Whether children turn out as a good thing
Or as something to cause pain, are spared
1070   Many troubles in lacking this knowledge.
And those who have in their homes
The sweet presence of children, I see that their lives
Are all wasted away by their worries.
First they must think how to bring them up well and

1075 How to leave them something to live on.
    And then after this whether all their toil
    Is for those who will turn out good or bad,
    Is still an unanswered question.
    And of one more trouble, the last of all,
1080 That is common to mortals I tell.
    For suppose you have found them enough for their living,
    Suppose that the children have grown into youth
    And have turned out good, still, if God so wills it,
    Death will away with your children's bodies,
1085 And carry them off into Hades.
    What is our profit, then, that for the sake of
    Children the gods should pile upon mortals
    After all else
    This most terrible grief of all?

  [*Enter Medea, from the spectators' right.*]

MEDEA: Friends, I can tell you that for long I have waited
    For the event. I stare toward the place from where
    The news will come. And now, see one of Jason's servants
    Is on his way here, and that labored breath of his
    Shows he has tidings for us, and evil tidings.

  [*Enter, also from the right, the Messenger.*]

MESSENGER: Medea, you who have done such a dreadful thing,
    So outrageous, run for your life, take what you can,
    A ship to bear you hence or chariot on land.
MEDEA: And what is the reason deserves such flight as this?
MESSENGER: She is dead, only just now, the royal princess,
1100 And Creon dead, too, her father, by your poisons.
MEDEA: The finest words you have spoken. Now and hereafter
    I shall count you among my benefactors and friends.
MESSENGER: What! Are you right in the mind? Are you not mad,
    Woman? The house of the king is outraged by you.
1105 Do you enjoy it? Not afraid of such doings?
MEDEA: To what you say I on my side have something too
    To say in answer. Do not be in a hurry, friend,
    But speak. How did they die? You will delight me twice
    As much again if you say they died in agony.
MESSENGER: When those two children, born of you, had entered in,
    Their father with them, and passed into the bride's house,
    We were pleased, we slaves who were distressed by your wrongs.
    All through the house we were talking of but one thing,
    How you and your husband had made up your quarrel.
1115 Some kissed the children's hands and some their yellow hair,
    And I myself was so full of my joy that I
    Followed the children into the women's quarters.
    Our mistress, whom we honor now instead of you,
    Before she noticed that your two children were there,

1120	Was keeping her eye fixed eagerly on Jason.
	Afterwards, however, she covered up her eyes,
	Her cheek paled, and she turned herself away from him,
	So disgusted was she at the children's coming there.
	But your husband tried to end the girl's bad temper,
1125	And said "You must not look unkindly on your friends.
	Cease to be angry. Turn your head to me again.
	Have as your friends the same ones as your husband has.
	And take these gifts, and beg your father to reprieve
	These children from their exile. Do it for my sake."
1130	She, when she saw the dress, could not restrain herself.
	She agreed with all her husband said, and before
	He and the children had gone far from the palace,
	She took the gorgeous robe and dressed herself in it,
	And put the golden crown around her curly locks,
1135	And arranged the set of the hair in a shining mirror,
	And smiled at the lifeless image of herself in it.
	Then she rose from her chair and walked about the room,
	With her gleaming feet stepping most soft and delicate,
	All overjoyed with the present. Often and often
1140	She would stretch her foot out straight and look along it.
	But after that it was a fearful thing to see.
	The color of her face changed, and she staggered back,
	She ran, and her legs trembled, and she only just
	Managed to reach a chair without falling flat down.
1145	An aged woman servant who, I take it, thought
	This was some seizure of Pan or another god,
	Cried out "God bless us," but that was before she saw
	The white foam breaking through her lips and her rolling
	The pupils of her eyes and her face all bloodless.
1150	Then she raised a different cry from that "God bless us,"
	A huge shriek, and the women ran, one to the king,
	One to the newly wedded husband to tell him
	What had happened to his bride; and with frequent sound
	The whole of the palace rang as they went running.
1155	One walking quickly round the course of a race-track
	Would now have turned the bend and be close to the goal,
	When she, poor girl, opened her shut and speechless eye,
	And with a terrible groan she came to herself.
	For a twofold pain was moving up against her.
1160	The wreath of gold that was resting around her head
	Let forth a fearful stream of all-devouring fire,
	And the finely woven dress your children gave to her,
	Was fastening on the unhappy girl's fine flesh.
	She leapt up from the chair, and all on fire she ran,
1165	Shaking her hair now this way and now that, trying
	To hurl the diadem away; but fixedly
	The gold preserved its grip, and, when she shook her hair,
	Then more and twice as fiercely the fire blazed out.

1170

Till, beaten by her fate, she fell down to the ground,
Hard to be recognized except by a parent.
Neither the setting of her eyes was plain to see,
Nor the shapeliness of her face. From the top of
Her head there oozed out blood and fire mixed together.
Like the drops on pine-bark, so the flesh from her bones

1175

Dropped away, torn by the hidden fang of the poison.
It was a fearful sight; and terror held us all
From touching the corpse. We had learned from what had happened.
But her wretched father, knowing nothing of the event,
Came suddenly to the house, and fell upon the corpse,

1180

And at once cried out and folded his arms about her,
And kissed her and spoke to her, saying, "O my poor child,
What heavenly power has so shamefully destroyed you?
And who has set me here like an ancient sepulcher,
Deprived of you? O let me die with you, my child!"

1185

And when he had made an end of his wailing and crying,
Then the old man wished to raise himself to his feet;
But, as the ivy clings to the twigs of the laurel,
So he stuck to the fine dress, and he struggled fearfully.
For he was trying to lift himself to his knee,

1190

And she was pulling him down, and when he tugged hard
He would be ripping his aged flesh from his bones.
At last his life was quenched, and the unhappy man
Gave up the ghost, no longer could hold up his head.
There they lie close, the daughter and the old father,

1195

Dead bodies, an event he prayed for in his tears.
As for your interests, I will say nothing of them,
For you will find your own escape from punishment.
Our human life I think and have thought a shadow,
And I do not fear to say that those who are held

1200

Wise among men and who search the reasons of things
Are those who bring the most sorrow on themselves.
For of mortals there is no one who is happy.
If wealth flows in upon one, one may be perhaps
Luckier than one's neighbor, but still not happy.

[*Exit.*]

CHORUS: Heaven, it seems, on this day has fastened many
Evils on Jason, and Jason has deserved them.
Poor girl, the daughter of Creon, how I pity you
And your misfortunes, you who have gone quite away
To the house of Hades because of marrying Jason.

MEDEA: Women, my task is fixed: as quickly as I may
To kill my children, and start away from this land,
And not, by wasting time, to suffer my children
To be slain by another hand less kindly to them.
Force every way will have it they must die, and since

1215

This must be so, then I, their mother, shall kill them.

Oh, arm yourself in steel, my heart! Do not hang back
From doing this fearful and necessary wrong.
Oh, come, my hand, poor wretched hand, and take the sword,
Take it, step forward to this bitter starting point,
1220 And do not be a coward, do not think of them,
How sweet they are, and how you are their mother. Just for
This one short day be forgetful of your children,
Afterward weep; for even though you will kill them,
They were very dear—Oh, I am an unhappy woman!

[*With a cry she rushes into the house.*]

CHORUS: O Earth, and the far shining
Ray of the Sun, look down, look down upon
This poor lost woman, look, before she raises
The hand of murder against her flesh and blood.
Yours was the golden birth from which
1230 She sprang, and now I fear divine
Blood may be shed by men.
O heavenly light, hold back her hand,
Check her, and drive from out the house
The bloody Fury raised by fiends of Hell.

1235 Vain waste, your care of children;
Was it in vain you bore the babes you loved,
After you passed the inhospitable strait
Between the dark blue rocks, Symplegades?
O wretched one, how has it come,
1240 This heavy anger on your heart,
This cruel bloody mind?
For God from mortals asks a stern
Price for the stain of kindred blood
In like disaster falling on their homes.

[*A cry from one of the children is heard.*]

CHORUS: Do you hear the cry, do you hear the children's cry?
O you hard heart, O woman fated for evil!
ONE OF THE CHILDREN [*from within*]: What can I do and how escape my mother's
hands?
ANOTHER CHILD [*from within*]: O my dear brother, I cannot tell. We are lost.
CHORUS: Shall I enter the house? Oh, surely I should
1250 Defend the children from murder.
A CHILD [*from within*]: O help us, in God's name, for now we need your help.
Now, now we are close to it. We are trapped by the sword.
CHORUS: O your heart must have been made of rock or steel,
You who can kill
1255 With your own hand the fruit of your own womb.
Of one alone I have heard, one woman alone
Of those of old who laid her hands on her children,
Ino, sent mad by heaven when the wife of Zeus

Drove her out from her home and made her wander;
1260   And because of the wicked shedding of blood
Of her own children she threw
Herself, poor wretch, into the sea and stepped away
Over the sea-cliff to die with her two children.
What horror more can be? O women's love,
1265   So full of trouble,
How many evils have you caused already!

[*Enter Jason, with attendants.*]

JASON: You women, standing close in front of this dwelling,
Is she, Medea, she who did this dreadful deed,
Still in the house, or has she run away in flight?
1270   For she will have to hide herself beneath the earth,
Or raise herself on wings into the height of air,
If she wishes to escape the royal vengeance.
Does she imagine that, having killed our rulers,
She will herself escape uninjured from this house?
1275   But I am thinking not so much of her as for
The children—her the king's friends will make to suffer
For what she did. So I have come to save the lives
Of my boys, in case the royal house should harm them
While taking vengeance for their mother's wicked deed.

CHORUS: O Jason, if you but knew how deeply you are
Involved in sorrow, you would not have spoken so.

JASON: What is it? That she is planning to kill me also?

CHORUS: Your children are dead, and by their own mother's hand.

JASON: What! That is it? O woman, you have destroyed me!

CHORUS: You must make up your mind your children are no more.

JASON: Where did she kill them? Was it here or in the house?

CHORUS: Open the gates and there you will see them murdered.

JASON: Quick as you can unlock the doors, men, and undo
The fastenings and let me see this double evil,
1290   My children dead and her—Oh her I will repay.

[*His attendants rush to the door. Medea appears above the house in a chariot
drawn by dragons. She has the dead bodies of the children with her.*]

MEDEA: Why do you batter these gates and try to unbar them,
Seeking the corpses and for me who did the deed?
You may cease your trouble, and, if you have need of me,
Speak, if you wish. You will never touch me with your hand,
1295   Such a chariot has Helius, my father's father,
Given me to defend me from my enemies.

JASON: You hateful thing, you woman most utterly loathed
By the gods and me and by all the race of mankind,
You who have had the heart to raise a sword against
1300   Your children, you, their mother, and left me childless—
You have done this, and do you still look at the sun
And at the earth, after these most fearful doings?

I wish you dead. Now I see it plain, though at that time
I did not, when I took you from your foreign home
1305   And brought you to a Greek house, you, an evil thing,
A traitress to your father and your native land.
The gods hurled the avenging curse of yours on me.
For your own brother you slew at your own hearthside,
And then came aboard that beautiful ship, the Argo.
1310   And that was your beginning. When you were married
To me, your husband, and had borne children to me,
For the sake of pleasure in the bed you killed them.
There is no Greek woman who would have dared such deeds,
Out of all those whom I passed over and chose you
1315   To marry instead, a bitter destructive match,
A monster, not a woman, having a nature
Wilder than that of Scylla in the Tuscan sea.
Ah! no, not if I had ten thousand words of shame
Could I sting you. You are naturally so brazen.
1320   Go, worker in evil, stained with your children's blood.
For me remains to cry aloud upon my fate,
Who will get no pleasure from my newly wedded love,
And the boys whom I begot and brought up, never
Shall I speak to them alive. Oh, my life is over!

MEDEA: Long would be the answer which I might have made to
These words of yours, if Zeus the father did not know
How I have treated you and what you did to me.
No, it was not to be that you should scorn my love,
And pleasantly live your life through, laughing at me;
1330   Nor would the princess, nor he who offered the match,
Creon, drive me away without paying for it.
So now you may call me a monster, if you wish,
A Scylla housed in the caves of the Tuscan sea.
I too, as I had to, have taken hold of your heart.

JASON: You feel the pain yourself. You share in my sorrow.
MEDEA: Yes, and my grief is gain when you cannot mock it.
JASON: O children, what a wicked mother she was to you!
MEDEA: They died from a disease they caught from their father.
JASON: I tell you it was not my hand that destroyed them.
MEDEA: But it was your insolence, and your virgin wedding.
JASON: And just for the sake of that you chose to kill them.
MEDEA: Is love so small a pain, do you think, for a woman?
JASON: For a wise one, certainly. But you are wholly evil.
MEDEA: The children are dead. I say this to make you suffer.
JASON: The children, I think, will bring down curses on you.
MEDEA: The gods know who was the author of this sorrow.
JASON: Yes, the gods know indeed, they know your loathsome heart.
MEDEA: Hate me. But I tire of your barking bitterness.
JASON: And I of yours. It is easier to leave you.
MEDEA: How then? What shall I do? I long to leave you too.
JASON: Give me the bodies to bury and to mourn them.

MEDEA: No, that I will not. I will bury them myself,
Bearing them to Hera's temple on the promontory;
So that no enemy may evilly treat them
1355 By tearing up their grave. In this land of Corinth
I shall establish a holy feast and sacrifice
Each year for ever to atone for the blood guilt.
And I myself go to the land of Erechtheus
To dwell in Aegeus' house, the son of Pandion.
1360 While you, as is right, will die without distinction,
Struck on the head by a piece of the Argo's timber,
And you will have seen the bitter end of my love.

JASON: May a Fury for the children's sake destroy you,
And justice, Requitor of blood.

MEDEA: What heavenly power lends an ear
To a breaker of oaths, a deceiver?

JASON: Oh, I hate you, murderess of children.

MEDEA: Go to your palace. Bury your bride.

JASON: I go, with two children to mourn for.

MEDEA: Not yet do you feel it. Wait for the future.

JASON: Oh, children I loved!

MEDEA: I loved them, you did not.

JASON: You loved them, and killed them.

MEDEA: To make you feel pain.

JASON: Oh, wretch that I am, how I long
To kiss the dear lips of my children!

MEDEA: Now you would speak to them, now you would kiss them.
Then you rejected them.

JASON: Let me, I beg you,
Touch my boys' delicate flesh.

MEDEA: I will not. Your words are all wasted.

JASON: O God, do you hear it, this persecution,
1380 These my sufferings from this hateful
Woman, this monster, murderess of children?
Still what I can do that I will do:
I will lament and cry upon heaven,
Calling the gods to bear me witness
1385 How you have killed my boys and prevent me from
Touching their bodies or giving them burial.
I wish I had never begot them to see them
Afterward slaughtered by you.

CHORUS: Zeus in Olympus is the overseer
1390 Of many doings. Many things the gods
Achieve beyond our judgment. What we thought
Is not confirmed and what we thought not god
Contrives. And so it happens in this story.

[*Curtain.*]

RESONANCE

Friedrich Nietzsche: from *The Birth of Tragedy*[1]

We shall do a great deal for the science of esthetics, once we perceive not merely by logical inference, but with the immediate certainty of intuition, that the continuous development of art is bound up with the *Apollonian* and *Dionysian* duality: just as procreation depends on the duality of the sexes, involving perpetual strife with only periodically intervening reconciliations. The terms Dionysian and Apollonian we borrow from the Greeks, who disclose to the discerning mind the profound mysteries of their view of art, not, to be sure, in concepts, but in the impressively clear figures of their gods. Through Apollo and Dionysus, the two art-deities of the Greeks, we come to recognize that in the Greek world there existed a sharp opposition, in origin and aims, between the Apollonian art of sculpture, and the non-plastic, Dionysian, art of music. These two distinct tendencies run parallel to each other, for the most part openly at variance; and they continually incite each other to new and more powerful births, which perpetuate an antagonism, only superficially reconciled by the common term "Art"; till at last, by a metaphysical miracle of the Hellenic will, they appear coupled with each other, and through this coupling eventually generate the art-product, equally Dionysian and Apollonian, of Attic tragedy.

In order to grasp these two tendencies, let us first conceive of them as the separate art-worlds of *dreams* and *drunkenness.* These physiological phenomena present a contrast analogous to that existing between the Apollonian and the Dionysian. It was in dreams, says Lucretius, that the glorious divine figures first appeared to the souls of men; in dreams the great shaper beheld the splendid corporeal structure of superhuman beings; and the Hellenic poet, if questioned about the mysteries of poetic inspiration, would likewise have suggested dreams and he might have given an explanation like that of Hans Sachs in the *Mastersingers:*

> *"Mein Freund, das grad' ist Dichters Werk,*
> *dass er sein Träumen deut' und merk'.*
> *Glaubt mir, des Menschen wahrster Wahn*
> *wird ihm im Traume aufgethan:*
> *all' Dichtkunst und Poëterei*
> *ist nichts als Wahrtraum-Deuterei."*[2]

---

1. Translated by Clifton P. Fadiman. Friedrich Nietzsche (1844–1900) provides a point of view on Euripides from the 19th century. This eccentric classicist, philologist, and philosopher, who ended his life in insanity, began his academic career in 1872 with the scandalous *Birth of Tragedy from the Spirit of Music,* a hymn to Nietzsche's then hero Richard Wagner, who fused what Nietzsche called the Apollonian and Dionysian strains in art, as did the greatest Athenian tragedians such as Aeschylus. Nietzsche's polemical text was despised and denounced by the most authoritative classicists of his day as he insisted on elements of disorder, orgiastic unreason, and even despair that his contemporaries didn't wish to see amid the beauties of classical culture. Their response turned Nietzsche against the discipline of classics, but his text has had great impact on the interpretation of the world of Athenian culture of the 5th and 4th centuries. In this excerpt, Nietzsche blames Euripides for the death of ancient tragedy.

2. From Wagner's opera *Der Meistersinger:* "The poet's task is this, my friend, to read his dream and comprehend. / The truest human fancy seems / to be revealed to us in dreams: / all poems and versification / are but true dreams' interpretation."

The beautiful appearance of the dream-worlds, in creating which every man is a perfect artist, is the prerequisite of all plastic art, and in fact, as we shall see, of an important part of poetry also. In our dreams we delight in the immediate apprehension of form; all forms speak to us; none are unimportant, none are superfluous. But, when this dream-reality is most intense, we also have, glimmering through it, the sensation of its appearance: at least this is my experience, as to whose frequency, aye, normality, I could adduce many proofs, in addition to the sayings of the poets. Indeed, the man of philosophic mind has a presentiment that underneath this reality in which we live and have our being, is concealed another and quite different reality, which, like the first, is an appearance; and Schopenhauer actually indicates as the criterion of philosophical ability the occasional ability to view men and things as mere phantoms or dream-pictures. Thus the esthetically sensitive man stands in the same relation to the reality of dreams as the philosopher does to the reality of existence; he is a close and willing observer, for these pictures afford him an interpretation of life, and it is by these processes that he trains himself for life. And it is not only the agreeable and friendly pictures that he experiences in himself with such perfect understanding: but the serious, the troubled, the sad, the gloomy, the sudden restraints, the tricks of fate, the uneasy presentiments, in short, the whole Divine Comedy of life, and the Inferno, also pass before him, not like mere shadows on the wall—for in these scenes he lives and suffers—and yet not without that fleeting sensation of appearance. And perhaps many will, like myself, recall that amid the dangers and terrors of dream-life they would at times, cry out in self-encouragement, and not without success. "It is only a dream! I will dream on!" I have likewise heard of persons capable of continuing one and the same dream for three and even more successive nights: facts which indicate clearly that our innermost beings, our common subconscious experiences, express themselves in dreams because they must do so and because they take profound delight in so doing.

This joyful necessity of the dream-experience has been embodied by the Greeks in their Apollo: for Apollo, the god of all plastic energies, is at the same time the soothsaying god. He, who (as the etymology of the name indicates) is the "shining one," the deity of light, is also ruler over the fair appearance of the inner world of fantasy. The higher truth, the perfection of these states in contrast to the incompletely intelligible everyday world, this deep consciousness of nature, healing and helping in sleep and dreams, is at the same time the symbolical analogue of the soothsaying faculty and of the arts generally, which make life possible and worth living. But we must also include in our picture of Apollo that delicate boundary, which the dream-picture must not overstep—lest it act pathologically (in which case appearance would impose upon us as pure reality). We must keep in mind that measured restraint, that freedom from the wilder emotions, that philosophical calm of the sculptor-god. His eye must be "sunlike," as befits his origin; even when his glance is angry and distempered, the sacredness of his beautiful appearance must still be there. And so, in one sense, we might apply to Apollo the words of Schopenhauer when he speaks of the man wrapped in the veil of Mâyâ:[3] *Welt als Wille und Vorstellung,* I. p. 416: "Just as in a stormy sea, unbounded in every direction, rising and falling with howling mountainous waves, a sailor sits in a boat and trusts in his frail barque: so in the midst of a world of sorrows the individual sits quietly, supported by and trusting in his

---

3. Hindu concept of illusion.

principium individuationis."[4] In fact, we might say of Apollo, that in him the unshaken faith in this *principium* and the calm repose of the man wrapped therein receive their sublimest expression; and we might consider Apollo himself as the glorious divine image of the *principium individuationis,* whose gestures and expression tell us of all the joy and wisdom of "appearance," together with its beauty.

In the same work Schopenhauer has depicted for us the terrible *awe* which seizes upon man, when he is suddenly unable to account for the cognitive forms of a phenomenon, when the principle of reason, in some one of its manifestations, seems to admit of an exception. If we add to this awe the blissful ecstasy which rises from the innermost depths of man, aye, of nature, at this very collapse of the *principium individuationis,* we shall gain an insight into the nature of the *Dionysian,* which is brought home to us most intimately perhaps by the analogy of *drunkenness.* It is either under the influence of the narcotic draught, which we hear of in the songs of all primitive men and peoples, or with the potent coming of spring penetrating all nature with joy, that these Dionysian emotions awake, which, as they intensify, cause the subjective to vanish into complete self-forgetfulness. So also in the German Middle Ages singing and dancing crowds, ever increasing in number, were whirled from place to place under this same Dionysian impulse. In these dancers of St. John and St. Vitus, we rediscover the Bacchic choruses of the Greeks, with their early history in Asia Minor, as far back as Babylon and the orgiastic Sacaea. There are some, who, from obtuseness, or lack of experience, will deprecate such phenomena as "folk-diseases," with contempt or pity born of the consciousness of their own "healthy-mindedness." But, of course, such poor wretches can not imagine how anemic and ghastly their so-called "healthy-mindedness" seems in contrast to the glowing life of the Dionysian revellers rushing past them.

Under the charm of the Dionysian not only is the union between man and man reaffirmed, but Nature which has become estranged, hostile, or subjugated, celebrates once more her reconciliation with her prodigal son, man. Freely earth proffers her gifts, and peacefully the beasts of prey approach from desert and mountain. The chariot of Dionysus is bedecked with flowers and garlands; panthers and tigers pass beneath his yoke. Transform Beethoven's "Hymn to Joy" into a painting; let your imagination conceive the multitudes bowing to the dust, awestruck—then you will be able to appreciate the Dionysian. Now the slave is free; now all the stubborn, hostile barriers, which necessity, caprice or "shameless fashion" have erected between man and man, are broken down. Now, with the gospel of universal harmony, each one feels himself not only united, reconciled, blended with his neighbor, but as one with him; he feels as if the veil of Mâyâ had been torn aside and were now merely fluttering in tatters before the mysterious Primordial Unity. In song and in dance man expresses himself as a member of a higher community; he has forgotten how to walk and speak; he is about to take a dancing flight into the air. His very gestures bespeak enchantment. Just as the animals now talk, just as the earth yields milk and honey, so from him emanate supernatural sounds. He feels himself a god, he himself now walks about enchanted, in ecstasy, like to the gods whom he saw walking about in his dreams. He is no longer an artist, he has become a work of art: in these paroxysms of intoxication the artistic power of all

---

4. Principle of individuation.

nature reveals itself to the highest gratification of the Primordial Unity. The noblest clay, the most costly marble, man, is here kneaded and cut, and to the sound
of the chisel strokes of the Dionysian world-artist rings out the cry of the Eleusinian mysteries: "Do ye bow in the dust, O millions? Do you divine your creator, O
world?"

* * *

We must understand Greek tragedy as the Dionysian chorus, disburdening itself
again and again in an Apollonian image-world. The choric parts, therefore, with
which tragedy is interlaced, are in a sense the maternal womb of the entire so-called
dialogue, that is, of the whole stage-world, of the drama proper. In several successive
outbursts this primal basis of tragedy releases this vision of the drama, which is a
dream-phenomenon throughout, and, as such, epic in character: on the other hand,
however, as the objectification of a Dionysian state, it represents not the Apollonian
redemption in appearance, but, conversely, the dissolution of the individual and his
unification with primordial existence. And so the drama becomes the Apollonian embodiment of Dionysian perceptions and influences, and therefore separates itself by a
tremendous gap from the epic.

* * *

Through tragedy the myth attains its most vital content, its most expressive form;
it rises once more like a wounded hero, and its whole excess of strength, together with
the philosophic calm of the dying, burns in its eyes with a last powerful gleam.

What didst thou mean, O impious Euripides, in seeking once more to subdue this
dying one to your service? Under thy ruthless hands it died: and then thou madest use
of counterfeit, masked myth, which like the ape of Heracles could but trick itself out in
the old finery. And as myth died in thy hands, so too died the genius of music; though
thou didst greedily plunder all the gardens of music—thou didst attain but a counterfeit, masked music. And as thou hast forsaken Dionysus, Apollo hath also forsaken
thee; rouse up all the passions from their haunts and conjure them into thy circle,
sharpen and whet thy sophistical dialectic for the speeches of thy heroes—thy very heroes have but counterfeit, masked passions, and utter but counterfeit, masked words.

Greek tragedy met an end different from that of her older sister arts: she died by
suicide, in consequence of an irreconcilable conflict. Accordingly she died tragically,
while all the others passed away calmly and beautifully at a ripe old age. If it be consonant with a happy natural state to take leave of life easily, leaving behind a fair posterity, the closing period of these older arts exhibits such a happy natural state: slowly
they sink from sight, and before their dying eyes already stand their fairer progeny,
who impatiently, with a bold gesture, lift up their heads. But when Greek tragedy
died, there rose everywhere the deep feeling of an immense void. Just as the Greek
sailors in the time of Tiberius once heard upon a lonesome island the thrilling cry,
"Great Pan is dead": so now through the Hellenic world there sounded the grievous
lament: "Tragedy is dead! Poetry itself has perished with her! Away with you, ye
pale, stunted epigones! Away to Hades, that ye may for once eat your fill of the
crumbs of your former masters!"

And when after this death a new Art blossomed forth which revered tragedy as
her ancestress and mistress, it was observed with horror that she did indeed bear the
features of her mother, but that they were the very features the latter had exhibited in
her long death-struggle. It was Euripides who fought this death-struggle of tragedy.
* * * When the poet recanted, his tendency had already conquered. Dionysus had

already been scared from the tragic stage; he had been seared by a demonic power speaking through Euripides. For even Euripides was, in a sense, only a mask: the deity that spoke through him was neither Dionysus nor Apollo. It was an altogether new-born demon. And it was called *Socrates*. Thus we have a new antithesis—the Dionysian and the Socratic; and on that antithesis the art of Greek tragedy was wrecked. In vain does Euripides seek to comfort us by his recantation. It avails not: the most magnificent temple lies in ruins.

Aristophanes
c. 455–c. 386 B.C.E.

Obscene and witty, larded with topical jokes, satire, and mockery directed toward an Athenian audience, Aristophanes' comedies are notoriously difficult to translate and, until very recently, they were probably illegal to translate literally. Once upon a time, translators resorted to Latin to convey only to the learned the especially obscene passages of an Aristophanic play. Like the tragedians, the comic writers competed for the privilege of staging their plays, trained their choruses and actors, and then competed again for prizes at festivals. Aristophanes is the only comic writer of the fifth century B.C.E. whose whole plays have survived; only fragments exist from other comedies. In the course of Aristophanes' comedies, we encounter much detail from everyday Athenian life. We hear slaves talk of beatings and sellers in the marketplace complain about their customers and argue about being cheated; we learn that the Athenians love to eat fish but find it expensive and sometimes unavailable in wartime; and we hear of the prices charged by prostitutes for various sexual positions. Women characters complain of sexual deprivation and talk of dildos and of their devotion to wine. Although pederasty (the erotic relationship between men and boys) was taken for granted in many classical texts, Aristophanes mocks men who are still passive sexual partners of other men in adulthood and includes in his ridicule Agathon, a tragic playwright, parodying his literary style and accusing him of effeminacy.

The members of his audience were fair game too; Aristophanes targets gluttons, the sexually unusual, and politicians for special mockery, and his plays often stage fantastic versions of actual events. During the Peloponnesian War, Aristophanes' comedy reached new heights. In the play *Acharnians* from 425 B.C.E., for example, the symbolically named central character Dikaiopolis ("City of Justice") arranges his own private peace with the Spartans and conducts trade and business on his own. Aristophanes exhibits a hatred of the war, some sympathy for the Spartans and their way of life, and in general scorns both aristocratic decadence and what he sees as the weakness of democracy—the susceptibility of the *demos,* the people, to charismatic or demagogic leaders. He saves a special degree of loathing and mockery for the tanner's son Cleon, a favorite of the people during the Peloponnesian War. Cleon was a politician who opposed peace with Sparta and attacked a now-lost comedy of Aristophanes, *Babylonians,* as a slander against Athens. Because Cleon was a new politician, not a member of the old aristocracy, he disgusted Aristophanes, who found him an ideal target for his critique of much that had gone wrong in Athens. In *Wasps,* Aristophanes finds fault with the Athenian jury system, which gave the older citizens a wage for serving on juries and, in his view, led to an excess of lawsuits, and he also mocks the social-climbing *nouveau riche* who cultivated aristocratic tastes. He prefers peasant farmers, the backbone of the Athenian *polis:* simple, rustic men without pretensions to politics, wealth, or empire.

The comedies of Aristophanes incorporate elements of everyday life and then set their characters in vastly improbable circumstances such as the separate peace of *Acharnians* or a journey to Cloudcuckooland, a world above the earth inhabited entirely by birds, or to the underground land of the dead in *Frogs,* a comedy that delights in parodying Euripidean excess. In *Peace* the central character flies into the heavens on a dung beetle. One of Aristophanes' plays, *Clouds,* which is more grounded in ordinary reality, ridicules Socrates and his school, the Thinkery, which resembles an early version of a university, and portrays the philosopher as concerned with such matters as the measurement of flea leaps, obtained by manufacturing tiny wax booties for the fleas and counting how many booties make up a leap. Satirizing the know-nothing peasant as well as the thinker, *Clouds* presents an early version of anti-intellectualism and a fear of new thinking that confuses Socrates with his opponents, the sophists; this play may have contributed to popular resentment toward Socrates and his execution by the Athenians.

Plots in Aristophanes' plays yield to the local pleasures of jokes and mockery; often the fantastic situation of the play resolves itself somehow in time, and the participants revel at its end in riotous dance or in the sharing of a voluptuous female body by various claimants. Jokes include many references to the body and its functions, especially sexual ones. Aristophanes uses a vast array of metaphors to describe both male and female sexual organs and positions. The female body is compared, for example, to an oven, in a metaphor that occurs in other Greek material. Aristophanes extends the metaphor with jokes about women's bodies scorched from intercourse and bowls and dishes licked clean by lovers.

Most of Aristophanes' comedies belong to the fifth century B.C.E. and to what scholars call "Old Comedy," a genre of fantastic plots, discontinuities, wild obscenity, and political bite. Two of his later plays, sometimes called "Middle Comedy," *The Women at the Assembly* and *Wealth,* introduce changes, skipping the *parabasis* or direct address to the audience, and changing the role of the chorus. Subsequent New Comedy by later writers introduced romance elements, centering on private life and stock figures such as the clever slave and prefiguring later developments in its heir, the comedy of Rome.

Aristophanes produced *Lysistrata* in 411 B.C.E.; the name may refer to an actual priestess of Athena whose name is recorded in an inscription. Greek women were often seen as lustful, shamelessly sexual, and prone to drunkenness, and Aristophanes uses these stereotypes to great effect here. The circumstances of the play, a sex strike conducted by a Panhellenic alliance of women, doesn't refer to any actual event, but the very impossibility of the situation yields comic effects. The Athenians and Spartans, deadly enemies, find their women united in a utopian effort to end the Peloponnesian War and return all their men to their proper place in the marriage bed. Aristophanes, whose Dikaiopolis negotiates his own private peace treaty with the Spartans, here finds another way of expressing his and the city's exhaustion with war. The characters of the play, in general robustly heterosexual, suffer from unsatisfied lust, which is explored in some detail. The hearty and buxom Spartan Lampito, her body an object of female interest, joins with Lysistrata, Myrrhine, and other women from throughout Greece to force the men to their knees. Lysistrata braces those colleagues who try to desert the cause; the women have taken the Acropolis, the shrine of the virgin warrior goddess Athena, and they defend it, in a metaphor for their own bodies, against the lusty attacks of a united chorus of old men. In the final scene, the victorious women seize the men by their erections, reconcile Spartans with Athenians, divide up the private and public parts of the body of Reconciliation herself, and prepare to return to a world of peace and married bliss. Off the comic stage, the Peloponnesian War continued for seven more years.

Lysistrata[1]

Speaking Characters

LYSISTRATA, *an Athenian woman*

CALONICE, *an Athenian wife*

MYRRHINE, *an Athenian wife*

LAMPITO, *a Spartan woman*

MAGISTRATE, *an Athenian bureaucrat*

OLD WOMEN, *three helpers of Lysistrata*

ROD, *Myrrhine's husband*

SPARTAN HERALD

SPARTAN AMBASSADOR

ATHENIAN AMBASSADOR

ATHENIAN, *friend of the Ambassador*

Mute Characters

ATHENIAN WIVES

FOREIGN WIVES

POLICEWOMAN WITH WIVES

SLAVES WITH MAGISTRATE

POLICE WITH MAGISTRATE

ATHENIAN OLD WOMEN

NURSE WITH ROD

BABY WITH ROD

RECONCILIATION, *a naked girl*

SPARTAN HUSBANDS

ATHENIAN HUSBANDS

DOORKEEPER

Chorus

OLD WAR-VETERANS, *twelve*

OLD WIVES, *twelve*

SCENE 1

LYSISTRATA: If I'd invited them to drink some wine
      or talk about the kids or go out dancing,
      you'd hear the sound of high heels everywhere.
      But now there's not a single wife in sight.
5   Well, here's my next-door neighbor, anyway.
      Hi, Calonice.

CALONICE: Hi to you, Lysistrata.
      Hey, why the dirty looks? Cheer up, kiddo.
      Don't frown, you'll wrinkle up your pretty face.

LYSISTRATA: I'm angry, Calonice, deeply hurt,
10   in fact offended by the wives, by *us*,
      because, according to our husbands we're
      the best at clever schemes—

CALONICE: And that's the truth.

LYSISTRATA: —but when I tell them all to meet me here,
      to scheme about the most important things,
15   they're sleeping in and don't show up.

CALONICE: They'll show.
      It's not so easy getting out this early.

---

1. Translated by Jeffrey Henderson.

We've got to do our husbands little favors,
    we've got to get the servants out of bed,
    we've got to wash and feed and burp the kids.
LYSISTRATA: But they've got more important things to do
    than those!
CALONICE: OK, Lysistrata, suppose
    you tell me why we're meeting here. The deal.
    Is it a big one?
LYSISTRATA: Very big.
CALONICE: Not hard as well?
LYSISTRATA: It's very hard.
CALONICE: Then why aren't we all here?
LYSISTRATA: No, no, not that: if it were that, they'd come.
    It's something I've been thinking hard *about:*
    on sleepless nights I've tossed it back and forth.
CALONICE: I guess it must be pretty limp by now.
LYSISTRATA: It's limp all right! So limp that the salvation
30   of all of Greece lies in the women's hands!
CALONICE: In women's hands? We're goners then for sure!
LYSISTRATA: The nation's fate is in our hands alone!
    The very existence of the Spartan people—
CALONICE: It's best they *don't* exist, in my opinion.
LYSISTRATA: and all of Thebes completely obliterated—
CALONICE: Not all of Thebes: please save the caviar!
LYSISTRATA: and I don't even want to mention Athens:
    You know what I could say: you fill it in.
    But all the women, if they'd only come,
40   the Theban women and the Spartan women
    and us, together we could rescue Greece!
CALONICE: But what can women do that's sensible,
    or grand? We're good at putting make-up on,
    designer clothes and wigs and necklaces,
45   imported gowns and fancy lingerie!
LYSISTRATA: And that's exactly what will save us all:
    the little gowns, the perfumes, and the slippers,
    the make-up and the see-through lingerie!
CALONICE: And how do you figure that?
LYSISTRATA: No man alive
50   will want to lift his spear against another—
CALONICE: I guess I better go and buy some clothes!
LYSISTRATA: or lift his shield—
CALONICE: I'll put my best dress on!
LYSISTRATA: or draw his sword.
CALONICE: I've got to buy some slippers.
LYSISTRATA: So don't you think the women should have come?
CALONICE: Have come? They should have taken wings and flown!
LYSISTRATA: But look around, our fellow Athenians
    are late as always, chronically delayed.
    But I'd have thought the women from the beach towns

and the islands—

CALONICE: Lighten up, I know they're coming:
60   the island girls are good at riding topside.
LYSISTRATA: But what about the women from that town
        that's always being burnt? I thought that they
        would be the first.
CALONICE: That shipping magnate's wife,
        at any rate, is coming: she packed her schooner.
65   But look, I see some women coming now!
LYSISTRATA: And there's another bunch!
CALONICE: But what's that smell?
        What's *their* town?
LYSISTRATA: Garlicville.
CALONICE: I might have guessed:
        they must have walked right through it on their way.
MYRRHINE: I hope we're not too late, Lysistrata.
70   Well. What's the matter?
LYSISTRATA: I'm upset, Myrrhine,
        when a woman's late for such important meetings.
MYRRHINE: I couldn't find my girdle: it was dark.
        But now we're here: so tell us what's important!
LYSISTRATA: Let's cool our heels a little while longer,
75   until the Thebans and the Spartans have a chance
        to get here.
MYRRHINE: Sure, let's wait, you're running things.
        Hey, hold it, here's the Spartan Lampito!
LYSISTRATA: Lampito, darling, greetings from us all.
        What a gorgeous specimen, you lovely thing!
80   What healthy skin, what firmness of physique!
        You could take on a bull!
LAMPITO: Is not impossible.
        I go to gym, I make my buttocks hard.[2]
CALONICE: I've never seen a pair of boobs like that!
LAMPITO: You feel them: like blue-ribbon ox, you think!
LYSISTRATA: And this young lady here, where's she come from?
LAMPITO: Distinguished comrade from collective farm
        of Thebes.
MYRRHINE: I knew she had to be from Thebes:
        she looks so natural and organic.
CALONICE: Yes,
        her organs have a cultivated look.
LYSISTRATA: And who is this one?
LAMPITO: Representative

---

2. Spartans were known as blunt talkers who lived in a military state and spoke a rough dialect of Greek; they were the Athenians' rivals in the drawn-out Peloponnesian War, with other city-states rallying around the two sides. The translator gives Lampito a stereotyped Russian mode of speech, using the Cold War rivalry of U.S. and U.S.S.R. as a modern equivalent to the struggles of Athens and Sparta.

from Gulf.

CALONICE: She's got some pretty gulfs herself.
Here's one in front, and here's another one.

LAMPITO: Well: who convenes this revolutionary cell
of women?

LYSISTRATA: I did.

LAMPITO: Please to tell us then
95 agenda of the meeting.

CALONICE: Yes, my dear,
we all would like to know what's so important.

LYSISTRATA: I'll tell you in a sec. But first I'll ask
you all a little question.

CALONICE: Go ahead.

LYSISTRATA: The fathers of your kids: they're off at war.
100 You miss them, right? I know that each of you
has got a husband fighting in the war.

CALONICE: My husband's been away for five whole months.
The northern front. He's guarding his lieutenant.

MYRRHINE: Mine's in the south, been gone for *seven* months.

LAMPITO: And mine, no sooner he come home from war,
he take his shield and mobilize again.

LYSISTRATA: And how about our lovers? They're gone too.
And since we don't get imports any more,
we can't even buy a decent twelve-inch dildo.
110 Well, it's not the real thing, but at least it's something.
So, are you ready, if I had a plan in mind,
to help me end the war?

CALONICE: By God, I'm ready!
I'd even pawn my best designer jeans
and use the proceeds only to celebrate!

MYRRHINE: And you could cut me up just like a pizza,
and everyone would get a slice of it!

CALONICE: And I would climb the highest Spartan mountain:
from there I see where they have hidden peace!

LYSISTRATA: All right, I'll tell you. No need keeping secrets.
120 Well, women, if we're really serious
and want to make our husbands end the war,
we must swear off—

CALONICE: Off what?

LYSISTRATA: You'll do it, then?

CALONICE: We'll do it, even if it means our death!

LYSISTRATA: All right, here goes: we've got to swear off fucking. ✓
125 Hey, where are you going? What's this backing off?
You shake your heads, you make a pickle-face.
How come you're all so pale? How come you're crying?
Are you with me or not? What do you want to do?

CALONICE: I'm out. I guess I'll let the war drag on.

MYRRHINE: Me too. I guess I'll let the war drag on.

LYSISTRATA: This from you, Ms. Pizza? You just said

you wanted us to slice you up in pieces.

CALONICE: If there's anything else at all, that's fine. Through fire
I would even walk. But as for fucking, no.

135 There's nothing like it, dear Lysistrata.

LYSISTRATA: And you?

WIFE: I guess I'll walk through fire too.

LYSISTRATA: Oh, what a low and shameless race are we!
No wonder men write tragedies about us.
We're nothing but a diaper and a bed.

140 But Lampito, comrade, surely you'll be willing.
If you alone would join me, we could do it!
What do you say?

LAMPITO: Is definitely hard
for women to sleep alone without the penis.
But nevertheless we must. We need the peace.

LYSISTRATA: Oh, dearest comrade, manliest of women!

CALONICE: Look, *if* we really swear off . . . what you say,
which God forbid, would that be really likely
to bring peace?

LYSISTRATA: I am absolutely positive.
If we go home, and get ourselves made up,

150 and slip on one of our imported gowns
with nothing underneath, and show some crotch,
our husbands will get hard and want to screw;
but if we keep away and don't go near them,
they'll soon enough make peace, you have my word.

LAMPITO: Remember Helen of Troy, whose warrior husband
looked at her naked tits and dropped his sword![3]

CALONICE: But what if our husbands pay us no attention?

LYSISTRATA: As the saying goes, you've got to use your head.

CALONICE: But that's no good, I wouldn't stoop to that.

160 And they might resort to violence, and drag us off
to the bedroom.

LYSISTRATA: Then you'll have to grab the door-jamb.

CALONICE: And if they beat us up?

LYSISTRATA: Then don't cooperate.
Men don't enjoy it when they have to force you.
And make them suffer otherwise as well.

165 They'll give. There's never been a happy man
who doesn't have a peaceful married life.

CALONICE: If you and Lampito want to, so do I.

LAMPITO: So: I am sure that we persuade our men
for peace with honor, nothing up the sleeve.

170 But Athenians are a democratic mob:
how you propose to get them to agree?

LYSISTRATA: Don't worry, I'll take care of the Athenians.

3. At the fall of Troy, Menelaos was about to kill Helen but stopped when she bared her breasts, overcoming him with her beauty.

LAMPITO: But the military and industrial complex,
     your capital funds stored on the citadel!
LYSISTRATA: I tell you, I've anticipated that.
     We're seizing the whole citadel today.
     The old women took on that assignment.
     They'll pretend to have religious business there.
     They're at it now, while we conclude our plans.
LAMPITO: I must admit, your plan sounds quite complete.
LYSISTRATA: Then, Lampito, let's swear an oath without
     delay, and then our plan will be official.
LAMPITO: Propose the oath, and we all swear to it.
LYSISTRATA: All right, then. Officeress! Where is she? Wake her up!
185   Put down your shield here. No, the other way.
     Now someone get a victim.
CALONICE: Say, Lysistrata,
     what sort of oath is this?
LYSISTRATA: What sort of oath?
     A slaughter in a shield, like tragic ones,
     the fatted calf: you know.
CALONICE: We can't do that,
190   we shouldn't use a shield if we want peace.
LYSISTRATA: What's *your* suggestion, smarty?
CALONICE: I suggest,
     we get a full-grown cock and slaughter that.
LYSISTRATA: You've got a one-track mind.
CALONICE: But then what *will*
     we swear on?
LYSISTRATA: Something's hit me. Want to hear?
195   Let's chuck the shield and get a giant wine-glass,
     and slaughter a great big bottle of red bordeaux,
     and swear we'll never fill the glass with water!
LAMPITO: Oh da!° One cannot quarrel with that oath.   *yes*
LYSISTRATA: So someone get the bottle and the glass.
MYRRHINE: Oh God, girls, take a look at all that glassware!
CALONICE: And just to touch this bottle makes me come!
LYSISTRATA: So put it down! Join hands, now, everyone.
     O Goddess of Persuasion, Conspiratorial Glass:
     receive this offering from the wives. Amen.
CALONICE: Behold the color of the gurgling blood.
LAMPITO: Perceive the sweetness of its fair aroma.
MYRRHINE: I'd like to be the first to take the oath.
CALONICE: Hey, not so fast, you've got to wait your turn.
LYSISTRATA: No! *All* hands on the glass. You also, Lampito.
210   Let one of you repeat the oath I make,
     and everybody else swear her allegiance.
     I won't allow my lover or my husband—
CALONICE: I won't allow my lover or my husband—
LYSISTRATA: to get near me with a hard-on. I can't hear you!
CALONICE: to get near me with a hard-on. Oh my God!

My knees are getting weak, Lysistrata!

LYSISTRATA: At home my life will be completely chaste.

CALONICE: At home my life will be completely chaste.

LYSISTRATA: I'll wear my sexiest dresses and cosmetics—

CALONICE: I'll wear my sexiest dresses and cosmetics—

LYSISTRATA: to make my man as horny as can be.

CALONICE: to make my man as horny as can be.

LYSISTRATA: But never will I willingly give in.

CALONICE: But never will I willingly give in.

LYSISTRATA: If he should get his way by violence—

CALONICE: If he should get his way by violence—

LYSISTRATA: I'll simply lie there uncooperative.

CALONICE: I'll simply lie there uncooperative.

LYSISTRATA: I will not wrap my legs around his back—

CALONICE: I will not wrap my legs around his back—

LYSISTRATA: nor will I crouch down like a lioness.

CALONICE: nor will I crouch down like a lioness.

LYSISTRATA: As I drink this wine, so will I keep this oath—

CALONICE: As I drink this wine, so will I keep this oath—

LYSISTRATA: but if I break it, may the wine be water.

CALONICE: but if I break it, may the wine be water.

LYSISTRATA: So say you one and all?

ALL: So say we all!

LYSISTRATA: All right, I'll do the honors.

CALONICE: Just make sure
you take one share: we must have solidarity.

LAMPITO: What's that?

LYSISTRATA: The signal: as I said before,
the ladies who would seize the citadel.
They've done it already! Listen, Lampito:
return to Sparta now, and start the strike.

245   And leave these women here as hostages.
The rest of us will enter the citadel
and lock the gates and barricade ourselves.

CALONICE: But don't you think the men will try to stop us?
And pretty quickly?

LYSISTRATA: They don't worry me.

250   They'll come with torches, shouting and making threats,
but they can't make us open up these gates
until they promise to honor our demands.

CALONICE: By Sex and Love they can't! For otherwise,
we're nothing but a weak and gutless gender.

MEN'S CHORUS

LEADER: Come on, sergeant, get a move on,
          even if your shoulder's raw
Hefting all this heavy wood and
          dragging all of it uphill.

CHORUS (1):[4] Incredible and shocking too
260   for wives to act like this!
    We fed and clothed them: now we find
      they're dirty terrorists!

    They seized the City Treasury
    and Offices of State.
265   They occupy our holy ground
      and won't unlock the gate!
LEADER: Butts in gear, men, double-time it,
      stack them right against the gate;
    then we'll pile them all around it,
270   sealing in the enemy troops:
    every single female traitor
      party to this coup d'etat.
    Then we'll make a giant bonfire:
      toss your flares at my command.
275   Death by burning is our verdict,
      starting with the bitch in charge.
CHORUS (1): While we're alive they'll never have
      the laugh on this old geezer!
    Remember when the Spartans first
280   attempted such a seizure?

    They came on big but went out small,
      their reputation shot.
    We didn't even let them keep
      a rag to wipe their snot!
LEADER: Ranks in order, siege positions,
      just the way we did it then.
    Let these women beat us now and
      all our reputation's gone.
CHORUS (2): The goal of our journey's around the bend.
290   but the steepest part's at the very end.
    Our shoulders are aching, we're out of fuel.
      It would have been smarter to bring a mule.

    But keep it moving all the same,
      and don't forget to fan the flame.
295   There's little point in climbing higher,
      then finding out we've lost our fire.
    God, the smoke!
CHORUS (2): The smoke's rushing out like a raving bitch
      and biting our eyes with an awful itch.
300   Can't see where we're going: it seems to us
      we're climbing the slopes of Vesuvius.

    But hurry onward anyhow:
      We've got to save the goddess now!

---

4. The Chorus divides in two groups to sing and dance.

    Our Purple Hearts aren't worth a dime
305   unless we help her out this time.
    God, the smoke!
LEADER: Now the fire's burning lively,
      now the gods are on our side.
    Stack the logs and set your torches,
310   then we'll charge the gate like rams,
    Open up, you wives, or else we'll
      burn the gates and smoke you out.
    Place the logs in orderly fashion.
      Ah, this smoke is terrible!
315   Can't the generals hear us? Won't they
      lift some logs? Our arms are dead.
    Pot of Coals, it's up to you now:
      furnish fire; I'll lead the charge.
    Victory Goddess, lend assistance,
320   help us beat these mutinous wives!

WOMEN'S CHORUS

WOMEN'S LEADER: I think I see the smoke and rising flames!
    The siege is underway. We've got to hurry!
CHORUS (3): Faster, faster, we've got to fly,
    or else our friends will surely die!
325 Some nasty elders have got a view
    to hold a female barbecue!

We started early but might be late:
    we had to fill our pitchers.
The well was jammed, we got delayed
330   by slaves and pushy bitches,

shouting, shoving, smashing pots,
    banging heads and raising knots.
Now we're here with pitchers filled
    to keep our friends from being grilled.
CHORUS (3): There they are, the demented bums!
    They're stacking logs to burn our chums,
shouting threats of an awful kind,
    to leave but ash and smoke behind.

O Goddess, spare the women's life!
340   They occupied your temple
to save the Greeks from war and strife
    and madness pure and simple.

Be our ally, help defend
    women fighting evil men.
345 Help us with our pitchers filled
    to keep our friends from getting grilled.
WOMEN'S LEADER: Hold it, girls! What's this I see here?
    Men, and evil bastards too.

MEN'S LEADER: What the hell is going on here?
350   Where's this swarm of women from?
WOMEN: Scared of us? We're not so many.
     Still, there's more where we came from.
MEN: Boys, do you hear all this babble?
     Someone bash her with a log.
WOMEN: Put your pitchers on the ground, girls:
     looks as if they want a fight.
MEN: How'd you like to have your mouth shut?
     Two or three punches ought to do.
WOMEN: Come on, hit me: I'm not moving.
360   I would love to chew your balls.
MEN: Quiet, or I'll bust your wrinkles!
WOMEN: Go ahead, just lift your hand.
MEN: What about my knuckles? What then?
WOMEN: Want to have your guts pulled out?
MEN: Tragic poets have a saying:
     nothing's wilder than a woman!
WOMEN: Come on, girls, let's lift our pitchers.
MEN: What's this water for, you bitch?
WOMEN: What's this fire, you mausoleum?
MEN: Just a pyre for your friends.
WOMEN: I'm about to douse your pyre.
MEN: Douse it?
WOMEN: That's exactly right.
MEN: How'd you like your hair on fire?
WOMEN: Get some soap: I've got your bath.
MEN: Bath, you crone?
WOMEN: You really need one.
MEN: Listen to her!
WOMEN: I've a right.
MEN: Quiet!
WOMEN: You're not judge and jury now.
MEN: Burn her hair!
WOMEN: And now the bath!
MEN: Goddamn!
WOMEN: I hope we didn't scald you.
MEN: Scald us? Stop! We've had enough!
WOMEN: Maybe now you'll start to blossom.
MEN: No, we'll wither up instead.
WOMEN: You brought the fire: warm yourselves.

SCENE 2

MAGISTRATE: I hear our spoiled wives are out of hand.
     Another phony festival for their wine-god,
     a noisy rooftop party for Adonis,[1]
     just like the one that spoiled our assembly.

1. Beautiful youth loved by the goddess Aphrodite, killed by a wild boar, and mourned by the women of the city.

           d, foolish politician moved
           icily, while his wife was dancing
         ig for Adonis. When he said,
        aster allied troops for this armada,
      ife was on the rooftop getting drunk
     d yelling "Oh doomed youth!" But he persisted,
    ne goddamned stubborn hotheaded son of a bitch![2]
    That's just the kind of mischief wives can make!

MEN'S LEADER: And wait till I tell you what they did to *us*.
    They treated us like slaves and dumped their pitchers
15   all over us and soaked our clothes through,
    so anyone would say we pissed our pants!

MAGISTRATE: It serves you right, I swear by the salty sea-god.
    We men have only got ourselves to blame.
    We virtually teach our wives to misbehave,
20   and so they're always nurturing their plots.
    What do we say when we visit the marketplace?
    "Oh, goldsmith, about that locket I bought from you.
    My wife was having a ball the other night
    and it seems this bolt here slipped right out of its hole.
25   I've got to leave, I'm travelling up to Bangor.
    I'd be grateful if you'd visit her some night
    with the proper tool and fix the hole that needs it."
    Another husband visits his local shoemaker,
    a half-grown boy with a very full-grown cock.
30   "Say, shoemaker, about this pair of slippers:
    my wife complains the orifice grips too tight;
    her skin is very soft. While I'm at work,
    please loosen up her orifice a bit."
    It's this complacency that leads to trouble,
35   so here I am, a supplier for the army,
    in need of public funds, and now I find
    the women have shut me out of the treasury!
    I'm wasting time. You slaves, bring on the crowbars!
    I'll put a stop to all this female foolery.
40   You bozo, look alive! And you as well!
    Stop wondering if there're any bars around.
    Pick up those crowbars, take them to the gate,
    and pry it open. Here, I'll show you how,
    I'll help you pry.

LYSISTRATA: No need for any prying.
45   I'm coming out myself. No need for crowbars.
    We don't need force, but rather brains and sense.

MAGISTRATE: That so, you bitch? I'm calling a policeman.
    Arrest this woman, put the handcuffs on.

LYSISTRATA: By the goddess, if he lays a hand on me,
50   policeman or no policeman, he'll regret it.

---

2. The expedition against Sicily was a major defeat for Athens in the war.

MAGISTRATE: Can you be scared of her? Go on and grab her.
    And you there, help him out. Hogtie the woman!
OLD WOMAN A: By the goddess, if you even raise your hand
    to her, I'll beat you till you shit your pants!
MAGISTRATE: What, shit my pants? Another policeman here!
    Grab this one first, the one with the dirty mouth.
OLD WOMAN B: By the goddess, if you lay a fingertip
    on her, you'll need an icebag for both eyes.
MAGISTRATE: Where'd *she* come from? Police! Arrest this woman!
60   Whoever's on this outing I'll arrest.
OLD WOMAN C: By the goddess, if you make a move toward her,
    I'll pull your hair out until you're bloody bald.
MAGISTRATE: My god, I'm out of cops! I'm in a fix.
    I *cannot* let myself be screwed by women!
65   We need a full-scale charge. Attention, Huns!
    Prepare to charge!
LYSISTRATA: As you will quickly see,
    we too have troops, four companies of women:
    they're fully armed and on alert inside.
MAGISTRATE: Go forward, Huns, and twist their arms behind them!
LYSISTRATA: Come forward, allied women, on the double!
    You market-women, meter-maids, bag-ladies!
    You check-out girls, mud-wrestlers, waitresses!
    Attack them, stomp them, chew them, beat them up!
    Cease fire! Stand at ease, don't chase them down!
MAGISTRATE: Alas, my Huns are utterly defeated.
LYSISTRATA: But what did you expect? Did you imagine
    that we were slaves, or did you think that women
    can't show courage?
MAGISTRATE: Courage, yes indeed,
    provided there's a lot of booze inside 'em.
MEN'S LEADER: Why waste your breath, my Magistrate,
    why argue with these bitches?
    You know the kind of bath we took
    without that kind of soft soap.
WOMEN'S LEADER: Dear sir, it's impolite to raise
85   your hand against your neighbors.
    Try that again, we'll punch you out,
    though we prefer decorum.
    We promise to be meek as girls,
    so don't stir up a mare's nest.
MEN'S CHORUS (4): King of the gods, these women are beasts!
    We need a plan, to say the least!
    Let's try to find out
    what they're angry about,
    why they're raising hell
95   on our sacred citadel.
MEN'S LEADER: Now question her and test her answers,
    and don't be buffaloed.

It's bad enough they've gone this far;
    we mustn't let it go!

MAGISTRATE: First I'd like to know the reason
    why you took the citadel.

LYSISTRATA: Confiscation of the money:
    thus we put a stop to war.

MAGISTRATE: Money's causing war?

LYSISTRATA: Exactly:

105   also the political mess.
    Generals and politicians
      argue war so they can steal.
    Go ahead and fight, but henceforth
      no more money leaves this place.

MAGISTRATE: *You* will keep it.

LYSISTRATA: No, we'll save it.

MAGISTRATE: Save it?

LYSISTRATA: What's so strange in that?
    Don't we manage household money?

MAGISTRATE: Not the same.

LYSISTRATA: How so?

MAGISTRATE: It's war!

LYSISTRATA: Stop the war.

MAGISTRATE: Then who will save us?

LYSISTRATA: *We* will.

MAGISTRATE: You?

LYSISTRATA: That's right.

MAGISTRATE: My god!

LYSISTRATA: What's your choice?

MAGISTRATE: You're mad!

LYSISTRATA: *Be* angry.
    Nonetheless we must.

MAGISTRATE: No way!

LYSISTRATA: Must.

MAGISTRATE: If I refuse?

LYSISTRATA: I'd like that!

MAGISTRATE: Dare you speak of war and peace?

LYSISTRATA: Yes.

MAGISTRATE: So make it fast.

LYSISTRATA: I'll do that.
    Calm yourself.

MAGISTRATE: It's difficult:
    itchy fists.

OLD WOMAN A: You risk a beating.

MAGISTRATE: Shut up, bag. *You* talk.

LYSISTRATA: I will.
    All along we kept our silence,

125   acquiesced as nice wives should—
    or else!—although we didn't like it.
    You would escalate the war;

we would ask you so politely,
    even though it hurt inside,
130   "Darling, what's the latest war-news?
    What did all you men decree?
    Anything about a treaty?"
    Then you'd say, "What's that to you?
    Shut up!" And I'd shut up.

OLD WOMAN B: Not me!

MAGISTRATE: Then I'd smack you!

LYSISTRATA: There you are.
    Then we'd hear some even worse news,
        so we'd say, "How stupid, dear!"
    Then you'd give us dirty looks and
        say, "Go mend my cloak or else!
140   War is strictly for the menfolk."

MAGISTRATE: Right we were.

LYSISTRATA: You stupid fool!
    We were quite prepared to warn you;
        you refused to hear advice.
    Then disaster. Throughout the city
145   "All our boys are gone!" you cried.
    That's when all the wives decided
        we must act to save the Greeks.
    Thus we're here: no point in waiting.
        Want to hear some good advice?
150   Shut your mouth the way *we* used to,
        let us save you from yourselves.

MAGISTRATE: You save *us?* That's madness!

LYSISTRATA: Shut up!

MAGISTRATE: Me shut up for you? You skirt!
    Let me die before that happens!

LYSISTRATA: It's my skirt that bothers you?
    Give the man a skirt and bonnet:
        Maybe that will shut him up.

OLD WOMAN C: Here's a sewing basket also!

LYSISTRATA: Now he needs some chewing gum.
160   Put a little lipstick on him,
        stuff your hankies down his shirt.
    War is strictly for the women!

WOMEN'S LEADER: Women arise, let go your jars.
    It's time to help these friends of ours.

WOMEN'S CHORUS (4): I'm dancing forever, I'll never retreat,
    never be tired or get cold feet!
    I'm ready to strive
    for the cause of the wives,
    who are decent, smart,
170   patriotic, bold of heart!

WOMEN'S LEADER: Most valiant child of bold fore-mothers,
    no slow-down or retreat!

     You've got him where you want him now:
          you're in the driver's seat!
LYSISTRATA: Goddess of sex and sweet desire,
          breathe upon our breasts and flanks,
     give our husbands lasting hard-ons,
          help us make them leave the ranks.
MAGISTRATE: What's your plan?
LYSISTRATA: My first requirement:
180   soldiers leave the marketplace.
OLD WOMAN A: Hear, hear!
LYSISTRATA: They strut about in armor,
          pushing shoppers, smashing goods.
MAGISTRATE: Manly men!
LYSISTRATA: But pretty comic,
          stacking burgers on their shields.
OLD WOMAN B: God, I've seen those grand lieutenants
          use their helmets for a bowl.
     Mercenaries slap the salesgirls,
          never even pay their bill!
MAGISTRATE: *You* can stop these wartime hardships,
190   I'm to gather?
LYSISTRATA: Sure!
MAGISTRATE: And how?
LYSISTRATA: Open up your sewing basket:
          see the skein of tangled wool?
     Put it to the spindle this way,
          wind it here, now wind it there.
195   Thus the war can be unravelled,
          making truces here, and there.
MAGISTRATE: Skiens and spindles? I don't get it.
LYSISTRATA: Sense and skill is all you need.
MAGISTRATE: Show me.
LYSISTRATA: Gladly. First you wash the
200   city as we wash the wool,
          cleaning out the bullshit. Then we
          pluck away the parasites;
     break up strands that clump together,
          forming special interest groups;
205   Here's a bozo: squeeze his head off.
          Now you're set to card the wool:
     use your basket for the carding,
          the basket of solidarity.
     There we put our migrant workers,
210   foreign friends, minorities,
     immigrants and wage-slaves, every
          person useful to the state.
     Don't forget our allies, either,
          languishing like separate strands.
215   Bring it all together now, and

make one giant ball of yarn.
>   Now you're ready: weave a brand new
>   suit for all the citizens.

MAGISTRATE: War is not the same as wool-balls!
220   What do women know of war?

LYSISTRATA: Even more than you do, asshole.
>   First of all we make the children,
>   Then we send them off to war, then—

MAGISTRATE: That's enough! I take your point.

LYSISTRATA: What about young wives? They waste their
>   prime of life in solitude.
>   What about the girls who'll grow old
>   long before they find a man?

MAGISTRATE: Men get old too.

LYSISTRATA: That's quite different.
230   Men can always get a girl,
>   even greybeards. Girls don't have that
>   luxury. Their time is short.
>   Men won't marry older girls: they
>   pine away in spinsterhood.

MAGISTRATE: Lucky men! For us it's easy:
>   all we need is in our pants!

LYSISTRATA: Time for you to die, old geezer.
>   Fetch your coffin. Here's a grave-site.
>   We'll arrange the funeral.
240   Put a lily in his hand.

OLD WOMAN C: Here's a wreath.

OLD WOMAN A: And here's a bible.

LYSISTRATA: What are you waiting for? You're dead!
>   Off to the big bureaucracy in the sky.
245   You're holding up St. Peter.[3]

MAGISTRATE: You haven't heard the last of this. Outrageous!
>   By god, I'll show the other magistrates
>   exactly what you've done to me. So there!

LYSISTRATA: I hope you won't complain about your funeral.
250   We did our best. I tell you what: we'll hold
>   a proper service at your grave: a dance!

MEN'S CHORUS

MEN'S LEADER: Wake up men, defend our manhood!
>   Strip for action! Dance away!

CHORUS (5): There's more to this outbreak
255   than you might guess:
>   we're sure that these women
>   are terrorists!

The Spartans have managed
>   to infiltrate

---

3. In the original, Charon, underworld ferryman.

260   our houses and women:
    and next the state!

    The citadel-seizure
      we understand:
    They're putting an end to
265   our pension plan!
LEADER: Outrageous that these women dare to prate
    of war and peace and governing the state!
    And then they tell us we should make a deal
    with Spartans, who are slipperier than an eel!
270   It's nothing but a plan for tyranny.
    While I'm alive they won't do that to me.
    I'll fight these women with my dying breath.
    For I say, Give me liberty or give me death!
    I'm standing tall, a loyal patriot:
275   if you don't like it I'll kick you in the butt!

WOMEN'S CHORUS

WOMEN'S LEADER: You'll soon be running home to mommy.
    Strip for action, girls, and dance!
CHORUS (5): A debt to our country
      we must repay:
280   so we've good advice for
      you all today.

    We're healthy and happy
      and well-to-do,
    and all our successes
285   we owe to you.

    Our schools and our temples,
      our social lives:
    they all helped to make us
      your perfect wives.
LEADER: With good advice we want to pay you back.
    Don't worry that it comes from Jill not Jack.
    Consider it on its merits. Anyway,
    we bear the children and deserve our say.
    What contribution do these old men make?
295   They never seem to give, but only take.
    We pay for all their laws, their wars, their theft.
    And they'll keep taking till there's nothing left.
    Old men, I warn you: better hold your peace.
    You make a sound, we'll kick you in the teeth!

MEN'S CHORUS (6)

300   I've seen a lot of arrogance,
      but this outdoes it all.
    We've got to beat them down to size

if we've still got the balls.
LEADER: Take your shirts off, you're not tacos!
305   Let them whiff your manly smell!
CHORUS: We once were Athenian raiders,
    we dealt mercilessly with traitors.
        Let's do it again,
        pretend we're young men,
310   not washed-up old alligators!
LEADER: We can't afford to let them get the jump,
    for women are a match for any hump.
    They might build submarines and strike below:
    we wouldn't know just when to expect the blow.
315   We'd hate to face equestrian encounters,
    for women are indomitable mounters.
    You'll never shake them off once they get on:
    just look at pictures of the Amazons![4]
    We must move now to make their plot a wreck,
320   so let's move out and grab them by the neck!

WOMEN'S CHORUS (6)

Go on and get our fire going,
    and pull the bitch's tail!
Then all your buddies get to hear
    how loud you weep and wail.
LEADER: Take your skirts off, don't be modest!
    Let them whiff an angry sow!
CHORUS: We wait for the note of your clarion,
    you nattering octogenarian!
        Just give us a chance
330   to pull down your pants
    and deliver your balls by caesarean.
LEADER: And anyway your efforts are for naught:
    the wives are carrying out a foolproof plot.
    Pass all the laws you want and call for war:
335   the decent folks will only hate you more.
    Just yesterday I had a picnic planned
    for a lovely visitor from a foreign land,
    in fact a pot of Theban caviar!
    But nothing doing: that's against your law.
340   You'll keep on regulating us, no doubt,
    till someone picks you up and throws you out.

SCENE 3

Hail, leader of our common enterprise!
    But why emerge? How come you look so sad?
LYSISTRATA: The wives reveal their baseness and grow weak.
    It's got me down, I don't know what to do.

---

4. Mythical women warriors.

LEADER: What's that you say?

LYSISTRATA: It's true, it's true.

LEADER: Let's hear it all: we're friends that you can trust.

LYSISTRATA: A shame to speak but risky to keep quiet.

LEADER: Don't hide a crisis that affects us all!

LYSISTRATA: I'll make it short: they're dying to get laid.

LEADER: Oh gods!

LYSISTRATA: I doubt the gods can get us out of this.
          I certainly can't keep on withholding wives
          from husbands: they're determined to escape.

15   I caught one by that grotto with a shovel,
          scraping away and widening her hole.
          Another one was climbing on that pulley,
          pulling herself off. And another one
          got on a giant bird, said "take me to

20   a whorehouse!" Luckily I grabbed her hair.
          And every excuse for going home there is,
          they make. I think that's one of them right now.
          Hey you, where to?

WIFE A: I've got to run back home.
          My bolts of woolen cloth, the finest kind,

25   are very much in need of moth-balls.

LYSISTRATA: Moth-balls?
          Get back in there!

WIFE: I swear I'll come right back.
          Just let me spread my wool out on the bed.

LYSISTRATA: You won't be spreading anything, nor be leaving.

WIFE: But then my wool will go to waste!

LYSISTRATA: So be it.

WIFE B: Oh stupid me, forgetting to tenderize
          the meat. I've got to go and beat it.

LYSISTRATA: Here's
          another who forgot to beat her meat.
          Get back inside!

WIFE: I swear I'll be right back.
          Just let me roll it in my hands a bit.

LYSISTRATA: No! Keep your hands to yourself. If you do this,
          then all the wives will want to do the same.

WIFE C: O Goddess of Labor, hold my pains a while,
          till I can get to a proper birthing place!

LYSISTRATA: What's all this yelling?

WIFE: I'm having a baby now!

LYSISTRATA: But yesterday you were skinny.

WIFE: Not today.
          I've got to see the doctor, dear Lysistrata:
          please send me home.

LYSISTRATA: Let's have a look at you.
          What's this? It sounds like metal.

WIFE: It's a boy!

LYSISTRATA: I'd swear you've got some hollow metal thing
45   beneath your dress. Let's pull it up and see.
          You card! You've got Athena's helmet there!
          Are you still pregnant?
WIFE: Yes indeed I am.
LYSISTRATA: Then what's the helmet for?
WIFE: In case the baby
          comes while I'm still here. Then I'd deliver it
50   into the helmet, like a nesting bird.
LYSISTRATA: Preposterous, an obvious excuse.
          You'll have to exercise the nesting option.
WIFE C: I can't get any sleep here on the citadel,
          not since I saw the Goddess' sacred snake!
WIFE D: I can't sleep either. I toss and turn all night,
          what with the hooting of the sacred owls.
LYSISTRATA: Enough! I won't hear any more excuses!
          You miss your husbands, fine. But don't you know
          they miss you too? I'm sure the nights they spend
60   are miserably lonely. Please hold out,
          please bear with me a little while longer.
          I've got a prophecy here predicting victory,
          provided we stay together. Want to hear it?
WIFE A: Let's hear the prophecy.
LYSISTRATA: Be quiet then.
65   Yea, when the birds shall hole up in a single place,
          fleeing the eagles and keeping themselves quite chaste,
          then shall their problems be solved, they'll be on top,
          so says the King of the Gods—
WIFE B: We'll be on top?
LYSISTRATA: But: if the birds start to argue and fly away
70   down from the citadel holy, all will say:
          no bird more disgusting and shameless lives today!
WIFE: A pretty explicit prophecy. My god!
LYSISTRATA: So let's hear no more talk of backing out.
          We'll all go back inside, for what a shame,
75   dear friends, if we betray the prophecy.

MEN'S CHORUS (7)

          I want to tell you all a tale.
              I heard it as a lad.
          Once there was a man called Black,
              who lived as a nomad.

80   A faithful dog his company,
              he hunted and he roamed,
          he made his nets and set his traps
              but never would go home.

          Because he hated women so,
85   and that's where he was wise.

> We follow Black's example in
>   that women we despise!

MEN'S LEADER: How about a kiss, old ghoul?

WOMEN'S LEADER: Wash your mouth out first, you fool!

MEN'S LEADER: I've got something for you here.

WOMEN'S LEADER: All I see is pubic hair.

MEN'S LEADER: That's right, I'm bushy down below.

> But manly men are always so!
>   Whenever I display my buns,
95   the enemy drops his spear and runs!

WOMEN'S CHORUS (7)

> Our hero answers all your tales
>   about that other dope.
> His name was Timon and he was
>   a total misanthrope.

100   He wandered in the mountains too,
>   and acted very mean.
> If anybody crossed his path
>   he'd pick their carcass clean.

> He couldn't stand men's evil ways,
105   but women he enjoyed.
> We too stand up for principles,
>   of which you are devoid.

WOMEN'S LEADER: You want me to re-do your nose?

MEN'S LEADER: No way, it doesn't need your blows.

WOMEN'S LEADER: So what about a stomping, then?

MEN'S LEADER: Your bush resembles a pig-pen.

WOMEN'S LEADER: You liar! That's a blatant slander!

> Just go ahead and take a gander:
>   my hair may be as white as snow,
115   but I keep myself well-groomed below.

SCENE 4

LYSISTRATA: Hey, women, women, come and take a look!
> Come quick!

WIFE: What's happening? What's the fuss about?

LYSISTRATA: A man is coming. By the look of him
> he's suffering from satyriasis.[1]

5   O Goddess of Love and Pangs of Sweet Desire,
> make this man's journey straight and very upright!

WIFE: Where is he, whoever it is?

LYSISTRATA: He's by that cave.

WIFE: I see him now! Who is he?

LYSISTRATA: Anyone know?

MYRRHINE: Oh god, I do! That's my own husband, Rod!

---

1. Permanent erection.

LYSISTRATA: You've got to light his fire, get him hot,
        do everything that turns him on, except
        the thing you're under oath not to. OK?
MYRRHINE: Don't worry, I can do it.
LYSISTRATA: Very well.
        While you get ready I'll try to get *him* ready
15   and warm him up a bit. Now out of sight!
ROD: O woe is me! I've got a terrible cramp!
        It's like I'm being broken on the rack!
LYSISTRATA: Who enters our defense perimeter?
ROD: Me.
LYSISTRATA: A man?
ROD: Just look!
LYSISTRATA: In that case please depart.
ROD: Who's telling me to leave?
LYSISTRATA: The daytime guard.
ROD: I've come for Myrrhine. Tell her that I'm here!
LYSISTRATA: You give me orders? Who do you think you are?
ROD: Her husband, Rodney Balling, from Bangtown.
LYSISTRATA: A lovely name! You know, we consider it
25   our very favorite topic of conversation.
        Your wife has little else upon her lips.
        She'll eat bananas, or a peanut, sighing,
        "If only this were really Balling!"
ROD: God!
LYSISTRATA: Yes sir! And any time the conversation turns
30   to men, your wife speaks up forthwith and says,
        "Compared to Balling, nothing else exists!"
ROD: Please, call her out!
LYSISTRATA: Got anything for me?
ROD: Indeed I do. You're very welcome, too.
        What's mine is yours. How's this? It's what I've got.
LYSISTRATA: I think I'll call your wife. Hold on.
ROD: Be quick!
        I have no joy or pleasure in my life
        since my Myrrhine up and left the house.
        I open up the door and start to cry,
        it looks so empty! Then I try to eat,
40   but I can hardly taste the food. I'm horny!
MYRRHINE: I love him dearly, but he doesn't want
        to love me back! Don't make me see him! Please!
ROD: Oh Pussikins, my darling, what's the matter?
        Come down here!
MYRRHINE: I'm not coming anywhere!
ROD: You won't obey me when I say to come?
MYRRHINE: I fail to see a reason for your summons.
ROD: A reason? Don't you see what shape I'm in?
MYRRHINE: Goodbye.
ROD: No, wait! Perhaps you'll want to hear

from Junior. Come on, yell for mommy, kid.

BABY: Mommy! Mommy! Mommy!

ROD: Well, what's the matter? Don't you pity him?
You know he's been six days without your breasts!

MYRRHINE: I feel for Junior, but it's very clear
you don't.

ROD: Get down here, woman, and see your child!

MYRRHINE: O motherhood, what a drag! I'll be right down.

ROD: She seems much sexier and even younger
than I remember. Very tasty looking!
She acted tough, and very haughty too,
but that just makes me want her even more!

MYRRHINE: Poor sweetie pie! With such a lousy father.
I'll kiss and cuddle you, my darling child.

ROD: The hell you think you're doing, listening to
those women? You only piss me off and hurt
yourself as well.

MYRRHINE: Don't lay your hands on me!

ROD: You know our home's an utter mess. You just
let everything go.

MYRRHINE: It doesn't bother me.

ROD: It doesn't bother you that all your clothes
were dragged away by chickens?

MYRRHINE: Not at all.

ROD: And worse, your sacred duty as my mate
70   has been neglected! Thus you must return.

MYRRHINE: I'm going nowhere till you swear on oath
to vote to end the war.

ROD: I'll maybe do that,
if it's appropriate.

MYRRHINE: Then maybe I'll go home,
if it's appropriate. But now I'm sworn to stay.

ROD: OK, at least lie down with me awhile.

MYRRHINE: I won't. But I don't say I wouldn't like to.

ROD: You would? Then why not do it, pussy mine?

MYRRHINE: Oh really, Rod, in front of Junior here?

ROD: Of course not. Nurse, take Junior home at once.
80   All right, the kid's no longer in our way.
Let's do it!

MYRRHINE: Do it where, you silly man?
It's public here!

ROD: You're right. Hey, there's a cave.

MYRRHINE: I must be pure to re-enter the citadel.

ROD: Then purify yourself in the sacred spring there.

MYRRHINE: But what about my oath? I won't be perjured.

ROD: A women's oath means nothing. I'm not worried.

MYRRHINE: Well, let me get a bed.

ROD: But I don't need one:
the ground's OK by me.

MYRRHINE: I wouldn't dream
     of making you lie there (though you deserve it).
ROD: She really loves me, that's quite obvious.
MYRRHINE: Your bed, sir. Lie right down, I'll tuck you in.
     But I forgot, what is it, yes, a mattress.
ROD: A mattress? None for me, thanks.
MYRRHINE: I'm uncomfortable
     on box-springs.
ROD: Give me just a little kiss?
MYRRHINE: OK.
ROD: Oh lordy! Get the mattress quick!
MYRRHINE: And here it is. Stay down while I undress.
     But I forget, what is it, yes, a pillow.
ROD: But I'm all set, I need no pillow.
MYRRHINE: I do.
ROD: It's like a restaurant where they serve no food.
MYRRHINE: Lift up, now, up. Well, now I think I'm set.
ROD: I know I am! Come here to papa, darling!
MYRRHINE: I'm taking off my bra. But don't forget,
     don't lie to me about your vote for peace.
ROD: May lightning strike me!
MYRRHINE: You don't have a blanket.
ROD: It's not a blanket I want! I want to get fucked!
MYRRHINE: That's just what's going to happen. Back in a flash.
ROD: That woman drives me nuts with all her bedding.
MYRRHINE: Get up now.
ROD: But I've already got it up!
MYRRHINE: You want some perfume?
ROD: Thank you, no, I don't.
MYRRHINE: But I do, if it's all the same to you.
ROD: Then get the goddamned perfume. Holy Zeus!
MYRRHINE: Hold out your hand. And save a bit for me.
ROD: I don't like perfume as a general rule,
     unless it smells like love is in the air.
MYRRHINE: Oh silly me, I must have brought Brand X.
ROD: No, wait, I like it!
MYRRHINE: You're just being polite.
ROD: God damn the guy who first invented perfume!
MYRRHINE: I found some good stuff. Here's the tube.
ROD: Here's mine!
     Come on now, let's lie down, there's nothing more
120   to fetch.
MYRRHINE: You're right, I will, I'll be right there.
     I'm taking off my shoes. Remember, dear,
     your promise to vote for peace.
ROD: I surely will.
     Where are you? Hey Myrrhine! Where's my pussikins?
     She pumped me up and dropped me flat. I'm ruined!

DUET

125   What'll I do? No one to screw!
            I've lost the sexiest girl I knew.
        My cock is an orphan,
            it couldn't be worse.
        I'll just have to get him
130   a practical nurse.
MEN'S LEADER: Frightful deceit! Pity on you!
        We cannot imagine what to do.
        What balls can endure
            being treated this way,
135   without any chance of
            an actual lay?
ROD: Oh god, the cramps attack anew!
LEADER: A dirty bitch did this to you!
ROD: Oh no, she's really sweet and kind.
LEADER: That bitch? You must have lost your mind!
ROD: You're right, a bitch
            is what she is!
        I'll put a curse
            upon that miz!

145   I pray for a tornado,
            with lightning bolts and all,
        to lift her into heaven
            and then to let her fall.

        Way down and down she's falling,
150   above a giant rock.
        And when she's almost on it,
            I pray she hits my cock!
SPARTAN HERALD: Direct me, please, to party headquarters.
        Where are your commissars? You please will speak.
ROD: The hell are you? A man or a Freudian nightmare?
SPARTAN HERALD: I'm Herald from Sparta, you very cute young man.
        I come with orders to propose a treaty.
ROD: Then why have you got that tommy-gun in there?
SPARTAN HERALD: Is not a weapon.
ROD: Turn around, let's see.
160   What's pushing out your trousers? What's in there,
        your lunch-box?
SPARTAN HERALD: This young man is obviously
        intoxicated.
ROD: That's a hard-on, rogue!
SPARTAN HERALD: Do not be silly, please: is no such thing.
ROD: Then what do you call that?
SPARTAN HERALD: Is my attache case.
ROD: If that's the case, then I've got one just like it.
        But let's come clean, OK? I know what's up.
        How fare you all in happy Sparta, sir?

SPARTAN HERALD: Not well. The comrades rise, also the allies.
      We all have hard-on. Have a pussy shortage.
ROD: What's wrong? Some difficulty with your five
      year plan?
SPARTAN HERALD: Oh no, was dissidents. Was Lampito.
      She lead the women comrades in a plot.
      They take an oath of solidarity,
      keep men away from warm and furry place.
ROD: What happened?
SPARTAN HERALD: Now we suffer! Walk around
      like men with hernia problem, all bent over.
      The women won't permit to touch the pussy,
      till each and every party member swear
      to make bilateral disarmament.
ROD: So this is global, a vast conspiracy
      devised by women! Now I see it all!
      Go quickly back to Sparta for the truce.
      Arrange to send ambassadors with full powers.
      And I will so instruct our leaders here,
185   to name ambassadors. I'll show them this!
SPARTAN HERALD: I fly away. You offer good advice.

CHORAL DIALOGUE

MEN'S LEADER: No animal exists more stubborn than a woman.
      Not even fire, nor any panther, is quite as shameless.
WOMEN'S LEADER: You seem to understand this, but still you keep on fighting.
190   It's possible, bad man, to have our lasting friendship.
MEN'S LEADER: I'll never cease to loathe the female sex!
WOMEN'S LEADER: That's up to you, I guess. But meanwhile I don't like
      the sight of you undressed. Just look at you, how silly!
      I simply must come over and put your shirt back on.
MEN'S LEADER: By god, I'd have to say that's no bad thing you did.
      And now I'm sorry I took it off before, in anger.
WOMEN'S LEADER: And now you look like a man again, and not so comic.
      And if you hadn't been so hostile, I'd have removed
      that bug in your eye, which I can see is still in there.
MEN'S LEADER: So that's what's been rubbing me the wrong way. Here's my ring.
      Please dig it out of my eye, and then I want to see it.
      By god, that thing's been biting at my eye a long time.
WOMEN'S LEADER: You're very welcome. Stand still! What a grumpy man!
      Great gods, it's huge, a genuinely king-sized gnat.
205   And there it comes. Look at it. Isn't it Brobdingnagian?[2]
MEN'S LEADER: You've helped me out a lot. That thing's been digging wells.
      And now that it's removed, my eyes are streaming tears.
WOMEN'S LEADER: There, there, you naughty man, I'll wipe your tears away,
      and kiss you.
MEN'S LEADER: I don't want a kiss!

---

2. Huge.

WOMEN'S LEADER: I'll kiss you anyway!

MEN'S LEADER: You got me, damn you. Women know how to get what they want.
That ancient adage puts it well and sums it up:
women are bad, you can't live with 'em, you can't live without 'em.
But now let's have a truce. We promise never again
to flout you; and you promise never again to hit us.

215   So now let's get together and sing a happy song!

CHORUS (8): No citizen need fear from us
the slightest castigation.
In recent times we've had our fill
of trial and tribulation.

220   Instead, if any man and wife
should need some extra dough,
we'll gladly let you have what's in
our piggy banks at home.

And when the war is over with,

225   don't bother to repay,
for what we have to loan you now
is nothing anyway.

CHORUS (8): Tomorrow night we'll have a feast,
a real celebrity ball.

230   We'll roast a pig and make some soup:
we'll have enough for all.

So get up early, bathe the kids,
and bathe yourselves as well.
Then come on over, walk right in:

235   you needn't ring the bell.

Then straight on to the dining room,
as if it were your own.
We'll treat you just as you'd treat us:
there'll be nobody home.

SCENE 5

CHORUS LEADER: Here they come, ambassadors from
Sparta. Look, I see their beards.
What's around their waists? They might be
wearing pig-pens under there.

5   Ambassadors from Sparta, first: our greetings.
Then tell us, please, what seems to be the matter?

SPARTAN AMBASSADOR: No use to waste a lot of time describing.
Is best to show condition we are in.

LEADER: Oh my! Your problem's big and very hard.

10   It looks to me like runaway inflation.

SPARTAN AMBASSADOR: Unspeakable. What can one say? We wish
to talk of peace on any reasonable terms.

LEADER: And now I see our own ambassadors.

They look like wrestlers hunkered down like that.
15   Their pants appear to walk ahead of them.
        They suffer from a dislocated boner.
ATHENIAN AMBASSADOR: Can anyone direct me to Lysistrata?
        It's obvious we need to find her fast.
LEADER: Their syndrome seems to be the same as *theirs*.
20   These spasms: are they worse in the wee hours?
ATHENIAN AMBASSADOR: They're always bad and getting even badder!
        Unless we get a treaty pretty quick,
        we'll have to start resorting to each other!
LEADER: You'll cover up, if you've got any sense.
25   Some fundamentalist might chop it off.
ATHENIAN AMBASSADOR: God, yes, good thinking.
SPARTAN AMBASSADOR: Da, is very straight
        advice. Come on, let's pull the trousers up.
ATHENIAN AMBASSADOR: So: greetings, Spartans. Shameful situation!
SPARTAN AMBASSADOR: Da, comrade, terrible, but would be worse,
30   if decadent religious ones had seen us.
ATHENIAN AMBASSADOR: All right then, Spartans, time to play our cards.
        The reason for your visit?
SPARTAN AMBASSADOR: Negotiation
        for peace.
ATHENIAN AMBASSADOR: That's very good. We want the same.
        So now we've got to call Lysistrata,
35   for she alone can be our arbitrator.
SPARTAN AMBASSADOR: Lysistratos, Lysistrata, whoever.
ATHENIAN AMBASSADOR: It doesn't look as if we need to call her.
        She must have heard us: here she comes herself.
LEADER: Hail the bravest of all women!
40   Now you must be more besides:
        Firm but soft, high-class but low-brow,
            Strict but lenient, versatile.

        Delegates from every city,
            captured by your potent charms,
45   Come before you and request your
            arbitration of their cause.
LYSISTRATA: My task will not be difficult, since they're all
        aroused and not at one another's throats.
        How ripe are they? Where's Reconciliation?
50   Take hold of the Spartans first, and bring them here.
        Be gentle with your hand and don't pull hard,
        don't grab and yank the way men handle women,
        but use a woman's touch, like home sweet home.
        They won't extend a hand? Go farther down.
55   Now do the same for our Athenians.
        Whatever they extend, take hold of that.
        Now, men of Sparta, stand here on my left,
        and you stand on my right. Both parties listen.

I'm female, yes, but still I've got a brain.
60   I'm not so badly off for judgment, either.
My father and some other elders, too,
have given me a first-rate education.
In no uncertain terms I must reproach you,
both sides, and rightly. Don't you share a cup
65   at common altars, for common gods, like brothers,
at the Olympic games, Thermophylai and Delphi?[1]
I needn't list the many, many others.
The world is full of foreigners you could fight,
but it's Greek men and cities you destroy!
70   And that's the first reproach I have for you.

SPARTAN AMBASSADOR: My hard-on's absolutely killing me!

LYSISTRATA: Now, Spartans, my next reproach is aimed at you.
You must remember, not so long ago,
you sent a man to Athens begging us,
75   on bended knee and whiter than a ghost,
to send an army? All your slaves were up
in arms when that big earthquake hit you.
We sent you help, four thousand infantry,
a force that saved your entire country for you.
80   And now you pay the Athenians back by ravaging
their country, after all they did for yours?

ATHENIAN AMBASSADOR: That's right, Lysistrata, they're in the wrong!

SPARTAN AMBASSADOR: We're wrong: but take a look at that sweet ass!

LYSISTRATA: Do you Athenians think I'll let you off?
85   You must remember, not so long ago,
when you wore rags, oppressed by tyranny,
and Spartans routed the army of occupation,
destroying the tyrant's men and all his allies,
and drove them out on a single glorious day,
90   and set you free, and then replaced your rags
with clothes befitting democratic people?

SPARTAN AMBASSADOR: I never saw so well-endowed a woman!

ATHENIAN AMBASSADOR: I never saw a better-looking pussy!

LYSISTRATA: Considering all these mutual benefactions,
95   why prosecute the war and make more trouble?
Why not make peace? What keeps you still apart?

SPARTAN AMBASSADOR: We must demand this promontory here
return to us.

LYSISTRATA: Which one?

SPARTAN AMBASSADOR: This one in back:
we count on having, we can almost feel it.

ATHENIAN AMBASSADOR: By the God of Earthquakes, that you'll never get!

LYSISTRATA: You'll give it up, sir.

ATHENIAN AMBASSADOR: What do we get, then?

---

1. Sites of a famous battle and of the Apollo oracle.

LYSISTRATA: You'll ask for something that's of equal value.
ATHENIAN AMBASSADOR: Let's see now, I know, give us first of all
     the furry triangle here, the gulf that runs
105   behind it, also the two connecting legs.
SPARTAN AMBASSADOR: My dear ambassador, you want it all!
LYSISTRATA: You'll give it. Don't be squabbling over legs.
ATHENIAN AMBASSADOR: I'm set to strip and do a little ploughing!
SPARTAN AMBASSADOR: Me first: before one ploughs one spreads manure!
LYSISTRATA: When peace is made you'll both do all you want.
     For now, are each of these items to your liking?
     If so you'd best confer with all your allies.
ATHENIAN AMBASSADOR: Confer with allies? Too hard up for that.
     They'll go along with us. I'm sure they're just
115   as anxious to start fucking.
SPARTAN AMBASSADOR: Also ours,
     is certain.
ATHENIAN AMBASSADOR: Every Greek is fond of fucking.
LYSISTRATA: You argue well. And now for ratification.
     The women on the citadel will host
     the banquet, for we brought our picnic boxes.
120   You'll swear your oaths and make your pledges there.
     And then let everybody take his wife
     and go on home.
ATHENIAN AMBASSADOR: What are we waiting for?
SPARTAN AMBASSADOR: Please, lead the way.
ATHENIAN AMBASSADOR: You'd best start running them!
CHORUS (8): Fine gowns, embroidered shawls, kid gloves,
125   and lots of golden rings:
     if you've a debutante at home,
       you needn't buy these things.

     We've got a closet in the house,
       we've got a jewelry box.
130   They're neither of them sealed so tight
       we couldn't pick the locks.

     So come around, feel free to take
       whatever you can find.
     But you won't find much unless you have
135   a sharper eye than mine.
CHORUS (8): All those with many mouths to feed
       but nothing to provide:
     we bought a peck of wheat and made
       some bread to put aside.

140   So anyone who's poor can bring
       a basket or a tray.
     We've told our slaves to fetch the bread
       and give it all away.

     One thing we should have told you first:

145   you can't get near the door.
       We've got a giant doberman
           who doesn't like the poor.

SCENE 6

ATHENIAN AMBASSADOR: Open up the gate you! Should have got out of my way!
       You slaves, quit loafing. How'd you like your hair
       burned off? Slave-beating: what a stale routine!
       Director, I won't do it. Ask the audience?
5   All right, to please you I'll go through with it.
ATHENIAN: We're right behind you, glad to help you out.
       Get lost, you slaves! Your hair's in serious danger!
ATHENIAN AMBASSADOR: Get lost: we'd like the Spartans to depart
       from their banquet without stumbling over you.
ATHENIAN: I've never seen a banquet quite like this.
       The Spartans were delightful company.
       And we were pretty clever over drinks.
ATHENIAN AMBASSADOR: That's right. You can't be clever when you're sober.
       I'm going to propose new legislation,
15   that diplomats conduct their business drunk.
       As things now stand, we go to Sparta sober,
       then look for ways to stir up lots of trouble.
       And so whatever they say we never hear it,
       but hunt for hidden meaning in what they don't say,
20   and then make contradictory reports.
       But now we're straightened out. If someone made
       a toast to workers rather than to profits,
       we cheered him anyway and raised our glasses.
       What's this? Those slaves are coming back again.
25   We told you: bugger off, you whipping posts!
ATHENIAN: That's right: the Spartans are emerging now.
SPARTAN AMBASSADOR: Comrade musician, ready the Spartan bagpipes.
       For now I dance and sing a happy song
       to honor jointly both our superpowers.
ATHENIAN AMBASSADOR: A splendid treat: some genuine Spartan music!
       I love to see you Spartans sing and dance.
SPARTAN AMBASSADOR: Holy Memory, reveal
           the glory days of yore:
       how Spartans and Athenians
35   won the Persian war.

       Athens met them on the sea,
           and Sparta held the land,
       although the Persian forces were
           more numerous than sand.

40   All the gods that helped us then,
           we bid you visit us again,
       to help us celebrate our peace
           and see that it will never cease.

Now let mutual friendship reign,
45   let's never fight a war again.
Put a stop to competition,
    end all mutual suspicion.

Hear our prayer, gods, loud and clear.
    Witness what we promise here.

ATHENIAN AMBASSADOR: Well, now that everything has turned out well,
    reclaim your wives here, Spartans. These are yours,
    Athenians. Every husband join his wife,
    and wife her husband. Then let's have a dance
    and ask the gods to bless us, promising
55   never again to make the same mistakes.

Form up the dance, the Graces call,
    summon Apollo, who heals us all,
    Artemis his twin sister too,
    Bacchos with his maenad crew,[1]
60   Father Zeus with lightning crowned,
    Hera, Zeus' wife renowned.
    Summon every force above,
    join us in our dance of love,
    peace and freedom are at hand,
65   thanks to Aphrodite's plan!

CHORUS: What can we say?
    horray, horray!
    We also pray
    you liked the play!

ATHENIAN AMBASSADOR: Hey Spartan, what about another song?

SPARTAN AMBASSADOR: To Sparta, Muse, my song will roam,
    where Apollo has his southern home,
    where Athena's house has brazen portals,
    where Zeus' twin sons, knights immortal,
75   gallop by Eurotas River,[2]
    setting Spartan hearts aquiver,
    where heavenly dancers leap and shout,
    like colts the maidens frisk about,
    raising dust, tossing their manes,
80   possessed by Bacchus, all insane,
    led by Zeus' holy child,
    Helen, women's nonpareil.

Hold your hair up with your hand,
    beat your feet throughout the land,
85   help the dancers make some noise,
    sing a song of joyous praise
    for Athena of Athens, for Spartan Athena
    of the House of Bronze!

---

1. God of wine, with maddened women attendants.   2. Sparta's major river.

Lady Writing a Love Letter, temple sculpture, Khajuraho, India, c. 1000 C.E.

Early South Asia

— ᚨ◈ᚨ —

WHERE IS "SOUTH ASIA"?

People who live in "South Asia" today began to think that this is where they live only recently, when new international political relations created a conceptual region with this name, made up of eight nation-states: Afghanistan (though this is sometimes omitted), Bangladesh, Bhutan, India, the Maldive Islands, Nepal, Pakistan, and Sri Lanka. For most of history no one thought they lived in South Asia. Instead, some lived in *Al-Hind,* as the geographers who wrote in Arabic named it in the later centuries of the first millennium; earlier, others lived in what they called *Bharata Varsha* ("Realm of the Descendents of Bharata"), according to scholars such as the sage Brihaspati who wrote in Sanskrit:

> The earth is 5,000,000 leagues in extent. It contains seven continents and is surrounded by seven oceans. In the middle is the Land of Action, and in the middle of this land is the Rose Apple Tree atop golden Mount Meru. To the north is Mount Himalaya, to the south, extending nine thousand leagues, is the area called Bharata, where good and bad action bear their fruit, and political governance is found. It is a thousand leagues from Badarika in the Himalayas, where the holy Ganga river rises, down to the Bridge that Rama built to the island of Lanka. Seven hundred leagues separate Dvaraka on the western coast, where the god Krishna dwells, from Purushottama-Shalagrama, the great city Puri, on the eastern.

Still others believed they lived in far larger and more complex spaces (see Color Plate 6 for an illustration of one such cosmological map). And some people who live outside what is now called "South Asia" conceived of themselves as living inside it. For example, a "Mount Meru" existed in Java, part of what is now Indonesia, while a "Field of the Kurus," site of the *Mahabharata* war (page 809), was to be found in Khmer country, in today's Cambodia.

It is probable, however, that few people in their everyday lives actually thought of themselves as living even in *Bharata Varsha* or *Al-Hind,* and certainly not in *India,* however much the contours of Brihaspati's space may agree with those of the present-day nation-state. "India" was what Greek and Roman geographers called the region, derived like "Hind" from "Indus," the name of a river in the northwest. And it was this name that was bequeathed to European humanist scholars and the colonialists who came a little later—starting with the Portuguese in the late fifteenth century (see Camões's the *Lusiads* in Volume C) and ending with the English, who in 1947 abandoned their "Indian Empire," which was subsequently divided into several of the nations listed above. In the earlier period, people in the region probably saw themselves as living in this village or that, sometimes in the realm of one overlord or another, but rarely in larger spheres. Yet sometimes political power, with its dreams of vast empire, and Sanskrit (and, later, Persian) literary culture, which spread across vast spaces, must have made the names of these and other larger regions come alive in the minds of subjects and readers.

KINGSHIP TO THE HORIZONS

The history of early South Asia until around 500 B.C.E. is obscure and contested. Complex, probably literate urban cultures had existed in the northwest, in the Indus Valley and its environs, from about 2500 to 1500 B.C.E. How these cultures came to an end is not yet fully understood, but when they did end, literacy and urban existence ended with them. The millennium that followed appears to have been dominated by the cultures of shifting cultivators and nomads. Some of these peoples had recently entered the subcontinent from areas to the west, bringing entirely new languages and religious practices that were to be widely assimilated. We don't know much about the history of political power, either, in this period until the middle of the first millennium B.C.E., when city life resumed and when, around the middle of the third century B.C.E., the first written documents in South Asia were produced, at the court of an emporer named Ashoka.

Ashoka was the third king of the Maurya dynasty, the first rulers about whom we possess solid historical information. Greek ambassadors coming in the wake of Alexander the Great's failed invasion (around 320 B.C.E.) visited the Maurya court in Magadha (today's Bihar) and left accounts. More important, a new Indian writing system—based ultimately on Phoenician principles but modified with remarkable skill to suit local language realities—was created at this time, probably by scholars in the chancellery of Ashoka in order to spread the king's moral message (page 857). After this point, documentary evidence becomes much more plentiful. As a result, we know

The Indian political theory of the day spoke of power radiating outward infinitely— "kingship to the horizon". . . .

a good deal about Ashoka's vision of power. It was adopted in part from the Achaemenids, the dynasty that ruled in Persia from about 550 to 330 B.C.E., but also much adapted: Ashoka too sought to build an empire, but it was very unlike the Persian model and those that followed it, such as the Roman Empire. The Indian political theory of the day spoke of power radiating outward infinitely— "kingship to the horizons"—but they were not unbounded horizons, as in the Persian case (Xerxes, for example, wanted "to extend the Persian territory as far as God's heaven reaches"). Ashoka sought a limited universality, if we can put it that way: there was a zone beyond which political power was thought not to extend—as Brihaspati makes clear in the excerpt cited earlier—even when cultural and economic power extended much farther, as it most certainly did for all of recorded history in the region.

The Maurya Empire vanished in the second century B.C.E., and about the events of the period that follow we have a only a shadowy idea. In southern India, kingdoms now came into being that we can name and place: Chera, Pandya, Chola, ruling from west to east, respectively, in peninsular India, and the Satavahanas, ruling to their north. These polities seem to have been among the first to support the production of written expressive texts, or "literature" (the Mauryas, by contrast, like the Achaemenids they imitated made no literary history at all). In the north of the subcontinent, new claimants for power, the Shakas (Scythians) and Kushanas, entered from central and western Asia. They, too, had notions of rule borrowed from Persian models, but in accordance with the new South Asian paradigm, the empire they sought was a limited one. They also patronized literature, but in ways that were to change the rules of the game of literary culture in the region.

When the Guptas established their polity around 320 C.E. and extended it far outward from the core area around today's Patna (in southern Bihar), many of these tendencies of power and culture found their most coherent expression yet:

> *Om.* Hail! The prosperous Samudragupta, the great overlord of lords, exterminator of all kings, without adversary equal to him on earth, whose fame is tasted by the waters of the four oceans. . . .

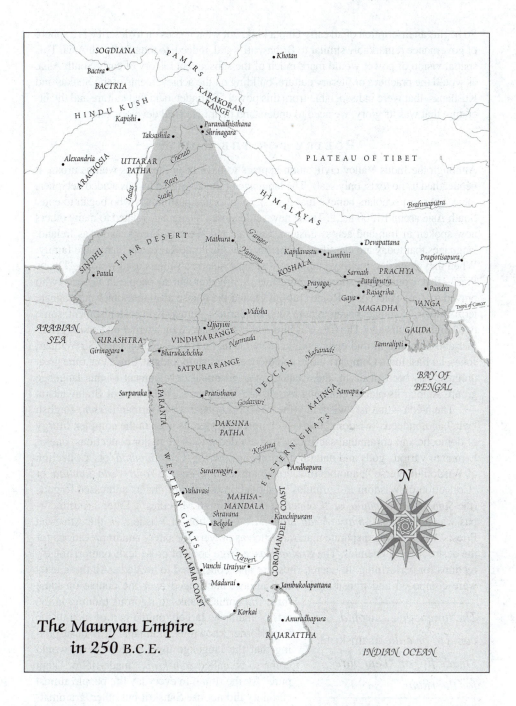

SOGDIANA

Bactra

BACTRIA

• Khotan

P A M I R S

KARAKORAM
RANGE

H I N D U   K U S H

Kapishi •

Taksashila •

Puranadhisthana •
• Shrinagara

PLATEAU OF TIBET

• Alexandria

ARACHOSIA

UTTARA
PATHA

Chenab

Ravi

Sutlej

Indus

H I M A L A Y A S

Brahmaputra

SINDHU

T H A R   D E S E R T

• Patala

Mathura •

Ganges

Yamuna

KOSHALA

Kapilavastu •
• Lumbini

Devapattana •

Prayaga •

Sarnath •
Pataliputra
• Rajagriha
Gaya •
MAGADHA

PRACHYA

Pragjotisapura •

VANGA

• Pundra

GAUDA

Tropic of Cancer

ARABIAN
SEA

SURASHTRA

Girinagara •

Vidisha •

Ujjayini •

VINDHYA RANGE

Narmada

Bharukachchha •

SATPURA RANGE

Mahanadi

Tamralipti •

BAY OF
BENGAL

Surparaka •

APARANTA

Pratisthana •

D E C C A N

Godavari

KALINGA

Samapa •

DAKSINA
PATHA

Krishna

EASTERN GHATS

W E S T E R N   G H A T S

Suvarnagiri •

Vahavasi •

MAHISA-
MANDALA

Shravana
Belgola •

Andhapura
•

Kanchipuram •

COROMANDEL COAST

N

MALABAR COAST

Kaveri

Vanchi Uraiyur •

Madurai •

Jambukolapattana •

Korkai •

• Anuradhapura

RAJARATTHA

INDIAN OCEAN

The Mauryan Empire
in 250 B.C.E.

So begins an inscription of an early Gupta king, but what it goes on to describe is a sphere of governance remarkably similar to Brihaspati's and, indeed, to today's South Asia. This spatial vision of power would mark much of the subsequent history of early South Asia, as would the practices of literary culture, building on the achievements of the Shakas and Kushanas, that were indissociable from this power. To understand that culture and the literature that was its glory, we need to understand their historical development.

POETRY FOR THE POLITY

Although the Indus Valley civilization appears to have been literate as well as urban, it bequeathed us no texts, only seals. The language of these seals so far has eluded decipherment, but most scholars believe that it wasn't that of the pastoralists who began to enter South Asia around 1500 B.C.E. These new settlers used a language related to many others now spoken in Iran and across Eastern, Central, and Western Europe as far as Ireland, languages that today are classified as members of the "Indo-European" language family. When they prayed to the Sky Father, for example, the new settlers used words—"Dyaus Pitā"—that would have sounded more than faintly familiar to people in Greece (who prayed to Zeus Patēr) or in Rome (Jup-piter), and the phrase even resembles our cognate term "father." Scholars began to note such similarities, with growing astonishment, some two hundred years ago. The first was Sirajuddin Ali Khan Arzu, a writer on Persian grammar and literature in mid-eighteenth-century Delhi, and, a generation later, Sir William Jones, an East India Company judge and pioneer English Indologist. Since that time great progress has been made in understanding the historical development of this language group. Among its oldest remaining texts is the Veda, the sacred works of Brahmanism.

The Veda—that is, "wisdom" (the word is cognate with German *wissen,* English "wit," and, indeed, "wisdom" itself)—comprises materials used in the complex liturgy of domestic and communal sacrifices. It is divided into three major collections: one of hymns to various gods and natural phenomena (the *Rig-Veda Samhita,* or "Collection of Wisdom in Verse"); another of sacred mantras in prose (the *Yajur-Veda Samhita,* or "Collection of Wisdom in Formulas"); and a compilation of chants addressed to gods (the *Sama-Veda Samhita,* or "Collection of Wisdom in Melodies"). Later a fourth corpus was added, the *Atharva-Veda Samhita* ("Collection of Wisdom of the Atharvan Priests"), containing disparate materials such as prayers for safety and imprecations for the destruction of enemies. The *Brahmanas,* a large body of prose texts comprising directions for performing the sacred rites, are also considered to be Veda. All these texts were composed and transmitted orally, almost unchanged over the course of some three millennia, thanks to rigorous training in the arts of memory, largely on the part of men of the social order known as Brahmans. It is unsurprising that the language used in these texts would come to be called *samskrita,* "made fit" or "kept pure" for the ritual. In everyday life people almost certainly did not use Sanskrit but other, grammatically less complex dialects related to Sanskrit. Later, some of these were formalized as literary languages with regional variations called the Prakrits (literally, the "natural" idioms). In addition to Sanskrit and the Prakrits, the languages of the Dravidian family—Kannada, Malayalam, Tamil, and Telugu—are found in southern India. These came into special prominence in literary culture from about 1000 C.E. onward (see

The language . . . would come to be called samskrita, *"made fit" or "kept pure" for the ritual.*

"Vernacular Writing in South Asia" in Volume C), though Tamil has a much older textual history.

Much of the Veda is in verse, often the same eleven-syllable meter found in ancient Greek poetry such as Sappho's (re-created in the English translation "He looks to me to be in heaven," page 565); the composers were called *kavi*, "seer," which became the term for "poet." These and other continuities notwithstanding, before the modern period people in South Asia were very careful to distinguish the sacred Veda from what later would be called *kavya* (literally, the "work of the *kavi*"), for which "literature" in our contemporary sense is a good translation. *Kavya* itself was something that had yet to be invented during the Vedic period (the millennium beginning around 1500 B.C.E.). Once invented it was widely acknowledged to be something new and radically different from the Veda. The story of the invention of literature recounted in the first book of the Sanskrit epic poem the *Ramayana* of Valmiki is provided in this volume on page 909; another key moment in the process comes in the fifth book of the poem when Hanuman, the monkey scout in the service of the hero Rama, at last discovers Rama's queen, Sita. She is being held captive in the distant kingdom of the overlord of demons, Ravana, who had abducted her after disguising himself as a Brahman mendicant and winning her trust when she was left alone. Hanuman puzzles over what language to use to speak with her:

> If like a Brahman I address Sita using Sanskrit speech
> she may think I am Ravana, and will be frightened.
> Far better to speak human language, one that will make sense to her.

It is no accident that in this first recorded use of the word "Sanskrit" for the language, allusion is made to its monopolization by a particular social group, the Brahmans, and also to the peculiar restrictions on its use that distinguished it from "human language." These features make perfect sense if we keep in mind the liturgical functions of early Sanskrit. It is, however, Sanskrit that Hanuman uses to speak to Sita, and with this, the poet who has him do so transformed the world of literary culture in South Asia for centuries to come.

The *Ramayana* has been known as the first poem (*adi-kavya*) since at least the second century C.E., and we should take this designation seriously. It embodies the tradition's own historical judgment, and this understanding has significance whether or not modern scholarship can prove it to be based on hard fact. In the form we know it from manuscripts still available, the *Ramayana* was almost certainly composed in the late Maurya epoch, around 200 B.C.E.. The poem shares much of the political perspective of Ashoka, and it reflects on its oral origins (when describing its invention as literature) in a way unlikely in a world truly ignorant of writing, which as we saw was almost certainly invented at Ashoka's court.

The Ramayana *has been known as the first poem since at least the second century C.E., and we should take this designation seriously.*

The second great epic of South Asia, the *Mahabharata,* ascribed to the sage Vyasa, is usually assigned to the genre of history (in Sanskrit, *itihasa*) rather than poetry. It is probable that the *Mahabharata* came into being a century or two before Ashoka though it continued to grow through addition of materials for some centuries even after Valmiki's work was completed. Like the *Ramayana,* it has as its principal theme the meaning of power as well as the extent of power—the nature of kingly rule and the limits of the world within which this rule makes sense. Consider how, at the midpoint of the epic (whose name means "The Great Battle of the Men of Bharata"), on the eve of the battle in which his ninety-nine sons will die, the blind old king addresses his confidant and asks him to describe Bharata Varsha:

> Oh Sanjaya! Brave kings are ready to die for land. They do not cease from killing but instead fill to overcrowding the house of the dead, in their quest for lordship over earth. What virtues must this earth possess, Sanjaya, speak to me of them—speak to me of this Bharata Varsha, where these armies have gathered, the land my son Duryodhana covets and the sons of Pandu, the land to which my own heart is attached. Speak to me of it!

There follows one of the most complete of the early geographies of South Asia.

In providing what the nineteenth-century philosopher G. W. F. Hegel, without too much anachronism, called "the entire matter of a nation," these Sanskrit epic traditions bear comparison with the ancient Greek (see the *Iliad* and the *Odyssey,* pages 201 and 259), for example, or medieval Iberian (see *The Poem of the Cid,* in Volume B). Like these works, the *Ramayana* and *Mahabharata* may deal with particular peoples in particular places, but they contemplate problems that no one anywhere has escaped: war and the perceived need to kill in order to live; duty; family; love. Yet the responses offered by the two South Asian epics to these problems are entirely dissimilar. Many readers today prefer the more steely-eyed, if more agonized, vision of the *Mahabharata,* which leaves us at the end—when the victors, all their kinsmen slain, set out on a death march to the north—with the taste of ashes in our mouths. But societies can't live by such hard realism alone, and the more utopian vision of the *Ramayana,* where victory brings unending peace and prosperity, seems a necessary supplement. For that very reason, perhaps, it has proved even more consequential in Indian history than the harrowing tale of the *Mahabharata.*

> *Many readers today prefer the more steely-eyed, if more agonized, vision of the* Mahabharata, *which leaves us at the end . . . with the taste of ashes in our mouths.*

It was because they framed core human problems that Valmiki and Vyasa could offer later writers so vast a store of themes—again as in Greece, where the tragedians were said to eat "crumbs from the great table of Homer." None of these themes was more celebrated than the story of Shakuntala, which the dramatist Kalidasa (fourth-fifth century C.E.) rewrote for the new courtly world of the Guptas (see page 944). However, this later literature was very slow to develop. After the Maurya period, rulers everywhere continued to follow Ashoka in eschewing the holy language of Sanskrit for their records and instead using Prakrit. This was also the language used for literature in courts in south-central India such as the Satavahana. Much of this Prakrit literature has been lost, but what has been preserved, such as *The Seven Hundred Songs of Hala* (see page 938), shows how remarkable and how sophisticated in its simplicity this poetry was. At courts in peninsular India, the literary language in the early centuries of the Common Era appears to have been Tamil. Everywhere we see an avoidance outside the ritual domain of the use of Sanskrit whether for political inscription or literature. This practice came to an end at the courts of the Shakas and Kushanas, who began to issue records in the language and to support poets, especially Buddhist poets such as Ashvaghosha, who wrote in Sanskrit.

Commencing in these early centuries C.E. and continuing in undiminished vigor for a thousand years, Sanskrit poets and scholars produced literature and theory about literature that dominated the cultural scene in South Asia up to and even beyond the vernacular revolutions in the early centuries of the second millennium, when regional languages began to replace Sanskrit for literary and political purposes. And for all these centuries Sanskrit literary culture exercised a power unlike any other in the region: it radiated across much of Asia, influencing the way literature was written from Tibet at the roof of the world to the island of Bali in the Pacific, offering new themes (some from the *Ramayana* itself; see page 864) and new theorems (especially in the domains of metrics and rhetoric) to poets and scholars as distant as China.

> *... Sanskrit literary culture exercised a power unlike any other in the region ... influencing the way literature was written from Tibet at the roof of the world to the island of Bali in the Pacific ...*

LITERATURE AND THE CRITIC

> The poet may make the poem
> but the critic knows its true power.
> Who better appreciates a woman's beauty,
> her father or her lover?

This old saying, still current among traditional Sanskrit scholars in India, expresses one of the most striking features of the literary traditions of early South Asia: their astonishing erudition. The body of reflection on this literature that developed in the centuries after it was created was due to two principal factors. First, the very invention of literature stimulated inquiry into what made it new and so different from the Veda. Second, remarkably sophisticated forms of language analysis had been developed for understanding the Veda—phonetics, metrics, lexicology, and, above all, grammar and hermeneutics—and when these were directed toward the examination of literature, they produced insights of an equally sophisticated sort. It was this critical reflection on literature as much as the literature itself that attracted the attention of scholars across Asia, as it still attracts ours.

Many theorists today reject the idea that "literature" is some essential feature of a text rather than something existing only in the eye of the beholder. We read the works of Plato as philosophy but also as dramatic dialogues, a novel of Tolstoy's as history, and the histories of Michelet as novels. But while the idea of a literary essence has been questioned in modernity, thinkers in early South Asia had no doubt about its existence; they only differed on what precisely this essence was. Everyone accepted two broad distinctions in the world of textuality, one of function and the other of form. The Veda was said to act like a master in giving us commands; ancient lore and legends (*purana*) like a friend in offering us advice; and literature like a lover in seducing us. To these various functions corresponds a set of formal distinctions. In the Veda, the words of the text themselves have central importance (indeed, a mantra is said to be potent in its very wording even if we don't understand what it says); in ancient lore, meaning has primacy, however it may be worded (it was thought that the same idea could be expressed in different words); in literature, both word and meaning are equally significant.

All scholars agreed, then, that literature constituted a unique kind of text and functioned as a kind of language different from other kinds; the hard question concerned the specifics of this constitution. In trying to answer it, scholars for centuries scrutinized every dimension of poetic language, developing brilliant analyses of the texture of poetic language (especially what were thought of as regional styles), of figures of speech (metaphor, metonymy, and so on), of levels of meaning (denotation, connotation, and suggestion), and of the ways in which language is able to create an emotional experience in the very text itself as well as in the reader or listener (what they called *rasa,* or "taste," something referring not to the judgment of literature as in English but to the emotional experience in or of literature). They examined genre and tried to order the features that distinguished the great types of literature: drama (both historical and fictional), courtly epic, lyric poetry, the tale, the prose biography, and the mixed prose-verse novel. And they analyzed character, providing complex ways to categorize the kinds of heroes and heroines appearing in literary texts and their normative traits: the four kinds of hero (the romantic, the proud, the dignified, and the serene) and the three kinds of heroine (one's own wife, another's, and the courtesan, each of whom can be naive, middling, or sophisticated). In addition to this careful ordering of the stuff of literature, they produced a vast range of handbooks for poets: treatises on metrics, dictionaries (separate works on synonyms, homonyms, words of one syllable, and the like), and grammars galore.

In the thought world of early South Asia, no practice was believed to be possible without the mastery of theory. And so no poet simply looked into his or her heart and wrote; each one was expected to possess vast learning. As a seventh-century critic put it, "There is no kind of speech or discourse, no principle or art that does not find a place in the making of literature. How heavy the writer's burden!" But this is a burden, he went on to add, that all poets take up voluntarily: "It is no sin or crime or sign of weakness not to be a poet. To be a bad poet, however, is to come face to face with death." Nonetheless, like Vatsyayana, the great authority on the art of love, the critic understood there were moments in our experience of literature beyond which "gone is system, and gone is thought," and that only silence is appropriate in the face of certain poems. The sixth-century writer Bhartrihari offers us an example:

> *As a seventh-century critic put it . . . "To be a bad poet is to come face to face with death."*

> I never rightly fixed my thoughts
> on the foot of God to end rebirth,
> I gained no moral strength of the sort
> to force open the gate of heaven,
> not even in my dreams did I embrace
> the full breasts of a woman—I did
> nothing but act as an axe to lay waste
> the forest of my mother's youth.

LEARNING NEW WAYS OF LIVING AND DYING

Many stories are told about this Bhartrihari, and they are richly suggestive of the conceptual and emotional world of early South Asia. He is said to have entered into the Buddhist monastic order, quit, and then entered again only to quit once more, poised in an awful balance between asceticism and eroticism—crying out, at the end of his life, "My face is wrinkled, my hair is gray, my legs are weak . . . the only thing still young is my desire!" The mention of Buddhism and the claims of spiritual life opens up an important dimension of early South Asia that we need to register both for what it can and what it cannot tell us about its literature.

The world of Vedic culture was one of punctilious observance of calendrical sacrifices. In time, perhaps around the middle of the first millennium B.C.E., many thinkers began to sense that sacrifice by itself might not encompass the ultimate meaning of human existence, and a true crisis of belief ensued. One response to this crisis was ascetic renunciation and physical self-mortification, which probably drew on archaic practices of bodily discipline and self-denial that had nothing to do with Vedic culture. Another response, among those who remained within the general ambit of ritualism, was a new and profound reflection on life and death; for the first time, we encounter the ideas of redeath and rebirth, or transmigration (*samsara*), in accordance with deeds committed in the previous life (*karma*). The texts in Sanskrit that these thinkers composed, including the Upanishads, played an important role in a more general critique of religious life that emerged among a wide range of spiritual masters on the margins of or outside the Vedic world. Chief among these was Siddhartha Gautama Shakyamuni, the Buddha or "Awakened One" (fourth century B.C.E.), whose new doctrine was summarized in "The Four Noble Truths":

"Suffering" (or "sorrow," *duhkha*): Suffering is an essential part of human life, and we are condemned to experience it over and over in the endless cycle of transmigration;

"The Arising of Suffering": Suffering comes into being under specific circumstances;

"The Ending of Suffering": Because suffering has an origin it must have an end;

"The Way to the Ending of Suffering": There is a real way to stop suffering, and to escape the cycle of rebirth: the teachings of the Buddha.

To this doctrine the Buddha wedded distinctive forms of meditation and new social practices—including the establishment of the monastic community, a sort of parallel society—to produce the most compelling alternative religious vision in the subcontinent, one that, within a very few centuries, was to spread across Asia like wildfire.

Theorists of the Vedic tradition, for their part, sought to synthesize many of these tendencies into a doctrine called—with the now-customary fourfold division—"the four life-goals" and "the four life-stages." According to these idealized schemas, a full human existence required evenhanded consideration of all the major human needs—physical (the goal of desire), socio-economic (that of power and wealth), moral (that of righteousness), and spiritual (that of emancipation from rebirth)—and appropriate times for their satisfaction were apportioned (in studentship, householdership, retirement from society, and wandering mendicancy). Around and about all these more philosophical, even abstract, ways of thinking about life were far more intimate practices of spiritual attachment to gods of various kinds. The world of old India was teeming with the divine, in visible nature, below the earth, and in the heavens above. "How many deities are there?" the great Upanishadic sage Yajnavalkya was once asked. "Thirty-three thousand three hundred and thirty-three," he answered in a reply that captures at once this plenitude and the very folly of any attempt at quantification. Chief among the deities were Brahma, Vishnu, and Shiva, who later, according to a more ideal ordering, were sometimes merged into a kind of

"How many deities are there?" the great Upanishadic sage Yajnavalkya was once asked. "Thirty-three thousand three hundred and thirty-three," he answered...

triple godhead. Brahma bore resonance from the old Vedic world and was often regarded not just as a kind of embodiment of the Veda—the word *brahma* sometimes actually connotes "Veda"—but as the creator god (since all creation requires knowledge, and the creation of the universe requires total knowledge, which the Veda purports to provide). Vishnu was seen as the sustainer of the cosmos (see Color plate 7, where Vishnu is shown reposing on the cosmic serpent Shesha), and a theory of his *avatara,* or descent, into earthly forms was developed. The theory of avatars made it possible to absorb once-independent divinities (such as Krishna) into a single pan-Indian deity and to explain the god's active role in the functioning of the universe. The third chief god, Shiva, was viewed as the dissolver—a beneficent destroyer, since all things must end. He may be the most complex of all these deities in both his history and character. He combined features of eroticism and asceticism where the true complexity of human life—the life that the poet Bhartrihari expresses most poignantly—could find its most perfect divine projection.

Religious thinking from these various traditions has naturally conditioned South Asian literary culture in many overt and subtle ways. Consider two of the masterpieces of Sanskrit literature, Valmiki's *Ramayana* and Kalidasa's *Shakuntala.* It may have been only centuries after the composition of the *Ramayana* that the hero came to be considered an avatar of Vishnu, but in the very core of the narrative can be found a vision of a divine king: it is only the conjunction of his godly nature with political power that can arrest the energies of chaos depicted with awesome force in the *Mahabharata.* Kalidasa's drama is a tale about love and loss and recovery, but the drama's narrative is also constructed according to the template of Shiva mythology with, again, important connotations for the exercise of political power and the special importance of the Realm of the Descendants of Bharata. But if religious sentiment plays an undeniably significant role in Sanskrit literature, we must be careful not to exaggerate its shaping power. Among the earliest courtly poems in Sanskrit are those on the life of the Buddha produced by the poet Ashvaghosha (probably around 150 C.E.), but when Ashvaghosha and other Buddhists wrote Sanskrit literature, they did so as poets first and Buddhists second. It is hard to identify a "Buddhist aesthetic"; what we have instead is a Sanskrit aesthetic, which transcended religious affiliation: as the great scholar-king Bhoja noted around 1050, "Literature is for all creeds."

> As the great scholar-king Bhoja noted . . . "Literature is for all creeds."

Beyond this, there were vast realms of literary culture in early South Asia as far removed from the spiritual as it is possible to go. The early Tamil poets, who wrote of the "interior landscape" and the "external landscape" (the affairs of the heart and of the world), the literary theoreticians who contemplated the nature of meaning and expressive emotion, the erotic and confessional poets, and the writers of comic novels and farcical plays all understood that literature was very much a cultural and social practice of this world, parallel at times to the divine but different—and one that had its own unique powers. As one anonymous Sanskrit poet wrote,

> The gods are in heaven and we live here on earth.
> Who is there then to answer our question:
> Which is sweeter, the taste of poetry,
> or the drink of immortality?

PRONUNCIATIONS:
  Atharva-Veda Samhita: uh-THAHR-wuh-VAY-duh SUM-hi-TAH

Bharata Varsha: BHAH-ruh-tuh VAHR-shuh
dharma: DHAHR-muh
duhkha: DOOH-khuh
itihasa: ee-tee-HAH-suh
Kalidasa: KAH-lee-DAH-suh
kavya: KAHV-yuh
Mahabharata: muh-HAH-BHAH-ruh-tuh
purana: poor-AH-nuh
Ramayana: RAH-MAH-yuh-nuh
rasa: RUH-suh
Rig-Veda Samhita: REEG-VAY-duh SUM-hi-TAH
samsara: sum-SAH-ruh
Sama-Veda Samhita: SAH-muh-VAY-duh SUM-hi-TAH
Shakuntala, the play: SHAH-koon-tuh-luh
Shakuntala, the heroine: shuh-KOON-tuh-LAH
Yajur-Veda Samhita: yuh-joor-VAY-duh SUM-hi-TAH

⊷ ⊠ ⊷

The Mahabharata of Vyasa
c. 4th century B.C.E.–c. 2nd century B.C.E.

"The law is a subtle thing," the venerable grandfather Bhishma repeatedly declares in the *Mahabharata,* and with this he expresses the central problem of the central and most problematic work in the history of Indian literature. The *Mahabharata,* or "Great Battle of the Men of Bharata," is indeed great both for its size and its argument. It has traditionally been calculated · to contain 100,000 quatrains (of thirty-two syllables each), which makes it about seven times the size of the *Iliad* and *Odyssey* combined (with their 30,000 sixteen-syllable lines). Even more decidedly than the Greek and other foundational epics, the *Mahabharata* seeks to offer a total account of a culture. The text itself announces at the start, "Whatever is found here may well be found elsewhere; what is not here is nowhere." The scholar and translator J. A. B. van Buitenen drew an apt analogy for the work from the tradition of European literature: he invites us to imagine a combined text including the *Iliad,* somewhat more loosely structured; an abbreviated version of the *Odyssey* (the *Mahabharata* contains a version of the *Ramayana*); quite a bit of Hesiod's account of the birth of the gods; some sequences adapted from Herodotus's history; many passages adapted and transformed from the pre-Socratic philosophers; Socrates by way of Plato by way of Plotinus, the third-century pantheist; and a generous selection of the Gospels by way of moralizing stories. This would seem absurd in the West, he adds, but the *Mahabharata* actually exists. And, we should quickly note, it exists not as a jumbled anthology but with parts conjoined into a narrative whole that never loses sight of the story it has to tell.

DHARMA

It is a great story, too—if one of the most harrowing in world literature—that the *Mahabharata* tells. Its theme is the nature and fundamental contradictions of political power, and in recounting the struggle for the throne between two groups of first cousins, the poem shows how thoroughly power is permeated by uncertainty and even paradox. The more the cousins strive to understand the law, to understand *dharma*—what is right, what one's duty is—the more confused the law appears to them; the more intense their quest for peace, the more inevitable the war between them; and the more secure their hold on victory, the more the victors realize they have lost. "We now live," they say at the moment of their triumph, "dead in life."

Section of a frieze depicting a battle from the *Mahabharata,* from Angkor Wat, Cambodia, early twelfth century. This 159-foot bas relief is part of a half-mile-long frieze.

COMPOSITION AND GENRE

Everything about the *Mahabharata* is as subtle as the problem of *dharma.* We have little idea when or where the text was composed, or who its author was. In fact, this is a work that complicates the very notions of "text," "composition," and "author." Vedic texts, the earliest Sanskrit works of India dating to the last centuries of the second millennium B.C.E., mention the names of some of the characters of the story and even refer to a struggle among brothers very similar to what is found in the *Mahabharata.* But the work that we can reconstruct from manuscript sources is nowhere near that old. Most scholars believe the *Mahabharata* grew slowly, with subsidiary tales being added to a core story over a period as long as four or five centuries beginning around 400 to 300 B.C.E. Some kind of editorial activity, which served to unify the text by committing parts of it to written form, was probably undertaken in the early centuries C.E. Although the poem continued to grow in different regional traditions, for long stretches of text there is reasonably close agreement among the hundreds of manuscripts that exist.

Where to place the *Mahabharata* among the various Indian literary genres is as complicated as anything about the work. It calls itself *itihasa,* a historical narrative of "the way things really were." And, in fact, it is consistently cited by later authors as defining that genre. Yet it contains large portions that are clearly meant as treatises on law or political thought or theology, and it calls itself another "Veda" as if to establish itself as a source of transcendental and timeless truth. Like the Homeric poems, it provided the materials for many literary adaptations, especially drama; writers from early medieval times such as Kalidasa (see page 944), have mined it for their own purposes, though the *Mahabharata* has also been regarded as a unified poem, with a distinctive aesthetic character of its own.

LOCATION AND AUTHORSHIP

The story itself centers on Hastinapura, the City of the Elephant, home to the ancient Kuru lineage from which the heroes were descended. Hastinapura is an imaginary town that can vaguely be placed in the area of today's Delhi. It is possible that the *Mahabharata* was originally produced in this general region, if we may even speak this way about something that was more a process than a product. But in many ways the *Mahabharata* is unlocalizable: the work has spread across South Asia (and much of Southeast Asia), just as the wars and the wanderings it recounts involved all of South Asia.

The *Mahabharata* itself ascribes its origins to a single author, Krishna Dvaipayana Vyasa. He is a creator in two senses: of the tale itself and of two of the tale's main characters. Pandu and Dhritarashtra, the fathers of the warring parties, are both his sons by the wives of a deceased half-brother. The peculiar paternity of Pandu and Dhritarashtra is only the first in a long series of twists and turns in the plot of the *Mahabharata*. Indeed, if it can be said to be "about" any one thing, the *Mahabharata* is about these twists and turns themselves and how they mark human life in general but especially life lived with others. For it is in living with others that we confront the biggest conundrum of all, and the focus of the *Mahabharata*'s anxieties: political power. "Man is slave to power," says the great epic, in one of its defining statements, "but power is slave to no one."

THE PUZZLE OF POWER

The puzzle of power, especially its transfer, is encountered at every step in the narrative, including the births of Pandu and Dhritarashtra. Both have physical defects: Pandu is afflicted with a skin disease (his name means "The white one"), and Dhritarashtra is blind; both are therefore not fully qualified for kingship. But Pandu rules briefly and then retires to the forest, where his five sons are born—fathered not by him (he was under a curse) but by various deities: his wife Kunti bears three sons: Yudhisthira (who is the son of Dharma, or Law); Bhima (son of Wind); and Arjuna (son of Indra). His wife Madri bears the twins Nakula and Sahadeva (sons of the Ashwins, the divine Horsemen). In Pandu's absence Dhritarashtra rules as quasi regent, fathering ninety-nine sons of his own with his wife, Gandhari, starting with Duryodhana and Duhshasana. Upon the death of their father, the Pandavas return from the forest, marry in common the princess of Panchala, Draupadi (an arrangement that puzzled many later thinkers), and eventually seek to establish an independent kingdom, thereby provoking the fear and anger of Duryodhana.

In the first selection offered here, Duryodhana challenges Yudhisthira to play a game of dice against the sly Shakuni, Duryodhana's maternal uncle. Some scholars have interpreted this episode as a relic of the ancient Vedic royal consecration. But in the *Mahabharata* itself it is clearly represented more as a metaphor and as a symptom: the metaphor that power itself is a gamble and a symptom of the human frailties even in Yudhisthira, the very son of Dharma. Even while his elders, especially his father's half-brother, Vidura, desperately try to stop the match, Yudhisthira continues to lose catastrophically—first his fortune, then his brothers, then himself, and finally their common wife. Draupadi is dragged into the assembly hall like a slave girl and publicly humiliated as the Pandavas' political authority has been humiliated (she is, after all, an incarnation of Shri, the goddess of royalty). And as her braided hair is undone, so too are set loose destructive energies that will not be contained until nearly everyone lies dead on the battlefield, and Draupadi's braid is at last tied up again.

Few parts of the *Mahabharata* illustrate this dense web of social complexity so well as the story of the temptation of the great warrior Karna. After the disastrous dice game, a compromise is reached whereby the Pandavas will retain half their wealth provided they undergo forest exile for twelve years, with a thirteenth year spent out of exile but in disguise. Having fulfilled these conditions, the Pandavas seek their share of the kingdom, but when Duryodhana refuses, war seems inevitable. In a final attempt at peace, first Krishna as an emissary of the Pandavas and then their mother, Kunti, reveal to Karna his true identity, in an attempt to win him over to the Pandava side. Abandoned at birth and raised by a low-caste couple, Karna was once publicly insulted by Arjuna and thereafter received continual support from Duryodhana. Karna's refusal to betray his benefactor even for the throne of Hastinapura, even in the certain knowledge that he would die fighting on the wrong side, marks the point of no return from the battle on "the field of Kuru, the field of sacred duty."

THE *BHAGAVAD GITA*

With these words begins the *Bhagavad Gita* ("Song of the Blessed One"). Although often read as an independent work, the *Gita* presupposes the whole dense narrative background of the *Mahabharata*. The tension we feel at its start—the armies standing poised on the battlefield, where the law of the warrior class is put into practice—is stretched to the breaking point if we have read the thousands of preceding lines. For then we will have seen the countless examples of confusion about the succession to kingship and the repeated and ever more desperate attempts to avoid what, eventually, presents itself to Arjuna's terrified gaze at the start of the *Gita:* brothers lined up in battle against brothers and fathers against sons, none of them fully knowing what is the right thing to do.

This is the context we should keep in mind for this justly celebrated poem, probably the most famous work of Indian literature. Arjuna's hesitation is, in our eyes, perfectly understandable; less so, at first glance, may be the advice he is given by his charioteer. Arjuna is told to kill, and the charioteer who counsels him is none other than Krishna, the divine being whose role in the *Mahabharata* is so ambiguous that scholars have long considered him—and most of the *Gita*—to be a later addition. But as we see when we consider the *Ramayana* (page 864), such divine presences cannot be removed from the narrative by any textual criticism based on manuscript evidence, or by any critical reading remotely consonant with the logic of the narrative or the unanimous understanding of traditional readers. Krishna enunciates a new code of conduct—the disinterested execution of one's duties even if violent—that has moved many readers for centuries, while puzzling others and prompting continual reinterpretation (as in the case of Mahatma Gandhi, the great exponent of nonviolent resistance). Perhaps we should expect nothing less from this enigmatic god. While Krishna's advice seems sensible in the abstract, in practice it can lead, as the *Mahabharata* itself shows us, to unmitigated misery.

THE ETHICAL ARGUMENT

The last and by no means least of the subtleties with which the *Mahabharata* confronts us is how to interpret its ethical argument. If it seeks above all to show how uncertain so much of life can be—like a throw of the dice—it is also shatteringly honest about confronting that uncertainty. Modern readers come to the text with presuppositions very different from those of ancient Indians and with very different histories in our memory. We are right to be cautious in our judgment about the meanings of such a work and to weigh them against other assessments. One astute reader of the *Mahabharata* was Anandavardhana, a ninth-century literary critic (a selection from his remarkable treatise on poetry is given below, page 920). For Ananda, the solution the *Mahabharata* offers to the problem of power is to demonstrate that there is in fact no solution:

> The main effect of Vyasa's work is to produce a sense of irreversible aversion to life. The world is sinking in a vast sea of delusion and he wants to rescue us; as he proclaims in the *Mahabharata* itself, "The more we see the system of the world fail, and fail so miserably / The more we come to feel a sense of disengagement." The story of the Pandavas is an elaborate tale on the theme of ignorance. The work tells us that we must not lust after empty forms of power, or focus on mere things like military might or even correct political or social behavior. Vyasa seeks to stimulate devotion to a higher principle beyond the worldly, and to do so he has thrown into question all of worldly existence.

This is a shattering kind of knowledge, which no society can take seriously and still endure. Perhaps it is for this reason that the *Mahabharata* was often viewed as a dangerous text in India (even having a complete manuscript in the house was thought to bring bad luck). Its insight into the terrible fragility of social and political life was too hard to live with; later versions, adaptations, and parallel epics sought to revise it. But they never replaced it, and its awesome power reverberates across the ages.

WHO'S WHO IN THE *MAHABHARATA*

Krishna Dvaipayana Vyasa: KRISH-nuh DWAI-PAH-yuh-nuh VYAH-suh; father of Pandu and Dhritarashtra, and author of the *Mahabharata*

Bhishma: BHEESH-muh; the Bharata patriarch and great-uncle of Pandu and Dhritarashtra
Pandu: PAAN-doo; father of the five Pandavas (PAHN-duh-vuhs), in their order of birth:

> *Yudhishthira:* yu-DHISH-thi-ruh
>
> *Bhimasena:* BHEE-muh-SAY-nuh, also known as Vrikodara, "Wolf-belly"
>
> *Arjuna:* AR-joo-nuh, also known as Dhanamjaya, "Victor of wealth"
>
> *Nakula:* NUH-koo-luh
>
> *Sahadeva:* suh-huh-DAY-vuh

Kunti: KOON-tee; mother of Yudhishthira, Bhimasena, and Arjuna
Madri: MAH-dree; mother of Nakula and Sahadeva
Draupadi: DROW-puh-dee; the common wife of the five Pandavas
Karna: KAR-nuh; the son of Kunti (by the Sun)
Dhritarashtra: dhri-tuh-RAHSH-truh; the blind king, brother of Pandu, and king of Bharata
  (BHAHR-uh-tuh). *Hastinapura* (huhs-tee-NAH-poor-uh; sometimes HAHS-tee-nuh-POO-
  ruh) "City of the Elephant," Dhritarashtra's capital.
Gandhari: GAN-DHAH-ree; wife of Dhritarashtra
Duryodhana: door-YODH-uh-nuh; eldest son of Dhritarashtra
Duhshasana: dooh-SHAH-suh-nuh; brother of Duryodhana
Vidura: VI-door-uh; the half-brother of Pandu and Dhritarashtra; fathered through a slave
  girl, he is sometimes called "Half-caste."
Shakuni: SHUH-koo-nee; brother of Gandhari and uncle of Duryodhana; as son of the
  Gandharan king Subala, he is also known as "Saubala"
Krishna Vasudeva: KRISH-nuh VAH-SOO-DAY-vuh; the god Vishnu, descended to earth in
  human form; brother-in-law and close advisor of Arjuna
Bhagavad Gita: BHUH-guh-vuhd GEE-tuh; Song of the Blessed One (i.e., Krishna
  Vasudeva)

from THE MAHABHARATA

from BOOK 2[1]

[THE FRIENDLY DICE GAME]

52

Vaiśampāyana[2] *spoke:*	Then Vidura set forth with noble steeds swift and strong, well broken to the car. Compelled by order of King Dhṛtarāṣṭra, he journeyed to the five wise Pāṇḍavas.
	He flew along the road; he reached the royal city. The wise counselor entered and was honored by the priests.
	He came to the king's citadel as bright as Kubera's[3] palace, and approached the son of Law, the Law itself, Yudhiṣṭhira.
	Yudhiṣṭhira the king, invincible, ever firm in truth and great of soul, then greeted Vidura with all respect and asked of Dhṛtarāṣṭra and his sons.
Yudhiṣṭira spoke:	I see your heart, O half-caste, is unhappy.

1. Translated by Daniel H. H. Ingalls.
2. A student of Krishna Dvaipayana Vyasa, who recited
the *Mahabharata* during a long rite held for King Janame-
jaya, the great-grandson of Arjuna.
3. God of wealth.

And yet, the news you bring is good, I trust?
His sons, I trust, obey the ancient king;
the Kuru tribesmen follow his command?

Vidura spoke:
The ancient king is well, as are his children:
He sits among his godlike family
happy with virtuous and obedient sons,
knowing no sorrow, self-reliant, strong.

But this is the message given me by the king,
bidding me first ask your health and welfare:
"Your cousins have built a court as fair as yours
that I would gladly have you see, my son.

"Come to it, Pāṇḍava, with your four brothers
and enjoy yourself at a friendly game of dice.
We will rejoice to see you, as will also
the Kuru lords whom we have brought together."

You will see the stocks of dice provided there
by Dhṛtarāṣṭra the magnificent,
and all the players that he has assembled.
Such was I bid to ask you. Pray accept.

Yudhiṣṭhira:
If we should gamble, I fear there will be quarrels.
What man, aware of what it leads to, gambles?
But I ask you what you think the proper course,
for all of us take counsel by your word.

Vidura:
I know that gambling is the source of evil
and I made great efforts to prevent it;
in spite of which the king has sent me.
Hear and choose with wisdom what is best.

Yudhiṣṭhira:
What other gamblers will attend the game
in addition to the sons of Dhṛtarāṣṭra?
I ask you, Vidura; tell me who they are,
those others brought together by the king.

Vidura:
The king of Gāndhāra, Śakuni, O king,
that gambler swift of hand who knows his dice;
Prince Vivimśati and Citrasena,
Purumitra, true to his word, and Jaya.[4]

Yudhiṣṭhira:
Fearful gamblers have been brought together,
experts in the art, who use deceit.
But the world, they say, is in the power of fate;
I will not fail to gamble with the experts.

For how can I refuse to come
when Dhṛtarāṣṭra sends his bidding?
—a son must wish what his father bids—
So I accept the invitation.

4. Four sons of Dhritarashtra.

But with Śakuni I have no wish to gamble
and will not do so unless he challenges.
Only if challenged I will not refuse,
for so I have sworn as my eternal vow.

Vaiśampāyana: So spoke the King of Law to Vidura
and bid with haste make ready for the journey.
Next morning he departed with his men,
and with his ladies led by Draupadī.

"Fate takes along our wits as a bright light takes our vision,
and we are in the power of fate as if bound to it by cords."

So spoke Yudhiṣṭhira in setting forth with the half-caste;
the invitation did not please the enemy-taming king.

The slayer of foes mounted the car that Bāhlika[5] had given;
surrounded by his brothers the son of Law drove forth,

drove shining with royal glory and accompanied by brahmins,
summoned by Dhṛtarāṣṭra and by the hour of fate.

He drove to Hāstinapura to Dhṛtarāṣṭra's palace
and there the lawful Pāṇḍava met the ancient king.

He met the teacher Droṇa, and Bhīṣma, Karṇa, Kṛpa,[6]
greeting each in his degree and greeting Droṇa's son.

And there the great-armed king met also Somadatta
together with Duryodhana, Śakuni, and Śalya.[7]

He met Jayadratha and Kuru lords by hundreds,
and all the other kings that had assembled there.

Then the great-armed king accompanied by his brothers
entered the inner chamber of learned Dhṛtarāṣṭra.

He saw Queen Gāndhārī with daughters-in-law beside her,
bright as the star Rohiṇī among its lesser stars.

He greeted Queen Gāndhārī and in return was greeted.
He saw the king his uncle blind except in wit.

The old king kissed his head and the heads of the kneeling princes,
the younger sons of Pāṇḍu, Bhīma and the rest.

There was joy among the Kurus at the coming of their cousins
to see these handsome Pāṇḍavas, these tigers among men.

* * *

The happy night had passed. They said their morning prayers

---

5. An ancestor in the Kuru lineage.
6. Drona and Kripa were preceptors to the young princes in the science of weapons.

7. Prince Somadatta fought on the side of the sons of Dhritarashtra, as did Shalya, though he was a maternal uncle of the Pandavas.

and entered the fair court where the gamblers stood in wait.

53

Śakuni:	The carpet is laid, Yudhiṣṭhira; all wait upon your coming. The dice are put in place; let us set the rules of play.
Yudhiṣṭhira:	Dicing is deception. It needs no warrior's courage; it needs no ruler's judgment. Why praise dicing, king?
	For men accord no honor to the deceptions of a gambler. Do not beat us, Śakuni, by such dishonest means.
Śakuni:	He alone can long endure at gambling who can reckon numbers and recognize deceit, who never tires in moving of the dice, who has the wit to understand the play.
	It is the way you draw the dice that wins and only that, when you will call it fate. Let us gamble, king, and no more hesitate; set stakes and make no more delay.
Yudhiṣṭhira:	I would rather heed the words of Devala[8] the holy, who ever visits our battles, those gates to heaven's world.
	"That sort of play is evil where gamblers use deception. To win by rightful war is the proper sort of play.
	"Nobles do not act like slaves; they do not use deception. An honest and straightforward fight is the way of real men."
	We seek to use our wealth in aid of worthy brahmins; whether one win or lose, it is wrong to gamble with such wealth.
	I like not wealth or pleasure when purchased by deception; even when the gambler is honest, I do not praise the game.
Śakuni:	The learned fights the ignorant: by deceit, Yudhiṣṭhira? the wise against the foolish: who calls out deceit?
	Just so you fight me here. But if you find deception, or if you are afraid, of course you may withdraw.
Yudhiṣṭhira:	Challenged, I will not refuse, for I have made that promise; and fate is strong, O Śakuni; I stand at its command.
	So say in this assembly with whom am I to gamble? Who can set stakes against me? Let the play begin.
Duryodhana:	O lord of tribes, it is I will stake my gold and jewels; but for my sake my uncle, Śakuni, will dice.

---

8. A sage to whom a number of Vedic hymns are ascribed.

Yudhiṣṭhira: It is wrong that one should gamble on another's wager;
you know as well as I. But take him if you wish.

Vaiśampāyana: As the game was about to begin, many kings and nobles
followed Dhṛtarāṣṭra into the fair court.

Bhīṣma, Droṇa, Kṛpa, and wise Vidura
came with the others, but they were not so glad of heart.

Singly and in couples the lion-necked heroes
seated themselves on the many brilliant thrones.

The court was then resplendent with these assembled nobles,
as heaven is resplendent with its assembled gods,

for all of them were brilliant, Veda-knowing heroes.
Then straightaway began the friendly game of dice.

Yudhiṣṭhira: I have a pearl necklace born of the deep ocean,
costly and fair, Duryodhana, and the pearls are set in gold.

This is my wager, king. What have you that is equal?
If not, I have won first turn to draw from the stock of dice.

Duryodhana: Indeed I too have pearls and many kinds of treasure.
I am no miser with my wealth. See, I have won the draw.

Vaiśampāyana: Then Śakuni drew the dice, who knew the art of dicing.
"I have won," said Śakuni to King Yudhiṣṭhira.

54

Yudhiṣṭhira: I have lost the stock of dice by my pride of gambling;
but let us keep on playing though you draw a thousand times.

I have a hundred jars; each holds a thousand *niṣkas:*[9]
a bottomless hoard of yellow metal, numberless bits of gold.
Such wealth I have, O king, with which I wager you.

Vaiśampāyana: So he spoke; and Śakuni said simply "I have won."

Yudhiṣṭhira: I have the car that brought us, worth a thousand others,
an easy-rolling chariot covered with tiger skin,

decked with golden bells, with perfect wheels and trappings,
a car of victory that thunders like the sea.

It is drawn by eight white horses each worth a prince's
ransom,
so swift that you would say their feet never touch the ground.
Such wealth I have, O king, with which I wager you.

Vaiśampāyana: The gambler heard the words; he used deceit in dealing.
"I have won," said Śakuni to King Yudhiṣṭhira.

9. A type of coin.

Yudhiṣṭhira: I have must-elephants, a thousand, fully furnished
with golden girths, head-ornaments, warpaint and
       golden chains,

well trained as royal mounts and unperturbed in battle.
Their tusks are long as plowshares; each leads eight mighty
cows

and all are breakers of castles, black and big as mountains.
Such wealth I have, O king, with which I wager you.

Vaiśampāyana: Śakuni looked and smiled at the Pāṇḍava so speaking.
"I have won," said Śakuni to King Yudhiṣṭhira.

Yudhiṣṭhira: I have a hundred thousand slave girls, young and handsome,
decked out in bracelets, anklets, golden necklaces,

wearing expensive garlands and finest sandal ointment;
all dressed in gold and pearls and finely woven clothes.

Well skilled in dance and song, they wait at my direction
upon my brahmin guests and ministers and kings.
Such wealth I have, O king, with which I wager you.

Vaiśampāyana: The gambler heard the words; he used deceit in dealing.
"I have won," said Śakuni to King Yudhiṣṭhira

Yudhiṣṭhira: Of well trained servant boys I have as many thousand,
richly dressed in cloaks, obedient and polite,

intelligent and skillful youths with polished earrings
who ever stand with dish in hand to serve my many guests.
Such wealth I have, O king, with which I wager you.

Vaiśampāyana: The gambler heard the words; he used deceit in dealing.
"I have won," said Śakuni to King Yudhiṣṭhira.

Yudhiṣṭhira: I have as many chariots, with flags and golden trappings,
each with well trained horses and a driver skilled in war.

To every driver I pay out each month in wages
a thousand pieces; and this, whether in peace or war.
Such wealth I have, O king, with which I wager you.

Vaiśampāyana: The evil, spiteful Śakuni heard the words of wager.
"I have won," said Śakuni to King Yudhiṣṭhira.

Yudhiṣṭhira: I have the partridge-speckled horses of the heavenly
       Gandharvas
that Citraratha[1] gave to my brother Arjuna.
Such wealth I have, O king, with which I wager you.

Vaiśampāyana: The gambler heard the words; he used deceit in dealing.
"I have won," said Śakuni to King Yudhiṣṭhira.

---

1. A king of the *gandharvas* (celestial musicians and singers) who gave Arjuna 400 horses at Yudhiṣṭhira's royal consecration.

Yudhiṣṭhira: I have many ten thousands of carriages and wagons
that stand ever ready, yoked to animals of every sort:

to oxen specially picked from every breed by thousands,
oxen that drink cream and are fed on finest rice

all of them deep-chested, more than sixty thousand.
Such wealth I have, O king, with which I wager you.

Vaiśampāyana: The gambler heard the words; he used deceit in dealing.
"I have won," said Śakuni to King Yudhiṣṭhira.

Yudhiṣṭhira: I have four hundred barrels bound with hoops of copper,
each a five-bushel barrel filled with beaten gold.
Such wealth I have, O king, with which I wager you.

Vaiśampāyana: The gambler heard the words; he used deceit in dealing.
"I have won," said Śakuni to King Yudhiṣṭhira.

55

Vidura   Your majesty! I must speak out. Attend to what I say
[to Dhṛtarāṣṭra]: although my words be bitter as a sick man's medicine.

Your son Duryodhana when he was born
cried out a strange cry, a jackal's bark:
bad omen to the race of Bhāratas
and evil presage of your future fate.

Duryodhana has been a jackal living in your palace
and you deaf to the omen. Remember Kāvya's words:[2]

"The honey-reaper climbs the cliff and, so he gets his honey,
marks not the fatal drop to rock and stream below."

Your son is drunk on dicing as deep as any drunkard
and fails to heed the danger of angering these lords.

You know how the Andhakas and Yādavas and Bhojas[3]
left their kinsman Kaṃsa[4] for his unseemly acts to kings;

he being killed at their behest by foe-destroying Krishna,
the kinsmen all rejoiced and lived happily thereby.

Give your command that Arjuna restrain Duryodhana
that by this evil one's restraint we all may live in peace.

Buy peacocks for a crow; for a jackal purchase tigers:
win to your side the Pāṇḍavas and escape the sea of grief.

"Give up one man for a family; give a family for a city,
a city for a country, and the wide world for your Self."

2. Kavya ("sagely"), also known as Shukra and Ushanas and sometimes considered the political counselor to the antigods, is a mythological authority in diverse fields of traditional learning.

3. Closely related clans for whom Krishna, foremost of the Yadavas, acted as leader in this particular instance.
4. King of Mathura and Krishna's treacherous maternal uncle and implacable foe.

By these words Kāvya urged that Jambha[5] be abandoned,
Kāvya who knew all things and overcame all foes.

You know of the gold-spitting birds—how the hunter caught them
and reared them in his house until he strangled them.

Thus by greed for gold what might have given profit
for future as for present use was all at once destroyed.

Harm not the Pāṇḍavas in hope of present profit
lest like the greedy hunter you live to have regrets.

Take from the Pāṇḍavas one flower at a time,
acting the part of gardener, treating them with love.

Be not a charcoal-burner, to burn your trees entirely,
lest you with your sons and ministers and army be destroyed.

For who, O Bhārata, could fight the united sons of Pāṇḍu?
Not even the Lord of Maruts with the heavenly Marut host.[6]

56[7]

Gambling is the root of future quarrels,
of opposing factions and of war.
By his gambling the son of Dhṛtarāṣṭra
has opened up the dam of enmity.

The Kuru family, descendents of Pratīpa,[8]
will come to no good end through Duryodhana's offense.

He drives peace from the kingdom in his intoxication,
as a mad bull that butts until it breaks its horns.

The man, though he be brave and wise himself,
who shuts his eyes and trusts another's sight
is like to suffer shipwreck, as the captain
who lets an untaught pilot steer the ship.

Your son is gambling with Yudhiṣṭhira
and you are glad to see him win;
but the joke has gone too far: a fight will come
by which many a man will be destroyed.

You would make up, perhaps, but do not say so;
the word of peace remains within your heart.
But come to terms with King Yudhiṣṭhira
and win back Arjuna by words of kindness.

5. An *asura* (antigod) eventually slain by Indra. The divine preceptor Kavya, knowing the fate of Jambha, had encouraged the *asuras* to abandon him at birth.
6. The lord of the Maruts (the wind deities) is Indra, king of the gods.
7. Vidura continues as speaker in this section.
8. Great-great-grandfather of the Pandavas and Kauravas.

O scions of Śantanu and of Pratīpa,
let not the words of Kāvya go unheard:
a fire that may prove a conflagration
must quickly be put out before it spreads.

For should Yudhiṣṭhira the Invincible,
beaten by tricks of dice, unleash his wrath
and take to battle with his Pāṇḍavas,
you would find no spot of refuge on the earth.

Your wealth was great before the game, as great
as any heart could wish. Why win wealth
by gambling with the Pāṇḍavas, O king,
when by kindness you could win themselves?

We know how the son of Subala can gamble,
how the mountain king knows all the tricks of dice.
Let Śakuni go back from whence he came,
the mountain king who fights by unfair means.

57

Duryodhana:

As always, you applaud my enemies
and secretly malign the Dhārtarāṣṭras.[9]
I know you, Vidura, and whom you love
and how you wish to make me out a fool.

A disappointed courtier is soon known
by how he fits together praise and blame.
Your tongue reveals your secret inclination
and cannot hide your disaffected heart.

I have taken a serpent into my embrace,
have fed a cat that scratches him that feeds it.
Disloyalty was ever held a sin;
have you no fear of sin, O Vidura?

I have won great riches from my enemy,
so give me no harsh words on that account.
I see you would consort with them that hate me
and in your folly have come to hate me too.

By use of grudging words a man turns traitor,
hiding his shame in praise of the other side.
Does the shame of joining them not bother you
that you speak out so freely what you feel?

Don't put me down; I know this heart of yours.
Go study your words of wisdom with old men
and rather try to keep your reputation

9. The sons of Dhritarashtra.

than meddle in what is none of your affair.

Don't put me down as though you were the master
and evermore be giving me harsh words.
I ask you, Vidura, for no advice.
Stay clear of me and don't wear out my patience.

There is one master only and no other
that rules a man from the time he leaves the womb;
just as He teaches water to run downhill
so He has set me on the course I run.

If a man would break a rock with his head or would
    feed a serpent,
he does whatever he does only at His command.

To cure a man by force wins only enmity.
The wise man who would keep a friend must overlook his
    faults.

He who starts up a fire, unless he runs before it,
will soon find himself with nothing left but ash.

I will keep no agent from the other camp,
most surely not a man who does me harm.
Leave the court! I am not one to keep
a whoring wife by trying to appease her.

Vidura: How quick to end the friendship of a master
who drops a man for nothing more than this!
The hearts of kings are marvellously agile
at turning favor into punishment.

You are wise, you think, young king, and I am stupid.
Such thinking shows a man of little wit:
for who is stupid if it is not he
that makes a friend and then abandons him?

One cannot lead a fool to his advantage,
nor lead a wanton girl to a virtuous match.
I see that I can no more please my prince
than an old bridegroom can please a bride.

If what you want is merely acquiescence,
whether to your benefit or not,
go ask advice of women and of fools,
of men whose wit is lame or paralyzed.

A counselor to speak kind words is never hard to come by;
but few will speak, and few will hear, unkind and good advice.

He who stands on what is right, whether or not it pleases,
and gives unkind and good advice, he is the king's true friend.

Anger, that causes loss of fame when shown,
can yet be medicine; but so sharp and bitter

that only the good can swallow it.
Swallow your anger, king; control yourself.

I pray for fame and wealth for the Kuru kings, for
Dhṛtarāṣṭra together with his sons.
I bow to you; I bow to the old king;
and may the brahmins grant me too their blessing.

But snakes kill with their eyes; do not rouse their anger.
I speak of the Pāṇḍavas, king, and I speak in deadly earnest.

58

Śakuni:	Much wealth have you lost, Yudhiṣṭhira, that belonged to the sons of Pāṇḍu. Tell me, son of Kuntī, if any wealth remains.
Yudhiṣṭhira:	I have a treasure, Śakuni, greater than man can reckon. O son of Subala, why ask me to enumerate? It holds thousands and ten-thousands, hundred-thousands, millions, billions of precious things that can be put at stake. Such wealth I have, O king, with which I wager you.
Vaiśampāyana:	The gambler heard his words; he used deceit in dealing. "I have won," said Śakuni to King Yudhiṣṭhira.
Yudhiṣṭhira:	Horses, herds of many cows, goats and sheep unnumbered: whatever is of every breed, from the Indus River east. Such wealth I have, O king, with which I wager you.
Vaiśampāyana:	The gambler heard the words; he used deceit in dealing. "I have won," said Śakuni to King Yudhiṣṭhira.
Yudhiṣṭhira	Still left is my land and citadel with the wealth of all but brahmins, and the people too, O king, excepting only brahmins. Such wealth I have, O king, with which I wager you.
Vaiśampāyana	The gambler heard the words; he used deceit in dealing. "I have won," said Śakuni to King Yudhiṣṭhira.
Yudhiṣṭhira	The jewelry that decks the persons of my brothers: their earrings and their necklaces and all their ornaments. Such wealth I have, O king, with which I wager you.
Vaiśampāyana	The gambler heard the words; he used deceit in dealing. "I have won," said Śakuni to King Yudhiṣṭhira.
Yudhiṣṭhira	This dark-skinned, red-eyed youth, mighty of arm and shoulder: I wager Nakula together with his wealth.
Śakuni	Prince Nakula is dear to you, O King Yudhiṣṭhira. When I have won him from you, what wager will remain?

Vaiśampāyana:	Śakuni so spoke and put his hand to the dice. "I have won," said Śakuni to King Yudhiṣṭhira.
Yudhiṣṭhira:	With Sahadeva, teacher of the law, who has won the name of wisdom in the world: with this dear prince, as if he were not dear, I make unwillingly with you my wager.
Vaiśampāyana:	The gambler heard the words; he used deceit in dealing. "I have won," said Śakuni to King Yudhiṣṭhira.
Śakuni:	Dear to you, O king, were these two sons of Mādrī; but Arjuna and Bhīma I think are dearer still.
Yudhiṣṭhira:	You act against the law; you pay no heed to reason in seeking thus to pluck every blossom that I love.
Śakuni:	A drunkard falls in a pit; a madman runs at tree trunks. You are the best and eldest, king; I make my bow to you. But stranger things than they have seen, than they have even dreamed of, will gamblers say, like madmen, when they play at dice.
Yudhiṣṭhira:	With this prince who slays our foes in battle and leads us like a ship across the sea: with this world-hero unworthy to be wagered, with Arjuna, O Śakuni, I wager.
Vaiśampāyana:	The gambler heard the words; he used deceit in dealing. "I have won," said Śakuni to King Yudhiṣṭhira.
Śakuni:	I have won the bowman of the Pāṇḍavas, the warrior who shoots with either hand. Now wager me with your beloved Bhīma, the only wager, Pāṇḍava, that's left.
Yudhiṣṭhira:	With our leader, the fore-leader of our troops, like bolt-weaponed Indra conqueror of demons, the great frowning warrior of sidelong glance, lion-shouldered, intolerant of insult, in strength unequalled, crusher of the foe and foremost wielder of the battle club: with this great prince unworthy to be wagered, with Prince Bhīma, Śakuni, I wager.
Vaiśampāyana:	The gambler heard the words; he used deceit in dealing. "I have won," said Śakuni to King Yudhiṣṭhira.
Śakuni:	You have lost much wealth: horses, elephants, and brothers. Tell me, son of Kuntī, if any wealth remains.
Yudhiṣṭhira:	I am the chief of all and well loved of my brothers; If beaten I will work for you myself in servitude.

Vaiśampāyana:	The gambler heard the words; he used deceit in dealing. "I have won," said Śakuni to King Yudhiṣṭhira.
Śakuni:	This was most ill done to lose yourself at wager; when wealth remains, O king, it is ill to lose oneself.
Vaiśampāyana:	He spoke and with proud glance herded his captives singly, drawing to him the heroes that had stood at stake.
Śakuni:	There still is left your dear queen, a single unwon wager. Set Draupadī at stake; by her win back yourself.
Yudhiṣṭhira:	The mean of tall and short; the mean of black and gold, whose eyes are lit by passion: with her I wager you.

Whose eyes are autumn lotuses, whose breath is the
    autumn lotus,
whose beauty is that of Śrī[1] who lives in the autumn lotus;

a woman of such kindliness and of such perfect beauty,
of such consummate virtue, as ever man could wish;

whose careful management extends to my meanest shepherd,
ever the first to wake, ever the last to sleep;

the sweat upon whose face smells of jasmine flowers;
long-haired, narrow-waisted, smooth-skinned, loving-eyed:

with this fair-waisted queen, the daughter of Pāñcāla,
with dear-limbed Draupadī: come, I wager you.

Vaiśampāyana:	So spoke the King of Law and at his words there mounted a cry of horror from the elders of the court.

All began to speak; the court was in an uproar.
Bhīṣma, Droṇa, Kṛpa, were overwhelmed with grief.

Vidura held his head as if fainting from a blow;
he sat with lowered face, breath hissing like a snake.

But Dhṛtarāṣṭra was glad. He asked over and over
"Has he won, has my son won?" unable to hide his joy.

Karṇa was overjoyed and Duḥśāsana exulted;
but others at the court could not hold back their tears.

Śakuni was sure of himself. As though without reflection
he approached the dice once more, and said simply "I have
    won."

59

Duryodhana:	Come, half-caste! Bring Draupadī to court: the dear consort of the Pāṇḍavas.

---

1. The goddess of royal power, well-being, and beauty.

We'll put her straight to work. It will be a pleasure
to watch her clean the floor with servant girls.

Vidura: Fool! you put a noose around your neck
and yet are unaware of what you do:
a simpleton that teeters on a cliff,
a boy that would show off by teasing tigers.

The snakes are on your head, their fangs filled with poison;
stir them not up, you fool, or you will soon be dead:

Queen Draupadī I think has not become your servant;
the king was not her master when he made the bet.

This young king is like the bamboo tree
that comes in fruit only in time to perish.
For gambling brings on deadly enmity:
he knows it not but he is ripe for death.

Be not spiteful. Turn not the knife in the wound,
nor summon payment from a helpless man.
Speak not that word by which, although
another trembles, you go yourself to hell.

We call it "overspeaking" when a word
so falls upon another's tenderness
that day and night he suffers from the pain.
A wise man guards himself from overspeech.

You know of the goat—the thieves had lost the knife
until the goat by digging with his hoof
revealed the means of cutting his own throat.
So you: don't dig at hatred that may kill you:

Some men are silent, saying not a word
of village dweller or of forester;
but when a holy man appears in town,
perfect in wisdom, they bark at him like dogs.

You do not realize, Duryodhana,
that at this dice game you have opened up
a gateway sloping down to hell, through which
how many Kuru lords must follow you!

Gourds may sink and stones may float,
ships may lose themselves on water,
but this stupid son of Dhṛtarāṣṭra
will never heed my good advice.

The end is near. Destruction of the Kurus,
cruel and all-devouring, will ensue
from this one prince who spurns the words of Kāvya,
the advice of friends, and only grows in greed.

60

Vaiśampāyana:	Duryodhana cried out, "I spurn your words,"
	and turned away from the half-caste with contempt.
	His eyes sought out the usher of the court,
	to whom among those noble lords he spoke.
	"You, usher, bring us Draupadī.
	You are not frightened of the Pāṇḍavas.
	The half-caste here opposes me from fear
	and from his never having wished me well."
	He spoke. The bard who served the court as usher
	left quickly in obedience to the king.
	As a dog might steal into a pride of lions
	he made his way to the Pāṇḍavas' chief queen.
The Usher:	Yudhiṣṭhira, mad with dicing,
	has lost you to Duryodhana.
	So come to Dhṛtarāṣṭra's chamber;
	I am to lead you to your work.
Draupadī:	O usher, how can such a thing be true?
	What son of kings would put his wife at wager?
	Was the king out of his mind with dicing,
	or was it that no other wealth remained?
The Usher:	It was when no other wealth remained
	that King Yudhiṣṭhira put up the wager;
	for first the king had wagered his four brothers
	and next himself; last of all were you.
Draupadī:	Go now, bard's son, to the court and ask my lord this question:
	whether he first lost himself or whether first lost me.
	Find out the answer and come back; then lead me as you say.
Vaiśampāyana:	He went straight to the court and told Yudhiṣṭhira her
	question:
	"Draupadī asks of whom you were master when you lost,
	'whether you first lost yourself, or whether first lost me.'"
	As though he were in a swoon Yudhiṣṭhira sat silent.
	He said no word to the bard's son, whether of good or ill.
Duryodhana:	Let Kṛṣṇā Draupadī come here and ask her question,
	here in the court where all may hear both her words and his.
Vaiśampāyana:	Again at the king's command he went to the royal harem
	and said to Draupadī, trembling as he spoke:
The Usher:	The courtiers, lady, order you to come
	and I fear destruction for the Kauravas.
	The worthless king will not keep fortune long
	if my lady Draupadī goes down to court.

Draupadī: The Ordainer surely has ordained it thus,
                     for both the wise and foolish feel his hand.
                     But he has given us one highest law
                     and he will give me peace if I obey it.

Vaiśampāyana: Yudhiṣṭhira now understood Duryodhana's intention.
                     He therefore sent a messenger well known to Draupadī.

                     In single garment, with knot turned down, weeping and in
                       her period,
                     the daughter of Pañcāla kings knelt before her uncle.

                     From where he stood Duryodhana observed
                     the expression of their faces. To the bard's son
                     he spoke exultant: "Bring her here, right here,
                     where the lords may speak to her directly."

                     The bard was subject to Duryodhana
                     but feared the anger of the highborn queen.
                     He faltered in obedience and asked,
                     "What shall I say to the lady Draupadī?"

Duryodhana: Duḥśāsana! My foolish usher
                     trembles with fear of Wolfbelly Bhīma.
                     Go bring us Draupadī yourself.
                     What can her helpless husbands do?

Vaiśampāyana: The younger prince heard his brother's words
                     and rose with anger-reddened eyes.
                     He strode up to the audience chamber
                     and thus addressed Queen Draupadī.

                     "Come, Pāñcālī; come! You have been won.
                     Look without shame on King Duryodhana.
                     Your love belongs to the Kurus; the lovely prize
                     is fairly won. Come down with me to the court."

                     Mindless what to do, the queen arose
                     and passed a hand across her bloodless face,
                     then ran in desperation toward the chambers
                     of the royal ladies of the Kauravas.

                     With speed Duḥśāsana ran after,
                     cursing at her in his wrath.
                     By her hair he seized the fleeing queen,
                     by her long and wavy, jet-black hair.

                     That hair that had been bathed in holy water
                     at ending of a royal consecration
                     the sons of Pāṇḍu now could not protect
                     from insult at a Dhārtarāṣṭra's hand.

                     Duḥśāsana seized and pulled her toward the court
                     as the wind pulls at the thrashing plantain tree,
                     Pāñcāla's daughter of the jet-black hair,

a married queen, like a woman without a man.

With slender body bending at his force
she whispered, "No! I wear a single garment;
I am unclean! You cannot be so vile
as to bring me in this state before the court."

To which he answered, seizing with rough hand
the soft black tresses of the trembling queen,
"Call on what gods you wish: not Krishna, Jiṣṇu,
Hari, Nara,[2] shall stop my taking you.

"Be you unclean, it makes no difference;
or in a single garment or stark naked.
You have been won at dice and are our slave
and masters do with slave girls as they wish."

Her hair fell dissheveled, her garment slipped
as she was shaken by Duḥśāsana.
In deep shame and burning indignation
the beautiful queen spoke with lowered voice.

Draupadī:

Here present in the court are learned men,
men like Indra, who perform the rites,
my elders and lords the equal of my elders;
they must not see me in my present state.

This is an outrage! You are being shameful!
Stop stripping me! Stop pulling me about!
These sons of kings will not permit such wrong
even if all the gods should give you aid.

The royal son of Law stands in the law,
and law is subtle: only the wise can grasp it.
But even at my lord's command I will not
give up honor and commit a sin.

This is a villainy to drag me so
among the Kurus when I am unclean.
But does no one cry out shame upon you?
Surely it cannot be that they approve.

Shame! Shame! The law of Bhāratas,[3]
the warrior code of honor is destroyed
when all the Kurus gathered here at court
see how the law of Kurus is transgressed.

Droṇa and Bhīṣma must have lost their strength
together with the great-souled Vidura.
Do not the elders of the Kauravas

---

2. Various manifestations of the god Vishnu.
3. Literally, "descendents of Bharata," the legendary universal emperor (usually held to be the king born of the union of Shakuntala and Dushyanta—see page 946). The term is used loosely for the ruling elite.

perceive the unlawful conduct of their king?

Vaiśampāyana: The queen spoke these pitiable words
and cast a glance upon her hero husbands,
raising the anger of the Pāṇḍava hearts
to blazing fire by her sidelong glance.

Not their lost kingdom; not the wealth,
not all the lost gems of highest price,
gave Pāṇḍu's sons such pain as Draupadī
gave by that one anguished sidelong glance.

from Book 5[1]

[THE TEMPTATION OF KARNA]

Dhṛtarāṣṭra said:

Saṃjaya,[2] before Madhusūdana[3] rode out amidst princes and councilors, he had Karṇa mount his chariot. What did that slayer of enemy heroes say to Rādheya[4] inside the chariot, what blandishments did Govinda offer the *sūta's* son? Relate to me what Kṛṣṇa, with his voice roaring like a flood or a cloud, said to Karṇa, whether gently or sharply?

Saṃjaya said:

Hear from me, Bhārata, what Madhusūdana of the boundless spirit had to say to Rādheya in the course of their conversing, in words that were smooth and gentle, friendly, informed with Law, truthful, and helpful, to be cherished in the heart.

Vāsudeva said:

Rādheya, you have attended to brahmins learned in the Veda, and you have questioned them about truths without demurring. You, Karṇa, know the sempiternal sayings of the Veda, and you are well-grounded in the subtleties of the scriptures regarding the Law.

Now, those who know the scriptures teach that the son born to a woman before her marriage is as much counted the son of her wedded husband as the son she bears in marriage. You, Karṇa, were born that way: under Law you are the son of Pāṇḍu. Under the constraint of the books of the Law, come with me and you shall be a king. The Pārthas[5] are your kin on your father's side, the Vṛṣṇis[6] on your mother's side: recognize, bull among men, both these lineages of your kinsmen!

Come with me today, my son; the Pāṇḍavas shall have to recognize you as the Kaunteya senior to Yudhiṣṭhira. The five Pāṇḍavas shall clasp your feet as your brothers, and so shall the five sons of Draupadī, and the unvanquished son[7] of

---

1. Translated by J. A. B. van Buitenen.
2. A *suta,* or bard, and the trusted counselor of King Dhritarashtra.
3. A wide range of epithets is used for Krishna. Some refer to his kinship ties (Vāsudeva, "the son of Vasudeva"; Madhava, "of the Madhu tribe"; Varshaneya, "of the Vrishni people"; and Dasharha, "of the Dasharha people") or to his deeds (Madhusudana, "destroyer of the demon Madhu" or Govinda, "lord of cows"), whereas others are of more obscure origin or meaning (Acyuta, Hrishikesha,

Janardana, Keshava, and Shauri).
4. Son of the unmarried Kunti and the sun god, Karna was abandoned at birth and discovered by the *suta* (son of a Kshatriya by a Brahman woman) Adhiratha and his wife, Radha. He was given the name Vashusena but is also referred to as Rādheya ("son of Radha").
5. The Pandavas.
6. A clan of the Yadavas, to which Kunti belongs.
7. Abhimanyu, the son of Arjuna and Subhadra, Krishna's sister. His death is poignantly recounted later in the epic.

Subhadrā. The kings and the sons of kings who have trooped together in the Pāṇḍava's cause, and all the Andhaka-Vṛṣṇis shall clasp your feet. Baronesses and daughters of kings shall bring golden, silver, and earthen vessels, herbs, all seeds, all gems and shrubs for your inauguration. And at the sixth turn you shall lie with Draupadī!

Today brahmins representing all four Vedas shall consecrate you, assisted by the very priest of the Pāṇḍavas, while you are seated on the tiger skin: so shall the five Pāṇḍava brothers, bulls among men, the Draupadeyas, the Pāñcālas, and Cedis.[8] I my-self shall consecrate you King and Lord of the Land, and Kuntī's son Yudhiṣṭhira shall be your Young King. Kuntī's law-spirited son Yudhiṣṭhira shall mount the chariot of state behind you, holding the white fan.

Kaunteya![9] Mighty Bhīmasena Kaunteya himself shall hold the grand white umbrella over you, the King consecrated! Arjuna shall drive the chariot drawn by his white horses, tinkling with hundreds of bells and covered with tiger hides. Abhimanyu, Nakula, Sahadeva, and the five Draupadeyas shall always be at your beck and call.

The Pāñcālas will follow your banner, and the great warrior Śikhaṇḍin,[1] and I myself will follow you; and all the Andhaka-Vṛṣṇis, the Dāśārhas, and Daśārṇas[2] shall be your retinue, lord of the people! Enjoy your kingship, with your Pāṇḍava brothers, amidst prayers and oblations and manifold benisons. The Draviḍas and Kuntalas shall be your vanguard with the Āndhras, Tālacaras, Cūcupas, and Veṇupas. Bards and minstrels shall today sing your praises in many a song. And the Pāṇḍavas shall proclaim the Triumph of Vasuṣeṇa.

You, Kaunteya, surrounded by the Pārthas as the moon by the stars, reign over the realm and bestow blessing on Kuni! Your friends shall shudder with joy, your enemies with fear. Today, let there be brotherhood between you and your Pāṇḍava brothers!

Karṇa said:

I have no doubt at all, Keśava, that you are speaking to me out of friendship and affection, and so as a friend have my best interests at heart, Vārṣṇeya. I understand it all: under the Law, under the constraints of the scriptures concerning the Law I am, as you hold, the son of Pāṇḍu, Kṛṣṇa. An unmarried maiden conceived me by the Sun, Janārdana, and at the behest of the Sun she abandoned me at birth. Yes, Kṛṣṇa, under Law I was born the son of Pāṇḍu. But Kuntī cast me out as though I had been stillborn! And Adhiratha, a *sūta,* no sooner did he see me than he carried me to his home, Madhusūdana, and proffered me to Rādhā, with *love!* Out of *love* for me the milk of Rādhā's breasts poured forth at once, and she accepted my piss and shit, Mādhava! How could a man like me deny her the ancestral offering? A man who knows the Law and always took care to listen to the scriptures on the Law? Adhiratha, the *sūta,* thinks of me as his son, and my *love* demands that I think of him as my father.

He had my birth rites performed, Mādhava, by the rules found in Scripture, out of love for his son, Janārdana. He had the brahmins name me Vasuṣeṇa, and when I was old enough, he married me to wives, Keśava. I have sons and grandsons by them, Janārdana, and my heart has bonds of love with them, Kṛṣṇa!

---

8. The Draupadeyas (the five sons of Draupadi), the Panchalas, and the Chedis are all allies of the Pandavas.
9. Literally, "born of Kunti."
1. A daughter of king Drupada and sister of Draupadi who changed sex in order to slay Bhishma in battle. (In Shikhandin's former life Bhishma had abducted her and given her in marriage to his half-brother.)
2. Here and in the rest of the paragraph are named some of the clans and peoples assembled from different regions of the subcontinent to fight on the side of the Pandavas.

Govinda, neither joy nor fear, nor all of earth nor piles of gold can make me a traitor to my word. For thirteen years I have enjoyed unrivaled royal power in Dhṛtarāṣṭra's lineage by relying on Duryodhana. I have offered up much and often, but always with *sūtas*. I have performed domestic and marital rites, but always with *sūtas*. Duryodhana has raised arms and prepared for war with the Pāṇḍavas, because he relies on me, Kṛṣṇa of the Vṛṣṇis. Therefore he has confidently chosen me to be the main opponent of the Left-handed Archer[3] in a chariot duel in the war, Acyuta. Neither death nor capture, neither fear nor greed can make me break my promise to the sagacious Dhārtarāṣṭra, Janārdana. If I now refuse to enter the chariot duel with the Left-handed Archer, Hṛṣīkeśa, it will bring both me and the Pārtha disgrace in the world.

No doubt you mean well, Madhusūdana, and no doubt, either, that the Pāṇḍavas will accomplish everything, with your guidance. So you should suppress word of our taking counsel here, best of men; that would be best, I think, joy of all the Yādavas. If the law-spirited king of strict vows knows that I am Kuntī's first-born son, he will not accept the kingdom; and if I were then to obtain this large, prosperous kingdom, I would hand it over to Duryodhana, Madhusūdana, enemy-tamer! Let the law-spirited Yudhiṣṭhira be king forever, he who has Hṛṣīkeśa as his guide, Dhanaṃjaya as his warrior. His is the earth who has the great warrior Bhīmasena, Nakula, Sahadeva, the Draupadeyas, O Mādhava, and Uttamaujas, Yudhāmanyu, Satyadharman, Somaki, Caidya and Cekitāna, the unvanquished Śikhaṇḍin, the firefly-colored Kekaya brothers, the rainbow-hued Kuntibhoja, that great warrior, and Bhīmasena's uncle, and the warrior Senājit, Śankha son of Virāṭa,[4] and you as his treasury, Janārdana. Great is this gathering of the baronage[5] that has been achieved, Keśava. And this kingdom, blazing and renowned among all kings, has now been won.

Vārṣṇeya, the Dhārtarāṣṭra will hold a grand sacrifice of war. Of this sacrifice you shall be the Witness, Janārdana, and you shall be the Adhvaryu priest at the ritual. The Terrifier with the monkey standard stands girt as the Hotar; Gāṇḍīva will be the ladle; the bravery of men the sacrificial butter. The *aindra, pāśupata, brāhma,* and *sthūṇākarṇa*[6] missiles will be the spells employed by the Left-handed Archer. Saubhadra, taking after his father, if not overtaking him, in prowess, will act perfectly as the Grāvastut priest. Mighty Bhīma will be the Udgātar and Prastotar, that tigerlike man who with his roars on the battlefield finishes off an army of elephants. The eternal king, law-spirited Yudhiṣṭhira, well-versed in recitations and oblations, will act as the Brahmán. The sounds of the conches, the drums, the kettledrums, and the piercing lion roars will be the Subrahmaṇyā invocation. Mādrī's two glorious sons Nakula and Sahadeva of great valor will fill the office of the Śamitar priest. The clean chariot spears with their spotted staffs will serve as the sacrificial poles at this sacrifice, Janārdana. The eared arrows, hollow reeds, iron shafts and calf-tooth piles, and the javelins will be the Soma jars, and the bows the strainers. Swords will be the potsherds, skulls the Purodāśa cakes, and blood will be the oblation at this sacrifice, Kṛṣṇa. The spears and bright clubs will be the kindling and enclosing sticks; the

---

3. Arjuna. He wields the Gandiva bow and bears on his battle standard the figure of the monkey god. He also goes by the epithet Dhanamjaya ("Victor of wealth").
4. Uttamaujas, Yudhamanyu, and Satyadharman are Panchala princes. Somaki, Chaidya, and Chekitana belong to clans allied with the Pandavas, as does Shankha, the son of Virata at whose court the Pandavas had lived in dis-

guise for one year, the five Kekaya brothers, Kuntibhoja (the adoptive father of Kunti), and the king Senajit.
5. In this selection "baronage" and "baron" are used to translate the Sanskrit *kshatra* and *kshatriya,* terms for the warrior class.
6. Magic weapons of divine make.

pupils of Droṇa and Kṛpa Śāradvata the Sadasyas.[7] The arrows shot by the Gāṇḍiva bowman, the great warriors, and Droṇa and his son will be the pillows. Sātyaki shall act as Pratiprasthātar, the Dhārtarāṣṭra as the Sacrificer, his great army as the Wife. Mighty Ghaṭotkaca will be the Śamitar when this Overnight Sacrifice is spun out, strong-armed hero. Majestic Dhṛṣṭadyumna shall be the sacrificial fee when the fire rite takes place, he who was born from the fire.

The insults I heaped on the Pāṇḍavas, to please Duryodhana, those I regret. When you see me cut down by the Left-handed Archer, it will be the Re-piling of the Fire of their sacrifice. When the Pāṇḍava drinks the blood of Duḥśāsana, bellowing his roar, it will be the Soma draught. When the two Pāñcālyas fell Droṇa and Bhīṣma, that will be the Conclusion of the sacrifice, Janārdana. When the mighty Bhīmasena kills Duryodhana, then the great sacrifice of the Dhārtarāṣṭra will end. The weeping of the gathered daughters-in-law and granddaughters-in-law, whose masters, sons, and protectors have been slain, with the mourning of Gāndhārī at the sacrificial site now teeming with dogs, vultures, and ospreys, will be the Final Bath of this sacrifice, Janārdana.[8]

May these barons, old in learning and days, O bull among barons, not die a useless death for your sake, Madhusūdana. Let the full circle of the baronage find their death by the sword on the Field of the Kurus, holiest in all three worlds, Keśava. Ordain here, lotus-eyed Vārṣṇeya, what you desire, so that the baronage in its totality may ascend to heaven.

As long as the mountains will stand and the rivers flow, Janārdana, so long and forevermore shall last the sound of the fame of this war. Brahmins shall in their gatherings narrate the Great War of the Bhāratas, proclaiming the glory of the barons.

Keśava, lead the Kaunteya to the battle, and keep this council of ours secret, enemy-burner.

Saṃjaya said:
Having heard Karṇa's reply, Keśava, slayer of enemy heroes, smiled; then he laughed and said, "Does the offer of a kingdom not tempt you, Karṇa? Do you not wish to rule the earth I am giving you?

> There is not a shadow of doubt remaining
> That victory's sure of the Pāṇḍavas:
> The Pāṇḍava's banner of Triumph is out.
> The terrible king of the apes has been raised!

> Celestial art did Bhauvana[9] fashion:
> It is raised like the banner of Indra himself;
> It shows many creatures that terrify,
> Celestial creatures that horrify.

---

7. The pupils of the masters Drona and Kripa Sharadvata are both the Pandavas and Kauravas, represented as the *sadasyas*, attendees or assistants, of the sacrifice battle.
8. The metaphor of the hallowed Vedic rites performed to propitiate the gods and secure well-being powerfully calls forth Karna's dark forebodings of war and destruction. The most important of the various priests of the sacrifice were the Hotar, the singer of *Rig Veda* hymns; the Adhvaryu, who did the practical work of the sacrifice while pronouncing various sacred formulas from the *Yajur Veda;* and the Udgatar, singer of the *Sama Veda*. The Pratiprashastar, Prastotar, and Gravastut performed other parts of the liturgy. A common sacrificial offering was the *purodasha*, cakes made of ground rice and offered in small, skull-like cups. An especially solemn moment of the sacrifice was the drinking of soma, an intoxicating beverage of uncertain composition.
9. Another name of Vishvakarman, chief artisan of the gods.

> It is never entangled in rocks or trees,
> Upward and across it stretches a league;
> The illustrious flag of Dhanaṃjaya, Karṇa,
> Is raised with a glow that resembles the fire's.

When you see the man of the white horses on the battlefield with Kṛṣṇa driving his chariot, employing the missiles of Indra, Fire, and Wind, and hear the whip-crack of Gāṇḍīva as of a thunderbolt, then there will be no more Kṛta Age, no more Tretā, no more Dvāpara.[1] When you see Kuntī's son Yudhiṣṭhira on the battlefield, protecting his grand-army with spells and oblations, unassailable like the sun burning the host of the enemy, then there will be no more Kṛta, no more Tretā, no more Dvāpara. When you see the mighty Bhīmasena on the battlefield, dancing his war dance after drinking Duḥśāsana's blood, like a rutting elephant that has killed a challenging tusker, then there will be no more Kṛta, no more Tretā, no more Dvāpara. When you see Mādrī's warrior sons on the battlefield, routing the army of the Dhārtarāṣṭras like elephants, shattering the chariots of enemy heroes as they plunge into the clash of arms, then there will be no more Kṛta, no more Tretā, no more Dvāpara. When you see on the battlefield Droṇa, Śāṃtanava, Kṛpa, King Suyodhana, and Jayadratha Saindhava[2] storming to the attack and halted by the Left-handed Archer, then there will be no more Kṛta, no more Tretā, no more Dvāpara.

Go hence, Karṇa, and say to Droṇa, Śāṃtanava, and Kṛpa: this is a propitious month, with fodder and fuel plentifully at hand, abounding with ripe grains and plants, with plenty of fruit and hardly any mosquitoes. There is no mud, the water is tasty, the weather is pleasant, neither too hot nor too cold. Seven days from now it will be New Moon: let then the battle be joined, for they say that that is the Day of Indra.

Likewise say to all the kings who have come to battle, 'I shall accomplish for you all that you desire.' The kings and princes who follow Duryodhana's orders will, in finding their death by the sword, attain to the highest goal."

Saṃjaya said:

Upon hearing Keśava's words, benevolent and propitious, Karṇa paid homage to Kṛṣṇa Madhusūdana, and said, "Why, strong-armed man, did you seek to delude me when you knew already? The total destruction that looms for the earth is caused by Śakuni, me, Duḥśāsana, and Dhṛtarāṣṭra's son King Duryodhana. There is no doubt, Kṛṣṇa, that a great battle impends between the Pāṇḍavas and Kurus, grisly and mired in blood. The kings and princes who follow Duryodhana's orders will journey to Yama's realm,[3] burned by the fire of the weapons in the war. Many nightmarish dreams are being seen, Madhusūdana, and dreadful portents and calamitous omens, hair-raising and manifold, which presage that victory will be Yudhiṣṭhira's and defeat Duryodhana's, Vārṣṇeya. The luminous planet Saturn is sharply threatening the

---

1. The first three of the four ages (*yugas*) that make up a cosmic cycle of creation and decay. The Kali age, the last and worst, commenced in the aftermath of the great Bharata war.

2. Suyodhana is another name of Duryodhana. Shantanava ("son of Shantanu") is Bhishma. Jayadratha, king of the Sindhus, is the brother-in-law and ally of Duryodhana.
3. The place of the dead.

constellation Rohiṇī, menacing the creatures even more. Mars, in retrograde position to Jyeṣṭhā, is aiming for Anurādhā,[4] Madhusūdana, as though pleading for the peace of friendship.

Surely great danger is at hand for the Kurus, Kṛṣṇa, for the planet threatens Citrā in particular, Vārṣṇeya. The spot on the moon is distorted, while Rāhu is about to attack the sun. Meteors are falling from the sky with hurricanes and earthquakes. The elephants are trumpeting, the horses are shedding tears and take no pleasure in water and fodder, Mādhava. When such portents appear, they say a horrendous danger is near that will destroy the creatures, strong-armed one. Horses, elephants, and men are eating little in all the armies of the Dhārtarāṣṭra, Keśava, yet their feces are massive. The wise say that that is a sign of defeat, Madhusūdana. They say, Kṛṣṇa, that the mounts of the Pāṇḍavas are in good spirits and that the wild beasts are circumambulating their camp, a sign of victory, but all animals go the reverse way around the Dhārtarāṣṭra, Keśava, and there are also disembodied voices, a sign of his defeat. Peacocks, flower birds, wild geese, cranes, *cātakas*, and *jīvamjīvaka* flocks follow the Pāṇḍavas, while vultures, crows, *baḍas*, kites, ghouls, jackals, and swarms of mosquitoes follow the Kauravas.

In the Dhārtarāṣṭra's armies there is no sound of drums, but the drums of the Pāṇḍavas sound forth unstruck. The wells in the Dhārtarāṣṭra's camp gurgle like bullocks, presaging his defeat. The God rains a rain of flesh and blood. A brilliant Gandharva city hovers nearby with walls, moats, ramparts, and handsome gate towers. A black mace obfuscates the sun at dawn and dusk, predicting great danger, and a single jackal howls horrifyingly, a sign of Duryodhana's defeat. Black-necked birds hover terrifyingly, then fly into the dusk, a sign of his defeat. He hates first of all the brahmins, Madhusūdana, and then his elders and loyal retainers, a sign of his defeat. The eastern horizon is blood-red, the southern darkling like swords, and the western mud-colored like an unbaked pot, Madhusūdana. All the horizons of the Dhārtarāṣṭra are on fire, Mādhava, and with these portentous signs they foredoom great danger.

I had a dream in which I saw Yudhiṣṭhira and his brothers ascend to a thousand-pillared palace, Acyuta. All wore white turbans and white robes, and I saw that they all had beautiful stools. In my vision I saw you drape the blood-fouled earth with entrails, Kṛṣṇa Janārdana. A boundlessly august Yudhiṣṭhira mounted a pile of bones and joyously ate rice mixed with ghee from a gold platter. I saw Yudhiṣṭhira swallow the earth which you had served him—clearly he shall enjoy the rule of the earth. Wolf-Belly of the terrible feats had climbed a steep mountain and with his club in hand the tigerlike man seemed to survey this earth—clearly he shall destroy us all in a great battle. I know, Hṛṣīkeśa, that where there is Law there is triumph. Dhanaṃjaya carrying Gāṇḍiva had mounted a white elephant, together with you, Hṛṣīkeśa, blazing with sublime luster. All of you shall—about that I have no doubts—slaughter all the kings led by Duryodhana in battle, Kṛṣṇa. Nakula, Sahadeva, and the great warrior Sātyaki, decked with pure bracelets and necklaces, wearing white garlands and robes, tigerlike man, had mounted on men, the three stately men wearing white umbrellas and robes. In the Dhārtarāṣṭra's armies too I saw three white-turbaned men, Janārdana Keśava—know who they are: Aśvatthāman, Kṛpa, and Kṛtavarman Sātvata. All other

4. Anuradha and Jyestha are the 17th and 18th of the 27th lunar houses.

kings wore red turbans, Mādhava. Mounted on a camel cart, O strong-armed Janārdana, Bhiṣma and Droṇa accompanied by me and the Dhārtarāṣṭra traveled to the region ruled by Agastya, Lord Janārdana: soon we shall reach the dwelling of Yama; I and the other kings and the circle of barons shall doubtless enter the fire of Gāṇḍīva.

Kṛṣṇa said:

Of a certainty, the destruction of the earth is now near, for my words do not reach your heart, Karṇa. When the destruction of all creatures is at hand, bad policy disguised as good does not stir from the heart, my friend.

Karṇa said:

Perhaps we shall see you again, strong-armed Kṛṣṇa, if we escape alive from the great battle, the carnage of heroes. Or surely we shall meet in heaven, Kṛṣṇa—yes, there we shall meet again next, prince sans blame.

Saṃjaya said:

Speaking thus, Karṇa clasped the Mādhava tightly; then, dismissed by Keśava, he came down from the pit of the chariot. Riding his own gold-adorned chariot, Rādheya dejectedly returned with us. Keśava rode off with Sātyaki[5] at a fast pace, again and again urging his charioteer, "Go! Go!"

Vaiśaṃpāyana said:

When Kṛṣṇa's diplomacy had failed and he had departed from the Kurus for the Pāṇḍavas, the Steward went to Pṛthā and spoke softly in sorrow, "You know, mother of living sons, that my heart always inclines to kindliness. I may shout, but Suyodhana does not take my advice. Yonder, King Yudhiṣṭhira, armed with the Cedis, Pāñcālas, and Kekayas, with Bhīma and Arjuna, Kṛṣṇa, Yuyudhāna, and the twins, and encamped at Upaplavya, still only wishes for Law out of love for his kinsmen, like a weak man although he is strong. King Dhṛtarāṣṭra here, on the other hand, while old in years does not make peace. Infected by the madness of his son, he walks the path of lawlessness. Because of the bad judgment of Jayadratha, Karṇa, Duḥśāsana, and Saubala the breach goes on. But the Law and its consequences will overtake those who lawlessly stole that most law-loving kingdom. Who would not run a fever when the Kurus steal the Law by force? When Keśava comes back without peace, the Pāṇḍavas shall arm for battle, and the bad policy of the Kurus will become the assassin of heroes. I worry and worry, and find no sleep by day or night."

Listening to his words, which were spoken by one who meant well, Kuntī, sick with grief herself, sighed aloud and reflected in her mind, "Accursed be this wealth for the sake of which there will be great carnage in the slaughter of kinsmen, for there will only be defeat in this family war. If the Pāṇḍavas, Cedis, Pāñcālas, and the Yādavas together fight the Bhāratas, what could be worse than that? I do see that there is evil in war, surely, but so is defeat in war evil. For the dispossessed it is better to die, for there is no victory in the killing of kin. Grandfather Śāṃtanava and the Teacher, master of warriors, and Karṇa increase my fears in the cause of the Dhārtarāṣṭra. Droṇa the Teacher would never willingly fight with his pupils for personal gain, and why would Grandfather not have good feelings toward the Pāṇḍavas? It is only *he* who perversely follows the folly of the evil-hearted Dhārtarāṣṭra, who always has hated the Pāṇḍavas wickedly. Karṇa is obdurate in a great cause, and always strong enough to visit disaster on the Pāṇḍavas; and that burns me now. Today I hope

---

5. Yuyudhana, a kinsmen of Krishna and one of the principal allies of the Pandavas.

to soften Karṇa's heart toward the Pāṇḍavas, when I approach him and show him the truth.

"When the blessed Durvāsas[6] was satisfied and granted me the boon of conjuring up Gods, while I lived honorably in father Kuntibhoja's house, I thought in many ways with beating heart, right there in the king's women's quarters, about the strength and weakness of spells and the power of a brahmin's word. I thought and thought, being both a woman and a child, protected by my trusted nurse and surrounded by my friends, shunning mistakes and guarding my father's good name, "How can I do something good for myself and yet not sin?" thinking of the brahmin and bowing to him. Then, on having attained the boon that enabled such a course I, out of curiosity and childishness, being just a girl, made God the Sun come to me. Why should he whom I carried as a girl, not obey my word, which is proper and good for his brothers, when he has been received back as my son?"

When Kuntī had taken this ultimate decision, she embarked upon her task and went to the river Bhāgīrathī.[7] On the bank of the Ganges Pṛthā heard the sound of her compassionate and truthful son's recitations. She stood miserably behind her son, who faced east with his hands raised, and waited for the recitation to end. She, wedded wife of a Kauravya, a Princess of the Vṛṣṇis, stood in the shade of Karṇa's upper garment like a withered garland of lotuses, hurting from the heat of the sun. He prayed until the heat reached his back, being strict in his vows; then he turned around and saw Kuntī. He saluted her and waited for her to speak with folded hands, as was proper, this proud and splendid man, first of the upholders of the Law.

  Karṇa said:
I, Karṇa, son of Rādhā and Adhiratha, salute you. Why has your ladyship come? Tell me what I must do for you.
  Kuntī said:
You are the son of Kuntī, not of Rādhā, nor is Adhiratha your father. You have not been born in the line of *sūtas,* Karṇa. Learn what I am telling you. I gave birth to you before I was married. You are my first-born whom I carried in my womb in the palace of Kuntibhoja. You are a *Pārtha,* my son! He, the God who makes light and spreads heat, he Virocana[8] begot you on me, Karṇa, to be the greatest of swordsmen. The child of a God, with inborn earrings and armor, you were borne by me in my father's house, covered with glory, invincible son. It is not at all right for you, son, innocently to serve the Dhārtarāṣṭras without knowing your real brothers. In the decisions of Law *that* is reckoned the fruit of the Law of men that as parents—and also as a one-eyed mother—they rest content with their son. Cut yourself off from the Dhārtarāṣṭras and enjoy Yudhiṣṭhira's fortune, the fortune once won by Arjuna and then greedily stolen by scoundrels. Let the Kurus today witness the meeting of Karṇa and Arjuna in a spirit of brotherhood. Let Karṇa and Arjuna be like Rāma and Janārdana.[9] When the two of you are united in spirit, what could you not achieve in the world! Surrounded by your five brothers, you shall surely shine forth, Karṇa, like Brahmā surrounded by the Vedas and their

---

6. An irascible sage, infamous in Sanskrit literature for his curses.
7. The Ganges. Brought down from heaven by King Bhagiratha's prayers, the river is often called Bhagirathi,

"daughter of Bhagiratha."
8. The sun god.
9. Krisha and his brother Balarama Balarama.

Branches. Endowed with virtues, the eldest and the best among relations who are the best, your title will no longer be that of the son of a *sūta;* you shall be a heroic *Pārtha!*

Vaiśaṃpāyana said:

Thereupon Karṇa heard a voice that issued from the sun, affectionate and not to be gainsaid, which the sun uttered like a father: "Pṛthā has spoken the truth, Karṇa, obey your mother's word. The greatest good will befall you, tiger among men, if you do as she says." And thus addressed by his mother, and by his father the Sun himself, Karṇa's mind did not falter, for he stood fast by the truth.

Karṇa said:

It is not that I do not believe the words you have spoken, *kṣatriya* lady, or deny that for me the gateway to the Law is to carry out your behest. But the irreparable wrong you have done me by casting me out has destroyed the name and fame I could have had. Born a *kṣatriya,* I have yet not received the respect due a baron. What enemy could have done me greater harm than you have? When there was time to act you did not show me your present compassion. And now you have laid orders on me, the son to whom you denied the sacraments. You have never acted in my interest like a mother, and now, here you are, enlightening me solely in your own interest.

Who would not tremble before a Dhanaṃjaya aided by a Kṛṣṇa? Who would not call me a coward, if I now joined the Pārthas? I who never had been known as their brother now stand revealed as one, at the hour of battle. If I now go to the Pāṇḍavas, what will the baronage call me? The Dhārtarāṣṭras have let me share in all their comforts and have honored me much at all times: how could I, *I* betray them now? Now that they are embroiled in a feud with the others, they attend to me at all times and honor me as much as the Vasus honor Vāsava. How could I shatter their hopes now, if they think that with my prowess they can engage their enemies? How could I desert them now when they see in me the boat they need to cross over this impassable battle and find the farther shore of this shoreless ocean? Now the hour has struck for all the men who have lived off the Dhārtarāṣṭra, and I have to discharge my duty heedless of my life. Those evil men who, after having been well supported to their heart's content, pay no heed to what has been done for them and fecklessly undo past benefactions when the time of duty arrives, wicked despoilers of their kings and thieves of their masters' riceball, gain neither this world nor the next.

Yes, I shall fight your sons in the cause of Dhṛtarāṣṭra's son with all my power and strength—I will *not* lie to you. While trying to persevere in the humane conduct that becomes a decent man, I will *not* carry out your word, beneficial though it may be. Yet, your effort with me shall not lack fruit. I shall not kill your sons in the battle, though I can withstand and slay them—that is, your sons Yudhiṣṭhira, Bhīma and the twins, excepting Arjuna. Arjuna I shall fight in Yudhiṣṭhira's army. In killing Arjuna on the battlefield I shall find my reward, or reap fame if the Left-handed Archer kills me. So never shall your sons number less than five, glorious woman: either without Arjuna but with Karṇa, or with Arjuna, if I am killed.

Vaiśaṃpāyana said:

Having heard Karṇa's answer, Kuntī shuddered from sorrow; and embracing her son, she said to Karṇa, who was unfaltering in his fortitude, "So it must be then—the Kauravas will go to their perdition, as you have said, Karṇa. Fate is all-powerful. But promise me, enemy-plougher: the safety you have granted your four brothers, of that pledge you will acquit yourself! Good health and good luck," said Pṛthā to Karṇa. Pleased, Karṇa saluted her. Then both went their separate ways.

from Book 6[1]

from THE BHAGAVAD GITA

The First Teaching

ARJUNA'S DEJECTION

Dhritarashtra: Sanjaya, tell me what my sons
and the sons of Pandu did when they met,
wanting to battle on the field of Kuru,
on the field of sacred duty?

Sanjaya: Your son Duryodhana, the king,
seeing the Pandava forces arrayed,   5
approached his teacher Drona
and spoke in command.

"My teacher, see
the great Pandava army arrayed   10
by Drupada's son,[2]
your pupil, intent on revenge.

Here are heroes, mighty archers
equal to Bhima and Arjuna in warfare,
Yuyudhana, Virata, and Drupada,   15
your sworn foe on his great chariot.

Here too are Dhrishtaketu,[3] Cekitana,
and the brave king of Benares;
Purujit, Kuntibhoja,
and the manly king of the Shibis.   20

Yudhamanyu is bold,
and Uttamaujas is brave;
the sons of Subhadra and Draupadi
all command great chariots.

Now, honored priest, mark   25
the superb men on our side
as I tell you the names
of my army's leaders.

They are you and Bhishma,
Karna and Kripa, a victor in battles,   30

1. Translated by Barbara Stoler Miller.
2. Drupada's son, Dhrishtadyumna, and one of the foremost generals in the Pandava forces. He was destined to slay Drona, his father's arch enemy, from whom he had learned the science of weapons.
3. A king of the Chedis and ally of the Pandavas.

your own son Ashvatthama,
Vikarna,[4] and the son of Somadatta.[5]

Many other heroes also risk
their lives for my sake,
bearing varied weapons   35
and skilled in the ways of war.

Guarded by Bhishma, the strength
of our army is without limit;
but the strength of their army,
guarded by Bhima, is limited.   40

In all the movements of battle,
you and your men,
stationed according to plan,
must guard Bhishma well!"

Bhishma, fiery elder of the Kurus,   45
roared his lion's roar
and blew his conch horn,
exciting Duryodhana's delight.

Conches and kettledrums,
cymbals, tabors, and trumpets   50
were sounded at once
and the din of tumult arose.

Standing on their great chariot
yoked with white stallions,
Krishna and Arjuna, Pandu's son,   55
sounded their divine conches.

Krishna blew Pancajanya, won from a demon;
Arjuna blew Devadatta, a gift of the gods;
fierce wolf-bellied Bhima blew Paundra,
his great conch of the east.   60

Yudhishthira, Kunti's son, the king,
blew Anantavijaya, conch of boundless victory;
his twin brothers Nakula and Sahadeva
blew conches resonant and jewel toned.

The king of Benares, a superb archer,   65
and Shikhandin on his great chariot,
Drishtadyumna, Virata, and indomitable Satyaki,
all blew their conches.

Drupada, with his five grandsons,
and Subhadra's strong-armed son,   70
each in his turn blew

---

4. One of the sons of Dhritarashtra.   5. Bhurishravas, who would be slain by the Vrishni warrior Satyaki.

their conches, O King.

The noise tore the hearts
of Dhritarashtra's sons,
and tumult echoed   75
through heaven and earth.

Arjuna, his war flag a rampant monkey,
saw Dhritarashtra's sons assembled
as weapons were ready to clash,
and he lifted his bow.   80

He told his charioteer:

    "Krishna,
    halt my chariot
    between the armies!

    Far enough for me to see   85
    these men who lust for war,
    ready to fight with me
    in the strain of battle.

    I see men gathered here,
    eager to fight,   90
    bent on serving the folly
    of Dhritarashtra's son."

    When Arjuna had spoken,
    Krishna halted
    their splendid chariot   95
    between the armies.

    Facing Bhishma and Drona
    and all the great kings,
    he said, "Arjuna, see
    the Kuru men assembled here!"   100

    Arjuna saw them standing there:
    fathers, grandfathers, teachers,
    uncles, brothers, sons,
    grandsons, and friends.

    He surveyed his elders   105
    and companions in both armies,
    all his kinsmen
    assembled together.

    Dejected, filled with strange pity,
    he said this: 110
    "Krishna, I see my kinsmen
    gathered here, wanting war.

    My limbs sink,
    my mouth is parched,

my body trembles,   115
the hair bristles on my flesh.

The magic bow slips
from my hand, my skin burns,
I cannot stand still,
my mind reels.   120

I see omens of chaos,
Krishna; I see no good
in killing my kinsmen
in battle.

Krishna, I seek no victory,   125
or kingship or pleasures.
What use to us are kingship,
delights, or life itself?

We sought kingship, delights,
and pleasures for the sake of those   130
assembled to abandon their lives
and fortunes in battle.

They are teachers, fathers, sons,
and grandfathers, uncles, grandsons,
fathers and brothers of wives,   135
and other men of our family.

I do not want to kill them
even if I am killed, Krishna;
not for kingship of all three worlds,
much less for the earth!   140

What joy is there for us, Krishna,
in killing Dhritarashtra's sons?
Evil will haunt us if we kill them,
though their bows are drawn to kill.

Honor forbids us to kill   145
our cousins, Dhritarashtra's sons;
how can we know happiness
if we kill our own kinsmen?

The greed that distorts their reason
blinds them to the sin they commit   150
in ruining the family, blinds them
to the crime of betraying friends.

How can we ignore the wisdom
of turning from this evil
when we see the sin   155
of family destruction, Krishna?

When the family is ruined,
the timeless laws of family duty

perish; and when duty is lost,
chaos overwhelms the family.   160

In overwhelming chaos, Krishna,
women of the family are corrupted;
and when women are corrupted,
disorder is born in society.

This discord drags the violators   165
and the family itself to hell;
for ancestors fall when rites
of offering rice and water lapse.

The sins of men who violate
the family create disorder in society   170
that undermines the constant laws
of caste and family duty.

Krishna, we have heard
that a place in hell
is reserved for men   175
who undermine family duties.

I lament the great sin
we commit when our greed
for kingship and pleasures
drives us to kill our kinsmen.   180

If Dhritarashtra's armed sons
kill me in battle when I am unarmed
and offer no resistance,
it will be my reward."

Saying this in the time of war,   185
Arjuna slumped into the chariot
and laid down his bow and arrows,
his mind tormented by grief.

The Second Teaching

PHILOSOPHY AND SPIRITUAL DISCIPLINE

Sanjaya:	Arjuna sat dejected,
	filled with pity,
	his sad eyes blurred by tears.
	Krishna gave him counsel.

Lord Krishna:	Why this cowardice	5
	in time of crisis, Arjuna?	
	The coward is ignoble, shameful,	
	foreign to the ways of heaven.	

Don't yield to impotence!
It is unnatural in you!   10

| | Banish this petty weakness from your heart. | |
| | Rise to the fight, Arjuna! | |

Arjuna: Krishna, how can I fight
                against Bhishma and Drona
                with arrows   15
                when they deserve my worship?

                It is better in this world
                to beg for scraps of food
                than to eat meals
                smeared with the blood   20
                of elders I killed
                at the height of their power
                while their goals
                were still desires.

                We don't know which weight   25
                is worse to bear—
                our conquering them
                or their conquering us.
                We will not want to live
                if we kill   30
                the sons of Dhritarashtra
                assembled before us.

                The flaw of pity
                blights my very being;
                conflicting sacred duties   35
                confound my reason.
                I ask you to tell me
                decisively—Which is better?
                I am your pupil.
                Teach me what I seek!   40

                I see nothing
                that could drive away
                the grief
                that withers my senses;
                even if I won kingdoms   45
                of unrivaled wealth
                on earth
                and sovereignty over gods.

Sanjaya: Arjuna told this
                to Krishna—then saying,   50
                "I shall not fight,"
                he fell silent.

                Mocking him gently,
                Krishna gave this counsel

as Arjuna sat dejected,   55
between the two armies.

Lord Krishna: You grieve for those beyond grief,
and you speak words of insight;
but learned men do not grieve
for the dead or the living.   60

Never have I not existed,
nor you, nor these kings;
and never in the future
shall we cease to exist.

Just as the embodied self   65
enters childhood, youth, and old age,
so does it enter another body;
this does not confound a steadfast man.

Contacts with matter make us feel
heat and cold, pleasure and pain.   70
Arjuna, you must learn to endure
fleeting things—they come and go!

When these cannot torment a man,
when suffering and joy are equal
for him and he has courage,   75
he is fit for immortality.

Nothing of nonbeing comes to be,
nor does being cease to exist;
the boundary between these two
is seen by men who see reality.   80

Indestructible is the presence
that pervades all this;
no one can destroy
this unchanging reality.

Our bodies are known to end,   85
but the embodied self is enduring,
indestructible, and immeasurable;
therefore, Arjuna, fight the battle!

He who thinks this self a killer
and he who thinks it killed,   90
both fail to understand;
it does not kill, nor is it killed.

It is not born,
it does not die;
having been,   95
it will never not be;
unborn, enduring,

constant, and primordial,
it is not killed
when the body is killed.   100

Arjuna, when a man knows the self
to be indestructible, enduring, unborn,
unchanging, how does he kill
or cause anyone to kill?

As a man discards   105
worn-out clothes
to put on new
and different ones,
so the embodied self
discards   110
its worn-out bodies
to take on other new ones.

Weapons do not cut it,
fire does not burn it,
waters do not wet it,   115
wind does not wither it.

It cannot be cut or burned;
it cannot be wet or withered;
it is enduring, all-pervasive,
fixed, immovable, and timeless.   120

It is called unmanifest,
inconceivable, and immutable;
since you know that to be so,
you should not grieve!

If you think of its birth   125
and death as ever-recurring,
then too, Great Warrior,
you have no cause to grieve!

Death is certain for anyone born,
and birth is certain for the dead;   130
since the cycle is inevitable,
you have no cause to grieve!

Creatures are unmanifest in origin,
manifest in the midst of life,
and unmanifest again in the end.   135
Since this is so, why do you lament?

Rarely someone
sees it,
rarely another
speaks it,   140
rarely anyone

hears it—
even hearing it,
no one really knows it.

The self embodied in the body   145
of every being is indestructible;
you have no cause to grieve
for all these creatures, Arjuna!

Look to your own duty;
do not tremble before it;   150
nothing is better for a warrior
than a battle of sacred duty.

The doors of heaven open
for warriors who rejoice
to have a battle like this   155
thrust on them by chance.

If you fail to wage this war
of sacred duty,
you will abandon your own duty
and fame only to gain evil.   160

People will tell
of your undying shame,
and for a man of honor
shame is worse than death.

The great chariot warriors will think   165
you deserted in fear of battle;
you will be despised
by those who held you in esteem.

Your enemies will slander you,
scorning your skill   170
in so many unspeakable ways—
could any suffering be worse?

If you are killed, you win heaven;
if you triumph, you enjoy the earth;
therefore, Arjuna, stand up   175
and resolve to fight the battle!

Impartial to joy and suffering,
gain and loss, victory and defeat,
arm yourself for the battle,
lest you fall into evil.   180

Understanding is defined in terms of philosophy;
now hear it in spiritual discipline.
Armed with this understanding, Arjuna,
you will escape the bondage of action.

No effort in this world
is lost or wasted;
a fragment of sacred duty
saves you from great fear.   185

This understanding is unique
in its inner core of resolve;   190
diffuse and pointless are the ways
irresolute men understand.

Undiscerning men who delight
in the tenets of ritual lore
utter florid speech, proclaiming,   195
"There is nothing else!"

Driven by desire, they strive after heaven
and contrive to win powers and delights,
but their intricate ritual language
bears only the fruit of action in rebirth.   200

Obsessed with powers and delights,
their reason lost in words,
they do not find in contemplation
this understanding of inner resolve.

Arjuna, the realm of sacred lore   205
is nature—beyond its triad of qualities,
dualities, and mundane rewards,
be forever lucid, alive to your self.

For the discerning priest,
all of sacred lore   210
has no more value than a well
when water flows everywhere.

Be intent on action,
not on the fruits of action;
avoid attraction to the fruits   215
and attachment to inaction!

Perform actions, firm in discipline,
relinquishing attachment;
be impartial to failure and success—
this equanimity is called discipline.   220

Arjuna, action is far inferior
to the discipline of understanding;
so seek refuge in understanding—pitiful
are men drawn by fruits of action.

Disciplined by understanding,   225
one abandons both good and evil deeds;
so arm yourself for discipline—

discipline is skill in actions.

Wise men disciplined by understanding
relinquish the fruit born of action;   230
freed from these bonds of rebirth,
they reach a place beyond decay.

When your understanding passes beyond
the swamp of delusion,
you will be indifferent to all   235
that is heard in sacred lore.

When your understanding turns
from sacred lore to stand fixed,
immovable in contemplation,
then you will reach discipline.   240

Arjuna:

Krishna, what defines a man
deep in contemplation whose insight
and thought are sure? How would he speak?
How would he sit? How would he move?

Lord Krishna:

When he gives up desires in his mind,   245
is content with the self within himself,
then he is said to be a man
whose insight is sure, Arjuna.

When suffering does not disturb his mind,
when his craving for pleasures has vanished,   250
when attraction, fear, and anger are gone,
he is called a sage whose thought is sure.

When he shows no preference
in fortune or misfortune
and neither exults nor hates,   255
his insight is sure.

When, like a tortoise retracting
its limbs, he withdraws his senses
completely from sensuous objects,
his insight is sure.   260

Sensuous objects fade
when the embodied self abstains from food;
the taste lingers, but it too fades
in the vision of higher truth.

Even when a man of wisdom   265
tries to control them, Arjuna,
the bewildering senses
attack his mind with violence.

Controlling them all,
with discipline he should focus on me;   270

when his senses are under control,
his insight is sure.

Brooding about sensuous objects
makes attachment to them grow;
from attachment desire arises,   275
from desire anger is born.

From anger comes confusion;
from confusion memory lapses;
from broken memory understanding is lost;
from loss of understanding, he is ruined.   280

But a man of inner strength
whose senses experience objects
without attraction and hatred,
in self-control, finds serenity.

In serenity, all his sorrows   285
dissolve;
his reason becomes serene,
his understanding sure.

Without discipline,
he has no understanding or inner power;   290
without inner power, he has no peace;
and without peace where is joy?

If his mind submits to the play
of the senses,
they drive away insight,   295
as wind drives a ship on water.

So, Great Warrior, when withdrawal
of the senses
from sense objects is complete,
discernment is firm.   300

When it is night for all creatures,
a master of restraint is awake;
when they are awake, it is night
for the sage who sees reality.

As the mountainous depths   305
of the ocean
are unmoved when waters
rush into it,
so the man unmoved
when desires enter him   310
attains a peace that eludes
the man of many desires.

When he renounces all desires
and acts without craving,

possessiveness,
or individuality, he finds peace.   315

This is the place of the infinite spirit;
achieving it, one is freed from delusion;
abiding in it even at the time of death,
one finds the pure calm of infinity.   320

❧ TRANSLATIONS: THE *BHAGAVAD GITA* ❧

No Sanskrit work has been translated more often than the *Bhagavad Gita*. It was the first text rendered directly into a European language, and scores of versions have appeared in English alone. This proliferation is no doubt due largely to the popularity and importance of the work, but the repeated attempts also seem to be tacit acknowledgment that translation success has been elusive.

There are several reasons for the mixed results. The main one is probably the difficulty of explaining the book's complex conceptual universe to Western readership. Another reason, less obvious, lies in the formal grounds of this complexity: the work is a hybrid of two textual modes, the epic and the philosophical, with their two highly differentiated registers. The *Gita*'s hybridity remains an obstacle to translators, few of whom are equally proficient in both the story world of the Indian epic and the thought world of ancient India.

Looking at three English versions of the *Gita* suggests something of the translation challenges it presents. The scene in question shows the hero Arjuna gazing upon the ranks of the enemy army, which includes his grandfather, cousins, and teachers (page 841), while Krishna, his counselor and friend (and hidden deity), tries to encourage him (page 843). Arjuna's despair is expressed with a sublimity that would be familiar to readers of Homer; Krishna responds in a voice of almost Kantian rationality. We start with the version of the text's first English translator, Charles Wilkins (1785):

Arjuna: I would rather beg my bread about the world, than be the
            murderer of my preceptors, to whom such awful reverence
            is due. Should I destroy such friends as these, I should par-
            take of possessions, wealth, and pleasures, polluted with
            their blood. We know not whether it would be better that
            we should defeat them, or they us; for those, whom having
            killed, I should not wish to live, are even the sons and people
            of Dhreetarashtra who are here drawn up before us.

Krishna: Thou grievest for those who are unworthy to be lamented,
            whilst thy sentiments are those of the wise men. The wise
            neither grieve for the dead nor for the living. I myself never
            was not, nor thou, nor all the princes of the earth; nor shall
            we ever hereafter cease *to be* . . . A thing imaginary hath no
            existence, whilst that which is true is a stranger to non-entity.

By those who look into the principles of things, the design of
each is seen.

The second translation is from Sir Edwin Arnold's popular Victorian version,
The Song Celestial (1885):

Arjuna: Better to live on beggar's bread
With those we love alive
Than taste their blood in rich feasts spread
And guiltily survive!
Ah! were it worse—who knows?—to be
Victor or vanquished here,
When those confront us angrily
Whose death leaves living drear?

Krishna: Thou grievest where no grief should be! thou speak'st
Words lacking wisdom! for the wise in heart
Mourn not for those that live, nor those that die.
Nor I, nor thou, nor any one of these,
Ever was not, nor ever will not be,
For ever and for ever afterwards. . . .
. . . That which is
Can never cease to be; that which is not
Will not exist. To see this truth of both
Is theirs who part essence from accident,
Substance from shadow.

The last is a recent attempt (2000) by Stephen Mitchell, not a Sanskritist but
a professional translator who assembled an interpretive version from existing
renderings:

Arjuna: It would be better to spend the rest of my life as a pauper,
begging for food, than to kill these honored teachers. If
I killed them, all my earthly pleasures would be smeared
with blood. And we do not know which is worse, winning
this battle or losing it, since if we kill Dhritarashtra's men
we will not wish to remain alive.

Krishna: Although you mean well, Arjuna,
your sorrow is sheer delusion.
Wise men do not grieve
for the dead or for the living.

Never was there a time
when I did not exist, or you,
or these kings; nor will there come
a time when we cease to be . . .

Nonbeing can never be;
being can never not be.

> Both these statements are obvious
> to those who have seen the truth

While Wilkins could handle the epic idiom reasonably well, he was at sea in the philosophical—"A thing imaginary hath no existence, whilst that which is true is a stranger to non-entity" is almost meaningless. At the end of the eighteenth century nothing whatever was known of the Samkhya philosophy that informs much of the poem. Mitchell's sources have figured this out, though the readers may still be puzzled by the discussion of "being" and "non-being" in the context of the battlefield. It's only the traditional commentaries that remind us that true "being" here refers to consciousness (the "self"), whereas everything material (such as the body) is ultimately subsumed in "nonbeing."

Arnold strives for greater fluidity with his versified version in the manner of Tennyson, though meter and rhyme, as often, force unnecessary additions ("theirs who part essence from accident, / Substance from shadow," for example, translates the simple Sanskrit *tattvadarśibhi,* "those who see truly"). Yet Arnold's fluidity came at the cost of much of the complexity and sheer *difference* of the original. For his part, Mitchell seems to have addressed the text's hybridity by using prose for the narrative portions and verse for the philosophical, but while the verse is forceful and economic (if sometimes too economic), the prose seems perfunctory. Like Arnold, Mitchell misses telling points of the epic vision of life without which we cannot understand Krishna's arguments. When he writes "It would be better to spend the rest of my life as a pauper" (Arnold's "Better to live on beggar's bread"), we are misled into believing that Arjuna is juxtaposing personal impoverishment with self-enrichment through victory in war. But if the *Mahabharata* is about anything, it is about the exigencies of *dharma*, about the social and moral obligations placed upon people by their position in the social order. What Arjuna is asking here is whether it might not be better to completely opt out of that order, become a wandering ascetic and beg mendicant's alms (something in fact forbidden to kings) than to execute the awful duties that it required of him—such as killing his kin.

This is precisely the conundrum that Krishna will address in the rest of the *Gita*. And it is a conundrum intensified by Arjuna's describing his esteemed elders (not his teachers) as *arthakāmān.* Both Arnold and Mitchell simply leave this detail out; Wilkins tries to convey something of the original ("[I should partake of possessions,] wealth, and pleasures"), but he was following a desperate interpretation incited precisely by discomfort at what the text is really saying. For Arjuna is explaining that his elders are "greedy for power": as the *Mahabharata* repeatedly declares, greed for power is inseparable from the possession of power. Arjuna recognizes this terrible truth, and shudders at the thought of continuing the cycle. That over the course of the *Gita* Krishna should finally convince him to do so, and with horrific consequences, challenges Wilkins' (and many later readers') conceptions of ethical discourse and of ancient Eastern wisdom alike.

RESONANCES

Kautilya: from *The Treatise on Power*[1]

[ON MAINTAINING POWER]

A king protects the kingdom (only) when (he is himself) protected from persons near him and from enemies, first from his wives and sons. Protection from wives we shall explain in "Regulations for the Royal Residence."

As to protection from sons, however:

"He should guard against princes right from their birth. For, princes devour their begetters, being of the same nature as crabs. Before love (for them) is produced in the father, silent punishment for them is best;" says Bhāradvāja.[2]

"This is cruel, (as it involves) the killing of innocent persons and the destruction of the Kṣatriya race," says Viśālākṣa. "Therefore, confinement in one place is best."

"This is danger as from a snake," say the followers of Parāśara. "For, the prince, realising 'through fear of my valour my father has confined me,' might get the father himself in his power. Therefore, making him stay in a frontier fortress is best."

"This is danger as from a (fighting) ram," says Piśuna. "For, realising that alone to be the means of his return, he might become the ally of the frontier chief. Therefore, making him stay in the fortress of a neighbouring (vassal) price, far removed from his own territory, is best."

"This is the position of a calf (for the prince)," says Kaunapadanta. "For, the neighbouring prince might milk his father as (one milks) a cow with the help of the calf. Therefore, making him stay with the kinsmen of his mother is best."

"This is the position of a flag (for the prince)," says Vātavyādhi. "For, with him as the flag, his mother's kinsmen would be making demands like Aditikauśikas.[3] Therefore, he should let him free to indulge in vulgar pleasures. For, sons kept engrossed in pleasures do not become hostile to the father."

"This is living death," says Kauṭilya. For, like a piece of wood eaten by worms, the royal family, with its princes undisciplined, would break the moment it is attacked. Therefore, when the chief queen is in her period, priests should offer a

---

1. Translated by R. P. Kangle. While the *Mahabharata* itself offers a number of general discourses on kingly duty, the first systematic account of statecraft in India is *The Treatise on Power*. It is attributed to Kautilya, the legendary counselor to Chandragupta Maurya, the king who defeated Alexander the Great and founded a powerful empire in northern India at the end of the 4th century B.C.E. In the shape we have it today, the text is more recent (probably 2nd or 3rd century C.E.), but it clearly represents a long tradition of reflection on the topics of governance. It offers the purest calculation of power anywhere in premodern Indian political thought. Many of its postulates—for example, that the enemy of one's enemy is one's friend—have been consequential in history. In form it is an early and influential example of the genre known as *shastra*, a treatise of systematic knowledge. The *Treatise* often seems to re-create the scene of a debate, where alternative views are weighed before a settled conclusion is reached.

As is the case with the *Mahabharata*, the problem of the transfer of power in royal succession is the major theme of the selection offered here. Although this transfer is framed primarily as one affecting father and son (and in this capacity it serves especially well to illuminate the opening of the *Ramayana*, page 864), the policies offered are meant to have a wide application. Again, the maintenance of political power, subjected to the closest calculation of risk and opportunity, is the supreme value, a harsh sun before which all other concerns including kinship and its natural affections simply melt away.

2. Little beyond their names is known about Bharadvaja and the other scholars of political thought with whom Kautilya is in dialogue throughout the *Treatise*.

3. Probably a class of mendicants who display images of deities when soliciting donations.

caru-oblation[4] to Indra and Bṛhaspati.[5] When she is pregnant, a children's specialist should arrange for the nourishment of the foetus and for delivery. When she has given birth, the chaplain should perform the sacraments for the son. When he is ready for it, experts should train him.

"And one of the secret agents should tempt him with hunting, gambling, wine and women, (suggesting to him,) 'Attack your father and seize the kingdom.' Another secret agent should dissuade him from that," say the followers of Āmbhi.

"This awakening of one not awake is highly dangerous," says Kauṭilya. For, a fresh object absorbs whatever it is smeared with. Similarly, this prince, immature in intellect, understands as the teaching of the science whatever he is told. Therefore, he should instruct him in what conduces to spiritual and material good, not in what is spiritually and materially harmful.

On the contrary, secret agents, declaring "We belong to you," should guard him. If in the exuberance of youth he were to entertain a longing for the wives of others, they should produce abhorrence in him through unclean women posing as noble ladies in lonely houses at night time. If he were to long for wine, they should frighten him with drugged liquor. If he were to long for gambling, they should create aversion in him through deceitful players. If he were to long for hunting, they should frighten him through agents disguised as highway robbers. If he were to entertain the idea of attacking his father, they should enter into his confidence (by pretending to agree) and then dissuade him (saying), "The king should not be attacked; if the attack fails, (there will be) death; if it succeeds, (there will be) a fall in hell (for you), an uproar and (your) annihilation by the subjects as of a single clod of earth."

They should inform (the king) if the prince is disaffected. He should put an only, favourite son (if disaffected) in prison. If he has many sons, he should send (the disaffected son) to the frontier or some other region where he may not become as a child in the womb (for the people there) or a commodity for sale (for those people) or a (source of) disturbance. If he is possessed of the excellences of self, he should install him in the position of the commander-in-chief or the crown prince.

One possessed of sagacity, one with intellect requiring to be goaded and one of evil intellect—these are the different kinds of sons. He who, when taught, understands spiritual and material good and practises the same is one possessed of sagacity. He who understands but does not practise (them) is one with intellect requiring to be goaded. He who is ever full of harm and hates spiritual and material good is one of evil intellect.

If such be the only son, he should endeavour to get a son born of him. Or, he should get sons begotten on an appointed daughter.

An old or a diseased king, however, should get a child begotten on his wife by one of the following, (viz.), his mother's kinsman, a member of his own family, and a virtuous neighbouring prince. But he should not install on the throne an only son, if undisciplined.

---

4. A mixture of rice and grain boiled for presentations to the gods.

5. Indra is the king of the gods, and Brihaspati is their

Brahman counselor. The latter is also credited with founding one of the major schools of political thought.

Of many (sons, who are undisciplined) confinement in one place (is best); (however), the father should be beneficently disposed towards the sons. Except in case of a calamity, sovereignty passing on to the oldest son is praised.

Or, the kingdom should belong to the (royal) family; for, a family oligarchy is difficult to conquer, and remains on the earth for ever without (having to face) the danger of a calamity befalling the king.

* * *

The disciplined prince, who finds living difficult, should obey his father when appointed to an unworthy task, except when it is dangerous to life or rouses the subjects (against him) or involves a heinous sin.

If he is assigned some agreeable task, he should ask for an officer to supervise his work. And under supervision of the officer, he should carry out the task assigned with special zest. And he should get despatched to his father the normal produce of the work as well as any (extra) gain received as a present.

If (the father is) even then not pleased and shows affection for another son or wife (other than his mother), he should ask for leave to repair to the forest. Or, in case of fear of imprisonment or death, he should seek refuge with a neighbouring prince who is justly behaved, pious, truthful in speech, not given to breach of faith and welcomes and honours those who have approached him (for help). Staying there and becoming enriched with treasure and troops, he should enter into marriage relations with heroic men, make contacts with forest chieftains and win over seducible parties (from his father's kingdom).

If he has to act alone, he should maintain himself by working mines and factories for gold-smelting, colouring gems and manufacturing gold and silver articles. Or, he should secretly rob the wealth of heretical corporations or the wealth of temples except that to be used by Brahmins learned in the Vedas or the wealth of rich widows after entering into their confidence, and plunder caravans and sailing vessels after cheating (the men) by administering a stupefying drink. Or, he should practise "the stratagems for the conquest of an enemy town." Or, he should act after securing the support of persons from the side of his mother. Or, with his appearance changed by disguising himself as an artisan, an artist, a minstrel, a physician, a professional story-teller or a heretical monk, (and) accompanied by associates in the same disguise, he should enter by taking advantage of some vulnerable point, and, striking the king with weapon or poison, announce, "I am that prince; this kingdom is to be enjoyed jointly; a single person does not deserve to enjoy it; those who desire to serve me, them will I reward with double food and wages."

Thus ends (the topic of) the conduct of a prince in disfavour.

But sons of principal officers acting as secret agents should bring the prince in disfavour (to the king) after securing his consent; or, the mother, if she enjoys favour, (should bring him). If he is given up (as incorrigible), secret agents should kill him with weapon or poison. If not given up, they should make him addicted to women of the same character or to drinking or hunting, and seizing him at night, should bring him (to the king).

And when he has come, he should conciliate him by the (offer of the) kingdom, saying "After me, (this is yours)." Then he should confine him in one place (if still recalcitrant); but if he has (other) sons, he should kill him.

Ashoka: from *Inscriptions*[1]

ROCK EDICT 13

The Kaliṅga country[2] was conquered by King Priyadarśī,[3] Beloved of the Gods, in the eighth year of his reign. One hundred and fifty thousand persons were carried away captive, one hundred thousand were slain, and many times that number died.

Immediately after the Kalingas had been conquered, King Priyadarśī became intensely devoted to the study of Dharma, to the love of Dharma, and to the inculcation of Dharma.

The Beloved of the Gods, conqueror of the Kaliṅgas, is moved to remorse now. For he has felt profound sorrow and regret because the conquest of a people previously unconquered involves slaughter, death, and deportation.

But there is a more important reason for the King's remorse. The Brāhmaṇas and Śramaṇas [the priestly and ascetic orders] as well as the followers of other religions and the householders—who all practiced obedience to superiors, parents, and teachers, and proper courtesy and firm devotion to friends, acquaintances, companions, relatives, slaves, and servants—all suffer from the injury, slaughter, and deportation inflicted on their loved ones. Even those who escaped calamity themselves are deeply afflicted by the misfortunes suffered by those friends, acquaintances, companions, and relatives for whom they feel an undiminished affection. Thus all men share in the misfortune, and this weighs on King Priyadarśī's mind.

[Moreover, there is no country except that of the Yōnas (that is, the Greeks) where Brahmin and Buddhist ascetics do not exist] and there is no place where men are not attached to one faith or another.

Therefore, even if the number of people who were killed or who died or who were carried away in the Kaliṅga war had been only one one-hundredth or one one-thousandth of what it actually was, this would still have weighed on the King's mind.

King Priyadarśī now thinks that even a person who wrongs him must be forgiven for wrongs that can be forgiven.

King Priyadarśī seeks to induce even the forest peoples who have come under his dominion [that is, primitive peoples in the remote sections of the conquered territory] to adopt this way of life and this ideal. He reminds them, however, that he exercises the power to punish, despite his repentance, in order to induce them to desist from their crimes and escape execution.

---

1. Translated by N. A. Nikam and Richard McKeon. Ashoka Maurya was a grandson of Chandragupta, who around 270 B.C.E. ascended the imperial throne—or rather, according to legend, waded to the throne through the blood of his brothers, as if putting into practice the terrible lessons of both Vyasa and his own father's counselor, Kautilya. Soon after becoming king he waged a brutal war against the country of Kalinga, on the southeast coast of India. It was the revulsion at the violence of this war that caused his great transformation: he turned to Buddhism and its creed of nonviolence.

Ashoka is important because of the new ethic he sought to bring to the conduct of statecraft and for the crucial state support he offered Buddhism. He is also, in a sense, the first person recorded in Indian history. In order to promulgate his new political ethics, Ashoka ordered inscriptions bearing his message to be set up all over the subcontinent and as far as Iran. But to carry out this order, a writing system was required, and it seems likely that one was invented in his chancellery. This script, the first in India (or the first since the end of the Indus Valley civilization, page 799), traveled even farther than his message, becoming the basis of virtually all the writing systems of South and Southeast Asia and profoundly changing the course of Indian literary history.

2. An area roughly equal to today's state of Orissa in eastern India.

3. An epithet of Ashoka (literally, "Of lovely countenance").

For King Priyadarśī desires security, self-control, impartiality, and cheerfulness for all living creatures.

King Priyadarśī considers moral conquest [that is, conquest by Dharma (*Dharma-vijaya*) the most important conquest. He has achieved this moral conquest repeatedly both here and among the peoples living beyond the borders of his kingdom, even as far away as six hundred *yojanas* [about three thousand miles], where the Yōna [Greek] king Antiyoka rules, and even beyond Antiyoka in the realms of the four kings named Turamaya, Antikini, Maka, and Alikasudara,[4] and to the south among the Cholas and Pāṇḍyas[5] [in the southern tip of the Indian peninsula] as far as Ceylon.

Here in the King's dominion also, among the Yānas [inhabitants of a northwest frontier province, probably Greeks] and the Kambōjas [neighbors of the Yōnas], among the Nābhakas and Nābhapaṅktis [who probably lived along the Himalayan frontier], among the Bhojas and Paitryaṅikas, among the Andhras and Paulindas [all peoples of the Indian peninsula], everywhere people heed his instructions in Dharma.

Even in countries which King Priyadarśī's envoys have not reached, people have heard about Dharma and about his Majesty's ordinances and instructions in Dharma, and they themselves conform to Dharma and will continue to do so.

Wherever conquest is achieved by Dharma, it produces satisfaction. Satisfaction is firmly established by conquest by Dharma [since it generates no opposition of conquered and conqueror]. Even satisfaction, however, is of little importance. King Priyadarśī attaches value ultimately only to consequences of action in the other world.

This edict on Dharma has been inscribed so that my sons and great-grandsons who may come after me should not think new conquests worth achieving. If they do conquer, let them take pleasure in moderation and mild punishments. Let them consider moral conquest the only true conquest.

This is good, here and hereafter. Let their pleasure be pleasure in morality [*Dharma-rati*]. For this alone is good, here and hereafter.

ROCK EDICT 4

For many hundreds of years in the past, slaughter of animals, cruelty to living creatures, discourtesy to relatives, and disrespect for priests and ascetics have been increasing.

But now, because of King Priyadarśī's practice of Dharma, the sound of war drums has become the call to Dharma [rather than to war], summoning the people to exhibitions of the chariots of the gods, elephants, fireworks, and other divine displays.

King Priyadarśī's inculcation of Dharma has increased, beyond anything observed in many hundreds of years, abstention from killing animals and from cruelty to living beings, kindliness in human and family relations, respect for priests and ascetics, and obedience to mother and father and elders.

The practice of Dharma has been promoted in this and other ways. King Priyadarśī will continue to promote the practice of Dharma. His sons, grandsons, and great-grandsons to the end of time will ever promote the practice of Dharma; standing firm themselves in Dharma, they will instruct the people in Dharma and moral conduct.

---

4. These names refer, respectively, to Antiochus II "Theos," who ruled Syria from 261 to 246 B.C.E.; Ptolemy II of Egypt (285–247 B.C.E.); Antigones Gonatas of Macedonia (278–239 B.C.E.); Magas of Cyrene (a land west of Egypt) (300–258 B.C.E.); and Alexander of Epirus (c. 270–258 B.C.E.).

5. Two dynasties of southern India.

For instruction in Dharma is the best of actions. The practice of Dharma is impossible for the immoral man. To increase this practice, even to forestall its diminution, is laudable.

This edict has been inscribed in order to inspire my descendants to work for the promotion and to prevent the decline of Dharma. King Priyadarśī commanded this record to be made twelve years after his coronation.

from PILLAR EDICT 7

King Priyadarśī, the Beloved of the Gods, speaks as follows:

In the past, kings have thought about ways of increasing the people's devotion to Dharma, but the people did not make progress enough in morality.

Concerning this, King Priyadarśī says:

This occurred to me. Since in the past kings have thought about ways of increasing the people's devotion to Dharma, but the people did not make progress enough in morality, how can the people be induced to follow Dharma strictly? How can progress in morality be increased sufficiently? How can I raise them up by the promotion of Dharma?

Pursuing this subject, King Priyadarśī says:

This occurred to me. I shall issue proclamations on Dharma, and I shall order instruction in Dharma to be given to the people. Hearing these proclamations and instructions, the people will conform to Dharma; they will raise themselves up and will make progress by the promotion of Dharma. To this end I have issued proclamations on Dharma, and I have instituted various kinds of moral and religious instruction.

My highest officials, who have authority over large numbers of people, will expound and spread the precepts of Dharma. I have instructed the provincial governors, too, who are in charge of many hundred thousand people, concerning how to guide people devoted to Dharma.

King Priyadarśī says:

Having come to this conclusion, therefore, I have erected pillars proclaiming Dharma. I have appointed officers charged with the spread of Dharma, called *Dharma-mahāmātras.* I have issued proclamations on Dharma. * * *
Whatever good deeds I have done the people have imitated, and they have followed them as a model. In doing so, they have progressed and will progress in obedience to parents and teachers, in respect for elders, in courtesy to priests and ascetics, to the poor and distressed, and even to slaves and servants. * * *
This edict on Dharma has been inscribed in order that it may endure and be followed as long as [my] sons and great-grandsons [shall reign and] as long as the sun and moon [shall shine]. For one who adheres to it will attain happiness in this world and hereafter. I ordered this edict inscribed twenty-seven years after my coronation.

ROCK EDICT 8

In the past, kings used to go on pleasure tours (*vihār-yātrās*). On these tours, they hunted and indulged in other pastimes.

King Priyadarśī, however, became enlightened in wisdom (*saṁbuddha*) ten years after his coronation. Since then his tours have been moral-tours (*Dharmayātrās*).

He visits priests and ascetics and makes gifts to them; he visits the aged and gives them money; he visits the people of rural areas, instructing them in Dharma and discussing it with them.

King Priyadarśī takes great pleasure in these tours, far more than could result from other tours.

BRAHMAGIRI ROCK EDICT II

King Priyadarśī says:

One should obey one's father and mother. One should respect the supreme value and sacredness of life. One should speak the truth. One should practice these virtues of Dharma.

In the same way, pupils should honor their teachers, and in families one should behave with fitting courtesy to relatives. This is the traditional rule of Dharma, and it is conducive to long life. Men should act according to it.

Written by Chapaḍa the Scribe.

KALIṄGA EDICT 21

King Priyadarśī says:

I command that the following instructions be communicated to my officials at Samāpā:

Whenever something right comes to my attention, I want it put into practice and I want effective means devised to achieve it. My principal means to do this is to transmit my instructions to you.

All men are my children. Just as I seek the welfare and happiness of my own children in this world and the next, I seek the same things for all men.

Unconquered peoples along the borders of my dominions may wonder what my disposition is toward them. My only wish with respect to them is that they should not fear me, but trust me; that they should expect only happiness from me, not misery; that they should understand further that I will forgive them for offenses which can be forgiven; that they should be induced by my example to practice Dharma; and that they should attain happiness in this world and the next.

I transmit these instructions to you in order to discharge my debt [to them] by instructing you and making known to you my will and my unshakable resolution and commitment. You must perform your duties in this way and establish their confidence in the King, assuring them that he is like a father to them, that he loves them as he loves himself, and that they are like his own children.

Having instructed you and informed you of my will and my unshakable resolution and commitment, I will appoint officials to carry out this program in all the provinces. You are able to inspire the border peoples with confidence in me and to advance their welfare and happiness in this world and the next. By doing so, you will also attain heaven and help me discharge my debts to the people.

This edict has been inscribed here so that my officials will work at all times to inspire the peoples of neighboring countries with confidence in me and to induce them to practice Dharma.

This edict must be proclaimed every four months [at the beginning of the three seasons—hot, rainy, and cold] on Tiṣya days [i.e., when the moon is in the constellation containing Tiṣya, Sirius]; it may also be proclaimed in the intervals between those days; and on appropriate occasions it may be read to individuals.

By doing this, you will be carrying out my commands.

The Ramayana of Valmiki

c. 200 B.C.E.

A teller of tales, so the story goes, was once reciting the *Ramayana*. He got to the part where Prince Rama explains to Sita, his wife, that she must stay in the city of Ayodhya and not accompany him into forest exile. After trying to dissuade him without success, Sita cries out, "Thousands of *Ramayanas* have been composed before this, and there isn't one in which Sita doesn't go with her husband!" The argument is persuasive, and Rama agrees to take her along.

Thousands of *Ramayanas?* Yes, quite likely, if we include all the versions from across Asia in all the different regional languages over the past two thousand years, to say nothing of the countless modern films, performance genres, and forms of popular culture ranging from peasant songs to comic books. And many of these versions are as self-aware as the little story recounted above, as far as their relationship to other tellings and their social, political, or historical location. The fact is indisputable: the story of Rama—his banishment to the forest on the eve of his coronation, the abduction of his wife, Sita, by the demon king Ravana, his defeat of the enemy and recovery of Sita—has had an impact on the literary imagination of India and wider Asia that is more intense and enduring than any other narrative, bar none. *Ramayanas* are found from Kashmir to Tibet to China (a famous Chinese adaptation, Wu Ch'eng-en's *Journey to the West,* can be found in Volume C) and from Sri Lanka to Thailand, Laos, and Java. And it isn't just literary imagination that has been influenced by the story. The different *Ramayanas,* each of them making a particular argument appropriate for its own time and place, have contributed to shaping the spheres of religion, politics, and everyday morality to a degree unmatched by any other work in Indian history.

The version of the *Ramayana* to which many retellings explicitly or implicitly respond—retellings are always responses—is the Sanskrit work of Valmiki. As is so often the case in early Sanskrit literature, we have no reliable historical knowledge about the author, and dating his poem has proved to be difficult. The *Ramayana* contains an account of its own creation: it presents itself as the "first literary work" (*kavya*), a thing said to be previously unknown in Indian culture (see Perspectives: What Is "Literature"?, page 908). But what its newness actually consists of is not entirely clear. The text itself links its novelty with the metrical form of the poem, but the verse structure used for most of the work is far older than the *Ramayana* of Valmiki could possibly be. Its self-identification as the first poem, along with everything else we know about it, suggests a relatively late date. Although tradition holds that the events of the *Mahabharata* took place in the Second Age from the present, whereas the *Ramayana* took place in the third, previous age, the *Ramayana* is later than the core text of the Bharata epic (c. 300 B.C.E.) since Valmiki knows the main story and has used it to deftly structure his own narrative. His thought world has features in common with that of King Ashoka, who issued his inscriptions in the middle of the third century B.C.E. (page 857). And the history of Sanskrit literature, as "literature" comes to be defined in the Sanskrit tradition, begins only around the start of the Common Era. All these considerations point toward 200 B.C.E. or so as the likeliest period of the creation of the poem that came to bear Valmiki's name.

AUTHORSHIP

Some scholars dispute the proposition that any one person created the *Ramayana*. The manuscript history of the work clearly reveals substantial variation owing to a period of oral transmission. And like the *Mahabharata,* Valmiki's text was subject to continual expansion; an entire book, the seventh and last, was added at some point (perhaps along with the greater part of the first). Yet the oral variation of the *Ramayana* remains a variation of one and the same poem. The

A contemporary Indian comic book rendering depicts the death of Ravana in Valmiki's *Ramayana*.

text was probably more or less memorized (the poem itself says as much) and was committed to writing at different times and places; it was assuredly not composed anew with each telling, as occurred in other oral epic traditions, such as the Serbo-Croatian. A single voice can clearly be heard in Books 2 through 6, a voice of a sort that had never been heard before in Sanskrit.

There is a degree of literary artistry present in every level of the text—from the cohesiveness and sustained momentum of the grand narrative all the way down to the individual image—that is consistent across the poem and quite unlike anything else found in earlier Sanskrit works. One small example of this occurs in Book 3: Rama has gone off to hunt a magic deer, which in reality is a demon sent by Ravana, who had gotten word of Sita's beauty, to lure Rama away from the hermitage where he is living out his exile. Rama's younger brother, Lakshmana, told to guard Sita, has reluctantly left her alone after hearing what he thinks is Rama's cry for help (it is, of course, the demon's cry). This is Ravana's opening, and Valmiki describes his approach with the unobtrusive skill of a meticulous artist, using a half dozen different verbs of motion to bring our apprehension slowly to a climax:

> Assuming the guise of a wandering mendicant, he turned his steps toward Vaidehi . . .
> Clad in a soft saffron robe, with topknot, parasol, and sandals . . . he approached Vaidehi . . .
> Both brothers had left her, and in his pride of power he advanced upon her . . .
> Ten-necked Ravana had waited for an opening . . . In the guise of a beggar he drew near to Vaidehi . . .
> As Vaidehi sat grieving for her husband, the unholy Ravana in the guise of a holy man edged closer to her . . .
> The blackhearted stalker of the night stole ever closer to Vaidehi

This kind of expressive care is in evidence throughout the poem, and often achieves a level of artistry with which the aesthetic of the *Mahabharata* narrative—powerful, even overwhelming in its own right—has nothing in common.

THE *RAMAYANA* AND THE *MAHABHARATA*

There are many other differences between these two defining works of Indian culture, but the most telling are at the level of argument and ethic. In fact, Valmiki's poem can be read as a response to the apocalyptic vision of social and political disintegration encountered in the *Mahabharata*. The basic narrative problem is identical to that found in the other text: when their aged father, King Dasharatha, declares his intention to abdicate, the two brothers Rama and Bharata would be expected to contest the succession of power. But no struggle ensues, since Rama is ready to withdraw and Bharata is ready to submit to Rama (it is almost as if no one wants the kingship). Again, like Draupadi, wife of the five Pandava brothers in the *Mahabharata*, Sita is the target of a violent attack. In this case, however, it is not a brother who attacks her but a (literally) demonized outsider, Ravana, king of the *rakshasas*, imaginary beings who embody all that is most feared—and perhaps most desired—by traditional Indian readers. In these two episodes we glimpse a major transformation in the epic narrative tradition that is the ongoing concern of Valmiki's work: the conundrum of power is solved, and its dangerous energies are displaced from brothers to Others.

Key to this transformation is the character of Rama. Almost from their first acquaintance with the poem, Western scholars without exception believed that the hero's divinity was the result of later revision. The original *Ramayana*, they thought, must have been a tale of a simple human hero struggling against evil; the text was eventually appropriated by devotees of the god Vishnu, who turned the work into a theological tract. This long-held interpretation has been shown to be false. The divinity of Rama—not as the major god Vishnu, but as an undoubtedly transcendent being—is a constitutive part of the poem, not only textually but logically. Now that a reasonably complete picture of the manuscript history of the work is available, it has become clear that no textual criticism allows for the removal of all references to Rama's divinity; it is an inexpugnable part of the text. The logic of the story shows what kind of divinity this is, one similar to the semi-divine status of epic heroes such as Gilgamesh (see page 59) and Achilles (see page 201), but far transcending it. When the demon king Ravana accepts the wish he has been granted from the great god Shiva, he couches it in terms he believes will ensure his immortality: he asks to be invincible to gods, demigods, men, and animals. What he fails to include in his list is what proves to be his undoing: a life-form that is part man and part god. Just such a being is Rama, both man and god at once. And this, as the text powerfully suggests, is what all real kings are supposed to be.

This mode of being also points toward a mode of behaving that enables Rama to escape the paralyzing moral dilemma of the *Mahabharata,* most starkly in evidence in the *Bhagavad Gita* (page 839). Can any acceptable definition of *dharma*—right, law, duty—require the slaughter of one's kinsmen? The *Mahabharata* has no workable answer to this horrific predicament; not even the doctrine of the *Bhagavad Gita,* the disinterested execution of one's *dharma,* seems an adequate response. Instead, the *Mahabharata* only shows what happens when the logic especially of the duty of the warrior is allowed to follow its course. This is precisely what Rama rejects. He juxtaposes the warrior's duty (Kshatriya *dharma*) to a higher law, that of hierarchical obedience—of son to father, younger brother to elder brother. This ethic, already emphasized in the edicts of Ashoka (see page 857) ensures peace among the contestants to power, and, in the end, a utopian reign in the kingdom. Equally important is that those who in any way oppose this vision are not truly human; they are demonic beings and can with justice be destroyed.

Because of its success in framing moral problems, Valmiki's *Ramayana* has long been held to provide models of conduct for the everyday lives of everyday people; even today, opinion polls show that Sita is the most influential figure in the lives of young Indian girls. As an old proverb advises, "Act like Rama, and never like Ravana." No one was ever told to "act like Krishna"; it is what Krishna and other such deities say, not what they do, that readers and listeners are told to follow. But the *Ramayana* offers positive paradigms for life, and no other work remotely approximates it for the didactic force it has exercised throughout India's history.

The story of Valmiki's invention of poetry appears on page 909.

WHO'S WHO IN THE *RAMAYANA*
   Dasharatha: DUH-shuh-RUH-thuh; king of Ayodhya (uh-YOH-dhyah)
   His four sons:
      Rama: RAH-muh
      Bharata: BHUH-ruh-tuh
      Lakshmana: LUHK-shmuh-nuh
      Shatrughna: SHUH-troo-ghnuh
   Kausalya: kow-SUHL-yah; mother of Rama
   Kaikeyi: kai-KAY-yee; mother of Bharata
   Sumitra: su-MEE-trah; mother of Lakshmana and Shatrughna
   Sita: SEE-TAH; wife of Rama

THE RAMAYANA OF VALMIKI

from BOOK 2[1]

[THE EXILE OF RAMA]

SARGA 7

Now, Kaikeyī's family servant, who had lived with her from the time of her birth, had happened to ascend to the rooftop terrace that shone like the moon.

---

1. Translated by Sheldon Pollock.

From the terrace Mantharā could see all Ayodhyā[2]—the king's way newly sprinkled, the lotuses and waterlilies strewn about, the costly ornamental pennants and banners, the sprinkling of sandalwood water, and the crowds of freshly bathed people.

Seeing a nursemaid standing nearby, Mantharā asked, "Why is Rāma's mother so delighted and giving away money to people, when she has always been so miserly? Tell me, why are the people displaying such boundless delight? Has something happened to delight the lord of earth? What is he planning to do?"

Bursting with delight and out of sheer gladness the nursemaid told the hunchback Mantharā about the greater majesty in store for Rāghava:

"Tomorrow on Puṣya day[3] King Daśaratha is going to consecrate Rāma Rāghava[4] as prince regent, the blameless prince who has mastered his anger."

When she heard what the nursemaid said, the hunchback was furious and descended straightway from the terrace that was like the peak of Mount Kailāsa.[5]

Consumed with rage, the malevolent Mantharā approached Kaikeyī as she lay upon her couch, and she said:

"Get up, you foolish woman! How can you lie there when danger is threatening you? Don't you realize that a flood of misery is about to overwhelm you?

"Your beautiful face has lost its charm. You boast of the power of your beauty, but it has proved to be as fleeting as a river's current in the hot season."

So she spoke, and Kaikeyī was deeply distraught at the bitter words of the angry, malevolent hunchback.

"Mantharā," she replied, "is something wrong? I can tell by the distress in your face how sorely troubled you are."

Hearing Kaikeyī's gentle words the wrathful Mantharā spoke—and a very clever speaker she was.

The hunchback grew even more distraught, and with Kaikeyī's best interests at heart, spoke out, trying to sharpen her distress and turn her against Rāghava:

"Something is very seriously wrong, my lady, something that threatens to ruin you. For King Daśaratha is going to consecrate Rāma as prince regent.

"I felt myself sinking down into unfathomable danger, stricken with grief and sorrow, burning as if on fire. And so I have come here, with your best interests at heart.

---

2. The capital of the kingdom of Kosala, in what is today the Indian state of Uttar Pradesh.

3. A favorable alignment of the constellation Pushya (consisting of the three stars of Cancer) marks an auspicious day on which important ceremonies are held.

4. Rama (literally, "descendent of Raghu," Rama's paternal great-grandfather).

5. A mountain in the Himalayan range, said to be the dwelling place of the great god Shiva.

"When you are sorrowful, Kaikeyī, I am too, and even more, and, when you prosper, so do I. There is not the slightest doubt of this.

"You were born into a family of kings, you are a queen of the lord of earth. My lady, how can you fail to know that the ways of kings are ruthless?

"Your husband talks of righteousness, but he is deceiving you; his words are gentle but he is cruel. You are too innocent to understand, and so he has utterly defrauded you like this.

"When expedient, your husband reassures you, but it is all worthless. Now that there is something of real worth he is ready to bestow it upon Kausalyā.

"Having got Bharata[6] out of the way by sending him off to your family, the wicked man shall tomorrow establish Rāma in unchallenged kingship.

"He is an enemy pretending to be your husband. He is like a viper, child, whom you have taken to your bosom and lovingly mothered.

"For what an enemy or a snake would do if one ignored them, King Daśaratha is now doing to you and your son.

"The man is evil, his assurances false, and, by establishing Rāma in the kingship, dear child who has always known comfort, he will bring ruin upon you and your family.

"Kaikeyī, the time has come to act, and you must act swiftly, for your own good. You must save your son, yourself, and me, my enchanting beauty."

After listening to Mantharā's speech, the lovely woman rose from the couch and presented the hunchback with a lovely piece of jewelry.

And, when she had given the hunchback the jewelry, Kaikeyī, most beautiful of women, said in delight to Mantharā,

"What you have reported to me is the most wonderful news. How else may I reward you, Mantharā, for reporting such good news to me?

"I draw no distinction between Rāma and Bharata, and so I am perfectly content that the king should consecrate Rāma as king.

"You could not possibly tell me better news than this, or speak more welcome words, my well-deserving woman. For what you have told me I will give you yet another boon, something you might like more—just choose it!"

SARGA 8

But Mantharā was beside herself with rage and sorrow. She threw the jewelry away and said spitefully:

6. Bharata and his younger brother Shatrughna were sent off to their maternal uncle's home by Dasharatha himself.

"You foolish woman, how can you be delighted at such a moment? Are you not aware that you stand in the midst of a sea of grief?

"It is Kausalyā who is fortunate; it is her son the eminent brahmans will consecrate as the powerful prince regent tomorrow, on Puṣya day.

"Once Kausalyā secures this great object of joy, she will cheerfully eliminate her enemies. And you will have to wait on her with hands cupped in reverence, like a serving woman.

"Delight is truly in store for Rāma's exalted women, and all that is in store for your daughters-in-law is misery, at Bharata's down-fall."

Seeing how deeply distressed Mantharā was as she spoke, Queen Kaikeyī began to extol Rāma's virtues:

"Rāma knows what is right, his gurus have taught him self-restraint. He is grateful, truthful, and honest, and as the king's eldest son, he deserves to be prince regent.

"He will protect his brothers and his dependents like a father; and long may he live! How can you be upset, hunchback, at learning of Rāma's consecration?

"Surely Bharata as well, the bull among men, will obtain the kingship of his fathers and forefathers after Rāma's one hundred years.

"Why should you be upset, Mantharā, when we have prospered in the past, and prosper now, and shall have good fortune in the future? For he obeys me even more scrupulously than he does Kausalyā."

When she heard what Kaikeyī said, Mantharā was still more sorely troubled. She heaved a long and hot sigh and then replied:

"You are too simple-minded to see what is good for you and what is not. You are not aware that you are sinking in an ocean of sorrow fraught with disaster and grief.

"Rāghava will be king, Kaikeyī, and then the son of Rāghava, while Bharata will be debarred from the royal succession altogether.

"For not all the sons of a king stand in line for the kingship, my lovely. Were all of them to be so placed, grave misfortune would ensue.

"That is why kings place the powers of kingship in the hands of the eldest, faultless Kaikeyī, however worthy the others.

"Like a helpless boy that son of yours, the object of all your motherly love, will be totally excluded from the royal succession and from its pleasures as well.

"Here I am, come on your behalf, but you pay me no heed. Instead, you want to reward me in token of your rival's good luck!

"Surely once Rāma secures unchallenged kingship he will have Bharata sent off to some other country—if not to the other world!

"And you had to send Bharata, a mere boy, off to your brother's, though knowing full well that proximity breeds affection, even in insentient things.

"Now, Rāghava will protect Lakṣmaṇa, just as Saumitri will protect Rāma, for their brotherly love is as celebrated as that of the Aśvins.

"And so Rāma will do no harm to Lakṣmaṇa, but he will to Bharata without question.

"So let your son go straight from Rājagṛha[7] to the forest. That is the course I favor, and it is very much in your own best interests.

"For in this way good fortune may still befall your side of the family—if, that is, Bharata secures, as by rights he should, the kingship of his forefathers.

"Your child has known only comfort, and, at the same time, he is Rāma's natural enemy. How could the one, with his fortunes lost, live under the sway of the other, whose fortunes are thriving?

"Like the leader of an elephant herd attacked by a lion in the forest, your son is about to be set upon by Rāma, and you must save him.

"Then, too, because of your beauty's power you used to spurn your co-wife, Rāma's mother, so proudly. How could she fail to repay that enmity?

"When Rāma secures control of the land, Bharata will be lost for certain. You must therefore devise some way of making your son the king and banishing his enemy this very day."

SARGA 9

So Mantharā spoke, and Kaikeyī, her face glowing with rage, heaved a long and burning sigh and said to her:

"Today, at once, I will have Rāma banished to the forest, and at once have Bharata consecrated as prince regent.

"But now, Mantharā, think: In what way can Bharata, and not Rāma, secure the kingship?"

So Queen Kaikeyī spoke, and the malevolent Mantharā answered her, to the ruin of Rāma's fortunes:

"Well then, I shall tell you, Kaikeyī—and pay close attention—how your son Bharata may secure sovereign kingship."

7. The capital city of Kekaya in Kashmir, the kingdom from which Kaikeyī hails.

Hearing Manthara's words, Kaikeyī half rose from her sumptuous couch and exclaimed:

"Tell me the way, Manthara! How can Bharata, and not Rāma, secure the kingship?"

So the queen spoke, and the malevolent hunchback answered her, to the ruin of Rāma's fortunes:

"When the gods and *asuras* were at war, your husband went with the royal seers to lend assistance to the king of the gods, and he took you along. He set off toward the south, Kaikeyī, to the Daṇḍakas and the city called Vaijayanta. It was there that Timidhvaja ruled, the same who is called Śambara, a great *asura* of a hundred magic powers. He had given battle to Śakra, and the host of gods could not conquer him.[8]

"In the great battle that followed, King Daśaratha was struck unconscious, and you, my lady, conveyed him out of battle. But there, too, your husband was wounded by weapons, and once again you saved him, my lovely. And so in his gratitude he granted you two boons.

"Then, my lady, you said to your husband. 'I shall choose my two boons when I want them,' and the great king consented. I myself was unaware of this, my lady, until you yourself told me, long ago.

"You must now demand these two boons of your husband: the consecration of Bharata and the banishment of Rāma for fourteen years.

"Now go into your private chamber, daughter of Aśvapati, as if in a fit of rage. Put on a dirty garment, lie down on the bare ground, and don't speak to him, don't even look at him.

"Your husband has always adored you, I haven't any doubt of it. For your sake the great king would even go through fire.

"The king could not bring himself to anger you, nor even bear to look at you when you are angry. He would give up his own life to please you.

"The lord of the land is powerless to refuse your demand. Dull-witted girl, recognize the power of your beauty.

"King Daśaratha will offer gems, pearls, gold, a whole array of precious gifts—but pay no mind to them.

"Just keep reminding Daśaratha of those two boons he granted at the battle of the gods and *asuras*. Illustrious lady, you must not let this opportunity pass you by.

---

8. The battle between the gods and *asuras,* or antigods, forms part of many ancient legends. In earlier Sanskrit works, Shambara is the enemy of Indra, the king of the gods, who is also known as Shakra (literally, "the able one"). The city Vaijayanta and the name Timidhvaja are obscure.

"When the great king Rāghava helps you up himself and offers you a boon, then you must ask him for this one, first making sure he swears to it: 'Banish Rāma to the forest for nine years and five, and make Bharata king of the land, the bull among kings.'

"In this way Rāma will be banished and cease to be 'the pleasing prince,' and your Bharata, his rival eliminated, will be king.

"And by the time Rāma returns from the forest, your steadfast son and his supporters will have struck deep roots and won over the populace.

"I think it high time you overcame your timidity. You must forcibly prevent the king from carrying out Rāma's consecration."

And so Mantharā induced her to accept such evil by disguising it as good, and Kaikeyī, now cheered and delighted, replied:

"Hunchback, I never recognized your excellence, nor how excellent your advice. Of all the hunchbacks in the land there is none better at devising plans.

"You are the only one who has always sought my advantage and had my interests at heart. I might never have known, hunchback, what the king intended to do.

"There are hunchbacks who are misshapen, crooked and hideously ugly—but not you, you are lovely, you are bent no more than a lotus in the breeze.

"Your chest is arched, raised as high as your shoulders, and down below your waist, with its lovely navel, seems as if it had grown thin in envy of it.

"Your girdle-belt beautifies your hips and sets them jingling. Your legs are set strong under you, while your feet are long.

"With your wide buttocks, Mantharā, and your garment of white linen, you are as resplendent as a wild goose when you go before me.

"And this huge hump of yours, wide as the hub of a chariot wheel—your clever ideas must be stored in it, your political wisdom and magic powers.

"And there, hunchback, is where I will drape you with a garland made of gold, once Bharata is consecrated and Rāghava has gone to the forest.

"When I have accomplished my purpose, my lovely, when I am satisfied, I will anoint your hump with precious liquid gold.

"And for your face I will have them fashion an elaborate and beautiful forehead mark of gold and exquisite jewelry for you, hunchback.

"Dressed in a pair of lovely garments you shall go about like a goddess; with that face of yours that challenges the moon, peerless in visage; and you shall strut holding your head high before the people who hate me.

"You too shall have hunchbacks, adorned with every sort of ornament, to humbly serve you, hunchback, just as you always serve me."

Being flattered in this fashion, she replied to Kaikeyī, who still lay on her luxurious couch like a flame of fire on an altar:

"One does not build a dike, my precious, after the water is gone. Get up, apprise the king, and see to your own welfare!"

Thus incited, the large-eyed queen went with Manthara to her private chamber, puffed up with the intoxicating power of her beauty.

There the lovely lady removed her pearl necklace, worth many hundred thousands, and her other costly and beautiful jewelry.

And then, under the spell of the hunchback Manthara's words, the golden Kaikeyī got down upon the floor and said to her:

"Hunchback, go inform the king that I will surely die right here unless Bharata receives as his portion the land and Rāghava, as his, the forest."

And uttering these ruthless words, the lady put all her jewelry aside and lay down upon the ground bare of any spread, like a fallen *kiṃnara* woman.[9]

Her face enveloped in the darkness of her swollen rage, her fine garlands and ornaments stripped off, the wife of the lord of men grew distraught and took on the appearance of a darkened sky, when all the stars have set.

Sarga 10

Now, when the great king had given orders for Rāghava's consecration, he gladly entered the inner chamber to tell his beloved wife the good news.

But when the lord of the world saw her fallen on the ground and lying there in a posture so ill-befitting her, he was consumed with sorrow.

The guileless old man saw her on the floor, that guileful young wife of his, who meant more to him than life itself.

He began to caress her affectionately, as a great bull elephant in the wilderness might caress his cow wounded by the poisoned arrow of a hunter lurking in the forest.

And, as he caressed his lotus-eyed wife with his hands, sick with worry and desire, he said to her:

"I do not understand, my lady, why you should be angry. Has someone offended you, or shown you disrespect, that you should lie here in the dust, my precious, and

---

9. *Kinnaras* ("part-man") are obscure mythical creatures; female *kinnaras* are renowned for their beauty.

cause me such sorrow? What reason have you to lie upon the floor as if possessed by a spirit, driving me to distraction, when you are so precious to me?

"I have skilled physicians, who have been gratified in every way. They will make you well again. Tell me what hurts you, my lovely.

"Is there someone to whom you would have favor shown, or has someone aroused your disfavor? The one shall find favor at once, the other incur my lasting disfavor.

"Is there some guilty man who should be freed, or some innocent man I should execute? What poor man should I enrich, what rich man impoverish?

"I and my people, we all bow to your will. I could not bring myself to thwart any wish of yours, not if it cost me my life. Tell me what your heart desires, for all the earth belongs to me, as far as the wheel of my power reaches."

So he spoke, and now encouraged she resolved to tell her hateful plan. She then commenced to cause her husband still greater pain.

"No one has mistreated me, my lord, or shown me disrespect. But there is one wish I have that I should like you to fulfill.

"You must first give me your promise that you are willing to do it. Then I shall reveal what it is I desire."

So his beloved Kaikeyī spoke, and the mighty king, hopelessly under the woman's power, said to her with some surprise:

"Do you not yet know, proud lady, that except for Rāma, tiger among men, there is not a single person I love as much as you?

"Take hold of my heart, rip it out, and examine it closely, my lovely Kaikeyī; then tell me if you do not find it true.

"Seeing that I have the power, you ought not to doubt me. I will do what will make you happy, I swear to you by all my acquired merit."

His words filled her with delight, and she made ready to reveal her dreadful wish, which was like a visitation of death:

"Let the three and thirty gods, with Indra at their head, hear how you in due order swear an oath and grant me a boon.

"Let the sun and moon, the sky, the planets, night and day, the quarters of space, heaven and earth, let all the *gandharvas* and *rākṣasas,* the spirits that stalk the night, the household gods in every house, and all the other spirits take heed of what you have said.[1]

---

1. *Gandharvas* are heavenly beings renowned for their musical skills. *Rakshasas,* often called "stalkers of the night," are demonic creatures known to eat humans and disrupt the sacrifices of forest ascetics.

"This mighty king, who is true to his word and knows the ways of righteousness, in full awareness grants me a boon—let the deities give ear to this for me."

Thus the queen ensnared the great archer and called upon witnesses. She then addressed the king, who in his mad passion had granted her a boon.

"I will now claim the two boons you once granted me, my lord. Hear my words, your Majesty.

"Let my son Bharata be consecrated with the very rite of consecration you have prepared for Rāghava.

"Let Rāma withdraw to Daṇḍaka wilderness[2] and for nine years and five live the life of an ascetic, wearing hides and barkcloth garments and matted hair.[3]

"Let Bharata today become the uncontested prince regent, and let me see Rāghava depart this very day for the forest."

When the great king heard Kaikeyī's ruthless demands, he was shaken and unnerved, like a stag at the sight of a tigress.

The lord of men gasped as he sank down upon the bare floor. "Oh damn you!" he cried in uncontrollable fury before he fell into a stupor, his heart crushed by grief.

Gradually the king regained his senses and then, in bitter sorrow and anger, he spoke to Kaikeyī, with fire in his eyes:

"Malicious, wicked woman, bent on destroying this House! Evil woman, what evil did Rāma or I ever do to you?

"Rāghava has always treated you just like his own mother. What reason can you have for trying to wreck his fortunes, of all people?

"It was sheer suicide to bring you into my home. I did it unwittingly, thinking you a princess—and not a deadly poisonous viper.

"When praise for Rāma's virtues is on the lips of every living soul, what crime could I adduce as pretext for renouncing my favorite son?

"I would sooner renounce Kausalyā, or Sumitrā, or sovereignty, or life itself, than Rāma, who so cherishes his father.

"The greatest joy I know is seeing my first-born son. If I cannot see Rāma, I shall lose my mind.

---

2. The country of King Dandaka was laid waste by Indra's curse or, according to another source, the curse of a Brahman whose daughter was raped by the king.

3. As a mark of renunciation, forest-dwelling ascetics are said to wear "barkcloth" (perhaps cloth woven of bast fiber) and to leave their hair unkempt.

"The world might endure without the sun, or crops without water, but without Rāma life could not endure within my body.

"Enough then, give up this scheme, you evil-scheming woman. I beg you! Must I get down and bow my head to your feet?"

His heart in the grip of a woman who knew no bounds, the guardian of the earth began helplessly to cry, and as the queen extended her feet he tried in vain to touch them, and collapsed like a man on the point of death.

SARGA 11

The king lay there, in so unaccustomed a posture, so ill-befitting his dignity, like Yayāti himself, his merit exhausted, fallen from the world of the gods.[4] But the woman was unafraid, for all the fear she awoke. She was misfortune incarnate and had yet to secure her fortunes. Once more she tried to force him to fulfill the boon.

"You are vaunted, great king, as a man true to his word and firm in his vows. How then can you be prepared to withhold my boon?"

So Kaikeyī spoke, and King Daśaratha, faltering for a moment, angrily replied:

"Vile woman, mortal enemy! Will you not be happy, will you not be satisfied until you see me dead, and Rāma, the bull among men, gone to the forest?

"To satisfy Kaikeyī Rāma must be banished to the forest, but if I keep my word in this, then I must be guilty of another lie. My infamy will be unequaled in the eyes of the people and my disgrace inevitable."

While he was lamenting like this, his mind in a whirl, the sun set and evening came on.

To the anguished king lost in lamentation, the night, adorned with the circlet of the moon, no longer seemed to last a mere three watches.

Heaving burning sighs, aged King Daśaratha sorrowfully lamented in his anguish, his eyes fixed upon the sky.

"I do not want you to bring the dawn—here, I cup my hands in supplication. But no, pass as quickly as you can, so that I no longer have to see this heartless, malicious Kaikeyî, the cause of this great calamity."

But with this, the king cupped his hands before Kaikeyī and once more, begging her mercy, he spoke:

"Please, I am an old man, my life is nearly over. I am desolate, I place myself in your hands. Dear lady, have mercy on me for, after all, I am king.

4. A legendary emperor who through ascetic discipline reached heaven, only to be expelled by Indra because of his pride.

"Truly it was thoughtless of me, my fair-hipped lady, to have said those things just now. Have mercy on me, please, my child. I know you have a heart."

So the pure-hearted king lamented, frantically and piteously, his eyes reddened and dimmed by tears, but the malicious, black-hearted woman only listened and made no reply.

And as the king stared at the woman he loved but could not appease, whose demand was so perverse—for the exile of his own son—he once again was taken faint, overcome with grief, and dropped unconscious to the floor.

* * *

SARGA 16

Rāma saw his father, with a wretched look and his mouth all parched, slumped upon his lovely couch, Kaikeyī at his side.

First he made an obeisance with all deference at his father's feet and then did homage most scrupulously at the feet of Kaikeyī.

"Rāma!" cried the wretched king, his eyes brimming with tears, but he was unable to say anything more or to look at him.

As if his foot had grazed a snake, Rāma was seized with terror to see the expression on the king's face, one more terrifying than he had ever seen before.

For the great king lay heaving sighs, racked with grief and remorse, all his senses numb with anguish, his mind stunned and confused.

It was as if the imperturbable, wave-wreathed ocean had suddenly been shaken with perturbation, as if the sun had been eclipsed, or a seer had told a lie.

His father's grief was incomprehensible to him, and the more he pondered it, the more his agitation grew, like that of the ocean under a full moon.

With his father's welfare at heart, Rāma struggled to comprehend, "Why does the king not greet me, today of all days?

"On other occasions, when Father might be angry, the sight of me would calm him. Why then, when he looked at me just now, did he instead become so troubled?

"He seems desolate and grief-stricken, and his face has lost its glow." Doing obeisance to Kaikeyī, Rāma spoke these words:

"I have not unknowingly committed some offense, have I, to anger my father? Tell me, and make him forgive me.

"His face is drained of color, he is desolate and does not speak to me. It cannot be, can it, that some physical illness or mental distress afflicts him? But it is true, well-being is not something one can always keep.

"Some misfortune has not befallen the handsome prince Bharata, has it, or courageous Śatrughna, or one of my mothers?

"I should not wish to live an instant if his majesty, the great king, my father, were angered by my failure to satisfy him or do his bidding.

"How could a man not treat him as a deity incarnate, in whom he must recognize the very source of his existence in this world?

"Can it be that in anger you presumed to use harsh words with my father, and so threw his mind into such turmoil?

"Answer my questions truthfully, my lady: What has happened to cause this unprecedented change in the lord of men?

"At the bidding of the king, if enjoined by him, my guru, father, king, and benefactor, I would hurl myself into fire, drink deadly poison, or drown myself in the sea.

"Tell me then, my lady, what the king would have me do. I will do it, I promise. Rāma need not say so twice."

The ignoble Kaikeyī then addressed these ruthless words to Rāma, the upright and truthful prince:

"Long ago, Rāghava, in the war of the gods and *asuras,* your father bestowed two boons on me, for protecting him when he was wounded in a great battle.

"By means of these I have demanded of the king that Bharata be consecrated and that you, Rāghava, be sent at once to Daṇḍaka wilderness.

"If you wish to ensure that your father be true to his word, and you to your own, best of men, then listen to what I have to say.

"Abide by your father's guarantee, exactly as he promised it, and enter the forest for nine years and five.

"Forgo the consecration and withdraw to Daṇḍaka wilderness, live there seven years and seven, wearing matted hair and barkcloth garments.

"Let Bharata rule this land from the city of the Kosalans, with all the treasures it contains, all its horses, chariots, elephants."

When Rāma, slayer of enemies, heard Kaikeyī's hateful words, like death itself, he was not the least disconcerted, but only replied,

"So be it. I shall go away to live in the forest, wearing matted hair and barkcloth garments, to safeguard the promise of the king.

"But I want to know why the lord of earth, the invincible tamer of foes, does not greet me as he used to?

"You need not worry, my lady. I say it to your face: I shall go to the forest—rest assured—wearing barkcloth and matted hair.

"Enjoined by my father, my benefactor, guru, and king, a man who knows what is right to do, what would I hesitate to do in order to please him?

"But there is still one thing troubling my mind and eating away at my heart: that the king does not tell me himself that Bharata is to be consecrated.

"For my wealth, the kingship, Sītā, and my own dear life I would gladly give up to my brother Bharata on my own, without any urging.

"How much more readily if urged by my father himself, the lord of men, in order to fulfill your fond desire and safeguard his promise?

"So you must reassure him. Why should the lord of earth keep his eyes fixed upon the ground and fitfully shed these tears?

"This very day let messengers depart on swift horses by order of the king to fetch Bharata from his uncle's house.

"As for me, I shall leave here in all haste for Daṇḍaka wilderness, without questioning my father's word, to live there fourteen years."

Kaikeyī was delighted to hear these words of Rāma's, and trusting them implicitly, she pressed Rāghava to set out at once.

"So be it. Men shall go as messengers on swift horses to bring home Bharata from his uncle's house.

"But since you are now so eager, Rāma, I do not think it wise to linger. You should therefore proceed directly from here to the forest.

"That the king is ashamed and does not address you himself, that is nothing, best of men, you needn't worry about that.

"But so long as you have not hastened from the city and gone to the forest, Rāma, your father shall neither bathe nor eat."

"Oh curse you!" the king gasped, overwhelmed with grief, and upon the gilt couch he fell back in a faint.

Rāma raised up the king, pressed though he was by Kaikeyī—like a horse whipped with a crop—to make haste and depart for the forest.

Listening to the ignoble Kaikeyī's hateful words, so dreadful in their consequences, Rāma remained unperturbed and only said to her,

"My lady, it is not in the hopes of gain that I suffer living in this world. You should know that, like the seers, I have but one concern and that is righteousness.

"Whatever I can do to please this honored man I will do at any cost, even if it means giving up my life.

"For there is no greater act of righteousness than this: obedience to one's father and doing as he bids.

"Even unbidden by this honored man, at your bidding alone I shall live for fourteen years in the desolate forest.

"Indeed, Kaikeyī, you must ascribe no virtue to me at all if you had to appeal to the king, when you yourself are so venerable in my eyes.

"Let me only take leave of my mother, and settle matters with Sītā. Then I shall go, this very day, to the vast forest of the Daṇḍakas.

"You must see to it that Bharata obeys Father and guards the kingdom, for that is the eternal way of righteousness."

When his father heard Rāma's words, he was stricken with such deep sorrow that he could not hold back his sobs in his grief and broke out in loud weeping.

Splendid Rāma did homage at the feet of his unconscious father and at the feet of that ignoble woman, Kaikeyī; then he turned to leave.

Reverently Rāma circled his father and Kaikeyī, and, withdrawing from the inner chamber, he saw his group of friends.

Lakṣmaṇa, the delight of Sumitrā, fell in behind him, his eyes brimming with tears, in a towering rage.

Reverently circling the equipment for the consecration, but careful not to gaze at it, Rāma slowly went away.

The loss of the kingship diminished his great majesty as little as night diminishes the loveliness of the cool-rayed moon, beloved of the world.

Though he was on the point of leaving his native land and going to the forest, he was no more discomposed than one who has passed beyond all things of this world.

Holding back his sorrow within his mind, keeping his every sense in check, and fully self-possessed he made his way to his mother's residence to tell her the sad news.

As Rāma entered her residence, where joy still reigned supreme, as he reflected on the sudden wreck of all his fortunes, even then he showed no sign of discomposure, for fear it might endanger the lives of those he loved.

from Book 3[1]

[THE ABDUCTION OF SITA]

SARGA 42

After instructing his brother the mighty prince, delight of the Raghus,[2] strapped on his gold-hilted sword.

He then strapped on a pair of quivers and took up his proper ornament—the bow with triple curve—and set off at a rapid pace.

The deer spied the lord of kings rushing toward him and he led him on, now timorously hiding, now showing himself again.

With sword strapped on and taking up his bow, Rāma ran toward the deer, imagining he saw his form shimmering before him.

At one moment he would spot him running through the deep forest, temptingly near, and would take his bow in hand, only to look once more and find the deer beyond the range of his arrow. In one stretch of forest he came into sight leaping through the air in frightful panic, and then he passed into another stretch and out of sight.

Like the disk of the autumn moon veiled in tatters of cloud, he was seen one instant and gone the next.

Now appearing, now disappearing, he drew Rāghava far away, and helplessly deluded by him Kākutstha[3] flew into a rage.

Then the deer halted in exhaustion and withdrew to a shady spot in the meadow, not far away, where Rāma spotted him surrounded by other animals of the forest.

Seeing the deer mighty Rāma was determined to kill him. The powerful prince nocked his sturdy bow and drew it back with power.

Aiming at the deer he shot a gleaming, flaming arrow fashioned by Brahmā[4] that glared like a snake as it darted forth.

1. Translated by Sheldon Pollock.
2. Rama.
3. Rama (literally, "a descendant of Kakutstha," an ances-

tor in Rama's lineage).
4. Rama had earlier received the god Brahma's heavenly weapons from the sage Agastya.

The supreme arrow penetrated the illusory deer form and like a bolt of lightning pierced the heart, Mārīca's heart.[5]

The deer leaped high as a palm tree and with a ghastly shriek fell to the ground, tormented by the arrow, his life ebbing away. And as Mārīca lay there dying, the shape he had assumed began to disappear.

Knowing the time had come, in Rāghava's own voice he cried out, "Oh Sītā! Oh Lakṣmaṇa!"

Pierced to the quick by an arrow unlike any other, Mārīca once more took on the form of a massive *rākṣasa,* giving up the deer form and his life.

Struck by the arrow, he became a *rākṣasa* once more, with huge fangs, a necklace of gold, sparkling earrings, and every other ornament to adorn him.

Seeing that dreadful sight, the *rākṣasa* fallen on the ground, Rāma thought suddenly of Sītā and recalled what Lakṣmaṇa had said.[6]

"With his dying breath this *rākṣasa* cried out at the top of his voice, 'Oh Sītā! Oh Lakṣmaṇa!' How will Sītā react to hearing this?

"And great-armed Lakṣmaṇa, what will be his state of mind?" As these thoughts came to righteous Rāma, the hair on his body bristled with dread.

Then Rāma's consternation gave way to a feeling of fear that shot through him with sharp pangs: The deer he had slain was in fact a *rākṣasa,* the voice it had used was his own.

He killed another dappled deer and taking the meat hurriedly retraced his steps to Janasthāna.[7]

SARGA 43

Now, when Sītā heard that cry of distress, in her husband's own voice, coming from the forest, she said to Lakṣmaṇa, "Go and find out what has happened to Rāghava.

"My heart—my very life—is jarred from its place by the sound of his crying in deep distress that I heard so clearly.

"You must rescue your brother, who cries out in the forest. Run to your brother at once, for he needs help! The *rākṣasas* have him in their power, like a bull fallen among lions." So she spoke, but Lakṣmaṇa, heeding his brother's command, did not go.

5. The *rakshasa* compelled by Ravana to assume the form of a bejeweled deer in order to draw Rama away from the hermitage.
6. At the first sight of the magical deer, Lakshmana had a premonition that it must be a *rakshasa.*
7. The region of the Dandaka forest located near Rama's hermitage.

Then the daughter of Janaka[8] angrily said to him, "You wear the guise of a friend to your brother, Saumitri,[9] but act like his foe, refusing to aid him in his extremity. You hope Rāma perishes, Lakṣmaṇa, isn't that so? And it is all because of me.

"I think you would be happy should some disaster befall your brother. You have no real affection for him, so you stand there calmly with the splendid prince gone from sight.

"For with him in danger and me here, how could I prevent what you came here with the sole intention of doing?"

So Sītā, princess of Videha, spoke, overwhelmed with tears and grief, and Lakṣmaṇa replied to her as she stood there frightened as a doe.

"My lady, there is no one, god or man, *gandharva,* great bird, or *rākṣasa, piśāca, kinnara,* beast, or dreaded *dānava*—no one, fair lady, who could match Rāma, the peer of Vāsava, in battle.[1]

"Rāma cannot be killed in battle. You must not talk this way, for I dare not leave you in the forest with Rāghava gone.

"His power cannot be withstood, not by any powers however vast, not by all three worlds up in arms, or the deathless gods themselves, their lord included.

"Let your heart rest easy, do not be alarmed. Your husband will soon return, after killing that splendid deer.

"That was clearly not his voice, or any belonging to a god. It was the magic of that *rākṣasa,* unreal as a mirage.

"You were entrusted to my safekeeping, shapely Vaidehī,[2] by the great Rāma. I dare not leave you here alone.

"Then too, dear lady, because of the slaughter at Janasthāna, where Khara perished, we have earned the hostility of the night-stalkers.[3]

"*Rākṣasas* delight in causing trouble, Vaidehī, they make all kinds of noises in the deep forest. You need not worry."

Though what he said was true, Sītā was enraged by Lakṣmaṇa's words. Her eyes blazed bright red as she made this harsh reply:

8. Sita is the adopted daughter of King Janaka of Mithila in Videha country, where he discovered her as a baby in a furrowed field.

9. Lakshmana (literally, "son of Sumitra").

1. *Pishacas* and *danavas* are two more categories of non-human beings. "Vasava" is an epithet of Indra, king of the gods.

2. Sita (literally, "woman of Videha").

3. The *rakshasa* Khara, a brother of Ravana, was killed when he and his 14,000 soldiers attacked Rama.

"Ignoble, cruel man, disgrace to your House! How pitiful this attempt of yours. I feel certain you are pleased with all this, and that is why you can talk the way you do.

"It is nothing new, Lakṣmaṇa, for rivals to be so evil, cruel rivals like you always plotting in secret.

"You treacherously followed Rāma to the forest, the two of you alone: You are either in the employ of Bharata or secretly plotting to get me.

"I am married to Rāma, a husband dark as a lotus, with eyes like lotus petals. How could I ever give my love to some ordinary man?

"I would not hesitate to take my life before your very eyes, Saumitri, for I could not live upon this earth one moment without Rāma."

Such were the words Sītā spoke to Lakṣmaṇa, so harsh they made his hair bristle with horror. But he controlled himself, and with hands cupped in reverence he addressed her:

"I dare not answer, Maithilī,[4] for you are a deity in my eyes. And yet inappropriate words from a woman come as nothing new.

"This is the nature of women the whole world over: Women care nothing for righteousness, they are flighty, sharp-tongued, and divisive.

"May all the inhabitants of the forest give ear and bear me witness how my words of reason met so harsh a reply from you.

"Curse you and be damned, that you could so suspect me, when I am only following the orders of my guru. How like a woman to be so perverse!

"I am going to Kākutstha. I wish you well, fair woman. May the spirits of the forest, each and every one, protect you, large-eyed lady.

"How ominous the portents that manifest themselves to me! I pray I find you here when I return with Rāma."

Now, when Lakṣmaṇa addressed her in this fashion, Janaka's daughter began to weep. Overwhelmed with tears she hotly replied:

"Parted from Rāma I will drown myself in the Godāvarī,[5] Lakṣmaṇa, I will hang myself or hurl my body upon some rocky place.

"Or I will drink deadly poison or throw myself into a blazing fire. I would never touch any man but Rāghava, not even with my foot!"

---

4. Sita (literally, "woman of Mithila").   5. A river in the southern region of India.

Such were the insults Sītā hurled at Lakṣmaṇa in her sorrow, and sorrowfully she wept and struck her belly with her fists.

At the sight of large-eyed Sītā so deeply anguished and weeping, Saumitri was beside himself and tried to comfort her, but she would say nothing more to her husband's brother.

Then, cupping his hands in reverence and bowing slightly, Lakṣmaṇa, the self-respecting prince, said goodbye to Sītā. And as he set forth to find Rāma, he turned around again and again and looked back at Maithilī.

SARGA 44

Rāghava's younger brother, angered by her harsh words and sorely longing for Rāma, set forth without further delay.

This was the opening ten-necked Rāvaṇa had been waiting for, and he took advantage of it at once. Assuming the guise of a wandering mendicant, he turned his steps toward Vaidehī.

Clad in a soft saffron robe, with topknot, parasol, and sandals, and goodly staff and water pitcher hanging at his left shoulder—disguised like this, as a mendicant—he approached Vaidehī.

Both brothers had left her, and in his pride of power he advanced upon her, like total darkness advancing upon the twilight, when both sun and moon have left.

He gazed at the glorious young princess as ominously as a planet might gaze upon the star Rohiṇī when the hare-marked moon is absent.[6]

At the appearance of the dreaded, evil creature, the trees that grew in Janasthāna stopped rustling and the wind died down.

At the sight of him peering around with his blood-red eyes, the swift current of the Godāvarī river began to slacken in fear.

Ten-necked Rāvaṇa had waited for an opening, and Rāma had given him one. In the guise of a beggar he drew near to Vaidehī.

As Vaidehī sat grieving for her husband, the unholy Rāvaṇa in the guise of a holy man edged closer to her, like the sluggish planet, Saturn, closing in on Citrā, the sparkling star.

Like a deep well concealed by grass, the evil one in the guise of a holy man stood watching Vaidehī, illustrious wife of Rāma—the beautiful woman with lovely teeth

---

6. The planet is Mercury and the star-cluster Rohini is the beloved of the moon. In Sanskrit literature, dramatic moments are often rendered through astronomical tropes because of the prominence given to astral phenomena in traditional Indian rituals and beliefs.

and lips, and a face like the full moon—as she sat in the leaf hut tormented with grief and tears.

The blackhearted stalker of the night stole ever closer to Vaidehī, the woman dressed in garments of yellow silk, and with eyes like lotus petals.

With arrows of Manmatha, god of love, lodged deep within his heart, and the sounds of the *vedas*[7] on his lips, the overlord of *rākṣasas* appeared before the deserted hut and courteously spoke.

Rāvaṇa began singing her praises, that loveliest of women in the three worlds, a radiant beauty, like the goddess Śrī herself without the lotus.

"Who are you, golden woman dressed in garments of yellow silk, wearing a lovely lotus garland, and like a lotus pond yourself?

"Are you the goddess Modesty or Fame? Are you Śrī or lovely Lakṣmī or perhaps an *apsaras,* lovely lady? Could you be Prosperity, shapely woman, or easygoing Pleasure?[8]

"Your teeth are bright white, tapered, and even; your eyes are large and clear, rosy at the corner, black in the center.

"Your hips are full and broad, your thighs smooth as an elephant's trunk. And these, your delightful breasts, how round they are, so firm and gently heaving; how full and lovely, smooth as two palm fruits, with their nipples standing stiff and the rarest gems to adorn them.

"Graceful lady with your lovely smile, lovely teeth, and lovely eyes, you have swept my heart away like a river in flood that sweeps away its banks.

"Your waist I could compass with my fingers; how fine is your hair, how firm your breasts. No goddess, no *gandharva* woman, no *yakṣa* or *kinnara* woman, no mortal woman so beautiful have I ever seen before on the face of this earth.[9]

"Your beauty, unrivaled in all the worlds, your delicacy and youth, and the fact of your living here in the woods stir the deepest feelings in me.

"I urge you to go home, this is no place for you to be living. For this is the lair of dreaded *rākṣasas,* who can change their form at will.

"In the most delightful palaces, in luxuriant, fragrant city gardens is where you should be strolling.

---

7. Ancient wisdom texts.
8. Shri and Lakshmi, goddesses of royalty and wealth, are normally taken to be one and the same, and the consort of Vishnu. *Apsaras* are celestial nymphs.
9. *Yakshas* are yet another category of divine beings whose women are famous for their beauty.

"To my mind you deserve the finest garlands and beverages and raiment, and the finest husband, lovely black-eyed lady.

"Could you be one of the Rudras or Maruts, sweet-smiling, shapely woman, or one of the Vasus, perhaps? You look like a goddess to me.

"But *gandharvas* do not pass this way, nor do gods or *kinnaras,* for this is the lair of *rākṣasas.* How is it you have come here?

"There are monkeys here, lions, panthers, and tigers, apes, hyenas, and flesh-eating birds. How is it you do not fear them?

"And the dreaded elephants that go running wild, maddened by rut—how is it you do not fear them, lovely lady, all alone in the deep wilderness?

"Who are you, to whom do you belong, where do you come from, my precious, and why are you wandering all alone through Daṇḍaka, the haunt of dreaded *rākṣasas?*"

Such was the praise evil Rāvaṇa lavished on Vaidehī. But seeing he had come in the garb of a brahman, Maithilī honored him with all the acts of hospitality due a guest.

First she brought forward a cushion and offered water for his feet, and then she called him when food was ready, for he looked kindly enough.

When Maithilī observed that he had come in the garb of a twice-born[1]—a brahman with a begging bowl and saffron robe; when she saw these accoutrements, it was impossible to refuse him, and so she extended him an invitation befitting a brahman.

"Here is a cushion, brahman, please be seated and accept this water for your feet. Here I have made ready for you the best fare the forest has to offer. You may partake of it freely."

So Maithilī extended him a cordial invitation, and as Rāvaṇa gazed at her, the wife of the lord of men, he confirmed his resolve to take her by force, and with that, consigned himself to death.

Her husband in his honest garb had gone to hunt the magic deer, and she waited for him and Lakṣmaṇa, scanning the horizon. But she saw neither Rāma nor Lakṣmaṇa—only the deep, green forest.

SARGA 45

When Rāvaṇa came in the guise of a mendicant to carry off Vaidehī, he had first put some questions to her. Of her own accord she now began to tell her story.

For Sītā had thought a moment: "He is a brahman and my guest. If I do not reply he will curse me." She then spoke these words:

1. A term used primarily of Brahmans. (They are said to be born a second time when initiated into studentship by their teacher.)

"I am the daughter of Janaka, the great king of Mithilā. My name is Sītā, may it please the best of twice-born, and I am the wife of Rāma.

"For twelve years I lived in the house of Rāghava, enjoying such pleasures as mortals enjoy. I had all I could desire.

"Then, in the thirteenth year, the king in concert with his kingly counselors approved the royal consecration of my husband.

"But just as the preparations for Rāghava's consecration were under way, a mother-in-law of mine named Kaikeyī asked her husband for a boon.

"You see, Kaikeyī had already married my father-in-law for a consideration. So she had two things she now could ask of her husband, the best of kings and a man who always kept his word: One was the consecration of Bharata, the other, my husband's banishment.

"'From this day forth I will not eat, or drink, or sleep, I will put an end to my life if Rāma is consecrated.'

"Such were Kaikeyī's words, and though my father-in-law, who had always shown her respect, begged her with offers of commensurate riches, she would not do what he begged of her.

"Rāma, my mighty husband, was then twenty-five years old, and I had just passed my eighteenth birthday.

"His name is renowned throughout the world, his eyes are large, his arms strong. He is virtuous, honest, truthful, and devoted to the welfare of all people.

"When Rāma came into his father's presence for the consecration to begin, it was Kaikeyī who addressed my husband, in a rush of words:

"'Listen to me, Rāghava, and hear what your father has decreed. The kingship is to be given to Bharata uncontested.

"'As for you, you are to live in the forest for nine years and five. Go into banishment, Kākutstha, and save your father from falsehood.'

"Without a trace of fear my husband Rāma answered Kaikeyī, 'So be it,' and in firm compliance with his vow did just as she had told him.

"For Rāma has taken a solemn vow, brahman, one never to be broken: always to give and not receive, to tell the truth and not lie.

"Rāma has a constant companion, his half brother Lakṣmaṇa, a tiger among men and mighty slayer of enemies in battle.

"This brother Lakṣmaṇa, who keeps to the ways of righteousness, firm in his vows, followed bow in hand when Rāma went into banishment with me.

"And so the three of us were driven from the kingdom for the sake of Kaikeyī. Thus it is under compulsion, best of twice-born, that we now wander the dense forest.

"Rest a moment; or you can even pass the night here if you like. My husband will soon return bringing an abundance of food from the forest.

"But can you just tell me your name, your clan, and family? How is it that you, a brahman, wander all alone in Daṇḍaka wilderness?"

So Sītā, wife of Rāma, spoke, and powerful Rāvaṇa, overlord of *rākṣasas,* made a reply that froze her blood:

"I am he who terrifies the worlds, with all their gods, *asuras,* and great serpents. I am Rāvaṇa, Sītā, supreme lord of the hosts of *rākṣasas.*

"Now that I have set eyes on you, flawless, golden lady dressed in silk, I shall no longer take any pleasure in my own wives.

"From one place and another I have carried off many splendid women. May it please you to become chief queen over every one of them.

"In the middle of the ocean lies my vast city Laṅkā, perched upon a mountain peak and ringed by the sea.

"There, my radiant Sītā, you shall stroll with me through the forests, never longing for this life you are leading in the wilderness.

"Five thousand slave women all adorned with ornaments shall wait upon you hand and foot, Sītā, if you become my wife."

So Rāvaṇa spoke, but Janaka's daughter, that faultless beauty, angrily and with utter contempt for the *rākṣasa* replied:

"I am faithful to Rāma, my husband, the equal of great Indra, unshakable as a great mountain, imperturbable as the great sea.

"I am faithful to Rāma, the great-armed, great-chested prince, who moves with the boldness of a lion, a lionlike man, a lion among men.

"I am faithful to Rāma, the king's most cherished son, a great-armed, mighty prince of wide renown and strict self-control, whose face is like the full moon.

"As for you, you are a jackal in the presence of a lioness, to come here seeking me, whom you can never have. You could no more touch me than touch the radiance of the sun.

"You must be seeing many a golden tree of death, ill-fated Rāvaṇa, if you seek to gain the beloved wife of Rāghava.

"You are seeking to pluck the fang from the mouth of a poisonous snake, the tooth from the mouth of a hungry lion in pursuit, the foe to all beasts.

"You are seeking to carry off Mandara, greatest of mountains, in your hand, to drink the *kālakūṭa* poison and take no harm of it.[2]

"You are rubbing your eye with a needle, licking a razor with your tongue, if you seek to violate the beloved wife of Rāghava.

"You are seeking to cross the ocean with a boulder tied around your neck, to take into your hands the very sun and moon, if you seek to assault the beloved wife of Rāghava.

"You have seen a blazing fire and seek to carry it away in a cloth, if you seek to carry off the virtuous wife of Rāma.

"You are seeking to walk atop a row of iron-headed spears, if you seek to violate the proper wife of Rāma.

"As different as a lion and a jackal in the forest, the ocean and a ditch, rare wine and gruel, so different are Dāśarathi and you.

"As different as gold and lead, sandalwood paste and slime, a bull elephant and a cat in the forest, so different are Dāśarathi[3] and you.

"As different as Garuda, the son of Vinatā,[4] and a crow, a peacock and a gull, a vulture and a crane in the forest, so different are Dāśarathi and you.

"As long as Rāma walks the earth, mighty as thousand-eyed Indra, armed with his bow and arrow, you may take me but could never enjoy me, no more than a fly the diamond chip it swallows."

Such were the words the good woman addressed to the evil nightstalker, but a shudder passed through her body, and she began to quiver like a slender plantain tree tossed by the wind.

And when Rāvaṇa, mighty as Death himself, observed how Sītā was trembling, he thought to frighten her still further by telling of his House, his power, the name he had won for himself, and the deeds he had done.

---

2. The legendary Mt. Mandara was made the churning stick when the gods and antigods churned the milk ocean for the drink of immortality. The cosmic serpent used as the twirling string spewed forth the terrible *kalakuta* poison, which Shiva swallowed to protect the world.
3. Rama (literally "descendent of Dasharatha").
4. King of birds and the mount of the god Vishnu.

SARGA 46

Even as Sītā was speaking in this manner, Rāvaṇa flew into a passion, and knitting his brow into a frown he harshly replied:

"I am half brother to Vaiśravaṇa,[5] lovely lady. My name is Rāvaṇa, if you please, the mighty ten-necked one.

"In fear of me the gods, *gandharvas, piśācas,* great birds, and serpents flee in terror, as all things born are put to flight by fear of Death.

"In connection with some issue between us Vaiśravaṇa, my half brother, and I came into conflict. In a rage I attacked and defeated him in battle.

"Tormented by fear of me he left his own prosperous realm and now dwells on Kailāsa, highest of mountains, with only men to convey him.

"For the aerial chariot that flies where one desires, the lovely Puṣpaka, once belonged to him. But I took it by force of arms, my beauty, and now ride upon it through the sky.

"At the mere sight of my face, Maithilī, once my anger has been provoked, the gods with Indra at their head flee in terror.

"In my presence the wind blows cautiously, and the sun's hot rays turn cold in fear.

"The leaves on the trees stop rustling, and the rivers slacken their current wherever I am, wherever I go.

"On the further shore of the ocean lies my lovely city, Laṅkā, grand as Indra's Amarāvatī, thronged with dreaded *rākṣasas.*

"It is a lovely, dazzling city ringed by a white rampart, with gateways made of gold and towers of cat's-eye beryl.

"It is crowded with elephants, horses, and chariots, the sound of pipes resounds there, and its gardens are beautiful, filled with trees bearing any fruit one wants.

"Living there with me, proud princess Sītā, you shall forget what it was like to have been a mortal woman.

"Enjoying not only the pleasures mortals enjoy, lovely lady, but divine pleasures, too, you shall soon forget that short-lived mortal, Rāma.

"So meager is his power that King Daśaratha, in order to enthrone a favored son, was able to drive him into the forest, first-born though he was.

5. Kubera, god of wealth. In his more common, wrathful form, Ravana has ten necks and twenty arms.

"What use is this witless Rāma to you, large-eyed woman, a miserable ascetic who lets himself be deposed from the kingship?

"The lord of all *rākṣasas* has come here in person, of his own accord. Do not reject him, whom the arrows of Manmatha, god of love, have so badly wounded.

"For if you do reject me, timid lady, you shall live to regret it, just like Urvaśī after she spurned Purūravas."[6]

So he spoke, but Vaidehī was overcome with rage—her eyes grew red, and though all alone in that deserted spot, she made this harsh reply to the lord of *rākṣasas:*

"How can you want to commit such an outrage, you who claim Vaiśravaṇa as brother, a god to whom all beings pay homage?

"The *rākṣasas* shall inevitably perish, Rāvaṇa, all who have you for their king, a cruel, imprudent, intemperate king.

"A man might abduct Indra's wife, úacī herself, and still hope to save his life, but he who carries me off, the wife of Rāma, has no life left to save.

"One might steal the incomparable úacī from the hand that wields the thunderbolt and long remain alive. But violate a woman like me, *rākṣasa,* and even drinking the nectar of immortality will be no escape for you."

Sarga 47

Hearing Sītā's words the awesome ten-necked Rāvaṇa struck his hands together and made ready to assume his massive form.

Again he addressed Maithilī, and far more severely than before: "It seems you did not hear, madwoman, when I spoke of my strength and valor.

"I can lift the earth in my arms while standing in the sky; I can drink up the ocean, I can slay Death in battle.

"I can shatter the earth with my sharp arrows, madwoman, or bring the sun to a halt. I can take on any form at will. You see before you a husband ready to grant your every wish."

And as Rāvaṇa spoke thus in his wild rage, his yellow-rimmed eyes turned fiery red.

Then suddenly Rāvaṇa, younger brother to Vaiśravaṇa, abandoned the kindly form of beggar and assumed his true shape, one such as Doom itself must have.

With eyes flaming bright red, with earrings of burnished gold, with bow and arrows, he became once more the majestic ten-faced stalker of the night.

6. The celestial nymph Urvashi fell in love with the mortal king Pururavas. The reference here to her misfortune when she left Pururavas is unclear.

He had thrown off the guise of mendicant and assumed his own form again, the colossal shape of Rāvaṇa, overlord of *rākṣasas*.

With eyes flaming bright red in his rage, lowering like a bank of storm clouds, clad in a red garment Rāvaṇa stood before Maithilī, staring at her, perfect jewel of a woman, with her jet-black hair, her sunlike radiance, and the fine clothes and ornaments that she wore. And he said:

"If you seek a husband whose fame has spread throughout the three worlds, shapely woman, be mine. I am a lord worthy of you.

"Love me forever. I shall be a lover to win your praise, and never, my beauty, will I do anything to displease you. Give up this love for a mortal being, and bestow your love on me.

"What possible virtues could make you love this short-lived Rāma, a failure, stripped of kingship? You think you are so smart, but what a fool you really are!

"He is a simpleton, who at the bidding of a woman abandoned his kingdom and loved ones to come and live in this forest, the haunt of wild beasts."

And so speaking to Sītā, princess of Mithilā, who deserved the same kindness she always showed others, Rāvaṇa seized her as the planet Budha might seize the star Rohiṇī in the sky.

With his left hand he seized lotus-eyed Sītā by her hair and with his right hand by her thighs.

With his long arms and sharp fangs he resembled a mountain peak; seeing him advancing like Death himself, the spirits of the forest fled overpowered by fear.

Then with a dreadful rumble Rāvaṇa's great chariot came into view, that unearthly chariot fashioned by magic, with wheels of gold, and harnessed with asses.

With loud, harsh threats he then clutched Vaidehī to his breast and boarded the chariot.

Caught in Rāvaṇa's grip and wild with despair, the glorious Sītā screamed at the top of her voice, crying, "Rāma!" But Rāma was far away in the forest.

Filled with desire for one who was filled with loathing for him, Rāvaṇa flew up holding her writhing like a serpent queen.

As the lord of *rākṣasas* carried her off through the sky, she screamed shrilly like a woman gone mad, in agony, or delirious:

"Oh great-armed Lakṣmaṇa, you have always sought favor with your guru. Don't you know that I am being carried off by a *rākṣasa*, who can change his form at will?

"And you, Rāghava, you renounced all life's pleasures, everything of value, for the sake of righteousness. Don't you see me being carried off in defiance of all that is right?

"And surely, slayer of enemies, you are the one to discipline wrongdoers. Why then don't you punish so evil a creature as Rāvaṇa?

"But no, the result of wrongdoing is not seen right away. Time is a factor in this, as in the ripening of grain.

"And as for you, Doom must have robbed you of your senses to do what you have done. Disaster shall befall you at the hands of Rāma, a terrible disaster that will end your life.

"Ah, now Kaikeyī and all her family must be satisfied. Rāma's lawful wife has been taken from him, that glorious prince whom nothing but righteousness could satisfy.

"Janasthāna, I call on you and you *karṇikāra* trees in full blossom: Tell Rāma at once that Rāvaṇa is carrying off Sītā.

"I greet you, Mount Prasravaṇa,[7] with your flower garlands and massive peaks: Quickly tell Rāma that Rāvaṇa is carrying off Sītā.

"I greet you, Godāvarī river, alive with the call of geese and cranes: Tell Rāma at once that Rāvaṇa is carrying off Sītā.

"And you spirits that inhabit the different trees of this forest, I salute you all: Tell my husband that I have been carried off.

"All creatures that live in this place, I appeal to you for help, all you flocks of birds and herds of beasts: Tell my husband that the woman he loves more than life itself is being carried off, that Sītā has been carried away, helpless, by Rāvaṇa.

"Once the powerful, great-armed prince discovers where I am—albeit in the other world—he shall come in all his valor and bring me home, were it Vaivasvata himself, god of death, who had carried me off.

* * *

from Book 6[1]

[The Death of Ravana]

from Sarga 96

The great battle raged all night long as the gods, *dānavas, yakṣas, piśācas,* great serpents, and *rākṣasas* stood watching.

---

7. A peak in the Vindhya range in central India, where Rama, Sita, and Lakshmana spent time during their exile.

1. Translated by Robert Goldman, Barend A. van Nooten, and Sally Sutherland Goldman.

Indeed the duel between Rāma and Rāvaṇa went on day and night not pausing for an hour or even a moment.

SARGA 97

But then Mātali[2] alerted Rāghava, saying, "Why, heroic prince, do you merely match him blow for blow, as if you knew no better?

"In order to kill him, my lord, you must shoot him with the missile of Grandfather Brahmā. For the moment ordained by the gods for his destruction is now at hand."

Alerted by Mātali's words, Rāma drew forth that blazing arrow which, as he did so, made a hissing sound like that of a snake.

It had been given to him earlier by the mighty and blessed seer Agastya. It was a mighty arrow, the gift of Brahmā and unfailing in battle.

Brahmā whose power is immeasurable had fashioned it long ago for the sake of Indra and had presented it to that lord of the gods, who was eager to conquer the three worlds.

Pavana, the god of the wind, resided in its feathers; Pāvaka, the god of fire, and Bhâskara, the sun god, were in its arrowhead. Its shaft was made of cosmic space; and the mountains Meru and Mandara lent it their weight.

Radiant in its appearance, beautifully feathered, and adorned with gold, it was fashioned with the radiant energy of all the elements, and it was as brilliant as the sun.

It looked like the smoking fire of doom and glistened like a venomous snake. It could shatter hosts of chariots, elephants, and horses; and its effects were instantaneous.

It could shatter gateways and their iron beams and even mountains. With its shaft drenched with the blood of various creatures and smeared with their marrow it was truly frightful.

Roaring deafeningly and charged with the power of the thunderbolt, it was the scourge of many hosts. Dreadful, hissing like a serpent, it inspired terror in all beings.

It was fearsome and looked like Yama, the god of death. It provided a constant supply of food to flocks of cranes and vultures, *rākṣasas,* and packs of jackals.

Fletched with the various, beautiful and variegated feathers of Garuda, it brought joy to the monkey chiefs and despair to the *rākṣasas.*

Then strong and mighty Rāma invoked that great, unequalled arrow—an arrow that robbed one's enemies of their glory but brought joy to oneself. It was destined to

---

2. As Ravana fought from a chariot while Rama was on foot, Indra, king of the gods, dispatched his charioteer Matali to provide Rama with a comparable conveyance.

destroy that menace to the Ikṣvākus[3] and all the worlds; and Rāma placed it on his bow in the manner prescribed in the *veda*.

Filled with fury and exerting himself to the utmost, he bent the bow fully and loosed the arrow towards Rāvaṇa, tearing at his vitals.

As unstoppable as the thunderbolt and released by those arms of adamant, it struck Rāvaṇa's breast, inevitable as death.

Loosed with tremendous speed the deadly arrow pierced evil-minded Rāvaṇa's heart.

Drenched with blood the fatal arrow swiftly entered the earth, carrying with it the life breaths of Rāvaṇa.

Once the arrow had accomplished its purpose in killing Rāvaṇa, it obediently returned to its quiver, glistening with its still-wet blood.

Meanwhile the bow and arrows of him who had been struck down so swiftly slipped from his grasp along with his life breaths as he lay dying.

The lord of the sons of chaos, once so swift and splendid, fell lifeless to the ground from his chariot like Vṛtra[4] smitten by the thunderbolt.

Seeing him fallen to the ground, the surviving rangers of the night, their lord slain, fled terrified in all directions.

But as for the monkeys, whose weapons were trees, when they saw that ten-necked Rāvaṇa had been slain and that Rāghava was victorious, they pursued the *rākṣasas,* roaring loudly.

Hard pressed by the jubilant monkeys, their protector slain, the *rākṣasas* fled in fear to Laṅkā, their piteous faces drenched with tears.

Then the rejoicing monkeys, acting the part of victors, roared triumphantly, proclaiming Rāghava's victory and the death of Rāvaṇa.

The auspicious kettledrums of the thirty gods then resounded in the heavens; and a pleasant breeze blew, wafting a divine fragrance.

Then an extraordinary and delightful shower of blossoms fell from the sky to the earth, covering Rāma's chariot.

The beautiful voice of the great gods filled with the praise of Rāghava could be heard in the heavens crying, "Well done! Well done!"

---

3. The family name of the royal dynasty of Ayodhya.   4. A demon slain by Indra, who as the god of rain wields a thunderbolt.

Now that fierce Rāvaṇa, the terror of all the worlds, had been slain, great joy filled the gods and celestial bards.

Then, having slain that bull among *rākṣasas,* Rāghava, in great delight, fulfilled the wishes of Sugrīva and mighty Aṅgada.[5]

The hosts of the Māruts[6] regained tranquility, the directions were limpid, and the sky grew clear. The earth ceased its trembling, and soft breezes blew, while the sun, the bringer of day, shone with a steady light.

Sugrīva, Vibhīṣaṇa,[7] and the rest of splendid Rāghava's close allies, together with Lakṣmaṇa, gathered around him on the battlefield in the joy of victory and paid him homage with all due ceremony.

And the mighty prince, the delight of the king of the Raghu dynasty, having slain his enemy, became true to his vow. Surrounded by his kinsmen and armies there on the field of battle, he looked as resplendent as Indra surrounded by the hosts of the thirty gods.

* * *

[*After the killing of Rāvaṇa, Sītā is recovered and brought before Rāma.*]

[THE FIRE ORDEAL OF SITA]

SARGA 103

Looking at Maithilī who stood so meekly beside him, Rāma began to speak as rage simmered in his heart.

"So here you are, my lady. I have won you back after conquering my enemy in battle. I did all this in accordance with the demands of manly valor.

"I have wiped clean the affront and so my wrath is appeased. For I have eliminated both the insult and my enemy at the same time.

"Today I have demonstrated my manly valor. Today my efforts have borne fruit. Today, having fulfilled my vow, I am once more master of myself.

"You were carried off by that wanton *rākṣasa* when you were left alone, but now through manly action I have expunged that affront caused by fate.

"Of what use to anyone is a weakling who cannot wipe clean an insult through his own power?

"The leaping of the ocean and the razing of Laṅkā—today those praiseworthy deeds of Hanumān have borne fruit.

5. Sugriva is the monkey king of Kishkindha who aided Rama in the recovery of Sita. Angada is his nephew and successor.

6. The wind gods.

7. The virtuous *rakshasa* brother of Ravana, who allies himself with Rama.

"And today the efforts of Sugrīva and his army through their valor in battle and their beneficial counsel to me have borne fruit as well.

"And the efforts of my devoted Vibhīṣaṇa, who abandoned his worthless brother and came to me of his own accord, have likewise borne fruit."

Now as Rāma was saying these words in this fashion, Sītā, who looked like a wide-eyed doe, was overcome with tears.

But as Rāma gazed upon her, his anger flared up once more, like a blazing fire drenched with melted butter.

Knitting his brows on his forehead and glancing at her from the corner of his eye, he spoke harshly to Sītā there in the midst of the monkeys and rākṣasas.

"In wiping away this affront, Sītā, I have accomplished all that a man could do. In my wrath, I have won you back from the hands of my enemy just as through his austerities, the contemplative sage Agastya won back the southern lands that had been inaccessible to all living beings.

"Please understand that I did not undertake this great war effort—now brought to completion through the valor of my allies—on your account. Instead I did all this in order to protect my reputation and in every way to wipe clean the insult and disgrace to my illustrious lineage.

"Since, however, your virtue is now in doubt, your presence has become as unbearable to me as a bright lamp to a man afflicted with a disease of the eye.

"Go, therefore, as you please with my permission, daughter of Janaka, in any of the ten directions. I have no further use for you, my lady.

"For what powerful man born in a respectable family—his heart tinged with affection—would take back a woman who had lived in the house of another man?

"How could I who boast of my noble lineage possibly take you back—just risen from Rāvaṇa's lap and gazed upon by his lustful eye?

"I have restored my reputation; and that is the purpose for which I won you back. I have no further interest in you. Go from here wherever you like.

"I have made up mind in saying this, my lady. Choose Lakṣmaṇa or Bharata as you please.

"Or, Sītā, turn your heart to Sugrīva, lord of the monkeys, or the rākṣasa lord Vibhīṣaṇa, whichever pleases you.

"For surely, Sītā, once he had seen you with your heavenly beauty so enchanting, Rāvaṇa would not long have left you unmolested while you were dwelling in his house."

When Maithilī, who deserved to hear only kind words, had heard those cruel words of her beloved after so long a time, she shed tears and trembled violently like a *vallarī* creeper struck down by the trunk of a mighty elephant.

Sarga 104

When Vaidehī was addressed in this cruel and horrifying manner by the furious Rāghava, she was deeply wounded.

Hearing those cutting words of her husband before that great multitude, words such as she had never heard before, Maithilī was overcome with shame.

Pierced, as it were, by those verbal barbs, the daughter of Janaka, seemed to shrink within herself and gave way to bitter tears.

Wiping her tear-stained face, she replied softly to her husband in a faltering voice:

"How can you, heroic prince, speak to me with such cutting and improper words, painful to the ears, as some vulgar man might speak to his vulgar wife?

"I am not as you think of me, great armed prince. You must believe in me, for I swear to you by my own virtue.

"You harbor suspicion against all women because of the conduct of the vulgar ones. If you really knew me, you would abandon your suspicion.

"If I touched another's body against my will, lord, it was not by my choice. It is fate that was to blame here.

"My heart, which I control, was always devoted to you. But I was helpless. What could I have done regarding my body, which was in the power of another?

"If, my love, you do not truly know me despite our long-nurtured love and intimacy, then surely I am lost forever.

"When you dispatched the heroic Hanumān to search for me, why, heroic prince, did you not repudiate me then, while I was still in Laṅkā?

"No sooner had I heard your message, heroic prince, then abandoned by you, I would have abandoned my own life right before the eyes of that monkey lord.

"Then you would not have had to risk your life in a useless effort nor would your allies have had to undergo hardships to no purpose.

"But now, tiger among men, you give way to anger like some lesser man, thinking of me only as a typical woman.

"Since I am named after Janaka, you fail to take into account that I was born from the Goddess Earth, nor, though you know my conduct well, do you give it proper consideration.

"You give no weight to the fact that you took my hand when we were both still children. My devotion, my virtuous conduct—all that you have set aside."

When she had spoken in this fashion, Sītā turned weeping to Lakṣmaṇa, who stood there despondent and brooding, and spoke, her voice choked with tears.

"Build me a pyre, Saumitri, the only cure for this calamity. I cannot bear to live under the cloud of this false allegation.

"Rejected in the assembly of the people by my husband, who is not satisfied with my virtues, I shall enter the fire, bearer of oblations, so that I may follow the only path proper for me."

When Lakṣmaṇa, slayer of heroic foes, had been addressed in this fashion by Vaidehī, he glared at Rāghava's face, gripped by indignation.

But, sensing Rāma's intentions, which were betrayed by his facial expression, mighty Saumitri, ever obedient to Rāma's wishes, built the pyre.

Then reverently circumambulating Rāma, who stood with his face downcast, Vaidehī approached the blazing fire, eater of oblations.

After making her obeisance to the gods and the brahmans, Maithilī cupped her hands in reverence and facing Agni, god of fire, said this:

"Since my heart has never once strayed from Rāghava, so may the purifying fire, witness of all the world, protect me in every way."

When she had spoken in this fashion, Vaidehī reverently circumambulated the fire, eater of oblations. Then she entered the blazing flames, with a fearless heart.

The vast crowd assembled there, filled with children and the aged, watched as Maithilī entered the fire, eater of oblations.

As Sītā entered the fire, a vast and prodigious cry of, "Alas! Alas!" arose from the rākṣasas and monkeys.

* * *

[*The gods appear to ask how Rāma, who is chief among the gods, could remain unmoved as Sītā throws herself into the fire. Led by Brahmā they then remind Rāma of his divinity and utter a hymn of praise to him.*]

SARGA 106

Upon hearing that auspicious speech uttered by Grandfather Brahmā, the shining god of fire took Vaidehī on his lap and rose.

She resembled the rising sun and was adorned with ornaments of burnished gold. She was young and wore red garments and her hair was dark and curling. Her garland and ornaments were undamaged. Her mind was calm and her appearance unchanged. Taking Vaidehī on his lap the shining god of fire presented her to Rāma.

Then the purifying god of fire, witness of all the world, spoke to Rāma, saying, "Here is your Vaidehī, Rāma. She has committed no sin.

"She is of pure conduct and high moral character and has never betrayed you in word, thought, imagination, or glance.

"When you had left her alone she was carried off, helpless and sorrowful, from the deserted forest by the *rākṣasa* Rāvaṇa, arrogant in his power.

"Hidden and imprisoned in the inner apartments, thinking only of you and having you for her only recourse, she was guarded by hordes of hideous *rākṣasa* women, dreadful to behold.

"Although she was enticed and threatened in various ways, Maithilī would not even think of the *rākṣasa,* since her heart was utterly devoted to you.

"You must take her back, Rāghava, for her heart is pure and she is free from sin. Say no more, I am giving you an order."

When mighty Rāma, steadfast and firm in his valor, had been addressed in this fashion, that best of those who maintain righteousness, replied to that foremost among the thirty gods.

"Unquestionably Sītā needed to be proven innocent before the three worlds, since the auspicious woman had long dwelt in Rāvaṇa's inner apartments.

"For had I not put Jānakī to the test, the virtuous would say of me, 'Daśaratha's son Rāma is a lustful fool.'

"I know full well that Janaka's daughter Maithilī could give her heart to no other, since she is devoted to me and obeys my every thought.

"But in order that the three worlds too should have faith in her, I, whose ultimate recourse is truth, took no notice as Vaidehī entered the fire, eater of oblations.

"Rāvaṇa could no more have violated that wide-eyed lady, protected by her own blazing energy, than could the mighty ocean violate its boundary.

"That evil-minded brute was incapable of assaulting Maithilī even in his thoughts. For she is as unapproachable as a blazing flame of fire.

"This auspicious woman was not destined to rule over Rāvaṇa's inner apartments. For she is as inseparable from me as is its radiance from the sun.

"Janaka's daughter Maithilī has been proven innocent before the three worlds, and I am no more able to give her up than is a self-controlled man his good reputation.

"Moreover, I must follow the good advice that all of you affectionate friends, respected throughout the world, have uttered for my own good."

When he had uttered these words, powerful Rāma, praised by his mighty companions for the feat he had accomplished, was reunited with his beloved. Then Rāghava, who well deserved it, experienced happiness.

◈

RESONANCES

from *A Public Address, 1989. The Birthplace of God Cannot Be Moved!*[1]

Victory to Lord Vishvanatha of Kashi!
Victory to the birthplace of Lord Krishna!
Victory to our Hindu traditions and the ancient Vedic religion!
Victory to Lord Mahavira and the Lord Buddha!
Victory to the great religious warriors Banda Bairagi and Guru Govind Singh!
Victory to Mother India!
Victory to Mother Ganga![2]

Esteemed religious teachers, wise seers, mothers and sisters who love the God Rama, my brothers, we consider it an honor to have been invited to this holy city to speak to you about the birthplace of Rama, about our religion, our culture, all of these things. Seers are assembled here, but today they are not here to enlighten us about spiritual matters. Holy men are assembled here, but today it isn't to recite the *Bhagavata Purana* that they have come. Today Vishvamitra[3] has come, and he is looking for Rama. The minister Chanakya[4] has come, and he is looking for Chandragupta. Dadhichi[5] has come, and he is ready to sacrifice his own body to make the god Indra's formidable thunderbolt weapon.

---

1. Translated by Allison Busch. The story of Rama reentered history dramatically in the 1980s. Religious groups in association with political and paramilitary organizations were attempting to mobilize the populace to "liberate the birthplace" of Rama in Ayodhya—a very real town in the northern state of Uttar Pradesh—as part of a larger initiative to reorder India according to principles associated with the majority Hindu community. A Muslim shrine constructed in the 16th century by a general of Babur, founder of the Mughal empire (see Volume D), was alleged to have been built on the ruins of a medieval temple commemorating Rama's birthplace. Various Hindu groups demanded that a new temple be built in place of the mosque. Demonstrations and speeches, such as the anonymous one translated here that argues against any suggestion of compromise, stirred up public passion to such an extent that on 6 December 1992, a large mob gathered in Ayodhya and demolished the structure. This was a historic moment, the first major breach of the mutual respect for Muslim and Hindu religious monuments and antiquities since India's independence in 1947; the significance of this event for the future of the nation-state continues to be vigorously debated. Stories can have consequences.

2. Lord Vishvanatha, more commonly known as "Shiva," is the patron deity of Varanasi, also called "Kashi," on the banks of the Ganga (the Ganges River). Krishna, an avatar of Vishnu, is said to have been born in Mathura. Mahavira and Buddha (both 5th century B.C.E.) were the founders of Jainism and Buddhism, respectively, the two most prominent heterodox religious movements of the 1st millennium B.C.E. Banda Bairagi (d. 1716) espoused the Sikh faith and joined the tenth Guru of Sikhism, Guru Govind Singh, in his military campaigns in the southern plains against Mughal forces in an era of imperial disintegration.

3. A sage who, in the first book of the *Ramayana* of Valmiki, takes Rama into the surrounding wilderness to slay the demons that had been defiling holy sacrifices and harassing ascetics.

4. The chief minister of the Chandragupta Maurya (r. 321–268 B.C.E.), Chanakya is often identified with Kautilya, author of *The Treatise on Power*, page 854.

5. A pious sage known for having sacrificed his life in order to offer his bones to the gods. The bones were later fashioned into the thunderbolt with which the god Indra defeated many demons.

We are here to tell you about Rama, about Lakshmana. We are here to tell you about the bravery of the freedom fighter Bhagat Singh.[6] We are here to tell you about Maharana Pratap Singh, and the glories of Shivaji.[7]

India has a long tradition of sages coming to the rescue in a time of crisis. There was a time when the demon Ravana was harassing the world. In those days India had three rulers. There was king Dasharatha, but he was too busy with all of his religious sacrifices to be an effective ruler. There was King Janaka, but he too was a man of an overly spiritual bent. And then there was King Vali, who was too caught up in the pleasures of this world.

The poet Tulsidas brings up this dilemma: "All the kings were chagrined—how could this wicked demon be killed?" Although there were already three kings to rule the land, it was a wise sage who took charge in this difficult situation. He emerged from his lofty meditations to enter the realm of human action. He saw us through our hour of need.

Today it is just such a sage, following in the footsteps of the great sages before him, who has come into our midst to tell you what it is your country, your society, your religion, your culture needs. We have come to remind you that it is not so much the perpetrator of injustice that is at fault, as the one that puts up with it. Holy men have come here to spur our brave young men into action, to tell them that now is not the time to let us down. Don't let your mother ever say of you that her sons failed her in her hour of need.

And now the hour of need has come. We need your youth, your vigor, your faith. The blood of your heroic ancestors is coursing through your veins. We have seen enough of that kind of Hindu who stands as a paragon of tolerance in the world. We have seen enough of those Hindus who get up at the pulpit and spout universalist teachings. We have seen enough of those Hindus who preach that Allah and Ishvar are one. * * *

It's the same old story. They commit murder and nobody utters a peep. If we voice even the tiniest complaint, then it is we who are to blame. We are not even allowed to talk about the injustices being perpetrated against us. Why are we treated like pariahs in our own home? This isn't any particular person's fault. Collectively we act like a bunch of political eunuchs. It isn't the fault of the appeasement policy toward Muslims, either. It is our own fault that even though we number hundreds of millions we have never united ourselves. We have not tried to mobilize our strength, we have forgotten what it means to have pride in our culture. We have sold off our self-respect in the auction house of politics. * * *

A society that has forgotten what it means to value its heritage, a society that doesn't know what self-respect or pride is, might as well stand back and watch as politics tramples its culture underfoot. I don't need to tell you that this is happening to us. There is only one solution. The solution to our problems is for Hindus to band together. We need to break down the barriers of caste, we need to reconcile our language and regional differences. We need to be tightly bound, like fingers gathered into a fist. Hindus have traditionally shied away from using force, but now it's high

6. A militant Sikh nationalist and socialist revolutionary who founded the Young India Council in 1926 and was simultaneously active in the Hindustan Socialist Republican Association. He was executed by the British colonial government in 1932 for terrorist activities.
7. The Rajput ruler Maharana Pratap Singh (r. 1572–1597) is remembered for his chivalry and bravery in fighting against Akbar's forces in an attempt to maintain sovereignty over the Rajasthan area. Shivaji (r. 1674–1680) and the Maratha kingdom he led posed a formidable threat to the Mughal Empire.

time you started defending yourselves. You have lived like corpses already for too long, now you have to die in the fight for life. Do not shy away from death. You may have to embrace death in order to live. * * *

Our country's leaders are power-hungry. All they really care about is getting themselves elected. The politicians—those in power and the opposition, too—just care about appeasing the Muslims. * * * V. P. Singh has made sure that not one of our workers can participate in the Rama temple campaign. Well, all we have to say to this is that we don't want Rajiv's rule, we don't want V. P. Singh's rule.[8] It's Rama's rule that we want, and Hanuman is ready for action.

My Hindu brothers, you've shown enough sympathy for the rest of the world. You have always been a peace-loving people, the type to take pity on everybody else. Don't you know that this kind of pacifism can backfire, and those whom you treat with kindness and respect may one day turn around and stab you in the back? Our sages have resolved that the time has come for Hindus to start being concerned about themselves. Think about your children and future generations. Cast off the cloak of cowardice and weakness. It's time to adopt the ways of bravery and heroism. You just stood by and watched as the Somnath temple was looted, you didn't say a word.[9] The Somnath temple was destroyed before your very eyes, and you didn't retaliate. Many have come and attacked you, and you didn't defend yourselves. And what have you received in return for this pacifism? How have your gentle ways been rewarded? People have mistaken your good will, your kind-heartedness, your generosity for cowardice and weakness.

No Hindu has ever razed a mosque to the ground, but what did we get in return for our gentleness? Muhammad Gauri came, Mahmud of Gazni came.[1] Invaders kept on coming, one after the other. They attacked us and tried to destroy our culture. They demolished our temples, they violated the honor of our mothers and sisters—do you want to see this kind of appalling history repeated? * * *

My heroic brothers, I don't need to tell you that you should be wary of this country's leaders and all their antics. You'll recall that years ago before the creation of Pakistan there was all of this political rhetoric about "unity." When people began to talk of partition, our country's foremost leaders used to say they would rather die than see such a thing happen. But they did let it happen—our motherland was hacked in two and today separatist sentiments still plague us. In the Punjab we have the Khalistan movement, and secessionist movements have taken the northeast by storm.[2] Politicians may contest elections on the issue of unity, but what they're really doing is tearing our country apart. Soon all that will be left of U. P. is a tiny fragment—but their election campaigns will still consist of unity slogans. * * *

It doesn't matter how many times you shout out slogans about unity, or raising the living standards of the lower castes, or eradicating poverty. We're not going to be able to keep our country together with just a bunch of slogans. It's sacrifice we need,

8. Rajiv Gandhi became the prime minister of India under the secularist Congress Party after the assassination of his mother, Indira Gandhi, in 1984. Vishvanath Pratap Singh ruled as prime minister from 1989 to 1990, implementing affirmative action policies in favor of low castes, which upper castes held to be profoundly threatening to their interests.
9. Mahmud of Ghazni culminated a series of raids on Indian temple towns by plundering the Somnath temple on the western coast of India in 1026 C.E.

1. Mahmud of Ghazni used his plunder to further strengthen the Ghaznavid kingdom in central Asia. By contrast, the conquest of Muhammad Gauri in 1192 led to the establishment of an enduring political entity in India, the Delhi Sultanate.
2. The Khalistan movement called for a sovereign homeland for Sikhs in the state of Punjab in western India. In Assam and neighboring states in the northeast, tribal groups in particular have long sought autonomy.

not slogans. And our opportunistic leaders are not capable of sacrifice. Sacrifice can only come from those who truly love their country.

My brothers, I know that you love your country. That's why I am telling you to get ready for action. Seeing our country's crisis, these sages have gathered here to help us. The policy of appeasing special interest groups has brought our country to the brink of ruin. These leaders are just greedy for votes and they don't care one bit about India's future. None of your leaders has the guts to raise his hand in parliament and stick up for the issue of Rama's birthplace. Because it takes strength of character to speak the truth and that's something our leaders no longer have. It's been forty-two years since Independence. We may have made some progress in this country, but we've also had major setbacks. All the ideals that our forefathers sacrificed so much to preserve are vanishing before our eyes!

> Look at what's going on in the world, look at what things have come to.
> Is there anything that isn't for sale?
> Minds and bodies are for sale.
> Our parliament was sold off long ago. Now the nation itself is up for sale.
> Our natural resources are being plundered.
> Youth is for sale. Now religion is for sale.
> The honor and integrity of our elders are up for grabs now.
> Everything is for sale—people would sell their very own soul if they could.
> Go ask your sisters and mothers—their brothers and sons are for sale.
> What a strange place we live in—brides and bridegrooms are for sale.
> Leaders of today, take a good look around you.
> We are hurtling towards destruction. Is there anyone who can save us now?

In this day and age people think nothing of abandoning truth in their grab for power. They'd sacrifice all our religious principles, the heritage of our ancestors. * * *

But the truth about Lord Rama's birthplace is something that can't be denied. The birthplace of Rama has always belonged to the Hindus. It still does, and it always will. We won't rest until we build a magnificent temple at Rama's birthplace. My brothers, your confused leaders are demanding proof of the existence of Rama. Tell them that one of our most basic everyday greetings to one another is "Victory to Lord Rama!" When we are tired from a long day at work, we get relief from our weariness by calling out to Rama. Sometimes we may be overwhelmed by sorrow, but we say his name and we feel peace. Our very life originates in Rama, and when we die the pall bearers carry us away shouting, "The only sure thing in life is the name of Rama!"

And they are still demanding proof of Rama's existence? Tell the whole world that this country is Rama's, the very air we breathe is Rama's. And the Lord Rama has set an example for us—that we fight our enemies. We have never tried to interfere with anybody else's rights, we have always treated others with respect. But when justice became a mockery, then even the great monkey king Vali[3] had to be destroyed. And Rama gave the order to charge forth and wipe out the tyrant Ravana. When Hanuman on his own was able to reduce Lanka to ashes,[4] then surely we should not shrink from the task of defending Rama's birthplace.

3. Rama killed the monkey king Vali to consolidate his alliance with Vali's brother and rival, Sugriva.
4. In the *Ramayana* of Valmiki, the valorous monkey scout Hanuman is apprehended soon after locating Sita. Ravana orders his tail to be set on fire, but Hanuman escapes and with his burning tail sets the capital on fire.

How can people oppose the god Rama and still consider themselves Indian? That's just not possible! Shout it out so that the whole world can hear! It's not only India—the entire world knows that this country belongs to that supreme Lord Rama, king of Ayodhya. My fellow Rama devotees, political leaders like Chandrashekhar[5] tell us that we should build our temple elsewhere, as though it were possible simply to move our God's birthplace. I would say to him, "Chandrashekhar, are you able to trade in your father for someone else?" No, he can't just go out and get a new father. And we are supposed to change the birthplace of the Father of the World?

Other leaders say, "Do you have to build a temple there? How about installing a commemorative plaque or something?" Well, what the hell are we supposed to commemorate? That a certain plunderer named Babur invaded India? That he attacked us, and demolished our temple and with it our sense of self-respect? Is that what our leaders want to commemorate? * * * Some of your leaders actually do have eyes to see, and they agree that the birthplace of Rama belongs to the Hindus, but they are too afraid to speak up about it.

My brothers, it's time to get ready for action. These sages have come today to spur you to action. Those good-for-nothing cowards can't do anything to protect your India. We are waiting for brave men who will fight, who will be able to protect this country's pride and honor.

That is why I am telling you to bind yourselves together like fists. Your powers are too diffuse, you need to gather your forces. There are caste barriers among you—you must eradicate those. There are language and regional barriers—be rid of them. You have to bind yourselves together like fists, you have to protect your honor and your self-respect. * * *

We don't have a problem with those Muslims who love India, Muslims like Rahim or Raskhan.[6] We welcome them with open arms. But we will not tolerate the Baburs and the Aurangzebs.[7] This is the truth, I don't care how much it hurts, you must listen to it! Let it pierce you like an arrow in the heart! I don't care if this will make you angry, or make you break into a sweat. How long can we remain quiet and avoid confrontation? We are boiling over with rage—how long can we put up with this? We don't want anything to do with those hypocrites who have hacked off the arms of our motherland, who heap curses upon our Lord Rama and extol the glories of Babur the invader. There's no room in India for such as they. They should get out, this isn't their India. * * *

An election is around the corner. Suddenly you're going to see a lot of politicians claiming to be supporters of Rama and trying to garner votes on this issue. You're going to have to watch out for false supporters spewing slogans about Rama. In the *Ramayana* there was that false ascetic Kalanemi[8] who tried to kill Hanuman. That's what these fellows are like. * * *

Why are you so afraid of death? Death is something we're all going to have to face some day, there's no escaping that. What kind of death do you want, a dog's

---

5. The prime minister of India under the Janata Dal Party during 1990 and 1991.

6. Abdur Rahim Khankhana and Sujan Raskhan (late 16th and early 17th centuries) composed poetry in Hindi. Raskhan also composed verses in praise of the Hindu god Krishna.

7. Babur (1483–1530) was founder of the Mughal empire (see Volume D). Aurangzeb (r. 1658–1707) was the most orthodox-minded of the Mughal rulers and the most oppressive toward non-Muslim faiths.

8. A demon uncle of Ravana according to some *Ramayana* traditions.

death or a hero's death? Hindus aren't going to let their principles be mocked. It's time to forget about turning the other cheek. We've had enough of Hindu tolerance and pacifism. You're going to have to start fighting back.

This is the message that these holy men have come here to deliver. They have come to spur you to action. You must protect our motherland, and victory will be yours. We will not rest until we have built a magnificent temple at the site of Rama's birthplace. I'm not addressing this to the sons of Ravana, and for supporters of Rama there really isn't any need. But let me just ask everybody here to hold up their hands and to pledge an oath to Lord Rama.

> We pledge ourselves to Lord Rama!
> We pledge ourselves to Lord Rama!
> We pledge ourselves to Lord Rama!
> Victory to India!
> Victory to Lord Rama!

Daya Pawar, Sambhaji Bhagat, and Anand Patwardhan: *We Are Not Your Monkeys*[1]

The rulers who controlled all knowledge

And claimed the *Ramayana*
to be India's history

Called us many names:

5 "Demons," "Low castes," "Untouchables"

But we were the aborigines of this land

Listen to our story

Today we call ourselves
Dalits—the oppressed

10 Once Aryans[2] on their horses
invaded this land

And we who were natives
became the displaced

1. Translated by Anand Patwardhan. While the *Ramayana* of Valmiki has offered influential models of conduct to generations of men and women, it has also at times been regarded with considerable suspicion and resentment. Its ideal of gender relationships, for example—exemplified in the fire ordeal Sita faces (see page 895) or, worse, her abandonment by Rama when rumors begin to circulate in Ayodhya about her chastity (in Book 7)—has been viewed as a distorted one, increasingly so in the contemporary world. (When Hindu refugee women from Sind who had been raped during the Partition of India in 1947 were abandoned on the streets of Bombay by their husbands "because that is what Rama would have done," a modern Marathi poet was moved to compose a new version of the *Ramayana* with a different ending.) Similarly, many historically oppressed communities in South Asia

believe themselves to have been humiliatingly represented as the demons or animals of the tale. "We Are Not Your Monkeys" gives voice to this sentiment among today's Dalits (formerly known as "Untouchables") of the state of Maharashtra in western India. That Valmiki almost certainly had not intended any such simplistic identification is less important than the fact that people have often been made to feel he did. Something of this complex relationship between literature and power in a world of inequality was noted by critic Walter Benjamin when he observed that there is no document of civilization that is not at the same time a document of barbarism.
2. The Sanskrit term *arya* was typically applied to men of the upper social orders in early South Asia. It took on racial connotations in the works of 19th-century Orientalists and 20th-century fascists.

O Rama, O Rama!

15   You became the gods
And we the demons

You portrayed our Hanuman
as a monkey

O Rama, you representative
20   of Aryans

You enslaved us
to form a monkey army

Those you could not subjugate
you deemed as *Rakshasas*—demons

25   But we were the *Rakshaks*—protectors
of the forest

To keep your racial purity
you invented the hierarchy of caste

Through your "Laws of Manu"[3]
30   you trampled on the rights of women

You made your wife Sita undergo
An ordeal by fire to prove her chastity

Such was your male law
O Rama

35   When Shambuka the "untouchable"[4]
Tried to gain knowledge

You beheaded him O Rama

Thus did you crush those that tried
To rise above their caste

40   Days passed
Years and aeons went by

But our lives remained the same

We skin your cattle
So you can wear shoes

45   We clean your gutters
So you can stay clean

Do you ask then O Rama

What our caste is?
What our religion is?

---

3. An influential ancient work of Hindu customary law, the *Laws of Manu* is attributed in Hindu thought to one of the progenitors of the human race.

4. In the seventh book of Valmiki's *Ramayana,* Rama kills the low-caste Shambuka for engaging in ascetic practices reserved for the high caste.

50 Independence dawned

And with it began the rule
of the Constitution

The author of the Constitution

Dr. B. R. Ambedkar[5]
55 himself born as an "untouchable"

Framed the Constitution
around secular ideals

The castle of caste privilege
Began to crumble

60 No longer could the elite

Skim the milk
of religious exploitation

But poverty grew
And to divert the attention of the poor

65 A new enemy was found

Muslims were targeted
And "taught a lesson"

To destroy Lanka, O Rama
You formed us into a monkey army

70 And today you want us
The working majority

To form a new monkey army
And attack Muslims

But be warned

75 Be warned you purveyors
Of self-serving religion

We will be your monkeys no more

We will sing songs of humanity

And we will make you human as well

80 We will make you human.

⚜

---

5. Bhimrao Ramji Ambedkar (1891–1956), scholar, social activist, and politician, helped draft India's constitution and was the preeminent voice of the Dalits against caste discrimination.

⇌ PERSPECTIVES ⇌
What Is "Literature"?

Reflection on the nature of language and texts has been long and deep in India. It was probably first prompted by the prominence of the Veda in the life of Brahmanical communities: the desire to understand this body of archaic material and to reason out its sacred character stimulated the development of linguistic and other forms of careful analysis as early as 500 B.C.E. Systematic thought on literature, however, began only in the early centuries of the Common Era, following the development of Sanskrit poetry or *kavya* (see page 803). We have seen that one well-known typology divides the major textual forms of Sanskrit into three categories, depending on how they communicate the moral message thought to lie at the heart of each. "Revealed texts" (the Vedas) command us to act, as a master commands a servant; "accounts of the past" (such as the *Mahabharata* and the collections of ancient lore, *puranas*) advise us to act, as one friend advises another; literature seduces us to act, as a lover seduces the beloved. A second typology distinguishes texts according to their dominant language feature. In revealed texts the specific wording is dominant: if a sacred formula (*mantra*) is changed in the least way, the power of the text would be neutralized. In the *Mahabharata* and related texts, meaning is dominant and remains unaffected even if the wording is changed. In literature what is dominant is the peculiar combination of wording and meaning.

Identifying the specific difference of literature— "the soul of poetry," as it was put—was thus as important to early Indian thinkers as to modern literary critics, and many of their answers were strikingly similar as they began to develop them in the systematic treatises on literature produced from the seventh century on. There was no doubt that such a "soul" existed, however uncertain its exact nature may have been. No Indian theorist believed, as many do today, that "literature" can be whatever this or that reader or institution chooses to treat as literature. For the earliest Indian critics, literature's defining trait was thought to lie in some feature of language usage. This could be the special attention given to qualities of sound, such as the use of "soft" sounds for love poems, or more generally alliteration, assonance, and the like. Or it could be the use of figures of speech such as simile ("her face is like the moon"), metaphor ("her face is the moon itself"), and the dozens of subvarieties identified with remarkable acuity (*denial*, "that cannot be her face, it must be the moon"; *superiority*, "the moon has a dark spot, her face is unblemished," and so on). Or the literary could be understood through deeper perceptions about the nature of linguistic meaning. This line of thinking, based on the analysis of the very language of literature, reached its height among theorists in the later medieval period, beginning with Anandavardhana in the mid-ninth century. Other theorists focused their attention, first, on the nature of human experience in literature—how literature "fixes emotions, making them more permanently perceptible," as the American New Critics put it; later, others explored the reader's response to literature—what we in fact are experiencing when we have an aesthetic experience, a problem that has preoccupied scholars in the West, too, since the time of Aristotle. Or they reflected on the particular social worlds in which literature is made and through which it circulates. For a thousand years they argued over the nature of literature, suggesting at once the importance of the question and the elusiveness of the answer.

⊶ ⊷

The Ramayana of Valmiki

c. 200 B.C.E.

Valmiki's masterpiece marks a watershed not only in the way people of early South Asia understood their political world (see page 861) but also in the literary forms they used to write about that understanding. His epic is fully aware of its own novelty: it calls itself "the first poem," and it provides a detailed account of its own originality in the suggestive prologue given here. Valmiki recounts how a sage first passes on to him a tale about the doings of the great prince Rama—an entirely matter-of-fact story, which comes to Valmiki as if out of nowhere, precisely as folktales and legends are passed along in an unself-conscious culture. Valmiki next experiences a transformative moment of personal sorrow—*shoka,* or grief—when he sees a hunter kill a bird in the act of mating. Spontaneously he utters a curse in a form of language wholly unfamiliar to him, which he names *shloka,* or verse. The great deity Brahma, symbol of Sanskrit learning, then manifests himself to Valmiki and urges him to compose the whole story of Rama in the new form he has just invented. In deep meditation, Valmiki discovers all that has happened in Rama's life, even in private, and creates his monumental poem. This he transmits to two young performers—they turn out to be Rama's twin sons, who in the course of their travels wind up reciting the poem in their father's presence, as if to confirm its veracity.

If we ask what exactly is "first" about the first poem, this prologue points to several distinctive features. The *Ramayana* is in fact a grand elaboration of a popular tale into an extended narrative, and the sophisticated narrative technique (including the omniscient narrator) marks the work as the first of its kind in South Asia, as does the poem's highly self-conscious use of language, even though the verse form that Valmiki is said to have invented was actually very ancient. The *Ramayana* may also be the first text in which the Sanskrit language, long restricted to religious functions, was used for a story about human events and human emotions. The prologue also inaugurates the theme that "the poetry is in the pity": that the specific power of literature lies in its *rasa,* the expression of emotion. This aesthetic value would mark the writing of Sanskrit literature and the thinking about it for much of its history.

For more on Valmiki, see his principal listing, page 861.

from The Ramayana of Valmiki

[THE INVENTION OF POETRY][1]

from *Sarga 1*

Vālmīki, the ascetic, questioned the eloquent Nārada,[2] bull among sages, always devoted to asceticism and study of the sacred texts.

"Is there a man in the world today who is truly virtuous? Who is there who is mighty and yet knows both what is right and how to act upon it? Who always speaks the truth and holds firmly to his vows?

"Who exemplifies proper conduct and is benevolent to all creatures? Who is learned, capable, and a pleasure to behold?

"Who is self-controlled, having subdued his anger? Who is both judicious and free from envy? Who, when his fury is aroused in battle, is feared even by the gods?

"This is what I want to hear, for my desire to know is very strong. Great seer, you must know of such a man."

---

1. Translated by Robert P. Goldman.

2. A celebrated divine sage, often serving as a messenger between gods and men.

When Nārada, who was familiar with all the three worlds, heard Vālmīki's words, he was delighted. "Listen," he replied and spoke these words:

"The many virtues you have named are hard to find. Let me think a moment, sage, before I speak. Hear now of a man who has them all.

"His name is Rāma and he was born in the House of Ikṣvāku.[3] All men know of him, for he is self-controlled, mighty, radiant, steadfast, and masterful. * * *

"His people are pleased and joyful, contented, well-fed, and righteous. They are also free from physical and mental afflictions and the danger of famine.

"Nowhere in his realm do men experience the death of a son. Women are never widowed and remain always faithful to their husbands.

"Just as in the Golden Age, there is no danger whatever of fire or wind, and no creatures are lost in floods.

"He performs hundreds of Horse Sacrifices involving vast quantities of gold.[4] And, in accordance with custom, he donates tens and hundreds of millions of cows to the learned.

"Rāghava[5] is establishing hundreds of royal lines and has set the four social orders each to its own work in the world." * * *

Sarga 2

When the great and eloquent sage had heard his words, the righteous man and his disciples did Nārada great honor.

After the divine seer Nārada had been duly honored by the sage, he took his leave and receiving it, flew off into the sky.

Once Nārada had departed for the world of the gods, the sage went after a while to the bank of the Tamasā river, not far from the Jāhnavī, the Ganges.[6]

Upon reaching the Tamasā riverbank, the great sage spied a bathing spot that was free from mud and spoke to the disciple who stood beside him.

"Bharadvāja, look at this lovely bathing place so free from mud. Its waters are as lucid as the mind of a good man.

"Set down the water jar, dear boy, and give me my barkcloth robe, for I will bathe here at this excellent bathing spot of the Tamasā."

---

3. The family name of the royal house in Ayodhya, the capital of the Kosala kingdom. The original Ikshvaku was a son of Manu Vaivasvata, the son of the Sun, and the first of the Solar Kings.
4. A king claimed paramountcy over all the territory through which his horse wandered unopposed. Gold

would be distributed to priests who later sacrificed the horse.
5. A clan name of Rama's (descendent of Raghu).
6. The epithet for the Ganges, "daughter of Jahnu," refers to a king who in anger swallowed the river and only discharged it when appeased by gods and sages.

Addressed in this fashion by the great Vālmīka, Bharadvāja, always attentive to his guru, gave him his barkcloth robe.

Taking the barkcloth from his disciple's hands, he walked about, his senses tightly controlled, looking all about him at the vast forest.

Nearby, that holy man saw an inseparable pair of sweet-voiced *krauñca* birds wandering about.

But even as he watched, a Niṣāda[7] hunter, filled with malice and intent on mischief, struck down the male of the pair.

Seeing him struck down and writhing on the ground, his body covered with blood, his mate uttered a piteous cry.

And the pious seer, seeing the bird struck down in this fashion by the Niṣāda, was filled with pity.

Then, in the intensity of this feeling of compassion, the brahman thought, "This is wrong." Hearing the *krauñca* hen wailing, he uttered these words:

"Since, Niṣāda, you killed one of this pair of *krauñcas,* distracted at the height of passion, you shall not live for very long."

And even as he stood watching and spoke in this way, this thought arose in his heart, "Stricken with grief for this bird, what is this I have uttered?"

But upon reflection, that wise and thoughtful man came to a conclusion. Then that bull among sages spoke these words to his disciple:

"Fixed in metrical quarters, each with a like number of syllables, and fit for the accompaniment of stringed and percussion instruments, the utterance that I produced in this access of *śoka,* grief, shall be called *śloka,* poetry, and nothing else."

But the delighted disciple had memorized that unsurpassed utterance even as the sage was making it, so that his guru was pleased with him.

At last the sage took the prescribed ritual bath at the bathing spot and still pondering this matter, went back.

His disciple, the obedient and learned Bharadvāja, took up his guru's brimming water pot and followed behind him.

The sage, who knew the ways of righteousness, entered his ashram with his disciple, seated himself, and began to discuss various other matters, still lost in profound thought.

7. An ancient forest-dwelling people.

Then the mighty four-faced lord Brahmā[8] himself, the maker of the worlds, came to see the bull among sages.

Seeing him, Vālmīki rose quickly and without a word. He stood subdued and greatly wonderstruck, his hands cupped in reverence.

Then he worshiped the god, offering water for his feet, the welcome offering, a seat, and hymns of praise. When he had made the prescribed prostration before him, he asked after his continuing well-being.

Once the holy lord was seated in a place of honor, he motioned the great seer Vālmīki also to a seat.

But even though the Grandfather of the worlds himself sat there before him, Vālmīki, his mind once more harking back to what had happened, lapsed again into profound thought:

"That wicked man, his mind possessed by malice, did a terrible thing in killing such a sweet-voiced *krauñca* bird for no reason."

Grieving once more for the *krauñca* hen, given over wholly to his grief and lost in his inner thought, he sang the verse again right there before the god.

With a smile, Brahmā spoke to the bull among sages, "This is a *śloka* that you have composed. You needn't be perplexed about this.

"Brahman, it was by my will alone that you produced this elegant speech. Greatest of seers, you must now compose the entire history of Rāma.

"You must tell the world the story of the righteous, virtuous, wise, and steadfast Rāma, just as you heard it from Nārada, the full story, public and private, of that wise man. For all that befell wise Rāma, Saumitri,[9] the *rākṣasas,* and Vaidehī,[1] whether in public or private, will be revealed to you, even those events of which you are ignorant.

"No utterance of yours in this poem shall be false. Now compose the holy story of Rāma fashioned into *ślokas* to delight the heart.

"As long as the mountains and rivers shall endure upon the earth, so long will the story of the *Rāmāyaṇa* be told among men.

"And as long as the story of Rāma you compose is told, so long will you live on in my worlds above and below."

When the holy lord Brahmā had spoken in this fashion, he vanished on the spot, and the sage Vālmīki and his disciples were filled with wonder.

---

8. The creator god, who with his four mouths simultaneously recites the four Vedas.
9. "Son of Sumitra," a name of Rama's younger brother

Lakshmana.
1. "Daughter of Videha," a name of Rama's wife, Sita, who was daughter of the king of Videha country.

Then all his disciples chanted that *sloka* again. Delighted and filled with wonder, they said over and over again:

"The *soka*, grief, that the great seer sang out in four metrical quarters, all equal in syllables, has, by virtue of its being repeated after him, become *sloka*, poetry."

Then the contemplative Vālmīki conceived this idea: "Let me compose an entire poem, called the *Rāmāyaṇa*, in verses such as these."

And thus did the renowned sage with enormous insight compose this poem that adds to the glory of the glorious Rāma, with hundreds of *slokas* equal in syllables, their words noble in sound and meaning, delighting the heart.

from *Sarga 3*

And so it came about that the righteous man, having learned the entire substance of that story, exemplary of righteousness, the tale of wise Rāma, sought to make it public.

First the sage sipped water in the prescribed fashion. Then seated on *darbha* grass with the tips pointed east and cupping his hands reverently, he sought through profound meditation the means of access to this tale.

Rāma's birth, his great strength and kindliness to all, the people's love for him, his forbearance, gentleness, and truthful nature ∗ ∗ ∗ all of this did the holy seer Vālmīki render into poetry. Even those events that had not yet befallen Rāma on earth were rendered in the latter portion of his poem.

Sarga 4

It was after Rāma had regained his kingdom that the holy and self-controlled seer Vālmīki composed this entire history in such wonderful words.

When the wise master had finished it, including the sections dealing with the future and final events, he thought, "Who should perform it?"

And as the great contemplative seer was pondering this, Kuśa and Lava[2] in the guise of sages came and touched his feet.

He looked at the two glorious brothers, Kuśa and Lava, who lived in his ashram, for they were sons of the king, familiar with the ways of righteousness, and had sweet voices.

Perceiving that they were well grounded in the *vedas* and had excellent memories, he accepted them as students of vedic exegesis.

---

2. The twin sons of Rama and Sita. Valmiki had provided refuge to the pregnant Sita after she was banished by Rama from the Kosala kingdom.

A man who always fulfilled his vows, he taught them the whole of this great poem, the *Rāmāyaṇa,* which is the tale of Sītā and the slaying of Paulastya. It is sweet both when recited and when sung in the three tempos to the seven notes of the scale, and it is eminently suitable for the accompaniment of both stringed and percussion instruments.

The two disciples sang the poem, which is replete with all the poetic sentiments: the humorous, the erotic, the piteous, the wrathful, the heroic, the terrifying, the loathsome, and the rest.

The brothers, beautiful as *gandharvas,*[3] had beautiful voices and were well versed in the *gandharvas'* musical art. They were expert in both articulation and modulation.

Gifted with beauty and auspicious marks, they spoke with sweet voices. Like twin reflections they seemed, born of the same image, Rāma's body.

That unsurpassed tale is exemplary of righteousness, and so the two blameless sons of the king learned the entire poem by heart.

And when they had done so, the two great and gifted men, who understood its essence and were marked by every auspicious sign, sang it as they had been instructed, with single-minded concentration before assemblies of seers, brahmans, and good men.

Now on one occasion the two sang the poem in the presence of some pure-minded seers who were seated in an assembly.

When the sages heard it, their eyes were clouded with tears and filled with the greatest wonder, they all said to the two, "Excellent, excellent!"

All the sages, glad at heart and loving righteousness, praised Kuśa and Lava as they sang, for they were worthy of praise:

"Ah, the sweetness of the singing and especially the poetry! Even though this all took place so long ago, it is as though it were happening before our very eyes."

Then the two of them together, entering fully into the emotion of the story, sang it with the full range of notes, sweetly and with feeling.

Praised in this fashion by those great seers, who were themselves to be extolled for their asceticism, they sang more sweetly still and with still greater feeling.

One sage there, delighted, gave them a water jar. Another, a man of great renown, gave them a barkcloth mantle.

---

3. A class of demigods famous as the singers and musicians of the gods in heaven.

This wondrous tale that the sage told and that he completed in perfect sequence is the great source of inspiration for poets.

Now it happened that on one occasion, the elder brother of Bharata saw there those two singers who were being praised everywhere on the roads and royal highways.

And Rāma, the destroyer of his enemies, brought the brothers, Kuśa and Lava, to his own dwelling where he honored them, for they were worthy of honor.

Then lord Rāma, chastiser of his foes, seated on a heavenly throne of gold with his ministers and brothers sitting nearby, looked at the two beautiful youths with their lutes and spoke to Lakṣmaṇa, Śatrughna, and Bharata.

"Let us listen to this tale, whose words and meaning alike are wonderful, as it is sweetly sung by these two godlike men.

"For although these two sages, Kuśa and Lava, are great ascetics, they bear all the marks of kings. Moreover, it is said that the profound tale they tell is highly bene-ficial, even for me. Listen to it."

Then at a word from Rāma, the two of them began to sing in the full perfection of the *mārga* mode. And right there in the assembly, even Rāma, in his desire to experi-ence it fully, gradually permitted his mind to become enthralled.

┉ ≡♦≣ ┉

Rajashekhara
early 900s

A quite different story from the *Ramayana* concerning the birth of literature comes from an un-finished encyclopedic treatise written by Rajashekhara, a playwright, literary theorist, and much-anthologized poet belonging to the first half of the tenth century. Again, the invention of metrical speech is held to distinguish "literature" in an important way (Valmiki's first verse has now become something of poetic charm), but there the similarity between the two stories ends. Rajashekhara is concerned not with literature as such but with literature as the expression of a particular world, both social and spatial. Poetry Man—he is modeled on the ancient Vedic Pri-mal Man—wanders through this world and thereby creates the regional types of Sanskrit litera-ture, comprising different literary styles and different musical modes and costuming for drama. But it all remains Sanskrit literature, and it belongs to one particular world only. (This is, of course, factually incorrect, given the spread of Sanskrit literary culture to Southeast Asia, Tibet, and beyond. See the introduction to Early South Asia, page 799.) Poetry Man's marriage to Poetics Woman may suggest to us a more general relationship between literary creativity (Poetry Man) and the disciplining of this creation through metrics, rhetoric, aesthetics, and the like (Poetics Woman), which has more universal application in the history of literature. But for Rajashekhara, Sanskrit literature itself comes into being in a particular world and has relevance only there. The relationship thought to exist between literary language and locale exerted powerful effects elsewhere, especially in the form of modern European nationalism. As the nineteenth-century German philosopher Gottfried Herder put it, "All events in the human sphere, like all productions of nature, are decreed solely by time, locality, and national character." As Rajashekhara's work shows, this theme has a long and complex history.

PRONUNCIATION:
Rajashekhara: RAH-juh-SHAY-kuh-ruh

from *Inquiry into Literature*[1]

[POETRY MAN WEDS POETICS WOMAN]

I once heard from my teacher the following ancient and auspicious tale:

Once upon a time, the students of Brihaspati, counselor to the gods, put a question to him in the course of their lessons: "You said that your own guru was Kavyapurusha, "Poetry Man," the son of Sarasvati, Goddess of Speech. Who was he?" Brihaspati answered them as follows:

Long ago Sarasvati performed ascetic penance on Snowy Mountain, in hopes she might give birth to a son. Lord Brahma was pleased by this, and said to her, "I will create a son for you." And in due course she gave birth to Poetry Man. No sooner was he born than he paid homage at her feet and spoke the following metrical speech:

> All the universe is made of language
> and objects are its magic transformation.
> Here am I, mother, your transformation, Poetry
> incarnate, I who now clasp your feet.

The Goddess, seeing the stamp of versification—something previously unique to the language of the Veda[2]—now present in the realm of everyday speech, embraced him with joy, and whispered to him, "Child, inventor of metrical speech, you surpass even me, your mother and the mother of all that is made of language. How true what people say, that to be outdone by one's own son is like having a second. Before your birth, the learned knew only prose, not verse. Today, metrical speech, which you have discovered on your own, begins its life. What praises you deserve. Your body consists of words and meanings, your mouth consists of Sanskrit, your arm of Prakrit, your groin of Apabhramsha, your feet of Paishacha, your chest of mixed language.[3] You are balanced, clear, sweet, noble, and forceful. Your speech is brilliant utterance, your soul aesthetic feeling, your hair the different meters, your wit question-answer poems, riddles, and the like, while alliteration, simile, and the other figures of speech adorn you. The Veda itself, which gives voice to things to come, has praised you thus:

> Four horns he has, three feet, two heads, seven hands;
> thrice-bound he roars; a great god
> who has entered the mortal world.

Powerful being though you may really be, pretend you are not so now, and take on the ways of a child."

With this, she placed him on the couch-like bench of a large boulder under a tree and went to bathe in the heavenly Ganges. At that very moment, the great sage

1. Translated by Sheldon Pollock.
2. The versified texts of the Veda were reserved for sacred liturgy.
3. Regarding Prakrit, see pages 802–803. Apabhramsha

was another literary dialect used especially for pastoral poetry. Paishacha was said to be the language of a single text, the "Great Tale," a lost story collection. "Mixed language" is a mélange of the four, used in Sanskrit drama.

Ushanas,[4] who had come out to gather fuel and sacred *kusha* grass, found the child lying overcome by heat in the noonday sun. Wondering who might be the parent of this unprotected child he brought him to his own ashram. When after a moment Sarasvateya[5] revived, he bestowed on him metrical speech. And then suddenly Ushanas proclaimed, to the astonishment of all those present:

> Day after day the poets milk her,
> yet she is never milked dry!
> May Sarasvati, dairy cow of poetry,
> be ever present in our hearts.[6]

Then Ushanas taught that knowledge to his students. From that time on wise men have referred to Ushanas as Kavi or the "wise one," and it is by way of allusion to him that poets are designated *kavi* in everyday usage. This word for "poet" is derived from the verbal root *kav,* which literally means "to describe," and "poetry" (*kavya*) means literally "the object [produced by the poet]." The compound "Poetry Man," for its part, is used figuratively in reference to Sarasvateya because he is no other than poetry itself.

The Goddess of Speech soon returned and, failing to find her son, she wept from the very depths of her heart. Now, Valmiki, the best of sages, happened to be passing by. Humbly he told her what had happened and showed the Blessed Goddess the ashram of Ushanas, son of Bhrigu. With her breasts moist with milk she embraced her son and kissed him on the head; and out of good will toward Valmiki, son of Pracetas,[7] she secretly made over metrical language to him, too. Later, after she had dismissed him, he came upon the sight of a young curlew crying mournfully for his mate, whom a Nishada hunter had killed. And filled with grief (*shoka*) the poet uttered this first verse (*shloka*), in a voice that wailed mournfully:

> May you never find happiness in all your living years, Nishada,
> for killing one of these curlews in the act of making love.

Then the Goddess, with divine vision, granted a secret power to this very verse: Any poet who should recite it first, this one verse, before reciting any other, would become a son to Sarasvati herself. For his part, the great sage, from whom this utterance first emerged, composed the history called the *Ramayana.* Dvaipayana Vyasa, reciting the same verse first and by reason of its power, composed the collection of one hundred thousand verses called the *Mahabharata.*

Now, some time later, when two distinguished Brahman sages were having a dispute about scripture, the Self-existent God Brahma, ever diplomatic, referred the question to Sarasvati for judgment. Hearing of the goings on, her son was ready to accompany her, but she refused to allow him. "For one like you who has not received permission from Paramesthin Brahma, Lord Who stands on high" she said, "the voyage to His world can be perilous," and so turning him back she set out on her own. Poetry Man stalked off in anger, and when he did, his best friend, Kumara, began to cry and scream. "Be still, Kumara, my child," said Shiva's wife Uma to him, "I'll put a stop to this." And she fell to thinking. "The only bond that holds people back is

---

4. A sage famous for his authority in political and religious matters and therefore called "Kavi," or sage-poet, in Vedic texts. He is the son of Bhrigu, ancestor of a famous family of brahman seers called the "Bhargavas."

5. Poetry Man ("son of Sarasvati").

6. The verse provides at once an example of poetic utterance in the metaphoric mode while expressing the infinitely generative nature of poetic figures.

7. A legendary sage and lawgiver.

love. I will create a special woman to keep Sarasvati's son in thrall." She then gave birth to Sahityavidya, "Poetics Woman," and she instructed her as follows, "This is your lawful husband, who has stalked off in anger. Follow him and bring him back. And you sages who are present, perfected in the science of literary art, go sing the deeds of these two, Poetry and Poetics. This will prove to be a treasure-store of literature for you." The blessed Uma then fell silent, and they all set out as directed.

They went first to the east, where are found the peoples of eastern Bihar, central Bengal, the Ganges delta, Burma, and Chota Nagpur. As the daughter of Uma tried to entice Poetry Man she put on different kinds of dress in the different regions, and this was imitated by the women of the various places. In that first place the costume was named after Orissa and Magadha, and was praised by the sages as follows:

> Woven necklaces on chests wet with sandalwood paste,
> scarves kissing the parted hair, a glimpse of the breasts,
> bodies the hue of *durva* grass from the use of aloe—
> may such costume ever regale the women of Bengal.

And the men of that country also adopted the attire Sarasvateya himself happened to be wearing, and it became the male costume specific to Orissa and Magadha. As for the dance and music-making and so on that she performed, that became the *bharati* mode, and the sages praised it as they had done earlier. And what he spoke when as yet not under her thrall, incomparable though she was—verses dense with compounds and alliteration, and filled with repeated use of words in their conventionally restricted etymological signification—that became known as the literary Path of Bengal. And the sages praised it as they had done earlier. In due course I shall discuss the nature of modes and literary Paths.

Next he went north to the country of Panchala, where are found the peoples of the Ganges plain, the region of Mathura, the environs of Delhi, Kashmir, Punjab, and Balkh. As the daughter of Uma tried to entice Poetry Man, it went as before. Her costume there was called the central Panchala, and was praised by the sages as follows:

> Cheeks with flashing sparkles of dangling earrings,
> bright necklaces gently swinging hanging down to the midriff,
> garments billowing out from hips to ankles—
> pay homage to the costume of the women of Kanauj.

This time Sarasvateya's interest was peeked. As before, the men of that country also adopted the attire he was wearing then. As for the partial dance, vocal and instrumental music, and graceful gesture that she displayed, that became the *sattvati* mode, and because it had sinuous movements it was also called the *arabhati*. The sages gave praise as they had done earlier. And what Sarasvateya spoke when partly in her thrall, incomparable though she was—verses with partial compounds and modest alliteration, and filled with metaphorical expressions—that became known as the Path of Panchala.

Next he went west to the country of Avanti, where are found the peoples of Ujjain, Bhopal, Surat, Malwa, Abu, Broach. As the daughter of Uma tried to entice Poetry Man, it went as before. Her costume there was called the *avanti*—it is midway between the central Panchala and the southern costume. Accordingly, too, there are two modes there, the *sattvati* of the north and the *kaishiki* of the south. And it was praised by the sages as follows:

> The men and women wear the costume of Panchala,
> and that of the south—may they all find pleasure in it!

> The recitation and gestures, too, of men and women
> in the land of Avanti combine both Paths.

Next he reached the southern region, where are found the peoples of the western Ghats, the Maikal range, northern Karnakata, Kerala, Maharashtra, southern Karnataka, north coastal Andhra/Orissa. As the daughter of Uma tried to entice Poetry Man, it went as before. Her costume there was called the Southern. And it was praised by the sages as follows:

> Coiffeur of braided hair curly down to the root,
> foreheads marked with fragrant saffron powder,
> the knot of skirts made tight by tucking at the waist—
> long live the costume of the women of Kerala.

This time Sarasvateya fell deeply in love with her. As before, the men of that country also adopted the attire he was wearing then. As for the complex dance, vocal and instrumental music and graceful gesture she manifested, that became the *kaishiki* mode. The sages gave praise as they had done earlier. And what Sarasvateya spoke when altogether enthralled by her—verses with moderate alliteration and no compounds, and only infrequent use of words in their etymological signification—became known as the Path of Vidarbha. And the sages praised it as they had done earlier. * * *

In the country of Vidarbha there is city called Vatsagulma, where the God of Love often comes to play. There the son of Sarasvati married the daughter of Uma by the rite of the love-marriage. The bride and groom in due course left that place, and enjoying themselves in the different regions on the way returned to Snowy Mountain, where Uma and Sarasvati, now kin by marriage, were dwelling. The young couple made obeisance to them, and their mothers gave them their blessing and had them take up their dwellings, in the form of imagination, in the minds of poets.

By their creation of this pair they have made a heavenly world for poets, a place where poets, while continuing to dwell in the mortal world with a body made of poetry, may rejoice for all ages with a body divine.

> Thus the Self-Existent Brahma created Poetry Man.
> And the poet who understands his ways,
> and those of Poetics Woman,
> will rejoice in this world and the world beyond.

Anandavardhana
mid-800s

Anandavardhana's *Light on Suggestion* marks the high point in Sanskrit linguistic analysis of the soul of literature. Anandavardhana argued that there are degrees of literariness. The literary qualities earlier thinkers had identified were real enough but only ornaments on the body of the literary text, not its soul. Something truly essential must exist that distinguishes the best literature from all other kinds of verbal communication. Anandavardhana believed he discovered this in something he named *dhvani*, literally "sound" or "echo," but used in the sense of "suggestion." He found this phenomenon first and most manifestly visible in early Prakrit poetry (see Love in a Courtly Language, page 930), but he believed it to be a feature of poetic language as such. Consider the phrase "a village on the Ganges." We don't take this phrase literally because villages (in India at least!) are built *next* to rivers, not on them. In everyday language use, such figures of speech imply nothing; in literature, however, where aesthetic effects are sought and expected, innumerable *suggestions* are generated when we reflect on why the poet said "on" rather than "on the bank of," perhaps to suggest how the village partakes of the river's special qualities: coolness, holiness, and so on.

The expressive power at work in this elementary example can be generalized, according to Anandavardhana, to account for all of the most distinctive phenomena of literary expression. *Dhvani* can invert the surface meaning of a statement: when a young woman tells a wandering ascetic that he can "go his rounds freely" on the bank of the Goda since a lion has killed the dog that used to harass him (page 923), her invitation is to be taken as a prohibition, implying her desire to protect her rendezvous place on the river and also suggesting her cleverness in indicating this without saying it. *Dhvani* can suggest a figure of speech like a simile, as when warriors are said to delight more in the round, protruding temples of the enemy elephants they slay than in the breasts of their wives. And *dhvani* alone communicates *rasa,* which can never be directly expressed (one does not make a poem erotic by declaring, "This is an erotic poem"), and it can do so in very complex ways. When a wife, grieving for her husband slain in the Bharata war, spots his severed hand and laments, "Here is the hand that once loosened the belt of my skirt," the dominant *rasa* of pity is made more complex by the "suggested *rasa*" of the erotic. The elements of a literary text can no longer be thought of as detachable ornaments; on the contrary, they can be considered literary only to the extent they contribute to the overall effect of the text. And that the literary text has such a unified meaning or impact is something Anandavardhana seems also to have been the first to argue, as he does even in the case of the sprawling *Mahabharata.*

On this understanding, then, "literature" is that kind of language use that invites us to really listen, to hear echoes in every word and in the work itself as a whole, to hear what is meant even when it isn't said.

PRONUNCIATIONS:
Anandavardhana: AH-nuhn-duh-VAHR-dhuh-nuh
dhvani: DHVUH-nee

from Light on Suggestion[1]

[MEANING WITHOUT SAYING]

K[2] Some have said that the soul of poetry, which has been handed down from the past by wise men as "suggestion" (*dhvani*), does not exist; others, that it is an associated meaning (*bhākta*), while some have said that its nature lies outside the scope of speech: of this [suggestion] we shall here state the true nature in order to delight the hearts of sensitive readers.

A By wise men, that is, by those who know the essence of poetry named "suggestion" (*dhvani*), which has been handed down from the past through a succession [of wise men], that is to say, has been made fully known far and wide: this [entity], in spite of its being clearly apparent to the hearts of sensitive readers, some have claimed to be non-existent.

1. Translated by Daniel H. H. Ingalls, Jeffrey M. Masson, and M. V. Patwardhan.
2. "K" refers to a *karika,* or summary verse; and "A"
refers to *Aloka* ("Light"), its exposition. Both are now attributed to Anandavardhana.

The following alternative ideas are possible for those who deny the existence of suggestion.

1.1 A

A Here some might contend that poetry is nothing more than what is embodied in word and meaning. The means of beautifying this pair that lie in sound, such as alliteration, and those that lie in meaning, such as simile, are well known. Also well known are [those qualities] such as sweetness, which possess certain properties of phoneme and arrangement. The *vṛttis,* which have been described by some writers under such names as *upanāgarikā,* and which are not different in function from these [figures and qualities] also have reached our ears.[3] So also the styles (*rītis*) such as the Vaidarbhī.[4] What is this thing called *dhvani* that it should differ from these?

1.1 B

A Others might say: There is no such thing as *dhvani.* For a type of poetry that falls outside our well-known system would no longer be poetry. The correct definition of poetry is that which consists of sounds and meaning which delight the heart of a sensitive audience. To a method which differs from the system which has been laid down this [definition] is inapplicable. Moreover, if you were to confer the title of "sensitive audience" on some few persons who belong to your persuasion and on that basis assign to *dhvani* the title of poetry, you would not thereby gain the assent of the general body of educated men.

1.1 C

A Still others might argue for its non-existence in another way. *Dhvani* simply cannot be something entirely new because, being something that falls within the area of beauty, it must be included in the means of beautifying poetry that have been mentioned [in earlier works on poetics]. It is trivial to single out one of these means and merely give it a new name. Moreover, as the possibilities of speech are limitless, there may well be some small variety that has not been dealt with by the well-known compilers of definitions for poetry. Even so, we cannot see any justification here [for the proponents of *dhvani*] to close their eyes in the fond imagination that they are sensitive critics and to dance about chanting *"dhvani, dhvani."* Others, great men too, have shown in the past different varieties of beauty in poetry by the thousand and continue to do so. But we do not find them acting in this indecorous fashion. As a matter of fact, *dhvani* is mere prattle. It is simply not possible to put forward anything as a definition of *dhvani* that can bear critical examination. In this vein someone has written a verse on the matter:

> A fool will take a poem that has no content
> to make the heart rejoice, no ornament,
> no words to show the author's skill,
> no striking turn of speech;
> and tell you with delight

---

3. A *vritti* is mode of gesture and speech; *upanagarika* (literally, "sub-urban") is a kind of alliteration formed of mellifluous-sounding letters.
4. One of three or four ostensible regional styles that

evolved in Sanskrit poetry, generally known for its moderate alliteration and absence of complicated compounds. "Poetry Man Weds Poetics Woman" allegorically accounts for their origins.

that this same poem is full of *dhvani.*
If you who are wise should ask him, I am sure
he could not tell you what this *dhvani* is.

1.1 D

A "Others say that it is an associated meaning (*bhākta*)": others say that this soul of poetry which we call *dhvani* is [merely] secondary usage (*guṇavṛtti*).[5] And although the authors of definitions for poetry have not given the specific name *dhvani* to secondary usage nor to any other sort of thing, still, in showing how secondary usage is employed in poetry, they have at least touched on the process of *dhvani* even if they have not actually defined it. It is with this in mind that [the *Kārikā*] states, "Others say that it is an associated meaning."

1.1 E

A Finally some, whose minds have shied away from attempting a definition, have declared that the true nature of *dhvani* lies outside the realm of speech, that it can only be felt and that only by a sensitive reader. Therefore, in view of such disagreements, we shall state its true nature in order to delight the hearts of sensitive readers. For the nature of this *dhvani,* which is the secret of all good poets' poetry, which despite its extraordinary beauty has not been opened to view by the subtle minds of the ancient makers of definitions of poetry, which, moreover, is clearly seen to be at work in such great poems as the *Rāmāyaṇa* and the *Mahābhārata,* will here be revealed so that the bliss [which arises] in the hearts of sensitive readers on their noticing it in [the poems that form] the object of their attention, may take firm hold in their hearts.

1.2

K Meaning, which has been praised by sensitive critics and determined to be the soul of poetry, is traditionally held to have two varieties, the literal and the implied.

A Meaning, which is praised by sensitive critics as being essential to a poem and therefore what the soul is to a body already charming by the configuration of graceful and appropriate parts, has two varieties, the literal and the implied.

1.3

K Of these [two varieties] the literal meaning is well known and has been analysed by others into many figures such as simile. We shall therefore not expatiate upon it here.

1.4

K On the other hand, the suggested is something different, found in the works of great poets. It is that which appears as [something] separate from the well-known elements

---

5. Opponents of the *dhvani* theory argued it was nothing more than what was already known as "associated" or "secondary usage," two different terms for what we would call figurative speech in general, and metaphor and metonymy in particular.

[of poetry], just as charm in a woman [is something that appears different from the well-known individual parts of her body].

A The suggested, on the other hand, is something which is found in the speech of great poets, different from the literal meaning. It is that which is well-known to sensitive readers and is separate from the known, ornamented, elements [of poetry], after they have been examined, being thus like charm in women. For just as charm is a certain something in women, a feast to the eyes of the discriminating, distinct from all the parts of the body after they have been examined, just so is this [suggested] meaning.

For this meaning, implied by force of the literal sense, will be shown to be divisible into several categories: a simple thing, a figure of speech, a *rasa,* etc. In each of these varieties what is suggested is different from the literal meaning. Thus, even the first variety is totally different from the literal sense. For sometimes where the literal meaning is an injunction, the suggested meaning takes the form of a prohibition.

For example:

> Go your rounds freely, gentle monk;
> the little dog is gone.
> Just today from the thickets by the Godā
> came a fearsome lion and killed him.

Sometimes when the literal meaning is a prohibition, this [suggested meaning] takes the form of an injunction (or invitation), as in:

> Mother-in-law sleeps here, I there:
> look, traveler, while it is light.
> For at night when you cannot see
> you must not fall into my bed.

Sometimes the literal meaning is in the form of an injunction, while the suggested meaning takes a form that is neither [injunction nor prohibition]. Thus,

> Go, and let the sighs and tears
> be mine; nor let them rise
> from you as well, tortured,
> being without her, by your hateful courtesy.

Sometimes the literal meaning is in the form of a prohibition, while the suggested meaning takes a form that is neither [prohibition nor injunction]. Thus,

> Turn back, I beg you. You are making trouble
> for other ladies stealing to their lovers.
> The moonlight of your countenance destroys
> their covering darkness, wretched woman.[6]

---

6. As the "wretched" woman of this poem is its addressee, the suggested meaning of the poem, as stated, is neither prohibition nor injunction, but praise.

Sometimes the suggested meaning is made to be directed to a person (or persons) different from that (or those) to whom the literal meaning is directed. Thus:

> Who wouldn't be angry to see
> his dear wife with her lower lip
> bitten?
> You scorned my warning to smell
> the bee-holding lotus. Now you must
> suffer.

1.5

K It is just this meaning that is the soul of poetry. And so it was that, long ago, grief, arising in the first poet from the separation of the pair of curlews, became verse.[7]

A It is just this [inner] meaning that is the essence of a poem, which has [outward] beauty in its wealth of direct meaning, word, and structure. And so it was that the grief (*śoka*) of the first poet, Vālmīki, born of the wailing of the cock curlew desolated by loss of its slain mate, turned into verse (*śloka*). For grief is the basic emotion of the flavor of compassion (*karuṇarasa*) [which, as has been said, appears only as suggested].

1.6

K Sarasvatī, [working] within great poets, in pouring forth this sweet matter [viz., the emotions and flavors] reveals a special, vibrant, genius, which is superhuman.

A The divine speech of great poets, in pouring forth this essential matter, reveals a special, vibrant, genius, which is superhuman. Thus it is in this world, where there has been a long succession of poets of every possible kind, that only two or three, or maybe five or six, such as Kālidāsa, can be counted as great poets.

A Here is another proof of the existence of a suggested meaning:

1.7

K It is not understood by the mere knowledge of grammar and dictionaries. It is understood only by those who know the true nature of poetic meaning.

A Because this [suggested] sense is understood only by those who know the nature of poetic meaning. If this meaning were denotative, one would get to it by a knowledge of literal, denotative meanings and the words that convey them. But this meaning is beyond the range of those who have taken pains only on the definitions of words and who have paid no attention to the study of poetic meaning, just as the character of the notes is beyond the range of those who know the definitions of music but are not good singers.

Having thus proven the existence of a suggested meaning which differs from the direct meaning, he goes on to show the greater importance of the suggested:

1.8

K This meaning and whatever particular word has the capability of conveying it are the meaning and the word which should be carefully scrutinized (or recognized) by a great poet.

---

7. The allusion is to Valmiki's invention of poetry in the *Ramayana* (see page 909).

A The suggested meaning and the particular word that has the capability of conveying it, not just any word: this word and meaning should be scrutinized (or recognized) by a great poet. It is by the proper use of the suggested sense and the word that suggests it that a great poet deserves his name, not by mere structuring of the denoting word and the denoting meaning.

Now, although a correct choice of suggested meaning and suggestive word is more important, it is right that poets should first turn their attention to the correct choice of denoted meaning and denoted word.

1.9

K Just as a man who wishes to see will take pains with the flame of the lamp as a means thereto, just so will a man who cares for this [suggested meaning] take pains [first] with the denoted sense.

A For just as a man, although the object of his wish is to see, will take pains with the flame of the lamp as a means thereto, for it is impossible to see without the flame of the lamp, just so will a man who cares for the suggested meaning take pains with the denoted sense.

So far the author has described the communicating poet's engagement with the suggested meaning. In order to describe the engagement of the recipient audience he goes on to say:

1.10

K Just as the sentence-meaning is apprehended through the meaning of the words, just so is the apprehending of this matter preceded by the denoted sense.

A For just as the sentence meaning is understood through the meaning of the words, just so is the understanding of the suggested meaning preceded by an understanding of the denoted sense.

A Now the author shows that the greater importance of the suggested meaning is not impugned by the fact that it is apprehended after the apprehension of the denoted meaning.

1.11

K Just as the meaning of an individual word, by force of its capability, acts toward conveying the sentence meaning, but is no longer distinguished after its activity is completed * * *

A Just as the meaning of an individual word, by force of its capability, acts toward revealing the sentence meaning, but is no longer distinguished apart [from the sentence meaning] after its activity is completed * * *

1.12

K Just so does the suggested sense flash forth in an instant in the minds of intelligent auditors who are averse to the literal sense and in quest of the real meaning.

A Having thus shown the existence of the suggested meaning as distinct from the literal, he puts it to use in the matter at issue.

1.13

K The type of poetry which the wise call *dhvani* is that in which sense or word, subordinating their own meaning, suggest that [suggested] meaning.

A The type of poetry which the wise call *dhvani* is that in which sense, viz., a particular literal sense, or word, viz., a particular denotative word, suggests that meaning.

This shows that the habitat of *dhvani* is different from that of causes of beauty in the denotative sense and word, such as simile and alliteration.

The objection that "there is no such thing as *dhvani* because what falls outside our well-known system would no longer be poetry" is injust, for it is only to the makers of definitions [of poetry] that *dhvani* is not well known. When poetry itself is examined, one finds that *dhvani* is the poetic essence that delights the heart of the sensitive audience. Whatever differs from it is mere *citra* (display), as we shall show in what follows.

[THE SUGGESTED MEANING OF THE EPICS]

A And now, although it has been stated time and again, the point is repeated because it is so essential:

4.5

K While this relationship of suggestor and suggested is capable of great variety, the poet should concentrate on that one type that achieves *rasa*.

A While words are capable of a varied relationship of suggestor and suggested and this is the source of their infinity of meaning, the poet who seeks to obtain an original meaning should concentrate his effort on the one relation which achieves *rasa*. For all original poetry is achieved by a poet whose mind attends closely to a suggested sense consisting of a *rasa, bhāva,* or the false or improper correlate of one of these, and on the suggestors, as we have described them, in the form of words, sentences, texture, or complete works. And so it is that in such works as the *Rāmāyaṇa* and *Mahābhārata* the battle scenes, etc., although they occur repeatedly, always appear new. Furthermore, one primary *rasa,* being woven into a work, gives it special meaning and extra beauty. Do you ask for an example? As in the *Rāmāyaṇa* and the *Mahābhārata.*

In the *Rāmāyaṇa* the *karuṇarasa* (flavor of compassion or tragic mood) is prepared by the first of poets himself, where he says that his "grief became verse." He carries out the same *rasa* throughout his composition up to Rāma's final, irreversible separation from Sītā.

Again, in the *Mahābhārata,* which has the form of a didactic work[1] although it contains poetic beauty, the great sage who was its author, by his furnishing a conclusion that dismays our hearts by the miserable end of the Vṛṣṇis and Pāṇḍavas,[2] shows that the primary aim of his work has been to produce a disenchantment with

---

1. A *shastra,* or work of systematic thought.
2. The Vrishni was the clan to which Krishna belonged. Through a series of curses, its members slaughtered each other in a drunken brawl. Krishna himself died when accidentally shot in the heel by a hunter. The Pandavas, after some years in power, renounced the world. All but

Yudhishthira died on a march north into the great Sand Desert, and when Yudhishthira arrives in heaven, he finds his ignoble and spiteful cousin, Duryodhana, against whom the war had been fought, resplendent upon a celestial throne.

the world and that he has intended his primary subject to be liberation from worldly life and the *rasa* of peace. This has been partly revealed indeed by others in their commenting on the work. The most compassionate of sages [Bhīṣma] himself asserts the same when he seeks, by imparting the light of his pure knowledge, to rescue the world from the cruel illusion in which it is plunged. He expresses it in many ways, as in the following:

> The more the world's affairs
> go wrong for us and lose their substance,
> the more will disenchantment with them
> grow, there is no doubt.

[*Mahābhārata* 12.168.4]

The ultimate meaning of the *Mahābhārata* thus appears very clearly: the two subjects intended by the author as primary are the *rasa* of peace and the human goal of liberation.[3] The other *rasas* and other human goals are subordinated to these; and how there may be a relation of principal and subordinate among the *rasas* is a matter we have already explained. It is no contradiction to this to concede that if we disregard the ultimate inner truth, there may be beauty in a subordinate *rasa* or human aim [in the *Mahābhārata*] regarded for the moment as paramount, just as there is beauty in the body [although it is in truth subordinate to the soul].

An objection may be raised that all the contents of the *Mahābhārata* are summarized in the Introductory Summary and that these subjects [liberation and the *rasa* of peace] are not mentioned there. Rather, it is specifically stated in that Introduction that the *Mahābhārata* will inform us of all human aims and that it contains all the *rasas*. To this it may be replied. It is true that the predominance of the *rasa* of peace and the predominance of liberation over other human aims are not specifically stated in the *Anukramaṇī*.[4] But they are shown by suggestion, as in this sentence:

> And the blessed Vāsudeva,
> the everlasting, is here glorified.

[*Mahābhārata* 1.1.193 ab]

For the meaning intended to be hereby suggested is as follows. The adventures of the Pāṇḍavas and others which are here recounted, since they come to a miserable conclusion, represent the elaboration of worldly illusion, whereas it is the blessed Vāsudeva, representing ultimate truth, who is here glorified. Purify your minds, therefore, in blessed God, the all-highest. Form no passion for insubstantial glories, nor let your minds dwell whole-heartedly on virtues such as statesmanship, modesty, courage, or the like, so as to regard them as sufficient in themselves. The word "and," graced with the full powers of a suggestor, appears clearly to be hinting that one should look farther [in the book] and see the worthlessness of all worldly life. The verses which immediately follow, "for He is the truth," etc. [*MBh.* 1.1.193 c] are seen to reveal within themselves the same sense.

3. The *rasa* of peace is developed out of the stable emotion of indifference to the world; liberation from the cycle of rebirth, or *moksha,* is one of the four life goals in traditional Indian society.

4. The "Introductory Summary" or table of contents with which the *Mahabharata* begins.

This sense is beautiful because it is concealed. The poet-creator Kṛṣṇad-vaipāyana has made it perfectly clear, however, by composing the *Harivaṃśa*[5] as a conclusion to his *Mahābhārata*. Since this sense stirs us toward an intense devotion (*bhakti*) to that other truth that lies beyond worldly life, all worldly activity appears now as a preliminary goal, to be rejected. He describes the power of gods, places of pilgrimage, and of ascetecism, only because these are the means of attaining the highest Brahma, because the various gods and sacred objects are epiphanies of that Brahma. Even the narrative of the adventures of the Pāṇḍavas, since its purpose is to generate a disenchantment with the world, since this disenchantment is a cause of liberation, and since liberation has been described in the *Gītā* and other works as the chief means of attaining the Blessed One: even this narrative is indirectly a means of attaining the highest Brahma.

What is intended [by the word Vāsudeva in the *Mahābhārata* verse just quoted] is the highest Brahma, the abode of unlimited power, known under such designations as "Vāsudeva" and made famous under that name in the *Gītā* and other passages; the original whole, which possesses all the forms which were copied by the appearance at Mathurā.[6] But the appearance at Mathurā, being a partial incarnation, is not meant, as it is excluded by the adjective "everlasting." And [there is no reason for limiting the epithet Vāsudeva to the son of Vasudeva], because we find the epithet used in such works as the *Rāmāyaṇa* of a still different incarnation. Furthermore, this sense [of the epithet as referring to an eternal entity] has been determined by the grammarians themselves.

By that [one] sentence exhibited in the Introductory Summary, which shows that everything other than the Blessed One is transient, we are already informed that the *Mahābhārata* as a work of doctrine considers the one supreme goal of man to be liberation and as a work of poetry intends the *rasa* of peace, which is a strengthening of the happiness that derives from the cessation of desire, to be the predominant *rasa*. As this matter is most essential, it is given by suggestion rather than by direct statement, for an essential matter carries far greater luster by not being stated in so many words. For it is common knowledge among intelligent and well-educated circles that one should suggest rather than state in so many words the matter which one has most at heart.

Accordingly, it is clear that in writing a poem one gains freshness and a large measure of beauty for the work by means of such factors as the predominant *rasa*. That is why we may see in literature a composition possessed of great beauty if it assembles its matter in harmony with a *rasa,* even if it lacks any particular figures of speech. For example:

> Victorious is the great sage,
> the prince of yogis, born of a water jar,
> who in one cupped handfull saw
> the Divine Fish and the Divine Tortoise.

Here the vision of the fish and the tortoise in the palm of Agastya's hand, being in conformity with the *rasa* of wonder, adds a great beauty to the stanza, for the vision

5. The *Harivamsha* ("Lineage of Vishnu") is a supplement of the *Mahabharata* and like it is ascribed to Krishna Dvaipayana Vyasa. The work emphasizes the divinity of Krishna as an *avatara* of Vishnu, a status that is obscure in certain episodes of the great epic.
6. A city in northern India, ruled by Kamsa, Krishna's uncle and deadly enemy, whom Krishna killed.

of the divine fish and tortoise, being an original touch, is more in conformity with the *rasa* of wonder than the [suggested] presence of the whole ocean in one palm of his hand. For a matter that is trite through being known to everyone, though it may be a marvel, does not give us a sense of wonder. Nor need the mention of an original trait in harmony with the *rasa* be limited to the *rasa* of wonder. It may harmonize with other *rasas.* For example,

> Lucky man! Her side,
> which you accidentally touched
> as you brushed past her on the street,
> still perspires, bristles, trembles.

From this stanza, as one thinks about it, there arises a perception in the highest degree of *rasa,* which would not appear at all from the mere fact, being perceived, that the lady after touching you perspires, bristles and trembles.

We have thus described how a fresh color is given to the matter of poetry by use of the various types of predominant suggestion (*dhvani*). A freshness of the poetic matter may also arise from using a subordinated suggestion of any of the three kinds.[7] But I have given no example of these in fear that my book would become too long. The sensitive reader can easily supply them for himself.

❦ CROSSCURRENTS: WHAT IS "LITERATURE"? ❦

- The readings in this section come from one of the great early traditions of organized reflection on the nature of literature, first by poets and then by systematic critical thinkers. The *Ramayana*'s poetic presentation of Valmiki's poetic activity can be compared with Homer's depiction of the bard Demodocus—and the story-telling activity of Odysseus himself—on the island of Phaeacia in Book 8 of the *Odyssey* (page 342). What differing aesthetic and social understandings of literature do the two epic texts express?

- The Sanskrit theorists were particularly concerned with poetry and drama, the reigning forms of literature in their culture. Other early treatises on literature were produced elsewhere in the ancient and medieval world: Aristotle's *Poetics* (page 691) discuss the construction of drama, while in the Tang Dynasty a variety of Chinese thinkers discussed poetry (see "What Is Literature" in Volume B). What differences are involved when drama rather than lyric poetry is taken as the starting point for a consideration of literature?

- Works such as "Rajashekhara's Weds Poetics Woman" envision a close, harmonious relation between criticism and artistic production, and more generally between literature and society, but modern poets and critics have often had a more combative relation to society—and to each other. How do these early Sanskrit discussions compare with the poetic and critical writings of Baudelaire (Volume E) and with the literary manifestos that open Volume F?

➤ END OF PERSPECTIVES: WHAT IS "LITERATURE"? ➤

---

7. The suggestion of a narrative element, a figure of speech, or an aesthetic mood.

LOVE IN A COURTLY LANGUAGE

The old division of text types that describes literature as acting like a lover (page 805) is especially apt, given that much of the most remarkable Indian literature is love poetry. The difficulty of speaking of "Indian literature" in general—especially in the later medieval period, given the plethora of languages and themes—seems lessened in the case of love poetry. Many features are shared across South Asian languages including forms, themes, aesthetics, and what might be called the social text out of which the poetry emerges and to which it owes so many fundamental aspects of its meaning.

Although rarely made clear in translation, the form of the oldest Sanskrit poetic literature, the epic, is the individual stanza consisting of four lines (usually of eight syllables each); each stanza typically contains a complete thought. Here, for example, is the second verse of *The Ramayana of Valmiki*:

ko nv asmin sāṃprataṃ loke	Who now at present in the world
guṇavān kaś ca vīryavān	is virtuous, who is brave,
dharmajñaś ca kṛtajñaś ca	knowing what is right and appreciative,
satyavākyo dṛḍhavrataḥ	true to his word and firm in his vows?

This same quatrain structure, but usually with longer lines, remained the basic building block of all later Sanskrit poetry (and, with some slight differences, Prakrit poetry as well). These quatrains could be combined into longer narratives, but sometimes they were meant from the start to be freestanding, to constitute complete literary works in their own right. What helped make this extraordinary concentration possible was a widely shared set of conventions, especially concerning character types, and the intense use of the expressive capacities of language, especially "suggestion," where meaning without saying was developed as the highest form of expressivity (see page 919). We might assume that the tradition's constraints on individual creativity would have been stultifying, but, in fact, the more rigid form, theme, and genre became, the more keenly poets felt the challenge to distinguish themselves, and so the more subtle and exquisitely refined their individual variations became (a situation well exemplified in the later Urdu *ghazal* poetry of Mir; see Volume D).

What marks much of this poetry so powerfully, in addition to the poets' allegiance to inherited forms and precedents, is their goal of generating a *rasa,* or a representation of an emotion, that was as pure as possible. Keeping this objective in mind may help us understand a striking feature of virtually all premodern Indian poetry: it is entirely stripped of references to particular persons, places, or times. Here you will find nothing comparable to Catullus's "Lesbia, let us live" (page 1246) or Yeats's "Easter 1916" (see Volume F). But it is important to remember that this kind of anonymity is an affirmative choice on the part of the poets. Any of the thousands of eulogies of kings found in inscriptions suffices to demonstrate that in early South Asia, individual people and locales and events could be directly described when it was felt appropriate to do so. In most poetry, however, especially love poetry, the aim was to express human emotion in a way permitting the sensitive reader to experience it as a pure distillate of aesthetic pleasure. In view of this objective, historical detail would only decrease what the Indian theorists consider one of poetry's most important effects: the imaginative identification of the reader with the character.

The "social text" to which so much of this poetry refers was also discussed by Indian thinkers in the late-medieval period. As we saw, the female characters of love poetry (poets are far less interested in the male) are divided into three types: one's own wife, another man's wife, and the courtesan. All were further categorized as innocent, average, or sophisticated, and again according to the various possible relationships in which they might find themselves, with respect either to "love enjoyed" or "love frustrated" (the two main divisions of erotic poetry): the woman waiting for her lover to arrive for a rendezvous, the woman whose lover is away on travels, the woman whose lover has been unfaithful, the woman who directs love anger at her lover, either sincerely or merely to provoke him, and so on. Shared knowledge of such conventions between poet and reader made it possible to communicate a great deal in a short verse even while—especially while—leaving much unsaid.

--- ⚔ ---

The Tamil Anthologies
2nd–3rd centuries

Among the finest literary creations in the Tamil language of South India is a corpus of some 2,400 poems collected in eight anthologies attributed to poets, both male and female, working in the poetic academies associated with the royal courts of ancient Tamil country in peninsular India. This body of literature has had a complicated history. Many features of its language, style, and reference suggest a date of composition in the early centuries of the Common Era. While these poems certainly continued to be read, commented upon and copied in certain circles—some medieval and early-modern Tamil poetry was clearly indebted to them—they gradually came to fall out of the canon known to many Tamil literati. It was not until their publication in the late nineteenth and early twentieth centuries by such scholars as U. V. Caminataiyar (Swaminatha Iyer) that these poems were made available to wider audiences and occasioned a fundamental rethinking of the literary history of Tamil and its relationship to Sanskrit and Prakrit literature.

Many formal and narrative conventions are shared among these literatures, and the question of inventor and borrower remains an open one. The poems in the anthologies are categorized as belonging either to the "interior"—the private world (*akam* in Tamil)—or to the "exterior"—the public domain (*puram*). The selections offered here are largely drawn from the "interior" group. Each poem depicts a moment in the story of two lovers that is described by one of the lovers or by someone who knows them, such as the girl's close friend, her fostermother, or another lover of the man's. An especially striking feature of the many *akam* poems is the way in which the poet uses landscape as a mirror of the emotional lives of the characters.

from THE TAMIL ANTHOLOGIES[1]

Ōrampokiyar: What Her Girl Friend Said
when he sent a flattering minstrel on his behalf

Dear man from the city
of portia trees and rice fields[1]
where

    the small barbus fish
5   slips sometimes
    from the heron's beak
    and dives into the water
    but fears ever after
    the white bud of the lotus,

1. Translated by A. K. Ramanujan. The poet's name precedes each title. Traditional Tamil theories of *akam* and *puram* poetics allow for *tinaimayakkam*, or "overlapping of genres." This and the two following poems provide examples of such overlaps.
1. In *akam* poetics, agricultural lowlands—such as those of rice fields—and freshwater fish are especially emblematic of a lover's infidelity.

10   since one of your minstrels
was a liar,
all your minstrels must seem liars
to the women you abandon.

Anonymous: What Her Girl Friend Said to Him

trying to dissuade him from his long journey[1]

As they carry the white paddy of their land
to barter it for the salt of another,
crossing the long roads in carts
through sands white as moonlight,

5   taking whole families
who hate to be left behind,

the exodus of the salt merchants
leaves a city empty.
                    Seashore man,
you must be dense indeed:

10   what with the nasty cold wind
blowing through everything
and the misery of evenings
in your absence,

she is a water lily

15   in a dry bed
trampled by white herons
overfed on a whole shoal of fish.

She'll not last a day, believe me,
and you don't even think of it.

Kapilar: What She Said

"O your hair," he said,
"it's like rainclouds[1]
moving between
branches of lightning.

5   It parts five ways
between gold ornaments,
braided with a length of flowers
and the fragrant screwpine.

"O your smiles, your glistening teeth,

10   words sheer honey,
mouth red as coral,
O fair brow,
I want to tell you

---

1. The poem gives a series of places, animals, peoples, times, and activities associated with the anxiety of separation from a loved one.

1. The rainy season is associated with patient waiting and domesticity.

something,
15   listen, stop and listen,"

he said, and stopped me.

Came close,
to look closer
at my brow, my hands, my eyes,
20   my walk, my speech,
and said, searching
for metaphors:

    "Amazed, it grows small, but it isn't the crescent.
    Unspotted, it isn't the moon.
25   Like bamboo, yet it isn't on a hill.
    Lotuses, yet there's no pool.
    Walk mincing, yet no peacock.
    The words languish, yet you're not a parrot,"

and so on.

30   On and on he praised my parts
with words gentle and sly,
looked for my weakening
like a man with a net
stalking an animal,

35   watched me
as my heart melted,
stared at me
like a butcher at his prey,

O he saluted me, saluted me,
40   touched me O he touched me,
a senseless lusting elephant
no goad could hold back.

Salute and touch,
and touch again he did,

45   but believe me, friend,
I still think he is not really

a fool by nature.

Kapilar: What She Said to Her Girl Friend

O you, you wear flowers of gold,
their colors made in fire,
complete with pollen,
while the flowers on creeper[1] and branch

---

1. The creeper is a vine of particular significance in *puram* poetry of which the *akam* counterpart is the jasmine flower. Whereas in *puram* the creeper suggests preparations for war and invasion, in *akam* the jasmine connotes patient longing. The common theme shared by these plants in traditional Tamil poetics is separation. In this poem, the suggestion is that the man has been tested by the contrived negligence and perhaps even infidelity of the woman.

5   are parched, waterless.
Your lovely forearm stacked
with jeweled bracelets,
shoulders soft as a bed of down,

is it right not to let me
10   live at your feet?
                    he said.

And didn't let go at that,
but stayed on to grab
all my hair
scented with lemon grass,
15   my hair-knot held together
by the gold shark's-mouth,[2]
and with a finger
he twisted tight
the garland in my hair
20   and smelled it too.

Not only that, he took
my fingers
        (unfolding now
        like crocus buds,
25   I suppose)

to cover his bloodshot eyes
and fetched a huge sigh,
blowing hot like a blacksmith
into his bellows.

30   And,

        like a deluded bull-elephant
        fondling with his trunk
        his beloved female,

he fondled my young painted breasts
35   till the paint rubbed off
on his rough hands.
Then he stroked me all over,
just about everywhere.

Yet friend,
40   with that act of his
I was rid
of all my troubles.

And I tell you this
only so that you can go
45   and persuade Mother:

2. The shark's-mouth is a particular kind of hair clip.

May the sweet smells
of my marriage in our house
cling to no man
but him,
50   and that will be good.

It will guarantee a lasting place for us
in this world that doesn't last.

Uruttiran: What She Said to Her Girl Friend,
and what her girl friend said in reply

"Friend,
like someone who gets drunk secretly
on hard liquor
till his body begins to ooze with it,
5   and goes on to brag shamelessly
till listeners shiver,
and then gets caught
with the stolen liquor in his hand,

I too got caught
10   with my secret in my hands:

my goatherd lover's
string of jasmine
that I'd twined in my hair
fell before my foster-mother
15   as she loosened my hair
to smear it with butter,

and embarrassed her
before Father, Mother,
and others in the house.

20   And she
didn't ask a thing about it,
or get angry,
but like someone
shaking off a live coal
25   she shook it off
and moved into the backyard.

Then I
dried my hair perfumed with sandal,
knotted it,
30   and picking up the end
of my blue flower-border dress
        that comes down to the floor
I tiptoed in fear
and hid
35   in the thick of the forest."

"O you got scared because of that?
No fears. Even as you wore
your young man's garlands,
they too have conspired
40   to give you to him.

They'll pour soft sand
in the wide yard,
put curtains all around,
and make a wedding there
45   very soon.
          Not only all day today,
but all night yesterday,
we've been scheming
to do just that."

Maturaittamiḻkkūtta Kaṭuvaṉ Mallaṉar: What the Servants Said to Him
as he returned home

In encampments,

powerful elephants have fought the war,
the thunder of drums
resounds on the battleground,
5   the king has raised his victory banners.

Herds of cows and calves
come leaping into the forest
as herdsmen raise flutes
to their lips.

10   Your henchmen go rushing ahead,
the charioteer reins hard
to keep on the path
the fast-paced steeds with flying manes,

and when you return, my lord,

15   wounds praised by poets,
garlands on your chest,
wearing cool fragrant sandal,
smooth powders,

and enter
20   your house in triumphant joy,

where will it go, where
will it find a place,
                that pallor
on the brow of our lady,
with eyes, lined with kohl,
25   darker than blue-dark flowers?

Vanmanipputi: What She Said to Her Girl Friend

On beaches washed by seas
older than the earth,
in the groves filled with bird-cries,
on the banks shaded by a *punnai*
5   clustered with flowers,
        when we made love
my eyes saw him
and my ears heard him;

my arms grow beautiful
10   in the coupling
and grow lean
as they come away.
        What shall I make of this?

The Seven Hundred Songs of Hala

2nd or 3rd century C.E.

The Seven Hundred Songs of Hala is an anthology probably assembled at the court of a large kingdom that ruled over much of south-central India (the Satavahana empire, c. 225 B.C.E.–250 C.E.). A number of these verses are ascribed to individuals; but for the most part we know nothing about the poets named, and virtually all of their other works have disappeared. And little is known of Hala, the king who is credited with producing the anthology itself.

The language of these poems is Prakrit. The term *prakrita* means "natural," or "basic," and when used in reference to language, it connotes a state of grammatical simplicity in contrast to Sanskrit, the linguistically elaborated or "refined" register. Yet Prakrit, too, was a literary language, never spoken in the streets in the form we find it in poetry. Nor was it ever tied to a particular region, any more than Sanskrit was; it was used for literature throughout India. That said, Prakrit did have definite associations with the non-urban and non-urbane world; it seems best to think of it as the literary representation of a country dialect. And this is something *The Seven Hundred Songs* illustrates very well, since these poems are about village life and love—or more precisely, about village life and love as imagined by courtly poets.

Many of these poems can be immediately understood and appreciated by contemporary readers, but there is an important type of Prakrit verse that presents intriguing problems of interpretation due to its concentration of meaning. Consider the following:

When she bends to touch
    Her mother-in-law's feet
And two bangles slip
    From her thin hands, tears
Come to the cold woman's eyes.

These seemingly simple lines play on the system of literary convention and on a broader social text. Since it was (and is) common in India for married couples to live with the husband's family, the mother-in-law is represented as a constant and sometimes forbidding presence to a young wife, who must show her absolute deference, for example by touching her feet. A woman separated from her husband is often depicted as wasting away for sorrow: her wrists will become thin, and her bangles—a symbol of marriage, rather like a wedding ring in the West—will slip from her hands. But as in all good poetry, literary and social conventions don't fully explain the meaning here, as the last line intimates: has her mother-in-law, only now and for the first time, become convinced of her daughter-in-law's true affection for her son? Or is she thinking back on her own past, about the love she herself once felt for her husband and how she pined away in his absence?

At work here is a kind of "suggestion," what later thinkers will call *dhvani*, or "echo." It was precisely this capacity of poetry for suggestion at various levels that the great critic Anandavardhana was later to develop into a new, unified theory of literariness (see page 919); and this is a hallmark of the Prakrit poems. It is easier to see how suggestion functions in the following poem:

> Mother-in-law sleeps here, I there;
> look, traveler, while it is light.
> For at night when you cannot see
> you must not fall into my bed.

We know from the verse that the woman is married, but she forgoes mentioning her husband. He is likely to be away on business like the traveler who comes and asks for a place to spend the night. The visitor is told to be careful, at nightfall when it becomes hard to see, that he does not get into the wrong bed. But we know—because this is a poem, not a mere statement of directions—that the woman doesn't mean what she is saying. The wrong bed is any bed except the woman's, and the traveler is being invited to sleep with her. If we reflect for a moment on how the speaker communicates her wishes, we relish our ability to get the meaning we assume her listening mother-in-law cannot get; we also come to understand something of the young woman's cleverness, audacity, and desire.

from THE SEVEN HUNDRED SONGS OF HALA

At night, cheeks blushed[1]

At night, cheeks blushed
    With joy, making me do
A hundred different things,
    And in the morning too shy
5 To even look up. I don't believe
    It's the same woman.

After a quarrel

After a quarrel,
    The breath suppressed,
Their ears attentive,
    The lovers feign sleep:
5 Let's see who
    Holds out longer.

His form

His form
    In my eyes,

---

1. Translated by Arvind Krishna Mehrotra.

His touch
     In my limbs,
5   His words
     In my ears,
His heart
     In my heart:
Now who's
10   Separated?

While the bhikshu[1]

While the *bhikshu*
     Views her navel
And she
     His handsome face,
5   Crows lick clean
     Both ladle and alms bowl.

Though he's wronged me

Though he's wronged me,
     I visit him:
Fires break out,
     We still light fire.

Tight lads in fields

Tight° lads in fields,   *tipsy*
     A month in spring,
A cuss for a husband,
     Liquor in the rack,
5   And she young, free-hearted:
     Asking her to be faithful
Is asking her to die.

He finds the missionary position

He finds the missionary position
     Tiresome, and grows suspicious
If I suggest another:
     Friend, what's the way out?

When she bends to touch

When she bends to touch
     Her mother-in-law's feet
And two bangles slip

1. A holy man who lives from alms.

His heart

In my heart;

Now who

Separated,

5   From her thin hands, tears
      Come to the cold woman's eyes.

As though she'd glimpsed

As though she'd glimpsed
The mouth of a buried
    Pot of gold,

Her joy on seeing
5   Under her daughter's
    Wind-blown skirt

A tooth-mark
    Near the crotch.

And the

Those men

Those men,
    This once rich village,
And days of my youth

Are now stories
5   That sometimes
Reach my ears too.

Tight lads in fields.

Tight lads in fields,

A tumult in

A

Labour in the rice.

And she, young, free-hearted,

He finds the missionary position

+ ⊷⊹⊱ +

The Hundred Poems of Amaru

7th century

A curious story is told in medieval India about Amaru. He is said to have been a powerful king with a vast harem, and as he lay dying, the great ascetic and philosopher Shankaracharya entered his body by means of his yogic powers and reanimated it. Shankara, a lifelong celibate, proceeded to learn the ways of desire in company with the king's wives, complementing his mastery of things spiritual. He then wrote *The Hundred Poems* in order to demonstrate his mastery of the art of love.

This striking story suggests that traditional readers not only thought *The Hundred Poems* the most perfect expression of the erotic mood (*rasa*) in Sanskrit but also heard a single authorial voice in the various poems. Medieval and modern scholarly opinion fully share the first view; one literary critic of the ninth century wrote that an individual Amaru verse "speaks volumes." It is almost certain, however, that, like *The Seven Hundred Songs of Hala,* the poems of Amaru represent a collection of texts from various poets. Yet their shared interest in a particular form and content has made them seem to many readers to be the work of one poet. A large number of these verses are found in other anthologies, where they are ascribed to many different poets, both men and women, though once again, we know nothing about most of these beyond their names.

One exception is Dharmakirti, an important Buddhist philosopher of the seventh century to whom several verses in *The Hundred Poems* are attributed (including "She is the child, but

I the one of timid heart"). Virtually all of his poetic oeuvre has disappeared, marking one of the saddest losses in Sanskrit literary history. Dharmakirti was by no means unusual in combining philosophical and poetical talents; on the contrary, he is typical of a cultural environment that knew nothing of the conflict of *logos* and *mythos,* reason and imagination, bemoaned in the West from the time of Plato onward. This happy combination produced poetry of uncommon intelligence and sophistication, as *The Hundred Poems of Amaru* demonstrates on nearly every page.

from THE HUNDRED POEMS OF AMARU

She is the child, but I the one of timid heart[1]

She is the child, but I the one of timid heart;
the woman, but I the coward;
her hips are heavy, but it's I who cannot run;
the high and heavy breasts are hers, but it's I am weary.
5   A wonder it is that in everything
I have grown subject to another's weaknesses.

You will return in an hour?

"You will return in an hour?
Or at noon? Or after?
Or at least some time today!"
With such words the young bride, choked with tears,
5   delayed her love's departure for a land
distant by a hundred days.

As he came to bed the knot fell open of itself

As he came to bed the knot fell open of itself,
the dress held only somehow to my hips
by the strands of the loosened girdle.
So much I know, my dear;
5   but when within his arms, I can't remember who he was
or who I was, or what we did or how.

The sheets, marked here with betel

The sheets, marked here with betel
and darkened there with aloe paste,
with scattering of powder here
and lacquer footprints there,
5   while in their ruffled folds
are flowers from her hair,
proclaim enjoyment of a woman
in every posture.

1. Translated by Daniel H. H. Ingalls.

At first our bodies knew a perfect oneness

At first our bodies knew a perfect oneness,
but then grew two with you as lover
and I, unhappy I, the loved.
Now you are husband, I the wife,
5 what's left except of this my life,
too hard to break, to reap the bitter fruit,
your broken faith.

Your palm erases from your cheek the painted ornament

Your palm erases from your cheek the painted ornament
and sighs have drunk the ambrosial flavor of your lip;
the tears that choke you agitate your breast.
Anger has become your lover, stubborn one, in place of me.

They lay upon the bed each turned aside

They lay upon the bed each turned aside
and suffering in silence;
though love still dwelt within their hearts
each feared a loss of pride.
5 But then from out the corner of their eyes
the sidelong glances met
and the quarrel broke in laughter as they turned
and clasped each other's neck.

If you are angry with me, you of lotus eyes

If you are angry with me, you of lotus eyes,
let anger be your lover; there's no help.
But give me back the kisses I have given;
give back with interest all of my embraces.

You listened not to words of friends

You listened not to words of friends,
you heeded not your relatives' advice;
but when your dearest fell before your feet
you struck him with the lily from your ear.
5 So now the moon is burning hot
and sandalpaste turns into fire,
the nights each last a thousand years
and the lotus necklace weighs like iron.

At day's end as the darkness crept apace

At day's end as the darkness crept apace
the saddened traveler's wife had gazed
as far as eye could reach along the quiet road.

She takes one step returning to the whitewashed house,
5   then thinking, "At this very moment he may come,"
she turns her head and quickly looks again.

She let him in[1]

She let him in
she did not turn away from him
there was no anger in her words
she simply looked straight at him
5   as though there had never been
anything between them

Held her

Held her
tight to me
breasts pressed flat
all of her skin
5   reached
and with wanting alone
her clothes by themselves fell down
her legs No
don't oh
10   god don't
too much oh
yes
she was saying I
could hardly hear her
15   after that did she
fall asleep did she die
did she vanish into me
did she totally dissolve
into me

Lush clouds in

Lush clouds in
dark sky of tears she saw *my love*
if you leave me now she
said and could not say more
5   twisting my shirt
toe gripping dust
after that what she
did all words
are helpless to repeat and
10   they know it and give up

[END OF LOVE IN A COURTLY LANGUAGE]

1. Translated by W. S. Merwin and Jeffrey M. Masson.

Kalidasa

4th–5th centuries C.E.

A verse long in circulation among traditional scholars in India declares that of all the works of Sanskrit dramatic literature, Kalidasa's *Shakuntala* is the best; of the seven acts of the play, the fourth is the best; of all the verses contained in the fourth act, the group of four spoken by Shakuntala's foster father are the best; and of these, the very best is this:

> My heart is touched with sadness
> since Shakuntala must go today,
> my throat is choked with sobs,
> my eyes are dulled by worry—
> if a disciplined ascetic
> suffers so deeply from love,
> how do fathers bear the pain
> of each daughter's parting?'

As contemporary readers trying to find their bearings on a work of literature from a distant time and place, we need to take seriously what the indigenous tradition has taken seriously including their evaluations seriously as well (even if, as here, we are never told explicitly what the grounds of such evaluations are). Yet traditions are not all-knowing, and great works are more complex than any reader or group of readers, however traditional, can grasp. This is something well illustrated by Kalidasa's *Shakuntala*.

Kalidasa is the most celebrated Sanskrit poet of early India, a stature achieved within two centuries of his death and unchallenged ever since. We cannot determine the dates of his life with absolute certainty, but all evidence suggests he wrote during the height of the Gupta Empire in the late fourth and early fifth centuries. His most ambitious work, *The Dynasty of Raghu (Raghu-vamsha),* a courtly epic on the ancestors and successors of Rama, alludes clearly to the career of the emperor Samudra Gupta (r. c. 330–380). Kalidasa's other works include *Birth of the Divine Prince Kumara (Kumara-sambhava),* a magnificent courtly epic on the love and marriage of the gods Shiva and Parvati; a narrative poem, the *Cloud Messenger (Megha-duta);* and two other plays besides *Shakuntala.* So large and varied a corpus of literary texts from so early a period has been preserved for no other Sanskrit poet. And this is no accident. No other Sanskrit poet has explored the primal human needs of power and desire, and fundamental aspects of Indian life and history, with the intensity of vision and expressive mastery that Kalidasa displays.

SANSKRIT DRAMA

Like so many other features of Sanskrit literary history, the origins of drama are irrecoverable. Although we have no evidence of direct connections between Sanskrit and Greek drama, scholars for generations have tried to demonstrate some kind of formative relationship. There are curious facts: that Sanskrit drama so often derives its materials from the epic tradition, as was the case in Greece; that the theater curtain is called the *yavanika* (probably from *yavana,* "Ionian"—that is, Greek); and that Greek women appear in the retinue of kings in Sanskrit drama. Obviously none of this need indicate direct and formal influence. But Hellenic kings did rule in northwestern India for some centuries beginning around 300 B.C.E., and the remains of a Greek theater have been excavated at Ai Khanum in what today is northern Afghanistan. Other scholars have believed that Sanskrit drama preserves archaic Vedic elements, and thus they argue for a long history of the genre. Yet according to the evidence that we actually possess, Sanskrit drama is no older than the first century C.E. Kalidasa acknowledges ancient predecessors; some that are preserved, however, are probably more recent works attributed to the ancient authors. The only extant dramatic compositions genuinely earlier than Kalidasa's are the allegorical dramas composed around 150 C.E. by the Buddhist poet Ashvaghosha, a writer whose poems demonstrably influenced Kalidasa. So far as we can judge, however, nothing in the surviving fragments of Ashvaghosha's plays prefigures the kind of artistry that Kalidasa brought to Sanskrit drama.

In its mature form the Sanskrit drama was a complex work of art, a "total artwork," if we may borrow Richard Wagner's notion. Instrumental music, song, dance, mime, and costume were all part of the performance. What is left to us today in the manuscripts of these works is hardly more than the libretto, so to speak. We should bear in mind that when reading the play, we are experiencing only a fraction of the comprehensive aesthetic impact the work was designed to deliver. We also need to learn to adjust to the objectives specific to the Sanskrit theater, for in some ways these differ fundamentally from what our experience of Western drama leads us to expect.

RASA

Consider the problems of moral choice and fate. Both are certainly as central to the Sanskrit theater as they are to the ancient Greek, but it is less common for choice and destiny to be placed front and center in motivated action, especially in conflict between characters, such as Oedipus and Tiresias (see page 618), or Antigone (page 656) and Creon. Instead, these problems are transmuted into possibilities for the literary representation of emotion, what is known as *rasa* (see page 920). Thus, in plays based on the *Ramayana,* while the hero Rama is confronted with choices to be made and is driven by a certain fate, what is of paramount interest to traditional writers and readers is the way choice and fate contribute to the mood of pity pervading the story: pity over Rama's loss of father, kingship, wife, and so on. The experience of pity predominates in the critical estimation, inseparable though it obviously is from the problem of moral choice. Similarly, in *Shakuntala,* suffering doesn't emerge from decisions taken and consequences confronted and doesn't lead to knowledge, the hallmark of the Greek theater, where *pathein mathein,* "to suffer is to learn." Suffering is displayed for the sake of relishing—in that strange, disengaged engagement of the art experience—the state of suffering.

The emphasis on *rasa* rather than on choice and action can narrow the scope for heroic agency in Sanskrit drama. The original version of the story of Shakuntala appears in the epic *Mahabharata,* and it is instructive to consider the kinds of changes that Kalidasa has introduced. The *Mahabharata*'s Shakuntala has greater autonomy and power, while instead of the motif of the sage's curse and the ring of recognition we find the plot hinging on the "kingship brideprice." This refers to a promise made by a royal groom to the bride's family that her son will succeed to the kingship, in preference to any other heir the king may have. In the *Mahabharata* the king's refusal to recognize Shakuntala is a function of this agreement. He requires the validation of a divine voice to prove to all concerned that the son is in fact his own, and therefore merits the status of heir-apparent. In Kalidasa's play, by contrast, the couple is caught unawares by a curse that baffles the king and stymies Shakuntala as she seeks her rightful due. Yet the diminution of agency seems to be exactly what the playwright is aiming at: The main characters of the play are not normal human agents at all. Shakuntala may appear to stand for Young Woman as such—she has appeared this way to generations of modern readers, Indian and European—but she is far more than this. As the daughter of a celestial nymph and a powerful, earthly sage-king, a girl who has grown up among ascetics in the forest, she clearly has something to do with the force of nature itself in a kind of potential state. Dushyanta, too, is no ordinary man, but a king and, as such, a kind of god-man, according to traditional Indian thought. More than this, he is an embodiment of the great god Shiva, and one to whom Indra himself, king of the gods, must turn in order to defeat demonic evil (Act 6). The union and reunion of these two remarkable beings are not accidental either, and what seems to be the troubled progress of human love is slowly revealed in the course of the play and, decisively at its conclusion, to be part of a cosmic plan.

Careful readers will see that the playwright has correlated this idea of cosmic design with the balanced structural design of his drama: there is an unmistakable symmetry of action that balances Acts 1 and 7, 2 and 6, and 3 and 5, each latter act recapitulating events, motifs, and even phrases from the former in a kind of counterpoint. The design of the drama thus can be said to recapitulate the design of a destiny through which the human-divine king is to be joined with the elemental power of nature in order to produce a son who will rule the four quarters of the world. Indeed, the son, Bharata, will give his name to that world as a whole—it was from about the time of Kalidasa that the Indian subcontinent had come to be called *Bharatavarsha*, or the Realm of the Descendents of Bharata.

These structural features and their implications were never discussed in Indian antiquity. But the traditional readers who counted Kalidasa as India's greatest poet and *Shakuntala* his greatest work were likely to have felt this deeply etched pattern. They understood that the playwright was giving voice not only to universal truths—about human love, family, and the separation of parent and child through marriage that is as poignant as it is inevitable—but also to specific truths about the world in which they lived, its past and its future, running in complex but perceptible currents beneath the play's surface narrative. One later Sanskrit poet put this well:

> It took me a long time
> to fathom, as it were,
> the deep, sweet flood
> of Kalidasa's muse.

PRONUNCIATIONS:
    Ashvaghosha: UHSH-vuh-GHOH-shuh
    Bharata: BHUH-ruh-tuh
    Dushyanta (Duṣyanta): doosh-YUHN-tuh
    Kalidasa: KAH-lee-DAH-suh
    Shakuntala (Śakuntalā): shuh-KOON-tuh-LAH (the heroine)
    Shakuntala: SHAH-koon-tuh-luh (the play)

Note: In the spellings used in this translation, the sound *sh* is shown by the letters ś and ṣ as well as sh, reflecting nuances in Sanskrit. "Śakuntalā" is pronounced "Shakuntala" and "Viṣṇu" is pronounced "Vishnu."

Śakuntalā and the Ring of Recollection[1]

Characters

Players in the Prologue
DIRECTOR, *director of the players and manager of the theater*
ACTRESS, *the lead actress*

Principal Roles
KING, Duṣyanta, *the hero; ruler of Hastināpura; a royal sage of the lunar dynasty of Puru*
ŚAKUNTALĀ, *the heroine; daughter of the royal sage Viśvāmitra and the celestial nymph Menakā; adoptive daughter of the ascetic Kaṇva*
BUFFOON, Māḍhavya, *the king's comical brahman companion*

---

1. Translated by Barbara Stoler Miller.

Members of Kaṇva's Hermitage

ANASŪYĀ and PRIYAṀVADĀ, *two young female ascetics; friends of Śakuntalā*
KAṆVA, *foster father of Śakuntalā and master of the hermitage; a sage belonging to the lineage of the divine creator Marīci, and thus related to Mārīca*
GAUTAMĪ, *the senior female ascetic*
ŚĀRṄGARAVA and ŚĀRADVATA, *Kaṇva's disciples*
VARIOUS INHABITANTS OF THE HERMITAGE, *a monk with his two pupils, two boy ascetics (named Gautama and Nārada), a young disciple of Kaṇva, a trio of female ascetics*

Members of the King's Forest Retinue

CHARIOTEER, *driver of the king's chariot*
GUARD, Raivataka, *guardian of the entrance to the king's quarters*
GENERAL, *commander of the king's army*
KARABHAKA, *royal messenger*

VARIOUS ATTENDANTS, INCLUDING GRECO-BACTRIAN BOW-BEARERS

Members of the King's Palace Retinue

CHAMBERLAIN, Vātāyana, *chief officer of the king's household*
PRIEST, Somarāta, *the king's religious preceptor and household priest*
DOORKEEPER, Vetravatī, *the female attendant who ushers in visitors and presents messages*
PARABHṚTIKĀ and MADHUKARIKĀ, *two maids assigned to the king's garden*
CATURIKĀ, *a maidservant*

City Dwellers

MAGISTRATE, *the king's low-caste brother-in-law; chief of the city's policemen*
POLICEMEN, Sūcaka *and* Jānuka
FISHERMAN, *an outcaste*

Celestials

MĀRĪCA, *a divine sage; master of the celestial hermitage in which Śakuntalā gives birth to her son; father of Indra, king of the gods, whose armies Duṣyanta leads*
ADITI, *wife of Mārīca*
MĀTALI, *Indra's charioteer*
SĀNUMATĪ, *a nymph; friend of Śakuntalā's mother Menakā*
VARIOUS MEMBERS OF MĀRĪCA'S HERMITAGE, *two female ascetics, Mārīca's disciple Gālava*
BOY, Sarvadamana, *son of Śakuntalā and Duṣyanta; later known as Bharata*

Offstage Voices

VOICE OFFSTAGE, *from the backstage area or dressing room; behind the curtain, out of view of the audience. The voice belongs to various players before they enter the stage, such as the monk, Śakuntalā's friends, the buffoon, Mātali; also to figures who never enter the stage, such as the angry sage Durvāsas, the two bards who chant royal panegyrics*

VOICE IN THE AIR, *a voice chanting in the air from somewhere offstage: the bodiless voice of Speech quoted in Sanskrit by Priyaṁvadā; the voice of a cuckoo who represents the trees of the forest blessing Śakuntalā in Sanskrit; the voice of Haṁsapadikā singing a Prakrit love song*

Aside from Duṣyanta, Śakuntalā, and the buffoon, most of the characters represent types that reappear in different contexts within the play itself, an aspect of the circular structure of the play in which complementary relations are repeated. In terms of their appearance, the following roles might be played by the same actor or actress:

Kaṇva—Mārīca
Gautamī—Aditi
Anasūyā and Priyaṁvadā—
Sānumatī and Caturikā—
Two Ascetic Women in the hermitage of Mārīca
Charioteer—Mātali
Monk—Śārṅgarava
General—Chamberlain
Karabhaka—Priest

The setting of the play shifts from the forest hermitage (Acts 1–4) to the palace (Acts 5–6) to the celestial hermitage (Act 7). The season is early summer when the play begins and spring during the sixth act; the passage of time is otherwise indicated by the birth and boyhood of Śakuntalā's son.

ACT 1

The water that was first created,
the sacrifice-bearing fire, the priest,
the time-setting sun and moon,
audible space that fills the universe,
what men call nature, the source of all seeds,
the air that living creatures breathe—
through his eight embodied forms,
may Lord Śiva come to bless you![2]

Prologue

DIRECTOR [*looking backstage*]: If you are in costume now, madam, please come on stage!

ACTRESS: I'm here, sir.

DIRECTOR: Our audience is learned. We shall play Kālidāsa's new drama called *Śakuntalā and the Ring of Recollection*. Let the players take their parts to heart!

ACTRESS: With you directing, sir, nothing will be lost.

DIRECTOR: Madam, the truth is:

I find no performance perfect
until the critics are pleased;
the better trained we are
the more we doubt ourselves.

ACTRESS: So true . . . now tell me what to do first!

DIRECTOR: What captures an audience better than a song?
Sing about the new summer season and its pleasures:

---

2. The sublime creative and destructive powers of the god Shiva are often alluded to in Kalidasa's works. Shiva's eight embodied forms are enumerated within this opening verse: water, fire, ether, earth, air, the sun, the moon, and the ritual sacrificer.

To plunge in fresh waters
swept by scented forest winds
and dream in soft shadows
of the day's ripened charms.

ACTRESS [*singing*]: Sensuous women
in summer love
weave
flower earrings
from fragile petals
of mimosa
while wild bees
kiss them gently.

DIRECTOR: Well sung, madam! Your melody enchants the audience. The silent theater is like a painting. What drama should we play to please it?

ACTRESS: But didn't you just direct us to perform a new play called *Śakuntalā and the Ring of Recollection?*

DIRECTOR: Madam, I'm conscious again! For a moment I forgot.

The mood of your song's melody
carried me off by force,
just as the swift dark antelope
enchanted King Duṣyanta.

[*They both exit; the prologue ends. Then the king enters with his charioteer, in a chariot, a bow and arrow in his hand, hunting an antelope.*]

CHARIOTEER [*watching the king and the antelope*]:
I see this black buck move
as you draw your bow
and I see the wild bowman Śiva,
hunting the dark antelope.

KING: Driver, this antelope has drawn us far into the forest. There he is again:

The graceful turn of his neck
as he glances back at our speeding car,
the haunches folded into his chest
in fear of my speeding arrow,
the open mouth dropping
half-chewed grass on our path—
watch how he leaps, bounding on air,
barely touching the earth.

[*He shows surprise.*]
Why is it so hard to keep him in sight?

CHARIOTEER: Sir, the ground was rough. I tightened the reins to slow the chariot and the buck raced ahead. Now that the path is smooth, he won't be hard to catch.

KING: Slacken the reins!

CHARIOTEER: As you command, sir.

[*He mimes the speeding chariot.*]
Look!

Their legs extend as I slacken the reins,
plumes and manes set in the wind, ears angle back;
our horses outrun their own clouds of dust,
straining to match the antelope's speed.

KING: These horses would outrace the steeds of the sun.

What is small suddenly looms large,
split forms seem to reunite,
bent shapes straighten before my eyes—
from the chariot's speed
nothing ever stays distant or near.

CHARIOTEER: The antelope is an easy target now.

[*He mimes the fixing of an arrow.*]

VOICE OFFSTAGE: Stop! Stop, king! This antelope belongs to our hermitage! Don't kill him!

CHARIOTEER [*listening and watching*]: Sir, two ascetics are protecting the black buck from your arrow's deadly aim.

KING [*showing confusion*]: Rein in the horses!

CHARIOTEER: It is done!

[*He mimes the chariot's halt. Then a monk enters with two pupils, his hand raised.*]

MONK: King, this antelope belongs to our hermitage.

Withdraw your well-aimed arrow! Your weapon
should rescue victims, not destroy the innocent!

KING: I withdraw it.

[*He does as he says.*]

MONK: An act worthy of the Puru dynasty's[3] shining light!

Your birth honors
the dynasty of the moon!
May you beget a son
to turn the wheel of your empire![4]

THE TWO PUPILS [*raising their arms*]: May you beget a son to turn the wheel of your empire!

KING [*bowing*]: I welcome your blessing.

MONK: King, we were going to gather firewood. From here you can see the hermitage of our master Kaṇva on the bank of the Mālinī river. If your work permits, enter and accept our hospitality.

When you see the peaceful rites of devoted ascetics,
you will know how well your scarred arm protects us.

---

3. Kings in early South Asia traced their origins either to the moon or the sun. Puru was the legendary founder of the lunar dynasty.

4. The wheel was the symbol of imperial power, and the emperor was called "Turner of the Wheel" (*cakravartin*).

KING: Is the master of the community there now?

MONK: He went to Somatīrtha,[5] the holy shrine of the moon, and put his daughter Śakuntalā in charge of receiving guests. Some evil threatens her, it seems.

KING: Then I shall see her. She will know my devotion and commend me to the great sage.

MONK: We shall leave you now.

[*He exits with his pupils.*]

KING: Driver, urge the horses on! The sight of this holy hermitage will purify us.

CHARIOTEER: As you command, sir.

[*He mimes the chariot's speed.*]

KING [*looking around*]: Without being told one can see that this is a grove where ascetics live.

CHARIOTEER: How?

KING: Don't you see—

> Wild rice grains under trees
> where parrots nest in hollow trunks,
> stones stained by the dark oil
> of crushed iṅgudī nuts,
> trusting deer who hear human voices
> yet don't break their gait,
> and paths from ponds streaked
> by water from wet bark cloth.

CHARIOTEER: It is perfect.

KING [*having gone a little inside*]: We should not disturb the grove! Stop the chariot and let me get down!

CHARIOTEER: I'm holding the reins. You can dismount now, sir.

KING [*dismounting*]: One should not enter an ascetics' grove in hunting gear. Take these!

[*He gives up his ornaments and his bow.*]

Driver, rub down the horses while I pay my respects to the residents of the hermitage!

CHARIOTEER: Yes, sir!

[*He exits.*]

KING: This gateway marks the sacred ground. I will enter.

[*He enters, indicating he feels an omen.*]

> The hermitage is a tranquil place,
> yet my arm is quivering . . .
> do I feel a false omen of love
> or does fate have doors everywhere?

VOICE OFFSTAGE: This way, friends!

5. A sacred place on the west coast of India.

KING [*straining to listen*]: I think I hear voices to the right of the grove. I'll find out.

[*Walking around and looking.*]

Young female ascetics with watering pots cradled on their hips are coming to water the saplings.

[*He mimes it in precise detail.*]

This view of them is sweet.

> These forest women have beauty
> rarely seen inside royal palaces—
> the wild forest vines far surpass
> creepers in my pleasure garden.

I'll hide in the shadows and wait.

[*Śakuntalā and her two friends enter, acting as described.*]

ŚAKUNTALĀ: This way, friends!

ANASŪYĀ: I think Father Kaṇva cares more about the trees in the hermitage than he cares about you. You're as delicate as a jasmine, yet he orders you to water the trees.

ŚAKUNTALĀ: Anasūyā, it's more than Father Kaṇva's order. I feel a sister's love for them.

[*She mimes the watering of trees.*]

KING [*to himself*]: Is this Kaṇva's daughter? The sage does show poor judgment in imposing the rules of the hermitage on her.

> The sage who hopes to subdue
> her sensuous body by penances
> is trying to cut firewood
> with a blade of blue-lotus leaf.

Let it be! I can watch her closely from here in the trees.

[*He does so.*]

ŚAKUNTALĀ: Anasūyā, I can't breathe! Our friend Priyaṁvadā tied my bark dress too tightly! Loosen it a bit!

ANASŪYĀ: As you say.

[*She loosens it.*]

PRIYAṀVADĀ [*laughing*]: Blame your youth for swelling your breasts. Why blame me?

KING: This bark dress fits her body badly, but it ornaments her beauty . . .

> A tangle of duckweed adorns a lotus,
> a dark spot heightens the moon's glow,
> the bark dress increases her charm—
> beauty finds its ornaments anywhere.

ŚAKUNTALĀ [*looking in front of her*]: The new branches on this mimosa tree are like fingers moving in the wind, calling to me. I must go to it!

[*Saying this, she walks around.*]

PRIYAṀVADĀ: Wait, Śakuntalā! Stay there a minute! When you stand by this mimosa tree, it seems to be guarding a creeper.

ŚAKUNTALĀ: That's why your name means "Sweet-talk."

KING: "Sweet-talk" yes, but Priyaṁvadā speaks the truth about Śakuntalā:

> Her lips are fresh red buds,
> her arms are tendrils,
> impatient youth is poised
> to blossom in her limbs.

ANASŪYĀ: Śakuntalā, this is the jasmine creeper who chose the mango tree in marriage,[6] the one you named "Forestlight." Have you forgotten her?

ŚAKUNTALĀ: I would be forgetting myself!

[*She approaches the creeper and examines it.*]

The creeper and the tree are twined together in perfect harmony. Forestlight has just flowered and the new mango shoots are made for her pleasure.

PRIYAṀVADĀ [*smiling*]: Anasūyā, don't you know why Śakuntalā looks so lovingly at Forestlight?

ANASŪYĀ: I can't guess.

PRIYAṀVADĀ: The marriage of Forestlight to her tree makes her long to have a husband too.

ŚAKUNTALĀ: You're just speaking your own secret wish.

[*Saying this, she pours water from the jar.*]

KING: Could her social class be different from her father's? There's no doubt!

> She was born to be a warrior's bride,
> for my noble heart desires her—
> when good men face doubt,
> inner feelings are truth's only measure.

Still, I must learn everything about her.

ŚAKUNTALĀ [*flustered*]: The splashing water has alarmed a bee. He is flying from the jasmine to my face.

[*She dances to show the bee's attack.*]

KING [*looking longingly*]: Bee, you touch the quivering
> corners of her frightened eyes,
> you hover softly near
> to whisper secrets in her ear;
> a hand brushes you away,
> but you drink her lips' treasure—
> while the truth we seek defeats us,
> you are truly blessed.

ŚAKUNTALĀ: This dreadful bee won't stop. I must escape.

---

6. A reference to a form of marriage whereby a young woman, normally a princess, would choose her husband in a public ceremony.

[*She steps to one side, glancing about.*]

Oh! He's pursuing me . . . Save me! Please save me! This mad bee is chasing me!

BOTH FRIENDS [*laughing*]: How can we save you? Call King Duṣyanta. The grove is under his protection.

KING: Here's my chance. Have no fear . . .

[*With this half-spoken, he stops and speaks to himself.*]

Then she will know that I am the king . . . Still, I shall speak.

ŚAKUNTALĀ [*stopping after a few steps*]: Why is he still following me?

KING [*approaching quickly*]:
> While a Puru king rules the earth
> to punish evildoers,
> who dares to molest
> these innocent young ascetics?

[*Seeing the king, all act flustered.*]

ANASŪYĀ: Sir, there's no real danger. Our friend was frightened when a bee attacked her.

[*She points to Śakuntalā.*]

KING [*approaching Śakuntalā*]: Does your ascetic practice go well?

[*Śakuntalā stands speechless.*]

ANASŪYĀ: It does now that we have a special guest. Śakuntalā, go to our hut and bring the ripe fruits. We'll use this water to bathe his feet.

KING: Your kind speech is hospitality enough.

PRIYAMVADĀ: Please sit in the cool shadows of this shade tree and rest, sir.

KING: You must also be tired from your work.

ANASŪYĀ: Śakuntalā, we should respect our guest. Let's sit down.

[*All sit.*]

ŚAKUNTALĀ [*to herself*]: When I see him, why do I feel an emotion that the forest seems to forbid?

KING [*looking at each of the girls*]: Youth and beauty complement your friendship.

PRIYAMVADĀ [*in a stage whisper*]: Anasūyā, who is he? He's so polite, fine looking, and pleasing to hear. He has the marks of royalty.

ANAYSŪYĀ: I'm curious too, friend. I'll just ask him. [*Aloud.*] Sir, your kind speech inspires trust. What family of royal sages[7] do you adorn? What country mourns your absence? Why does a man of refinement subject himself to the discomfort of visiting an ascetics' grove?

ŚAKUNTALĀ [*to herself*]: Heart, don't faint! Anasūyā speaks your thoughts.

KING [*to himself*]: Should I reveal myself now or conceal who I am? I'll say it this way.

---

7. A royal sage is a man of the warrior (*kshatriya*) social order who through penances and virtuous deeds comes to be regarded as a sage.

[*Aloud.*]

Lady, I have been appointed by the Puru king as the officer in charge of religious matters. I have come to this sacred forest to assure that your holy rites proceed unhindered.

ANASŪYĀ: Our religious life has a guardian now.

[*Śakuntalā mimes the embarrassment of erotic emotion.*]

BOTH FRIENDS [*observing the behavior of Śakuntalā and the king; in a stage whisper*]: Śakuntalā, if only your father were here now!

ŚAKUNTALĀ [*angrily*]: What if he were?

BOTH FRIENDS: He would honor this distinguished guest with what he values most in life.

ŚAKUNTALĀ: Quiet! Such words hint at your hearts' conspiracy. I won't listen.

KING: Ladies, I want to ask about your friend.

BOTH FRIENDS: Your request honors us, sir.

KING: Sage Kaṇva has always been celibate, but you call your friend his daughter. How can this be?

ANASŪYĀ: Please listen, sir. There was a powerful royal sage of the Kauśika clan . . .

KING: I am listening.

ANASŪYĀ: He begot our friend, but Kaṇva is her father because he cared for her when she was abandoned.

KING: "Abandoned"? The word makes me curious. I want to hear her story from the beginning.

ANASŪYĀ: Please listen, sir. Once when this great sage was practicing terrible austerities on the bank of the Gautamī river, he became so powerful that the jealous gods sent a nymph named Menakā to break his self-control.

KING: The gods dread men who meditate.

ANASŪYĀ: When springtime came to the forest with all its charm, the sage saw her intoxicating beauty . . .

KING: I understand what happened then. She is the nymph's daughter.

ANASŪYĀ: Yes.

KING: It had to be!

No mortal woman could give birth to such beauty—
lightning does not flash out of the earth.

[*Śakuntalā stands with her face bowed. The king continues speaking to himself.*]

My desire is not hopeless. Yet, when I hear her friends teasing her about a bridegroom, a new fear divides my heart.

PRIYAṂVADĀ [*smiling, looking at Śakuntalā, then turning to the king*]: Sir, you seem to want to say more.

[*Śakuntalā makes a threatening gesture with her finger.*]

KING: You judge correctly. In my eagerness to learn more about your pious lives, I have another question.

PRIYAṂVADĀ: Don't hesitate! Ascetics can be questioned frankly.

KING: I want to know this about your friend:

Will she keep the vow of hermit life

only until she marries . . .
or will she always exchange
loving looks with deer in the forest?

PRIYAMVADĀ: Sir, even in her religious life, she is subject to her father, but he does intend to give her to a suitable husband.

KING [*to himself*]: His wish is not hard to fulfill.

Heart, indulge your desire—
now that doubt is dispelled,
the fire you feared to touch
is a jewel in your hands.

ŚAKUNTALĀ [*showing anger*]: Anasūyā, I'm leaving!

ANASŪYĀ: Why?

ŚAKUNTALĀ: I'm going to tell Mother Gautamī that Priyaṁvadā is talking nonsense.

ANASŪYĀ: Friend, it's wrong to neglect a distinguished guest and leave as you like.

[*Śakuntalā starts to go without answering.*]

KING [*wanting to seize her, but holding back, he speaks to himself*]: A lover dare not act on his impulsive thoughts!

I wanted to follow the sage's daughter,
but decorum abruptly pulled me back;
I set out and returned again
without moving my feet from this spot.

PRIYAMVADĀ [*stopping Śakuntalā*]: It's wrong of you to go!

ŚAKUNTALĀ [*bending her brow into a frown*]: Give me a reason why!

PRIYAMVADĀ: You promised to water two trees for me.
Come here and pay your debt before you go!

[*She stops her by force.*]

KING: But she seems exhausted from watering the trees:

Her shoulders droop, her palms
are red from the watering pot—
even now, breathless sighs
make her breasts shake;
beads of sweat on her face
wilt the flower at her ear;
her hand holds back
disheveled locks of hair.

Here, I'll pay her debt!

[*He offers his ring. Both friends recite the syllables of the name on the seal and stare at each other.*]

Don't mistake me for what I am not! This is a gift from the king to identify me as his royal official.

PRIYAMVADĀ: Then the ring should never leave your finger. Your word has already paid her debt.

[*She laughs a little.*]

Śakuntalā, you are freed by this kind man . . . or perhaps by the king. Go now!

ŚAKUNTALĀ [*to herself*]: If I am able to . . .

[*Aloud.*]

Who are you to keep me or release me?

KING [*watching Śakuntalā*]: Can she feel toward me what I feel toward her? Or is my desire fulfilled?

> She won't respond directly to my words,
> but she listens when I speak;
> she won't turn to look at me,
> but her eyes can't rest anywhere else.

VOICE OFFSTAGE: Ascetics, be prepared to protect the creatures of our forest grove! King Duṣyanta is hunting nearby!

> Dust raised by his horses' hooves
> falls like a cloud of locusts swarming
> at sunset over branches of trees
> where wet bark garments hang.

> In terror of the chariots, an elephant
> charged into the hermitage
> and scattered the herd of black antelope,
> like a demon foe of our penances—
> his tusks garlanded with branches
> from a tree crushed by his weight,
> his feet tangled in vines
> that tether him like chains.

[*Hearing this, all the girls are agitated.*]

KING [*to himself*]: Oh! My palace men are searching for me and wrecking the grove. I'll have to go back.

BOTH FRIENDS: Sir, we're all upset by this news. Please let us go to our hut.

KING [*showing confusion*]: Go, please. We will try to protect the hermitage.

[*They all stand to go.*]

BOTH FRIENDS: Sir, we're ashamed that our bad hospitality is our only excuse to invite you back.

KING: Not at all. I am honored to have seen you.

[*Śakuntalā exits with her two friends, looking back at the king, lingering artfully.*]

I have little desire to return to the city. I'll join my men and have them camp near the grove. I can't control my feelings for Śakuntalā.

> My body turns to go,
> my heart pulls me back,
> like a silk banner
> buffeted by the wind.

[*All exit.*]

ACT 2

[*The buffoon enters, despondent.*]

BUFFOON [*sighing*]: My bad luck! I'm tired of playing sidekick to a king who's hooked on hunting. "There's a deer!" "There's a boar!" "There's a tiger!" Even in the summer midday heat we chase from jungle to jungle on paths where trees give barely any shade. We drink stinking water from mountain streams foul with rusty leaves. At odd hours we eat nasty meals of spit-roasted meat. Even at night I can't sleep. My joints ache from galloping on that horse. Then at the crack of dawn, I'm woken rudely by a noise piercing the forest. Those sons of bitches hunt their birds then. The torture doesn't end—now I have sores on top of my bruises. Yesterday, we lagged behind. The king chased a buck into the hermitage. As luck would have it, an ascetic's daughter called Śakuntalā caught his eye. Now he isn't even thinking of going back to the city. This very dawn I found him wide-eyed, mooning about her. What a fate! I must see him after his bath.

[*He walks around, looking.*]

Here comes my friend now, wearing garlands of wild flowers. Greek women[1] carry his bow in their hands. Good! I'll stand here pretending my arms and legs are broken. Maybe then I'll get some rest.

[*He stands leaning on his staff. The king enters with his retinue, as described.*]

KING [*to himself*]: My beloved will not be easy to win,
　　　but signs of emotion revealed her heart—
　　　even when love seems hopeless,
　　　mutual longing keeps passion alive.

[*He smiles.*]

A suitor who measures his beloved's state of mind by his own desire is a fool.

　　　She threw tender glances
　　　though her eyes were cast down,
　　　her heavy hips swayed
　　　in slow seductive movements,
　　　she answered in anger
　　　when her friend said, "Don't go!"
　　　and I felt it was all for my sake . . .
　　　but a lover sees in his own way.

BUFFOON [*still in the same position*]: Dear friend, since my hands can't move to greet you, I have to salute you with my voice.
KING: How did you cripple your limbs?
BUFFOON: Why do you ask why I cry after throwing dust in my eyes yourself?
KING: I don't understand.

---

1. A stock reference in Sanskrit drama, a vague reminiscence of the Greek presence in northwest India for some centuries from about 300 B.C.E., and perhaps, even more vaguely, of the legend of the Amazon women.

BUFFOON: Dear friend, when a straight reed is twisted into a crooked reed, is it by its own power, or is it the river current?

KING: The river current is the cause.

BUFFOON: And so it is with me.

KING: How so?

BUFFOON: You neglect the business of being a king and live like a woodsman in this awful camp. Chasing after wild beasts every day jolts my joints and muscles till I can't control my own limbs anymore. I beg you to let me rest for just one day!

KING: [*to himself*] He says what I also feel. When I remember Kaṇva's daughter, the thought of hunting disgusts me.

> I can't draw my bowstring
> to shoot arrows at deer
> who live with my love
> and teach her tender glances.

BUFFOON: Sir, you have something on your mind. I'm crying in a wilderness.

KING [*smiling*]: Yes, it is wrong to ignore my friend's plea.

BUFFOON: Live long!

[*He starts to go.*]

KING: Dear friend, stay! Hear what I have to say!

BUFFOON: At your command, sir!

KING: When you have rested, I need your help in some work that you will enjoy.

BUFFOON: Is it eating sweets? I'm game!

KING: I shall tell you. Who stands guard?

GUARD [*entering*]: At your command, sir!

KING: Raivataka! Summon the general!

[*The guard exits and reenters with the general.*]

GUARD: The king is looking this way, waiting to give you his orders. Approach him, sir!

GENERAL [*looking at the king*]: Hunting is said to be a vice, but our king prospers:

> Drawing the bow only hardens his chest,
> he suffers the sun's scorching rays unburned,
> hard muscles mask his body's lean state—
> like a wild elephant, his energy sustains him.

[*He approaches the king.*]

Victory, my lord! We've already tracked some wild beasts. Why the delay?

KING: Mādhavya's censure of hunting has dampened my spirit.

GENERAL [*in a stage whisper, to the buffoon*]: Friend, you stick to your opposition! I'll try to restore our king's good sense.

[*Aloud.*]

This fool is talking nonsense. Here is the king as proof:

> A hunter's belly is taut and lean,
> his slender body craves exertion;
> he penetrates the spirit of creatures

> overcome by fear and rage;
> his bowmanship is proved
> by arrows striking a moving target—
> hunting is falsely called a vice.
> What sport can rival it?

BUFFOON [*angrily*]: The king has come to his senses. If you keep chasing from forest to forest, you'll fall into the jaws of an old bear hungry for a human nose . . .

KING: My noble general, we are near a hermitage; your words cannot please me now.

> Let horned buffaloes plunge into muddy pools!
> Let herds of deer huddle in the shade to eat grass!
> Let fearless wild boars crush fragrant swamp grass!
> Let my bowstring lie slack and my bow at rest!

GENERAL: Whatever gives the king pleasure.

KING: Withdraw the men who are in the forest now and forbid my soldiers to disturb the grove!

> Ascetics devoted to peace
> possess a fiery hidden power,
> like smooth crystal sunstones
> that reflect the sun's scorching rays.

GENERAL: Whatever you command, sir!

BUFFOON: Your arguments for keeping up the hunt fall on deaf ears!

[*The general exits.*]

KING [*looking at his retinue*]: You women, take away my hunting gear! Raivataka, don't neglect your duty!

RETINUE: As the king commands!

[*They exit.*]

BUFFOON: Sir, now that the flies are cleared out, sit on a stone bench under this shady canopy. Then I'll find a comfortable seat too.

KING: Go ahead!

BUFFOON: You first, sir!

[*Both walk about, then sit down.*]

KING: Mādhavya, you haven't really used your eyes because you haven't seen true beauty.

BUFFOON: But you're right in front of me, sir!

KING: Everyone is partial to what he knows well, but I'm speaking about Śakuntalā, the jewel of the hermitage.

BUFFOON [*to himself*]: I won't give him a chance!

[*Aloud.*]

Dear friend, it seems that you're pursuing an ascetic's daughter.

KING: Friend, the heart of a Puru king wouldn't crave a forbidden fruit . . .

> The sage's child is a nymph's daughter,

rescued by him after she was abandoned,
like a fragile jasmine blossom
broken and caught on a sunflower pod.

BUFFOON [*laughing*]: You're like the man who loses his taste for dates and prefers sour tamarind! How can you abandon the gorgeous gems of your palace?

KING: You speak this way because you haven't seen her.

BUFFOON: She must be delectable if you're so enticed!

KING: Friend, what is the use of all this talk?

The divine creator imagined perfection
and shaped her ideal form in his mind—
when I recall the beauty his power wrought,
she shines like a gemstone among my jewels.

BUFFOON: So she's the reason you reject the other beauties!

KING: She stays in my mind:

A flower no one has smelled,
a bud no fingers have plucked,
an uncut jewel, honey untasted,
unbroken fruit of holy deeds—
I don't know who is destined
to enjoy her flawless beauty.

BUFFOON: Then you should rescue her quickly! Don't let her fall into the arms of some ascetic who greases his head with ingudī oil!

KING: She is someone else's ward and her guardian is away.

BUFFOON: What kind of passion did her eyes betray?

KING: Ascetics are timid by nature:

Her eyes were cast down in my presence,
but she found an excuse to smile—
modesty barely contained the love
she could neither reveal nor conceal.

BUFFOON: Did you expect her to climb into your lap when she'd barely seen you?

KING: When we parted her feelings for me showed despite her modesty.

"A blade of kuśa grass
pricked my foot,"
the girl said for no reason
after walking a few steps away;
then she pretended to free
her bark dress from branches
where it was not caught
and shyly glanced at me.

BUFFOON: Stock up on food for a long trip! I can see you've turned that ascetics' grove into a pleasure garden.

KING: Friend, some of the ascetics recognize me. What excuse can we find to return to the hermitage?

BUFFOON: What excuse? Aren't you the king? Collect a sixth of their wild rice as tax!

KING: Fool! These ascetics pay tribute that pleases me more than mounds of jewels.

Tribute that kings collect
from members of society decays,
but the share of austerity
that ascetics give lasts forever.

VOICE OFFSTAGE: Good, we have succeeded!

KING [*listening*]: These are the steady, calm voices of ascetics.

GUARD [*entering*]: Victory, sir! Two boy ascetics are waiting near the gate.

KING: Let them enter without delay!

GUARD: I'll show them in.

[*He exits; reenters with the boys.*]

Here you are!

FIRST BOY: His majestic body inspires trust. It is natural when a king is virtually a sage.

His palace is a hermitage
with its infinite pleasures,
the discipline of protecting men
imposes austerities every day—
pairs of celestial bards praise
his perfect self-control,
adding the royal word "king"
to "sage," his sacred title.

SECOND BOY: Gautama, is this Duṣyanta, the friend of Indra?[2]

FIRST BOY: Of course!

SECOND BOY: It is no surprise that this arm of iron
rules the whole earth bounded by dark seas—
when demons harass the gods, victory's hope
rests on his bow and Indra's thunderbolt.

BOTH BOYS [*coming near*]: Victory to you, king!

KING [*rising from his seat*]: I salute you both!

BOTH BOYS: To your success, sir!

[*They offer fruits.*]

KING [*accepting their offering*]: I am ready to listen.

BOTH BOYS: The ascetics know that you are camped nearby and send a petition to you.

KING: What do they request?

BOTH BOYS: Demons are taking advantage of Sage Kaṇva's absence to harass us. You must come with your charioteer to protect the hermitage for a few days!

KING: I am honored to oblige.

BUFFOON [*in a stage whisper*]: Your wish is fulfilled!

KING [*smiling*]: Raivataka, call my charioteer! Tell him to bring the chariot and my bow!

GUARD: As the king commands!

---

2. The king of the Vedic pantheon and a warrior god whose weapon is the thunderbolt.

[*He exits.*]

BOTH BOYS [*showing delight*]:
> Following your ancestral duties
> suits your noble form—
> the Puru kings are ordained
> to dispel their subjects' fear.

KING [*bowing*]: You two return! I shall follow.

BOTH BOYS: Be victorious!

[*They exit.*]

KING: Mādhavya, are you curious to see Śakuntalā?

BUFFOON: At first there was a flood, but now with this news of demons, not a drop is left.

KING: Don't be afraid! Won't you be with me?

BUFFOON: Then I'll be safe from any demon . . .

GUARD [*entering*]: The chariot is ready to take you to victory . . . but Karabhaka has just come from the city with a message from the queen.

KING: Did my mother send him?

GUARD: She did.

KING: Have him enter then.

GUARD: Yes.

[*He exits; reenters with Karabhaka.*]

Here is the king. Approach!

KARABHAKA: Victory, sir! Victory! The queen has ordered a ceremony four days from now to mark the end of her fast. Your Majesty will surely give us the honor of his presence.

KING: The ascetics' business keeps me here and my mother's command calls me there. I must find a way to avoid neglecting either!

BUFFOON: Hang yourself between them the way Triśaṅku[3] hung between heaven and earth.

KING: I'm really confused . . .

> My mind is split in two
> by these conflicting duties,
> like a river current split
> by boulders in its course.

[*Thinking.*]

Friend, my mother has treated you like a son. You must go back and report that I've set my heart on fulfilling my duty to the ascetics. You fulfill my filial duty to the queen.

BUFFOON: You don't really think I'm afraid of demons?

KING [*smiling*]: My brave brahman, how could you be?

BUFFOON: Then I can travel like the king's younger brother.

3. A king who sought to ascend to heaven with his physical body intact, with the help of the sage Vishvamitra. When the gods resisted his arrival in their midst, Vishvamitra created another whole starry heaven and threatened to produce even another Indra and host of gods. The gods compromised by allowing the newly created stars to persist forever and to revolve around Trishanku as if he had attained heaven in bodily form.

KING: We really should not disturb the grove! Take my whole entourage with you!

BUFFOON: Now I've turned into the crown prince!

KING [*to himself*]: This fellow is absent-minded. At any time he may tell the palace women about my passion. I'll tell him this:

[*taking the buffoon by the hand, he speaks aloud*]

Dear friend, I'm going to the hermitage out of reverence for the sages. I really feel no desire for the young ascetic Śakuntalā.

> What do I share with a rustic girl
> reared among fawns, unskilled in love?
> Don't mistake what I muttered
> in jest for the real truth, friend!

[*All exit.*]

ACT 3

[*A disciple of Kaṇva enters, carrying kuśa grass for a sacrificial rite.*]

DISCIPLE: King Duṣyanta is certainly powerful. Since he entered the hermitage, our rites have not been hindered.

> Why talk of fixing arrows?
> The mere twang of his bowstring
> clears away menacing demons
> as if his bow roared with death.

I'll gather some more grass for the priests to spread on the sacrificial altar.

[*Walking around and looking, he calls aloud.*]

Priyaṁvadā, for whom are you bringing the ointment of fragrant lotus root fibers and leaves?

[*Listening.*]

What are you saying? Śakuntalā is suffering from heat exhaustion? They're for rubbing on her body? Priyaṁvadā, take care of her! She is the breath of Father Kaṇva's life. I'll give Gautamī this water from the sacrifice to use for soothing her.

[*He exits; the interlude ends. Then the king enters, suffering from love, deep in thought, sighing.*]

KING: I know the power ascetics have
> and the rules that bind her,
> but I cannot abandon my heart
> now that she has taken it.

[*Showing the pain of love.*]

Love, why do you and the moon both contrive to deceive lovers by first gaining our trust?

> Arrows of flowers and cool moon rays
> are both deadly for men like me—

the moon shoots fire through icy rays
and you hurl thunderbolts of flowers.

[*Walking around.*]

Now that the rites are concluded and the priests have dismissed me, where can I
rest from the weariness of this work?

[*Sighing.*]

There is no refuge but the sight of my love. I must find her.

[*Looking up at the sun.*]

Śakuntalā usually spends the heat of the day with her friends in a bower of vines on
the Mālinī riverbank. I shall go there.

[*Walking around, miming the touch of breeze.*]

This place is enchanted by the wind.

> A breeze fragrant with lotus pollen
> and moist from the Mālinī waves
> can be held in soothing embrace
> by my love-scorched arms.

[*Walking around and looking.*]

> I see fresh footprints
> on white sand in the clearing,
> deeply pressed at the heel
> by the sway of full hips.

> I'll just look through the branches.

[*Walking around, looking, he becomes joyous.*]

My eyes have found bliss! The girl I desire is lying on a stone couch strewn with
flowers, attended by her two friends. I'll eavesdrop as they confide in one another.

[*He stands watching. Śakuntalā appears as described, with her two friends.*]

BOTH FRIENDS [*fanning her affectionately*]: Śakuntalā, does the breeze from this lotus
leaf please you?
ŚAKUNTALĀ: Are you fanning me?

[*The friends trade looks, miming dismay.*]

KING [*deliberating*]: Śakuntalā seems to be in great physical pain. Is it the heat or is it
what is in my own heart?

[*Miming ardent desire.*]

My doubts are unfounded!

> Her breasts are smeared with lotus balm,
> her lotus-fiber bracelet hangs limp,
> her beautiful body glows in pain—
> love burns young women like summer heat,
> but its guilt makes them more charming.

PRIYAṀVADĀ [*in a stage whisper*]: Anasūyā, Śakuntalā has been pining since she first saw the king. Could he be the cause of her sickness?

ANASŪYĀ: She must be suffering from lovesickness. I'll ask her . . .

[*Aloud.*]

Friend, I have something to ask you. Your pain seems so deep . . .

ŚAKUNTALĀ [*raising herself halfway*]: What do you want to say?

ANASŪYĀ: Śakuntalā, though we don't know what it is to be in love, your condition reminds us of lovers we have heard about in stories. Can you tell us the cause of your pain? Unless we understand your illness, we can't begin to find a cure.

KING: Anasūyā expresses my own thoughts.

ŚAKUNTALĀ: Even though I want to, suddenly I can't make myself tell you.

PRIYAṀVADĀ: Śakuntalā, my friend Anasūyā means well. Don't you see how sick you are? Your limbs are wasting away. Only the shadow of your beauty remains . . .

KING: What Priyaṁvadā says is true:

> Her checks are deeply sunken,
> her breasts' full shape is gone,
> her waist is thin, her shoulders bent,
> and the color has left her skin—
> tormented by love,
> she is sad but beautiful to see,
> like a jasmine creeper
> when hot wind shrivels its leaves.

ŚAKUNTALĀ: Friends, who else can I tell? May I burden you?

BOTH FRIENDS: We insist! Sharing sorrow with loving friends makes it bearable.

KING:
> Friends who share her joy and sorrow
> discover the love concealed in her heart—
> though she looked back longingly at me,
> now I am afraid to hear her response.

ŚAKUNTALĀ: Friend, since my eyes first saw the guardian of the hermits' retreat, I've felt such strong desire for him!

KING: I have heard what I want to hear.

> My tormentor, the god of love,
> has soothed my fever himself,
> like the heat of late summer
> allayed by early rain clouds.

ŚAKUNTALĀ: If you two think it's right, then help me to win the king's pity. Otherwise, you'll soon pour sesame oil and water on my corpse . . .

KING: Her words destroy my doubt.

PRIYAṀVADĀ [*in a stage whisper*]: She's so dangerously in love that there's no time to lose. Since her heart is set on the ornament of the Puru dynasty, we should rejoice that she desires him.

ANASŪYĀ: What you say is true.

PRIYAṀVADĀ [*aloud*]: Friend, by good fortune your desire is in harmony with nature. A great river can only descend to the ocean. A jasmine creeper can only twine around a mango tree.

KING: Why is this surprising when the twin stars of spring serve the crescent moon?

ANASŪYĀ: What means do we have to fulfill our friend's desire secretly and quickly?

PRIYAMVADĀ: "Secretly" demands some effort. "Quickly" is easy.

ANASŪYĀ: How so?

PRIYAMVADĀ: The king was charmed by her loving look; he seems thin these days from sleepless nights.

KING: It's true . . .

> This golden armlet
> slips to my wrist
> without touching the scars
> my bowstring has made;
> its gemstones are faded
> by tears of secret pain
> that every night wets my arm
> where I bury my face.

PRIYAMVADĀ [*thinking*]: Compose a love letter and I'll hide it in a flower. I'll deliver it to his hand on the pretext of bringing an offering to the deity.

ANASŪYĀ: This subtle plan pleases me. What does Śakuntalā say?

ŚAKUNTALĀ: I'll try my friend's plan.

PRIYAMVADĀ: Then compose a poem to declare your love!

ŚAKUNTALĀ: I'm thinking, but my heart trembles with fear that he'll reject me.

KING [*delighted*]: The man you fear will reject you

> waits longing to love you, timid girl—
> a suitor may lose or be lucky,
> but the goddess always wins.

BOTH FRIENDS: Why do you belittle your own virtues? Who would cover his body with a piece of cloth to keep off cool autumn moonlight?

ŚAKUNTALĀ [*smiling*]: I'm trying to follow your advice.

[*She sits thinking.*]

KING: As I gaze at her, my eyes forget to blink.

> She arches an eyebrow,
> struggling to compose the verse—
> the down rises on her cheek,
> showing the passion she feels.

ŚAKUNTALĀ: I've thought of a verse, but I have nothing to write it on.

PRIYAMVADĀ: Engrave the letters with your nail on this lotus leaf! It's as delicate as a parrot's breast.

ŚAKUNTALĀ [*miming what Priyaṁvadā described*]: Listen and tell me if this makes sense!

BOTH FRIENDS: We're both paying attention.

ŚAKUNTALĀ [*singing*]: I don't know
> your heart,
> but day and night
> for wanting you,
> love violently

tortures
my limbs,
cruel man.

KING [*suddenly revealing himself*]:

Love torments you, slender girl,
but he completely consumes me—
daylight spares the lotus pond
while it destroys the moon.

BOTH FRIENDS [*looking, rising with delight*]: Welcome to the swift success of love's desire!

[*Śakuntalā tries to rise.*]

KING: Don't exert yourself!

Limbs lying among crushed petals
like fragile lotus stalks
are too weakened by pain
to perform ceremonious acts.

ANASŪYĀ: Then let the king sit on this stone bench!

[*The king sits; Śakuntalā rises in embarrassment.*]

PRIYAMVADĀ: The passion of two young lovers is clear. My affection for our friend makes me speak out again now.

KING: Noble lady, don't hesitate! It is painful to keep silent when one must speak.

PRIYAMVADĀ: We're told that it is the king's duty to ease the pain of his suffering subjects.

KING: My duty, exactly!

PRIYAMVADĀ: Since she first saw you, our dear friend has been reduced to this sad condition. You must protect her and save her life.

KING: Noble lady, our affection is shared and I am honored by all you say.

ŚAKUNTALĀ [*looking at Priyamvadā*]: Why are you keeping the king here? He must be anxious to return to his palace.

KING: If you think that my lost heart
could love anyone but you,
a fatal blow strikes a man
already wounded by love's arrows!

ANASŪYĀ: We've heard that kings have many loves. Will our dear friend become a sorrow to her family after you've spent time with her?

KING: Noble lady, enough of this!

Despite my many wives,
on two the royal line rests—
sea-bound earth
and your friend.

BOTH FRIENDS: You reassure us.

PRIYAMVADĀ [*casting a glance*]: Anasūyā, this fawn is looking for its mother. Let's take it to her!

[*They both begin to leave.*]

ŚAKUNTALĀ: Come back! Don't leave me unprotected!

BOTH FRIENDS: The protector of the earth is at your side.

ŚAKUNTALĀ: Why have they gone?

KING: Don't be alarmed! I am your servant.

> Shall I set moist winds in motion
> with lotus-leaf fans to cool your pain,
> or rest your soft red lotus feet
> on my lap to stroke them, my love?

ŚAKUNTALĀ: I cannot sin against those I respect!

[*Standing as if she wants to leave.*]

KING: Beautiful Śakuntalā, the day is still hot.

> Why should your frail limbs
> leave this couch of flowers
> shielded by lotus leaves
> to wander in the heat?

[*Saying this, he forces her to turn around.*]

ŚAKUNTALĀ: Puru king, control yourself! Though I'm burning with love, how can I give myself to you?

KING: Don't fear your elders! The father of your family knows the law. When he finds out, he will not blame you.

> The daughters of royal sages often marry
> in secret and then their fathers bless them.[1]

ŚAKUNTALĀ: Release me! I must ask my friends' advice!

KING: Yes, I shall release you.

ŚAKUNTALĀ: When?

KING:
> Only let my thirsting mouth
> gently drink from your lips,
> the way a bee sips nectar
> from a fragile virgin blossom.

[*Saying this, he tries to raise her face. Śakuntalā evades him with a dance.*]

VOICE OFFSTAGE: Red goose, bid farewell to your gander! Night has arrived!

ŚAKUNTALĀ [*flustered*]: Puru king, Mother Gautamī is surely coming to ask about my health. Hide behind this tree!

KING: Yes.

[*He conceals himself and waits. Then Gautamī enters with a vessel in her hand, accompanied by Śakuntalā's two friends.*]

BOTH FRIENDS: This way, Mother Gautamī!

GAUTAMĪ [*approaching Śakuntalā*]: Child, does the fever in your limbs burn less?

ŚAKUNTALĀ: Madam, I do feel better.

---

1. Marriage by mutual consent (termed the *gandharva* form of marriage) was permitted to the warrior order.

GAUTAMĪ: Kuśa grass and water will soothe your body.

[*She sprinkles Śakuntalā's head.*]

Child, the day is ended. Come, let's go back to our hut!

[*She starts to go.*]

ŚAKUNTALĀ [*to herself*]: My heart, even when your desire was within reach, you were bound by fear. Now you'll suffer the torment of separation and regret.

[*Stopping after a few steps, she speaks aloud.*]

Bower of creepers, refuge from my torment, I say goodbye until our joy can be renewed . . .

[*Sorrowfully, Śakuntalā exits with the other women.*]

KING [*coming out of hiding*]: Fulfillment of desire is fraught with obstacles.

> Why didn't I kiss her face
> as it bent near my shoulder,
> her fingers shielding lips
> that stammered lovely warning?

Should I go now? Or shall I stay here in this bower of creepers that my love enjoyed and then left?

> I see the flowers her body pressed
> on this bench of stone,
> the letter her nails inscribed
> on the faded lotus leaf,
> the lotus-fiber bracelet
> that slipped from her wrist—
> my eyes are prisoners
> in this empty house of reeds.

VOICE IN THE AIR: King!

> When the evening rituals begin,
> shadows of flesh-eating demons swarm
> like amber clouds of twilight,
> raising terror at the altar of fire.

KING: I am coming.

[*He exits.*]

ACT 4

[*The two friends enter, miming the gathering of flowers.*]

ANASŪYĀ: Priyaṁvadā, I'm delighted that Śakuntalā chose a suitable husband for herself, but I still feel anxious.

PRIYAṀVADĀ: Why?

ANASŪYĀ: When the king finished the sacrifice, the sages thanked him and he left. Now that he has returned to his palace women in the city, will he remember us here?

PRIYAMVADĀ: Have faith! He's so handsome, he can't be evil. But I don't know what Father Kaṇva will think when he hears about what happened.

ANASŪYĀ: I predict that he'll give his approval.

PRIYAMVADĀ: Why?

ANASŪYĀ: He's always planned to give his daughter to a worthy husband. If fate accomplished it so quickly, Father Kaṇva won't object.

PRIYAMVADĀ [looking at the basket of flowers]: We've gathered enough flowers for the offering ceremony.

ANASŪYĀ: Shouldn't we worship the goddess who guards Śakuntalā?

PRIYAMVADĀ: I have just begun.

[She begins the rite.]

VOICE OFFSTAGE: I am here!

ANASŪYĀ [listening]: Friend, a guest is announcing himself.

PRIYAMVADĀ: Śakuntalā is in her hut nearby, but her heart is far away.

ANASŪYĀ: You're right! Enough of these flowers!

[They begin to leave.]

VOICE OFFSTAGE: So . . . you slight a guest . . .

> Since you blindly ignore
> a great sage like me,
> the lover you worship
> with mindless devotion
> will not remember you,
> even when awakened—
> like a drunkard who forgets
> a story he just composed!

PRIYAMVADĀ: Oh! What a terrible turn of events! Śakuntalā's distraction has offended someone she should have greeted.

[Looking ahead.]

Not just an ordinary person, but the angry sage Durvāsas[1] himself cursed her and went away in a frenzy of quivering, mad gestures. What else but fire has such power to burn?

ANASŪYĀ: Go! Bow at his feet and make him return while I prepare the water for washing his feet!

PRIYAMVADĀ: As you say.

[She exits.]

ANASŪYĀ [after a few steps, she mimes stumbling]: Oh! The basket of flowers fell from my hand when I stumbled in my haste to go.

---

1. An irascible ascetic, son of the legendary sage Atri and his wife Anasuya (namesake of the female ascetic in the play), who was infamous in Sanskrit literature for his curses.

[*She mimes the gathering of flowers.*]

PRIYAṀVADĀ [*entering*]: He's so terribly cruel! No one could pacify him! But I was able to soften him a little.

ANASŪYĀ: Even that is a great feat with him! Tell me more!

PRIYAṀVADĀ: When he refused to return, I begged him to forgive a daughter's first offense, since she didn't understand the power of his austerity.

ANASŪYĀ: Then? Then?

PRIYAṀVADĀ: He refused to change his word, but he promised that when the king sees the ring of recollection, the curse will end. Then he vanished.

ANASŪYĀ: Now we can breathe again. When he left, the king himself gave her the ring engraved with his name. Śakuntalā will have her own means of ending the curse.

PRIYAṀVADĀ: Come friend! We should finish the holy rite we're performing for her.

[*The two walk around, looking.*]

Anasūyā, look! With her face resting on her hand, our dear friend looks like a picture. She is thinking about her husband's leaving, with no thought for herself, much less for a guest.

ANASŪYĀ: Priyaṁvadā, we two must keep all this a secret between us. Our friend is fragile by nature; she needs our protection.

PRIYAṀVADĀ: Who would sprinkle a jasmine with scalding water?

[*They both exit; the interlude ends. Then a disciple of Kaṇva enters, just awakened from sleep.*]

DISCIPLE: Father Kaṇva has just returned from his pilgrimage and wants to know the exact time. I'll go into a clearing to see what remains of the night.

[*Walking around and looking.*]

It is dawn.

> The moon sets over the western mountain
> as the sun rises in dawn's red trail—
> rising and setting, these two bright powers
> portend the rise and fall of men.
>
> When the moon disappears, night lotuses
> are but dull souvenirs of its beauty—
> when her lover disappears, the sorrow
> is too painful for a frail girl to bear.

ANASŪYĀ [*throwing aside the curtain and entering*]: Even a person withdrawn from worldly life knows that the king has treated Śakuntalā badly.

DISCIPLE: I'll inform Father Kaṇva that it's time for the fire oblation.

[*He exits.*]

ANASŪYĀ: Even when I'm awake, I'm useless. My hands and feet don't do their work. Love must be pleased to have made our innocent friend put her trust in a liar . . . but perhaps it was the curse of Durvāsas that changed him . . . otherwise, how could the king have made such promises and not sent even a message by now? Maybe we should send the ring to remind him. Which of these ascetics who practice austerities can we ask? Father Kaṇva has just returned from his pilgrim-age. Since we feel that our friend was also at fault, we haven't told him that Śakun-talā is married to Duṣyanta and is pregnant. The problem is serious. What should we do?

PRIYAṂVADĀ [entering, with delight]: Friend, hurry! We're to celebrate the festival of Śakuntalā's departure for her husband's house.

ANASŪYĀ: What's happened, friend?

PRIYAṂVADĀ: Listen! I went to ask Śakuntalā how she had slept. Father Kaṇva em-braced her and though her face was bowed in shame, he blessed her: "Though his eyes were filled with smoke, the priest's oblation luckily fell on the fire. My child, I shall not mourn for you . . . like knowledge given to a good student I shall send you to your husband today with an escort of sages."

ANASŪYĀ: Who told Father Kaṇva what happened?

PRIYAṂVADĀ: A bodiless voice was chanting when he entered the fire sanctuary.

[Quoting in Sanskrit.]

> Priest, know that your daughter
> carries Duṣyanta's potent seed
> for the good of the earth—
> like fire in mimosa wood.

ANASŪYĀ: I'm joyful, friend. But I know that Śakuntalā must leave us today and sor-row shadows my happiness.

PRIYAṂVADĀ: Friend, we must chase away sorrow and make this hermit girl happy!

ANASŪYĀ: Friend, I've made a garland of mimosa flowers. It's in the coconut-shell box hanging on a branch of the mango tree. Get it for me! Meanwhile I'll prepare the special ointments of deer musk, sacred earth, and blades of dūrvā grass.

PRIYAṂVADĀ: Here it is!

[Anasūyā exits; Priyaṃvadā gracefully mimes taking down the box.]

VOICE OFFSTAGE: Gautamī! Śārṅgarava and some others have been appointed to es-cort Śakuntalā.

PRIYAṂVADĀ [listening]: Hurry! Hurry! The sages are being called to go to Hastināpura.

ANASŪYĀ [reentering with pots of ointments in her hands]: Come, friend! Let's go!

PRIYAṂVADĀ [looking around]: Śakuntalā stands at sunrise with freshly washed hair while the female ascetics bless her with handfuls of wild rice and auspicious words of farewell. Let's go to her together.

[The two approach as Śakuntalā enters with Gautamī and other female ascetics, and strikes a posture as described. One after another, the female ascetics address her.]

FIRST FEMALE ASCETIC: Child, win the title "Chief Queen" as a sign of your husband's high esteem!

SECOND FEMALE ASCETIC: Child, be a mother to heroes!

THIRD FEMALE ASCETIC: Child, be honored by your husband!

BOTH FRIENDS: This happy moment is no time for tears, friend.

[Wiping away her tears, they calm her with dance gestures.]

PRIYAMVADĀ: Your beauty deserves jewels, not these humble things we've gathered in the hermitage.

[*Two boy ascetics enter with offerings in their hands.*]

BOTH BOYS: Here is an ornament for you!

[*Everyone looks amazed.*]

GAUTAMĪ: Nārada, my child, where did this come from?

FIRST BOY: From Father Kaṇva's power.

GAUTAMĪ: Was it his mind's magic?

SECOND BOY: Not at all! Listen! You ordered us to bring flowers from the forest trees for Śakuntalā.

> One tree produced this white silk cloth,
> another poured resinous lac to redden her feet—
> the tree nymphs produced jewels in hands
> that stretched from branches like young shoots.

PRIYAMVADĀ [*watching Śakuntalā*]: This is a sign that royal fortune will come to you in your husband's house.

[*Śakuntalā mimes modesty.*]

FIRST BOY: Gautama, come quickly! Father Kaṇva is back from bathing. We'll tell him how the trees honor her.

SECOND BOY: As you say.

[*The two exit.*]

BOTH FRIENDS: We've never worn them ourselves, but we'll put these jewels on your limbs the way they look in pictures.

ŚAKUNTALĀ: I trust your skill.

[*Both friends mime ornamenting her. Then Kaṇva enters, fresh from his bath.*]

KAṆVA: My heart is touched with sadness
  since Śakuntalā must go today,
  my throat is choked with sobs,
  my eyes are dulled by worry—
  if a disciplined ascetic
  suffers so deeply from love,
  how do fathers bear the pain
  of each daughter's parting?

[*He walks around.*]

BOTH FRIENDS: Śakuntalā, your jewels are in place; now put on the pair of silken cloths.

[*Standing, Śakuntalā wraps them.*]

GAUTAMĪ: Child, your father has come. His eyes filled with tears of joy embrace you. Greet him reverently!

ŚAKUNTALĀ [*modestly*]: Father, I welcome you.

KAṆVA: Child,

May your husband honor you
the way Yayāti honored Śarmiṣṭhā.
As she bore her son Puru,[2]
may you bear an imperial prince.

GAUTAMĪ: Sir, this is a blessing, not just a prayer.
KAṆVA: Child, walk around the sacrifical fires!

[*All walk around; Kaṇva intoning a prayer in Vedic meter.*]

Perfectly placed around the main altar,
fed with fuel, strewn with holy grass,
destroying sin by incense from oblations,
may these sacred fires purify you!
You must leave now!

[*Looking around.*]

Where are Śārṅgarava and the others?
DISCIPLE [*entering*]: Here we are, sir!
KAṆVA: You show your sister the way!
ŚĀRṄGARAVA: Come this way!

[*They walk around.*]

KAṆVA: Listen, you trees that grow in our grove!

Until you were well watered
she could not bear to drink;
she loved you too much
to pluck your flowers for her hair;
the first time your buds bloomed,
she blossomed with joy—
may you all bless Śakuntalā
as she leaves for her husband's house.

[*Miming that he hears a cuckoo's cry.*]

The trees of her forest family
have blessed Śakuntalā—
the cuckoo's melodious song
announces their response.
VOICE IN THE AIR: May lakes colored by lotuses mark her path!
May trees shade her from the sun's burning rays!
May the dust be as soft as lotus pollen!
May fragrant breezes cool her way!

[*All listen astonished.*]

GAUTAMĪ: Child, the divinities of our grove love you like your family and bless you.
We bow to you all!

---

2. The legendary King Yayati fell in love with Sharmishtha, daughter of the king of the antigods, who was acting as his chief queen's maid, and they married by the *gandharva* rite. Puru, the youngest among the sons she bore him, succeeded to the throne.

ŚAKUNTALĀ [*bowing and walking around; speaking in a stage whisper*]: Priyaṁvadā, though I long to see my husband, my feet move with sorrow as I start to leave the hermitage.

PRIYAṀVADĀ: You are not the only one who grieves. The whole hermitage feels this way as your departure from our grove draws near.

> Grazing deer
> drop grass,
> peacocks
> stop dancing,
> vines loose
> pale leaves
> falling
> like tears.

ŚAKUNTALĀ [*remembering*]: Father, before I leave, I must see my sister, the vine Forestlight.

KAṆVA: I know that you feel a sister's love for her. She is right here.

ŚAKUNTALĀ: Forestlight, though you love your mango tree, turn to embrace me with your tendril arms! After today, I'll be so far away . . .

KAṆVA: Your merits won you the husband
I always hoped you would have
and your jasmine has her mango tree—
my worries for you both are over.

Start your journey here!

ŚAKUNTALĀ [*facing her two friends*]: I entrust her care to you.

BOTH FRIENDS: But who will care for us?

[*They wipe away their tears.*]

KAṆVA: Anasūyā, enough crying! You should be giving
Śakuntalā courage!

[*All walk around.*]

ŚAKUNTALĀ: Father, when the pregnant doe who grazes near my hut gives birth, please send someone to give me the good news.

KAṆVA: I shall not forget.

ŚAKUNTALĀ [*miming the interrupting of her gait*]: Who is clinging to my skirt?

[*She turns around.*]

KAṆVA: Child,

> The buck whose mouth you healed with oil
> when it was pierced by a blade of kuśa grass
> and whom you fed with grains of rice—
> your adopted son will not leave the path.

ŚAKUNTALĀ: Child, don't follow when I'm abandoning those I love! I raised you when you were orphaned soon after your birth, but now I'm deserting you too. Father will look after you. Go back!

[*Weeping, she starts to go.*]

KANVA: Be strong!

> Hold back the tears that blind
> your long-lashed eyes—
> you will stumble if you cannot see
> the uneven ground on the path.

ŚĀRNGARAVA: Sir, the scriptures prescribe that loved ones be escorted only to the water's edge. We are at the shore of the lake. Give us your message and return!

ŚAKUNTALĀ: We shall rest in the shade of this fig tree.

[*All walk around and stop; Kaṇva speaks to himself.*]

What would be the right message to send to King Duṣyanta?

[*He ponders.*]

ŚAKUNTALĀ [*in a stage whisper*]: Look! The wild goose cries in anguish when her mate is hidden by lotus leaves. What I'm suffering is much worse.

ANASŪYĀ: Friend, don't speak this way!

> This goose spends
> every long night
> in sorrow
> without her mate,
> but hope lets her
> survive
> the deep pain
> of loneliness.

KANVA: Śārngarava, speak my words to the king after you present Śakuntalā!

ŚĀRNGARAVA: As you command, sir!

KANVA: Considering our discipline,

> the nobility of your birth
> and that she fell in love with you
> before her kinsmen could act,
> acknowledge her with equal rank
> among your wives—
> what more is destined for her,
> the bride's family will not ask.

ŚĀRNGARAVA: I grasp your message.

KANVA: Child, now I must instruct you. We forest hermits know something about worldly matters.

ŚĀRNGARAVA: Nothing is beyond the scope of wise men.

KANVA: When you enter your husband's family:

> Obey your elders, be a friend to the other wives!
> If your husband seems harsh, don't be impatient!
> Be fair to your servants, humble in your happiness!
> Women who act this way become noble wives;
> sullen girls only bring their families disgrace.

But what does Gautamī think?

GAUTAMĪ: This is good advice for wives, child. Take it all to heart!

KAṆVA: Child, embrace me and your friends!

ŚAKUNTALĀ: Father, why must Priyaṁvadā and my other friends turn back here?

KAṆVA: They will also be given in marriage. It is not proper for them to go there now. Gautamī will go with you.

ŚAKUNTALĀ [*embracing her father*]: How can I go on living in a strange place, torn from my father's side, like a vine torn from the side of a sandalwood tree growing on a mountain slope?

KAṆVA: Child, why are you so frightened?

> When you are your husband's honored wife,
> absorbed in royal duties and in your son,
> born like the sun to the eastern dawn,
> the sorrow of separation will fade.

[*Śakuntalā falls at her father's feet.*]

Let my hopes for you be fulfilled!

ŚAKUNTALĀ [*approaching her two friends*]: You two must embrace me together!

BOTH FRIENDS [*embracing her*]: Friend, if the king seems slow to recognize you, show him the ring engraved with his name!

ŚAKUNTALĀ: Your suspicions make me tremble!

BOTH FRIENDS: Don't be afraid! It's our love that fears evil.

ŚĀRṄGARAVA: The sun is high in the afternoon sky. Hurry, please!

ŚAKUNTALĀ [*facing the sanctuary*]: Father, will I ever see the grove again?

KAṆVA:
> When you have lived for many years
> as a queen equal to the earth
> and raised Duṣyanta's son
> to be a matchless warrior,
> your husband will entrust him
> with the burdens of the kingdom
> and will return with you
> to the calm of this hermitage.

GAUTAMĪ: Child, the time for our departure has passed. Let your father turn back! It would be better, sir, if you turn back yourself. She'll keep talking this way forever.

KAṆVA: Child, my ascetic practice has been interrupted.

ŚAKUNTALĀ: My father's body is already tortured by ascetic practices. He must not grieve too much for me!

KAṆVA [*sighing*]:
> When I see the grains of rice
> sprout from offerings you made
> at the door of your hut,
> how shall I calm my sorrow!

[*Śakuntalā exits with her escort.*]

BOTH FRIENDS [*watching Śakuntalā*]: Śakuntalā is hidden by forest trees now.

KAṆVA: Anasūyā, your companion is following her duty. Restrain yourself and return with me!

BOTH FRIENDS: Father, the ascetics' grove seems empty without Śakuntalā. How can we enter?

KAṆVA: The strength of your love makes it seem so.

[*Walking around in meditation.*]

Good! Now that Śakuntalā is on her way to her husband's family, I feel calm.

> A daughter belongs to another man—
> by sending her to her husband today,
> I feel the satisfaction
> one has on repaying a loan.

[*All exit.*]

ACT 5

[*The king and the buffoon enter; both sit down.*]

BUFFOON: Pay attention to the music room, friend, and you'll hear the notes of a song strung into a delicious melody . . . the lady Haṁsapadikā is practicing her singing.

KING: Be quiet so I can hear her!

VOICE IN THE AIR [*singing*]:
> Craving sweet
> new nectar,
> you kissed
> a mango bud once—
> how could you
> forget her, bee,
> to bury your joy
> in a lotus?

KING: The melody of the song is passionate.

BUFFOON: But did you get the meaning of the words?

KING: I once made love to her. Now she reproaches me for loving Queen Vasumatī. Friend Mādhavya, tell Haṁsapadikā that her words rebuke me soundly.

BUFFOON: As you command!

[*He rises.*]

But if that woman grabs my hair tuft, it will be like a heavenly nymph grabbing some ascetic . . . there go my hopes of liberation![1]

KING: Go! Use your courtly charm to console her.

BUFFOON: What a fate!

[*He exits.*]

KING [*to himself*]: Why did hearing the song's words fill me with such strong desire? I'm not parted from anyone I love . . .

> Seeing rare beauty,
> hearing lovely sounds,

---

1. In this context, liberation from the cycle of death and rebirth through sexual abstinence.

even a happy man
becomes strangely uneasy . . .
perhaps he remembers,
without knowing why,
loves of another life
buried deep in his being.

[*He stands bewildered. Then the king's chamberlain enters.*]

CHAMBERLAIN: At my age, look at me!

Since I took this ceremonial bamboo staff
as my badge of office in the king's chambers
many years have passed; now I use it
as a crutch to support my faltering steps.

A king cannot neglect his duty. He has just risen from his seat of justice and though I am loath to keep him longer, Sage Kaṇva's pupils have just arrived. Authority to rule the world leaves no time for rest.

The sun's steeds were yoked before time began,
the fragrant wind blows night and day,
the cosmic serpent[2] always bears earth's weight,
and a king who levies taxes has his duty.

Therefore, I must perform my office.

[*Walking around and looking.*]

Weary from ruling them like children,
he seeks solitude far from his subjects,
like an elephant bull who seeks cool shade
after gathering his herd at midday.

[*Approaching.*]

Victory to you, king! Some ascetics who dwell in the forest at the foothills of the Himālayas have come. They have women with them and bring a message from Sage Kaṇva. Listen, king, and judge!

KING [*respectfully*]: Are they Sage Kaṇva's messengers?

CHAMBERLAIN: They are.

KING: Inform the teacher Somarāta that he should welcome the ascetics with the prescribed rites and then bring them to me himself. I'll wait in a place suitable for greeting them.

CHAMBERLAIN: As the king commands.

[*He exits.*]

KING [*rising*]: Vetravatī, lead the way to the fire sanctuary.

DOORKEEPER: Come this way, king!

KING [*walking around, showing fatigue*]: Every other creature is happy when the object of his desire is won, but for kings success contains a core of suffering.

2. The cosmic snake Shesha is represented in traditional lore as the support upon which the world rests.

High office only leads to greater greed;
just perfecting its rewards is wearisome—
a kingdom is more trouble than it's worth,
like a royal umbrella one holds alone.

TWO BARDS OFFSTAGE: Victory to you, king!

FIRST BARD: You sacrifice your pleasures every day
    to labor for your subjects—
    as a tree endures burning heat
    to give shade from the summer sun.

SECOND BARD: You punish villains with your rod of justice,
    you reconcile disputes, you grant protection—
    most relatives are loyal only in hope of gain,
    but you treat all your subjects like kinsmen.

KING: My weary mind is revived.

[*He walks around.*]

DOORKEEPER: The terrace of the fire sanctuary is freshly washed and the cow is waiting to give milk for the oblation. Let the king ascend!
KING: Vetravatī, why has Father Kaṇva sent these sages to me?

    Does something hinder their ascetic life?
    Or threaten creatures in the sacred forest?
    Or do my sins stunt the flowering vines?
    My mind is filled with conflicting doubts.

DOORKEEPER: I would guess that these sages rejoice in your virtuous conduct and
come to honor you.

[*The ascetics enter; Śakuntalā is in front with Gautamī; the chamberlain and the
king's priest are in front of her.*]

CHAMBERLAIN: Come this way, sirs!
ŚĀRṄGARAVA: Śāradvata, my friend:

    I know that this renowned king is righteous
    and none of the social classes follows evil ways,
    but my mind is so accustomed to seclusion
    that the palace feels like a house in flames.

ŚĀRADVATA: I've felt the same way ever since we entered the city.

    As if I were freshly bathed, seeing a filthy man,
    pure while he's defiled, awake while he's asleep,
    as if I were a free man watching a prisoner,
    I watch this city mired in pleasures.

ŚAKUNTALĀ [*indicating she feels an omen*]: Why is my right eye twitching?
GAUTAMĪ: Child, your husband's family gods turn bad fortune into blessings!

[*They walk around.*]

PRIEST [*indicating the king*]: Ascetics, the guardian of sacred order has left the seat of
justice and awaits you now. Behold him!

ŚĀRṄGARAVA: Great priest, he seems praiseworthy, but we expect no less.

> Boughs bend, heavy with ripened fruit,
> clouds descend with fresh rain,
> noble men are gracious with wealth—
> this is the nature of bountiful things.

DOORKEEPER: King, their faces look calm. I'm sure that the sages have confidence in what they're doing.

KING [*seeing Śakuntalā*]:   Who is she? Carefully veiled
> to barely reveal her body's beauty,
> surrounded by the ascetics
> like a bud among withered leaves.

DOORKEEPER: King, I feel curious and puzzled too. Surely her form deserves closer inspection.

KING: Let her be! One should not stare at another man's wife!

ŚAKUNTALĀ [*placing her hand on her chest, she speaks to herself*]: My heart, why are you quivering? Be quiet while I learn my noble husband's feelings.

PRIEST [*going forward*]: These ascetics have been honored with due ceremony. They have a message from their teacher. The king should hear them!

KING: I am paying attention.

SAGES [*raising their hands in a gesture of greeting*]: May you be victorious, king!

KING: I salute you all!

SAGES: May your desires be fulfilled!

KING: Do the sages perform austerities unhampered?

SAGES: Who would dare obstruct the rites
> of holy men whom you protect—
> how can darkness descend
> when the sun's rays shine?

KING: My title "king" is more meaningful now. Is the world blessed by Father Kaṇva's health?

SAGES: Saints control their own health. He asks about your welfare and sends this message . . .

KING: What does he command?

ŚĀRṄGARAVA: At the time you secretly met and married my daughter, affection made me pardon you both.

> We remember you to be a prince of honor;
> Śakuntalā is virtue incarnate—
> the creator cannot be condemned
> for mating the perfect bride and groom.

And now that she is pregnant, receive her and perform your sacred duty together.

GAUTAMĪ: Sir, I have something to say, though I wasn't appointed to speak:

> She ignored her elders
> and you failed to ask her kinsmen—
> since you acted on your own,
> what can I say to you now?

ŚAKUNTALĀ: What does my noble husband say?

KING: What has been proposed?

ŚAKUNTALĀ [*to herself*]: The proposal is as clear as fire.

ŚĀRṄGARAVA: What's this? Your Majesty certainly knows the ways of the world!

> People suspect a married woman who stays
> with her kinsmen, even if she is chaste—
> a young wife should live with her husband,
> no matter how he despises her.

KING: Did I ever marry you?

ŚAKUNTALĀ [*visibly dejected, speaking to herself*]: Now your fears are real, my heart!

ŚĀRṄGARAVA: Does one turn away from duty in contempt
> because his own actions repulse him?

KING: Why ask this insulting question?

ŚĀRṄGARAVA: Such transformations take shape
> when men are drunk with power.

KING: This censure is clearly directed at me.

GAUTAMĪ: Child, this is no time to be modest. I'll remove your veil. Then your husband will recognize you.

   [*She does so.*]

KING [*staring at Śakuntalā*]: Must I judge whether I ever married
> the flawless beauty they offer me now?
> I cannot love her or leave her, like a bee
> near a jasmine filled with frost at dawn.

   [*He shows hesitation.*]

DOORKEEPER: Our king has a strong sense of justice. Who else would hesitate when beauty like this is handed to him?

ŚĀRṄGARAVA: King, why do you remain silent?

KING: Ascetics, even though I'm searching my mind, I don't remember marrying this lady. How can I accept a woman who is visibly pregnant when I doubt that I am the cause?

ŚAKUNTALĀ [*in a stage whisper*]: My lord casts doubt on our marriage. Why were my hopes so high?

ŚĀRṄGARAVA: It can't be!

> Are you going to insult the sage
> who pardons the girl you seduced
> and bids you keep his stolen wealth,
> treating a thief like you with honor?

ŚĀRADVATA: Śārṅgarava, stop now! Śakuntalā, we have delivered our message and the king has responded. He must be shown some proof.

ŚAKUNTALĀ [*in a stage whisper*]: When passion can turn to this, what's the use of reminding him? But, it's up to me to prove my honor now.

   [*Aloud.*]

My noble husband . . .

[*She breaks off when this is half-spoken.*]

Since our marriage is in doubt, this is no way to address him. Puru king, you do wrong to reject a simple-hearted person with such words after you deceived her in the hermitage.

KING [*covering his ears*]: Stop this shameful talk!

> Are you trying to stain my name
> and drag me to ruin—
> like a river eroding her own banks,
> soiling water and uprooting trees?

ŚAKUNTALĀ: Very well! If it's really true that fear of taking another man's wife turns you away, then this ring will revive your memory and remove your doubt.

KING: An excellent idea!

ŚAKUNTALĀ [*touching the place where the ring had been*]: I'm lost! The ring is gone from my finger.

[*She looks despairingly at Gautamī.*]

GAUTAMĪ: The ring must have fallen off while you were bathing in the holy waters at the shrine of the goddess near Indra's grove.

KING [*smiling*]: And so they say the female sex is cunning.

ŚAKUNTALĀ: Fate has shown its power. Yet, I will tell you something else.

KING: I am still obliged to listen.

ŚAKUNTALĀ: One day, in a jasmine bower, you held a lotus-leaf cup full of water in your hand.

KING: We hear you.

ŚAKUNTALĀ: At that moment the buck I treated as my son approached. You coaxed it with the water, saying that it should drink first. But he didn't trust you and wouldn't drink from your hand. When I took the water, his trust returned. Then you jested, "Every creature trusts what its senses know. You both belong to the forest."

KING: Thus do women further their own ends by attracting eager men with the honey of false words.

GAUTAMĪ: Great king, you are wrong to speak this way. This child raised in an ascetics' grove doesn't know deceit.

KING: Old woman,

> When naive female beasts show cunning,
> what can we expect of women who reason?
> Don't cuckoos let other birds nurture
> their eggs and teach the chicks to fly?

ŚAKUNTALĀ [*angrily*]: Evil man! you see everything distorted by your own ignoble heart. Who would want to imitate you now, hiding behind your show of justice, like a well overgrown with weeds?

KING [*to himself*]: Her anger does not seem feigned; it makes me doubt myself.

> When the absence of love's memory
> made me deny a secret affair with her,
> this fire-eyed beauty bent her angry brows

and seemed to break the bow of love.

[*Aloud.*]

Lady, Duṣyanta's conduct is renowned, so what you say is groundless.

ŚAKUNTALĀ: All right! I may be a self-willed wanton woman! But it was faith in the Puru dynasty that brought me into the power of a man with honey in his words and poison in his heart.

[*She covers her face and weeps.*]

ŚĀRṄGARAVA: A willful act unchecked always causes pain.

> One should be cautious
> in forming a secret union—
> unless a lover's heart is clear,
> affection turns to poison.

KING: But sir, why do you demean me with such warnings? Do you trust the lady?

ŚĀRṄGARAVA [*scornfully*]: You have learned everything backwards.

> If you suspect the word of one
> whose nature knows no guile,
> then you can only trust
> people who practice deception.

KING: I presume you speak the truth. Let us assume so. But what could I gain by deceiving this woman?

ŚĀRṄGARAVA: Ruin.

KING: Ruin? A Puru king has no reason to want his own ruin!

ŚĀRADVATA: Śārṅgarava, this talk is pointless. We have delivered our master's message and should return.

> Since you married her, abandon her or take her—
> absolute is the power a husband has over his wife.

GAUTAMĪ: You go ahead.

[*They start to go.*]

ŚAKUNTALĀ: What? Am I deceived by this cruel man and then abandoned by you?

[*She tries to follow them.*]

GAUTAMĪ [*stopping*]: Śārṅgarava my son, Śakuntalā is following us, crying pitifully. What will my child do now that her husband has refused her?

ŚĀRṄGARAVA [*turning back angrily*]: Bold woman, do you still insist on having your way?

[*Śakuntalā trembles in fear.*]

> If you are what the king says you are,
> you don't belong in Father Kaṇva's family—
> if you know that your marriage vow is pure,
> you can bear slavery in your husband's house.

Stay! We must go on!

KING: Ascetic, why do you disappoint the lady too?

> The moon only makes lotuses open,
> the sun's light awakens lilies—
> a king's discipline forbids him
> to touch another man's wife.

ŚĀRṄGARAVA: If you forget a past affair because of some present attachment, why do you fear injustice now?

KING [to the priest]: Sir, I ask you to weigh the alternatives:

> Since it's unclear whether I'm deluded
> or she is speaking falsely—
> should I risk abandoning a wife
> or being tainted by another man's?

PRIEST [deliberating]: I recommend this . . .

KING: Instruct me! I'll do as you say.

PRIEST: Then let the lady stay in our house until her child is born. If you ask why: the wise men predict that your first son will be born with the marks of a king who turns the wheel of empire. If the child of the sage's daughter bears the marks, congratulate her and welcome her into your palace chambers. Otherwise, send her back to her father.

KING: Whatever the elders desire.

PRIEST: Child, follow me!

ŚAKUNTALĀ: Mother earth,[3] open to receive me!

[Weeping, Śakuntalā exits with the priest and the hermits. The king, his memory lost through the curse, thinks about her.]

VOICE OFFSTAGE: Amazing! Amazing!

KING [listening]: What could this be?

PRIEST [reentering, amazed]: King, something marvelous has occurred!

KING: What?

PRIEST: When Kaṇva's pupils had departed,

> The girl threw up her arms and wept,
> lamenting her misfortune . . . then . . .

KING: Then what?

PRIEST: Near the nymph's shrine a ray of light
in the shape of a woman carried her away.

[All mime amazement.]

KING: We've already settled the matter. Why discuss it further?

PRIEST [observing the king]: May you be victorious!

[He exits.]

KING: Vetravatī, I am bewildered. Lead the way to my chamber!

---

3. Mother Earth is a frequent savior of heroines in Sanskrit literature; the most famous instance concerns Sita (see *The Ramayana of Valimiki*, page 861).

DOORKEEPER: Come this way, my lord!

[*She walks forward.*]

KING: I cannot remember marrying
the sage's abandoned daughter,
but the pain my heart feels
makes me suspect that I did.

[*All exit.*]

ACT 6

[*The king's wife's brother, who is city magistrate, enters with two policemen leading a man whose hands are tied behind his back.*]

BOTH POLICEMEN [*beating the man*]: Speak, thief! Where'd you steal this handsome ring with the king's name engraved in the jewel?

MAN [*showing fear*]: Peace, sirs! I wouldn't do a thing like that.

FIRST POLICEMAN: Don't tell us the king thought you were some famous priest and gave it to you as a gift!

MAN: Listen, I'm a humble fisherman who lives near Indra's grove.

SECOND POLICEMAN: Thief, did we ask you about your caste?

MAGISTRATE: Sūcaka, let him tell it all in order! Don't interrupt him!

BOTH POLICEMEN: Whatever you command, chief!

MAN: I feed my family by catching fish with nets and hooks.

MAGISTRATE [*mocking*]: What a pure profession!

MAN: The work I do
may be vile
but I won't deny
my birthright—
a priest
doing his holy rites
pities the animals
he kills.

MAGISTRATE: Go on!

MAN: One day as I was cutting up a red carp, I saw the shining stone of this ring in its belly. When I tried to sell it, you grabbed me. Kill me or let me go! That's how I got it!

MAGISTRATE: Jānuka, I'm sure this ugly butcher's a fisherman by his stinking smell. We must investigate how he got the ring. We'll go straight to the palace.

BOTH POLICEMEN: Okay. Go in front, you pickpocket!

[*All walk around.*]

MAGISTRATE: Sūcaka, guard this villain at the palace gate! I'll report to the king how we found the ring, get his orders, and come back.

BOTH POLICEMEN: Chief, good luck with the king!

[*The magistrate exits.*]

FIRST POLICEMAN: Jānuka, the chief's been gone a long time.

SECOND POLICEMAN: Well, there are fixed times for seeing kings.

FIRST POLICEMAN: Jānuka, my hands are itching to tie on his execution garland.

[*He points to the man.*]

MAN: You shouldn't think about killing a man for no reason.

SECOND POLICEMAN [*looking*]: I see our chief coming with a letter in his hand. It's probably an order from the king. You'll be thrown to the vultures or you'll see the face of death's dog again . . .[1]

MAGISTRATE [*entering*]: Sūcaka, release this fisherman! I'll tell you how he got the ring.

FIRST POLICEMAN: Whatever you say, chief!

SECOND POLICEMAN: The villain entered the house of death and came out again.

[*He unties the prisoner.*]

MAN [*bowing to the magistrate*]: Master, how will I make my living now?

MAGISTRATE: The king sends you a sum equal to the ring.

[*He gives the money to the man.*]

MAN [*bowing as he grabs it*]: The king honors me.

FIRST POLICEMAN: This fellow's certainly honored. He was lowered from the execution stake and raised up on a royal elephant's back.

SECOND POLICEMAN: Chief, the reward tells me this ring was special to the king.

MAGISTRATE: I don't think the king valued the stone, but when he caught sight of the ring, he suddenly seemed to remember someone he loved, and he became deeply disturbed.

FIRST POLICEMAN: You served him well, chief!

SECOND POLICEMAN: I think you better served this king of fish.

[*Looking at the fisherman with jealousy.*]

MAN: My lords, half of this is yours for your good will.

FIRST POLICEMAN: It's only fair!

MAGISTRATE: Fisherman, now that you are my greatest and dearest friend, we should pledge our love over kadamba-blossom wine. Let's go to the wine shop!

[*They all exit together; the interlude ends. Then a nymph named Sānumatī enters by the skyway.*]

SĀNUMATĪ: Now that I've performed my assigned duties at the nymph's shrine, I'll slip away to spy on King Duṣyanta while the worshipers are bathing. My friendship with Menakā makes me feel a bond with Śakuntalā. Besides, Menakā asked me to help her daughter.

[*Looking around.*]

Why don't I see preparations for the spring festival in the king's palace? I can learn everything by using my mental powers, but I must respect my friend's request. So be it! I'll make myself invisible and spy on these two girls who are guarding the pleasure garden.

---

1. Yama, the god of death, is accompanied by two four-eyed dogs who guard the way of the dead [translator's note].

[*Sānumatī mimes descending and stands waiting. Then a maid servant named Parabhṛtikā, "Little Cuckoo," enters, looking at a mango bud. A second maid, named Madhukarikā, "Little Bee," is following her.*]

FIRST MAID: Your pale green stem
　　　tinged with pink
　　　is a true sign
　　　that spring has come—
　　　I see you,
　　　mango-blossom bud,
　　　and I pray
　　　for a season of joy.

SECOND MAID: What are you muttering to yourself?

FIRST MAID: A cuckoo goes mad when she sees a mango bud.

SECOND MAID [*joyfully rushing over*]: Has the sweet month of spring come?

FIRST MAID: Now's the time to sing your songs of love.

second maid: Hold me while I pluck a mango bud and worship the god of love.

FIRST MAID: Only if you'll give me half the fruit of your worship.

second maid: That goes without saying . . . our bodies may be separate, but our lives are one . . .

[*Leaning on her friend, she stands and plucks a mango bud.*]

The mango flower is still closed, but this broken stem is fragrant.

[*She makes the dove gesture with her hands.*]

　　　Mango-blossom bud,
　　　I offer you to Love
　　　as he lifts
　　　his bow of passion.
　　　Be the first
　　　of his flower arrows
　　　aimed at lonely girls
　　　with lovers far away!

[*She throws the mango bud.*]

CHAMBERLAIN [*angrily throwing aside the curtain and entering*]: Not now, stupid girl! When the king has banned the festival of spring, how dare you pluck a mango bud!

BOTH MAIDS [*frightened*]: Please forgive us, sir. We don't know what you mean.

CHAMBERLAIN: Did you not hear that even the spring trees and the nesting birds obey the king's order?

　　　The mango flowers bloom without spreading pollen,
　　　the red amaranth buds, but will not bloom,
　　　cries of cuckoo cocks freeze though frost is past,
　　　and out of fear, Love holds his arrow half-drawn.

BOTH MAIDS: There is no doubt about the king's great power!

FIRST MAID: Sir, several days ago we were sent to wait on the queen by Mitrāvasu, the king's brother-in-law. We were assigned to guard the pleasure garden. Since we're newcomers, we've heard no news.

CHAMBERLAIN: Let it be! But don't do it again!

BOTH MAIDS: Sir, we're curious. May we ask why the spring festival was banned?

SĀNUMATĪ: Mortals are fond of festivals. The reason must be serious.

CHAMBERLAIN: It is public knowledge. Why should I not tell them? Has the scandal of Śakuntalā's rejection not reached your ears?

BOTH MAIDS: We only heard from the king's brother-in-law that the ring was found.

CHAMBERLAIN [to himself]: There is little more to tell.

   [Aloud.]

When he saw the ring, the king remembered that he had married Śakuntalā in secret and had rejected her in his delusion. Since then the king has been tortured by remorse.

> Despising what he once enjoyed,
> he shuns his ministers every day
> and spends long sleepless nights
> tossing at the edge of his bed—
> when courtesy demands that
> he converse with palace women,
> he stumbles over their names,
> and then retreats in shame.

SĀNUMATĪ: This news delights me.

CHAMBERLAIN: The festival is banned because of the king's melancholy.

BOTH MAIDS: It's only right.

VOICE OFFSTAGE: This way, sir!

CHAMBERLAIN [listening]: The king is coming. Go about your business!

BOTH MAIDS: As you say.

   [Both maids exit. Then the king enters, costumed to show his grief, accompanied by the buffoon and the doorkeeper.]

CHAMBERLAIN [observing the king]: Extraordinary beauty is appealing under all conditions. Even in his lovesick state, the king is wonderful to see.

> Rejecting his regal jewels,
> he wears one golden bangle
> above his left wrist;
> his lips are pale with sighs,
> his eyes wan from brooding at night—
> like a gemstone ground in polishing,
> the fiery beauty of his body
> makes his wasted form seem strong.

SĀNUMATĪ [seeing the king]: I see why Śakuntalā pines for him though he rejected and disgraced her.

KING [walking around slowly, deep in thought]:
> This cursed heart slept
> when my love came to wake it,
> and now it stays awake
> to suffer the pain of remorse.

SĀNUMATĪ: The girl shares his fate.

BUFFOON [*in a stage whisper*]: He's having another attack of his Śakuntalā disease. I doubt if there's any cure for that.

CHAMBERLAIN [*approaching*]: Victory to the king! I have inspected the grounds of the pleasure garden. Let the king visit his favorite spots and divert himself.

KING: Vetravatī, deliver a message to my noble minister Piśuna: "After being awake all night, we cannot sit on the seat of justice today. Set in writing what your judgment tells you the citizens require and send it to us!"

DOORKEEPER: Whatever you command!

[*She exits.*]

KING: Vātāyana, attend to the rest of your business!

CHAMBERLAIN: As the king commands!

[*He exits.*]

BUFFOON: You've cleared out the flies. Now you can rest in some pretty spot. The garden is pleasant now in this break between morning cold and noonday heat.

KING: Dear friend, the saying "Misfortunes rush through any crack" is absolutely right:

> Barely freed by the dark force
> that made me forget Kaṇva's daughter,
> my mind is threatened by an arrow
> of mango buds fixed on Love's bow.

BUFFOON: Wait, I'll destroy the love god's arrow with my wooden stick.

[*Raising his staff, he tries to strike a mango bud.*]

KING [*smiling*]: Let it be! I see the majesty of brahman bravery. Friend, where may I sit to divert my eyes with vines that remind me of my love?

BUFFOON: Didn't you tell your maid Caturikā, "I'll pass the time in the jasmine bower. Bring me the drawing board on which I painted a picture of Śakuntalā with my own hand!"

KING: Such a place may soothe my heart. Show me the way!

BUFFOON: Come this way!

[*Both walk around; the nymph Sānumatī follows.*]

The marble seat and flower offerings in this jasmine bower are certainly trying to make us feel welcome. Come in and sit down!

[*Both enter the bower and sit.*]

SĀNUMATĪ: I'll hide behind these creepers to see the picture he's drawn of my friend. Then I'll report how great her husband's passion is.

[*She does as she says and stands waiting.*]

KING: Friend, now I remember everything. I told you about my first meeting with Śakuntalā. You weren't with me when I rejected her, but why didn't you say anything about her before? Did you suffer a loss of memory too?

BUFFOON: I didn't forget. You did tell me all about it once, but then you said, "It's all a joke without any truth." My wit is like a lump of clay, so I took you at your word . . . or it could be that fate is powerful . . .

SĀNUMATĪ: It is!

KING: Friend, help me!

BUFFOON: What's this? It doesn't become you! Noblemen never take grief to heart. Even in storms, mountains don't tremble.

KING: Dear friend, I'm defenseless when I remember the pain of my love's bewilderment when I rejected her.

> When I cast her away, she followed her kinsmen,
> but Kaṇva's disciple harshly shouted, "Stay!"
> The tearful look my cruelty provoked
> burns me like an arrow tipped with poison.

SĀNUMATĪ: The way he rehearses his actions makes me delight in his pain.

BUFFOON: Sir, I guess that the lady was carried off by some celestial creature or other.

KING: Who else would dare to touch a woman who worshiped her husband? I was told that Menakā is her mother. My heart suspects that her mother's companions carried her off.

SĀNUMATĪ: His delusion puzzled me, but not his reawakening.

BUFFOON: If that's the case, you'll meet her again in good time.

KING: How?

BUFFOON: No mother or father can bear to see a daughter parted from her husband.

> KING: Was it dream or illusion or mental confusion,
> or the last meager fruit of my former good deeds?
> It is gone now, and my heart's desires are
> like riverbanks crumbling of their own weight.

BUFFOON: Stop this! Isn't the ring evidence that an unexpected meeting is destined to take place?

KING [looking at the ring]: I only pity it for falling from such a place.

> Ring, your punishment is proof
> that your fate is as flawed as mine—
> you were placed in her lovely fingers,
> glowing with crimson nails, and you fell.

SĀNUMATĪ: The real pity would have been if it had fallen into some other hand.

BUFFOON: What prompted you to put the signet ring on her hand?

SĀNUMATĪ: I'm curious too.

KING: I did it when I left for the city. My love broke into tears and asked, "How long will it be before my noble husband sends news to me?"

BUFFOON: Then? What then?

KING: Then I placed the ring on her finger with this promise:

> One by one, day after day,
> count each syllable of my name!
> At the end, a messenger will come
> to bring you to my palace.

But in my cruel delusion, I never kept my word.

SĀNUMATĪ: Fate broke their charming agreement!

BUFFOON: How did it get into the belly of the carp the fisherman was cutting up?

KING: While she was worshiping at the shrine of Indra's wife, it fell from her hand into the Gaṅgā.[2]

BUFFOON: It's obvious now!

SĀNUMATĪ: And the king, doubtful of his marriage to Śakuntalā, a female ascetic, was afraid to commit an act of injustice. But why should such passionate love need a ring to be remembered?

KING: I must reproach the ring for what it's done.

BUFFOON [to himself]: He's gone the way of all madmen . . .

KING: Why did you leave her delicate finger
          and sink into the deep river?

Of course . . .

          A mindless ring can't recognize virtue,
          but why did I reject my love?

BUFFOON [to himself again]: Why am I consumed by a craving for food?

KING: Oh ring! Have pity on a man whose heart is tormented because he abandoned his love without cause! Let him see her again!

[Throwing the curtain aside, the maid Caturikā enters, with the drawing board in her hand.]

CATURIKĀ: Here's the picture you painted of the lady.

[She shows the drawing board.]

BUFFOON: Dear friend, how well you've painted your feelings in this sweet scene! My eyes almost stumble over the hollows and hills.

SĀNUMATĪ: What skill the king has! I feel as if my friend were before me.

KING: The picture's imperfections are not hers,
          but this drawing does hint at her beauty.

SĀNUMATĪ: Such words reveal that suffering has increased his modesty as much as his love.

BUFFOON: Sir, I see three ladies now and they're all lovely to look at. Which is your Śakuntalā?

SĀNUMATĪ: Only a dim-witted fool like this wouldn't know such beauty!

KING: You guess which one!

BUFFOON: I guess Śakuntalā is the one you've drawn with flowers falling from her loosened locks of hair, with drops of sweat on her face, with her arms hanging limp and tired as she stands at the side of a mango tree whose tender shoots are gleaming with the fresh water she poured. The other two are her friends.

KING: You are clever! Look at these signs of my passion!

          Smudges from my sweating fingers
          stain the edges of the picture
          and a tear fallen from my cheek

---

2. The Ganges River. Worshiping at the shrine of Shachi, Indra's wife, is appropriate for a woman who hopes to win the affections of a kingly husband.

has raised a wrinkle in the paint.

Caturikā, the scenery is only half-drawn. Go and bring my paints!

CATURIKĀ: Noble Mādhavya, hold the drawing board until I come back!

KING: I'll hold it myself.

[*He takes it, the maid exits.*]

> I rejected my love when she came to me,
> and now I worship her in a painted image—
> having passed by a river full of water,
> I'm longing now for an empty mirage.

BUFFOON [*to himself*]: He's too far gone for a river now! He's looking for a mirage!

[*Aloud.*]

Sir, what else do you plan to draw here?

SĀNUMATĪ: He'll want to draw every place my friend loved.

KING: I'll draw the river Mālinī
> flowing through Himālaya's foothills
> where pairs of wild geese nest in the sand
> and deer recline on both riverbanks,
> where a doe is rubbing her left eye
> on the horn of a black buck antelope
> under a tree whose branches
> have bark dresses hanging to dry.

BUFFOON [*to himself*]: Next he'll fill the drawing board with mobs of ascetics wearing long grassy beards.

KING: Dear friend, I've forgotten to draw an ornament that Śakuntalā wore.

BUFFOON: What is it?

SĀNUMATĪ: It will suit her forest life and her tender beauty.

KING: I haven't drawn the mimosa flower on her ear,
> its filaments resting on her cheek,
> or the necklace of tender lotus stalks,
> lying on her breasts like autumn moonbeams.

BUFFOON: But why does the lady cover her face with her red lotus-bud fingertips and stand trembling in fear?

[*Looking closely.*]

That son-of-a-bee who steals nectar from flowers is attacking her face.

KING: Drive the impudent rogue away!

BUFFOON: You have the power to punish criminals. You drive him off!

KING: All right! Bee, favored guest of the flowering vines, why do you frustrate yourself by flying here?

> A female bee waits on a flower,
> thirsting for your love—
> she refuses to drink
> the sweet nectar without you.

SĀNUMATĪ: How gallantly he's driving him away!

BUFFOON: When you try to drive it away, this creature becomes vicious.

KING: Why don't you stop when I command you?

> Bee, if you touch the lips of my love
> that lure you like a young tree's virgin buds,
> lips I gently kissed in festivals of love,
> I'll hold you captive in a lotus flower cage.

BUFFOON: Why isn't he afraid of your harsh punishment?

> [*Laughing, he speaks to himself.*]

He's gone crazy and I'll be the same if I go on talking like this.

> [*Aloud.*]

But sir, it's just a picture!

KING: A picture? How can that be?

SĀNUMATĪ: When I couldn't tell whether it was painted, how could he realize he was looking at a picture?

KING: Dear friend, are you envious of me?

> My heart's affection made me feel
> the joy of seeing her—
> but you reminded me again
> that my love is only a picture.

> [*He wipes away a tear.*]

SĀNUMATĪ: The effects of her absence make him quarrelsome.

KING: Dear friend, why do I suffer this endless pain?

> Sleepless nights prevent our meeting in dreams;
> her image in a picture is ruined by my tears.

SĀNUMATĪ: You have clearly atoned for the suffering your rejection caused Śakuntalā.

CATURIKĀ [*entering*]: Victory my lord! I found the paint box and started back right away . . . but I met Queen Vasumatī with her maid Taralikā on the path and she grabbed the box from my hand, saying, "I'll bring it to the noble lord myself!"

BUFFOON: You were lucky to get away!

CATURIKĀ: The queen's shawl got caught on a tree. While Taralikā was freeing it, I made my escape.

KING: Dear friend, the queen's pride can quickly turn to anger. Save this picture!

BUFFOON: You should say, "Save yourself!"

> [*Taking the picture, he stands up.*]

If you escape the woman's deadly poison, then send word to me in the Palace of the Clouds.

> [*He exits hastily.*]

SĀNUMATĪ: Even though another woman has taken his heart and he feels indifferent to the queen, he treats her with respect.

DOORKEEPER [*entering with a letter in her hand*]: Victory, king!

KING: Vetravatī, did you meet the queen on the way?

DOORKEEPER: I did, but when she saw the letter in my hand, she turned back.

KING: She knows that this is official and would not interrupt my work.

DOORKEEPER: King, the minister requests that you examine the contents of this letter. He said that the enormous job of reckoning the revenue in this one citizen's case had taken all his time.

KING: Show me the letter!

[*The girl hands it to him and he reads barely aloud.*]

What is this? "A wealthy merchant sea captain named Dhanamitra has been lost in a shipwreck and the laws say that since the brave man was childless, his accumulated wealth all goes to the king." It's terrible to be childless! A man of such wealth probably had several wives. We must find out if any one of his wives is pregnant!

DOORKEEPER: King, it's said that one of his wives, the daughter of a merchant of Ayodhyā, has performed the rite to ensure the birth of a son.

KING: The child in her womb surely deserves his paternal wealth. Go! Report this to my minister!

DOORKEEPER: As the king commands!

[*She starts to go.*]

KING: Come here a moment!

DOORKEEPER: I am here.

KING: Is it his offspring or not?

> When his subjects lose a kinsman,
> Duṣyanta will preserve the estates—
> unless there is some crime.
> Let this be proclaimed.

DOORKEEPER: It shall be proclaimed loudly.

[*She exits; reenters.*]

The king's order will be as welcome as rain in the right season.

KING [*sighing long and deeply*]: Families without offspring whose lines of succession are cut off lose their wealth to strangers when the last male heir dies. When I die, this will happen to the wealth of the Puru dynasty.

DOORKEEPER: Heaven forbid such a fate!

KING: I curse myself for despising the treasure I was offered.

SĀNUMATĪ: He surely has my friend in mind when he blames himself.

> KING: I abandoned my lawful wife, the holy ground
> where I myself planted my family's glory,
> like earth sown with seed at the right time,
> ready to bear rich fruit in season.

SĀNUMATĪ: But your family's line will not be broken.

CATURIKĀ [*in a stage whisper*]: The king is upset by the story of the merchant. Go and bring noble Mādhavya from the Palace of the Clouds to console him!

DOORKEEPER: A good idea!

[*She exits.*]

KING: Duṣyanta's ancestors are imperiled.

> Our fathers drink the yearly libation
> mixed with my childless tears,
> knowing that there is no other son
> to offer the sacred funeral waters.

[*He falls into a faint.*]

CATURIKĀ [*looking at the bewildered king*]: Calm yourself, my lord!

SĀNUMATĪ: Though a light shines, his separation from Śakuntalā keeps him in a state of dark depression. I could make him happy now, but I've heard Indra's consort consoling Śakuntalā with the news that the gods are hungry for their share of the ancestral oblations and will soon conspire to have her husband welcome his lawful wife. I'll have to wait for the auspicious time, but meanwhile I'll cheer my friend by reporting his condition.

[*She exits, flying into the air.*]

VOICE OFFSTAGE: Help! Brahman-murder!

KING [*regaining consciousness, listening*]: Is it Māḍhavya's cry of pain? Who's there?

DOORKEEPER: King, your friend is in danger. Help him!

KING: Who dares to threaten him?

DOORKEEPER: Some invisible spirit seized him and dragged him to the roof of the Palace of the Clouds.

KING [*getting up*]: Not this! Even my house is haunted by spirits.

> When I don't even recognize
> the blunders I commit every day,
> how can I keep track
> of where my subjects stray?

VOICE OFFSTAGE: Dear friend! Help! Help!

KING [*breaking into a run*]: Friend, don't be afraid! I'm coming!

VOICE OFFSTAGE [*repeating the call for help*]: Why shouldn't I be afraid? Someone is trying to split my neck in three, like a stalk of sugar cane.

KING [*casting a glance*]: Quickly, my bow!

BOW-BEARER [*entering with a bow in hand*]: Here are your bow and quiver.

[*The king takes his bow and arrows.*]

VOICE OFFSTAGE: I'll kill you as a tiger kills struggling prey!

> I'll drink fresh blood from your tender neck!
> Take refuge now in the bow Duṣyanta lifts
> to calm the fears of the oppressed!

KING [*angrily*]: How dare you abuse my name? Stop, carrion-eater! Or you will not live!

[*He strings his bow.*]

Vetravatī, lead the way to the stairs!

DOORKEEPER: This way, king.

[*All move forward in haste.*]

KING [*searching around*]: There is no one here!

VOICE OFFSTAGE: Help! Help! I see you. Don't you see me?
I'm like a mouse caught by a cat! My life is hopeless!

KING: Don't count on your powers of invisibility! My magical arrows will find you. I aim this arrow:

> It will strike its doomed target
> and spare the brahman it must save—
> a wild goose can extract the milk
> and leave the water untouched.[3]

[*He aims the arrow. Then Indra's charioteer Mātali enters, having released the buffoon.*]

MĀTALI: King!

> Indra sets demons as your targets;
> draw your bow against them!
> Send friends gracious glances
> rather than deadly arrows!

KING [*withdrawing his arrow*]: Mātali, welcome to great Indra's charioteer!

BUFFOON [*entering*]: He tried to slaughter me like a sacrifical beast and this king is greeting him with honors!

MĀTALI [*smiling*]: Your Majesty, hear why Indra has sent me to you!

KING: I am all attention.

MĀTALI: There is an army of demons descended from one-hundred-headed Kālanemi, known to be invincible . . .

KING: I have already heard it from Nārada,[4] the gods' messenger.

MĀTALI: He is invulnerable to your friend Indra,

> so you are appointed to lead the charge—
> the moon dispels the darkness of night
> since the sun cannot drive it out.

Take your weapon, mount Indra's chariot, and prepare for victory!

KING: Indra favors me with this honor. But why did you attack Mādhavya?

MĀTALI: I'll tell you! From the signs of anguish Your Majesty showed, I knew that you were despondent. I attacked him to arouse your anger.

> A fire blazes when fuel is added;
> a cobra provoked raises its hood—
> men can regain lost courage
> if their emotions are roused.

KING [*in a stage whisper*]: Dear friend, I cannot disobey a command from the lord of heaven. Inform my minister Piśuna of this and tell him this for me:

---

3. The royal goose is credited with the ability to drink only the milk when it is mixed with water.

4. A divine sage who often communicated between gods and mortals.

Concentrate your mind on guarding my subjects!
My bow is strung to accomplish other work.

BUFFOON: Whatever you command!

[*He exits.*]

MĀTALI: Mount the chariot, Your Majesty!

[*The king mimes mounting the chariot; all exit.*]

ACT 7

[*The king enters with Mātali by the skyway, mounted on a chariot.*]

KING: Mātali, though I carried out his command, I feel unworthy of the honors Indra
gave me.

MĀTALI [*smiling*]: Your Majesty, neither of you seems satisfied.

You belittle the aid you gave Indra
in face of the honors he conferred,
and he, amazed by your heroic acts,
deems his hospitality too slight.

KING: No, not so! When I was taking leave, he honored me beyond my heart's desire
and shared his throne with me in the presence of the gods:

Indra gave me a garland of coral flowers
tinged with sandalpowder from his chest,
while he smiled at his son Jayanta,
who stood there barely hiding his envy.

MĀTALI: Don't you deserve whatever you want from Indra?

Indra's heaven of pleasures has twice
been saved by rooting out thorny demons—
your smooth-jointed arrows have now done
what Viṣṇu once did with his lion claws.[1]

KING: Here too Indra's might deserves the praise.

When servants succeed in great tasks,
they act in hope of their master's praise—
would dawn scatter the darkness
if he were not the sun's own charioteer?

MĀTALI: This attitude suits you well!

[*He moves a little distance.*]

Look over there, Your Majesty! See how your own glorious fame has reached the
vault of heaven!

Celestial artists are drawing your exploits

---

1. In his fourth avatar Vishnu took on a form part-man, part-lion, and thereby was able to slay the otherwise invulnerable
demon.

on leaves of the wish-granting creeper
with colors of the nymphs' cosmetic paints,
and bards are moved to sing of you in ballads.

KING: Mātali, in my desire to do battle with the demons, I did not notice the path we took to heaven as we climbed through the sky yesterday. Which course of the winds are we traveling?

MĀTALI: They call this path of the wind Parivaha[2]—
freed from darkness by Viṣṇu's second stride,
it bears the Gaṅgā's three celestial streams
and turns stars in orbit, dividing their rays.

KING: Mātali, this is why my soul, my senses, and my heart feel calm.

[He looks at the chariot wheels.]

We've descended to the level of the clouds.

MĀTALI: How do you know?

KING: Crested cuckoos fly between the spokes,
lightning flashes glint off the horses' coats,
and a fine mist wets your chariot's wheels—
all signs that we go over rain-filled clouds.

MĀTALI: In a moment you'll be back in your own domain, Your Majesty.

KING [looking down]: Our speeding chariot makes the mortal world appear fantastic. Look!

Mountain peaks emerge as the earth descends,
branches spread up from a sea of leaves,
fine lines become great rivers to behold—
the world seems to hurtle toward me.

MĀTALI: You observe well!

[He looks with great reverence.]

The beauty of earth is sublime.

KING: Mātali, what mountain do I see stretching into the eastern and western seas, rippled with streams of liquid gold, like a gateway of twilight clouds?

MĀTALI: Your Majesty, it is called the "Golden Peak," the mountain of the demigods, a place where austerities are practiced to perfection.

Mārīca,[3] the descendant of Brahmā,
a father of both demons and gods,
lives the life of an ascetic here
in the company of Aditi, his wife.

KING: One must not ignore good fortune! I shall perform the rite of circumambulating the sage.

---

2. This wind (one of seven cosmic winds) was produced when Vishnu in his Dwarf avatar grew great and bestrode the universe. The Ganges River flows in heaven before descending to earth. The stars mentioned are the Big Dipper.

3. The ancient seer Marica, also known as "Kashyapa," was husband to Aditi and Diti, and thus the father of most gods and antigods.

MĀTALI: An excellent idea!

[*The two mime descending.*]

KING [*smiling*]:   The chariot wheels make no sound,
      they raise no clouds of dust,
      they touch the ground unhindered—
      nothing marks the chariot's descent.

MĀTALI: It is because of the extraordinary power that you and Indra both possess.
KING: Mātali, where is Mārīca's hermitage?

MĀTALI [*pointing with his hand*]:   Where the sage stands staring at the sun,
      as immobile as the trunk of a tree,
      his body half-buried in an ant hill,
      with a snake skin on his chest,
      his throat pricked by a necklace
      of withered thorny vines,
      wearing a coil of long matted hair
      filled with nests of śakunta birds.

KING: I do homage to the sage for his severe austerity.
MĀTALI [*pulling hard on the chariot reins*]: Great king, let us enter Mārīca's her-
mitage, where Aditi nurtures the celestial coral trees.
KING: This tranquil place surpasses heaven. I feel as if I'm bathing in a lake of nectar.
MĀTALI [*stopping the chariot*]: Dismount, Your Majesty!
KING [*dismounting*]: Mātali, what about you?
MĀTALI: I have stopped the chariot. I'll dismount too.

[*He does so.*]

This way, Your Majesty!

[*He walks around.*]

You can see the grounds of the ascetics' grove ahead.
KING: I am amazed!

      In this forest of wish-fulfilling trees
      ascetics live on only the air they breathe
      and perform their ritual ablutions
      in water colored by golden lotus pollen.
      They sit in trance on jeweled marble slabs
      and stay chaste among celestial nymphs,
      practicing austerities in the place
      that others seek to win by penances.

MĀTALI: Great men always aspire to rare heights!

[*He walks around, calling aloud.*]

O venerable Śākalya, what is the sage Mārīca doing now? What do you say? In response to Aditi's question about the duties of a devoted wife, he is talking in a
gathering of great sages' wives.
KING [*listening*]: We must wait our turn.

MĀTALI [*looking at the king*]: Your Majesty, rest at the foot of this aśoka tree. Meanwhile, I'll look for a chance to announce you to Indra's father.

KING: As you advise . . .

[*He stops.*]

MĀTALI: Your Majesty, I'll attend to this.

[*He exits.*]

KING [*indicating he feels an omen*]:
        I have no hope for my desire.
        Why does my arm throb in vain?
        Once good fortune is lost,
        it becomes constant pain.

VOICE OFFSTAGE: Don't be so wild! Why is his nature so stubborn?

KING [*listening*]: Unruly conduct is out of place here. Whom are they reprimanding?

[*Looking toward the sound, surprised.*]

Who is this child, guarded by two female ascetics? A boy who acts more like a man.

        He has dragged this lion cub
        from its mother's half-full teat
        to play with it, and with his hand
        he violently tugs its mane.

[*The boy enters as described, with two female ascetics.*]

BOY: Open your mouth, lion! I want to count your teeth!

FIRST ASCETIC: Nasty boy, why do you torture creatures we love like our children? You're getting too headstrong! The sages gave you the right name when they called you "Sarvadamana, Tamer-of-everything."

KING: Why is my heart drawn to this child, as if he were my own flesh? I don't have a son. That is why I feel tender toward him . . .

SECOND ASCETIC: The lioness will maul you if you don't let go of her cub!

BOY [*smiling*]: Oh, I'm scared to death!

[*Pouting.*]

KING: This child appears to be
           the seed of hidden glory,
           like a spark of fire
           awaiting fuel to burn.

FIRST ASCETIC: Child, let go of the lion cub and I'll give you another toy!

BOY: Where is it? Give it to me!

[*He reaches out his hand.*]

KING: Why does he bear the mark of a king who turns the wheel of empire?

        A hand with fine webs connecting the fingers
        opens as he reaches for the object greedily,
        like a single lotus with faint inner petals
        spread open in the red glow of early dawn.

SECOND ASCETIC: Suvratā, you can't stop him with words! The sage Mārkaṇḍeya's son left a brightly painted clay bird in my hut. Get it for him!

FIRST ASCETIC: I will!

[*She exits.*]

BOY: But until it comes I'll play with this cub.

KING: I am attracted to this pampered boy . . .

> Lucky are fathers whose laps give refuge
> to the muddy limbs of adoring little sons
> when childish smiles show budding teeth
> and jumbled sounds make charming words.

SECOND ASCETIC: Well, he ignores me.

[*She looks back.*]

Is one of the sage's sons here?

[*Looking at the king.*]

Sir, please come here! Make him loosen his grip and let go of the lion cub! He's tormenting it in his cruel child's play.

KING [*approaching the boy, smiling*]: Stop! You're a great sage's son!

> When self-control is your duty by birth,
> why do you violate the sanctuary laws
> and ruin the animals' peaceful life,
> like a young black snake in a sandal tree?

SECOND ASCETIC: Sir, he's not a sage's son.

KING: His actions and his looks confirm it. I based my false assumption on his presence in this place.

[*He does what she asked; responding to the boy's touch, he speaks to himself.*]

> Even my limbs feel delighted
> from the touch of a stranger's son—
> the father at whose side he grew
> must feel pure joy in his heart.

SECOND ASCETIC [*examining them both*]: It's amazing! Amazing!

KING: What is it, madam?

SECOND ASCETIC: This boy looks surprisingly like you. He doesn't even know you, and he's acting naturally.

KING [*fondling the child*]: If he's not the son of an ascetic, what lineage does he belong to?

SECOND ASCETIC: The family of Puru.

KING [*to himself*]: What? His ancestry is the same as mine . . . so this lady thinks he resembles me. The family vow of Puru's descendants is to spend their last days in the forest.

> As world protectors they first choose
> palaces filled with sensuous pleasures,

but later, their homes are under trees
and one wife shares the ascetic vows.

[*Aloud.*]

But mortals cannot enter this realm on their own.

SECOND ASCETIC: You're right, sir. His mother is a nymph's child. She gave birth to him here in the hermitage of Mārīca.

KING [*in a stage whisper*]: Here is a second ground for hope!

[*Aloud.*]

What famed royal sage claims her as his wife?

SECOND ASCETIC: Who would even think of speaking the name of a man who rejected his lawful wife?

KING [*to himself*]: Perhaps this story points to me. What if I ask the name of the boy's mother? No, it is wrong to ask about another man's wife.

FIRST ASCETIC [*returning with a clay bird in her hand*]: Look, Sarvadamana, a śakunta! Look! Isn't it lovely?

BOY: Where's my mother?

BOTH ASCETICS: He's tricked by the similarity of names. He wants his mother.

SECOND ASCETIC: Child, she told you to look at the lovely clay śakunta bird.

KING [*to himself*]: What? Is his mother's name Śakuntalā? But names can be the same. Even a name is a mirage . . . a false hope to herald despair.

BOY: I like this bird!

[*He picks up the toy.*]

FIRST ASCETIC [*looking frantically*]: Oh, I don't see the amulet-box on his wrist!

KING: Don't be alarmed! It broke off while he was tussling with the lion cub.

[*He goes to pick it up.*]

BOTH ASCETICS: Don't touch it! Oh, he's already picked it up!

[*With their hands on their chests, they stare at each other in amazement.*]

KING: Why did you warn me against it?

FIRST ASCETIC: It contains the magical herb called Aparājitā, honored sir. Mārīca gave it to him at his birth ceremony. He said that if it fell to the ground no one but his parents or himself could pick it up.

KING: And if someone else does pick it up?

FIRST ASCETIC: Then it turns into a snake and strikes.

KING: Have you two seen it so transformed?

BOTH ASCETICS: Many times.

KING [*to himself, joyfully*]: Why not rejoice in the fulfillment of my heart's desire?

[*He embraces the child.*]

SECOND ASCETIC: Suvratā, come, let's tell Śakuntalā that her penances are over.

[*Both ascetics exit.*]

BOY: Let me go! I want my mother!

KING: Son, you will greet your mother with me.

BOY: My father is Duṣyanta, not you!

KING: This contradiction confirms the truth.

[*Śakuntalā enters, wearing the single braid of a woman in mourning.*]

ŚAKUNTALĀ: Even though Sarvadamana's amulet kept its natural form instead of changing into a snake, I can't hope that my destiny will be fulfilled. But maybe what my friend Sānumatī reports is right.

KING [*looking at Śakuntalā*]: It is Śakuntalā!

> Wearing dusty gray garments,
> her face gaunt from penances,
> her bare braid hanging down—
> she bears with perfect virtue
> the trial of long separation
> my cruelty forced on her.

ŚAKUNTALĀ [*seeing the king pale with suffering*]: He doesn't resemble my noble husband. Whose touch defiles my son when the amulet is protecting him?

BOY [*going to his mother*]: Mother, who is this stranger who calls me "son"?

KING: My dear, I see that you recognize me now. Even my cruelty to you is transformed by your grace.

ŚAKUNTALĀ [*to herself*]: Heart, be consoled! My cruel fate has finally taken pity on me. It is my noble husband!

KING:
> Memory chanced to break my dark delusion
> and you stand before me in beauty,
> like the moon's wife Rohiṇī[4]
> as she rejoins her lord after an eclipse.

ŚAKUNTALĀ: Victory to my noble husband! Vic . . .

[*She stops when the word is half-spoken, her throat choked with tears.*]

KING: Beautiful Śakuntalā,

> Even choked by your tears,
> the word "victory" is my triumph
> on your bare pouting lips,
> pale-red flowers of your face.

BOY: Mother, who is he?

ŚAKUNTALĀ: Child, ask the powers of fate!

KING [*falling at Śakuntalā's feet*]:
> May the pain of my rejection
> vanish from your heart;
> delusion clouded my weak mind
> and darkness obscured good fortune—

---

4. According to Sanskrit literary convention, the star cluster Rohini is the beloved of the moon.

> a blind man tears off a garland,
> fearing the bite of a snake.

ŚAKUNTALĀ: Noble husband, rise! Some crime I had committed in a former life surely came to fruit and made my kind husband indifferent to me.

[*The king rises.*]

But how did my noble husband come to remember this woman who was doomed to pain?

KING: I shall tell you after I have removed the last barb of sorrow.

> In my delusion I once ignored
> a teardrop burning your lip—
> let me dry the tear on your lash
> to end the pain of remorse!

[*He does so.*]

ŚAKUNTALĀ [*seeing the signet ring*]: My noble husband, this is the ring!

KING: I regained my memory when the ring was recovered.

ŚAKUNTALĀ: When it was lost, I tried in vain to convince my noble husband who I was.

KING: Let the vine take back this flower as a sign of her union with spring.

ŚAKUNTALĀ: I don't trust it. Let my noble husband wear it!

[*Mātali enters.*]

MĀTALI: Good fortune! This meeting with your lawful wife and the sight of your son's face are reasons to rejoice.

KING: The sweet fruit of my desire! Mātali, didn't Indra know about all this?

MĀTALI: What is unknown to the gods? Come, Your Majesty! The sage Mārīca grants you an audience.

KING: Śakuntalā, hold our son's hand! We shall go to see Mārīca together.

ŚAKUNTALĀ: I feel shy about appearing before my elders in my husband's company.

KING: But it is customary at a joyous time like this. Come! Come!

[*They all walk around. Then Mārīca enters with Aditi; they sit.*]

MĀRĪCA [*looking at the king*]: Aditi, this is king Duṣyanta,
> who leads Indra's armies in battle;
> his bow lets your son's thunderbolt
> lie ready with its tip unblunted.

ADITI: He bears himself with dignity.

MĀTALI: Your Majesty, the parents of the gods look at you with affection reserved for a son. Approach them!

KING: Mātali, the sages so describe this pair:

> Source of the sun's twelve potent forms,
> parents of Indra, who rules the triple world,
> birthplace of Viṣṇu's primordial form,
> sired by Brahmā's sons, Marīci and Dakṣa.

MĀTALI: Correct!

KING [*bowing*]: Indra's servant, Duṣyanta, bows to you both.

MĀRĪCA: My son, live long and protect the earth!

ADITI: My son, be an invincible warrior!

ŚAKUNTALĀ: I worship at your feet with my son.

MĀRĪCA: Child, with a husband like Indra
　　　　and a son like his son Jayanta,
　　　　you need no other blessing.
　　　　Be like Indra's wife Paulomī!

ADITI: Child, may your husband honor you and may your child live long to give both families joy! Be seated!

[*All sit near Mārīca.*]

MĀRĪCA [*pointing to each one*]:
　　　　By the turn of fortune,
　　　　virtuous Śakuntalā, her noble son,
　　　　and the king are reunited—
　　　　faith and wealth with order.

KING: Sir, first came the success of my hopes, then the sight of you. Your kindness is unparalleled.

　　　　First flowers appear, then fruits,
　　　　first clouds rise, then rain falls,
　　　　but here the chain of events is reversed—
　　　　first came success, then your blessing.

MĀTALI: This is the way the creator gods give blessings.

KING: Sir, I married your charge by secret marriage rites. When her relatives brought her to me after some time, my memory failed and I sinned against the sage Kaṇva, your kinsman. When I saw the ring, I remembered that I had married his daughter. This is all so strange!

　　　　Like one who doubts the existence
　　　　of an elephant who walks in front of him
　　　　but feels convinced by seeing footprints,
　　　　my mind has taken strange turns.

MĀRĪCA: My son, you need not take the blame. Even your delusion has another cause. Listen!

KING: I am attentive.

MĀRĪCA: When Menakā took her bewildered daughter from the steps of the nymphs' shrine and brought her to my wife, I knew through meditation that you had rejected this girl as your lawful wife because of Durvāsas' curse, and that the curse would end when you saw the ring.

KING [*sighing*]: So I am freed of blame.

ŚAKUNTALĀ [*to herself*]: And I am happy to learn that I wasn't rejected by my husband without cause. But I don't remember being cursed. Maybe the empty heart of love's separation made me deaf to the curse . . . my friends did warn me to show the ring to my husband . . .

MĀRĪCA: My child, I have told you the truth. Don't be angry with your husband!

> You were rejected when the curse
> that clouded memory made him cruel,
> but now darkness is lifted
> and your power is restored—
> a shadow has no shape
> in a badly tarnished mirror,
> but when the surface is clean
> it can easily be seen.

KING: Sir, here is the glory of my family!

[He takes the child by the hand.]

MĀRĪCA: Know that he is destined to turn the wheel of your empire!

> His chariot will smoothly cross
> the ocean's rough waves
> and as a mighty warrior
> he will conquer the seven continents.
> Here he is called Sarvadamana,
> Tamer-of-everything;
> later when his burden is the world,
> men will call him Bharata, Sustainer.

KING: Since you performed his birth ceremonies, we can hope for all this.

ADITI: Sir, let Kaṇva be told that his daughter's hopes have been fulfilled. Menakā, who loves her daughter, is here in attendance.

ŚAKUNTALĀ [to herself]: The lady expresses my own desire.

MĀRĪCA: He knows everything already through the power of his austerity.

KING: This is why the sage was not angry at me.

MĀRĪCA: Still, I want to hear his response to this joyful reunion. Who is there?

DISCIPLE [entering]: Sir, it is I.

MĀRĪCA: Gālava, fly through the sky and report the joyous reunion to Kaṇva in my own words: "The curse is ended. Śakuntalā and her son are embraced by Duṣyanta now that his memory is restored."

DISCIPLE: As you command, sir!

[He exits.]

MĀRĪCA: My son, mount your friend Indra's chariot with your wife and son and return to your royal capital!

KING: As you command, sir!

MĀRĪCA: My son, what other joy can I give you?

KING: There is no greater joy, but if you will:

> May the king serve nature's good!
> May priests honor the goddess of speech!
> And may Śiva's dazzling power
> destroy my cycle of rebirths!

[All exit.]

RESONANCES

Kuntaka: from *The Life-Force of Literary Beauty*[1]

> When a poet is constructing a plot of his own, based though it might be on a
> well-known source, if he succeeds in infusing even a small streak of originality,
> the beauty gained thereby will be singular.
> Even an episode too can shine forth as the vital essence of the work as a
> whole, brimful of sentiments reaching their utmost limit.

As in the simile given in the next passage, the original art of construction manifested by a poet will appear as singularly appealing to connoisseurs, in the field of
plot-construction. The author[2] adds that this applies even to plots based on traditional
stories. The simile given is:—"Even as an episode too can shine forth as the vital
essence of the work as a whole." The works meant are literary forms like the literary
epic (*mahākāvya* running to several cantos). "Brimful of sentiments reaching their utmost limit" is a description of their fullness of literary sentiments like the erotic.

The gist is this:—Even in a well-known plot based on epics like the Mahābhārata
which may be described as a store-house of renowned and varied stories and as an
ocean full of sentiments, since there is no other consideration to decide between the
relative beauty of the several stories contained therein, a poet should select only such
themes as are capable of evoking sentiments and moods and generating a sense of
wonder in the readers. He should see also that the theme so selected will give full
scope for the exquisitely aesthetic, original and matchless inventive power of his genius. When a poet thus achieves such an exquisite artistic beauty in his episode, he
succeeds in delighting the assemblies of all poets and tasteful critics.

In a whole literary work also, such an attainment of aesthetic effect owing its origin to the original inventive power of the poet will present a new shade of charm even
like a new touch-up given by a painter to an old broken portrait.

In the play, *Abhijñāna-Śākuntalā,* we see (in the hero) a recollection of the sweet
feeling of Śakuntalā's matchless beauty in her exquisite youth as soon as he sees her
(when she removes her veil) in a way which does not rule out the possibility of rejecting her as a wife of another person. Śakuntalā does everything to revive his memory
by relating intimate incidents of their first honeymoon when both were filled with
deep love for each other, the incidents which are at once so intimate and delicate that
they are bound to infuse confidence. The reason why Duṣyanta is unable to recognise
her even after listening to it is a mystery left unexplained in the original Mahābhārata.

---

1. Translated by K. Krishnamoorthy. Kuntaka was a literary theorist who wrote in late-10th-century Kashmir.
Like many others before him he sought to identify the
essence, or "life-force," of literariness, and he discovered
this in what he called *vakrokti,* here meaning something
like "striking expression." His principal interest in
Shakuntala lies at the most elevated end of this concept
of *vakrokti*: in analyzing Kalidasa's rewriting of the epic
narrative, he is concerned to understand how the changes
introduced in the plot assist in the development of *rasa,*
the highest form of striking expression. Although the action as earlier presented in the *Mahabharata* is in fact
highly motivated, Kuntaka understood it to be otherwise,

calling Dushyanta's failure to recognize Shakuntala "a
mystery left unexplained in the original *Mahabharata.*"
He holds that Kalidasa's introducing the motifs of the
curse, the king's amnesia, and the ring of recognition cor-
rects a serious aesthetic flaw in the epic prototype. In this
Kuntaka agrees with many other medieval Indian critics
who believed that poetry has vastly different objectives
from those of history or legend and that revising plots in
the service of *rasa* is not only possible but necessary.
2. Kuntaka refers to himself as "the author," since his
work consists of a commentary on a series of memorial
verses that he composed, including the lines that begin
this passage.

For explaining it adequately with a cogent reason, the poet has invented the episode of the curse of sage Durvāsas. Durvāsas is a sage blind to all soft feeling and highly irate by temperament, one who flies into a rage even at the slightest fault. In that episode of Durvāsas, it is seen that Śakuntalā is completely overwhelmed by the unbearably deep pangs of her first separation from her lover; and as she is lying in her cottage in such a state, there comes this great sage at her door-step, flies into a fit of anger at being unnoticed and pronounces a curse:—

> Since you blindly ignore
> a great sage like me,
> the lover you worship
> with mindless devotion
> will not remember you,
> even when awakened—
> like a drunkard who forgets
> a story he just composed!

Such was the curse flung on Śakuntalā. And at once the sage was moving out. Yet when he was appealed to by the two friends of Śakuntalā, the great sage yields to the extent of limiting the duration of his curse to the sight of the signet ring given by the king to his beloved. And when the daughter of sage Kaṇva is on her way to meet her beloved, the ring which adorned her tender shoot-like finger slips down without her notice somewhere in the waters of a meandering river which she had entered for bathing. And mistaking the glittering glow of the ruby set in the ring for a juicy lump of flesh, a fish swallows it. In course of time, the fish gets killed by a fisherman who catches it and the ring recovered by him is at last presented to the king himself. Such an art of plot-construction may surely be regarded as the best repository of literary sentiments. Thanks to it, the entire play has acquired a unique beauty. Again, in proper time, we have the incident of the song outwardly reviling the bee,[3] whose inner significance is caught by the king, though his memory has been blacked out by the curse of the sage; deep down in his mind we notice that traces are still left of the old love in Duṣyanta on account of which he is very much upset:—

> Seeing rare beauty,
> hearing lovely sounds,
> even a happy man
> becomes strangely uneasy . . .
> perhaps he remembers,
> without knowing why,
> loves of another life
> buried deep in his being.

Here the beauty of such a recollection of Śakuntalā (so deep down in the layers of his subconscious), at once guileless and charming, appeals very much to the hearts of connoisseurs. What is more, she is turned down later, her story and ring of recognition are dismissed as false; the account of her marriage with him and pregnancy given by Sage Kaṇva's disciple is discredited and the King is seen in a fit of anger. Then, even transgressing the limits of natural shyness, her veil is removed from her face

---

3. The reference is to *Shakuntala*, page 979: "Craving sweet / new nectar, / you kissed / a mango bud once— / how could you / forget her, bee, / to bury your joy / in a lotus?"

suddenly. Yet the king is under the illusion that she is another's wife. Though her effervescent youthful charm, superior to that of all the women seen by him so far, impresses him very much as much as her narration, sweet like the strains from a lyre, of intimate incidents of her association to bring back his memory, incidents such as excursions in the forest grove, still he shows the rudeness of rejecting Śakuntalā. Such rudeness too becomes understandable only by the intensity of his later repentance at the termination of the curse, a repentance which is indicative of the depth of his unmitigated love for her in his heart. And it is most appealing to the connoisseurs. And in devising the end of the curse, the poet prefaces it with a description of the intense wretchedness of the King's mental state, who is suffering feverishly the pangs of unbearable separation after the dawn of his memory of the forgotten incidents. Synchronising with it comes the recovery of the lost ring too which again delights the readers very much. The chamberlain of the King observes:—

> Rejecting his regal jewels,
> he wears one golden bangle
> above his left wrist;
> his lips are pale with sighs,
> his eyes wan from brooding at night—
> like a gemstone ground in polishing,
> the fiery beauty of his body
> makes his wasted form seem strong.
>
> Despising what he once enjoyed,
> he shuns his ministers every day
> and spends long sleepless nights
> tossing at the edge of his bed—
> when courtesy demands that
> he converse with palace women,
> he stumbles over their names,
> and then retreats in shame.

Here the epithets given to the king are full of artistic beauty. There is artistic beauty of "number" instanced in the word names[4] (where the plural number is idiomatically used to refer to a single name of a rival). These add to our aesthetic appeal. When the king looking at the picture of his beloved drawn by himself, speaks gallantly of his sweet recollection with the deep impress of his darling:—

> Bee, if you touch the lips of my love
> that lure you like a young tree's virgin buds,
> lips I gently kissed in festivals of love,
> I'll hold you captive in a lotus flower cage.

the speech directly appeals to our hearts even as he is speaking.

If this exquisite episode invented by the genius of the poet were not to be there in the play, the unbearable fact of the King's forgetting his wife without any reason would have become a source of blemish as much in the play as in the original story of the Mahābhārata itself.

---

4. Kuntaka strives to find "striking expression" everywhere, even in the use of the plural "names": calling one mistress by the name of another is a common peccadillo in Sanskrit love poetry. Logically the singular would be expected; the plural is presumably used to indicate the frequency of his slip.

The expression in the *Kārikā,* "a small streak of originality,"[5] should be understood in a two-fold manner: Firstly, something which never existed before might be invented. Secondly, that which lacks propriety as it exists in the source should be modified suitably. The object in both cases remaining the same, namely, aesthetic effect on readers.

Johann Wolfgang Goethe: On *Shakuntala*[1]

> If you long for springtime flowers or autumn fruit,
> for something that charms, enchants, sates, and sustains,
> for a single word for heaven and earth, I say
> "Shakuntala"—and no more need be said. (1791)

* * *

We would be most ungrateful if we failed to mention Indian compositions as well. Especially those that should be admired for escaping in a perfectly felicitous and natural manner from conflict between the most abstruse philosophy on the one hand and the most outlandish religion on the other, and for taking from both only so much as conduces to inner depth and outer dignity.

We must give pride of place to *Shakuntala,* since for so many years we have been lost in admiration of this work. Feminine purity, guiltless forbearance, male forgetfulness, maternal separation, father and mother reunited through their son: the most natural of all states of affairs, but which here float, like life-giving clouds, in the regions of miracles between heaven and earth, elevated by poetry—an entirely ordinary drama of nature, but one presented by the gods themselves, and the children of gods. (1817)

* * *

It is hardly possible to give an accounting of this day. Who has not had the experience of casually picking up a book to read and found it irresistibly carrying him along, and exerting the greatest influence on his entire life? And had its ultimate effect at that very first moment, so that later rereading and studious contemplation could scarcely add to the impact? Once this happened to me, with *Shakuntala*—and doesn't the same sort of thing happen to us with certain very special people? (1817)

* * *

[*Goethe has been contrasting three types of translation: the prosaic, the parodic, and the authentic.*] One may recall the most remarkable applause with which we Germans

---

5. See the verse that begins this excerpt.
1. Translated by Sheldon Pollock. When Sir William Jones, a judge in the service of the East India Company, first translated *Shakuntala* in 1789, it caused a sensation in European literary circles. The excitement likely had much to do with what it demonstrated for the first time: that a rich literature existed in India. The country was long known as the birthplace of philosophical wisdom, but little of its remarkable nonreligious poetry or drama had reached the West. *Shakuntala* was thus a revelation of the new. But it was also evidence of how ancient Indian culture and civility were, and thus of the irrationality of European colonial rule, which was then in the course of consolidation.

No one fell under the spell of the play more powerfully

than Johann Wolfgang Goethe, the great German poet and dramatist. He returned to the work repeatedly throughout his life, famously adapting some of its conventions such as the "meta-play" at its opening for the "Prelude on the Stage" in his *Faust* (see Volume E). Given here are a poem and remarks scattered through Goethe's writings (with the date of each passage, where known, given at the end). Goethe interpreted the work as a sentimental education, a view that resonates to some degree with the traditional Indian interpretation. But his sympathetic understanding faltered when he confronted the "monstrous gods" and "absurd theology" in Kalidasa's work. Think what Kalidasa might have been, says Goethe, if only like Shakespeare he had been born a Protestant!

greeted that sort of translation of the *Shakuntala*.[2] The joy this occasioned can be ascribed to the plain prose to which the poem was reduced. Yet it is now high time we had a translation of the third kind, one in harmony with the different dialects and modes of speech of the original—rhythmical, metrical, and prosaic—and one that naturalized the poem in all its particularities and made it once again a source of joy. Since at present a manuscript of this eternal work is available in Paris, a German living in that city could render us immortal service by such a feat of translation. (1819)

* * *

Shakuntala: Here the poet appears in his highest function. It is only because he is a representative of the most natural circumstances, the most civilized ways of life, the purest moral standards, the most dignified majesty and sincerest worship of God that he is able to venture upon things that mark the most vulgar and ridiculous contrast. * * * It is another of the happier circumstances enabling the free and pure development of Shakespeare's great talent, that he was born a Protestant. He would otherwise have had, like Kalidasa and Calderon, to glorify the greatest absurdities.[3]

Rabindranath Tagore: from *Sakuntala: Its Inner Meaning*[1]

Goethe, the master-poet of Europe, has summed up his criticism of *Sakuntala* in a single quatrain;[2] he has not taken the poem to pieces. This quatrain seems to be a small thing like the flame of a candle, but it lights up the whole drama in an instant and reveals its inner nature. In Goethe's words, *Sakuntala* blends together the young year's blossoms and the fruits of its maturity; it combines heaven and earth in one.

We are apt to pass over this eulogy lightly as a mere poetical outburst. We are apt to consider that it only means in effect that Goethe regarded *Sakuntala* as fine poetry. But it is not really so. His stanza breathes not the exaggeration of rapture, but the deliberate judgment of a true critic. There is a special point in his words. Goethe says expressly that *Sakuntala* contains the history of a development,—the development of flower into fruit, of earth into heaven, of matter into spirit.

In truth there are unions in *Sakuntala;* and the motif of the play is the progress from the earlier union of the First Act, with its earthly, unstable beauty and romance, to the higher union in the heavenly hermitage of eternal bliss described in the last Act. This drama was meant not for dealing with a particular passion, not for developing a particular character, but for translating the whole subject from one world to another,—to elevate love from the sphere of physical beauty to the eternal heaven of moral beauty.

2. The prose version of Georg Forster in 1791 (from the English translation of Sir William Jones, 1789).
3. The five selections given here are from: *Goethes Werke,* Weimar, 1891, vol. 4, pt. 1, page 122; 1904, vol. 42, pt. 2, page 50; 1904, vol. 31, page 20; 1888, vol. 7, page 238; 1904, vol. 42, pt. 2, page 247–48.
1. Translator anonymous. Rabindranath Tagore (1861–1941) occupies a place in the literary and cultural history of modern-day Bengal for which it is hard to find parallels in other societies. Prolific poet, novelist, short-story writer (see Volume E), public intellectual, and recipient of the Nobel Prize in literature (1913), Tagore shaped the thinking of his contemporaries in India with unparalleled effect, and his views on India's most famous play merit consideration. It may prove hard for contemporary readers to be persuaded by his argument that

Shakuntala is about sexual sin and redemption. After all, Shakuntala's love is fated and countenanced by the cosmic powers, and Dushyanta is the perfect king; their behavior is certainly not viewed as blameworthy in the terms of the drama itself. But Tagore was motivated both by the recent arrival of Victorian morality in late-colonial Bengal and, perhaps more importantly, by the search for a new moral order suited to the longed-for independence of India. This makes it less curious that he should discover the highest value of the play to be in its supposed interest in tempering freedom by restraint. His argument is a salutary reminder of how all of us interpret literature—until disciplined by history—out of a location in our own present.
2. See page 1012.

With the greatest ease Kalidas has effected this junction of earth with heaven. His earth so naturally passes into heaven that we do not mark the boundary-line between the two. In the First Act the poet has not concealed the gross earthiness of the fall of Sakuntala: he has clearly shown, in the conduct of the hero and the heroine alike, how much desire contributed to that fall. He has fully painted all the blandishments, playfulness and flutterings of the intoxicating sense of youth, the struggle between deep bashfulness and strong self-expression.

This is a proof of the simplicity of Sakuntala: she was not prepared beforehand for the outburst of passion which the occasion of Dushyanta's visit called forth; she had not learned how to restrain herself, how to hide her feelings. Sakuntala had not known Cupid before; hence her heart was bare of armour, and she could not distrust either the sentiment of love or the character of her lover. The daughter of the hermitage was off her guard, just as the deer there knew not fear. * * *

At the beginning we see Sakuntala is self-forgetful and obedient to Nature's impulses like the plants and flowers; at the end we see the deeper feminine soul,—sober, patient under ill, intent on austerities, strictly regulated by the sacred laws of piety. With matchless art Kalidas has placed his heroine on the meeting-point of action and calmness, of Nature and Law, of river and ocean, as it were. Her father was a hermit, but her mother was an *apsara,* a nymph. Her birth was the outcome of interrupted austerities, but her nurture was in a hermitage, which is just the spot where nature and austerities, beauty and restraint, are harmonised.[3] There is none of the conventional bonds of society there, yet we have the harder regulations of religion. Her Gandharva marriage,[4] too, was of the same type; it had the wildness of Nature joined to the social tie of wedlock. The drama stands alone and unrivalled in all literature, because it depicts how restraint can be harmonised with freedom. All its joys and sorrows, unions and partings, proceed from the conflict of these two forces. * * *

Our rebellious passions raise storms. In this drama Kalidas has extinguished the volcanic fire of tumultuous passion by means of the tears of the penitent heart. But he has not dwelt too long on the disease; he has just given us a glimpse of it and then dropped the veil. The desertion of Sakuntala by the polygamous Dushyanta, which in real life would have happened as a natural consequence of his character, is here brought about by the curse of Durvasa. Otherwise, the desertion would have been extremely cruel and pathetic and would have destroyed the peace and harmony of the whole play. But the poet has left a small rent in the veil through which we can get an idea of the royal sin. It is in the Fifth Act. Just before Sakuntala arrives at court and is repudiated by her husband, the poet momentarily draws aside the curtain from the King's love-affairs. Queen Hansapadika is singing to herself in her music room:[5]

"O honey-bee, having sucked the mango blossoms in your search for new honey, you have clean forgotten your recent loving welcome by the lotus."

This tear-stained song of a stricken heart in the royal harem gives us a rude shock, especially as our heart was hitherto filled with Dushyanta's love-passages with Sakuntala. Only in the preceding Act we saw Sakuntala setting out for her husband's home in a very holy, sweet, and tender mood, carrying with herself the blessings of the hoary sage Kanva and the good wishes of the whole forest world. And now a stain

---

3. Recall that Shakuntala was born of celestial nymph Menaka and Vishvamitra, a king who had become an ascetic. Abandoned at birth, Shakuntala was found by the sage Kanva, who adopted her as his daughter.
4. Consisting simply in the mutual consent of the man and woman.

5. The verse here attributed to Hansapadika appears in the translation of the play included in this anthology as the singing of the voice in the Air (*Shakuntala,* page 946).

falls on the picture we had so hopefully formed of the home of love to which she was going.

When the Jester asked, "What means this song?" Dushyanta smiled and said, "We desert our lasses after a short spell of love-making, and therefore I have deserved this strong rebuke from Queen Hansapadika." This indication of the fickleness of royal love is not purposeless at the beginning of the Fifth Act. With masterly skill the poet here shows that what Durvasa's curse had brought about had its seeds in human nature. * * *

What is easily gained is as easily lost. Therefore, the poet has made the two lovers undergo a long and austere *tapasya*[6] that they may gain each other truly, eternally. If Dushyanta had accepted Sakuntala when she was first brought to his court, she would have only added to the number of Hansapadikas, occupied a corner of the royal harem, and passed the rest of her life in neglect, gloom and uselessness. * * *

Thus has Kalidas burnt away vice in the internal fire of the sinner's heart; he has not tried to conceal it from the outside. When the curtain drops on the last Act, we feel that all the evil has been destroyed as on a funeral pyre, and the peace born of a perfect and satisfactory fruition reigns in our hearts. He has made the physical union of Dushyanta and Sakuntala tread the path of sorrow, and thereby chastened and sublimated it into a moral union. Hence did Goethe rightly say that Sakuntala combines the blossoms of Spring with the fruits of Autumn; it combines Heaven and Earth. Truly in Sakuntala there is one Paradise lost and another regained. * * *

The poet has shown here, * * * that the Beauty that goes hand in hand with Moral Law is eternal, that the calm, controlled and beneficent form of Love is its best expression, that Beauty is truly charming under restraint and decays quickly when it gets wild and unfettered. * * *

On the foundation of the hermitage of recluses Kalidas has built the home of the householder. He has rescued the relation of the sexes from the sway of lust and enthroned it in the holy and pure seat of asceticism. In the sacred books of the Hindus the ordered relation of the sexes has been defined by strict injunctions and laws. Kalidas has demonstrated that relation by means of the elements of Beauty. The Beauty that he adores is lit up by grace, modesty and goodness; in its range it embraces the whole universe. It is fulfilled by renunciation, gratified by sorrow, and rendered eternal by religion. In the midst of this Beauty, the impetuous, unruly love of man and woman has restrained itself and attained to a profound peace, like a wild torrent merged in the ocean of Goodness. Therefore is such love higher and more wonderful than wild and unrestrained passion.

⟨∞⟩

---

6. Ascetic practices.

Terra-cotta soldiers from the tomb of the first Qin Dynasty emperor (r. 247–210 B.C.E.). As many as 7,000 life-size statues may have been produced to accompany the emperor after death in the vast underground necropolis he built for himself outside the capital of Xi'an. Construction began upon his ascension to the imperial throne at the age of 13. The tomb, which replicates the emperor's earthly domain, has not yet been completely excavated.

China: The Classical Tradition

━━━━━●━▷◁▷◁●━━━━━

Though not the earliest civilization in human history, China's has certainly been the longest continuing one, a record supported by material evidence and historical documents extending back in time at least five thousand years. The foundations for this remarkable power of endurance were laid early on but were articulated most clearly in the period we refer to as Early China, which corresponds approximately to the first millennium B.C.E. The philosopher Confucius (551–479) lived at its midpoint and is the central figure in this history. His own perspective, however, was one that looked backward over many centuries, and his legacy survives to the present day.

Well-preserved pottery and other artifacts attest to the existence of several developed Neolithic cultures at multiple sites along the Yellow River in northern China, with at least one on the Yangzi River to the south as well. Although one of these cultures is dated to the fifth millennium B.C.E., the majority appear to have flourished during the third. This is also the beginning of a prehistoric mythological record constructed by later generations, who credited a series of sage emperors with innovations and principles that were instrumental in the development of Chinese civilization and that established abiding norms of ethical and political practice. Fu Xi, for example, was said to have taught humans how to hunt and fish using nets, to domesticate animals and each other (through marriage), to raise silkworms, and to cook. His study of chicken tracks inspired his invention of writing, and he also devised the eight trigrams whose manipulation and interpretation were to become central in the later divination text, the *Book of Changes* (*Yi jing*). After Fu Xi, Shen Nong was credited with developing instruction in how to plow, raise crops, use herbs for medicinal purposes, and exchange goods at markets. Shortly after that Huang Di, or the Yellow Emperor, was said to have introduced techniques of clearing forest and brush and of cattle breeding; under his enlightened rule wheeled vehicles, pottery, shipbuilding, and armor were also invented, and musical notes were standardized. Three later emperors further exemplified principles of sage rule. Yao, recognizing that his own son was unfit, chose a more qualified commoner to succeed him, establishing the primacy of merit over birth in governance. This commoner, Shun, became in turn a paragon of filial piety by remaining solicitous of parents who were constantly trying to do him in. And his successor, Yu, embodied the ideal ruler's tireless dedication to the welfare of his populace by toiling for years to harness the devastating flooding of the Yellow River by dredging natural irrigation channels.

However historically uncertain this mythical lineage may be, the accomplishments of this sequence of cultural heroes highlight aspects and values of Chinese civilization from its very beginnings that were both formative and enduring. These include the importance of agriculture, writing, ritual, and the arts; an insistence on respect for one's parents and ancestors; and the conviction that morality, rather than genealogy, validated one's right to govern. Moreover, the very transformation of what may have been supernatural figures into benevolent patriarchs—real historical beings—reflects what was to become a powerful rationalizing impulse in the culture. Indeed, early Chinese culture does not appear to have been preoccupied with a supernal realm different in kind from that of the human world or concerned about struggles with deities or their interventions into human lives. Despite the many legends about mythic characters, there is little in the way of fully articulated mythologies but rather a focus on events in real historical time, in which both life and the afterlife were firmly situated.

BONES OF THE CULTURE

Yu was the founder of the legendary Xia dynasty at the beginning of the second millennium B.C.E. Definitive evidence of the historical existence of this dynasty has not yet been found although it is being actively sought by Chinese archeologists. The actual historical record begins with the Shang dynasty (c. 1550–1040 B.C.E.), which developed in the central Yellow River basin, when Sumer had long since disappeared and Egypt was already an old civilization. The burial sites of the last Shang kings were discovered near Anyang in Henan Province early in the twentieth century. They reveal evidence of a centralized, hierarchical society whose king used an extensive administrative structure to rule over what had been a loose confederation of states, deploying the agricultural surplus of the population for massive projects of construction, bronze-casting, and warfare. The many ritual jades and bronze vessels excavated from the cross-shaped pit tombs attest both to the sophistication of Shang production techniques and the conviction that such artifacts would prove useful after death.

Equally revealing have been the inscriptions on animal bones and turtle shells also unearthed at these burial sites, which record divinations undertaken by the king. In a process called *scapulimancy,* heat was applied to a bone or shell, and the resulting pattern of cracks was "read" as an answer to whatever question had been posed. A record of the process, sometimes with its subsequent verification, was then inscribed on the object.

What the kings generally sought was either information—about the harvest, the weather, childbirth, illness, or other troubles—or justification of a plan, such as an administrative appointment or a military invasion. The written record is typically a laconic one:

> Crack-making on day 16, it was divined: It will rain.
> The king, reading the cracks, said: It will rain, on day 19.
> On day 19, it really did rain.

But the inscriptions on these oracle bones nonetheless provide much valuable information about prevalent concerns and values. Almost all meticulously dated, they attest to the king's worries about the disposition of his ancestors, the wisdom of his decisions, the general welfare of the populace, and the importance of keeping a written record. The Shang cared deeply about timeliness and good order, about pleasing the dead, about ensuring the continuity of the family line through male descendants, about according with the forces of nature and the wishes of a supreme being known as "Di," and about deciphering the hidden meaning of events. Other practices of the Shang, such as slavery and human sacrifice, were abandoned by their successors, but these beliefs persisted in some form long after the dynasty's demise. Moreover, the script incised on the oracle bones, as well as on

The Shang cared deeply about timeliness and good order, about pleasing the dead, [and] about ensuring the continuity of the family line through male descendants . . .

An oracle bone inscription from the reign of Wu Ding (died c. 1189 B.C.E.). Wu Ding's diviners typically inquired about such issues as harvests, hunts, childbearing, dreams, and omens. Here the prognostication, based on reading the cracks, is equivocal regarding the imminent birth of Lady Hao's child. The outcome, however, was judged a negative one: "After 31 days she gave birth; it was not good; it was a girl."

later Shang bronzes, exhibits structural principles that the Chinese language retained, even as it evolved. Rather than employing an alphabet or syllabary, it employs characters that were once pictographs, as well as combinations of symbols representing both sound and meaning; the vast majority of words now are phonetic compounds of this second type. The table on page 1020 illustrates the development of some common early characters from their pictorial origins.

However varied regional pronunciations of the language may have become, its written form remained relatively impervious to these dialectal differences and was instrumental in ensuring the continuity of the culture. Although developed later than cuneiform or hieroglyphics, Chinese writing has never been totally unreadable by the literate, though admittedly it is subject to conflicting interpretations and endless argument.

	Shang bone script	Zhou bronze script	Warring States script	Seal script	Clerical script (Han)
1. 'child'					
2. 'cloud'					
3. 'water'					
4. 'year'					
5. 'silk'					
6. 'be born'					
7. 'eye'					
8. 'fruit'					
9. 'tripod'					
10. 'deer'					
11. 'wise'					
12. 'buy'					

A historical table of Chinese script. The first four columns illustrate the evolution of ancient Chinese script from its earliest surviving examples on Shang oracle bones. During the Han dynasty in the first century B.C.E., a clerical script was adopted as the official form for all purposes. In what was probably the most important development in the history of Chinese writing, formerly pictographic elements became more abstract and conventionalized in the interests of convenience and standardization. Unlike the earlier forms, Han clerical script can still be read with relative ease today.

A NEW MANDATE

The last ruler of the Shang was dissolute and tyrannical, and was therefore rightfully overthrown by the Zhou people to the west around 1040 B.C.E. So explained the new rulers to those whom they had conquered, invoking the term "Mandate of Heaven" to justify their revolt. Having once enjoyed Heaven's blessing of their benevolent rule, the Shang had evidently forfeited its sanction because of cruel and barbarous behavior, and the Mandate had therefore passed to the Zhou to establish a new dynasty. It traced its ancestry to a Lord Millet (Hou Ji), whose father's rule was said to have preceded that of the sage king Yao. The authority and legitimacy of its founding King Wen are celebrated in a ritual hymn from the sixth-century B.C.E. anthology, the *Book of Songs:*

> August is Wen the king:
> Reverenced in his glittering light.
> Great indeed was the Mandate of Heaven.
> The grandsons and sons of the Shang,
> Shang's grandsons and sons,
> Their numbers were countless.
> But Di on high gave His mandate,
> And by Zhou they were subdued.

For the Zhou the notion of Heaven (Tian) represented a relatively abstract, universalized concept of cosmic moral order and power that gradually took the place of the Shang's more anthropomorphic Di. There was otherwise no sharp break in the civilization. Like the Shang, the Zhou were an agrarian people who maintained a strong commitment to ancestor worship. Typical city structures centered on a palace-temple complex that emphasized the centrality of the royal family and its ancestral line. Unlike the sprawling cities of Mesopotamia, regulated layouts of cities in ancient China maintained a more focused, unitary authority in which merchants and artisans played but a minor political role. The ruling family consolidated its power by establishing relatives and supporters with land in surrounding regions, although allegiance was based on kinship

Unlike the sprawling cities of Mesopotamia, regulated layouts of cities in ancient China maintained a more focused, unitary authority . . .

obligations rather than on the contractual bonds of feudal Europe and came to be undergirded by a more centralized bureaucracy as well. The dynasty's prosperity and stability were short-lived, however, and within three centuries it had become weak enough that a non-Chinese tribe succeeded in sacking the capital near modern-day Xi'an in 770 B.C.E. Thus ended what historians would refer to as the Western Zhou. A new capital of a revived Eastern Zhou was established near Luoyang farther down the Yellow River, but the empire existed henceforth in name only, as its increasingly powerful feudal states engaged in a long struggle to take its place.

THE SEARCH FOR ORDER

The five centuries of the Eastern Zhou's nominal rule are traditionally divided into two eras known as the Spring and Autumn period (722–481 B.C.E.) and the Warring States period (403–221 B.C.E.). The latter term is self-explanatory, and the former is

China in 250 B.C.E.
(the Warring States Period)

the name of a terse chronicle of events in the northeastern state of Lu, birthplace of
Confucius and attributed to his hand. As the efforts of its larger subject states to take
advantage of the weakened Zhou dynasty became increasingly rapacious, a number of
strategists and thinkers turned their attention to solutions for the warfare and chaos
that threatened both political and social stability.

The duchy of Lu was most closely identified with ancient Zhou traditions, and
for its native son Confucius, the remedy for contemporary troubles lay in a return to
those values, which centered on the primacy of a family-based morality and the extension of its ideal behaviors to all other relationships. For him there was nothing new
in this message, as he insisted: "I transmit but do not innovate; I am truthful in what I
say and devoted to antiquity." The founding ideals of the Zhou dynasty in his view retained their nobility and a legitimacy possessed by no contemporary contender for dominion. As he stated, "The Zhou is resplendent in culture, having before it the example of the two previous dynasties. I am for the Zhou." And the most important ruling
principle was a simple one: "If a man is correct in his own person, then there will be
obedience without orders being given; but if he is not correct in his own person, there
will not be obedience even though orders are given." Government was for the good of
the governed, and the government must be good. The sayings of and about Confucius

collected in *The Analects* are replete with illustrations of governing by moral example, whose
practice itself is rooted in being a dutiful child
and exemplary father, in respecting one's ancestors, and in becoming an ancestor oneself through
parenthood. Other normative principles of behav-

Priorities of the group took precedence over those of the individual . . .

ior were also based on the family as model: priorities of the group took precedence
over those of the individual or of other units, and social harmony was most easily
achieved when individuals recognized their proper roles within a hierarchical structure; but each role carried with it a set of attendant responsibilities. And ritual and
learning were both essential and efficacious in fulfilling one's obligations and realizing one's potential for moral action.

Confucius was but one of many voices contending to be heard and not, evidently,
among the most persuasive at the time. Indeed, he was recognized as someone "who
keeps working towards a goal whose realization he knows to be hopeless." His best-
known disciple, Mencius (385?–312? B.C.E.), sought to anchor the Confucian ethical
mandates in a more fully articulated theory of the innate goodness of human nature.
Its realization did, however, require both the proper environment and cultivation:

> Heaven has not sent down men whose endowment differs so greatly. The difference is due
> to what ensnares their hearts. Take the barley for example. Sow the seeds and cover them
> with soil. The place is the same and the time of sowing is also the same. The plants shoot
> up and by the summer solstice they all ripen. If there is any unevenness, it is because the
> soil varies in richness and there is no uniformity in the fall of rain and dew and the amount
> of human effort devoted to tending it. Now things of the same kind are all alike. Why
> should we have doubts when it comes to man? The sage and I are of the same kind.

The format of Mencius's discussions suggests that agreement on these notions
was by no means universal, for they are couched as conversations and arguments with
a variety of speakers. Indeed, by the Warring States period, it was said that "a hundred
schools" of thought were contending for the attention of rulers who were, in turn, looking for advice that might enhance their chances of success on the political battlefield.

Among the most important early thinkers to take issue with Confucian values were
the Daoists, who emphasized seeking harmony with the Way of the cosmos and therefore
privileged the natural over the human. Moreover, whereas some Daoists such as Laozi
participated in the ongoing discussions focused on effective governance, Zhuangzi and
others advocated turning one's back on political engagement altogether. His justification
for such a rejection was framed in both subtle argumentation and whimsical anecdotes
whose thoroughgoing relativity undermined active commitment of any sort. Still other
thinkers who accepted basic Confucian beliefs in the absoluteness of ethical values and
of government by moral example became less sanguine than their predecessors about the
larger context within which they functioned. For Xunzi, a third-century B.C.E. thinker, for
example, the inculcation of such values through ritual and education was crucial because
human nature was not inclined to be good. Culture and civilization represented a real triumph, then, over the cruder appetites and passions to which humans are susceptible.

Xunzi's most famous student, Han Fei (d. 233 B.C.E.), argued that even more
stringent methods were required to control the unfortunate predilections of the populace: not the power of example but only the power of power—of laws, rewards, and
punishments—would succeed in ordering the state. Confucius may have been loved

and respected, he pointed out, but "only seventy people became his devoted pupils." Why? Because "people are submissive to power and few of them can be influenced by doctrines of righteousness." His advice to rulers was unequivocal:

> The tiger is able to subdue the dog because of its claws and fangs. If the tiger abandons its claws and fangs and lets the dog use them, it will be subdued by the dog. Similarly, the ruler controls his ministers through punishment and rewards. If the ruler abandons his punishment and rewards and lets his ministers use them, he will be controlled by the ministers. . . .

It would be difficult to imagine a more radical departure from Confucian tenets, but Han Fei's lessons were clear and practical. His Legalist teachings proved of interest to the king of Qin, whose victory over rival states to succeed the Zhou was imminent, and they were instrumental in establishing his rule as the first emperor of China.

IMPERIAL CONSOLIDATIONS

In any event the Qin dynasty was remarkably and mercifully short-lived, lasting only from 221 to 206 B.C.E. The first emperor worked indefatigably to unify his domain and accomplished many feats for which succeeding rulers could only be grateful, including standardizing the writing system, weights and measures, coinage, and the width of carriage axles (so that carts could travel in the same ruts). He engaged in numerous construction projects including the Great Wall and planned to centralize imperial authority through officials appointed and dispatched throughout the country by the emperor, creating a bureaucracy drawing on but also challenging the powerful families who enjoyed hereditary control of land, a struggle that shaped Chinese politics for centuries. The Qin emperor's efforts to unify and control cultural life were even more drastic and devastating: in 213 B.C.E. he decreed that almost all classical texts were to be burned, and only a few works deemed of practical utility—on medicine, divination, and agriculture—escaped this fate. The many expeditions he dispatched in search of elixirs of immortality proved less useful than the elaborate mausoleum he built outside modern-day Xi'an—from which thousands of terra-cotta figures have been excavated—for what turned out to be an early death (see page 1016). Civil war then erupted, ending when a victorious general from the state of Han established a new dynasty that not only lasted for four hundred years but also remained for later generations the paragon of imperial power.

[E]ven more drastic and devastating: the Qin emperor decreed that almost all classical texts were to be burned . . .

While rejecting the excesses of the Qin, the Han dynasty (206 B.C.E.–220 C.E.) benefited from the centralizing efforts of its despised predecessor and developed its administrative structure even further. Its rulers promoted Confucianism as state orthodoxy and implemented a rudimentary civil service competition in an attempt to match merit with responsibility. Five classical texts were also identified as the canon of the culture. Each of "the Five Classics" was associated in some way with Confucius, although later scholars have agreed that the links are tenuous at best. The *Book of Changes* (*Yijing* or *I Ching*) is a text used to interpret sixty-four hexagrams (patterns of six lines) connected to a divination process employing milfoil stalks that probably dates to the late Shang; Confucius was the supposed author of one of its most important affiliated commentaries. The *Book of Documents* (*Shujing* or *Shangshu*) was purported to contain pronouncements and other utterances of rulers and ministers dating back to the sage king Yao; though it was traditionally said to have been edited by Confucius, many sections are now agreed to be forgeries of a much later date. The *Book of Songs* (*Shijing*) is an anthology of some three hundred poems that were composed across much of the Zhou dynasty and which were thought to have been compiled and edited by Confucius. The fourth classic contains ritual texts of which the *Record of Rites* (*Liji*) is the most important; it addresses issues of decorum both large and small and was supposedly collected and edited by Confucius as well. And, fifth, the *Spring and Autumn Annals* chronicled events in Confucius's home state of Lu from 722 to 481 B.C.E.

Not only were court officials appointed to oversee their study, but the Five Classics became required reading for any educated person and, especially, for an aspiring bureaucrat. Each of them left much leeway for interpretation, an opportunity that generated endless shelves of annotation and commentary over the course of many centuries. In addition to centralizing the structures of government and the curriculum, the Han expanded its territory and foreign trade and memorialized its power by building impressive palaces and imperial parks. One of its most important contributions was the first comprehensive history of China, *The Grand Scribe's Records* (*Shiji*), completed at court by Sima Qian (c. 145–90 B.C.E.). An exemplar of Confucian values himself, Sima Qian combed all available documents to chronicle the civilization's already substantial heritage, which culminated in the Han. And as Confucius looked back to the early Zhou, so all later dynasties would look back to the Han as the quintessential embodiment of imperial and cultural unity.

SPELLING AND PRONUNCIATION GUIDE

Chinese names and places are generally spelled using the system of Romanization developed in China known as *pinyin*, which is now internationally accepted. However, many translators employ an older system known as Wade-Giles, which has been retained for those texts. The following chart lists some of the approximate sound values and equivalents.

Pinyin	Wade-Giles	Pronunciation
a	a	as in *father*
ai	ai	as in *ice*
an		after *i* or *y,* as in *hen*
ao	ao	as in *cow*
e	e	as in *fun,* except after *i* or *y,* in which case, as in *yes*
ei	ei	as in *feint*
i	i	as in *machine,* except as below
i		after *zh, ch, sh, z, c, s, r:* between a short *i* and a vocalized *r*
	ih	between a short *i* and a vocalized *r*
in	in	as in *tin*
iu	iu	between *eo* of *Leo* and *you*
o	o	as in *paw*
ou	ou	as in *owe*
u	u	as in *too*

Pinyin	Wade-Giles	Pronunciation
u	ü	*u* after *j, q, x, y* (pinyin), *ü* elsewhere: like German *ü* or French *tu*
c	ts', tz'	as in *Watson*
j	ch	*j*
q	ch'	*ch*
	j	between *r* and a French *j* as in *je*
k	k	as in *gun*
	k'	*k*
	p	as in *bun*
	p'	*p*
t		*d*
	t'	*t*
x	hs	between *s* and *sh*
z	ts, tz	like *ds* in *suds*
zh	ch	*j*

The Book of Songs

1000–600 B.C.E.

The *Book of Songs* (*Shi jing*, or Classic of Poetry), compiled by the sixth century B.C.E., is the oldest anthology in China, whose literary tradition begins with the lyric. According to one historical tradition, the poems were collected by Zhou dynasty officials as evidence for contemporary mores to be presented to the ruler, but the prevailing account of the text's compilation appears in the *Grand Scribe's Records* of Sima Qian. There we are told that it was edited by none other than Confucius himself, who selected its 305 songs from a larger group of over three thousand stored in the archives of the Zhou feudal states, edited their musical accompaniments (now lost), and arranged them in their present order. However unlikely, this attribution remained unquestioned until modern times, and already by the fourth century B.C.E. the anthology had been canonized as one of the five Confucian classics. This ensured the text's preservation, and its inclusion in the educational curriculum of the elite (more specifically, on the civil service examination), and brought a scholarly attention that generated many volumes of commentary over the ages.

The poems were most likely composed between 1000 and 600 B.C.E. Many appear to be simple folk songs, whereas others reveal a more aristocratic and literary origin, and some are clearly temple hymns to the dynasty's ruling house. All but six are anonymous, and the majority treat themes familiar to folk and ballad traditions worldwide: friendship, courtship, marriage, and death; planting, harvesting, hunting, and fishing; and the glories and sorrows of war. The natural images with which many poems open (sometimes repeated elsewhere) offer a cue to what follows, but their often enigmatic quality has elicited centuries of scholarly speculation. Unlike most early poetry in other cultures, the *Book of Songs* features a great deal of rhyme, and the most common form employs three stanzas of four (or six) four-syllable lines each.

The numbers assigned to the poems refer to their sequence in the standard edition from the second century B.C.E. The poems are grouped into four sections of varying size, of which the first and largest contains 160 "Airs of the States" (*Guo feng*). *Feng* literally means "wind" but can also denote "customs" and is closely related to a word meaning "to criticize," and the

States represent fifteen of the Zhou feudal domains. These are among the latest of the poems in the anthology and among the most accessible; all but the last six included here are from this group. The next seventy-four poems, "Lesser Elegances" (*xiao ya*), treat similar subjects drawn from daily life but sometimes placed within a more elite context; poems 166, 189, and 234 belong to this section. The thirty-one "Greater Elegances" (*da ya*) that follow (including poems 238 and 245) are sometimes difficult to distinguish from the preceding group but tend to include the longest poems in the anthology, narratives of historical and legendary events and figures. Finally, the forty "Hymns" (*song*), of which 283 is an example, may be among the oldest works in the collection. They were said to have been used in ritual performances by the Zhou rulers and two other feudal courts; many lack both rhyme and divisions into stanzas.

Traditions of reading the *Book of Songs* are important for understanding not only the collection itself but also later presumptions about all literature, and poetry in particular. The *Songs* are the most frequently cited work in Confucius's *Analects,* and other early texts demonstrate that the poems were often quoted in political and diplomatic discussions to convey opinions obliquely but effectively. Such trust in the poems' didactic utility, coupled with the fact that some clearly are accounts of actual events, led early scholars to assume that the entire anthology was commenting either directly or indirectly on history. The premises for this belief are articulated most clearly in what is known as the "Great Preface" to the collection: poetry (or song, the two being interchangeable) expresses naturally and spontaneously what is in one's heart or mind, and the impulse arises from the external world of nature, society, and the body politic, which are linked by correlative networks. Any poetic expression could therefore be assumed to implicate something larger than the individual, construed as a response to a particular set of circumstances in a particular context. Thus poem 5, "Locusts," was read as praise of the Zhou queen, whose freedom from jealousy and willingness to allow the king other consorts produced, happily, a multitude of progeny. Such interpretations may represent far-fetched distortions of the poems' original import, but they also provided valuable explanations for often perplexing vignettes. These practices also dignified texts that might otherwise have been devalued or lost (much as allegory served the Hebrew Bible's *Song of Songs*), and they continued to shape the later poetic and critical tradition in profound ways.

The linguistic difficulty of the *Book of Songs* has challenged both traditional Chinese commentators and translators into Western languages. Arthur Waley's translations offer the best compromise between philological accuracy and poetic fluency, but they may be usefully compared with two alternatives. Swedish sinologist Bernhard Karlgren (1889–1978) translated the poems into philologically accurate prose. The poet Ezra Pound (1885–1972), who knew no Chinese but considered himself a Confucian, sought to highlight the resemblance of the *Songs* to English ballads and was said by T. S. Eliot to have been "the inventor of Chinese poetry for our time." Alternative versions by Karlgren and Pound are provided for poems 23, 94, and 166.

from THE BOOK OF SONGS[1]

1 The Ospreys Cry

"Fair, fair," cry the ospreys
On the island in the river.
Lovely is this noble lady,
Fit bride for our lord.

5   In patches grows the water mallow;
To left and right one must seek it.
Shy was this noble lady;

---

1. Translated by Arthur Waley.

Day and night he sought her.

Sought her and could not get her;
10   Day and night he grieved.
Long thoughts, oh, long unhappy thoughts,
Now on his back, now tossing on to his side.

In patches grows the water mallow;
To left and right one must gather it.
15   Shy is this noble lady;
With great zither and little we hearten her.

In patches grows the water mallow;
To left and right one must choose it.
Shy is this noble lady;
20   With bells and drums we will gladden her.

5 Locusts

The locusts' wings say "throng, throng";
Well may your sons and grandsons
Be a host innumerable.

The locusts' wings say "bind, bind";
5   Well may your sons and grandsons
Continue in an endless line.

The locusts' wings say "join, join";[1]
Well may your sons and grandsons
Be forever at one.

20 Plop Fall the Plums

Plop fall the plums; but there are still seven.
Let those gentlemen that would court me
Come while it is lucky!

Plop fall the plums; there are still three.
5   Let any gentleman that would court me
Come before it is too late!

Plop fall the plums, in shallow baskets we lay them
Any gentleman who would court me
Had better speak while there is time.

23 In the Wilds Is a Dead Doe

In the wilds there is a dead doe;
With white rushes we cover her.
There was a lady longing for the spring;
A fair knight seduced her.

---

1. The three noises that the locusts' wings make are being punned upon and interpreted as omens.

5   In the wood there is a clump of oaks,
       And in the wilds a dead deer
       With white rushes well bound;
       There was a lady fair as jade.

       "Heigh, not so hasty, not so rough;
10   Heigh, do not touch my handkerchief.
       Take care, or the dog will bark."

✺

RESONANCES

Translation by Bernhard Karlgren: In the wilds there is a dead deer

1. In the wilds there is a dead deer, with white grass one wraps it up; there is a girl having spring feelings, a fine gentleman entices her.—2. In the forest there are low shrubby trees, in the wilds there is a dead deer; with white grass one wraps it up and binds it; there is a girl like a jade.—3. Slowly! Gently! Do not move my kerchief; do not make the dog bark!

Translation by Ezra Pound: Lies a dead deer on younder plain

       Lies a dead deer on younder plain
       whom white grass covers,
       A melancholy maid in spring
                                is luck
5   for
                                lovers.

       Where the scrub elm skirts the wood,
       be it not in white mat bound,
       as a jewel flawless found,
10   dead as doe is maidenhood.

       Hark!
       Unhand my girdle-knot,
                       stay, stay, stay
                       or the dog
15   may
                       bark.

✺

26 Cypress Boat[1]

       Tossed is that cypress boat,
       Wave-tossed it floats.
       My heart is in turmoil, I cannot sleep.
       But secret is my grief.

---

1. Traditional commentators believe that this is a song of a woman being married against her will.

5   Wine I have, all things needful
       For play, for sport.

       My heart is not a mirror,
       To reflect what others will.
       Brothers too I have;
10   I cannot be snatched away.
       But lo, when I told them of my plight
       I found that they were angry with me.

       My heart is not a stone;
       It cannot be rolled.
15   My heart is not a mat;
       It cannot be folded away.
       I have borne myself correctly
       In rites more than can be numbered.

       My sad heart is consumed, I am harassed
20   By a host of small men.
       I have borne vexations very many,
       Received insults not few.
       In the still of night I brood upon it;
       In the waking hours I rend my breast.

25   O sun, ah, moon,
       Why are you changed and dim?
       Sorrow clings to me
       Like an unwashed dress.
       In the still of night I brood upon it,
30   Long to take wing and fly away.

41 Northern Wind

       Cold blows the northern wind,
       Thick falls the snow.
       Be kind to me, love me,
       Take my hand and go with me.
5   Yet she lingers, yet she havers!°   *hesitates*
       There is no time to lose.

       The north wind whistles,
       Whirls the falling snow.
       Be kind to me, love me,
10   Take my hand and go home with me.
       Yet she lingers, yet she havers!
       There is no time to lose.

       Nothing is redder than the fox,
       Nothing blacker than the crow.
15   Be kind to me, love me,

Take my hand and ride with me.
Yet she lingers, yet she havers!
There is no time to lose.

42 Of Fair Girls

Of fair girls the loveliest
Was to meet me at the corner of the Wall.
But she hides and will not show herself;
I scratch my head, pace up and down.

5   Of fair girls the prettiest
Gave me a red flute.
The flush of that red flute
Is pleasure at the girl's beauty.

She has been in the pastures and brought for me rush-wool,
10   Very beautiful and rare.
It is not you that are beautiful;
But you were given by a lovely girl.

45 Cypress Boat

Unsteady is that cypress boat
In the middle of the river.
His two locks looped over his brow[1]
He swore that truly he was my comrade,
5   And till death would love no other.
Oh, mother, ah, Heaven,
That a man could be so false!

Unsteady is that boat of cypress-wood
By that river's side.
10   His two locks looped over his brow
He swore that truly he was my mate,
And till death would not fail me.
Oh, mother, ah, Heaven,
That a man could be so false!

76 I Beg of You, Zhong Zi

I beg of you, Zhong Zi,
Do not climb into our homestead,
Do not break the willows we have planted.
Not that I mind about the willows,
5   But I am afraid of my father and mother.
Zhong Zi I dearly love;

---

1. A sign that he has not yet come of age.

But of what my father and mother say
Indeed I am afraid.

I beg of you, Zhong Zi,
10   Do not climb over our wall,
Do not break the mulberry-trees we have planted.
Not that I mind about the mulberry-trees,
But I am afraid of my brothers.
Zhong Zi I dearly love;
15   But of what my brothers say
Indeed I am afraid.

I beg of you, Zhong Zi,
Do not climb into our garden,
Do not break the hard-wood we have planted.
20   Not that I mind about the hard-wood,
But I am afraid of what people will say.
Zhong Zi I dearly love;
But of all that people will say
Indeed I am afraid.

82 The Lady Says

The lady says: "The cock has crowed";
The knight says: "Day has not dawned."
"Rise, then, and look at the night;
The morning star is shining.
5   You must be out and abroad,
Must shoot the wild-duck and wild-geese.

When you have shot them, you must bring them home
And I will dress them for you,
And when I have dressed them we will drink wine
10   And I will be yours till we are old.
I will set your zithers before you;
All shall be peaceful and good.

Did I but know those who come to you,
I have girdle-stones of many sorts to give them;
15   Did I but know those that have followed you,
I have girdle-stones of many sorts as presents for them.
Did I know those that love you,
I have girdle-stones of many sorts to requite them."

94 Out in the Bushlands a Creeper Grows

Out in the bushlands a creeper grows,
The falling dew lies thick upon it.
There was a man so lovely,
Clear brow well rounded.
5   By chance I came across him,
And he let me have my will.

Out in the bushlands a creeper grows,
The falling dew lies heavy on it.
There was a man so lovely,
10   Well rounded his clear brow.
By chance I came upon him:
"Oh, Sir, to be with you is good."

RESONANCES

Translation by Bernhard Karlgren:
In the open grounds there is the creeping grass

1. In the open grounds there is the creeping grass, the falling dew is plentiful; there is a beautiful person, the clear forehead how beautiful! We met carefree and happy, and so my desire was satisfied.—2. In the open grounds there is the creeping grass, the falling dew is ample; there is a beautiful person, how beautiful the clear forehead! We met carefree and happy; "together with you I shall live happily."

Translation by Ezra Pound: Mid the bind-grass on the plain

Mid the bind-grass on the plain
that the dew makes wet as rain
I met by chance my clear-eyed man,
                    then my
                    joy began.

Mid the wild grass dank with dew
lay we the full night thru,
          that clear-eyed man and I
          in mutual felicity.

96 The Cock Has Crowed

THE LADY: The cock has crowed;
          It is full daylight.

THE LOVER: It was not the cock that crowed,
          It was the buzzing of those green flies.

THE LADY: The eastern sky glows;
          It is broad daylight.

THE LOVER: That is not the glow of dawn,
          But the rising moon's light.
          The gnats fly drowsily;
          It would be sweet to share a dream with you.

THE LADY: Quick! Go home!
          Lest I have cause to hate you!

113 Big Rat

Big rat, big rat,
Do not gobble our millet!
Three years we have slaved for you,
Yet you take no notice of us.
5   At last we are going to leave you
And go to that happy land;
Happy land, happy land,
Where we shall have our place.

Big rat, big rat,
10   Do not gobble our corn!
Three years we have slaved for you,
Yet you give us no credit.
At last we are going to leave you
And go to that happy kingdom;
15   Happy kingdom, happy kingdom,
Where we shall get our due.

Big rat, big rat,
Do not eat our rice-shoots!
Three years we have slaved for you.
20   Yet you did nothing to reward us.
At last we are going to leave you
And go to those happy borders;
Happy borders, happy borders
Where no sad songs are sung.

119 Tall Pear-Tree

Tall stands that pear-tree;
Its leaves are fresh and fair.
But alone I walk, in utter solitude.
True indeed, there are other men;
5   But they are not like children of one's own father.
Heigh, you that walk upon the road,
Why do you not join me?
A man that has no brothers,
Why do you not help him?

10   Tall stands that pear-tree;
Its leaves grow very thick.
Alone I walk and unbefriended.
True indeed, there are other men;
But they are not like people of one's own clan.
15   Heigh, you that walk upon the road,
Why do you not join me?
A man that has no brothers,
Why do you not help him?

123 Tall Is the Pear-Tree

Tall is the pear-tree
That is on the left side of the road.
Ah, that good lord
At last has deigned to visit me.
5   To the depths of my heart I love him.
Had I but drink and food for him!

Tall is the pear-tree
That is at the turn of the road.
Ah, that good lord
10   At last is willing to come and play with me.
To the depths of my heart I love him.
Had I but drink and food for him!

143 Moon Rising

A moon rising white
Is the beauty of my lovely one.
Ah, the tenderness, the grace!
Heart's pain consumes me.

5   A moon rising bright
Is the fairness of my lovely one.
Ah, the gentle softness!
Heart's pain wounds me.

A moon rising in splendor
10   Is the beauty of my lovely one.
Ah, the delicate yielding!
Heart's pain torments me.

154 The Seventh Month

In the seventh month the Fire ebbs;
In the ninth month I hand out the coats.
In the days of the First, sharp frosts;
In the days of the Second, keen winds.
5   Without coats, without serge,
How should they finish the year?
In the days of the Third they plough;
In the days of the Fourth out I step
With my wife and children,
10   Bringing hampers to the southern acre
Where the field-hands come to take good cheer.

In the seventh month the Fire ebbs;
In the ninth month I hand out the coats.
But when the spring days grow warm
15   And the oriole sings
The girls take their deep baskets

And follow the path under the wall
To gather the soft mulberry-leaves:
"The spring days are drawing out;
20   They gather the white aster in crowds.
A girl's heart is sick and sad
Till with her lord she can go home."

In the seventh month the Fire ebbs;
In the eighth month they pluck the rushes,
25   In the silk-worm month they gather the mulberry-leaves,
Take that chopper and bill
To lop the far boughs and high,
Pull toward them the tender leaves.
In the seventh month the shrike cries;
30   In the eighth month they twist thread,
The black thread and the yellow:
"With my red dye so bright
I make a robe for my lord."

In the fourth month the milkwort is in spike,
35   In the fifth month the cicada cries.
In the eighth month the harvest is gathered,
In the tenth month the boughs fall.
In the days of the First we hunt the raccoon,
And take those foxes and wild-cats
40   To make furs for our Lord.
In the days of the Second is the great Meet;
Practice for deeds of war.
The boar one year old we keep;
The three-year-old we offer to our lord.

45   In the fifth month the locust moves its leg,
In the sixth month the grasshopper shakes its wing,
In the seventh month, out in the wilds;
In the eighth month, in the farm,
In the ninth month, at the door.
50   In the tenth month the cricket goes under my bed.
I stop up every hole to smoke out the rats,
Plugging the windows, burying the doors:
"Come, wife and children,
The change of the year is at hand.
55   Come and live in this house."

In the sixth month we eat wild plums and cherries,
In the seventh month we boil mallows and beans.
In the eighth month we dry the dates,
In the tenth month we take the rice
60   To make with it the spring wine,
So that we may be granted long life.
In the seventh month we eat melons,
In the eighth month we cut the gourds,

In the ninth month we take the seeding hemp,
65   We gather bitter herbs, we cut the ailanthus for firewood,
That our husbandmen may eat.

In the ninth month we make ready the stack-yards,
In the tenth month we bring in the harvest,
Millet for wine, millet for cooking, the early and the late,
70   Paddy and hemp, beans and wheat.
Come, my husbandmen,
My harvesting is over,
Go up and begin your work in the house,
In the morning gather thatch-reeds,
75   In the evening twist rope;
Go quickly on to the roofs.
Soon you will be beginning to sow your many grains.

In the days of the Second they cut the ice with tingling blows;
In the days of the Third they bring it into the cold shed.
80   In the days of the Fourth very early
They offer lambs and garlic.
In the ninth month are shrewd frosts;
In the tenth month they clear the stack-grounds.
With twin pitchers they hold the village feast,
85   Killing for it a young lamb.
Up they go into their lord's hall,
Raise the drinking-cup of buffalo-horn:
"Hurray for our lord; may he live for ever and ever!"

166 May Heaven Guard

May Heaven guard and keep you
In great security,
Make you staunch and hale;
What blessing not vouchsafed?
5   Give you much increase,
Send nothing but abundance.

May Heaven guard and keep you,
Cause your grain to prosper,
Send you nothing that is not good.
10   May you receive from Heaven a hundred boons,
May Heaven send down to you blessings so many
That the day is not long enough for them all.

May Heaven guard and keep you,
Cause there to be nothing in which you do not rise higher,
15   Like the mountains, like the uplands,
Like the ridges, the great ranges,
Like a stream coming down in flood;
In nothing not increased.
Lucky and pure are your viands of sacrifice

20   That you use in filial offering,
        Offerings of invocation, gift-offerings, offering in dishes and offering of
            first-fruits
        To dukes and former kings.
        Those sovereigns say: "We give you
        Myriad years of life, days unending."

25   The Spirits are good,
        They will give you many blessings.
        The common people are contented,
        For daily they have their drink and food.
        The thronging herd, the many clans
30   All side with you in deeds of power.

        To be like the moon advancing to its full,
        Like the sun climbing the sky,
        Like the everlastingness of the southern hills,
        Without failing or falling,
35   Like the pine-tree, the cypress in their verdure—
        All these blessings may you receive!

RESONANCES

Translation by Bernhard Karlgen: Heaven protects and secures you

1. Heaven protects and secures you, doing it very solidly; it causes you to be richly endowed; what felicity is not heaped (on you); it causes you to have much (increase:) prosperity, so that there is nothing that is not (numerous:) abundant.—2. Heaven protects and
secures you; it causes you to (cut:) reap your grain, so that to the last straw there is nothing that is not (proper:) good; you receive the hundred emoluments from Heaven, it sends
down to you a far-reaching felicity; only the days are not sufficient (to hold so much
blessing).—3. Heaven protects and secures you, so that there is nothing that does not rise
prosperingly; like a mountain, like a hill, like a ridge, like a range, like a river at its highest flood, so that there is nothing that is not increased.—4. Auspicious and pure are your
sacrificial wine and food; with them you make filial offerings; you perform summer,
spring, winter and autumn sacrifices, to princes and former kings; the (dead) lords say:
"We predict for you a myriad years of life, without limit."—5. The Spirits are good, they
bestow upon you much felicity; the people are simple, daily they enjoy their drink and
food; all the numerous (people of) the hundred clans everywhere practise your virtue.—
6. Like the moon's advancing to the full, like the rising of the sun (a), like the longevity
of the Southern mountains, which are never injured, never falling, like the luxuriance of
the fir and the cypress, there is nothing that will not be (continued:) ever-lasting for you.

Translation by Ezra Pound: Heaven conserve thy course in quietness

        Heaven conserve thy course in quietness,
        Solid thy unity, thy weal endless
        that all the crops increase and nothing lack

in any common house.

5   Heaven susteyne thy course in quietness
that thou be just in all, and reap
so, as it were at ease, that every day
seem festival.

Heaven susteyne thy course in quietness
10   To abound and rise as mountain hill and range
constant as rivers flow that all augment
steady th' increase in ever cyclic change.

Pure be the victuals of thy sacrifice
throughout the year as autumns move to springs,
15   above the fane to hear "ten thousand years"
spoke by the manes of foregone dukes and kings.

Spirits of air assign felicity:
thy folk be honest, in food and drink delight;
dark-haired the hundred tribes concord
20   in act born of thy true insight.

As moon constant in phase; as sun to rise;
as the south-hills nor crumble nor decline;
as pine and cypress evergreen the year
be thy continuing line.

∞

189 The Beck

Ceaseless flows that beck,
Far stretch the southern hills.
May you be sturdy as the bamboo,
May you flourish like the pine,
5   May elder brother and younger brother
Always love one another,
Never do evil to one another.

To give continuance to foremothers and forefathers
We build a house, many hundred cubits of wall;
10   To south and west its doors.
Here shall we live, here rest,
Here laugh, here talk.

We bind the frames, creak, creak;
We hammer the mud, tap, tap,
15   That it may be a place where wind and rain cannot enter,
Nor birds and rats get in,
But where our lord may dwell.

As a halberd, even so plumed,
As an arrow, even so sharp,
20   As a bird, even so soaring,

As wings, even so flying
Are the halls to which our lord ascends.

Well leveled is the courtyard,
Firm are the pillars,
25   Cheerful are the rooms by day,
Softly gloaming by night,
A place where our lord can be at peace.

Below, the rush-mats; over them the bamboo-mats.
Comfortably he sleeps,
30   He sleeps and wakes
And interprets his dreams.
"Your lucky dreams, what were they?"
"They were of black bears and brown,
Of serpents and snakes."

35   The diviner thus interprets it:
"Black bears and brown
Mean men-children.
Snakes and serpents
Mean girl-children."

40   So he bears a son,
And puts him to sleep upon a bed,
Clothes him in robes,
Gives him a jade scepter to play with.
The child's howling is very lusty;
45   In red greaves shall he flare,
Be lord and king of house and home.
Then he bears a daughter,

And puts her upon the ground,
Clothes her in swaddling-clothes,
50   Gives her a loom-whorl to play with.
For her no decorations, no emblems;
Her only care, the wine and food,
And how to give no trouble to father and mother.

234 What Plant Is Not Faded?

What plant is not faded?
What day do we not march?
What man is not taken
To defend the four bounds?

5   What plant is not wilting?
What man is not taken from his wife?
Alas for us soldiers,
Treated as though we were not fellow-men!

Are we buffaloes, are we tigers
10   That our home should be these desolate wilds?

Alas for us soldiers,
Neither by day nor night can we rest!

The fox bumps and drags
Through the tall, thick grass.
15   Inch by inch move our barrows
As we push them along the track.

238 Oak Clumps

Thick grow the oak clumps;
We make firewood of them, we stack them.
Great is the magnificence of the lord king;
On either hand are those that speed for him.

5   Great is the magnificence of the lord king;
On either hand are those that hold up scepters before him,
Hold up scepters in solemn state,
As befits doughty knights.

Spurt goes that boat on the Jing;
10   A host of oarsmen rows it.
When the King of Zhou goes forth,
His six armies are with him.

How it stands out, the Milky Way,
Making a blazon in the sky!
15   Long life to the King of Zhou,
And a portion for his people!

Chiseled and carved are his emblems,
Of bronze and jade are they made.
Ceaseless are the labors of our king
20   Fashioning the network of all the lands.

245 Birth to the People

She who in the beginning gave birth to the people,
This was Jiang Yuan.
How did she give birth to the people?
Well she sacrificed and prayed
5   That she might no longer be childless.
She trod on the big toe of God's footprint,
Was accepted and got what she desired.
Then in reverence, then in awe
She gave birth, she nurtured;
10 And this was Hou Ji.°   *"Lord Millet" (a grain)*

Indeed, she had fulfilled her months,
And her first-born came like a lamb
With no bursting or rending,
With no hurt or harm.
15 To make manifest His magic power

God on high gave her ease.
So blessed were her sacrifice and prayer
That easily she bore her child.

Indeed, they[1] put it in a narrow lane;
20   But oxen and sheep tenderly cherished it.
Indeed, they put it in a far-off wood;
But it chanced that woodcutters came to this wood.
Indeed, they put it on the cold ice;
But the birds covered it with their wings.
25   The birds at last went away,
And Hou Ji began to wail.

Truly far and wide
His voice was very loud.
Then sure enough he began to crawl;
30   Well he straddled, well he reared,
To reach food for his mouth.
He planted large beans;
His beans grew fat and tall.
His paddy-lines were close set,
35   His hemp and wheat grew thick,
His young gourds teemed.

Truly Hou Ji's husbandry
Followed the way that had been shown.
He cleared away the thick grass,
40   He planted the yellow crop.
It failed nowhere, it grew thick,
It was heavy, it was tall,
It sprouted, it eared,
It was firm and good,
45   It nodded, it hung—
He made house and home in Tai.

Indeed, the lucky grains were sent down to us,
The black millet, the double-kerneled,
Millet pink-sprouted and white.
50   Far and wide the black and the double-kerneled
He reaped and acred;
Far and wide the millet pink and white
He carried in his arms, he bore on his back,
Brought them home, and created the sacrifice.

55   Indeed, what are they, our sacrifices?
We pound the grain, we bale it out,
We sift, we tread,
We wash it—soak, soak;

---

1. The ballad does not tell us who exposed the child. According to one version it was the mother herself; according to another, her husband [translator's note].

We boil it all steamy.
60   Then with due care, due thought
      We gather southernwood, make offering of fat,
      Take lambs for the rite of expiation,
      We roast, we broil,
      To give a start to the coming year.

65   High we load the stands,
      The stands of wood and of earthenware.
      As soon as the smell rises
      God on high is very pleased:
      "What smell is this, so strong and good?"
70   Hou Ji founded the sacrifices,
      And without blemish or flaw
      They have gone on till now.

283 So They Appeared

      So they appeared before their lord the king
      To get from him their emblems,
      Dragon-banners blazing bright,
      Tuneful bells tinkling,
5   Bronze-knobbed reins jangling—
      The gifts shone with glorious light.
      Then they showed them to their shining ancestors
      Piously, making offering,
      That they might be vouchsafed long life,
10   Everlastingly be guarded.
      Oh, a mighty store of blessings!
      Glorious and mighty, those former princes and lords
      Who secure us with many blessings,
      Through whose bright splendors
15   We greatly prosper.

❧

RESONANCES

Confucius: from *The Analects*[1]

1.15. Zigong said: "'Poor without servility; rich without arrogance.' How is that?"
The Master said: "Not bad, but better still: 'Poor, yet cheerful; rich, yet considerate.'"
Zigong said: "In the *Poems,* it is said: 'Like carving horn, like sculpting ivory, like

1. Translated by Simon Leys. Passages from Confucius's *Analects* represent some of the earliest critical material on the *Book of Songs,* translated here as the *Poems.* If, as early scholars wished to believe, Confucius compiled the *Book of Songs,* he had remarkably little to say about the collection in his *Analects.* These scattered passages vary considerably in their focus; some offer brief remarks about a specific poem in the anthology; others use a song as a means of commenting on something else; and still others indicate his interest in the collection's general ethical propriety and practical utility. Later writers concerned with asserting the didactic function of literature draw frequently upon these passages.

cutting jade, like polishing stone.' Is this not the same idea?" The Master said: "Ah, one can really begin to discuss the *Poems* with you! I tell you one thing, and you can figure out the rest."

2.2. The Master said: "The three hundred *Poems* are summed up in one single phrase: 'Think no evil.'"

3.8. Zixia asked: "What do these verses mean:

> Oh, the dimples of her smile!
> Ah, the black and white of her beautiful eyes!
> It is on plain white silk that colors shine."[2]

The Master said: "Painting starts from a plain white silk." Zixia said: "Ritual is something that comes afterward?" The Master said: "Ah, you really opened my eyes! It is only with a man like you that one can discuss the *Poems*!"

3.20. The Master said: "The poem *The Ospreys* is gay without lasciviousness and sad without bitterness."[3]

8.3. Master Zeng was ill. He called his disciples and said: "Look at my feet! Look at my hands! It is said in the *Poems:*

> Trembling and shaking,
> As if on the edge of an abyss,
> As if treading on thin ice.[4]

But now, my little ones, I know that I have safely reached port."

8.8. The Master said: "Draw inspiration from the *Poems;* steady your course with the ritual; find your fulfillment in music."

8.15. The Master said: "When Zhi, the music master, is conducting, at the opening passage and the finale of *The Ospreys,* what fullness flows to the ear!"

13.5. The Master said: "Consider a man who can recite the three hundred *Poems;* you give him an official post, but he is not up to the task; you send him abroad on a diplomatic mission, but he is incapable of simple repartee. What is the use of all his vast learning?"

16.13. Chen Ziqin asked Confucius's son: "Have you received any special teaching from your father?" The other replied: "No. Once, as he was standing alone, and I was discreetly crossing the courtyard, he asked me: 'Have you studied the *Poems?*' I replied: 'No.' He said: 'If you do not study the *Poems,* you will not be able to hold your own in any discussion.' I withdrew and studied the *Poems.* Another day, as he was again standing alone and I was discreetly crossing the courtyard, he asked me: 'Have you studied the ritual?' I replied: 'No.' He said: 'If you do not study the ritual,

---

2. The first two lines, but not the third, appear in poem 58 of the *Songs* anthology.

3. This refers to the first poem, "The Ospreys Cry" (see

page 1027).

4. This is from poem 195 in the *Songs* anthology.

you will not be able to take your stand in society.' I withdrew and studied the ritual. These are the two teachings I received."

Chen Ziqin went away delighted and said: "I asked one thing, and learned three. I learned about the *Poems,* I learned about the ritual, and I learned how a gentleman maintains distance from his son."

17.9. The Master said: "Little ones, why don't you study the *Poems*? The *Poems* can provide you with stimulation and with observation, with a capacity for communion, and with a vehicle for grief. At home, they enable you to serve your father, and abroad, to serve your lord. Also, you will learn there the names of many birds, animals, plants, and trees."

17.10. The Master said to his son: "Have you worked through the first and the second part of the *Poems*? Whoever goes into life without having worked through the first and the second part of the *Poems* will remain stuck, as if facing a wall."

Wei Hong: from Preface to the Book of Songs[1]

"The Ospreys Cry" is about the queen's virtue.[2] It is the beginning of the Airs of the State (*feng*), used to influence all under heaven and order relations between husband and wife. Thus it can be used among the people in the country and among the officials of state.

Feng (wind/air) means to influence or criticize and to instruct. One criticizes in order to stimulate and instructs in order to transform.

Poetry[3] is where the intent of the heart goes. What within the heart is intent is poetry when emitted in words. Feelings are moved within and take shape in words. When words are insufficient then one sighs; when sighing is insufficient then one sings to prolong the feelings; when singing is insufficient, one unconsciously gestures with the hands and dances, tapping the feet.

Feelings are emitted in sounds, and when sounds become a pattern, that is called a tone. The tones of a well-governed world are peaceful and joyous, its government harmonious. The tones of a disorderly state are resentful and angry, its government perverse. The tones of a doomed state are mournful and longing, its people in dire straits. Thus for correcting successes and failures, for arousing heaven and earth, and for moving ghosts and spirits, nothing surpasses poetry. The former kings used it to regulate relations between husband and wife, to perfect filial piety and respect, to substantiate human bonds, to make moral instruction attractive and to change popular mores.

---

1. Translated by Pauline Yu. What is commonly known as the "Great Preface" (*Da xu*) to the *Book of Songs* is taken from an introduction to the first poem in the anthology, "The Ospreys Cry," which is in turn part of a set of prefaces written to each of the 305 poems. Its authorship is uncertain. Attributed to one of Confucius's disciples, Zixia, it is more likely to be associated with a 1st-century C.E. scholar named Wei Hong, although it is clearly drawn from a body of shared traditions about the collection.

Like the other prefaces, the "Great Preface" offers a specific commentary on the poem to which it is attached, but its more general statements on the nature of the *Songs* exerted an early and lasting influence on subsequent conceptions about poetry in general and how it should be read. Later texts would make explicit the tacit assumption here that the "intent" or emotion that moves within represents a natural response to the stimulus of the external

world, be it that of nature or the body politic. The "Great Preface" emphasizes the political and takes for granted that the internal emotion will naturally find some externally correlative form or action. As song, furthermore, it will spontaneously reflect, affect, and effect political and cosmic order. The pervasive power of this assumption throughout much of the tradition should not be underestimated—that a seamless connection between the individual and the world enables the poem simultaneously to reveal feelings, provide an index of governmental stability, and serve as a didactic tool.

2. According to commentators, this refers to the consort of King Wen, founder of the Zhou dynasty (c. 1140 B.C.E.). This is part of a commentary to the first poem in the *Book of Songs*.

3. The word *shi* refers to the *Book of Songs* and then, by extension, to all poetry.

Therefore there are six principles in poetry (the *Book of Songs*). The first is called the air, the second description, the third comparison, the fourth evocative image, the fifth the elegance and the sixth the hymn.[4] The superior uses the air to transform the inferior; the inferior uses the air to criticize the superior.[5] By emphasizing patterns and admonishing indirectly, the speaker does not offend and the hearer is sufficiently chastised; thus this is called *feng*. * * *

Therefore, "The Ospreys Cry" takes delight in finding a virtuous young woman as a match for the lord and is concerned about presenting worth without being seduced by appearance. It feels deeply about chaste beauty, longs for worth and talent and harbors no ill will toward the good. This is the meaning of "The Ospreys Cry."

Confucius
551–479 B.C.E.

"Ever since man came into this world, there has never been one greater than Confucius." So declared the fourth-century B.C.E. thinker Mencius, who developed his predecessor's key ideas in ways that would prove instrumental in securing their influence throughout the course of Chinese history. About this great man himself, however, we know remarkably little. Confucius lived during the waning years of the Zhou dynasty in China, when the ruling house had lost virtually all of its power to a ravenous set of competing kingdoms headed by more or less distant relatives. Warfare, economic growth, and social change had destabilized social and political structures and the language that had come to justify them, putting into question the actual and the conceptual bases of received authority.

Confucius probably belonged to the lower ranks of a hereditary nobility whose status was in jeopardy; he was a native of the state of Lu, which supported the legitimacy and rituals of the Zhou rulers. He attributed the social chaos of his time to a falling away from these practices and devoted his life to the attempt to restore them. Failing to secure appointment as a political counselor despite extensive travels to one feudal state after another, he settled for a job as a professional teacher, probably China's first, back home in Lu. *The Analects* (*Lun yu*), best understood as "selected sayings," comprise quotations, conversations, and anecdotes often centering on his response to a specific question. Compiled by multiple generations of later students, it has come down to us in twenty sections or books, of which 3–8 and 11–15 are agreed by scholars to be the oldest and 16–20 the newest. Loosely organized at best, the text contains occasionally repeated passages and material that might even be considered anti-Confucian. By the first century B.C.E., however, *The Analects* were taken as the key to the thoughts of Confucius, who had become identified as the fundamental shaper and transmitter of the cultural heritage.

Obsessed with the prevailing chaos around him, Confucius sought a remedy in a renewal of values and behavior embodied for him in an idealized vision of the founders of the Zhou dynasty. Followers of Confucius were to become known as *ru*, a term evoking a respect for traditional scholarship and ritual. He explicitly disavowed any claims to being an innovator, but many implications of his teachings were in fact quite novel. He articulated his ideas within the

4. The first, fifth, and sixth of these terms refer to categories of the *Songs* and the remaining three to rhetorical devices.

5. Here, as above, the author is playing on the multiple meanings of the word *feng*: "wind," "air," "to influence," and "to criticize."

context of human relationships, both large and small. Although clearly mindful of notions of heaven and destiny that in earlier eras were probably associated with divine or cosmic forces, Confucius focused not on "gods and spirits" but rather on the realm of the concrete and human. And rather than consider morality in the abstract, he sought to explicate the actions of a specific individual in a particular context. For him, principles of mutual respect and obligation rooted in the family were extended to the community and the body politic, creating a social order consisting of a specific set of appropriate roles, a hierarchical relationship among them, and a governing code of conduct. A key concept is that of the *junzi,* or "gentleman," a term that had denoted social nobility but that Confucius transformed into a state of moral excellence that is attainable, in principle, by almost anyone. Equally important is the term *ren,* translated here as "humanity" and "goodness," which is rooted etymologically in a notion of "human-heartedness," or what it means to be one human being associating with another. Ethical behavior is grounded in a refusal to do to another what one would not want done to oneself and is manifested in respect for one's elders and observance of ritual decorum. It can be learned, cultivated, performed, and, ultimately, perfected when precept and behavior become one.

Traditions (now largely discounted) linked Confucius with the compilation of the Five Classics that became identified as canonical: the *Book of Songs, Book of Documents, Book of Changes,* the *Records of Rites,* and the *Spring and Autumn Annals* (a chronicle of Confucius's home state of Lu). By the beginning of the second millennium, *The Analects* had joined them on the classical curriculum for the imperial civil service examination, the most important entry into the career of choice for the literate elite in the government bureaucracy. Rote, uncomprehending memorization of the text as a child would be followed by a lifetime of reflection and, even more important, action upon its meaning. That generations of scholars in China were to aspire to this goal, seeing the educated person as morally superior but obliged to serve others, is owing in no small measure to the lessons of the text itself.

from The Analects[1]

1.1. The Master[2] said: "To learn something and then to put it into practice at the right time: is this not a joy? To have friends coming from afar: is this not a delight? Not to be upset when one's merits are ignored: is this not the mark of a gentleman?"

1.2. Master You[3] said: "A man who respects his parents and his elders would hardly be inclined to defy his superiors. A man who is not inclined to defy his superiors will never foment a rebellion. A gentleman works at the root. Once the root is secured, the Way unfolds. To respect parents and elders is the root of humanity."

1.3. The Master said: "Clever talk and affected manners are seldom signs of goodness."

1.4. Master Zeng[4] said: "I examine myself three times a day. When dealing on behalf of others, have I been trustworthy? In intercourse with my friends, have I been faithful? Have I practiced what I was taught?"

1.5. The Master said: "To govern a state of middle size, one must dispatch business with dignity and good faith; be thrifty and love all men; mobilize the people only at the right times."

1. Translated by Simon Leys.
2. "The Master" is Confucius himself.
3. Confucius's disciple Zhong You (d. 480 B.C.E.), also

known as Zilu.
4. Another disciple, Zeng Can, who played a prominent role in early Confucianism.

1.6. The Master said: "At home, a young man must respect his parents; abroad, he must respect his elders. He should talk little, but with good faith; love all people, but associate with the virtuous. Having done this, if he still has energy to spare, let him study literature."

1.16. The Master said: "Don't worry if people don't recognize your merits; worry that you may not recognize theirs."

2.1 The Master said: "He who rules by virtue is like the polestar, which remains unmoving in its mansion while all the other stars revolve respectfully around it."

2.3. The Master said: "Lead them by political maneuvers, restrain them with punishments: the people will become cunning and shameless. Lead them by virtue, restrain them with ritual: they will develop a sense of shame and a sense of participation."

2.4. The Master said: "At fifteen, I set my mind upon learning. At thirty, I took my stand. At forty, I had no doubts. At fifty, I knew the will of Heaven. At sixty, my ear was attuned. At seventy, I follow all the desires of my heart without breaking any rule."

2.5. Lord Meng Yi asked about filial piety. The Master said: "Never disobey."
As Fan Chi was driving him in his chariot, the Master told him: "Meng Yi asked me about filial piety and I replied: 'Never disobey.'" Fan Chi said: "What does that mean?" The Master said: "When your parents are alive, serve them according to the ritual. When they die, bury them according to the ritual, make sacrifices to them according to the ritual."

2.6. Lord Meng Wu asked about filial piety. The Master said: "The only time a dutiful son ever makes his parents worry is when he is sick."

2.7. Ziyou[5] asked about filial piety. The Master said: "Nowadays people think they are dutiful sons when they feed their parents. Yet they also feed their dogs and horses. Unless there is respect, where is the difference?"

2.8. Zixia[6] asked about filial piety. The Master said: "It is the attitude that matters. If young people merely offer their services when there is work to do, or let their elders drink and eat when there is wine and food, how could this ever pass as filial piety?"

2.9. The Master said: "I can talk all day to Yan Hui[7]—he never raises any objection, he looks stupid. Yet, observe him when he is on his own: his actions fully reflect what he learned. Oh no, Hui is not stupid!"

2.11. The Master said: "He who by revising the old knows the new, is fit to be a teacher."

2.12. The Master said: "A gentleman is not a pot."[8]

---

5. The disciple Yan Yan, about whom little is known except that he was one of Confucius's younger students.
6. Bu Shang, a disciple who played a major role in the transmission of the Confucian classics.

7. Also known as Yan Yuan, one of Confucius's most gifted and favorite disciples.
8. That is, he is not a specialist, in the way a vessel is designed for one specific purpose.

2.13. Zigong[9] asked about the true gentleman. The Master said: "He preaches only what he practices."

2.14. The Master said: "The gentleman considers the whole rather than the parts. The small man considers the parts rather than the whole."

2.15. The Master said: "To study without thinking is futile. To think without studying is dangerous."

2.16. The Master said: "To attack a question from the wrong end—this is harmful indeed."

2.17. The Master said: "Zilu, I am going to teach you what knowledge is. To take what you know for what you know, and what you do not know for what you do not know, that is knowledge indeed."

2.18. Zizhang[1] was studying in the hope of securing an official position. The Master said: "Collect much information, put aside what is doubtful, repeat cautiously the rest; then you will seldom say something wrong. Make many observations, leave aside what is suspect, apply cautiously the rest; then you will seldom have cause for regret. With few mistakes in what you say and few regrets for what you do, your career is made."

2.19. Duke Ai asked: "What should I do to win the hearts of the people?" Confucius replied: "Raise the straight and set them above the crooked, and you will win the hearts of the people. If you raise the crooked and set them above the straight, the people will deny you their support."

2.20. Lord Ji Kang asked: "What should I do in order to make the people respectful, loyal, and zealous?" The Master said: "Approach them with dignity and they will be respectful. Be yourself a good son and a kind father, and they will be loyal. Raise the good and train the incompetent, and they will be zealous."

4.1. The Master said: "It is beautiful to live amidst humanity. To choose a dwelling place destitute of humanity is hardly wise."

4.3. The Master said: "Only a good man can love people and can hate people."

4.4. The Master said: "Seeking to achieve humanity leaves no room for evil."

4.5. The Master said: "Riches and rank are what every man craves; yet if the only way to obtain them goes against his principles, he should desist from such a pursuit. Poverty and obscurity are what every man hates; yet if the only escape from them goes against his principles, he should accept his lot. If a gentleman forsakes humanity, how can he make a name for himself? Never for a moment does a

9. Duanmu Si, the only one of the three best-known disciples to survive Confucius. He was a successful merchant and diplomat.

1. Zhuansun Shi, another disciple about whom little is known.

gentleman part from humanity; he clings to it through trials, he clings to it through tribulations."

4.6. The Master said: "I have never seen a man who truly loved goodness and hated evil. Whoever truly loves goodness would put nothing above it; whoever truly hates evil would practice goodness in such a way that no evil could enter him. Has anyone ever devoted all his strength to goodness just for one day? No one ever has, and yet it is not for want of strength—there may be people who do not have even the small amount of strength it takes, but I have never seen any."

4.8. The Master said: "In the morning hear the Way; in the evening die content."

4.9. The Master said: "A scholar sets his heart on the Way; if he is ashamed of his shabby clothes and coarse food, he is not worth listening to."

4.10. The Master said: "In the affairs of the world, a gentleman has no parti pris: he takes the side of justice."

4.14. The Master said: "Do not worry if you are without a position; worry lest you do not deserve a position. Do not worry if you are not famous; worry lest you do not deserve to be famous."

4.15. The Master said: "Shen, my doctrine has one single thread running through it." Master Zeng Shen replied: "Indeed."
The Master left. The other disciples asked: "What did he mean?" Master Zeng said: "The doctrine of the Master is: Loyalty and reciprocity, and that is all."

4.16. The Master said: "A gentleman considers what is just; a small man considers what is expedient."

4.18. The Master said: "When you serve your parents, you may gently remonstrate with them. If you see that they do not take your advice, be all the more respectful and do not contradict them. Let not your efforts turn to bitterness."

4.19. The Master said: "While your parents are alive, do not travel afar. If you have to travel, you must leave an address."

4.20. The Master said: "If three years after his father's death, the son does not alter his father's ways, he is a good son indeed."

4.21. The Master said: "Always keep in mind the age of your parents. Let this thought be both your joy and your worry."

4.25. The Master said: "Virtue is not solitary; it always has neighbors."

5.7. The Master said: "The Way does not prevail. I shall take a raft and put out to sea. I am sure Zilu will accompany me." Hearing this, Zilu was overjoyed. The Master said: "Zilu is bolder than I. Still, where would we get the timber for our craft?"

5.10. Zai Yu[2] was sleeping during the day. The Master said: "Rotten wood cannot be carved; dung walls cannot be troweled. What is the use of scolding him?"

The Master said: "There was a time when I used to listen to what people said and trusted that they would act accordingly, but now I listen to what they say and watch what they do. It is Zai Yu who made me change."

5.11. The Master said: "I have never seen a man who was truly steadfast." Someone replied: "Shen Cheng?" The Master said: "Shen Cheng is driven by his desires. How could he be called steadfast?"

5.14. When Zilu had learned one thing, his only fear was that he might learn another one before he had the chance to practice the first.

5.20. Lord Ji Wen always thought thrice before acting. Hearing this, the Master said: "Twice is enough."

5.27. The Master said: "Alas, I have never seen a man capable of seeing his own faults and of exposing them in the tribunal of his heart."

5.28. The Master said: "In a hamlet of ten houses, you will certainly find people as loyal and faithful as I, but you will not find one man who loves learning as much as I do."

6.3. Duke Ai asked: "Which of the disciples has a love of learning?" Confucius replied: "There was Yan Hui who loved learning; he never vented his frustrations upon others; he never made the same mistake twice. Alas, his allotted span of life was short: he is dead. Now, for all I know, there is no one with such a love of learning."

6.11. The Master said: "How admirable was Yan Hui! A handful of rice to eat, a gourd of water for drink, a hovel for your shelter—no one would endure such misery, yet Yan Hui's joy remained unaltered. How admirable was Yan Hui!"

6.17. The Master said: "Who would leave a house without using the door? Why do people seek to walk outside the Way?"

6.18. The Master said: "When nature prevails over culture, you get a savage; when culture prevails over nature, you get a pedant. When nature and culture are in balance, you get a gentleman."

6.23. The Master said: "The wise find joy on the water, the good find joy in the mountains. The wise are active, the good are quiet. The wise are joyful, the good live long."

6.27. The Master said: "A gentleman enlarges his learning through literature and restrains himself with ritual; therefore, he is not likely to go wrong."

2. Also known as Zai Wo, a disciple who tended to disappoint Confucius.

6.29. The Master said: "The moral power of the Middle Way is supreme, and yet it is not commonly found among the people anymore."

7.1. The Master said: "I transmit, I invent nothing. I trust and love the past. In this, I dare to compare myself to our venerable Peng."

7.7. The Master said: "I never denied my teaching to anyone who sought it, even if he was too poor to offer more than a token present for his tuition."

7.8. The Master said: "I enlighten only the enthusiastic; I guide only the fervent. After I have lifted up one corner of a question, if the student cannot discover the other three, I do not repeat."

7.12. The Master said: "If seeking wealth were a decent pursuit, I too would seek it, even if I had to work as a janitor. As it is, I'd rather follow my inclinations."

7.13. Matters which the Master approached with circumspection: fasting; war; illness.

7.14. When the Master was in Qi, he heard the Coronation Hymn of Shun. For three months, he forgot the taste of meat. He said: "I never imagined that music could reach such a point."

7.15. Ran Qiu[3] said: "Does our Master support the Duke of Wei?" Zigong said: "Well, I am going to ask him."
   Zigong went in and asked Confucius: "What sort of people were Boyi and Shuqi?"—"They were virtuous men of old."—"Did they complain?"—"They sought goodness, they got goodness. Why should they have complained?"
   Zigong left and said to Ran Qiu: "Our Master does not support the Duke of Wei."[4]

7.18. Occasions when the Master did not use dialect: when reciting the *Poems* and the *Documents,* and when performing ceremonies. In all these occasions, he used the correct pronunciation.

7.19. The Governor of She asked Zilu about Confucius. Zilu did not reply. The Master said: "Why did you not say 'He is the sort of man who, in his enthusiasm, forgets to eat, in his joy forgets to worry, and who ignores the approach of old age'?"

7.20. The Master said: "For my part, I am not endowed with innate knowledge. I am simply a man who loves the past and who is diligent in investigating it."

7.21. The Master never talked of: miracles; violence; disorders; spirits.

---

3. Another disciple, also known as Ran You.
4. The Duke of Wei had taken power after the death of his grandfather when his father was forced to flee the state after a failed attempt to kill his own father's notorious wife.

The Duke's father was awaiting an opportunity to oust his son. Boyi and Shuqi were two brothers whose biographies appear prominently in Sima Qian's *Grand Scribe's Records.*

7.22. The Master said: "Put me in the company of any two people at random—they will invariably have something to teach me. I can take their qualities as a model and their defects as a warning."

7.23. The Master said: "Heaven vested me with moral power. What do I have to fear from Huan Tui?"[5]

7.26. The Master said: "A saint, I cannot hope to meet. I would be content if only I could meet a gentleman."
The Master said: "A perfect man, I cannot hope to meet. I would be content if only I could meet a principled man. When Nothing pretends to be Something, Emptiness pretends to be Fullness, and Penury pretends to be Affluence, it is hard to have principles."

7.29. The people of Huxiang were deaf to all teaching; but a boy came to visit the Master. The disciples were perplexed. The Master said: "To approve his visit does not mean approving what he does besides. Why be so finicky? When a man makes himself clean before a visit, we appreciate his cleanliness, we do not endorse his past or his future."

7.30. The Master said: "Is goodness out of reach? As soon as I long for goodness, goodness is at hand."

7.34. The Master said: "I make no claims to wisdom or to human perfection—how would I dare? Still, my aim remains unflagging and I never tire of teaching people." Gongxi Chi[6] said: "This is precisely what we disciples fail to emulate."

7.35. The Master was severely ill. Zilu asked leave to pray. The Master said: "Is there such a practice?" Zilu said: "Oh yes, and the invocation goes like this: 'We pray you, Spirits from above and Spirits from below.'" The Master said: "In that case, I have been praying for a long time already."

8.4. Master Zeng was ill. Lord Mengjing came to visit him. Master Zeng said: "When a bird is about to die, his song is sad; when a man is about to die, his words are true. In following the Way, a gentleman pays special attention to three things: in his attitude, he eschews rashness and arrogance; in his expression, he clings to good faith; in his speech, he eschews vulgarity and nonsense. As to the details of liturgy, leave these to the sextons."

8.9. The Master said: "You can make the people follow the Way, you cannot make them understand it."

8.17. The Master said: "Learning is like a chase in which, as you fail to catch up, you fear to lose what you have already gained."

---

5. Tradition has it that this was said when Huan Tui, minister of war in the state of Song, attempted to kill Confucius.

6. Also known as Gongxi Hua, another disciple who was said to have been in charge of Confucius's funeral.

9.2. A man from Daxiang said: "Your Confucius is really great! With his vast learning, he has still not managed to excel in any particular field." The Master heard of this and said to his disciples: "Which skill should I cultivate? Shall I take up charioteering? Shall I take up archery? All right, I shall take up charioteering."

9.4. The Master absolutely eschewed four things: capriciousness, dogmatism, willfulness, self-importance.

9.5. The Master was trapped in Kuang. He said: "King Wen is dead; is civilization not resting now on me? If Heaven intends civilization to be destroyed, why was it vested in me? If Heaven does not intend civilization to be destroyed, what should I fear from the people of Kuang?"

9.11. Yan Hui said with a sigh: "The more I contemplate it, the higher it is; the deeper I dig into it, the more it resists; I saw it in front of me, and then suddenly it was behind me. Step by step, our Master really knows how to entrap people. He stimulates me with literature, he restrains me with ritual. Even if I wanted to stop, I could not. Just as all my resources are exhausted, the goal is towering right above me; I long to embrace it, but cannot find the way."

9.13. Zigong said: "If you had a precious piece of jade, would you hide it safely in a box, or would you try to sell it for a good price?" The Master said: "I would sell it! I would sell it! All I am waiting for is the right offer."

9.14. The Master wanted to settle among the nine barbarian tribes of the East. Someone said: "It is wild in those parts. How would you cope?" The Master said: "How could it be wild, once a gentleman has settled there?"

9.16. The Master said: "I have never found it difficult to serve my superiors abroad and my elders at home; or to bury the dead with due reverence; or to hold my wine."

9.17. The Master stood by a river and said: "Everything flows like this, without ceasing, day and night."

9.18. The Master said: "I have never seen anyone who loved virtue as much as sex."

9.20. The Master said: "What was unique in Yan Hui was his capacity for attention whenever one spoke to him."

9.21. The Master said of Yan Hui: "Alas, I watched his progress, but did not see him reach the goal."

9.22. The Master said: "There are shoots that bear no flower, and there are flowers that bear no fruit."

9.24. The Master said: "How could words of admonition fail to win our assent? Yet the main thing should be actually to amend our conduct. How could words of praise fail to delight us? Yet the main thing should be actually to understand their purpose. Some people show delight but no understanding, or they assent without changing their ways—I really don't know what to do with them."

9.29. The Master said: "The wise are without perplexity; the good are without sorrow; the brave are without fear."

9.30. The Master said: "There are people with whom you may share information, but not share the Way. There are people with whom you may share the Way, but not share a commitment. There are people with whom you may share a commitment, but not share counsel."

9.31.

> The cherry tree
> Waves its blossoms.
> It is not that I do not think of you
> But your house is so far away!

The Master said: "He does not really love her; if he did, would he mind the distance?"

11.10. Yan Hui died. The Master wailed wildly. His followers said: "Master, such grief is not proper." The Master said: "In mourning such a man, what sort of grief would be proper?"

11.11. Yan Hui died. The disciples wanted to give him a grand burial. The Master said: "This is not right."

The disciples gave him a grand burial. The Master said: "Yan Hui treated me as his father, and yet I was not given the chance to treat him as my son. This is not my fault, but yours, my friends."

11.12. Zilu asked how to serve the spirits and gods. The Master said: "You are not yet able to serve men, how could you serve the spirits?"

Zilu said: "May I ask you about death?" The Master said: "You do not yet know life, how could you know death?"

11.22. Zilu asked: "Should I practice at once what I have just learned?" The Master said: "Your father and your elder brother are still alive; how could you practice at once what you have just learned?"

Ran Qiu asked: "Should I practice at once what I have just learned?" The Master said: "Practice it at once."

Gongxi Chi said: "When Zilu asked if he should practice at once what he had just learned, you told him to consult first with his father and elder brother. When Ran Qiu asked if he should practice at once what he had just learned, you told him to practice it at once. I am confused; may I ask you to explain?" The Master said: "Ran Qiu is slow, therefore I push him; Zilu has energy for two, therefore I hold him back."

12.1. Yan Hui asked about humanity. The Master said: "The practice of humanity comes down to this: tame the self and restore the rites. Tame the self and restore the rites for but one day, and the whole world will rally to your humanity. The practice of humanity comes from the self, not from anyone else."

Yan Hui said: "May I ask which steps to follow?" The Master said: "Observe the rites in this way: don't look at anything improper; don't listen to anything improper; don't say anything improper; don't do anything improper."

Yan Hui said: "I may not be clever, but with your permission, I shall endeavor to do as you have said."

12.2. Ran Yong asked about humanity. The Master said: "When abroad, behave as if in front of an important guest. Lead the people as if performing a great ceremony. What you do not wish for yourself, do not impose upon others. Let no resentment enter public affairs; let no resentment enter private affairs."

Ran Yong said: "I may not be clever, but with your permission I shall endeavor to do as you have said."

12.5. Sima Niu[7] was grieving: "All men have brothers; I alone have none." Zixia said: "I have heard this: life and death are decreed by fate, riches and honors are allotted by Heaven. Since a gentleman behaves with reverence and diligence, treating people with deference and courtesy, all within the Four Seas are his brothers. How could a gentleman ever complain that he has no brothers?"

12.7. Zigong asked about government. The Master said: "Sufficient food, sufficient weapons, and the trust of the people." Zigong said: "If you had to do without one of these three, which would you give up?"—"Weapons."—"If you had to do without one of the remaining two, which would you give up?"—"Food; after all, everyone has to die eventually. But without the trust of the people, no government can stand."

12.10. Zizhang asked how to accumulate moral power and how to recognize emotional incoherence. The Master said: "Put loyalty and faith above everything, and follow justice. That is how one accumulates moral power. When you love someone, you wish him to live; when you hate someone, you wish him to die. Now, if you simultaneously wish him to live and to die, this is an instance of incoherence."

> If not for the sake of wealth,
> Then for the sake of change . . .

12.11. Duke Jing of Qi asked Confucius about government. Confucius replied: "Let the lord be a lord; the subject a subject; the father a father; the son a son." The Duke said: "Excellent! If indeed the lord is not a lord, the subject not a subject, the father not a father, the son not a son, I could be sure of nothing anymore—not even of my daily food."

12.18. Lord Ji Kang was troubled by burglars. He consulted with Confucius. Confucius replied: "If you yourself were not covetous, they would not rob you, even if you paid them to."

---

7. A brother of Huan Tui, who made an attempt on Confucius's life.

12.19. Lord Ji Kang asked Confucius about government, saying: "Suppose I were to kill the bad to help the good: how about that?" Confucius replied: "You are here to govern; what need is there to kill? If you desire what is good, the people will be good. The moral power of the gentleman is wind, the moral power of the common man is grass. Under the wind, the grass must bend."

13.3. Zilu asked: "If the ruler of Wei were to entrust you with the government of the country, what would be your first initiative?" The Master said: "It would certainly be to rectify the names." Zilu said: "Really? Isn't this a little farfetched? What is this rectification for?" The Master said: "How boorish can you get! Whereupon a gentleman is incompetent, thereupon he should remain silent. If the names are not correct, language is without an object. When language is without an object, no affair can be effected. When no affair can be effected, rites and music wither. When rites and music wither, punishments and penalties miss their target. When punishments and penalties miss their target, the people do not know where they stand. Therefore, whatever a gentleman conceives of, he must be able to say; and whatever he says, he must be able to do. In the matter of language, a gentleman leaves nothing to chance."

13.9. The Master was on his way to Wei, and Ran Qiu was driving. The Master said: "So many people!" Ran Qiu said: "Once the people are many, what next should be done?"—"Enrich them."—"Once they are rich, what next should be done?"—"Educate them."

13.10. The Master said: "If a ruler could employ me, in one year I would make things work, and in three years the results would show."

13.11. The Master said: "'When good men have been running the country for a hundred years, cruelty can be overcome, and murder extirpated.' How true is this saying!"

13.15. Duke Ding asked: "Is there one single maxim that could ensure the prosperity of a country?" Confucius replied: "Mere words could not achieve this. There is this saying, however: 'It is difficult to be a prince, it is not easy to be a subject.' A maxim that could make the ruler understand the difficulty of his task would come close to ensuring the prosperity of the country."
"Is there one single maxim that could ruin a country?"
Confucius replied: "Mere words could not achieve this. There is this saying, however: 'The only pleasure of being a prince is never having to suffer contradiction.' If you are right and no one contradicts you, that's fine; but if you are wrong and no one contradicts you—is this not almost a case of 'one single maxim that could ruin a country'?"

13.20. Zigong asked: "How does one deserve to be called a gentleman?" The Master said: "He who behaves with honor, and, being sent on a mission to the four corners of the world, does not bring disgrace to his lord, deserves to be called a gentleman."
"And next to that, if I may ask?"
"His relatives praise his filial piety and the people of his village praise the way he respects the elders."
"And next to that, if I may ask?"

"His word can be trusted; whatever he undertakes, he brings to completion. In this, he may merely show the obstinacy of a vulgar man; still, he should probably qualify as a gentleman of lower category."

"In this respect, how would you rate our present politicians?"

"Alas! These puny creatures are not even worth mentioning!"

13.24. Zigong asked: "What would you think of a man, if all the people in his village liked him?" The Master said: "This is not enough."—"And what if all the people in the village disliked him?"—"This is not enough. It would be better if the good people in the village were to like him, and the bad people to dislike him."

13.25. The Master said: "It is easy to work for a gentleman, but not easy to please him. Try to please him by immoral means, and he will not be pleased; but he never demands anything that is beyond your capacity. It is not easy to work for a vulgar man, but easy to please him. Try to please him, even by immoral means, and he will be pleased; but his demands know no limits."

13.26. The Master said: "A gentleman shows authority, but no arrogance. A vulgar man shows arrogance, but no authority."

14.4. The Master said: "A virtuous man is always of good counsel; a man of good counsel is not always virtuous. A good man is always brave: a brave man is not always good."

14.6. The Master said: "Gentlemen may not always achieve the fullness of humanity. Small men never achieve the fullness of humanity."

14.23. The Master said: "A gentleman reaches up. A vulgar man reaches down."

14.24. The Master said: "In the old days, people studied to improve themselves. Now they study in order to impress others."

14.27. The Master said: "A gentleman would be ashamed should his deeds not match his words."

14.28. The Master said: "A gentleman abides by three principles which I am unable to follow: his humanity knows no anxiety; his wisdom knows no hesitation; his courage knows no fear." Zigong said: "Master, you have just drawn your own portrait."

14.29. Zigong was criticizing other people. The Master said: "Zigong must have already reached perfection, which affords him a leisure I do not possess."

14.30. The Master said: "It is not your obscurity that should distress you, but your incompetence."

14.35. The Master said: "No one understands me!" Zigong said: "Why is it that no one understands you?" The Master said: "I do not accuse Heaven, nor do I blame men; here below I am learning, and there above I am being heard. If I am understood, it must be by Heaven."

14.38. Zilu stayed for the night at the Stone Gate. The gatekeeper said: "Where are you from?" Zilu said: "I am from Confucius's household."—"Oh, is that the one who keeps pursuing what he knows is impossible?"

15.16. The Master said: "With those who cannot say 'What should I do? what should I do?,' I really do not know what I should do."

15.24. Zigong asked: "Is there any single word that could guide one's entire life?" The Master said: "Should it not be *reciprocity?* What you do not wish for yourself, do not do to others."

15.27. The Master said: "Clever talk ruins virtue. Small impatiences ruin great plans."

15.36. The Master said: "In the pursuit of virtue, do not be afraid to overtake your teacher."

17.2. The Master said: "What nature put together, habit separates."

17.19. The Master said: "I wish to speak no more." Zigong said: "Master, if you do not speak, how would little ones like us still be able to hand down any teachings?" The Master said: "Does Heaven speak? Yet the four seasons follow their course and the hundred creatures continue to be born. Does Heaven speak?"

17.20. Ru Bei wanted to see Confucius. Confucius declined on the grounds of illness. As Ru Bei's messenger was leaving, the Master took up his zithern and sang loudly enough for him to hear.

17.21. Zai Yu asked: "Three years mourning for one's parents—this is quite long. If a gentleman stops all ritual practices for three years, the practices will decay; if he stops all musical performances for three years, music will be lost. As the old crop is consumed, a new crop grows up, and for lighting the fire, a new lighter is used with each season. One year of mourning should be enough." The Master said: "If after only one year, you were again to eat white rice and to wear silk, would you feel at ease?"—"Absolutely."—"In that case, go ahead! The reason a gentleman prolongs his mourning is simply that, since fine food seems tasteless to him, and music offers him no enjoyment, and the comfort of his house makes him uneasy, he prefers to do without all these pleasures. But now, if you can enjoy them, go ahead!"

Zai Yu left. The Master said: "Zai Yu is devoid of humanity. After a child is born, for the first three years of his life, he does not leave his parents' bosom. Three years mourning is a custom that is observed everywhere in the world. Did Zai Yu never enjoy the love of his parents, even for three years?"

17.24. Zigong said: "Does a gentleman have hatreds?" The Master said: "Yes. He hates those who dwell on what is hateful in others. He hates those inferiors who slander their superiors. He hates those whose courage is not tempered by civilized manners. He hates the impulsive and the stubborn." He went on: "And you? Don't you have your own hatreds?"— "I hate the plagiarists who pretend to be learned. I hate the arrogant who pretend to be brave. I hate the malicious who pretend to be frank."

17.25. The Master said: "Women and underlings are especially difficult to handle: be friendly, and they become familiar; be distant, and they resent it."

17.26. The Master said: "Whoever, by the age of forty, is still disliked, will remain so till the end."

18.5. Jieyu, the Madman of Chu, went past Confucius, singing:

> Phoenix, oh Phoenix!
> The past cannot be retrieved,
> But the future still holds a chance.
>   Give up, give up!
> The days of those in office are numbered!

Confucius stopped his chariot, for he wanted to speak with him, but the other hurried away and disappeared. Confucius did not succeed in speaking to him.

18.6. Changju and Jieni were ploughing together. Confucius, who was passing by, sent Zilu to ask where the ford was. Changju said: "Who is in the chariot?" Zilu said: "It is Confucius." "The Confucius from Lu?"—"Himself."—"Then he already knows where the ford is."

Zilu then asked Jieni, who replied: "Who are you?"—"I am Zilu."—"The disciple of Confucius, from Lu?"—"Yes."—"The whole universe is swept along by the same flood; who can reverse its flow? Instead of following a gentleman who keeps running from one patron to the next, would it not be better to follow a gentleman who has forsaken the world?" All the while he kept on tilling his field.

Zilu came back and reported to Confucius. Rapt in thought, the Master sighed: "One cannot associate with birds and beasts. With whom should I keep company, if not with my own kind? If the world were following the Way, I would not have to reform it."

⟞ PERSPECTIVES ⟞
Daoism and Its Ways

Other schools of thought in early China promoted ethical ways of living, but only Daoism is literally the school of the Way (*dao*). Daoism developed during the tumultuous era known as the Warring States period (403–221 B.C.E.), a time of civil unrest during which lively and intense philosophical debates swirled concerning the best way to manage a state and one's own life. In contrast to Confucianism's focus on human relationships and responsibilities in society and government, Daoism views nature, and a life lived in accordance with its principles, as the key to wisdom, happiness, and survival. At its simplest level it glorifies the virtues of an existence that is as free from the trammels of civilization and its burdens as possible, with figures such as fishermen and woodcutters serving as idealized models of individual reclusion. From a more spiritual perspective, it calls for an intuitive understanding of the Way of nature, the cosmic principle underlying all phenomena. This, by definition, cannot be defined, for it transcends all categories of language and thought, and like mystical traditions elsewhere, Daoist writings confront the challenge of expressing the ineffable by employing suggestive images and parables to illustrate the nature of the Way and to point toward an ideal integration with it. Despite their typical rejection of direct, declarative statements, Daoism's foundational texts, the *Dao De Jing* and the *Zhuangzi,* do hint at the value of a supple, noncoercive, and spontaneous stance that will both accord with the Way and enable one to merge with it.

What is to be gained by transcending the boundary between self and other? At its most basic, one of Daoism's many apparent paradoxes states that losing one's sense of self is the secret to self-preservation. Learning how to negotiate a world fraught with perils is clearly paramount in Daoist thought, even though the texts assert the ultimate meaninglessness of a distinction between life and death. This impulse motivated later obsessive searches for the secret to immortality, whether through alchemy, elixirs, diet, exercises, or sexual practices, and the development of elaborate ritual practices and a pantheon of deities. These are often referred to as "popular" or "religious" Daoism and are distinguished from the more "philosophical" traditions represented in the texts below, although they share many basic impulses.

For an educated class mindful of Confucianism's insistence on government service, Daoism provided a compelling argument in favor of turning one's back on potentially dangerous engagements. This proved particularly useful during the period of disunion following the collapse of the Han dynasty in 220 C.E., when a rapid succession of ruling families for over three centuries made allegiances risky at best. Daoism also served as a valuable counterweight to Confucianism's subordination of the individual to collective forms and behaviors, providing a safety valve from the pressures of conforming to established roles. And its often equally unconstrained language injected an important element of levity, fancy, and fantasy to both philosophical debate and much artistic production. Discussions of inspiration and aesthetics were especially indebted to examples supplied by early Daoist texts. Daoism is best viewed, however, as a complement to Confucianism rather than its mutually exclusive alternative, for unlike religious systems with jealous gods, aspects of both schools of thought have been embraced simultaneously and creatively by generations of scholars.

⊷ ⫴◈⫴ ⊶

Dao De Jing
6th–3rd centuries B.C.E.

Although the *Dao De Jing* has been translated into Western languages more often than any other ancient Chinese text, we know very little about its origins. The historian Sima Qian in his

Grand Scribe's Records lists a number of received traditions about its author: he was a native of the state of Chu named Li Dan, known as "Laozi" ("Old Master," another title for the text), and an older contemporary of Confucius who was an archivist in the state of Zhou; he lived to the age of 160 years or more, having set forth his teachings in this work and cultivated the Way; he taught ritual to Confucius, who likened him to a dragon; he headed west upon sensing the decline of the Zhou rulers, left the work now known as the *Dao De Jing* with the Keeper of the Pass on the road out of China, and vanished. There is, however, no documented evidence of the text's existence prior to the third century B.C.E., and scholars now agree that it is most likely a work of composite authorship—an anthology of multiple layers—with "Old Master" serving as a general reference to sages of a quietist bent.

The *Dao De Jing* ("*The Classic of the Way and Its Power*") appears to be a handbook for a wise and minimalist ruler, but it also provides advice for any individual seeking to achieve harmony with the Way of nature. Unlike other texts of the many philosophical "schools" contending for adherents at this time, the *Dao De Jing* makes no reference to historical or fictional events or characters. However, Confucian values of moral righteousness, zealous self-cultivation, and political activism provide a foil for the Daoist text's emphasis on a primitive simplicity, yielding and inaction, and doing nothing contrary to nature. Principles embodied in the behavior of water and the feminine, it is suggested, provide the key to survival in perilous times.

The *Dao De Jing's* evocative imagery and rhythmic language, frequently rhymed, have appealed to generations of readers seeking both inspiration and practical advice. Scholars have been equally attracted by the mysteries of the text's descriptions of the ineffable and the boldness of its challenge: "My words are very easy to understand and very easy to put into practice, yet amongst men there is no one who is able to understand them and there is no one who is able to put them into practice" (35 / LXX). It was the subject of more commentaries than any other classical text and was included on the curriculum for the civil service examination during the Tang dynasty (618–907 C.E.), when it acquired its current title and canonical status.

from Dao De Jing[1]

4 / XL

> Reversal is the movement of the way;
> Weakness is the use of the way.
> The creatures in the world are born from Something, and
> Something from Nothing.

6 / XLIII

The most submissive thing in the world can ride roughshod over the most unyielding in the world—that which is without substance entering that which has no gaps.

That is why I know the benefit of taking no action. The teaching that uses no words, the benefit of taking no action, these are beyond the understanding of all but a very few in the world.

8 / XLV

> Great perfection seems chipped,
> Yet use will not wear it out;

---

1. Translated by D. C. Lau. This version reflects new information about the text based on archeological excavations. The Roman numerals indicate the earlier and more common sequence of the chapters.

Laozi Riding an Ox, c. 1600 C.E. Laozi (or Lao-Tzu) was credited with the authorship of the *Dao De Jing,* and during the Six Dynasties period (3rd–6th century C.E.), he was both deified and said to have converted the Buddha to Daoism. One of the many representations of his journey westward from China on this mission, this image was published in a Ming dynasty encyclopedia.

Great fullness seems empty,
Yet use will not drain it;
5   Great straightness seems bent;
Great skill seems awkward;
Great surplus seems deficient;
Great eloquence seems tongue-tied.
Restlessness overcomes the cold; stillness overcomes the heat.
10   Limpid and still,
One can be a leader in the empire.

10 / XLVII

By not setting foot outside the door
One knows the whole world;
By not looking out of the window
One knows the way of heaven.
The further one goes
The less one knows.
Hence the sage knows without having to stir,
Identifies without having to see [it],
Accomplishes without having to do it.

19 / LVI

One who knows does not say it; one who says does not know it.
   Block the openings,
   Shut the doors,
   Soften the glare,
   Follow along old wheel tracks;
   Blunt the point,
   Untangle the knots.
This is known as dark identity.
   Thus you cannot get close to it, nor can you keep it at arm's length; you cannot
bestow benefit on it, nor can you do it harm; you cannot ennoble it, nor can you
debase it.
   Hence it is the most valued in the empire.

23 / LX

Governing a large state is like boiling a small fish.
   When the empire is ruled in accordance with the way, the spirits are not potent.
Or, rather, it is not that they are not potent, but that in their potency they do not
harm men. It is not only they who, in their potency, do not harm men, the sage, too,
does not harm them. Now as neither does any harm, each attributes the merit to the
other.

24 / LXI

A large state is the lower reaches of a river—the female of the world. In the inter-
course of the world, the female always gets the better of the male by stillness. It is be-
cause of her stillness that it is fitting for her to take the lower position.
   Hence the large state, by taking the lower position, annexes the small state;
   The small state, by taking the lower position, is annexed by the large state.
   Thus the one, by taking the lower position, annexes;
   The other, by taking the lower position, is annexed.
   Thus all that the large state wants is to take the other under its wing;
   All that the small state wants is to have its services accepted by the other.
   Now if they both get their desire,
   It is fitting that the large should take the lower position.

30 / LXXX

Reduce the size and population of the state. Ensure that even though there are tools ten times or a hundred times better than those of other men the people will not use them; ensure also that they will look on death as a grave matter and give migration a wide berth.

They have ships and carts but will not go on them; they have armour and weapons but will have no occasion to make a show of them.

Bring it about that the people will return to the use of the knotted rope,

Will find relish in their food,

And beauty in their clothes,

Will be happy in the way they live.

And be content in their abode.

Though adjoining states are within sight of one another, and the sound of dogs barking and cocks crowing in one state can be heard in another, yet the people of one state will grow old and die without having had any dealings with those of another.

31 / LXXXI

Truthful words are not beautiful; beautiful words are not truthful.

He who knows has no wide learning; he who has wide learning does not know.

He who is good does not have much; he who has much is not good.

The sage has no hoard. Having bestowed all he has on others, he has yet more; having given all he has to others, he is richer still.

Hence the way of heaven does not harm but benefits; the way of man does not contend but is bountiful.

36 / LXXI

To know yet to think that one does not know is the best;

Not to know yet to think that one knows will put one in difficulty.

That the sage meets with no difficulty is because he is alive to difficulty. That is why he meets with no difficulty.

41 / LXXVI

A man is supple and weak when alive, but hard and stiff when dead. The myriad creatures and grass and trees are pliant and fragile when alive, but dried and shrivelled when dead. Thus it is said, the hard and the strong are the comrades of death; the supple and the weak are the comrades of life.

Hence a weapon that is strong will not vanquish;

A tree that is strong will come to its end;

Thus the strong and big takes the lower position;

The supple and weak takes the upper position.

43 / LXXVIII

In the world there is nothing more submissive and weak than water. Yet for attacking that which is unyielding and strong nothing can take precedence over it. This is because there is nothing that can take its place.

The weak overcomes the unbending,

And the submissive overcomes the strong,
This everyone in the world knows yet no one can put it into practice.
Hence in the words of the sage,
One who takes on himself the abuse hurled against the state
Is called a ruler worthy of offering sacrifices to the gods of earth and millet;
One who takes on himself the calamities of the state
Is called a king worthy of dominion over the entire empire.
Straightforward words seem paradoxical.

45 / I

The way can be spoken of,
  But it will not be the constant way;
  The name can be named,
  But it will not be the constant name.
  The nameless was the beginning of the myriad creatures;
  The named was the mother of the myriad creatures.
  Hence constantly rid yourself of desires in order to observe its subtlety;
  But constantly allow yourself to have desires in order to observe what it is after.
  These two have the same origin but differ in name.
  They are both called dark,
  Darkness upon darkness
  The gateway to all that is subtle.

47 / III

Not to honour men of excellence will keep the people from contention; not to value
goods that are hard to come by will keep the people from theft; not to display what is
desirable will keep the people from being unsettled.

Hence in his rule, the sage empties their minds but fills their bellies, weakens
their purpose but strengthens their bones.

He constantly keeps the people innocent of knowledge and free from desire, and
causes the clever not to dare.

He simply takes no action and everything is in order.

48 / IV

The way is empty, yet when used there is something that does not make it
    full.
Deep, it is like the ancestor of the myriad creatures.
Blunt the sharpness;
Untangle the knots;
Soften the glare;
Follow along old wheel tracks.
Darkly visible, it only seems as if it were there.
I know not whose son it is.
It images the forefather of God.

50 / VI

The spirit of the valley never dies;
This is called the dark female.
The entry into the dark female
Is called the root of heaven and earth.
Tenuous, it seems as if it were there,
Yet use will never exhaust it.

54 / X

When carrying on your head your perplexed bodily soul can you hold in
    your arms the One
And not let go?
In concentrating your breath can you become as supple
As a babe?
5   Can you polish your dark mirror
And leave no blemish?
In loving the people and bringing life to the state
Are you capable of not resorting to knowledge?
When the gates of heaven open and shut
10   Are you capable of keeping to the role of the female?
When your discernment penetrates the four quarters
Are you capable of not resorting to knowledge?
It gives them life and rears them.
It gives them life without claiming to possess them;
15   It is the steward yet exercises no authority over them.
Such is called dark virtue.

55 / XI

Thirty spokes
Share one hub.
Make the nothing therein appropriate, and you will have the use of the cart. Knead
clay in order to make a vessel. Make the nothing therein appropriate, and you will
have the use of the clay vessel. Cut out doors and windows in order to make a room.
Make the nothing therein appropriate, and you will have the use of the room.

    Thus we gain by making it Something, but we have the use by making it Nothing.

62 / XVIII

Thus when the great way falls into disuse
There are benevolence and rectitude;
When cleverness emerges
There is great hypocrisy;
When the six relations are at variance
There are the filial;
When the state is benighted
There are true subjects.

63 / XIX

Exterminate the sage, discard the wise,
And the people will benefit a hundredfold;
Exterminate benevolence, discard rectitude,
And the people will return to being filial;
Exterminate ingenuity, discard profit,
And there will be no more thieves and bandits.
Concerning these three sayings,
It is thought that the text leaves yet something to be desired
And there should, therefore, be something to which it is attached:
Exhibit the unadorned and embrace the uncarved block,
Have little thought of self and as few desires as possible.

69 / XXV

There is a thing confusedly formed,
Born before heaven and earth.
Silent and void
It stands alone and does not change,
Goes round and does not weary.
It is capable of being the mother of heaven and earth.
As yet I do not know its name.
I style it "the way."
I give it the makeshift name of "great."
Being great, it is described as receding,
Receding, it is described as far away,
Being far away, it is described as turning back.
The way is great; heaven is great; earth is great, and the king is great.
Within the realm there are four greats and the king counts as one.
Man models himself on earth,
Earth on heaven,
Heaven on the way,
And the way on that which is naturally so.

━━◆═━━

Zhuangzi
4th century B.C.E.

The *Zhuangzi* ("Master Zhuang") is a text identified with a certain Zhuang Zhou (or Chuang Tzu in the older spelling), about whom very little is known. According to the historian Sima Qian, he was a native of the state of Meng who served sometime during the fourth century B.C.E. as an official in a royal garden. Of the thirty-three chapters in the work that bears his name, the first seven are generally agreed to have actually been written by him, with the remainder by other hands over an undetermined period of time. Rich in anecdote, parable, irreverent wit, and clever wordplay, the text offers vivid insights into the major issues in the lively philosophical debates swirling about a country wracked by disunity and war.

Like the *Dao de jing,* with which it has been linked since the first century B.C.E., the *Zhuangzi* is concerned with attaining harmony with the *dao,* or Way. Unlike the former text, however, it turns its back on political engagement of any sort. At its most basic level it counters Confucian righteous activism with the advantages of retreat from society. But its method for achieving a spontaneous integration with the natural course of things also rests on challenging the entire system of signification—the framework and conventions by which words acquire and keep their meanings. Nothing is immune from this critique, as in the following well-known anecdote from the text:

> The fish trap exists because of the fish; once you've gotten the fish, you can forget the trap. The rabbit snare exists because of the rabbit; once you've gotten the rabbit, you can forget the snare. Words exist because of meaning; once you've gotten the meaning, you can forget the words. Where can I find a man who has forgotten words so I can have a word with him?

The *Zhuangzi* never hesitates to question its own assertions, and it extends this challenge to all other sets of absolutes as well. Its many unconventional characters revel in paradoxes and delight in undermining accepted values, which are usually couched within binary oppositions such as beauty versus ugliness or utility versus uselessness. Only by recognizing the relativity of all conceptual, verbal, logical, and moral distinctions can we hope to attain a union with the cosmic principle. The text's insistence on jolting us out of traditional habits of thought and its aesthetic delight at skepticism are expressed with a playful inventiveness that has few peers in the literary tradition; the *Zhuangzi* has even inspired contemporary comic books. And its advocacy of a spontaneous, free, and tranquil life at one with nature has long provided important inspiration and models for artistic creativity in general, and an artlessness beyond art.

PRONUNCIATION:

Zhuangzi: JWAHNG-dzi

from **Zhuangzi**[1]

from *Free and Easy Wandering*

In the northern darkness there is a fish and his name is K'un.[2] The K'un is so huge I don't know how many thousand li he measures. He changes and becomes a bird whose name is P'eng. The back of the P'eng measures I don't know how many thousand li across and, when he rises up and flies off, his wings are like clouds all over the sky. When the sea begins to move, this bird sets off for the southern darkness, which is the Lake of Heaven.

The *Universal Harmony* records various wonders, and it says: "When the P'eng journeys to the southern darkness, the waters are roiled for three thousand li. He beats the whirlwind and rises ninety thousand li, setting off on the sixth-month gale." Wavering heat, bits of dust, living things blowing each other about—the sky looks very blue. Is that its real color, or is it because it is so far away and has no end? When the bird looks down, all he sees is blue too.

If water is not piled up deep enough, it won't have the strength to bear up a big boat. Pour a cup of water into a hollow in the floor and bits of trash will sail on it like

---

1. Translated by Burton Watson, from whom these footnotes are adapted.
2. *K'un* (kun) means fish roe. So Zhuangzi begins with a

paradox—the tiniest fish imaginable is also the largest fish imaginable.

boats. But set the cup there and it will stick fast, for the water is too shallow and the boat too large. If wind is not piled up deep enough, it won't have the strength to bear up great wings. Therefore when the P'eng rises ninety thousand li, he must have the wind under him like that. Only then can he mount on the back of the wind, shoulder the blue sky, and nothing can hinder or block him. Only then can he set his eyes to the south.

The cicada and the little dove laugh at this, saying, "When we make an effort and fly up, we can get as far as the elm or the sapanwood tree, but sometimes we don't make it and just fall down on the ground. Now how is anyone going to go ninety thousand li to the south!"

If you go off to the green woods nearby, you can take along food for three meals and come back with your stomach as full as ever. If you are going a hundred li, you must grind your grain the night before; and if you are going a thousand li, you must start getting the provisions together three months in advance. What do these two creatures understand? Little understanding cannot come up to great understanding; the short-lived cannot come up to the long-lived.

How do I know this is so? The morning mushroom knows nothing of twilight and dawn; the summer cicada knows nothing of spring and autumn. They are the short-lived. South of Ch'u there is a caterpillar which counts five hundred years as one spring and five hundred years as one autumn. Long, long ago there was a great rose of Sharon that counted eight thousand years as one spring and eight thousand years as one autumn. They are the long-lived. Yet P'eng-tsu[3] alone is famous today for having lived a long time, and everybody tries to ape him. Isn't it pitiful!

* * *

Hui Tzu[4] said to Chuang Tzu, "The king of Wei gave me some seeds of a huge gourd. I planted them, and when they grew up, the fruit was big enough to hold five piculs. I tried using it for a water container, but it was so heavy I couldn't lift it. I split it in half to make dippers, but they were so large and unwieldy that I couldn't dip them into anything. It's not that the gourds weren't fantastically big—but I decided they were no use and so I smashed them to pieces."

Chuang Tzu said, "You certainly are dense when it comes to using big things! In Sung there was a man who was skilled at making a salve to prevent chapped hands, and generation after generation his family made a living by bleaching silk in water. A traveler heard about the salve and offered to buy the prescription for a hundred measures of gold. The man called everyone to a family council. 'For generations we've been bleaching silk and we've never made more than a few measures of gold,' he said. 'Now, if we sell our secret, we can make a hundred measures in one morning. Let's let him have it!' The traveler got the salve and introduced it to the king of Wu, who was having trouble with the state of Yüeh. The king put the man in charge of his troops, and that winter they fought a naval battle with the men of Yüeh and gave them a bad beating.[5] A portion of the conquered territory was awarded to the man as a fief. The salve had the power to prevent chapped hands in either case; but one man used it to get a fief, while the other one never got beyond silk bleaching—because they used it in different ways. Now you had a gourd big enough to hold five piculs. Why didn't you think of making it into a great tub so you could go floating around the rivers and

---

3. The Chinese Methuselah.
4. A logician who relies on pure intellect.

5. By preventing the soldiers' hands from chapping, the salve made it easier for them to handle their weapons.

lakes, instead of worrying because it was too big and unwieldy to dip into things! Obviously you still have a lot of underbrush in your head!"

Hui Tzu said to Chuang Tzu, "I have a big tree of the kind men call *shu*. Its trunk is too gnarled and bumpy to apply a measuring line to, its branches too bent and twisty to match up to a compass or square. You could stand it by the road and no carpenter would look at it twice. Your words, too, are big and useless, and so everyone alike spurns them!"

Chuang Tzu said, "Maybe you've never seen a wildcat or a weasel. It crouches down and hides, watching for something to come along. It leaps and races east and west, not hesitating to go high or low—until it falls into the trap and dies in the net. Then again there's the yak, big as a cloud covering the sky. It certainly knows how to be big, though it doesn't know how to catch rats. Now you have this big tree and you're distressed because it's useless. Why don't you plant it in Not-Even-Anything Village, or the field of Broad-and-Boundless, relax and do nothing by its side, or lie down for a free and easy sleep under it? Axes will never shorten its life, nothing can ever harm it. If there's no use for it, how can it come to grief or pain?"

Discussion on Making All Things Equal

Tzu-ch'i of South Wall sat leaning on his armrest, staring up at the sky and breathing—vacant and far away, as though he'd lost his companion.[1] Yen Ch'eng Tzu-yu, who was standing by his side in attendance, said, "What is this? Can you really make the body like a withered tree and the mind like dead ashes? The man leaning on the armrest now is not the one who leaned on it before!"

Tzu-ch'i said, "You do well to ask the question, Yen. Now I have lost myself. Do you understand that? You hear the piping of men, but you haven't heard the piping of earth. Or if you've heard the piping of earth, you haven't heard the piping of Heaven!"

Tzu-yu said, "May I venture to ask what this means?"

Tzu-ch'i said, "The Great Clod[2] belches out breath and its name is wind. So long as it doesn't come forth, nothing happens. But when it does, then ten thousand hollows begin crying wildly. Can't you hear them, long drawn out? In the mountain forests that lash and sway, there are huge trees a hundred spans around with hollows and openings like noses, like mouths, like ears, like jugs, like cups, like mortars, like rifts, like ruts. They roar like waves, whistle like arrows, screech, gasp, cry, wail, moan, and howl, those in the lead calling out *yeee!,* those behind calling out *yuuu!* In a gentle breeze they answer faintly, but in a full gale the chorus is gigantic. And when the fierce wind has passed on, then all the hollows are empty again. Have you never seen the tossing and trembling that goes on?"

Tzu-yu said, "By the piping of earth, then, you mean simply [the sound of] these hollows, and by the piping of man [the sound of] flutes and whistles. But may I ask about the piping of Heaven?"

Tzu-ch'i said, "Blowing on the ten thousand things in a different way, so that each can be itself—all take what they want for themselves, but who does the sounding?"

1. The word "companion" may refer to his associates, his   2. The earth.
wife or his body.

Great understanding is broad and unhurried; little understanding is cramped and busy. Great words are clear and limpid; little words are shrill and quarrelsome. In sleep, men's spirits go visiting; in waking hours, their bodies hustle. With everything they meet they become entangled. Day after day they use their minds in strife, sometimes grandiose, sometimes sly, sometimes petty. Their little fears are mean and trembly; their great fears are stunned and overwhelming. They bound off like an arrow or a crossbow pellet, certain that they are the arbiters of right and wrong. They cling to their position as though they had sworn before the gods, sure that they are holding on to victory. They fade like fall and winter—such is the way they dwindle day by day. They drown in what they do—you cannot make them turn back. They grow dark, as though sealed with seals—such are the excesses of their old age. And when their minds draw near to death, nothing can restore them to the light.

Joy, anger, grief, delight, worry, regret, fickleness, inflexibility, modesty, willfulness, candor, insolence—music from empty holes, mushrooms springing up in dampness, day and night replacing each other before us, and no one knows where they sprout from. Let it be! Let it be! [It is enough that] morning and evening we have them, and they are the means by which we live. Without them we would not exist; without us they would have nothing to take hold of. This comes close to the matter. But I do not know what makes them the way they are. It would seem as though they have some True Master, and yet I find no trace of him. He can act—that is certain. Yet I cannot see his form. He has identity but no form.

The hundred joints, the nine openings, the six organs, all come together and exist here [as my body]. But which part should I feel closest to? I should delight in all parts, you say? But there must be one I ought to favor more. If not, are they all of them mere servants? But if they are all servants, then how can they keep order among themselves? Or do they take turns being lord and servant? It would seem as though there must be some True Lord among them. But whether I succeed in discovering his identity or not, it neither adds to nor detracts from his Truth.

Once a man receives this fixed bodily form, he holds on to it, waiting for the end. Sometimes clashing with things, sometimes bending before them, he runs his course like a galloping steed, and nothing can stop him. Is he not pathetic? Sweating and laboring to the end of his days and never seeing his accomplishment, utterly exhausting himself and never knowing where to look for rest—can you help pitying him? I'm not dead yet! he says, but what good is that? His body decays, his mind follows it—can you deny that this is a great sorrow? Man's life has always been a muddle like this. How could I be the only muddled one, and other men not muddled?

If a man follows the mind given him and makes it his teacher, then who can be without a teacher? Why must you comprehend the process of change and form your mind on that basis before you can have a teacher? Even an idiot has his teacher. But to fail to abide by this mind and still insist upon your rights and wrongs—this is like saying that you set off for Yüeh today and got there yesterday. This is to claim that what doesn't exist exists. If you claim that what doesn't exist exists, then even the holy sage Yü couldn't understand you, much less a person like me!

Words are not just wind. Words have something to say. But if what they have to say is not fixed, then do they really say something? Or do they say nothing? People suppose that words are different from the peeps of baby birds, but is there any difference, or isn't there? What does the Way rely upon, that we have true and false? What do words rely upon, that we have right and wrong? How can the Way go away and not exist? How can words exist and not be acceptable? When the Way relies on little accomplishments and words rely on vain show, then we have the rights and wrongs of the Confucians and the Mo-ists.[3] What one calls right the other calls wrong; what one calls wrong the other calls right. But if we want to right their wrongs and wrong their rights, then the best thing to use is clarity.

Everything has its "that," everything has its "this." From the point of view of "that" you cannot see it, but through understanding you can know it. So I say, "that" comes out of "this" and "this" depends on "that"—which is to say that "this" and "that" give birth to each other. But where there is birth there must be death; where there is death there must be birth. Where there is acceptability there must be unacceptability; where there is unacceptability there must be acceptability. Where there is recognition of right there must be recognition of wrong; where there is recognition of wrong there must be recognition of right. Therefore the sage does not proceed in such a way, but illuminates all in the light of Heaven. He too recognizes a "this," but a "this" which is also "that," a "that" which is also "this." His "that" has both a right and a wrong in it; his "this" too has both a right and a wrong in it. So, in fact, does he still have a "this" and "that"? Or does he in fact no longer have a "this" and "that"? A state in which "this" and "that" no longer find their opposites is called the hinge of the Way. When the hinge is fitted into the socket, it can respond endlessly. Its right then is a single endlessness and its wrong too is a single endlessness. So, I say, the best thing to use is clarity.

To use an attribute to show that attributes are not attributes is not as good as using a nonattribute to show that attributes are not attributes. To use a horse to show that a horse is not a horse is not as good as using a non-horse to show that a horse is not a horse.[4] Heaven and earth are one attribute; the ten thousand things are one horse.

What is acceptable we call acceptable; what is unacceptable we call unacceptable. A road is made by people walking on it; things are so because they are called so. What makes them so? Making them so makes them so. What makes them not so? Making them not so makes them not so. Things all must have that which is so; things all must have that which is acceptable. There is nothing that is not so, nothing that is not acceptable.

For this reason, whether you point to a little stalk or a great pillar, a leper or the beautiful Hsi-shih, things ribald and shady or things grotesque and strange, the Way makes them all into one. Their dividedness is their completeness; their completeness is their impairment. No thing is either complete or impaired, but all are made into one again. Only the man of far-reaching vision knows how to make them into one. So he has no use [for categories], but relegates all to the constant. The constant is the useful; the useful is the passable; the passable is the successful; and with success, all is accomplished. He relies upon this alone, relies upon it and does not know he is doing so. This is called the Way.

But to wear out your brain trying to make things into one without realizing that they are all the same—this is called "three in the morning." What do I mean by "three in the morning"? When the monkey trainer was handing out acorns, he said, "You get three in the morning and four at night." This made all the monkeys furious. "Well,

3. An early philosophical school linked with the 5th-century B.C.E. thinker Mozi, known for his ascetic opposition to Confucian ritual, for a purely utilitarian justification of morality, and for a doctrine of universal love, as opposed to Confucius's conviction that affection was

more naturally proportional to degrees of relationship.
4. A reference to the statements of the logician Kung-sun Lung, "A white horse is not a horse" and "Attributes are not attributes in and of themselves."

then," he said, "you get four in the morning and three at night." The monkeys were all delighted. There was no change in the reality behind the words, and yet the monkeys responded with joy and anger. Let them, if they want to. So the sage harmonizes with both right and wrong and rests in Heaven the Equalizer. This is called walking two roads.

The understanding of the men of ancient times went a long way. How far did it go? To the point where some of them believed that things have never existed—so far, to the end, where nothing can be added. Those at the next stage thought that things exist but recognized no boundaries among them. Those at the next stage thought there were boundaries but recognized no right and wrong. Because right and wrong appeared, the Way was injured, and because the Way was injured, love became complete. But do such things as completion and injury really exist, or do they not?

There is such a thing as completion and injury—Mr. Chao playing the lute is an example. There is such a thing as no completion and no injury—Mr. Chao not playing the lute is an example.[5] Chao Wen played the lute; Music Master K'uang waved his baton; Hui Tzu leaned on his desk. The knowledge of these three was close to perfection. All were masters, and therefore their names have been handed down to later ages. Only in their likes they were different from him [the true sage]. What they liked, they tried to make clear. What he is not clear about, they tried to make clear, and so they ended in the foolishness of "hard" and "white."[6] Their sons, too, devoted all their lives to their fathers' theories, but till their death never reached any completion. Can these men be said to have attained completion? If so, then so have all the rest of us. Or can they not be said to have attained completion? If so, then neither we nor anything else have ever attained it.

The torch of chaos and doubt—this is what the sage steers by. So he does not use things but relegates all to the constant. This is what it means to use clarity.

Now I am going to make a statement here. I don't know whether it fits into the category of other people's statements or not. But whether it fits into their category or whether it doesn't, it obviously fits into some category. So in that respect it is no different from their statements. However, let me try making my statement.

There is a beginning. There is a not yet beginning to be a beginning. There is a not yet beginning to be a not yet beginning to be a beginning. There is being. There is nonbeing. There is a not yet beginning to be nonbeing. There is a not yet beginning to be a not yet beginning to be nonbeing. Suddenly there is nonbeing. But I do not know, when it comes to nonbeing, which is really being and which is nonbeing. Now I have just said something. But I don't know whether what I have said has really said something or whether it hasn't said something.

There is nothing in the world bigger than the tip of an autumn hair,[7] and Mount T'ai is tiny. No one has lived longer than a dead child, and P'eng-tsu died young. Heaven and earth were born at the same time I was, and the ten thousand things are one with me.

---

5. Chao Wen was a famous lute (*ch'in*) player. But his playing was only a pale and partial reflection of the ideal music, which was thereby injured and impaired, just as the unity of the Way was injured by the appearance of love—i.e., man's likes and dislikes. Hence, when he refrained from playing the lute, there was neither completion nor injury.

6. The logicians Hui Tzu and Kung-sun Lung spent much time discussing the relationship between attributes such as "hard" and "white" and the things to which they pertain.

7. The strands of animal fur were believed to grow particularly fine in autumn; hence "the tip of an autumn hair" indicates something extremely tiny.

We have already become one, so how can I say anything? But I have just *said* that we are one, so how can I not be saying something? The one and what I said about it make two, and two and the original one make three. If we go on this way, then even the cleverest mathematician can't tell where we'll end, much less an ordinary man. If by moving from nonbeing to being we get to three, how far will we get if we move from being to being? Better not to move, but to let things be!

The Way has never known boundaries; speech has no constancy. But because of [the recognition of a] "this," there came to be boundaries. Let me tell you what the boundaries are. There is left, there is right, there are theories, there are debates, there are divisions, there are discriminations, there are emulations, and there are contentions. These are called the Eight Virtues. As to what is beyond the Six Realms,[8] the sage admits its existence but does not theorize. As to what is within the Six Realms, he theorizes but does not debate. In the case of the *Spring and Autumn*,[9] the record of the former kings of past ages, the sage debates but does not discriminate. So [I say,] those who divide fail to divide; those who discriminate fail to discriminate. What does this mean, you ask? The sage embraces things. Ordinary men discriminate among them and parade their discriminations before others. So I say, those who discriminate fail to see.

The Great Way is not named; Great Discriminations are not spoken; Great Benevolence is not benevolent; Great Modesty is not humble; Great Daring does not attack. If the Way is made clear, it is not the Way. If discriminations are put into words, they do not suffice. If benevolence has a constant object, it cannot be universal. If modesty is fastidious, it cannot be trusted. If daring attacks, it cannot be complete. These five are all round, but they tend toward the square.[1]

Therefore understanding that rests in what it does not understand is the finest. Who can understand discriminations that are not spoken, the Way that is not a way? If he can understand this, he may be called the Reservoir of Heaven. Pour into it and it is never full, dip from it and it never runs dry, and yet it does not know where the supply comes from. This is called the Shaded Light.

So it is that long ago Yao said to Shun, "I want to attack the rulers of Tsung, K'uai, and Hsü-ao. Even as I sit on my throne, this thought nags at me. Why is this?"

Shun replied, "These three rulers are only little dwellers in the weeds and brush. Why this nagging desire? Long ago, ten suns came out all at once and the ten thousand things all lighted up. And how much greater is virtue than these suns!"[2]

Nieh Ch'üeh asked Wang Ni, "Do you know what all things agree in calling right?"

"How would I know that?" said Wang Ni.

"Do you know that you don't know it?"

"How would I know that?"

"Then do things know nothing?"

"How would I know that? However, suppose I try saying something. What way do I have of knowing that if I say I know something I don't really not know it? Or what way do I have of knowing that if I say I don't know something I don't really in

8. Heaven, earth and the four directions, i.e., the universe.
9. Perhaps a reference to the Confucian Spring and Autumn Annals.
1. All are originally perfect, but may become "squared,"
i.e., impaired, by the misuses mentioned.
2. Here virtue is to be understood in a good sense, as the power of the way.

fact know it? Now let me ask *you* some questions. If a man sleeps in a damp place, his back aches and he ends up half paralyzed, but is this true of a loach? If he lives in a tree, he is terrified and shakes with fright, but is this true of a monkey? Of these three creatures, then, which one knows the proper place to live? Men eat the flesh of grass-fed and grain-fed animals, deer eat grass, centipedes find snakes tasty, and hawks and falcons relish mice. Of these four, which knows how food ought to taste? Monkeys pair with monkeys, deer go out with deer, and fish play around with fish. Men claim that Mao-ch'iang and Lady Li were beautiful, but if fish saw them they would dive to the bottom of the stream, if birds saw them they would fly away, and if deer saw them they would break into a run. Of these four, which knows how to fix the standard of beauty for the world? The way I see it, the rules of benevolence and righteousness and the paths of right and wrong are all hopelessly snarled and jumbled. How could I know anything about such discriminations?"

Nieh Ch'üeh said, "If you don't know what is profitable or harmful, then does the Perfect Man likewise know nothing of such things?"

Wang Ni replied, "The Perfect Man is godlike. Though the great swamps blaze, they cannot burn him; though the great rivers freeze, they cannot chill him; though swift lightning splits the hills and howling gales shake the sea, they cannot frighten him. A man like this rides the clouds and mist, straddles the sun and moon, and wanders beyond the four seas. Even life and death have no effect on him, much less the rules of profit and loss!"

Chü Ch'üeh-tzu said to Chang Wu-tzu, "I have heard Confucius say that the sage does not work at anything, does not pursue profit, does not dodge harm, does not enjoy being sought after, does not follow the Way, says nothing yet says something, says something yet says nothing, and wanders beyond the dust and grime. Confucius himself regarded these as wild and flippant words, though I believe they describe the working of the mysterious Way. What do you think of them?"

Chang Wu-tzu said, "Even the Yellow Emperor would be confused if he heard such words, so how could you expect Confucius to understand them? What's more, you're too hasty in your own appraisal. You see an egg and demand a crowing cock, see a crossbow pellet and demand a roast dove. I'm going to try speaking some reckless words and I want you to listen to them recklessly. How will that be? The sage leans on the sun and moon, tucks the universe under his arm, merges himself with things, leaves the confusion and muddle as it is, and looks on slaves as exalted. Ordinary men strain and struggle; the sage is stupid and blockish. He takes part in ten thousand ages and achieves simplicity in oneness. For him, all the ten thousand things are what they are, and thus they enfold each other.

"How do I know that loving life is not a delusion? How do I know that in hating death I am not like a man who, having left home in his youth, has forgotten the way back?

"Lady Li was the daughter of the border guard of Ai.[3] When she was first taken captive and brought to the state of Chin, she wept until her tears drenched the collar of her robe. But later, when she went to live in the palace of the ruler, shared his couch with him, and ate the delicious meats of his table, she wondered why she had ever wept. How do I know that the dead do not wonder why they ever longed for life?

---

3. She was taken captive by Duke Hsien of Chin in 671 B.C.E., and later became his consort.

"He who dreams of drinking wine may weep when morning comes; he who dreams of weeping may in the morning go off to hunt. While he is dreaming he does not know it is a dream, and in his dream he may even try to interpret a dream. Only after he wakes does he know it was a dream. And someday there will be a great awakening when we know that this is all a great dream. Yet the stupid believe they are awake, busily and brightly assuming they understand things, calling this man ruler, that one herdsman—how dense. Confucius and you are both dreaming! And when I say you are dreaming, I am dreaming, too. Words like these will be labeled the Supreme Swindle. Yet, after ten thousand generations, a great sage may appear who will know their meaning, and it will still be as though he appeared with astonishing speed.

"Suppose you and I have had an argument. If you have beaten me instead of my beating you, then are you necessarily right and am I necessarily wrong? If I have beaten you instead of your beating me, then am I necessarily right and are you necessarily wrong? Is one of us right and the other wrong? Are both of us right or are both of us wrong? If you and I don't know the answer, then other people are bound to be even more in the dark. Whom shall we get to decide what is right? Shall we get someone who agrees with you to decide? But if he already agrees with you, how can he decide fairly? Shall we get someone who agrees with me? But if he already agrees with me, how can he decide? Shall we get someone who disagrees with both of us? But if he already disagrees with both of us, how can he decide? Shall we get someone who agrees with both of us? But if he already agrees with both of us, how can he decide? Obviously, then, neither you nor I nor anyone else can decide for each other. Shall we wait for still another person?

"But waiting for one shifting voice [to pass judgment on] another is the same as waiting for none of them. Harmonize them all with the Heavenly Equality, leave them to their endless changes, and so live out your years. What do I mean by harmonizing them with the Heavenly Equality? Right is not right; so is not so. If right were really right, it would differ so clearly from not right that there would be no need for argument. If so were really so, it would differ so clearly from not so that there would be no need for argument. Forget the years; forget distinctions. Leap into the boundless and make it your home!"

Penumbra said to Shadow, "A little while ago you were walking and now you're standing still; a little while ago you were sitting and now you're standing up. Why this lack of independent action?"

Shadow said, "Do I have to wait for something before I can be like this? Does what I wait for also have to wait for something before it can be like this? Am I waiting for the scales of a snake or the wings of a cicada? How do I know why it is so? How do I know why it isn't so?"[4]

Once Chuang Chou dreamt he was a butterfly, a butterfly flitting and fluttering around, happy with himself and doing as he pleased. He didn't know he was Chuang Chou. Suddenly he woke up and there he was, solid and unmistakable Chuang Chou. But he didn't know if he was Chuang Chou who had dreamt he was a butterfly, or a

---

4. That is, to ordinary men the shadow appears to depend upon something else for its movement, just as the snake depends on its scales and the cicada on its wings. But do such causal views of action really have any meaning?

butterfly dreaming he was Chuang Chou. Between Chuang Chou and a butterfly there must be *some* distinction! This is called the Transformation of Things.

* * *

from *The Secret of Caring for Life*

Cook Ting was cutting up an ox for Lord Wen-hui. At every touch of his hand, every heave of his shoulder, every move of his feet, every thrust of his knee—zip! zoop! He slithered the knife along with a zing, and all was in perfect rhythm, as though he were performing the dance of the Mulberry Grove or keeping time to the Ching-shou music.[1]

"Ah, this is marvelous!" said Lord Wen-hui. "Imagine skill reaching such heights!"

Cook Ting laid down his knife and replied, "What I care about is the Way, which goes beyond skill. When I first began cutting up oxen, all I could see was the ox itself. After three years I no longer saw the whole ox. And now—now I go at it by spirit and don't look with my eyes. Perception and understanding have come to a stop and spirit moves where it wants. I go along with the natural makeup, strike in the big hollows, guide the knife through the big openings, and follow things as they are. So I never touch the smallest ligament or tendon, much less a main joint.

"A good cook changes his knife once a year—because he cuts. A mediocre cook changes his knife once a month—because he hacks. I've had this knife of mine for nineteen years and I've cut up thousands of oxen with it, and yet the blade is as good as though it had just come from the grindstone. There are spaces between the joints, and the blade of the knife has really no thickness. If you insert what has no thickness into such spaces, then there's plenty of room—more than enough for the blade to play about it. That's why after nineteen years the blade of my knife is still as good as when it first came from the grindstone."

"However, whenever I come to a complicated place, I size up the difficulties, tell myself to watch out and be careful, keep my eyes on what I'm doing, work very slowly, and move the knife with the greatest subtlety, until—flop! the whole thing comes apart like a clod of earth crumbling to the ground. I stand there holding the knife and look all around me, completely satisfied and reluctant to move on, and then I wipe off the knife and put it away."

"Excellent!" said Lord Wen-hui. "I have heard the words of Cook Ting and learned how to care for life!"

* * *

from *The Way of Heaven*

Men of the world who value the Way all turn to books. But books are nothing more than words. Words have value; what is of value in words is meaning. Meaning has something it is pursuing, but the thing that it is pursuing cannot be put into words and handed down. The world values words and hands down books but, though the world values them, I do not think them worth valuing. What the world takes to be value is not real value.

What you can look at and see are forms and colors; what you can listen to and hear are names and sounds. What a pity!—that the men of the world should suppose

---

1. Identified as compositions from the time of legendary kings.

that form and color, name and sound are sufficient to convey the truth of a thing. It is because in the end they are not sufficient to convey truth that "those who know do not speak, those who speak do not know." But how can the world understand this!

Duke Huan was in his hall reading a book. The wheelwright P'ien, who was in the yard below chiseling a wheel, laid down his mallet and chisel, stepped up into the hall, and said to Duke Huan, "This book Your Grace is reading—may I venture to ask whose words are in it?"

"The words of the sages," said the duke.

"Are the sages still alive?"

"Dead long ago," said the duke.

"In that case, what you are reading there is nothing but the chaff and dregs of the men of old!"

"Since when does a wheelwright have permission to comment on the books I read?" said Duke Huan. "If you have some explanation, well and good. If not, it's your life!"

Wheelwright P'ien said, "I look at it from the point of view of my own work. When I chisel a wheel, if the blows of the mallet are too gentle, the chisel slides and won't take hold. But if they're too hard, it bites in and won't budge. Not too gentle, not too hard—you can get it in your hand and feel it in your mind. You can't put it into words, and yet there's a knack to it somehow. I can't teach it to my son, and he can't learn it from me. So I've gone along for seventy years and at my age I'm still chiseling wheels. When the men of old died, they took with them the things that couldn't be handed down. So what you are reading there must be nothing but the chaff and dregs of the men of old."

* * *

from *Autumn Floods*

The time of the autumn floods came and the hundred streams poured into the Yellow River. Its racing current swelled to such proportions that, looking from bank to bank or island to island, it was impossible to distinguish a horse from a cow. Then the Lord of the River[1] was beside himself with joy, believing that all the beauty in the world belonged to him alone. Following the current, he journeyed east until at last he reached the North Sea. Looking east, he could see no end to the water.

The Lord of the River began to wag his head and roll his eyes. Peering far off in the direction of Jo,[2] he sighed and said, "The common saying has it, 'He has heard the Way a mere hundred times but he thinks he's better than anyone else.' It applies to me. In the past, I heard men belittling the learning of Confucius and making light of the righteousness of Po Yi,[3] though I never believed them. Now, however, I have seen your unfathomable vastness. If I hadn't come to your gate, I would have been in danger. I would forever have been laughed at by the masters of the Great Method!"

Jo of the North Sea said, "You can't discuss the ocean with a well frog—he's limited by the space he lives in. You can't discuss ice with a summer insect—he's bound to a single season. You can't discuss the Way with a cramped scholar—he's shackled

1. The god of the Yellow River.
2. The sea god.
3. Po Yi (Bo Yi), who relinquished his kingdom to his brother and later chose to die of starvation rather than serve a ruler he considered unjust, was regarded as a model of righteousness.

by his doctrines. Now you have come out beyond your banks and borders and have seen the great sea—so you realize your own pettiness. From now on it will be possible to talk to you about the Great Principle.

"Of all the waters of the world, none is as great as the sea. Ten thousand streams flow into it—I have never heard of a time when they stopped—and yet it is never full. The water leaks away at Wei-lü[4]—I have never heard of a time when it didn't—and yet the sea is never empty. Spring or autumn, it never changes. Flood or drought, it takes no notice. It is so much greater than the streams of the Yangtze or the Yellow River that it is impossible to measure the difference. But I have never for this reason prided myself on it. I take my place with heaven and earth and receive breath from the yin and yang. I sit here between heaven and earth as a little stone or a little tree sits on a huge mountain. Since I can see my own smallness, what reason would I have to pride myself?

"Compare the area within the four seas with all that is between heaven and earth—is it not like one little anthill in a vast marsh? Compare the Middle Kingdom with the area within the four seas—is it not like one tiny grain in a great storehouse? When we refer to the things of creation, we speak of them as numbering ten thousand—and man is only one of them. We talk of the Nine Provinces where men are most numerous, and yet of the whole area where grain and foods are grown and where boats and carts pass back and forth, man occupies only one fraction. Compared to the ten thousand things, is he not like one little hair on the body of a horse? What the Five Emperors passed along, what the Three Kings fought over, what the benevolent man grieves about, what the responsible man labors over—all is no more than this![5] Po Yi gained a reputation by giving it up; Confucius passed himself off as learned because he talked about it. But in priding themselves in this way, were they not like you a moment ago priding yourself on your flood waters?"

"Well then," said the Lord of the River, "if I recognize the hugeness of heaven and earth and the smallness of the tip of a hair, will that do?"

"No indeed!" said Jo of the North Sea. "There is no end to the weighing of things, no stop to time, no constancy to the division of lots, no fixed rule to beginning and end. Therefore great wisdom observes both far and near, and for that reason recognizes small without considering it paltry, recognizes large without considering it unwieldy, for it knows that there is no end to the weighing of things. It has a clear understanding of past and present, and for that reason it spends a long time without finding it tedious, a short time without fretting at its shortness, for it knows that time has no stop. It perceives the nature of fullness and emptiness, and for that reason it does not delight if it acquires something nor worry if it loses it, for it knows that there is no constancy to the division of lots. It comprehends the Level Road, and for that reason it does not rejoice in life nor look on death as a calamity, for it knows that no fixed rule can be assigned to beginning and end."

"Calculate what man knows and it cannot compare to what he does not know. Calculate the time he is alive and it cannot compare to the time before he was born. Yet man takes something so small and tries to exhaust the dimensions of something so large! Hence he is muddled and confused and can never get anywhere. Looking at it this way, how do we know that the tip of a hair can be singled out as the measure of

---

4. Said to be a huge fiery stone against which the sea water turns to steam.
5. The Five Emperors were five legendary rulers, of whom the Yellow Emperor, Yao, and Shun are the most famous. The Three Kings were the founders of the Three Dynasties: the Hsia, the Shang and the Chou.

the smallest thing possible? Or how do we know that heaven and earth can fully encompass the dimensions of the largest thing possible?"

The Lord of the River said, "Men who debate such matters these days all claim that the minutest thing has no form and the largest thing cannot be encompassed. Is this a true statement?"

Jo of the North Sea said, "If from the standpoint of the minute we look at what is large, we cannot see to the end. If from the standpoint of what is large we look at what is minute, we cannot distinguish it clearly. The minute is the smallest of the small, the gigantic is the largest of the large, and it is therefore convenient to distinguish between them. But this is merely a matter of circumstance. Before we can speak of coarse or fine, however, there must be some form. If a thing has no form, then numbers cannot express its dimensions, and if it cannot be encompassed, then numbers cannot express its size. We can use words to talk about the coarseness of things and we can use our minds to visualize the fineness of things. But what words cannot describe and the mind cannot succeed in visualizing—this has nothing to do with coarseness or fineness.

"Therefore the Great Man in his actions will not harm others, but he makes no show of benevolence or charity. He will not move for the sake of profit, but he does not despise the porter at the gate. He will not wrangle for goods or wealth, but he makes no show of refusing or relinquishing them. He will not enlist the help of others in his work, but he makes no show of being self-supporting, and he does not despise the greedy and base. His actions differ from those of the mob, but he makes no show of uniqueness or eccentricity. He is content to stay behind with the crowd, but he does not despise those who run forward to flatter and fawn. All the titles and stipends of the age are not enough to stir him to exertion; all its penalties and censures are not enough to make him feel shame. He knows that no line can be drawn between right and wrong, no border can be fixed between great and small. I have heard it said, 'The Man of the Way wins no fame, the highest virtue wins no gain,[6] the Great Man has no self.' To the most perfect degree, he goes along with what has been allotted to him."

The Lord of the River said, "Whether they are external to things or internal, I do not understand how we come to have these distinctions of noble and mean or of great and small."

Jo of the North Sea said, "From the point of view of the Way, things have no nobility or meanness. From the point of view of things themselves, each regards itself as noble and other things as mean. From the point of view of common opinion, nobility and meanness are not determined by the individual himself.

"From the point of view of differences, if we regard a thing as big because there is a certain bigness to it, then among all the ten thousand things there are none that are not big. If we regard a thing as small because there is a certain smallness to it, then among the ten thousand things there are none that are not small. If we know that heaven and earth are tiny grains and the tip of a hair is a range of mountains, then we have perceived the law of difference.

"From the point of view of function, if we regard a thing as useful because there is a certain usefulness to it, then among all the ten thousand things there are none that are not useful. If we regard a thing as useless because there is a certain uselessness to it, then among the ten thousand things there are none that are not useless. If we know that east and west are mutually opposed but that one cannot do without the other, then we can estimate the degree of function.

---

6. A play on the words *te* (virtue) and *te* (gain, or acquisition).

"From the point of view of preference, if we regard a thing as right because there is a certain right to it, then among the ten thousand things there are none that are not right. If we regard a thing as wrong because there is a certain wrong to it, then among the ten thousand things there are none that are not wrong. If we know that Yao and Chieh each thought himself right and condemned the other as wrong, then we may understand how there are preferences in behavior.

"In ancient times Yao abdicated in favor of Shun and Shun ruled as emperor; K'uai abdicated in favor of Chih and Chih was destroyed.[7] T'ang and Wu fought and became kings; Duke Po fought and was wiped out.[8] Looking at it this way, we see that struggling or giving way, behaving like a Yao or like a Chieh, may be at one time noble and at another time mean. It is impossible to establish any constant rule.

"A beam or pillar can be used to batter down a city wall, but it is no good for stopping up a little hole—this refers to a difference in function. Thoroughbreds like Ch'i-chi and Hua-liu could gallop a thousand li in one day, but when it came to catching rats they were no match for the wildcat or the weasel—this refers to a difference in skill. The horned owl catches fleas at night and can spot the tip of a hair, but when daylight comes, no matter how wide it opens its eyes, it cannot see a mound or a hill—this refers to a difference in nature. Now do you say that you are going to make Right your master and do away with Wrong, or make Order your master and do away with Disorder? If you do, then you have not understood the principle of heaven and earth or the nature of the ten thousand things. This is like saying that you are going to make Heaven your master and do away with Earth, or make Yin your master and do away with Yang. Obviously it is impossible. If men persist in talking this way without stop, they must be either fools or deceivers!

"Emperors and kings have different ways of ceding their thrones; the Three Dynasties had different rules of succession. Those who went against the times and flouted custom were called usurpers; those who went with the times and followed custom were called companions of righteousness. Be quiet, be quiet, O Lord of the River! How could you understand anything about the gateway of nobility and meanness or the house of great and small?"

"Well then," said the Lord of the River, "what should I do and what should I not do? How am I to know in the end what to accept and what to reject, what to abide by and what to discard?"

Jo of the North Sea said, "From the point of view of the Way, what is noble or what is mean? These are merely what are called endless changes. Do not hobble your will, or you will be departing far from the Way! What is few, or what is many? These are merely what are called boundless turnings. Do not strive to unify your actions, or you will be at sixes and sevens with the Way! Be stern like the ruler of a state—he grants no private favor. Be benign and impartial like the god of the soil at the sacrifice—he grants no private blessing. Be broad and expansive like the endlessness of the four directions—they have nothing which bounds or hedges them. Embrace the ten thousand things universally—how could there be one you should give special support to? This is called being without bent. When the ten thousand things are unified and equal, then which is short and which is long?

7. In 316 B.C.E., King K'uai of Yen was persuaded to imitate Yao by ceding his throne to his minister Tzu Chih. In no time the state was torn by internal strife and three years later it was invaded and annexed by the state of Ch'i.
8. T'ang and Wu were the founders of the Shang and

Chou dynasties, respectively. Duke Po was a scion of the royal family of Ch'u who led an unsuccessful revolt against its ruler and was defeated and forced to commit suicide in 479 B.C.E.

"The Way is without beginning or end, but things have their life and death—you cannot rely upon their fulfillment. One moment empty, the next moment full—you cannot depend upon their form. The years cannot be held off; time cannot be stopped. Decay, growth, fullness, and emptiness end and then begin again. It is thus that we must describe the plan of the Great Meaning and discuss the principles of the ten thousand things. The life of things is a gallop, a headlong dash—with every movement they alter, with every moment they shift. What should you do and what should you not do? Everything will change of itself, that is certain!"

"If that is so," said the Lord of the River, "then what is there valuable about the Way?"

Jo of the North Sea said, "He who understands the Way is certain to have command of basic principles. He who has command of basic principles is certain to know how to deal with circumstances. And he who knows how to deal with circumstances will not allow things to do him harm. When a man has perfect virtue, fire cannot burn him, water cannot drown him, cold and heat cannot afflict him, birds and beasts cannot injure him. I do not say that he makes light of these things. I mean that he distinguishes between safety and danger, contents himself with fortune or misfortune, and is cautious in his comings and goings. Therefore nothing can harm him.

"Hence it is said: the Heavenly is on the inside, the human is on the outside. Virtue resides in the Heavenly. Understand the actions of Heaven and man, base yourself upon Heaven, take your stand in virtue, and then, although you hasten or hold back, bend or stretch, you may return to the essential and speak of the ultimate."

"What do you mean by the Heavenly and the human?"

Jo of the North Sea said, "Horses and oxen have four feet—this is what I mean by the Heavenly. Putting a halter on the horse's head, piercing the ox's nose—this is what I mean by the human. So I say: do not let what is human wipe out what is Heavenly; do not let what is purposeful wipe out what is fated; do not let [the desire for] gain lead you after fame. Be cautious, guard it, and do not lose it—this is what I mean by returning to the True."

* * *

Once, when Chuang Tzu was fishing in the P'u River, the king of Ch'u sent two officials to go and announce to him: "I would like to trouble you with the administration of my realm."

Chuang Tzu held on to the fishing pole and, without turning his head, said, "I have heard that there is a sacred tortoise in Ch'u that has been dead for three thousand years. The king keeps it wrapped in cloth and boxed, and stores it in the ancestral temple. Now would this tortoise rather be dead and have its bones left behind and honored? Or would it rather be alive and dragging its tail in the mud?"

"It would rather be alive and dragging its tail in the mud," said the two officials.

Chuang Tzu said, "Go away! I'll drag my tail in the mud!"

* * *

━━◆Ξ━━

Liezi
4th century C.E.

The *Zhuangzi* and other early texts refer to a certain Liezi who could ride the wind, but about this individual nothing more is known. Scholars now agree that the eight chapters of the book that bears his name were probably not compiled before 300 C.E. The *Book of Liezi* is the most important Daoist text after the *Dao de jing* and the *Zhuangzi*. Its fondness for the apt anecdote links it especially closely to the latter text; some of its material is in fact very similar, and the two texts also both include Confucius freely among their cast of characters. The passages that follow illustrate the virtues of acting spontaneously and responsively in harmony with the Way of nature, with particular reference to artistic production, and describe the hazards of failing to do so.

from The Book of Liezi[1]

Confucius was looking at Lü-liang waterfall. The water dropped two hundred feet, streaming foam for thirty miles; it was a place where fish and turtles and crocodiles could not swim, but he saw a man swimming there. Taking him for someone in trouble who wanted to die, he sent a disciple along the bank to pull him up. But after swimming a few hundred yards the man came out, and strolled along singing under the bank with his hair hanging down his back. Confucius proceeded to question him:

"I thought you were a ghost, but now I can look you over I see you are human. May I ask whether you have a Way to tread in water?"

"No, I have no Way. I began in what is native to me, grew up in what is natural to me, matured by trusting destiny. I enter the vortex with the inflow and leave with the outflow, follow the Way of the water instead of imposing a course of my own; this is how I tread it."

"What do you mean by 'beginning in what is native to you, growing up in what is natural to you, maturing by trusting destiny'?"

"Having been born on land I am safe on land—this is native to me. Having grown up in the water I am safe in the water—this is natural to me. I do it without knowing how I do it—this is trusting destiny."

* * *

There was a man living by the sea-shore who loved seagulls. Every morning he went down to the sea to roam with the seagulls, and more birds came to him than you could count in hundreds. His father said to him:

"I hear the seagulls all come roaming with you. Bring me some to play with."

Next day, when he went down to the sea, the seagulls danced above him and would not come down.

Therefore it is said: "The utmost in speech is to be rid of speech, the utmost doing is Doing Nothing."

* * *

When Hu Pa played the lute, the birds danced and the fishes bounded. Wen of Cheng heard this story, and left his family to travel as an apprentice with Music-master Hsiang. He would lay his fingers on the strings to tune them but for three years did not finish a piece.

"You may as well go home," said Music-master Hsiang.

Wen put aside his lute with a sigh and answered:

"It is not the strings that I cannot tune, nor the piece that I cannot finish. What I have in mind is not in the strings, what I am aiming at is not in the notes. Unless I grasp it inwardly in my heart, it will not answer from the instrument outside me. That

1. Translated by A. C. Graham.

is why I dare not put out my hand to stir the strings. Let me stay a little longer and see if I do better later."

Soon afterwards he saw Music-master Hsiang again.

"How are you getting on with the lute?" Hsiang asked.

"I've got it, let me show you."

Then, during the spring, he touched the Autumn string and called up the note of the eighth month;[2] a cool wind came suddenly, and fruit ripened on the bushes and trees. When autumn came he touched the Spring string and aroused the note of the second month; a warm breeze whirled gently, and the bushes and trees burst into flower. During the summer he touched the Winter string and called up the note of the eleventh month; frost and snow fell together and the rivers and lakes abruptly froze. When winter came he touched the Summer string, and aroused the note of the fifth month; the sunshine burned fiercely and the hard ice melted at once. When he was coming to the end he announced the Kung string and played the other four together; a fortunate wind soared, auspicious clouds drifted, the sweet dew fell, the fresh springs bubbled.

Then Music-master Hsiang slapped his chest and stepped high, saying:

"Sublime, your playing! Even the Music-master K'uang performing the *ch'ing-chiao* music, and Tsou Yen blowing the pitch-tubes,[3] had nothing to add to this. They would have to put their lutes under their arms, take their pipes in their hands, and follow behind you."

* * *

Po Ya was a good lute-player, and Chung Tzǔ-ch'i was a good listener. Po Ya strummed his lute, with his mind on climbing high mountains; and Chung Tzǔ-ch'i said:

"Good! Lofty, like Mount T'ai!"

When his mind was on flowing waters, Chung Tzǔ-ch'i said:

"Good! Boundless, like the Yellow River and the Yangtse!"

Whatever came into Po Ya's thoughts, Chung Tzǔ-ch'i always grasped it. Po Ya was roaming on the North side of Mount T'ai; he was caught in a sudden storm of rain, and took shelter under a cliff. Feeling sad, he took up his lute and strummed it; first he composed an air about the persistent rain, then he improvised the sound of crashing mountains. Whatever melody he played, Chung Tzǔ-ch'i never missed the direction of his thought. Then Po Ya put away his lute and sighed:

"Good! Good! How well you listen! What you imagine is just what is in my mind. Is there nowhere for my notes to flee to?"

Xi Kang
223–262 C.E.

An accomplished poet and musician, Xi Kang was known for his outspokenness and his fondness for debate. He was said to have exercised these talents with a group of scholars dubbed the

2. Chinese music has a pentatonic scale in which the notes (excluding the first, "Kung") are associated with the four seasons. Its absolute pitch depends on semitones blown through 12 pitch-tubes of standard lengths, associated with the 12 months. Each piece of music prescribes the semitone to which the Kung string is to be tuned [transla-

tor's note].

3. K'uang's performance of the *ch'ing-chiao* caused a drought that lasted three years. Tsou Yen, by blowing the pitch-tubes, warmed the climate of a country in the far north.

"Seven Sages of the Bamboo Grove." According to later legends, these gentlemen retreated to the country to drink, write, play the zither, and argue about philosophical issues of common interest. Central among these was Daoism, whose fine points, implications, and relationships to Confucianism and Buddhism inspired lively discussions known as "pure conversation" because of their often abstract nature. Xi retired permanently from a minor office in 249 when a change in government eliminated the protection and advantage he had previously been afforded by his marriage to a princess in the former ruling family.

In this letter to Shan Tao (205–283 C.E.), another of the Seven Sages, Xi responds to his friend's recommendation for another post and explains why he is constitutionally and philosophically opposed to political engagement. Although it is of doubtful authenticity, the letter reflects attitudes documented in other sources. Even in retirement, however, Xi proved vulnerable: trumped-up charges of sedition were manufactured by someone he had once offended, and he was executed in 262.

PRONUNCIATION:
  Xi Kang: SHE KAHNG

from Letter to Shan T'ao[1]

Some time ago you spoke of me to your uncle, the Prefect of Ying-ch'uan, and I must say I found your estimate of me just. But I wondered how you could have come to so accurate an understanding without really knowing what my principles are. Last year when I came back from Hotung, Kung-sun Ch'ung and Lü An said you had proposed me as your successor in office. Nothing came of it, but your proposal made it obvious you really did not understand me at all.

You are versatile: you accept most things and are surprised at little. I, on the other hand, am by nature straightforward and narrow-minded: there are lots of things that I cannot put up with. It was only chance that made us friends. * * * Hence I am writing to make clear what may and may not be done.

It used to be that when in my reading I came across people resolutely above the world, I rather doubted their existence, but now I am convinced that they really do exist after all. One can be so constituted that there are things one cannot endure; honest endorsement cannot be forced. * * *

Thus there are those who stick to the court and never emerge and those who enter the wilderness and never come back.

Moreover, I am filled with admiration when I read the biographies of the recluses Shang Tzu-p'ing and T'ai Hsiao-wei[2] and can imagine what sort of men they were. Add to that the fact that I lost my father when young, was spoiled by my mother and elder brother and never took up the study of the classics. I was already wayward and lazy by nature, so that my muscles became weak and my flesh flabby. I would commonly go half a month without washing my face, and until the itching became a considerable annoyance, I would not wash my hair. When I had to urinate, if I could stand it I would wait until my bladder cramped inside before I got up.

Further, I was long left to my own devices, and my disposition became arrogant and careless, my bluntness diametrically opposed to etiquette; laziness and rudeness

---

1. Translated by J. R. Hightower.

2. Both men resisted repeated entreaties to enter government service.

reinforcing one another. But my friends were indulgent, and did not attack me for my faults.

Besides, my taste for independence was aggravated by my reading of Chuang Tzu and Lao Tzu; as a result any desire for fame or success grew daily weaker, and my commitment to freedom increasingly firmer. In this I am like the wild deer, which captured young and reared in captivity will be docile and obedient. But if it be caught when full-grown, it will stare wildly and butt against its bonds, dashing into boiling water or fire to escape. You may dress it up with a golden bridle and feed it delicacies, and it will but long the more for its native woods and yearn for rich pasture. * * *

Furthermore, in society there are prescribed courtesies, and the court has its rules. When I consider the matter carefully, there are seven things I could never stand and two things which would never be condoned. I am fond of lying late abed, and the herald at my door would not leave me in peace: this is the first thing I could not stand. I like to walk, singing, with my lute in my arms, or go fowling or fishing in the woods. But surrounded by subordinates, I would be unable to move freely—this is the second thing I could not stand. When I kneel for a while I become as though paralyzed and unable to move. Being infested with lice, I am always scratching. To have to bow and kowtow to my superiors while dressed up in formal clothes—this is the third thing I could not stand. I have never been a facile calligrapher and do not like to write letters. Business matters would pile up on my table and fill my desk. To fail to answer would be bad manners and a violation of duty, but I would not long be able to force myself to do it. This is the fourth thing I could not stand. I do not like funerals and mourning, but these are things people consider important. Far from forgiving my offence, their resentment would reach the point where they would like to see me injured. Although in alarm I might make the effort, I still could not change my nature. If I were to bend my mind to the expectations of the crowd, it would be dissembling and dishonest, and even so I would not be sure to go unblamed—this is the fifth thing I could not stand. I do not care for the crowd and yet I would have to serve together with such people. Or on occasions when guests fill the table and their clamor deafens the ears, their noise and dirt contaminating the place, before my very eyes they would indulge in their double-dealings. This is the sixth thing I could not stand. My heart cannot bear trouble, and official life is full of it. One's mind is bound with a thousand cares, one's thoughts are involved with worldly affairs. This is the seventh thing I could not stand.

Further, I am always finding fault with T'ang and Wu Wang, or running down the Duke of Chou and Confucius.[3] If I did not stop this in society, it is clear that the religion of the times would not put up with me. This is the first thing which would never be condoned. I am quite ruthless in my hatred of evil, and speak out without hesitation, whenever I have the occasion. This is the second thing which would never be condoned.

To try to control these nine weaknesses with a disposition as narrow and niggling as mine could only result in my falling ill, if indeed I were able to avoid trouble with the authorities. Would I be long in the world of men? Besides, I have studied in

3. Tang was the founder of the Shang dynasty, and Wu Wang, to whom the Duke of Zhou was principal advisor, founded the Zhou dynasty.

the esoteric lore of the Taoist masters, where a man's life can be indefinitely prolonged through eating herbs, and I firmly believe this to be so. To wander among the
hills and streams, observing fish and birds, is what gives my heart great pleasure.
Once I embarked on an official career, this is something I would have to give up
forthwith. Why should I relinquish what gives me pleasure for something that fills
me with dread?

What is esteemed in human relationships is the just estimate of another's inborn
nature, and helping him to realize it. When you see a straight piece of wood, you do
not want to make it into a wheel, nor do you try to make a rafter of a crooked piece,
and this is because you would not want to pervert its heaven-given quality, but rather
see that it finds its proper place. Now all the four classes of people have each their
own occupation, in which each takes pleasure in fulfilling his own ambition. It is only
the man of understanding who can comprehend all of them. In this you have only to
seek within yourself to know that one may not, out of one's own preference for formal clothes, force the people of Yüeh to wear figured caps, or, because one has a taste
for putrid meat, try to feed a phoenix a dead rat.

Of late I have been studying the techniques of prolonging one's life, casting out
all ideas of fame and glory, eliminating tastes, and letting my mind wander in stillness: what is most worthwhile to me is Inaction. Even if there were not these nine
concerns, I could still pay no attention to your wishes. But beyond this, my mind
tends toward melancholy, increasingly so of late, and I am personally convinced that I
would not be able to stand any occupation in which I took no pleasure. I really know
myself in this respect. If worse comes to worst and there is no way out, then I shall
simply die. But you have no grudge against me that you should cause me to lie lifeless
in the gutter.

I am continually unhappy over the recent loss of the company of my mother and
elder brother. My daughter is thirteen, my son eight years old—neither grown to maturity, and I am in ill health. This is another fact that pains me so much I cannot bear
to speak further of it.

Today I only wish to stay on in this out-of-the-way lane and bring up my
children and grandchildren, on occasion relaxing and reminiscing with old
friends—a cup of unstrained wine, a song to the lute: this is the sum of my desires
and ambitions.

If you keep on relentlessly nagging me, it can only be because you are anxious
to get someone for the post who will be of use to the world. But you have always
known what an irresponsible, bungling sort of person I am, not at all up on current
affairs. I know myself that I am in all respects inferior to our modern men of ability.
If you think me unlike ordinary men in that I alone do not find pleasure in fame and
distinction, this is closest to my true feelings and deserves to be considered. If a
man of great ability and endowments, able to turn his hand to anything, were able to
be without ambition, he would be worth your respect. But one like me, frequently
ill, who wants to stay out of office so as to take care of himself for the remaining
years of his life—in me it is rather a deficiency. There is not much point in praising
a eunuch for his chastity. If you insist on my joining you in the king's service, expecting that we will rise together and will be a joy and help to one another, one fine
day you will find that the pressure has driven me quite mad. Only my bitterest enemy would go so far. The rustic who took such pleasure in the warm sun on his
back, or the one who so esteemed the flavor of celery that they wanted to bring these
things to the attention of the Most High; this showed them to be well-meaning, but it

also showed their complete ignorance. I hope you will not do as they did. This being the way I feel about it, I have written to explain it to you and at the same time to say farewell.

Liu Yiqing
403–444 C.E.

Compiled around 430 C.E. under the aegis of Prince Liu Yiqing of the Liu Song dynasty, *A New Account of the Tales of the World* recounts conversations, anecdotes, and descriptions of over six hundred individuals who lived during the first two centuries of the period of political disunion known as the Six Dynasties (220–589). The thirty-six-chapter anthology provides valuable and often quite amusing glimpses into the lifestyles of the rich and famous in early China, as well as illuminating insights into their understanding of important texts, issues, and doctrines. Chapter 23, "The Free and Unrestrained," from which the following selections are taken, focuses on the group known as the "Seven Sages of the Bamboo Grove" (see the introduction to Xi Kang, page 1085). Scholars now believe that the identification of this group is most likely a nostalgic construct of mid-fourth-century literati. The best-known poet of the seven was Ruan Ji (210–263), whose poems often explored Daoist themes and whose eccentric and ritual-flouting behavior was similarly inspired. Liu Ling (d. after 265) was well known as a wine drinker of prodigious capacity whose refusal to conform to social norms and attunement to the Way of nature expressed itself most graphically in his frequent nudity.

PRONUNCIATION:
   Liu Yiqing: lee-OH EE-ching

from A New Account of the Tales of the World[1]

While Juan Chi was in mourning for his mother (ca. 255), he was once present at a party at the house of Prince Wen of Chin (Ssu-ma Chao) where he was helping himself to meat and wine. The commandant of the capital province, Ho Tseng, who was also present, said to Prince Wen, "Your Excellency is now ruling the realm with filial devotion, yet Juan Chi, during an important period of mourning, has appeared openly among Your Lordship's guests drinking wine and eating meat. You should banish him beyond the sea to set right the teaching on public morals."

Prince Wen replied, "Here is Juan Chi, emaciated and depressed like this, yet you're unable to grieve with him. What's the reason? Furthermore, 'when one is ill, to drink wine and eat meat' is definitely in accord with the mourning rites."

Chi continued drinking and devouring his food without interruption, his spirit and expression completely self-possessed.

Liu Ling was once suffering from a hangover, and, being extremely thirsty, asked his wife for some wine. His wife, who had poured out all the wine and smashed the vessels, pleaded with tears in her eyes, saying, "You're drinking far too much. It's no way to preserve your life. You'll have to stop it."

Ling said, "A very good idea. But I'm unable to stop by myself. It can only be done if I pray to the ghosts and spirits and take an oath that I'll stop it. So you may get ready the wine and meat for the sacrifice."

1. Translated by Richard B. Mather.

His wife said, "As you wish," and setting out wine and meat before the spirits, requested Ling to pray and take his oath. Ling knelt down and prayed,

> "Heaven produced Liu Ling
> And took 'wine' for his name.
> At one gulp he will down a gallon—
> Five dipperfuls to ease the hangover.
> As for his wife's complaint,
> Be careful not to listen."

Whereupon he drained the wine and ate up the meat, and before he knew it was already drunk again. * * *

On many occasions Liu Ling, under the influence of wine, would be completely free and uninhibited, sometimes taking off his clothes and sitting naked in his room. Once when some persons saw him and chided him for it, Ling retorted, "I take heaven and earth for my pillars and roof, and the rooms of my house for my pants and coat. What are you gentlemen doing in my pants?"

Juan Chi's sister-in-law was once returning to her parents' home, and Chi went to see her to say good-bye. When someone chided him for this, Chi replied, "Were the rites established for people like me?"

* * *

When Juan Chi was in mourning for his mother, P'ei K'ai went to pay him a visit of condolence. Juan was drunk at the time and was sitting with disheveled hair, his legs sprawled apart, not weeping. When P'ei arrived he put down a mat for himself on the floor, and after his weeping and words of condolence were completed, he departed.

Someone asked P'ei, "Generally when one offers condolences, the host weeps and the guest simply pays his respects. Since Juan was not weeping, why did *you* weep?"

P'ei replied, "Juan is a man beyond the realm of ordinary morality and therefore pays no homage to the rules of propriety. People like you and me are still within the realm of custom, so we live our lives after the pattern set by etiquette." His contemporaries sighed in admiration over the way both men had found their true center.

❀ CROSSCURRENTS: DAOISM AND ITS WAYS ❀

- The Daoist texts in this section frequently employ paradoxical examples and parables as ways to convey philosophical and ethical ideas. How do these often enigmatic illustrations compare with Socrates' sly use of examples in Plato's *Apology* (page 709) and with Jesus's use of parables in Luke's gospel (page 1272)?

- The image of the *dao*—the "way" or "path"—has been used in many cultures as a means to embody narratives of spiritual journeying and development. How does the idea of a spiritual journey play out in Dante's *Divine Comedy* (with its opening in the middle of "our life's way," Volume B), Farid al-Din al-Attar's *Conference of the Birds* (Volume B), Geoffrey Chaucer's *Canterbury Tales* (Volume B), and Matsuo Bashō's *Narrow Road to the Deep North* (Volume D)?

- Daoist texts often emphasize the value of withdrawing from society into a close communion with nature, in contrast to Confucian ideals of social engagement and good governance. How do the dynamics of social engagement and aesthetic and political withdrawal compare in Kalidasa's *Sakuntala* (page 946), Han-Shan's poetry (Volume B), and ideas of nature as seen in Wordsworth and other Romantic poets (Volume E)?

END OF PERSPECTIVES: DAOISM AND ITS WAYS

Marble statue of Augustus Caesar, c. 20 B.C.E.

Rome and the Roman Empire

❋━┼━⊰♦⊱━┼━❋

"What else is all history," contended the fourteenth-century Florentine poet Petrarch, "if not the praise of Rome?" There were many people then and more today who might take issue with Petrarch's enthusiasm, but it is a fact that the Roman empire indelibly marked the history and culture of the modern world. Three-fourths of the vocabulary of the English language is of Latin or Greek derivation. The French and the American revolutions and the governments resulting from them were inspired by and modeled on the Roman republic. Until the middle of the twentieth century, a classical education was required for membership in the ranks of the social elites of Europe and America. The Roman empire shaped the social, political, and legal organization of the Western world. Through its literature and its translations and adaptations of the Greek tradition, it defined what we know today as classical culture. By adopting Christianity as its official religion in the fourth century, the empire provided the institutional framework and temporal authority that allowed the Catholic Church to expand and endure far beyond its Mediterranean origins.

> *"What else is all history . . . if not the praise of Rome?"*
>
> —FRANCIS PETRARCH

Moreover, whatever Petrarch may have thought, the fame of Rome has always derived from blame as well as from praise. It is notorious for the excesses of emperors such as Caligula and Nero, recorded in detail by historians of the time; for its civil wars, assassinations, and suicides by decree; for its highly trained and brutally efficient legionaries; and for its insatiable thirst for the spectacles of the circus: gladiators dueling to the death, the slaughter of wild beasts (as many as eleven thousand in a single day) by gladiators, and the slaughter of Christians and other criminals by wild beasts in front of crowds matching or exceeding in number those at modern football stadiums. The poets, historians, orators, and moralists of the several centuries before and following the birth of Christ, when Rome was at the height of its power, have left an incomparable record of praise and blame for this complex society, usually with both sentiments intermingled ambivalently in the same text. No one could afford to be indifferent about Rome.

THE MYTHIC PAST

According to tradition, Rome was founded in 753 B.C.E. by Romulus on the Palatine, one of the seven hills that dominated the topography of the ancient city. Legend had it that Romulus and his brother Remus were twin sons of the god Mars, suckled by a she-wolf. An even more fictitious legend popularized in the first century B.C.E. by the historian Livy and the poet Virgil attributed the genesis of the Roman people to the twelfth-century arrival on Italian shores of Aeneas, the Trojan hero who was said to have escaped the destruction by the Greeks of his ancestral city in Asia Minor. Aeneas's son Ascanius and their descendants supposedly ruled the region of Latium until Romulus took over the succession from his grandfather's usurper. The dual myth of origin expressed the double identity of the imperial city. On the one hand, it saw itself as grounded in the *mores maiorum,* the strict morality and customs of its rustic

Latin ancestors. On the other hand, it saw itself as the cosmopolitan center of the world, steeped in the ancient and cultured traditions of the Hellenistic east.

The *mores maiorum* were most closely associated with the republic, which had been instituted when local magistrates expelled the last of the Tarquin kings and gained independence from the Etruscan Empire in 510 B.C.E.; it lasted more or less until the principate of Augustus in 27 B.C.E. The republic was governed by a Senate composed of the patrician classes. Over the next few centuries, the poorer or plebeian classes gradually wrested a certain amount of power and privilege. The wealthiest of these eventually joined with the patricians to form a class of nobles that dominated appointments and government. Membership in the Senate was restricted in number, required possession of a fixed amount of property, and was granted for life. Below the senators was the equestrian class (so called because they were wealthy enough to provide their own horses), whose numbers filled the civil and military service and who became a powerful political force during the late republic. Poorer citizens also served in the army as privates or junior officers. Rome was liberal in making citizens out of freed slaves and out of the communities it conquered as it expanded its influence through Italy and beyond. Like the many slaves, women had no political rights, although they did have legal ones, and of course exerted influence indirectly through men.

According to Ennius (239–169 B.C.E.), the most prominent figure of early Latin literature, "The Roman republic endures through its old-fashioned mores and men." Republican ideology put a premium on gravity, dignity, austerity, integrity, fortitude, and disciplined obedience to the tradition. For women, "old-fashioned mores" meant modesty, chastity, and subordination to the family of her father or her husband. Roman religion was originally animistic and remained highly localized, based on the worship of ancestors, household gods, and heroes of the fatherland. As Livy noted, "We have a city founded with due augury and auspice, no place within it but is permeated with religious observance and divine presence." The herdsman's life of the city's legendary founder, for instance, was memorialized in an often-rebuilt straw-roofed "hut of Romulus" on the Palatine hill. During the empire an additional hut of Romulus could be found on the Capitoline hill, the most sacred spot in ancient Rome and the site of the temple of Jupiter Capitolinus, which housed Jupiter, Juno, and Minerva, the three most important gods in the Roman pantheon. Time and again, later Romans would invoke the virtue of the past, grandly expressed in the bold statue of Caesar Augustus on page 1092. In Book 8 of the *Aeneid* Virgil's hero visits the Arcadian king Evander's hut on the Palatine hill, where centuries later Rome would be located:

> Conversing of such matters, going toward
> Austere Evander's house, they saw his cattle
> Lowing everywhere in what is now
> Rome's Forum and her fashionable quarter,
> Carinae. As they came up to the door,
> Evander said:
>   "In victory Hercules
> Bent for this lintel, and these royal rooms
> Were grand enough for him. Friend, have the courage

Fight of the Gladiators, mosaic, Rome, Italy, 4th century C.E.

> To care little for wealth, and shape yourself,
> You too, to merit godhead. Do not come
> Disdainfully into our needy home."

Virgil gave his Aeneas a strong resemblance to Caesar Augustus; Evander's words serve to recall the mighty emperor to the fundamental traits of his ancestors' virtue.

Roman citizens were expected to devote their lives to their country. This meant fighting in the army—Rome was an expansionist power from the early days of the republic—and serving in government. As the famous lawyer and orator Cicero, staunch defender of the republican tradition, put it, "The Roman people hate private luxury but love public magnificence." Money was poured into great public works, such as the Colosseum where gladiators and prisoners faced wild beasts; victorious generals were feted with grand "triumphs"; martyrs and heroes of the republic were memorialized in statuary throughout the city. To be sure, the very insistence of so many writers on the austere virtue of the legendary past suggests that many wealthy and powerful Romans were in frequent need of admonition. Nevertheless, seldom has an ideology of self-restraint and self-sacrifice been more successfully employed. Nor is it difficult in this context to understand how the later empire and its citizenry would adapt so readily to the ascetic demands of early Christianity.

THE WORLD CITY

Rome was the center of religion, government, and cultural life from the early days of the republic until the division of the empire between east and west in the fourth century C.E. By the first century B.C.E., it had grown from a tiny republic to the dominant power in the Mediterranean; the capital city had some 250,000 inhabitants. Hellenistic architects from the ancient cities of Greece and the Near East had helped to transform the provincial town into the first giant city in world history. By 100 C.E., over a million people lived there, far more than in any other city for another seven centuries. Because it developed in an unplanned manner and because there was no form of public transportation, the city was extraordinarily densely

Notwithstanding the overcrowding and the immense problems in feeding its population and disposing of their waste, the city's allure was irresistible.

Ippolito Caffi, *The Roman Forum,* 1841. This is one of four murals painted by Caffi (1809–1866) on the walls of a café in Padua. Patriots sat beneath this image of ancient Roman grandeur as they plotted their 1848 uprising against the Austrians who were ruling northern Italy.

populated. Over eighty percent of the inhabitants lived in five- or six-story *insulae,* or apartment blocks; the lucky few lived in spacious and lavish freestanding houses. Notwithstanding the overcrowding and the immense problems in feeding its population and disposing of their waste, the city's allure was irresistible. As the poet Ovid attested from unhappy exile on the Black Sea, the city (*urbs*) of Rome and the world (*orbis*) were one and the same: *Romanae spatium est urbis et orbis idem.*

Drainage and water supply were a priority from early on. The Tarquins had first built the *cloaca maxima* to drain the Forum valley between the Capitoline and Palatine hills. By the late republic, this great central sewer had been enclosed; its tunnel ran nearly a kilometer and would be large enough for the imperial administrator Agrippa to cruise through on a tour of inspection. Later sources list 144 public latrines within the city, in addition to those in the many baths. Water was brought in vast quantities via aqueducts, the first of which was built in 312 B.C.E. By the early second century C.E., there were ten major aqueducts to assuage the city's thirst for water. Most outlets, whether public or private, flowed freely round the clock, approximately one million liters a day. Nearly a quarter of this water went directly into the emperor's personal service area, a third was for public use, and the rest was for private use. The average Roman household used as much water in one day as a modern household uses in two months. Although water reached only the ground floor of most *insulae,* nearly every courtyard had its own tap and cistern.

Public baths were central to the social life of Rome and its provincial towns and grew progressively larger and more spectacular as the empire expanded. Basic features included a changing room, an unheated *frigidarium* with a cold plunge pool, and a very warm *caldarium* with a hot plunge pool. By the first century B.C.E., wall heating

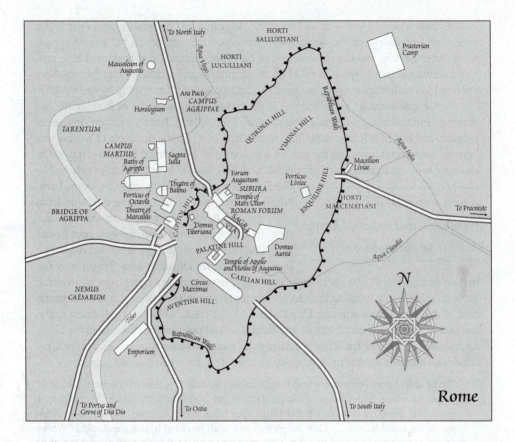

and an increased water supply permitted an elaborately graded system, wet and dry sweating rooms, large cold swimming pools and even heated ones. The Caracalla baths, whose ruins can still be visited, could hold up to 1,500 persons and included art galleries, libraries, and exercise halls. It was in sumptuous baths such as these that two aspiring writers encounter their dinner host, the nouveau riche freedman Trimalchio, in the *Satyricon* of Petronius:

> We entered the baths where we began sweating at once and we went immediately into the cold water. Trimalchio had been smothered in perfume and was already being rubbed down, not with linen towels, but with bath-robes of the finest wool. As this was going on, three masseurs sat drinking Falernian [wine] in front of him. . . . Wrapped in thick scarlet felt he was put in a litter. Four couriers with lots of medals went in front, as well as a go-cart in which his favorite boy was riding. . . . As he was carried off, a musician with a tiny set of pipes took his place by Trimalchio's head and whispered a tune in his ear the whole way.

Display of wealth was an important aspect of the baths, but they also served the practical purpose of keeping a notoriously fastidious people clean.

The streets of Rome were extremely narrow, unlit at night, made of dirt, and strewn with filth and refuse. *Insulae* were built mostly of wood frames, often hastily and in slipshod manner, and highly susceptible to fire and to collapse. The ground floors were occupied by workshops, shops and baths, so they were extremely noisy as well as dirty and dangerous. As the satirist Juvenal complained, "The wagons thundering past through these narrow twisting streets, the oaths of draymen caught in a traffic jam, would rouse a dozing seal—or an emperor." Augustus and his successors in particular undertook impressive public works—not just aqueducts and drains but temple repair, some street paving, and the construction of basilicas, circuses, and bridges. These provided additional public space as relief for those middle- and working-class city dwellers confined to *insulae* apartments and gave further opportunity for display by the wealthy.

Public space equally permitted one of the most striking activities of Roman life: listening to and observing its extraordinary range of inhabitants. Nearly everyone in late republican and imperial Rome came from somewhere else. Although the poet Catullus was born in Verona and served on the staff of a governor in Asia Minor, he had no qualms in mocking his rival Egnatius as a provincial, with "untrimmed beard, and teeth polished in the Spanish / manner—with urine." Cicero, Livy, Virgil, Horace, and Ovid all came to Rome from other parts of Italy. Later writers arrived from farther afield: Tacitus from Gaul, the epic poet Lucan from Córdoba in Spain, and Apuleius and Augustine from North Africa. Spanish-born Trajan was the first emperor (98–117 C.E.) born outside of Italy; later emperors came from all over the Mediterranean, often bringing their local customs and beliefs with them, as in the extreme case of the Syrian-born emperor Elagabalus (218–22 C.E.), hereditary High Priest to the sun god of Emesa; his exotic rituals and bizarre sexual practices contributed to his being assassinated in short order. Even in earlier days, many Romans were exiles. As the Córdoba-born moralist Seneca (c. 4 B.C.E.–65 C.E.) wrote to his mother on the subject:

> "To be absent from one's native land is unbearable," you say. Come now, observe this mass of people for whom the buildings of this great city scarce afford sufficient space. A great part of this crowd are absent from their native lands. They flock from towns and colonies, from every part of the world indeed. . . . Give orders that each shall be called by name and asked "Where do you come from?" You shall see that the greater part have left behind the place where they were born and come to this city, the greatest, the most beautiful city perhaps, but not their own.

Marginal note: Nearly everyone in late republican and imperial Rome came from somewhere else.

THE POETRY OF ROME: ELEGY AND SATIRE

The satirist Juvenal complained that there was no money in writing poetry. In Rome, at least, there was fame in it, and social acceptance. Several emperors were known as patrons of the arts, but writing was generally either integral to political activity—oratory and letter writing—or conducted in one's leisure or by those with independent incomes. All educated Romans were bilingual in Latin and Greek, and most higher education (rhetoric and philosophy) was conducted in Greek by teachers of Hellenistic origin. Unlike Homer in the Hellenistic world, there was no archetypal Roman poet. Rather, Latin literature grew out of imitation and translation from the Greek. Consequently, Roman writers developed a highly sophisticated system of allusion and reference. Because of their intimate familiarity with the Greek and Hellenistic traditions, they could make complex poetic and political arguments through slight variations in a conventional image, use of a term, character, or place-name closely associated with another poet, or similarities between a historical character and a contemporary figure. Latin required neither articles nor pronouns and had a flexible word order; it was a practical, pragmatic, and precise language, but it also offered a far greater potential for ambiguity of meaning, wordplay, and allusion than, for instance, most modern European languages. These qualities were ideally suited to an urban elite in a volatile and highly self-conscious society.

Most Latin literature was composed to be read aloud, but scrolls were status objects, and there was a vigorous publishing trade in classical Rome. Writing took place in one of three forms. Papyrus, made from the pith of an Egyptian marsh plant that was pounded into layers, was widely used in the east. More common in Italy and less expensive were parchment or vellum, made from the skins of cattle, sheep, or goats. All of these materials would be written upon with ink made from soot and water then stored in rolls up to sixteen feet in length. Wooden leaf tablets, thin enough to fold, could also be written on in ink. Alternatively, wooden stylus tablets with a recessed surface covered in colored wax could be inscribed with a bronze or iron stylus and were reusable (see Color Plate 9). By the fourth century, the parchment book or codex, bound on one edge, had replaced the scroll.

> *Most Latin literature was composed to be read aloud, but scrolls were status objects, and there was a vigorous publishing trade in classical Rome.*

Perhaps the most Roman of all literary genres were the erotic elegy and the satire. The elegy was transformed from its Greek model by the addition of an apparently autobiographical first-person narrator. The erotic poet was single-minded in his pursuit of love and generally turned his back on the traditionally public duties of the Roman citizen; Ovid would be banished in part for his apparent celebration of this new ethos in the elegies collected in the *Amores* (c. 20 B.C.E.) and later writings such as *The Art of Love* (c. 1 B.C.E.). A major influence on this poetry was Catullus (84–54 B.C.E.), whose school of "neoteric" poets was self-consciously modern, stressing emotionality, confessional detail, linguistic polish, and negligible subject matter over the rustic virtues of dignity, gravity, and civic duty. The neoterics preferred novelty and Alexandrian urbanity to old Roman virtue, and, like Ovid after them, they situated their amours firmly within their beloved city. Catullus paints a vivid if stylized portrait of late-republic Rome: its literati and social climbers, its courtesans and whores, its banquets and bar rooms. In one poem he skewers Ascanius for stealing napkins (it was customary to bring your own when you dined out); in another he mocks Victius for his bad breath; we have already encountered Egnatius's exotic dental hygiene.

As Catullus's many barbs about dining protocol make clear, eating was as important in Roman society as bathing. Dining was a setting for amorous encounters and also an important opportunity for the networking, deal making, and philosophizing that were central to the social life of the ruling class and its hangers-on. Readers of Plato's *Symposium* will be familiar with the traditional Greek combination of eating, drinking, and dialoguing. In Roman literature, discussions of food, as the scholar Emily Gower has observed, nearly always implied issues of taste, lifestyle, and philosophy. This is especially the case in the genre of satire, the very name of which derives from the term for a "full dish." Roman satire was a mixed bag of descriptions, observations, and exaggerations of contemporary life, using the language of ordinary conversation in a much less obviously polished verse than that of the elegy. There were two culinary traditions at stake in food metaphors: the communal meal as a symbolic re-enactment of social hierarchies—there was a strict protocol for seating the customary nine persons on the three couches surrounding the Roman table—and the Saturnalia, the December festival during which social distinctions were ignored and slaves were allowed temporary license to do as they liked.

In the *Satires* of Virgil's friend and contemporary Horace (65–8 B.C.E.), for instance, *sal* refers to both salt and wit, *jus* to both gravy and the law, and the poet's famous dictum on moderation—*iam satis est,* "that's quite enough"—applies an oft-broken law of dining to a stoic view of the world at large. Later satirists such as Petronius and Juvenal explore more fully the potential of excess, Petronius in his vivid portrait of the outrageously saturnalian feast thrown by the ex-slave Trimalchio, Juvenal in his hyperbolic indignation at a bloated imperial city: "What way out is there now your funds are exhausted and your gullet ever-swelling, your debts engulfing your whole inheritance in a stomach capacious enough for mounds of silver, flocks and estates?" Like the elegy, the satire focuses primarily on individuals in nonofficial settings. Despite its capacity for character assassination, it seldom ventures into political territory or *ad hominem* attacks. Ovid, exiled by Augustus for "a poem and an indiscretion"; Juvenal, banished by Domitian; and Petronius, forced by Nero to commit suicide, were all well aware that many subjects were off-limits to the poets of imperial Rome.

IMPERIUM SINE FINE

In the first book of the *Aeneid,* Jupiter prophesies that the land to be granted to the descendants of Aeneas will be an *imperium sine fine,* an empire without either temporal or geographical end. Virgil wrote these lines under the patronage of the first Roman emperor, Caesar Augustus (formerly Octavian), who reigned from 27 B.C.E. until 14 C.E. As the historian Tacitus later wrote, Augustus "seduced everyone with the sweetness of peace." The restrictions of the *princeps* seemed to many a small price to pay for putting an end to a hundred years of civil strife under the late republic and stabilizing a world now dominated by Rome. Until the late second century, the republic had done its fighting primarily against outside forces, most notably the Carthaginians, whose capital city they had razed at the end of the third Punic War in 146 B.C.E. Most scholars date the onset of internal trouble to attempts by two Roman tribunes, the Gracchi brothers, to deal with growing social inequality by measures such as land redistribution and the offer of citizenship to all Latins. Their challenge to constitutional order in the 130s and 120s caused a series of both reforms and grabs for power that climaxed in the dictatorship of Julius Caesar in 49 B.C.E. As with most leaders before and after, Caesar's power was based in the army he controlled and the reputation his victories had given him, most notably his subjugation of Gaul. When Caesar was assassinated in 44 C.E. by a group of republican senators, war broke out among his heirs and rivals, most notably his adopted son, Octavian, and Mark Antony. Octavian defeated Mark Antony and Antony's ally and lover, Cleopatra, at the decisive battle of Actium in 31 B.C.E., and the way was paved for him to become sole ruler.

The Roman Empire was a complex combination of military prowess and political savvy. The Roman legions were highly trained and well equipped and fought with disciplined efficiency. Repeated opposition, especially from rival powers, was savagely repressed, as in the leveling of Carthage. For the most part, however, defeated peoples retained a fair measure of autonomy as long as they paid the heavy taxes levied upon them by the central authority in Rome. The legionaries constructed carefully planned and laid-out provincial capitals throughout Roman territory, the origins of modern cities such

> *The Roman Empire was a complex combination of military prowess and political savvy.*

as London, Paris, and Córdoba. They also built an extensive network of paved roads to allow rapid movement of persons and goods between Rome and the provinces, and they constructed aqueducts to transport water. Local peoples were usually allowed to preserve their own languages, customs, and religions. At the same time, they were gradually incorporated into Roman culture through citizenship: all Latins by 90 B.C.E., wealthy provincials and legionary recruits in Italy and then in the east by the late first century C.E., and all freedmen and -women throughout the empire in 212 C.E. (although by this time it meant much less than it once had).

Expansion continued through the fourth century. At its height, the borders of Rome extended into Scotland in the British Isles and as far north as the Rhine and the Danube rivers in Europe, circling the Mediterranean from Gaul, Spain, North Africa, and Egypt through Palestine, Syria, Asia Minor, Greece, and the Balkans. Although the empire was increasingly destabilized from within and threatened from without, continued expansion was essential for establishing a new emperor's reputation and for bringing in new revenue from taxes and plunder including slaves, who were generally culled from "barbarian" peoples, those not sharing the language and customs of the Latins. The office of emperor carried increasingly autocratic powers and godlike status. It did not, however, provide either job security or assurance of succession. The preferred mode of inheritance was through an adopted son,

> *The office of emperor carried increasingly autocratic powers and godlike status. It did not, however, provide either job security or assurance of succession.*

but that didn't always work: in 69 C.E., for instance, the "year of four emperors," as Tacitus reported in shock, "The city was devastated by fires, the most ancient shrines were destroyed and the Capitol itself was fired by the hands of Roman citizens." The military played an increasingly prominent role in choosing emperors, and succession often meant no more than a series of military coups. The need for military support also contributed to the eventual fall of Rome as later emperors depended more and more on mercenaries from Germanic tribes to augment their forces.

HISTORY AND EPIC

The primary genres of Roman expansion were history and epic. While history included its fair share of mythmaking and epic was generally based on historical events, the genres remained distinct. Roman historiography began in the *Annales,* a year-by-year record of the republic from its earliest days. The influence of this chronological approach is evident in the *Histories* and *Annals* of Tacitus, which narrate events of the late first and early second centuries C.E., and Livy's monumental record of Rome *ab urbe condita,* "from the founding of the city." There were other forms of historiography, such as the supremely entertaining biographies in the *Lives of the Caesars* of Suetonius (70–160 C.E.), but the primary model was Livy's idealization of the ancient Roman character through a vivid chronicle of the deeds of its inhabitants through the death of Augustus, about a quarter of which has survived. Rome was a record-keeping society, setting down numerous laws and treaties and copious oratory and correspondence. Its historiographers' concern with memorializing the past and their consciousness of the ideological power of historical narrative was especially influential on post-medieval writers, not least of whom was the celebrated chronicler Edward Gibbon, whose

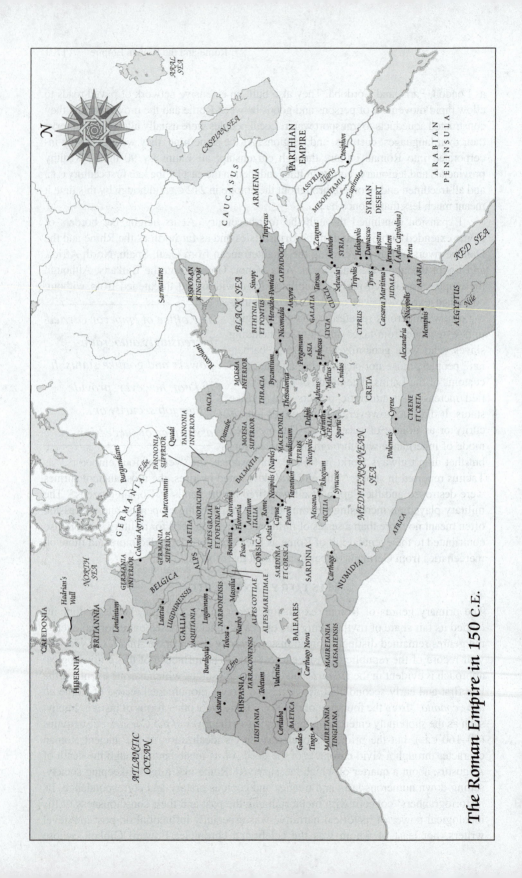

The Roman Empire in 150 C.E.

magnum opus, *The Decline and Fall of the Roman Empire* (1776–1788), molded the reception of Rome and its legacy for many generations.

While historiography developed a distinctly Roman form, epic remained self-consciously indebted to its Greek antecedents, most notably the Homeric poems the *Iliad* and the *Odyssey*. Epic had strict formal rules governing meter, language, and subject matter. The paradigm was Virgil's *Aeneid,* which transferred the archaic, orally composed, and mythic Homeric poems into a world simultaneously mythic and historical, archaic and contemporary. Rehearsing the matter both of the *Iliad*—the Trojan War—and the *Odyssey*—the difficult voyage home—the *Aeneid* created a monumental national epic for a new emperor and a new empire, pleading with both to return to their roots as well in the *mos maiorum* and its Stoic principles. There had been some precedent for the *Aeneid,* but what followed it was a veritable explosion of epics concerning other episodes of Roman history and Greek myth, including Lucan's dark and violent account of the civil war that had brought Julius Caesar to power. Two of the most enduring works of Latin literature—Lucretius's Epicurean account of the way of the natural world, *On the Nature of Things* (c. 54 B.C.E.), and Ovid's protean retelling of the entire corpus of Greek and Roman mythology, the *Metamorphoses* (2–8 C.E.)—brought the monumental scope and elevated style of epic to bear on subject matter and narrative forms that creatively stretched the epic's boundaries. Reaching its peak at the end of the republic and in the first centuries of the empire, Latin epic and historiography reflected the new preeminence of Rome in their scope and ambition. Still, the accomplishments of the empire were never recounted without at least a hint of ambivalence as to the sacrifice and suffering they entailed.

THE ETERNAL CITY IN RUINS

As first-century writers such as Lucan and Petronius made clear, the golden age of Augustus didn't last long (if it ever existed at all), and the empire was always a very complicated place in which to live. It endured by name until the fall of Constantinople to the Ottoman Turks in 1453, but from a Roman point of view it was all over by 410. The conversion of emperor Constantine in 324 that had inaugurated the spread of Christianity throughout western Europe was also responsible for the shift of imperial power eastward. A primary reason for the construction of Constantinople on the straits of the Bosphorus was to establish a Christian empire in a city free of the pagan temples and traditions that saturated Rome. Rome remained the seat of traditional religious practice, upheld by the old senate, which led a pagan revival in the fourth century. This revival reached its apogee with the accession of the emperor Julian (361–363), known as "the Apostate." Following his initiation as a neoplatonic theurgist, or performer of divine operations, Julian during his brief reign initiated a policy of religious toleration and outright administrative discrimination in favor of pagan individuals and communities.

> *. . . the golden age of Augustus didn't last long (if it ever existed at all), and the empire was always a very complicated place in which to live.*

Constantine had already built the first Saint Peter's in Rome, and the decades following his death saw a struggle within the city for religious supremacy and an external struggle with Constantinople as the capital of Christianity. The basis for Rome's preeminence was the traditional belief that Saint Peter, foremost of the twelve apostles and considered the church's first pope, had spent his last years and been martyred in Rome. Nevertheless, the most influential Christian figure of the time was probably Ambrose (340–397), bishop of the imperial capital of Milan in northern Italy, who excommunicated the emperor Theodosius in 390. Alexandria (in Egypt) and Antioch (in Syria) were the other patriarchal seats of the early church; during the same period the influence of Augustine in the North African bishopric of Hippo was also growing. The newly Christianized empire was awash with doctrinal controversy. Arianism, which denied the divinity of Jesus, had been declared a heresy in 325 and vigorously suppressed. It survived in the north, however, where an Arianist bishop had converted many of the Goths. For Christians, then, the northern invaders were not pagans but heretics.

Partially acculturated into a western empire that was rapidly being eclipsed by the east, the Goths used a combination of force and negotiation to extract concessions for several decades before Alaric finally led them into Rome in 410. Evidently not everyone was sorry for the change. According to the Christian priest Salvanius (c. 400–c. 480), many in Gaul felt that "the enemy is more lenient to them than the tax collectors," and already in the third century, the Gallic provinces had successfully broken away from the empire for a period of more than ten years. Nevertheless, the symbolism of Rome in the hands of northern barbarians sent shock waves throughout the empire. The church father Jerome, who while in Rome had commenced work on the Vulgate, his enduring Latin translation of the Bible, lamented from Palestine that "the head of the Roman empire was cut off, and, to speak more truly, the entire world perished with that single city." Rome continued to decline, and by the middle of the ninth century it had only seventeen thousand inhabitants. As the power of the medieval

> ... *ever since Alaric the ruins and past of Rome have overshadowed its present.*

papacy grew from that point, so did the city revive, but ever since Alaric the ruins and the past of Rome have overshadowed its present. From Dante and Petrarch through Shakespeare and Montaigne to Thomas Mann and Sigmund Freud, few Western writers have been able to resist the allure of those ruins.

Rome dominated Western culture and society through the Middle Ages, but rule by the Germanic tribes was far less centralized. It was also often at odds with the Eastern, or Byzantine, Empire, which remained wealthy, powerful, and unified for centuries more, taking back parts of Adriatic Italy from the Goths. Although their Arianism created tension with many of their orthodox Christian subjects, the Germanic rulers tended to maintain Roman administrators. Western emperors remained in at least putative power for most of the fifth century, but even rulers who replaced them, such as the Ostrogoth Theodoric (493–526), retained Roman-style adminstration, presented their rule as a continuation of the empire, and cultivated good relations with the papacy. Theodoric also shared with his Roman predecessors an intolerance for dissent. The philosopher-poet Boethius served as Theodoric's consul and bureaucrat for many years before he was implicated in a senatorial conspiracy and executed around 524. His *Consolation of Philosophy,* written in prison, has sometimes been called the last work of classical learning and sometimes the first of the Middle Ages. For just as it had several beginnings, there were many possible endings for classical Rome and many ways in which it was transformed, slowly and unevenly, into part of medieval Europe. As it faded in reality, what the Augustan poets had first celebrated as "the eternal city" grew ever-more powerful in memory.

PRONUNCIATIONS:

Actium: ACT-ee-um	*Juno:* JOO-noh
Caesar Augustus: SEE-zahr aw-GUH-stuhs	*Jupiter:* JOO-pi-tur
Caligula: ka-LI-geu-la	*Livy:* LI-vee
Cicero: SI-se-roh	*Minerva:* mi-NUR-vah
Cleopatra: klee-oh-PAH-trah	*Romulus:* ROM-you-luhs
Domitian: DO-mi-zhuhn	*Tiber:* TAI-bur

━━━━ ✖◆✖ ━━━━

Virgil
70–19 B.C.E.

From shortly after his death until just a few centuries ago, Publius Vergilius Maro was commonly regarded not only as the poet of Rome and the Roman Empire but also as a philosopher, prophet, sage, and even magician. One result of the legends surrounding Virgil was that the *Aeneid* was customarily used as a book of divination. Seeking guidance, readers would close their eyes, open the pages at random, and point a blind finger at a line of poetry by which they would direct their actions from that moment onward. In his medieval epic poem *The Divine Comedy,* Dante gave a similar authority to the *Aeneid,* invoking its words and its author as guide to the perilous task of journeying through the afterlife (see Volume B). Virgil would perhaps not have been surprised by such responses to the *Aeneid,* for seldom has a work of literature been so self-consciously focused on the effect it would have on its readers, on its culture, and on posterity.

There are several ways in which the *Aeneid* signals these intentions. The first is the thoroughness with which it revisits and revises the two founding epics of ancient Greece, the *Iliad* and the *Odyssey.* Because it sets its action during the aftermath of the Trojan War and because the path of its hero, Aeneas, follows in the trail of Odysseus's journey, the *Aeneid* operates as a Roman sequel to Homer. Because it switches allegiance, glorifying Troy and denigrating the Greek forces, it significantly reinterprets the Homeric epics as well. And because it tells its tale of the legendary past with one eye always fixed on the meaning of that past for the Roman present under the rule of Emperor Augustus, the *Aeneid* displays a consciousness of its place in history quite alien to the oral tradition represented by the Homeric poems.

LIFE AND WORKS

Born in 70 B.C.E. near the small Italian town of Mantua, Virgil came of age during a traumatic period of Roman history, nearly a century of recurring civil war. When Octavian defeated the forces of Marc Antony and Cleopatra in 31 B.C.E. and acceded soon after to the reins of empire as Augustus Caesar, he inaugurated a long-desired stretch of peace and stability as well as an end to the cherished tradition of the republic over which so much blood had been spilled. Both emotions are strongly registered in the ancient world depicted in the *Aeneid,* balanced as it is between repeated prophecies of the destined glories of Rome to come and the enormous suffering and hardship that will be required to get there. So the opening to Book 1 concludes majestically but also with a touch of exhaustion: "So hard and huge a task it was to found the Roman people."

Following the publication of his first collection of poetry, the *Bucolics,* or *Eclogues* (42–39 B.C.E.)—ten fairly short, loose adaptations of the Greek pastoral poems of Theocritus—Virgil found himself, like his younger friend Horace, a member of Octavian's inner circle by virtue of the patronage and friendship of Maecenas, an influential member of the aristocracy and one of Octavian's ministers. Over the next years, Virgil slowly polished his second collection, the *Georgics,* four books of verse concerning farming and beekeeping but equally immersed in mythology and contemporary events. Octavian reportedly ordered a preview reading of the barely completed *Georgics* by their author in 29 B.C.E.; Virgil's canonical status has never been in doubt since. He spent the last ten years of his life at work on the *Aeneid.* Apparently not yet satisfied with its form at the end of his life, he left orders for it to be burned. Augustus countermanded the order, consigning the manuscript to Virgil's colleague Varius to prepare it for publication (i.e., copying and circulation in manuscript form). It immediately became a school text, used for teaching grammar, verse, and philosophy; commented and glossed repeatedly; and frequently imitated, although for the most part timorously and from afar. Because the fourth of his *Eclogues* includes an enigmatic prophecy of a savior to come, Virgil was also rapidly assimilated as a forerunner of Christianity, and the *Aeneid* functioned throughout late antiquity and the Middle Ages as a linking text between Christian doctrine and the classical tradition, most famously in Dante's work.

The Story of the *Aeneid*

The *Aeneid* is composed of twelve books containing a total of just under ten thousand lines in the traditional six-beat meter of epic. The first six books recount the difficult journey of Aeneas from the defeated city of Troy to the shores of Italy, where he is fated to found Rome. The poem plunges *in medias res*—into the middle of the story—with Aeneas's fleet nearly destroyed by a storm roused by the goddess Juno, who bears various grudges against the Trojans and is determined to prevent or at least delay their ambitions. They manage to land safely on the North African coast, where they are taken in by Queen Dido, herself an exile engaged in building Carthage, a city that would much later become the opponent of Rome in three brutal conflicts, the so-called Punic Wars of the third and second centuries B.C.E. In Books 2 and 3, Aeneas tells Dido and her court the story of the fall of Troy and the early stages of his journey. Then, following the machinations of his mother, Venus, the pair conduct a short-lived but passionate affair that ends in catastrophe when Aeneas is ordered by the gods to return to his fated duty. Following further difficulties, Aeneas decides after a dream vision to journey into the underworld to meet and consult with the shade of his father, Anchises. In the Elysian Fields, Anchises shows Aeneas the souls waiting to return to the world above and sketches out his descendants in a prophetic history of Rome dating all the way through the recent civil war and the time of Augustus.

The final six books of the poem describe the war that awaits Aeneas after he lands in Latium on the coast of Italy. A series of broken treaties and much maneuvering by Juno and Venus lead to a conflict between the Trojans and their allies and the local king, Turnus, and his allies. Although traditionally neglected in favor of the more varied material of the first six books, the "Iliadic" second half of the *Aeneid* offers a sustained meditation on the costs of civil war and the pros and cons of empire building. The poem ends abruptly, offering not the closure of Aeneas's impending marriage with the Latinian princess Lavinia or his promised deification but his summary execution of Turnus as the defeated leader pleads for mercy.

Like much else in the poem, the ending has prompted debate over the years as to how we are meant to interpret Aeneas's action. This would appear to be a consistent artistic strategy throughout the poem. The *Aeneid* possesses a typological structure, constantly sending the reader back and forth between the legendary period of the poem's setting and the contemporary period of its composition. The character and choices of Aeneas constantly reflect on those of the current ruler, Augustus, who had recently concluded a civil war himself. The Dido episode is not only a tragic rendition of the conflict between individual desire and public duty but also a complex foreshadowing of the three Punic Wars, which ended in the destruction of Carthage by Rome in 146 B.C.E. The sympathy that Virgil imparts to Dido in this episode casts a shadow on the later episode, just as the wrath to which Aeneas succumbs in killing Turnus implicates in some way the character of Augustus. Virgil never makes a direct equation between past and present, nor does he give straightforward, symbolic meaning to any specific episodes. Instead, he sets up a framework of correspondences between the past and the present that invites the reader to seek meaning through a chain of comparisons.

Virgil and the Homeric Epics

A similar relationship exists with the Homeric epics, with which Virgil assumed his readers would be intimately familiar. One of Virgil's goals in rewriting episodes from the *Iliad* and the

Odyssey was to define what was specifically Roman about his own characters and epic. In Book 2, for example, the bloody encounter between Troy's ruler Priam and Achilles' son Pyrrhus can be compared to the concluding book of the *Iliad,* where Priam persuades Achilles to relent in his anger and return the body of Priam's son, Hektor, for proper burial (see page 238). In Virgil's account of the fall of Troy, Pyrrhus first slaughters another of Priam's sons before the father's eyes at the family altar and then butchers the aged man himself. The story is striking on its own terms, but the additional resonance of the Homeric comparison places the issues of heroism, piety, loss, exile, and fathers and sons in especially sharp relief.

On the level of language, the *Aeneid* also shuttles its readers back and forth between the ancient world of the Homeric epic and Virgil's contemporary world. He borrows techniques of oral composition to give his poem an archaic feel, heightening its effect of sublime distance from everyday life. Characters are referred to repeatedly by epithets such as "pious Aeneas" or "faithful Achates"; particular formulae such as "marvelous to tell" are repeated; different forces receive lengthy catalogues of names and lineage. The epic hexameter, a line composed of six equal parts, or "feet," is weighty and serious, although carefully varied to avoid monotony. Like the Greek, Latin meter was based on the length of vowels, determined by default (certain vowels are long by rule) and by placement (vowels are usually long when followed by two consonants, for example). The dactyl was the standard foot (long—short—short), but various of the six dactyls in a line could be changed to spondees (long—long) according to certain rules. In the previously cited line, "So hard and huge a task it was to found the Roman people" (Book 1, line 33), for example, an opening spondee and two more in the center lay a heavy stress on the solemn meaning of the line and on the key adjective, "Roman," in its middle:

> tāntǣ mōlĭs ĕrāt / Rōmānăm // cōndĕrĕ gēnt^xĕm.[1]

Word order in Latin is extremely flexible, allowing *Romanam* to come in the middle, and for the act of founding to be flanked by the adjective and noun being founded; a word-by-word rendering of the translator's language would read: "So hard and huge—task—was—Roman—to found—people."

PATTERNS OF MEANING

At the same time that Virgil strove to echo Homer, he also grounded his poem in the language and experience of his own day. He coined a good number of new words, and especially in his use of simile he was frequently and self-consciously anachronistic. The very first simile of the poem, for example, compares Neptune calming the waves to a veteran quieting a rioting crowd in the Roman Forum, a space that wouldn't be created until hundreds of years after the time in which the poem is set. Later in Book 1, we find Aeneas looking down on the rising walls of Carthage, marveling at the laws being enacted and the "magistrates and sacred senate" being chosen, as if Carthage were already modern Rome. Virgil chooses here to use the traditional epic device of a natural simile to describe a human phenomenon, comparing the scene to "bees in early summer." Here he also alludes to the final book of his previous work, the *Georgics,* which uses a long treatise on beekeeping to comment on the proper functioning of Roman society. The *Aeneid* can be read as a self-contained epic tale of exile and war, but the more one follows its many threads backward to Greek literature and forward to contemporary Rome, the deeper and more satisfying that tale becomes.

Virgil equally encourages and rewards the reader who follows the imagery forward and backward within the body of the poem. There are myriad formal patterns in the *Aeneid;* one of the most striking and most disturbing is the set of attributes Virgil associates with many of the female characters in the poem, beginning with the goddess Juno, whose implacably "black rage" determines that every time it seems a resolution has finally been reached, all hell will break loose once again.

---

1. A long vowel is marked by "‾" and a short one by "ˇ"; "/" marks a strong caesura, or pause, when a word ends after the first, long vowel in the foot (most commonly occurring, as here, in the 3rd foot); "//" marks a diaeresis, or a pause, when the end of a foot coincides with the end of a word; the final "ˣ" marks the last vowel, always read as long regardless.

A divine, overpowering, and contagious anger that descends thematically from the rage of Achilles in the *Iliad* and before that, the fury of the goddess Ishtar in *The Epic of Gilgamesh* (see page 77), Juno's rage (*ira*) has a terrifying effect on every character it infects. It transforms the steady and pious ruler Dido into a raving fury; it causes the Trojan women to torch their own fleet; through the fury Allecto it feeds Turnus's seething fire of injustice and the passions of the Latin queen Amata. It is particularly associated with imagery of fire and serpents, and although Virgil never quite identifies it with a feminine force per se, he certainly relates it to forces of uncontrollable emotion usually undergone by female characters in the mythological tradition before him.

The split between male and female is a primary opposition in a poem built around oppositions. Like all of the polarities we find in the poem, however, it becomes more complicated the more we study its details; after all, the last person in the poem to be overcome with *ira* is Aeneas himself in the final scene, even though Juno has agreed finally to give up her own wrath. Because of so many built-in cross-references and so much historical mirroring, the *Aeneid* is readily allegorized into symbolic meanings. This is particularly the case with the gods, who drive most of the poem's plot, causing events to occur by their conflicting machinations. The gods were also pretty much an archaism by the time Virgil was writing, at least in the sense of divine figures who interacted openly with mortals. Here, too, Virgil seems careful not to reduce them to a single meaning. There are moments when the gods behave like the distanced immortals of legend, moments when they react with petty human emotions, moments when they insist on the traditional virtues of Roman society, and moments when they appear irreligious and well-nigh immoral. Virgil's human characters, too, straddle a space between heroic, sometimes tragic paradigms of humanity and fully fleshed individuals with idiosyncratic, subjective takes on the world around them. Witness Aeneas's reaction when his father wants to show him his heroic future, the great tradition of Rome he is destined to sire. Rather than embrace his heroic role, Aeneas responds in the baffled tone of a long-suffering trooper who cannot imagine anyone being eager about anything related to the cruel world above:

> "Must we imagine,
> Father, there are souls that go from here
> Aloft to upper heaven, and once more
> Return to bodies' dead weight? The poor souls,
> How can they crave our daylight so?"

It is not just because of its philosophical and prophetic gravity that the *Aeneid* has laid such a claim on posterity; it is because Virgil was able to balance that gravity through a constant reminder of how it must have felt weighing on the hearts and minds of those required to sacrifice themselves to the goals they were responsible for achieving.

A selection from Virgil's *Georgics* appears as a Resonance to Francis Petrarch in Volume C.

PRONUNCIATIONS:
Aeneas: eh-NEE-uhs
Aeneid: eh-NEE-id
Allecto: ah-LEC-toh
Amata: ah-MAH-tah
Anchises: an-KAI-seez
Ascanius: as-KAY-nee-uhs
Dido: DAI-doh
Eclogues: EH-klogs
Elysian: eh-LEE-zhuhn
Lavinia: lah-VI-nee-uh
Pyrrhus: PIR-ruhs
Turnus: TUR-nuhs

from AENEID[1]

from Book 1

[A FATEFUL HAVEN]

I sing of warfare and a man at war.[2]
From the sea-coast of Troy in early days
He came to Italy by destiny,
To our Lavinian western shore,
A fugitive, this captain, buffeted
Cruelly on land as on the sea
By blows from powers of the air—behind them
Baleful Juno[3] in her sleepless rage.
And cruel losses were his lot in war,
Till he could found a city and bring home
His gods to Latium, land of the Latin race,
The Alban lords, and the high walls of Rome.
Tell me the causes now, O Muse, how galled
In her divine pride, and how sore at heart
From her old wound, the queen of gods compelled him—
A man apart, devoted to his mission—
To undergo so many perilous days
And enter on so many trials. Can anger
Black as this prey on the minds of heaven?
Tyrian settlers in that ancient time
Held Carthage, on the far shore of the sea,
Set against Italy and Tiber's mouth,
A rich new town, warlike and trained for war.[4]
And Juno, we are told, cared more for Carthage
Than for any walled city of the earth,
More than for Samos,[5] even. There her armor
And chariot were kept, and, fate permitting,
Carthage would be the ruler of the world.
So she intended, and so nursed that power.
But she had heard long since
That generations born of Trojan blood
Would one day overthrow her Tyrian walls,
And from that blood a race would come in time
With ample kingdoms, arrogant in war,

5

10

15

20

25

30

---

1. Translated by Robert Fitzgerald.
2. Virgil echoes the opening lines of Homer's *Iliad* and *Odyssey*. As does Homer, he begins in the midst of events; we find out how this situation arose only in Books 2 and 3.
3. Female counterpart of Jupiter in Roman religion, identified with the Greek Hera.

4. The historical Carthage was founded by Phoenicians from the eastern Mediterranean island harbor of Tyre around the 9th or 8th century B.C.E. on the northeast coast of Tunisia. All of the North African coastal zone, and sometimes all of Africa, was known to the Greeks as "Libya."
5. Ionian island, legendary birthplace of Hera.

35 For Libya's ruin: so the Parcae spun.[6]
 In fear of this, and holding in memory
 The old war she had carried on at Troy
 For Argos'° sake (the origins of that anger,   *the Greeks*
 That suffering, still rankled: deep within her,
40 Hidden away, the judgment Paris gave,[7]
 Snubbing her loveliness; the race she hated;
 The honors given ravished Ganymede),[8]
 Saturnian Juno,[9] burning for it all,
 Buffeted on the waste of sea those Trojans
45 Left by the Greeks and pitiless Achilles,[1]
 Keeping them far from Latium. For years
 They wandered as their destiny drove them on
 From one sea to the next: so hard and huge
 A task it was to found the Roman people.

50 They were all under sail in open water
 With Sicily just out of sight astern,
 Lighthearted as they plowed the whitecapped sea
 With stems of cutting bronze. But never free
 Of her eternal inward wound, the goddess
55 Said to herself:
      "Give up what I began?
 Am I defeated? Am I impotent
 To keep the king of Teucrians[2] from Italy?
 The Fates forbid me, am I to suppose?
 Could Pallas° then consume the Argive° fleet   *Athena / Greek*
60 With fire, and drown the crews,
 Because of one man's one mad act—the crime
 Of Ajax, son of Oïleus?[3] She—yes, she!—
 Hurled out of cloudland lancing fire of Jove,
 Scattered the ships, roughed up the sea with gales,
65 Then caught the man, bolt-struck, exhaling flames,
 In a whirlwind and impaled him on a rock.
 But I who walk as queen of all the gods,
 Sister and wife of Jove,[4] I must contend
 For years against one people! Who adores
70 The power of Juno after this, or lays
 An offering with prayer upon her altar?"

6. The Fates, who were represented as three old women spinning.
7. According to Greek myth, Hera and Athena (Roman: Minerva) supported the Greeks in the Trojan War because Paris had chosen Aphrodite as the most beautiful goddess in return for her promise to grant him Helen as a prize.
8. Son of Troy's founder, Tros. Because of his great beauty, he was carried off by Zeus to be his cupbearer on Mt. Olympus.
9. "Saturnian" because she was the daughter of Cronos, who was identified with the Roman god Saturnus.

1. Champion of the Greeks and the hero of the *Iliad*.
2. Teucer was a legendary king in the region of Troy whose daughter Zeus's son Dardanus married. Because of him the Trojans are sometimes called "Teucri" ("Teucrians") or from "Dardanus," "Dardanians."
3. Minor hero of the *Iliad*, said by legend to be hated by Athena because he had disrupted Athena's statue when he dragged Cassandra from it before raping her.
4. Another name for Jupiter, chief of the gods in Roman religion, who is identified with the Greek Zeus, the brother and husband of Hera.

Smouldering, putting these questions to herself,
The goddess made her way to stormcloud country,
Aeolia, the weather-breeding isle.
75 Here in a vast cavern King Aeolus[5]
Rules the contending winds and moaning gales
As warden of their prison. Round the walls
They chafe and bluster underground. The din
Makes a great mountain murmur overhead.
80 High on a citadel enthroned,
Scepter in hand, he mollifies their fury,
Else they might flay the sea and sweep away
Land masses and deep sky through empty air.
In fear of this, Jupiter hid them away
85 In caverns of black night. He set above them
Granite of high mountains—and a king
Empowered at command to rein them in
Or let them go. To this king Juno now
Made her petition:
                              "Aeolus, the father
90 Of gods and men decreed and fixed your power
To calm the waves or make them rise in wind.
The race I hate is crossing the Tuscan° sea,   *Tyrrhenian*
Transporting Ilium° with her household gods[6]—   *Troy*
Beaten as they are—to Italy.
                              Put new fury
95 Into your winds, and make the long ships founder!
Drive them off course! Throw bodies in the sea!
I have fourteen exquisite nymphs, of whom
The loveliest by far, Deïopëa,[7]
Shall be your own. I'll join you two in marriage,
100 So she will spend all future years with you,
As you so well deserve,
And make you father of her lovely children."

Said Aeolus:
                              "To settle on what you wish
Is all you need to do, your majesty.
105 I must perform it. You have given me
What realm I have. By your good offices
I rule with Jove's consent, and I recline
Among the gods at feasts, for you appoint me
Lord of wind and cloud."
                              Spearhaft reversed,

---

5. Ruler of the winds who aids Odysseus in Homer's
Odyssey, Book 10. Later tradition made him a deity.
6. The Penates, or household gods, were Roman spirits
connected with the inner part of the house—in essence,
the souls of the ancestors of the race.

7. In Greek mythology, nymphs were divinities of trees,
mountains, and rivers, who were personified as young and
beautiful women. Deïopëa was a sea nymph from the region of Cyrene, a major Greek colony in Africa.

110　He gave the hollow mountainside a stroke,
　　And, where a portal opened, winds in ranks,
　　As though drawn up for battle, hurtled through,
　　To blow across the earth in hurricane.
　　Over the sea, tossed up from the sea-floor,
115　Eastwind and Southwind, then the wild Southwest
　　With squall on squall came scudding down,
　　Rolling high combers shoreward.
　　　　　　　　　　　　　　　Now one heard
　　The cries of men and screech of ropes in rigging
　　Suddenly, as the stormcloud whipped away
120　Clear sky and daylight from the Teucrians'° eyes,　　　　*Trojans'*
　　And gloom of night leaned on the open sea.
　　It thundered from all quarters, as it lightened
　　Flash on flash through heaven. Every sign
　　Portended a quick death for mariners.
125　Aeneas on the instant felt his knees
　　Go numb and slack, and stretched both hands to heaven,
　　Groaning out:
　　　　　　　　"Triply lucky, all you men
　　To whom death came before your fathers' eyes
　　Below the wall at Troy! Bravest Danaan,°　　　　　*Greek*
130　Diomedes, why could I not go down
　　When you had wounded me, and lose my life
　　On Ilium's battlefield?[8] Our Hector lies there,
　　Torn by Achilles' weapon; there Sarpedon,
　　Our giant fighter, lies; and there the river
135　Simoïs washes down so many shields
　　And helmets, with strong bodies taken under!"[9]

　　As he flung out these words, a howling gust
　　From due north took the sail aback and lifted
　　Wavetops to heaven; oars were snapped in two;
140　The prow sheered round and left them broadside on
　　To breaking seas; over her flank and deck
　　A mountain of grey water crashed in tons.
　　Men hung on crests; to some a yawning trough
　　Uncovered bottom, boiling waves and sand.
145　The Southwind caught three ships and whirled them down
　　On reefs, hidden midsea, called by Italians
　　"The Altars"—razorbacks just under water.
　　The Eastwind drove three others from deep water
　　Into great shoals and banks, embedding them
150　And ringing them with sand, a desperate sight.

8. Diomedes was one of the principal Achaean warriors in the *Iliad*; in Book 5 he fought Aeneas. He appears in Book 11 of the *Aeneid*, where he refuses to join the forces massed against Aeneas. "Danaans" is a word used by Homer and other poets to mean the Greeks.

9. Hector was the leader of the Trojans, killed by Achilles (*Iliad*, bk. 22); Sarpedon, a son of Zeus and an ally of the Trojans, was killed by Achilles's companion Patroclus (*Iliad*, bk. 16); Simoïs was a river of Troy.

Before Aeneas' eyes a toppling billow
Struck the Lycians' ship, Orontës' ship,
Across the stern, pitching the steersman down
And overboard. Three times the eddying sea
155   Carried the ship around in the same place
Until the rapid whirlpool gulped it down.
A few men swimming surfaced in the welter.
So did shields, planks, precious things of Troy.
Ilioneus' good ship, brave Achatës' ship,
160   The ship that carried Abas, and the one
Aletës sailed in, hale in his great age,
Were all undone by the wild gale: their seams
Parted and let the enemy pour in.
During all this, Neptune[1] became aware
165   Of hurly-burly and tempest overhead,
Bringing commotion to the still sea-depth
And rousing him. He lifted his calm brow
Above the surface, viewing the great sea,
And saw Aeneas' squadron far and wide
170   Dispersed over the water, saw the Trojans
Overwhelmed, the ruining clouds of heaven,
And saw his angry sister's hand in all.
He called to him Eastwind and South and said:

"Are you so sure your line is privileged?
175   How could you dare to throw heaven and earth
Into confusion, by no will of mine,
And make such trouble? You will get from me—
But first to calm the rough sea; after this,
You'll pay a stricter penalty for your sins.
180   Off with you! Give this message to your king:
Power over the sea and the cruel trident
Were never his by destiny, but mine.
He owns the monstrous rocks, your home, Eastwind.
Let Aeolus ruffle in that hall alone
185   And lord it over winds shut in their prison."

Before the words were out, he quieted
The surging water, drove the clouds away,
And brought the sunlight back. Cymothoë
And Triton,[2] side by side, worked to dislodge
190   The grounded ships; then Neptune with his trident
Heaved them away, opened the miles of shoals,
Tempered the sea, and in his car departed
Gliding over the wave-tops on light wheels.

When rioting breaks out in a great city,
195   And the rampaging rabble goes so far

---

1. Roman version of the Greek sea god, Poseidon, brother of Zeus and Hera.

2. Cymothoë was one of the Nereids, or sea maidens. Triton was a son of Poseidon.

That stones fly, and incendiary brands—
For anger can supply that kind of weapon—
If it so happens they look round and see
Some dedicated public man, a veteran
200   Whose record gives him weight, they quiet down,
Willing to stop and listen.
Then he prevails in speech over their fury
By his authority, and placates them.
Just so, the whole uproar of the great sea
205   Fell silent, as the Father of it all,
Scanning horizons under the open sky,
Swung his team around and gave free rein
In flight to his eager chariot.[3]

                        Tired out,
Aeneas' people made for the nearest land,
210   Turning their prows toward Libya. There's a spot
Where at the mouth of a long bay an island
Makes a harbor, forming a breakwater
Where every swell divides as it comes in
And runs far into curving recesses.
215   There are high cliffs on this side and on that,
And twin peaks towering heavenward impend
On reaches of still water. Over these,
Against a forest backdrop shimmering,
A dark and shaggy grove casts a deep shade,
220   While in the cliffside opposite, below
The overhanging peaks, there is a cave
With fresh water and seats in the living rock,
The home of nymphs. Here never an anchor chain,
Never an anchor's biting fluke need hold
225   A tired ship.

                Aeneas put in here,
With only seven ships from his full number,
And longing for the firm earth underfoot
The Trojans disembarked, to take possession
Of the desired sand-beach. Down they lay,
230   To rest their brinesoaked bodies on the shore.
Achatës promptly struck a spark from flint
And caught it in dry leaves; he added tinder
Round about and waved it for a flame-burst.
Then they brought out the grain of Ceres, tainted
235   By sea water, and Ceres' implements,
And, weary of their troubles, made all ready
To dry and grind with millstones what they had.[4]

---

3. The first of the poem's epic similes, intentionally anachronistic in its comparison of Neptune to a "public man" placating a rioting crowd, embodying the Roman ideal of the *vir pietate gravis*, the man solemn and weighty with piety.

4. The Italian goddess Ceres was identified with the Greek Demeter, goddess of agriculture and fertility—hence the word "cereal" for edible grains. Her implements are the millstones and other tools for grinding grain.

Meanwhile, Aeneas climbed one of the peaks
For a long seaward view, hoping to sight
240 Gale-worn Antheus and the Phrygian° biremes,[5]   *Trojan*
Capys, or high poops bearing Caïcus' arms.
He found no ship in sight, but on the shore
Three wandering stags.[6] Behind them whole herds followed,
Grazing in a long line down the valleys.
245 Planting his feet, he took in hand the bow
And arrows carried by his aide, Achatës,
Then, aiming for the leaders with heads high
And branching antlers, brought them first to earth.
Next he routed the whole herd,
250 Driving them with his shafts through leafy places,
Shooting and shooting till he won the hunt
By laying seven carcasses on the ground,
A number equal to his ships. Then back
To port he went, and parcelled out the game
255 To his ships' companies. There he divided
The wine courtly Acestës had poured out
And given them on the Sicilian shore—
Full jugs of it—when they were about to sail.[7]
By this and by a simple speech Aeneas
260 Comforted his people:
                              "Friends and companions,
Have we not known hard hours before this?
My men, who have endured still greater dangers,
God will grant us an end to these as well.
You sailed by Scylla's rage, her booming crags,
265 You saw the Cyclops' boulders.[8] Now call back
Your courage, and have done with fear and sorrow.
Some day, perhaps, remembering even this
Will be a pleasure. Through diversities
Of luck, and through so many challenges,
270 We hold our course for Latium, where the Fates
Hold out a settlement and rest for us.
Troy's kingdom there shall rise again. Be patient:
Save yourselves for more auspicious days."

So ran the speech. Burdened and sick at heart,
275 He feigned hope in his look, and inwardly
Contained his anguish. Now the Trojan crews
Made ready for their windfall and their feast.
They skinned the deer, bared ribs and viscera,

5. Rowing ships with two levels of oars.
6. Many classical commentators interpreted the three stags as a figure representing the three Punic Wars that Rome would fight with Carthage.
7. Acestës was a Sicilian king who had hosted the Trojans in Sicily on their way to Carthage; he welcomes them again at his shores in Book 5.

8. The monster Scylla was traditionally said to be located across from the whirlpool of Charybdis in the straits of Messina between the island of Sicily and the boot of Italy. The Cyclops were one-eyed giants whom tradition placed on Sicily. Both monsters are encountered by Odysseus; Aeneas recounts both adventures in Book 3 of the *Aeneid*.

Then one lot sliced the flesh and skewered it
280   On spits, all quivering, while others filled
Bronze cooking pots and tended the beach fires.
All got their strength back from the meal, reclining
On the wild grass, gorging on venison
And mellowed wine. When hunger had been banished,
285   And tables put away, they talked at length
In hope and fear about their missing friends:
Could one believe they might be still alive,
Or had they suffered their last hour,
Never again to hear a voice that called them?
290   Aeneas, more than any, secretly
Mourned for them all—for that fierce man, Orontës,
Then for Amycus, then for the bitter fate
Of Lycus, for brave Gyas, brave Cloanthus.

It was the day's end when from highest air
295   Jupiter looked down on the broad sea
Flecked with wings of sails, and the land masses,
Coasts, and nations of the earth. He stood
On heaven's height and turned his gaze toward Libya,
And, as he took the troubles there to heart,
300   Venus[9] appealed to him, all pale and wan,
With tears in her shining eyes:
                                   "My lord who rule
The lives of men and gods now and forever,
And bring them all to heel with your bright bolt,
What in the world could my Aeneas do,
305   What could the Trojans do, so to offend you
That after suffering all those deaths they find
The whole world closed to them, because of Italy?
Surely from these the Romans are to come
In the course of years, renewing Teucer's line,
310   To rule the sea and all the lands about it,
According to your promise. What new thought
Has turned you from them, Father? I consoled myself
For Troy's fall, that grim ruin, weighing out
One fate against another in the scales.[1]
315   But now, when they have borne so many blows,
The same misfortune follows them. Great king,
What finish to their troubles will you give?
After Antenor slipped through the Achaeans
He could explore Illyrian coves and reach
320   In safety the Liburnians' inland kingdoms

9. Goddess of love, Aphrodite to the Greeks, daughter
of Zeus and Dione. She was the mother of Aeneas by
Anchises, a member of the royal house of Troy. In the
Iliad, she rescues Aeneas from duels with Diomedes and
Achilles.
1. The image of Zeus weighing two fates on the golden
scales appears twice in the *Iliad* (8.69 and 22.209).

And source of the Timavus.[2] Through nine openings
With a great rumble in the mountain wall
It bursts from the ground there and floods the fields
In a rushing sea. And yet he chose that place
325   For Padua and new homes for Teucrians,
Gave them a name, set up the arms of Troy,
And now rests in his peace. As for ourselves,
Your own children, whom you make heirs of heaven,
Our ships being lost (this is unspeakable!),
330   We are forsaken through one enemy's rage
And kept remote from Italy. Is this
The palm for loyalty? This our power restored?"

He smiled at her, the father of gods and men,
With that serenity that calms the weather,[3]
335   And lightly kissed his daughter. Then he said:

"No need to be afraid, Cytherëa.[4]
Your children's destiny has not been changed.
As promised, you shall see Lavinium's walls[5]
And take up, then, amid the stars of heaven
340   Great-souled Aeneas.[6] No new thought has turned me.
No, he, your son—now let me speak of him,
In view of your consuming care, at length,
Unfolding secret fated things to come[7]—
In Italy he will fight a massive war,
345   Beat down fierce armies, then for the people there
Establish city walls and a way of life.
When the Rutulians[8] are subdued he'll pass
Three summers of command in Latium,
Three years of winter quarters. But the boy,
350   Ascanius, to whom the name of Iulus
Now is added—Ilus while Ilium stood[9]—
Will hold the power for all of thirty years,
Great rings of wheeling months. He will transfer
His capital from Lavinium and make
355   A fortress, Alba Longa.[1] Three full centuries

2. A spring in northern Italy. In mythology, Antenor was an elderly and upright counselor in Troy during the siege. In Roman times, he was said to have settled at the head of the Adriatic, where he founded Padua. The Liburni were an Illyrian (Balkan) people on the northeast coast of the Adriatic, famous as seafarers and pirates in Roman times.
3. In Greek mythology, Zeus was the god of the sky and the weather.
4. Venus. Cythera is an island off the Peloponnese that in Greek myth was the birthplace of Aphrodite, who had a sanctuary there.
5. The large town founded where Aeneas will first land in Latium.
6. Jove predicts the eventual deification of Aeneas. A hero-cult of Aeneas existed by the 3rd century B.C.E.

7. The next 44 lines contain the first of the poem's prophecies linking Aeneas's legendary voyage with actual as well as mythical events in more recent Roman history.
8. The subjects of Turnus, Aeneas's rival in Italy.
9. Ascanius was Aeneas's son. The Julian clan (whose members included Julius Caesar and Augustus) called him "Iulus" and claimed descent from him. According to Virgil, they derived the name from "Ilus," the founder of Troy.
1. A city in the Alban hills about 13 miles southeast of Rome. Tradition placed the founding of Alba Longa c. 1152 B.C.E. It lost its primacy in Latium not long after the founding of Rome.

That kingdom will be ruled by Hector's race,
Until the queen and priestess, Ilia,[2]
Pregnant by Mars, will bear twin sons to him.
Afterward, happy in the tawny pelt

360   His nurse, the she-wolf, wears, young Romulus
Will take the leadership, build walls of Mars,
And call by his own name his people Romans.
For these I set no limits, world or time,
But make the gift of empire without end.

365   Juno, indeed, whose bitterness now fills
With fear and torment sea and earth and sky,
Will mend her ways, and favor them as I do,
Lords of the world, the toga-bearing Romans.
Such is our pleasure. As the years fall away,

370   An age comes when Assaracus' royal house
Will bring to servitude Thessalian Phthia,
Renowned Mycenae, too; and subjugate
Defeated Argos.[3] From that comely line
The Trojan Caesar comes, to circumscribe

375   Empire with Ocean, fame with heaven's stars.
Julius his name, from Iulus handed down:
All tranquil shall you take him heavenward
In time, laden with plunder of the East,
And he with you shall be invoked in prayer.[4]

380   Wars at an end, harsh centuries then will soften,
Ancient Fides and Vesta, Quirinus
With Brother Remus, will be lawgivers,[5]
And grim with iron frames, the Gates of War
Will then be shut: inside, unholy Furor,

385   Squatting on cruel weapons, hands enchained
Behind him by a hundred links of bronze,
Will grind his teeth and howl with bloodied mouth."[6]

That said, he sent the son of Maia[7] down
From his high place to make the land of Carthage,

390   The new-built town, receptive to the Trojans,
Not to allow Queen Dido, all unknowing

2. According to Roman legend, Ilia was a Vestal Virgin who bore two sons to the war god Mars (Greek: Ares). She was thrown into the river Tiber by her usurping uncle, and Romulus and Remus were raised by a she-wolf.
3. Jove predicts Trojan revenge in the form of the eventual Roman conquest of Greece. At the time of Homer, Phthia was the kingdom of Achilles, Mycenae of Agamemnon, and Argos of Diomedes. Greece and Macedonia became the Roman province of Achaea in 146 B.C.E.
4. Virgil presents the claim of the *gens Iulia* to descent from Ascanius and predicts the career of either Julius Caesar (100–44 B.C.E.) or his adopted son, Julius Caesar Octavianus (63 B.C.E.–14 C.E.), known also as "Augustus." Julius Caesar was officially deified as Divus Iulius in 42 B.C.E.; Virgil predicts the deification of Augustus, which

occurred after the poet's death, at the time of the emperor's funeral.
5. Fides was the Roman personification of Faith, and Vesta was the goddess of the hearth. Quirinus was the local deity of the Sabine community who settled on the Quirinal hill, later identified with Romulus.
6. In times of complete peace, the temple of Janus Geminus (the god of doors and gates) in the Forum in Rome would be closed, most famously in 29, following Augustus's victory in the civil war. *Furor,* the Latin word for fury or rage, personifies the irrationality of war, especially of the civil variety.
7. Hermes, the messenger of the gods, identified in Roman religion with Mercury, was originally a god of trade.

As to the fated future, to exclude them.
Through the vast air with stroking wings he flew
And came down quickly on the Libyan coast,
395   Performing Jove's command, so that at once
Phoenicians put aside belligerence
As the god willed. Especially the queen
Took on a peaceful mood, an open mind
Toward Teucrians.
                    But the dedicated man,
400   Aeneas, thoughtful through the restless night,
Made up his mind, as kindly daylight came,
To go out and explore the strange new places,
To learn what coast the wind had brought him to
And who were living there, men or wild creatures—
405   For wilderness was all he saw—and bring
Report back to his company. The ships
He hid beneath a hollowed rocky cliff
And groves that made a vault, trees all around
And deep shade quivering. He took his way
410   With only one man at his side, Achatës,
Hefting two hunting spears with broad steel points.
Then suddenly, in front of him,
His mother crossed his path in mid-forest,
Wearing a girl's shape and a girl's gear—
415   A Spartan girl, or like that one of Thrace,
Harpalycë,[8] who tires horses out,
Outrunning the swift Hebrus. She had hung
About her shoulders the light, handy bow
A huntress carries, and had given her hair
420   To the disheveling wind; her knees were bare,
Her flowing gown knotted and kirtled up.
She spoke first:
               "Ho, young fellows, have you seen—
Can you say where—one of my sisters here,
In a spotted lynx-hide, belted with a quiver,
425   Scouting the wood, or shouting on the track
Behind a foam-flecked boar?"
                       To Venus then
The son of Venus answered:
                       "No, I've heard
Or seen none of your sisters—only, how
Shall I address you, girl? Your look's not mortal,
430   Neither has your accent a mortal ring.
O Goddess, beyond doubt! Apollo's sister?[9]
One of the family of nymphs? Be kind,

8. A mythical Thracian princess raised by her father to be a warrior.
9. Artemis, the daughter of Zeus and Leto, was a virgin and huntress who was identified with the Italian moon goddess, Diana.

Whoever you may be, relieve our trouble,
Tell us under what heaven we've come at last,
435   On what shore of the world are we cast up,
Wanderers that we are, strange to this country,
Driven here by wind and heavy sea.
By my right hand many an offering
Will be cut down for you before your altars."
440   Venus replied:
                    "Be sure I am not fit
For any such devotion. Tyrian girls
Are given to wearing quivers and hunting boots
Of crimson, laced on the leg up to the knee.
This is the Punic kingdom that you see,
445   The folk are Tyrian, the town Agenor's.[1]
But neighboring lands belong to Libya,
A nation hard to fight against in war.
The ruler here is Dido,[2] of Tyre city,
In flight here from her brother—a long tale
450   Of wrong endured, mysterious and long.
But let me tell the main events in order.
Her husband was Sychaeus, of all Phoenicians
Richest in land, and greatly loved by her,
Ill-fated woman. Her father had given her,
455   A virgin still, in marriage, her first rite.
Her brother, though, held power in Tyre—Pygmalion,
A monster of wickedness beyond all others.
Between the two men furious hate arose,
And sacrilegiously before the altars,
460   Driven by a blind lust for gold, Pygmalion
Took Sychaeus by surprise and killed him
With a dagger blow in secret, undeterred
By any thought of Dido's love. He hid
What he had done for a long time, cozening° her,   *deceiving*
465   Deluding the sick woman with false hope.
But the true form of her unburied husband
Came in a dream: lifting his pallid face
Before her strangely, he made visible
The cruel altars and his body pierced,
470   Uncovering all the dark crime of the house.

He urged her then to make haste and take flight,
Leaving her fatherland, and to assist the journey
Revealed a buried treasure of old time,
Unknown to any, a weight of gold and silver.
475   Impelled by this, Dido laid her plans

---

1. In Greek mythology, Agenor was the Phoenician king
of Tyre and the father of Cadmus and Europa.
2. Dido was originally the name of a Phoenician goddess
but was later given to Elissa, the legendary daughter of
Belus of Tyre, whose story Venus tells here.

To get away and to equip her company.
All who hated the tyrant, all in fear
As bitter as her own, now came together,
And ships in port, already fitted out,
480 They commandeered, to fill with gold: the riches
Pygmalion had itched for went to sea,
And captaining the venture was a woman.
They sailed to this place where today you'll see
Stone walls going higher and the citadel
485 Of Carthage, the new town. They bought the land,
Called Drumskin from the bargain made, a tract
They could enclose with one bull's hide.[3]
What of yourselves? From what coast do you come?
Where are you bound?"
                              Then to the questioner
490 He answered sighing, bringing out the words
From deep within him:
                              "Goddess, if I should tell
Our story from the start, if you had leisure
To hear our annals of adversity,
Before I finished, the fair evening star
495 Would come to close Olympus and the day.
From old Troy—if the name of Troy has fallen
Perhaps upon your ears—we sailed the seas,
And yesterday were driven by a storm,
Of its own whim, upon this Libyan coast.
500 I am Aeneas, duty-bound, and known
Above high air of heaven by my fame,
Carrying with me in my ships our gods
Of hearth and home, saved from the enemy.
I look for Italy to be my fatherland,
505 And my descent is from all-highest Jove.
With twenty ships I mounted the Phrygian° sea,   *Aegean*
As my immortal mother showed the way.
I followed the given fates. Now barely seven
Ships are left, battered by wind and sea,
510 And I myself, unknown and unprovisioned,
Cross the Libyan wilderness, an exile
Driven from Europe and from Asia—"

But Venus chose to hear no more complaints
And broke in, midway through his bitterness:

515 "Whoever you are, I doubt Heaven is unfriendly
To you, as you still breathe life-giving air
On your approach to the Tyrian town. Go on:
Betake yourself this way to the queen's gate.

---

3. According to legend, a Libyan king granted Dido as much land as she could cover with a bull's hide. By cutting the hide into narrow strips, she obtained enough space to found Carthage.

Your friends are back. This is my news for you:
520   Your ships were saved and brought to shore again
By winds shifting north, or else my parents
Taught me augury to no purpose. Look:
See the twelve swans in line rejoicing there!
Jove's eagle, like a bolt out of the blue,
525   Had flurried them in open heaven, but now
They seem to be alighting one by one
Or looking down on those already grounded.
As they disport themselves, with flapping wings,
After their chanting flight about the sky,
530   Just so your ships and your ships' companies
Are either in port or entering under sail.
Go on then, where the path leads, go ahead!"

On this she turned away. Rose-pink and fair
Her nape shone, her ambrosial hair exhaled
535   Divine perfume, her gown rippled full length,
And by her stride she showed herself a goddess.
Knowing her for his mother, he called out
To the figure fleeting away:
                              "You! cruel, too!
Why tease your son so often with disguises?
540   Why may we not join hands and speak and hear
The simple truth?"
                    So he called after her,
And went on toward the town. But Venus muffled
The two wayfarers in grey mist, a cloak
Of dense cloud poured around them, so that no one
545   Had the power to see or to accost them,
Make them halt, or ask them what they came for.
Away to Paphos[4] through high air she went
In joy to see her home again, her shrine
And hundred altars where Sabaean incense[5]
550   Fumed and garlands freshened the air.
                                          Meanwhile
The two men pressed on where the pathway led,
Soon climbing a long ridge that gave a view
Down over the city and facing towers.
Aeneas found, where lately huts had been,
555   Marvelous buildings, gateways, cobbled ways,
And din of wagons. There the Tyrians
Were hard at work: laying courses for walls,
Rolling up stones to build the citadel,
While others picked out building sites and plowed
560   A boundary furrow. Laws were being enacted,

4. City-kingdom on the island of Cyprus and home of one of the most famous Aphrodite cults.   5. The Sabaeans were one of the chief peoples of Arabia, famous for precious spices and perfumes.

Magistrates and a sacred senate chosen.
Here men were dredging harbors, there they laid
The deep foundation of a theatre,
And quarried massive pillars to enhance
565   The future stage—as bees in early summer
In sunlight in the flowering fields
Hum at their work, and bring along the young
Full-grown to beehood; as they cram their combs
With honey, brimming all the cells with nectar,
570   Or take newcomers' plunder, or like troops
Alerted, drive away the lazy drones,
And labor thrives and sweet thyme scents the honey.
Aeneas said: "How fortunate these are
Whose city walls are rising here and now!"[6]

575   He looked up at the roofs, for he had entered,
Swathed in cloud—strange to relate—among them,
Mingling with men, yet visible to none.
In mid-town stood a grove that cast sweet shade
Where the Phoenicians, shaken by wind and sea,
580   Had first dug up that symbol Juno showed them,
A proud warhorse's head:[7] this meant for Carthage
Prowess in war and ease of life through ages.
Here being built by the Sidonian[8] queen
Was a great temple planned in Juno's honor,
585   Rich in offerings and the godhead there.
Steps led up to a sill of bronze, with brazen
Lintel, and bronze doors on groaning pins.
Here in this grove new things that met his eyes
Calmed Aeneas' fear for the first time.
590   Here for the first time he took heart to hope
For safety, and to trust his destiny more
Even in affliction. It was while he walked
From one to another wall of the great temple
And waited for the queen, staring amazed
595   At Carthaginian promise, at the handiwork
Of artificers and the toil they spent upon it:
He found before his eyes the Trojan battles
In the old war, now known throughout the world—
The great Atridae, Priam, and Achilles,
600   Fierce in his rage at both sides. Here Aeneas
Halted, and tears came.
                              "What spot on earth,"

---

6. The founding of Carthage was traditionally dated to 814 or 813 B.C.E., some four centuries after the destruction of Troy. This makes the meeting between Dido and Aeneas chronologically tricky but allows a profound symmetry between the two cities being founded by two exiles.
7. Tanit, the great goddess of Carthage, was identified early on with Juno. It was she who, according to legend, had led the Tyrians to the spot where they dug up a horse's head, a divine portent of the future site of their city.
8. Phoenician. Sidon was a Phoenician city on the coast of modern Lebanon.

He said, "what region of the earth, Achatës,
Is not full of the story of our sorrow?
Look, here is Priam. Even so far away
605   Great valor has due honor; they weep here
For how the world goes, and our life that passes
Touches their hearts. Throw off your fear. This fame
Insures some kind of refuge."9
                      He broke off
To feast his eyes and mind on a mere image,
610   Sighing often, cheeks grown wet with tears,
To see again how, fighting around Troy,
The Greeks broke here, and ran before the Trojans,
And there the Phrygians ran, as plumed Achilles
Harried them in his warcar. Nearby, then,
615   He recognized the snowy canvas tents
Of Rhesus,1 and more tears came: these, betrayed
In first sleep, Diomedes devastated,
Swording many, till he reeked with blood,
Then turned the mettlesome horses toward the beachhead
620   Before they tasted Trojan grass or drank
At Xanthus2 ford.
                And on another panel
Troilus,3 without his armor, luckless boy,
No match for his antagonist, Achilles,
Appeared pulled onward by his team: he clung
625   To his warcar, though fallen backward, hanging
On to the reins still, head dragged on the ground,
His javelin scribbling S's in the dust.
Meanwhile to hostile Pallas'° shrine   *Athena's*
The Trojan women walked with hair unbound,
630   Bearing the robe of offering, in sorrow,
Entreating her, beating their breasts. But she,
Her face averted, would not raise her eyes.4
And there was Hector, dragged around Troy walls
Three times, and there for gold Achilles sold him,
635   Bloodless and lifeless.5 Now indeed Aeneas
Heaved a mighty sigh from deep within him,
Seeing the spoils, the chariot, and the corpse
Of his great friend, and Priam, all unarmed,
Stretching his hands out.
                He himself he saw

9. The scenes from the Trojan War on the temple walls that Virgil recounts here constitute the poem's first use of the classical rhetorical figure of *ekphrasis,* the verbal description of a work of visual art. The scenes also serve to preview Aeneas's own account of the fall of Troy in Book 2.
1. A Thracian ally of the Trojans who was victimized by Odysseus and Diomedes in the night raid of the *Iliad,* Book 10, described here.
2. A river of Troy; its god was a son of Zeus.
3. One of the sons of Hecuba and Priam, king of Troy.

Non-Homeric sources told of his ambush by Achilles and slaughter at the altar of Apollo.
4. Like Hera, Athena sided with the Greeks; in this scene from the *Iliad,* Trojan women attempt unsuccessfully to appease her anger.
5. Achilles dragged Hector's body around the city in the *Iliad,* Book 22 (the scene is described in further detail in bk. 2); he ransomed the body to Hector's father, Priam, in the *Iliad,* Book 24.

640   In combat with the first of the Achaeans,[6]
        And saw the ranks of Dawn, black Memnon's arms;[7]
        Then, leading the battalion of Amazons
        With half-moon shields, he saw Penthesilëa
        Fiery amid her host, buckling a golden
645   Girdle beneath her bare and arrogant breast,
        A girl who dared fight men, a warrior queen.[8]
        Now, while these wonders were being surveyed
        By Aeneas of Dardania, while he stood
        Enthralled, devouring all in one long gaze,
650   The queen paced toward the temple in her beauty,
        Dido, with a throng of men behind.

[*Under Venus's influence, Dido welcomes Aeneas and his people. At dinner, Venus sends down Cupid to take the shape of Ascanius and awaken love for Aeneas in Dido. Dido asks Aeneas to recount the story of the fall of Troy and of his travels thereafter.*]

from Book 2

[HOW THEY TOOK THE CITY]

        The room fell silent, and all eyes were on him,
        As Father Aeneas from his high couch began:

        "Sorrow too deep to tell, your majesty,
        You order me to feel and tell once more:
5   How the Danaans leveled in the dust
        The splendor of our mourned-forever kingdom—
        Heartbreaking things I saw with my own eyes
        And was myself a part of. Who could tell them,
        Even a Myrmidon or Dolopian
10   Or ruffian of Ulysses, without tears?[1]
        Now, too, the night is well along, with dewfall
        Out of heaven, and setting stars weigh down
        Our heads toward sleep. But if so great desire
        Moves you to hear the tale of our disasters,
15   Briefly recalled, the final throes of Troy,
        However I may shudder at the memory
        And shrink again in grief, let me begin.[2]

        Knowing their strength broken in warfare, turned
        Back by the fates, and years—so many years—

---

6. The duel with Achilles in the *Iliad,* Book 20, from which Aeneas's mother rescues him.
7. A mythical king of Ethiopia, son of Aurora, goddess of Dawn, and Priam's brother Tithonus; he arrived after Hector's death and was killed by Achilles.
8. A mythical Amazon queen who led an army to aid Priam after Hector's death; she was killed by Achilles.

1. The Myrmidons were the subjects of Achilles, and the Dolopians were the subjects of Phoenix, who raised Achilles; in the *Aeneid,* Ulysses (Odysseus) is the archvillain of the Homeric Greeks.
2. Although the *Iliad* strongly foreshadows the fall of Troy, it doesn't recount the events themselves, which are filled in by post-Homeric poems.

20   Already slipped away, the Danaan captains
      By the divine handicraft of Pallas built
      A horse of timber, tall as a hill,
      And sheathed its ribs with planking of cut pine.
      This they gave out to be an offering
25   For a safe return by sea, and the word went round.
      But on the sly they shut inside a company
      Chosen from their picked soldiery by lot,
      Crowding the vaulted caverns in the dark—
      The horse's belly—with men fully armed.

30   Offshore there's a long island, Tenedos,
      Famous and rich while Priam's kingdom lasted,
      A treacherous anchorage now, and nothing more.
      They crossed to this and hid their ships behind it
      On the bare shore beyond. We thought they'd gone,
35   Sailing home to Mycenae³ before the wind,
      So Teucer's town is freed of her long anguish,
      Gates thrown wide! And out we go in joy
      To see the Dorian° campsites, all deserted,   *Greek*
      The beach they left behind. Here the Dolopians
40   Pitched their tents, here cruel Achilles lodged,
      There lay the ships, and there, formed up in ranks,
      They came inland to fight us. Of our men
      One group stood marveling, gaping up to see
      The dire gift of the cold unbedded goddess,
45   The sheer mass of the horse.
                                      Thymoetes shouts
      It should be hauled inside the walls and moored
      High on the citadel—whether by treason
      Or just because Troy's fate went that way now.
      Capys opposed him; so did the wiser heads:
50   'Into the sea with it,' they said, 'or burn it,
      Build up a bonfire under it,
      This trick of the Greeks, a gift no one can trust,
      Or cut it open, search the hollow belly!'

      Contrary notions pulled the crowd apart.
55   Next thing we knew, in front of everyone,
      Laocoön⁴ with a great company
      Came furiously running from the Height,
      And still far off cried out: 'O my poor people,
      Men of Troy, what madness has come over you?
60   Can you believe the enemy truly gone?
      A gift from the Danaans, and no ruse?
      Is that Ulysses' way, as you have known him?
      Achaeans must be hiding in this timber,

---

3. The kingdom of Agamemnon, leader of the Greeks.   4. A Trojan prince, brother of Anchises, and a priest of
Poseidon.

Or it was built to butt against our walls,
65   Peer over them into our houses, pelt
The city from the sky. Some crookedness
Is in this thing. Have no faith in the horse!
Whatever it is, even when Greeks bring gifts
I fear them, gifts and all.'
                                        He broke off then
70   And rifled his big spear with all his might
Against the horse's flank, the curve of belly.
It stuck there trembling, and the rounded hull
Reverberated groaning at the blow.
If the gods' will had not been sinister,
75   If our own minds had not been crazed,
He would have made us foul that Argive den
With bloody steel, and Troy would stand today—
O citadel of Priam, towering still!

But now look: hillmen, shepherds of Dardania,
80   Raising a shout, dragged in before the king
An unknown fellow with hands tied behind—
This all as he himself had planned,
Volunteering, letting them come across him,
So he could open Troy to the Achaeans.
85   Sure of himself this man was, braced for it
Either way, to work his trick or die.
From every quarter Trojans run to see him,
Ring the prisoner round, and make a game
Of jeering at him. Be instructed now
90   In Greek deceptive arts: one barefaced deed
Can tell you of them all.
As the man stood there, shaken and defenceless,
Looking around at ranks of Phrygians,
'Oh god,' he said, 'what land on earth, what seas
95   Can take me in? What's left me in the end,
Outcast that I am from the Danaans,
Now the Dardanians will have my blood?'

The whimpering speech brought us up short; we felt
A twinge for him. Let him speak up, we said,
100   Tell us where he was born, what news he brought,
What he could hope for as a prisoner.
Taking his time, slow to discard his fright,
He said:
                'I'll tell you the whole truth, my lord,
No matter what may come of it. Argive
105   I am by birth, and will not say I'm not.
That first of all: Fortune has made a derelict
Of Sinon, but the bitch
Won't make an empty liar of him, too.
Report of Palamedes may have reached you,

110   Scion of Belus' line, a famous man
    Who gave commands against the war.[5] For this,
    On a trumped-up charge, on perjured testimony,
    The Greeks put him to death—but now they mourn him,
    Now he has lost the light. Being kin to him,
115   In my first years I joined him as companion,
    Sent by my poor old father on this campaign,
    And while he held high rank and influence
    In royal councils, we did well, with honor.
    Then by the guile and envy of Ulysses—
120   Nothing unheard of there!—he left this world,
    And I lived on, but under a cloud, in sorrow,
    Raging for my blameless friend's downfall.
    Demented, too, I could not hold my peace
    But said if I had luck, if I won through
125   Again to Argos, I'd avenge him there.
    And I roused hatred with my talk; I fell
    Afoul now of that man. From that time on,
    Day in, day out, Ulysses
    Found new ways to bait and terrify me,
130   Putting out shady rumors among the troops,
    Looking for weapons he could use against me.
    He could not rest till Calchas served his turn[6]—
    But why go on? The tale's unwelcome, useless,
    If Achaeans are all one,
135   And it's enough I'm called Achaean, then
    Exact the punishment, long overdue;
    The Ithacan° desires it; the Atridae[7]   *Ulysses*
    Would pay well for it.'
                     Burning with curiosity,
    We questioned him, called on him to explain—
140   Unable to conceive such a performance,
    The art of the Pelasgian.[8] He went on,
    Atremble, as though he feared us:
                     'Many times
    The Danaans wished to organize retreat,
    To leave Troy and the long war, tired out.
145   If only they had done it! Heavy weather
    At sea closed down on them, or a fresh gale
    From the Southwest would keep them from embarking,
    Most of all after this figure here,
    This horse they put together with maple beams,
150   Reached its full height. Then wind and thunderstorms

---

5. Palamedes was a proverbially clever hero, hated by Odysseus because he had exposed the madness Odysseus feigned to avoid going to Troy. In revenge, Odysseus forged a letter from Priam to Palamedes offering gold to betray the Greeks and buried a sum of gold in Palamedes' quarters. Palamedes was stoned to death by the army.

6. Calchas was a seer with the Greek army in Troy (*Iliad*, bks.1 and 2).
7. The house of Atreus, the father of Agamemnon and Menelaus, the king of Sparta.
8. Greeks: the Pelasgians were mythical pre-Hellenic inhabitants of Greece.

Rumbled in heaven. So in our quandary
We sent Eurypylus[9] to Phoebus'° oracle,   *Apollo's*
And he brought back this grim reply:

'Blood and a virgin slain
155   You gave to appease the winds, for your first voyage
Troyward, O Danaans.[1] Blood again
And Argive blood, one life, wins your return.'

When this got round among the soldiers, gloom
Came over them, and a cold chill that ran
160   To the very marrow. Who had death in store?
Whom did Apollo call for? Now the man
Of Ithaca haled Calchas out among us
In tumult, calling on the seer to tell
The true will of the gods. Ah, there were many
165   Able to divine the crookedness
And cruelty afoot for me, but they
Looked on in silence. For ten days the seer
Kept still, kept under cover, would not speak
Of anyone, or name a man for death,
170   Till driven to it at last by Ulysses' cries—
By prearrangement—he broke silence, barely
Enough to designate me for the altar.
Every last man agreed. The torments each
Had feared for himself, now shifted to another,
175   All could endure. And the infamous day came,
The ritual, the salted meal, the fillets . . .
I broke free, I confess it, broke my chains,
Hid myself all night in a muddy marsh,
Concealed by reeds, waiting for them to sail
180   If they were going to.
                    Now no hope is left me
Of seeing my home country ever again,
My sweet children, my father, missed for years.
Perhaps the army will demand they pay
For my escape, my crime here, and their death,
185   Poor things, will be my punishment. Ah, sir,
I beg you by the gods above, the powers
In whom truth lives, and by what faith remains
Uncontaminated to men, take pity
On pain so great and so unmerited!'

190   For tears we gave him life, and pity, too.
Priam himself ordered the gyves° removed   *shackles*
And the tight chain between. In kindness then

9. A minor Iliadic figure related to the cults of Artemis and Dionysus, the god of wine and intoxication.
1. When the Greeks were unable to raise a fair wind to sail to Troy, Artemis, whom Agamemnon had offended, demanded that he sacrifice his daughter, Iphigenia, to appease her anger.

He said to him:
              'Whoever you may be,
The Greeks are gone; forget them from now on;

195   You shall be ours. And answer me these questions:
Who put this huge thing up, this horse?
Who designed it? What do they want with it?
Is it religious or a means of war?'

These were his questions. Then the captive, trained
200   In trickery, in the stagecraft of Achaea,
Lifted his hands unfettered to the stars.
'Eternal fires of heaven,' he began,
'Powers inviolable, I swear by thee,
As by the altars and blaspheming swords
205   I got away from, and the gods' white bands
I wore as one chosen for sacrifice,
This is justice, I am justified
In dropping all allegiance to the Greeks—
As I had cause to hate them; I may bring
210   Into the open what they would keep dark.
No laws of my own country bind me now.
Only be sure you keep your promises
And keep faith, Troy, as you are kept from harm
If what I say proves true, if what I give
215   Is great and valuable.
                   The whole hope
Of the Danaans, and their confidence
In the war they started, rested all along
In help from Pallas. Then the night came
When Diomedes and that criminal,
220   Ulysses, dared to raid her holy shrine.
They killed the guards on the high citadel
And ripped away the statue, the Palladium,
Desecrating with bloody hands the virginal
Chaplets of the goddess.[2] After that,
225   Danaan hopes waned and were undermined,
Ebbing away, their strength in battle broken,
The goddess now against them. This she made
Evident to them all with signs and portents.
Just as they set her statue up in camp,
230   The eyes, cast upward, glowed with crackling flames,
And salty sweat ran down the body. Then—
I say it in awe—three times, up from the ground,
The apparition of the goddess rose

---

2. The Trojan Palladium was a small wooden image of an armed Athena that fell from heaven in answer to the prayer of Ilus, Troy's founder. Because it protected the city from capture, Diomedes and Odysseus carried it off. According to later Roman tradition, this was only a copy, and Aeneas brought the original with him to Lavinium, from which it eventually reached Rome.

<pre>
      In a lightning flash, with shield and spear atremble.
235   Calchas divined at once that the sea crossing
      Must be attempted in retreat—that Pergamum³
      Cannot be torn apart by Argive swords
      Unless at Argos first they beg new omens,
      Carrying homeward the divine power
240   Brought overseas in ships. Now they are gone
      Before the wind to the fatherland, Mycenae,
      Gone to enlist new troops and gods. They'll cross
      The water again and be here, unforeseen.
      So Calchas read the portents. Warned by him,
245   They set this figure up in reparation
      For the Palladium stolen, to appease
      The offended power and expiate the crime.
      Enormous, though, he made them build the thing
      With timber braces, towering to the sky,
250   Too big for the gates, not to be hauled inside
      And give the people back their ancient guardian.
      If any hand here violates this gift
      To great Minerva, then extinction waits,
      Not for one only—would god it were so—
255   But for the realm of Priam and all Phrygians.
      If this proud offering, drawn by your hands,
      Should mount into your city, then so far
      As the walls of Pelops'⁴ town the tide of Asia
      Surges in war: that doom awaits our children.'

260   This fraud of Sinon, his accomplished lying,
      Won us over; a tall tale and fake tears
      Had captured us, whom neither Diomedes
      Nor Larisaean⁵ Achilles overpowered,
      Nor ten long years, nor all their thousand ships.

265   And now another sign, more fearful still,
      Broke on our blind miserable people,
      Filling us all with dread. Laocoön,
      Acting as Neptune's priest that day by lot,
      Was on the point of putting to the knife
270   A massive bull before the appointed altar,
      When ah—look there!
      From Tenedos, on the calm sea, twin snakes—
      I shiver to recall it—endlessly
      Coiling, uncoiling, swam abreast for shore,
275   Their underbellies showing as their crests
</pre>

---

3. The citadel of Troy; often used to refer to the city as a whole.
4. The father of Atreus, who gave his name to the Peloponnese, the southern part of Greece.

5. Larissa was the mother of Phthia, hero of the Thessalian kingdom ruled by Achilles. The chief city of Thessaly, in the northeast part of Greece, was named after her.

Reared red as blood above the swell; behind
They glided with great undulating backs.
Now came the sound of thrashed seawater foaming;
Now they were on dry land, and we could see
280   Their burning eyes, fiery and suffused with blood,
Their tongues a-flicker out of hissing maws.
We scattered, pale with fright. But straight ahead
They slid until they reached Laocoön.
Each snake enveloped one of his two boys,
285   Twining about and feeding on the body.
Next they ensnared the man as he ran up
With weapons: coils like cables looped and bound him
Twice round the middle; twice about his throat
They whipped their back-scales, and their heads towered,
290   While with both hands he fought to break the knots,
Drenched in slime, his head-bands black with venom,
Sending to heaven his appalling cries
Like a slashed bull escaping from an altar,
The fumbled axe shrugged off. The pair of snakes
295   Now flowed away and made for the highest shrines,
The citadel of pitiless Minerva,
Where coiling they took cover at her feet
Under the rondure of her shield. New terrors
Ran in the shaken crowd: the word went round
300   Laocoön had paid, and rightfully,
For profanation of the sacred hulk
With his offending spear hurled at its flank.

‘The offering must be hauled to its true home,’
They clamored. ‘Votive prayers to the goddess
305   Must be said there!’
                              So we breached the walls
And laid the city open. Everyone
Pitched in to get the figure underpinned
With rollers, hempen lines around the neck.
Deadly, pregnant with enemies, the horse
310   Crawled upward to the breach. And boys and girls
Sang hymns around the towrope as for joy
They touched it. Rolling on, it cast a shadow
Over the city’s heart. O Fatherland,
O Ilium, home of gods! Defensive wall
315   Renowned in war for Dardanus’s people!
There on the very threshold of the breach
It jarred to a halt four times, four times the arms
In the belly thrown together made a sound—
Yet on we strove unmindful, deaf and blind,
320   To place the monster on our blessed height.
Then, even then, Cassandra’s lips unsealed
The doom to come: lips by a god’s command

Never believed or heeded by the Trojans.[6]
So pitiably we, for whom that day
325 Would be the last, made all our temples green
With leafy festal boughs throughout the city.

As heaven turned, Night from the Ocean stream
Came on, profound in gloom on earth and sky
And Myrmidons in hiding. In their homes
330 The Teucrians lay silent, wearied out,
And sleep enfolded them. The Argive fleet,
Drawn up in line abreast, left Tenedos
Through the aloof moon's friendly stillnesses
And made for the familiar shore. Flame signals
335 Shone from the command ship. Sinon, favored
By what the gods unjustly had decreed,
Stole out to tap the pine walls and set free
The Danaans in the belly. Opened wide,
The horse emitted men; gladly they dropped
340 Out of the cavern, captains first, Thessandrus,
Sthenelus and the man of iron, Ulysses;
Hand over hand upon the rope, Acamas, Thoas,
Neoptolemus and Prince Machaon,[7]
Menelaus and then the master builder,
345 Epeos, who designed the horse decoy.
Into the darkened city, buried deep
In sleep and wine, they made their way,
Cut the few sentries down,
Let in their fellow soldiers at the gate,
350 And joined their combat companies as planned.

That time of night it was when the first sleep,
Gift of the gods, begins for ill mankind,
Arriving gradually, delicious rest.
In sleep, in dream, Hector appeared to me,
355 Gaunt with sorrow, streaming tears, all torn—
As by the violent car on his death day—
And black with bloody dust,
His puffed-out feet cut by the rawhide thongs.
Ah god, the look of him! How changed
360 From that proud Hector who returned to Troy
Wearing Achilles' armor, or that one
Who pitched the torches on Danaan ships;[8]
His beard all filth, his hair matted with blood,
Showing the wounds, the many wounds, received

6. Cassandra was the daughter of Priam and Hecuba. A post-Homeric tradition recounts that Apollo gave her prophetic powers in return for sexual favors. When she reneged on her promise, he decreed that her prophecies would always be disbelieved.
7. Greek champions. Acamas was son of Theseus, and Neoptolemus (also known as Pyrrhus) was son of Achilles.
8. In the *Iliad*, Books 11–17, Hector leads the Trojan forces to the Greek ships, which they threaten to set alight. He then defeats Patroclus and strips him of Achilles's armor.

365   Outside his father's city walls. I seemed
       Myself to weep and call upon the man
       In grieving speech, brought from the depth of me:

       'Light of Dardania, best hope of Troy,
       What kept you from us for so long, and where?
370   From what far place, O Hector, have you come,
       Long, long awaited? After so many deaths
       Of friends and brothers, after a world of pain
       For all our folk and all our town, at last,
       Boneweary, we behold you! What has happened
375   To ravage your serene face? Why these wounds?'

       He wasted no reply on my poor questions
       But heaved a great sigh from his chest and said:
       'Ai! Give up and go, child of the goddess,
       Save yourself, out of these flames. The enemy
380   Holds the city walls, and from her height
       Troy falls in ruin. Fatherland and Priam
       Have their due; if by one hand our towers
       Could be defended, by this hand, my own,
       They would have been. Her holy things, her gods
385   Of hearth and household Troy commends to you.
       Accept them as companions of your days;
       Go find for them the great walls that one day
       You'll dedicate, when you have roamed the sea.'

       As he said this, he brought out from the sanctuary
390   Chaplets and Vesta, Lady of the Hearth,
       With her eternal fire.
                              While I dreamed,
       The turmoil rose, with anguish, in the city.
       More and more, although Anchises' house
       Lay in seclusion, muffled among trees,
395   The din at the grim onset grew; and now
       I shook off sleep, I climbed to the roof top
       To cup my ears and listen. And the sound
       Was like the sound a grassfire makes in grain,
       Whipped by a Southwind, or a torrent foaming
400   Out of a mountainside to strew in ruin
       Fields, happy crops, the yield of plowing teams,
       Or woodlands borne off in the flood; in wonder
       The shepherd listens on a rocky peak.
       I knew then what our trust had won for us,
405   Knew the Danaan fraud: Deïphobus'[9]
       Great house in flames, already caving in
       Under the overpowering god of fire;

---

9. The son of Priam and Hecuba and Hector's dearest brother; he marries Helen after Paris's death. Aeneas discovers his gruesome fate in full when he encounters him in the Underworld in Book 6.

410   Ucalegon's already caught nearby;
       The glare lighting the straits beyond Sigeum;
       The cries of men, the wild calls of the trumpets.

                              * * *

       What was the fate of Priam, you may ask.[1]
660   Seeing his city captive, seeing his own
       Royal portals rent apart, his enemies
       In the inner rooms, the old man uselessly
       Put on his shoulders, shaking with old age,
       Armor unused for years, belted a sword on,
665   And made for the massed enemy to die.
       Under the open sky in a central court
       Stood a big altar; near it, a laurel tree
       Of great age, leaning over, in deep shade
       Embowered the Penatës.° At this altar   *household gods*
670   Hecuba and her daughters, like white doves
       Blown down in a black storm, clung together,
       Enfolding holy images in their arms.
       Now, seeing Priam in a young man's gear,
       She called out:
                          'My poor husband, what mad thought
675   Drove you to buckle on these weapons?
       Where are you trying to go? The time is past
       For help like this, for this kind of defending,
       Even if my own Hector could be here.
       Come to me now: the altar will protect us,
680   Or else you'll die with us.'
                                  She drew him close,
       Heavy with years, and made a place for him
       To rest on the consecrated stone.
                                       Now see
       Politës,[2] one of Priam's sons, escaped
       From Pyrrhus'° butchery and on the run   *Neoptolemus's*
685   Through enemies and spears, down colonnades,
       Through empty courtyards, wounded. Close behind
       Comes Pyrrhus burning for the death-stroke: has him,
       Catches him now, and lunges with the spear.
       The boy has reached his parents, and before them
690   Goes down, pouring out his life with blood.
       Now Priam, in the very midst of death,
       Would neither hold his peace nor spare his anger.

       'For what you've done, for what you've dared,' he said,
       'If there is care in heaven for atrocity,
695   May the gods render fitting thanks, reward you

---

1. The death of Priam is closely modeled after the ransom
of Hector's body in the *Iliad,* Book 24, a comparison
Priam himself makes to Achilles's son here.

2. A fast runner, Politës plays a minor role in the *Iliad* as a
scout.

As you deserve. You forced me to look on
At the destruction of my son: defiled
A father's eyes with death. That great Achilles
You claim to be the son of—and you lie—
700 Was not like you to Priam, his enemy;
To me who threw myself upon his mercy
He showed compunction, gave me back for burial
The bloodless corpse of Hector, and returned me
To my own realm.'
                        The old man threw his spear
705 With feeble impact; blocked by the ringing bronze,
It hung there harmless from the jutting boss.
Then Pyrrhus answered:
                        'You'll report the news
To Pelidës,° my father; don't forget   *Achilles*
My sad behavior, the degeneracy
710 Of Neoptolemus. Now die.'
                        With this,
To the altar step itself he dragged him trembling,
Slipping in the pooled blood of his son,
And took him by the hair with his left hand.
The sword flashed in his right; up to the hilt
715 He thrust it in his body.
                        That was the end
Of Priam's age, the doom that took him off,
With Troy in flames before his eyes, his towers
Headlong fallen—he that in other days
Had ruled in pride so many lands and peoples,
720 The power of Asia.
                        On the distant shore
The vast trunk headless lies without a name.

For the first time that night, inhuman shuddering
Took me, head to foot. I stood unmanned,
And my dear father's image came to mind
725 As our king, just his age, mortally wounded,
Gasped his life away before my eyes.
Creusa[3] came to mind, too, left alone;
The house plundered; danger to little Iulus.
I looked around to take stock of my men,
730 But all had left me, utterly played out,
Giving their beaten bodies to the fire
Or plunging from the roof.
                        It came to this,
That I stood there alone. And then I saw
Lurking beyond the doorsill of the Vesta,
735 In hiding, silent, in that place reserved,

---

3. Aeneas's wife, a daughter of Priam, and mother of Ascanius (Iulus).

The daughter of Tyndareus.° Glare of fires   *Helen*
Lighted my steps this way and that, my eyes
Glancing over the whole scene, everywhere.
That woman, terrified of the Trojans' hate
740   For the city overthrown, terrified too
Of Danaan vengeance, her abandoned husband's
Anger after years—Helen, that Fury
Both to her own homeland and Troy, had gone
To earth, a hated thing, before the altars.
745   Now fires blazed up in my own spirit—
A passion to avenge my fallen town
And punish Helen's whorishness.
                              'Shall this one
Look untouched on Sparta and Mycenae
After her triumph, going like a queen,
750   And see her home and husband, kin and children,
With Trojan girls for escort, Phrygian slaves?
Must Priam perish by the sword for this?
Troy burn, for this? Dardania's littoral°   *shore*
Be soaked in blood, so many times, for this?
755   Not by my leave. I know
No glory comes of punishing a woman,
The feat can bring no honor. Still, I'll be
Approved for snuffing out a monstrous life,
For a just sentence carried out. My heart
760   Will teem with joy in this avenging fire,
And the ashes of my kin will be appeased.'

So ran my thoughts. I turned wildly upon her,
But at that moment, clear, before my eyes—
Never before so clear—in a pure light
765   Stepping before me, radiant through the night,
My loving mother came: immortal, tall,
And lovely as the lords of heaven know her.
Catching me by the hand, she held me back,
Then with her rose-red mouth reproved me:
                                        'Son,
770   Why let such suffering goad you on to fury
Past control? Where is your thoughtfulness
For me, for us? Will you not first revisit
The place you left your father, worn and old,
Or find out if your wife, Creusa, lives,
775   And the young boy, Ascanius—all these
Cut off by Greek troops foraging everywhere?
Had I not cared for them, fire would by now
Have taken them, their blood glutted the sword.
You must not hold the woman of Laconia,[4]

4. The southeast district of the Peloponnesus, controlled by Sparta, the kingdom of Helen's husband, Menelaus.

780 That hated face, the cause of this, nor Paris.
The harsh will of the gods it is, the gods,
That overthrows the splendor of this place
And brings Troy from her height into the dust.
Look over there: I'll tear away the cloud
785 That curtains you, and films your mortal sight,
The fog around you.—Have no fear of doing
Your mother's will, or balk at obeying her.—
Look: where you see high masonry thrown down,
Stone torn from stone, with billowing smoke and dust,
790 Neptune is shaking from their beds the walls
That his great trident pried up, undermining,
Toppling the whole city down.[5] And look:
Juno in all her savagery holds
The Scaean Gates, and raging in steel armor
795 Calls her allied army from the ships.
Up on the citadel—turn, look—Pallas Tritonia°   *Athena*
Couched in a stormcloud, lightening, with her Gorgon![6]
The Father° himself empowers the Danaans,   *Jove*
Urges assaulting gods on the defenders.
800 Away, child; put an end to toiling so.
I shall be near, to see you safely home.'

She hid herself in the deep gloom of night,
And now the dire forms appeared to me
Of great immortals, enemies of Troy.
805 I knew the end then: Ilium was going down
In fire, the Troy of Neptune going down,
As in high mountains when the countrymen
Have notched an ancient ash, then make their axes
Ring with might and main, chopping away
810 To fell the tree—ever on the point of falling,
Shaken through all its foliage, and the treetop
Nodding; bit by bit the strokes prevail
Until it gives a final groan at last
And crashes down in ruin from the height.

815 Now I descended where the goddess guided,
Clear of the flames, and clear of enemies,
For both retired; so gained my father's door,
My ancient home. I looked for him at once,
My first wish being to help him to the mountains;
820 But with Troy gone he set his face against it,
Not to prolong his life, or suffer exile.

---

5. Poseidon and Apollo had originally built the walls of
Troy at the behest of Ilus's son, Laomedon.
6. The Gorgons were three female monsters with hideous
faces, glaring eyes, and snakes for hair. A Gorgon's head
turned whatever met its gaze to stone. Athena was generally represented in armor with the Gorgon's head on her
shield.

'The rest of you, all in your prime,' he said,
'Make your escape; you are still hale and strong.
If heaven's lords had wished me a longer span
825 They would have saved this home for me. I call it
More than enough that once before I saw
My city taken and wrecked, and went on living.
Here is my death bed, here. Take leave of me.
Depart now. I'll find death with my sword arm.
830 The enemy will oblige; they'll come for spoils.
Burial can be dispensed with. All these years
I've lingered in my impotence, at odds
With heaven, since the Father of gods and men
Breathed high winds of thunderbolt upon me
835 And touched me with his fire.'[7]

               He spoke on
In the same vein, inflexible. The rest of us,
Creusa and Ascanius and the servants,
Begged him in tears not to pull down with him
Our lives as well, adding his own dead weight
840 To the fates' pressure. But he would not budge,
He held to his resolve and to his chair.
I felt swept off again to fight, in misery
Longing for death. What choices now were open,
What chance had I?

             'Did you suppose, my father,
845 That I could tear myself away and leave you?
Unthinkable; how could a father say it?
Now if it please the powers above that nothing
Stand of this great city; if your heart
Is set on adding your own death and ours
850 To that of Troy, the door's wide open for it:
Pyrrhus will be here, splashed with Priam's blood;
He kills the son before his father's eyes,
The father at the altars.

             My dear mother,
Was it for this, through spears and fire, you brought me,
855 To see the enemy deep in my house,
To see my son, Ascanius, my father,
And near them both, Creusa,
Butchered in one another's blood? My gear,
Men, bring my gear. The last light calls the conquered.
860 Give me back to the Greeks. Let me take up
The combat once again. We shall not all
Die this day unavenged.'

             I buckled on

---

7. According to the myth, when Anchises broke his vow to Aphrodite not to reveal her identity as the mother of his child, he was lamed by a thunderbolt.

Swordbelt and blade and slid my left forearm
Into the shield-strap, turning to go out,
865   But at the door Creusa hugged my knees,
Then held up little Iulus to his father.

'If you are going out to die, take us
To face the whole thing with you. If experience
Leads you to put some hope in weaponry
870   Such as you now take, guard your own house here.
When you have gone, to whom is Iulus left?
Your father? Wife?—one called that long ago.'

She went on, and her wailing filled the house,
But then a sudden portent came, a marvel:
875   Amid his parents' hands and their sad faces
A point on Iulus' head seemed to cast light,
A tongue of flame that touched but did not burn him,
Licking his fine hair, playing round his temples.
We, in panic, beat at the flaming hair
880   And put the sacred fire out with water;
Father Anchises lifted his eyes to heaven
And lifted up his hands, his voice, in joy:

'Omnipotent Jupiter, if prayers affect you,
Look down upon us, that is all I ask,
885   If by devotion to the gods we earn it,
Grant us a new sign, and confirm this portent!'
The old man barely finished when it thundered
A loud crack on the left. Out of the sky
Through depths of night a star fell trailing flame
890   And glided on, turning the night to day.
We watched it pass above the roof and go
To hide its glare, its trace, in Ida's wood;[8]
But still, behind, the luminous furrow shone
And wide zones fumed with sulphur.
                                    Now indeed
895   My father, overcome, addressed the gods,
And rose in worship of the blessed star.

'Now, now, no more delay. I'll follow you.
Where you conduct me, there I'll be.
                            Gods of my fathers,
Preserve this house, preserve my grandson. Yours
900   This portent was. Troy's life is in your power.
I yield. I go as your companion, son.'
Then he was still. We heard the blazing town
Crackle more loudly, felt the scorching heat.

---

8. Ida was a range of mountains in southern Phrygia from the summit of which Zeus was said to have watched the Trojan War.

'Then come, dear father. Arms around my neck:
905 I'll take you on my shoulders, no great weight.
Whatever happens, both will face one danger,
Find one safety. Iulus will come with me,
My wife at a good interval behind.
Servants, give your attention to what I say.
910 At the gate inland there's a funeral mound
And an old shrine of Ceres the Bereft;
Near it an ancient cypress, kept alive
For many years by our fathers' piety.
By various routes we'll come to that one place.
915 Father, carry our hearthgods, our Penatës.
It would be wrong for me to handle them—
Just come from such hard fighting, bloody work—
Until I wash myself in running water.'

When I had said this, over my breadth of shoulder
920 And bent neck, I spread out a lion skin
For tawny cloak and stooped to take his weight.
Then little Iulus put his hand in mine
And came with shorter steps beside his father.
My wife fell in behind. Through shadowed places
925 On we went, and I, lately unmoved
By any spears thrown, any squads of Greeks,
Felt terror now at every eddy of wind,
Alarm at every sound, alert and worried
Alike for my companion and my burden.
930 I had got near the gate, and now I thought
We had made it all the way, when suddenly
A noise of running feet came near at hand,
And peering through the gloom ahead, my father
Cried out:
                'Run, boy; here they come; I see
935 Flame light on shields, bronze shining.'
                                              I took fright,
And some unfriendly power, I know not what,
Stole all my addled wits—for as I turned
Aside from the known way, entering a maze
Of pathless places on the run—
                                Alas,
940 Creusa, taken from us by grim fate, did she
Linger, or stray, or sink in weariness?
There is no telling. Never would she be
Restored to us. Never did I look back
Or think to look for her, lost as she was,
945 Until we reached the funeral mound and shrine
Of venerable Ceres. Here at last
All came together, but she was not there;
She alone failed her friends, her child, her husband.

Out of my mind, whom did I not accuse,
950   What man or god? What crueller loss had I
Beheld, that night the city fell? Ascanius,
My father, and the Teucrian Penates,
I left in my friends' charge, and hid them well
In a hollow valley.
                I turned back alone
955   Into the city, cinching my bright harness.
Nothing for it but to run the risks
Again, go back again, comb all of Troy,
And put my life in danger as before:
First by the town wall, then the gate, all gloom,
960   Through which I had come out—and so on backward,
Tracing my own footsteps through the night;
And everywhere my heart misgave me: even
Stillness had its terror. Then to our house,
Thinking she might, just might, have wandered there.
965   Danaans had got in and filled the place,
And at that instant fire they had set,
Consuming it, went roofward in a blast;
Flames leaped and seethed in heat to the night sky.
I pressed on, to see Priam's hall and tower.
970   In the bare colonnades of Juno's shrine
Two chosen guards, Phoenix[9] and hard Ulysses,
Kept watch over the plunder. Piled up here
Were treasures of old Troy from every quarter,
Torn out of burning temples: altar tables,
975   Robes, and golden bowls. Drawn up around them,
Boys and frightened mothers stood in line.
I even dared to call out in the night;
I filled the streets with calling; in my grief
Time after time I groaned and called Creusa,
980   Frantic, in endless quest from door to door.
Then to my vision her sad wraith appeared—
Creusa's ghost, larger than life, before me.
Chilled to the marrow, I could feel the hair
On my head rise, the voice clot in my throat;
985   But she spoke out to ease me of my fear:

'What's to be gained by giving way to grief
So madly, my sweet husband? Nothing here
Has come to pass except as heaven willed.
You may not take Creusa with you now;
990   It was not so ordained, nor does the lord
Of high Olympus give you leave. For you

---

9. The son of Amyntor, who took shelter with Achilles's father, Peleus, after quarrelling with his father. Made the king of the Dolopians, he reared Achilles and went with him to Troy as an old man.

Long exile waits, and long sea miles to plough.
You shall make landfall on Hesperia
Where Lydian Tiber flows,[1] with gentle pace,
995   Between rich farmlands, and the years will bear
Glad peace, a kingdom, and a queen for you.
Dismiss these tears for your beloved Creusa.
I shall not see the proud homelands of Myrmidons
Or of Dolopians, or go to serve
1000   Greek ladies, Dardan lady that I am
And daughter-in-law of Venus the divine.
No: the great mother of the gods detains me
Here on these shores. Farewell now; cherish still
Your son and mine.'
                              With this she left me weeping,
1005   Wishing that I could say so many things,
And faded on the tenuous air. Three times
I tried to put my arms around her neck,
Three times enfolded nothing, as the wraith
Slipped through my fingers, bodiless as wind,
1010   Or like a flitting dream.
                              So in the end
As night waned I rejoined my company.
And there to my astonishment I found
New refugees in a great crowd: men and women
Gathered for exile, young—pitiful people
1015   Coming from every quarter, minds made up,
With their belongings, for whatever lands
I'd lead them to by sea.
                              The morning star
Now rose on Ida's ridges, bringing day.
Greeks had secured the city gates. No help
1020   Or hope of help existed.
So I resigned myself, picked up my father,
And turned my face toward the mountain range."

[*Book 3: Aeneas's wanderings. After a winter's preparation, the Trojan survivors set out in search of their promised new home. They attempt unsuccessfully to settle in Thrace and Crete. After several years, Aeneas receives a detailed prophecy from Helenus, a son of Priam and Hecuba who has married Hector's wife, Andromache, and settled in Epirus. They cross over to Italy and sail on to Sicily, where they pick up one of Ulysses' men near Mount Aetna, the haunt of the Cyclops. They make their way around the south coast of Sicily to Drepanum, where Anchises dies.*]

---

1. Hesperia, "the Western land," is a poetic name for Italy; the Tiber is the chief river of central Italy and flows through Rome.

Book 4

[THE PASSION OF THE QUEEN]

The queen, for her part, all that evening ached
With longing that her heart's blood fed, a wound
Or inward fire eating her away.
The manhood of the man, his pride of birth,
5 Came home to her time and again; his looks,
His words remained with her to haunt her mind,
And desire for him gave her no rest.

                          When Dawn
Swept earth with Phoebus' torch° and burned away   *the sun*
Night-gloom and damp, this queen, far gone and ill,
10 Confided to the sister of her heart:
"My sister Anna, quandaries and dreams
Have come to frighten me—such dreams!

                         Think what a stranger
Yesterday found lodging in our house:
How princely, how courageous, what a soldier.
15 I can believe him in the line of gods,
And this is no delusion. Tell-tale fear
Betrays inferior souls. What scenes of war
Fought to the bitter end he pictured for us!
What buffetings awaited him at sea!
20 Had I not set my face against remarriage
After my first love died and failed me, left me
Barren and bereaved—and sick to death
At the mere thought of torch and bridal bed—
I could perhaps give way in this one case
25 To frailty. I shall say it: since that time
Sychaeus, my poor husband, met his fate,
And blood my brother shed stained our hearth gods,
This man alone has wrought upon me so
And moved my soul to yield. I recognize
30 The signs of the old flame, of old desire.
But O chaste life, before I break your laws,
I pray that Earth may open, gape for me
Down to its depth, or the omnipotent
With one stroke blast me to the shades, pale shades
35 Of Erebus[1] and the deep world of night!
That man who took me to himself in youth
Has taken all my love; may that man keep it,
Hold it forever with him in the tomb."

At this she wept and wet her breast with tears.
40 But Anna answered:
                  "Dearer to your sister

---

1. Primeval darkness, sprung from Chaos, the father of Day by his sister, Night.

Than daylight is, will you wear out your life,
Young as you are, in solitary mourning,
Never to know sweet children, or the crown
Of joy that Venus brings? Do you believe
This matters to the dust, to ghosts in tombs?
Granted no suitors up to now have moved you,
Neither in Libya nor before, in Tyre—
Iarbas[2] you rejected, and the others,
Chieftains bred by the land of Africa
Their triumphs have enriched—will you contend
Even against a welcome love? Have you
Considered in whose lands you settled here?
On one frontier the Gaetulans, their cities,
People invincible in war—with wild
Numidian horsemen, and the offshore banks,
The Syrtës; on the other, desert sands,
Bone-dry, where fierce Barcaean nomads range.[3]
Or need I speak of future wars brought on
From Tyre, and the menace of your brother?
Surely by dispensation of the gods
And backed by Juno's will, the ships from Ilium
Held their course this way on the wind.
Sister,
What a great city you'll see rising here,
And what a kingdom, from this royal match!
With Trojan soldiers as companions in arms
By what exploits will Punic glory grow!
Only ask the indulgence of the gods,
Win them with offerings, give your guests ease,
And contrive reasons for delay, while winter
Gales rage, drenched Orion[4] storms at sea,
And their ships, damaged still, face iron skies."

This counsel fanned the flame, already kindled,
Giving her hesitant sister hope, and set her
Free of scruple. Visiting the shrines
They begged for grace at every altar first,
Then put choice rams and ewes to ritual death
For Ceres Giver of Laws, Father Lyaeus,
Phoebus, and for Juno most of all
Who has the bonds of marriage in her keeping.[5]

2. The Libyan king with whom Dido made the bargain of the bull's hide.

3. The Berber inhabitants of Numidia, west and south of Carthaginian territory, were nomadic herdsmen who had become warlike by the Second Punic War. The Syrtës were dangerous shoals and shallows of the Libyan continental shelf.

4. A mighty hunter who was eventually transformed into the constellation known by his name.

5. "Lyaeus" was a frequent poetic cult title for Bacchus; "pater" ("father") was often used for gods and heroes as a mark of respect. One of the roles Juno took from Hera was the protector of marriage.

80   Dido herself, splendidly beautiful,
      Holding a shallow cup, tips out the wine
      On a white shining heifer, between the horns,
      Or gravely in the shadow of the gods
      Approaches opulent altars. Through the day
85   She brings new gifts, and when the breasts are opened
      Pores over organs, living still, for signs.
      Alas, what darkened minds have soothsayers!
      What good are shrines and vows to maddened lovers?
      The inward fire eats the soft marrow away,
90   And the internal wound bleeds on in silence.

      Unlucky Dido, burning, in her madness
      Roamed through all the city, like a doe
      Hit by an arrow shot from far away
      By a shepherd hunting in the Cretan woods—
95   Hit by surprise, nor could the hunter see
      His flying steel had fixed itself in her;
      But though she runs for life through copse and glade
      The fatal shaft clings to her side.
                              Now Dido
      Took Aeneas with her among her buildings,
100   Showed her Sidonian wealth, her walls prepared,
      And tried to speak, but in mid-speech grew still.
      When the day waned she wanted to repeat
      The banquet as before, to hear once more
      In her wild need the throes of Ilium,
105   And once more hung on the narrator's words.
      Afterward, when all the guests were gone,
      And the dim moon in turn had quenched her light,
      And setting stars weighed weariness to sleep,
      Alone she mourned in the great empty hall
110   And pressed her body on the couch he left:
      She heard him still, though absent—heard and saw him.
      Or she would hold Ascanius in her lap,
      Enthralled by him, the image of his father,
      As though by this ruse to appease a love
115   Beyond all telling.
                        Towers, half-built, rose
      No farther; men no longer trained in arms
      Or toiled to make harbors and battlements
      Impregnable. Projects were broken off,
      Laid over, and the menacing huge walls
120   With cranes unmoving stood against the sky.

      As soon as Jove's dear consort saw the lady
      Prey to such illness, and her reputation
      Standing no longer in the way of passion,

Saturn's daughter[6] said to Venus:

               "Wondrous!

125   Covered yourself with glory, have you not,
You and your boy, and won such prizes, too.
Divine power is something to remember
If by collusion of two gods one mortal
Woman is brought low.

                    I am not blind.

130   Your fear of our new walls has not escaped me,
Fear and mistrust of Carthage at her height.
But how far will it go? What do you hope for,
Being so contentious? Why do we not
Arrange eternal peace and formal marriage?

135   You have your heart's desire: Dido in love,
Dido consumed with passion to her core.
Why not, then, rule this people side by side
With equal authority? And let the queen
Wait on her Phrygian lord, let her consign

140   Into your hand her Tyrians as a dowry."

Now Venus knew this talk was all pretence,
All to divert the future power from Italy
To Libya; and she answered:

                   "Who would be
So mad, so foolish as to shun that prospect

145   Or prefer war with you? That is, provided
Fortune is on the side of your proposal.
The fates here are perplexing: would one city
Satisfy Jupiter's will for Tyrians
And Trojan exiles? Does he approve

150   A union and a mingling of these races?
You are his consort: you have every right
To sound him out. Go on, and I'll come, too."

But regal Juno pointedly replied:
"That task will rest with me. Just now, as to

155   The need of the moment and the way to meet it,
Listen, and I'll explain in a few words.
Aeneas and Dido in her misery
Plan hunting in the forest, when the Titan
Sun[7] comes up with rays to light the world,

160   While beaters in excitement ring the glens
My gift will be a black raincloud, and hail,
A downpour, and I'll shake heaven with thunder.
The company will scatter, lost in gloom,

---

6. Saturn was identified with the Greek Cronos, father of Hera, Zeus, Hestia, Demeter, Poseidon, and Hades.

7. The Greek sun god Helios was the son of the Titan Hyperion; Helios became identified by the Greeks with Apollo, the god of prophecy, by the time of Euripides.

As Dido and the Trojan captain come
165   To one same cavern. I shall be on hand,
And if I can be certain you are willing,
There I shall marry them and call her his.
A wedding, this will be."
                                        Then Cytherëa,
Not disinclined, nodded to Juno's plea,
170   And smiled at the stratagem now given away.

Dawn came up meanwhile from the Ocean stream,
And in the early sunshine from the gates
Picked huntsmen issued: wide-meshed nets and snares,
Broad spearheads for big game, Massylian[8] horsemen
175   Trooping with hounds in packs keen on the scent.
But Dido lingered in her hall, as Punic
Nobles waited, and her mettlesome hunter
Stood nearby, cavorting in gold and scarlet,
Champing his foam-flecked bridle. At long last
180   The queen appeared with courtiers in a crowd,
A short Sidonian cloak edged in embroidery
Caught about her, at her back a quiver
Sheathed in gold, her hair tied up in gold,
And a brooch of gold pinning her scarlet dress.
185   Phrygians came in her company as well,
And Iulus, joyous at the scene. Resplendent
Above the rest, Aeneas walked to meet her,
To join his retinue with hers. He seemed—
Think of the lord Apollo in the spring
190   When he leaves wintering in Lycia
By Xanthus torrent, for his mother's isle
Of Delos, to renew the festival;
Around his altars Cretans, Dryopës,
And painted Agathyrsans raise a shout,
195   But the god walks the Cynthian ridge alone
And smooths his hair, binds it in fronded laurel,
Braids it in gold; and shafts ring on his shoulders.[9]
So elated and swift, Aeneas walked
With sunlit grace upon him.
                                        Soon the hunters,
200   Riding in company to high pathless hills,
Saw mountain goats shoot down from a rocky peak
And scamper on the ridges; toward the plain
Deer left the slopes, herding in clouds of dust
In flight across the open lands. Alone,
205   The boy Ascanius, delightedly riding

8. The Massyli were a people of northern Africa.
9. Xanthus was the major river of the region of Lycia in southwest Asia Minor, where there was an important sanctuary of Leto, the mother of Apollo. Delos is a small island in the Aegean, mythological birthplace of Apollo and Artemis, an important center of worship, and the seat of an oracle of Apollo. Cynthia is a mountain of Delos. Cretans, Dryopës, and Agathyrsans were peoples associated with the cult of Apollo.

His eager horse amid the lowland vales,
Outran both goats and deer. Could he only meet
Amid the harmless game some foaming boar,
Or a tawny lion down from the mountainside!

210 Meanwhile in heaven began a rolling thunder,
And soon the storm broke, pouring rain and hail.
Then Tyrians and Trojans in alarm—
With Venus' Dardan grandson—ran for cover
Here and there in the wilderness, as freshets
215 Coursed from the high hills.
                              Now to the self-same cave
Came Dido and the captain of the Trojans.
Primal Earth herself and Nuptial Juno
Opened the ritual, torches of lightning blazed,
High Heaven became witness to the marriage,
220 And nymphs cried out wild hymns from a mountain top.

That day was the first cause of death, and first
Of sorrow. Dido had no further qualms
As to impressions given and set abroad;
She thought no longer of a secret love
225 But called it marriage. Thus, under that name,
She hid her fault.
                   Now in no time at all
Through all the African cities Rumor[1] goes—
Nimble as quicksilver among evils. Rumor
Thrives on motion, stronger for the running,
230 Lowly at first through fear, then rearing high,
She treads the land and hides her head in cloud.
As people fable it, the Earth, her mother,
Furious against the gods, bore a late sister
To the giants Coeus and Enceladus,[2]
235 Giving her speed on foot and on the wing:
Monstrous, deformed, titanic. Pinioned, with
An eye beneath for every body feather,
And, strange to say, as many tongues and buzzing
Mouths as eyes, as many pricked-up ears,
240 By night she flies between the earth and heaven
Shrieking through darkness, and she never turns
Her eye-lids down to sleep. By day she broods,
On the alert, on rooftops or on towers,
Bringing great cities fear, harping on lies
245 And slander evenhandedly with truth.
In those days Rumor took an evil joy
At filling countrysides with whispers, whispers,

---

1. Rumor appears in Hesiod as a Greek god whose work is "never quite in vain"; Virgil portrays her as midway between a god and an allegory of the social effects of rumor (*fama*).

2. According to Hesiod, the giants were sons of Ge (Earth). After the defeat of their rebellion against the gods, the giants were buried under volcanoes in Greece and Italy, Enceladus under Aetna in Sicily.

Gossip of what was done, and never done:
How this Aeneas landed, Trojan born,
250   How Dido in her beauty graced his company,
Then how they reveled all the winter long
Unmindful of the realm, prisoners of lust.

These tales the scabrous goddess put about
On men's lips everywhere. Her twisting course
255   Took her to King Iarbas, whom she set
Ablaze with anger piled on top of anger.
Son of Jupiter Hammon by a nymph,
A ravished Garamantean,[3] this prince
Had built the god a hundred giant shrines,
260   A hundred altars, each with holy fires.
Alight by night and day, sentries on watch,
The ground enriched by victims' blood, the doors
Festooned with flowering wreaths. Before his altars
King Iarbas, crazed by the raw story,
265   Stood, they say, amid the Presences,°   *spirits*
With supplicating hands, pouring out prayer:
"All powerful Jove, to whom the feasting Moors
At ease on colored couches tip their wine,
Do you see this? Are we then fools to fear you
270   Throwing down your bolts? Those dazzling fires
Of lightning, are they aimless in the clouds
And rumbling thunder meaningless? This woman
Who turned up in our country and laid down
A tiny city at a price, to whom
275   I gave a beach to plow—and on my terms—
After refusing to marry me has taken
Aeneas to be master in her realm.
And now Sir Paris with his men, half-men,
His chin and perfumed hair tied up
280   In a Maeonian bonnet, takes possession.[4]
As for ourselves, here we are bringing gifts
Into these shrines—supposedly your shrines—
Hugging that empty fable."
                              Pleas like this
From the man clinging to his altars reached
285   The ears of the Almighty. Now he turned
His eyes upon the queen's town and the lovers
Careless of their good name; then spoke to Mercury,
Assigning him a mission:
                              "Son, bestir yourself,
Call up the Zephyrs,° take to your wings and glide.   *winds*
290   Approach the Dardan captain where he tarries

3. An African people; Hammon was a Libyan god identified with Jupiter.
4. Iarbas compares Aeneas to Paris, the abductor of Helen,
who was regarded as unmanly, more interested in seduction than warfare. "Maeonia" was an old name for Lydia
and denotes the Asiatic origin of the Trojans.

Rapt in Tyrian Carthage, losing sight
Of future towns the fates ordain. Correct him,
Carry my speech to him on the running winds:
No son like this did his enchanting mother
295 Promise to us, nor such did she deliver
Twice from peril at the hands of Greeks.
He was to be the ruler of Italy,
Potential empire, armorer of war;
To father men from Teucer's noble blood
300 And bring the whole world under law's dominion.
If glories to be won by deeds like these
Cannot arouse him, if he will not strive
For his own honor, does he begrudge his son,
Ascanius, the high strongholds of Rome?
305 What has he in mind? What hope, to make him stay
Amid a hostile race, and lose from view
Ausonian[5] progeny, Lavinian lands?
The man should sail: that is the whole point.
Let this be what you tell him, as from me."

310 He finished and fell silent. Mercury
Made ready to obey the great command
Of his great father, and he first tied on
The golden sandals, winged, that high in air
Transport him over seas or over land
315 Abreast of gale winds; then he took the wand
With which he summons pale souls out of Orcus
And ushers others to the undergloom,
Lulls men to slumber or awakens them,
And opens dead men's eyes.[6] This wand in hand,
320 He can drive winds before him, swimming down
Along the stormcloud. Now aloft, he saw
The craggy flanks and crown of patient Atlas,[7]
Giant Atlas, balancing the sky
Upon his peak—his pine-forested head
325 In vapor cowled, beaten by wind and rain.
Snow lay upon his shoulders, rills cascaded
Down his ancient chin and beard a-bristle,
Caked with ice. Here Mercury of Cyllenë[8]
Hovered first on even wings, then down
330 He plummeted to sea-level and flew on
Like a low-flying gull that skims the shallows
And rocky coasts where fish ply close inshore.

---

5. Italian. From an ancient name for central and southern Italy.
6. In addition to his role as messenger, Mercury was the conductor of souls of the dead to the underworld. Orcus was an infernal deity in Greek mythology, identified in Roman religion with Dis, god of the underworld.

7. The Atlas mountains run through northern Africa; Greek mythology made them a Titan's son who was punished by having to support the skies on his head and hands.
8. Hermes was born on Mt. Cyllenë in Arcadia.

So, like a gull between the earth and sky,
The progeny of Cyllenë, on the wing
335 From his maternal grandsire, split the winds
To the sand bars of Libya.
                              Alighting tiptoe
On the first hutments, there he found Aeneas
Laying foundations for new towers and homes.
He noted well the swordhilt the man wore,
340 Adorned with yellow jasper; and the cloak
Aglow with Tyrian dye upon his shoulders—
Gifts of the wealthy queen, who had inwoven
Gold thread in the fabric. Mercury
Took him to task at once:[9]
                              "Is it for you
345 To lay the stones for Carthage's high walls,
Tame husband that you are, and build their city?
Oblivious of your own world, your own kingdom!
From bright Olympus he that rules the gods
And turns the earth and heaven by his power—
350 He and no other sent me to you, told me
To bring this message on the running winds:
What have you in mind? What hope, wasting your days
In Libya? If future history's glories
Do not affect you, if you will not strive
355 For your own honor, think of Ascanius,
Think of the expectations of your heir,
Iulus, to whom the Italian realm, the land
Of Rome, are due."
                              And Mercury, as he spoke,
Departed from the visual field of mortals
360 To a great distance, ebbed in subtle air.
Amazed, and shocked to the bottom of his soul
By what his eyes had seen, Aeneas felt
His hackles rise, his voice choke in his throat.
As the sharp admonition and command
365 From heaven had shaken him awake, he now
Burned only to be gone, to leave that land
Of the sweet life behind. What can he do? How tell
The impassioned queen and hope to win her over?
What opening shall he choose? This way and that
370 He let his mind dart, testing alternatives,
Running through every one. And as he pondered
This seemed the better tactic: he called in
Mnestheus, Sergestus and stalwart Serestus,
Telling them:
                              "Get the fleet ready for sea,

---

9. Mercury repeats Jove's speech word for word. This is one of the many ways Virgil mimics Homeric oral conventions.

375   But quietly, and collect the men on shore.
      Lay in ship stores and gear."
                                    As to the cause
      For a change of plan, they were to keep it secret,
      Seeing the excellent Dido had no notion,
      No warning that such love could be cut short;
380   He would himself look for the right occasion,
      The easiest time to speak, the way to do it.
      The Trojans to a man gladly obeyed.

      The queen, for her part, felt some plot afoot
      Quite soon—for who deceives a woman in love?
385   She caught wind of a change, being in fear
      Of what had seemed her safety. Evil Rumor,
      Shameless as before, brought word to her
      In her distracted state of ships being rigged
      In trim for sailing. Furious, at her wits' end,
390   She traversed the whole city, all aflame
      With rage, like a Bacchantë driven wild
      By emblems shaken, when the mountain revels
      Of the odd year possess her, when the cry
      Of Bacchus rises and Cithaeron calls
395   All through the shouting night.[1] Thus it turned out
      She was the first to speak and charge Aeneas:

      "You even hoped to keep me in the dark
      As to this outrage, did you, two-faced man,
      And slip away in silence? Can our love
400   Not hold you, can the pledge we gave not hold you,
      Can Dido not, now sure to die in pain?
      Even in winter weather must you toil
      With ships, and fret to launch against high winds
      For the open sea? Oh, heartless!
                                        Tell me now,
405   If you were not in search of alien lands
      And new strange homes, if ancient Troy remained,
      Would ships put out for Troy on these big seas?
      Do you go to get away from me? I beg you,
      By these tears, by your own right hand, since I
410   Have left my wretched self nothing but that—
      Yes, by the marriage that we entered on,
      If ever I did well and you were grateful
      Or found some sweetness in a gift from me,
      Have pity now on a declining house!
415   Put this plan by, I beg you, if a prayer

---

1. Bacchantës, or maenads, were initiates in the cult of Bacchus (Greek: Dionysus), usually women, whose ritual behavior when possessed by their god was characterized by wild dancing and ecstatic behavior. The most famous and most extreme portrait of Dionysiac behavior was in Euripides' play *The Bacchae,* where king Pentheus is torn apart by his mother on Mt. Cithaeron when he refuses to recognize the new god.

Is not yet out of place.
Because of you, Libyans and nomad kings
Detest me, my own Tyrians are hostile;
Because of you, I lost my integrity
420   And that admired name by which alone
I made my way once toward the stars.
                                    To whom
Do you abandon me, a dying woman,
Guest that you are—the only name now left
From that of husband? Why do I live on?
425   Shall I, until my brother Pygmalion comes
To pull my walls down? Or the Gaetulan
Iarbas leads me captive? If at least
There were a child by you for me to care for,
A little one to play in my courtyard
430   And give me back Aeneas, in spite of all,
I should not feel so utterly defeated,
Utterly bereft."
                         She ended there.
The man by Jove's command held fast his eyes
And fought down the emotion in his heart.
435   At length he answered:
                              "As for myself, be sure
I never shall deny all you can say,
Your majesty, of what you meant to me.
Never will the memory of Elissa°   *Dido*
Stale for me, while I can still remember
440   My own life, and the spirit rules my body.
As to the event, a few words. Do not think
I meant to be deceitful and slip away.
I never held the torches of a bridegroom,
Never entered upon the pact of marriage.
445   If Fate permitted me to spend my days
By my own lights, and make the best of things
According to my wishes, first of all
I should look after Troy and the loved relics
Left me of my people. Priam's great hall
450   Should stand again; I should have restored the tower
Of Pergamum for Trojans in defeat.
But now it is the rich Italian land
Apollo tells me I must make for: Italy,
Named by his oracles.[2] There is my love;
455   There is my country. If, as a Phoenician,
You are so given to the charms of Carthage,
Libyan city that it is, then tell me,
Why begrudge the Teucrians new lands

2. Aeneas recounted this episode to Dido as part of his wanderings in Book 3.

For homesteads in Ausonia? Are we not
460 Entitled, too, to look for realms abroad?
Night never veils the earth in damp and darkness,
Fiery stars never ascend the east,
But in my dreams my father's troubled ghost
Admonishes and frightens me. Then, too,
465 Each night thoughts come of young Ascanius,
My dear boy wronged, defrauded of his kingdom,
Hesperian lands of destiny. And now
The gods' interpreter, sent by Jove himself—
I swear it by your head and mine—has brought
470 Commands down through the racing winds! I say
With my own eyes in full daylight I saw him
Entering the building! With my very ears
I drank his message in! So please, no more
Of these appeals that set us both afire.
475 I sail for Italy not of my own free will."

During all this she had been watching him
With face averted, looking him up and down
In silence, and she burst out raging now:

"No goddess was your mother. Dardanus
480 Was not the founder of your family.
Liar and cheat! Some rough Caucasian cliff
Begot you on flint. Hyrcanian tigresses[3]
Tendered their teats to you. Why should I palter?
Why still hold back for more indignity?
485 Sigh, did he, while I wept? Or look at me?
Or yield a tear, or pity her who loved him?
What shall I say first, with so much to say?
The time is past when either supreme Juno
Or the Saturnian father viewed these things
490 With justice. Faith can never be secure.
I took the man in, thrown up on this coast
In dire need, and in my madness then
Contrived a place for him in my domain,
Rescued his lost fleet, saved his shipmates' lives.
495 Oh, I am swept away burning by furies!
Now the prophet Apollo, now his oracles,
Now the gods' interpreter, if you please,
Sent down by Jove himself, brings through the air
His formidable commands! What fit employment
500 For heaven's high powers! What anxieties
To plague serene immortals! I shall not
Detain you or dispute your story. Go,
Go after Italy on the sailing winds,

3. Caucasian and Hyrcanian (referring to regions near the Caspian Sea) are used as epitomes of Asian barbarism and savagery in contrast to the Roman civility claimed by Aeneas.

Look for your kingdom, cross the deepsea swell!
505 If divine justice counts for anything,
I hope and pray that on some grinding reef
Midway at sea you'll drink your punishment
And call and call on Dido's name!
From far away I shall come after you
510 With my black fires, and when cold death has parted
Body from soul I shall be everywhere
A shade° to haunt you! You will pay for this,   *spirit*
Unconscionable! I shall hear! The news will reach me
Even among the lowest of the dead!"

515 At this abruptly she broke off and ran
In sickness from his sight and the light of day,
Leaving him at a loss, alarmed, and mute
With all he meant to say. The maids in waiting
Caught her as she swooned and carried her
520 To bed in her marble chamber.
                                        Duty-bound,
Aeneas, though he struggled with desire
To calm and comfort her in all her pain,
To speak to her and turn her mind from grief,
And though he sighed his heart out, shaken still
525 With love of her, yet took the course heaven gave him
And went back to the fleet. Then with a will
The Teucrians fell to work and launched the ships
Along the whole shore: slick with tar each hull
Took to the water. Eager to get away,
530 The sailors brought oar-boughs out of the woods
With leaves still on, and oaken logs unhewn.
Now you could see them issuing from the town
To the water's edge in streams, as when, aware
Of winter, ants will pillage a mound of spelt
535 To store it in their granary; over fields
The black battalion moves, and through the grass
On a narrow trail they carry off the spoil;
Some put their shoulders to the enormous weight
Of a trundled grain, while some pull stragglers in
540 And castigate delay; their to-and-fro
Of labor makes the whole track come alive.
At that sight, what were your emotions, Dido?
Sighing how deeply, looking out and down
From your high tower on the seething shore
545 Where all the harbor filled before your eyes
With bustle and shouts! Unconscionable Love,
To what extremes will you not drive our hearts!
She now felt driven to weep again, again
To move him, if she could, by supplication,
550 Humbling her pride before her love—to leave

Nothing untried, not to die needlessly.

"Anna, you see the arc of waterfront
All in commotion: they come crowding in
From everywhere. Spread canvas calls for wind,
555   The happy crews have garlanded the sterns.
If I could brace myself for this great sorrow,
Sister, I can endure it, too. One favor,
Even so, you may perform for me.
Since that deserter chose you for his friend
560   And trusted you, even with private thoughts,
Since you alone know when he may be reached,
Go, intercede with our proud enemy.
Remind him that I took no oath at Aulis
With Danaans to destroy the Trojan race;[4]
565   I sent no ship to Pergamum.° Never did I   *Troy*
Profane his father Anchises' dust and shade.
Why will he not allow my prayers to fall
On his unpitying ears? Where is he racing?
Let him bestow one last gift on his mistress:
570   This, to await fair winds and easier flight.
Now I no longer plead the bond he broke
Of our old marriage, nor do I ask that he
Should live without his dear love, Latium,
Or yield his kingdom. Time is all I beg,
575   Mere time, a respite and a breathing space
For madness to subside in, while my fortune
Teaches me how to take defeat and grieve.
Pity your sister. This is the end, this favor—
To be repaid with interest when I die."

580   She pleaded in such terms, and such, in tears,
Her sorrowing sister brought him, time and again.
But no tears moved him, no one's voice would he
Attend to tractably. The fates opposed it;
God's will blocked the man's once kindly ears.
585   And just as when the north winds from the Alps
This way and that contend among themselves
To tear away an oaktree hale with age,
The wind and tree cry, and the buffeted trunk
Showers high foliage to earth, but holds
590   On bedrock, for the roots go down as far
Into the underworld as cresting boughs
Go up in heaven's air: just so this captain,
Buffeted by a gale of pleas
This way and that way, dinned all the day long,
595   Felt their moving power in his great heart,

4. Aulis was the launching point of the Greek expedition to Troy.

And yet his will stood fast; tears fell in vain.

On Dido in her desolation now
Terror grew at her fate. She prayed for death,
Being heartsick at the mere sight of heaven.
600   That she more surely would perform the act
And leave the daylight, now she saw before her
A thing one shudders to recall: on altars
Fuming with incense where she placed her gifts,
The holy water blackened, the spilt wine
605   Turned into blood and mire. Of this she spoke
To no one, not to her sister even. Then, too,
Within the palace was a marble shrine
Devoted to her onetime lord, a place
She held in wondrous honor, all festooned
610   With snowy fleeces and green festive boughs.
From this she now thought voices could be heard
And words could be made out, her husband's words,
Calling her, when midnight hushed the earth;
And lonely on the rooftops the night owl
615   Seemed to lament, in melancholy notes,
Prolonged to a doleful cry. And then, besides,
The riddling words of seers in ancient days,
Foreboding sayings, made her thrill with fear.
In nightmare, fevered, she was hunted down
620   By pitiless Aeneas, and she seemed
Deserted always, uncompanioned always,
On a long journey, looking for her Tyrians
In desolate landscapes—
                                        as Pentheus gone mad
Sees the oncoming Eumenidës and sees
625   A double sun and double Thebes appear,[5]
Or as when, hounded on the stage, Orestës
Runs from a mother armed with burning brands,
With serpents hellish black,
And in the doorway squat the Avenging Ones.[6]

630   So broken in mind by suffering, Dido caught
Her fatal madness and resolved to die.
She pondered time and means, then visiting
Her mournful sister, covered up her plan
With a calm look, a clear and hopeful brow.

635   "Sister, be glad for me! I've found a way
To bring him back or free me of desire.

5. Here Virgil cites a scene from the *Bacchae* of Euripides in which Dionysus has driven mad Pentheus, King of Thebes, causing him to see the world double as the Bacchantes approach to tear him to pieces. Virgil equates them with the Furies (Eumenides), female powers of the underworld who punish blood guilt.

6. Son of Clytemnestra and Agamemnon, Orestes kills his mother and her lover to revenge her murder of his father. He is then pursued by the Furies (the Avenging Ones). Virgil's description comes from the *Oresteia* of Aeschylus.

Near to the Ocean boundary, near sundown,
The Aethiops' farthest territory lies,
Where giant Atlas turns the sphere of heaven
640   Studded with burning stars. From there
A priestess of Massylian stock has come;
She had been pointed out to me: custodian
Of that shrine named for daughters of the west,
Hesperidës; and it is she who fed
645   The dragon, guarding well the holy boughs
With honey dripping slow and drowsy poppy.[7]
Chanting her spells she undertakes to free
What hearts she wills, but to inflict on others
Duress of sad desires; to arrest
650   The flow of rivers, make the stars move backward,
Call up the spirits of deep Night.[8] You'll see
Earth shift and rumble underfoot and ash trees
Walk down mountainsides. Dearest, I swear
Before the gods and by your own sweet self,
655   It is against my will that I resort
For weaponry to magic powers. In secret
Build up a pyre in the inner court
Under the open sky, and place upon it
The arms that faithless man left in my chamber,
660   All his clothing, and the marriage bed
On which I came to grief—solace for me
To annihilate all vestige of the man,
Vile as he is: my priestess shows me this."

While she was speaking, cheek and brow grew pale.
665   But Anna could not think her sister cloaked
A suicide in these unheard-of rites;
She failed to see how great her madness was
And feared no consequence more grave
Than at Sychaeus' death. So, as commanded,
670   She made the preparations. For her part,
The queen, seeing the pyre in her inmost court
Erected huge with pitch-pine and sawn ilex,°   *holm oak*
Hung all the place under the sky with wreaths
And crowned it with funereal cypress boughs.
675   On the pyre's top she put a sword he left
With clothing, and an effigy on a couch,
Her mind fixed now ahead on what would come.
Around the pyre stood altars, and the priestess,
Hair unbound, called in a voice of thunder

---

7. The garden tended by the Hesperides, the daughters of Hesperus (West) and Atlas, was traditionally located beyond the Atlas mountains at the western border of the Ocean. The garden contained a tree of golden apples given by Earth to Hera following her marriage. The tree was guarded by a dragon, who was slain by Hercules.
8. Another tradition made the Hesperides the daughters of Night and Erebus. As is his custom, Virgil combines elements of different versions of the myth in Dido's description.

680   Upon three hundred gods, on Erebus,
        On Chaos, and on triple Hecatë,
        Three-faced Diana.[9] Then she sprinkled drops
        Purportedly from the fountain of Avernus.[1]
        Rare herbs were brought out, reaped at the new moon
685   By scythes of bronze, and juicy with a milk
        Of dusky venom; then the rare love-charm
        Or caul torn from the brow of a birthing foal
        And snatched away before the mother found it.
        Dido herself with consecrated grain
690   In her pure hands, as she went near the altars,
        Freed one foot from sandal straps, let fall
        Her dress ungirdled, and, now sworn to death,
        Called on the gods and stars that knew her fate.
        She prayed then to whatever power may care
695   In comprehending justice for the grief
        Of lovers bound unequally by love.

        The night had come, and weary in every land
        Men's bodies took the boon of peaceful sleep.
        The woods and the wild seas had quieted
700   At that hour when the stars are in mid-course
        And every field is still; cattle and birds
        With vivid wings that haunt the limpid lakes
        Or nest in thickets in the country places
        All were asleep under the silent night.
705   Not, though, the agonized Phoenician queen:
        She never slackened into sleep and never
        Allowed the tranquil night to rest
        Upon her eyelids or within her heart.
        Her pain redoubled; love came on again,
710   Devouring her, and on her bed she tossed
        In a great surge of anger.
                                    So awake,
        She pressed these questions, musing to herself:

        "Look now, what can I do? Turn once again
        To the old suitors, only to be laughed at—
715   Begging a marriage with Numidians
        Whom I disdained so often? Then what? Trail
        The Ilian ships and follow like a slave
        Commands of Trojans? Seeing them so agreeable,
        In view of past assistance and relief,
720   So thoughtful their unshaken gratitude?
        Suppose I wished it, who permits or takes

---

9. Hecatë was a sinister goddess associated with magic, witchcraft, the night, the underworld, and crossroads, which she haunted. She was frequently depicted with three faces representing her three aspects and sometimes identified with Artemis (Roman: Diana).

1. A lake near Cumae and Naples. Near it is a cave reputed to contain an entrance to the underworld (see bk. 6). Avernus was used by Virgil and others to refer to the underworld in general.

Aboard their proud ships one they so dislike?
Poor lost soul, do you not yet grasp or feel
The treachery of the line of Laömedon?
725 What then? Am I to go alone, companion
Of the exultant sailors in their flight?
Or shall I set out in their wake, with Tyrians,
With all my crew close at my side, and send
The men I barely tore away from Tyre
730 To sea again, making them hoist their sails
To more sea-winds? No: die as you deserve,
Give pain quietus° with a steel blade.   *rest*
                                        Sister,
You are the one who gave way to my tears
In the beginning, burdened a mad queen
735 With sufferings, and thrust me on my enemy.
It was not given me to lead my life
Without new passion, innocently, the way
Wild creatures live, and not to touch these depths.
The vow I took to the ashes of Sychaeus
740 Was not kept."
                        So she broke out afresh
In bitter mourning. On his high stern deck
Aeneas, now quite certain of departure,
Everything ready, took the boon of sleep,
In dream the figure of the god returned
745 With looks reproachful as before: he seemed
Again to warn him, being like Mercury
In every way, in voice, in golden hair,
And in the bloom of youth.
                        "Son of the goddess,
Sleep away this crisis, can you still?
750 Do you not see the dangers growing round you,
Madman, from now on? Can you not hear
The offshore westwind blow? The woman hatches
Plots and drastic actions in her heart,
Resolved on death now, whipping herself on
755 To heights of anger. Will you not be gone
In flight, while flight is still within your power?
Soon you will see the offing boil with ships
And glare with torches; soon again
The waterfront will be alive with fires,
760 If Dawn comes while you linger in this country.
Ha! Come, break the spell! Woman's a thing
Forever fitful and forever changing."

At this he merged into the darkness. Then
As the abrupt phantom filled him with fear,
765 Aeneas broke from sleep and roused his crewmen:
"Up, turn out now! Oarsmen, take your thwarts!
Shake out sail! Look here, for the second time

> A god from heaven's high air is goading me
> To hasten our break away, to cut the cables.

770

> Holy one, whatever god you are,
> We go with you, we act on your command
> Most happily! Be near, graciously help us,
> Make the stars in heaven propitious ones!"

> He pulled his sword aflash out of its sheath

775

> And struck at the stern hawser.° All the men   *mooring cable*
> Were gripped by his excitement to be gone,
> And hauled and hustled. Ships cast off their moorings,
> And an array of hulls hid inshore water
> As oarsmen churned up foam and swept to sea.

780

> Soon early Dawn, quitting the saffron bed
> Of old Tithonus,[2] cast new light on earth,
> And as air grew transparent, from her tower
> The queen caught sight of ships on the seaward reach
> With sails full and the wind astern. She knew

785

> The waterfront now empty, bare of oarsmen.
> Beating her lovely breast three times, four times,
> And tearing her golden hair,
>
>   "O Jupiter,"
> She said, "will this man go, will he have mocked
> My kingdom, stranger that he was and is?

790

> Will they not snatch up arms and follow him
> From every quarter of the town? And dockhands
> Tear our ships from moorings? On! Be quick
> With torches! Give out arms! Unship the oars!
> What am I saying? Where am I? What madness

795

> Takes me out of myself? Dido, poor soul,
> Your evil doing has come home to you.
> Then was the right time, when you offered him
> A royal scepter. See the good faith and honor
> Of one they say bears with him everywhere

800

> The hearthgods of his country! One who bore
> His father, spent with age, upon his shoulders!
> Could I not then have torn him limb from limb
> And flung the pieces on the sea?[3] His company,
> Even Ascanius could I not have minced

805

> And served up to his father at a feast?[4]
> The luck of battle might have been in doubt—
> So let it have been! Whom had I to fear,

2. In Greek mythology, Tithonus, a son of Laomedon and the brother of Priam, was loved by Eos (Roman: Aurora), the goddess of Dawn. She begged Zeus to make Tithonus immortal but forgot to ask for eternal youth for him as well.
3. As Medea did to her brother, Apsyrtus, to aid her escape with her lover, Jason. In revenge for Jason's later betrayal of her, she killed their two children as well. See Euripides' *Medea* (page 729).

4. When Procne, daughter of a legendary king of Athens, discovered that her husband, Tereus, had raped and mutilated her sister, Philomela, she killed their son, Itys, and served him to his father as punishment. Agamemnon's father, Atreus, served his brother Thyestes' son to him as punishment for sleeping with Atreus's wife (see *Agamemnon*, pages 637 and 645).

Being sure to die? I could have carried torches
Into his camp, filled passage ways with flame,
810 Annihilated father and son and followers
And given my own life on top of all!
O Sun, scanning with flame all works of earth,
And thou, O Juno, witness and go-between
Of my long miseries; and Hecatë,
815 Screeched for at night at crossroads in the cities;
And thou, avenging Furies, and all gods
On whom Elissa dying may call: take notice,
Overshadow this hell with your high power,
As I deserve, and hear my prayer!
820 If by necessity that impious wretch
Must find his haven and come safe to land,
If so Jove's destinies require, and this,
His end in view, must stand, yet all the same
When hard beset in war by a brave people,
825 Forced to go outside his boundaries
And torn from Iulus, let him beg assistance,
Let him see the unmerited deaths of those
Around and with him, and accepting peace
On unjust terms, let him not, even so,
830 Enjoy his kingdom or the life he longs for,
But fall in battle before his time and lie
Unburied on the sand! This I implore,
This is my last cry, as my last blood flows.
Then, O my Tyrians, besiege with hate
835 His progeny and all his race to come:
Make this your offering to my dust. No love,
No pact must be between our peoples; No,
But rise up from my bones, avenging spirit!
Harry with fire and sword the Dardan countrymen
840 Now, or hereafter, at whatever time
The strength will be afforded. Coast with coast
In conflict, I implore, and sea with sea,
And arms with arms: may they contend in war,
Themselves and all the children of their children!"[5]

845 Now she took thought of one way or another,
At the first chance, to end her hated life,
And briefly spoke to Barcë, who had been
Sychaeus' nurse; her own an urn of ash
Long held in her ancient fatherland.
                                        "Dear nurse,
850 Tell Sister Anna to come here, and have her
Quickly bedew herself with running water

---

5. Virgil creates a myth of the origins of the conflict between Carthage and Rome. More immediately, he motivates the difficulty faced by the Trojans when they reach Latium in defeating an obviously inferior foe.

Before she brings our victims for atonement.
Let her come that way. And you, too, put on
Pure wool around your brows. I have a mind
855 To carry out that rite to Stygian Jove[6]
That I have readied here, and put an end
To my distress, committing to the flames
The pyre of that miserable Dardan."

At this with an old woman's eagerness
860 Barcë hurried away. And Dido's heart
Beat wildly at the enormous thing afoot.
She rolled her bloodshot eyes, her quivering cheeks
Were flecked with red as her sick pallor grew
Before her coming death. Into the court
865 She burst her way, then at her passion's height
She climbed the pyre and bared the Dardan sword—
A gift desired once, for no such need.
Her eyes now on the Trojan clothing there
And the familiar bed, she paused a little,
870 Weeping a little, mindful, then lay down
And spoke her last words:
                                           "Remnants dear to me
While god and fate allowed it, take this breath
And give me respite from these agonies.
I lived my life out to the very end
875 And passed the stages Fortune had appointed.
Now my tall shade goes to the under world.
I built a famous town, saw my great walls,
Avenged my husband, made my hostile brother
Pay for his crime. Happy, alas, too happy,
880 If only the Dardanian keels had never
Beached on our coast." And here she kissed the bed.
"I die unavenged," she said, "but let me die.
This way, this way, a blessed relief to go
Into the undergloom. Let the cold Trojan,
885 Far at sea, drink in this conflagration
And take with him the omen of my death!"

Amid these words her household people saw her
Crumpled over the steel blade, and the blade
Aflush with red blood, drenched her hands. A scream
890 Pierced the high chambers. Now through the shocked city
Rumor went rioting, as wails and sobs
With women's outcry echoed in the palace
And heaven's high air gave back the beating din,
As though all Carthage or old Tyre fell
895 To storming enemies, and, out of hand,

6. Dis, god of the underworld, "ruler of the Styx."

Flames billowed on the roofs of men and gods.
Her sister heard the trembling, faint with terror,
Lacerating her face, beating her breast,
Ran through the crowd to call the dying queen:

900 "It came to this, then, sister? You deceived me?
The pyre meant this, altars and fires meant this?
What shall I mourn first, being abandoned? Did you
Scorn your sister's company in death?
You should have called me out to the same fate!

905 The same blade's edge and hurt, at the same hour,
Should have taken us off. With my own hands
Had I to build this pyre, and had I to call
Upon our country's gods, that in the end
With you placed on it there, O heartless one,

910 I should be absent? You have put to death
Yourself and me, the people and the fathers
Bred in Sidon, and your own new city.
Give me fresh water, let me bathe her wound
And catch upon my lips any last breath

915 Hovering over hers."
                              Now she had climbed
The topmost steps and took her dying sister
Into her arms to cherish, with a sob,
Using her dress to stanch the dark blood flow.
But Dido trying to lift her heavy eyes

920 Fainted again. Her chest-wound whistled air.
Three times she struggled up on one elbow
And each time fell back on the bed. Her gaze
Went wavering as she looked for heaven's light
And groaned at finding it. Almighty Juno,

925 Filled with pity for this long ordeal
And difficult passage, now sent Iris[7] down
Out of Olympus to set free
The wrestling spirit from the body's hold.
For since she died, not at her fated span

930 Nor as she merited, but before her time
Enflamed and driven mad, Proserpina
Had not yet plucked from her the golden hair,
Delivering her to Orcus of the Styx.[8]
So humid Iris through bright heaven flew

935 On saffron-yellow wings, and in her train
A thousand hues shimmered before the sun.
At Dido's head she came to rest.
                              "This token

---

7. The goddess of the rainbow, and also messenger of the gods, especially Hera/Juno.
8. Proserpina (Greek: Persephone) was the goddess of the underworld and the wife of Dis (Greek: Hades). In sacrifices, the hair of the victim would be removed and offered as first fruits. When men and women died at their appointed time, Proserpina herself was said to cut their locks for a similar reason; however, she cannot do this for the untimely dead, so Iris is sent out of special compassion in her place.

Sacred to Dis I bear away as bidden
And free you from your body."
                                        Saying this,
940   She cut a lock of hair. Along with it
Her body's warmth fell into dissolution,
And out into the winds her life withdrew.

[*Leaving Carthage, the Trojans stop again at Drepinum in Sicily, where they conduct
funeral games for the anniversary of Anchises' death. The games—naval and foot
races, boxing, and archery—are interrupted when the women of Troy, goaded by
Juno, set fire to the ships. Anchises visits Aeneas in a dream, telling him that he must
descend to the underworld to meet him. The helmsman Palinurus is lost at sea during
the night.*]

from **Book 6**

[THE WORLD BELOW]

So grieving, and in tears, he gave the ship
Her head before the wind, drawing toward land
At the Euboian settlement of Cumae.[1]
Ships came about, prows pointing seaward, anchors
5   Biting to hold them fast, and rounded sterns
Indented all the water's edge. The men
Debarked in groups, eager to go ashore
Upon Hesperia. Some struck seeds of fire
Out of the veins of flint, and some explored
10   The virgin woods, lairs of wild things, for fuel,
Pointing out, too, what streams they found.
                                        Aeneas,
In duty bound, went inland to the heights
Where overshadowing Apollo dwells
And nearby, in a place apart—a dark
15   Enormous cave—the Sibyl feared by men.[2]
In her the Delian god of prophecy°   *Apollo*
Inspires uncanny powers of mind and soul,
Disclosing things to come. Here Trojan captains
Walked to Diana of the Crossroads' wood
20   And entered under roofs of gold.[3] They say
That Daedalus, when he fled the realm of Minos,
Dared to entrust himself to stroking wings
And to the air of heaven—unheard-of path—

1. Settlers from the Greek island of Euboea founded a colony at Cumae, ten miles northwest of Naples, c. 740 B.C.E.
2. Sibyls were prophetic women, usually inspired by the god Apollo, whose oracles were often collected and preserved. Most celebrated were the books of the Cumaean sibyl kept in Rome and consulted by the senate in times of crisis.
3. The Cumaean sibyl Deiphobë was the priestess of both Apollo and Hecate ("Diana of the Crossroads").

On which he swam away to the cold North
25 At length to touch down on that very height
Of the Chalcidians.[4] Here, on earth again
He dedicated to you, Phoebus Apollo,
The twin sweeps of his wings; here he laid out
A spacious temple. In the entrance way
30 Androgeos' death appeared, then Cecrops' children
Ordered to pay in recompense each year
The living flesh of seven sons.[5] The urn
From which the lots were drawn stood modeled there.[6]
And facing it, upon the opposite door,
35 The land of Crete, emergent from the sea;
Here the brutish act appeared: Pasiphaë
Being covered by the bull in the cow's place,
Then her mixed breed, her child of double form,
The Minotaur, get of unholy lust.[7]
40 Here, too, that puzzle of the house of Minos,
The maze none could untangle, until, touched
By a great love shown by a royal girl,
He, Daedalus himself, unravelled all
The baffling turns and dead ends in the dark,
45 Guiding the blind way back by a skein unwound.[8]
In that high sculpture you, too, would have had
Your great part, Icarus, had grief allowed.
Twice your father had tried to shape your fall
In gold, but twice his hands dropped.[9]
                                    Here the Trojans
50 Would have passed on and gazed and read it all,
Had not Achatës, whom they had sent ahead,
Returned now with the priestess of Apollo
And of Diana, goddess of the Crossroads—
Deiphobë, the Sibyl, Glaucus' daughter.
55 Thus she addressed the king:
                            "The hour demands
No lagging over sights like these. Instead,
You should make offering of seven young bulls
From an ungelded herd, and seven again

4. Daedalus was a legendary Athenian artist, craftsman, and inventor and builder for King Minos of Crete of the labyrinth in which the Minotaur was housed. Trapped on Minos's island kingdom, Daedalus made wings of wax and feathers and escaped through the air. The most famous version is Ovid's in the *Metamorphoses,* Book 8 (see page 1227).
5. After Androgeos dies an untimely death in Attica, the region of Greece ruled by Athens, his father, Minos, extracts an annual tribute of seven youths and seven maidens to be thrown to the Minotaur in its labyrinth. The Athenians are called "Cecrops' children" here after the legendary first king of Athens.
6. The victims were chosen by lot drawn from an urn, a standard ancient procedure.

7. Pasiphaë, daughter of the Sun, was married to Minos. When Minos refused to sacrifice to Poseidon a beautiful bull he had promised him, the god caused Pasiphaë to fall in love with the bull, which she seduced, hidden within an artificial cow created by Daedalus. The Minotaur—half-man, half-bull—was the result of this union.
8. The legendary king of Athens, Theseus, traveled to Crete as one of the sacrificial youths, killed the Minotaur, and escaped from the labyrinth with the help of a spool of thread given him by Minos's daughter, Ariadne, with whom he fled.
9. Daedalus's son, Icarus, fled with him, but Icarus flew too close to the sun, causing the wax of his wings to melt, and he fell to his death in the sea.

Well-chosen ewes."
    With these words for Aeneas—
60 Orders his men were quick to act upon—
The priestess called them to her lofty shrine.
The cliff's huge flank is honeycombed, cut out
In a cavern perforated a hundred times,
Having a hundred mouths, with rushing voices
65 Carrying the responses of the Sibyl.[1]
Here, as the men approached the entrance way,
The Sibyl cried out:
    "Now is the time to ask
Your destinies!"
    And then:

     "The god! Look there!
The god!"
    And as she spoke neither her face
70 Nor hue went untransformed, nor did her hair
Stay neatly bound: her breast heaved, her wild heart
Grew large with passion. Taller to their eyes
And sounding now no longer like a mortal
Since she had felt the god's power breathing near,
75 She cried:
    "Slow, are you, in your vows and prayers?
Trojan Aeneas, are you slow? Be quick,
The great mouths of the god's house, thunderstruck,
Will never open till you pray."
    Her lips
Closed tight on this. A chill ran through the bones
80 Of the tough Teucrians, but their king poured out
Entreaties from his deepest heart:
    "O Phoebus,
God who took pity on the pain of Troy,
Who guided Paris' hand, his Dardan shaft,
Against the body of Aiacidës,[2]
85 As you led on I entered all those seas
Washing great lands, and then the distant tribe
Of the Massylians at the Syrtës' edge.
Now we take hold at last of Italy
That slipped away so long. Grant that the fortune
90 Of Troy shall have pursued us this far only!
And all you gods and goddesses as well
Who took offence at Ilium and our pride,
At last, and rightly, you may spare

1. A cave believed to have been that of the Sibyl has been discovered and excavated on the site of the ancient Cumae. It consists of a quadrangular chamber approached by a corridor in the side of the mountain 125 yards long and 60 feet high.

2. Paris, with the help of Apollo, caused the death of Achilles with an arrow in his heel, the only vulnerable part of his body. Aiacidës (or Aeacidës) means a descendant of Aeacus, the grandfather of Achilles.

Pergamum's children. Most holy prophetess,
95   Foreknowing things to come, I ask no kingdom
Other than fate allows me; let our people
Make their settlement in Latium
With all Troy's wandering gods and shaken powers.
Then I shall dedicate a temple here
100   To Phoebus and Diana of the Crossroads,
Ordering festal days in Phoebus' name.
A holy place awaits you in my kingdom
Where I shall store your prophecies, your dark
Revelations to my people, and appoint
105   A chosen priesthood for you, gracious one.[3]
But now commit no verses to the leaves
Or they may be confused, shuffled and whirled
By playing winds: chant them aloud, I pray."

Then he fell silent. But the prophetess
110   Whom the bestriding god had not yet broken
Stormed about the cavern, trying to shake
His influence from her breast, while all the more
He tired her mad jaws, quelled her savage heart,
And tamed her by his pressure. In the end
115   The cavern's hundred mouths all of themselves
Unclosed to let the Sibyl's answers through:

"You, sir, now quit at last of the sea's dangers,
For whom still greater are in store on land,
The Dardan race will reach Lavinian country—
120   Put that anxiety away—but there
Will wish they had not come. Wars, vicious wars
I see ahead, and Tiber foaming blood.
Simoïs, Xanthus, Dorians encamped—
You'll have them all again, with an Achilles,
125   Child of Latium, he, too, goddess-born.[4]
And nowhere from pursuit of Teucrians
Will Juno stray, while you go destitute,
Begging so many tribes and towns for aid.
The cause of suffering here again will be
130   A bride foreign to Teucrians, a marriage
Made with a stranger.[5]
                          Never shrink from blows.
Boldly, more boldly where your luck allows,
Go forward, face them. A first way to safety
Will open where you reckon on it least,

---

3. Originally stored in the temple of Capitoline Jupiter, the Sibylline books were moved to the temple of Palatine Apollo, constructed by Augustus in 28 B.C.E. in the neighborhood of Rome where the emperor himself lived.
4. The prophecy of Apollo establishes the war of the second half of the *Aeneid* in terms of the *Iliad,* with Turnus, the son of the nymph Venilia, as the new Achilles.
5. Apollo's prediction echoes Dido's curse, quite aptly as it concerns the betrothal of Aeneas to Lavinia, daughter of Latinus, the king of Latium.

135   From a Greek city."[6]
                            These were the sentences
         In which the Sibyl of Cumae from her shrine
         Sang out her riddles, echoing in the cave,
         Dark sayings muffling truths, the way Apollo
         Pulled her up raging, or else whipped her on,
140   Digging the spurs beneath her breast. As soon
         As her fit ceased, her wild voice quieted,
         The great soldier, Aeneas, began to speak:

         "No novel kinds of hardship, no surprises,
         Loom ahead, Sister. I foresaw them all,
145   Went through them in my mind. One thing I pray for:
         Since it is here they say one finds the gate
         Of the king of under world, the shadowy marsh
         That wells from Acheron,[7] may I have leave
         To go to my dear father's side and see him.
150   Teach me the path, show me the entrance way.
         Through fires, and with a thousand spears behind,
         I brought him on these shoulders, rescued him
         Amid our enemies. He shared my voyage,
         Bore all the seas with me, hard nights and days
155   Of menace from the sea and sky, beyond
         The strength and lot of age, frail though he was.
         Indeed, he prayed this very prayer; he told me
         That I should come to you and beg it humbly.
         Pity a son and father, gracious lady,
160   All this is in your power. Hecatë
         Gave you authority to have and hold
         Avernus wood. If Orpheus could call
         His wife's shade up, relying on the strings
         That sang loud on his Thracian lyre; if Pollux
165   Redeemed his brother, taking his turn at death,
         So often passing back and forth; why name
         The heroes, Theseus and Hercules?[8]
         By birth I too descend from Jove on high—"

         While in these terms he prayed and pressed the altar,
170   Breaking in, the Sibyl said:
                            "Offspring
         Of gods by blood, Trojan Anchises' son,

---

6. Evander, whose aid Aeneas will seek in Book 8, was supposedly an Arcadian who with his countrymen founded a colony on the banks of the Tiber river.
7. A river in Epirus (northwest Greece) that breaks through an impenetrable gorge to form the Acherusian swamps. After Homer named it a river of Hades in the *Odyssey,* the Acheron became identified with the underworld.
8. Mythological figures who descended to the underworld and returned (Virgil pointedly omits Odysseus). The

singer Orpheus went to Hades to recover his wife, Eurydice, only to lose her again when he could not resist looking behind him (see *Metamorphoses,* page 1230). Castor and Pollux were twin brothers of Helen. When Castor was killed, his brother asked to die also. Touched by such devotion, Zeus granted that they should spend alternate days in Hades and in Heaven. Theseus and a companion were imprisoned in Hades until rescued by Hercules, who found them there while fetching Cerberus as the twelfth of his Twelve Labors.

The way downward is easy from Avernus.
Black Dis's door stands open night and day.
But to retrace your steps to heaven's air,
175　There is the trouble, there is the toil. A few
Whom a benign Jupiter has loved or whom
Fiery heroism has borne to heaven,
Sons of gods, could do it. All midway
Are forests, then Cocytus,[9] thick and black,
180　Winds through the gloom. But if you feel such love,
And such desire to cross the Stygian water
Twice, to view the night of Tartarus twice[1]—
If this mad effort's to your liking, then
Consider what you must accomplish first.
185　A tree's deep shade conceals a bough whose leaves
And pliant twigs are all of gold, a thing
Sacred to Juno of the lower world.°　　　　　　　　　　　*Proserpina*
The whole grove shelters it, and thickest shade
In dusky valleys shuts it in. And yet
190　No one may enter hidden depths
Below the earth unless he picks this bough,
The tree's fruit, with its foliage of gold.[2]
Proserpina decreed this bough, as due her,
Should be given into her own fair hands
195　When torn away. In place of it a second
Grows up without fail, all gold as well,
Flowering with metallic leaves again.
So lift your eyes and search, and once you find it
Pull away the bough. It will come willingly,
200　Easily, if you are called by fate.
If not, with all your strength you cannot conquer it,
Cannot lop it off with a sword's edge.
A further thing is this: your friend's dead body—
Ah, but you *don't* know!—lies out there unburied,
205　Polluting all your fleet with death
While you are lingering, waiting on my counsel
Here at my door. First give the man his rest,
Entomb him; lead black beasts to sacrifice;
Begin with these amends. Then in due course
210　You'll see the Stygian forest rise before you,
Regions not for the living."[3]

---

9. One of the tributaries of the Acheron in Epirus, later considered a river of the world below.
1. That is, now and when he dies. Tartarus generally refers to the deepest part of the underworld, a place of punishment.
2. Aeneas's journey combines aspects of the heroic descent through personal prowess with religious ritual, perhaps through personal knowledge of rites used in the mysteries of Proserpina. In necromancy and mystery cults, some form of magical token was usually required for admittance to the realm of the dead or conversation with them.
3. The burial of Misenus bears many traces of rituals of human sacrifice said also to be required for converse with the dead.

                                She fell silent,
        Closing her lips. With downcast face and eyes
        Aeneas turned from the cavern to the shore,
        Dark matters on his mind. Steadfast Achatës
215   Walked beside him with deliberate pace
        And equal anxieties. The two exchanged
        In shifting conversation many guesses
        As to that friend, now dead, now to be buried,
        So the prophetess had said—then suddenly
220   As they came down to the dry beach they saw
        Misenus, robbed of life by early death,
        Their own Misenus, a son of Aeolus,
        Never surpassed at rousing fighting men
        With brazen trumpet, setting Mars afire.
225   Once he had been great Hector's adjutant,
        Going forward at Hector's side in battle,
        Brilliant with trumpet and with spear as well.
        After Achilles took the life of Hector,
        This gallant soldier joined Dardan Aeneas
230   In allegiance to no lesser cause. That day
        By chance, as he blew notes on a hollow shell,
        Making the sea sing back, in his wild folly
        He dared the gods to rival him. Then Triton,[4]
        Envious, if this can be believed,
235   Caught him and put him under in the surf
        Amid the rocks off shore.
                                All who were there
        Clamored around the body in lament,
        Aeneas, the good captain, most of all.
        In haste then, even as they wept, they turned
240   To carry out the orders of the Sibyl,
        Racing to pile up logs for the altar-pyre
        And build it sky-high. Into the virgin forest,
        Thicket of wild things, went the men, and down
        The pitch pines came, the bitten ilex rang
245   With axe blows, ash and oak were split with wedges,
        Mighty rowans were trundled down the slopes.

        Aeneas himself went first in all this labor,
        Cheering his fellows on, with implements
        Like theirs in hand; but grimly in his heart
250   He wondered, studying the unmeasured forest,
        And fell to prayer:
                                "If only the golden bough
        Might shine for us in such a wilderness!
        As all the prophetess foretold was true—

---

4. In Greek myth a merman, a son of Poseidon who is commonly shown blowing on a conch shell. He appears as Poseidon's aide in Book 1.

Misenus, in your case only too true."

255　The words were barely uttered when two doves
　　In casual flight out of the upper air
　　Came down before the man's eyes to alight
　　On the green grass, and the great hero knew
　　These birds to be his mother's. Joyously
260　He prayed:
　　　　　　"O be my guides, if there's a way.
　　Wing on, into that woodland where the bough,
　　The priceless bough, shadows the fertile ground.
　　My divine mother, do not fail your son
　　In a baffling time."
　　　　　　　　　　Then he stood still to see
265　What signs the doves might give, or where their flight
　　Might lead him. And they fed, and then flew on,
　　Each time as far as one who came behind
　　Could keep in view. Then when they reached the gorge
　　Of sulphurous Avernus, first borne upward
270　Through the lucent air, they glided down
　　To their desired rest, the two-hued tree
　　Where glitter of gold filtered between green boughs.
　　Like mistletoe that in the woods in winter
　　Thrives with yellowish berries and new leaves—
275　A parasite on the trunk it twines around—
　　So bright amid the dark green ilex shone
　　The golden leafage, rustling in light wind.
　　Aeneas at once briskly took hold of it
　　And, though it clung, greedily broke it off,
280　Then carried it to the Sibyl's cave.
　　　　　　　　　　　　　　　Meanwhile
　　The Teucrians on the shore wept for Misenus,
　　Doing for thankless dust the final honors.
　　First they built up a giant pyre, enriched
　　With pitch pine and split oak, with somber boughs
285　Alongside and dark cypresses in front.
　　On top they made a blazon of bright arms.
　　One group set water boiling over flames,
　　Then washed the cold corpse and anointed it,
　　Groaning loud, and laid it out when mourned
290　On a low couch, with purple robes thrown over it,
　　A hero's shrouding. Bearers then took up
　　As their sad duty the great bier. With eyes
　　Averted in their fathers' ancient way
　　They held the torch below.
　　　　　　　　　　　　Heaped offerings
295　Blazed up and burned—food, incense, oil in bowls.
　　And when the flame died and the coals fell in,
　　They gave a bath of wine to the pyre's remnant,

Thirsty ash; then picking out the bones
Corynaeus enclosed them in an urn.
300   The same priest with pure water went three times
Around the company, asperging them
With cleansing drops from a ripe olive sprig,
And spoke the final words. Faithfully then
Aeneas heaped a great tomb over the dead,
305   Placing his arms, his oar, his trumpet there
Beneath a promontory, named for him,
Misenum now and always, age to age.[5]
All this accomplished, with no more ado
He carried out the orders of the Sibyl.

310   The cavern was profound, wide-mouthed, and huge,
Rough underfoot, defended by dark pool
And gloomy forest. Overhead, flying things
Could never safely take their way, such deathly
Exhalations rose from the black gorge
315   Into the dome of heaven. The priestess here
Placed four black bullocks, wet their brows with wine,
Plucked bristles from between the horns and laid them
As her first offerings on the holy fire,
Calling aloud to Hecatë, supreme
320   In heaven and Erebus. Others drew knives
Across beneath and caught warm blood in bowls.
Aeneas by the sword's edge offered up
To Night, the mother of the Eumenidës,
And her great sister, Earth, a black-fleeced lamb,
325   A sterile cow to thee, Proserpina.
Then for the Stygian king he lit at night
New altars where he placed over the flames
Entire carcasses of bulls, and poured
Rich oil on blazing viscera.[6] Only see:
330   Just at the light's edge, just before sunrise,
Earth rumbled underfoot, forested ridges
Broke into movement, and far howls of dogs
Were heard across the twilight as the goddess
Nearer and nearer came.
                              "Away, away,"
335   The Sibyl cried, "all those unblest, away!
Depart from all the grove! But you, Aeneas,
Enter the path here, and unsheathe your sword.
There's need of gall and resolution now."

She flung herself wildly into the cave-mouth,
340   Leading, and he strode boldly at her heels.

---

5. Here Virgil provides an origin for Misenum, the north-ern headland of the bay of Naples.

6. To gain permission for their descent, the sibyl sacri-fices to the underworld gods, by contrast with the Olympian or "heavenly" gods of the world above.

Gods who rule the ghosts; all silent shades;
And Chaos and infernal Fiery Stream,
And regions of wide night without a sound,
May it be right to tell what I have heard,
345   May it be right, and fitting, by your will,
That I describe the deep world sunk in darkness
Under the earth.[7]
              Now dim to one another
In desolate night they walked on through the gloom,
Through Dis's homes all void, and empty realms,
350   As one goes through a wood by a faint moon's
Treacherous light, when Jupiter veils the sky
And black night blots the colors of the world.

Before the entrance, in the jaws of Orcus,
Grief and avenging Cares have made their beds,
355   And pale Diseases and sad Age are there,
And Dread, and Hunger that sways men to crime,
And sordid Want—in shapes to affright the eyes—
And Death and Toil and Death's own brother, Sleep,
And the mind's evil joys; on the door sill
360   Death-bringing War, and iron cubicles
Of the Eumenidës, and raving Discord,
Viperish hair bound up in gory bands.[8]
In the courtyard a shadowy giant elm
Spreads ancient boughs, her ancient arms where dreams,
365   False dreams, the old tale goes, beneath each leaf
Cling and are numberless. There, too,
About the doorway forms of monsters crowd—
Centaurs, twiformed Scyllas, hundred-armed
Briareus, and the Lernaean hydra
370   Hissing horribly, and the Chimaera
Breathing dangerous flames, and Gorgons, Harpies,
Huge Geryon, triple-bodied ghost.[9]
Here, swept by sudden fear, drawing his sword,
Aeneas stood on guard with naked edge
375   Against them as they came. If his companion,
Knowing the truth, had not admonished him
How faint these lives were—empty images
Hovering bodiless—he had attacked
And cut his way through phantoms, empty air.[1]

380   The path goes on from that place to the waves
Of Tartarus's Acheron. Thick with mud,
A whirlpool out of a vast abyss

---

7. An important component of mystery religions was the secrecy of their rituals, not to be revealed to the uninitiated.

8. Here Virgil combines traditional underworld deities—the Furies and Discord—with allegorical personifications

of the ills of the world.

9. Monsters out of Greek mythology, placed by Virgil at the threshold of Dis.

1. A Roman reminder of the power of the mind over the trials of the world.

Boils up and belches all the silt it carries
Into Cocytus. Here the ferryman,
385   A figure of fright, keeper of waters and streams,
Is Charon, foul and terrible, his beard
Grown wild and hoar, his staring eyes all flame,
His sordid cloak hung from a shoulder knot.
Alone he poles his craft and trims the sails
390   And in his rusty hull ferries the dead,
Old now—but old age in the gods is green.[2]

Here a whole crowd came streaming to the banks,
Mothers and men, the forms with all life spent
Of heroes great in valor, boys and girls
395   Unmarried, and young sons laid on the pyre
Before their parents' eyes—as many souls
As leaves that yield their hold on boughs and fall
Through forests in the early frost of autumn,
Or as migrating birds from the open sea
400   That darken heaven when the cold season comes
And drives them overseas to sunlit lands.
There all stood begging to be first across
And reached out longing hands to the far shore.

But the grim boatman now took these aboard,
405   Now those, waving the rest back from the strand.
In wonder at this and touched by the commotion,
Aeneas said:
          "Tell me, Sister, what this means,
The crowd at the stream. Where are the souls bound?
How are they tested, so that these turn back,
410   While those take oars to cross the dead-black water?"

Briefly the ancient priestess answered him:

"Cocytus is the deep pool that you see,
The swamp of Styx beyond, infernal power
By which the gods take oath and fear to break it.
415   All in the nearby crowd you notice here
Are pauper souls, the souls of the unburied.
Charon's the boatman. Those the water bears
Are souls of buried men. He may not take them
Shore to dread shore on the hoarse currents there
420   Until their bones rest in the grave, or till
They flutter and roam this side a hundred years;
They may have passage then, and may return
To cross the deeps they long for."
                              Anchises' son
Had halted, pondering on so much, and stood

---

2. Charon was the mythological ferryman who carried shades across the river (usually Acheron) that marked the entrance to Hades proper.

425   In pity for the souls' hard lot. Among them
      He saw two sad ones of unhonored death,
      Leucaspis and the Lycian fleet's commander,
      Orontës, who had sailed the windy sea
      From Troy together, till the Southern gale
430   Had swamped and whirled them down, both ship and men.
      Of a sudden he saw his helmsman, Palinurus,
      Going by, who but a few nights before
      On course from Libya, as he watched the stars,
      Had been pitched overboard astern.[3] As soon
435   As he made sure of the disconsolate one
      In all the gloom, Aeneas called:
                                    "Which god
      Took you away from us and put you under,
      Palinurus? Tell me. In this one prophecy
      Apollo, who had never played me false,
440   Falsely foretold you'd be unharmed at sea
      And would arrive at the Ausonian coast.
      Is the promise kept?"
                          But the shade said:
                                    "Phoebus' caldron
      Told you no lie, my captain, and no god
      Drowned me at sea. The helm that I hung on to,
445   Duty bound to keep our ship on course,
      By some great shock chanced to be torn away,
      And I went with it overboard. I swear
      By the rough sea, I feared less for myself
      Than for your ship: with rudder gone and steersman
450   Knocked overboard, it might well come to grief
      In big seas running. Three nights, heavy weather
      Out of the South on the vast water tossed me.
      On the fourth dawn, I sighted Italy
      Dimly ahead, as a wave-crest lifted me.
455   By turns I swam and rested, swam again
      And got my footing on the beach, but savages
      Attacked me as I clutched at a cliff-top,
      Weighted down by my wet clothes. Poor fools,
      They took me for a prize and ran me through.
460   Surf has me now, and sea winds, washing me
      Close inshore.
                    By heaven's happy light
      And the sweet air, I beg you, by your father,
      And by your hopes of Iulus' rising star,
      Deliver me from this captivity,
465   Unconquered friend! Throw earth on me—you can—
      Put in to Velia port! Or if there be

---

3. A bargain between Venus and Neptune at the end of Book 5 made the loss of Palinurus Neptune's price for the safe arrival of the Trojans in Italy. Palinurus gives a more human explanation for his death here.

Some way to do it, if your goddess mother
Shows a way—and I feel sure you pass
These streams and Stygian marsh by heaven's will—
470   Give this poor soul your hand, take me across,
Let me at least in death find quiet haven."
When he had made his plea, the Sibyl said:
"From what source comes this craving, Palinurus?
Would you though still unburied see the Styx
475   And the grim river of the Eumenidës,
Or even the river bank, without a summons?
Abandon hope by prayer to make the gods
Change their decrees. Hold fast to what I say
To comfort your hard lot: neighboring folk
480   In cities up and down the coast will be
Induced by portents to appease your bones,
Building a tomb and making offerings there
On a cape forever named for Palinurus."[4]

The Sibyl's words relieved him, and the pain
485   Was for a while dispelled from his sad heart,
Pleased at the place-name. So the two walked on
Down to the stream. Now from the Stygian water
The boatman, seeing them in the silent wood
And headed for the bank, cried out to them
490   A rough uncalled-for challenge:
                                                    "Who are you
In armor, visiting our rivers? Speak
From where you are, stop there, say why you come.
This is the region of the Shades, and Sleep,
And drowsy Night. It breaks eternal law
495   For the Stygian craft to carry living bodies.
Never did I rejoice, I tell you, letting
Alcidës° cross, or Theseus and Pirithous,   *Hercules*
Demigods by paternity though they were,
Invincible in power. One forced in chains
500   From the king's own seat the watchdog of the dead
And dragged him away trembling.[5] The other two
Were bent on carrying our lady off
From Dis's chamber."[6]
                                    This the prophetess
And servant of Amphrysian Apollo[7]
505   Briefly answered:
                                    "Here are no such plots,

---

4. In another explanatory myth, the sibyl promises that a nearby cape will preserve the name and fame of the lost helmsman.
5. On his descent to the underworld to fulfill the last of his twelve labors, Hercules bound the three-headed watchdog Cerberus and dragged him to the world above as a prize.
6. Theseus and Pirithous were imprisoned by Hades when they undertook an ill-fated expedition to kidnap Proserpina. Theseus was rescued by Hercules; Pirithous was not.
7. Often Virgil encapsulates a mythical episode into an epithet. Here, he uses "Amphrysian" because Apollo at one time was constrained to serve as a herdsman to Admetus by the river Amphrysus in Thessaly.

So fret no more. These weapons threaten nothing.
Let the great watchdog at the door howl on
Forever terrifying the bloodless shades.
Let chaste Proserpina remain at home
510   In her uncle's house.[8] The man of Troy, Aeneas,
Remarkable for loyalty, great in arms,
Goes through the deepest shades of Erebus
To see his father.
                    If the very image
Of so much goodness moves you not at all,
515   Here is a bough"—at this she showed the bough
That had been hidden, held beneath her dress—
"You'll recognize it."
                    Then his heart, puffed up
With rage, subsided. They had no more words.
His eyes fixed on the ancient gift, the bough,
520   The destined gift, so long unseen, now seen,
He turned his dusky craft and made for shore.
There from the long thwarts where they sat he cleared
The other souls and made the gangway wide,
Letting the massive man step in the bilge.
525   The leaky coracle° groaned at the weight   *small boat*
And took a flood of swampy water in.
At length, on the other side, he put ashore
The prophetess and hero in the mire,
A formless ooze amid the grey-green sedge.
530   Great Cerberus barking with his triple throat
Makes all that shoreline ring, as he lies huge
In a facing cave. Seeing his neck begin
To come alive with snakes, the prophetess
Tossed him a lump of honey and drugged meal
535   To make him drowse. Three ravenous gullets gaped
And he snapped up the sop. Then his great bulk
Subsided and lay down through all the cave.
Now seeing the watchdog deep in sleep, Aeneas
Took the opening: swiftly he turned away
540   From the river over which no soul returns.[9]

Now voices crying loud were heard at once—
The souls of infants wailing. At the door
Of the sweet life they were to have no part in,
Torn from the breast, a black day took them off
545   And drowned them all in bitter death. Near these
Were souls falsely accused, condemned to die.
But not without a judge, or jurymen,

---

8. In Greek myth, Persephone (Roman: Proserpina) was
the daughter of Demeter and Zeus, who like her husband
Hades were children of Cronos and Rhea.

9. The souls Aeneas sees in this part of the underworld are
those who met untimely deaths.

Had these souls got their places: Minos reigned
As the presiding judge, moving the urn,
550   And called a jury of the silent ones
To learn of lives and accusations.[1] Next
Were those sad souls, benighted, who contrived
Their own destruction, and as they hated daylight,
Cast their lives away. How they would wish
555   In the upper air now to endure the pain
Of poverty and toil! But iron law
Stands in the way, since the drear hateful swamp
Has pinned them down here, and the Styx that winds
Nine times around exerts imprisoning power.
560   Not far away, spreading on every side,
The Fields of Mourning came in view, so called
Since here are those whom pitiless love consumed
With cruel wasting, hidden on paths apart
By myrtle woodland growing overhead.
565   In death itself, pain will not let them be.
He saw here Phaedra, Procris, Eriphylë
Sadly showing the wounds her hard son gave;
Evadnë and Pasiphaë, at whose side
Laodamia walked, and Caeneus,
570   A young man once, a woman now, and turned
Again by fate into the older form.[2]
Among them, with her fatal wound still fresh,
Phoenician Dido wandered the deep wood.
The Trojan captain paused nearby and knew
575   Her dim form in the dark, as one who sees,
Early in the month, or thinks to have seen, the moon
Rising through cloud, all dim. He wept and spoke
Tenderly to her:
                    "Dido, so forlorn,
The story then that came to me was true,
580   That you were out of life, had met your end
By your own hand. Was I, was I the cause?
I swear by heaven's stars, by the high gods,
By any certainty below the earth,
I left your land against my will, my queen.
585   The gods' commands drove me to do their will,
As now they drive me through this world of shades,
These mouldy waste lands and these depths of night.
And I could not believe that I would hurt you
So terribly by going. Wait a little.
590   Do not leave my sight.
Am I someone to flee from? The last word

---

1. With his brother Rhadamanthus, the legendary king of Crete acted as judge of the living and the dead (see *Odyssey,* bk. 11). The "silent ones" are the dead.

2. Legendary women who died as a consequence of passion—sometimes licit, sometimes illicit, some by their own hand, some by that of their loved ones.

Destiny lets me say to you is this."

Aeneas with such pleas tried to placate
The burning soul, savagely glaring back,
595 And tears came to his eyes. But she had turned
With gaze fixed on the ground as he spoke on,
Her face no more affected than if she were
Immobile granite or Marpesian stone.³
At length she flung away from him and fled,
600 His enemy still, into the shadowy grove
Where he whose bride she once had been, Sychaeus,
Joined in her sorrows and returned her love.
Aeneas still gazed after her in tears,
Shaken by her ill fate and pitying her.

605 With effort then he took the given way,
And they went on, reaching the farthest lands
Where men famous in war gather apart.
Here Tydeus came to meet him, and then came
Parthenopaeus, glorious in arms,
610 Adrastus then, a pallid shade.⁴ Here too
Were Dardans long bewept in the upper air,
Men who died in the great war. And he groaned
To pick these figures out, in a long file,
Glaucus, Medon, Thersilochus, besides
615 Antenor's three sons, then the priest of Ceres
Polyboetës, then Idaeus, holding
Still to his warcar, holding his old gear.⁵
To right and left they crowd the path and stay
And will not have enough of seeing him,
620 But love to hold him back, to walk beside him,
And hear the story of why he came.
                                    Not so
Agamemnon's phalanx, chiefs of the Danaans:
Seeing the living man in bronze that glowed
Through the dark air, they shrank in fear. Some turned
625 And ran, as once, when routed, to the ships,
While others raised a battle shout, or tried to,
Mouths agape, mocked by the whispering cry.
Here next he saw Deïphobus, Priam's son,⁶
Mutilated from head to foot, his face
630 And both hands cruelly torn, ears shorn away,
Nose to the noseholes lopped by a shameful stroke.

---

3. Marpessus was a Greek mountain famed for a marble with a luminous quality.
4. Legendary warriors of the generation before the Trojan War, three of the Seven against Thebes who challenged the gods—including Tydeus, the father of Diomedes.
5. Names of Trojans or their allies. Glaucus, with Sarpedon, was leader of the Lycians and killed by Ajax in the *Iliad*. Idaeus was Hector's herald and charioteer.
6. Deïphobus had married Helen after the death of Paris. The mutilation of his body serves as further evidence of Greek disregard for the traditional rules of war.

Barely knowing the shade who quailed before him
Covering up his tortured face, Aeneas
Spoke out to him in his known voice:
                    "Deïphobus,

635   Gallant officer in high Teucer's line,
Who chose this brutal punishment, who had
So much the upper hand of you? I heard
On that last night that you had fallen, spent
After a slaughter of Pelasgians—

640   Fallen on piled-up carnage. It was I
Who built on Rhoeteum Point an empty tomb
And sent a high call to your soul three times.
Your name, your armor, marks the place. I could not
Find you, friend, to put your bones in earth

645   In the old country as I came away."

And Priam's son replied:
                    "You left undone
Nothing, my friend, but gave all ritual due
Deïphobus, due a dead man's shade. My lot
And the Laconian woman's° ghastly doing   Helen's

650   Sank me in this hell. These are the marks
She left me as her memorial. You know
How between one false gladness and another
We spent that last night—no need to remind you.
When the tall deadly horse came at one bound,

655   With troops crammed in its paunch, above our towers,
She made a show of choral dance and led
Our Phrygian women crying out on Bacchus
Here and there—but held a torch amid them,
Signalling to Danaans from the Height.

660   Worn by the long day, heavily asleep,
I lay in my unlucky bridal chamber,
And rest, profound and sweet, most like the rest
Of death, weighed on me as I lay. Meanwhile
She, my distinguished wife, moved all my arms

665   Out of the house—as she had slipped my sword,
My faithful sword, out from beneath my pillow—
Opened the door and called in Menelaus,
Hoping no doubt by this great gift to him,
Her lover, to blot old infamy out. Why hold back

670   From telling it? The two burst in the bedroom,
Joined by that ringleader of atrocity,
Ulysses, of the windking's line.[7] O gods,
If with pure lips I pray, requite the Greeks
With equal suffering! But you, now tell me

---

7. Deïphobus alludes rather maliciously to a legend that Ulysses was the bastard son of Aeolus's son Sisyphus, a legendary thief punished in Tartarus.

675   What in the world has brought you here alive:
        Have you come from your sea wandering, and did heaven
        Direct you? How could harrying fortune send you
        To these sad sunless homes, disordered places?"

        At this point in their talk Aurora,° borne   *goddess of Dawn*
680   Through high air on her glowing rosy car
        Had crossed the meridian: should they linger now
        With stories they might spend the allotted time.
        But at Aeneas' side the Sibyl spoke,
        Warning him briefly:
                    "Night comes on, Aeneas,
685   We use up hours grieving. Here is the place
        Where the road forks: on the right hand it goes
        Past mighty Dis's walls, Elysium way,
        Our way; but the leftward road will punish
        Malefactors, taking them to Tartarus."
690   Deïphobus answered her:
                    "No need for anger,
        Reverend lady. I'll depart and make
        The tally in the darkness full again.
        Go on, sir, glory of us all! Go on,
        Enjoy a better destiny."
                    He spoke,
695   And even as he spoke he turned away.
        Now of a sudden Aeneas looked and saw
        To the left, under a cliff, wide buildings girt
        By a triple wall round which a torrent rushed
        With scorching flames and boulders tossed in thunder,
700   The abyss's Fiery River.[8] A massive gate
        With adamantine° pillars faced the stream,   *unyielding*
        So strong no force of men or gods in war
        May ever avail to crack and bring it down,
        And high in air an iron tower stands
705   On which Tisiphonë,[9] her bloody robe
        Pulled up about her, has her seat and keeps
        Unsleeping watch over the entrance way
        By day and night. From the interior, groans
        Are heard, and thud of lashes, clanking iron,
710   Dragging chains. Arrested in his tracks,
        Appalled by what he heard, Aeneas stood.

        "What are the forms of evil here? O Sister,
        Tell me. And the punishments dealt out:
        Why such a lamentation?"
                    Said the Sibyl:
715   "Light of the Teucrians, it is decreed

---

8. Also known as Phlegethon, one of the five rivers of the   9. One of the Furies.
underworld.

That no pure soul may cross the sill of evil.
When, however, Hecatë appointed me
Caretaker of Avernus wood, she led me
Through heaven's punishments and taught me all.
720   This realm is under Cretan Rhadamanthus'[1]
Iron rule. He sentences. He listens
And makes the souls confess their crooked ways,
How they put off atonements in the world
With foolish satisfaction, thieves of time,
725   Until too late, until the hour of death.
At once the avenger girdled with her whip,
Tisiphonë, leaps down to lash the guilty,
Vile writhing snakes held out on her left hand,
And calls her savage sisterhood.[2] The awaited
730   Time has come, hell gates will shudder wide
On shrieking hinges. Can you see her now,
Her shape, as doorkeeper, upon the sill?
More bestial, just inside, the giant Hydra
Lurks with fifty black and yawning throats.[3]
735   Then Tartarus itself goes plunging down
In darkness twice as deep as heaven is high
For eyes fixed on etherial Olympus.
Here is Earth's ancient race, the brood of Titans,
Hurled by the lightning down to roll forever
740   In the abyss.[4] Here, too, I saw those giant
Twins of Aloeus who laid their hands
Upon great heaven to rend it and to topple
Jove from his high seat,[5] and I saw, too,
Salmoneus[6] paying dearly for the jape
745   Of mimicking Jove's fire, Olympus' thunder:
Shaking a bright torch from a four-horse car
He rode through Greece and his home town in Elis,
Glorying, claiming honor as a god—
Out of his mind, to feign with horses' hoofs
750   On bronze the blast and inimitable bolt.
The father almighty amid heavy cloud
Let fly his missile—no firebrand for him
Nor smoky pitchpine light—and spun the man
Headlong in a huge whirlwind.
                                        One had sight
755   Of Tityos, too, child of all-mothering Earth,[7]

1. Along with his brother, Minos, a judge of the dead.
2. Furies were traditionally depicted with snakes for hair.
3. The Hydra was a monster with 50 heads; wherever one was chopped off, two more would grow. It was killed by Hercules as one of his Twelve Labors.
4. The 12 Titans, including Rhea and Cronos, were children of the primeval couple Ge and Uranus, blasted by the thunderbolts of their own child, Zeus.

5. Otus and Ephialtes were giant sons of Aloeus who attacked the gods by piling mountain upon mountain to climb to heaven. Zeus destroyed them.
6. A king in Greek myth and ancestor of Jason and Pelias, two of the Argonauts.
7. A giant son of Ge (Earth) who was killed by Apollo and Artemis for threatening their mother, Leto.

His body stretched out over nine whole acres
While an enormous vulture with hooked beak
Forages forever in his liver,
His vitals rife with agonies. The bird,
760 Lodged in the chest cavity, tears at his feast,
And tissues growing again get no relief.
As for the Lapiths, need I tell: Ixion,
Pirithoüs, and the black crag overhead
So sure to fall it seems already falling.[8]
765 Golden legs gleam on the feasters' couches,
Dishes in royal luxury prepared
Are laid before them—but the oldest Fury
Crouches near and springs out with her torch,
Her outcry, if they try to touch the meal.
770 Here come those who as long as life remained
Held brothers hateful, beat their parents, cheated
Poor men dependent on them; also those
Who hugged their newfound riches to themselves
And put nothing aside for relatives—
775 A great crowd, this—then men killed for adultery,
Men who took arms in war against the right,
Not scrupling to betray their lords. All these
Are hemmed in here, awaiting punishment.
Best not inquire what punishment, what form
780 Of suffering at their last end overwhelms them.
Some heave at a great boulder, or revolve,
Spreadeagled, hung on wheel-spokes.[9] Theseus
Cleaves to his chair and cleaves to it forever.[1]
Phlegyas in his misery teaches all souls
785 His lesson, thundering out amid the gloom:
'Be warned and study justice, not to scorn
The immortal gods.'[2] Here's one who sold his country,
Foisted a tyrant on her, set up laws
Or nullified them for a price; another
790 Entered his daughter's room to take a bride
Forbidden him. All these dared monstrous wrong
And took what they dared try for. If I had
A hundred tongues, a hundred mouths, a voice
Of iron, I could not tell of all the shapes
795 Their crimes had taken, or their punishments."

---

8. According to Greek myth, Ixion committed several crimes including the attempted rape of Hera, which resulted in the race of Centaurs, horse-men. Pirithous was the son by Zeus of Ixion's wife. At his wedding, the famous battle between his people, the Lapiths, and their neighbors, the Centaurs, occurred. After descending with Theseus to carry off Persephone as his wife, Pirithous never returned.

9. The traditional punishments of Sisyphus and Ixion,

respectively.

1. When Theseus and Pirithous attempted to kidnap Persephone, they unknowingly sat down on the Chair of Forgetfulness, where they were stuck for four years, tormented by Furies, until the arrival of Hercules. Virgil extends the punishment for eternity.

2. Phlegyas was a Thessalian king and by some accounts the father of Ixion.

All this he heard from her who for long years
Had served Apollo. Then she said:
                                    "Come now,
Be on your way, and carry out your mission.
Let us go faster. I can see the walls
800   The Cyclops' forges built[3] and, facing us,
The portico and gate where they command us
To leave the gifts required."
                            On this the two
In haste strode on abreast down the dark paths
Over the space between, and neared the doors.
805   Aeneas gained the entrance, halted there,
Asperged his body with fresh water drops,
And on the sill before him fixed the bough.

Now that at last this ritual was performed,
His duty to the goddess done, they came
810   To places of delight, to green park land,
Where souls take ease amid the Blessed Groves.
Wider expanses of high air endow
Each vista with a wealth of light. Souls here
Possess their own familiar sun and stars.[4]
815   Some train on grassy rings, others compete
In field games, others grapple on the sand.
Feet moving to a rhythmic beat, the dancers
Group in a choral pattern as they sing.
Orpheus, the priest of Thrace, in his long robe
820   Accompanies, plucking his seven notes
Now with his fingers, now with his ivory quill.
Here is the ancient dynasty of Teucer,
Heroes high of heart, beautiful scions,
Born in greater days: Ilus, Assaracus,
825   And Dardanus, who founded Troy.[5] Aeneas
Marvels to see their chariots and gear
Far off, all phantom: lances fixed in earth,
And teams unyoked, at graze on the wide plain.
All joy they took, alive, in cars and weapons,
830   As in the care and pasturing of horses,
Remained with them when they were laid in earth.
He saw, how vividly! along the grass
To right and left, others who feasted there

3. In addition to the savage one-eyed giants of the *Odyssey* and the *Aeneid,* Book 3, Hesiod told of three divine craftsmen Cyclops, giant sons of Ge and Uranus, who made Zeus's divine thunderbolt, among many other great works including the walls of Elysium described here.
4. Although they are underground, the Elysian Fields magically share the attributes of the world above: light, air, sun, and stars.
5. Dardanus, a son of Zeus and a daughter of Atlas, began the Dardanian people when he married the daughter of the local king, Teucer. Ilus, the founder of the city of Troy, and Assaracus were his grandsons, the former the grandfather of Priam, the latter of Anchises, and thus greatgrandfather of Aeneas.

And chorused out a hymn praising Apollo,
835 Within a fragrant laurel grove, where Po[6]
Sprang up and took his course to the world above,
The broad stream flowing on amid the forest.
This was the company of those who suffered
Wounds in battle for their country; those
840 Who in their lives were holy men and chaste
Or worthy of Phoebus in prophetic song;
Or those who bettered life, by finding out
New truths and skills; or those who to some folk
By benefactions made themselves remembered.
845 They all wore snowy chaplets on their brows.
To these souls, mingling on all sides, the Sibyl
Spoke now, and especially to Musaeus,[7]
The central figure, toward whose towering shoulders
All the crowd gazed:
                    "Tell us, happy souls,
850 And you, great seer, what region holds Anchises,
Where is his resting place? For him we came
By ferry across the rivers of Erebus."
And the great soul answered briefly:
                                   "None of us
Has one fixed home. We walk in shady groves
855 And bed on riverbanks and occupy
Green meadows fresh with streams. But if your hearts
Are set on it, first cross this ridge; and soon
I shall point out an easy path."
                              So saying,
He walked ahead and showed them from the height
860 The sweep of shining plain. Then down they went
And left the hilltops.
                      Now Aeneas' father
Anchises, deep in the lush green of a valley,
Had given all his mind to a survey
Of souls, till then confined there, who were bound
865 For daylight in the upper world. By chance
His own were those he scanned now, all his own
Descendants, with their futures and their fates,
Their characters and acts. But when he saw
Aeneas advancing toward him on the grass,
870 He stretched out both his hands in eagerness
As tears wetted his cheeks. He said in welcome:

"Have you at last come, has that loyalty
Your father counted on conquered the journey?

---

6. The Po is Italy's longest river, rising in the Alps and entering the Adriatic some 400 miles eastward near Ravenna.

7. Musaeus (literally, "of the Muses") was a mythical singer closely associated with Eleusis and the singer Orpheus; like Orpheus, he was said to have invented hexameter and perhaps the alphabet.

Am I to see your face, my son, and hear
875   Our voices in communion as before?
I thought so, surely; counting the months I thought
The time would come. My longing has not tricked me.
I greet you now, how many lands behind you,
How many seas, what blows and dangers, son!
880   How much I feared the land of Libya
Might do you harm."
                                    Aeneas said:
                                                "Your ghost,
Your sad ghost, father, often before my mind,
Impelled me to the threshold of this place.
My ships ride anchored in the Tuscan° sea.   *Tyrhhenian*
885   But let me have your hand, let me embrace you,
Do not draw back."
                            At this his tears brimmed over
And down his cheeks. And there he tried three times
To throw his arms around his father's neck,
Three times the shade untouched slipped through his hands,
890   Weightless as wind and fugitive as dream.
Aeneas now saw at the valley's end
A grove standing apart, with stems and boughs
Of woodland rustling, and the stream of Lethe[8]
Running past those peaceful glades. Around it
895   Souls of a thousand nations filled the air,
As bees in meadows at the height of summer
Hover and home on flowers and thickly swarm
On snow-white lilies, and the countryside
Is loud with humming. At the sudden vision
900   Shivering, at a loss, Aeneas asked
What river flowed there and what men were those
In such a throng along the riverside.
His father Anchises told him:
                                        "Souls for whom
A second body is in store: their drink
905   Is water of Lethe, and it frees from care
In long forgetfulness. For all this time
I have so much desired to show you these
And tell you of them face to face—to take
The roster of my children's children here,
910   So you may feel with me more happiness
At finding Italy."
                        "Must we imagine,
Father, there are souls that go from here
Aloft to upper heaven, and once more

---

8. Underworld river of forgetfulness.

Return to bodies' dead weight? The poor souls,
915 How can they crave our daylight so?"

                                    "My son,
I'll tell you, not to leave you mystified,"
Anchises said, and took each point in order:[9]

First, then, the sky and lands and sheets of water,
The bright moon's globe, the Titan sun and stars,
920 Are fed within by Spirit, and a Mind
Infused through all the members of the world
Makes one great living body of the mass.[1]
From Spirit come the races of man and beast,
The life of birds, odd creatures the deep sea
925 Contains beneath her sparkling surfaces,
And fiery energy from a heavenly source
Belongs to the generative seeds of these,
So far as they are not poisoned or clogged
By mortal bodies, their free essence dimmed
930 By earthiness and deathliness of flesh.
This makes them fear and crave, rejoice and grieve.[2]
Imprisoned in the darkness of the body
They cannot clearly see heaven's air; in fact
Even when life departs on the last day
935 Not all the scourges of the body pass
From the poor souls, not all distress of life.
Inevitably, many malformations,
Growing together in mysterious ways,
Become inveterate. Therefore they undergo
940 The discipline of punishments and pay
In penance for old sins: some hang full length
To the empty winds, for some the stain of wrong
Is washed by floods or burned away by fire.[3]
We suffer each his own shade. We are sent
945 Through wide Elysium, where a few abide
In happy lands, till the long day, the round
Of Time fulfilled, has worn our stains away,
Leaving the soul's heaven-sent perception clear,
The fire from heaven pure. These other souls,
950 When they have turned Time's wheel a thousand years,
The god calls in a crowd to Lethe stream,
That there unmemoried they may see again
The heavens and wish re-entry into bodies."

---

9. Anchises' speech blends elements from Platonic, Orphic-Pythagorean, and Stoic philosophy and was fundamental in establishing Virgil's later reputation as privy to the secrets of life and death.
1. Stoic philosophy held that the *anima mundi*, or spirit of the world, had emanated the universe from its primordial fiery ether. Human souls are detached from this ether and only when purified can return again to it.
2. According to Plato, the harmful contagion of the soul by the body brings fears, desires, sorrow, and joy.
3. In Pythagorean doctrine, souls must undergo cycles of purgation and transmigration until cleansed.

Anchises paused. He drew both son and Sibyl
955   Into the middle of the murmuring throng,
Then picked out a green mound from which to view
The souls as they came forward, one by one,
And to take note of faces.[4]

                   "Come," he said,
"What glories follow Dardan generations
960   In after years, and from Italian blood
What famous children in your line will come,
Souls of the future, living in our name,
I shall tell clearly now, and in the telling
Teach you your destiny. That one you see,
965   The young man leaning on a spear unarmed,
Has his allotted place nearest the light.
He will be first to take the upper air,
Silvius, a child with half Italian blood
And an Alban name, your last born, whom your wife,
970   Lavinia, late in your great age will rear
In forests to be king and father of kings.[5]
Through him our race will rule in Alba Longa.[6]
Next him is Procas, pride of the Trojan line,
And Capys, too, then Numitor, then one
975   Whose name restores you: Silvius Aeneas,
Both in arms and piety your peer,
If ever he shall come to reign in Alba.[7]
What men they are! And see their rugged forms
With oakleaf crowns shadowing their brows. I tell you,
980   These are to found Nomentum, Gabii,
Fidenae town, Collatia's hilltop towers,
Pometii, Fort Inuus, Bola, Cora—
Names to be heard for places nameless now.[8]
Then Romulus, fathered by Mars, will come
985   To make himself his grandfather's° companion,   *Numitor*
Romulus, reared by his mother, Ilia,
In the blood-line of Assaracus.[9] Do you see
The double plume of Mars fixed on his crest,
See how the father of the gods himself

---

990   Now marks him out with his own sign of honor?[1]
        Look now, my son: under his auspices
        Illustrious Rome will bound her power with earth,
        Her spirit with Olympus. She'll enclose
        Her seven hills with one great city wall,[2]
995   Fortunate in the men she breeds. Just so
        Cybelë Mother, honored on Berecynthus,[3]
        Wearing her crown of towers, onward rides
        By chariot through the towns of Phrygia,
        In joy at having given birth to gods,
1000   And cherishing a hundred grandsons, heaven
        Dwellers with homes on high.
                                    Turn your two eyes
        This way and see this people, your own Romans.
        Here is Caesar, and all the line of Iulus,
        All who shall one day pass under the dome
1005   Of the great sky: this is the man, this one,
        Of whom so often you have heard the promise,
        Caesar Augustus, son of the deified,[4]
        Who shall bring once again an Age of Gold
        To Latium, to the land where Saturn reigned
1010   In early times.[5] He will extend his power
        Beyond the Garamants° and Indians,   *Africans*
        Over far territories north and south
        Of the zodiacal stars, the solar way,
        Where Atlas,[6] heaven-bearing, on his shoulder
1015   Turns the night-sphere, studded with burning stars.
        At that man's coming even now the realms
        Of Caspia and Maeotia tremble,[7] warned
        By oracles, and the seven mouths of Nile[8]
        Go dark with fear. The truth is, even Alcidës°   *Hercules*
1020   Never traversed so much of earth—I grant

1. With Jupiter, Mars was the chief Italian god, later equated with the Greek war god Ares. The legend of Romulus and Remus made Mars their father and his sacred animal, the she-wolf, their nurse.
2. Rome is dominated by seven hills. The settlement of Romulus and Remus was on the Palatine hill; all seven hills were first enclosed by the Wall of Servius, assigned by legend to King Servius Tullius (6th century) and now dated to the 4th century during the Republic.
3. Mt. Berecynthus was a cult place of Cybele, the Great Mother goddess of Asia Minor, identified by the Greeks with Rhea and introduced into Rome in 204 B.C.E., where her cult was under control of the same priesthood as the Sibylline books.
4. The *gens Iulia*, or Julius clan, claimed descent from Iulus (Ascanius). Octavian (63 B.C.E.–14 C.E.) was the adopted son of Julius Caesar (100–44 B.C.E.), who was deified in 42 B.C.E. Octavian was the first Roman emperor and received the honorary title Augustus ("sacred," "venerable") in 27 C.E.

5. According to Hesiod and other poets, the Golden Age was the period during which Cronos ruled the world, men lived without strife, labor, or injustice, and the earth gave forth its fruits in abundance. The Romans identified Cronos with Saturn, an Italian god of agriculture, by legend an early king of Rome, who introduced agriculture to the region and founded the citadel on the Capitol, at the foot of which his temple stood.
6. Greek myth placed Atlas somewhere in the extreme west of the earth.
7. Caspia was the land around the Central Asian Caspian Sea; Maeotia was the land around the Sea of Azov, north of the Black Sea. The Roman empire never extended quite this far, although its influence certainly may have.
8. The river Nile in Egypt drains into the Mediterranean through a vast and rich delta. Octavian defeated the forces of Mark Antony and Cleopatra at Actium in 31 B.C.E.; he captured Egypt's capital Alexandria and brought it into the empire the following year.

That he could shoot the hind with brazen hoofs
Or bring peace to the groves of Erymanthus,
Or leave Lerna affrighted by his bow.[9]
Neither did he who guides his triumphal car
1025   With reins of vine-shoots twisted, Bacchus, driving
Down from Nysa's height his tiger team.[1]
Do we lag still at carrying our valor
Into action? Can our fear prevent
Our settling in Ausonia?

[*Anchises then points out the future kings of Rome and great men of the early Republic, interpolating Julius Caesar among them. He concludes with young Marcellus, the
nephew and assumed-to-be adopted heir of Augustus, the hope of the future of Rome,
who had died at the age of 20 in 23 B.C.E.*]

1205   After Anchises had conducted him
To every region and had fired his love
Of glory in the years to come, he spoke
Of wars that he must fight, of Laurentines,[2]
And of Latinus' city, then of how
1210   He might avoid or bear each toil to come.

There are two gates of Sleep, one said to be
Of horn, whereby the true shades pass with ease,
The other all white ivory agleam
Without a flaw, and yet false dreams are sent
1215   Through this one by the ghosts to the upper world.[3]
Anchises now, his last instructions given,
Took son and Sibyl there and let them go
By the Ivory Gate.
                            Aeneas made his way
Straight to the ships to see his crews again,
1220   Then sailed directly to Caieta's port.[4]
Bow anchors out, the sterns rest on the beach.

[*Aeneas disembarks at the mouth of the Tiber, and the fulfillment of certain signs
leads him to recognize the land promised him. He makes a pact with King Latinus,
which Juno disrupts by sending the Fury Allecto to assail Latinus's wife, Amata, and
the Rutulian leader, Turnus. The pact is broken, and a powerful alliance of Italian
peoples marches on the Trojan camp. Following divine advice, Aeneas sails up the
Tiber in search of aid, where he finds Evander, king of a small nation of Arcadians on*]

9. Three of the Twelve Labors of Hercules were to slay
the Hydra, which lived in the marshes of Lerna near
Argos, and to capture the Hind of Ceryneia in Arcadia
and the Boar of Erymanthus, a high mountain also in Arcadia (see Color Plate 4).
1. Dionysus was represented with vine shoots and ivy and
often either riding or driving a team of tigresses, as in the
Bacchae of Euripides. Nysa was the legendary mountain
on which he was said to have been raised by nymphs.

2. Latinus's community in Latium.
3. The twin Gates of Dreams derive from the *Odyssey*,
Book 19. The prophetic and admonitory nature of dreams
was accepted by most ancients, although only certain
dreams were held to be significant. There has been much
debate over the significance of Aeneas's departure via the
Ivory Gate of false dreams.
4. Caieta (now Gaeta) is 58 kilometers northwest of
Cumae.

the site where Rome one day will be. Evander is honoring Hercules, who had once visited them and disposed of Cacus, a local nuisance.]

from **Book 8**

[EVANDER]

405 When they had carried out the ritual
They turned back to the town. And, slowed by age,
The king walked, keeping Aeneas and his son
Close by his side, with talk of various things
To make the long path easy. Marveling,
410 Aeneas gladly looked at all about him,
Delighted with the setting, asking questions,
Hearing of earlier men and what they left.
Then King Evander, founder unaware
Of Rome's great citadel,[1] said:
                              "These woodland places
415 Once were homes of local fauns and nymphs
Together with a race of men that came
From tree trunks, from hard oak: they had no way
Of settled life, no arts of life, no skill
At yoking oxen, gathering provisions,
420 Practising husbandry, but got their food
From oaken boughs and wild game hunted down.
In that first time, out of Olympian heaven,
Saturn came here in flight from Jove in arms,
An exile from a kingdom lost; he brought
425 These unschooled men together from the hills
Where they were scattered, gave them laws, and chose
The name of Latium, from his latency
Or safe concealment in this countryside.[2]
In his reign were the golden centuries
430 Men tell of still, so peacefully he ruled,
Till gradually a meaner, tarnished age
Came on with fever of war and lust of gain.
Then came Ausonians and Sicanians,[3]
And Saturn's land now often changed her name,
435 And there were kings, one savage and gigantic,
Thybris, from whom we afterborn Italians
Named the river Tiber. The old name,
Albula, was lost.[4] As for myself,
In exile from my country, I set out

1. The Pallanteum on the Palatine, where Romulus would build his city and Augustus had a palace.
2. Evander retells the myth of Saturn's gift of agriculture to Latium and the Golden Age to which Anchises alluded in Book 6. According to Greek myth, Cronos (Saturn) was a Titan expelled by his son, Zeus (Jove).
3. The Ausonians were a people from central Italy; the Sicanians were from central Sicily.
4. The Tiber formed the border between Latium and the Sabine people to the north.

440   For the sea's end, but Fortune that prevails
            In everything, Fate not to be thrown off,
            Arrested me in this land—solemn warnings
            Came from my mother, from the nymph Carmentis,
            Backed by the god Apollo, to urge me here."[5]

445   Just after this, as he went on he showed
            The altar and the gate the Romans call
            Carmental,[6] honoring as of old the nymph
            And prophetess Carmentis, first to sing
            The glory of Pallanteum and Aeneas'
450   Great descendants.[7] Then he showed the wood
            That Romulus would make a place of refuge,
            Then the grotto called the Lupercal
            Under the cold crag, named in Arcadian fashion
            After Lycaean Pan.[8] And then as well
455   He showed the sacred wood of Argiletum,
            "Argus' death," and took oath by it, telling
            Of a guest, Argus, put to death.[9] From there
            He led to our Tarpeian site and Capitol,
            All golden now, in those days tangled, wild
460   With underbrush—but awesome even then.[1]
            A strangeness there filled country hearts with dread
            And made them shiver at the wood and Rock.

            "Some god," he said, "it is not sure what god,
            Lives in this grove, this hilltop thick with leaves.
465   Arcadians think they've seen great Jove himself
            Sometimes with his right hand shaking the aegis
            To darken sky and make the storm clouds rise
            Towering in turmoil.[2] Here, too, in these walls
            Long fallen down, you see what were two towns,
470   Monuments of the ancients. Father Janus
            Founded one stronghold, Saturn the other,

---

5. Carmentis (Greek: Themis) was a nymph and prophetess who brought writing to Latium. Greek myth regarded Evander as her son by Hermes, which made him a distant relation of Aeneas through Dardanus.

6. In Rome, Carmentis had her own priest, a two-day festival in January, and a shrine at the foot of the Capitoline hill, near the Porta Carmentalis, the "altar and the gate" described here as already standing.

7. The name Carmentis derives from the Latin word *carmen*, or religious utterance, a term that also came to mean "song" and then "poem." Carmentis was also identified with the Muses. Pallanteum was an Arcadian city often cited as the origin of the name of the Palatine hill.

8. The *ficus Ruminalis* was the fig tree under which the she-wolf was said to have suckled the twins; the Lupercal was the cave on the north side of the Palatine where the twins had ostensibly been found. Both could still be visited in Virgil's day. The god Pan originated from Mount Lykaion in Arcadia. He was a shepherd god and protector

of shepherds and is identified here with "Lycaeus," the god of wolves.

9. In Virgil's time, Argiletum was a district of artisans and shopkeepers extending from the south of the Quirinal to the Forum. Argus was evidently a guest of Evander who met his death because he was suspected of conspiring against his host.

1. The Tarpeian Rock was a steep cliff on the Capitoline hill from which traitors and murderers were thrown. The hill itself was the focal point of Roman religion and seen by ancient Romans as the heart of their empire. First built in the 6th century, the temple of Jupiter Capitolinus on its summit was one of the most striking sights of antiquity, especially after it was rebuilt in the 1st century B.C.E. with a golden head.

2. The *genius loci*, or spirit of the place, serves to sanction both the piety and the imperial ambitions of future Romans.

Named Janiculum and Saturnia."[3]

Conversing of such matters, going toward
Austere Evander's house, they saw his cattle
475   Lowing everywhere in what is now
Rome's Forum and her fashionable quarter,
Carinae.[4] As they came up to the door,
Evander said:
            "In victory Hercules
Bent for this lintel, and these royal rooms
480   Were grand enough for him. Friend, have the courage
To care little for wealth, and shape yourself,
You too, to merit godhead. Do not come
Disdainfully into our needy home."[5]

Even as he spoke, he led under the gabled
485   Narrow roof Aeneas' mighty figure
And made him rest where on strewn leaves he spread
A Libyan bearskin. Swiftly Night came on
To fold her dusky wings about the earth.

[*The two leaders make an alliance, and Evander entrusts his son, Pallas, to Aeneas's
care in the war. Aeneas collects further allies, and his mother presents him with a suit
of armor made by Vulcan, including a shield adorned with scenes from the future history of Rome. Turnus seizes on Aeneas's absence to attack the Trojan camp, nearly
succeeding in taking it. The return of Aeneas with his allies tips the balance in the
other direction. Turnus kills Pallas in single combat, stripping him of his sword belt,
which he dons as a token of his victory. Further battles ensue, including the death of
the virgin warrior Camilla on the Latin side. Turnus accepts decisive single combat
with Aeneas, but Juno persuades his sister, the nymph Juturna, to cause the truce to
fail, and the seemingly endless battle recommences.*]

from Book 12

[THE DEATH OF TURNUS]

Omnipotent Olympus' king meanwhile
1070   Had words for Juno, as she watched the combat
Out of a golden cloud. He said:
                 "My consort,
What will the end be? What is left for you?

3. A prominent ridge on the west bank of the Tiber at
Rome, the Janiculum was early on associated with Janus,
the god of door and gate, and site of an early defensive
outpost. Legend made Saturn the founder of "Saturnia"
on the Capitoline hill.

4. The double vision of past and present on the Palatine allows Virgil to combine two Roman virtues: the strict traditional morals of the rustic Italians and the sophisticated
and cosmopolitan wealth of imperial Rome. Originally a
marketplace, the Forum was the center of social and political life. The Carinae was where the emperor lived.

5. According to a Roman myth, Hercules stopped at the
site of future Rome while engaged in his labors. Cacus, a
local thief or monster, stole the cattle of Geryon and was
slain by Hercules for his trouble. Aeneas has arrived on
the anniversary of the deed. Hercules and Aeneas are par-
alleled throughout the *Aeneid* because both heroes were
persecuted by Juno. Both figures can also be identified
with Emperor Augustus, a likely target of Evander's
words of humility here at the future site of the imperial
palace.

You yourself know, and say you know, Aeneas
Born for heaven, tutelary° of this land,   *protector*
1075   By fate to be translated to the stars.
What do you plan? What are you hoping for,
Keeping your seat apart in the cold clouds?
Fitting, was it, that a mortal archer
Wound an immortal? That a blade let slip
1080   Should be restored to Turnus, and new force
Accrue to a beaten man? Without your help
What could Juturna do?[1] Come now, at last
Have done, and heed our pleading, and give way.
Let yourself no longer be consumed
1085   Without relief by all that inward burning;
Let care and trouble not forever come to me
From your sweet lips. The finish is at hand.
You had the power to harry men of Troy
By land and sea, to light the fires of war
1090   Beyond belief, to scar a family
With mourning before marriage. I forbid
Your going further."[2]
                           So spoke Jupiter,
And with a downcast look Juno replied:

"Because I know that is your will indeed,
1095   Great Jupiter, I left the earth below,
Though sore at heart, and left the side of Turnus.
Were it not so, you would not see me here
Suffering all that passes, here alone,
Resting on air. I should be armed in flames
1100   At the very battle-line, dragging the Trojans
Into a deadly action. I persuaded
Juturna—I confess—to help her brother
In his hard lot, and I approved her daring
Greater difficulties to save his life,
1105   But not that she should fight with bow and arrow.
This I swear by Styx' great fountainhead
Inexorable, which high gods hold in awe.[3]
I yield now and for all my hatred leave
This battlefield. But one thing not retained
1110   By fate I beg for Latium, for the future
Greatness of your kin: when presently
They crown peace with a happy wedding day—
So let it be—and merge their laws and treaties,
Never command the land's own Latin folk

---

1. Jupiter is referring to earlier incidents in the war involving divine meddling. The water nymph Juturna was
the sister and protectress of Turnus.
2. Jupiter outlines the limits of Juno's power against fate,
which legislates the outcome of events but not necessarily

the way in which they unroll.
3. It was customary for the Olympian gods to swear on
the river Styx. Such oaths were held by the gods to be inviolable.

1115   To change their old name, to become new Trojans,
       Known as Teucrians; never make them alter
       Dialect or dress. Let Latium be.
       Let there be Alban kings for generations,
       And let Italian valor be the strength
1120   Of Rome in after times. Once and for all
       Troy fell, and with her name let her lie fallen."[4]

       The author of men and of the world replied
       With a half-smile:
                 "Sister of Jupiter
       Indeed you are, and Saturn's other child,
1125   To feel such anger, stormy in your breast.
       But come, no need; put down this fit of rage.
       I grant your wish. I yield, I am won over
       Willingly. Ausonian folk will keep
       Their fathers' language and their way of life,
1130   And, that being so, their name. The Teucrians
       Will mingle and be submerged, incorporated.
       Rituals and observances of theirs
       I'll add, but make them Latin, one in speech.
       The race to come, mixed with Ausonian blood,
1135   Will outdo men and gods in its devotion,
       You shall see—and no nation on earth
       Will honor and worship you so faithfully."[5]

       To all this Juno nodded in assent
       And, gladdened by his promise, changed her mind.
1140   Then she withdrew from sky and cloud.
                         That done,
       The Father set about a second plan—
       To take Juturna from her warring brother.
       Stories are told of twin fiends, called the Dirae,[6]
       Whom, with Hell's Megaera, deep Night bore
1145   In one birth. She entwined their heads with coils
       Of snakes and gave them wings to race the wind.
       Before Jove's throne, a step from the cruel king,
       These twins attend him and give piercing fear
       To ill mankind, when he who rules the gods
1150   Deals out appalling death and pestilence,
       Or war to terrify our wicked cities.[7]
       Jove now dispatched one of these, swift from heaven,
       Bidding her be an omen to Juturna.
       Down she flew, in a whirlwind borne to earth,

---

4. Virgil provides an explanation for the disappearance of any historical trace of the Trojan origins of Rome.

5. The temple of Jupiter Capitolinus was dedicated to Jupiter, Juno, and Minerva.

6. The Latin word for the Furies, whom the tragedian Aeschylus called the daughters of Night. Megaera was one of the three Furies named in antiquity.

7. Here, rather than summoned from the underworld, the Furies are depicted as acting in the service of Olympian justice.

1155   Just like an arrow driven through a cloud
From a taut string, an arrow armed with gall
Of deadly posion, shot by a Parthian[8]—
A Parthian or a Cretan—for a wound
Immedicable; whizzing unforeseen
1160   It goes through racing shadows: so the spawn
Of Night went diving downward to the earth.

On seeing Trojan troops drawn up in face
Of Turnus' army, she took on at once
The shape of that small bird that perches late
1165   At night on tombs or desolate roof-tops
And troubles darkness with a gruesome song.[9]
Shrunk to that form, the fiend in Turnus' face
Went screeching, flitting, flitting to and fro
And beating with her wings against his shield.
1170   Unstrung by numbness, faint and strange, he felt
His hackles rise, his voice choke in his throat.
As for Juturna, when she knew the wings,
The shriek to be the fiend's, she tore her hair,
Despairing, then she fell upon her cheeks
1175   With nails, upon her breast with clenched hands.

"Turnus, how can your sister help you now?
What action is still open to me, soldierly
Though I have been? Can I by any skill
Hold daylight for you? Can I meet and turn
1180   This deathliness away? Now I withdraw,
Now leave this war. Indecent birds, I fear you;
Spare me your terror. Whip-lash of your wings
I recognize, that ghastly sound, and guess
Great-hearted Jupiter's high cruel commands.
1185   Returns for my virginity, are they?
He gave me life eternal—to what end?
Why has mortality been taken from me?
Now beyond question I could put a term
To all my pain, and go with my poor brother
1190   Into the darkness, his companion there.
Never to die? Will any brook of mine
Without you, brother, still be sweet to me?
If only earth's abyss were wide enough
To take me downward, goddess though I am,
1195   To join the shades below!"
                              So she lamented,
Then with a long sigh, covering up her head
In her grey mantle, sank to the river's depth.

---

8. The Parthians held an empire in what is now eastern
Iran.

9. The Fury takes the form of an owl, a bird closely associated with death.

Aeneas moved against his enemy
And shook his heavy pine-tree spear. He called
1200   From his hot heart:
            "Rearmed now, why so slow?
Why, even now, fall back? The contest here
Is not a race, but fighting to the death
With spear and sword. Take on all shapes there are,
Summon up all your nerve and skill, choose any
1205   Footing, fly among the stars, or hide
In caverned earth—"
                    The other shook his head,
Saying:
        "I do not fear your taunting fury,
Arrogant prince. It is the gods I fear
And Jove my enemy."
                    He said no more,
1210   But looked around him. Then he saw a stone,
Enormous, ancient, set up there to prevent
Landowners' quarrels. Even a dozen picked men
Such as the earth produces in our day
Could barely lift and shoulder it. He swooped
1215   And wrenched it free, in one hand, then rose up
To his heroic height, ran a few steps,
And tried to hurl the stone against his foe—
But as he bent and as he ran
And as he hefted and propelled the weight
1220   He did not know himself. His knees gave way,
His blood ran cold and froze. The stone itself,
Tumbling through space, fell short and had no impact.

Just as in dreams when the night-swoon of sleep
Weighs on our eyes, it seems we try in vain
1225   To keep on running, try with all our might,
But in the midst of effort faint and fail;
Our tongue is powerless, familiar strength
Will not hold up our body, not a sound
Or word will come: just so with Turnus now:
1230   However bravely he made shift to fight
The immortal fiend blocked and frustrated him.
Flurrying images passed through his mind.
He gazed at the Rutulians, and beyond them,
Gazed at the city, hesitant, in dread.
1235   He trembled now before the poised spear-shaft
And saw no way to escape; he had no force
With which to close, or reach his foe, no chariot
And no sign of the charioteer, his sister.[1]

---

1. In an earlier scene in Book 12, where Juturna replaces Turnus's charioteer and spirits him away from the scene of battle.

At a dead loss he stood. Aeneas made
1240   His deadly spear flash in the sun and aimed it,
Narrowing his eyes for a lucky hit.
Then, distant still, he put his body's might
Into the cast. Never a stone that soared
From a wall-battering catapult went humming
1245   Loud as this, nor with so great a crack
Burst ever a bolt of lightning. It flew on
Like a black whirlwind bringing devastation,
Pierced with a crash the rim of sevenfold shield,
Cleared the cuirass'° edge, and passed clean through   *breastplate's*
1250   The middle of Turnus' thigh. Force of the blow
Brought the huge man to earth, his knees buckling,
And a groan swept the Rutulians as they rose,
A groan heard echoing on all sides from all
The mountain range, and echoed by the forests.
1255   The man brought down, brought low, lifted his eyes
And held his right hand out to make his plea:

"Clearly I earned this, and I ask no quarter.
Make the most of your good fortune here.
If you can feel a father's grief—and you, too,
1260   Had such a father in Anchises—then
Let me bespeak your mercy for old age
In Daunus,° and return me, or my body,   *Turnus's father*
Stripped, if you will, of life, to my own kin.
You have defeated me. The Ausonians
1265   Have seen me in defeat, spreading my hands.
Lavinia is your bride. But go no further
Out of hatred."
                    Fierce under arms, Aeneas
Looked to and fro, and towered, and stayed his hand
Upon the sword-hilt. Moment by moment now
1270   What Turnus said began to bring him round
From indecision. Then to his glance appeared
The accurst swordbelt surmounting Turnus' shoulder,
Shining with its familiar studs—the strap
Young Pallas wore when Turnus wounded him
1275   And left him dead upon the field; now Turnus
Bore that enemy token on his shoulder—
Enemy still. For when the sight came home to him,
Aeneas raged at the relic of his anguish
Worn by this man as trophy. Blazing up
1280   And terrible in his anger, he called out:

"You in your plunder, torn from one of mine,
Shall I be robbed of you? This wound will come
From Pallas: Pallas makes this offering

And from your criminal blood exacts his due."

1285 He sank his blade in fury in Turnus' chest.
Then all the body slackened in death's chill,
And with a groan for that indignity
His spirit fled into the gloom below.

⁂

RESONANCES

Horace: Ode 1. 24: Why should our grief for a man so loved[1]

Why should our grief for a man so loved
know any shame or limit? Teach us sad songs,
Melpomene. Your father gave you a clear voice
    and with it the lyre.[2]

5   So a sleep that will not end bears down
upon Quintilius.[3] Honour, incorruptible Honesty,
sister of Justice, and naked Truth—
    when will they ever see his equal?

Many good men will weep at his death,
10 but none weep more than you, Virgil. You ask the gods
for Quintilius, but your piety counts for nothing.
    They did not give him on such terms.

What if you were to tune a sweeter lyre than Thracian Orpheus[4]
and trees came to listen? Would blood come back
15 into the empty shade which Mercury has once herded
    into his black flock

with fearful crook?[5] Prayers do not easily
persuade him to open the gates of death.
It is hard. But, by enduring, we can make lighter
20   what the gods forbid us to change.

---

1. Translated by David West. Horace was a few years younger than Virgil and owed to his well-connected friend his entry into Roman society, the patronage of Maecenas, and his first success as a poet. In this ode, as in the ones later in this volume (page 1256), Horace begins with an event in his life and draws poetic imagery and philosophical lessons from it. He weaves in allusions to Virgil's poetry and takes for granted their shared stoic viewpoint, inviting the reader to share with them in learning from life's calamities.
2. Horace invokes Melpomene, the Muse of tragedy, and the daughter of Zeus and Mnemosyne. The lyre was U-shaped and four- or seven-stringed, the standard instrument

of poet-singers.
3. A Roman patrician and friend of Horace and Virgil who died in 24 or 23 B.C.E.
4. Legendary pre-Homeric poet whose singing persuaded Hades to release the dead Eurydice. When he lost her a second time, he retired to the wilds in grief, where his lamenting songs moved beasts, rocks, and trees. Virgil recounts the story in detail in Book 4 of the *Georgics*.
5. Mercury (Greek: Hermes), inventor of the lyre, was also the traditional guide of souls to the underworld. Compare this version of the power of music over death with the more playful version of Ode 2.13 (page 1258).

Macrobius: from *Saturnalia*[1]

Book 1, Chapter 24

As Praetextatus[2] ended his discourse, the company for a while regarded him in wide-eyed wonder and amazement. Then one of the guests began to praise his memory, another his learning, and all his knowledge of the observances of religion; for he alone, they declared, knew the secrets of the nature of godhead, he alone had the intelligence to apprehend the divine and the ability to expound it. But Evangelus interrupted, saying: I am certainly full of admiration for a capacity to understand the powers of all those mighty deities, but to call on our poet of Mantua[3] to corroborate every statement in a theological exposition would seem to suggest partiality rather than a reasoned judgment. For my part, should I not take it that Vergil was imitating some other poet when he referred to the sun and moon as "Liber and kindly Ceres," hearing the names so used but not knowing why?[4] Unless, perhaps, just as the Greeks are immoderate in their praise of all that is Greek, we too would turn even our poets into philosophers, although Cicero himself, who maintained that he was as devoted to philosophy as to oratory, cannot discuss the nature of the gods or fate, or divination, without impairing his reputation as an orator, by his unmethodical treatment of these subjects.[5]

Cicero, replied Symmachus,[6] is proof against your criticism, Evangelus, but we shall consider him later. At present we are concerned with Vergil, and I should be glad if you would tell us whether, in your judgment, his works are fit only for the instruction of schoolboys, or whether you would admit that their contents can serve higher ends; for it seems to me that for you Vergil's verse is, still, what it was for the rest of us in boyhood, when our masters would read it to us and we would recite it to them.

I should rather put it this way, Symmachus, said Evangelus. When we were boys we had an uncritical admiration for Vergil, because our masters, as well as the inexperience of our youth, did not allow us to see his faults. That he had faults no one can honestly deny. In fact he admitted as much himself, for on his deathbed he bequeathed his *Aeneid* to the flames; and why should he have done this unless he was anxious to keep from posterity something which he knew would damage his reputation? And how

---

1. Translated by Percival Vaughan Davies. Ambrosius Theodosius Macrobius (*fl.* late 4th or early 5th century C.E.) was roughly contemporary to Augustine and wrote for the same educated, patrician audience but with the opposite intent. Macrobius was at the heart of what is known as the "pagan revival," a defense of old Roman values and religious beliefs that regarded Virgil as its guiding light. The *Saturnalia* recounts the dialogues among several literary figures, including Servius, author of an important commentary on the *Aeneid,* and a probably fictitious ignoramus named Evangelus, that took place over three days in the year 384 during banquets at the houses of some leading members of the Roman aristocracy. The selections included here indicate the extraordinary esteem in which Virgil and his poems were held in the late Roman Empire and the wide variety of qualities attributed to them.

2. Vettius Agorius Praetextatus (c. 320–84 C.E.), the host of the first day of the Saturnalia, was a pagan senator and a resolute opponent of Christianity. He held many important state offices as well as priesthoods in traditional public cults and in the Oriental mystery cults of Isis, Magna Mater (Cybele), and Mithras.

3. Virgil was born in 70 B.C.E. in a village near Mantua,

then part of Cisalpine Gaul.

4. A reference to *Georgics* 1.7. Liber was an Italian god of fertility and wine who was identified with Dionysus. Ceres was a goddess of growth identified with Demeter. Evangelus argues that Virgil used their names as personifications of wine and grain rather than as references to their cultic qualities.

5. Marcus Tullius Cicero (106–43 B.C.E.) was Rome's greatest orator and an important political figure of the late republic. His writings on rhetoric and his eclectic philosophy were equally influential on pagan Romans and on early Christians such as Augustine. Evangelus refers especially to the book *On Divination,* published shortly after Caesar's murder, which was critical of the Stoic reliance on divination.

6. Quintus Aurelius Symmachus (c. 340–402 C.E.), the host of the third day, was a Roman senator, orator, and letter writer and prefect of Rome from 384–385. He had a successful literary career and was a leading advocate of the pagan religious cause against the Christian emperors. His religious energies were focused on the maintenance of Roman public cults and priesthoods.

right he was! For he was ashamed to think what the verdict on him would be, if any should come to read of a goddess begging from her only husband—and that a husband by whom, as well she knew, she had not had a child—a gift of arms for her son,[7] or if countless other passages should come to light in which the poet had offended against good taste—whether by his use of Greek and outlandish expressions or by the faulty arrangement of his work.

All shuddered as they heard these words, and Symmachus retorted: Vergil's renown, Evangelus, is such that no one can add to it by praise or detract from it by disparagement. And, as for your carping criticisms, anyone from the lowest ranks of the grammarians can answer them, so that there is no need to put our friend Servius, who, to my mind, surpasses the teachers of former times in learning, to the trouble of rebutting such charges. But since, outstanding poet though he is, his poetic skill displeases you, tell me whether his rhetorical powers meet with your approval, for they are very great.[8]

Evangelus at first smiled but then replied: True indeed! All that remains for you people to do now is to proclaim Vergil an orator as well. And I am not surprised, for not so long ago you were canvassing his promotion to a place among the philosophers.

If, in your opinion, said Symmachus, Vergil should be regarded as having no thought for anything but poetry (although you go so far as to grudge him the name of poet), listen to what he has himself to say about the many kinds of learning which his work entailed. For there is a letter of his, addressed to Augustus, which begins with these words: "I am getting many letters from you" (and goes on) "as for my Aeneas, if I now had anything worthy of your attention, I should gladly send it; but the subject on which I have embarked is so vast that I think I must have been almost mad to have entered upon it; all the more so since, as you know, there are other and much more important studies which claim from me a share in the work."[9] What Vergil says here is consistent with that wealth of material which almost all the literary critics carelessly pass by with (as the proverb says) "dusty feet"—as though a grammarian were permitted to understand nothing beyond the meanings of words. Thus those fine fellows have set hard and fast bounds to their science, like the tracts fixed and defined by the augurs;[1] and, if anyone were to dare to overstep these prescribed limits, he would have to be deemed guilty of as heinous an offense as if he had peered into the temple from which all males are banned.[2] But we, who claim to have a finer taste, shall not suffer the secret places of this sacred poem to remain concealed, but we shall examine the approaches to its hidden meanings and throw open its inmost shrine for the worship of the learned. I should be sorry to seem to be anxious to undertake the whole work single-handed, and I propose therefore only to point out the most forcible of the rhetorical devices and conceits that are to be found in Vergil's work, leaving Eusebius,[3] that most eloquent of orators, to deal with Vergil's skill in oratory, a theme which—thanks to his learning, and experience as a teacher—he will handle better

---

7. Evangelus refers to *Aeneid*, Book 8, where Venus requests arms for her illegitimate son, Aeneas, from her husband, Vulcan, who in a famous mythological episode had also trapped her in bed with Mars.

8. Rhetoric is the art and effect of words, whether applied to poetry, as here, or in its purest form as oratory, the art of public speaking.

9. In his account of Virgil's life, the Roman historian Suetonius refers to letters from Augustus; this letter is

perhaps in reply to one of those.

1. The official Roman diviners read auspices, which were signs from the sky or from birds in flight. The first step was to mark off a *templum*, a rectangular space in which the auspices were to be sought.

2. The Bona Dea ("Good Goddess") had an annual nocturnal ceremony in Rome from which men were rigorously excluded.

3. A Greek rhetorician.

than I. As for the rest of you here, I would earnestly beg that each of you contribute, as it were to a common feast, anything that he may have noted as particularly striking about the poet's genius.

These words aroused great, and general, enthusiasm, each of the company wishing to hear the others and overlooking the fact that he too would himself be called on to make a like contribution. Mutual encouragement led to ready and willing assent, and, turning to Praetextatus, all begged him to give his opinion first, to be followed by the rest in the order in which they happened to be sitting.

Of all the high qualities for which Vergil is praised, said Vettius, my constant reading of his poems leads me, for my part, to admire the great learning with which he has observed the rules of the pontifical law[4] in many different parts of his work. One might well suppose that he had made a special study of this law, and if my discourse does not prove unequal to so lofty a topic, I undertake to show that our Vergil may fairly be regarded as a Pontifex Maximus.[5]

Flavianus[6] was the next to speak. I find in our poet, he said, such knowledge of augural law that, even if he were unskilled in all other branches of learning, the exhibition of this knowledge alone would win him high esteem.

I, added Eustathius,[7] should give the highest praise to his use of Greek models—a cautious use and one which may even have the appearance of being accidental, since he sometimes skillfully conceals the debt, although at other times he imitates openly—did I not admire even more his knowledge of astronomy and of the whole field of philosophy, and the sparing and restrained way in which he makes occasional, and everywhere praiseworthy, use of this knowledge in his poems.

Furius Albinus was placed on the other side of Praetextatus, and next to him Caecina.[8] Both spoke highly of the way in which Vergil strove to profit by the work of earlier writers, Furius referring to lines and passages, Caecina to single words.

Avienus[9] said: I shall not take it upon myself to dare to praise any single virtue in Vergil's work, but I shall listen to what the rest of you have to say, and, if any remark of yours or anything in my long reading of the poet suggests an observation, I shall make it, as the occasion for it may arise. But bear in mind that it is to our friend Servius that we must go for an explanation of any obscurity, since of all literary critics he is far the greatest.[1]

These proposals were unanimously accepted, and Praetextatus, seeing that all were looking toward him, said: Philosophy, the discipline of disciplines, is the gods' unequaled gift to man.[2] It must therefore have the honor of being our first topic. Let Eustathius remember, then, that all other discourses give place to his and that he is to open the discussion. You, Flavianus, will follow him. I shall find it refreshing to listen

4. Sacred law.

5. Leading member of the priestly college and, from the reign of Augustus, something like a "high priest," a position always held by the emperor until refused by the Christian Gratian (375–383). The position was thus a pressing issue at the time of the *Saturnalia*'s composition, c. 384.

6. Virius Nicomachus Flavianus (c. 340–394 C.E.), the host of the second day, was a distinguished senator and historian. As praetorian prefect under the usurper Eugenius (392–394 C.E.), Flavianus conducted a full-scale pagan revival in Rome.

7. A philosopher-technician, connoisseur of the three schools (Academic, Stoic, and Peripatetic), and perhaps the Neoplatonic philosopher Eustathius of Cappadocius.

8. Furius Albinus and Caecina were two of the three members of the Albini at the Saturnalia (the third, Caecina's son Decius, was 15 at the time and expected to hold his tongue). Furius Albinus was prefect of Rome from 389–391. Caecina was of the same generation as Symmachus, a consulary of Numidia in 365, and a priest of Vesta.

9. Possibly the Avienus who dedicated a collection of 42 fables to Macrobius.

1. Still young at this date, Servius was the author of a celebrated commentary on the *Aeneid* that is still studied today.

2. Roman philosophy was primarily concerned with ethics and included what we would now call theology.

to the two of you, and some respite from talking will enable me to recover strength to speak.

Meanwhile the head slave (whose duty it was to burn incense before the household gods, to arrange for the provision of food, and to direct the tasks of the domestic servants) had come to inform his master that the household staff had finished the customary yearly feast; for in houses where religious usages are observed it is the practice at the Saturnalia to compliment the slaves by first providing for them a dinner prepared as though for the master, and it is not until this meal is over that the table is spread again for the head of the household.[3] And so it was that the chief servant entered to announce the hour of dinner and to summon the masters to it. Then, said Praetextatus, our friend Vergil must be kept for a more suitable time of day, and let us devote a fresh morning to a systematic examination of his poetry. Now the hour reminds us that my table is to have the honor of your company. But Eustathius, and after him Nicomachus, must not forget that at tomorrow's discussion the duty of speaking first is reserved for them.

My meeting with you all, added Flavianus, is in accordance with the ruling which we have already approved, that my household gods are to have the privilege and pleasure of entertaining this distinguished gathering tomorrow. All agreed, and they went in to dinner in high spirits, recalling to one another with approval the topics which they had debated together.

from *Book 2, Chapter 1*

When dinner was now over and the diners, having eaten sparingly of a modest number of dishes, were growing merry, though the cups were small, Avienus said: In similar lines and with the change of but a few words Vergil has well and shrewdly hit off the difference between a riotous and a sober meal. For of the din which attends the splendor and magnificence of a royal banquet he writes:

> When first there came a lull in the feast [*Aeneid* 1.723]

but, when his heroes sit down to a simple repast, he makes no reference to a lull, because there had been no previous clamor, and says instead:

> When hunger had been banished by the feast. [*Aeneid* 1.216]

This dinner of ours has combined the moderation of the heroic age with the good taste of our own; it is sober yet elegant, carefully planned without being lavish. And for all Plato's eloquence I have no hesitation in comparing it with—nay, in preferring it to—Agathon's banquet,[1] for our host is no whit inferior to Socrates in character and is at the same time more influential in public life than the philosopher; and, as for the rest of you, my friends, your practice of all the virtues is too well known for anyone to regard you as comparable with any comic poet or with Alcibiades (a man whose courage was directed to criminal ends) or with any other in that large company.

Hush! said Praetextatus. Respect, I beg you, the honored name of Socrates, although you can say what you like about the rest of the guests at that banquet, for these distinguished friends of ours would by general consent be regarded as superior to them. But tell me, Avienus, what have you in mind in making this comparison?

---

3. The fundamental principle of the Saturnalia was the inversion of social order. Consequently, the slaves dine before their master and are allowed temporary liberty to do as they like.

1. Plato's *Symposium* (c. 384–369 B.C.E.) describes an Athenian banquet that supposedly takes place at the house of the tragedian Agathon. The participants include the philosopher Socrates and the controversial politician and general Alcibiades; the topic is love.

Just this, said he, that, in spite of their high brows, one of those people was prepared to call for the admission of a lute player, that a girl artificially made up to enhance her charms might beguile their philosophic conversation with pleasant tunes and suggestive dances.[2] The purpose on that occasion was to celebrate Agathon's success in the theater; but we, for our part, are failing to introduce any pleasurable relaxation in doing honor to the god whose festival this is.[3] And yet I am well aware that none of you sees any particular merit in wearing a sad and gloomy countenance, nor do you greatly admire the man Crassus, who (as Cicero tells us, on the authority of Lucilius), laughed but once in all his life.[4]

Praetextatus replied that his household gods were not accustomed to take any pleasure in a cabaret show and that such a show would ill become so serious a gathering. But Symmachus rejoined: "At the Saturnalia, best of days," as the poet of Verona says,[5] I take it that we should neither imitate the Stoics and repel pleasure as a foe nor follow the Epicureans and make pleasure the highest good.[6] Let us then make humor without impropriety our aim.

❧

✦ ✠ ✦

Ovid

43 B.C.E.–18 C.E.

The poet Publius Ovidius Naso had the misfortune to experience the extremes of life in imperial Rome: after some years at the height of fame in the center of the world, he was abruptly exiled to the far reaches of the empire, on the weather-beaten shore of the Black Sea, where, he complained bitterly, the barbarous inhabitants couldn't even understand Latin and he lived in fear for his life. While we will never know the precise reasons behind this precipitous change in fortunes, the usual explanation that he was accused of immorality does at least resonate with the irreverent and unpredictable tone of Ovid's poetry. For example, the erotic verses that first made his name—the *Loves* (sometime after 20 B.C.E.), *The Art of Love* (c. 1 B.C.E.), and *Remedy of Love* (1 B.C.E.–1 C.E.)—sometimes celebrate and sometimes satirize the single-minded pursuit of sexual pleasure. The *Metamorphoses* (2–8 C.E.), Ovid's *magnum opus*, recounts the history of the world from the first creation through the reign of Augustus. It too is a double-edged work, a collection of wondrous transformations and beautiful myths but also a chronicle of the disaster and suffering of mortals and the misdeeds perpetrated by the ancient gods.

Much about the *Metamorphoses* can be viewed as a response to Virgil's epic of the founding of Rome, the *Aeneid* (19 B.C.E.), and to Virgil's status as the preeminent poet of his time. Ovid was seventeen years Virgil's junior and spent his formative years under the peace of Augustus rather than the tumultuous years of civil war that forged Virgil's poetry. Consequently,

---

2. In addition to dancing girls, Plato's *Symposium* concludes with every participant dead drunk except for Socrates, who holds his wine better than anyone else.

3. The Saturnalia was the merriest festival of the year, a time of eating, drinking, playing, and a fair degree of license. The connection with Saturn is unclear, but it was later explained by making him the god of liberation.

4. Marcus Crassus was a praetor in 105 B.C.E. Lucilius (180–102 B.C.E.) was known as the inventor of the Roman genre of the satire.

5. Catullus, "the poet of Verona," writes this in poem 14.

6. Roman philosophers were divided between Epicureans and Stoics; the latter had prevailed.

where Virgil's concern had been how best to represent the costs of war and the demands of peace, Ovid's was how to compose a great work when Virgil's had already been written. There are many underlying similarities in theme and structure. Both poems employ hexameter, the six-footed meter characteristic of classical epic; both are also epic in length, although Ovid divides his poem into fifteen books rather than the *Aeneid*'s twelve or the twenty-four of the Homeric poems. Both poems place the Roman Empire of Augustus at the end point of their narratives, and both refer to their lord and patron as a god. Moreover, the *Metamorphoses* includes within its historical trajectory the *Aeneid*'s material—the fall of Troy and the difficult journey of Aeneas from Troy to found Rome. Nevertheless, these similarities serve more to emphasize the differences than to efface them.

Ovid calls his poem a "book of changes" in the opening verses, and it is truly a dazzling compendium of transformations. Nothing is stable in the world of the *Metamorphoses*. There is no unifying protagonist, no single character who makes more than a few cameo appearances, and no continuity of setting or chronology. Ovid took as his raw material basically everything that had been written in Greek and Latin up to that point, with a particular focus on the many myths about the interaction, primarily erotic, between the Olympian gods and the mortals of the ancient world. Rather than link his many episodes in any consistently causal manner, Ovid chose a looser range of associations: sometimes there is a similarity in type of transformation; sometimes the tale of one family's child will lead to the story of another child of the same generation; and sometimes one story frames a series of further, unrelated tales. So when Orpheus loses Eurydice and sits down to sing of his sorrows, he sings about other transformations. Part of the artistry of the *Metamorphoses* lies in the way it encourages us to seek meanings and connections not just along the chain of its interlinked tales but between the different levels of its sets of tales inside tales, or between the different parts of a myth split up and scattered throughout the poem for the reader to reconstruct.

In the *Aeneid,* the reader is constantly being reminded of the role played by each event in the grand narrative of the founding of Rome. The *Metamorphoses,* by contrast, is resolutely focused on how a particular event looks and feels to its participants. We are given but a single glimpse of the weaver Arachne, but it is the defining moment of her life: her weaving duel with the goddess Minerva. Ovid paints the duel in great detail, especially the fabrics themselves, for they too tell cautionary tales of transformation. Minerva weaves scenes of contest, "the sorry fate" of mortals who challenged gods; Arachne responds with scenes of divine deception and abuse of mortals. The climax of nearly every episode is the transformation scene, where Ovid shows the full range of his powers of description and variation, always catching in words the moment of change, the moment when the person being transformed is neither one thing nor the other. Here is Arachne's metamorphosis into a spider:

> Touched by the bitter lotion, all her hair
> Falls off and with it go her nose and ears.
> Her head shrinks tiny; her whole body's small;
> Instead of legs slim fingers line her sides.
> The rest is belly; yet from that she sends
> A fine-spun thread and, as a spider, still
> Weaving her web, pursues her former skill.

Characteristically, the change is both beautiful and horrible, and Arachne is both utterly transformed and yet strangely still herself.

The closest thing to a guiding philosophy in the *Metamorphoses,* a program that would gather its disparate gems into a fixed setting, is the speech of the Greek mathematician Pythagoras in Book 15. This speech, the longest in the poem, asserts what looks like a general moral: "Nothing retains its form; new shapes from old / Nature, the great inventor, ceaselessly / Contrives." For Pythagoras, the principle of change implies the transmigration of souls from one body to the next; every thing and every creature on the earth is sentient, and the world's souls are constantly migrating from one being to another. Pythagoras, consequently, is a vegetarian. Many scholars have taken Pythagoras seriously as the voice of the author and argued that his speech gives shape and substance to the poem; many others have argued that it is just another Ovidian parody of a blowhard who takes himself too seriously. Strong arguments can be made both ways, and we need not exclude the possibility that Ovid has perversely placed the secrets of his poem's meaning in the mouth of a character he may also have thought was ridiculous. There is great pleasure to be found in the endless invention and playfulness of the *Metamorphoses* and great satisfaction in its profound glimpses of human emotions and tragedy. Perhaps its most enduring quality, however, and what has made it such an influential compendium of myth over the past two millennia, is the myriad combinations and recombinations of the extremes of experience that Ovid achieves at every turn in his exploration of the meanings of change in our lives.

PRONUNCIATIONS:

Arachne: ah-RAK-nee
Daedalus: DEH-dah-luhs
Echo: EH-koh
Eurydice: yur-RI-di-see
Ganymede: GA-ni-meed
Hyacinth: HAI-uh-sinth
Icarus: IH-kah-ruhs
Metamorphoses: me-tuh-MOR-foh-seez
Minotaur: MI-nah-tawr
Narcissus: nahr-SI-suhs
Orpheus: OR-fee-uhs
Ovid: AH-vid
Phaethon: FAY-tuhn
Pygmalion: pig-MAY-lee-uhn
Pythagoras: pi-THA-gor-uhs
Tiresias: tai-REE-see-uhs

from METAMORPHOSES[1]

from BOOKS 1 AND 2

[PROLOGUE]

Of bodies changed to other forms I tell;
You Gods, who have yourselves wrought every change,
Inspire my enterprise and lead my lay
In one continuous song from nature's first
5   Remote beginnings to our modern times.

[PHAETHON][2]

His° peer in pride and years was Phaethon,   *Epaphus's*
Child of the Sun,° whose arrogance one day   *Apollo*
And boasts of his high parentage were more

---

1. Translated by A. D. Melville.
2. The first book of the *Metamorphoses* describes Creation and the first establishment of the world's order. Following a battle with giants and a global deluge, human relations with the gods take on their familiar pattern.

Jupiter (Jove) seduces the maiden Io, whom he changes into a heifer to hide her from his jealous wife Juno. Io's son with Jove, Epaphus, becomes close friends with Phaethon, son of the sun god Apollo and the earthly princess Clymene. Phaethon's story follows.

Than Epaphus could bear. "You fool," he said,
755   "To credit all your mother says; that birth
You boast about is false." Then Phaethon
Flushed (though shame checked his rage) and took those taunts
To Clymene, his mother. "And to grieve
You more, dear mother, I so frank," he said,
760   "So fiery, stood there silent. I'm ashamed
That he could so insult me and that I
Could not repulse him. But, if I indeed
Am sprung from heavenly stock, give me sure proof
Of my high birth, confirm my claim to heaven."
765   He threw his arms around his mother's neck,
And begged her by his own and Merops' life,
His sisters' hopes of marriage, to provide
Some token that that parentage was true.
And Clymene, moved whether by his words
770   Or anger at the insult to herself,
Held out her arms to heaven and faced the Sun
And cried, "By this great glorious radiance,
This beaming blaze, that hears and sees us now,
I swear, dear child, that he, the Sun, on whom
775   You gaze, the Sun who governs all the globe,
He is your father. If I lie, let him
Deny his beams, let this light be the last
My eyes shall ever see! And you may find
Your father's home with no long toil. The place
780   From which he rises borders our own land.
Go, make the journey if your heart is set,
And put your question to the Sun himself."
Then up flashed Phaethon at his mother's words;
Heaven filled his happy thoughts; and journeying
785   Through his own Ethiopians and the lands
Of India beneath their burning skies,
He quickly reached his father's rising-place.

    The palace of the Sun rose high aloft
On soaring columns, bright with flashing gold
And flaming bronze; the pediments were clothed
With sheen of ivory; the double doors
5   Dazzled with silver—and the artistry
Was nobler still. For Vulcan had engraved[3]
The world's great orb, the seas that ring the world,
The sky that hangs above; and in the waves
The sea-gods dwelt, Aegaeon,° his huge arms   *Briareus, a 100-armed giant*
10   Entwined around the backs of giant whales,
Ambiguous Proteus,[4] Triton with his horn;

---

3. The first of Ovid's many examples of ecphrasis, or verbal descriptions of visual art, these doors were, like the
shields of Achilles in Homer and of Aeneas in Virgil,
created by the god of fire and the forge, Vulcan.
4. A sea god and a seer who could take any shape he
desired. Aegaeon was a 100-armed giant.

And Doris and her daughters might be seen,
And some were swimming, some on fishes rode,
Or sat on rocks to dry their sea-green hair.
15   Nor were their looks the same, nor yet diverse,
But like as sisters should be. On the land
People and cities, woods and beasts were graven,
Rivers and nymphs and rural deities,
And, set above them, the bright signs of heaven,
20   In glory shining, six upon each door.
     Then Phaethon, climbing the steep ascent,
Entered his father's palace (fatherhood
Uncertain still) and made his way direct
Into the presence and there stood afar,
25   Unable to approach the dazzling light.
Enrobed in purple vestments Phoebus° sat,   *Apollo*
High on a throne of gleaming emeralds.
Attending him on either side stood Day
And Month and Year and Century, and Hours
30   Disposed at equal intervals between.
Young Spring was there, with coronet of flowers,
And naked Summer, garlanded with grain;
Autumn was there with trampled vintage stained,
And icy Winter, rime° upon his locks.   *hoarfrost*
35   Enthroned amidst, the Sun who sees all things
Beheld the boy dismayed by sights so strange,
And said "What purpose brings, faring so far,
My son, a son no father would deny,
To this high citadel?" The boy replied
40   "O thou, Creation's universal light,
Phoebus, my father, if to use that name
Thou givest me leave, and Clymene spoke truth
And hides no guilt, give proof that all may know
I am thy son indeed, and end for ever
45   The doubt that grieves me." Then his father laid
Aside the dazzling beams that crowned his head
And bade him come and held him to his heart:
"Well you deserve to be my son," he said,
"Truly your mother named your lineage;
50   And to dispel all doubt, ask what you will
That I may satisfy your heart's desire;
And that dark marsh by which the gods make oath,[5]
Though to my eyes unknown, shall seal my troth."°   *truth*
He scarce had ended when the boy declared
55   His wish—his father's chariot for one day
With licence to control the soaring steeds.
     Grief and remorse flooded his father's soul,

---

5. It was customary of the gods to swear their oaths on the underworld river Styx, the "dark marsh" of Apollo's words.

And bitterly he shook his glorious head:
"Rash have your words proved mine! Would that I might
60 Retract my promise, Phaethon! This alone
I would indeed deny you. Yet at least
I may dissuade you. Dangerous is your choice;
You seek a privilege that ill befits
Your growing years and strength so boyish still.
65 Mortal your lot—not mortal your desire;
This, to which even the gods may not aspire,
In ignorance you claim. Though their own powers
May please the gods, not one can take his stand
Above my chariot's flaming axle-tree
70 Save I. Even he whose hand hurls thunderbolts,
Olympus' mighty lord, may never drive
My team—and who is mightier than Jove?
      Steep is the way at first, which my steeds scarce
Can climb in morning freshness; in mid sky
75 The altitude is greatest and the sight
Of land and sea below has often struck
In my own heart an agony of fear.
The final part drops sheer; then above all
Control must be assured, and even she
80 Whose waters lie below to welcome me,
Tethys, waits fearful lest I headlong fall.
Besides, in constant flux the sky streams by,
Sweeping in dizzy whirl the stars on high.
I drive against this force, which overcomes
85 All things but me, and on opposing course
Against its rushing circuit make my way.
Suppose my chariot yours: what then? Could you
Confront the spinning poles and not be swept
Away by the swift axis of the world?
90 Perhaps you fancy cities of gods are there
And groves and temples rich with offerings.
No! Wild beasts lie in wait and shapes of fear!
And though you keep your course and steer aright,
Yet you shall meet the Bull, must brave his horns,
95 And face the Archer and the ravening Lion,
The long curved circuit of the Scorpion's claws,
The Crab whose claws in counter-menace wave.[6]
My horses too, when fire within their breasts
Rages, from mouth and nostrils breathing flames,
100 Are hard to hold; even I can scarce restrain
Their ardent hearts, their necks that fight the rein.
But, O my son, amend, while time remains,
Your choice, so may my gift not be your doom.

---

6. Apollo mentions five of the 12 signs of the zodiac: Taurus, Sagittarius, Leo, Scorpio, and Cancer.

Sure proof you seek of fatherhood; indeed
105   My dread sure proof affords: a father's fear
Proves me your father. Look into my eyes!
Would you could look into my heart and see
And understand your father's agony!
See, last, how rich the world around you lies,
110   The bounty of the lands, the seas, the skies;
Choose what you will of these—it shall be yours.
But this alone, not this! Bane truly named
Not glory, Phaethon—bane this gift not boon!
Why fold me in your arms, fond foolish boy?
115   By Styx I swore and I shall not refuse,
Whate'er your choice: but oh! more wisely choose!"
    So the Sun warned; but Phaethon would not yield
And held his purpose, burning with desire
To drive the chariot. Then his father, slow
120   And pausing as he might, led out the boy
To that high chariot, Vulcan's masterwork.
Gold was the axle, gold the shaft, and gold
The rolling circles of the tyres; the spokes
In silver order stood, and on the harness
125   Patterns of gorgeous gems and chrysolites[7]
Shone gleaming in the glory of the Sun.
And while the daring boy in wonder gazed,
Aurora, watchful in the reddening dawn,
Threw wide her crimson doors and rose-filled halls;
130   The stars took flight, in marshalled order set
By Lucifer° who left his station last.   *the morning star*
Then, when the Sun perceived the morning star
Setting and saw the world in crimson sheen
And the last lingering crescent of the moon
135   Fade in the dawn, he bade the nimble Hours
Go yoke his steeds, and they, swift goddesses,
Fastened the jingling harness and the reins,
As from the lofty stalls the horses came,
Filled with ambrosial food and breathing flame.
140   Then on his son's young face the father smeared
A magic salve to shield him from the heat,
And set the flashing sunbeams on his head,
And with a heavy heart and many a sigh,
That told of grief to come, addressed the boy:
145   "If this advice at least you will obey,
Spare, child, the whip and rein them hard; they race
Unurged; the task's to hold them in their zeal.
Avoid the road direct through all five zones;
On a wide slanting curve the true course lies

7. A green-colored, translucent precious stone.

150 Within the confines of three zones; beware
    Alike the southern pole and northern Bear.
    Keep to this route; my wheeltracks there show plain.
    Press not too low nor strain your course too high;
    Too high, you'll burn heaven's palaces; too low,
155 The earth; the safest course lies in between.
    And neither rightwards towards the twisting Snake
    Nor leftwards swerve to where the Altar lies.[8]
    Hold in the midst! To fortune I resign
    The rest to guide with wiser wit than yours.
160   See, dewy night upon the Hesperian° shore   *western*
    Even while I speak has reached her goal. No more
    May we delay; our duty calls; the day
    Dawns bright, all shadows fled. Come take the reins!
    Or take, if yet your stubborn heart will change,
165 My counsel, not my chariot, while you may,
    While still on firm foundations here you stand
    Before you mount between my chariot wheels,
    So ignorant, so foolish!—and let me
    Give the world light that you may safely see."
170   But Phaethon mounted, light and young and proud,
    And took the reins with joy, and looking down,
    Thanked his reluctant father for the gift.
    Meanwhile the four swift horses of the Sun,
    Aethon, Eous, Pyrois and Phlegon,
175 Kick at the gates, neighing and snorting fire,
    And Tethys then, her grandson's fate undreamt,
    Draws back the bars and makes the horses free
    Of all the boundless heavens. Forth they go,
    Tearing away, and cleave with beating hooves
180 The clouds before them, and on wings outride
    The winds that westwards from the morning blow.
    But lightly weighs the yoke; the chariot moves
    With ease unwonted, suspect buoyancy;
    And like a ship at sea unballasted
185 That pitches in the waves for lack of weight,
    The chariot, lacking now its usual load,
    Bounced driverless, it seemed, in empty leaps.
    The horses in alarm ran wild and left
    The well-worn highway. Phaethon, dazed with fear,
190 Could neither use the reins nor find the road,
    Nor were it found could make the team obey.
    Then first the sunbeams warmed the freezing Bear,
    Who sought vain refuge in forbidden seas;
    The Snake that numb and harmless hitherto
195 Lay next the icy pole, roused by the heat,

8. Constellations of the north (the Snake) and the south (the Altar).

In newly kindled rage began to burn;
The Wagoner too, it's said, fled in dismay,
Though slow and hampered by his lumbering wain.
    And when poor hapless Phaethon from the height
200   Of highest heaven looked down and saw below,
Far, far below the continents outspread,
His face grew pale, his knees in sudden fear
Shook, and his eyes were blind with light so bright.
Would he had never touched his father's steeds,
205   Nor learnt his birth, nor won his heart's desire!
Oh, to be known as Merops' son! Too late!
He's swept away as when a barque is driven
Before the northern gales and in despair
The master leaves the helm, resigns his charge
210   To heaven. What shall he do? The sky behind
Stretches away so far; yet more in front.
He measures each in turn; ahead he sees
The west that fate ordains he shall not reach,
Then looks back to the east. Dazed and in doubt
215   He cannot hold the reins or let them fall
Or even recall the horses' names. And then
He sees in panic strewn across the sky
Monstrous gigantic shapes of beasts of prey.
There is a place in which the Scorpion's claws
220   Curve in a double arc, with tail and legs
On either side crossing two signs of heaven;
Sweating black venom, there before his eyes,
Circling its tail to strike, the creature lies.
His senses reel; he drops the reins aghast.
225   And when the reins fall loose upon their backs,
The horses swerve away and, unrestrained,
Gallop through tracts of air unknown and race
Headlong, out of control, running amok
Amid the stars fixed in the vault of heaven,
230   Hurtling the chariot where no road had run.
And now they climb to highest heaven, now plunge
Sheer in breakneck descent down to the earth.
The moon in wonder sees her brother's team[9]
Running below her own; the scalding clouds
235   Steam; the parched fields crack deep, all moisture dried,
And every summit flames; the calcined° meads   *scorched to dust*
Lie white; the leaf dies burning with the bough
And the dry corn its own destruction feeds.
These are but trifles. Mighty cities burn
240   With all their ramparts; realms and nations turn

9. The sun god Apollo and the moon goddess Diana were twin children of Jupiter and the Titaness Latona (Greek: Leto).

To ashes; mountains with their forests blaze.[1]
Athos is burning, Oeta is on fire,
And Tmolus and proud Taurus and the crest
Of Ida, dry, whose springs were once so famed,
245   And virgin Helicon and Haemus, still
Unknown, unhonoured. Etna burns immense
In twofold conflagration; Eryx flames
And Othrys and Parnassus' double peaks;
Cynthus and Dindyma and Mycale
250   And Rhodope, losing at last her snows,
And Mimas and Cithaeron's holy hill.
Caucasus burns; the frosts of Scythia
Fail in her need; Pindus and Ossa blaze
And, lordlier than both, Olympus flames
255   And the airy Alps and cloud-capped Apennines.
Then Phaethon saw the world on every side
Ablaze—heat more than he could bear. He breathed
Vapours that burned like furnace-blasts, and felt
The chariot glow white-hot beneath his feet.
260   Cinders and sparks past bearing shoot and swirl
And scorching smoke surrounds him; in the murk,
The midnight murk, he knows not where he is
Or goes; the horses whirl him where they will.
     The Aethiops then turned black, so men believe,
265   As heat summoned their blood too near the skin.
Then was Sahara's dusty desert formed,
All water scorched away. Then the sad nymphs
Bewailed their pools and springs;[2] Boeotia mourned
Her Dirce lost, Argos Amymone,
270   Corinth Pirene; nor were rivers safe
Though fortune's favour made them broad and deep
And their banks far apart; in middle stream
From old Peneus rose the drifting steam,
From Erymanthus and Swift Ismer
275   And Mysian Caicu and the Don;
Maeander playing on his winding way;
Tawny Lycormas, Xanthus doomed to burn
At Troy a second time; Melas of Thrace,
That sable stream; Eurotas, Sparta's pride.
280   Euphrates burned, river of Babylon,
Phasis, Danube and Ganges were on fire,
Orontes burned and racing Thermodon;
Alpheus boiled, fire scorched Spercheus' banks.
The gold that Tagus carries in his sands
285   Ran molten in the flames, and all the swans
That used to charm the Lydian banks with song

---

1. The list that follows includes many of the most celebrated mountains of the ancient world.

2. This list catalogues streams and rivers of the ancient world.

Huddled in mid Cayster sweltering.
The Nile in terror to the world's end fled
And hid his head, still hidden; his seven mouths
290 Gaped dusty, seven vales without a stream.
The same disaster dried the Thracian rivers,
Hebrus and Strymon, dried the lordly flow
Of western waters, Rhone and Rhine and Po,
And Tiber, promised empire of the world.[3]
295 Earth everywhere splits deep and light strikes down
Into the Underworld and fills with fear
Hell's monarch and his consort; the wide seas
Shrink and where ocean lay a wilderness
Of dry sand spreads; new peaks and ranges rise,
300 Long covered by the deep, and multiply
The scattered islands of the Cyclades.[4]
The fishes dive; the dolphins dare not leap
Their curving course through the familiar air,
And lifeless seals float supine on the waves;
305 Even Nereus, fathoms down, in his dark caves,
With Doris and her daughters, felt the fire.
Thrice from the waters Neptune raised his arm
And frowning face; thrice fled the fiery air.
    But Mother Earth, encompassed by the seas,
310 Between the ocean and her shrinking streams,
That cowered for refuge in her lightless womb,
Lifted her smothered head and raised her hand
To shield her tortured face; then with a quake,
A mighty tremor that convulsed the world,
315 Sinking in shallow subsidence below
Her wonted place, in solemn tones appealed:
"If this thy pleasure and my due, why now,
Greatest of gods, lie thy dread lightnings still?
If fire destroy me, let the fire be thine:
320 My doom were lighter dealt by thy design!
Scarce can my throat find voice to speak" (the smoke
And heat were choking her). "See my singed hair!
Ash in my eyes, ash on my lips so deep!
Are these the fruits of my fertility?
325 Is this for duty done the due return?
That I endure the wounds of pick and plough,
Year-long unceasing pain, that I supply
Grass for the flocks and crops, sweet sustenance,
For humankind and incense for you gods?
330 But, grant my doom deserved, what have the seas
Deserved and what thy brother°? Why shrinks the main,   *Neptune*
His charge, and from the sky so far recoils?
And if no grace can save thy brother now,

335 Nor me, pity thine own fair sky! Look round!
See, each pole smokes; if there the fire should gain,
Your royal roofs will fall. Even Atlas fails,
His shoulders scarce sustain the flaming sky.[5]
If land and sea, if heaven's high palaces
340 Perish, prime chaos will us all confound!
Save from the flames whatever's still alive,
And prove you mean Creation to survive!"
  Then Earth could speak no more, no more endure
The fiery heat and vapour, and sank back
345 To her deep caverns next the Underworld.
But the Almighty Father, calling the gods
And him who gave the chariot to attest
Creation doomed were now his aid not given,
Mounted the highest citadel of heaven,
350 Whence he was wont to veil the lands with clouds
And roll his thunders and his lightnings hurl.
But then no clouds had he the lands to veil,
Nor rain to send from heaven to soothe their pain.
He thundered; and poising high his bolt to blast,
355 Struck Phaethon from the chariot and from life,
And fire extinguished fire and flame quenched flame.
The horses in wild panic leapt apart,
Burst from the traces and flung off the yoke.
There lie the reins, the sundered axle there,
360 Here the spokes dangle from a shattered wheel,
And far and wide the signs of wreckage fly.
And Phaethon, flames ravaging his auburn hair,
Falls headlong down, a streaming trail of light,
As sometimes through the cloudless vault of night
365 A star, though never falling, seems to fall.
Eridanus[6] receives him, far from home,
In his wide waters half a world away,
And bathes his burning face. The Hesperian° nymphs   *western*
Bury his smouldering body in a tomb
370 And on a stone engrave this epitaph:
"Here Phaethon lies, his father's charioteer;
Great was his fall, yet did he greatly dare."

from Book 3

[Tiresias]

While down on earth as destiny ordained
These things took place, and Bacchus, babe twice born,

---

5. The Titan brother of Prometheus was responsible for holding up the heavens.

6. A mythical river in northern or western Europe that was eventually identified with the Italian river Po.

Was cradled safe and sound,¹ it chanced that Jove,
Well warmed with nectar, laid his weighty cares
5   Aside and, Juno too in idle mood,
The pair were gaily joking, and Jove said
"You women get more pleasure out of love
Than we men do, I'm sure." She disagreed.
So they resolved to get the views of wise
10 Tiresias.² He knew both sides of love.
For once in a green copse when two huge snakes
Were mating, he attacked them with his stick,
And was transformed (a miracle!) from man
To woman; and spent seven autumns so;
15 Till in the eighth he saw the snakes once more
And said "If striking you has magic power
To change the striker to the other sex,
I'll strike you now again." He struck the snakes
And so regained the shape he had at birth.
20 Asked then to give his judgement on the joke,
He found for Jove; and Juno (so it's said)
Took umbrage beyond reason, out of all
Proportion, and condemned her judge to live
In the black night of blindness evermore.
25 But the Almighty Father (since no god
Has right to undo what any god has done)
For his lost sight gave him the gift to see
What things should come, the power of prophecy,
An honour to relieve that penalty.

[NARCISSUS AND ECHO]

30 So blind Tiresias gave to all who came
Faultless and sure reply and far and wide
Through all Boeotia's cities³ spread his fame.
To test his truth and trust the first who tried
Was wave-blue water-nymph Liriope,
35 Whom once Cephisus in his sinuous flow
Embracing held and ravished. In due time
The lovely sprite bore a fine infant boy,
From birth adorable, and named her son
Narcissus; and of him she asked the seer,
40 Would he long years and ripe old age enjoy,
Who answered "If he shall himself not know."
For long his words seemed vain; what they concealed

---

1. Bacchus (Greek: Dionysus) was the son of Jove and Cadmus's daughter Semele. He is called "twice born" because after his mother was killed by a trick of the jealous Juno, Jove sewed him up in his thigh. The god of wine and intoxication, Bacchus was associated with the ecstatic rituals of his Bacchantes, or female followers.

2. The resident seer of Thebes, Tiresias is the most celebrated prophet of classical myth and literature. Odysseus consults his ghost in the *Odyssey,* and Tiresias plays a central role in *Oedipus the King.*

3. Boeotia was a region of central Greece. Thebes, in the south, was its dominant city.

The lad's strange death and stranger love revealed.
          Narcissus now had reached his sixteenth year
45 And seemed both man and boy; and many a youth
          And many a girl desired him, but hard pride
          Ruled in that delicate frame, and never a youth
          And never a girl could touch his haughty heart.
          Once as he drove to nets the frightened deer
50 A strange-voiced nymph observed him, who must speak
          If any other speak and cannot speak
          Unless another speak, resounding Echo.
          Echo was still a body, not a voice,
          But talkative as now, and with the same
55 Power of speaking, only to repeat,
          As best she could, the last of many words.
          Juno had made her so; for many a time,
          When the great goddess might have caught the nymphs
          Lying with Jove upon the mountainside,
60 Echo discreetly kept her talking till
          The nymphs had fled away; and when at last
          The goddess saw the truth, "Your tongue," she said,
          "With which you tricked me, now its power shall lose,
          Your voice avail but for the briefest use."
65 The event confirmed the threat: when speaking ends,
          All she can do is double each last word,
          And echo back again the voice she's heard.
               Now when she saw Narcissus wandering
          In the green byways, Echo's heart was fired;
70 And stealthily she followed, and the more
          She followed him, the nearer flamed her love,
          As when a torch is lit and from the tip
          The leaping sulphur grasps the offered flame.
          She longed to come to him with winning words,
75 To urge soft pleas, but nature now opposed;
          She might not speak the first but—what she might—
          Waited for words her voice could say again.
               It chanced Narcissus, searching for his friends,
          Called "Anyone here?" and Echo answered "Here!"
80 Amazed he looked all round and, raising his voice,
          Called "Come this way!" and Echo called "This way!"
          He looked behind and, no one coming, shouted
          "Why run away?" and heard his words again.
          He stopped and, cheated by the answering voice,
85 Called "Join me here!" and she, never more glad
          To give her answer, answered "Join me here!"
          And graced her words and ran out from the wood
          To throw her longing arms around his neck.
          He bolted, shouting "Keep your arms from me!
90 Be off! I'll die before I yield to you."
          And all she answered was "I yield to you."

Shamed and rejected in the woods she hides
And has her dwelling in the lonely caves;
Yet still her love endures and grows on grief,

95   And weeping vigils waste her frame away;
Her body shrivels, all its moisture dries;
Only her voice and bones are left; at last
Only her voice, her bones are turned to stone.
So in the woods she hides and hills around,

100   For all to hear, alive, but just a sound.
        Thus had Narcissus mocked her; others too,
Hill-nymphs and water-nymphs and many a man
He mocked; till one scorned youth, with raised hands, prayed,
"So may *he* love—and never win his love!"

105   And Nemesis[4] approved the righteous prayer.
        There was a pool, limpid and silvery,
Whither no shepherd came nor any herd,
Nor mountain goat; and never bird nor beast
Nor falling branch disturbed its shining peace;

110   Grass grew around it, by the water fed,
And trees to shield it from the warming sun.
Here—for the chase and heat had wearied him—
The boy lay down, charmed by the quiet pool,
And, while he slaked his thirst, another thirst

115   Grew; as he drank he saw before his eyes
A form, a face, and loved with leaping heart
A hope unreal and thought the shape was real.
Spellbound he saw himself, and motionless
Lay like a marble statue staring down.

120   He gazes at his eyes, twin constellation,
His hair worthy of Bacchus or Apollo,
His face so fine, his ivory neck, his cheeks
Smooth, and the snowy pallor and the blush;
All he admires that all admire in him,

125   Himself he longs for, longs unwittingly,
Praising is praised, desiring is desired,
And love he kindles while with love he burns.
How often in vain he kissed the cheating pool
And in the water sank his arms to clasp

130   The neck he saw, but could not clasp himself!
Not knowing what he sees, he adores the sight;
That false face fools and fuels his delight.
You simple boy, why strive in vain to catch
A fleeting image? What you see is nowhere;

135   And what you love—but turn away—you lose!
You see a phantom of a mirrored shape;
Nothing itself; with you it came and stays;

4. Nemesis personified the concept of divine retribution for human pride; she was also worshipped as a goddess.

With you it too will go, if you can go!
     No thought of food or rest draws him away;
140 Stretched on the grassy shade he gazes down
On the false phantom, staring endlessly,
His eyes his own undoing. Raising himself
He holds his arms towards the encircling trees
And cries "You woods, was ever love more cruel!
145 You know! For you are lovers' secret haunts.
Can you in your long living centuries
Recall a lad who pined so piteously?
My joy! I see it; but the joy I see
I cannot find" (so fondly love is foiled!)
150 "And—to my greater grief—between us lies
No mighty sea, no long and dusty road,
Nor mountain range nor bolted barbican.°   *fortification*
A little water sunders us. He longs
For my embrace. Why, every time I reach
155 My lips towards the gleaming pool, he strains
His upturned face to mine. I surely could
Touch him, so slight the thing that thwarts our love.
Come forth, whoever you are! Why, peerless boy,
Elude me? Where retreat beyond my reach?
160 My looks, my age—indeed it cannot be
That you should shun—the nymphs have loved me too!
Some hope, some nameless hope, your friendly face
Pledges; and when I stretch my arms to you
You stretch your arms to me, and when I smile
165 You smile, and when I weep, I've often seen
Your tears, and to my nod your nod replies,
And your sweet lips appear to move in speech,
Though to my ears your answer cannot reach.
Oh, I am he! Oh, now I know for sure
170 The image is my own; it's for myself
I burn with love; I fan the flames I feel.
What now? Woo or be wooed? Why woo at all?
My love's myself—my riches beggar me.
Would I might leave my body! I could wish
175 (Strange lover's wish!) my love were not so near!
Now sorrow saps my strength; of my life's span
Not long is left; I die before my prime.
Nor is death sad for death will end my sorrow;
Would he I love might live a long tomorrow!
180 But now we two—one soul—one death will die."
     Distraught he turned towards the face again;
His tears rippled the pool, and darkly then
The troubled water veiled the fading form,
And, as it vanished, "Stay," he shouted, "stay!
185 Oh, cruelty to leave your lover so!
Let me but gaze on what I may not touch

And feed the aching fever in my heart."
Then in his grief he tore his robe and beat
His pale cold fists upon his naked breast,
190   And on his breast a blushing redness spread
Like apples, white in part and partly red,
Or summer grapes whose varying skins assume
Upon the ripening vine a blushing bloom.
And this he saw reflected in the pool,
195   Now still again, and could endure no more.
But as wax melts before a gentle fire,
Or morning frosts beneath the rising sun,
So, by love wasted, slowly he dissolves
By hidden fire consumed. No colour now,
200   Blending the white with red, nor strength remains
Nor will, nor aught that lately seemed so fair,
Nor longer lasts the body Echo loved.
But she, though angry still and unforgetting,
Grieved for the hapless boy, and when he moaned
205   "Alas," with answering sob she moaned "alas,"
And when he beat his hands upon his breast,
She gave again the same sad sounds of woe.
His latest words, gazing and gazing still,
He sighed "alas! the boy I loved in vain!"
210   And these the place repeats, and then "farewell,"
And Echo said "farewell." On the green grass
He drooped his weary head, and those bright eyes
That loved their master's beauty closed in death.
Then still, received into the Underworld,
215   He gazed upon himself in Styx's pool.
His Naiad sisters wailed and sheared their locks
In mourning for their brother; the Dryads too
Wailed[5] and sad Echo wailed in answering woe.
And then the brandished torches, bier and pyre
220   Were ready—but no body anywhere;
And in its stead they found a flower—behold,
White petals clustered round a cup of gold![6]

from Book 6

[ARACHNE]

Pallas[1] had listened to the tale she told
With warm approval of the Muses' song

---

5. Naiads are freshwater nymphs, or minor female deities, often daughters of river gods; hence their kinship to the river's son, Narcissus. Dryads are tree nymphs.
6. Narcissus is a genus of fragrant, bulbous flowers including the daffodil, jonquil, and the poet's narcissus,

which most closely matches Ovid's description.
1. Minerva (Greek: Pallas Athena) was born fully formed from the head of Jove. She was the goddess of crafts, wisdom, and war. She was also the patroness of the Greek city-state of Athens.

And of their righteous rage.[2] Then to herself—
"To praise is not enough; I should have praise
5   Myself, not suffer my divinity
To be despised unscathed." She had in mind
Arachne's doom, the girl of Lydia,[3]
Who in the arts of wool-craft claimed renown
(So she had heard) to rival hers. The girl
10 Had no distinction in her place of birth
Or pedigree, only that special skill.
Her father was Idmon of Colophon,
Whose trade it was to dye the thirsty wool
With purple of Phocaea.[4] She had lost
15 Her mother, but she too had been low-born
And matched her husband. Yet in all the towns
Of Lydia Arachne's work had won
A memorable name, although her home
Was humble and Hypaepae where she lived
20 Was humble too. To watch her wondrous work
The nymphs would often leave their vine-clad slopes
Of Tmolus, often leave Pactolus' stream,
Delighted both to see the cloth she wove
And watch her working too; such grace she had.
25 Forming the raw wool first into a ball,
Or fingering the flock and drawing out
Again and yet again the fleecy cloud
In long soft threads, or twirling with her thumb,
Her dainty thumb, the slender spindle, or
30 Embroidering the pattern—you would know
Pallas had trained her. Yet the girl denied it
(A teacher so distinguished hurt her pride)
And said, "Let her contend with me. Should I
Lose, there's no forfeit that I would not pay."
35   Pallas disguised herself as an old woman.
A fringe of false grey hair around her brow,
Her tottering steps supported by a stick,
And speaking to the girl, "Not everything
That old age brings," she said, "we'd wish to avoid.
40 With riper years we gain experience.
Heed my advice. Among the world of men
Seek for your wool-craft all the fame you will,
But yield the goddess place, and humbly ask
Pardon for those rash words of yours; she'll give
45 You pardon if you ask." With blazing eyes
Arachne stared at her and left her work.

2. The nine Muses, goddesses of the arts, especially music and poetry, made their home on Helicon, a mountain in southwest Boeotia. They have just finished relating to Minerva their singing contest with the Pierides, nine daughters of Pierus of Pella in Macedonia. To punish their presumption, the Muses had transformed the sisters into magpies.
3. A region in Asia Minor, now western Turkey.
4. Colophon and Phocaea were Ionian cities in western Asia Minor.

She almost struck her; anger strong and clear
Glowed as she gave the goddess (in disguise)
Her answer: "You're too old, your brain has gone.
50   You've lived too long, your years have done for you.
Talk to your daughters, talk to your sons' wives!
My own advice is all I need. Don't think
Your words have any weight. My mind's unchanged.
Why doesn't Pallas come herself? Why should
55   She hesitate to match herself with me?"
Then Pallas said, "She's come!" and threw aside
The old crone's guise and stood revealed. The nymphs
And Lydian women knelt in reverence.
Only Arachne had no fear. Yet she
60   Blushed all the same; a sudden colour tinged
Her cheeks against her will, then disappeared;
So when Aurora rises in the dawn,
The eastern sky is red and, as the sun
Climbs, in a little while is pale again.

65   She stood by her resolve, setting her heart,
Her stupid heart, on victory, and rushed
To meet her fate. Nor did the child of Jove
Refuse or warn her further or postpone
The contest. Then, with no delay, they both,
70   Standing apart, set up their separate looms
And stretched the slender warp. The warp is tied
To the wide cross-beam; a cane divides the threads;
The pointed shuttles carry the woof through,
Sped by their fingers. When it's through the warp,
75   The comb's teeth, tapping, press it into place.
Both work in haste, their dresses girdled tight
Below their breasts; the movements of their arms
Are skilled and sure; their zeal beguiles their toil.
Here purple threads that Tyrian vats have dyed[5]
80   Are woven in, and subtle delicate tints
That change insensibly from shade to shade.
So when the sunshine strikes a shower of rain,
The bow's huge arc will paint the whole wide sky,
And countless different colours shine, yet each
85   Gradation dupes the gaze, the tints that touch
So similar, the extremes so far distinct.
Threads too of golden wire were woven in,
And on the loom an ancient tale was traced.[6]
    The rock of Mars in Cecrops' citadel[7]

---

5. Tyre was a city of the Phoenicians in the ancient Middle East. An important trading center, it founded colonies in Cyprus and Carthage and was famed for its purple dye and its glass.

6. Athena weaves the tale of her dispute with the sea god Neptune (Greek: Poseidon) over who should be the patron deity of Athens.

7. The Areopagus, or "Hill of Mars," was the meeting place of the ancient council of Athens, which took its name from it. Cecrops was the legendary founder of the city.

90   Is Pallas' picture and that old dispute
About the name of Athens. Twelve great gods,
Jove in their midst, sit there on lofty thrones,
Grave and august, each pictured with his own
Familiar features: Jove in regal grace,

95   The Sea-god standing, striking the rough rock
With his tall trident, and the wounded rock
Gushing sea-brine, his proof to clinch his claim.
Herself she gives a shield, she gives a spear
Sharp-tipped, she gives a helmet for her head;

100   The aegis guards her breast,[8] and from the earth,
Struck by her spear, she shows an olive tree,
Springing pale-green with berries on the boughs;
The gods admire; and Victory ends the work.
Yet to provide examples to instruct

105   Her rival what reward she should expect
For her insensate daring, she designed
In each of the four corners four small scenes
Of contest, brightly coloured miniatures.
There in one corner Thracian Rhodope

110   And Haemon, icy mountains now, but once
Mortals, who claimed the names of gods most high.[9]
Another showed the Pygmy matron's doom,
Her pitiable doom, when Juno won
The contest and transformed her to a crane

115   And made her fight her folk, her kith and kin.[1]
Antigone she pictured too, who once
Challenged the royal consort of great Jove.
And Juno changed her to a bird, and Troy
Availed her nothing nor Laomedon,

120   Her father—no! with snowy feathers clothed,
In self-applause she claps her stork's loud bill.[2]
In the last corner Cinyras, bereaved,
Embraced the temple steps, his daughters' limbs,
And lying on the marble seemed to weep.[3]

125   All round the border ran an olive-branch,
The branch of peace. That was the end, and she
Finished her picture with her own fair tree.°   *the olive*
       Arachne shows Europa cheated by
The bull's disguise, a real bull you'd think,

8. The aegis was a goatskin cloak or breastplate with tassels. Worn by Minerva, it terrified her enemies and granted protection from attack.

9. Rhodope and Haemon were an incestuous brother-and-sister pair who called themselves "Jove" and "Juno" (who were also brother and sister). They were transformed into mountains in Thrace, a region in the southeastern Balkans.

1. Oenoe was a pygmy, one of a race of dwarves located by Greek mythology variously in Thrace, India, the Nile, or elsewhere. The battle between the pygmies and the cranes was a common topic in ancient art and poetry.

2. Antigone (not to be confused with the Theban daughter of Oedipus and Jocasta) was the sister of Priam and daughter of Laomedon of Troy. This is the only known account of her dispute with Juno.

3. Cinyras was an Assyrian king; this is the only known account of his daughter's presumption toward Juno.

130   And real sea.[4] The girl was gazing at
         The shore she'd left and calling to her friends,
         Seeming to dread the leaping billows' touch,
         Shrinking and drawing up her feet in fear.
         Asterie in the struggling eagle's clutch
135   She wove, and pictured Leda as she lay
         Under the white swan's wings, and added too
         How Jove once in a satyr's guise had got
         Antiope with twins, and, as Amphitryon,
         Bedded Alcmena; in a golden shower
140   Fooled Danae, Aegina in a flame,
         And as a shepherd snared Mnemosyne,
         And as a spotted serpent Proserpine.[5]
         Neptune she drew, changed to a savage bull
         For love of Canace; and Neptune too
145   Sired, as Enipeus, the Aloidae;
         Bisaltes' child he cheated as a ram;
         The corn's most gracious mother, golden-haired,
         Suffered him as a horse, and, as a bird,
         The snake-tressed mother of the flying steed;
150   And poor Melantho knew him as a dolphin.[6]
         To all of them Arachne gave their own
         Features and proper features of the scene.
         She wove too Phoebus in a herdsman's guise,
         And how he sometimes wore a lion's skin,
155   Sometimes hawk's plumage; how he fooled Isse,
         Macareus' daughter, as a shepherd;[7] how
         Bacchus with bunches of false grapes deceived
         Erigone, and Saturn, as a horse,
         Begot the centaur Chiron.[8] Round the edge
160   A narrow band of flowers she designed,
         Flowers and clinging ivy intertwined.
            In all that work of hers Pallas could find,

4. Arachne's weaving offers a lengthy list of the gods' se-
ductions or rapes of mortals, a number of which Ovid
recounts in more detail elsewhere in the poem. Europa
was abducted by Jove, who was disguised as a white bull.
5. Asterie was a Titan's daughter; Leda was the mother
of Helen, Castor, and Pollux; Antiope bore the Theban
twins Amphion and Zethus; Jove fathered Hercules on
Alcmena, disguised as her husband, the king of Thebes;
Danae bore the hero Perseus; Aegina was a daughter of
the river god Asopus, and Aeacus, the son of the union,
was the grandfather of both Achilles and Ajax; Jove's
seduction of Mnemosyne yielded the nine Muses;
Proserpine (Greek: Persephone) was Jove's daughter by
Ceres (Greek: Demeter), and their son was the second
Dionysus, Dionysus-Zagreus.
6. Neptune's amours: Canace was a daughter of Aeolus of
Thessaly and the sister of Macareus; the Thessalian river
god Enipeus was Tyro's lover, a story Ovid combines

with Neptune's siring the giants Otus and Ephialtes on
Aloeus's wife, Iphimedia; Neptune turned himself into a
ram and Bisaltes's daughter Theophane into a ewe, and
their offspring was the Ram with the Golden Fleece; in
Arcadia, Ceres was said to have mated as a mare with
Neptune in horse shape; raped in Athena's temple by
Neptune, the girl Medusa had her hair transformed into
serpents, and the winged horse Pegasus emerged when
Perseus cut off her head; Melantho was the daughter of
Deucalion and Pyrrha.
7. As a shepherd, Apollo seduces Isse, or Amphisse, the
daughter of Macareus and his sister, Canace.
8. Erigone was a daughter of Icarius, who was killed by
shepherds unfamiliar with the novel effects of Bacchus's
grapevines; both became stars in the heavens. The sea
nymph Philyra, loved by Saturn as horse and mare, gave
birth to the wise centaur Chiron, the teacher of Asclepius,
Jason, and Achilles among others.

Envy could find, no fault. Incensed at such
Success the warrior goddess, golden-haired,
165   Tore up the tapestry, those crimes of heaven,
And with the boxwood shuttle in her hand
(Box of Cytorus)⁹ three times, four times, struck
Arachne on her forehead. The poor wretch,
Unable to endure it, bravely placed
170   A noose around her neck; but, as she hung,
Pallas in pity raised her. "Live!" she said,
"Yes, live but hang, you wicked girl, and know
You'll rue the future too: that penalty
Your kin shall pay to all posterity!"
175   And as she turned to go, she sprinkled her
With drugs of Hecate,¹ and in a trice,
Touched by the bitter lotion, all her hair
Falls off and with it go her nose and ears.
Her head shrinks tiny; her whole body's small;
180   Instead of legs slim fingers line her sides.
The rest is belly; yet from that she sends
A fine-spun thread and, as a spider, still
Weaving her web, pursues her former skill.

from Book 8

[THE MINOTAUR: DAEDALUS AND ICARUS]

Minos reached harbour in the isle of Crete¹
155   And, disembarking, paid his vows to Jove,
A hundred bulls, and hung the spoils of war
To adorn his palace walls. His dynasty's
Disgrace had grown; the monstrous hybrid beast
Declared the queen's obscene adultery.²
160   To rid his precincts of this shame the king
Planned to confine him shut away within
Blind walls of intricate complexity.
The structure was designed by Daedalus,
That famous architect.³ Appearances
165   Were all confused; he led the eye astray
By a mazy multitude of winding ways,
Just as Maeander plays among the meads
Of Phrygia and in its puzzling flow

9. Cytorus is a mountain in northern Asia Minor that is proverbial for its box trees, which produced a hard and fine-grained wood.

1. A sinister goddess associated with magic, witchcraft, the night, the underworld, and crossroads.

1. Minos, a son of Europa and Jove, was king of the island-kingdom of Crete.

2. Inspired with the love of a bull sent by the sea god Nep-tune, Minos's wife, Pasiphaë, had the inventor Daedalus create a wooden cow covered with a leather hide. The bull impregnated her inside this contraption, and she gave birth to the Minotaur, a man with the head of a bull.

3. A member of the royal family of Athens, Daedalus came to Crete after he had been banished for the murder of Perdix, out of fear that his sister's son would prove to be the greater inventor.

170 Glides back and forth and meets itself and sees
Its waters on their way and winds along,
Facing sometimes its source, sometimes the sea.[4]
So Daedalus in countless corridors
Built his bafflement, and hardly could himself
Make his way out, so puzzling was the maze.

175 Within this labyrinth Minos shut fast
The beast, half bull, half man, and fed him twice
On Attic blood, lot-chosen each nine years,
Until the third choice mastered him.[5] The door,
So difficult, which none of those before

180 Could find again, by Ariadne's aid
Was found, the thread that traced the way rewound.
Then Theseus, seizing Minos' daughter,[6] spread
His sails for Naxos, where, upon the shore,
That cruel prince abandoned her and she,

185 Abandoned, in her grief and anger found
Comfort in Bacchus' arms.[7] He took her crown
And set it in the heavens to win her there
A star's eternal glory; and the crown
Flew through the soft light air and, as it flew,

190 Its gems were turned to gleaming fires, and still
Shaped as a crown their place in heaven they take
Between the Kneeler and him who grasps the Snake.[8]

  Hating the isle of Crete and the long years
Of exile, Daedalus was pining for

195 His native land, but seas on every side
Imprisoned him. "Though land and sea," he thought,
"The king may bar to me, at least the sky
Is open; through the sky I'll set my course.[9]
Minos may own all else; he does not own

200 The air." So then to unimagined arts
He set his mind and altered nature's laws.

  Row upon row of feathers he arranged,
The smallest first, then larger ones, to form
A growing graded shape, as rustic pipes

205 Rise in a gradual slope of lengthening reeds;
Then bound the middle and the base with wax
And flaxen threads, and bent them, so arranged,
Into a gentle curve to imitate

---

4. Maeander was in southern Asia Minor; its name was synonymous with the idea of a winding river.
5. Every nine years, Minos exacted a tribute of seven young men and seven young women from Athens to feed the Minotaur. The third time, the Athenian hero (and later king) Theseus joined the tribute.
6. Ariadne, Minos's daughter, fell in love with Theseus and offered to help him in return for leaving with him and becoming his wife. Daedalus revealed to her the secret of the labyrinth.

7. Naxos is an island in the Cyclades between Crete and Athens.
8. One version of the myth relates that Bacchus married her, and she was transformed into the constellation Corona Borealis, or the Crown, in the stars between the Kneeler, or Hercules, and the Snake, once the guardian dragon of the Hesperides.
9. Daedalus had been imprisoned with his son, Icarus, by Minos for telling Ariadne how to escape from the labyrinth.

Wings of a real bird. His boy stood by,
210 Young Icarus, who, blithely unaware
He plays with his own peril, tries to catch
Feathers that float upon the wandering breeze,
Or softens with his thumb the yellow wax,
And by his laughing mischief interrupts
215 His father's wondrous work. Then, when the last
Sure touch was given, the craftsman poised himself
On his twin wings and hovered in the air.
    Next he prepared his son. "Take care," he said,
"To fly a middle course, lest if you sink
220 Too low the waves may weight your feathers; if
Too high, the heat may burn them. Fly half-way
Between the two. And do not watch the stars,
The Great Bear or the Wagoner or Orion,
With his drawn sword, to steer by. Set your course
225 Where I shall lead." He fixed the strange new wings
On his son's shoulders and instructed him
How he should fly; and, as he worked and warned,
The old man's cheeks were wet, the father's hands
Trembled. He kissed his son (the last kisses
230 He'd ever give) and rising on his wings
He flew ahead, anxious for his son's sake,
Just like a bird that from its lofty nest
Launches a tender fledgeling in the air.
Calling his son to follow, schooling him
235 In that fatal apprenticeship, he flapped
His wings and watched the boy flapping behind.
    An angler fishing with his quivering rod,
A lonely shepherd propped upon his crook,
A ploughman leaning on his plough, looked up
240 And gazed in awe, and thought they must be gods
That they could fly. Delos and Paros lay
Behind them now; Samos, great Juno's isle,
Was on the left, Lebinthos on the right
And honey-rich Calymne,[1] when the boy
245 Began to enjoy his thrilling flight and left
His guide to roam the ranges of the heavens,
And soared too high. The scorching sun so close
Softened the fragrant wax that bound his wings;
The wax melted; his waving arms were bare;
250 Unfledged, they had no purchase on the air!
And calling to his father as he fell,
The boy was swallowed in the blue sea's swell,
The blue sea that for ever bears his name.[2]
His wretched father, now no father, cried

1. Islands in the Aegean between Crete and Asia Minor.   2. The Icarian Sea surrounds the island of Icaria, near Samos in the Aegean Sea.

255 "Oh, Icarus, where are you? Icarus,
 Where shall I look, where find you?" On the waves
 He saw the feathers. Then he cursed his skill,
 And buried his boy's body in a grave,
 And still that island keeps the name he gave.

from Book 10

[ORPHEUS AND EURYDICE]

 Thence Hymen° came, in saffron mantle clad,   *god of marriage*
 At Orpheus'[1] summons through the boundless sky
 To Thessaly, but vain the summons proved.
 True he was present, but no hallowed words
5 He brought nor happy smiles nor lucky sign;
 Even the torch he held sputtered throughout
 With smarting smoke, and caught no living flame
 For all his brandishing. The ill-starred rite
 Led to a grimmer end. The new-wed bride,°   *Eurydice*
10 Roaming with her gay Naiads through the grass,
 Fell dying when a serpent struck her heel.
 And when at last the bard of Rhodope°   *Thrace*
 Had mourned his fill in the wide world above,
 He dared descend through Taenarus' dark gate
15 To Hades[2] to make trial of the shades;
 And through the thronging wraiths and grave-spent ghosts
 He came to pale Persephone and him,
 Lord of the shades, who rules the unlovely realm,
 And as he struck his lyre's sad chords he said:
20 "Ye deities who rule the world below,
 Whither we mortal creatures all return,
 If simple truth, direct and genuine,
 May by your leave be told, I have come down
 Not with intent to see the glooms of Hell,
25 Nor to enchain the triple snake-haired necks
 Of Cerberus,[3] but for my dear wife's sake,
 In whom a trodden viper poured his venom
 And stole her budding years. My heart has sought
 Strength to endure; the attempt I'll not deny;
30 But love has won, a god whose fame is fair
 In the world above; but here I doubt, though here
 Too, I surmise; and if that ancient tale
 Of ravishment is true, you too were joined

---

1. The son of Apollo and the Muse Calliope, the Thracian Orpheus was the preeminent singer of classical myth. Voyaging with the Argonauts, he outsang the Sirens. His journey to the underworld to rescue Eurydice was at the root of an important mystery cult, and many hymns, most of them related to Dionysus, were attributed to Orpheus.

2. Taenarum, the central of the three southern fingers of the Peloponnesus, was known to contain a cave leading to the underworld, used by Hercules, among others.

3. The three-headed dog Cerberus was the legendary guardian of the underworld.

In love.[4] Now by these regions filled with fear,
35   By this huge chaos, these vast silent realms,
Reweave, I implore, the fate unwound too fast
Of my Eurydice. To you are owed
Ourselves and all creation; a brief while
We linger; then we hasten, late or soon,
40   To one abode; here one road leads us all;
Here in the end is home; over humankind
Your kingdom keeps the longest sovereignty.
She too, when ripening years reach their due term,
Shall own your rule. The favour that I ask
45   Is but to enjoy her love; and, if the Fates
Will not reprieve her, my resolve is clear
Not to return: may two deaths give you cheer."
        So to the music of his strings he sang,
And all the bloodless spirits wept to hear;
50   And Tantalus forgot the fleeing water,
Ixion's wheel was tranced; the Danaids
Laid down their urns; the vultures left their feast,
And Sisyphus sat rapt upon his stone.[5]
Then first by that sad singing overwhelmed,
55   The Furies' cheeks, it's said, were wet with tears;[6]
And Hades' queen and he whose sceptre rules
The Underworld could not deny the prayer,
And called Eurydice. She was among
The recent ghosts and, limping from her wound,
60   Came slowly forth; and Orpheus took his bride
And with her this compact that, till he reach
The world above and leave Avernus' vale,[7]
He look not back or else the gift would fail.
        The track climbed upwards, steep and indistinct,
65   Through the hushed silence and the murky gloom;
And now they neared the edge of the bright world,
And, fearing lest she faint, longing to look,
He turned his eyes—and straight she slipped away.
He stretched his arms to hold her—to be held—
70   And clasped, poor soul, naught but the yielding air.
And she, dying again, made no complaint
(For what complaint had she save she was loved?)

4. Pluto (Greek: Hades) had snatched his niece Proserpine, the daughter of Jove and Ceres, down to the underworld to be his queen.

5. Celebrated underworld punishments. Tantalus, a son of Jove, sat at the gods' table but for revealing their secrets was punished by the torment of food and drink always just out of his reach. Ixion, the king of the Lapithae and the father of Pirithous, was bound to a wheel for the attempted rape of Juno. The 50 daughters of Danaus, the king of Argos, killed their husbands on their collective wedding night, for which they were forced eternally to carry water in leaky urns. Prometheus was punished for

his theft of fire by having his liver eternally eaten by a vulture. Sisyphus, a son of Aeolus and the founder of Corinth, was renowned for his cunning and trickery; he was punished for them as well, forced to roll a boulder up a hill that would always escape him just as he reached the summit.

6. Born like the Giants from Earth and the blood of Uranus's severed genitals, the Furies were female powers of the underworld who punished transgressions.

7. Avernus, near Naples, was another reputed entrance to the underworld.

And breathed a faint farewell, and turned again
Back to the land of spirits whence she came.
75   The double death of his Eurydice
Stole Orpheus' wits away; (like him who saw
In dread the three-necked hound of Hell with chains
Fast round his middle neck, and never lost
His terror till he lost his nature too
80   And turned to stone; or Olenos, who took
Upon himself the charge and claimed the guilt
When his ill-starred Lethaea trusted to
Her beauty, hearts once linked so close, and now
Two rocks on runnelled Ida's mountainside).
85   He longed, he begged, in vain to be allowed
To cross the stream of Styx a second time.
The ferryman repulsed him.[8] Even so
For seven days he sat upon the bank,
Unkempt and fasting, anguish, grief and tears
90   His nourishment, and cursed Hell's cruelty.
Then he withdrew to soaring Rhodope
And Haemus battered by the northern gales.
      Three times the sun had reached the watery Fish
That close the year,[9] while Orpheus held himself
95   Aloof from love of women, hurt perhaps
By ill-success or bound by plighted troth.
Yet many a woman burned with passion for
The bard, and many grieved at their repulse.
It was his lead that taught the folk of Thrace
100   The love for tender boys, to pluck the buds,
The brief springtime, with manhood still to come.
      There was a hill, and on the hill a wide
Level of open ground, all green with grass.
The place lacked any shade. But when the bard,
105   The heaven-born bard, sat there and touched his strings,
Shade came in plenty. Every tree was there:[1]
Dodona's holy durmast, poplars once
The Sun's sad daughters, oaks with lofty leaves,
Soft limes, the virgin laurel and the beech;[2]
110   The ash, choice wood for spearshafts, brittle hazels,
The knotless fir, the ilex curving down
With weight of acorns, many-coloured maples,
The social plane, the river-loving willow,

---

8. It was the task of Charon to ferry newly arrived souls
across the river Styx.
9. Three years have passed. The twelfth and final sign of
the zodiac, Pisces ("the Fish"), marks the end of winter
(mid-February to mid-March).
1. The catalogue of trees includes several whose transformations Ovid has already described.
2. Dodona in Epirus was said to be the oldest Greek

oracle; the durmast, or oak, was her sacred tree. The sun's
three daughters were Phaethon's sisters, who wept so
long at his tomb that they were transformed into poplars.
The river Peneus's daughter, Daphne, was changed by her
father into a laurel to escape the advances of Apollo; he
chose the laurel as his tree and its wreath as the victor's
crown.

The water-lotus, box for ever green,
115 Thin tamarisks and myrtles double-hued,
Viburnums bearing berries of rich blue.
Twist-footed ivy came and tendrilled vines,
And vine-clad elms, pitch-pines and mountain-ash,
Arbutus laden with its blushing fruit,
120 Lithe lofty palms, the prize of victory,
And pines, high-girdled, in a leafy crest,
The favourite of Cybele, the gods'
Great mother, since in this tree Attis doffed
His human shape and stiffened in its trunk.[3]

125 Amid the throng the cone-shaped cypress stood,
A tree now, but in days gone by a boy,
Loved by that god who strings both lyre and bow.[4]
Once, sacred to the nymphs who dwell among
Carthaea's fields,[5] there was a giant stag,
130 Whose spreading antlers shed a screen of shade
Upon his head. Those antlers gleamed with gold
And from his silky neck a collar hung
Over his shoulders, set with precious stones.
Upon his brow, secured by slender strings,
135 A silver medal swayed, given at his birth,
And round his hollow temples, gleaming bright,
From either ear a pearly pendant hung.
Quite fearless, all his natural shyness lost,
He often visited the homes of men,
140 And he'd let even strangers stroke his neck.
But of them all he was the favourite
Of Cyparissus, Cea's° fairest lad.   *Ceos*
And he it was who used to lead the stag
To pasture and the waters of the spring.
145 Flowers of many colours he would weave
Around his horns or, mounted on his back,
A happy cavalier, ride up and down,
Guiding his tender mouth with crimson reins.
    It was high noon upon a summer's day;
150 The sun's bright beams were burning as the Crab,
That loves the shore-line, spread his curving claws,[6]
The stag lay down upon the grass to rest
And breathed the coolness of the spinney's° shade.   *thicket, small wood*
There, unaware, with his sharp javelin
155 Young Cyparissus pierced him to the heart.
And as he saw him dying of the wound,
So cruel, he resolved to die himself.

---

3. Attis was a Phrygian, or Lydian, youth beloved of
Cybele, the Anatolian fertility goddess, who castrated
himself in a fit of madness.
4. Cyparissus, an invention of Ovid's, loved by Apollo.

5. Carthaea was a city on the island of Ceos between
Greece and Asia Minor.
6. The zodiac sign of Cancer, June 19 to July 21, the beginning of summer.

What words of comfort did not Phoebus give!
What warnings not to yield to grief so sore,
160 So ill-proportioned! Still he groaned and begged
A last boon from the gods, that he might mourn
For evermore. And now, with endless sobs,
With lifeblood drained away, his limbs began
To take a greenish hue; his hair that curled
165 Down from his snowy brow rose in a crest,
A crest of bristles, and as stiffness spread
A graceful spire gazed at the starry sky.
Apollo groaned and said in sorrow "I
Shall mourn for you, for others you shall mourn;
170 You shall attend when men with grief are torn."[7]

[ORPHEUS'S SONG: GANYMEDE, HYACINTH, PYGMALION]

Such was the grove the bard assembled. There
He sat amid a company of beasts,
A flock of birds, and when he'd tried his strings
And, as he tuned, was satisfied the notes,
175 Though different, agreed in harmony,
He sang this song: "From Jove, great Mother Muse,[8]
Inspire my song: to Jove all creatures bow;
Jove's might I've often hymned in days gone by.
I sang the giants in a graver theme
180 And bolts victorious in Phlegra's plains.[9]
But now I need a lighter strain, to sing
Of boys beloved of gods and girls bewitched
By lawless fires who paid the price of lust.
    The King of Heaven once was fired with love
185 Of Ganymede,[1] and something was devised
That Jove would rather be than what he was.
Yet no bird would he deign to be but one
That had the power to bear his thunderbolts.[2]
At once his spurious pinions° beat the breeze   wings
190 And off he swept the Trojan lad; who now,
Mixing the nectar, waits in heaven above
(Though Juno frowns) and hands the cup to Jove.
    Hyacinth, too, Apollo would have placed
In heaven had the drear° Fates given time   dreary
195 To place him there. Yet in the form vouchsafed
He is immortal. Year by year, when spring
Drives winter flying and the Ram succeeds
The watery Fish, he rises from the earth

---

7. The cypress tree has long been associated with mourning, death, and burial.
8. Orpheus was the son of Calliope, the Muse of epic poetry.
9. The battle with the Giants took place on the plain of Phlegra in Thrace.

1. Ganymede was a brother of Ilos, the founder of Troy. Both were sons of Tros, a grandson of Jove.
2. The eagle was closely associated with Jove and was said to fetch his thunderbolts after he threw them.

And in the greensward° brings his bloom to birth.³   *grassy ground*

200   Hyacinth was my father's favourite,
      And Delphi, chosen centre of the world,
      Lost its presiding god, who passed his days
      Beside Eurotas° in the martial land   *Sparta's river*
      Of unwalled Sparta, and no more esteemed
205   Zither or bow. Forgetting his true self,
      He was content to bear the nets, to hold
      The hounds in leash and join the daylong chase
      Through the rough mountain ridges, nourishing
      His heart's desire with long companionship.

210   One day, near noon, when the high sun midway
      Between the night past and the night to come
      At equal distance stood from dawn and dusk,
      They both stripped off their clothes and oiled their limbs,
      So sleek and splendid, and began the game,
215   Throwing the discus; and Apollo first
      Poised, swung and hurled it skywards through the air,
      Up, soaring up, to cleave the waiting clouds.
      The heavy disk at longest last fell back
      To the familiar earth, a proof of skill,
220   And strength with skill. Then straightway Hyacinth,
      Unthinking, in the excitement of the sport,
      Ran out to seize it, but it bounded back
      From the hard surface full into his face.
      The god turned pale, pale as the boy himself,
225   And catching up the huddled body, tried
      To revive him, tried to staunch the tragic wound
      And stay the fading soul with healing herbs.
      His skill was vain; the wound was past all cure.
      And as, when in a garden violets
230   Or lilies tawny-tongued or poppies proud
      Are bruised and bent, at once they hang their heads
      And, drooping, cannot stand erect and bow
      Their gaze upon the ground; so dying lies
      That face so fair and, all strength ebbed away,
235   His head, too heavy, on his shoulder sinks.

      "My Hyacinth," Apollo cried, "laid low
      And cheated of youth's prime! I see your wound,
      My condemnation, you my grief and guilt!
      I, I have caused your death; on my own hand,
240   My own, your doom is written. Yet what wrong
      Is mine unless to join the game with you
      Were wrong or I were wrong to love you well?

---

3. Pisces ("Fish") is the last month of the solar year (mid-February to mid-March); Aries ("the Ram") is the first of the new year (mid-March to mid-April). Although not the same as the modern hyacinth, the name also refers here to a flower, to be described below.

Oh, would for you—or with you—I might give
My life! But since the laws of fate forbid,
245   You shall be with me always; you shall stay
For ever in remembrance on my lips,
And you my lyre and you my song shall hymn.
A new flower you shall be with letters marked
To imitate my sobs, and time shall come
250   When to that flower the bravest hero born
Shall add his name on the same petals writ."
      So with prophetic words Apollo spoke,
And lo! the flowing blood that stained the grass
Was blood no longer; and a flower rose
255   Gorgeous as Tyrian dye, in form a lily,
Save that a lily wears a silver hue,
This richest purple. And, not yet content,
Apollo (who had wrought the work of grace)
Inscribed upon the flower his lament,
260   AI AI, AI AI, and still the petals show
The letters written there in words of woe.
And Sparta's pride in Hyacinth, her son,
Endures undimmed; with pomp and proud display
Each year his feast returns in the ancient way.[4]
265   But should you ask ore-laden Amathus
If her Propoetides have brought her pride,
She would reject alike both them and those
Whose brows twin horns made hideous, whence their name,
Cerastae.[5] Once an altar stood before
270   Their doors to Jove, the God of Hospitality.
A newcomer who did not know their guilt,
Seeing that altar stained with blood, would think
That suckling calves or lambs of Amathus
Were offered there. It was the blood of guests!
275   Kind Venus, outraged by these wicked rites,
Prepared to leave her cities and the land
Of Cyprus. "Yet," she said, "these towns of mine,
These charming places, what have they done wrong?
Rather this impious race shall pay the price
280   By death or exile or some means half-way
Between the two, and that, what can it be
Except to change their shape to something new?"
What change to choose, she wondered; then, her eyes
Lighting upon their horns, she realized
285   Those could be left to them, and she transformed
Their bulky bodies into savage bulls.
      Even so the obscene Propoetides had dared

4. The three-day festival honoring Apollo and Hyacinth   closely associated with the goddess Venus. "Cerastae" is
was an important date in the Spartan year.   Greek for "horned." Both stories are apparently Ovid's
5. Amathus was a port city on the island of Cyprus,   invention.

Deny Venus' divinity. For that
The goddess' rage, it's said, made them the first
290 Strumpets to prostitute their bodies' charms.
As shame retreated and their cheeks grew hard,
They turned with little change to stones of flint.

Pygmalion[6] had seen these women spend
Their days in wickedness, and horrified
295 At all the countless vices nature gives
To womankind lived celibate and long
Lacked the companionship of married love.
Meanwhile he carved his snow-white ivory
With marvellous triumphant artistry
300 And gave it perfect shape, more beautiful
Than ever woman born. His masterwork
Fired him with love. It seemed to be alive,
Its face to be a real girl's, a girl
Who wished to move—but modesty forbade.
305 Such art his art concealed. In admiration
His heart desired the body he had formed.
With many a touch he tries it—is it flesh
Or ivory? Not ivory still, he's sure!
Kisses he gives and thinks they are returned;
310 He speaks to it, caresses it, believes
The firm new flesh beneath his fingers yields,
And fears the limbs may darken with a bruise.
And now fond words he whispers, now brings gifts
That girls delight in—shells and polished stones,
315 And little birds and flowers of every hue,
Lilies and coloured balls and beads of amber,
The tear-drops of the daughters of the Sun.[7]
He decks her limbs with robes and on her fingers
Sets splendid rings, a necklace round her neck,
320 Pearls in her ears, a pendant on her breast;
Lovely she looked, yet unadorned she seemed
In nakedness no whit less beautiful.
He laid her on a couch of purple silk,
Called her his darling, cushioning her head,
325 As if she relished it, on softest down.
     Venus' day came, the holiest festival
All Cyprus celebrates; incense rose high
And heifers, with their wide horns gilded, fell
Beneath the blade that struck their snowy necks,
330 Pygmalion, his offering given, prayed
Before the altar, half afraid, "Vouchsafe,
O Gods, if all things you can grant, my bride
Shall be"—he dared not say my ivory girl—

6. A king of Cyprus.
7. Mourning at the tomb of their fallen brother Phaethon, the Heliades, or daughters of the Sun, were transformed into trees. Their resinous tears hardened into amber.

"The living likeness of my ivory girl."
335　And golden Venus (for her presence graced
　　　Her feast) knew well the purpose of his prayer;
　　　And, as an omen of her favouring power,
　　　Thrice did the flame burn bright and leap up high.
　　　And he went home, home to his heart's delight,
340　And kissed her as she lay, and she seemed warm;
　　　Again he kissed her and with marvelling touch
　　　Caressed her breast; beneath his touch the flesh
　　　Grew soft, its ivory hardness vanishing,
　　　And yielded to his hands, as in the sun
345　Wax of Hymettus[8] softens and is shaped
　　　By practised fingers into many forms,
　　　And usefulness acquires by being used.
　　　His heart was torn with wonder and misgiving,
　　　Delight and terror that it was not true!
350　Again and yet again he tried his hopes—
　　　She was alive! The pulse beat in her veins!
　　　And then indeed in words that overflowed
　　　He poured his thanks to Venus, and at last
　　　His lips pressed real lips, and she, his girl,
355　Felt every kiss, and blushed, and shyly raised
　　　Her eyes to his and saw the world and him.
　　　The goddess graced the union she had made,
　　　And when nine times the crescent moon had filled
　　　Her silver orb, an infant girl was born,
360　Paphos,[9] from whom the island takes its name.

from Book 11

[THE DEATH OF ORPHEUS]

　　　While Orpheus sang his minstrel's songs and charmed
　　　The rocks and woods and creatures of the wild
　　　To follow, suddenly, as he swept his strings
　　　In concord with his song, a frenzied band
5　　Of Thracian women, wearing skins of beasts,
　　　From some high ridge of ground caught sight of him.[1]
　　　"Look!" shouted one of them, tossing her hair
　　　That floated in the breeze, "Look, there he is,
　　　The man who scorns us!" and she threw her lance
10　Full in Apollo's minstrel's face, but, tipped
　　　With leaves, it left a bruise but drew no blood.
　　　Another hurled a stone; that, in mid air,
　　　Was vanquished by the strains of voice and lyre

---

8. A mountain in Attica near Athens.
9. A city-kingdom in Cyprus.
1. Maenads, or Bacchantes, were followers of Bacchus

(Greek: Dionysus), intoxicated by the god's power. They dressed in panther skins and carried a *thyrsos*, or ivy-covered staff.

And grovelled at his feet, as if to ask
15 Pardon for frenzy's daring. Even so
The reckless onslaught swelled; their fury knew
No bounds; stark madness reigned. And still his singing
Would have charmed every weapon, but the huge
Clamour, the drums, the curving Phrygian fifes,°   *small flutes*
20 Hand-clapping, Bacchic screaming drowned the lyre.
And then at last, his song unheard, his blood
Reddened the stones. The Maenads first pounced on
The countless birds still spellbound by his song,
The snakes, the host of creatures of the wild,
25 His glory and his triumph. Next they turned
Their bloody hands on Orpheus, flocking like
Birds that have seen a midnight owl abroad
By day, or in the amphitheatre
Upon the morning sand a pack of hounds
30 Round a doomed stag. They rushed upon the bard,
Hurling their leaf-dressed lances, never meant
For work like that; and some slung clods, some flints,
Some branches torn from trees. And, lest they lack
Good weapons for their fury, as it chanced,
35 Oxen were toiling there to plough the land
And brawny farmhands digging their hard fields
Not far away, and sweating for their crop.
Seeing the horde of women, they fled and left
Their labour's armoury, and all across
40 The empty acres lay their heavy rakes,
Hoes and long-handled mattocks. Seizing these,
Those frantic women tore apart the oxen
That threatened with their horns, and streamed to slay
The bard. He pleaded then with hands outstretched
45 And in that hour for the first time his words
Were useless and his voice of no avail.
In sacrilege they slew him. Through those lips
(Great Lord of Heaven!) that held the rocks entranced,
That wild beasts understood, he breathed his last,
50 And forth into the winds his spirit passed.
     The sorrowing birds, the creatures of the wild,
The woods that often followed as he sang,
The flinty rocks and stones, all wept and mourned
For Orpheus; forest trees cast down their leaves,
55 Tonsured in grief, and rivers too, men say,
Were swollen with their tears, and Naiads wore,
And Dryads too, their mourning robes of black
And hair dishevelled. All around his limbs
Lay scattered. Hebrus'[2] stream received his head

2. A Thracian river that flowed into the Aegean Sea.

60   And lyre, and floating by (so wonderful!)
       His lyre sent sounds of sorrow and his tongue,
       Lifeless, still murmured sorrow, and the banks
       Gave sorrowing reply. And then they left
       Their native river, carried out to sea,
65   And gained Methymna's shore on Lesbos' isle.[3]
       There, as his head lay on that foreign sand,
       Its tumbled tresses dripping, a fierce snake
       Threatened, until at last Apollo came
       To thwart it as it struck and froze to stone
70   That serpent's open mouth and petrified,
       Just as they were, its jaws that gaped so wide.
            The ghost of Orpheus passed to the Underworld,
       And all the places that he'd seen before
       He recognized again and, searching through
75   The Elysian fields, he found Eurydice
       And took her in his arms with leaping heart.
       There hand in hand they stroll, the two together;
       Sometimes he follows as she walks in front,
       Sometimes he goes ahead and gazes back—
80   No danger now—at his Eurydice.

from Book 15

[PYTHAGORAS]

       A man lived here, a Samian by birth,
60   But he had fled from Samos and its masters
       And, hating tyranny, by his own choice
       Became an exile.[1] Though the gods in heaven
       Live far removed, he approached them in his mind,
       And things that nature kept from mortal sight
65   His inward eye explored. When meditation
       And vigils of long study had surveyed
       All things that are, he made his wisdom free
       For all to share; and he would teach his class,
       Hanging in silent wonder on his words,
70   The great world's origin, the cause of things,
       What nature is, what god, and whence the snow,
       What makes the lightning, whether thunder comes
       From Jove or from the winds when clouds burst wide,
       Why the earth quakes, what ordinance controls
75   The courses of the stars, and the whole sum

---

3. Methymna was a city on Lesbos, a large island off the
coast of Asia Minor.
1. Pythagoras was born on the island of Samos in the
mid-6th century B.C.E. He left for Croton, a Greek colony
in southern Italy, around 530. He was held to have

brought to Greece the doctrine of the transmigration of
souls on which Ovid has him speak here. He was also
credited with important discoveries in music, astronomy,
and mathematics, including the Pythagorean theorem.

Of nature's secrets. He was first to ban
As food for men the flesh of living things:
These are the doctrines he was first to teach,
Wise words, though wisdom powerless to persuade:[2]

* * *

"Now since the sea's great surges sweep me on,
All canvas spread, hear me! In all creation
Nothing endures, all is in endless flux,
Each wandering shape a pilgrim passing by.
180 And time itself glides on in ceaseless flow,
A rolling stream—and streams can never stay,
Nor lightfoot hours. As wave is driven by wave
And each, pursued, pursues the wave ahead,
So time flies on and follows, flies and follows,
185 Always, for ever new. What was before
Is left behind; what never was is now;
And every passing moment is renewed.
You see how day extends as night is spent,
And this bright radiance succeeds the dark;
190 Nor, when the tired world lies in midnight peace,
Is the sky's sheen the same as in the hour
When on his milk-white steed the Morning Star
Rides forth, or when, bright harbinger of day,
Aurora gilds the globe to greet the sun.
195 The sun's round shield at morning when he climbs
From earth's abyss glows red, and when he sinks
To earth's abyss at evening red again,
And at his zenith gleaming bright, for there
The air is pure and earth's dross far away.
200 Nor can the queenly moon ever retain
Her shape unchanged, but always, as her orb
Waxes or wanes, tomorrow, she must shine
Larger or smaller than she is today.
Again, you notice how the year in four
205 Seasons revolves, completing one by one
Fit illustration of our human life.
The young springtime, the tender suckling spring,
Is like a child; the swelling shoots so fresh,
So soft and fragile, fill the farmers' hearts
210 With hope and gladness. Flowers are everywhere;
Their colours dance across the fostering fields,
While the green leaves still lack their strength and pride.
Spring passes, and the year, grown sturdier,
Rolls on to summer like a strong young man;
215 No age so sturdy, none so rich, so warm.

2. Vegetarianism was one of the tenets of the ancient cult of Pythagoreanism. After arguing that vegetarianism hearkens back to the Golden Age, Pythagoras goes on to dismiss the fear of death: because of the transmigration of souls, nothing dies.

Then autumn follows, youth's fine fervour spent,
Mellow and ripe, a temperate time between
Youth and old age, his temples flecked with grey.
And last, with faltering footsteps, rough and wild,
220   His hair, if any, white, old winter comes.
       Our bodies too are always, endlessly
Changing; what we have been, or are today,
We shall not be tomorrow. Years ago
We hid, mere seeds and promise, in the womb;
225   Nature applied her artist's hands to free
Us from our swollen mother's narrow home,
And sent us forth into the open air.
Born to the shining day, the infant lies
Strengthless, but soon on all fours like the beasts
230   Begins to crawl, and then by slow degrees,
Weak-kneed and wobbling, clutching for support
Some helping upright, learns at last to stand.
Then swift and strong he traverses the span
Of youth, and when the years of middle life
235   Have given their service too, he glides away
Down the last sunset slope of sad old age—
Old age that saps and mines and overthrows
The strength of earlier years. Milo, grown old,
Sheds tears to see how shrunk and flabby hang
240   Those arms on which the muscles used to swell,
Massive like Hercules; and, when her glass
Shows every time-worn wrinkle, Helen weeps
And wonders why she twice was stolen for love.[3]
Time, the devourer, and the jealous years
245   With long corruption ruin all the world
And waste all things in slow mortality.
      The elements themselves do not endure;
Examine how they change and learn from me.
The everlasting universe contains
250   Four generative substances; of these
Two, earth and water, sink of their own weight;
Two, air and fire (fire purer still than air),
Weightless, unburdened, seek the heights above.
Though spaced apart, all issue from each other
255   And to each other fall. So earth, reduced,
Is rarefied to water; moisture, thinned,
Dissolves to air and wind; air, losing weight,
So light, so insubstantial, flashes up
To empyrean fire. Then they return
260   In reverse order as the skein° unwinds.   *bundle of yarn*

3. Milo was a wrestler from Croton who won many victories at the Olympic and the Pythian Games and a disciple of
Pythagoras. Helen was first carried off by Theseus and then later, after she had married Menelaus, by Paris of Troy.

Thus fire, condensed, passes to heavier air,
Air into water, water in its turn
Compressed, conglobed, solidifies to earth.
   Nothing retains its form; new shapes from old
265   Nature, the great inventor, ceaselessly
Contrives. In all creation, be assured,
There is no death—no death, but only change
And innovation; what we men call birth
Is but a different new beginning; death
270   Is but to cease to be the same. Perhaps
This may have moved to that and that to this,
Yet still the sum of things remains the same.

* * *

   "So—lest I range too far and my steeds lose
Their course—the earth and all therein, the sky
455   And all thereunder change and change again.
We too ourselves, who of this world are part,
Not only flesh and blood but pilgrim souls,
Can make our homes in creatures of the wild
Or of the farm. These creatures might have housed
460   Souls of our parents, brothers, other kin,
Or men at least, and we must keep them safe,
Respected, honoured, lest we gorge ourselves
On such a banquet as Thyestes ate.[4]
How vilely he's inured, how wickedly
465   He fits himself to kill his human kin,
He who can slit his calf's throat, hear its cries
Unmoved, who has the heart to kill his kid
That screams like a small child, or eat the bird
His hand has reared and fed! How far does this
470   Fall short of murder? Where else does it lead?
No! Let the oxen plough and owe their death
To length of days; let the sheep give their shield
Against the north wind's fury; let the goats
Bring their full udders for your hand to milk.
475   Away with traps and snares and lures and wiles!
Never again lime twigs to cheat the birds,
Nor feather ropes to drive the frightened deer,
Nor hide the hook with dainties that deceive!
Destroy what harms; destroy, but never eat;
480   Choose wholesome fare and never feast on meat!

---

4. The sons of Thyestes were killed and served to their father in a meal by his brother, Atreus.

⇒ PERSPECTIVES ⇐

The Culture of Rome and the Beginnings of Christianity

To the sophisticated and powerful urban elite that controlled ancient Rome, the first Christians were superstitious bumpkins from a distant backwater. How could they suspect that this obscure cult would soon enough take over their empire? It is true that Rome had a generally tolerant policy for the assimilation of members of the farther reaches of its Empire, and the inhabitants of Judaea at times had received special consideration. Still, from early reactions through at least the fourth century it appears that resistance to Christianity was at least as much aesthetic and social as it was political and religious. The urbane poetry of Catullus and Horace gives a good impression of the values and attitudes of educated Romans around the time of the birth of Jesus. Both poets cultivate the persona of a well-connected member of the elite: the republican Catullus stresses the thrill-seeking vigor of the brash, young aesthete; Horace expresses the measured, Stoic outlook of the next generation under the reign of Augustus, where even death could become a subject for a lesson on proper living.

It is a far cry from the balanced ethic of Horace or the self-consciously cultivated passion of Catullus to the strident urgency and stern demands of Luke and Paul. Earliest Christianity was a sect of Judaism, regarding Jesus as the Christ, the fulfillment of the Hebrew prophets' promise of a Messiah. The first-century writings of Luke and Paul bear witness to the struggle to extricate an independent religion out of a complex web of forces: the legal and spiritual tradition of Judaism, the language and philosophy of Hellenism, the political yoke of the Empire, and the many other radical new forms of worship circulating around the eastern Mediterranean during the early centuries of the Common Era.

Strict asceticism and a rejection of material and familial ties were hallmarks of the Gospels—oral accounts of the "Good News" of Christ that began being written down near the end of the first century. The martyrdom that often resulted from this choice gave a positive meaning to the omnipresence of death for most of the inhabitants of the Empire. The Roman historians excerpted below give a good sense of the relative insignificance of the movement during these years. Still, its members could make excellent scapegoats, such as the "notoriously depraved Christians" who were falsely blamed by Nero for the great fire in Rome in 64. The decadent world portrayed so vividly by Petronius in the *Satyricon* is perhaps not exemplary of behavior under Nero, but it does suggest the world that Saul of Tarsus chose to leave behind when a vision of Christ converted him into the apostle Paul, eventually to be martyred on the Ostian Way outside Rome by Nero's command.

Juvenal's satires present a traditionally Roman response to a corrupt society; he attacks the miserable city from the point of view of classical Roman ethics and morality, while other writers like the second-century novelist Apuleius graphically depicted the instability of the changing world outside the capital city. Both traditions would find their home in Christian sermonizing, but joined to a rhetoric of separation and a language of mystery wholly alien to a rationalist like Juvenal—who chose, after all, to remain in the city he professed to hate—and with a gravity and an intensity of purpose lacking in Apuleius's ambling narrative *The Golden Ass.* The paradoxical formulations that punctuate the fire and brimstone of Paul's Epistles and the parables and miracles of Jesus recounted in Luke proved more potent and compelling antidotes to the crises of the late Empire. But as Augustine shows in his *Confessions,* the crux of Christianity's appeal lay in the unmatchable grip it had on the emotions—the passions and the disappointments of everyday suffering. Its debt to Rome was the means of channeling that visceral power into a form that would be intellectually and aesthetically palatable to those figures such

Chariot race at the Circus Maximus in Rome. As Juvenal asserted in his tenth *Satire,* "Luxury, more deadly than war, broods over the city . . . the people that once bestowed commands, consulships, legions, and all else, now concerns itself no more, and longs eagerly for just two things—bread and circuses."

as Emperor Constantine who were in a position finally to entrench it within an enduring framework of temporal power.

PRONUNCIATIONS:

Catullus: kah-TUHL-luhs
Encolpius: en-KOL-pee-uhs
Gitai: JEE-tai
Juvenal: JOO-ve-nahl
Petronius: pe-TROH-nee-uhs
Pliny: PLI-nee
Priapea: PRAI-ah-PAY-ah
Satyricon: sah-TI-ri-con
Suetonius: soo-eh-TOH-nee-uhs
Tacitus: TA-si-tuhs
Trajan: TRAY-juhn

Catullus
84–54 B.C.E.

In the small corpus of verse he completed before his untimely death at age 30, Gaius Valerius Catullus celebrated novelty, obscenity, youth, brevity, charm, wit, passion, and urbanity. His 113 poems, most of them quite short, reproduce everyday life and take us inside the mind of a young man-about-town in first-century Rome. Meals and journeys are described; friends are praised and heckled, enemies mocked and reviled; loves and disappointments are chronicled in graphic detail; and everywhere there is the writing, reciting, and criticism of poetry.

Born into a well-to-do family in Verona, Catullus soon made his way to the capital, where he moved among the preeminent political and literary figures of his day. He had a brother, whose sudden death in Asia Minor around 57 B.C.E. was the occasion of a sea voyage to the distant grave near Troy and a moving poem that strove "to speak in vain to your un-speaking ashes." He conducted a love affair with the powerful (and, according to Cicero, no-torious) Clodia, half-sister of the tribune Publius Clodius Pulcher and wife of Quintus Caecil-ius Metellus, consul in the year 60. This was the "Lesbia" to whom many of the poems refer and with whom the poet explores the extremes of passion; her name itself pays homage to the erotic lyrics of Sappho, the archaic Greek poet of the island of Lesbos (page 562; an imitation of one of her poems is included in the selection below, page 1247). Catullus's depiction of love is central to his portrayal of life as a paradoxical mix of emotions, a heady brew both sweet and sour in which despair and joy are inseparable. With its capacity to concentrate op-posites of emotion and sense perceptions into concrete feelings through a masterful control of language and meter, the lyric form allowed Catullus to render vividly the chaotic experience of an individual in the late Republic.

from POEMS[1]

3[1]

Cry out lamenting, Venuses & Cupids,
and mortal men endowed with Love's refinement:
the sparrow of my lady lives no longer!
Sparrow, the darling pet of my beloved,
5   that was more precious to her than her eyes were;
it was her little honey, and it knew her
as well as any girl knows her own mother;
it would not ever leave my lady's bosom
but leapt up, fluttering from yon to hither,
10   chirruping always only to its mistress.
It now flits off on its way, goes, gloom-laden
down to where—word is—there is no returning.
Damn you, damned shades of Orcus[2] that devour
all mortal loveliness, for such a lovely
15   sparrow it was you've stolen from my keeping!
O hideous deed! O poor little sparrow!
It's your great fault that my lady goes weeping,
reddening, ruining her eyes from sorrow.

5

Lesbia, let us live only for loving,
and let us value at a single penny

---

1. Translated by Charles Martin.
1. This poem is in the form of a mock threnody, or funeral dirge.

2. An infernal deity in Greek mythology. Identified in Ro-man religion with Dis, the god of the underworld.

all the loose flap of senile busybodies!
Suns when they set are capable of rising,
5 but at the setting of our own brief light
night is one sleep from which we never waken.
Give me a thousand kisses, then a hundred,
another thousand next, another hundred,
a thousand without pause & then a hundred,
10 until when we have run up our thousands
we will cry bankrupt, hiding our assets
from ourselves & any who would harm us,
knowing the volume of our trade in kisses.

13

You will dine well with me, my dear Fabullus,[1]
in a few days or so, the gods permitting.
—Provided you provide the many-splendored
feast, and invite your fair-complected° lady,   *complexioned*
5 your wine, your salt & all the entertainment!
Which is to say, my dear, if you bring dinner
you will dine well, for these days your Catullus
finds that his purse is only full of cobwebs.
But in return, you'll have from me Love's Essence,
10 —or what (if anything) is more delicious:
I'll let you sniff a certain charming fragrance
which Venuses & Cupids gave my lady;
one whiff of it, Fabullus, and you'll beg the
gods to transform you into nose, completely!

51[1]

To me that man seems like a god in heaven,
seems—may I say it?—greater than all gods are,
who sits by you & without interruption
     watches you, listens

5 to your light laughter, which casts such confusion
onto my senses, Lesbia, that when I
gaze at you merely, all of my well-chosen
     words are forgotten

as my tongue thickens & a subtle fire
10 runs through my body while my ears are deafened

---

1. Fabullus was a colleague in the Roman province of
Spain with Veranius, a friend of Catullus who, we are
told, sent the poet a set of fine napkins of Spanish linen as
a souvenir. The poem's number comes from its place in
the manuscript. It is not known if this order reflects the

author's intention.
1. A free translation of Sappho's poem "He looks to me to
be in heaven" (see page 565), in Sapphic strophes, with a
final stanza of his own.

by their own ringing & at once my eyes are
    covered in darkness!

Leisure, Catullus. More than just a nuisance,
leisure: you riot, overmuch enthusing.
15   Fabulous cities & their sometime kings have
    died of such leisure.

76[1]

If any pleasure can come to a man through recalling
    decent behavior in his relations with others,
not breaking his word, and never, in any agreement,
    deceiving men by abusing vows sworn to heaven,
5   then countless joys will await you in old age, Catullus,
    as a reward for this unrequited passion!
For all of those things which a man could possibly say or
    do have all been said & done by you already,
and none of them counted for anything, thanks to her vileness!
10   Then why endure your self-torment any longer?
Why not abandon this wretched affair altogether,
    spare yourself pain the gods don't intend you to suffer!
It's hard to break off with someone you've loved such a long time:
    it's hard, but you have to do it, somehow or other.
15   Your only chance is to get out from under this sickness,
    no matter whether or not you think you're able.
O gods, if pity is yours, or if ever to any
    who lay near death you offered the gift of your mercy,
look on my suffering: if my life seems to you decent,
20   then tear from within me this devouring cancer,
this heavy dullness wasting the joints of my body,
    completely driving every joy from my spirit!
Now I no longer ask that she love me as I love her,
    or—even less likely—that she give up the others:
25   all that I ask for is health, an end to this foul sickness!
    O gods, grant me this in exchange for my worship.

107

If ever something which someone with no expectation
    desired should happen, we are rightly delighted!
And so this news is delightful—it's dearer than gold is:
    you have returned to me, Lesbia, my desired!
Desired, yet never expected—but you *have* come back
    to me! A holiday, a day of celebration!

---

1. The mood, subject, and meter of this poem anticipate the classical Roman love elegies of Propertius, Tibullus, and Ovid.

What living man is luckier than I am? Or able
to say that anything could possibly be better?

〰 TRANSLATIONS: CATULLUS, POEM 85 〰

The compression and power of these two lines derive in large part from the elimination of adjectives and of images. The poet gives us only verbs of condensed sensation: *hate, love, do, feel, shiver.* Rather than explaining the paradox of the opening antithesis, *odi et amo,* this string of verbs heightens its effect. Half the verbs are active; half are passive: the poet hates and loves; he rules and is ruled by his lover and his love.

CATULLUS, POEM 85—LATIN ORIGINAL AND WORD-FOR-WORD TRANSLATION

I hate and I love why it I do   perhaps you ask
odi   et amo   quare id faciam fortasse requiris

I do not know but being done I feel it and I am tormented [literally "I am crucified"]
nescio   sed fieri   sentio et excrucior.

Poem 85 poses a serious challenge for translators due to its condensed form and the differences between English and Latin, an extremely compact language having verbs that do not require pronouns and objects that often do not require prepositions. Moreover, Latin word order is highly flexible. The original texts of the poems had no punctuation, so words could be arranged for maximum effect, something much more difficult to achieve in the linear syntax of English.

Landor and Lovelace translate the couplet into rhyming verse. Both add to the poem in order to make the rhyme work. Landor adds an entire line of explanation, to make the irrationality of passion somehow more rational. How does the use of end-rhyme affect the meaning of the poem?

I hate and love, wouldst thou the reason know?
I know not, but I burn and feel it so.
Richard Lovelace (1618–1657)

I love and hate. Ah! never ask why so!
I hate and love—and that is all I know.
I see 'tis folly, but I feel 'tis woe.
Walter Savage Landor (1775–1864)

Both Whigham and Pound render Catullus's Latin in hard-sounding one-syllable words that stress the inescapable nature of the speaker's dilemma. Both also work to capture the shift to the passive voice in the second line.

I hate and love. Why? You ask me but
It beats me. I feel it done to me, and ache.
Ezra Pound (1885–1972)

I hate and I love. And if you ask me how,
I do not know: I only feel it, and I'm torn in two.
Peter Whigham (1966)

Martin tempers the extreme syncopation of Whigham and Pound but aims for a similar matter-of-factness in the first line. His second line is more conversational, which makes the stark confession of the final clause, "and it shivers me," all the more effective.

> I hate & love. And if you should ask how I can do both,
> I couldn't say: but I feel it, and it shivers me.
> *Charles Martin (1990)*

The contemporary American poet Frank Bidart has done two radically different versions of poem 85; both take more liberties than any of the previous examples.

CATULLUS: ODI ET AMO

> I hate and love. Ignorant fish, who even
> Wants the fly while writhing.
> *Frank Bidart (1980)*

CATULLUS: EXCRUCIOR

> I hate and—love. the sleepless body hammering a nail nails
> itself, hanging crucified.
> *Frank Bidart (1997)*

What do you think justifies the metaphor of the fish caught on the line? In the 1997 poem, Bidart proves to be the only translator who literally translates the meaning of "excrucior." Do you think he is justified in making this word the focus of the poem?

~∞~

RESONANCE

from Priapea[1]

In your honor, Lord Priapus

In your honor, Lord Priapus,
I've dashed off these verses, fitter
for a garden than a bookshop.

---

1. Translated by Richard W. Hopper. The god Priapus, whose large, erect phallus was believed to avert evil and abet procreation, came to Rome from Greece and probably originated in Asia Minor. A cult was devoted to him, and carved wooden figures would be placed in gardens or orchards as watchmen and deterrents to theft. While Greek poetry dedicated to the god was frequently serious and religious in tone, the Roman *priapea* was generally a mocking combination of erotic and invective. The main corpus of 80 *carmina Priapea* ("Songs of Priapus") are of unknown authorship, although long numbered among the minor works of Virgil; they date from either the end of the 1st century B.C.E. or the 1st century C.E. Deliberately modest in their poetic aspirations, the four epigrams included here give a sense of Roman poetry at its loosest and most playful. Although these epigrams are closest perhaps to Catullus in their terse combination of wit, erudition, and obscenity, there are examples of *priapea* by many Latin poets including Virgil, Ovid, and Horace (see *Satire* 1.8, page 1252).

Nor, in trite poetic fashion,
5   have I summoned forth the Muses[2]
to this most deflowered setting.
I'd be heartless to conduct that
chaste Pierian assemblage[3]
to the pecker of Priapus.
10   Thus, whatever in my leisure
I have scribbled o'er your temple,
please accept as well intentioned.

The law which (as they say) Priapus coined

The law which (as they say) Priapus coined
for boys appears immediately subjoined:
"Come pluck my garden's contents without blame
if in your garden I can do the same."

You ask why I don't hide my filthy charms?

You ask why I don't hide my filthy charms?
Ask rather why no god conceals his arms.[1]
The Lord of Earth meant lightning to be seen,
nor is the trident's nature submarine.[2]
5   Nor Mars conceals his sword point from our eyes,
nor Pallas° warms her spear between her thighs.   *Athena*
Does Phoebus° blush to see his arrows fly?   *Apollo*
Diana bear her quiver on the sly?
Is Alcides'° holm-oaken staff covert?   *Hercules's*
10   The Winged God's° concealed beneath his shirt?   *Mercury's*
What pretext of concealment could command
the Wine God's° staff or Cupid's fiery brand?   *Bacchus's*
To fault me for a naked cock is senseless.
Without my weapon I'd be left defenseless.

Whichever one of you throwing a party at home

Whichever one of you throwing a party at home
doesn't endeavor to honor my name with a poem,
long may his wife or his girlfriend (so help me!) wear out
a fortunate rival, squeezed dry in lascivious rout.
And let the culprit himself spend his evenings alone,
harsh aphrodisiacs vainly inflating his bone.

❧

2. The nine Muses were goddesses who inspired poets to creation.
3. Pieria, near Mount Olympus, was the home of the Muses.

1. The lines that follow refer to Olympian gods (and one demigod, Alcides, or Hercules) and their principal weapons.
2. The trident was the weapon of the sea god Neptune.

——— ⚜ ———

Horace
65–8 B.C.E.

Son of a freedman farmer of modest means, Quintus Horatius Flaccus was by the end of his life a close acquaintance of Emperor Augustus. Through his often topical poetry and through his actions, Horace was intimately involved in the events of his day. In 42 B.C.E., he fought on the losing side of Caesar's murderers, Brutus and Cassius, at Philippi against Mark Antony and Octavian. His family farm was confiscated, but Horace eventually landed on his feet, gaining the patronage of the influential Etruscan noble and minister of Octavian, Maecenas, with the aid of his friend Virgil. In 33, Maecenas presented Horace with a farm in the rich Sabine country northeast of Rome. Horace published his *Satires* (*Sermones*) between 34 and 30 B.C.E., the *Epodes* in 30, three books of *Odes* in 23, the *Epistles* in 20, and a fourth book of *Odes* around 13.

The *Satires* are more conversational and occasional in form and subject matter, the *Odes* are more formal and morally instructive; but both are built around a series of oppositions: country versus city, a simple versus a complicated life, poverty versus wealth, past versus present, private versus public. Central to these oppositions is the Epicurean conception of the *aurea mediocritas,* or golden mean, the desire to avoid extremes in life and to focus on the simple pleasures of the present. Horace prides himself on puncturing pretensions and unreasonable behavior, including his own, as in Ode 2.13, where he berates a falling tree that has almost crushed him. The strategy of comic deflation allows Horace to introduce philosophical concerns with the lightest of touches. So the tree leads him to consider the underworld from which he has so narrowly escaped; and Ode 2.14 skips from a lament for his aging friend Postumus to the concluding image of his heir spilling his fine wine all over the floor.

from SATIRES

1.8 Once I was wood from a worthless old fig tree[1]

Once I was wood from a worthless old fig tree
when a handyman, hesitant between hassock° and Priapus,   *footstool*
decided on sanctity. So I'm a god,
the terrible terror of thieves and of birds.
5   For my right hand scares robbers as does the red-colored column
that operates out of my obscene crotch;
while importunate pigeons panicked at the reed
set high on my head don't harm the new gardens.
A co-slave would contract for corpses ejected
10   from the teeming tenements to be transported here
in a bargain-priced box; for built on this spot
was the cemetery for slaves where such as Nomentanus
and grandfather Grabby the gadfly lay buried.
The tomb bore this title: "A thousand feet front,
15   three hundred behind. The heirs can't inherit."[2]

---

1. Translated by Richard W. Hopper. Compare to the *Priapea* above.

2. It was common for graves to be preserved by being excluded from property inheritance.

Now healthful housing has been constructed
on the Esquiline, and the Esplanade is especially good for a stroll
(blanch-white bones used to blemish the prospect).[3]
But the footpads and fauna who frequent these regions
20   cannot make me nervous or nearly so anxious
as enchantresses and alchemists who charm human ghosts.
Once the moon has unmasked her modest face
I'm unable to interfere or even prevent them
from unburying bones and baleful plants.
25   I myself have caught sight of unsightly Canidia,
her black gown bunched up, barefoot, dishevelled,
and Sagana, her senior sister in howling.
Their pallor compounded the pair's fearful aspect.
They scratched furrows with their fingernails and fastened their teeth
30   in a black lamb whose blood boiled into a ditch
where ghosts could gather and grant responses.
One figure was fashioned from wool, one from wax.
The wool one worked better at wounding the lesser;
the waxen was waiting in woebegone fashion
35   soon to dissolve. One summoned: "Hecate!"
"Tissiphone!" thundered the other.[4] Think of the snakes,
the bustling of infernal bitches, the fair blushing moon
who, lest she be witness, withdrew behind a great tomb!
If I'm telling a tale may the white turds of the crows
40   pollute my pate; let them piss and crap on me—
Julius and gentle Pediata, and that jailbait Voranus.
Why pause for particulars? How piping up mournfully
the shades sounded out with Sagana in canon,
how they buried the beard of a wolf with the bite of a serpent,
45   how the fire flashed up from the figure of wax,
how I witnessed with horror but not without vengeance
the prayers and practices of this pair of Furies.
For just as a bladder goes "boom!" when it bursts, so I farted
through my fractured fig butt. They fled to the city.
50   You'd have let out a laugh at the ludicrous sight:
Canidia's custom-made teeth, the coiffure of Sagana,
their herbs and their armlets in orbit together.

1.5 Leaving the big city behind I found lodgings at Aricia[1]

Leaving the big city° behind I found lodgings at Aricia   *Rome*
in a smallish pub. With me was Heliodorus, the professor
of rhetoric, the greatest scholar in the land of Greece. From there
to Forum Appi crammed with bargees° and stingy landlords.   *bargemen*

3. The slave's cemetery that had dominated the Esquiline Field in Rome had been transformed by Maecenas into gardens.
4. Hecate was a sinister goddess associated with magic, witchcraft, the night, the underworld, and crossroads; Tissiphone was one of the Furies.
1. Translated by Niall Rudd.

5   Being lazy types we split this stretch into two, though speed-merchants
       do it in one. The Appian[2] is easier when you take it slowly.
       Here I declared war on my stomach because of the water
       which was quite appalling, and waited impatiently as the other travellers
       enjoyed their dinner.
                                    Now night was preparing to draw her shadows
10   over the earth and to sprinkle the heavens with glimmering lights
       when the lads started to shout at the boatmen, who replied in kind.[3]
       "Bring her over here!" "How many hundred are you going to pack in?"
       "Whoah, that's enough!"
                              While the fares are collected and the mule harnessed,
       a whole hour goes by. The blasted mosquitoes and the marsh
15   frogs make sleep impossible. The boatman, who has had a skinful
       of sour wine, sings of his distant loved one, and a traveller
       takes up the refrain. Weariness finally gets the better of the traveller
       and he nods off. The lazy boatman lets the mule graze;
       he ties the rope to a stone and lies on his back snoring.
20   When day dawns we realize the barge is making no progress.
       This is remedied when a furious passenger jumps ashore,
       seizes a branch of willow, and wallops the mule and the boatman
       on the head and back.
                            It was almost ten before we landed.
       We washed our hands and face in Feronia's holy spring.[4]
25   Then after breakfast we crawled three miles up to Anxur
       perched on its white rocks which can be seen from far and wide.
       This was where the admirable Maecenas was due to come,
       along with Cocceius; both were envoys on a mission of immense
       importance; both had experience in reconciling friends who had quarrelled.[5]
30   I went indoors to smear some black ointment on my eyes,
       which were rather bloodshot. Meanwhile Maecenas and Cocceius arrived,
       and also Fonteius Capito, a man of consummate charm
       and tact, who held a unique place in Antony's affections.

       We left Fundi with relief in the Praetorship° of Aufidius Luscus,   *control*
35   laughing at the regalia of that fatuous official—the toga complete
       with border, the broad-striped tunic, and the pan of glowing charcoal.
       Then, after a weary journey, we stopped at the Mamurras' city.
       Murena lent us his house, Capito provided the food.

       Dawn the next day found us in a state of high
40   excitement, for on reaching Sinuessa we were joined by Plotius, Varius,
       and Virgil.[6] No finer men have ever walked the face
       of the earth; and no one is more dearly attached to them all than I am.

---

2. Their route follows the Appian Way, most ancient of
the roads for which the Romans were celebrated. It ran
south from Rome to Brindisi in the heel of Italy, a major
port for travel to Greece and other eastern destinations.
3. This leg of the Appian Way was a canal that ran
through the Pomptine Marshes.
4. The local goddess, Feronia, had a temple and holy
spring near Anxur (modern Terracina).

5. Horace was on the trip as companion to Maecenas at an
important diplomatic meeting that took place in 38 or 37
between representatives of Octavian and Antony ("friends
who had quarrelled"). Lucius Cocceius Nerva was a
politician who had helped negotiate an earlier treaty.
6. Plotius Tucca and Lucius Varius would later edit the
Aeneid after Virgil's death in 19 B.C.E.

You can imagine how delighted we were and how warmly we greeted one
   another.
For me there's nothing in life to compare with the joy of friendship.
45 Near the Campanian Bridge accommodation was provided
by a small house, fuel and salt by official caterers.[7]
Then, at Capua, the mules laid down their packs early.
Maecenas went off to take exercise; Virgil and I had a sleep,
for ball-games are bad for inflamed eyes and dyspeptic stomachs.

50 Next we put up at a well-stocked villa belonging to Cocceius,
which overlooks the inns of Caudium. Now, O Muse,
recount in brief, I pray thee, the clash of Sarmentus the clown
with Messius Cicirrus, and from what lineage each entered
the fray. Messius comes of glorious stock—Oscans!
55 Sarmentus' lady owner is still alive.[8] With such
pedigrees they joined battle. Sarmentus was the first to strike:
"I declare you're the image of a wild horse!"
                                        "Right!" says Messius,
amid general laughter, and tosses his head.
                                        "Hey," says the other,
"If you can threaten us like that when your horn's cut off, what would you
   do
60 if it was still on your head?" (The point being that the left side
of his hairy brow was in fact disfigured by an ugly scar.)
After making a string of jokes about Messius' face and his Campanian
disease he begged him to do the dance of the shepherd Cyclops,
swearing he would have no need of a mask or tragic buskins.[9]

65 Cicirrus wasn't lost for an answer. Had Sarmentus got around to offering
his chain, as promised, to the household gods? His status of clerk
in no way diminished his mistress's claim on him. Finally, why
had he ever bothered to run away when a single pound of meal
would have been quite enough for a tiny miserable scrap like him?

70 We had great fun as the party continued into the night.

From there we went straight to Beneventum, where the fussy host very
   nearly
burnt his house down while turning some skinny thrushes on the fire.
For Vulcan fell out sideways through the old stove, and his darting
flame instantly shot up to lick the roof overhead.
75 Then, what a sight! greedy guests and frightened servants
snatching up the dinner and all struggling to put out the blaze.

From that point on Apulia began to bring into view
her old familiar hills.[1] They were scorched as usual by the Scirocco

---

7. Roman law required that traveling officials be provided
with accommodations and supplies along major roads.
8. Sarmentus was a freed slave of Maecenas's household,
and Messius descended from the ancient Oscan people of
Campania, the butts of many Roman jokes. Like many
comic duos, one is tiny, and the other huge. Horace

parodies the form of the epic combat.
9. The thick-soled boots and mask worn by tragic actors.
1. Apulia occupies the heel of southern Italy; Horace was
born there in the town of Venusia. The hot sirocco wind
blows there from northern Africa.

and we'd never have crawled across them had it not been for a house
80   near Trivicum which provided shelter—plus a lot of weepy smoke.
(Damp branches were burning in the stove, leaves and all.)

Here, like an utter fool, I stayed awake till midnight
waiting for a girl who broke her promise. Sleep eventually
overtook me, still keyed up for sex. Then scenes from a dirty
85   dream spattered my nightshirt and stomach as I lay on my back.

From there we bowled along in waggons for twenty-four miles
putting up at a little town which can't be identified in verse,
though it can very easily by its features: there they sell the most common
of all commodities—water, but their bread is quite unbeatable,
90   and a traveller, if he's wise, usually carries some with him on his journey;
for the sort you get at Canusium (founded of yore by Diomede
the bold)[2] is gritty, and your jug is no better off for water.
Here Varius said a sad good-bye to his tearful friends.

The following night we arrived at Rubi, worn out
95   after covering a long stretch of road damaged by heavy rain.
On the next day the weather was better but the road worse
all the way to the walls of Bari, famous for fish.

Then Gnatia, on whose construction the water-nymphs scowled, provided
fun and amusement by trying to persuade us that incense melts
100   without fire on the temple steps; Apella the Jew may believe it—
not me, for I have learned that the gods live a life of calm,
and that if nature presents some strange occurrence it is not
sent down by the gods in anger from their high home in the sky.

Brindisi marks the end of this long tale and journey.

from ODES[1]

1.25 The young bloods are not so eager now[2]

The young bloods are not so eager now
to rattle your closed shutters with volleys of pebbles
and disturb your sleep. The door that once
        moved so very easily

5   on its hinges, now hugs the threshold.
Less and less often do you hear the cry "I'm yours,
and dying for your love, Lydia, night after long night,
        and you lie there sleeping."

Your turn will come, when you are an old rag
10   in some lonely alley-way, weeping at the insolence of lovers

---

2. After the end of the Trojan War, the Greek hero
Diomedes was said to have gone to Apulia and was credited with the founding of several towns there.
1. Translated by David West.

2. Some take this poem as an attack on a specific woman
called "Lydia" for the occasion; others regard it as a formal exercise in the genre of the love poem. It is most
likely a bit of both.

as the wind from Thrace[3] holds wilder and wilder orgies
    between the old moon and the new,

and your burning love, the lust
that drives the mothers of horses to madness,
15   rages round your ulcerous liver.
    There will be no shortage of complaints

about cheerful youngsters who take
more pleasure in green ivy and dark myrtle,
and dedicate dry leaves to the east wind,
20   winter's crony.

1.9 You see Soracte standing white and deep

You see Soracte[1] standing white and deep
with snow, the woods in trouble, hardly able
    to carry their burden, and the rivers
    halted by sharp ice.

5   Thaw out the cold. Pile up the logs
on the hearth and be more generous, Thaliarchus,[2]
    as you draw the four-year-old Sabine[3]
    from its two-eared cask.

Leave everything else to the gods. As soon as
10   they still the winds battling it out
    on the boiling sea, the cypresses stop waving
    and the old ash trees.

Don't ask what will happen tomorrow.
Whatever day Fortune[4] gives you, enter it
15   as profit, and don't look down on love
    and dancing while you're still a lad,

while the gloomy grey keeps away from the green.
Now is the time for the Campus[5] and the squares
    and soft sighs at the time arranged
20   as darkness falls.

Now is the time for the lovely laugh from the secret corner
giving away the girl in her hiding-place,
    and for the token snatched from her arm
    or finger feebly resisting.

3. A kingdom between Macedonia and the west coast of the Black Sea, later a Roman province. Horace was at the battle of Philippi in Thrace.
1. An isolated mountain to the north of Rome that was home of the Hirpi, priests of the cult of Soranus, an underworld deity identified with Apollo, who also happened to be the special patron of Emperor Augustus.
2. Most of Horace's poems address real-life acquaintances; however, "Thaliarchus" is simply Greek for "master of the revels," an apt name for this poem, one of

several by Horace on the theme of *carpe diem,* or "seize the day."
3. A proverbially excellent wine from the region northeast of Rome where Horace's estate was located.
4. The goddess of chance or luck, of great importance in Roman religion.
5. The Campus Martius was a center of public life and leisure in 1st-century Rome, full of baths, theaters, and temples.

2.13 Not only did he plant you on an unholy day

Not only did he plant you on an unholy day,
whoever did it first, but he also tended you
    with sacrilegious hand—a tree to destroy
        his descendants and disgrace the district,

5   and I could believe he strangled his own father
and spattered one night the shrine of the gods
    of his house with the blood of a guest.
        He dealt in Colchian poisons[1]

and every crime devised in every corner
10   of the world—the man who planted you in my field,
    you evil timber, set to fall
        on your innocent master's head.[2]

No man can ever see for sure from hour to hour
what he should avoid. The Phoenician sailor shudders
15   at the Bosphorus and, clear of the straits, fails
    to see death coming from some other quarter.[3]

The soldier is afraid of arrows and the Parthian's swift flight.[4]
The Parthian fears chains and a Roman dungeon,
    but no man foretells the stroke of death which has carried off
20   the peoples of the earth, and always will.

How nearly did we see the kingdom
of dark Proserpina, and Aeacus in judgement,[5]
    and the seats of the holy set apart,
        and Sappho complaining

25   of her young countrywomen to her Aeolian lyre,
and you, Alcaeus, sounding in fuller tones
    with your golden plectrum the rigours of shipboard,
        the cruel rigours of exile, the rigours of war.[6]

The shades listen in wonderment and sacred silence
30   to the words of both, but with more willing ear
    the crowd packed shoulder to shoulder drinks in
        battles and expulsions of tyrants.

Little wonder, when the hundred-headed monster,
    struck dumb by the singing, lets down his black ears,
35   and coiling snakes come to life

---

1. That is, the poisons of Medea, a daughter of the king of
Colchis beyond the Black Sea, renowned for her powers
of witchcraft.
2. In 33 B.C.E., Horace's patron, Maecenas, presented him
with a farm in the rich Sabine country northeast of Rome,
providing him with financial security, raising him to the
class of the *equites,* and allowing him to devote himself to
his poetry.
3. The Phoenicians were legendary seafarers of the eastern Mediterranean coast. The Bosphorus is the narrow

strait linking the Sea of Marmara with the Black Sea, site
of Byzantium (present-day Istanbul).
4. The Parthian Empire occupied the territory east of the
Roman Empire across the Euphrates River. It had invaded
the Roman province of Syria in 37.
5. Proserpina (Greek: Persephone) was the goddess of the
underworld, and Aeacus was a judge.
6. Alcaeus (Alkaios) and Sappho were poets of Lesbos in
the 7th century B.C.E. (see pages 560–568).

in the hair of the Furies.

Even Prometheus and the father of Pelops
are cheated of their labour by the sweet music,
   and Orion neglects to drive the lions
40   and the timorous lynxes.[7]

2.14 Ah how quickly, Postumus, Postumus

Ah how quickly, Postumus, Postumus,[1]
the years glide by, and piety will not delay
   the wrinkles, and old age, and death, the unsubdued,
      pressing at their heels,

5   no, my friend, not if every day that passes you sacrificed
three hundred bulls to appease Pluto, the god
   who cannot weep, who confines Tityos
      and the three-bodied giant Geryon

in the prison of those gloomy waters
10   that we know all of us must cross[2]
   who feed upon the bounty of the earth,
      whether we be kings or poor tenant farmers.

In vain shall we avoid the bloody god of war
and the roaring breakers of the Adriatic.[3]
15   In vain autumn after long autumn shall we tremble
      for our health when the south wind blows.

We must go and see black Cocytus meandering
in its sluggish flow,[4] the infamous daughters of Danaus,
   and Sisyphus, son of Aeolus,
20   at his long sentence of hard labour.[5]

We must leave the earth, our home,
and the wife we love, and none of these trees you tend
   except the hated cypresses[6]
      will go with their short-lived master.

25   Your heir, worthier than yourself, will drink off
      the Caecuban[7] you laid down behind a hundred locks,

7. Mythological figures. Perhaps the underworld's watch-dog, Cerberus (more commonly portrayed with three heads), or perhaps the 100-headed monster Typhon, off-spring of Earth and Tartarus. The three Furies punished crimes committed on earth. Prometheus, Tantalus ("father of Pelops"), and Orion were punished eternally for trans-gressions against the gods in their earthly lives.

1. Perhaps Propertius Postumus, a relation of the poet Propertius.

2. Pluto was the god of the underworld, the Roman equiv-alent of the Greek Hades. The Giant Tityos was punished in the underworld for his attempted rape of Leto, the mother of Apollo and Diana; composed of three men joined together, Geryon was killed by the hero Hercules.

The Styx was the principal river of the underworld.

3. The sea located between Italy and the Balkans.

4. The Cocytus was another underworld river.

5. Mythical figures punished for their misdeeds on earth. Danaus's 50 daughters had killed their husbands on their wedding night. Sisyphus was a legendary trickster who was condemned to push up hill a boulder that always rolled down again just as he reached the top.

6. The cypress tree was traditionally associated by the Ro-mans with mortality, especially in the case of rich and im-portant men. Its branches were placed at the door of the mourning house, on the funeral altar, and on the pyre it-self; the cypress was also planted around graves.

7. A prized wine from a region of Latium.

and stain your paving with proud wine undiluted
and too good for the banquets of priests.

Petronius
d. 65 C.E.

The *Satyricon* is a closely observed and persuasively authentic satire of everyday life in the late Roman Empire—and under the reign of Nero, there was no shortage of material. Its author has never been conclusively identified, but it is generally assumed that he was the same Gaius Petronius whose biography was memorably sketched by the historian Tacitus:

> He spent his days sleeping, his nights working and enjoying himself. Others achieve fame by energy, Petronius by laziness. Yet he was not, like others who waste their resources, regarded as dissipated or extravagant, but as a refined voluptuary. . . . He had been admitted into the small circle of Nero's intimates, as Arbiter of Taste: to the blasé emperor, smartness and elegance were restricted to what Petronius had approved.

Petronius soon fell out of favor, but his suicide was evidently as stylish as the life he had led:

> He severed his veins. Then, having them bound up again when the fancy took him, he talked with his friends—but not seriously, or so as to gain a name for fortitude. And he listened to them reciting, not discourses about the immortality of the soul or philosophy, but light lyrics and frivolous poems. Some slaves received presents—others were beaten. He appeared at dinner, and dozed, so that his death, if compulsory, might look natural.

Tacitus recounts that rather than the customary deathbed flatteries of the emperor, the Arbiter left behind a stinging indictment of his master's corruption, "giving names of each male and female bed-fellow and details of every lubricious novelty." Even though Tacitus's portrait may not be strictly factual, it reflects the character that the author of the *Satyricon* ought to have had.

Only fragments of the *Satyricon* have survived; it was structured around the sexual misadventures of a young antihero, Encolpius, as he traveled around the backwaters of Greece in pursuit of his fickle lover, the slave-boy Gitai. Both the portions that have survived and those that have been reconstructed tell the story of Encolpius in a series of random and chaotic episodes, with characters who appear and disappear without warning. There are no explicit morals, no clear lessons learned, and no obvious change or growth in the characters. It is not evident whether Petronius expects his reader to gain a positive insight from the dissolute world he depicts; what is clear is that nothing and no one is sacred.

The episode known as "Dinner with Trimalchio" is characteristic of Petronius's approach. It is a fundamentally accurate depiction of the excesses of a typical dinner party of the time, yet it nevertheless satirizes all involved. The host, Trimalchio, is a fabulously wealthy merchant trader seeking to elevate his social status by staging elaborate meals. Encolpius and his companion are posing as literati, cadging free meals by lending their artistic cachet to the occasion. The events of the meal combine slapstick misadventures with carefully drawn parodies of the rituals of the Roman banquet: the impossibly complicated dishes whose meanings have to be interpreted before they can be consumed, the nonstop literary references, and the malicious gossip. What elevates this episode beyond delicious parody is that Trimalchio is not merely a target for ridicule—even though he does indeed manage to do everything wrong—but a memorable individual, a fleshed-out character as vividly present to us today as he must have been to his Roman contemporaries.

from # Satyricon[1]

from ## Dinner with Trimalchio

Finally we took our places. Boys from Alexandria[2] poured iced water over our hands. Others followed them and attended to our feet, removing any hangnails with great skill. But they were not quiet even during this troublesome operation: they sang away at their work. I wanted to find out if the whole staff were singers, so I asked for a drink. In a flash a boy was there, singing in a shrill voice while he attended to me—and anyone else who was asked to bring something did the same. It was more like a musical comedy than a respectable dinner party.

Some extremely elegant hors d'oeuvre were served at this point—by now everyone had taken his place with the exception of Trimalchio, for whom, strangely enough, the place at the top was reserved.[3] The dishes for the first course included an ass of Corinthian bronze with two panniers, white olives on one side and black on the other. Over the ass were two pieces of plate, with Trimalchio's name and the weight of the silver inscribed on the rims. There were some small iron frames shaped like bridges supporting dormice sprinkled with honey and poppy seed. There were steaming hot sausages too, on a silver gridiron with damsons[4] and pomegranate seeds underneath.

We were in the middle of these elegant dishes when Trimalchio himself was carried in to the sound of music and set down on a pile of tightly stuffed cushions. The sight of him drew an astonished laugh from the guests. His cropped head stuck out from a scarlet coat; his neck was well muffled up and he had put round it a napkin with a broad purple stripe and tassels dangling here and there. On the little finger of his left hand he wore a heavy gilt ring and a smaller one on the last joint of the next finger. This I thought was solid gold, but actually it was studded with little iron stars.[5] And to show off even more of his jewellery, he had his right arm bare and set off by a gold armlet and an ivory circlet fastened with a gleaming metal plate.

After picking his teeth with a silver toothpick, he began: "My friends, I wasn't keen to come into the dining room yet. But if I stayed away any more, I would have kept you back, so I've deprived myself of all my little pleasures for you. However, you'll allow me to finish my game."

A boy was at his heels with a board of terebinth wood[6] with glass squares, and I noticed the very last word in luxury—instead of white and black pieces he had gold and silver coins. While he was swearing away like a trooper over his game and we were still on the hors d'oeuvre, a tray was brought in with a basket on it. There sat a wooden hen, its wings spread round it the way hens are when they are broody. Two slaves hurried up and as the orchestra played a tune they began searching through the straw and dug out peahens' eggs, which they distributed to the guests.

1. Translated by J. P. Sullivan.
2. The great Egyptian port city of Alexandria was associated in Roman culture with what they saw as the degeneracy and taste for luxury of the Eastern cultures.
3. Seating at the standard Roman banquet consisted of nine places, three on each of three sides of an open

square. Placement was strictly determined by custom, which Trimalchio ignores.
4. Plums.
5. Only equestrians, or men of free birth, were allowed to wear solid gold rings; Trimalchio is a freedman.
6. The costly wood of the turpentine tree.

Trimalchio turned to look at this little scene and said: "My friends, I gave orders for that bird to sit on some peahens' eggs. I hope to goodness they are not starting to hatch. However, let's try them and see if they are still soft."

We took up our spoons (weighing at least half a pound each) and cracked the eggs, which were made of rich pastry. To tell the truth, I nearly threw away my share, as the chicken seemed already formed. But I heard a guest who was an old hand say: "There should be something good here." So I searched the shell with my fingers and found the plumpest little figpecker, all covered with yolk and seasoned with pepper.

At this point Trimalchio became tired of his game and demanded that all the previous dishes be brought to him. He gave permission in a loud voice for any of us to have another glass of mead if we wanted it. Suddenly there was a crash from the orchestra and a troop of waiters—still singing—snatched away the hors d'oeuvre. However in the confusion one of the side-dishes happened to fall and a slave picked it up from the floor. Trimalchio noticed this, had the boy's ears boxed and told him to throw it down again. A cleaner came in with a broom and began to sweep up the silver plate along with the rest of the rubbish. Two long-haired Ethiopians followed him, carrying small skin bottles like those they use for scattering sand in the circus, and they poured wine over our hands—no one ever offered us water.

* * *

This was the sort of conversation flying round when Trimalchio came in, dabbed his forehead and washed his hands in perfume. There was a short pause, then he said:

"Excuse me, dear people, my inside has not been answering the call for several days now. The doctors are puzzled. But some pomegranate rind and resin in vinegar has done me good. But I hope now it will be back on its good behaviour. Otherwise my stomach rumbles like a bull. So if any of you wants to go out, there's no need for him to be embarrassed. None of us was born solid. I think there's nothing so tormenting as holding yourself in. This is the one thing even God Almighty can't object to. Yes, laugh, Fortunata,[7] but you generally keep me up all night with this sort of thing.

"Anyway, I don't object to people doing what suits them even in the middle of dinner—and the doctors forbid you to hold yourself in. Even if it's a longer business, everything is there just outside—water, bowls, and all the other little comforts. Believe me, if the wind goes to your brain it starts flooding your whole body too. I've known a lot of people die from this because they wouldn't be honest with themselves."

We thanked him for being so generous and considerate and promptly proceeded to bury our amusement in our glasses. Up to this point we'd not realized we were only in mid-stream, as you might say.

The orchestra played, the tables were cleared, and then three white pigs were brought into the dining-room, all decked out in muzzles and bells. The first, the master of ceremonies announced, was two years old, the second three, and the third six. I was under the impression that some acrobats were on their way in and the pigs were going to do some tricks, the way they do in street shows. But Trimalchio dispelled this impression by asking:

"Which of these would you like for the next course? Any clodhopper can do you a barnyard cock or a stew and trifles like that, but my cooks are used to boiling whole calves."

---

7. Trimalchio's wife, about whom the guests have just been maliciously gossiping.

He immediately sent for the chef and without waiting for us to choose he told him to kill the oldest pig.

He then said to the man in a loud voice:

"Which division are you from?"[8]

When he replied he was from number forty, Trimalchio asked:

"Were you bought or were you born here?"

"Neither," said the chef, "I was left to you in Pansa's will."[9]

"Well, then," said Trimalchio, "see you serve it up carefully—otherwise I'll have you thrown into the messenger's division."

So the chef, duly reminded of his master's magnificence, went back to his kitchen, the next course leading the way.

Trimalchio looked round at us with a gentle smile: "If you don't like the wine, I'll have it changed. It is up to you to do it justice. I don't buy it, thank heaven. In fact, whatever wine really tickles your palate this evening, it comes from an estate of mine which as yet I haven't seen. It's said to join my estates at Tarracina and Tarentum.[1] What I'd like to do now is add Sicily to my little bit of land, so that when I want to go to Africa, I could sail there without leaving my own property.[2]

"But tell me, Agamemnon,[3] what was your debate about today? Even though I don't go in for the law, still I've picked up enough education for home consumption. And don't you think I turn my nose up at studying, because I have two libraries, one Greek, one Latin. So tell us, just as a favour, what was the topic of your debate?"

Agamemnon was just beginning, "A poor man and a rich man were enemies . . ." when Trimalchio said: "What's a poor man?" "Oh, witty!" said Agamemnon, and then told us about some fictitious case or other. Like lightning Trimalchio said: "If this happened, it's not a fictitious case—if it didn't happen, then it's nothing at all."

We greeted this witticism and several more like it with the greatest enthusiasm.

"Tell me, my dear Agamemnon," continued Trimalchio, "do you remember the twelve labours of Hercules and the story of Ulysses—how the Cyclops tore out his thumb with a pair of pincers. I used to read about them in Homer, when I was a boy.[4] In fact, I actually saw the Sibyl at Cumae with my own eyes dangling in a bottle, and when the children asked her in Greek: 'What do you want, Sybil?' she used to answer: 'I want to die.'"[5]

He was still droning on when a server carrying the massive pig was put on the table. We started to express our amazement at this speed and swear that not even an ordinary rooster could be cooked so quickly, the more so as the pig appeared far larger than we remembered. Trimalchio looked closer and closer at it, and then shouted:

"What's this? Isn't this pig gutted? I'm damn certain it isn't. Call the chef in here, go on, call him!"

8. It was customary to divide slaves into groups of ten. Trimalchio plainly has far more than the usual 20.
9. The chef refers to the custom of leaving slaves to the emperor in one's will. Various aspects of Trimalchio's behavior (such as his superstition) echo that of Nero or emperors of the time in general.
1. Tarentum was in the heel of Italy, and Tarracina was north of Naples; Trimalchio's third estate would thus span southern Italy from east to west.
2. The scale of exaggeration grows: Sicily lies off the southwest coast of the Italian peninsula on the way to North Africa.

3. This Agamemnon, not to be confused with the king of Greek epic and tragedy, is a teacher of rhetoric and a subject of mockery.
4. The labors of Hercules are not actually recounted in Homer. Ulysses burned out the Cyclops's eye with a stake.
5. The Cumaean sibyl, who leads Aeneas through the underworld in Virgil's *Aeneid,* was said to have asked the god Apollo for immortality, forgetting to ask for eternal youth, and was doomed to grow older and older without ever dying. Her legend appears to have inspired a sideshow attraction in the towns of Trimalchio's youth.

The downcast chef stood by the table and said he'd forgotten it.

"What, you forgot!" shouted Trimalchio. "You'd think he'd only left out the pepper and cumin. Strip him!"

In a second the chef was stripped and standing miserably between two men with whips. But everyone began pleading for him:

"It does tend to happen," they said, "do let him off, please. If he does it any more, none of us will stand up for him again."

Personally, given my tough and ruthless temperament, I couldn't contain myself. I leaned over and whispered in Agamemnon's ear:

"How could anyone forget to clean a pig? I damn well wouldn't let him off if he forgot to clean a fish."

But not Trimalchio. His face relaxed into a smile.

"Well," he said, "since you have such a bad memory, gut it in front of us."

The chef recovered his shirt, took up a knife and with a nervous hand cut open the pig's belly left and right. Suddenly, as the slits widened with the pressure, out poured sausages and bloodpuddings.

The staff applauded this piece of ingenuity and gave a concerted cheer—"Hurray for Gaius!" The chef of course was rewarded with a drink and a silver crown, and was also given a drinking cup on a tray of Corinthian bronze.[6] Seeing Agamemnon staring hard at this cup, Trimalchio remarked:

"I'm the only person in the world with genuine Corinthian."

I was expecting him with his usual conceit to claim that all his plate came from Corinth. But he was not as bad as I thought.

"Perhaps you're wondering," he went on, "how I'm the only one with genuine Corinthian dishes. The simple reason is that the manufacturer I buy from is named Corinth—but what can be Corinthian, if you don't have a Corinth to get it from?

"You mustn't take me for a fool: I know very well where Corinthian metalwork first came from.[7] When Troy was captured that crafty snake Hannibal piled all the bronze, silver, and gold statues into one heap and set them on fire, and they were all melted to a bronze alloy. The metalworkers took this solid mass and made plates, dishes, and statuettes out of it.[8] That is how Corinthian plate was born, not really one thing or another, but everything in one. You won't mind my saying so, but I prefer glass—that's got no taste at all. If only it didn't break, I'd prefer it to gold, but it's poor stuff the way it is.

* * *

Finally the acrobats arrived. One was a silly idiot who stood there holding a ladder and made his boy climb up the rungs, give us a song and dance at the top, then jump through blazing hoops, and hold up a large wine-jar with his teeth.

Only Trimalchio was impressed by all this: art wasn't appreciated, he considered, but if there were two things in the world he really liked to watch, they were acrobats and horn-players. All the other shows were not worth a damn.

6. A prized bronze, treasured, among others, by Emperor Augustus.

7. Having played on his audience's expectations of his ignorance to make a joke, Trimalchio goes on to demonstrate that he has no idea where Corinthian metalwork originated.

8. Troy was sacked by the Greeks in the 12th century B.C.E.; Hannibal took Saguntum in Spain in 219 B.C.E. There was also a false story that Corinthian bronze was discovered during the sacking of the Greek city of Corinth in 146 B.C.E.

"As a matter of fact," he said, "once I even bought some comic-actors, but I preferred them putting on Atellan farces, and I told my conductor to keep his songs Latin."[9]

Just as he was saying this, the boy tumbled down on Trimalchio's couch. Everyone screamed, the guests as well as the servants—not because they were worried over such an awful person (they would happily have watched his neck being broken) but because it would have been a poor ending to the party if they had to offer their condolences for a comparative stranger. Trimalchio himself groaned heavily and leaned over his arm as though it were hurt. Doctors raced to the scene, but practically the first one there was Fortunata, hair flying and cup in hand, telling the world what a poor unfortunate thing she was. As for the boy who had fallen, he was already crawling round our feet, begging for mercy. I had an uneasy feeling that his pleadings might be the prelude to some funny surprise ending, as I still remembered the chef who had forgotten to gut his pig. So I began looking round the dining-room for some machine to appear out of the wall, especially after a servant was beaten for using white instead of purple wool to bandage his master's bruised arm.

Nor were my suspicions far out, because instead of punishment, there came an official announcement from Trimalchio that the boy was free, so that no one could say that such a great figure had been injured by a slave.

* * *

"Meantime, Stichus,[1] bring out the shroud and the things I want to be buried in. Bring some cosmetic cream too, and a sample from that jar of wine I want my bones washed in."

Stichus did not delay over it, but brought his white shroud and his formal dress into the dining-room . . . Trimalchio told us to examine them and see if they were made of good wool. Then he said with a smile:

"Now you, Stichus, see no mice or moths get at those—otherwise I'll burn you alive. I want to be buried in style, so the whole town will pray for my rest."

He opened a bottle of nard on the spot, rubbed some on all of us and said:

"I hope this'll be as nice when I'm dead as when I'm alive." The wine he had poured into a big decanter and he said:

"I want you to think you've been invited to my wake."[2]

The thing was becoming absolutely sickening, when Trimalchio, showing the effects of his disgusting drunkenness, had a fresh entertainment brought into the dining-room, some cornet players. Propped up on a lot of cushions, he stretched out along the edge of the couch and said: "Pretend I'm dead and say something nice."

The cornet players struck up a dead march. One man in particular, the slave of his undertaker (who was the most respectable person present) blew so loudly that he roused the neighbourhood. As a result, the fire brigade, thinking Trimalchio's house was on fire, suddenly broke down the front door and began kicking up their own sort of din with their water and axes.

Seizing this perfect chance, we gave Agamemnon the slip and escaped as rapidly as if there really were a fire.

---

9. Comic satires of provincial life, Atellan farces used stock-character stereotypes and were originally performed in Italian dialect rather than proper Latin.
1. A slave of Trimalchio.

2. The final example of Trimalchio's outrageous behavior is this staging of a mock-funeral, a practice attested to at the time.

Paul
c.10–c.67 C.E.

The earliest written records of Christianity, the Epistles of Paul present the daily activities, vivid personality, and combative theology of perhaps the single most influential figure in the history of the Church. The sensation of intensity and immediacy that imbues his letters conveys well the difficulties Paul faced in his untiring efforts on behalf of his nascent religion and the dramatic path he had taken to embrace it. Born around 10 C.E. at Tarsus in Cilicia on what is now the southern coast of Turkey, Saul (in Hebrew) or Paul (in Latin) came from an Aramaic-speaking Jewish family of the tribe of Benjamin that also possessed Roman citizenship. Tarsus was a center of Hellenistic culture, and Saul received a classical education but remained a fiercely devoted Pharisee, convinced of the finality and perfection of Mosaic law and the oral tradition surrounding it. He began his career disputing against the new Christians and even aiding in their persecution until the time of his conversion on the road to Damascus in around 35 C.E. Embracing his new faith with equal zeal, Paul traveled throughout Greece and Asia Minor tirelessly preaching and making converts. Imprisoned in Jerusalem, he was sent to Rome, where he stayed two years preaching the Gospel between two stretches of incarceration, the latter of which ended with his execution on Nero's order.

Paul's letters are masterpieces of rhetoric, each one carefully composed and tailored to meet the specific requirements of the congregation it addresses and to correct their particular errors. Their enduring importance to theologians and laypersons alike testifies to his ability to draw theological principles out of those everyday circumstances. In the celebrated Epistle to the Romans, which dates to between 54 and 58, Paul is concerned with two issues that he perceives as interrelated: the Jews' excessive reliance on the Law and thus on the surface orders and regulations of the Old Testament, and the sinner's inability to ignore the urges of the body, or superficial being. Paul needed to show that Christians could embrace the Hebrew Bible as revealed truth without having to follow the specific dictates it contained. At the same time, because Christianity was a Messianic belief, Paul also preached that believers must live their lives as if the world's end and the Last Judgment were imminent events. Paul presents the teachings he chooses to uphold and the longings he chooses to encourage as what is obvious and instinctive; the Law and the desires of the flesh he rejects by contrast as being dark and obscure. It is a somber and conflicted vision of a self divided that Paul employs to unshackle the chains of tradition and of sin that bind his fellow Christians: "I do not understand my own actions. For I do not do what I want, but I do the very thing I hate." The powerful philosophical dualism inherited from Platonic philosophy was to become deeply embedded in Western culture as an irrevocable split between sacred mind and sinful body. In many ways, Paul can be said to have invented the modern dilemma of a split consciousness, desperate and yet unable to control its own desires. It is a conception of the self that would have seemed utterly alien either to Petronius's self-indulgent Encolpius or to Virgil's stoic Aeneas.

Paul's theology of paradox is equally capable of memorably summoning up the possibility of a world beyond the imaginings of rationality, logic, or law, as in the extraordinary image of the First Epistle to the Corinthians, comparing our vision of the present world to looking through a glass, darkly (13:12). Rather than the lucid reflection of a solid reality, the world and the individuals within it are fundamentally unknowable and mysterious. Only in the presence of the Lord, face to face, he maintains, will it be possible either to truly know oneself or the world, and to be truly happy and at peace. Only at brief moments does Paul allow himself to divulge glimpses of the visions he must have had of better things. In the same letter to the Corinthians, he waxes eloquent on the positive virtue of *caritas,* the love of the new Christians: "Love bears all things, believes all things, hopes all things, endures all things. Love never ends" (13:7–8). In similar fashion, he wraps up the fervent exhortations of his Epistle to the Romans with a simple greeting, one by one to each of his brothers and sisters in Rome. Paul never loses sight of the practical objects of his millenarian calling. Perhaps this is the reason that, more than any classical writer, and more than any early Christian except his later devotee Saint Augustine, Paul makes us feel in his letters as if we know the man himself.

from Epistle to the Romans[1]

from *Chapter 1*

To all God's beloved in Rome, who are called to be saints:

Grace to you and peace from God our Father and the Lord Jesus Christ.

First, I thank my God through Jesus Christ for all of you, because your faith is proclaimed in all the world. For God is my witness, whom I serve with my spirit in the gospel of his Son, that without ceasing I mention you always in my prayers, asking that somehow by God's will I may now at last succeed in coming to you. For I long to see you, that I may impart to you some spiritual gift to strengthen you, that is, that we may be mutually encouraged by each other's faith, both yours and mine. I want you to know, brethren, that I have often intended to come to you (but thus far have been prevented), in order that I may reap some harvest among you as well as among the rest of the Gentiles. I am under obligation both to Greeks and to barbarians, both to the wise and to the foolish: so I am eager to preach the gospel to you also who are in Rome.

For I am not ashamed of the gospel: it is the power of God for salvation to every one who has faith, to the Jew first and also to the Greek. For in it the righteousness of God is revealed through faith for faith; as it is written, "He who through faith is righteous shall live."[2]

For the wrath of God is revealed from heaven against all ungodliness and wickedness of men who by their wickedness suppress the truth. For what can be known about God is plain to them, because God has shown it to them. Ever since the creation of the world his invisible nature, namely, his eternal power and deity, has been clearly perceived in the things that have been made.[3] So they are without excuse; for although they knew God they did not honor him as God or give thanks to him, but they became futile in their thinking and their senseless minds were darkened. Claiming to be wise, they became fools, and exchanged the glory of the immortal God for images resembling mortal man or birds or animals or reptiles.

Therefore God gave them up in the lusts of their hearts to impurity, to the dishonoring of their bodies among themselves, because they exchanged the truth about God for a lie and worshiped and served the creature rather than the Creator, who is blessed for ever! Amen.

For this reason God gave them up to dishonorable passions. Their women exchanged natural relations for unnatural, and the men likewise gave up natural relations with women and were consumed with passion for one another, men committing shameless acts with men and receiving in their own persons the due penalty for their error.

---

1. New Revised Standard Version.
2. Here Paul begins the distinction between faith, which applies to all people, and the traditional Law of Jews such as himself.

3. Paul describes the responsibility of those who lived before the teachings and the life of Jesus made the gospel evident to all.

And since they did not see fit to acknowledge God, God gave them up to a base mind and to improper conduct. They were filled with all manner of wickedness, evil, covetousness, malice. Full of envy, murder, strife, deceit, malignity, they are gossips, slanderers, haters of God, insolent, haughty, boastful, inventors of evil, disobedient to parents, foolish, faithless, heartless, ruthless. Though they know God's decree that those who do such things deserve to die, they not only do them but approve those who practice them. * * *

Chapter 7

Do you not know, brethren—for I am speaking to those who know the law—that the law is binding on a person only during his life? Thus a married woman is bound by law to her husband as long as he lives; but if her husband dies she is discharged from the law concerning the husband. Accordingly, she will be called an adulteress if she lives with another man while her husband is alive. But if her husband dies she is free from that law, and if she marries another man she is not an adulteress.

Likewise, my brethren, you have died to the law through the body of Christ, so that you may belong to another, to him who has been raised from the dead in order that we may bear fruit for God. While we were living in the flesh, our sinful passions, aroused by the law, were at work in our members to bear fruit for death. But now we are discharged from the law, dead to that which held us captive, so that we serve not under the old written code but in the new life of the Spirit.[4]

What then shall we say? That the law is sin? By no means! Yet, if it had not been for the law, I should not have known sin. I should not have known what it is to covet if the law had not said, "You shall not covet." But sin, finding opportunity in the commandment, wrought in me all kinds of covetousness. Apart from the law sin lies dead. I was once alive apart from the law, but when the commandment came, sin revived and I died; the very commandment which promised life proved to be death to me. For sin, finding opportunity in the commandment, deceived me and by it killed me. So the law is holy, and the commandment is holy and just and good.[5]

Did that which is good, then, bring death to me? By no means! It was sin, working death in me through what is good, in order that sin might be shown to be sin, and through the commandment might become sinful beyond measure. We know that the law is spiritual; but I am carnal, sold under sin. I do not understand my own actions. For I do not do what I want, but I do the very thing I hate. Now if I do what I do not want, I agree that the law is good. So then it is no longer I that do it, but sin which dwells within me. For I know that nothing good dwells within me, that is, in my flesh. I can will what is right, but I cannot do it. For I do not do the good I want, but the evil I do not want is what I do. Now if I do what I do not want, it is no longer I that do it, but sin which dwells within me.

So I find it to be a law that when I want to do right, evil lies close at hand. For I delight in the law of God, in my inmost self, but I see in my members another law at war with the law of my mind and making me captive to the law of sin which dwells in my members. Wretched man that I am! Who will deliver me from this body of death?

---

4. In Paul's eyes, with the resurrection of Christ, humanity became dead to the laws of the past. The new law is not written or literal, but spiritual, based in faith.

5. This is a good example of Paul's rhetoric of antithesis and paradox. Only with laws, he argues, can we become conscious of sins, and thus able to commit them, but only through recognizing sin as such can we be saved.

Thanks be to God through Jesus Christ our Lord! So then, I of myself serve the law of God with my mind, but with my flesh I serve the law of sin.[6]

Chapter 13

Let every person be subject to the governing authorities. For there is no authority except from God, and those that exist have been instituted by God. Therefore he who resists the authorities resists what God has appointed, and those who resist will incur judgment. For rulers are not a terror to good conduct, but to bad. Would you have no fear of him who is in authority? Then do what is good, and you will receive his approval, for he is God's servant for your good. But if you do wrong, be afraid, for he does not bear the sword in vain; he is the servant of God to execute his wrath on the wrongdoer. Therefore one must be subject, not only to avoid God's wrath but also for the sake of conscience. For the same reason you also pay taxes, for the authorities are ministers of God, attending to this very thing. Pay all of them their dues, taxes to whom taxes are due, revenue to whom revenue is due, respect to whom respect is due, honor to whom honor is due.

Owe no one anything, except to love one another; for he who loves his neighbor has fulfilled the law. The commandments, "You shall not commit adultery, You shall not kill, You shall not steal, You shall not covet," and any other commandment, are summed up in this sentence, "You shall love your neighbor as yourself."

Love does no wrong to a neighbor; therefore love is the fulfilling of the law.

Besides this you know what hour it is, how it is full time now for you to wake from sleep. For salvation is nearer to us now than when we first believed; the night is far gone, the day is at hand. Let us then cast off the works of darkness and put on the armor of light; let us conduct ourselves becomingly as in the day, not in reveling and drunkenness, not in debauchery and licentiousness, not in quarreling and jealousy. But put on the Lord Jesus Christ, and make no provision for the flesh, to gratify its desires.

from Chapter 15

I myself am satisfied about you, my brethren, that you yourselves are full of goodness, filled with all knowledge, and able to instruct one another.

But on some points I have written to you very boldly by way of reminder, because of the grace given me by God to be a minister of Christ Jesus to the Gentiles in the priestly service of the gospel of God, so that the offering of the Gentiles may be acceptable, sanctified by the Holy Spirit. In Christ Jesus, then, I have reason to be proud of my work for God. For I will not venture to speak of anything except what Christ has wrought through me to win obedience from the Gentiles, by word and deed, by the power of signs and wonders, by the power of the Holy Spirit, so that from Jerusalem and as far round as Illyricum[7] I have fully preached the gospel of Christ, thus making it my ambition to preach the gospel, not where Christ has already been named, lest I build on another man's foundation, but as it is written,

---

6. In this influential formulation, Paul maintains that following the letter of the Judaic Law will not lead to salvation because it only governs the flesh, which is irredeemably tainted by sin and death. Instead, the Romans to whom he writes must follow the rule of faith, "serve the law of God with [their] mind[s]."

7. The Roman name for the region across the Adriatic Sea from Italy.

> "They shall see who have never been told of him,
> and they shall understand who have never heard of him."

This is the reason why I have so often been hindered from coming to you. But now, since I no longer have any room for work in these regions, and since I have longed for many years to come to you, I hope to see you in passing as I go to Spain,[8] and to be sped on my journey there by you, once I have enjoyed your company for a little. At present, however, I am going to Jerusalem with aid for the saints. For Macedonia and Achaia[9] have been pleased to make some contribution for the poor among the saints at Jerusalem; they were pleased to do it, and indeed they are in debt to them, for if the Gentiles have come to share in their spiritual blessings, they ought also to be of service to them in material blessings. When therefore I have completed this, and have delivered to them what has been raised, I shall go on by way of you to Spain; and I know that when I come to you I shall come in the fulness of the blessing of Christ.

I appeal to you, brethren, by our Lord Jesus Christ and by the love of the Spirit, to strive together with me in your prayers to God on my behalf, that I may be delivered from the unbelievers in Judea,[1] and that my service for Jerusalem may be acceptable to the saints, so that by God's will I may come to you with joy and be refreshed in your company. The God of peace be with you all. Amen.

from *Chapter 16*

I commend to you our sister Phoebe, a deaconess of the church at Cenchreae,[2] that you may receive her in the Lord as befits the saints, and help her in whatever she may require from you, for she has been a helper of many and of myself as well.

Greet Prisca and Aquila,[3] my fellow workers in Christ Jesus, who risked their necks for my life, to whom not only I but also all the churches of the Gentiles give thanks; greet also the church in their house. Greet my beloved Epaenetus, who was the first convert in Asia for Christ.[4] Greet Mary, who has worked hard among you. Greet Andronicus and Junias; my kinsmen and my fellow prisoners; they are men of note among the apostles, and they were in Christ before me. Greet Ampliatus, my beloved in the Lord. Greet Urbanus, our fellow worker in Christ, and my beloved Stachys. Greet Apelles, who is approved in Christ. Greet those who belong to the family of Aristobulus. Greet my kinsman Herodion. Greet those in the Lord who belong to the family of Narcissus. Greet those workers in the Lord, Tryphaena and Tryphosa. Greet the beloved Persis, who has worked hard in the Lord. Greet Rufus, eminent in the Lord, also his mother and mine. Greet Asyncritus, Phlegon, Hermes, Patrobas, Hermas, and the brethren who are with them. Greet Philologus, Julia, Nereus and his sister, and Olympas, and all the saints who are with them. Greet one another with a holy kiss. All the churches of Christ greet you.

I appeal to you, brethren, to take note of those who create dissensions and difficulties, in opposition to the doctrine which you have been taught; avoid them. For

---

8. It is not known whether Paul managed to carry out his intention to preach the gospel in Spain between his first and his second captivities in Rome.
9. During the second of his three extended missionary journeys, Paul spread his faith around the Aegean Sea to Macedonia and to Achaia (Greece).
1. As is detailed in Acts 21, Paul's teaching that Jews need no longer follow the Law since the coming of Christ was highly controversial.

2. The eastern port of Corinth.
3. When all Jews were expelled by Emperor Claudius from Rome in 49 C.E., Prisca and her husband, Aquila, had settled in Corinth and then in Ephesus on the western coast of Asia Minor, the capital of the Roman province of Asia (see Acts 18:2). They would have been able to return following Claudius's death in 54.
4. Little or nothing is known about the rest of the Christians Paul salutes beyond what he says about them here.

such persons do not serve our Lord Christ, but their own appetites, and by fair and flattering words they deceive the hearts of the simple-minded. For while your obedience is known to all, so that I rejoice over you, I would have you wise as to what is good and guileless as to what is evil; then the God of peace will soon crush Satan under your feet. The grace of our Lord Jesus Christ be with you.

Luke
fl. 80–110 C.E.

Tradition has it that the author of the Gospel According to Luke and its sequel, the Acts of the Apostles, was a physician and the companion of Paul of Tarsus. What is certain is that he was a brilliant stylist, crafting a historical record of the life of Jesus and the ministry of his apostles that combines the sparsely dramatic narrative technique of the Hellenistic-Roman historians with the theological concerns of the Hebrew Bible. After Jesus's crucifixion in 30 C.E., the original Palestinian movement probably transmitted his sayings and the accounts of his miracles orally for several decades in the Aramaic language he had spoken. The first written sources we have are the Epistles of Paul, composed in Greek, that date from the 50s and 60s. At the same time that Paul was opening up what had been a Jewish reform movement to a larger, Gentile population, the Jewish wars led to the traumatic burning of the Temple in Jerusalem in 70 and the dispersal of the Jewish people. Over the next couple of decades, various gospels appeared to reconcile the growing outreach of the Jesus movement with the oral tradition of his life and sayings. Four of those gospels were eventually included as part of the New Testament, the contents of which were finally fixed as a canon only several centuries later: the three synoptic gospels (Mark, Matthew, and Luke), so called because they resemble each other in content, order of events, and the words of Jesus they include; and the Gospel According to John, several decades later in composition, which is steeped in Jewish and Hellenistic philosophy and derives from a different source.

Luke opens his Gospel by referring to the problem of the apparently conflicting reports circulating of the great events that have occurred; he promises to write "an orderly account." His Gospel gives the fullest record of Jesus's life, including the only accounts, for example, of some events in the life of John the Baptist, of the tale of the shepherds at Jesus's birth, and of the twelve-year-old Jesus confounding the rabbis in the Temple. Highly conscious of the need for the events of Jesus's life to conform to the many prophecies of the Messiah in the Hebrew Bible, Luke is equally concerned to incorporate the Pauline teaching that Jesus came as savior to Jew and Gentile alike. Jesus is not simply a universal savior, however; he has come especially for the outcasts of the world: its peasants, its poor, its sinners, and its women. This was a radical message, and traces of the political motivation for Jesus's crucifixion remain in the deal-making that surrounds Pontius Pilate's decision to let the execution proceed. All these secular powers, Luke implies, will pale before the new order to come.

The end of the world is an important context for the simply narrated events of Luke's chronicle, for he is at pains to demonstrate how the workings of the world fit into the divine plan for its end. The key lessons taught by this eschatological framework are both pragmatic and paradoxical. Jesus speaks either in simple imperatives—"Follow me!"—or in enigmatic parables. To the man who responds that first he must bury his father, Jesus answers, "Leave the dead to bury the dead." If the world is about to end, the natural impulse is to attend no longer to its pressing affairs but to the even more pressing affair of achieving eternal life. The concerns of Luke's Gospel are thus presented as basic needs—nourishment and survival—rather than intellectual or aesthetic ones; many of Jesus's parables and paradoxes underscore the argument that spiritual nourishment and survival after death are material and primary, rather than abstract

and secondary, needs. Jesus's first disciples are lowly fishermen; his miracles include multiply-
ing food at a wedding and raising a man from the dead. The central mystery of communion, the
transmutation of bread and wine into flesh and blood at the Last Supper, imparts one aspect of
this symbolism—he is nourishment—and his crucifixion and resurrection impart another: he is
life. And to prove that he has truly risen from the dead and not merely returned as an apparition,
the imagery comes full circle: the resurrection is accepted only when he proves himself able to
eat a piece of broiled fish. Never before had such simplicity of language and imagery been used
to convey such a profound theme. Luke and the other Gospel writers found a new style and
form to fit what they saw as a radically new religion.

Cast as the sequel to his Gospel, Acts makes Luke's historical intent even clearer because it
deals with events up to his own day, directly depicting the transformation of Jesus's life and teachings into Christianity through the apostles' preaching and miracle making and including especially
the work of the newly converted Paul. Palestine was a multilingual culture in transition from a
Hellenistic to a Roman base. Jesus and his followers spoke Aramaic and would not have read old
Hebrew, the language of the Hebrew Bible. Most educated Romans were bilingual in Greek and
Latin. The second generation of Jesus's followers were Easterners, still writing in Greek, which became the language of the New Testament. The famous episode of Pentecost illustrates this linguistic confusion, updating and reversing the Tower of Babel episode from Genesis, as the apostles are
inspired by holy flames to begin speaking in tongues, each of the spectators—Parthians, Medes,
Jews, Arabs, and many others—hearing them in his or her own language.

In Luke's account, the Jewish Saul (or Paul in Greek and Latin) becomes a model for the
conversion narrative that would be so important for the later saints' lives and for the spiritual
autobiography from Augustine through Dante and Saint Theresa and even into the modern
novel. At the same time, the focus on Paul makes his tumultuous life exemplary of the expanding scope of Christianity that is central to Paul's Epistles. Luke also successfully downplays the
full extent of Roman persecution, implicating the local Jewish leaders as Mark's and
Matthew's Gospels do, and implicitly arguing for the separation of religion from state control.
Paul's journey to Rome enacts the destined spread of the new religion, while his status as prisoner and his execution by Nero remind the reader that the true kingdom of God will be
achieved in fact only in the next life.

from The Gospel According to Luke[1]

Chapter 2

[JESUS'S BIRTH. JOHN THE BAPTIST]

In those days a decree went out from Emperor Augustus that all the world should be
registered. This was the first registration and was taken while Quirinius was governor
of Syria.[2] All went to their own towns to be registered. Joseph also went from the
town of Nazareth in Galilee to Judea, to the city of David called Bethlehem, because
he was descended from the house and family of David.[3] He went to be registered with
Mary, to whom he was engaged and who was expecting a child. While they were
there, the time came for her to deliver her child. And she gave birth to her firstborn
son and wrapped him in bands of cloth, and laid him in a manger, because there was
no place for them in the inn.

---

1. New Revised Standard Version.
2. Probably in about 6 B.C.E.

3. A journey of some 50 miles. Luke emphasizes Jesus's
descent from the Israelite king, David.

In that region there were shepherds living in the fields, keeping watch over their flock by night. Then an angel of the Lord stood before them, and the glory of the Lord shone around them, and they were terrified. But the angel said to them, "Do not be afraid; for see—I am bringing you good news of great joy for all the people: to you is born this day in the city of David a Savior, who is the Messiah, the Lord. This will be a sign for you: you will find a child wrapped in bands of cloth and lying in a manger." And suddenly there was with the angel a multitude of the heavenly host, praising God and saying,

> "Glory to God in the highest heaven,
>   and on earth peace among those whom he favors!"

When the angels had left them and gone into heaven, the shepherds said to one another, "Let us go now to Bethlehem and see this thing that has taken place, which the Lord has made known to us." So they went with haste and found Mary and Joseph, and the child lying in the manger. When they saw this, they made known what had been told them about this child; and all who heard it were amazed at what the shepherds told them. But Mary treasured all these words and pondered them in her heart. The shepherds returned, glorifying and praising God for all they had heard and seen, as it had been told them.

After eight days had passed, it was time to circumcise the child; and he was called Jesus, the name given by the angel before he was conceived in the womb.[4]

When the time came for their purification according to the law of Moses, they brought him up to Jerusalem to present him to the Lord (as it is written in the law of the Lord, "Every firstborn male shall be designated as holy to the Lord"), and they offered a sacrifice according to what is stated in the law of the Lord, "a pair of turtledoves or two young pigeons."[5]

Now there was a man in Jerusalem whose name was Simeon; this man was righteous and devout, looking forward to the consolation of Israel, and the Holy Spirit rested on him. It had been revealed to him by the Holy Spirit that he would not see death before he had seen the Lord's Messiah. Guided by the Spirit, Simeon came into the temple; and when the parents brought in the child Jesus, to do for him what was customary under the law, Simeon took him in his arms and praised God, saying,

> "Master, now you are dismissing your servant in peace,
>   according to your word;
> for my eyes have seen your salvation,
>   which you have prepared in the presence of all peoples,
> a light for revelation to the Gentiles
>   and for glory to your people Israel."

And the child's father and mother were amazed at what was being said about him. Then Simeon blessed them and said to his mother Mary, "This child is destined for the falling and the rising of many in Israel, and to be a sign that will be opposed so that the inner thoughts of many will be revealed—and a sword will pierce your own soul too."

---

4. The angel Gabriel had come to Mary to announce her pregnancy and to prophesy the birth of a son, Jesus, who would be king over Israel forever (1:26–38).

5. On the rites of purification, see Leviticus 12. According to Exodus 13, every firstborn male belonged to God but could be redeemed by a sacrifice.

There was also a prophet, Anna the daughter of Phanuel, of the tribe of Asher. She was of a great age, having lived with her husband seven years after her marriage, then as a widow to the age of eighty-four. She never left the temple but worshiped there with fasting and prayer night and day. At that moment she came, and began to praise God and to speak about the child to all who were looking for the redemption of Jerusalem.

When they had finished everything required by the law of the Lord, they returned to Galilee, to their own town of Nazareth. The child grew and became strong, filled with wisdom; and the favor of God was upon him.

Now every year his parents went to Jerusalem for the festival of the Passover. And when he was twelve years old, they went up as usual for the festival. When the festival was ended and they started to return, the boy Jesus stayed behind in Jerusalem, but his parents did not know it. Assuming that he was in the group of travelers, they went a day's journey. Then they started to look for him among their relatives and friends. When they did not find him, they returned to Jerusalem to search for him. After three days they found him in the temple, sitting among the teachers, listening to them and asking them questions. And all who heard him were amazed at his understanding and his answers. When his parents saw him they were astonished; and his mother said to him, "Child, why have you treated us like this? Look, your father and I have been searching for you in great anxiety." He said to them, "Why were you searching for me? Did you not know that I must be in my Father's house?" But they did not understand what he said to them. Then he went down with them and came to Nazareth, and was obedient to them. His mother treasured all these things in her heart.

And Jesus increased in wisdom and in years, and in divine and human favor.

Chapter 3

In the fifteenth year of the reign of Emperor Tiberius, when Pontius Pilate was governor of Judea, and Herod was ruler of Galilee, and his brother Philip ruler of the region of Ituraea and Trachonitis, and Lysanias ruler of Abilene,[6] during the high priesthood of Annas and Caiaphas,[7] the word of God came to John son of Zechariah in the wilderness.[8] He went into all the region around the Jordan, proclaiming a baptism of repentance for the forgiveness of sins, as it is written in the book of the words of the prophet Isaiah,

> "The voice of one crying out in the wilderness:
> 'Prepare the way of the Lord,
> make his paths straight.
> Every valley shall be filled,
> and every mountain and hill shall be made low,
> and the crooked shall be made straight,

6. Tiberius reigned from Augustus's death in 14 until 37; the "fifteenth year" would be 28–29. Judea was ruled by Roman governors from 6 C.E. on, by Pontius Pilate in particular from 26–36. Herod Antipas was the ruler of the tetrarchy, or lesser kingdom, of Galilee and Perea to the north and east of Judea. His brother Philip was the ruler of the tetrarchy across the river Jordan and to the northeast of Galilee. Abilene was a region farther to the north beyond Damascus.

7. During postexilic Judaism, the high priest was the spiritual and civil head of the nation, elected by the Romans from a select number of families. Annas was the high priest from 15–5 B.C.E., his son-in-law Caiaphas from 18–36 C.E.

8. The son of a priest and of a descendant of Aaron who was also a relative of Mary, John the Baptist is portrayed as a messianic prophet of the coming of Christ.

and the rough ways made smooth;
and all flesh shall see the salvation of God.'"[9]

John said to the crowds that came out to be baptized by him, "You brood of vipers! Who warned you to flee from the wrath to come? Bear fruits worthy of repentance. Do not begin to say to yourselves, 'We have Abraham as our ancestor';[1] for I tell you, God is able from these stones to raise up children to Abraham. Even now the ax is lying at the root of the trees; every tree therefore that does not bear good fruit is cut down and thrown into the fire."

And the crowds asked him, "What then should we do?" In reply he said to them, "Whoever has two coats must share with anyone who has none; and whoever has food must do likewise." Even tax collectors came to be baptized,[2] and they asked him, "Teacher, what should we do?" He said to them, "Collect no more than the amount prescribed for you." Soldiers also asked him, "And we, what should we do?" He said to them, "Do not extort money from anyone by threats or false accusation, and be satisfied with your wages."

As the people were filled with expectation, and all were questioning in their hearts concerning John, whether he might be the Messiah, John answered all of them by saying, "I baptize you with water; but one who is more powerful than I is coming; I am not worthy to untie the thong of his sandals. He will baptize you with the Holy Spirit and fire. His winnowing fork is in his hand, to clear his threshing floor and to gather the wheat into his granary; but the chaff[3] he will burn with unquenchable fire."

So, with many other exhortations, he proclaimed the good news to the people. But Herod the ruler, who had been rebuked by him because of Herodias, his brother's wife,[4] and because of all the evil things that Herod had done, added to them all by shutting up John in prison.

Now when all the people were baptized, and when Jesus also had been baptized and was praying, the heaven was opened, and the Holy Spirit descended upon him in bodily form like a dove. And a voice came from heaven, "You are my Son, the Beloved; with you I am well pleased."

Jesus was about thirty years old when he began his work. He was the son (as was thought) of Joseph son of Heli, son of Matthat, son of Levi, son of Melchi, son of Jannai, son of Joseph, son of Mattathias, son of Amos, son of Nahum, son of Esli, son of Naggai, son of Maath, son of Mattathias, son of Semein, son of Josech, son of Joda, son of Joanan, son of Rhesa, son of Zerubbabel, son of Shealtiel, son of Neri, son of Melchi, son of Addi, son of Cosam, son of Elmadam, son of Er, son of Joshua, son of Eliezer, son of Jorim, son of Matthat, son of Levi, son of Simeon, son of Judah, son of Joseph, son of Jonam, son of Eliakim, son of Melea, son of Menna, son of Mattatha, son of Nathan, son of David, son of Jesse, son of Obed, son of Boaz, son of Sala, son of Nahshon, son of Amminadab, son of Admin, son of Arni, son of Hezron, son of Perez, son of Judah, son of Jacob, son of Isaac, son of Abraham, son of Terah, son of Nahor, son of Serug, son of Reu, son of Peleg, son of Eber, son of Shelah, son of Cainan, son of Arphaxad, son of Shem, son of Noah, son of Lamech, son of

---

9. Isaiah 40:3–5.
1. The covenant between God and Abraham described in Genesis 17:4–8 and 22:18 applied to all of his descendants.
2. Publicans, or tax collectors for the Roman authorities, were considered traitors and classified with other undesirables such as prostitutes, public sinners, and gentiles, or non-Jews.
3. The husks, used for animal feed, in bricks, or burned for fuel.
4. Herodias had been the wife of Philip, her father's half-brother and Herod's brother.

Methuselah, son of Enoch, son of Jared, son of Mahalaleel, son of Cainan, son of Enos, son of Seth, son of Adam, son of God.[5]

Chapter 6

[TEACHINGS AND PARABLES]

One sabbath while Jesus was going through the grainfields, his disciples plucked some heads of grain, rubbed them in their hands, and ate them. But some of the Pharisees[1] said, "Why are you doing what is not lawful on the sabbath?" Jesus answered, "Have you not read what David did when he and his companions were hungry? He entered the house of God and took and ate the bread of the Presence, which it is not lawful for any but the priests to eat, and gave some to his companions?"[2] Then he said to them, "The Son of Man is lord of the sabbath."

On another sabbath he entered the synagogue and taught, and there was a man there whose right hand was withered. The scribes and the Pharisees watched him to see whether he would cure on the sabbath, so that they might find an accusation against him. Even though he knew what they were thinking, he said to the man who had the withered hand, "Come and stand here." He got up and stood there. Then Jesus said to them, "I ask you, is it lawful to do good or to do harm on the sabbath, to save life or to destroy it?" After looking around at all of them, he said to him, "Stretch out your hand." He did so, and his hand was restored. But they were filled with fury and discussed with one another what they might do to Jesus.

Now during those days he went out to the mountain to pray; and he spent the night in prayer to God. And when day came, he called his disciples and chose twelve of them, whom he also named apostles:[3] Simon, whom he named Peter, and his brother Andrew, and James, and John, and Philip, and Bartholomew, and Matthew, and Thomas, and James son of Alphaeus, and Simon, who was called the Zealot, and Judas son of James, and Judas Iscariot, who became a traitor.

He came down with them and stood on a level place, with a great crowd of his disciples and a great multitude of people from all Judea, Jerusalem, and the coast of Tyre and Sidon. They had come to hear him and to be healed of their diseases; and those who were troubled with unclean spirits were cured. And all in the crowd were trying to touch him, for power came out from him and healed all of them.

Then he looked up at his disciples and said:

> "Blessed are you who are poor,
>   for yours is the kingdom of God.
> "Blessed are you who are hungry now,
>   for you will be filled.

---

5. The traditional genealogy traces Jesus's descent from David although not through his ruling son, Solomon. Whereas Matthew's gospel, written for a Jewish community, traces Jesus's lineage back to Abraham, Luke goes all the way back to the Creator and the moment of creation itself.

1. An influential religious party that believed in the validity of the oral tradition as an intrinsic element of the Law of Moses. They were associated with scribes, laypeople, and the middle classes and held that the Lord could be worshiped beyond the confines of the Temple. Their rivals, the Sadducees, belonged to the high priestly aristocracy around the Temple in Jerusalem who believed only in the letter of the Pentateuch itself.

2. The bread of the presence was sacred bread baked in groups of 12 (Leviticus 24:5–9) and laid on a table as a memorial. They were eaten only by the priests, except for the episode recounted by Jesus when David and his men were fed by the priest Ahimelech (1 Samuel 21:5–7).

3. The word "apostle" comes from the Greek verb "to send," and was sometimes used to refer to a simple messenger.

"Blessed are you who weep now,
    for you will laugh.

"Blessed are you when people hate you, and when they exclude you, revile you, and defame you on account of the Son of Man. Rejoice in that day and leap for joy, for surely your reward is great in heaven; for that is what their ancestors did to the prophets.

"But woe to you who are rich,
    for you have received your consolation.
"Woe to you who are full now,
    for you will be hungry.
"Woe to you who are laughing now,
    for you will mourn and weep.

"Woe to you when all speak well of you, for that is what their ancestors did to the false prophets.

"But I say to you that listen, Love your enemies, do good to those who hate you, bless those who curse you, pray for those who abuse you. If anyone strikes you on the cheek, offer the other also; and from anyone who takes away your coat do not withhold even your shirt. Give to everyone who begs from you; and if anyone takes away your goods, do not ask for them again. Do to others as you would have them do to you.

"If you love those who love you, what credit is that to you? For even sinners love those who love them. If you do good to those who do good to you, what credit is that to you? For even sinners do the same. If you lend to those from whom you hope to receive, what credit is that to you? Even sinners lend to sinners, to receive as much again. But love your enemies, do good, and lend, expecting nothing in return. Your reward will be great, and you will be children of the Most High; for he is kind to the ungrateful and the wicked. Be merciful, just as your Father is merciful.

"Do not judge, and you will not be judged; do not condemn, and you will not be condemned. Forgive, and you will be forgiven; give, and it will be given to you. A good measure, pressed down, shaken together, running over, will be put into your lap; for the measure you give will be the measure you get back."

He also told them a parable: "Can a blind person guide a blind person? Will not both fall into a pit? A disciple is not above the teacher, but everyone who is fully qualified will be like the teacher. Why do you see the speck in your neighbor's eye, but do not notice the log in your own eye? Or how can you say to your neighbor, 'Friend, let me take out the speck in your eye,' when you yourself do not see the log in your own eye? You hypocrite, first take the log out of your own eye, and then you will see clearly to take the speck out of your neighbor's eye.

"No good tree bears bad fruit, nor again does a bad tree bear good fruit; for each tree is known by its own fruit. Figs are not gathered from thorns, nor are grapes picked from a bramble bush: The good person out of the good treasure of the heart produces good, and the evil person out of evil treasure produces evil; for it is out of the abundance of the heart that the mouth speaks.

"Why do you call me 'Lord, Lord,' and do not do what I tell you? I will show you what someone is like who comes to me, hears my words, and acts on them. That one is like a man building a house, who dug deeply and laid the foundation on rock; when a flood arose, the river burst against that house but could not shake it, because it had been well built. But the one who hears and does not act is like a man who built a house on the ground without a foundation. When the river burst against it, immediately it fell, and great was the ruin of that house."

Chapter 22

[JESUS'S TRIAL, DEATH, AND RESURRECTION]

Now the festival of Unleavened Bread, which is called the Passover, was near. The chief priests and the scribes were looking for a way to put Jesus to death, for they were afraid of the people.

Then Satan entered into Judas called Iscariot, who was one of the twelve; he went away and conferred with the chief priests and officers of the temple police about how he might betray him to them. They were greatly pleased and agreed to give him money. So he consented and began to look for an opportunity to betray him to them when no crowd was present.

Then came the day of Unleavened Bread, on which the Passover lamb had to be sacrificed. So Jesus sent Peter and John, saying, "Go and prepare the Passover meal for us that we may eat it." They asked him, "Where do you want us to make preparations for it?" "Listen," he said to them, "when you have entered the city, a man carrying a jar of water will meet you; follow him into the house he enters and say to the owner of the house, 'The teacher asks you, "Where is the guest room, where I may eat the Passover with my disciples?"'" He will show you a large room upstairs, already furnished. Make preparations for us there." So they went and found everything as he had told them; and they prepared the Passover meal.

When the hour came, he took his place at the table, and the apostles with him. He said to them, "I have eagerly desired to eat this Passover with you before I suffer; for I tell you, I will not eat it until it is fulfilled in the kingdom of God." Then he took a cup, and after giving thanks he said, "Take this and divide it among yourselves; for I tell you that from now on I will not drink of the fruit of the vine until the kingdom of God comes." Then he took a loaf of bread, and when he had given thanks, he broke it and gave it to them, saying, "This is my body, which is given for you. Do this in remembrance of me." And he did the same with the cup after supper, saying, "This cup that is poured out for you is the new covenant in my blood. But see, the one who betrays me is with me, and his hand is on the table. For the Son of Man is going as it has been determined, but woe to that one by whom he is betrayed!" Then they began to ask one another which one of them it could be who would do this.

A dispute also arose among them as to which one of them was to be regarded as the greatest. But he said to them, "The kings of the Gentiles lord it over them; and those in authority over them are called benefactors. But not so with you; rather the greatest among you must become like the youngest, and the leader like one who serves. For who is greater, the one who is at the table or the one who serves? Is it not the one at the table? But I am among you as one who serves.

"You are those who have stood by me in my trials; and I confer on you, just as my Father has conferred on me, a kingdom, so that you may eat and drink at my table in my kingdom, and you will sit on thrones judging the twelve tribes of Israel.

"Simon, Simon, listen! Satan has demanded to sift all of you like wheat, but I have prayed for you that your own faith may not fail; and you, when once you have turned back, strengthen your brothers." And he said to him, "Lord, I am ready to go with you to prison and to death!" Jesus said, "I tell you, Peter, the cock will not crow this day, until you have denied three times that you know me."

He said to them, "When I sent you out without a purse, bag, or sandals, did you lack anything?" They said, "No, not a thing." He said to them, "But now, the one who has a purse must take it, and likewise a bag. And the one who has no sword must sell his cloak and buy one. For I tell you, this scripture must be fulfilled in me, 'And he was counted among the lawless'; and indeed what is written about me is being fulfilled." They said, "Lord, look, here are two swords." He replied, "It is enough."

He came out and went, as was his custom, to the Mount of Olives;[1] and the disciples followed him. When he reached the place, he said to them, "Pray that you may not come into the time of trial." Then he withdrew from them about a stone's throw, knelt down, and prayed, "Father, if you are willing, remove this cup from me; yet, not my will but yours be done." [Then an angel from heaven appeared to him and gave him strength. In his anguish he prayed more earnestly, and his sweat became like great drops of blood falling down on the ground.][2] When he got up from prayer, he came to the disciples and found them sleeping because of grief, and he said to them, "Why are you sleeping? Get up and pray that you may not come into the time of trial."

While he was still speaking, suddenly a crowd came, and the one called Judas, one of the twelve, was leading them. He approached Jesus to kiss him; but Jesus said to him, "Judas, is it with a kiss that you are betraying the Son of Man?" When those who were around him saw what was coming, they asked, "Lord, should we strike with the sword?" Then one of them struck the slave of the high priest and cut off his right ear. But Jesus said, "No more of this!" And he touched his ear and healed him. Then Jesus said to the chief priests, the officers of the temple police, and the elders who had come for him, "Have you come out with swords and clubs as if I were a bandit? When I was with you day after day in the temple, you did not lay hands on me. But this is your hour, and the power of darkness!"

Then they seized him and led him away, bringing him into the high priest's house. But Peter was following at a distance. When they had kindled a fire in the middle of the courtyard and sat down together, Peter sat among them. Then a servant-girl, seeing him in the firelight, stared at him and said, "This man also was with him." But he denied it, saying, "Woman, I do not know him." A little later someone else, on seeing him, said, "You also are one of them." But Peter said, "Man, I am not!" Then about an hour later still another kept insisting, "Surely this man also was with him; for he is a Galilean." But Peter said, "Man, I do not know what you are talking about!" At that moment, while he was still speaking, the cock crowed. The Lord turned and looked at Peter. Then Peter remembered the word of the Lord, how he had said to him, "Before the cock crows today, you will deny me three times." And he went out and wept bitterly.

Now the men who were holding Jesus began to mock him and beat him; they also blindfolded him and kept asking him, "Prophesy! Who is it that struck you?" They kept heaping many other insults on him.

When day came, the assembly of the elders of the people, both chief priests and scribes, gathered together, and they brought him to their council. They said, "If you

---

1. A hill east of Jerusalem, separated from the city by the Kidron brook. The garden of Gethsemane was on its western slope.

2. These lines appear in some manuscripts but not others.

are the Messiah,[3] tell us." He replied, "If I tell you, you will not believe; and if I question you, you will not answer. But from now on the Son of Man will be seated at the right hand of the power of God." All of them asked, "Are you, then, the Son of God?" He said to them, "You say that I am." Then they said, "What further testimony do we need? We have heard it ourselves from his own lips!"

Chapter 23

Then the assembly rose as a body and brought Jesus before Pilate. They began to accuse him, saying, "We found this man perverting our nation, forbidding us to pay taxes to the emperor, and saying that he himself is the Messiah, a king." Then Pilate asked him, "Are you the king of the Jews?" He answered, "You say so." Then Pilate said to the chief priests and the crowds, "I find no basis for an accusation against this man." But they were insistent and said, "He stirs up the people by teaching throughout all Judea, from Galilee where he began even to this place."

When Pilate heard this, he asked whether the man was a Galilean. And when he learned that he was under Herod's jurisdiction, he sent him off to Herod, who was himself in Jerusalem at that time. When Herod saw Jesus, he was very glad, for he had been wanting to see him for a long time, because he had heard about him and was hoping to see him perform some sign. He questioned him at some length, but Jesus gave him no answer. The chief priests and the scribes stood by, vehemently accusing him. Even Herod with his soldiers treated him with contempt and mocked him; then he put an elegant robe on him, and sent him back to Pilate. That same day Herod and Pilate became friends with each other; before this they had been enemies.

Pilate then called together the chief priests, the leaders, and the people, and said to them, "You brought me this man as one who was perverting the people; and here I have examined him in your presence and have not found this man guilty of any of your charges against him. Neither has Herod, for he sent him back to us. Indeed, he has done nothing to deserve death. I will therefore have him flogged and release him."

Then they all shouted out together, "Away with this fellow! Release Barabbas for us!" (This was a man who had been put in prison for an insurrection that had taken place in the city, and for murder.) Pilate, wanting to release Jesus, addressed them again; but they kept shouting, "Crucify, crucify him!"[4] A third time he said to them, "Why, what evil has he done? I have found in him no ground for the sentence of death; I will therefore have him flogged and then release him." But they kept urgently demanding with loud shouts that he should be crucified; and their voices prevailed. So Pilate gave his verdict that their demand should be granted. He released the man they asked for, the one who had been put in prison for insurrection and murder, and he handed Jesus over as they wished.

As they led him away, they seized a man, Simon of Cyrene, who was coming from the country, and they laid the cross on him, and made him carry it behind Jesus. A great number of the people followed him, and among them were women who were beating their breasts and wailing for him. But Jesus turned to them and said, "Daughters of Jerusalem, do not weep for me, but weep for yourselves and for your children.

---

3. From the Hebrew word for "anointed one," which at this time referred to the descendant of David who would usher in the end of time, the Kingdom of God, and the salvation of his people.

4. Crucifixion was the standard punishment for slaves and noncitizens convicted of grave crimes, especially political or religious agitation.

For the days are surely coming when they will say, 'Blessed are the barren, and the wombs that never bore, and the breasts that never nursed.' Then they will begin to say to the mountains, 'Fall on us'; and to the hills, 'Cover us.' For if they do this when the wood is green, what will happen when it is dry?"

Two others also, who were criminals, were led away to be put to death with him. When they came to the place that is called The Skull, they crucified Jesus there with the criminals, one on his right and one on his left. [Then Jesus said, "Father, forgive them; for they do not know what they are doing."] And they cast lots to divide his clothing. And the people stood by, watching; but the leaders scoffed at him, saying, "He saved others; let him save himself if he is the Messiah of God, his chosen one!" The soldiers also mocked him, coming up and offering him sour wine, and saying, "If you are the King of the Jews, save yourself!" There was also an inscription over him, "This is the King of the Jews."[5]

One of the criminals who were hanged there kept deriding him and saying, "Are you not the Messiah? Save yourself and us!" But the other rebuked him, saying, "Do you not fear God, since you are under the same sentence of condemnation? And we indeed have been condemned justly, for we are getting what we deserve for our deeds, but this man has done nothing wrong." Then he said, "Jesus, remember me when you come into your kingdom." He replied, "Truly I tell you, today you will be with me in Paradise."

It was now about noon, and darkness came over the whole land until three in the afternoon, while the sun's light failed; and the curtain of the temple was torn in two. Then Jesus, crying with a loud voice, said, "Father, into your hands I commend my spirit." Having said this, he breathed his last. When the centurion saw what had taken place, he praised God and said, "Certainly this man was innocent." And when all the crowds who had gathered there for this spectacle saw what had taken place, they returned home, beating their breasts. But all his acquaintances, including the women who had followed him from Galilee, stood at a distance, watching these things.

Now there was a good and righteous man named Joseph, who, though a member of the council, had not agreed to their plan and action. He came from the Jewish town of Arimathea, and he was waiting expectantly for the kingdom of God. This man went to Pilate and asked for the body of Jesus. Then he took it down, wrapped it in a linen cloth, and laid it in a rock-hewn tomb where no one had ever been laid. It was the day of Preparation, and the sabbath was beginning. The women who had come with him from Galilee followed, and they saw the tomb and how his body was laid. Then they returned, and prepared spices and ointments.

On the sabbath they rested according to the commandment.

Chapter 24

But on the first day of the week,[6] at early dawn, they came to the tomb, taking the spices that they had prepared. They found the stone rolled away from the tomb, but when they went in, they did not find the body. While they were perplexed about this, suddenly two men in dazzling clothes stood beside them. The women were terrified and bowed their faces to the ground, but the men said to them, "Why do you look for

---

5. It was customary to place over the crucified person's head an inscription with his name and crime.   6. Sunday.

the living among the dead? He is not here, but has risen. Remember how he told you, while he was still in Galilee, that the Son of Man must be handed over to sinners, and be crucified, and on the third day rise again." Then they remembered his words, and returning from the tomb, they told all this to the eleven and to all the rest. Now it was Mary Magdalene, Joanna, Mary the mother of James, and the other women with them who told this to the apostles. But these words seemed to them an idle tale, and they did not believe them. But Peter got up and ran to the tomb; stooping and looking in, he saw the linen cloths by themselves; then he went home, amazed at what had happened.

Now on that same day two of them were going to a village called Emmaus, about seven miles from Jerusalem, and talking with each other about all these things that had happened. While they were talking and discussing, Jesus himself came near and went with them, but their eyes were kept from recognizing him. And he said to them, "What are you discussing with each other while you walk along?" They stood still, looking sad. Then one of them, whose name was Cleopas, answered him, "Are you the only stranger in Jerusalem who does not know the things that have taken place there in these days?" He asked them, "What things?" They replied, "The things about Jesus of Nazareth, who was a prophet mighty in deed and word before God and all the people, and how our chief priests and leaders handed him over to be condemned to death and crucified him. But we had hoped that he was the one to redeem Israel. Yes, and besides all this, it is now the third day since these things took place. Moreover, some women of our group astounded us. They were at the tomb early this morning, and when they did not find his body there, they came back and told us that they had indeed seen a vision of angels who said that he was alive. Some of those who were with us went to the tomb and found it just as the women had said; but they did not see him." Then he said to them, "Oh, how foolish you are, and how slow of heart to believe all that the prophets have declared! Was it not necessary that the Messiah should suffer these things and then enter into his glory?" Then beginning with Moses and all the prophets, he interpreted to them the things about himself in all the scriptures.

As they came near the village to which they were going, he walked ahead as if he were going on. But they urged him strongly, saying, "Stay with us, because it is almost evening and the day is now nearly over." So he went in to stay with them. When he was at the table with them, he took bread, blessed and broke it, and gave it to them. Then their eyes were opened, and they recognized him; and he vanished from their sight. They said to each other, "Were not our hearts burning within us while he was talking to us on the road, while he was opening the scriptures to us?" That same hour they got up and returned to Jerusalem; and they found the eleven and their companions gathered together. They were saying, "The Lord has risen indeed, and he has appeared to Simon!" Then they told what had happened on the road, and how he had been made known to them in the breaking of the bread.

While they were talking about this, Jesus himself stood among them and said to them, "Peace be with you." They were startled and terrified, and thought that they were seeing a ghost. He said to them, "Why are you frightened, and why do doubts arise in your hearts? Look at my hands and my feet; see that it is I myself. Touch me and see; for a ghost does not have flesh and bones as you see that I have." And when he had said this, he showed them his hands and his feet. While in their joy they were disbelieving and still wondering, he said to them, "Have you anything here to eat?" They gave him a piece of broiled fish, and he took it and ate in their presence.

Then he said to them, "These are my words that I spoke to you while I was still with you—that everything written about me in the law of Moses, the prophets, and the psalms must be fulfilled." Then he opened their minds to understand the scriptures, and he said to them, "Thus it is written, that the Messiah is to suffer and to rise from the dead on the third day, and that repentance and forgiveness of sins is to be proclaimed in his name to all nations, beginning from Jerusalem. You are witnesses of these things. And see, I am sending upon you what my Father promised; so stay here in the city until you have been clothed with power from on high."

Then he led them out as far as Bethany,[7] and, lifting up his hands, he blessed them. While he was blessing them, he withdrew from them and was carried up into heaven. And they worshiped him, and returned to Jerusalem with great joy; and they were continually in the temple blessing God.

from The Acts of the Apostles[1]

from *Chapter 1*

[PROLOGUE]

In the first book, Theophilus,[2] I wrote about all that Jesus did and taught from the beginning until the day when he was taken up to heaven, after giving instructions through the Holy Spirit to the apostles whom he had chosen. After his suffering he presented himself alive to them by many convincing proofs, appearing to them during forty days and speaking about the kingdom of God. While staying with them, he ordered them not to leave Jerusalem, but to wait there for the promise of the Father. "This," he said, "is what you have heard from me; for John baptized with water, but you will be baptized with the Holy Spirit not many days from now."

Chapter 2

[PETER ADDRESSES THE CROWD AT PENTECOST]

When the day of Pentecost[1] had come, they were all together in one place. And suddenly from heaven there came a sound like the rush of a violent wind, and it filled the entire house where they were sitting. Divided tongues, as of fire, appeared among them, and a tongue rested on each of them. All of them were filled with the Holy Spirit and began to speak in other languages, as the Spirit gave them ability.

Now there were devout Jews from every nation under heaven living in Jerusalem. And at this sound the crowd gathered and was bewildered, because each one heard them speaking in the native language of each. Amazed and astonished, they asked, "Are not all these who are speaking Galileans? And how is it that we hear, each of us, in our own native language? Parthians, Medes, Elamites, and residents of Mesopotamia, Judea and Cappadocia, Pontus and Asia, Phrygia and Pamphylia, Egypt and the parts of Libya belonging to Cyrene, and visitors from Rome,

7. A place on the eastern slope of the Mount of Olives.
1. New Revised Standard Version.
2. "The first book" is the Gospel According to Luke. "Theophilus" is Greek for "lover of God." It is probably the name of an influential patron, but it may simply refer in general to all Christians.
1. A religious festival that celebrated the end of the harvest.

both Jews and proselytes, Cretans and Arabs—in our own languages we hear them speaking about God's deeds of power." All were amazed and perplexed, saying to one another, "What does this mean?" But others sneered and said, "They are filled with new wine."

But Peter, standing with the eleven, raised his voice and addressed them, "Men of Judea and all who live in Jerusalem, let this be known to you, and listen to what I say. Indeed, these are not drunk, as you suppose, for it is only nine o'clock in the morning. No, this is what was spoken through the prophet Joel:

> 'In the last days it will be, God declares,
> that I will pour out my Spirit upon all flesh,
> and your sons and your daughters shall prophesy,
> and your young men shall see visions,
> and your old men shall dream dreams.
> Even upon my slaves, both men and women,
> in those days I will pour out my Spirit;
> and they shall prophesy.
> And I will show portents in the heaven above
> and signs on the earth below, blood, and fire, and smoky mist.
> The sun shall be turned to darkness
> and the moon to blood, before the coming of the Lord's great and glorious day.
> Then everyone who calls on the name of the Lord shall be saved.'

"You that are Israelites, listen to what I have to say: Jesus of Nazareth, a man attested to you by God with deeds of power, wonders, and signs that God did through him among you, as you yourselves know—this man, handed over to you according to the definite plan and foreknowledge of God, you crucified and killed by the hands of those outside the law.[2] But God raised him up, having freed him from death, because it was impossible for him to be held in its power. For David says concerning him,

> 'I saw the Lord always before me,
> for he is at my right hand so that I will not be shaken;
> therefore my heart was glad, and my tongue rejoiced;
> moreover my flesh will live in hope.
> For you will not abandon my soul to Hades,[3]
> or let your Holy One experience corruption.
> You have made known to me the ways of life;
> you will make me full of gladness with your presence.'

"Fellow Israelites, I may say to you confidently of our ancestor David that he both died and was buried, and his tomb is with us to this day. Since he was a prophet, he knew that God had sworn with an oath to him that he would put one of his descendants on his throne. Foreseeing this, David spoke of the resurrection of the Messiah, saying,

> 'He was not abandoned to Hades,
> nor did his flesh experience corruption.'

This Jesus God raised up, and of that all of us are witnesses. Being therefore exalted at the right hand of God, and having received from the Father the promise of the Holy

---

2. That is, the Romans, outside of Judaic law.
3. "Hades," the name for the underworld in Greek religion, was used in New Testament Greek to translate the Hebrew word *Sheol*, a subterranean space of death.

Spirit, he has poured out this that you both see and hear. For David did not ascend into the heavens, but he himself says,

> 'The Lord said to my Lord,
> "Sit at my right hand,
> until I make your enemies your footstool."'

Therefore let the entire house of Israel know with certainty that God has made him both Lord and Messiah, this Jesus whom you crucified."[4]

Now when they heard this, they were cut to the heart and said to Peter and to the other apostles, "Brothers, what should we do?" Peter said to them, "Repent, and be baptized every one of you in the name of Jesus Christ so that your sins may be forgiven; and you will receive the gift of the Holy Spirit. For the promise is for you, for your children, and for all who are far away, everyone whom the Lord our God calls to him." And he testified with many other arguments and exhorted them, saying, "Save yourselves from this corrupt generation." So those who welcomed his message were baptized, and that day about three thousand persons were added. They devoted themselves to the apostles' teaching and fellowship, to the breaking of bread and the prayers.

Awe came upon everyone, because many wonders and signs were being done by the apostles. All who believed were together and had all things in common; they would sell their possessions and goods and distribute the proceeds to all, as any had need. Day by day, as they spent much time together in the temple, they broke bread at home and ate their food with glad and generous hearts, praising God and having the goodwill of all the people. And day by day the Lord added to their number those who were being saved.

from *Chapter 9*

[THE CONVERSION OF PAUL]

Meanwhile Saul,[1] still breathing threats and murder against the disciples of the Lord, went to the high priest and asked him for letters to the synagogues at Damascus,[2] so that if he found any who belonged to the Way; men or women, he might bring them bound to Jerusalem. Now as he was going along and approaching Damascus, suddenly a light from heaven flashed around him. He fell to the ground and heard a voice saying to him, "Saul, Saul, why do you persecute me?" He asked, "Who are you, Lord?" The reply came, "I am Jesus, whom you are persecuting. But get up and enter the city, and you will be told what you are to do." The men who were traveling with him stood speechless because they heard the voice but saw no one. Saul got up from the ground, and though his eyes were open, he could see nothing; so they led him by the hand and brought him into Damascus. For three days he was without sight, and neither ate nor drank.

---

4. As Jesus did with his disciples after his resurrection, so Peter here tells the crowd how "the law of Moses, the prophets, and the psalms" have been "fulfilled" by recent events (Luke 24:44). The first passage is from Joel 2:28–32; the second is from Psalm 16:8–11 (David was the traditional author of Psalms).

1. The Jewish name of the apostle Paul.
2. A commercial center in Syria. It was the site of an early Christian community.

Now there was a disciple in Damascus named Ananias. The Lord said to him in a vision, "Ananias." He answered, "Here I am, Lord." The Lord said to him, "Get up and go to the street called Straight, and at the house of Judas look for a man of Tarsus named Saul. At this moment he is praying, and he has seen in a vision a man named Ananias come in and lay his hands on him so that he might regain his sight." But Ananias answered, "Lord, I have heard from many about this man, how much evil he has done to your saints in Jerusalem; and here he has authority from the chief priests to bind all who invoke your name." But the Lord said to him, "Go, for he is an instrument whom I have chosen to bring my name before Gentiles and kings and before the people of Israel; I myself will show him how much he must suffer for the sake of my name." So Ananias went and entered the house. He laid his hands on Saul and said, "Brother Saul, the Lord Jesus, who appeared to you on your way here, has sent me so that you may regain your sight and be filled with the Holy Spirit." And immediately something like scales fell from his eyes, and his sight was restored. Then he got up and was baptized, and after taking some food, he regained his strength.

For several days he was with the disciples in Damascus, and immediately he began to proclaim Jesus in the synagogues, saying, "He is the Son of God." All who heard him were amazed and said, "Is not this the man who made havoc in Jerusalem among those who invoked this name? And has he not come here for the purpose of bringing them bound before the chief priests?" Saul became increasingly more powerful and confounded the Jews who lived in Damascus by proving that Jesus was the Messiah.

After some time had passed, the Jews plotted to kill him, but their plot became known to Saul. They were watching the gates day and night so that they might kill him; but his disciples took him by night and let him down through an opening in the wall, lowering him in a basket.

When he had come to Jerusalem, he attempted to join the disciples; and they were all afraid of him, for they did not believe that he was a disciple. But Barnabas took him, brought him to the apostles, and described for them how on the road he had seen the Lord, who had spoken to him, and how in Damascus he had spoken boldly in the name of Jesus. So he went in and out among them in Jerusalem, speaking boldly in the name of the Lord.

Chapter 26

[PAUL DEFENDS HIMSELF BEFORE HEROD AGRIPPA]

Agrippa[1] said to Paul, "You have permission to speak for yourself." Then Paul stretched out his hand and began to defend himself:

"I consider myself fortunate that it is before you, King Agrippa, I am to make my defense today against all the accusations of the Jews, because you are especially familiar with all the customs and controversies of the Jews; therefore I beg of you to listen to me patiently.

"All the Jews know my way of life from my youth, a life spent from the beginning among my own people and in Jerusalem. They have known for a long time, if

---

1. Herod Agrippa (27–93 C.E.) was a great-grandson of Herod the Great and controlled various parts of Lebanon, Syria, and Galilee. Paul was arrested in the mid-50s, and had been in prison for two years at the time of this hearing.

they are willing to testify, that I have belonged to the strictest sect of our religion and lived as a Pharisee. And now I stand here on trial on account of my hope in the promise made by God to our ancestors, a promise that our twelve tribes hope to attain, as they earnestly worship day and night. It is for this hope, your Excellency, that I am accused by Jews! Why is it thought incredible by any of you that God raises the dead?

"Indeed, I myself was convinced that I ought to do many things against the name of Jesus of Nazareth. And that is what I did in Jerusalem; with authority received from the chief priests, I not only locked up many of the saints in prison, but I also cast my vote against them when they were being condemned to death. By punishing them often in all the synagogues I tried to force them to blaspheme; and since I was so furiously enraged at them, I pursued them even to foreign cities.

"With this in mind, I was traveling to Damascus with the authority and commission of the chief priests, when at midday along the road, your Excellency, I saw a light from heaven, brighter than the sun, shining around me and my companions. When we had all fallen to the ground, I heard a voice saying to me in the Hebrew language, 'Saul, Saul, why are you persecuting me? It hurts you to kick against the goads.' I asked, 'Who are you, Lord?' The Lord answered, 'I am Jesus whom you are persecuting. But get up and stand on your feet; for I have appeared to you for this purpose, to appoint you to serve and testify to the things in which you have seen me and to those in which I will appear to you. I will rescue you from your people and from the Gentiles—to whom I am sending you to open their eyes so that they may turn from darkness to light and from the power of Satan to God, so that they may receive forgiveness of sins and a place among those who are sanctified by faith in me.'

"After that, King Agrippa, I was not disobedient to the heavenly vision, but declared first to those in Damascus, then in Jerusalem and throughout the countryside of Judea, and also to the Gentiles, that they should repent and turn to God and do deeds consistent with repentance. For this reason the Jews seized me in the temple and tried to kill me. To this day I have had help from God, and so I stand here, testifying to both small and great, saying nothing but what the prophets and Moses said would take place: that the Messiah must suffer, and that, by being the first to rise from the dead, he would proclaim light both to our people and to the Gentiles."

While he was making this defense, Festus[2] exclaimed, "You are out of your mind, Paul! Too much learning is driving you insane!" But Paul said, "I am not out of my mind, most excellent Festus, but I am speaking the sober truth. Indeed the king knows about these things, and to him I speak freely; for I am certain that none of these things has escaped his notice, for this was not done in a corner. King Agrippa, do you believe the prophets? I know that you believe." Agrippa said to Paul, "Are you so quickly persuading me to become a Christian?" Paul replied, "Whether quickly or not, I pray to God that not only you but also all who are listening to me today might become such as I am—except for these chains."

Then the king got up, and with him the governor and Bernice[3] and those who had been seated with them; and as they were leaving, they said to one another, "This man is doing nothing to deserve death or imprisonment." Agrippa said to Festus, "This man could have been set free if he had not appealed to the emperor."[4]

---

2. Porcius Festus became the Roman procurator of Judea around 55 C.E.

3. A sister of Agrippa's.

4. As a Roman citizen, Paul had appealed to the emperor's tribunal in Rome.

Chapter 28

[PAUL REACHES ROME]

After we had reached safety, we then learned that the island was called Malta.[1] The natives showed us unusual kindness. Since it had begun to rain and was cold, they kindled a fire and welcomed all of us around it. Paul had gathered a bundle of brushwood and was putting it on the fire, when a viper, driven out by the heat, fastened itself on his hand. When the natives saw the creature hanging from his hand, they said to one another, "This man must be a murderer; though he has escaped from the sea, justice has not allowed him to live." He, however, shook off the creature into the fire and suffered no harm. They were expecting him to swell up or drop dead, but after they had waited a long time and saw that nothing unusual had happened to him, they changed their minds and began to say that he was a god.

Now in the neighborhood of that place were lands belonging to the leading man of the island, named Publius, who received us and entertained us hospitably for three days. It so happened that the father of Publius lay sick in bed with fever and dysentery. Paul visited him and cured him by praying and putting his hands on him. After this happened, the rest of the people on the island who had diseases also came and were cured. They bestowed many honors on us, and when we were about to sail, they put on board all the provisions we needed.

Three months later we set sail on a ship that had wintered at the island, an Alexandrian ship with the Twin Brothers as its figurehead.[2] We put in at Syracuse and stayed there for three days; then we weighed anchor and came to Rhegium. After one day there a south wind sprang up, and on the second day we came to Puteoli.[3] There we found believers and were invited to stay with them for seven days. And so we came to Rome. The believers from there, when they heard of us, came as far as the Forum of Appius and Three Taverns to meet us.[4] On seeing them, Paul thanked God and took courage.

When we came into Rome, Paul was allowed to live by himself, with the soldier who was guarding him.

Three days later he called together the local leaders of the Jews. When they had assembled, he said to them, "Brothers, though I had done nothing against our people or the customs of our ancestors, yet I was arrested in Jerusalem and handed over to the Romans. When they had examined me, the Romans wanted to release me, because there was no reason for the death penalty in my case. But when the Jews objected, I was compelled to appeal to the emperor—even though I had no charge to bring against my nation. For this reason therefore I have asked to see you and speak with you, since it is for the sake of the hope of Israel that I am bound with this chain." They replied, "We have received no letters from Judea about you, and none of the brothers coming here has reported or spoken anything evil about you. But we would like to hear from you what you think, for with regard to this sect we know that everywhere it is spoken against."

After they had set a day to meet with him, they came to him at his lodgings in great numbers. From morning until evening he explained the matter to them, testifying to the kingdom of God and trying to convince them about Jesus both from the law

---

1. In the central Mediterranean, south of Sicily. The prison ship has just survived a storm at sea.
2. Castor and Pollux, legendary twins of Greek and Roman myth.

3. Ports along the route to Rome.
4. Places on the Appian Way that ran through southern Italy to Rome.

of Moses and from the prophets. Some were convinced by what he had said, while others refused to believe. So they disagreed with each other; and as they were leaving, Paul made one further statement: "The Holy Spirit was right in saying to your ancestors through the prophet Isaiah,

> 'Go to this people and say,
> You will indeed listen, but never understand,
> and you will indeed look, but never perceive.
> For this people's heart has grown dull,
> and their ears are hard of hearing,
> and they have shut their eyes;
> so that they might not look with their eyes,
> and listen with their ears,
> and understand with their heart and turn—
> and I would heal them.'

Let it be known to you then that this salvation of God has been sent to the Gentiles; they will listen."

He lived there two whole years at his own expense and welcomed all who came to him, proclaiming the kingdom of God and teaching about the Lord Jesus Christ with all boldness and without hindrance.

⊶ ⸎⸎⸎ ⊷

Roman Reactions to Early Christianity

Palestine was conquered by Pompey in 63 B.C.E., and became part of the Roman province of Syria. Herod the Great, King of Judaea from 37 to 4 B.C.E., was an important ally to Rome, and his people were allowed unusual freedoms. Jesus was born at the end of Herod's reign, under the so-called Peace of Augustus; he was crucified in 30 C.E. during the reign of Augustus's successor, Tiberius, because he was seen as a political threat to the stability of the region. According to Suetonius, Jewish worshipers of "Chrestus" were already active (and unruly) in Rome under Claudius (41–54); a church was well established by the time of Paul's Epistle to the Romans in the mid-first century. Persecution was intermittent but often severe; as suggested by the Roman sources below, however, the prevailing attitude may have been to regard the new religion as just one particularly annoying sect among many.

⊶ ⸎⸎⸎ ⊷

Suetonius
c. 70–after 122 C.E.

A successful bureaucrat first patronized by Pliny the Younger, Suetonius prospered under Emperors Trajan and Hadrian before falling precipitously into disgrace in 122. Written in the early second century, his *Twelve Caesars* is a racy and richly anecdotal account of the lives of the rulers of Rome covering some two hundred years from Julius Caesar to Domitian. Here, he reports on the treatment of Jews and Christians in Rome under Tiberius, Claudius, and Nero.

from **The Twelve Caesars**[1]

[TIBERIUS][2]

He abolished foreign cults at Rome, particularly the Egyptian and Jewish, forcing all citizens who had embraced these superstitious faiths to burn their religious vestments and other accessories. Jews of military age were removed to unhealthy regions, on the pretext of drafting them into the army; the others of the same race or of similar beliefs were expelled from the city and threatened with slavery if they defied the order. Tiberius also banished all astrologers except such as asked for his forgiveness and undertook to make no more predictions. * * *

[CLAUDIUS][3]

It now became illegal for foreigners to adopt the names of Roman families, and any who usurped the rights of Roman citizens were executed in the Esquiline Field.[4] Tiberius had converted the provinces of Greece and Macedonia into a private domain of his own; Claudius gave them back to the Senate. He deprived the Lycians of national independence to punish their love of savage vendettas; but restored the Rhodians' independence to express his pleasure at their recantation of their faults.[5] In granting the Trojans, as founders of the Roman race, perpetual exemption from tribute, he supported his act by reading aloud an ancient letter written in Greek to King Seleucus, from the Senate and People of Rome, with a promise of loyal friendship on condition that Seleucus should "keep their Trojan kinsfolk free from all imposts."[6] Because the Jews at Rome caused continuous disturbances at the instigation of Chrestus,[7] he expelled them from the city. When the German envoys first visited the Theatre, they took their seats among the common people, but, noticing the Parthian and Armenian envoys seated with the Senators in the orchestra, went to join them—were they not just as brave and nobly born? Claudius admired their simple confidence and let them remain there. Augustus had been content to prohibit any Roman citizen in Gaul from taking part in the savage and terrible Druidic cult; Claudius abolished it altogether.[8] On the other hand, he attempted to transfer the Eleusinian Mysteries from Attica to Rome; and had the ruined Temple of Venus on Mount Eryx in Sicily restored at the expense of the Public Treasury.[9] Whenever he concluded a treaty with foreign rulers, he sacrificed a sow in the Forum, using the ancient formula of the Fetial priests.[1] Yet all these acts, and others like them—indeed, one might say, everything that Claudius did throughout his reign—were dictated by his wives and freedmen: he practically always obeyed their whims rather than his own judgment.

---

1. Translated by Robert Graves, revised by Michael Grant.
2. The adopted son of Augustus, Tiberius was the second Roman emperor, reigning from 14 to 37 C.E., near the end of which time Jesus was crucified.
3. Claudius was proclaimed emperor in 41 following the assassination of his nephew Caligula. He reigned for 13 years.
4. Site of a cemetery for slaves in Rome.
5. Lycia was a region in southwest Asia Minor; Rhodes is a large island off its coast.
6. Taxes or duties. According to Roman legend (and Virgil's *Aeneid*), Rome had been founded by the Trojan hero Aeneas. The kingdom founded by Seleucus, a general

under Alexander the Great, controlled much of Asia Minor and the Middle East. It had been conquered by Rome in 64 B.C.E.
7. Most likely a reference to Christ.
8. Druidism was the religion of the Celtic peoples of northern Europe.
9. The ancient Greek mystery cult of Eleusis was based at the sanctuary of Demeter in Attica near Athens. Eryx in Sicily was the site of a cult of Venus and is visited by Aeneas in Virgil's *Aeneid*.
1. The *Fetiales* were Latin priests who presided over the rituals associated with declaring wars and making treaties. The Forum was the main Roman square.

[NERO][2]

Nero introduced his own new style of architecture in the city: building out porches from the fronts of apartments and private houses to serve as fire-fighting platforms, and subsidizing the work himself. He also considered a scheme for extending the city wall as far as Ostia, and cutting a canal which would allow ships to sail straight up to Rome.[3]

During his reign a great many public abuses were suppressed by the imposition of heavy penalties, and among the equally numerous novel enactments were sumptuary laws limiting private expenditure; the substitution of a simple grain distribution for public banquets; and a decree restricting the food sold in wine-shops to green vegetables and dried beans—whereas before all kinds of snacks had been displayed. Punishments were also inflicted on the Christians, a sect professing a new and mischievous religious belief; and Nero ended the licence which the charioteers had so long enjoyed that they claimed it as a right: to wander down the streets, swindling and robbing the populace. He likewise expelled from the city all pantomime actors and their hangers-on.

Tacitus
c. 56–after 118 C.E.

Politician and celebrated orator under the reigns of Vespasian, Titus, Domitian, and Nerva, Tacitus held several high positions in the government in Rome and was posted to his birthplace of Gaul (or else to Germany), to Africa, and to Asia Minor. A close friend of Pliny the Younger, he is remembered for his *Germania,* a sympathetic study of the northern barbarians, and for his ambitious *Histories* and *Annals,* giving a detailed, continuous narrative of Roman history from the death of Augustus to the death of Domitian, of which about half has survived. Tacitus's skill in portraiture, command of narrative movement, and tragic sense of history are in evidence in the following brief account of the great fire in Rome in 64 C.E. and Nero's response to it.

from The Annals of Imperial Rome[1]

[THE BURNING OF ROME]

Disaster followed. Whether it was accidental or caused by the emperor's criminal act[2] is uncertain—both versions have supporters. Now started the most terrible and destructive fire which Rome had ever experienced. It began in the Circus, where it adjoins the hills.[3] Breaking out in shops selling inflammable goods, and fanned by the wind, the conflagration instantly grew and swept the whole length of the Circus. There were no walled mansions or temples, or any other obstructions which could arrest it. First, the fire swept violently over the level spaces. Then it climbed the hills—but returned to ravage the lower ground again. It outstripped every counter-measure.

---

2. Nero was the son of Agrippina, Claudius's wife and Caligula's sister. He reigned as emperor from 54 to 68.
3. Ostia was a port for the city of Rome at the mouth of the river Tiber.
1. Translated by Michael Grant.

2. Tacitus has been recounting some debauched banqueting by Nero and his cronies.
3. The fire began late at night in the middle of June 64 in the Circus Maximus, between the Palatine and Aventine hills.

The ancient city's narrow winding streets and irregular blocks encouraged its progress.

Terrified, shrieking women, helpless old and young, people intent on their own safety, people unselfishly supporting invalids or waiting for them, fugitives and lingerers alike—all heightened the confusion. When people looked back, menacing flames sprang up before them or outflanked them. When they escaped to a neighbouring quarter, the fire followed—even districts believed remote proved to be involved. Finally, with no idea where or what to flee, they crowded on to the country roads, or lay in the fields. Some who had lost everything—even their food for the day—could have escaped, but preferred to die. So did others, who had failed to rescue their loved ones. Nobody dared fight the flames. Attempts to do so were prevented by menacing gangs. Torches, too, were openly thrown in, by men crying that they acted under orders. Perhaps they had received orders. Or they may just have wanted to plunder unhampered.

Nero was at Antium.[4] He only returned to the city when the fire was approaching the mansion he had built to link the Gardens of Maecenas to the Palatine.[5] The flames could not be prevented from overwhelming the whole of the Palatine, including his palace. Nevertheless, for the relief of the homeless, fugitive masses he threw open the Field of Mars, including Agrippa's public buildings, and even his own Gardens.[6] Nero also constructed emergency accommodation for the destitute multitude. Food was brought from Ostia and neighbouring towns, and the price of corn was cut. Yet these measures, for all their popular character, earned no gratitude. For a rumour had spread that, while the city was burning, Nero had gone to his private stage and, comparing modern calamities with ancient, had sung of the destruction of Troy.

By the sixth day enormous demolitions had confronted the raging flames with bare ground and open sky, and the fire was finally stamped out. But before panic had subsided, or hope revived, flames broke out again in the more open regions of the city. Here there were fewer casualties; but the destruction of temples and pleasure arcades was even worse. This new conflagration caused additional ill-feeling because it started on Tigellinus' estate.[7] For people believed that Nero was ambitious to found a new city to be called after himself.

Of Rome's fourteen districts only four remained intact. Three were levelled to the ground. The other seven were reduced to a few scorched and mangled ruins. To count the mansions, blocks, and temples destroyed would be difficult. They included shrines of remote antiquity, the precious spoils of countless victories, Greek artistic masterpieces, and authentic records of old Roman genius. All the splendour of the rebuilt city did not prevent the older generation from remembering these irreplaceable objects. It was noted that the fire had started on July 19th, the day on which the Senonian Gauls had captured and burnt the city.[8]

But Nero profited by his country's ruin to build a new palace. Its wonders were not so much customary and commonplace luxuries like gold and jewels, but lawns

4. Antium (modern Anzio) was a fashionable resort in imperial times; Nero had rebuilt the harbor and imperial villa.

5. Maecenas, the advisor to Augustus and patron to Horace and Virgil, had built extensive gardens on the Esquiline (see Horace's Satire 1.8, page 1252). There were imperial properties here and on the Palatine.

6. Situated along the Tiber, the Campus Martius (Field of Mars) was a center of public life and leisure, full of theaters, temples, and baths, including a set just completed by Nero.

7. Ofidius Tigellinus was an advisor to Nero notorious for his indulgence of the emperor's more extreme tastes.

8. The Senones were said to have been leaders of the band of Gauls who had settled in Italy and took the city of Rome in 390 B.C.E.

and lakes and faked rusticity—woods here, open spaces and views there. With their cunning, impudent artificialities, Nero's architects and contractors outbid Nature.[9]

They also fooled away an emperor's riches. For they promised to dig a navigable canal from Lake Avernus to the Tiber estuary, over the stony shore and mountain barriers.[1] The only water to feed the canal was in the Pontine marshes. Elsewhere, all was precipitous or waterless. Moreover, even if a passage could have been forced, the labour would have been unendurable and unjustified. But Nero was eager to perform the incredible; so he attempted to excavate the hills adjoining Lake Avernus. Traces of his frustrated hopes are visible today. * * *

After consultation of the Sibylline books, prayers were addressed to Vulcan, Ceres, and Proserpina. Juno, too, was propitiated.[2] But neither human resources, nor imperial munificence, nor appeasement of the gods, eliminated sinister suspicions that the fire had been instigated. To suppress this rumour, Nero fabricated scapegoats—and punished with every refinement the notoriously depraved Christians (as they were popularly called). Their originator, Christ, had been executed in Tiberius' reign by the governor of Judaea, Pontius Pilatus. But in spite of this temporary setback the deadly superstition had broken out afresh, not only in Judaea (where the mischief had started) but even in Rome. All degraded and shameful practices collect and flourish in the capital.

First, Nero had self-acknowledged Christians arrested. Then, on their information, large numbers of others were condemned—not so much for incendiarism as for their anti-social tendencies. Their deaths were made farcical. Dressed in wild animals' skins, they were torn to pieces by dogs, or crucified, or made into torches to be ignited after dark as substitutes for daylight. Nero provided his Gardens for the spectacle, and exhibited displays in the Circus, at which he mingled with the crowd—or stood in a chariot, dressed as a charioteer. Despite their guilt as Christians, and the ruthless punishment it deserved, the victims were pitied. For it was felt that they were being sacrificed to one man's brutality rather than to the national interest.

Meanwhile Italy was ransacked for funds, and the provinces were ruined—unprivileged and privileged communities alike. Even the gods were included in the looting. Temples at Rome were robbed, and emptied of the gold dedicated for the triumphs and vows, the ambitions and fears, of generations of Romans. Plunder from Asia and Greece included not only offerings but actual statues of the gods. Two agents were sent to these provinces. One was an ex-slave, capable of any depravity. The other professed Greek culture, but no virtue from it percolated to his heart.

Seneca, rumour went, sought to avoid the odium of this sacrilege by asking leave to retire to a distant country retreat, and then—permission being refused—feigning a muscular complaint and keeping to his bedroom. According to some accounts, one of his former slaves acting on Nero's orders intended to poison Seneca, but he escaped—either because the man confessed or because Seneca's own fears caused him to live very simply on plain fruit, quenching his thirst with running water.[3]

9. Nero's famous Domus Aurea, or Golden House, its gardens, and an artificial lake occupied the center of Rome.
1. It was a good hundred miles to Lake Avernus, near Naples.
2. According to Roman legend, a sibyl, or prophetess, had offered a book of prophecies to the last of the ancient Roman kings. The three surviving books were housed in Nero's time in the temple of Palatine Apollo. With Vulcan's relation to fire, Ceres's to fertility, and Proserpina's to the underworld, they would be logical choices for prayer. Juno was a principal god of the city.
3. Seneca, the famous Stoic philosopher and tragedian, had been the young Nero's tutor and was the emperor's advisor and minister until he fell out of favor and withdrew from public life. A year after the fire he was compelled to take his life after being accused of conspiracy against the emperor.

At this juncture there was an attempted break-out by gladiators at Praeneste.[4] Their army guards overpowered them. But the Roman public, as always terrified (or fascinated) by revolution, were already talking of ancient calamities such as the rising of Spartacus.[5] Soon afterwards, a naval disaster occurred. This was not on active service; never had there been such profound peace. But Nero had ordered the fleet to return to Campania by a fixed date, regardless of weather. So, despite heavy seas, the steersmen started from Formiae. But when they tried to round Cape Misenum, a south-westerly gale drove them ashore near Cumae and destroyed numerous warships and smaller craft.[6]

✦ ⊱✦⊰ ✦

Pliny the Younger
c. 60–c. 112 C.E.

An influential and wealthy lawyer and politician, Pliny preserved in his ten books of letters a record of the most important figures and events of his day, including an eyewitness account of the eruption of Vesuvius that killed his uncle and namesake, the natural historian Pliny the Elder. Pliny's correspondence with the Emperor Trajan, whom he served as governor of the Asia Minor province Bithynia-Pontus around 110, provides a unique insight into the functioning of Roman provincial government. The letter included here suggests the complicated situation of Christians in Asia Minor and the lack of a fixed policy for dealing with them.

Letter to the Emperor Trajan[1]

It is my custom to refer all my difficulties to you, Sir, for no one is better able to resolve my doubts and to inform my ignorance.

I have never been present at an examination of Christians. Consequently, I do not know the nature or the extent of the punishments usually meted out to them, nor the grounds for starting an investigation and how far it should be pressed. Nor am I at all sure whether any distinction should be made between them on the grounds of age, or if young people and adults should be treated alike; whether a pardon ought to be granted to anyone retracting his beliefs, or if he has once professed Christianity, he shall gain nothing by renouncing it; and whether it is the mere name of Christian which is punishable, even if innocent of crime, or rather the crimes associated with the name.

For the moment this is the line I have taken with all persons brought before me on the charge of being Christians. I have asked them in person if they are Christians, and if they admit it, I repeat the question a second and third time, with a warning of the punishment awaiting them. If they persist, I order them to be led away for execution; for, whatever the nature of their admission, I am convinced that their stubbornness and unshakeable obstinacy ought not to go unpunished. There have been others similarly fanatical who are Roman citizens. I have entered them on the list of persons to be sent to Rome for trial.[2]

---

4. A town some 25 miles east-southeast of Rome (modern Palestrina).
5. Spartacus was a gladiator who led an impressive revolt and ravaged Italy during the late 70s B.C.E.
6. The region is the southern Adriatic coast between Rome and Naples.

1. Translated by Betty Radice.
2. Citizenship of Rome was conferred at this time on members of the elite in provincial cities all over the empire. Citizenship conveyed various privileges including certain legal rights.

Now that I have begun to deal with this problem, as so often happens, the charges are becoming more widespread and increasing in variety. An anonymous pamphlet has been circulated which contains the names of a number of accused persons. Among these I considered that I should dismiss any who denied that they were or ever had been Christians when they had repeated after me a formula of invocation to the gods and had made offerings of wine and incense to your statue (which I had ordered to be brought into court for this purpose along with the images of the gods),[3] and furthermore had reviled the name of Christ: none of which things, I understand, any genuine Christian can be induced to do.

Others, whose names were given to me by an informer, first admitted the charge and then denied it; they said that they had ceased to be Christians two or more years previously, and some of them even twenty years ago. They all did reverence to your statue and the images of the gods in the same way as the others, and reviled the name of Christ. They also declared that the sum total of their guilt or error amounted to no more than this: they had met regularly before dawn on a fixed day to chant verses alternately among themselves in honour of Christ as if to a god, and also to bind themselves by oath, not for any criminal purpose, but to abstain from theft, robbery and adultery, to commit no breach of trust and not to deny a deposit when called upon to restore it. After this ceremony it had been their custom to disperse and reassemble later to take food of an ordinary, harmless kind; but they had in fact given up this practice since my edict, issued on your instructions, which banned all political societies. This made me decide it was all the more necessary to extract the truth by torture from two slave-women, whom they call deaconesses. I found nothing but a degenerate sort of cult carried to extravagant lengths.

I have therefore postponed any further examination and hastened to consult you. The question seems to me to be worthy of your consideration, especially in view of the number of persons endangered; for a great many individuals of every age and class, both men and women, are being brought to trial, and this is likely to continue. It is not only the towns, but villages and rural districts too which are infected through contact with this wretched cult. I think though that it is still possible for it to be checked and directed to better ends, for there is no doubt that people have begun to throng the temples which had been almost entirely deserted for a long time; the sacred rites which had been allowed to lapse are being performed again, and flesh of sacrificial victims is on sale everywhere, though up till recently scarcely anyone could be found to buy it. It is easy to infer from this that a great many people could be reformed if they were given an opportunity to repent.

* ⊨◆⊨ *

Trajan
r. 98–117 C.E.

Probably born in Spain in 53, Trajan was adopted by Emperor Nerva as his son and co-ruler in 98, following distinguished service in Syria, Spain, and Germany. He became sole ruler after the infirm Nerva's death the same year and was known as a modest and judicious emperor. His measured reply to Pliny suggests the general character of his reign.

---

3. In provinces of Asia Minor including Pliny's station in Bithynia-Pontus, it had become custom to establish cults of living emperors.

Response to Pliny[1]

You have followed the right course of procedure, my dear Pliny, in your examination of the cases of persons charged with being Christians, for it is impossible to lay down a general rule to a fixed formula. These people must not be hunted out; if they are brought before you and the charge against them is proved, they must be punished, but in the case of anyone who denies that he is a Christian, and makes it clear that he is not by offering prayers to our gods, he is to be pardoned as a result of his repentance however suspect his past conduct may be. But pamphlets circulated anonymously must play no part in any accusation. They create the worst sort of precedent and are quite out of keeping with the spirit of our age.

[END OF ROMAN REACTIONS TO EARLY CHRISTIANITY]

❊ CROSSCURRENTS: THE CULTURE OF ROME ❊ AND THE BEGINNINGS OF CHRISTIANITY

- Augustine's *Confessions* (page 1298) is probably the most influential account of the conflict and eventual synthesis of the Roman Empire and the new religion of Christianity. In what ways does Augustine's depiction of his pre-conversion life in the Empire resemble those in Catullus, Horace, and Petronius? In what ways does it differ from them? In what ways does Augustine's relationship to the Christian texts differ from his relationship to classical texts?

- The status of Christianity and its relation to the classical tradition and to the new religion of Islam were central concerns throughout the Mediterranean region during the medieval era. The Qur'an (Volume B) sums up the relationship in Islam between the Hebrew and Christian bibles and the sacred text revealed to Muhammad. The vision of the afterlife in Dante's *Divine Comedy* (Volume B), sums up the complex relationship between Christianity, classical culture, and, in passing, Islam.

- The rise of vernacular writing during the early modern period also framed issues of language in terms of the canonical status of scripture and the often highly fraught question of translating sacred texts (see "Attacking and Defending the Vernacular Bible" in Volume C). Seminal South Asian vernacular narratives such as Wu Cheng 'En's *Journey to the West* used the arrival of a new religion (Buddhism) as the frame for an epic narrative combining adventure with spiritual instruction.

- The early modern age of exploration brought to the foreground the complex role of Christianity in the global expansion of European power. The tragic results of this process in Mesoamerica are highlighted in the Perspectives section "The Conquest and Its Aftermath" (Volume C). We also witness the conflict of colonization through a rubric of indigenous and Christian belief systems in Nigerian writer Chinua Achebe's 1958 novel *Things Fall Apart* (Volume F).

➤ END OF PERSPECTIVES: THE CULTURE OF ROME AND ➤
THE BEGINNINGS OF CHRISTIANITY

1. Translated by Betty Radice.

Augustine
354–430 C.E.

One of the Old Testament lessons Saint Augustine loved to cite concerned the gold taken by Moses and his people in their flight from Egypt to the Holy Land. Gold, he would argue, referred not only to the allure of worldly riches but to the wealth of classical literature and philosophy; hence, one could either succumb to the superficial brilliance of its rhetoric and its pagan ideas or one could transmute their splendor into the inner richness of spiritual peace. Throughout Augustine's writings, we witness a battle between a lifetime's immersion in the intellectual rigor and aesthetic power of Greek and Roman culture and a fervent belief in a Christianity that he found unsophisticated and illogical but that gave him inner tranquility nonetheless. He recorded the struggle on a personal level in his spiritual autobiography, the *Confessions*; in the *City of God,* he traced the same struggle on the stage of world history. For Augustine, Christianity meant not so much the defeat of the ancient world as its apotheosis, or raising up to God, just as the gold of the pagans could be remolded into the basis of a new and better world.

Aurelius Augustinus was born in 354 in the Roman town of Thagaste (now Souk Ahras in eastern Algeria). His father, Patricius, was a respectable but impoverished Roman citizen who died before Augustine was twenty. His mother, Monica, was a devout Christian; Augustine portrays his father by contrast as a worldly, distant pagan. The primary means for advancement in this society was education in the classics, and this was the direction in which Augustine's ambitious parents pushed him. He completed his education at Carthage, the biggest city in North Africa, full of literary associations with Virgil's Dido and Aeneas as well as the more fleshly temptations he would detail in the *Confessions*. His early career as a teacher of rhetoric took him from Carthage to Rome and finally Milan, residence of the western emperor, Valentinian. There, Augustine encountered the learned Bishop Ambrose, who taught a Christianity steeped in the philosophy of Neoplatonism, which conceived of the divine as a spiritual force wholly distinct from things of the material world. Pushed toward a society marriage, tormented by the requisite dismissal of a beloved mistress (the mother of his son, Adeodatus), Augustine chose instead in July 386 to convert, and he was baptized the following Easter. Three years later, back in Africa, he was persuaded to accept ordination as a priest in the coastal town of Hippo Regius, where he was made bishop a few years later. He devoted the rest of his life to his church duties and to writing and engaging in a series of fierce battles over questions of doctrine. In addition to the *Confessions* (397–401) and the *City of God* (413–427), the dozens of volumes of his collected works include extensive biblical commentaries, treatises on topics such as *The Trinity* and *On Christian Doctrine,* and copious writings against several movements he succeeded in declaring heretical. Probably the most influential of all the Church Fathers, Augustine died in 430, a year before Hippo was abandoned to the invading Vandals.

Education in Augustine's day was based on repetition and memorization. He knew Latin authors such as Cicero, Virgil, and Terence nearly by heart and later also the Bible, which he cited over forty thousand times in his writings. Teaching stressed imitating the perfection of the past rather than individual creation and innovation, a practice Augustine incorporated into his account of religious conversion as fundamentally a matter of finding the correct model to imitate. The crux of the *Confessions* was persuading his readers that the Christian model was indeed the best. As a bishop, Augustine preached to a popular audience, but as a writer he had a more select group of readers in mind. The educated, sophisticated elite of the Roman Empire would not be persuaded by the humble rhetoric and plain speaking of the Gospels; they expected their religion to be aesthetically pleasing and intellectually rigorous. This is the dilemma Augustine attributes to his own spiritual search in the *Confessions*. On the one hand, he is deeply dissatisfied with his life and rapidly disillusioned with each new philosophical or religious "answer" he happens upon. On the other hand, as a rhetorician, he is disdainful of the only teaching—the Scriptures—that seems to offer what he needs: "To me they seemed quite unworthy of comparison with the stately prose of Cicero." Later, as a logician, he found equally difficult to swallow the fundamental tenets of the Trinity—the three that is one—and the Incarnation, the doctrine that Jesus could be simultaneously human and divine.

Augustine's drive to reconcile new doctrine with classical tradition led him to create a highly original book, the fullest and most personal autobiography that had ever been written. In the *Confessions*, he uses several strategies to finesse the qualms of his readers. First, he tells the story in retrospect rather than from beginning to end, so that he is able always to comment upon his wayward past from the safe harbor in which he now finds himself. In this way he can show how each apparently errant step he took—into the "hissing cauldron of lust" in Carthage, for example—could also play a role in his eventual salvation. Second, he forges a style that is elegant and full of rhetorical flourishes in the classical manner, but bound together lyrically with a cluster of modest, everyday images drawn from the language of the Bible. At times, as in the opening sections, the prose is almost entirely woven out of unmarked citations from Scripture, especially the Book of Psalms. The humble imagery of these citations—the house, the tree, the book, the song, the child—recurs throughout as a refrain, to remind us that all the other flourishes are present only so as to lead us to the very simple realization that in fact opens the book in his declaration to God: "our heart is restless until it rests in you." Everything that follows is simply a proof of this first assertion, and herein lies Augustine's third strategy: he must refute all of the competing claims to fulfillment swirling around the Empire. There were many of them, and Augustine had the sense not simply to dismiss them but to show how seductive each of them was—the emotional satisfaction of poetry, the sensual pleasure of sexual dissipation, the clarity of Manicheeism, and the profundity of Neoplatonism—in order to demonstrate what was lacking and to prove that Christianity offered the good of each without the bad.

The Goths invaded Italy in 408 and sacked Rome in 410; wealthy Roman refugees began washing up on the shores of Africa, many of them neo-pagans profoundly affected by the shock of defeat. The twenty-two books of Augustine's magnum opus, the *City of God*, set out a vision of world history in which the fall of an empire and the loss of a way of life could be regarded as a minor element in the divine scheme. Like most early Christians, Augustine lived in the certainty that the end of the world, the second coming of the Messiah, and the Last Judgment were imminent. This lends an urgency (and sometimes a virulence) to even the most arcane theological arguments he makes; it adds emotional depth to the *City of God* and increases the pathos of his mother's death in the *Confessions*. For if what finally converted Augustine to the Christian faith was the promise of rest, we only need to look at the turbulence of his life to appreciate the intensity of his longing.

PRONUNCIATIONS:
  Augustine: AHW-gus-teen
  Boethius: boh-EE-thee-uhs

Confessions

The *Confessions* is divided into thirteen books, the first nine of which recount Augustine's life through his conversion and the subsequent death of his mother, Monica. Books 10–13 are set in the present and are more philosophical in tone, discussing memory, time, and the opening verses of Genesis. The selections from Book 11 give a good sense of how the second half relates to the first, for in Augustine's mind there is a profound analogy between the many levels of experience, from the recitation of a psalm to the confession of a life's story to God's narration of the world from creation to the end of things. Seen in this perspective, the earlier episodes such as his days in grammar school, the stealing of pears, and the student days in Carthage are not only incidents in Augustine's life but also significant moments in the pattern of God's plan.

Recurring images such as the allusions to Virgil's *Aeneid* in Books 1–5 and the multiple models of conversion in Book 8 stress the patterned nature of the events of Augustine's life. Mirroring effects such as the discussion of infancy in Book 1 and the child's song in Book 8 undercut the linear flow of time and ask us to seek other means of organizing a life's story. Sin, for Augustine, is the endless repetition of the same action with no tangible result; redemption is the escape from this temporal cycle. The narrative of the *Confessions* flows because its narrator has seen his way through its events; it repeats itself because he wants us to experience what it means to be mired in the world. In its vision of life as a series of moments of conversion, in its sense of individual experience as the fulcrum through which history takes on meaning, and especially in its revolutionizing of the autobiographical form, the *Confessions* has exerted an enormous influence over Western writing, from spiritual autobiographies to confessional writing to first-person fictional narratives such as Daniel Defoe's *Robinson Crusoe* and James Joyce's *Portrait of the Artist as a Young Man.*

from Confessions[1]

from *Book 1*

[INVOCATION AND INFANCY]

You are great, Lord, and highly to be praised:[2] *great is your power and your wisdom is immeasurable.* Man, a little piece of your creation, desires to praise you, a human being *bearing his mortality with him,* carrying with him the witness of his sin and the witness that you *resist the proud.* Nevertheless, to praise you is the desire of man, a little piece of your creation. You stir man to take pleasure in praising you, because you have made us for yourself, and our heart is restless until it rests in you.

Grant me Lord to know and understand which comes first—to call upon you or to praise you, and whether knowing you precedes calling upon you. But who calls upon you when he does not know you? For an ignorant person might call upon someone else instead of the right one. But surely you may be called upon in prayer that you may be known. Yet *how shall they call upon him in whom they have not believed? and how shall they believe without a preacher? They will praise the Lord who seek for him.*

In seeking him they find him, and in finding they will praise him. Lord, I would seek you, calling upon you—and calling upon you is an act of believing in you. You have been preached to us. My faith, Lord, calls upon you. It is your gift to me. You breathed it into me by the humanity of your Son, by the ministry of your preacher.[3]

How shall I call upon my God, my God and Lord? Surely when I call on him, I am calling on him to come into me. But what place is there in me where my God can enter into me? *God made heaven and earth.* Where may he come to me? Lord my God, is there any room in me which can contain you? Can heaven and earth, which you have made and in which you have made me, contain you? Without you, whatever exists would not exist. Then can what exists contain you? I also have being. So why do I request you to come to me when, unless you were within me, I would have no being at

1. Translated by Henry Chadwick.
2. Psalm 48:1. Augustine weaves the opening of his autobiography out of a tissue of quotations from the biblical book of Psalms, hymns of praise to God traditionally attributed to King David. His text is dotted with Bible quotations (given in italics), most often from the Gospels and

the letters of Paul, in addition to Psalms. Specific sources will be noted when the biblical context is particularly important.
3. By the Incarnation of Christ as well as by the ministry of Ambrose's teacher Bishop Ambrose, the powerful church leader and influential interpreter of the Bible.

all? I am not now possessed by Hades; yet even there are you: for *even if I were to go down to Hades, you would be present.* Accordingly, my God, I would have no being, I would not have any existence, unless you were in me. Or rather, I would have no being if I were not in you *of whom are all things, through whom are all things, in whom are all things.* Even so, Lord, even so. How can I call on you to come if I am already in you? Or where can you come from so as to be in me? Can I move outside heaven and earth so that my God may come to me from there? For God has said *I fill heaven and earth.*[4]

Do heaven and earth contain you because you have filled them? or do you fill them and overflow them because they do not contain you? Where do you put the overflow of yourself after heaven and earth are filled? Or have you, who contain all things, no need to be contained by anything because what you will you fill by containing it? We cannot think you are given coherence by vessels full of you, because even if they were to be broken, you would not be spilt. When you are *poured out* upon us, you are not wasted on the ground. You raise us upright. You are not scattered but reassemble us. In filling all things, you fill them all with the whole of yourself.

Is it that because all things cannot contain the whole of you, they contain part of you, and that all things contain the same part of you simultaneously? Or does each part contain a different part of you, the larger containing the greater parts, the lesser parts the smaller? Does that imply that there is some part of you which is greater, another part smaller? Or is the whole of you everywhere, yet without anything that contains you entire?[5]

Who then are you, my God? What, I ask, but God who is Lord? For *who is the Lord but the Lord,* or *who is God but our God?* Most high, utterly good, utterly powerful, most omnipotent, most merciful and most just, deeply hidden yet most intimately present, perfection of both beauty and strength, stable and incomprehensible, immutable and yet changing all things, never new, never old, making everything new and *leading* the proud *to be old without their knowledge;* always active, always in repose, gathering to yourself but not in need, supporting and filling and protecting, creating and nurturing and bringing to maturity, searching even though to you nothing is lacking: you love without burning, you are jealous in a way that is free of anxiety, you *repent* without the pain of regret, you are wrathful and remain tranquil. You will a change without any change in your design. You recover what you find, yet have never lost. Never in any need, you rejoice in your gains; you are never avaricious, yet you require interest. We pay you more than you require so as to make you our debtor, yet who has anything which does not belong to you? You pay off debts, though owing nothing to anyone; you cancel debts and incur no loss. But in these words what have I said, my God, my life, my holy sweetness? What has anyone achieved in words when he speaks about you?[6] Yet woe to those who are silent about you because, though loquacious with verbosity, they have nothing to say.[7]

Who will enable me to find rest in you? Who will grant me that you come to my heart and intoxicate it, so that I forget my evils and embrace my one and only good, yourself? What are you to me? Have mercy so that I may find words. What am I to you that you command me to love you, and that, if I fail to love you, you are angry

4. Jeremiah 23:24. The series of questions raises philosophical and theological debates as matters of personal urgency, in particular what sort of being God is and what limits, if any, there are to his existence and his power. The questions presume a rational inquiry; the paradoxes prepare for a resolution based on faith.
5. The 3rd century C.E. Neoplatonic philosopher Plotinus had written a treatise on the omnipresence of being, part of his work the *Enneads.*
6. The long string of antitheses represents the closest words can come to expressing the essence of the Lord. As Plotinus wrote, "We say what he is not, not what he is; if we can say what is true, that is by mantic inspiration" (5.3.14). Augustine attempts to combine "mantic inspiration" with rational language.
7. For Augustine, the "loquacious" whose words cannot approach the mystery of divine revelation, were usually pagan philosophers who rejected the irrational aspects of Christianity or else the Manichees, who saw the universe as divided between a good and an evil entity.

with me and threaten me with vast miseries? If I do not love you, is that but a little misery? What a wretch I am! In your mercies, Lord God, tell me what you are to me. *Say to my soul, I am your salvation.* Speak to me so that I may hear. See the ears of my heart are before you, Lord. Open them and *say to my soul, I am your salvation.* After that utterance I will run and lay hold on you. *Do not hide your face from me.* Lest I die, let me die so that I may see it.[8]

The house of my soul is too small for you to come to it. May it be enlarged by you. It is in ruins: restore it. In your eyes it has offensive features. I admit it, I know it; but who will clean it up? Or to whom shall I cry other than you? *Cleanse me from my secret faults, Lord, and spare your servant from sins to which I am tempted by others. I believe and therefore I speak. Lord, you know.* Have I not openly accused myself of *my faults,* my God, and *you forgave me the iniquity of my heart.* I do not *contend with you in a court of law,* for you are the truth. I do not deceive myself *lest my iniquity lie to itself.* Therefore I do not contend with you like a litigant because, *if you take note of iniquities, Lord, who shall stand?*

Nevertheless allow me to speak before your mercy, though I am but dust and ashes. Allow me to speak: for I am addressing your mercy, not a man who would laugh at me. Perhaps even you deride me, but you will turn and have mercy on me. What, Lord, do I wish to say except that I do not know whence I came to be in this mortal life or, as I may call it, this living death?[9] I do not know where I came from.[1] But *the consolations of your mercies* upheld me, as I have heard from the parents of my flesh, him from whom and her in whom you formed me in time. For I do not remember. So I was welcomed by the consolations of human milk; but it was not my mother or my nurses who made any decision to fill their breasts, but you who through them gave me infant food, in accordance with your ordinance and the riches which are distributed deep in the natural order. You also granted me not to wish for more than you were giving, and to my nurses the desire to give me what you gave them. For by an impulse which you control their instinctive wish was to give me the milk which they had in abundance from you. For the good which came to me from them was a good for them; yet it was not from them but through them. Indeed all good things come from you, O God, and *from my God is all my salvation.* I became aware of this only later when you cried aloud to me through the gifts which you bestow both inwardly in mind and outwardly in body. For at that time I knew nothing more than how to suck and to be quietened by bodily delights, and to weep when I was physically uncomfortable.[2]

Afterwards I began to smile, first in my sleep, then when awake. That at least is what I was told, and I believed it since that is what we see other infants doing. I do not actually remember what I then did.

Little by little I began to be aware where I was and wanted to manifest my wishes to those who could fulfil them as I could not. For my desires were internal; adults were external to me and had no means of entering into my soul. So I threw my limbs about and uttered sounds, signs resembling my wishes, the small number of signs of which I was capable but such signs as lay in my power to use: for there was no real

8. The heavenly vision is life, yet none can see God's face and live (Exodus 33:20).
9. A common sentiment of pagan philosophy as in the 1st century B.C.E. Roman Epicurean Lucretius's *On the Nature of Things* (3.869).
1. Neoplatonic philosophy upheld the soul's preexistence

and subsequent imprisonment in the body; Augustine never explicitly affirms or denies this doctrine.
2. Augustine searches for the first time in which God was present in his life but finds that even in infancy the baby is nourished through God.

resemblance. When I did not get my way, either because I was not understood or lest it be harmful to me, I used to be indignant with my seniors for their disobedience, and with free people who were not slaves to my interests; and I would revenge myself upon them by weeping. That this is the way of infants I have learnt from those I have been able to watch. That is what I was like myself and, although they have not been aware of it, they have taught me more than my nurses with all their knowledge of how I behaved.

My infancy is long dead and I am alive.[3] But you, Lord, live and in you nothing dies. You are before the beginning of the ages, and prior to everything that can be said to be "before." You are God and Lord of all you have created. In you are the constant causes of inconstant things. All mutable things have in you their immutable origins. In you all irrational and temporal things have the everlasting causes of their life. Tell me, God, tell your suppliant, in mercy to your poor wretch, tell me whether there was some period of my life, now dead and gone, which preceded my infancy? Or is this period that which I spent in my mother's womb? On that matter also I have learnt something, and I myself have seen pregnant women. What was going on before that, my sweetness, my God? Was I anywhere, or any sort of person? I have no one able to tell me that—neither my father nor my mother nor the experience of others nor my own memory. But you may smile at me for putting these questions. Your command that I praise you and confess you may be limited to that which I know.

So *I acknowledge you, Lord of heaven and earth,* articulating my praise to you for my beginnings and my infancy which I do not recall. You have also given mankind the capacity to understand oneself by analogy with others, and to believe much about oneself on the authority of weak women. Even at that time I had existence and life, and already at the last stage of my infant speechlessness I was searching out signs by which I made my thoughts known to others. Where can a living being such as an infant come from if not from you, God? Or can anyone become the cause of his own making? Or is there any channel through which being and life can be drawn into us other than what you make us, Lord? In you it is not one thing to be and another to live: the supreme degree of being and the supreme degree of life are one and the same thing.[4] You are being in a supreme degree and are immutable. In you the present day has no ending, and yet in you it has its end: *all these things have their being in you.* They would have no way of passing away unless you set a limit to them. Because *your years do not fail,* your years are one Today. How many of our days and days of our fathers have passed during your Today, and have derived from it the measure and condition of their existence? And others too will pass away and from the same source derive the condition of their existence. "But you are the same"; and all tomorrow and hereafter, and indeed all yesterday and further back, you will make a Today, you have made a Today.[5]

If anyone finds your simultaneity beyond his understanding, it is not for me to explain it. Let him be content to say *What is this?* So too let him rejoice and delight in finding you who are beyond discovery rather than fail to find you by supposing you to be discoverable.

Hear me, God. Alas for the sins of humanity! Man it is who says this, and you have pity on him, because you made him and did not make sin in him. Who reminds

---

3. Classical writers divided human life into distinct "ages," the first of which was *infantia*, which "died" when Augustine passed to the next age, *pueritia*, or boyhood.

4. As said by the philosopher Plotinus (3.6.6.15).
5. The relationship between human time ("our days") and eternity ("your Today") is discussed at length in Book 11.

me of *the sin of my infancy? for none is pure from sin before you, not even an infant of one day upon the earth.* Who reminds me? Any tiny child now, for I see in that child what I do not remember in myself. What sin did I then have? Was it wrong that in tears I greedily opened my mouth wide to suck the breasts? If I were to do that now, gasping to eat food appropriate to my present age, I would be laughed at and very properly rebuked. At the time of my infancy I must have acted reprehensibly; but since I could not understand the person who admonished me, neither custom nor reason allowed me to be reprehended. As we grow up, we eliminate and set aside such ways. But I have never seen anyone knowingly setting aside what is good when purging something of faults.[6]

Yet, for an infant of that age, could it be reckoned good to use tears in trying to obtain what it would have been harmful to get, to be vehemently indignant at the refusals of free and older people and of parents or many other people of good sense who would not yield to my whims, and to attempt to strike them and to do as much injury as possible? There is never an obligation to be obedient to orders which it would be pernicious to obey. So the feebleness of infant limbs is innocent, not the infant's mind. I have personally watched and studied a jealous baby. He could not yet speak and, pale with jealousy and bitterness, glared at his brother sharing his mother's milk. Who is unaware of this fact of experience? Mothers and nurses claim to charm it away by their own private remedies. But it can hardly be innocence, when the source of milk is flowing richly and abundantly, not to endure a share going to one's blood-brother, who is in profound need, dependent for life exclusively on that one food.

But people smilingly tolerate this behaviour, not because it is nothing or only a trivial matter, but because with coming of age it will pass away. You can prove this to be the case from the fact that the same behaviour cannot be borne without irritation when encountered in someone of more mature years.

You, Lord my God, are the giver of life and a body to a baby. As we see, you have endowed it with senses. You have co-ordinated the limbs. You have adorned it with a beautiful form, and for the coherence and preservation of the whole you have implanted all the instincts of a living being. You therefore command me to praise you for that and to *confess to you and to sing to your name, Most High*—God, you are omnipotent and good—even if that were all that you had made. No one else could do that except you, the one from whom every kind of being is derived. The supreme beauty, you give distinct form to all things and by your law impose order on everything. This period of my life, Lord, I do not remember having lived, but I have believed what others have told me and have assumed how I behaved from observing other infants. Despite the high probability of this assumption, I do not wish to reckon this as part of the life that I live in this world; for it is lost in the darkness of my forgetfulness, and is on the same level as the life I lived in my mother's womb. If *I was conceived in iniquity and in sins my mother nourished me in her womb,* I ask you, my God, I ask, Lord, where and when your servant was innocent? But of that time I say nothing more. I feel no sense of responsibility now for a time of which I recall not a single trace.[7]

[*Augustine describes his boyhood, including his introduction to the Church and the desire for baptism instilled in him by the fear of death. Monica, his mother, refuses to*

---

6. Augustine views children as naturally sinful rather than innocent, their behavior moderated only as they learn through "custom" and "reason."
7. God's creation is defined in Genesis as essentially beautiful and good, and so each individual as part of that creation must consequently have been made beautiful and good. Nevertheless, it is impossible to discover a time when the individual was not already tainted by sin.

baptize him, fearing that it would be too difficult to wash away all the sins he was likely to commit in the future.]

[GRAMMAR SCHOOL]

Even now I have not yet discovered the reasons why I hated Greek literature when I was being taught it as a small boy.[8] Latin I deeply loved, not at the stage of my primary teachers but at the secondary level taught by the teachers of literature called "grammarians." The initial elements, where one learns the three Rs of reading, writing, and arithmetic, I felt to be no less a burden and an infliction than the entire series of Greek classes. The root of this aversion must simply have been sin and the vanity of life, by which I was *mere flesh and wind going on its way and not returning.* Of course, those first elements of the language were better, because more fundamental. On that foundation I came to acquire the faculty which I had and still possess of being able to read whatever I find written, and to write myself whatever I wish. This was better than the poetry I was later forced to learn about the wanderings of some legendary fellow named Aeneas (forgetful of my own wanderings) and to weep over the death of a Dido who took her own life from love.[9] In reading this, O God my life, I myself was meanwhile dying by my alienation from you, and my miserable condition in that respect brought no tear to my eyes.

What is more pitiable than a wretch without pity for himself who weeps over the death of Dido dying for love of Aeneas, but not weeping over himself dying for his lack of love for you, my God, light of my heart, bread of the inner mouth of my soul, the power which begets life in my mind and in the innermost recesses of my thinking. I had no love for you and *committed fornication against you;* and in my fornications I heard all round me the cries *Well done, well done. For the friendship of this world is fornication against you,* and "Well done" is what they say to shame a man who does not go along with them. Over this I wept not a tear. I wept over Dido who "died in pursuing her ultimate end with a sword."[1] I abandoned you to pursue the lowest things of your creation. I was dust going to dust. Had I been forbidden to read this story, I would have been sad that I could not read what made me sad. Such madness is considered a higher and more fruitful literary education than being taught to read and write.

But now may my God cry out in my soul and may your truth tell me: "It is not so, it is not so. The best education you received was the primary." Obviously I much prefer to forget the wanderings of Aeneas and all that stuff than to write and read. It is true, veils hang at the entrances to the schools of literature; but they do not signify the prestige of élite teaching so much as the covering up of error.[2]

Let no critics shout against me (I am not afraid of them now) while I confess to you the longing of my soul, my God, and when I accept rebuke for my evil ways and

8. Although not fluent, Augustine could read Greek and was more proficient than he lets on here.
9. Although Augustine speaks about it disparagingly, Virgil's *Aeneid* was a formative influence on his writing, and he cites it frequently. The episode referred to here is the tragic love affair of Book 4. The opposition between the pointless wanderings of the pagan and the (eventually) fruitful wanderings of the convert Augustine is a fundamental one in the *Confessions.*
1. *Aeneid* 6.457.
2. During the Roman Empire, it was customary to hang veils before an entrance in a number proportionate to the importance of whomever or whatever they guarded. In addition to the attack on the use of poetic fictions for educational purposes, Augustine is also drawing a distinction between the direct and unadorned language of the Bible and the complex and often allegorical imagery he saw in classical poetry, "veils" covering up the "error" of the beliefs propounded in it. In addition to the foundation of the curriculum of grammar school, Virgil's poetry was also considered a sacred text of the pagan revival current during the 4th century (see Macrobius, *Saturnalia,* page 1202).

wish to love your good ways. Let there be no abuse of me from people who sell or buy a literary education. If I put the question to them whether the poet's story is true that Aeneas once came to Carthage, the uneducated will reply that they do not know, while the educated will say it is false. But if I ask with what letters Aeneas' name is spelled, all who have learnt to read will reply correctly in accordance with the agreement and convention by which human beings have determined the value of these signs. Similarly, if I ask which would cause the greater inconvenience to someone's life, to forget how to read and write or to forget these fabulous poems, who does not see what answer he would give, unless he has totally lost his senses? So it was a sin in me as a boy when I gave pride of place in my affection to those empty fables rather than to more useful studies, or rather when I hated the one and loved the other. But to me it was a hateful chant to recite "one and one is two," and "two and two are four"; delightful was the vain spectacle of the wooden horse full of armed soldiers and the burning of Troy and the very ghost of Creusa.[3]

from *Book 2*

[THE PEAR-TREE]

During my sixteenth year there was an interruption in my studies. I was recalled from Madauros,[1] the nearby town where I had first lived away from home to learn literature and oratory. During that time funds were gathered in preparation for a more distant absence at Carthage,[2] for which my father had more enthusiasm than cash, since he was a citizen of Thagaste with very modest resources.[3] To whom do I tell these things? Not to you, my God. But before you I declare this to my race, to the human race, though only a tiny part can light on this composition of mine. And why do I include this episode? It is that I and any of my readers may reflect on *the great depth* from which we have *to cry to you.* Nothing is nearer to your ears than *a confessing heart* and a life grounded in faith.[4] At that time everybody was full of praise for my father because he spent money on his son beyond the means of his estate, when that was necessary to finance an education entailing a long journey. Many citizens of far greater wealth did nothing of the kind for their children. But this same father did not care what character before you I was developing, or how chaste I was so long as I possessed a cultured tongue—though my culture really meant a desert uncultivated by you, God. You are the one true and good lord of your land, which is my heart.

In my sixteenth year idleness interposed because of my family's lack of funds. I was on holiday from all schooling and lived with my parents. The thorns of lust rose above my head, and there was no hand to root them out. Indeed, when at the bathhouse my father saw that I was showing signs of virility and the stirrings of adolescence, he was overjoyed to suppose that he would now be having grand-children, and told my mother so. His delight was that of the intoxication which makes the world oblivious of you, its Creator, and to love your creation instead of you. He was drunk with the invisible wine of his perverse will directed downwards to inferior things. But

---

3. Episodes in the fall of Troy narrated in Book 2 of the *Aeneid:* the enormous wooden horse that smuggles the Greek warriors into the city in its belly, the sacking of the city that ensues, and the ghost of Aeneas's first wife, which begs him to flee the city.
1. An intellectual center about 15 miles from Thagaste.
2. Capital of the Roman province of Numidia in northern

Africa.
3. Augustine's father, Patricius, was respectable but poor by Roman standards, owning a modest estate with a few slaves to keep the household and work the land.
4. In Romans 10:9, Paul describes verbal confession as a key step in revelation.

in my mother's heart you had already begun your temple and the beginning of *your holy habitation*. My father was still a catechumen and had become that only recently. So she shook with a pious trepidation and a holy fear.[5] For, although I had not yet become a baptized believer,[6] she feared the twisted paths along which walk those who turn their backs and not their face towards you.

Wretch that I am, do I dare to say that you, my God, were silent when in reality I was travelling farther from you? Was it in this sense that you kept silence to me? Then whose words were they but yours which you were chanting in my ears through my mother, your faithful servant? But nothing of that went down into my heart to issue in action. Her concern (and in the secret of my conscience I recall the memory of her admonition delivered with vehement anxiety) was that I should not fall into fornication, and above all that I should not commit adultery with someone else's wife. These warnings seemed to me womanish advice which I would have blushed to take the least notice of. But they were your warnings and I did not realize it. I believed you were silent, and that it was only she who was speaking, when you were speaking to me through her. In her you were scorned by me, by me her son, *the son of your handmaid, your servant*. But I did not realize this and went on my way headlong with such blindness that among my peer group I was ashamed not to be equally guilty of shameful behaviour when I heard them boasting of their sexual exploits. Their pride was the more aggressive, the more debauched their acts were; they derived pleasure not merely from the lust of the act but also from the admiration it evoked. What is more worthy of censure than vice? Yet I went deeper into vice to avoid being despised, and when there was no act by admitting to which I could rival my depraved companions, I used to pretend I had done things I had not done at all, so that my innocence should not lead my companions to scorn my lack of courage, and lest my chastity be taken as a mark of inferiority.

Such were the companions with whom I made my way through the streets of Babylon.[7] With them I rolled in its dung as if rolling *in spices and precious ointments*. To tie me down the more tenaciously to Babylon's belly, the *invisible enemy trampled on me*[8] and seduced me because I was in the mood to be seduced. The mother of my flesh already had fled from *the centre of Babylon*, but still lingered in the outskirts of the city.[9] Although she had warned me to guard my virginity, she did not seriously pay heed to what her husband had told her about me, and which she felt to hold danger for the future: for she did not seek to restrain my sexual drive within the limit of the marriage bond, if it could not be cut back to the quick. The reason why she showed no such concern was that she was afraid that the hope she placed in me could be impeded by a wife. This was not the hope which my mother placed in you for the life to come, but the hope which my parents entertained for my career that I might do well out of the study of literature. Both of them, as I realized, were very ambitious for me: my father because he hardly gave a thought to you at all, and his ambitions for me

5. Augustine portrays his parents here as embodying a strict opposition between flesh and spirit, earthly concerns and celestial ones. A catechumen is a convert to Christianity who is receiving training in doctrine and discipline before being baptized.
6. The sins of a pagan were more easily erased by conversion than those of a baptized Christian could be absolved.
7. In the Bible, Babylon (in southern Mesopotamia) was the proverbial city of pagan iniquity. Augustine uses it here to refer both literally to the North African streets he wandered with his companions and figuratively to his wandering through the earthly city of sin rather than toward the heavenly city of salvation.
8. Psalm 56:2. The "invisible enemy" is Satan.
9. Here, Babylon is primarily metaphorical. His mother lingers on the edges of the earthly city in order to maintain contact with her wayward son, and because she herself still retains earthly values such as ambitions for her son's career.

were concerned with mere vanities; my mother because she thought it would do no harm and would be a help to set me on the way towards you, if I studied the traditional pattern of a literary education. That at least is my conjecture as I try to recall the characters of my parents.

The reins were relaxed to allow me to amuse myself. There was no strict discipline to keep me in check, which led to an unbridled dissoluteness in many different directions. In all of this there was a thick mist shutting me off from the brightness of your face, my God, and my iniquity as it were *burst out from my fatness.*

Theft receives certain punishment *by your law,* Lord, and by *the law written in the hearts of men* which not even iniquity itself destroys. For what thief can with equanimity endure being robbed by another thief? He cannot tolerate it even if he is rich and the other is destitute. I wanted to carry out an act of theft and did so, driven by no kind of need other than my inner lack of any sense of, or feeling for, justice. Wickedness filled me. I stole something which I had in plenty and of much better quality. My desire was to enjoy not what I sought by stealing but merely the excitement of thieving and the doing of what was wrong. There was a pear tree near our vineyard laden with fruit, though attractive in neither colour nor taste. To shake the fruit off the tree and carry off the pears, I and a gang of naughty adolescents set off late at night after (in our usual pestilential way) we had continued our game in the streets. We carried off a huge load of pears. But they were not for our feasts but merely to throw to the pigs. Even if we ate a few, nevertheless our pleasure lay in doing what was not allowed.[1]

Such was my heart, O God, such was my heart. You had pity on it when it was at the bottom of the abyss.[2] Now let my heart tell you what it was seeking there in that I became evil for no reason. I had no motive for my wickedness except wickedness itself. It was foul, and I loved it. I loved the self-destruction, I loved my fall, not the object for which I had fallen but my fall itself. My depraved soul leaped down from your firmament to ruin. I was seeking not to gain anything by shameful means, but shame for its own sake.

There is beauty in lovely physical objects, as in gold and silver and all other such things. When the body touches such things, much significance attaches to the rapport of the object with the touch. Each of the other senses has its own appropriate mode of response to physical things. Temporal honour and the power of giving orders and of being in command have their own kind of dignity, though this is also the origin of the urge to self-assertion. Yet in the acquisition of all these sources of social status, one must not depart from you, Lord, nor deviate from your law. The life which we live in this world has its attractiveness because of a certain measure in its beauty and its harmony with all these inferior objects that are beautiful. Human friendship is also a nest of love and gentleness because of the unity it brings about between many souls. Yet sin is committed for the sake of all these things and others of this kind when, in consequence of an immoderate urge towards those things which are at the bottom end of the scale of good, we abandon the higher and supreme goods, that is you, Lord God,

1. The pear tree demands comparison with the apple in Eden; here, however, the fruit is unripe and fit only for swine. Augustine likens himself both to the unripe fruit, awaiting the proper time to be plucked by God, and to the swine, a reflection of his current bestial behavior.

2. Comparing his actions with the apparently incomprehensible rebellion of the angel Lucifer. In addition to its biblical echoes, this episode recalls the Roman historian Sallust's depiction of the famous conspirator Catiline (c. 108–62 B.C.E.), who attempted to overthrow the republic during the consulship of Cicero.

and *your truth and your law*.[3] These inferior goods have their delights, but not comparable to my God who has made them all. It is in him that the just person takes delight; he is the joy of those who are true of heart.

When a crime is under investigation to discover the motive for which it was done, the accusation is not usually believed except in cases where the appetite to obtain (or the fear of losing) one of those goods which we have called inferior appears a plausible possibility. They are beautiful and attractive even if, in comparison with the higher goods which give true happiness, they are mean and base. A man committed murder. Why? Because he loved another's wife or his property; or he wanted to acquire money to live on by plundering his goods; or he was afraid of losing his own property by the action of his victim; or he had suffered injury and burned with desire for revenge. No one would commit murder without a motive, merely because he took pleasure in killing. Who would believe that? It was said of one brutal and cruel man that he was evil and savage without reason.[4] Yet the preceding passage gave the motive: "lest disuse might make his hand or mind slow to react." Why did he wish for that? Why so? His objective was to capture the city by violent crimes to obtain honours, government, and wealth; to live without fear of the laws and without the difficulty of attaining his ambitions because of the poverty of his family estate and his known criminal record. No, not even Catiline himself loved his crimes; something else motivated him to commit them.

Wretch that I was, what did I love in you, my act of theft, that crime which I did at night in the sixteenth year of my life? There was nothing beautiful about you, my thieving. Indeed do you exist at all for me to be addressing you?

The fruit which we stole was beautiful because it was your creation, most beautiful of all Beings, maker of all things, the good God, God the highest good and my true good. The fruit was beautiful, but was not that which my miserable soul coveted. I had a quantity of better pears. But those I picked solely with the motive of stealing. I threw away what I had picked. My feasting was only on the wickedness which I took pleasure in enjoying. If any of those pears entered my mouth, my criminality was the piquant sauce. And now, Lord my God, I inquire what was the nature of my pleasure in the theft. The act has nothing lovely about it, none of the loveliness found in equity and prudence, or in the human mind whether in the memory or in the senses or in physical vitality. Nor was it beautiful in the way the stars are, noble in their courses, or earth and sea full of newborn creatures which, as they are born, take the place of those which die; not even in the way that specious vices have a flawed reflection of beauty.

Pride imitates what is lofty; but you alone are God most high above all things. What does ambition seek but honour and glory? Yet you alone are worthy of honour and are glorious for eternity. The cruelty of powerful people aims to arouse fear. Who is to be feared but God alone? What can be seized or stolen from his power? When or where or how or by whom? Soft endearments are intended to arouse love. But there are no caresses tenderer than your charity, and no object of love is more healthy than your truth, beautiful and luminous beyond all things. Curiosity appears to be a zeal for knowledge; yet you supremely know all. Ignorance and stupidity are given the names

3. According to this argument, all things of the world are good, and all desires derive from an impulse toward the good, but there is a gradation of this good; sin occurs when the lower aspects of the creation are desired for their own qualities rather than for what of the greater good they may contain.
4. Sallust, *The Catiline War*, chapter 16.

of simplicity and innocence; but there is no greater simplicity than in you. And what greater innocence than yours, whereas to evil men their own works are damaging? Idleness appears as desire for a quiet life; yet can rest be assured apart from the Lord? Luxury wants to be called abundance and satiety; but you are fullness and the inexhaustible treasure of incorruptible pleasure. Prodigality presents itself under the shadow of generosity; but you are the rich bestower of all good things. Avarice wishes to have large possessions; you possess everything. Envy contends about excellence; but what is more excellent than you? Anger seeks revenge; who avenges with greater justice than you? Fear quails before sudden and unexpected events attacking things which are loved, and takes precautions for their safety; to you is anything unexpected or sudden? Or who can take away from you what you love? There is no reliable security except with you. Regret wastes away for the loss of things which cupidity delighted in. Its wish would be that nothing be taken away, just as nothing can be taken from you.

So the soul fornicates when it is turned away from you and seeks outside you the pure and clear intentions which are not to be found except by returning to you. In their perverted way all humanity imitates you.[5] Yet they put themselves at a distance from you and exalt themselves against you. But even by thus imitating you they acknowledge that you are the creator of all nature and so concede that there is no place where one can entirely escape from you. Therefore in that act of theft what was the object of my love, and in what way did I viciously and perversely imitate my Lord? Was my pleasure to break your law, but by deceit since I had not the power to do that by force? Was I acting like a prisoner with restricted liberty who does without punishment what is not permitted, thereby making an assertion of possessing a dim resemblance to omnipotence? Here is a runaway slave fleeing his master and *pursuing a shadow*. What rottenness! What a monstrous life and what an abyss of death! Was it possible to take pleasure in what was illicit for no reason other than that it was not allowed?

from *Book 3*

[STUDENT AT CARTHAGE]

I came to Carthage and all around me hissed a cauldron of illicit loves. As yet I had never been in love and I longed to love; and from a subconscious poverty of mind I hated the thought of being less inwardly destitute. I sought an object for my love; I was in love with love, and I hated safety and *a path free of snares*. My hunger was internal, deprived of inward food, that is of you yourself, my God. But that was not the kind of hunger I felt. I was without any desire for incorruptible nourishment, not because I was replete with it, but the emptier I was, the more unappetizing such food became. So my soul was in rotten health. In an ulcerous condition it thrust itself to outward things, miserably avid to be scratched by contact with the world of the senses. Yet physical things had no soul. Love lay outside their range. To me it was sweet to love and to be loved, the more so if I could also enjoy the body of the beloved. I therefore polluted the spring water of friendship with the filth of concupiscence. I muddied its clear stream by the hell of lust, and yet, though foul and immoral, in my excessive vanity, I used to carry on in the manner of an elegant man about town. I rushed headlong into love, by which I was longing to be captured. *My God,*

---

5. In this definition, all sin is the perverse—*per* ("from") + *vertere* ("to turn")—imitation of the divine.

my mercy in your goodness you mixed in much vinegar with that sweetness. My love was returned and in secret. I attained the joy that enchains. I was glad to be in bondage, tied with troublesome chains, with the result that I was flogged with the red-hot iron rods of jealousy, suspicion, fear, anger, and contention.[1]

I was captivated by theatrical shows. They were full of representations of my own miseries and fuelled my fire. Why is it that a person should wish to experience suffering by watching grievous and tragic events which he himself would not wish to endure? Nevertheless he wants to suffer the pain given by being a spectator of these sufferings, and the pain itself is his pleasure. What is this but amazing folly? For the more anyone is moved by these scenes, the less free he is from similar passions. Only, when he himself suffers, it is called misery; when he feels compassion for others, it is called mercy. But what quality of mercy is it in fictitious and theatrical inventions? A member of the audience is not excited to offer help, but invited only to grieve. The greater his pain, the greater his approval of the actor in these representations. If the human calamities, whether in ancient histories or fictitious myths, are so presented that the theatregoer is not caused pain, he walks out of the theatre disgusted and highly critical. But if he feels pain, he stays riveted in his seat enjoying himself.[2]

Tears and agonies, therefore, are objects of love. Certainly everyone wishes to enjoy himself. Is it that while no one wants to be miserable, yet it is agreeable to feel merciful? Mercy cannot exist apart from suffering. Is that the sole reason why agonies are an object of love? This feeling flows from the stream of friendship; but where does it go? Where does it flow to? Why does it run down into the torrent of boiling pitch, the monstrous heats of black desires into which it is transformed? From a heavenly serenity it is altered by its own consent into something twisted and distorted. Does this mean mercy is to be rejected? Not in the least. At times, therefore, sufferings can be proper objects of love. But, my soul, be on your guard against uncleanness, under the protection of my God, *the God of our fathers, to be praised and exalted above all for all ages;* be on your guard against uncleanness. Even today I am not unmoved to pity. But at that time at the theatres I shared the joy of lovers when they wickedly found delight in each other, even though their actions in the spectacle on the stage were imaginary; when, moreover, they lost each other, I shared their sadness by a feeling of compassion. Nevertheless, in both there was pleasure. Today I have more pity for a person who rejoices in wickedness than for a person who has the feeling of having suffered hard knocks by being deprived of a pernicious pleasure or having lost a source of miserable felicity. This is surely a more authentic compassion; for the sorrow contains no element of pleasure.

Even if we approve of a person who, from a sense of duty in charity, is sorry for a wretch, yet he who manifests fraternal compassion would prefer that there be no cause for sorrow. It is only if there could be a malicious good will (which is impossible) that someone who truly and sincerely felt compassion would wish wretches to exist so as to be objects of compassion. Therefore some kind of suffering is commendable, but none is lovable. You, Lord God, lover of souls, show a compassion far purer and freer of mixed motives than ours; for no suffering injures you. *And who is sufficient for these things?*

---

1. Criminals were beaten with red-hot rods to obtain evidence.

2. This critique of the theory of tragic pity and fear leading to catharsis takes up a debate addressed by both Plato and Aristotle.

But at that time, poor thing that I was, I loved to suffer and sought out occasions for such suffering. So when an actor on stage gave a fictional imitation of someone else's misfortunes, I was the more pleased; and the more vehement the attraction for me, the more the actor compelled my tears to flow. There can be no surprise that an unhappy sheep wandering from your flock and impatient of your protection was infected by a disgusting sore.[3] Hence came my love for sufferings, but not of a kind that pierced me very deeply; for my longing was not to experience myself miseries such as I saw on stage. I wanted only to hear stories and imaginary legends of sufferings which, as it were, scratched me on the surface. Yet like the scratches of fingernails, they produced inflamed spots, pus, and repulsive sores. That was my kind of life, Surely, my God, it was no real life at all?

Your mercy faithfully hovered over me from afar. In what iniquities was I wasting myself! I pursued a sacrilegious quest for knowledge, which led me, a deserter from you, down to faithless depths and the fraudulent service of devils. The sacrifices I offered them were my evil acts. And in all this I experienced your chastisement. During the celebration of your solemn rites within the walls of your Church, I even dared to lust after a girl and to start an affair that would procure the fruit of death.[4] So you beat me with heavy punishments, but not the equivalent of my guilt; *O my God, my great mercy, my refuge* from the terrible dangers in which I was wandering. My stiff neck took me further and further away from you. I loved my own ways, not yours. The liberty I loved was merely that of a runaway.[5]

My studies which were deemed respectable had the objective of leading me to distinction as an advocate in the lawcourts, where one's reputation is high in proportion to one's success in deceiving people. The blindness of humanity is so great that people are actually proud of their blindness. I was already top of the class in the rhetor's school;[6] and was pleased with myself for my success and was inflated with conceit. Yet I was far quieter than the other students (as you know, Lord), and had nothing whatever to do with the vandalism which used to be carried out by the Wreckers. This sinister and diabolical self-designation was a kind of mark of their urbane sophistication. I lived among them shamelessly ashamed of not being one of the gang. I kept company with them and sometimes delighted in their friendship, though I always held their actions in abhorrence. The Wreckers used wantonly to persecute shy and unknown freshmen. Their aim was to persecute them by mockery and so to feed their own malevolent amusement. Nothing more resembles the behaviour of devils than their manner of carrying on. So no truer name could be given them than the Wreckers. Clearly they are themselves wrecked first of all and perverted by evil spirits, who are mocking them and seducing them in the very acts by which they love to mock and deceive others.

This was the society in which at a vulnerable age I was to study the textbooks on eloquence. I wanted to distinguish myself as an orator for a damnable and conceited purpose, namely delight in human vanity. Following the usual curriculum I had

---

3. This echoes Virgil's *Eclogue* 3.3; see also Luke 15:4ff. The parable of the lost sheep was a fundamental image of Christian conversion. The concluding detail of the "disgusting sore" is Augustine's own embellishment, making the state of being lost not only natural but an excessive suffering for its straying.

4. The "fruit of death" is sin (Romans 7:5). For Augustine, there could be no more egregiously misplaced desire

than to have sex in a church.

5. Augustine again likens himself to a runaway slave of the Lord. To run away from one's master was a grave offense in antiquity. Few individuals were powerful enough to shelter a runaway slave, but the church could provide temporary asylum under certain circumstances.

6. The school run by the teacher of rhetoric, or the art of public speaking.

already come across a book by a certain Cicero, whose language (but not his heart) almost everyone admires. That book of his contains an exhortation to study philosophy and is entitled *Hortensius*.[7] The book changed my feelings. It altered my prayers, Lord, to be towards you yourself. It gave me different values and priorities. Suddenly every vain hope became empty to me, and I longed for the immortality of wisdom with an incredible ardour in my heart. I began to rise up to return to you. For I did not read the book for a sharpening of my style, which was what I was buying with my mother's financial support now that I was 18 years old and my father had been dead for two years.[8] I was impressed not by the book's refining effect on my style and literary expression but by the content.

My God, how I burned, how I burned with longing to leave earthly things and fly back to you. I did not know what you were doing with me. For *with you is wisdom*. "Love of wisdom" is the meaning of the Greek word *philosophia*.[9] This book kindled my love for it. There are some people who use philosophy to lead people astray. They lend colour to their errors and paint them over by using a great and acceptable and honourable name. Almost all those who in the author's times and earlier behaved in this way are noted in that book and refuted. That text is a clear demonstration of the salutary admonition given by your Spirit through your good and devoted servant (Paul): "See that none deceives you by philosophy and vain seduction following human tradition; following the elements of this world and not following Christ; in him dwells all the fullness of divinity in bodily form."[1] At that time, as you know, light of my heart, I did not yet know these words of the apostle. Nevertheless, the one thing that delighted me in Cicero's exhortation was the advice "not to study one particular sect but to love and seek and pursue and hold fast and strongly embrace wisdom itself, wherever found."[2] One thing alone put a brake on my intense enthusiasm—that the name of Christ was not contained in the book. This name, by your mercy, Lord, this name of my Saviour your Son, my infant heart had piously drunk in with my mother's milk, and at a deep level I retained the memory. Any book which lacked this name, however well written or polished or true, could not entirely grip me.

I therefore decided to give attention to the holy scriptures and to find out what they were like. And this is what met me: something neither open to the proud nor laid bare to mere children; a text lowly to the beginner but, on further reading, of mountainous difficulty and enveloped in mysteries. I was not in any state to be able to enter into that, or to bow my head to climb its steps.[3] What I am now saying did not then enter my mind when I gave my attention to the scripture. It seemed to me unworthy in comparison with the dignity of Cicero. My inflated conceit shunned the Bible's restraint, and my gaze never penetrated to its inwardness. Yet the Bible was composed in such a way that as beginners mature, its meaning grows with them. I disdained to be a little beginner. Puffed up with pride, I considered myself a mature adult.

That explains why I fell in with men proud of their slick talk, very earthly-minded and loquacious. In their mouths were the devil's traps and a birdlime compounded of a mixture of the syllables of your name, and that of the Lord Jesus

---

7. Marcus Tullius Cicero (106–43 B.C.E.) was Rome's greatest orator, an important political figure of the late republic, and an extremely influential writer of rhetoric and philosophy. Composed near the end of Cicero's life, the *Hortensius* survives where it has been quoted by later writers such as Augustine. It argued that philosophy fulfilled a social purpose and that it could demonstrate the way to achieve happiness.

8. This is the first reference to the death of Patricius.
9. A sentence drawn from Cicero's *Hortensius*.
1. Colossians 2:8–9. The "good and devoted servant" is the apostle Paul.
2. Another sentence from the *Hortensius*.
3. The image of humility recalls the words of the Arcadian King Evander to Aeneas when inviting the latter into his humble abode (*Aeneid*, page 1109).

Christ, and that of the Paraclete, the Comforter, the Holy Spirit.[4] These names were never absent from their lips; but it was no more than sound and noise with their tongue. Otherwise their heart was empty of truth. They used to say "Truth, truth," and they had a lot to tell me about it; but there was never any truth in them. They uttered false statements not only about you who really are the Truth, but also about the elements of the world, your creation. On that subject the philosophers have said things which are true, but even them I would think to be no final authority for love of you, my supremely good Father, beauty of all things beautiful. Truth, truth: how in my inmost being the very marrow of my mind sighed for you! Those people used to sound off about you to me frequently and repeatedly with mere assertions and with the support of many huge tomes.[5] To meet my hunger, instead of you they brought me a diet of the sun and moon, your beautiful works— but they are your works, not you yourself, nor indeed the first of your works. For priority goes to your spiritual creation rather than the physical order, however heavenly and full of light.[6] But for myself, my hunger and thirst were not even for the spiritual creation but for you yourself, the truth *in whom there is no changing nor shadow caused by any revolving.* The dishes they placed before me contained splendid hallucinations. Indeed one would do better to love this visible sun, which at least is truly evident to the eyes, than those false mythologies which use the eyes to deceive the mind. Nevertheless, because I took them to be you, I ate—not indeed with much of an appetite, for the taste in my mouth was not that of yourself. You were not those empty fictions, and I derived no nourishment from them but was left more exhausted than before.

Food pictured in dreams is extremely like food received in the waking state; yet sleepers receive no nourishment, they are simply sleeping. But those fantasies had not the least resemblance to you as you have now told me, because they were physical images, fictional bodily shapes. But more certain objects of knowledge are the actually existing bodies which we see with our physical sight, whether they are celestial or earthly. We see them just as beasts and birds do, and they are more certain than the images we form of them. And yet again the pictures of these realities which our imagination forms are more reliable than the mythological pictures of vast and unlimited entities whose being, by an extension of our image-making of real objects, we may postulate, but which do not exist at all.[7] Such were the empty phantoms with which I was fed or rather was not fed.

But you, my love, for whom I faint *that I may receive strength,* you are not the bodies which we see, though they be up in heaven, nor even any object up there lying

---

4. These are the Manichees, members of a religion founded in Persia in the 3rd century c.e. by Mani. The 4th century marked its height in the West, but it was pretty much eradicated by the next century, following vigorous attack from the Christian church (including Augustine), which considered it a heresy of Christianity, and by the Roman state, which considered it a threat to its authority. Aiming to be a universal religion, Manicheeism was Gnostic at its core, teaching that existence was radically divided between Spirit and Matter, Good and Evil, and Light and Darkness; that life in the world is unbearably evil; and that the righteous soul must transcend the body and the material world to discover its true soul and the nature of God. The Manichees denied the humanity of Christ, believing only in his divine nature, and held that the third aspect of the Trinity, the Paraclete, or Holy Spirit, was a manifestation of Mani.

5. In contrast to the simply bound liturgical books of most of the mainstream Christian churches, those of the Manichees were beautifully bound and decorated.

6. Augustine maintained that Genesis 1:1 describes God's creation of a spiritual "heaven" and of unformed matter called "earth," which was given its shape in the second account of creation in Genesis. (See Book 12 of the *Confessions* as well his treatise *On Genesis Against the Manichees.*)

7. Because dreams seem so real, Augustine regards them with suspicion. Nevertheless, they can still be of use in advising people or leading them to convert. Here, their "image-making" is preferable to the "mythological pictures" of the Manichean cosmology.

beyond our sight. For you have made these bodies, and you do not even hold them to be among the greatest of your creatures. How far removed you are from those fantasies of mine, fantasies of physical entities which have no existence! We have more reliable knowledge in our images of bodies which really exist, and the bodies are more certain than the images. But you are no body. Nor are you soul, which is the life of bodies; for the life of bodies is superior to bodies themselves, and a more certain object of knowledge. But you are the life of souls, the life of lives. You live in dependence only on yourself, and you never change, life of my soul.

At that time where were you in relation to me? Far distant. Indeed I wandered far away, separated from you, not even granted to share in the husks of the pigs, whom I was feeding with husks.[8] How superior are the fables of the masters of literature and poets to these deceptive traps! For verses, poems, and "the flight of Medea" are certainly more useful than the Five Elements which take on different colours, each in accordance with one of the Five Caverns of Darkness—things which have no reality whatever and kill anyone who believes they have.[9] Verses and poetry I can transform into real nourishment. "Medea flying through the air" I might recite, but would not assert to be fact. Even if I heard someone reciting the passage, I would not believe it. Yet the other myths I did believe. Wretched man that I was, by what steps was I brought down to the depths of hell, there to toil and sweat from lack of truth! For I sought for you, my God (I confess to you who took pity on me even when I did not yet confess). In seeking for you I followed not the intelligence of the mind, by which you willed that I should surpass the beasts, but the mind of the flesh. But you were more inward than my most inward part and higher than the highest element within me.

I had stumbled on that bold-faced woman, lacking in prudence, who in Solomon's allegory sits on a chair outside her door and says "Enjoy a meal of secret bread and drink sweet stolen water."[1] She seduced me; for she found me living outside myself, seeing only with the eye of the flesh, and chewing over in myself such food as I had devoured by means of that eye.[2]

[*In Book 4, Augustine recounts the life of "vain desires" he led in Carthage, including the mistress who eventually bore him a son, Adeodatus; his consultation of astrologers; and the conversion of his friend, Nebridius, who was baptized without his knowledge while thought to be dying of a fever. He writes a first book, now lost,* On the Beautiful and the Fitting, *and encounters Aristotle's treatise* Ten Categories *but cannot find God within its classifications.*]

from *Book 5*

[*The Manichean bishop Faustus comes to Carthage, an encounter Augustine claims to have been awaiting during his nine years under the sway of the Manichees. He*

---

8. The image of the husks fed to pigs recalls both the episode of the pear tree and the parable of the Prodigal Son, who at his furthest from his father finds himself feeding on husks with the pigs (Luke 15:16).

9. Just as dreams are deceptive but may be useful, so poetic fables have the potential of being "transform[ed] into real nourishment." The magical flight of Medea from Jason after she has murdered their two children in vengeance for his betrayal (see Ovid's *Metamorphoses,* page 1208) was probably a standard subject for rhetorical exercises. The Five Elements are part of Manichean

doctrine on the generation of animals.

1. Proverbs 9:17. King Solomon was considered to have been the author of Proverbs as well as of the Song of Songs.

2. Just as he distinguishes between the "intelligence of the mind," directed upward, and the "mind of the flesh," directed downward, so too Augustine distinguishes between an eye of the flesh, which seeks only physical nourishment and satisfaction, and an eye able to see what is spiritual.

discovers that Faustus, while a smooth talker, is neither well educated in the liberal arts nor able to answer any of his questions. Augustine becomes disillusioned with the Manichean religion, one motivation for his decision to move to Rome.]

[ARRIVAL IN ROME]

You were at work in persuading me to go to Rome and to do my teaching there rather than at Carthage. The consideration which persuaded me I will not omit to confess to you because in this also your profoundly mysterious providence and your mercy very present to us are proper matters for reflection and proclamation. My motive in going to Rome was not that the friends who urged it on me promised higher fees and a greater position of dignity, though at that time these considerations had an influence on my mind. The principal and almost sole reason was that I had heard how at Rome the young men went quietly about their studies and were kept in order by a stricter imposition of discipline. They did not rush all at once and in a mob into the class of a teacher with whom they were not enrolled, nor were pupils admitted at all unless the teacher gave them leave. By contrast at Carthage the licence of the students is foul and uncontrolled. They impudently break in and with almost mad behaviour disrupt the order which each teacher has established for his pupils' benefit. They commit many acts of vandalism with an astonishing mindlessness, which would be punished under the law were it not that custom protects them. Thereby their wretched self-delusion is shown up. They act as if they were allowed to do what would never be permitted by your eternal law. They think they are free to act with impunity when by the very blindness of their behaviour they are being punished, and inflict on themselves incomparably worse damage than on others. When I was a student, I refused to have anything to do with these customs; as a professor I was forced to tolerate them in outsiders who were not my own pupils. So I decided to go where all informed people declared that such troubles did not occur. But it was you, *my hope and my portion in the land of the living* who wished me to change my earthly home for *the salvation of my soul.* You applied the pricks which made me tear myself away from Carthage, and you put before me the attractions of Rome to draw me there, using people who love a life of death, committing insane actions in this world, promising vain rewards in the next. To correct my *steps* you secretly made use of their and my perversity. For those who disturbed my serenity were blinded with a disgraceful frenzy. Those who invited me to go elsewhere had a taste only for this earth. I myself, while I hated a true misery here, pursued a false felicity there.

But you knew, God, why I left Carthage and went to Rome, and of that you gave no hint either to me or to my mother, who was fearfully upset at my going and followed me down to the sea. But as she vehemently held on to me calling me back or saying she would come with me, I deceived her. I pretended I had a friend I did not want to leave until the wind was right for him to sail. I lied to my mother—to such a mother—and I gave her the slip.[1] Even this you forgave me, mercifully saving me from the waters of the sea, when I was full of abominable filth, so as to bring me to the water of your grace.[2] This water was to wash me clean, and to dry the rivers flowing from my mother's eyes which daily before you irrigated the soil beneath her face.

---

1. The separation of Augustine and his mother, Monica, closely mirrors Aeneas's nocturnal abandonment of his lover Dido in Carthage to follow his destiny in Rome, the city he is to found (see the *Aeneid,* page 1144).

2. The contrast between the supposed dangers of the sea and the "grace" of the baptismal waters recalls the apostle Paul's lack of fear in the storm at sea during his voyage to Rome (Acts 27), further evoked in the subsequent paragraph.

Nevertheless since she refused to return home without me, with difficulty I persuaded her to stay that night in a place close to our ship, the memorial shrine to blessed Cyprian.[3] But that night I secretly set out; she did not come, but remained praying and weeping. By her floods of tears what was she begging of you, my God, but that you would not allow me to sail? Yet in your deep counsel you heard the central point of her longing, though not granting her what she then asked, namely that you would make me what she continually prayed for. The wind blew and filled our sails and the shore was lost to our sight. There, when morning came, she was crazed with grief, and with recriminations and groans she filled your ears. But you paid no heed to her cries. You were using my ambitious desires as a means towards putting an end to those desires, and the longing she felt for her own flesh and blood was justly chastised by the whip of sorrows.[4] As mothers do, she loved to have me with her, but much more than most mothers; and she did not understand that you were to use my absence as a means of bringing her joy. She did not know that. So she wept and lamented, and these agonies proved that there survived in her the remnants of Eve, seeking with groaning for the child she had brought forth in sorrow.[5] And yet after accusing me of deception and cruelty, she turned again to pray for me and to go back to her usual home. Meanwhile I came to Rome.

At Rome my arrival was marked by the scourge of physical sickness, and I was on the way to the underworld, bearing all the evils I had committed against you, against myself, and against others—sins both numerous and serious, in addition to the chain of original sin by which *in Adam we die*. You had not yet forgiven me in Christ for any of them, nor had he by his cross delivered me from the hostile disposition towards you which I had contracted by my sins. How could he deliver me from them if his cross was, as I had believed, a phantom?[6] Insofar as the death of his flesh was in my opinion unreal, the death of my soul was real. And insofar as the death of his flesh was authentic, to that extent the life of my soul, which disbelieved that, was inauthentic. The fevers became worse, and I was on my way out and dying. If at that time I had died, where was I going but into the fire and to the torments which, by your true order of justice, my deeds deserved? My mother did not know I was ill, but she was praying for me, though not beside me. But you are present everywhere. Where she was, you heard her, and where I was, you had mercy on me so that I recovered the health of my body. I still remained sick in my sacrilegious heart, for though in such great danger, I had no desire for your baptism. I did better as a boy when I begged for it from my devout mother, as I have recalled and confessed.[7] But I had grown in shame and in my folly used to laugh at the counsels of your medicine. Yet you did not allow me to die in this sad condition of both body and soul. If my mother's heart had suffered that wound, she would never have recovered. I cannot speak enough of the love she had for me. She suffered greater pains in my spiritual pregnancy than when she bore me in the flesh.

I do not see how she could have recovered if my death in those circumstances had like a scourge struck across the compassion of her love. Where would have been

---

3. The Carthaginian theologian and bishop Cyprian (c. 200–258) led the Christianization of Africa during a period of Roman persecution. Upon his execution, he became the first bishop-martyr of Africa.
4. Monica is duly chastised for her undue attachment to the son of her flesh rather than to the one of the spirit, as she will eventually be (Book 9, chapter 10).
5. Genesis 3:16. The Lord's curse on Eve for her disobedience was to suffer in bearing children. Monica's sufferings here refer to both the physical ones of her son's birth and the spiritual ones attending his belabored spiritual rebirth.
6. As they did not acknowledge the humanity of Christ, the Manichees interpreted his crucifixion as a symbol of general suffering rather than a historical event.
7. When very ill as a boy, Augustine had asked to be baptized, but his mother had refused, not believing him ready for such an irrevocable step (Book 1, chapter 11).

all her prayers, so frequent as to be ceaseless? Nowhere except with you. But, God of mercies, would you despise *the contrite and humble heart* of a chaste and sober widow, liberal in almsgiving, obedient and helpful in serving your saints, letting no day pass without making an oblation at your altar, twice a day at morning and at evening coming to your Church with unfailing regularity, taking no part in vain gossip and old wives' chatter, but wanting to hear you in your words and to speak to you in her prayers? Could you, who gave her this character, despise and repel from your assistance tears by which she sought of you, not gold and silver nor any inconstant or transitory benefit, but the salvation of her son's soul? No indeed, Lord, of course you were there and were hearing her petition, and were following through the order of events that you had predestinated. You could not have misled her in those visions and your responses, both those which I have already mentioned, and those which I have omitted. At her faithful breast she held on to them, and in her unceasing prayer she as it were presented to you your bond of promises. For *your mercy is for ever,* and you deign to make yourself a debtor obliged by your promises to those to whom you forgive all debts.

[*Augustine's next intellectual encounter is with the Academic philosophers, or Skeptics, most notably Plato. He complains about the Roman students' skill in avoiding paying for their lessons and soon obtains a government appointment to teach rhetoric in Milan, the residence of the emperor at the time and an important Christian center dominated by Bishop Ambrose. Augustine is impressed with Ambrose's power as a speaker but claims to have heard his meaning only in retrospect. His mother braves a hazardous sea journey to join him, and Augustine begins to prefer the Catholic Christian Church to other religions, deciding that its simple style and rhetoric indicate great profundity and humility rather than ignorance. He encounters a drunken beggar on the street who appears to enjoy life more than Augustine himself with all his ambitions. He introduces the character of his close childhood friend, Alypius, who is addicted to the circus games and who has followed Augustine to Italy. His mother desires him to marry, and in the process his longtime mistress is torn from him. He accepts most of Christian doctrine but is held back by his incapacity to account for the origin of evil. He encounters the books of Neoplatonism, which urge him to inner contemplation and "immaterial truth" but which don't accept the dual nature of Christ. He returns to the Epistles of Paul and finds that they combine the truths of Neoplatonism with a belief in the passion of Christ and divine grace. He is intellectually poised for conversion but unwilling to take the final leap of faith and renounce the pleasures of the flesh.*]

from *Book 8*

[PONTICIANUS]

Lord, my helper and redeemer, I will now tell the story, and confess to your name, of the way in which you delivered me from the chain of sexual desire, by which I was tightly bound, and from the slavery of worldly affairs. I went about my usual routine in a state of mental anxiety. Every day I sighed after you. I used to frequent your Church whenever I had time off from the affairs under whose weight I was groaning. With me was Alypius, unemployed in his work as a lawyer after a third period as assessor[1] and waiting for someone else to whom he could again sell his advice, just as I

---

1. An official who assists a judge or magistrate.

was selling the art of public speaking—if oratory is something that can be conveyed by teaching. Nebridius, however, had yielded to the pressure of his friendship with us and was assistant teacher to Verecundus, a close friend to all of us, a citizen of Milan and instructor in literature there. Verecundus was in urgent need of reliable assistance, and by right of friendship claimed from our group the supply he badly wanted. So Nebridius was not attracted to this work by desire for the profits; for had he so wished, he could have made more money on his own as teacher of literature. He was a most gentle and kind friend, and recognizing the duty of generosity would not scorn our request. He performed his task most prudently, and took care not to become known to important people, as this world reckons them, so avoiding anything likely to distract his mind. He wanted to keep his mind free and to devote as many hours as possible to the pursuit of wisdom by investigating some problem or listening to conversation.

One day when Nebridius was absent for a reason I cannot recall, Alypius and I received a surprise visit at home from a man named Ponticianus, a compatriot in that he was an African, holding high office at the court. He wanted something or other from us. We sat down together to converse. By chance he noticed a book on top of a gaming table which lay before us. He picked it up, opened it, and discovered, much to his astonishment, that it was the apostle Paul.[2] He had expected it to be one of the books used for the profession which was wearing me out. But then he smiled and looked at me in a spirit of congratulation. He was amazed that he had suddenly discovered this book and this book alone open before my eyes. He was a Christian and a baptized believer. He often prostrated himself before you, our God, at the Church with frequent and long times of prayer. When I had indicated to him that those scriptures were the subject of deep study for me, a conversation began in which he told the story of Antony the Egyptian monk, a name held in high honour among your servants, though up to that moment Alypius and I had never heard of him.[3] When he discovered this, he dwelt on the story instilling in us who were ignorant an awareness of the man's greatness, and expressing astonishment that we did not know of him. We were amazed as we heard of your wonderful acts very well attested and occurring so recently, almost in our own time, done in orthodox faith and in the Catholic Church. All of us were in a state of surprise, we because of the greatness of the story, he because we had not heard about it.

From there his conversation moved on to speak of the flocks in the monasteries and their manner of life well pleasing to you and the fertile deserts of the wilderness. Of these we knew nothing. There was a monastery full of good brothers at Milan outside the city walls, fostered by Ambrose, and we had not known of it. He developed the theme and talked on while we listened with rapt silence. Then it occurred to him to mention how he and three of his colleagues (the date I do not know but it was at Trier),[4] when the emperor was detained by a circus spectacle in the forenoon, went out for a walk in the gardens adjacent to the walls. There they strolled in couples, one as it turned out with Ponticianus, the other two separately wandering off on their

2. That is, a collection of the Epistles of the apostle Paul.
3. St. Anthony of Egypt (c. 251–356) was the founder of organized Christian monasticism. He lived in absolute solitude on a mountain by the river Nile from about 286 to 305, during which time he engaged in a legendary combat with the devil, withstanding a series of temptations in the form of visions either seductive or horrible. His "rule," or code of guidelines for monastic living, was compiled from writings and sayings attributed to him in the *Life of St. Anthony* by Athanasius of Alexandria.
4. The Roman town of Trier was founded in 15 B.C.E. on the site of a Germanic shrine. In the 3rd century it was an imperial seat and later the seat of the emperor responsible for Gaul and Britain. It became a bishopric in the 4th century and remained a center of Christianity north of the Alps after its capture by the Franks in the 5th century.

own. In their wanderings they happened on a certain house where there lived some of your servants, poor in spirit: *of such is the kingdom of heaven.* They found there a book in which was written the Life of Antony. One of them began to read it. He was amazed and set on fire, and during his reading began to think of taking up this way of life and of leaving his secular post in the civil service to be your servant. For they were agents in the special branch.[5] Suddenly he was filled with holy love and sobering shame. Angry with himself, he turned his eyes on his friend and said to him: "Tell me, I beg of you, what do we hope to achieve with all our labours? What is our aim in life? What is the motive of our service to the state? Can we hope for any higher office in the palace than to be Friends of the Emperor? And in that position what is not fragile and full of dangers? How many hazards must one risk to attain to a position of even greater danger?[6] And when will we arrive there? Whereas, if I wish to become God's friend, in an instant I may become that now." So he spoke, and in pain at the coming to birth of new life, he returned his eyes to the book's pages. He read on and experienced a conversion inwardly where you alone could see and, as was soon evident, his mind rid itself of the world. Indeed, as he read and turned over and over in the turbulent hesitations of his heart, there were some moments when he was angry with himself. But then he perceived the choice to be made and took a decision to follow the better course. He was already yours, and said to his friend: "As for myself, I have broken away from our ambition, and have decided to serve God, and I propose to start doing that from this hour in this place. If it costs you too much to follow my example, do not turn against me." His friend replied that he would join him and be associated with him for such great reward and for so great a service. And both men, already yours, were building their tower at the right cost of forsaking all their property and following you. Then Ponticianus and his companion who were walking through other parts of the garden in search of them, came to the same place and, on finding them, suggested returning home since the daylight had already begun to fade. But they told him of their decision and purpose, and how this intention had started and had become a firm resolve. They begged the others, if they did not wish to be associated with them, not to obstruct them. Ponticianus and his friend, however, did not change from their old career; nevertheless, as he told us, they wept for themselves. They offered their friends devout congratulations, and commended themselves to their prayers. Then, dragging their hearts along the ground, they went off into the palace. The others fixed their hearts on heaven and stayed at the house. Both had fiancées. When later their fiancées heard this, they also dedicated their virginity to you.[7]

This was the story Ponticianus told. But while he was speaking, Lord, you turned my attention back to myself. You took me up from behind my own back where I had placed myself because I did not wish *to observe myself,* and *you set me before my face* so that I should see how vile I was, how twisted and filthy, covered in sores and ulcers. And I looked and was appalled, but there was no way of escaping from myself. If I tried to avert my gaze from myself, his story continued relentlessly, and you once again placed me in front of myself; you thrust me before my own eyes so that I should

---

5. In addition to their roles as members of the secret imperial police, the "general agents" operated the *cursus publicus,* the efficient Roman postal system.

6. "Friends of the Emperor" were a select group of advisors to the emperor. They were highly exposed in the event of coups and conspiracies.

7. The accumulation of a story within a story, written text, and recounted experiences is characteristic of narrative in the late Empire; it also serves here to emphasize the importance of example and imitation in conversion and in the dissemination of Christianity.

discover my iniquity and hate it. I had known it, but deceived myself, refused to admit it, and pushed it out of my mind.

But at that moment the more ardent my affection for those young men of whom I was hearing, who for the soul's health had given themselves wholly to you for healing, the more was the detestation and hatred I felt for myself in comparison with them. Many years of my life had passed by—about twelve—since in my nineteenth year I had read Cicero's *Hortensius,* and had been stirred to a zeal for wisdom. But although I came to despise earthly success, I put off giving time to the quest for wisdom. For "it is not the discovery but the mere search for wisdom which should be preferred even to the discovery of treasures and to ruling over nations and to the physical delights available to me at a nod."[8] But I was an unhappy young man, wretched as at the beginning of my adolescence when I prayed you for chastity and said: "Grant me chastity and continence, but not yet." I was afraid you might hear my prayer quickly, and that you might too rapidly heal me of the disease of lust which I preferred to satisfy rather than suppress. I had gone along *evil ways* with a sacrilegious superstition, not indeed because I felt sure of its truth but because I preferred it to the alternatives, which I did not investigate in a devout spirit but opposed in an attitude of hostility.

I supposed that the reason for my postponing *from day to day* the moment when I would despise worldly ambition and follow you was that I had not seen any certainty by which to direct my course. But the day had now come when I stood naked to myself, and my conscience complained against me: "Where is your tongue? You were saying that, because the truth is uncertain, you do not want to abandon the burden of futility. But look, it is certain now, and the burden still presses on you. Yet wings are won by the freer shoulders of men who have not been exhausted by their searching and have not taken ten years or more to meditate on these matters." This is how I was gnawing at my inner self. I was violently overcome by a fearful sense of shame during the time that Ponticianus was telling his story. When he had ended his talk and settled the matter for which he came, he went home and I was left to myself. What accusations against myself did I not bring? With what verbal rods did I not scourge my soul so that it would follow me in my attempt to go after you! But my soul hung back. It refused, and had no excuse to offer. The arguments were exhausted, and all had been refuted. The only thing left to it was a mute trembling, and as if it were facing death it was terrified of being restrained from the treadmill of habit by which it suffered *sickness unto death.*

Then in the middle of that grand struggle in my inner house, which I had vehemently stirred up with my soul in the intimate chamber of my heart, distressed not only in mind but in appearance, I turned on Alypius and cried out: "What is wrong with us? What is this that you have heard? Uneducated people are *rising up and capturing heaven,* and we with our high culture without any heart—see where we roll in the mud of flesh and blood. Is it because they are ahead of us that we are ashamed to follow? Do we feel no shame at making not even an attempt to follow?" That is the gist of what I said, and the heat of my passion took my attention away from him as he contemplated my condition in astonished silence. For I sounded very strange. My uttered words said less about the state of my mind than my forehead, cheeks, eyes, colour, and tone of voice.

8. Drawn from Cicero's *Hortensius.*

Our lodging had a garden. We had the use of it as well as of the entire house, for our host, the owner of the house, was not living there.[9] The tumult of my heart took me out into the garden where no one could interfere with the burning struggle with myself in which I was engaged, until the matter could be settled. You knew, but I did not, what the outcome would be. But my madness with myself was part of the process of recovering health, and in the agony of death I was coming to life. I was aware how ill I was, unaware how well I was soon to be. So I went out into the garden. Alypius followed me step after step. Although he was present, I felt no intrusion on my solitude. How could he abandon me in such a state? We sat down as far as we could from the buildings. I was deeply disturbed in spirit, angry with indignation and distress that I was not entering into my pact and covenant with you, my God, *when all my bones were crying out* that I should enter into it and were exalting it to heaven with praises. But to reach that destination one does not use ships or chariots or feet. It was not even necessary to go the distance I had come from the house to where we were sitting. The one necessary condition, which meant not only going but at once arriving there, was to have the will to go—provided only that the will was strong and unqualified, not the turning and twisting first this way, then that, of a will half-wounded, struggling with one part rising up and the other part falling down.

Finally in the agony of hesitation I made many physical gestures of the kind men make when they want to achieve something and lack the strength, either because they lack the actual limbs or because their limbs are fettered with chains or weak with sickness or in some way hindered. If I tore my hair, if I struck my forehead, if I intertwined my fingers and clasped my knee, I did that because to do so was my will. But I could have willed this and then not done it if my limbs had not possessed the power to obey. So I did many actions in which the will to act was not equalled by the power. Yet I was not doing what with an incomparably greater longing I yearned to do, and could have done the moment I so resolved. For as soon as I had the will, I would have had a wholehearted will. At this point the power to act is identical with the will. The willing itself was performative of the action. Nevertheless, it did not happen. The body obeyed the slightest inclination of the soul to move the limbs at its pleasure more easily than the soul obeyed itself, when its supreme desire could be achieved exclusively by the will alone.

* * *

["Pick Up and Read"]

From a hidden depth a profound self-examination had dredged up a heap of all my misery and set it *in the sight of my heart.* That precipitated a vast storm bearing a massive downpour of tears. To pour it all out with the accompanying groans, I got up from beside Alypius (solitude seemed to me more appropriate for the business of weeping), and I moved further away to ensure that even his presence put no inhibition upon me. He sensed that this was my condition at that moment. I think I may have said something which made it clear that the sound of my voice was already choking with tears. So I stood up while in profound astonishment he remained where we were sitting. I threw myself down somehow under a certain figtree,[1] and let my tears flow

9. While clearly a real place, the "garden" within the "house" where they are lodging also reads as an allegory involving two sets of imagery—the house and the garden—carefully developed throughout the *Confessions.* The scene recalls both the original sin in the Garden of Eden and Augustine's difficulty in making the house of his soul a fit dwelling place for the Lord.
1. This recalls the fig tree of Eden (Genesis 3:7) and stresses the allegorical meaning of the garden.

freely. Rivers streamed from my eyes, *a sacrifice acceptable to you,* and (though not in these words, yet in this sense) I repeatedly said to you: "*How long, O Lord? How long, Lord, will you be angry to the uttermost? Do not be mindful of our old iniquities.*" For I felt my past to have a grip on me. It uttered wretched cries: "How long, how long is it to be?" "Tomorrow, tomorrow." "Why not now? Why not an end to my impure life in this very hour?"

As I was saying this and weeping in the bitter agony of my heart, suddenly I heard a voice from the nearby house chanting as if it might be a boy or a girl (I do not know which), saying and repeating over and over again "Pick up and read, pick up and read."[2] At once my countenance changed, and I began to think intently whether there might be some sort of children's game in which such a chant is used. But I could not remember having heard of one. I checked the flood of tears and stood up. I interpreted it solely as a divine command to me to open the book and read the first chapter I might find.[3] For I had heard how Antony happened to be present at the gospel reading, and took it as an admonition addressed to himself when the words were read: "Go, sell all you have, give to the poor, and you shall have treasure in heaven; and come, follow me."[4] By such an inspired utterance he was immediately *converted to you.* So I hurried back to the place where Alypius was sitting. There I had put down the book of the apostle when I got up. I seized it, opened it and in silence read the first passage on which my eyes lit: "Not in riots and drunken parties, not in eroticism and indecencies, not in strife and rivalry, but put on the Lord Jesus Christ and make no provision for the flesh in its lusts."[5]

I neither wished nor needed to read further. At once, with the last words of this sentence, it was as if a light of relief from all anxiety flooded into my heart. All the shadows of doubt were dispelled.

Then I inserted my finger or some other mark in the book and closed it. With a face now at peace I told everything to Alypius. What had been going on in his mind, which I did not know, he disclosed in this way. He asked to see the text I had been reading. I showed him, and he noticed a passage following that which I had read. I did not know how the text went on; but the continuation was "Receive the person who is weak in faith."[6] Alypius applied this to himself, and he made that known to me. He was given confidence by this admonition. Without any agony of hesitation he joined me in making a good resolution and affirmation of intention, entirely congruent with his moral principles in which he had long been greatly superior to me. From there we went in to my mother, and told her. She was filled with joy. We told her how it had happened. She exulted, feeling it to be a triumph, and blessed you who *are powerful to do more than we ask or think.* She saw that you had granted her far more than she had long been praying for in her unhappy and tearful groans.

The effect of your converting me to yourself was that I did not now seek a wife and had no ambition for success in this world. I stood firm upon that rule of faith on which many years before you had revealed me to her. You *changed her grief into joy* far more abundantly than she desired, far dearer and more chaste than she expected when she looked for grandchildren begotten of my body.

---

2. Rather than from the books or the stories of his learned friends, the final impulse toward conversion comes from a child's voice: "tolle lege, tolle lege."

3. The practice of divination by choosing a passage at random from a sacred book was widespread in antiquity; its commonest form in the later Empire was the *sortes*

Vergilianae, which used the writings of Virgil.

4. Matthew 19:21, Jesus's words to a young man who asks what he must do to achieve eternal life.

5. Romans 13:13–14 (see page 1269). The apostle Paul thus provides the apt words for Augustine's conversion.

6. Romans 14:1.

from *Book 9*

[Augustine gives up his teaching post and retires to the rural villa of the grammarian Verecundus in Cassiciacum some twenty miles northeast of Milan, surrounded by family and friends including his son, Adeodatus, now sixteen (he would die two years later). Augustine returns to Milan to be baptized.]

[MONICA'S DEATH]

You make people to live in a house in unanimity. So you made Evodius a member of our circle, a young man from my home town.[1] When he was a civil servant as an agent in the special branch, he was converted to you before we were. He was baptized and resigned his post on taking up your service. We were together and by a holy decision resolved to live together. We looked for a place where we could be of most use in your service; all of us agreed on a move back to Africa.

While we were at Ostia by the mouths of the Tiber, my mother died. I pass over many events because I write in great haste. Accept my confessions and thanksgivings, my God, for innumerable things even though I do not specifically mention them. But I shall not pass over whatever my soul may bring to birth concerning your servant, who brought me to birth both in her body so that I was born into the light of time, and in her heart so that I was born into the light of eternity. I speak not of her gifts to me, but of your gifts to her. She had not made herself or brought herself up. You created her, and her father and mother did not know what kind of character their child would have. She was trained *in your fear* by the discipline of your Christ, by the government of your only Son in a believing household through a good member of your Church. She used to speak highly not so much of her mother's diligence in training her as of a decrepit maidservant who had carried her father when he was an infant, in the way that infants are often carried on the back of older girls. Because of this long service and for her seniority and high moral standards in a Christian house, she was held in great honour by her masters. So she was entrusted with responsibility for her master's daughters and discharged it with diligence and, when necessary, was vehement with a holy severity in administering correction. In training them she exercised a discreet prudence. Outside those times when they were nourished by a most modest meal at their parents' table, even if they were burning with thirst, she allowed them to drink not even water, wishing to avert the formation of a bad habit. She used to add the wise word: "Now you drink water because it is not in your power to get wine. But when you come to have husbands and become mistresses of storerooms and cellars, water will seem dull stuff but the drinking habit will be unbreakable." By this method of laying down rules for behaviour and by her authoritative way of giving commands, she restrained the greedy appetite of a tender age, and brought the girls' thirst to respectable moderation, so that they should not later hanker after anything they ought not to touch.

Nevertheless, as your servant[2] told me her son, a weakness for wine gradually got a grip upon her. By custom her parents used to send her, a sober girl, to fetch wine from the cask. She would plunge the cup through the aperture at the top. Before she poured the wine into a jug, she used to take a tiny sip with the tip of her lips. She could not take more as she disliked the taste. What led her to do this was not an appetite for liquor but the surplus high spirits of a young person, which can overflow in

1. Later to become Bishop of Uzali in North Africa, Evodius accompanied Augustine from Rome to Africa
and is featured in two dialogues written by Augustine.
2. Monica.

playful impulses and which in children adults ordinarily try to suppress.[3] Accordingly, to that sip of wine she added more sips every day—for *he who despises small things gradually comes to a fall*—until she had fallen into the habit of gulping down almost full cups of wine. Where then was the wise old woman and her vehement prohibition? She could have had no strength against the secret malady unless your healing care, Lord, were watching over us. When father and mother and nurses are not there, you are present. You have created us, you call us, you use human authorities set over us to do something for the health of our souls. How did you cure her? How did you restore her health? You brought from another soul a harsh and sharp rebuke, like a surgeon's knife, from your secret stores, and with one blow you cut away the rottenness. The slavegirl who used to accompany her to the cask had a dispute with her young mistress which happened when they were alone together. Bitterly she insulted her by bringing up the accusation that she was a boozer. The taunt hurt. She reflected upon her own foul addiction, at once condemned it, and stopped the habit. Just as flattering friends corrupt, so quarrelsome enemies often bring us correction. Yet you reward them not for what you use them to achieve, but according to their intention. The maidservant in her anger sought to wound her little mistress, not to cure her. That is why she spoke in private—either because the time and place of the quarrel happened to find them alone together, or perhaps because she was afraid of the fact that she had come out with it so belatedly.

But you, Lord, ruler of heaven and earth, turn to your own purposes the deep torrents. You order the turbulent flux of the centuries. Even from the fury of one soul you brought healing to another. Thereby you showed that no one should attribute it to his own power if by anything he says he sets on the right path someone whom he wishes to be corrected.

* * *

The day was imminent when she was to depart this life (the day which you knew and we did not). It came about, as I believe by your providence through your hidden ways, that she and I were standing leaning out of a window overlooking a garden. It was at the house where we were staying at Ostia on the Tiber, where, far removed from the crowds, after the exhaustion of a long journey, we were recovering our strength for the voyage.

Alone with each other, we talked very intimately. *Forgetting the past and reaching forward to what lies ahead,* we were searching together in the presence of the truth which is you yourself. We asked what quality of life the eternal life of the saints will have, a life which *neither eye has seen nor ear heard, nor has it entered into the heart of man.* But with the mouth of the heart wide open, we drank in the waters flowing from your spring on high, *the spring of life* which is with you. Sprinkled with this dew to the limit of our capacity, our minds attempted in some degree to reflect on so great a reality.

The conversation led us towards the conclusion that the pleasure of the bodily senses, however delightful in the radiant light of this physical world, is seen by comparison with the life of eternity to be not even worth considering. Our minds were lifted up by an ardent affection towards eternal being itself. Step by step we climbed beyond all corporeal objects and the heaven itself, where sun, moon, and stars shed light on the earth. We ascended even further by internal reflection and dialogue and

---

3. Once again Augustine stresses not lack of will in the origin of the bad habit but the exercise of the will.

wonder at your works, and we entered into our own minds. We moved up beyond them so as to attain to the region of inexhaustible abundance where you feed Israel eternally with truth for food. There life is the wisdom by which all creatures come into being, both things which were and which will be. But wisdom itself is not brought into being but is as it was and always will be. Furthermore, in this wisdom there is no past and future, but only being, since it is eternal. For to exist in the past or in the future is no property of the eternal. And while we talked and panted after it, we touched it in some small degree by a moment of total concentration of the heart. And we sighed and left behind us *the firstfruits of the Spirit* bound to that higher world, as we returned to the noise of our human speech where a sentence has both a beginning and an ending. But what is to be compared with your word, Lord of our lives? It dwells in you without growing old and gives renewal to all things.[4]

Therefore we said: If to anyone the tumult of the flesh has fallen silent, if the images of earth, water, and air are quiescent, if the heavens themselves are shut out and the very soul itself is making no sound and is surpassing itself by no longer thinking about itself, if all dreams and visions in the imagination are excluded, if all language and every sign and everything transitory is silent—for if anyone could hear them, this is what all of them would be saying, "We did not make ourselves, we were made by him who abides for eternity"[5]—if after this declaration they were to keep silence, having directed our ears to him that made them, then he alone would speak not through them but through himself.[6] We would hear his word, not through the tongue of the flesh, nor through the voice of an angel, nor through the sound of thunder, nor through the obscurity of a symbolic utterance. Him who in these things we love we would hear in person without their mediation. That is how it was when at that moment we extended our reach and in a flash of mental energy attained the eternal wisdom which abides beyond all things. If only it could last, and other visions of a vastly inferior kind could be withdrawn! Then this alone could ravish and absorb and enfold in inward joys the person granted the vision. So too eternal life is of the quality of that moment of understanding after which we sighed. Is not this the meaning of *Enter into the joy of your Lord?* And when is that to be? Surely it is when *we all rise again, but are not all changed.*

I said something like this, even if not in just this way and with exactly these words. Yet, Lord, you know that on that day when we had this conversation, and this world with all its delights became worthless to us as we talked on, my mother said "My son, as for myself, I now find no pleasure in this life. What I have still to do here and why I am here, I do not know. My hope in this world is already fulfilled. The one reason why I wanted to stay longer in this life was my desire to see you a Catholic Christian before I die. My God has granted this in a way more than I had hoped. For I see you despising this world's success to become his servant.[7] What have I to do here?"

[The death of Monica concludes the narrative part of the Confessions. *In Book 10, Augustine analyzes at length the relationship between his memory and his search for*

---

4. The vision at Ostia serves to anticipate the fate of Monica's soul after her death, and thus lessen the sorrow of it, and also to develop the contemplative and speculative tone of the latter, postconversion books of the *Confessions.*

5. Psalms 80:3, 5.

6. Augustine describes the process and the goal of this

meditation: to experience the word of God directly without the distortion of any form of representation. This would be a taste of what eternal life must be like.

7. That is, to withdraw from worldly affairs to become an ascetic, Augustine's first activity after his conversion; later, he would take a more active role as Bishop of Hippo.

God in it through the act of confession. He enumerates the pleasures of the senses that continue to tempt him.]

from *Book 11*

[TIME, ETERNITY, AND MEMORY]

Lord, eternity is yours, so you cannot be ignorant of what I tell you. Your vision of occurrences in time is not temporally conditioned. Why then do I set before you an ordered account of so many things? It is certainly not through me that you know them. But I am stirring up love for you in myself and in those who read this, so that we may all say "Great is the Lord and highly worthy to be praised."[1] I have already affirmed this and will say it again: I tell my story for love of your love. We pray, and yet the truth says "Your Father knows what you need before you ask him."[2] Therefore I lay bare my feelings towards you, by confessing to you my miseries and *your mercies to us,* so that the deliverance you have begun may be complete. So I may cease to be wretched in myself and may find happiness in you. For you have called us to be *poor in spirit,* meek, mournful, hungering and thirsting for righteousness, merciful, pure in heart, and peacemakers.[3]

See, the long story I have told to the best of my ability and will responds to your prior will that I should make confession to you, my Lord God. For *you are good, for your mercy is for ever.* * * *

Stand firm, my mind, concentrate with resolution.[4] *God is our help, he has made us and not we ourselves.* Concentrate on the point where truth is beginning to dawn. For example, a physical voice begins to sound. It sounds. It continues to sound, and then ceases. Silence has now come, and the voice is past. There is now no sound. Before it sounded it lay in the future. It could not be measured because it did not exist; and now it cannot be measured because it has ceased to be. At the time when it was sounding, it was possible because at that time it existed to be measured. Yet even then it had no permanence. It came and went. Did this make it more possible to measure? In process of passing away it was extended through a certain space of time by which it could be measured, since the present occupies no length of time. Therefore during that transient process it could be measured. But take, for example, another voice. It begins to sound and continues to do so unflaggingly without any interruption. Let us measure it while it is sounding; when it has ceased to sound, it will be past and will not exist to be measurable. Evidently we may at that stage measure it by saying how long it lasted. But if it is still sounding, it cannot be measured except from the starting moment when it began to sound to the finish when it ceased. What we measure is the actual interval from the beginning to the end. That is why a sound which has not yet ended cannot be measured: one cannot say how long or how short it is, nor that it is equal to some other length of time or that in relation to another it is single or double or any such proportion. But when it has come to an end, then it will already have ceased to be. By what method then can it be measured?

Nevertheless we do measure periods of time. And yet the times we measure are not those which do not yet exist, nor those which already have no existence, nor those

---

1. Psalm 48:1. Augustine returns to the concerns of the opening paragraph. The reason for his confession and his ordering it chronologically as an autobiography is not to make it comprehensible to the Lord but as a story in His praise.

2. Matthew 6:8.
3. Summarizing the Sermon on the Mount in Matthew 5.
4. Augustine prepares his mind for an exercise in imagining the relationship between the divine and human perspectives on time.

which extend over no interval of time, nor those which reach no conclusions. So the times we measure are not future nor past nor present nor those in process of passing away. Yet we measure periods of time.

"God, Creator of all things"—*Deus Creator omnium*—the line consists of eight syllables, in which short and long syllables alternate.[5] So the four which are short (the first, third, fifth, and seventh) are single in relation to the four long syllables (the second, fourth, sixth and eighth).[6] Each of the long syllables has twice the time of the short. As I recite the words, I also observe that this is so, for it is evident to sense-perception. To the degree that the sense-perception is unambiguous, I measure the long syllable by the short one, and perceive it to be twice the length. But when one syllable sounds after another, the short first, the long after it, how shall I keep my hold on the short, and how use it to apply a measure to the long, so as to verify that the long is twice as much? The long does not begin to sound unless the short has ceased to sound. I can hardly measure the long during the presence of its sound, as measuring becomes possible only after it has ended. When it is finished, it has gone into the past. What then is it which I measure? Where is the short syllable with which I am making my measurement? Where is the long which I am measuring? Both have sounded; they have flown away; they belong to the past. They now do not exist. And I offer my measurement and declare as confidently as a practised sense-perception will allow, that the short is single, the long double—I mean in the time they occupy. I can do this only because they are past and gone. Therefore it is not the syllables which I am measuring, but something in my memory which stays fixed there.[7]

So it is in you, my mind, that I measure periods of time. Do not distract me; that is, do not allow yourself to be distracted by the hubbub of the impressions being made upon you. In you, I affirm, I measure periods of time. The impression which passing events make upon you abides when they are gone. That present consciousness is what I am measuring, not the stream of past events which have caused it. When I measure periods of time, that is what I am actually measuring. Therefore, either this is what time is, or time is not what I am measuring.

What happens when we measure silences and say that a given period of silence lasted as long as a given sound? Do we direct our attention to measuring it as if a sound occurred, so that we are enabled to judge the intervals of the silences within the space of time concerned? For without any sound or utterance we mentally recite poems and lines and speeches, and we assess the lengths of their movements and the relative amounts of time they occupy, no differently from the way we would speak if we were actually making sounds. Suppose someone wished to utter a sound lasting a long time, and decided in advance how long that was going to be. He would have planned that space of time in silence. Entrusting that to his memory he would begin to utter the sound which continues until it has reached the intended end. It would be more accurate to say the utterance has sounded and will sound. For the part of it which is complete has sounded, but what remains will sound, and so the action is being accomplished as present attention transfers the future into the past. The future diminishes as the past grows, until the future has completely gone and everything is in the past.

But how does this future, which does not yet exist, diminish or become consumed? Or how does the past, which now has no being, grow, unless there are three

5. A hymn written by Bishop Ambrose for Saturday vespers (evening services).
6. Latin meter is based on the length of syllables rather than on accent, as in English.

7. According to this analysis, time is not something that can be measured in the present, as an event is unfolding, but only when it is past and exists solely in the memory.

processes in the mind which in this is the active agent? For the mind expects and attends and remembers, so that what it expects passes through what has its attention to what it remembers. Who therefore can deny that the future does not yet exist? Yet already in the mind there is an expectation of the future. Who can deny that the past does not now exist? Yet there is still in the mind a memory of the past. None can deny that present time lacks any extension because it passes in a flash. Yet attention is continuous, and it is through this that what will be present progresses towards being absent. So the future, which does not exist, is not a long period of time. A long future is a long expectation of the future. And the past, which has no existence, is not a long period of time. A long past is a long memory of the past.

Suppose I am about to recite a psalm which I know. Before I begin, my expectation is directed towards the whole. But when I have begun, the verses from it which I take into the past become the object of my memory. The life of this act of mine is stretched two ways, into my memory because of the words I have already said and into my expectation because of those which I am about to say. But my attention is on what is present: by that the future is transferred to become the past. As the action advances further and further, the shorter the expectation and the longer the memory, until all expectation is consumed, the entire action is finished, and it has passed into the memory. What occurs in the psalm as a whole occurs in its particular pieces and its individual syllables. The same is true of a longer action in which perhaps that psalm is a part. It is also valid of the entire life of an individual person, where all actions are parts of a whole, and of the total history of *the sons of men*[8] where all human lives are but parts.

Because your mercy is more than lives, see how my life is a distension in several directions. *Your right hand upheld me* in my Lord, the Son of man who is mediator between you the One and us the many, who live in a multiplicity of distractions by many things; so *I might apprehend him in whom also I am apprehended,* and leaving behind the old days I might be gathered to follow the One, *forgetting the past* and moving not towards those future things which are transitory but to *the things which are before* me, not stretched out in distraction but extended in reach, not by being pulled apart but by concentration.[9] So I *pursue the prize of the high calling* where I *may hear the voice of praise* and *contemplate your delight* which neither comes nor goes. But now *my years pass in groans* and you, Lord, are my consolation. You are my eternal Father, but I am scattered in times whose order I do not understand. The storms of incoherent events tear to pieces my thoughts, the inmost entrails of my soul, until that day when, purified and molten by the fire of your love, I flow together to merge into you.

Then shall I find stability and solidity in you, in your truth which imparts form to me. I shall not have to endure the questions of people who suffer from a disease which brings its own punishment and want to drink more than they have the capacity to hold. They say "What was God doing before he made heaven and earth?", or "Why did he ever conceive the thought of making something when he had never made anything before?"[1] Grant them, Lord, to consider carefully what they are saying and to

8. Psalms 31:20. In Book 1, the *Confessions* opens up out of the recitation of psalms as the means of approaching God; here, Augustine uses the model of the recitation of a psalm, a song of praise, to make tangible the divine perspective of a human life and of the history of the world from the Creation to the Last Judgment. Paradoxically, God is neither ignorant nor powerless concerning the path it will take but neither has he already predetermined what will happen.

9. It is the multiple distractions of errant and transitory paths that render it impossible from the human perspective to perceive the single path that will, in the end, lead to the Lord and become history.

1. Underlying the discussion of time and memory was an ongoing debate over how and in what form God could have existed before he created the world; whether, in other words, there exists or existed anything prior to Him or outside of Him.

make the discovery that where there is no time, one cannot use the word "never." To say that God has never done something is to say that there is no time when he did it. Let them therefore see that without the creation no time can exist, and let them cease to speak that vanity. Let them also be *extended* towards *those things which are before,* and understand that before all times you are eternal Creator of all time. Nor are any times or created thing coeternal with you, even if there is an order of creation which transcends time.[2]

Lord my God, how deep is your profound mystery, and how far away from it have I been thrust by the consequences of my sins. Heal my eyes and let me rejoice with your light. Certainly if there were a mind endowed with such great knowledge and prescience that all things past and future could be known in the way I know a very familiar psalm, this mind would be utterly miraculous and amazing to the point of inducing awe. From such a mind nothing of the past would be hidden, nor anything of what remaining ages have in store, just as I have full knowledge of that psalm I sing. I know by heart what and how much of it has passed since the beginning, and what and how much remains until the end. But far be it from you, Creator of the universe, creator of souls and bodies, far be it from you to know all future and past events in this kind of sense. You know them in a much more wonderful and much more mysterious way. A person singing or listening to a song he knows well suffers a distension or stretching in feeling and in sense-perception from the expectation of future sounds and the memory of past sound. With you it is otherwise. You are unchangeably eternal, that is the truly eternal Creator of minds. Just as you knew heaven and earth in the beginning without that bringing any variation into your knowing, so you made heaven and earth in the beginning without that meaning a tension between past and future in your activity. Let the person who understands this make confession to you. Let him who fails to understand it make confession to you. How exalted you are, and *the humble in heart are your house. You lift up those who are cast down,* and those whom you raise to that summit which is yourself do not fall.

[*In the final two books of the* Confessions, *Augustine applies everything he has discovered thus far to an explanation of the Creation and of the first chapters of Genesis, resolving to his satisfaction the relationship of God to the material and temporal world.*]

❧

RESONANCES

Michel de Montaigne: from *Essays*[1]

To the Reader

This book was written in good faith, reader. It warns you from the outset that in it I have set myself no goal but a domestic and private one. I have had no thought of serving

2. Augustine refers here to the order of angels (*City of God* 12.16).

1. Translated by Donald Frame. In 1571 at the age of 38, tired of a public life of law and politics in war-torn southern France, Michel de Montaigne (1533–1592) retired to his family château to devote himself to private concerns. To commemorate his retreat, he had a medallion cast with the words *Que sais-je?* ("What do I know?") on one side and *Restraint* in Greek on the other. In the three volumes of *Essays* (a word he coined for the occasion) he published over the next 20 years, Montaigne adapted Augustine's model of the exploration of self in search of God and of spiritual rest into the exploration of self in search of self-knowledge and peace with the world. "To the Reader" opens the *Essays* with a confession of an endeavor as unexpected in the late 16th century as Augustine's was in his time. See Volume C for further selections from the *Essays*.

either you or my own glory. My powers are inadequate for such a purpose. I have dedicated it to the private convenience of my relatives and friends, so that when they have lost me (as soon they must), they may recover here some features of my habits and temperament, and by this means keep the knowledge they have had of me more complete and alive.

If I had written to seek the world's favor, I should have bedecked myself better, and should present myself in a studied posture. I want to be seen here in my simple, natural, ordinary fashion, without straining or artifice; for it is myself that I portray. My defects will here be read to the life, and also my natural form, as far as respect for the public has allowed. Had I been placed among those nations which are said to live still in the sweet freedom of nature's first laws, I assure you I should very gladly have portrayed myself here entire and wholly naked.[2]

Thus, reader, I am myself the matter of my book; you would be unreasonable to spend your leisure on so frivolous and vain a subject.

So farewell. Montaigne,[3] this first day of March, fifteen hundred and eighty.

Jean-Jacques Rousseau: from Confessions[1]

from *Book One*

I have resolved on an enterprise which has no precedent, and which, once complete, will have no imitator. My purpose is to display to my kind a portrait in every way true to nature, and the man I shall portray will be myself.

Simply myself. I know my own heart and understand my fellow man. But I am made unlike any one I have ever met; I will even venture to say that I am like no one in the whole world. I may be no better, but at least I am different. Whether Nature did well or ill in breaking the mould in which she formed me, is a question which can only be resolved after the reading of my book.

Let the last trump sound when it will, I shall come forward with this work in my hand, to present myself before my Sovereign Judge, and proclaim aloud: "Here is what I have done, and if by chance I have used some immaterial embellishment it has been only to fill a void due to a defect of memory. I may have taken for fact what was no more than probability, but I have never put down as true what I knew to be false.[2] I have displayed myself as I was, as vile and despicable when my behaviour was such, as good, generous, and noble when I was so. I have bared my secret soul as Thou thyself hast seen it, Eternal Being! So let the numberless legion of my fellow men gather round me, and hear my confessions. Let them groan at my depravities, and blush for my misdeeds. But let each one of them reveal his heart at the foot of Thy throne with equal sincerity, and may any man who dares, say 'I was a better man than he.'"

✧

2. Like Augustine, Montaigne treats his book as himself, but in addition to his actions and thoughts, he includes his "natural form," meaning both his body and his thoughts, as unencumbered as possible of the prejudices of human custom. The New World had recently been discovered by Europe, and its indigenous peoples were widely held to be in an equivalent state of nature to Adam and Eve in Eden before they gained knowledge of good and evil.
3. That is, the Château of Montaigne.
1. Translated by J. M. Cohen. Confession is a powerful device of rhetoric for guaranteeing the truth of a life story. In the prologue to his autobiography, Jean-Jacques

Rousseau (1712–1788), Enlightenment philosopher, political theorist, musician, novelist, and spiritual father of the French Revolution, imagines Christ himself absolving the writer for any distortions he may unwittingly have included. As with Augustine, the autobiography as confession is both universal and unique, both browbeating and self-congratulatory; the combination has become since Rousseau an indelible feature of life writing. For more on Rousseau, see Volumes D and E.
2. Like Montaigne but unlike Augustine, Rousseau feels it necessary to distinguish between an ideal of absolute truth and the relative truth represented by his *Confessions*.

BIBLIOGRAPHY

The Ancient World

Genesis • Bernard W. Anderson, ed., *Creation in the Old Testament*, 1984. • Eugene Combs, *The Foundations of Political Order in Genesis and the Chondogya Upanishad*, 1987. • R. Gilboa, *Intercourses in the Book of Genesis: Mythic Motifs in Creator-Created Relationships*, 1998. • Dorothy Irvin, *Mytharion: The Comparison of Tales from the Old Testament and the Ancient Near East*, 1978. • Jon D. Levenson, *Creation and the Persistence of Evil: The Jewish Drama of Divine Omnipotence*, 1988. • Terry J. Prewitt, *The Elusive Covenant: A Structural-Semiotic Reading of Genesis*, 1990. • Ellen van Wolde, *Stories of the Beginning: Genesis 1–11 and Other Creation Stories*, 1997. • Claus Westermann, *Genesis: An Introduction*, 1992.

The Ancient Near East

General • Bertil Albrektson, *History and the Gods*, 1967. • Cyril Aldred, *Akhenaten, Pharaoh of Egypt: A New Study*, 1968. • Robert Alter, *The Art of Biblical Narrative*, 1981. • Robert Alter, *The Art of Biblical Poetry*, 1985. • Robert Alter and Frank Kermode, eds., *The Literary Guide to the Bible*, 1987. • Jan Assmann, *The Mind of Egypt: History and Meaning in the Time of the Pharaohs*, 2002. • Jan Assmann, *The Search for God in Ancient Egypt*, 2001. • John Barton, *Reading the Old Testament: Method in Biblical Study*, 1984. • Jean Bottéro, *Mesopotamia: Writing, Reasoning and the Gods*, 1992. • Brevard Childs, *Introduction to the Old Testament as Scripture*, 1979. • Frank M. Cross, *Canaanite Myth and Hebrew Epic*, 1973. • Stephanie Dalley, *Myths from Mesopotamia*, 1989. • David Damrosch, *The Narrative Covenant: Transformations of Genre in the Growth of Biblical Literature*, 1987. • Michael Fishbane, *Biblical Interpretation in Ancient Israel*, 1985. • Benjamin Foster, *From Distant Days: Myths, Tales and Poetry of Ancient Mesopotamia*, 1995. • Henri Frankfort et al., *Before Philosophy*, 1954. • Northrop Frye, *The Great Code: The Bible and Literature*, 1982. • Norman Gottwald, *The Hebrew Bible: A Socio-Literary Introduction*, 1985. • James Kugel, *The Bible as It Was*, 1997. • James Kugel, *The Idea of Biblical Poetry*, 1981. • Amélie Kuhrt, *The Ancient Near East c. 3000–300 BC*, 1995. • Miriam Lichtheim, *Ancient Egyptian Literature*, 3 vols., 1975–1980. • Ilana Pardes, *The Biography of Ancient Israel: National Narratives in the Bible*, 2000. • J. N. Postgate, *Early Mesopotamia: Society and Economy at the Dawn of History*, 1992. • James B. Pritchard, *Ancient Near Eastern Texts Relating to the Old Testament*, 1976. • Paul Ricoeur, *The Symbolism of Evil*, 1969. • Herbert Schneidau, *Sacred Discontent: The Bible and Western Tradition*, 1976. • William K. Simpson, ed., *The Literature of Ancient Egypt*, 1973. • Daniel Snell, *Life in the Ancient Near East*, 1997. • Meir Sternberg, *The Poetics of Biblical Narrative*, 1985. • Joyce Tyldesley, *Daughters of Iris: Women of Ancient Egypt*, 1995. • John Van Seters, *In Search of History: Historiography in the Ancient World and the Origins of Biblical History*, 1983.

Perspectives: Death and Immortality • Bendt Alster, *Death in Mesopotamia*, 1980. • James G. Frazer, *The Golden Bough*, 1945. • Thorkild Jacobsen, *The Treasures of Darkness*, 1976. • Dimitri Meeks and Christine Favard-Meeks, *Daily Life of the Egyptian Gods*, 1996.

The Book of the Dead • Robert A. Armour, *Gods and Myths of Ancient Egypt*, 1986. • R.T. Rundle Clark, *Myth and Symbol in Ancient Egypt*, 1959. • A. H. Gardiner and K. Sethe, *Egyptian Letters to the Dead: Mainly from the Old and Middle Kingdom*, 1928. • Paul Hamlyn, *Egyptian Mythology*, 1965. • George Hart, *Egyptian Myths*, 1990.

The Descent of Ishtar to the Underworld • Rivkah Harris, "Inanna-Ishtar and Paradox and a Coincidence of Opposites," *History of Religions* 30:3 (1991), 261–78. • Gwendolyn Leick, *The Babylonians: An Introduction*, 2003. • Hugh R. Page, *The Myth of Cosmic Rebellion: A Study of Its Reflexes in Ugaritic and Biblical Literature*, 1996. • Alice Lenore Perlman, *Aherah and Astarte in the Old Testament and Ugaritic*

Literatures, 1978. • Diana White, trans. *The Descent of Ishtar*, 1993.

Perspectives: Strangers in a Strange Land • Rebecca Saunders, ed., *The Concept of the Foreign: An Interdisciplinary Dialogue*, 2003.

The Book of Ruth • Mishael Caspi, *The Book of Ruth: An Annotated Bibliography*, 1994. • Mishael Maswari Caspi and Rachel S. Havrelock, *Women on the Biblical Road: Ruth, Naomi, and the Female Journey*, 1996. • John J. Davis, *Conquest and Crisis: Studies in Joshua, Judges, and Ruth*, 1969. • J. Gordon Harris, *Joshua, Judges, Ruth*, 2000. • Marjo C. A. Korpel, *Structure of the Book of Ruth*, 2001. • Ilana Pardes, *Countertraditions in the Bible: A Feminist Approach*, 1992. • Johanna W. H. van Wijk-Bos, *Ruth and Esther: Women in Alien Lands*, 2001.

The Joseph Story • Robert Alter, *The Art of Biblical Narrative*, 1981. • Yiu-Wing Fung, *Victim and Victimizer: Joseph's Interpretation of His Destiny*, 2000. • Theo L. Hettema, *Reading for Good: Narrative Theology and Ethics in the Joseph Story from the Perspective of Ricoeur's Hermeneutics*, 1996. • W. Lee Humphreys, *Joseph and His Family: A Literary Study*, 1988. • Eric I. Lowenthal, *The Joseph Narrative in Genesis*, 1973. • Donald B. Redford, *Study of the Biblical Story of Joseph (Genesis 37–50)*, 1970. • Aaron Wildavsky, *Assimilation Versus Separation: Joseph the Administrator and the Politics of Religion in Biblical Israel*, 1993.

The Book of Job • Carol A. Newsom, *The Book of Job: A Contest of Moral Imaginations*, 2003. • Donal J. O'Connor, *Job: His Wife, His Friends, and His God*, 1995. • Marvin Pope, *The Book of Job*, 1975. • Paul S. Sanders, ed., *Twentieth-Century Interpretations of the Book of Job*, 1969. • Bruce Zuckerman, *Job, the*

Silent: A Study in Historical Counterpoint, 1991.

The Epic of Gilgamesh • David Damrosch, "Gilgamesh and Genesis," in *The Narrative Covenant*, 1987. • Andrew George, ed., *The Epic of Gilgamesh*, 1999. • Rivkah Harris, *Gender and Aging in Mesopotamia: The Gilgamesh Epic and Other Ancient Literature*, 2000. • Alexander Heidel, *The Gilgamesh Epic and Old Testament Parallels*, 1949. • Derrek Hines, *Gilgamesh*, 2002. • John Maier, ed., *Gilgamesh: A Reader*, 1997. • Benjamin Caleb Ray, "The Gilgamesh Epic: Myth and Meaning," in *Myth and Method*, eds. Laurie L. Patton and Wendy Doniger, 1996. • Jeffrey H. Tigay, *The Evolution of the Gilgamesh Epic*, 2002.

Poetry of Love and Devotion • David Damrosch, "Allegories of Love in Egyptian Poetry and the Song of Songs," *Stanford Literature Review* 5:1 (1988), 25–42. • Samuel N. Kramer, *The Sacred Marriage Rite: Aspects of Faith, Myth and Ritual in Ancient Sumer*, 1969. • Johannes C. de Moor and Wilfred G. E. Watson, eds., *Verse in Ancient Near Eastern Prose*, 1993. • D. Schmandt-Besserat, *The Legacy of Sumer*, 1977. • John Bradley White, *A Study of the Language of Love in the Song of Songs and Ancient Egyptian Poetry*, 1978.

The Song of Songs • Blaise Arminjon, *Cantata of Love: A Verse-by-Verse Reading of the Song of Songs*, 1988. • Ariel Bloch and Chana Bloch, *The Song of Songs: A New Translation with an Introduction and Commentary*, 1994. • Athalva Brenner and Carole R. Fontaine, eds., *The Song of Songs: A Feminist Companion to the Bible*, 2000. • Marvin Pope, *The Song of Songs*, 1977. • Luis Stadelmann, *Love and Politics: A New Commentary on the Song of Songs*, 1992.

Classical Greece

General • John Boardman, Jasper Griffin, and Oswyn Murray, eds., *The Oxford History of the Classical World*, 1986. • Paul Cartledge, *The Greeks*, 2002. • J. N. Davidson, *Courtesans and Fishcakes*, 1998. • Thomas R. Martin, *Ancient Greece*, 1996. • Robin Osborne, *Greece in the Making: 1200–479 BC*, 1996. • *Perseus* (database on ancient Greek civilization): www.perseus.tufts.edu • Jean-Pierre Vernant, ed., *The Greeks*, 1995.

Perspectives: Tyranny and Democracy • Michael Gagarin and Paul Woodruff, eds., *Early Greek Political Thought*, 1995. • Thomas Harrison, *Divinity and History*, 2000. • Joseph Mail, *Mythistory: The Making of a Modern Historiography*, 2003. • Arlene W. Saxonhouse, *Athenian Democracy*, 1996. • Norma Thompson, *Herodotus and the Origins of the Political Community*, 1996.

Plato ● W. K. C. Guthrie, *A History of Greek Philosophy,* vol. 3, 1969. ● A. Nightingale, *Genres in Dialogue,* 1995. ● R. B. Rutherford, *The Art of Plato,* 1995.

Solon ● I. M. Linforth, *Solon the Athenian,* 1919. ● P. B. Manville, *The Origins of Citizenship in Ancient Athens,* 1990.

Thucydides ● George Cawkwell, *Thucydides and the Peloponnesian War,* 1997. ● W. R. Connor, *Thucydides,* 1984. ● John H. Finley, *Thucydides,* 1947. ● Nicole Loraux, *The Invention of Athens,* 1986. ● Thucydides, *The Peloponnesian War,* trans. Lattimore, 1998. ● John E. Ziolkowski, *Thucydides and the Tradition of Funeral Speeches at Athens,* 1981.

Archaic Lyric Poetry ● Anne Burnett, *Three Archaic Poets: Archilochus, Alcaeus, Sappho,* 1983. ● C. Calame, *The Poetics of Eros in Ancient Greece,* 1999. ● D. L. Page, *Poetae Melici Graeci,* 1962.

Aeschylus ● *Aeschylus,* ed. M. L. West, 1990. ● *The Complete Greek Tragedies,* eds. D. Grene and R. Lattimore, 1954–1956. ● D. J. Conacher, *Aeschylus's Oresteia: A Literary Commentary,* 1987. ● Simon Goldhill, *Aeschylus: The Oresteia,* 1992. ● A. Lebeck, *The Oresteia,* 1982. ● Froma Zeitlin, *Playing the Other: Gender and Society in Classical Greek Literature,* 1996.

Aristophanes ● K. J. Dover, *Aristophanic Comedy,* 1972. ● V. Ehrenberg, *The People of Aristophanes,* 1951. ● David Konstan, *Greek Comedy and Ideology,* 1995. ● E. Segal, *Oxford Readings in Aristophanes,* 1996.

Aristotle ● J. Barnes, *Aristotle,* 1982. ● S. H. Halliwell, *Aristotle's Poetics,* 1986. ● G. E. R. Lloyd, *Aristotle,* 1968. ● A. Rorty, ed., *Essays on Aristotle's Poetics,* 1992.

Euripides ● Page duBois, *Centaurs and Amazons,* 1982. ● E. Segal, ed., *Euripides: A Collection of Critical Essays,* 1968.

Homer ● George Dimock, *The Unity of the Odyssey,* 1989. ● Nancy Felson-Rubin, *Regarding Penelope: From Character to Poetics,* 1994. ● Ralph Hexter, *A Guide to the Odyssey,* 1993. ● A. B. Lord, *The Singer of Tales,* 1960. ● Gregory Nagy, *The Best of the Achaeans,* 1979. ● Seth Schein, *The Mortal Hero: An Introduction to Homer's Iliad,* 1987. ● Seth Schein, *Reading the Odyssey,* 1991. ● W. G. Thalmann, *The Odyssey: An Epic of Return,* 1997.

Pindar ● Leslie Kurke, *The Traffic in Praise,* 1991. ● F. Nisetich, trans., *Pindar's Victory Odes,* 1980. ● W. H. Race, *Pindar,* 1986.

Sappho ● Paqe duBois, *Sappho Is Burning,* 1995. ● Denys Page, *Sappho and Alcaeus,* 1955. ● E. M. Voigt, *Sappho et Alcaeus,* 1971. ● *Sappho's Lyre: Archaic Lyric and Women Poets of Ancient Greece,* 1991. ● *If Not, Winter: Fragments of Sappho,* trans. Anne Carson, 2002.

Sophocles ● Harold Bloom, ed., *Sophocles's Oedipus Rex,* 1988. ● Helene B. Foley, *Female Acts in Greek Tragedy,* 2001. ● B. M. W. Knox, *Oedipus at Thebes,* 1957. ● Charles Segal, *Oedipus Tyrannus: Tragic Heroism and the Limits of Knowledge,* 1993. ● George Steiner, *Antigones,* 1984. ● J. -P. Vernant and P. Vidal-Naquet, *Myth and Tragedy in Ancient Greece,* trans. J. Lloyd, 1988.

Early South Asia

General ● Edward C. Dimock et al., eds. *Literatures of India: An Introduction,* 1974. ● Ainslie Embree, ed., *Sources of Indian Tradition,* 1988. ● David Ludden, *India and South Asia: A Short History,* 2002. ● Sheldon Pollock, ed., *Literary Cultures in History: Reconstructions from South Asia,* 2003. ● Sheldon Pollock, "Introduction," and "Sanskrit Literature from the Inside Out," in *Literary Cultures in History,* ed. S. Pollock,* 2003. ● Joseph Schwartzberg, ed., *A Historical Atlas of South Asia,* 1992. ● Romila Thapar, *Early India,* 2002. ● Susie Tharu and K. Lalitha, eds., *Women Writing in India, 600 B.C. to the Present,* 1991–1993. ● Herman Tieken, *Kavya in South India,* 2001.

Perspectives: What Is Literature? ● Edward Dimock et al., eds. *The Literatures of India, An Introduction,* 1974. ● Robert Goldman, *The*

Ramayana of Valmiki, vol. 1: *Balakanda,* 1984. • Daniel H. H. Ingalls, Jeffrey Moussaieff Masson, and M. V. Patwardhan, "Introduction," in *The Dhvanyaloka of Anandavardhana,* 1990. • Siegfried Lienhard, *A History of Classical Poetry: Sanskrit, Pali, Prakrit,* 1984. • Sheldon Pollock, "Sanskrit Literature from the Inside Out," in *Literary Cultures in History,* ed. S. Pollock, 2003.

Kalidasa • Robert E Goodwin, *The Playworld of Sanskrit Drama,* 1998. • K. Krishnamoorthy, *Kalidasa,* 1972. • Barbara Stoler Miller et al., trans., *Theatre of Memory: The Plays of Kalidasa,* 1984. • Walter Ruben, *Kalidasa: The Human Meaning of his Works*, 1957. • Romila Thapar, ed., *Sakuntala: Texts, Readings, Histories,* 1999.

Love in a Courtly Language • Norman Cutler, "Three Moments in the Genealogy of Tamil Literary Culture," in *Literary Cultures in History,* ed. S. Pollock, 2003. • Daniel H. H. Ingalls, trans., *An Anthology of Sanskrit Court Poetry,* 1965. • Arvind Krishna Mehrotra, trans., *The Absent Traveler, Prakrit Love Poetry from the Gathasaptasati of Satavahana Hala,* 1991. • W. S. Merwin and J. Moussaieff Masson, trans., *The Peacock's Egg: Love Poems from Ancient India,* 1977. • A. K. Ramanujan, trans., *Poems of Love and War: From the Eight Anthologies and the Ten Long Poems of Classical Tamil,* 1985. • Herman Tieken, *Kavya in South India,* 2001.

Mahabharata of Vyasa • John Brockington, *The Sanskrit Epics,* 1998. • J. A. B. van Buitenen, "The Indian Epics," in *Literatures of India,* eds. Edward Dimock et al., 1974. • J. A. B. van Buitenen et al., trans., *The Mahabharata,* 1973. • John Ross Carter and Mahinda Paliawadana, trans., *The Dhammpada,* 1987. • Robert P. Goldman and Sally Sutherland, eds. *The Epic Tradition,* 2004. • Alf Hiltebeital, *Rethinking the Mahabharata: A Reader's Guide to the Education of the Dharma King,* 2001. • R. P. Kangle, trans., *Arthasastra,* 1969. • N. A. Nikam and Richard McKeon, trans., *Edicts of Asoka,* 1959. • Pratap Chandra Roy, trans., *The Mahabharata of Krishna Dwaipayana Vyasa,* 1963–1965. • Arvind Sharma, ed. *Essays on the Mahabharata,* 1991.

Ramayana of Valmiki • John Brockington, *The Sanskrit Epics,* 1998. • Robert Goldman et al., trans., *The Ramayana of Valmiki: An Epic of Ancient India,* 1984–. • Robert P. Goldman and Sally Sutherland, eds., *The Epic Tradition,* 2004. • Sheldon Pollock, "Ramayana and Political Imagination in India," *Journal of Asian Studies* 52.2 (1993), 261–97. • A. K. Ramanujan, "Three Hundred Ramayanas: Five Examples and Three Thoughts on Translation," In *Many Ramayanas,* ed. Paula Richman, 1994. • Paula Richman, ed. *Many Ramayanas: The Diversity of a Narrative Tradition in South Asia,* 1991. • Paula Richman, ed. *Questioning Ramayanas: A South Asian Tradition,* 2000.

China: The Classical Tradition

General • Cyril Birch, *Anthology of Chinese Literature,* vol. I, 1965. • Anne Birrell, *Chinese Mythology,* 1993. • Wing-tsit Chan, *A Sourcebook in Chinese Philosophy,* 1963. • Raymond Dawson, ed., *The Legacy of China,* 1964. • William Theodore de Bary, ed., *Sources of Chinese Tradition,* 1999. • Patricia B. Ebrey, ed., *Chinese Civilization and Society: A Sourcebook,* 1981. • C. P. Fitzgerald, *China: A Short Cultural History,* 1967. • Yu-lan Fung, *A History of Chinese Philosophy,* 1953. • Jacques Gernet, *A History of Chinese Civilization,* 1982. • James Legge, trans., *The Chinese Classics,* 1892. • Michael Loewe and Edward Shaughnessy, eds., *The Cambridge History of Ancient China,* 1999. • Frederick Mote, *Intellectual Foundations of China,* 1971. • William Nienhauser, ed., *The Indiana Companion to Traditional Chinese Literature,* 1986. • Stephen Owen, *An Anthology of Chinese Literature, Beginnings to 1911,* 1996. • Paul Ropp, ed., *The Heritage of China,* 1990.

• Benjamin Schwartz, *The World of Thought in Ancient China,* 1985. • Burton Watson, *Early Chinese Literature,* 1962. • Arthur Waley, *Three Ways of Thought in Ancient China,* 1939. • Pauline Yu et al., eds., *Ways With Words: Writing About Reading Texts from Early China,* 2000.

Perspectives: Daoism and Its Ways • Herrlee Creel, *What Is Taoism?* 1960. • N. J. Girardot, *Myth and Meaning in Early Taoism: The Theme of Chaos (Hun-tun),* 1983. • Chad Hansen, *A Daoist Theory of Chinese Thought: A Philosophical Interpretation,* 1992. • Henri Maspero, *Taoism and Chinese Religion,* 1981. • Isabelle Robinet, *Taoism: Growth of a Religion,* trans. Phyllis Brooks, 1997. • Holmes Welch and Anna Seidel, eds., *Facets of Taoism,* 1979.

The Book of Songs • Joseph R. Allen, ed., *The Book of Songs,* trans. Arthur Waley, 1996.

• Marcel Granet, *Festivals and Songs of Ancient China,* 1932. • Bernhard Karlgren, trans., *The Book of Odes,* 1950. • William McNaughton, *The Book of Songs,* 1971. • Ezra Pound, trans., *The Confucian Odes,* 1954. • Haun Saussy, *The Problem of a Chinese Aesthetic,* 1993. • Steven Van Zoeren, *Poetry and Personality: Reading, Exegesis and Hermeneutics in Traditional China,* 1991. • Arthur Waley, trans., *The Book of Songs,* 1937. • C. H. Wang, *The Bell and the Drum,* 1974.

Confucius • Roger T. Ames and Henry Rosemont, trans., *The Analects of Confucius: A Philosophical Translation,* 1998. • Herrlee Creel, *Confucius: The Man and the Myth,* 1949. • Raymond Dawson, trans., *The Analects,* 1993. • Herbert Fingarette, *Confucius, the Secular as Sacred,* 1972. • David L. Hall and Roger T. Ames, *Thinking through Confucius,* 1987. • D. C. Lau, trans., *Confucius: The Analects,* 1979. • Simon Leys, trans., *The Analects of Confucius,* 1997. • Pertti Nikkilä, *Preference and Choice in the Confucian Analects,* 1997. • Yuri Pines, *Foundations of Confucian Thought,* 2002. • Edward L. Shaughnessy, *Before Confucius: Studies in the Creation of the Confucius Classics,* 1997. • Bryan W. Van Norden, ed., *Confucius and the Analects: New Essays,* 2002. • Arthur Waley, *The Analects of Confucius,* 1938.

Dao De Jing • Roger T. Ames and David L. Hall, *Daodejing: "Making This Life Significant": A Philosophical Translation,* 2003. • Robert G. Henricks, trans., *Lao-tzu: Tao-te Ching: A New Translation Based on the Recently Discovered Ma-wang-tui Texts,* 1989. • Robert G. Henricks, trans., *Lao Tzu's Tao Te Ching: A Translation of the Startling New Documents Found at Guodian,* 2000. • David Hinton, *Tao Te Ching,* 2000. • Max Kaltenmark, *Lao-Tzu and Taoism,* 1970. • Livia Kohn and Michael

LaFargue, *Lao-tzu and the Tao-te-ching,* 1998. • D. C. Lau, trans., *Tao Te Ching,* 1963. • Richard John Lynn, trans., *The Classic of the Way and Virtue: A New Translation of the Tao-te Ching of Laozi as Interpreted by Wang Bi,* 1999. • Moss Roberts, trans. and commentary, *Dao De Jing: The Book of the Way,* 2001. • Arthur Waley, *The Way and Its Power: A Study of the Tao Te Ching and Its Place in Chinese Thought,* 1958.

Liezi • Lionel Giles, trans., *Taoist Teachings: From the Book of Lieh Tzu,* 1925. • A. C. Graham, trans., *The Book of Lieh-Tzu,* 1990. • Léon Wieger, *Wisdom of the Daoist Masters: The Works of Lao Zi (Lao Tzu), Lie Zi (Lieh Tzu), Zhuang Zi (Chuang Tzu),* trans. from French by Derek Bryce, 1984. • Eva Wong, trans., *Lieh-tzu: A Taoist Guide to Practical Living,* 1995.

Liu Yiqing • Richard Mather, trans., *Shih-shuo Hsin-yü: A New Account of Tales of the World,* 2002. • Nanxiu Qian, *Spirit and Self in Medieval China: The Shih-shuo Hsin-yu and Its Legacy,* 2001.

Xi Kang • John Makeham, *Name and Actuality in Early Chinese Thought,* 1994.

Zhuangzi • Roger T. Ames, *Wandering at Ease in the Zhuangzi,* 1998. • A. C. Graham, trans., *Chuang Tzu: The Inner Chapters,* 1981. • Roger P. Hart, *The Inner Chapters of Zhuangzi: Interpretation and the Limits of Coherence,* 1991. • Paul Kjellberg and Philip J. Ivanhoe, eds., *Essays on Skepticism, Relativism and Ethics in the Zhuangzi,* 1996. • Victor H. Mair, *Experimental Essays on Chuang-tzu,* 1983. • Michael James Millner, *Roaming Freely Inside the Cage: Social Concern in Zhuangzi and Early Chinese Thought,* 2000. • Burton Watson, trans., *The Complete Works of Chuang Tzu,* 1970.

Rome and the Roman Empire

General • Alessandro Barchiesi, *The Poet and the Prince: Ovid and Augustan Discourse,* 1997. • Anthony A. Barrett, *Livia: First Lady of Imperial Rome,* 2002. • Mary Beard, John North, and Simon Price, *Religions of Rome,* vol. 1: *A History*; vol. 2: *A Sourcebook,* 1998. • John Boardman, Jasper Griffin, and Oswyn Murray, *The Oxford History of the Roman World,* 2001. • Anthony J. Boyle, ed., *Roman Epic.* New York: Routledge, 1993. • Susan Braund, *Roman Verse Satire,* 1992. • Caesar, *The*

Conquest of Gaul, trans. S. A. Handford, 1982. • Kitty Chisholm and John Ferguson, eds., *Rome, the Augustan Age: A Source Book,* 1981. • Peter Connolly and Hazel Dodge, *The Ancient City: Life in Classical Athens and Rome,* 1998. • Gian Biagio Conte, *Latin Literature: A History,* trans. Joseph B. Solodow, 1994. • Werner Eck, *The Age of Augustus,* trans. Deborah Lucas Schneider, 2003. • Catherine Edwards, *Writing Rome: Textual Approaches to the City.* New York: Cambridge

University Press, 1996. ● Elaine Fantham, Helene Peet Foley, Natalie Boymel Kampen, and H. A. Shapiro. *Women in the Classical World: Image and Text*, 1995. ● Diane Favro, *The Urban Image of Imperial Rome*, 1998. ● Dennis Feeney, *Literature and Religion at Rome: Cultures, Contexts, and Beliefs*, 1998. ● M. I. Finley, *The Ancient Economy*, 1999. ● Karl Galinsky, *Augustan Culture*, 1996. ● Edward Gibbon, *The History of the Decline and Fall of the Roman Empire*, 1776–1788. ● Emily Gowers, *The Loaded Table: Representations of Food in Roman Literature*, 1996. ● Jasper Griffin, *Latin Poets and Roman Life*, 1985. ● Thomas Habinek, *The Politics of Latin Literature*, 1998. ● Thomas Habinek and Alessandro Schiesaro, eds., *The Roman Cultural Revolution*, 1997. ● Judith P. Hallett and Marilyn B. Skinner, eds., *Roman Sexualities*, 1998. ● Philip R. Hardie, *The Epic Successors of Virgil: A Study in the Dynamics of a Tradition.* New York: Cambridge University Press, 1993. ● Fritz Heichelheim et al., *A History of the Roman People*, 2002. ● Peter V. Jones and Keith C. Sidwell, *The World of Rome: An Introduction to Roman Culture*, 1997. ● Josephus, *The Jewish War*, 1970. ● Livy, *History of Rome*, 14 vols. Loeb Classical Library, 1964–1970. ● Livy, *History of Rome from Its Foundation*, 4 vols., 1960–1982. ● R. O. A. M. Lyne, *The Latin Love Poets: From Catullus to Horace.* Oxford: Clarendon, 1980. ● Ramsay MacMullen, *Romanization in the Time of Augustus*, 2000. ● Plutarch, *The Parallel Lives*, 11 vols., trans. Bernadotte Perrin, Loeb Classical Library, 1967. ● David Quint, *Epic and Empire: Politics and Generic Form from Virgil to Milton.* Princeton: Princeton University Press, 1993. ● Nancy H. Ramage and Andrew Ramage, *Roman Art: From Romulus to Constantine*, 1991. ● Amy Richlin, *The Garden of Priapus: Sexuality and Aggression in Roman Humor*, 1992. ● Howard H. Scullard, *From the Gracchi to Nero: A History of Rome 133 B.C. to A.D. 68*, 1990. ● Ronald Syme, *The Roman Revolution*, 2002. ● Robert Turcan, *The Gods of Ancient Rome: Religion in Everyday Life from Archaic to Imperial Times*, 2001. ● Paul Veyne, *Roman Erotic Elegy: Love, Poetry and the West*, 1988. ● Paul Veyne, ed., *A History of Private Life: I. From Pagan Rome to Byzantium*, 1987. ● J. M. Wallace-Hadrill, *Augustan Rome*, 1993. ● Peter White, *Promised Verse: Poets in the Society of Augustan Rome*, 1993. ● Paul Zanker, *The Power of Images in the Age of Augustus*, 1988.

Perspectives: Roman Culture and the Beginnings of Christianity ● Peter Brown, *The Body and Society: Men, Women, and Sexual Renunciation in Early Chritistianity*, 1988. ● Peter Brown, *The World of Late Antiquity*, 1971.

● John B. Bury, *History of the Later Roman Empire*, 2 vols., 1958. ● Everett Ferguson, *Backgrounds of Early Christianity*, 1993. ● Robin Lane Fox, *Pagans and Christians*, 1987. ● Richard A. Horsley and John S. Hanson, *Bandits, Prophets, and Messiahs: Popular Movements in the Time of Jesus*, 1985. ● A. H. M. Jones, *The Later Roman Empire 284-602: A Social, Economic and Administrative Survey*, 3 vols., 1986. ● Santo Mazzarino, *The End of the Ancient World*, 1966.

Augustine ● R. H. Barrow, *Introduction to St. Augustine "City of God,"* 1970. ● Gerald Bonner, *St. Augustine: His Life and Controversies*, 1986. ● Peter Brown, *Augustine of Hippo*, 1967. ● Peter Brown, *Religion and Society in the Age of St. Augustine*, 1972. ● Kenneth Burke, *The Rhetoric of Religion: Studies in Logology*, 1970. ● Henry Chadwick, *Augustine*, 1986. ● Gillian Clark, *Saint Augustine: The Confessions*, 1993. ● Elizabeth De Mijolla, *Autobiographical Quests: Augustine, Montaigne, Rousseau, and Wordsworth*, 1994. ● Allan D. Fitzgerald, ed., *Augustine Through the Ages: An Encyclopedia*, 1999. ● Harald Hagendahl, *Augustine and the Latin Classics*, 2 vols. 1967. ● Ann Hartle, *The Modern Self in Rousseau's Confessions: A Reply to St. Augustine*, 1983. ● Christopher Kirwan, *Augustine*, 1989. ● Sabine MacCormack, *The Shadows of Poetry: Vergil in the Mind of Augustine*, 1998. ● Robert A. Markus, *Saeculum: History and Society in the Theology of St. Augustine*, 1988. ● Robert McMahon, *Augustine's Prayerful Ascent: An Essay on the Literary Form of the Confessions*, 1989. ● Robert J. O'Connell, *Soundings in St. Augustine's Imagination*, 1994. ● Gerard P. O'Daly, *Augustine's City of God: A Reader's Guide*, 1999. ● James J. O'Donnell, *Augustine*, 1985. ● John J. O'Meara, *The Young Augustine: The Growth of St. Augustine's Mind up to his Conversion*, 1954. ● John J. O'Meara, *Understanding Augustine*, 1997. ● Sarah Spence, *Rhetorics of Reason and Desire: Vergil, Augustine, and the Troubadours*, 1988. ● Eleonore Stump and Norman Katzmann, eds. *Cambridge Companion to Augustine*, 2001.

Catullus ● William Fitzgerald, *Catullan Provocations: Lyric Poetry and the Drama of Position*, 1995. ● Richard Jenkyns, *Three Classical Poets—Sappho, Catullus, and Juvenal*, 1982. ● Charles Martin, *Catullus*, 1992. ● Kenneth Quinn, *The Catullan Revolution*, 1959. ● Arthur Leslie Wheeler, *Catullus and the Traditions of Ancient Poetry*, 1934. ● T. P. Wiseman, *Catullus and His World: A Reappraisal*, 1985.

Horace ● David Armstrong, *Horace*, 1989. ● Steele Commager, *The Odes of Horace*,

1962. ● Eduard Fraenkel, *Horace,* 1957. ● Niall Rudd, ed., *Horace 2000: A Celebration. Essays for the Bimillennium,* 1993. ● Niall Rudd, ed., *The Satires of Horace,* 1966. ● David Alexander West, *Reading Horace,* 1967. ● L. P. Wilkinson, *Horace and His Lyric Poetry,* 1951.

Luke ● Robert Alter and Frank Kermode, eds., *The Literary Guide to the Bible,* 1987. ● C. K. Barrett, *The Acts of the Apostles: A Shorter Commentary,* 2002. ● H. J. Cadbury, *The Making of Luke—Acts,* 1958. ● Hans Conzelmann, *The Theology of St. Luke,* 1961. ● John Drury, *Tradition and Design in Luke's Gospel,* 1976. ● Joel B. Green et al., eds. *Dictionary of Jesus and the Gospels,* 1992. ● Ernst Haenchen, *The Acts of the Apostles: A Commentary,* 1971. ● Leander G. Keck and J. Louis Martyn, eds., *Studies in Luke—Acts: Studies Presented in Honor of Paul Schubert,* 1966. ● E. P. Sanders, *The Historical Figure of Jesus,* 1993. ● Charles H. Talbert, ed., *Luke—Acts: New Perspectives from the Society of Biblical Literature Seminar,* 1984. ● Robert C. Tannehill, *The Narrative Unity of Luke—Acts: A Literary Interpretation,* 2 vols., 1986.

Ovid ● Karl Galinsky, *Ovid's Metamorphoses: An Introduction to the Basic Aspects,* 1975. ● Philip Hardie, *Ovid's Poetics of Illusion,* 2002. ● Philip Hardie, ed., *The Cambridge Companion to Ovid,* 2002. ● P. E. Knox, *Ovid's Metamorphoses and the Traditions of Augustan Poetry,* 1986. ● Sara Mack, *Ovid,* 1988. ● Brooks Otis, *Ovid as an Epic Poet,* 1966. ● Joseph B. Solodow, *The World of Ovid's Metamorphoses,* 1988. ● Garth Tissol, *The Face of Nature: Wit, Narrative, and Cosmic Origins in Ovid's Metamorphoses,* 1997.

Paul ● Michael Goulder, "The Pauline Epistles," in *The Literary Guide to the Bible,* eds. Robert Alter and Frank Kermode, 1987. ● Anthony Tyrell Hanson, *Studies in Paul's Technique and Theology,* 1974. ● Gerald Hawthorne et al., eds. *Dictionary of Paul and His Letters,* 1993. ● Martin Hengel, with Roland Deines, *The Pre-Christian Paul,* trans. John Bowden, 1991. ● Martin Hengel, with Anna Maria Schwemer, *Paul Between Damascus and Antioch,* trans., John Bowden, 1997. ● Leander Keck, *Paul and His Letters,* 1988. ● Wayne A.

Meeks, *The First Urban Christians: The Social World of the Apostle Paul,* 1983. ● E. P. Sanders, *Paul,* 1991. ● E. P. Sanders, *Paul and Palestinian Judaism: A Comparison of Patterns of Religion,* 1977. ● Marion L. Soards, *The Apostle Paul: An Introduction to His Writings and Teaching,* 1987. ● Krister Stendahl, *Paul Among Jews and Gentiles: And Other Essays,* 1976. ● Stanley K. Stowers, *A Rereading of Romans: Justice, Jews, and Gentiles,* 1994.

Petronius ● Gian Biagio Conte, *The Hidden Author: An Interpretation of Petronius' "Satyricon,"* 1996. ● Niall W. Slater, *Reading Petronius,* 1990. ● J. P. Sullivan, *The "Satyricon" of Petronius: A Literary Study,* 1968. ● P. G. Walsh, *The Roman Novel: The "Satyricon" of Petronius and the "Metamorphoses" of Apuleius,* 1970.

Priapea ● *The Priapus Poems: Erotic Epigrams from Ancient Rome,* trans., introduction and commentary, Richard W. Hooper, 1999.

Roman Responses to Christianity ● Barry Baldwin, *Suetonius,* 1983. ● Julian Bennett, *Trajan, Optimum Princeps: A Life and Times,* 1997. ● Donald R. Dudley, *The World of Tacitus,* 1969. ● Ronald H. Martin, *Tacitus,* 1981. ● Ronald Symes, *Tacitus,* 2 vols., 1958. ● Andrew Wallace-Hadrill, *Suetonius, The Scholar and His Caesars,* 1983.

Virgil ● Francis Cairns, *Virgil's Augustan Epic,* 1989. ● Wendell Clausen, *Virgil's "Aeneid" and the Tradition of Hellenistic Poetry,* 1987. ● Steele Commager, ed., *Virgil: A Collection of Critical Essays,* 1966. ● Domenico Comparetti, *Virgil in the Middle Ages,* 1966. ● K. W. Gransden, *Virgil's "Iliad": An Essay on Epic Narrative,* 1984. ● Jasper Griffin, *Virgil,* 1986. ● P. R. Hardie, *Virgil's "Aeneid": Cosmos and Imperium,* 1986. ● S. J. Harrison, *Oxford Readings in Vergil's "Aeneid,"* 1990. ● W. R. Johnson, *Darkness Visible: A Study of Vergil's "Aeneid,"* 1976. ● Charles Martindale, ed., *The Cambridge Companion to Virgil,* 1997. ● Charles Martindale, ed., *Virgil and His Influence,* 1984. ● Michael C. J. Putnam, *Virgil's "Aeneid": Interpretation and Influence,* 1995. ● Kenneth Quinn, *Virgil's "Aeneid": A Critical Description,* 1968. ● David Slavitt, *Virgil,* 1992. ● Theodore Ziolkowski, *Virgil and the Moderns,* 1993.

CREDITS

Višnjić, Filip: "The Death of Kraljević Marko," by Filip Višnjić, from *Immanent Art: From Structure to Meaning in Traditional Oral Epic,* translated by John Miles Foley, 1991. Reprinted by permission of John M. Foley.

Walcott, Derek: From *Omeros* by Derek Walcott. Copyright © 1990 by Derek Walcott. Reprinted by permission of Farrar, Straus, and Giroux, LLC.

Wei Hong: From "The Preface to the Book of Songs, attributed to Wei Hong," translated by Pauline Yu. Reprinted by permission of Pauline Yu.

Xi Kang: "Letter to Shan Tao," from *Anthology of Chinese Literature,* edited by Cyril Birch. Copyright © 1965 by Grove Press, Inc. Used by permission of Grove/Atlantic, Inc.

Yeats, William Butler: "Leda and the Swan," reprinted with permission of Scribner, a division of Simon & Schuster, from *The Collected Poems of W. B. Yeats,* Revised Second Edition edited by Richard J. Finneran. Copyright © 1928 by Macmillan Publishing Company, renewed 1956 by Georgie Yeats.

Zhuangzi: From *The Complete Works of Chuang Tzu,* translated by Burton Watson. Copyright © 1968 Columbia University Press. Reprinted by permission of the publisher.

ILLUSTRATION CREDITS

Cover image: Detail from a funerary shroud with a portrait of the deceased between Anubis and Osiris. Egypt, 2nd century C.E. Pushkin Museum of Fine Arts, Moscow. Copyright © Scala/Art Resource, New York. **Inside front cover image:** *The World According to Herodotus.* AKG Images, London/AKG Images. **Page xxx:** Detail of stele inscribed with the Law Code of Hammurabi, c. 1750 B.C.E. Reunion des Musees Nationaux/Art Resource, New York. **Page 10:** The creation of heaven and earth, Egyptian papyrus from c. 1025 B.C.E. The British Museum Images. Copyright © The Trustees of The British Museum. **Page 12:** *Portrait of Mereruka*, Saqqara, Egypt, c. 2290 B.C.E. ARJ/Photos12.com. **Page 21:** *Spoils from the Temple in Jerusalem,* c. 81 C.E. Alinari/Art Resource, New York. **Page 57:** Impression from a stone cylinder seal, Babylonia, c. second millennium B.C.E. The British Museum Images. Copyright © The Trustees of The British Museum. **Page 103:** From the *Book of the Dead*, Papyrus of Ani, Thebes, c. 1250 B.C.E. The British Museum Images. Copyright © The Trustees of The British Museum. **Page 146:** Hebrew captives being taken into exile. Detail of a relief from the palace of Sennacherib at Nineveh, showing the Assyrian conquest of the fortified Hebrew town of Lachish in 701 B.C.E. Erich Lessing/Art Resource, New York. **Page 184:** Statue of Zeus or Poseidon from Cape Artemision, Greece, c. 450 B.C.E. National Archeological Museum. John Hios/AKG Images. **Page 187:** Amazon combat, vase painting, 5th century B.C.E. Bridgeman Art Library. **Page 404:** *Odysseus and the Sirens*, Etruscan red-figure amphora, c. 500 B.C.E. The British Museum Images. Copyright © The Trustees of The British Museum. **Page 563:** Sappho and Alkaios, red-figure vase, c. 500 B.C.E. Staatliche Antikensammlungen und Glyptothek, Munich, Germany. **Page 727:** Maenad cup by the Brygos Painter, mid-first millennium B.C.E. Staatliche Antikensammlung, Munich, Germany/Erich Lessing/Art Resource, New York. **Page 798:** *Lady Writing a Love Letter*, temple sculpture, Khajuraho, India, c. 1000 C.E. Indian Museum, Calcutta. **Page 810:** Section of a frieze depicting a battle from the *Mahabharata*, from Angkor Wat, Cambodia, early twelfth century. Michael Freeman. **Page 862:** Contemporary Indian comic book rendering depicts the death of Ravana in Valmiki's *Ramayana*. Amar Chitra Katha–Ramayana/Published by India Book House, Pvt. Ltd. **Page 1016:** Terra-cotta soldiers from the tomb of the first Qin Dynasty emperor (r. 247–210 B.C.E.). Laurent Lecat/Photos12.com. **Page 1019:** Oracle bone inscription from the reign of Wu Ding. From *The Cambridge History of Ancient China: From the Origins of Civilization to 221 B.C.,* edited by Michael Loewe and Edward L. Shaughnessy. Cambridge UK; New York: Cambridge University Press, New York, 1999. **Page 1020:** Historical table of Chinese script. From *Development of the Chinese Script*, by Jerry Norman. Cambridge: Cambridge University Press, 1988/New York Public Library, NY. **Page 1063:** *Laozi Riding an Ox*, c. 1600 C.E. National Palace Museum, Taipei, Taiwan/Bridgeman Art Library. **Page 1092:** Marble statue of Augustus Caesar, c. 20 B.C.E. Erich Lessing/Art Resource, New York. **Page 1095:** *Fight of the Gladiators*, mosaic, Rome, Italy, 4th century C.E. Galleria Borghese, Rome, Italy/Scala/Art Resource, New York. **Page 1096:** Ippolito Caffi, *The Roman Forum*, 1841. Museo di Roma, Roma/Dagli Orti. The Art Archive/Museo di Roma, Rome/Dagli Orti/The Art Archive Picture Desk, Inc./Kobal Collection. **Page 1245:** Chariot race at the Circus Maximus in Rome. Museo della Civilta Romana, Rome, Italy/Bridgeman Art Library.

FONTS CREDIT

The EuroSlavic, AfroRoman, Macron, TransIndic, Semitic Transliterator, and ANSEL fonts used to publish this work are available from Linguist's Software, Inc., P.O. Box 580, Edmonds, WA 98020-0580 USA, tel (425) 775-1130, www.linguistsoftware.com.

INDEX